LES LIVRES DE DROIT DE L'ACADÉMIE
THE LAW BOOKS OF THE ACADEMY

ISBN (volume broché/Soft-cover Volume) 978-90-04-26807-4
ISBN (volume relié/Hard-back Volume) 978-90-04-26805-0

Imprimé par/Printed by Triangle Bleu, Maubeuge, France

ONT PARU DANS LA MÊME COLLECTION
PUBLISHED IN THE SAME SERIES

Manuel sur les organisations internationales/A Handbook on International Organizations (1re éd./1st ed., 1988 ; 2e éd./2nd ed., 1998) (R.-J. Dupuy, dir. publ./ed.)

A Handbook on the New Law of the Sea (2 Vols.) (R.-J. Dupuy - D. Vignes, eds.)

La dette extérieure/The External Debt (D. Carreau - M. N. Shaw, dir. publ./eds.)

La succession d'Etats : la codification à l'épreuve des faits/ State Succession : Codification Tested against the Facts (P. M. Eisemann - K. Koskenniemi, dir. publ./eds.)

Les aspects internationaux des catastrophes naturelles et industrielles/The International Aspects of Natural and Industrial Catastrophes (D. D. Caron - Ch. Leben, dir. publ./eds.)

La politique de l'environnement: De la réglementation aux instruments économiques/Environmental Policy: From Regulation to Economic Instruments (M. Bothe - P. H. Sand, dir. publ./eds.)

Les sanctions économiques en droit international/Economic Sanctions in International Law (L. Picchio Forlati - L.-A. Sicilianos, dir. publ./eds.)

Les ressources en eau et le droit international/Water Resources and International Law (L. Boisson de Chazournes - S. M. A. Salman, dir. publ./eds.)

La sécurité alimentaire/Food Security and Food Safety (A. Mahiou - F. Snyder, dir. publ./eds.)

Les aspects nouveaux du droit des investissements internationaux/New Aspects of International Investment Law (Ph. Kahn - T. W. Wälde, dir. publ./eds.)

Le patrimoine culturel de l'humanité/The Cultural Heritage of Mankind (J. A. R. Nafziger - T. Scovazzi, dir. publ./eds.)

Terrorisme et droit international/Terrorism and International Law (M. J. Glennon - S. Sur, dir. publ./eds.)

Les règles et institutions du droit international humanitaire à l'épreuve des conflits armés récents/Rules and Institutions of International Humanitarian Law Put to the Test of Recent Armed Conflicts (M. J. Matheson - D. Momtaz, dir. publ./eds.)

La mise en œuvre du droit international de l'environnement/ Implementation of International Environmental Law (S. Maljean-Dubois - L. Rajamani, dir. publ./eds.)

Mesures de réparation et responsabilité à raison des actes des organisations internationales/Remedies and Responsibility for the Actions of International Organizations (Dan Sarooshi, dir. publ./ed.)

La criminalité en mer

Crimes at Sea

ACADÉMIE DE DROIT INTERNATIONAL DE LA HAYE
HAGUE ACADEMY OF INTERNATIONAL LAW

La criminalité en mer

Crimes at Sea

PUBLIÉ SOUS LA DIRECTION DE — EDITED BY

Efthymios D. PAPASTAVRIDIS

Kimberley N. TRAPP

2014

MARTINUS NIJHOFF PUBLISHERS
Leiden/Boston

... AVEC LA COLLABORATION DE :

. . . WITH THE CONTRIBUTION OF :

N. Abdoul
D. Batsalas
W. L. Cheah
H. Cherief
J. Coppens
S. F. Gahlen
A. Grymaneli
S. Guggisberg
A. Montas
K. Neri
G. A. Oanta
P. Sergis
I. Y. Tesfalidet
E. Williams

L'OUVRAGE ET LES AUTEURS

THE BOOK AND THE AUTHORS

Avant-Propos — Foreword

E. D. Papastavridis — K. N. Trapp

Introduction

Chapitre 1 — Chapter 1

Efthymios D. Papastavridis (Greece)

Director of Studies of the Centre, English-speaking Section. Lecturer, Democritus University of Thrace; Research Fellow, Academy of Athens.

Chapitre 2 — Chapter 2

Kimberley N. Trapp (Canada)

Directeur d'études de la section de langue française du Centre. Lecturer in Public International Law, Faculty of Laws, UCL.

Première partie — Part I

Chapitre 3 — Chapter 3

Sarah Fiona Gahlen (Allemagne)

Candidate au doctorat à l'International Max Planck Research School for Maritime Affairs, Hambourg. Titulaire d'une maîtrise en droit international et européen, Université de Rouen, et d'un LL.M. en droit commercial, King's College, Londres.

Chapitre 4 — Chapter 4

Gabriela A. Oanta (Romania)

PhD Lecturer in Public International Law and International Relations, and Academic Coordinator of the "University Master in Law : European Union Studies" at the University of A Coruña (Spain). Bachelor of Art in Law in Bucharest (Romania) and LL.M and PhD from A Coruña (Spain).

Chapitre 5 — Chapter 5

Aikaterini Grymaneli (Grèce)

Master 2 recherche en droit international public, Université Paris II (Panthéon-Assas).

Chapitre 6 — Chapter 6

Solène Guggisberg (Suisse)

Doctorante à la Bucerius Law School; chercheuse associée à l'International Max Planck Research School for Maritinus Affairs, Hambourg. Titulaire d'une licence en relations internationales de l'Institut des hautes études internationales et du développement, Genève, et d'un LL.M en droit international, Université d'Edimbourg.

Chapitre 7 — Chapter 7

Nasser Abdoul (Cameroun)

Docteur en droit international de l'Université de Douala (Cameroun). Diplômé de l'Académie internationale de droit constitutionnel (2007). Enseignant-chercheur à l'ISS Université de Maroua (Cameroun).

Chapitre 8 — Chapter 8

Cheah Wui Ling (Malaysia)

Assistant Professor, Faculty of Law of the National University of Singapore (NUS). Research Fellow, NUS Centre of International Law. Qualified lawyer, called to the New York Bar. Diploma in arbitration, Queen Mary, University of London. LL.B and LL.M, National University of Singapore. LL.M, Harvard. Diploma from the Academy of European Law (EUI).

Deuxième partie — Part II

Chapitre 9 — Chapter 9

Eniola Williams (Nigeria)

Bachelor of Laws (LL.B), University of Lagos, Akoka, Nigeria (1985), Bassister at Law (BL) (1986), Masters Degree in International Maritime Law (LLM) (1998), IMO International Maritime Law Institute, Malta (IMLI). Assistant General Manager, Legal, Nigerian Ports Authority. Currently research candidate at IMLI.

Troisième partie — Part III

Chapitre 10 — Chapter 10

Jasmine Coppens (Belgium)

Master in Law as well as Master in Maritime Sciences. Post-doctoral Researcher at the Maritime Institute of Ghent University, Belgium. PhD, "Migrants at Sea: A Legal Analysis of a Maritime Safety and Security Problem".

Chapitre 11 — Chapter 11

Dimitrios Batsalas (Greece)

LLM (Warwick), LLB (Democritus University of Thrace). Teaching and Research Assistant at the Democritus University of Thrace (2009-2012). Attorney-at-Law (Member of Naousa Bar, Greece).

Chapitre 12 — Chapter 12

Arnaud Montas (France)

Docteur en droit privé de l'Université de Nantes. Maître de conférences en droit privé et en sciences criminelles, faculté de droit de l'Université de Bretagne-Occidentale. Chercheur à l'UMR Amure, Institut universitaire européen de la mer.

Quatrième partie — Part IV

Chapitre 13 — Chapter 13

Hamza Cherief (France)

Docteur en droit international public. Chercheur associé au Centre de recherche en droit et en science politique (CREDESPO), Université de Bourgogne. Chercheur associé (2008-2011) pour le projet «Priv-War» de la Commission européenne. Assistant-ingénieur au Centre de recherche sur le droit des marchés et des investissements internationaux (CREDIMI), Université de Bourgogne.

Chapitre 14 — Chapter 14

Panagiotis Sergis (Greece)

HN, Hellenic Naval Academy (1995). Served as the Legal Advisor to the first Force Commander of the European Union operation, "Atalanta" (2008-2009). Law degree, University of Athens (2002), LLMs from the UoL (2004) and LSE (2005) and MSc in International Relations from the Panteion University, Athens (2008).

Cinquième partie — Part V

Chapitre 15 — Chapter 15

Kiara Neri (France)

Maître de conférences et enseignant-chercheur, Université Jean-Moulin Lyon III. Chercheur au Centre de droit international de la même université. Enseignant-chercheur, Université catholique de Lyon.

Chapitre 16 — Chapter 16

Isaias Yemane Tesfalidet (Eritrea)

J.S.D. Candidate at the Yale Law School in New Haven, Connecticut, United States. LL.B., University of Asmara, Faculty of Law (Eritrea), and LL.M., Yale Law School. Staff Attorney at the Office of the Legal Advisor to the Office of the President of Eritrea (2006-2009).

Bibliographie — Bibliography

R. J. W. Ridderhof, R. Steenhard

avec la collaboration de/with contribution by

L. E. Deeks

Bibliothèque du Palais de la Paix, La Haye/Peace Palace Library, The Hague.

Table analytique des matières — Analytical Index

Solène Guggisberg

Le présent ouvrage collectif est le fruit de recherches communes entreprises au sein du Centre d'étude et de recherche de droit international et de relations internationales de l'Académie, qui s'est terminé en septembre 2012, et ce sont les données connues à cette date qui ont été principalement exploitées. En outre, les opinions exprimées ci-après n'engagent que les auteurs et ne représentent pas nécessairement celles des organisations ou des services qui les emploient.

The present collective work is the result of joint research undertaken in the Centre for Studies and Research in International Law and International Relations of the Academy. It was completed in September 2012 and is based primarily on material available at that date. The opinions hereafter expressed are those of the authors and do not necessarily reflect those of the organizations or services for which they work.

TABLE DES MATIÈRES

CONTENTS

Avant-propos — Foreword XXXIII

Introduction

Les rapports des directeurs d'études 1

Introduction

The Reports of the Directors of Studies 1

Chapitre 1 — Chapter 1

CRIMES AT SEA: A LAW OF THE SEA PERSPECTIVE — REPORT OF THE DIRECTOR OF STUDIES OF THE ENGLISH-SPEAKING SECTION OF THE CENTRE 3

Section 1. Introduction 3
Section 2. LOSC and criminality at sea 5
Para. 1. Internal waters 5
Para. 2. Territorial waters 7
Para. 3. International straits 9
Para. 4. Contiguous zone 10
Para. 5. Exclusive Economic Zone (EEZ) 12
Para. 6. High seas 14
Section 3. Criminal activities challenging the public order of the oceans . . . 20
Para. 1, Maritime terrorism and the proliferation of Weapons of Mass Destruction (WMD) 20
A. Introduction 20
B. The law of the sea and maritime terrorism/proliferation of WMD . . 21
C. Other initiatives to counter maritime terrorism and the proliferation of WMD 23
Para. 2. Drug trafficking 27
A. Introductory remarks 27
B. Drug trafficking and the law of the sea 29
C. Other instruments to counter drug trafficking at sea 30

Para. 3. Smuggling of migrants and human trafficking at sea 34

A. Introductory remarks 34
B. Smuggling of migrants and the law of the sea 36
C. Other instruments countering the trafficking of human beings at sea 40

Para. 4. Piracy and armed robbery at sea 43

A. Introduction 43
B. The law of the sea and piracy 44
C. Armed robbery at sea 46

Para. 5. Illegal fishing 47

A. Introduction 47
B. Illegal fishing and the law of the sea 49
C. Regional fisheries management organizations 50

Para. 6. Pollution of maritime environment 51

A. Introduction 51
B. Maritime pollution and the law of the sea 51

Section 4. Concluding remarks 52

Chapitre 2 — Chapter 2

La criminalité en mer : l'approche du droit international — Rapport du directeur d'études de la section de langue française du centre 53

Section 1. Introduction 53
Section 2. Cadre général : Le droit international et les crimes en mer 54

Par. 1. La « juridiction »/« compétence » sous toutes ses formes 54

A. La compétence législative 55

i) Territorialité 55
ii) La compétence extraterritoriale 61

B. La compétence d'exécution 64

i) A moins que la CNUDM ne le prévoie 68
ii) Avec l'accord de l'Etat pavillonnaire ou de l'Etat territorial . . . 72
iii) Avec l'autorisation du Conseil de sécurité 73

C. Les différentes significations de « juridiction » 75

Par. 2. La responsabilité dans toutes ses formes 78

A. La responsabilité pénale individuelle 78

i) Des questions purement nationales 78
ii) Le droit international exigeant l'exercice de la compétence pénale nationale 79
iii) Les crimes internationaux à proprement parler 83

B. La responsabilité étatique 84

i) Les obligations de mise en application du droit pénal 85
ii) Les modalités de la mise en application du droit pénal 87

a) Compétence excessive 87
b) Les obligations de droits humains 90

C. Des mesures d'exécution imposées par le Conseil de sécurité 91

Section 3. Conclusion 92

Première partie
La répression 95

Part I
Suppression 95

Chapitre 3 — Chapter 3

LA COMPÉTENCE NATIONALE EN MATIÈRE DE POLLUTION MARINE 97

Section 1. Introduction 97
Section 2. La compétence nationale en matière criminelle face à la pollution marine dans le cadre du droit international 98
Par. 1. Des limites dans le droit de la mer 99
A. Les eaux intérieures 99
B. La mer territoriale 100
C. La zone économique exclusive (ZEE) 106
D. La haute mer 111
E. La suspension des poursuites suite à l'engagement des poursuites par l'Etat du pavillon 112
Par. 2. La relation entre les lois nationales et les règlements internationaux. 115
A. Le rôle de MARPOL 116
i) Le sanctionnement pénal des pollutions accidentelles par les hydrocarbures dans la ZEE 117
ii) Le degré de dol nécessaire pour un sanctionnement des rejets accidentels 121
iii) Les personnes visées comme potentiellement responsables . . . 123
iv) Le sanctionnement des infractions dites «documentaires» 125
B. A côté de MARPOL: des RNIGA relatives à la pollution marine à mettre en œuvre par les Etats côtiers?. 128
Section 3. La mise en œuvre de la compétence nationale en matière criminelle. 130
Par. 1. Difficultés d'enquête et de mise en œuvre de la responsabilité pénale 131
A. Les moyens d'investigation. 132
i) Les mesures et la surveillance en mer 132
ii) Les inspections portuaires et en mer 134
iii) Les informateurs et le «whistle-blowing» 135
B. Le degré de preuve exigé et l'établissement de l'élément psychologique 136
C. Les sanctions 138
i) Sanctions envers des personnes légales 139
ii) Sanctions civiles et procédures administratives 141
Par. 2. Les sanctions pénales: une réponse appropriée à la pollution marine? 142
A. La criminalisation des pollutions marines et la dimension humaine . 143
B. Des finalités atteintes? 144
i) Châtiment 144
ii) La valeur dissuasive 146
Section 4. Conclusion. 147

Chapitre 4— Chapter 4

Illegal fishing as a criminal act at sea 149

Section 1. Introduction 149
Section 2. Definition of illegal fishing as a criminal act at sea 154
Section 3. International legal framework for the prevention and suppression of illegal fishing. 158

Para. 1. Binding international instruments for the prevention and suppression of illegal fishing 159
A. The role of the coastal State 160
B. The role of the flag State 162
(i) First argument (a non-formalistic solution) 166
(ii) Second argument (a formalistic solution) 167
(iii) Third argument (mixed solution) 168
C. The role of the port State 170

Para. 2. Non-binding instruments in the field of fisheries. 171
Para. 3. New challenges in the fight against illegal fishing 179

Section 4. The enforcement jurisdiction in the international law of the sea for the prevention and suppression of illegal fishing 183
Section 5. Concluding remarks 195

Chapitre 5— Chapter 5

La compétence des tribunaux internes en matière de piraterie 199

Section 1. Introduction 199
Section 2. Les sources du droit international applicable en matière de piraterie 202

Par. 1. Définition de la piraterie 202
A. La définition de la piraterie en vertu du droit international général . . 202
B. Des définitions extensives ? 205
i) OMI 205
ii) BMI 206
iii) Conseil de sécurité 206

Par. 2. Autres conventions susceptibles d'application en matière de piraterie 207
A. La Convention pour la répression d'actes illicites contre la sécurité de la navigation maritime (SUA) 207
B. La Convention internationale contre la prise d'otages 210
C. La Convention des Nations Unies contre la criminalité transnationale organisée 211

Section 3. Pouvoir juridictionnel des Etats en matière de piraterie 213

Par. 1. La piraterie, entre droit international et droit interne 213
A. De la nécessité d'ériger la piraterie en crime dans le droit interne . . 213
B. Problèmes liés à la nécessité d'ériger la piraterie en infraction en droit interne 218
i) Les ambiguïtés de la définition reflétées dans des législations variables et une jurisprudence incohérente 218
ii) *Nullum crimen nulla poena sine lege stricta* 220

Par. 2. La compétence universelle en matière de piraterie 222
A. Raison d'être de la compétence universelle en matière de piraterie . . 222
i) Perte de nationalité. 222
ii) Atrocité du crime. 223
iii) *Locus delicti commissi* 224

B. Une compétence universelle facultative ? 224
i) Compétence universelle facultative en vertu de la Convention de Montego Bay 224
ii) Compétence en vertu des autres conventions 228
a) Une compétence obligatoire mais non universelle ou quasi universelle 228
b) L'apport de la clause *aut dedere aut judicare* 230
c) Compétence quasi universelle *inter partes* ? 231
d) Absence de hiérarchisation entre les diverses bases de compétence 232
C. Une compétence universelle limitée ? 233
i) Poursuites par l'Etat capteur et par un Etat entretenant un lien avec l'incident 233
ii) Transfèrement à un Etat tiers 235

Chapitre 6 — Chapter 6

LE TRAFIC ILLICITE DE MIGRANTS EN MER 239
Section 1. Introduction 239
Par. 1. Problématique 239
Par. 2. Différentiations 241
Section 2. Droits et obligations pertinents 244
Par. 1. Interceptions 244
Par. 2. Droits et obligations pertinents envers les personnes à bord 246
A. Criminalisation du trafic de migrants 246
B. Obligations envers les migrants 250
i) Non-refoulement 250
ii) Interdiction de l'expulsion collective 256
iii) Droit de quitter son propre pays et liberté de mouvement 257
Section 3. Approche zonale 258
Par. 1. Mer territoriale 258
A. Interception 258
B. Compétence pour criminaliser 259
C. Applicabilité des droits humains 262
Par. 2. Zone contiguë 263
A. Interception 263
B. Compétence pour criminaliser 263
C. Applicabilité des droits humains 265
Par. 3. Haute mer 265
A. Interception 265
B. Compétence pour criminaliser 269
C. Applicabilité des droits humains 273
Par. 4. Mer territoriale d'un autre Etat 276
A. Interception 276
B. Compétence pour criminaliser 278
C. Applicabilité des droits humains 278
Section 4. Conclusion — Efficacité du régime de la criminalisation du trafic en mer 280
Par. 1. Cohérence juridique 280
Par. 2. Utilité et faisabilité 283

Chapitre 7 — Chapter 7

LE VOL À MAIN ARMÉE EN MER 287

Section 1. Introduction 287
Section 2. L'imprécision du droit international en matière de vol à main armée en mer 291
Par. 1. L'inadéquation des sources classiques 291
A. Les conventions internationales et le vol à main armée en mer 291
i) La convention sur le droit de la mer 292
ii) La convention pour la répression d'actes illicites contre la sécurité de la navigation maritime (SUA) 293
B. La méconnaissance du vol à main armée par les autres sources classiques 294
i) La coutume internationale 295
ii) La jurisprudence internationale 295
Par. 2. L'éveil de nouvelles sources du droit international concernant le vol à main armé en mer 296
A. Les résolutions des principaux organes de l'ONU relatives aux vols à main armée 297
B. Les résolutions de l'OMI en matière de vol à main armée en mer . . 298
Section 3. La quête d'un cadre juridique adapté aux actes de vol à main armée en mer 300
Par. 1. La prégnance des droits nationaux dans la prévention et la répression des actes de vol à main armée contre les navires 300
A. La mise en place d'un dispositif juridique efficace en vue de prévenir et de réprimer les actes de vol à main armée contre les navires 301
B. La compétence juridictionnelle de l'Etat côtier en matière de vol à main armée contre les navires 302
Par. 2. Le respect du droit international en matière de lutte contre les actes de vol à main armée contre les navires 304
A. Le respect des droits de l'homme en matière de répression du vol à main armée contre les navires 304
B. La conformité au droit international humanitaire des mesures de répression 306
Section 4. Conclusion 307

Chapitre 8 — Chapter 8

EXTRADITION AND MUTUAL LEGAL ASSISTANCE IN THE PROSECUTION OF SERIOUS MARITIME CRIMES : A COMPARATIVE AND CRITICAL ANALYSIS OF APPLICABLE LEGAL FRAMEWORKS 311

Section 1. Introduction 311
Section 2. The legal framework of UNCLOS: interpreting UNCLOS provisions in favour of interstate co-operation 315
Section 3. Universal *aut dedere aut judicare* treaties: mandating interstate co-operation and limiting State discretion 320
Section 4. The UN Transnational Organized Crime Treaty regime: achieving conceptual and procedural clarity and regulating State discretion in interstate co-operation 325
Section 5. Contextual approaches: regional and locale-specific arrangements 330
Section 6. Conclusion: maximizing the potential of multiple frameworks to strengthen interstate co-operation 334

Deuxième partie
La prévention . . . 337

Part II
Prevention . . . 337

Chapitre 9 — Chapter 9

PRIVATE ARMED GUARDS IN THE FIGHT AGAINST PIRACY . . . 339

Section 1. Introduction . . . 339
Para. 1. Threat to maritime security/global response . . . 340
Para. 2. The observed gaps in past initiatives . . . 341
Para. 3. Emergence of the solution of private armed guards . . . 342
Para. 4. Terminology . . . 344
Para. 5. Definitions and distinctions . . . 345
A. Private Armed Guards/Privately Contracted Armed Security Personnel 345
B. Private Maritime Security Companies . . . 345
C. Escort vessels . . . 345
D. Vessel Protection Detachment . . . 346
E. Shiprider . . . 347
Para. 6. Scope . . . 347
Section 2. The general legal framework of PAG . . . 347
Para. 1. Legal and regulatory framework . . . 347
A. The Law of the Sea Convention . . . 348
B. IMO Convention/Resolution/Guidelines . . . 349
C. The UN Draft Convention . . . 351
D. BIMCO GUARDCON contract for employment of security guards . 352
E. National legislation and guidelines . . . 352
Para. 2. The relevant stakeholders and their obligations under international law . . . 353
A. Flag States . . . 353
B. Ship-owner . . . 353
C. Master . . . 355
D. Private Maritime Security Company . . . 355
E. Private Armed Guards/Privately Contracted Armed Security Personnel 356
F. Insurance . . . 357
Section 3. Operation of Private Armed Guards under international and national laws . . . 357
Para. 1. Jurisdiction . . . 357
A. High seas . . . 358
B. Internal waters/port . . . 358
C. Territorial waters/contiguous zones . . . 360
D. Innocent passage . . . 361
E. Straits used for international navigation . . . 362
Para. 2 Use of force by Private Armed Guards — regulation by national law . . . 363
Para. 3. Arrest of pirates . . . 364
Para. 4. Case law/incidents . . . 365
A. The *Almezaan* . . . 365
B. *MV Enrica Lexie* . . . 366
C. *Maersk Alabama* . . . 367
Para. 5. National practices . . . 368

Section 4. State responsibility and liability issues 371
Para. 1. State responsibility 371
Para. 2. Liability issues under international and national legislation 371
A. Rules for the use of force 371
Para. 3 Criminal and civil actions for breach by Private Armed Guards . . 375
Section 5. Conclusion 376
Para. 1. Emerging trend/recommendations/the way forward 376

Troisième partie
La protection et la sécurité 379

Part III
Protection and Security 379

Chapitre 10 — Chapter 10

SEARCH AND RESCUE 381

Section 1. Introduction 381
Section 2. Search and rescue 382
Para. 1, The duty to render assistance 382
Para. 2. The obligation to co-operate 387
Para. 3. Place of safety 392
Section 3. Regional Memorandum of Understanding for the Mediterranean on disembarkation 396
Para. 1, From an international to a regional approach 396
Para. 2. From an interagency to a maritime approach 401
Para. 3. Malta and the regional agreement 403
A. Malta : a distinct view on migrants at sea 403
B. Malta and the regional MoU : a mutual impact 407
Para. 4. Conclusion 408
Section 4. State responsibility 409
Para. 1. State responsibility of flag States and coastal States 409
Para. 2. An example : the left-to-die boat 414
Para. 3. Unmanned Aerial Vehicles : a solution ? 417
Section 5. Sanctions for the master and the ship-owner 419
Para. 1. Shipmaster 419
Para. 2. Ship-owner 421
Para. 3. When the rescuer becomes a smuggler 422
Section 6. Conclusion 426

Chapitre 11 — Chapter 11

MARITIME INTERDICTION AND HUMAN RIGHTS 429

Section 1. Introduction 429
Section 2. Conditions of permissibility 430
Para. 1. The legal framework 430
Para. 2. Questions of applicability 432
A. Extraterritorial application 432
B. Operations under international organizations 435
C. Private security companies 436

Section 3. Maritime interdiction operations as a threat to human rights 437
Para. 1. Prior to the interdiction 437
Para. 2. During the interdiction 438
Para. 3. After the boarding 439
A. Right to liberty and security of person 440
B. Other procedural guarantees 444
C. Right to property 447
D. *Non-refoulement* 447
Section 4. Should HR be perceived as a threat to MIOs ? 450
Section 5. Conclusions 454

Chapitre 12 — Chapter 12

La lutte contre la criminalité en mer à l'épreuve de la Cour européenne des droits de l'homme 457

Section 1. Introduction 457
Section 2. La Cour des droits de l'homme et les atteintes aux droits substantiels dans la lutte contre la criminalité en mer 459
Par. 1. L'interdiction de la torture et des peines ou traitements inhumains ou dégradants (art. 3) 460
Par. 2. La liberté d'expression (art. 10) 465
Par. 3. La protection de la propriété (Protocole nº 1, art. 1) 469
Section 3. La Cour des droits de l'homme et les atteintes aux droits procéduraux dans la lutte contre la criminalité en mer 472
Par. 1. Le droit à la liberté et à la sûreté (art. 5) 473
Par. 2. L'interdiction des expulsions collectives (Protocone nº 4, art. 4) . . 479
Section 4. Conclusion 481

Quatrième partie
Pénalisation internationale 483

Part IV
International Criminalization 483

Chapitre 13 — Chapter 13

La pénalisation de la prolifération maritime des armes de destruction massive 485

Section 1. Introduction 485
Section 2. 1. Le champ d'application des normes relatives à la prolifération maritime des armes de destruction massive 492
Par. 1. Le champ d'application *rationae personae* de la lutte contre la prolifération maritime des armes de destruction massive 492
Par. 2. Le champ d'application *rationae materiae* de la lutte contre la prolifération maritime des armes de destruction massive 495
Section 3. Le cadre légal de la lutte contre la prolifération maritime des armes de destruction massive 499
Par. 1. La compétence pénale de l'Etat sur les navires battant son propre pavillon. 500
Par. 2. La compétence pénale de l'Etat sur un navire battant pavillon étranger en haute mer. 501
Par. 3. La compétence de l'Etat sur les navires battant pavillon étranger dans les eaux soumises à sa souveraineté. 503

Section 4. Les équivoques de la pénalisation de la prolifération maritime des armes nucléaires 510
Par. 1. Le régime juridique de la lutte contre la prolifération étatique, la notion de situation objective conventionnelle. 512
Par. 2. Le maintien de l'avantage stratégique des puissances nucléaires «légitimes» dans le cadre de la lutte contre la prolifération maritime des ADM 514
Par. 3. L'extension en dehors du TNP des obligations de non-prolifération pesant sur les Etats dans le cadre de la lutte contre la prolifération maritime des ADM 517

Chapitre 14 — Chapter 14

WAR CRIMES DURING ARMED CONFLICTS AT SEA 523
Section 1. Introduction 523
Section 2. Existence of an "armed conflict". 525
Section 3. Regulating the naval warfare. 531
Section 4. Criminalization of violations of IHL 541
Section 5. The *Mavi Marmara* incident 547
Section 6. Conclusion. 552

Cinquième partie
Responsabilité et compétence 555
Part V
Responsibility and Jurisdiction 555

Chapitre 15 — Chapter 15

LA RESPONSABILITÉ DE L'ÉTAT DANS LE CADRE DES OPÉRATIONS D'INTERDICTION MARITIME 557
Section 1. Introduction 557
Section 2. Le fait générateur de la responsabilité : les opérations d'interdiction maritime 559
Par. 1. La violation d'une obligation internationale 561
A. La violation d'une obligation internationale issue du droit de la mer 562
i) La violation des obligations négatives de l'Etat. 562
a) La violation des obligations internationales de l'Etat par excès de compétence 563
b) La violation des obligations internationales de l'Etat par excès de pouvoir. 565
ii) La violation des obligations positives de l'Etat 567
a) La violation des obligations de *prévenir*. 567
b) La violation des obligations de *réprimer* 569
c) La violation des obligations *d'intervenir* 570
B. La violation d'une obligation issue du droit des conflits armés en mer 572
C. La violation d'une obligation internationale issue du droit international des droits de l'homme ou du droit des réfugiés 574
Par. 2. La responsabilité sans violation d'une obligation internationale de l'Etat 576
Section 3. L'attribution de la responsabilité à l'Etat en matière d'opération d'interdiction maritime 579

Par. 1. Le cas des opérations unilatérales : l'attribution de la responsabilité à l'Etat 579
A. La persistance d'une responsabilité de l'Etat du pavillon 580
B. L'attribution à l'Etat du comportement de personnes privées 584
i) En temps de paix 584
ii) En temps de guerre 588
Par. 2. Le cas des opérations multilatérales : les règles de répartition de la responsabilité 589
A. La répartition de la responsabilité entre Etats 589
B. La répartition de la responsabilité dans le cadre d'opérations décidées ou menées par des organisations internationales 590
i) La répartition de la responsabilité entre l'organisation internationale et ses Etats membres 590
ii) La répartition de la responsabilité entre organisations internationales impliquées dans des interdictions maritimes 593
Section 4. L'engagement de la responsabilité 595
Par. 1. L'engagement de la responsabilité par l'Etat lésé 596
A. L'Etat du pavillon. 596
B. L'Etat côtier. 599
Par. 2. L'engagement de la responsabilité par la personne privée victime du dommage 600
A. La personne privée destinataire des obligations de compensation. . . 600
B. La personne privée titulaire d'un recours juridictionnel. 603
Section 5. La réparation. 604
Par. 1. La réparation du préjudice de l'Etat 605
Par. 2. La réparation du préjudice des personnes privées 606
Section 6. Conclusion 608

Chapitre 16 — Chapter 16

SHIPRIDER INSTITUTION : QUESTIONS OF JURISDICTION AND STATE RESPONSIBILITY . . 609

Section 1. Introduction 609
Section 2. Shiprider institution in international law and practice 614
Para. 1. Shiprider agreements and international law 614
Para. 2. The basic shiprider model : law and practice 618
Section 3. Shiprider institution and questions of jurisdiction 622
Para. 1. Introduction 622
Para. 2. Shiprider operations : who exercises jurisdiction ? 624
Section 4. State responsibility. 626
Para. 1. Authority of shiprider as an organ of the State 626
Para. 2 The rules on State responsibility 627
Para. 3. The rules on State responsibility as applied to shiprider operations. 630
Section 5. Concluding remarks 632

Bibliographie sélective 635
Selected Bibliography 635

Table analytique des matières 699
Analytical index. 717

PRINCIPALES ABRÉVIATIONS

PRINCIPAL ABBREVIATIONS

1979 Hostages Convention	International Convention against the Taking of Hostages of 1979
1988 SUA Convention	Convention for the Suppression of Unlawful Acts against the Safety of Maritime Navigation of 1988
1988 Vienna Convention	United Nations Convention against Illicit Traffic in Narcotic Drugs and Psychotropic Substances of 1988
1993 FAO Compliance Agreement	Agreement to Promote Compliance with International Conservation and Management Measures by Fishing Vessels on the High Seas of 1993
1995 New York Agreement/ 1995 Fish Stocks Agreement	United Nations Agreement for the Implementation of the Provisions of the United Nations Convention on the Law of the Sea of 10 December 1982 relating to the Conservation and Management of Straddling Fish Stocks and Highly Migratory Fish Stocks of 1995
1999 TFC	International Convention for the Suppression of the Financing of Terrorism of 1999
2005 Model Scheme	Model Scheme on Port State Measures to Combat IUU Fishing adopted in 2005
2005 SUA Protocol	Illegal, Unreported and Unregulated Protocol of 2005 to the Convention for the Suppression of Unlawful Acts against the Safety of Maritime Navigation of 1988
2009 Agreement on Port State Measures	Agreement on Port State Measures to Prevent, Deter and Eliminate Illegal, Unreported and Unregulated Fishing of 2009
ACCT	ASEAN Convention on Counter-terrorism of 2007
ADM	Armes de destruction massive
AFDI	*Annuaire français de droit international*
AFM	Armed Forces of Malta
AGNU	Assemblée générale des Nations Unies

AIEA	Agence internationale de l'énergie atomique
AJIL	*American Journal of International Law*
BIMCO	Baltic and International Maritime Council
BMI	Bureau maritime international
BMPs	Best Management Practices
Caribbean Agreement	Agreement concerning Co-operation in Suppressing Illicit Maritime and Air Trafficking in Narcotic Drugs and Psychotropic Substances in the Caribbean Area of 2003
CARICOM Agreement	CARICOM Maritime and Airspace Security Cooperation Agreement of 2008
CCA	Conception, construction et armement des navires
CCAMLR	Commission on the Conservation of Antarctic Marine Living Resources of 1982
CDH	Conseil des droits de l'homme
CDI	Commission du droit international des Nations Unies
CEDH	Convention européenne des droits de l'homme de 1950 ou Cour européenne des droits de l'homme
CIJ	Cour internationale de Justice
CJCE	Cour de justice des Communautés européennes
CJUE	Cour de justice de l'Union européenne
CMB/CNUDM	Convention des Nations Unies sur le droit de la mer de 1982
COFI	Committee on Fisheries
COMSAR	IMO Sub-Committee on Radiocommunications and Search and Rescue
Convention contre la criminalité transnationale organisée	Convention des Nations Unies contre la criminalité transnationale organisée de 2000
Convention contre la prise d'otages	Convention internationale contre la prise d'otages de 1979
Convention de 1988/ Convention SUA	Convention pour la répression d'actes illicites contre la sécurité de la navigation maritime de 1988
Convention de Vienne	Convention des Nations Unies contre le trafic illicite de stupéfiants et de substances psychotropes de Vienne de 1988
CPI	Cour pénale internationale
CVDT	Convention de Vienne sur le droit des traités de 1969
Djibouti Code of Conduct	Code of Conduct concerning the Repression of Piracy and Armed Robbery against Ships in the Western Indian Ocean and the Gulf of Aden (of the IMO)
DTVIA	Drug Trafficking Vessel Interdiction Act
ECJ	European Court of Justice

ECtHR	European Court of Human Rights
EEZ	Exclusive Economic Zone
EJIL	*European Journal of International Law*
EUNAVFOR / EU NAVFOR	European Union Naval Force
EUROSUR	European Border Surveillance System
EUSC	European Union Satellite Centre
FAL	Facilitation Committee
FAL Convention	Convention on Facilitation of International Maritime Traffic of 1965
FAO	Food and Agriculture Organization of the United Nations
FAO Code of Conduct	FAO Code of Conduct for Responsible Fisheries of 1995
FIDH	Fédération internationale des ligues des droits de l'homme
FIR	Flight Information Region
FRONTEX	Agence européenne pour la gestion de la coopération opérationnelle aux frontières extérieures des Etats membres de l'Union européenne/European Agency for the Management of Operational Co-operation at the External Borders of the Members States of the European Union
GISTI	Groupe d'information et de soutien des immigrés
GMDSS	Global Maritime Distress and Safety System
GUARDCON	Security Guards on Vessels
HRA	High Risk Areas
IACs	International Armed Conflicts
IAMSAR Manual	International Aeronautical and Maritime Search and Rescue Manual
ICAO	International Civil Aviation Organization
ICC	International Criminal Court
ICJ	International Court of Justice
ICL	International Criminal Law
ICoC	International Code of Conduct for Private Security Service Providers
ICRC	International Committee of the Red Cross
ICS	International Chamber of Shipping
ICTR	International Criminal Tribunal for Rwanda
ICTY	International Criminal Tribunal for the former Yugoslavia
IHL	International Humanitarian Law
IJMCL	*International Journal of Marine and Coastal Law*
ILA	International Law Association
ILC	International Law Commission
ILC Articles Commentary	ILC Articles on Responsibility of States for Internationally Wrongful Acts with Commentaries of 2001

ILC (Draft) Articles	ILC (Draft) Articles on Responsibility of States for Internationally Wrongful Acts of 2001
IMB	International Maritime Bureau
IMO	International Maritime Organization
IMO Convention	Convention on the International Maritime Organization of 1948
IOM	International Organization for Migration
IPOA-IUU	International Plan of Action to Prevent, Deter and Eliminate Illegal, Unreported and Unregulated Fishing of 2001
ISO	International Organization for Standardization
ISP	Initiative de sécurité contre la prolifération
ISPS Code	International Ship and Port Facility Security Code
ITLOS	International Tribunal for the Law of the Sea
IUU	Illegal, Unreported, (and) Unregulated
JICJ	*Journal of International Criminal Justice*
JOCE	*Journal officiel des Communautés européennes*
LEDET(s)	Law Enforcement Detachments
LOSC	United Nations Convention on the Law of the Sea of 1982
MARPOL	Convention internationale pour la prévention de la pollution par les navires de 1973, telle que modifiée par le Protocole de 1978/International Convention for the Prevention of Pollution from Ships of 1973, as modified by the 1978 Protocol
MIOs	Maritime Interdiction Operations
MLA	Mutual Legal Assistance
Montego Bay Convention	United Nations Convention on the Law of the Sea of 1982
MoU(s)	Memorandum(a) of Understanding
MRCC	Maritime Rescue Coordination Centre
MSC	Maritime Safety Committee
NATO	North Atlantic Treaty Organization
NIACs	Non-International Armed Conflicts
OHCHR	Office of the United Nations High Commissioner for Human Rights
OILPOL	International Convention for the Prevention of Pollution of the Sea by Oil of 1954
OMI	Organisation maritime internationale
ONU	Organisation des Nations Unies
P&I	Protection & Indemnity
PACE	Parliamentary Assembly of the Council of Europe
PAG	Private Armed Guards
PCASP	Privately Contracted Armed Security Personnel
PMSC	Private Maritime Security Companies

Projet d'articles sur la responsabilité (de la CDI)	Projet d'articles sur la responsabilité de l'Etat pour fait internationalement illicite de 2001
Protocol I	Protocol Additional to the Geneva Conventions of 1949, and relating to the Protection of Victims of International Armed Conflicts of 1977
Protocol II	Protocol Additional to the Geneva Conventions of 1949, and relating to the Protection of Victims of Non-International Armed Conflicts of 1977
Protocole contre le trafic illicite de migrants	Protocole de 2000 contre le trafic illicite de migrants par terre, air et mer à la Convention des Nations Unies contre la criminalité internationale organisée
Protocole (SUA) de 2005	Protocole de 2005 à la Convention pour la répression d'actes illicites contre la sécurité de la navigation maritime de 1988
PSI	Proliferation Security Initiative
RCC	Rescue Co-ordination Centre
Refugee Convention	Convention relating to the Status of Refugees of 1951
RFMOs	Regional Fisheries Management Organisations
RGDIP	*Revue générale de droit international public*
RNIGA	Règles et normes internationales généralement acceptées
ROE	Rules of Engagement
RSA	*Recueil des sentences arbitrales*
RUDH	*Revue universelle des droits de l'homme*
RUF	Rules concerning/on the use of force
SAR	Search and Rescue
SAR Convention	International Convention on Maritime Search and Rescue of 1979
SC	Security Council (of the United Nations)
SMP	Sociétés militaires et de sécurité privées
Smuggling Protocol	Protocol against the Smuggling of Migrants by Land, Sea and Air of 2000, supplementing the United Nations Convention against Transnational Organized Crime
SOLAS (Convention)	International Convention for the Safety of Life at Sea of 1974
SOP(s)	Standard Operating Procedure(s) (for Shipmasters)
SRR	Search and Rescue Region(s)
SUA (Convention)	Convention pour la répression d'actes illicites contre la sécurité de la sécurité maritime de 1988/ Convention for the Suppression of Unlawful Acts against the Safety of Maritime Navigation of 1988
TEZ	Total Exclusion Zone
TIDM	Tribunal international du droit de la mer
TNP	Traité sur la non-prolifération des armes nucléaires de 1968

UE	Union européenne
UEO	Union de l'Europe occidentale
UNCLOS	United Nations Convention on the Law of the Sea of 1982
UNDOALOS	United Nations Division for Ocean Affairs and the Law of the Sea
UNHCR	Agence des Nations Unies pour les réfugiés
UNHCR	United Nations High Commissioner for Refugees
UNODC	Office des Nations Unies contre la drogue et le crime/United Nations Office on Drugs and Crime
UNTOC/2000 UNTOC	United Nations Convention against Transnational Organized Crime of 2000
USCG	US Coast Guard
VCLT	Vienna Convention on the Law of Treaties of 1969
VPDs	Vessel Protection Detachments
WMD	Weapon(s) of Mass Destruction
ZEE	Zone économique exclusive

AVANT-PROPOS

FOREWORD

LE CENTRE D'ÉTUDE et de recherche de droit international et de relations internationales a consacré sa session de 2012 à la question de « La criminalité en mer ». Lors de la fin du XXe et du début du XXIe siècle, la criminalité maritime est apparue comme un problème tant d'une importance pratique considérable que d'un grand intérêt académique. Une augmentation régulière dans l'éventail des crimes en mer a pris place, crimes à la fois communs et interconnectés, parmi lesquels on peut relever la piraterie et les attaques armées en mer, le trafic de migrants et la traite de personnes, le trafic de drogues et le crime organisé au sein de l'industrie halieutique. L'essor extraordinaire des activités criminelles organisées dans le contexte maritime ne génère pas seulement des préoccupations d'un type pratique, mais présente également un défi légal, trente ans après l'adoption de la « Constitution des océans », la Convention des Nations Unies sur le droit de la mer (1982). Que la décision du Curatorium de l'Académie pour le Centre de recherche 2012 se soit fixée sur ce sujet est donc un choix à la fois hautement pertinent et opportun.

Vingt participants dans les sections anglophone et francophone ont réalisé ce projet avec passion et talent. Le présent volume regroupe un certain nombre des excellents résultats de leur travail, illustrant les efforts dynamiques et industrieux de tous les participants durant leurs trois semaines au Centre. De manière collective, les chapitres de ce volume mettent en évidence, au niveau légal, les défis communs auxquels la coopération internationale doit faire face dans le domaine des crimes en mer et identifient nombre de potentielles faiblesses dans le droit international applicable.

Le Centre 2012 a été une expérience d'enseignement très gratifiante, en raison non seulement de la qualité des chercheurs, du magnifique cadre et de l'équipement de pointe de l'Académie, mais aussi de l'exceptionnel esprit de coopération entre les sections, francophone et anglophone, et entre tous les participants. Bien qu'un sujet différent ait été attribué à chacun d'entre eux, il s'est agi plus généralement d'un projet collégial. Cela s'est illustré à la fois par les discussions formelles dans les séminaires, où chacun a présenté son projet de chapitre et où de très fructueux échanges ont pris place au-delà des barrières linguistiques, et par celles, plus détendues, entre nouveaux amis dans les cafés et restaurants de La Haye. Dans cet esprit de coopération, nous avons aussi organisé avec grand succès deux séminaires joints (français/anglais) lors desquels tous les participants ont activement débattu de questions difficiles, telles que celles liées à la juridiction, à la piraterie et à la responsabilité.

Lors de notre séjour à La Haye, nous avons eu le privilège de décou-

THE CENTRE FOR STUDIES and Research in International Law and International Relations devoted its Session of 2012 to the issue of "Criminal Acts at Sea". The late twentieth and early twenty-first century has seen maritime criminality emerge as an issue of both great practical importance and academic interest. There has been a steady increase in the range of common and interlinked crimes at sea, including piracy and armed robbery at sea, migrant smuggling and trafficking in persons, drug trafficking, and organized crime within the fishing industry. This extraordinary growth in organized criminal activity in the maritime context is not just of practical concern, it also presents a legal challenge 30 years after the adoption of the "Constitution of the Oceans", the 1982 UN Convention on the Law of the Sea. It was thus a particularly insightful and propitious choice of the Curatorium of the Academy to set this topic for the 2012 Research Centre.

Twenty participants from French- and English-speaking sections carried out this project with passion and talent. The present volume includes some of the outstanding products of their work, reflecting the vibrant and industrious efforts of all the participants during their three weeks at the Centre. Collectively, the chapters in this volume underscore the common challenges in international co-operation at the legal level with respect to crimes at sea and identify a number of the potential shortcomings of the applicable international law.

The 2012 Centre has been the most gratifying of teaching experiences owing to the quality of the participating scholars, the beautiful surroundings and state of the art facilities of the Academy, but also in no small measure because of the exceptional spirit of co-operation between the French and English sections and all participants. Even though participants were each assigned a different topic, this was very much a collegiate enterprise, evident both in the formal seminars in which each participant presented a draft paper for discussion purposes (delightfully attended on a cross-lingual basis) and the more informal discussions between new friends in cafes and restaurants throughout The Hague. In this spirit of co-operation, we also organized two very successful joint (French/English) seminars, in which all participants actively engaged in discussing difficult questions of jurisdiction, piracy and responsibility.

During our time in The Hague, we also had the privilege of visiting the

vrir la base de la marine royale néerlandaise à Den Helder, visite qui nous a considérablement aidés à nous assurer que l'approche académique du programme restait connectée aux réalités pratiques de la mise en application, par la marine, des concepts abordés. Egalement très précieuse a été la « Matinée de réflexion », qui a pris place le dernier jour du Centre et lors de laquelle les participants ont présenté leur travail devant de très estimés collègues. Nous leur sommes extrêmement redevables de leurs commentaires pertinents.

Finalement, nous désirons exprimer notre extrême reconnaissance, tout d'abord et surtout au Curatorium de l'Académie de La Haye et au professeur Yves Daudet, qui nous ont confié cette grande responsabilité et cette belle opportunité, ainsi qu'à Mme Sophie de Sèze pour son aide inestimable toujours offerte avec gentillesse. Un mot de remerciement tout particulier doit aussi être adressé à M. Jeroen Vervliet et à ses collègues de la Bibliothèque du Palais de la Paix pour l'excellente bibliographie qu'ils ont préparée à l'intention des participants et pour leur aide enthousiaste tout au long du programme du Centre.

Kimberley N. TRAPP Efthymios D. PAPASTAVRIDIS

Mai 2013

Netherlands Royal Navy Base in Den Helder, which assisted us considerably in ensuring that the scholarly approach of the Hague Academy was alive to the practicalities of naval implementation at sea. Also extremely valuable was the "Matinée de réflexion" organized on the last day of the Centre, in which all the participants presented their work before esteemed colleagues, to whom we are greatly indebted for their insights.

We would also like to acknowledge our debt of gratitude, first and foremost to the Curatorium of the Hague Academy and to Professor Yves Daudet for entrusting us with this great responsibility and opportunity, and to Ms Sophie de Seze for her invaluable (and always kindly offered) assistance. A special word of thanks must also be given to Mr. Jeroen Vervliet and his colleagues at the Library of the Peace Palace for the excellent bibliography that they prepared for the use of the participants and for their enthusiastic assistance during the course of the Session.

Efthymios D. PAPASTAVRIDIS Kimberley N. TRAPP

May 2013

INTRODUCTION

Les rapports des directeurs d'études

The Reports of the Directors of Studies

1 Crimes at Sea: A Law of the Sea Perspective

Efthymios D. Papastavridis *

SECTION 1 INTRODUCTION

Back in 1982, when the contemporary "Constitution of the Oceans", the UN Convention on the Law of the Sea [1], was finally concluded, the problem of criminality at sea was not of primary concern. The division of jurisdictional competences between coastal and flag States seemed adequate to address the then maritime criminality: serious crimes within the internal or territorial waters as well as illicit fishing within the — then new — Exclusive Economic Zone (EEZ) were to be addressed by coastal States, whereas crimes committed on the high seas were to be addressed by flag States. International policing and assertion of jurisdiction by other States on the high seas were confined to a handful of crimes, such as piracy, the slave trade and unauthorized broadcasting.

More than 30 years later the picture is definitely not the same: there is an array of criminal activities at sea, including piracy and armed robbery at sea; maritime terrorism and proliferation of weapons of mass destruction (WMD); migrant smuggling and trafficking in persons; drug trafficking; organized crime within the fishing industry; oil bunkering —all of which challenge the public order of the oceans. These crimes occur in various maritime zones, but predominantly in areas beyond national jurisdiction. In response, States have entered in various multilateral and bilateral agreements and partnerships as well as have increased their policing activities, especially, on the high seas. Several partnerships in various forms have been established to this end, such as the Proliferation Security Initiative (PSI) [2] as well as numerous agree-

---

* Director of Studies of the Centre, English-speaking Section. Lecturer, Democritus University of Thrace; Research Fellow, Academy of Athens.

1. See United Nations Convention on the Law of the Sea, 1833 *UNTS* 397; entered into force 16 November 1994; as at 30 January 2013, LOSC has 165 parties, including the European Community; see at http://www.un.org/Depts/los/reference_files/chronological_lists_of_ratifications.htm#The United Nations Convention on the Law of the Sea (hereinafter, LOSC).

2. PSI is described on the website of the US Department of State as "a global effort that aims to stop trafficking of weapons of mass destruction (WMD), their

ments concluded concerning the interdiction of suspect vessels in this regard, such as the 2005 SUA Protocol[3] or the 2000 Smuggling Protocol[4].

All the above-mentioned illicit activities at sea are inextricably intertwined in the sense that not only do they involve activities of "organized criminal groups" within the meaning of the 2000 UN Convention against Transnational Organized Crime (UNTOC)[5], but often the same organized criminal groups are associated with more than one illicit activity. This poses significant hurdles both in respect of the prevention of such crimes and in respect of the applicable legal framework. It is not surprising that a naval asset engaged, for example, in a counter-piracy operation may encounter a fishing trawler that, while suspected of being engaged in piracy, is actually engaged in smuggling of migrants or drug trafficking. This may necessitate the application of different Rules of Engagement and may jeopardize the effectiveness of the operation in question. Evidently, an area with heightened and multifaceted transnational organized criminal activity, including illegal fishing, human trafficking, piracy, is West Africa.

It is for this reason that an increasing number of multipurpose maritime interdiction operations have been recently launched with a view to patrolling waters and countering all potential threats to maritime security. Such operations are pursuant either to international agreements, such as the 2008 CARICOM Maritime Security Agreement[6] or to inter-

---

delivery systems, and related materials to and from states and non-state actors of proliferation concern": see www.state.gov/t/isn/c10390.htm.

3. Protocol of 2005 to the Convention for the Suppression of Unlawful Acts against the Safety of Maritime Navigation, IMO Doc. LEG/CONF.15/21 (2005), available on the website of the US Department of State at www.state.gov/t/isn/trty/81727.htm (hereinafter, 2005 SUA Protocol). The 2005 SUA Protocol entered into force on 28 July 2010 and as at 30 April 2013 it had 23 parties; see the list of States parties available at http://www.imo.org/About/Conventions/StatusOfConventions/Documents/Status%20-%202013.pdf.

4. 2000 Protocol against the Smuggling of Migrants by Land, Sea and Air, supplementing the United Nations Convention against Transnational Organized Crime, 2241 *UNTS* 507 (entered into force 28 January 2004) (hereinafter, Smuggling Protocol). As at 10 May 2013, the Smuggling Protocol had 135 parties: see http://treaties.un.org/Pages/ViewDetails.aspx?src=TREATY&mtdsg_no=XVIII-12-b&chapter=18&lang=en.

5. "'Organized criminal group' shall mean a structured group of three or more persons, existing for a period of time and acting in concert with the aim of committing one or more serious crimes or offences established in accordance with this Convention, in order to obtain, directly or indirectly, a financial or other material benefit" (UNTOC; Article 2 *(a)*; reprinted in 40 *ILM* (2001), 335).

6. CARICOM Maritime and Airspace Security Cooperation Agreement, signed at Bolans, Antigua and Barbuda on 4 July 2008; available at www.caricom.org/jsp/secretariat/legal_instruments/agreement_maritime_airspace_security_cooperation.pdf (hereinafter, CARICOM Agreement).

agency co-operation agreements. The United States has been engaged in multipurpose operations in the Caribbean Sea as well as the Agency for the Management of Operational Cooperation at the External Borders of the European Union (FRONTEX) lately in the Mediterranean Sea[7].

In addition, the effective repression of transnational organized crime at sea will never be possible without having adequate and precise legislation in place. It is a common observation that very often States sign and ratify treaties, yet they fail in taking the appropriate legislative measures to give teeth to these international instruments. As a consequence, many incidents involving transnational organized crime at sea never reach a trial phase, while it is observed that often national courts assume a divergent and controversial standing in relation to some issues, e.g. drug trafficking[8].

These issues and many others were discussed extensively during the 2012 Centre for Research and Studies of the Hague Academy. This chapter serves as an introduction to the excellent research papers that are found in the present volume. It aims to set the scene for the analysis of the legal framework of "crimes at sea", focusing in particular on questions relating to international law of the sea. Accordingly, it will, first, have regard to the LOSC and its provisions concerning crimes at sea, especially from the perspective of the jurisdictional competences that each State has in the various maritime zones under LOSC. Then, the focus will shift to "maritime criminality" as such: each category of crimes at sea will be presented and the relevant measures taken by the international community will be canvassed. It must be noted, from the outset, that the relevant analysis will be restricted to what occurs at sea and not on dry land, since these questions are brilliantly explored elsewhere[9]. Also, needless to say, it will not be exhaustive in view of the research papers to follow in the Volume at hand.

SECTION 2 LOSC AND CRIMINALITY AT SEA

Paragraph 1 Internal Waters

States enjoy exclusive sovereignty in their internal waters, including ports. This means that no State is obliged to allow

7. For further information regarding FRONTEX, see its website: www.frontex.europa.eu. See also generally R. Weinzierl and U. Lisson, *Border Management and Human Rights: A Study of EU Law and the Law of the Sea*, Berlin, German Institute for Human Rights, 2007, and E. Papastavridis, "Fortress Europe and FRONTEX: Within or Without International Law?", 79 *Nordic Journal of International Law* (2010) 75.

8. See e.g. *United States* v. *Bellaizac-Hurtado and Others*, Case 11-14049 (11th Cir. 2012).

9. See K. Trapp, Chapter 2, *infra*.

foreign vessels into its internal waters and especially its ports, except in cases of distress[10], or where this is provided for in a bilateral or multilateral treaty[11].

With regard to jurisdiction over criminal acts, foreign ships entering a port are subject to the sovereignty of the coastal State; hence, the latter has criminal jurisdiction over them. This notwithstanding, the coastal State usually refrains from exercising criminal jurisdiction over matters involving solely the internal discipline of the ship[12]. Instead, it will exercise criminal jurisdiction in the following cases: (i) when an offence committed on board the ship is serious or it affects or is likely to affect the peace and the good order of the port; (ii) when the intervention of the coastal State is officially requested by the master of the vessel or the port consul of the flag State; (iii) when a non-crew member is involved; (iv) when matters which do not concern the "internal economy" of the foreign vessel, such as pollution, are involved[13].

It is evident that the illicit activities under scrutiny, like drug trafficking or maritime terrorism, will be subject to the jurisdiction of the port State. The latter has also a very significant role to play in fighting illegal fishing and serious maritime pollution. Suffice to mention with regard to illegal fishing Article 23 (1) of the 1995 Fish Stocks Agreement, providing that the port State has not only the right, but also the duty, to adopt measures in accordance with international law, with the aim of promoting "the effectiveness of subregional, regional and global conservation and management measures"[14] as well as the 2009 Agreement

10. See *inter alia*, R. R. Churchill and A. V. Lowe, *The Law of the Sea*, 3rd ed., Manchester, Manchester University Press, 1999, 63 (hereinafter: Churchill and Lowe), and R. Barnes, "Refugee Law at Sea", 53 *ICLQ* (2004), 58. See also Coppens, Chapter 10, *infra*, on the delivery of persons rescued at sea to a port of a place of safety.

11. See, e.g., 1956 Treaty of Friendship, Commerce and Navigation between the Netherlands and the United States of America, Article XIX (2); 285 *UNTS* 232.

12. For long time, theory oscillated between the Anglo-American and the French positions on the reasons why coastal States refrained from exercising jurisdiction over these matters; see G. Gidel, *Le droit international public de la mer*, Vol. 2: *Les eaux intérieures* (reprint), Paris, Douchemin, 1981, 87, and pp. 204-205; A. Clapham, *Brierly's Law of Nations*, 7th ed., Oxford, Oxford University Press, 2012, 215.

13. See M. Hayashi, "Jurisdiction over Foreign Commercial Ships in Ports: A Gap in the Law of the Sea Codification", 18 *Ocean Yearbook* (2004), 505.

14. See UN Agreement for the Implementation of the Provisions of the UNCLOS of 10 December 1982 relating to the Conservation and Management of Straddling Fish Stocks and Highly Migratory Fish Stocks, 1995, 2167 *UNTS* 88 (hereinafter, 1995 Fish Stocks Agreement). For commentary see M. Hayashi, "The 1995 Agreement on the Conservation and Management of Straddling and Highly Migratory Fish Stocks: Significance for the Law of the Sea Convention", 29 *Ocean & Coastal Management* (1995), 51.

on Port State Measures[15]. On the marine pollution front[16], reference should be made to Article 218 (1), LOSC, which sets out:

> "When a vessel is voluntarily within a port or at an off-shore terminal of a State, that State may undertake investigations and, where the evidence so warrants, institute proceedings in respect of any discharge from that vessel outside the internal waters, territorial sea or exclusive economic zone of that State in violation of applicable international rules and standards established through the competent international organization or general diplomatic conference."

Thus, the port State jurisdiction is innovative in the sense that the port State is entitled to take enforcement action against a vessel even where a violation was committed on the high seas or marine spaces under that State's jurisdiction. This port State control is enhanced by many global treaties in the field of pollution regulation and marine safety, such as the 1974 SOLAS Convention[17] and the MARPOL Convention[18]. In addition, port States have formulated regional institutions through Memoranda of Understanding (MoUs), which aim at the effective suppression of such illicit activities[19].

Paragraph 2 **Territorial Waters**

The coastal State exercises sovereignty over its territorial waters, subject, however, to certain restrictions, particularly the right of innocent passage, which ships of all States enjoy[20]. A vessel's passage is considered "innocent" where it is not prejudicial to the peace, good order or security of the coastal State (Article 19 (1), LOSC). LOSC includes a long list of activities and circumstances whereby innocence is deemed as lost, such as fishing, serious pollution, research (Article 19 (2), LOSC). If a foreign vessel engages in such activities the coastal State is

---

15. Agreement on Port State Measures to Prevent, Deter and Eliminate Illegal, Unreported and Unregulated Fishing, adopted in November 2009, Appendix V of the FAO Council, 137th Session, Rome, 28 September–2 October 2009. It has not yet entered into force. See further Oanta, Chapter 4, *infra*.

16. See further Gahlen, Chapter 3, *infra*.

17. International Convention for the Safety of Life at Sea, 1 November 1974, Annex, Chapter 1, Regulation 19, 1184 *UNTS* 2.

18. International Convention for the Prevention of Pollution from Ships of 1973, as modified by the 1978 Protocol, Regulation 11 of Annex I, 1340 *UNTS* 184.

19. See *inter alia* T. McDorman, "Regional Port State Control Agreements: Some Issues of International Law", 5 *Ocean and Coastal Law Journal* (2000) 207.

20. See *Corfu Channel (United Kingdom* v. *Albania)*, Judgment (Merits), *ICJ Reports 1949*, p. 1, p. 28.

entitled to take the necessary steps in its territorial sea to prevent passage which is not innocent in accordance with Article 25 (1). Coastal States may enact legislation only for the range of matters stipulated in Article 21, LOCS. This includes, among others, the safety of navigation, conservation of living resources, and violations of customs or immigration laws.

As regards criminal jurisdiction in general, given that the territorial sea is under the sovereignty of the coastal State, the latter may, in principle, exercise criminal jurisdiction over foreign vessels passing through the territorial sea[21]. Nonetheless, in order to pay due regard to the interests of navigation, Article 27, LOSC, sets out that the criminal jurisdiction of the coastal State "should not" be exercised on board a foreign vessel passing through the territorial sea, save only in the following cases:

> "*(a)* if the consequences of the crime extend to the coastal State; *(b)* if the crime is of a kind to disturb the peace of the country or the good order of the territorial sea; *(c)* if the assistance of the local authorities has been requested by the master of the ship or by a diplomatic agent or consular officer of the flag State; or *(d)* if such measures are necessary for the suppression of illicit traffic in narcotic drugs or psychotropic substances."

The restriction of criminal jurisdiction does not apply to offences on board a foreign ship passing through the territorial sea after leaving internal waters pursuant to Article 27 (2), LOSC.

It follows that the majority of the criminal activities, which are of interest for the international community, would be subject to the coastal State's jurisdiction if they are committed in the territorial waters: (i) *drug trafficking* is explicitly mentioned in Article 27 (1), LOSC; (ii) *smuggling migrants* to the coastal State[22]; and (iii) *illegal fishing* would be in contravention to the domestic laws of that State enacted in accordance with Article 21, LOSC; (iv) *acts of maritime terrorism* would undoubtedly disturb the peace and *ordre public* of the territorial sea (Article 27 (1) LOSC); (v) *piracy jure gentium* takes place on the high seas, albeit *armed robbery* would be criminalized under domestic legislation (Articles 21 and 27); and (vi) concerning the *pollution of marine environment*, Article 220 (2), LOSC provides that

> "Where there are clear grounds for believing that a vessel navigating in the territorial sea of a State has, during its passage

21. See, in general, I. Shearer, "Problems of Jurisdiction and Law Enforcement against Delinquent Vessels", 35 *ICLQ* (1986), 320, at 325-329.
22. See further Guggisberg, Chapter 6, *infra*.

> therein, violated laws and regulations of that State adopted in accordance with this Convention or applicable international rules and standards for the prevention, reduction and control of pollution from vessels, that State . . . may undertake physical inspection of the vessel relating to the violation and may, where the evidence so warrants, institute proceedings, including detention of the vessel, in accordance with its laws."[23]

The only thorny question may arise in respect of foreign vessels carrying illicit material, such as WMD components, and traversing the territorial sea bound to another State. In such cases, LOSC does not seem to afford a clear legal basis for the coastal State to interdict that vessel; only pursuant to other legal bases such as the Security Council (SC) resolution 1540 (2004) or the consent of the flag State[24]. On the other hand, it has been argued, for example, that coastal States may declare the transport of WMD and relevant software as a crime under their national criminal law pursuant to the protective principle and take enforcement action on the basis of Article 27 of LOSC[25].

Paragraph 3 **International Straits**

Less power to exert authority and jurisdiction is granted to the coastal State with respect to straits used for international navigation. Under LOSC, the regime of "non-suspendable innocent passage" through straits is supplemented by another entitlement, i.e. the right of transit passage[26]. The right of transit passage applies only to straits connecting high seas or EEZs with other areas of high seas or EEZs and as long as these are used for international navigation. There are also straits covered by particular treaty regimes (e.g. the Dardanelles)[27].

The LOSC grants the coastal State with the competence to adopt laws and regulations relating to transit passage. By virtue of Article 42 (1), those laws and regulations may be in respect of all or any of the following:

---

23. See further Gahlen, Chapter 3, *infra*.
24. See further discussion in Trapp, Chapter 2, *infra* and Cherief, Chapter 13, *infra*.
25. See, e.g., S. E. Logan, "The Proliferation Security Initiative Navigating the Legal Challenges", (2005) 14 *Journal of Transnational Law and Policy*, 253, 263.
26. See in general H. Caminos, "The Legal Regime of Straits in the 1982 United Nations Convention on the Law of the Sea", 205 *Recueil des cours* (1987), 13-245.
27. See, e.g., the Convention Regarding the Regime of Straits (1936); 31 *AJIL Supplement* (1937), 1-17.

> "*(a)* the safety of navigation and the regulation of maritime traffic, as provided in article 41; *(b)* the prevention, reduction and control of pollution, by giving effect to applicable international regulations regarding the discharge of oil, oily wastes and other noxious substances in the strait; *(c)* with respect to fishing vessels, the prevention of fishing, including the stowage of fishing gear; *(d)* the loading or unloading of any commodity, currency or person in contravention of the customs, fiscal, immigration or sanitary laws and regulations of States bordering straits".

It is submitted that the majority of crimes under scrutiny would be subject to both the legislative and enforcement jurisdiction of the coastal State, especially in view of the provision of Article 42 (1) *(d)* above. A recurring question again would be what about a vessel carrying WMD components or smuggling migrants in transit passage to another State? The answer again would be that the legal basis for any assertion of jurisdiction would not be afforded by LOSC, albeit by the SC resolution 1540 (2004) or another treaty, such as the 2000 Smuggling of Migrants Protocol (Article 8).

Paragraph 4 **Contiguous Zone**

It has been long accepted that coastal States may exercise certain police powers outside their territorial waters in a zone known as the contiguous zone[28], in relation to offences already committed, or in the process of being committed, there. Under Article 33, LOSC,

> "1. . . . the coastal State may exercise the control necessary to: *(a)* prevent infringement of its customs, fiscal, immigration or sanitary laws and regulations within its territory or territorial sea; *(b)* punish infringement of the above laws and regulations committed within its territory or territorial sea.
>
> 2. The contiguous zone may not extend beyond 24 nautical miles from the baselines from which the breadth of the territorial sea is measured."

As Shearer notes,

> "the first limb [of para. 1] applies to inward-bound ships and is anticipatory or preventive in character; the second limb [of para. 1], applying to outward-bound ships, gives more extensive

28. See generally S. Oda, "The Concept of the Contiguous Zone", 11 *ICLQ* (1962), 153.

> power and is analogous to the doctrine of hot pursuit . . . Since laws on the substantive subjects of customs, fiscal, immigration or sanitary matters cannot be applied in the contiguous zone, it follows that an offence cannot be committed until the boundary of the territorial waters is crossed by inward-bound ships. 'Control' therefore must be limited to such measures as inspections and warnings and cannot include arrest or forcible taking into port."[29]

Indeed, Article 33 literally means that the coastal State may exercise only enforcement, not legislative, jurisdiction within its contiguous zone; hence, action of the coastal State may only be taken concerning offences committed within the territory or territorial sea of the latter State and not in respect of anything done within the contiguous zone itself[30]. Moreover, it must be underscored that the contiguous zone would be either part of the high seas or part of the EEZ for States that have declared such zone.

As regards the crimes of our concern, the following comments are in order: coastal States may apprehend in the contiguous zone the outward ships that have committed the relevant offence within the territorial sea either pursuant to Article 33 (e.g. for crimes such as drug trafficking or smuggling of migrants) or pursuant to the doctrine of hot pursuit enshrined in Article 111 of LOSC and discussed later[31] (e.g. for crimes such illicit fishing or terrorism). Insofar as the inward ships are concerned, there seems to be a watershed difference, which, as stressed above, is that typically there has been no violation of the municipal laws of the coastal State. Thus, any assertion of jurisdiction, both prescriptive and enforcement, would have to be premised upon the relevant provisions of LOSC concerning the EEZ, if the coastal State has declared such a zone, or the high seas as well as upon other international agreements.

In more detail, as regards the crimes at sea addressed in this volume:

(i) *illegal fishing:* if the coastal State has declared an EEZ, it can exert jurisdiction under Article 73 (1), LOSC; if not, there has to be a multilateral or bilateral treaty to which both the coastal and the flag State of the delinquent vessel are parties[32], or the consent of the flag State;

(ii) *smuggling of migrants:* save the rare instance of the application of Article 60 (2), LOSC, namely when the smuggling vessel is located

29. Shearer, *supra* footnote 21, at 330.

30. Sir Gerald Fitzmaurice is a leading supporter of this view; see G. Fitzmaurice, "Some Results of the Geneva Conference on the Law of the Sea", 8 *ICLQ* (1959), 114.

31. See *infra* footnote 65 and accompanying text.

32. For example see Article 21 (1) of the1995 Fish Stocks Agreement.

within the safety zone around an artificial island or an installation of the coastal State within its EEZ, all other cases of smuggling of migrants either in the EEZ or on the high seas are to be regulated by other treaties[33];

(iii) *illegal pollution:* similar to illicit fishing, if the coastal State has declared an EEZ, it would suffice to exercise jurisdiction according to Article 56 (1) *(b)*, LOSC, if not, there are few treaties granting such rights[34];

(iv) *drug trafficking:* save again the rare instance of Article 60 (2), LOSC, there must be a bilateral or multilateral agreement granting such enforcement powers or the consent of the flag State;

(v) *maritime terrorism and proliferation of WMD:* there is no legal basis under LOSC for the seizure of an inward-bound ship suspected of being engaged in terrorist acts or carrying WMD material. The coastal State may enforce its jurisdiction pursuant to 2005 SUA Protocol or pursuant to the consent of the flag State.

(vi) *piracy:* beyond the limits of the territorial seas, all States, including the coastal State concerned, may intercept and seize the pirate vessel in accordance with Article 105, LOSC[35].

Paragraph 5 **Exclusive Economic Zone (EEZ)**

By virtue of Article 57, LOSC, coastal States may claim an EEZ up to 200 miles[36]. There, first and foremost, coastal States exercise sovereign rights for the purposes of "exploring and exploiting, conserving and managing" both its living and non-living resources (Art 56). In addition, coastal States enjoy jurisdiction over the establishment and use of artificial islands and installations, marine scientific research, and the preservation of the marine environment in the EEZ, in addition to other (Art. 56 *(b)* and *(c)*, LOSC). As to the juridical nature of the EEZ, it is described as a *sui generis* zone, i.e. a zone subject to a distinct jurisdictional framework and comprised of neither territorial seas nor high seas. Thus, Article 58, LOSC, provides that three of the freedoms of the high seas — i.e. navigation, over-flight, and the laying of cables and pipelines — are exercisable by all States within the EEZ in accordance with the general framework governing the high seas.

---

33. Arguably, certain cases of smuggling of migrants/human trafficking may be assimilated to slave trade.

34. A notable exception is the Protocol Relating to the Intervention on the High Seas in Cases of Pollution by Substances Other than Oil, 1313 *UNTS* 4.

35. See further Grymaneli, Chapter 5, *infra*.

36. On EEZ see generally D. Attard, *The Exclusive Economic Zone in International Law*, Oxford, Clarendon Press, 1987.

As far as the crimes in question are concerned,

(i) *illegal fishing:* it is evident that the coastal State may exercise jurisdiction by virtue of its sovereign rights in this regard. Article 73 (1), LOSC, sets forth that:

> "The coastal State may, in the exercise of its sovereign rights to explore, exploit, conserve and manage the living resources in the exclusive economic zone, take such measures, including boarding, inspection, arrest and judicial proceedings, as may be necessary to ensure compliance with the laws and regulations adopted by it in conformity with this Convention."

(ii) *marine pollution:* several provisions of Part XII of the Convention are relevant to enforcement in the EEZ. Article 210 (5), LOSC, allows the coastal State to "permit, regulate and control dumping in its EEZ". Moreover, national laws and regulations shall be "no less effective" than "global rules and standards", while specific power to enforce these laws and regulations in their EEZ is given to the coastal States by Article 216, LOSC, though that jurisdiction is concurrent with that of the flag State. Under Article 211 (5), LOSC, States may adopt laws and regulations on pollution from vessels conforming to "generally accepted international rules and standards established though the competent international organization" for the purpose of enforcement in their EEZ. Article 220 (3) allows the coastal State only to "require" the offending vessel to give information regarding its identity, route and details of the pollution incident. A series of enforcement measures, however, may be taken where the discharge causes or threatens "significant pollution of the marine environment", including boarding and physical inspection (Article 220 (5), LOSC) and where a discharge causes 'major damage or threat to major damage', namely arrest of the vessel (Article 220 (6), LOSC)[37].

(iii) *drug trafficking:* the coastal State may assert jurisdiction over foreign vessels suspected of being engaged in drug trafficking only with regard to such activities occurring on artificial islands or other installations pursuant to Article 60 (2), LOSC, which states that:

> "[t]he coastal State shall have exclusive jurisdiction over such artificial islands, installations and structures, including jurisdiction with regard to customs, fiscal, health, safety and immigration laws and regulations"[38].

---

37. See Shearer, *supra* footnote 21, at 335, and Gahlen, Chapter 3, *infra*.

38. See also *M/V Saiga No. 2* case (Judgment) (1999), para. 1127, 38 *ILM* 1323, 1351. This provision is similar to that of Article 80, LOSC, which pertains to such installations or islands located on the continental shelf.

A prerequisite for the assertion of such jurisdiction is, of course, the extension by the coastal State of its customs legislation, including legislation concerning drug trafficking, to such islands and installations. In all other cases of drug-trafficking in the EEZ, the regime of the high seas is applicable.

(iv) *smuggling of migrants:* similar to drug trafficking, the coastal State has explicit jurisdiction over such activity only if it takes place in the artificial islands and installations, provided the existence of the necessary legislation[39].

(v) *maritime terrorism and proliferation of WMD:* if the proliferation of WMD components happened to take place in an artificial island in the EEZ, it could be considered as a customs matter and the coastal State could exert jurisdiction. In all other cases, the jurisdictional authority for suppressing such acts could not to be found in LOSC, but in other agreements. Special reference should be made to 1988 SUA Protocol, which concerns directly the installations over the continental shelf[40].

(vi) *piracy:* the regime of the high seas is fully applicable in this respect.

Paragraph 6 **High Seas**

The premise of any discussion about the regime of the high seas is the fundamental principle of the freedom of the high seas, which is predominantly of a negative nature. According to the UN Memorandum on the Regime of the High Seas (1950):

> "The freedom of the high seas, essentially negative, may nevertheless contain positive consequences . . . All maritime flag-States have equal right to put the high seas to legitimate use. But the idea of the equality of usage comes only in second place. The essential idea underlying the principle of freedom of the high seas is the concept of the prohibition of interference in peacetime by ships flying one national flag with ships flying the flag of other nationalities."[41]

---

39. See further Guiggisberg, Chapter 6, *infra*.

40. Protocol for the Suppression of Unlawful Acts against the Safety of Fixed Platforms Located on the Continental Shelf, reprinted in 27 *ILM* (1988), 680; see also the 2005 Protocol for the Suppression of Unlawful Acts against the Safety of Fixed Platforms Located on the Continental Shelf; available at http://www.dipublico.com.ar/english/treaties/protocol-for-the-suppression-of-unlawful-acts-against-the-safety-of-fixed-platforms-located-on-the-continental-shelf-2005-2005-sua-fixed-platforms-protocol/.

41. Memorandum on the Regime of the High Seas, by the Secretariat (1950-II) (14 July 1950), UN doc. A/CN.4/32, reprinted in *Yearbook of the International Law Commission,* 67, 69 (translation). The Memorandum is believed to be the work of Gilbert Gidel.

From this prohibition of interference with non-national vessels flows the principle of exclusivity of flag-State jurisdiction, namely that ships on the high seas are, as a general rule, subject to the exclusive jurisdiction and authority of the State whose flag they lawfully fly[42]. This principle is firmly rooted in the axioms of State equality and of the freedom of the high seas[43]. Thus, it is generally accepted that no State can interfere with the shipping of another State unless the interfering State possesses an exceptional right clearly vested by customary law or pursuant to a particular treaty regime. Although the nature of this interference varies, justifiable acts of interference fall under two general rubrics: the right of approach *(droit de reconnaissance)* and the right of visit *(droit de visite)*.

On the one hand,

> "it is a universally recognised customary rule of international law that warships of all nations, in order to maintain the safety of the high seas, have the power to require suspicious private vessels on the high seas to show their flag"[44].

The right to approach, or *reconnaissance*, is limited to the right to approach a ship to identify her[45]. An approaching warship may request an encountered vessel to show her colours, which are prima facie evidence of her nationality[46]. Without evidence to counter this showing of nationality or further suspicions, a warship may not board the encoun-

42. See generally D. P. O'Connell, *The International Law of the Sea*, Vol. II (ed. I. A. Shearer), Oxford, Clarendon Press, 1984, p. 796; R. Jennings and A. Watts, *Oppenheim's International Law*, 9th ed., London, Longman, 1992, p. 737.

43. It was famously given judicial imprimatur in the dictum of Lord Stowell in the *Le Louis* case:

> "All nations being equal all have an equal right to the uninterrupted use of the unappropriated parts of the oceans for their navigation. In places where no local authority exists, where the subjects of all States meet upon a footing of entire equality and independence, no one State, or any of its subjects, has a right to assume or exercise authority over the subjects of another." *Le Louis,* 2 Dods, 210, 243, 165 Eng. Rep. (1817), 1464, 1475.

See also *"Lotus"* case (*France* v. *Turkey*), Judgment, *PCIJ, Ser. A, No. 10* (1927), 25.

44. *Oppenheim's International Law*, at p. 737.

45. The US Supreme Court has held:

> "In respect to ships of war . . . there is no reason why they may not approach any vessels descried at sea, for ascertaining their real characters. Such a right seems indispensable for the fair and discreet exercise of their authority." See *The Marianna Flora*, 24 US (11 Wheat.) (1826), 1, at 43.

46. See O. de Ferron, *Le droit international de la mer* (1958), pp. 108-109; Y. Van der Mensbrugghe, "Le pouvoir de police des Etats en haute mer", 11 *RBDI* (1975), 56, 61.

tered vessel and, *a fortiori*, may not proceed to examine her papers or perform a search[47].

On the other hand, "under extreme circumstances, the public ships of a state are competent to visit and search the vessel of another State"[48]. The acceptance of the peacetime right of visit *(droit de visite)* has been gradual and controversial, since it was originally conceived as a belligerent right which did not apply in time of peace, unless provided for under a customary or conventional exception to the general rule of non-interference[49]. The traditional non-conventional exceptions were piracy and the right of self-defence, while the conventional exceptions in the nineteenth and early twentieth centuries pertained to fisheries, the protection of submarine cables, the slave trade and anti-smuggling measures[50].

The right of visit is composed of two distinct operations: the *droit d'enquête du pavillon*, i.e. the right of boarding the vessel and of investigation of the flag, and the right of search *(perquisition)*[51].

> "A warship may employ the *droit d'enquête du pavillon* — the first element of the comprehensive *droit de visite* — to ascertain or verify the true nationality of a vessel she encounters upon the high seas. She may exercise her *droit d'enquête* against only those vessels she reasonably suspects of having engaged in some proscribed activity, which, under customary or conventional law, would permit the warship to proceed against the suspect vessel."[52]

To effect a stoppage, of course, the warship will hail the suspect vessel or, if this is impossible or ineffectual, fire across its bow[53]. The actual verification of the flag takes place aboard the suspect vessel,

---

47. See G. Gidel, *Le droit de la mer*, p. 289; François, *Regime of the High Seas*, UN doc. A.CN.A/17, reprinted in ILC *Yearbook* (1950-II), 36, 41; R. Reuland, "Interference with Non-National Ships on the High Seas", 22 *Vanderbilt Journal of Transnational Law* (1989), 1161, 1170.

48. Reuland, *supra* footnote 47, 1170.

49. Gidel wrote that "le droit de visite en temps de paix n'existe pas, sauf exceptions strictement limitées et résultant d'accords conventionnels"; G. Gidel, *Le droit de la mer*, Vol. I, Paris, Etablissements Mellottee Chateauroux, 1932, at p. 292.

50. See extensive discussion of these exceptions in Gidel, *supra* footnote 49, p. 301.

51. There is a certain discrepancy between the Anglo-Saxon and the French doctrines in the use of the relevant terms; for example, the former tend to speak only of a "right of visit and search" and they employ the terms *"reconnaissance"* and *"enquête du pavillon"* to designate what was called "the right of approach"; see *inter alia Oppenheim's International Law*, p. 737; Ortolan, *Règles internationales et diplomatie de la mer,* tome II, Paris, 1864, p. 233.

52. Reuland, *supra* footnote 43, at 1172.

53. See Ortolan, *supra* footnote 47, at 252, and R.-J. Dupuy and D. Vignes, *Traité du nouveau droit de lamer*, Paris, Economica, 1985, p. 371.

which requires that the warship will send a party under the command of an officer to the suspect vessel, who will examine the papers and documentation of the suspect vessel[54]. Only circumstances of extreme suspicion, however, will justify the search of the vessel, which may include a detailed inspection of all parts of the ship and its cargo and the questioning of the crew[55].

The 1958 High Seas Convention codified for the first time in a treaty the peacetime right of visit.[56] Article 22 of the High Seas Convention maintained the above distinction between the right of visit or *"droit d'enquête du pavillon"* and the right of search[57], whereas it remained silent on the question of the customary right of approach. This did not entail, however, that the right of approach ceased to exist, as it was clear that the ILC intended only to codify the right of visit as such. As far as the right of visit *(droit de visite)* as such is concerned, Article 22 of High Seas Convention, and later Article 110 of LOSC, which was primarily based on the former provision[58], set forth that it is accorded to warships against only those vessels reasonably suspected of having engaged in certain proscribed activities. These activities are: *(a)* piracy, *(b)* slave trading, *(c)* unauthorized broadcasting, *(d)* absence of nationality of the ship, or *(e)* though flying a foreign flag or refusing to show its flag, the ship is in reality of the same nationality as the warship[59].

It is true that not all of the above circumstances are relevant in the contemporary era; for example, both the "unauthorised broadcasting"[60] and the "slave trade"[61] provisions have minimal application, whereas,

54. See ILC, *Regime of the High Seas*, Draft Articles, A/CN4/79, Section II, reprinted in ILC *Yearbook* (1955-I), 27. See also L. B. Sohn, "International Law of the Sea and Human Rights Issues", in Clingan (ed.), *The Law of the Sea: What Lies Ahead?*, 1988, p. 56.

55. See *Oppenheim's International Law*, p. 738.

56. See Report of the ILC covering the work of its 8th session (A/3159), Art. 46, ILC *Yearbook* (1956-II), 283, and M. Nordquist (ed.), *UNCLOS 1982: A Commentary* (1993-II), p. 239 (hereinafter, Nordquist, *Commentary*).

57. See Article 22 of the 1958 Geneva Convention on the High Seas, 450 *UNTS* 52.

58. The only substantial changes were the inclusion in the grounds of interference of the "vessel without nationality" and unauthorized broadcasting. On the Third UN Conference on the Law of the Sea (UNCLOS III) in general see R. Platzöder, *Third United Nations Conference on the Law of the Sea*, London, Oceana Publications, 1982-1987 and on Article 110, in particular, see Nordquist, *Commentary*, 239-244.

59. See Churchill and Lowe, p. 203; Nordquist, *Commentary*, p. 237.

60. For a contemporary overview of the "unauthorized broadcasting" see D. Guilfoyle, *Shipping Interdiction and the Law of the Sea*, Cambridge, Cambridge University Press, 2009, pp. 161-171.

61. Nevertheless, it is argued that the relevant provision should be reinvigorated to suppress certain forms of human trafficking; see *infra* footnote 150 and accompanying text.

"piracy", once almost obsolete, has attained greater prominence lately, in view of the recent piratical activity off the coast of Somalia. As regards *(d)* "absence of nationality of the ship", it denotes stateless vessels, i.e. vessels lacking any claim to nationality under Article 91 of LOSC on the basis either of State registration or some other right to fly a State's flag. Under Article 92 (2), LOSC, vessels flying two or more flags according to convenience may also be assimilated to stateless vessels. It needs to be stressed here that in light of the wording of Article 91 (1)[62], vessels may hold nationality independent of registration. For example, "national legal systems commonly only require vessels of certain size to register, and smaller vessels may be entitled to fly the flag of their owner state's nationality without registration"[63]. This is important especially in relation to any exercise of enforcement jurisdiction over the vessel or the persons on board, in the sense that the lack of registration would not mean *ipso facto* that no State exercises jurisdiction over the vessel or the persons.

Furthermore, by virtue of Article 110 (1), other forms of interference can by conferred by treaty on a variety of subjects[64]. Accordingly, States have concluded numerous multilateral and bilateral agreements that provide for the right of visit on the high seas with a view to suppressing illegal activities, such as illegal fishing, drug trafficking, maritime terrorism and WMD. The above-mentioned illicit activities that have given rise to boarding agreements will be discussed in detail in the next Part.

Also, mention should be made to the doctrine of hot pursuit, which is another form of interference recognized by LOSC and customary law[65]. Under Article 111, LOSC,

> "The hot pursuit of a foreign ship may be undertaken when the competent authorities of the coastal State have good reason to believe that the ship has violated the laws and regulations of that State. Such pursuit must be commenced when the foreign ship or one of its boats is within the internal waters, the archipelagic waters, the territorial sea or the contiguous zone of the pursuing State, and may only be continued outside the territorial sea or the

62. "Every State shall fix the conditions for the grant of its nationality to ships, for the registration of ships in its territory, and for the right to fly its flag. Ships have the nationality of the State whose flag they are entitled to fly." Article 91 (1) LOSC.

63. Guilfoyle, *supra* footnote 60, at p. 95 with further references.

64. Both the High Seas Convention and LOSC contain the exception "where acts of interference derive from powers conferred by treaty"; see Articles 22 (1) and 110 (1) respectively.

65. On hot pursuit see *inter alia* N. Poulantzas, *The Right of Hot Pursuit in International Law*, 2nd ed., The Hague, Martinus Nijhoff, 2002.

> contiguous zone if the pursuit has not been interrupted . . . If the foreign ship is within a contiguous zone, as defined in article 33, the pursuit may only be undertaken if there has been a violation of the rights for the protection of which the zone was established.
>
> 2. The right of hot pursuit shall apply *mutatis mutandis* to violations in the exclusive economic zone or on the continental shelf, including safety zones around continental shelf installations, of the laws and regulations of the coastal State applicable in accordance with this Convention to the exclusive economic zone or the continental shelf, including such safety zones."

Finally, it is worth mentioning that although it is common ground that the LOSC does not directly bear on the law of naval warfare[66], this does not mean that the law of the sea does not have any impact on the law regulating armed conflict at sea. As Natalie Klein reports:

> "the arguments have varied from one extreme to the other — from considering that UNCLOS is not applicable during the armed conflict[67], to UNCLOS being applicable because the laws of naval warfare are no longer relevant with the changes in laws relating to when States may lawfully resort to force[68]. As may be expected, a more moderate position whereby 'the maritime rights and duties States enjoy in peacetime continue to exist, with minor exceptions, during armed conflict' is the most tenable view."[69]

Indeed, LOSC has an extensive impact on the rules defining the "regions" of naval operations, and especially the extent of these regions. Belligerent measures may be exercised on the high seas or in the territorial seas of belligerents, but not in areas under the sovereignty of neutral States[70].

66. While none of the 1958 Geneva Conventions expressly so provide, it is true that the International Law Commission, which prepared draft articles on the subject, intended the articles to apply in time of peace; see ILC *Yearbook* (1956-II), 256. The LOSC is similarly silent, although here, too, it was understood that the Conference was concerned with the peacetime law of the sea; see A. V. Lowe, "The Commander's Handbook on the Law of Naval Operations and the Contemporary Law of the Sea", in H. Robertson (ed.), *The Law of Naval Operations*, Newport, Naval War College Press, 1991, pp. 109, 132.

67. See *inter alia* B. Wilson and J. Kraska, "American Security and the Law of the Sea", 40 *Ocean Development and International Law* (2009), 268, 277.

68. See A. V. Lowe, *supra* footnote 66, at pp. 130-133.

69. N. Klein, *Maritime Security and the Law of the Sea,* Oxford, Oxford University Press, 2011, p. 259. See also G. K. Walker, "Self-defence, the Law of Armed Conflict and Port Security", 5 *South Carolina Journal of International Law and Business* (2009), 347.

70. See W. Heinegg (ed.), *Regions of Operations of Naval Warfare*, Bochum, Brockmeyer, 1995, pp. 19–29.

Belligerent measures, such as naval blockade, the belligerent right of visit and search, perfidy had been discussed during the 2012 Centre with the emphasis placed upon whether they could give rise to war crimes at sea. Sergis's chapter provides an excellent overview of this issue[71]. Notwithstanding the paucity of the relevant incidents, the *MV Marmara* episode off the Gaza strip gave some food for thought in this regard[72]. And it may be destined to give more food for thought, should the ICC initiate criminal proceedings against Israeli officials pursuant to the recent (on 14 May 2013) referral of the case to the ICC by Comoros[73].

SECTION 3 CRIMINAL ACTIVITIES CHALLENGING THE PUBLIC ORDER OF THE OCEANS

Paragraph 1 Maritime Terrorism and the Proliferation of Weapons of Mass Destruction (WMD)

A. Introduction

It was after the unprecedented terrorist attacks on the United States on 11 September 2001 that States and the international community as a whole were forced to take into serious consideration the threats posed by maritime terrorism and by the proliferation of Weapons of Mass Destruction (WMD)[74]. These threats have been the object of much public and academic concern as well as of numerous unilateral or multilateral efforts by individual States and by international organizations. Suffice it to refer to the Proliferation Security Initiative (PSI), which was initially conceived as a "collection of interdiction partnerships" among eleven core members[75], but it has subsequently expanded to a multifaceted international effort to combat the transfer of banned

71. See Sergis, Chapter 14, *infra*.

72. See *inter alia*, Report of the Secretary-General's Panel of Inquiry on 31 May 2010 (September 2011); D. Guilfoyle, "The *Mavi Marmara* Incident and Blockade in Armed Conflict", 81 *BYIL* (2011), 171, and Sergis, *op. cit.*

73. See further information at http://www.icc-cpi.int/iccdocs/otp/Referral-from-Comoros.pdf, and comments by D. Akande at http://www.ejiltalk.org/court-between-a-rock-and-a-hard-place-comoros-refers-israels-raid-on-gaza-flotilla-to-the-icc/ (15 May 2013).

74. See, e.g., the 2004 UN High-Level Panel Report emphasized that preventing the proliferation of nuclear, chemical, and biological weapons materials and their potential use must remain an urgent priority for collective security; see Report of the UN Secretary-General's High-Level Panel on Threats, Challenges and Change, (2004), p. 39. See further Cherief, Chapter 13, *infra*, examining the relationship between the regime applicable to the proliferation of weapons of areas destruction by non-State actors and the NPT.

75. See J. Garvey, "The International Institutional Imperative for Countering the Spread of WMD", 10 *Journal of Conflict and Security Law* (2005), 125, 129.

weapons and weapons technology, receiving the support of another eighty States[76]. In addition, reference should be made to the UN Security Council resolutions 1373 (2001)[77] and 1540 (2004)[78]; the IMO SOLAS Amendments[79], the 2005 SUA Protocol, and a plethora of other unilateral and bilateral measures in this regard[80].

B. The law of the sea and maritime terrorism/proliferation of WMD

As regards the law of the sea, it is true that there is no reference to terrorism, let alone WMD, in the LOSC. Nonetheless, as discussed above, LOSC can be used to find out which jurisdictional powers States have to prescribe and enforce laws concerning terrorist activities at sea. Accordingly, a coastal State has the power to enact and enforce laws concerning maritime terrorism and the proliferation of WMD in its internal waters, usually in its ports, and in its territorial waters. Such laws are also required by the relevant UN Security Council resolutions (1373 (2001) and 1540 (2004) on terrorism and WMD respectively). The question whether the coastal State can intercept a vessel flying a foreign flag and engaged in such activities was addressed in the previous Section. On the high seas, the most pertinent provision is Article 110 of LOSC; it is readily apparent that neither international terrorism nor the proliferation of WMD is contemplated by the Convention as a specific ground for the right to visit of a foreign vessel. As a result, the requisite legal basis should be either extrapolated from the grounds for interference that are enshrined in the above provision, or be sought in another legal framework.

First, it is clear that the unauthorized broadcasting and the slave-trade grounds are completely irrelevant to the present survey. Moreover, the "same nationality" ground seems not to raise any particular problems, since in this case the vessel will be susceptible to the full jurisdiction of the flag State pursuant to Article 92 of LOSC. The grounds of "the absence of nationality" as well as "piracy", however, merit scrutiny. As far as the former ground is concerned, it is very often the case that the

76. See US Department of State, Proliferation Security Initiative Participants (as of 10 September 2011), available at http://www.state.gov/t/isn/c27732.htm.

77. SC res. 1373 (28 September 2001) UN doc. S/RES/1373. See M. Happold, "Security Council Resolution 1373 and the Constitution of the UN", 16 *Leiden Journal of International Law* (2003) 93.

78. SC res. 1540 (27 April, 2004) UN doc. S/RES/1540. See also S. Sur, "La Resolution 1540 du Conseil de Securité (28 Avril 2004)", 104 *RGDIP* (2004), 855.

79. See *inter alia* G. Hesse, "Maritime Security in a Multilateral Context", 18 *International Journal of Marine and Coastal Law* (2003), 327.

80. See A. J. Roach, "Initiatives to Enhance Maritime Security at Sea", 28 *Marine Policy* (2004), 41.

transportation of persons involved in terrorist actions or of WMD and related materials is carried out using non-registered vessels, without name or flag, i.e. stateless vessels. To exemplify this, suffice to mention the *M/V So San* incident.

On 10 December, 2002, Spanish naval forces patrolling the Arabian Sea were alerted by US intelligence to the presence of a suspicious cargo vessel in the Indian Ocean en route from North Korea. While the suspect vessel, which displayed no flag, had initially undertaken evasive manœuvres, Spanish forces succeeded in intercepting and boarding the vessel 600 miles from the coast of Yemen. Upon searching the vessel, the inspecting team discovered a cache of 15 Scud missiles, although only the cement shipment was listed on the ship's manifest. Because the vessel which was later determined to be registered in Cambodia, as the *So San*, was not flying any flag, the Spanish authorities acted lawfully under the LOSC in boarding the ship. On the next day, however, the vessel was released with its cargo and was allowed to continue on to Yemen. Spain acknowledged the lack of authority for seizing the missiles since the sale between North Korea and Yemen as well as the transport of ballistic missiles by sea was not prohibited under any international instrument[81].

This incident highlights also the jurisdictional deficit of the above provision, i.e. the right to visit stateless vessels does not *ipso facto* entail the full extension of the jurisdictional powers of the boarding States. This runs counter to a significant strand of legal doctrine, which supports that the boarding States may also completely subject stateless vessels to their laws[82]. Nevertheless, as was demonstrated in the *M/V So San* episode, Article 110, LOSC, does not accord any further jurisdictional powers vis-à-vis stateless vessels than the right of visit. In the present case, the transport of ballistic missiles by sea is not prohibited under any international instrument and thus there is not any legal justification for the confiscation of the cargo and the arrest of the crew members. Nonetheless, there will be cases involving international terrorism where the visit of a stateless vessel will be followed by the arrest of the suspects pursuant to principles, such as the passive nationality[83].

81. See the detailed legal assessment in D. Guilfoyle, "The PSI: Interdicting Vessels in International Waters to Prevent the Spread of WMD?", 29 *Melbourne University Law Review* (2005), 733, 735.

82. This is in accord with the practice by the United Kingdom and the United States, that a stateless vessel may be seized by any State as it enjoys the protection of none; see: D. P. O'Connell, *The International Law of the Sea*, *supra* footnote 42, p. 756.

83. See *United States* v. *Yunis*, 681 F. Supp. 896, 902 (D.D.C. 1988), aff'd, 924 F. 2d 1086 (D.C. Cir. 1991); see also M. Halberstam, "Terrorism on the High Seas", 82 *AJIL* (1988), 269, at 297-298.

With regard to piracy, and whether it could be employed as justification for the visit of vessels involved in international terrorism, suffice to refer to the extended debate following the *Achille Lauro* incident[84], where the rules of piracy were arguably considered as the best legal vehicle to address the problem of maritime terrorism[85]. Nevertheless, the question of maritime terrorism, especially in cases like the *Achille Lauro*, where the two-ship requirement is missing, falls beyond the scope of piracy *jure gentium*. Nevertheless, there will be situations that despite the political ends involved, the lack of "a due authority" and "legitimate targets" will be decisive for the designation of certain terrorist acts concerned as *acta pirata* under customary law. For example, any such act by a recognized belligerent or rebel group against vessels of third States and not of the State towards which they are in revolt, regardless of its motive, would not fall within the "political ends" exception and thus if the other requirements of Article 101 of LOSC exist, it could be considered as piracy[86].

C. Other initiatives to counter maritime terrorism and the proliferation of WMD

Firstly, reference should be made to resolutions 1373 (2001) and 1540 (2004) on terrorism and WMD respectively, which marked a significant departure from the traditional understanding of the Council's role and powers under Chapter VII and the beginning of a new chapter of quasi-legislative action of the Council in these areas. In more detail and in chronological order, the Security Council passed resolution 1373 on 28 September 2001, only 17 days after the terrorist attacks on New York and Washington, DC. The resolution commences by "reconfirming that such acts, like any act of international terrorism, constitute a threat to international peace and security". In its operative paragraphs, resolution 1373 decides that all States shall prevent and suppress the financing of terrorist acts, including by criminalizing terrorist fund-raising and donation activities, and by freezing assets of known terrorist individuals or entities. It goes on that all States shall take necessary steps to prevent the commission of terrorist acts, deny safe haven to those who finance, plan or support terrorist acts, and

84. On the *Achille Lauro* incident see *inter alia* A. Cassese, *Terrorism, Politics and the Law, the Achille Lauro Affair*, Polity Press, 1989.

85. See, e.g., Y. Dinstein, "Terrorism and War of Liberation", in C. Bassiouni (ed.), *International Terrorism and Political Crimes*, 1975, p. 164.

86. See in this regard D. Guilfoyle, "Piracy off Somalia: UN Security Council Resolution 1816 and IMO Regional Counter-Piracy Efforts", 57 *ICLQ* (2008) 690, 693. See also *Castle John and Nenderlandse Stichting Sirius* v. *Nv Marjlo and Nv Parfin* (1986), 77 *ILR* 537.

ensure that any person who participates in terrorist acts is brought to justice[87].

On 28 April 2004 the Security Council passed resolution 1540. In this resolution, the Council undertook to address a number of fundamental loopholes in the existing non-proliferation treaties and regimes system. First, it centred its focus on non-State actors. Existing treaties and regimes assume that only States have the intention and capabilities to develop WMD[88]. The resolution addresses this non-State actor problem in paragraph 1, in which it provides that

> "all States shall refrain from providing any form of support to non-state actors that attempt to develop, acquire, manufacture, possess, transport, transfer or use nuclear, chemical or biological weapons and their means of delivery".

It is questioned whether these "generic" or legislative resolutions[89] may afford the requisite legal basis for interdiction operations in order to suppress non-State actors engaged in terrorist acts and/or in the proliferation of WMD. It is obvious that on the footing of the actual words used in the resolutions such a proposition finds no warrant. There is no explicit authorization for any interdiction operations on the high seas for the present purposes. Moreover, it is important to stress that in the drafting of what is now operative paragraph 10 of the SC resolution 1540, China was adamant in rejecting any reference to the word "interdiction", included in the tabled drafts[90]. In its final version, paragraph 10 calls upon all States, in accordance with national and international law, to "take cooperative action to prevent illicit trafficking in nuclear, chemical or biological weapons, their means of delivery and related materials". The exhortatory nature of the latter provision in conjunction with, on the one hand, the deletion of the word "interdiction" from the final draft and on the other, the explicit reference to international law, reflects the collective will of the Council in the resolution not to authorize any such operation[91]. It bears also reiterating that, in general, SC resolutions

---

87. See also S. Szurek, "La Lutte Internationale contre le Terrorisme", 109 *RGDIP* (2005), 5. See also Cherief, Chapter 13, *infra*.

88. See P. van Ham and O. Bosch, "Global Non-Proliferation and Counter-Terrorism: The Role of Resolution 1540 and Its Implications", in O. Bosch and P. Van Ham (eds.), *Global Non-Proliferation and Counter-Terrorism: The Impact of UNSCR 1540* (2007), pp. 3, 9.

89. See S. Talmon, "The Security Council as World Legislature", 99 *AJIL* (2005), 175, 190.

90. See UNSC Verbatim Record (22 April 2004), UN doc. S/PV.4950 (Resumption 1), at p. 6 and also comments in S. Logan, "The PSI Navigating the Legal Challenges", 14 *Journal of Transnational Law and Policy* (2005), 253, 270.

91. See *per* this view N. Klein, *Maritime Security and the Law of the Sea*, OUP, 2011, p. 283. *Contra* W. Heinegg, "Maritime Interception/Interdiction

under Chapter VII should be construed *stricto sensu* and any unilateral action involving the use or threat of force should not lightly be presumed[92].

Secondly, reference should be made to the role of the IMO and specifically to the revision of the SUA Convention and Protocol in 2005. While the original 1988 SUA Convention and Protocol provided for the arrest, detention, and extradition of alleged offenders with respect to certain categories of acts of violence committed on board or against unlawful shipping, it lacked an effective means to apprehend offenders[93]. "The inclusion of a procedure in the 2005 Protocol to allow states to board ships marks a shift from merely providing lawful bases to establish jurisdiction to creating the means to exercise jurisdiction."[94] Indeed, the 2005 SUA Protocol sets out in Article 8*bis* procedures by which States parties may request flag States of suspect vessels to permit boarding outside the territorial sea of any State and thus it represents the latest exception to the traditional rules relating to the exclusive jurisdiction of the flag State over its vessels when those vessels are on the high seas. Noteworthy also is that the 2005 Protocol and the above SC resolutions complement each other, in the sense that while resolution 1540 proscribes the manufacture, possession, transport of WMD by non-State actors, the Protocol comes to criminalize the use of the latter weapons for terrorist purposes.

This comprehensive list of offences enshrined in the new Article 3 of the 2005 SUA Protocol would be ineffective without the reciprocal framework for interdiction of State parties' vessels suspected of such offences on the high seas stipulated in Article 8 *bis*. In substance, Article 8 *bis* is premised on the scenario of a State party wishing to board a vessel that either flies the flag or displays marks of registry of another State party and is "located seaward of any State's territorial sea", i.e. on the high seas or in the EEZ[95]. According to Article 8 *bis* (5), a State party wishing to board a ship flying the flag of another Party should proceed to the following two requests: the first is simply the confirmation of nationality; only upon confirmation of nationality will

Operations within the Framework of Operation Enduring Freedom", in *Les nouvelles menaces contre la paix et la sécurité internationales*, Pedone, 2004, pp. 149, 158.

92. See E. Papastavridis, "Interpretation of Security Council Resolutions under Chapter VII in the Aftermath of the Iraqi Crisis", 56 *ICLQ* (2007), 83-117.

93. On SUA Convention and Protocol see also G. Plant, "The Convention for the Suppression of Unlawful Acts against the Safety of Maritime Navigation", 39 *ICLQ* (1990), 27.

94. N. Klein, "The Right of Visit and the 2005 SUA Protocol", 35 *Denver Journal of International Law and Policy* (2007), 287, 288.

95. See Article 8 *bis* (5).

the requesting Party ask for authorization to board and take appropriate measures, including stopping, boarding, searching of the ship and the searching and questioning of persons on board.

The 2005 SUA Protocol follows an approach similar to the other relevant treaties, i.e. it fully adheres to the principle of preferential flag State jurisdiction, with the sole exception of the consensual conferment of the jurisdiction to the requesting or another Party [96]. This conferment, however, is contingent upon the establishment of jurisdiction by the requesting or the other Parties pursuant to Article 6 of the SUA Convention. In addition, if the boarding State takes the alleged offenders in its territory, then it is obliged either to establish the requisite jurisdiction or extradite them (*aut dedere aut judicare* principle) [97].

Finally, we must have regard to the PSI and the relevant bilateral agreements. As regards the exact legal nature of the PSI, its authors have consistently characterized it as "an activity, not organization" and as "a collection of interdiction partnerships" [98], while academic doctrine share the same view designating it as an "international partnership of countries" [99], or a "loose alliance". In respect of the interdiction of suspect vessels on the high seas, it is submitted that the PSI does not afford by itself any legal basis for such interdiction operations. Despite concerns and assertions to the contrary [100], the PSI never purported to establish an autonomous legal authority for the interception of WMD shipments on the high seas and this was emphatically stated in the Statement of Interdiction Principles [101].

In view of the fact that the PSI falls short of providing a sufficient legal basis for interdictions on the high seas, the United States shifted its attention to concluding bilateral agreements that put in place a framework for consensual boardings of vessels flying the flag of the respective parties on the high seas. Accordingly, the United States has signed agreements with 11 major-flag States, namely Liberia, Panama, the Mar-

96. See Article 8 *bis* (8).

97. See Article 6 (4) of the SUA Convention. See further discussion Cheah, Chapter 8, *infra*.

98. Bureau of Non-proliferation, US Department of State, *PSI (Continued) Frequently Asked Questions (FAQ)*, 11 January 2005; available at http:// www.state.gov/t/np/rls/fs/32725.htm.

99. J. Garvey, "The International Institutional Imperative for Countering the Spread of Weapons of Mass Destruction: Assessing the Proliferation Security Initiative", 10 *Journal of Conflict and Security Law* (2005), 125, 129.

100. See in this respect A. Bergin, "The PSI: Implications for the Indian Ocean", *International Journal for Marine and Coastal Law* (2005), 85, at 87.

101. See D. Rothwell, "The Proliferation Security Initiative: Amending the Convention on the Law of the Sea by Stealth?", in D. Caron and H. N. Scheiber (eds.), *The Oceans in the Nuclear Age: Legacies and Risks*, Leiden, Martinus Nijhoff Pub., 2010, p. 285, at p. 287.

shall Islands, Croatia, Cyprus, Malta, Belize, Mongolia and Bahamas, St. Vincent and the Grenadines, and Antigua and Barbuda[102].

In summary, all these ship-boarding agreements refer to suspect vessels, defined as ships "used for commercial or private purposes in respect of which there are reasonable grounds to suspect it is engaged in proliferation by sea", the latter being described as the "transportation by ship of WMD, their delivery systems and related materials to and from States or non-State actors of proliferation concern". They all work within the framework of flag-State consent, upholding the requirement of flag-State permission to board a vessel on the high seas and the primacy of its jurisdiction to prosecute any offences discovered aboard.

Paragraph 2 **Drug Trafficking**

A. Introductory remarks

Although a wide variety of methods are utilized by drug traffickers in plying their trade, the use of private and commercial vessels has long been significant. This is particularly the case with drugs such as cocaine, opium and its derivatives, and cannabis, all regulated by the Single Convention on Narcotics Drugs, as amended[103], where transportation from source to consumer country frequently involves passage over ocean areas[104]. For example, given its relative widespread availability and low cost, the vast majority of marijuana and cocaine entering the United States from abroad is said to be transported by private vessels[105]. As is reported by the UN Office on Drugs and Crime (UNODC),

> "For the North American market, cocaine is typically transported from Colombia to Mexico or Central America by sea and then onwards by land to the United States and Canada. Cocaine is trafficked to Europe mostly by sea, often in container shipments. Colombia remains the main source of the cocaine found in Europe, but direct shipments from Peru and the Plurinational State of Bolivia are far more common than in the United States market."[106]

---

102. The text of all these agreements is available at http://www.state.gov/t/isn/c27733.htm.

103. See Single Convention on Narcotic Drugs (1961), 520 *UNTS* 151; as amended by the 1972 Protocol, 976 *UNTS* 3.

104. See P. Van der Kruit, *Maritime Drug Interdiction in International Law*, Utrecht, Druk OBT/TDS, 2007, p. 21

105. See W. Gilmore, "Narcotics Interdiction at Sea, US-UK Cooperation", *Marine Policy* (1989), 218.

106. See at www.unodc.org/unodc/en/drug-trafficking/index.html. The 2011 World Drugs Report-Executive Summary issued by the UNODC recorded that

> "since 2006 seizures have shifted towards the source areas in South

Also, the means employed by the drug-traffickers in Central America have become highly sophisticated: apart from "go-fast" vessels[107], they use semi-submersible vessels, which are almost impossible to be properly stopped and visited[108]. Such vessels are

> "both difficult for the Coast Guard to detect and easy for crew-members, who often prefer losing their cargo to being caught, to sink. At the first sign of the Coast Guard, drug traffickers can quickly sink the vessel and jump into the ocean, which destroys the evidence necessary to prosecute them for a drug offense . . ."[109]

This traffic by sea has led to various initiatives taken by those States most affected, such as the United States and European countries. Central to this has been the policy of interception of vessels not only in the territorial waters of the consumer States, but also on the high seas and even further in the territorial waters of the source or transit States. This policy has been effectuated either through informal means, i.e. *ad hoc* consent of the flag State or of the vessel's master (consensual boarding), or through bilateral and multilateral treaties, such as the Caribbean ship rider agreements[110] and the 1988 UN Convention against

---

America and away from the consumer markets in North America and West and Central Europe. The role of West Africa in cocaine trafficking from South America to Europe might have decreased if judged from seizures only, but there are other indications that traffickers may have changed their tactics, and the area remains vulnerable to a resurgence in trafficking of cocaine"; see www.unodc.org/documents/data-and-analysis/WDR2011/WDR2011-ExSum.pdf.

107. These are typically 25-50-ft open boats, powered by twin outbound engines and capable of sustaining speed of 20-40 knots in 1-3-ft seas. Such boats present significant detection problems and their high speed enables them to escape into foreign territorial waters when confronted by the possibility of interdiction on the high seas; see W. Gilmore, *Agreement concerning Co-operation in Suppressing Illicit Maritime and Air Trafficking in Narcotic Drugs and Psychotropic Substances in the Caribbean Area*, London, The Stationery Office, 2005, p. 2 (hereinafter, Gilmore, *Caribbean Agreement*).

108. It is reported that "One self-propelled semi-submersible vessel intercepted by the Coast Guard, for example, contained seven tons of cocaine, worth 187 million"; see A. Bennett, "The Sinking Feeling: Stateless Ships, Universal Jurisdiction, and the Drug Trafficking Vessel interdiction Act", 37 *Yale Journal of International Law* (2012), 433, 434.

109. *Ibid.*, 434.

110. The problem of maritime illicit traffic of narcotic drugs is particularly acute in the Caribbean region, where there are a number of contiguous nations separated by relatively narrow bodies of water which serve, for the smugglers, as natural "stepping stones" between source and consumer States. These nations provide the "quintessential drug trafficking havens due to their sparse populations and limited enforcement capability"; see K. Rattray, "Caribbean Drug Challenges", in M. Nordquist and J. N. Moore (eds.), *Ocean Policy: New Institutions, Challenges and Opportunities*, The Hague, Nijhoff, 1999, pp. 179, 185.

Illicit Traffic in Narcotic Drugs and Psychotropic Substances, respectively[111].

B. Drug trafficking and the law of the sea

The point of departure for the following assessment is necessarily the LOSC. The various provisions concerning the assertion of both legislative and enforcement jurisdiction in the various maritime zones have discussed previously. In relation to the high seas, it is evident on the face of Article 110 that drug trafficking is not contemplated by the Convention as a specific ground for the right to visit of a foreign vessel. The LOSC only refers to illicit drug trafficking on the high seas in Article 108 and only asks that States co-operate in its suppression[112].

In more detail, paragraph 1 sets out a general obligation for all States to co-operate, when the illicit traffic is "contrary to international conventions". This obligation depends on the content of the above-mentioned Drug Conventions as well as that it is an obligation of conduct rather than result[113]. On the other hand, paragraph 2 addresses the issue of providing assistance to suppress the traffic in question. Nevertheless, only the State "which has reasonable grounds for believing that the ship flying *its* flag is engaged in illicit traffic" in such drugs or substances "may request the co-operation of other States to suppress such traffic"[114]. As Sohn observes, "The opposite case of a State asking for cooperation of a State whose ship is suspected of smuggling drugs to other countries is noticeably not mentioned."[115] Consequently, Article 108 falls short of providing any enforcement mechanism to complement the obligation to co-operate enshrined in paragraph 1. This, in conjunction with the

111. See UN Convention against Illicit Traffic in Narcotic Drugs and Psychotropic Substances (Vienna, 19 December 1988), 21 *ILM* (1988) 1261 (hereinafter, 1988 Vienna Convention). As at 20 May 2013, the Convention had 188 States parties; see http://treaties.un.org/Pages/ViewDetails.aspx?src=TREATY&mtdsg_no=VI-19&chapter=6&lang=en. For commentary see inter alia UN Economic and Social Council, *Commentary on the UN Convention against Illicit Traffic in Narcotic Drugs and Psychotropic Substances 1988* (1998) (hereinafter, Vienna *Commentary*).

112. The provision in question was proposed for the first time by Malta at the 1971 session of the Sea-Bed Committee; see A/AC183/53, Art. 16, reproduced in SBC Report 1971, pp. 105, 123. See also Nordquist, *Commentary*, 224.

113. Cf. Bellayer-Roille writing that

> "Une obligation de coopération est donc bien inscrite dans cet article, mais il ne s'agit en réalité que d'une obligation d'une 'obligation théorique', reposant sur la bonne volonté des Etats et, a fortiori, sur leur capacité réelle de réaction"; *idem*, "La lutte contre le narcotrafic en mer Caraïbe", 111 *RGDIP* (2007), 355, 365.

114. Emphasis added; see Nordquist, *Commentary*, 224.

115. See Sohn, *supra* footnote 54, at p. 60.

absence of any explicit reference to drug trafficking in Article 110, LOSC, entails that in principle the LOSC and the respective customary law fail to furnish any basis for boarding drug smuggling vessels on the high seas [116].

In consequence, the only relevant heading under Article 110 of LOSC is the "absence of nationality", since none of the other grounds, i.e. piracy, slave trade, unauthorized broadcasting and the same nationality, would be applicable. Many drug traffickers operate in unregistered, stateless vessels, in which case Article 110 (1) *(d)* of LOSC applies. It is pursuant to this provision that warships or other duly authorised vessels of any State may exercise the right of visit on these vessels, but not to assert also jurisdiction, as explained above.

However, there is a case in which the statelessness of the vessel suffices not only for the boarding but also for the assertion of jurisdiction *per se*; this is the case of submersible or semi-submersible vessels according to the Drug Trafficking Vessel Interdiction Act (DTVIA), adopted by the US Congress in 2008 [117]. The DTVIA purports to address the practical difficulties posed by the use of such vessels by criminalizing the operation of a submersible or semi-submersible vessel without nationality and with the intent to evade detection. Unlike other relevant laws, the DTVIA does not use a vessel's statelessness solely as a jurisdictional hook, but makes the operation of a stateless vessel a key component of the substantive crime it proscribes [118]. In *United States* v. *Ibarguen-Mosquera,* the Eleventh Circuit upheld the DTVIA without noting any significant difference between the jurisdictional requirements of the DTVIA and of previous laws: in the words of the Court, "international law permits any nation to subject stateless vessels on the high seas to its jurisdiction . . . Jurisdiction exists solely as a consequence of the vessel's status as stateless. [119]

C. Other instruments to counter drug trafficking at sea

The most important multilateral instrument in this regard is the 1988 Vienna Convention, which contains provisions speci-

116. This was the reason that, for example, the boarding of the Honduran flagship *Fidelio*, loaded with several tones of hashish, by the Italian authorities on the high seas in 1986 was declared illegal by the Court of Appeal of Palermo in a Judgment of 30 June 1992; see further analysis in T. Scovazzi, "The Evolution of International Law of the Sea: New Issues and New Challenges", 286 *Recueil des cours* (2000), 39, 225.

117. 18 USCA, § 2285 (West, 2011).

118. Bennett, *supra* footnote 108, p. 434.

119. 634 F. 3d 1370 (llth Cir. 2011), at 1379 (quoting *Marino-Garcia* 6, 79 F. 2d at 1382). The 1lth Circuit also upheld the DTVIA in *United States* v. *Saac*, 632 F. 3d 1203, 1210-1211 (11th Cir. 2011).

fically directed to traffic at sea, including the right to board the vessels of other State parties engaged in illicit drug traffic. The Convention in question had been the outcome of protracted negotiations between States and various UN bodies since 1982[120]. In respect of the right to board the vessel, Article 17 (3) reads as follows:

> "A Party which has reasonable grounds to suspect that a vessel exercising the freedom of navigation in accordance with international law and flying the flag or displaying marks of registry of another Party is engaged in illicit traffic may so notify the flag State, request confirmation of registry and, if confirmed, request authorisation from the flag State to take appropriate measures in regard to that vessel."

This provision should be scrutinized in relation both to Article 17 as a whole, entitled "illicit traffic by sea", and to other key provisions of the Vienna Convention, with which it is inextricably linked. For example, while the focus of the article in question is on facilitating the exercise of enforcement jurisdiction in relation to suspect vessels, the overall effectiveness of the scheme is contingent upon the possession by States of appropriate prescriptive jurisdiction, which is accorded by Article 4[121].

The most significant remark is that Article 17 (3) requires the explicit "authorisation" of the flag State, a word which was included after lengthy informal consultations. As it is pointed out in the *travaux préparatoires*, this word was deliberately used to

> "stress the positive nature of the decision and of the action which the flag State in the exercise of its sovereignty was to take with regard to the vessel. It is entirely within the discretion of that State to decide whether to allow another party to act against its vessel."[122]

Apart from the need for the explicit authorization, the requesting party has, first, to notify the flag State, then, request confirmation of the registry and, lastly, request the authorization. This provision should be read in conjunction with paragraph 4, which stipulates that

> "the flag State *may* authorise the requesting State to *inter alia*: *(a)* board the vessel, *(b)* search the vessel and *(c)* if evidence

120. See in this respect W. Gilmore, "The 1988 United Nations Convention against Illicit Traffic in Narcotic Drugs and Psychotropic Substances", 15 *Marine Policy* (1991), 183, and F. Rouchereau, "La Convention des Nations Unies contre le traffic illicite de stupéfiants et de substances psychotropes", 36 *AFDI* (1988), 601.

121. See Vienna *Commentary*, at p. 323.

122. See *Official Records of the Vienna Convention, Summary Records of Committee II*, 29th meeting, para. 7.

of involvement in illicit traffic is found, take appropriate action with respect to the vessel, persons and cargo on board" [123].

In a regional context, reference should, first, be made to the 1995 Council of Europe Agreement [124]. This Agreement supplements and strengthens the relevant treaty framework in the European context, consisting, besides the Vienna Convention, of few bilateral treaties [125]. As a result, following Article 17, parties to the 1995 CoE Agreement undertake to co-operate to the fullest extent possible to interdict narcotics trafficking at sea. Action towards this end is envisaged in respect of private and commercial vessels located beyond the territorial sea of any State [126] and includes the right of visit of vessels flying the flag of another State party, which has given its explicit authorization to this end. It was agreed from the outset that, as with the Vienna Convention, action of this kind would be firmly based on the concept of authorization of the flag State, as well as that there is no obligation for a flag State to respond affirmatively to a request for authorization [127].

Another regional arrangement to be regarded is the Agreement concerning Co-operation in Suppressing Illicit Maritime and Air Trafficking in Narcotic Drugs and Psychotropic Substances in the Caribbean Area, concluded on 10 April 2003, at San José, Costa Rica, and entered into force on 18 September 2008 [128]. This Agreement may be said to have emerged from the extensive practical experience of the States and territories of the region, which has also materialized in an extensive network of bilateral agreements in respect of drug trafficking. In addition, it has

123. See Article 17 (4) (emphasis added).

124. 1995 Council of Europe Agreement on Illicit Traffic by Sea, implementing Article 17 of the UN Convention against Illicit Traffic in Narcotic Drugs and Psychotropic Substances, *European Treaty Series*, No. 156. The Agreement entered into force on 1 May 2000 and as of 20 May 2013 it had 15 States parties, http://www.conventions.coe.int/Treaty/Commun/ChercheSig.asp?NT=156&CM=8&DF=20/05/2013&CL=ENG. For the associated official Explanatory Report see Council of Europe Document CDPC (94) 22, Addendum of 27 June 1995, http://conventions.coe.int/Treaty/en/Reports/Html/156.htm (hereinafter, Explanatory Report).

125. See for further information on the negotiation W. Gilmore, "Narcotics Interdiction at Sea: The 1995 CoE Agreement", 20 *Marine Policy* (1995), 3.

126. As the Explanatory Report notes: "this would include the high seas, the contiguous zone and the EEZ within the meaning of the Montego Bay Convention and customary international law . . ."; at p. 25.

127. See also Article 17 of the 1995 Agreement.

128. See Gilmore, Caribbean Agreement. As of 19 April 2011, parties to the Agreement have been Belize, Costa Rica, Dominican Republic, France, Guatemala, Netherlands, Nicaragua, United States of America. Signatures subject to ratification: Haiti, Honduras, Jamaica, United Kingdom. See A. Roach and R. Smith, *Excessive Maritime Claims*, 3rd ed., Martinus Nijhoff, 2012, Appendix 16.

been significantly influenced by the special geographical circumstances of the Caribbean basin.

This Agreement, like the 1995 CoE Agreement in the European region, purports to enhance the effectiveness of Article 17 of the Vienna Convention in the Caribbean basin; however, it is far more innovative and ambitious than the latter, since it is based less on the Vienna Convention and more on the bilateral arrangements already in place in the region. Accordingly, this instrument contains detailed provisions concerning law enforcement operations of all State Parties in and over the territorial waters of the contracting States (Articles 11-15); a zone of coastal State sovereignty beyond the *ratione loci* reach both of the Vienna Convention and of the 1995 Agreement [129]. It directly addresses issues arising in illicit trafficking by air and regulates in some detail assistance by aircraft for the suppression of illicit traffic in zones of coastal State jurisdiction; issues on which the aforementioned treaties are largely silent. By virtue of Articles 11 and 13 (6), however, the previous authorization of the coastal State is a prerequisite for such operations, which, in any event, are subject to the authority of the coastal State and should be carried out by, or under the direction of, its law enforcement authorities [130]. Another innovative feature, which has been directly drawn from the bilateral treaties, is the already discussed "shiprider" institution, i.e. each Party is required to designate law enforcement officials to embark on the vessels of other Parties in order to facilitate the timely provision of authorizations and the exercise of relevant national law enforcement powers within zones of jurisdiction of the former Party (Article 9) [131].

Finally, as indicated above, there is an array of bilateral agreements, which include the right to visit foreign-flagged vessels suspected of illicit traffic in narcotic drugs on the high seas as well as in the territorial seas of the State Parties. The United States and many States in the Central and South American continent have concluded the majority of them. According to the latest International Narcotics Control Strategy Report (March 2012), "there are 44 maritime counterdrug bilateral agreements or operational procedures in place between the United States and partner nations" [132]. In general, they mirror the recent Caribbean

129. Article 1 *(h)* of the Agreement defines "waters of a Party" to mean the territorial sea and archipelagic waters of that Party. Importantly nonetheless, Article 15 provides a Party with the option of extending the application of the Agreement to some or all of its internal waters.

130. See Gilmore, *Caribbean Agreement*, at p. 23.

131. See further Tesfalidet, Chapter 16, *infra*.

132. See International Narcotics Control Strategy Report (Vol. I, 2012), at p. 52; available at http://www.state.gov/documents/organization/187109.pdf.

Agreement rather than the 1988 Vienna Convention or the 1995 CoE Agreement. They are noticeably flexible and practical, which, on the one hand, has considerable merits, while on the other, might create certain hazards for legal certainty and the rule of law in the oceans. This corresponds to their bilateral nature that enables the negotiating Parties to circumvent many of the procedural hurdles that unavoidably arise in a multilateral process when more than two jurisdictions are involved.

Paragraph 3 Smuggling of Migrants and Human Trafficking at Sea

A. *Introductory remarks*

For centuries people have often undertake very perilous journeys, putting their lives into serious danger as a way to safety for persons in fear of their lives, or a gateway for others in search for a better life[133]. The sea can be the location of exploitation of victims of trafficking in persons or the means by which they are transported from one place to another. Smuggling of migrants by sea is the most dangerous type of smuggling for the migrants concerned[134]. Fishing boats, merchant vessels, cargo ships can be both the location where the exploitation takes place or where rights of migrants are violated, and the means used by smugglers and traffickers for transportation. The oceans have also facilitated the "commerce" of human beings, traded like commodities from one country or continent to another. Trafficking in persons and the smuggling of migrants are a very profitable business and source of income for criminals and these crimes have concomitantly engaged the concern of the international community.

Given that the prime concern of most migrants is to flee from their country of origin, rather than to flee to any particular place, it is not surprising that they flee by whatever means possible, including overcrowded and unseaworthy vessels[135]. Such vessels will often be at risk of sinking and indeed many do sink, with the result that thousands of

133. Reports to IMO recount unimaginable means of transportation such as a small inflated raft for children of two metres length, carrying two migrants, a windsurfer with two migrants, an improvised raft (wooden door with plastic bottles tied to it) with two migrants etc.; see Second Biannual Report, IMO doc. MSC.3/Circ.2 (October 31, 2001); available at www.imo.org.

134. UNODC Issue Paper, "Smuggling of Migrants by Sea" (Vienna, 2011); available at http://www.unodc.org/documents/human-trafficking/Migrant-Smuggling/Issue-Papers/Issue_Paper_-_Smuggling_of_Migrants_by_Sea.pdf. See also Guggisburg, Chapter 6, *infra*.

135. See IMO Report, *supra* footnote 133.

lives are lost every year[136]. This was particularly noticeable in the period of the Arab Spring (since January 2011), in which there was an increase in departures of migrant boats from North Africa and, allegedly, at least as many as 1,500 persons have lost their lives while trying to cross the Mediterranean[137]. Such problem may also arise soon in relation to the flow of people from Syria, due to the ongoing civil strife[138]. The migrants traversing the Mediterranean Sea or other seas of the world can be qualified under many legal categories, but it is very often the case that they are victims of human trafficking or are being smuggled by transnational organized groups.

It is evident that in the contemporary era the focus of most, especially developed, States has predominantly shifted to preventing asylum-seekers or illicit migrants from reaching their territory. Amongst the "non-arrival" policies employed to this end[139], a primary role is attributed to interception, which has attained even more vigour recently in the light of the adoption of the Smuggling of Migrants Protocol, as well as of the relevant practice of States, like Australia[140], the United States[141] and various European States[142]. The latest example is manifestly the 2009 "push-back" operations conducted by Italy in co-operation with Libya in the central Mediterranean Sea[143].

---

136. See information and reports of dead or missing people up to 2011 in the UNHCR's website on asylum and migration, entitled "All in the Same boat: The Challenges of Mixed Migratio", available at http://www.unhcr.org/pages/4a1d406060.html.

137. See *inter alia* Report by T. Hammarberg, Commissioner for Human Rights of the Council of Europe (Strasbourg, 7 September 2011) — CommDH (2011)26, available at https://wcd.coe.int/wcd/ViewDoc.jsp?id=1826921. See also the allegations with respect to NATO vessels leaving people to die off the coast off Libya, at http://www.guardian.co.uk/world/2011/may/08/nato-ship-libyan-migrants (8 May 2011).

138. According to UNHCR, there are "more than 280,000 people registered or in need of humanitarian assistance and protection as of end of September [2012]"; see UN, Syrian Regional Response Plan, Second Revision (September 2012); available at http://data.unhcr.org/syrianrefugees/uploads/SyriaRRP.pdf.

139. See G. Goodwin-Gill and J. McAdam, *The Refugee in International Law*, 3rd ed., Oxford, Oxford University Press, 2007, p. 374.

140. Following the *Tampa* incident in 2001, the then Howard Government passed a series of laws — commonly referred to as "Pacific Strategy" (previously, "Solution") — "excising" various islands and coastal ports from the migration zone. See in this regard A. Schloenhardt (ed.), *Migrant Smuggling, Illegal Migration and Organized Crime in Australia and Asia Pacific Region*, Leiden, Martinus Nijhoff, 2003.

141. For interception operations recently launched in relation to Haiti, see B. Frelick, "Abundantly Clear: *Refoulement*", 19 *Georgetown International Law Journal* (2005), 245.

142. See UNHCR, "Selected Reference Materials, Rescue at Sea, Maritime Interception and Stowaways" (November 2006), available at www.unhcr.bg/other/law_of_the_sea.pdf.

143. See *infra* footnote 174 and accompanying text.

A central role in the interception of asylum-seekers or illicit migrants has been ascribed to FRONTEX, which was established in 2004 to help EU Member States in implementing community legislation on the surveillance of the EU borders, including maritime borders, and to co-ordinate their operational co-operation[144]. As officially stated by FRONTEX, the Agency "plans, coordinates, implements and evaluates joint operations conducted using Member States' staff and equipment at the external borders (sea, land and air)"[145]. Truly, many joint interception operations have been executed by EU Member States at sea[146]. Moreover, the operation capabilities of FRONTEX have been significantly enhanced by Regulation (EU) No. 1168/2011, which amended the Council Regulation (EC) No. 2007/2004 establishing FRONTEX. Under this Regulation, the Agency, *inter alia,* has the authority to plan, on its own, joint operations or pilot projects, while Member States should contribute with an appropriate number of skilled border guards and make them available for deployment on a semi-permanent basis[147].

B. Smuggling of migrants and the law of the sea

The LOSC refers to immigration matters in its provisions regarding innocent passage (Articles 19 (2) *(g)* and 21 (1) *(h)*, LOSC), the police powers within the contiguous zone (Article 33 (1), LOSC), transit passage (Article 42 (1) *(d)*, LOSC) and offshore installations and artificial islands within the EEZ or on the continental shelf (Articles 60 (2) and 80 (2), LOSC). On the high seas, the relevant provisions do not make any reference to smuggling of migrants or human trafficking and the latter are not contemplated by the Convention as a specific ground for the right to visit of a foreign vessel[148].

With regard to interception of vessel suspected of being engaged in such illicit activities, it is apt to consider first whether Article 110 can provide any justification for the boarding in question. On the face of this article, only the grounds of "the absence of nationality" as well as the "slave trade" merit a closer scrutiny. As far as the former ground is concerned, it is very often the case that the transportation of the persons in

144. See *supra* footnote 7.
145. See at http://frontex.europa.eu/about/mission-and-tasks.
146. Examples of recently accomplished operations include *inter alia*: JO EPN Hera 2009 (extended in 2010), on tackling illegal immigration coming from West African countries disembarking in Canary Islands; JO Operation POSEIDON 2009 (extended in 2010) in the Eastern Mediterranean Sea; see http://frontex.europa.eu/operations/archive-of-accomplished-operations.
147. See *inter alia* 2011 FRONTEX Regulation, Article 1 (5) amending Article 3 of Regulation No. 2007/2004.
148. See further Guggisberg, Chapter 6, *infra*.

question is carried out using non-registered small vessels, without name or flag, i.e. stateless vessels[149]. In a Study of the European Commission, it was noted that

> "Illegal immigration via [small craft aiming to reach the coast clandestinely] accounts for most of the illegal immigration by sea (over 70%–80% of detected illegal immigration by sea). These crossings involve small craft or dinghies which are not usually seaworthy and which are therefore jeopardising the lives of their occupants."[150]

It goes without saying that such small craft or "dinghies" would not be flying any flag. By virtue of the provision of Article 110 (1) *(d)* of LOSC, warships or other duly authorized vessels of any State may exercise the right of visit on these vessels[151]. Furthermore, as already noted, according to one strand of legal doctrine, the boarding States may also subject stateless vessels to their laws. A number of judicial pronouncements concerning stateless vessels in general support this line of reasoning[152]. Similarly, in the only reported case of illicit migrants on board such vessels before a national court, the *Pamuk and Others* case in 2001, the "stateless vessel" ground was considered by an Italian court as sufficient for the arrest and trial of illegal migrants on the high seas bound for the coast of Italy[153]. Nevertheless, in the present author's view, the right to visit such vessels does not *ipso facto* entail the full extension of the jurisdictional powers of the boarding States[154].

149. See, e.g., cases like the ones reported to the IMO, *supra* footnote 133, and N. Ronzitti, "Coastal State Jurisdiction over Refugees and Migrants at Sea", in N. Ando *et al.* (eds.), *Liber Amicorum Judge Shigeru Oda*, The Hague, Kluwer Law International, 2002, pp. 1271, 1274.

150. *Study on the International Law Instruments in Relation to Illegal Immigration by Sea*, SEC (2007) 691, 15 May 2007, Annex, para. 1.1.2.

151. The relevant provision was inserted for the first time in 1976 in the Revised Single Negotiating Text (A/CONF.62/WP.8/Part II, Art. 96, IV *Official Records*, p. 166), reprinted in IV Platzöder, p. 129. It should be noted that the insertion of the stateless vessels did not encounter any difficulties or objections; see also Nordquist, *Commentary*, 240.

152. See, e.g., the decision of the Privy Council in *Molvan* v. *Attorney-General for Palestine* [1948] AC 351. In that case the Council found that no breach of international law resulted when a British destroyer intercepted a ship carrying illegal immigrants bound for Palestine on the high seas and escorted into port, where the vessel was forfeited.

153. Italian customs officers had arrested on the high seas a flagless vessel transporting illegal immigrants who had been transferred, on the high seas, to another vessel directed to the Italian coast and had subsequently entered Italian territorial waters. See the decision of Tribunale di Crotone, 27 September 2001, *Pamuk et al.*, cited in *RDI* (2001), 1155, and for commentary, S. Trevisanut, "Droit de la mer", 133 *Journal du droit international* (2006) 1035.

154. Similar arguments were put forward in relation to maritime terrorism and drug trafficking.

The other possible legal basis afforded by the LOSC for interception of human beings on the high seas is suppression of the slave trade. It is beyond the scope of this chapter to refer in detail to this argument[155]; suffice it to say for the present purposes that it constitutes a novel proposition premised upon an evolutionary interpretation of the relevant texts, especially the LOSC. While there is an evident tendency in international judicial practice and doctrine to broadly interpret the relevant slavery provisions in order to include contemporary manifestations of slavery, there is no actual State practice or any judicial decision to buttress a corresponding interpretation of the relevant provision of the LOSC. Nonetheless, it is worth pursuing it for several reasons: first, it purports to address the problem of contemporary "slave trade", namely human trafficking, and secondly it does so without the need of new instruments. It also reflects the "positive" and humanitarian face of "interception", which is completely different than the current state practice of external immigration controls. Finally, it aims to fulfil the normative content of Article 99 of LOSC, namely the suppression of slavery in the legal order of the oceans[156].

Of relevance is obviously the duty to assist persons in distress at sea enshrined in Part VII of LOSC[157]. The duty to assist persons in distress at sea is a long-established rule of customary international law. It extends both to other vessels and coastal States in the vicinity. First, with regard to flag States, Article 98 (1) of UNCLOS provides that:

> "Every State shall require the master of a ship flying its flag, in so far as he can do so without serious danger to the ship, the crew, or the passengers . . . to render assistance to any person found at sea in danger of being lost . . . and to proceed to the rescue of persons in distress, if informed of their need for assistance, in so far as such action may be reasonably be expected of him."

Although the aforesaid provision is located in the part of UNCLOS concerning the high seas, it is submitted that the duty in question applies in all maritime zones. On the face of Article 98 (1), the responsibility to rescue and provide assistance rests initially with the master of the ship that comes to rescue and entails the duty to deliver the people on board

155. This argument has been put forward in E. Papastavridis, *The Interception of Vessels on the High Seas: Contemporary Challenges to the Legal Order of the Oceans*, Oxford, Hart Publishing, 2013, pp. 267-278.

156. *Ibid.*, at p. 267.

157. See detailed discussion in Coppens, Chapter 10, *infra*. For a discussion of the interaction between the duty to assist persons in distress at sea and criminal law enforcement against migrant smuggling, see Guggisberg, Chapter 6, *infra*.

to a place of safety. Every flag State must require the master of a ship flying its flag, both State and private vessels, to proceed with all possible speed to the rescue of persons in distress when informed of their need of assistance.

Secondly, with regard to coastal States, Article 98 (2) of UNCLOS stipulates:

> "Every coastal State shall promote the establishment, operation and maintenance of an adequate and effective search and rescue service regarding safety on and over the sea and, where circumstances so require, by way of mutual regional arrangements cooperate with neighbouring States for this purpose."

On the face of this provision, it is evident that UNCLOS sets out a general obligation of conduct on the part of coastal States to maintain search and rescue services as well as a general obligation of co-operation with other States to this end.

These laws are supplemented by other treaty instruments, for example the 1974 Safety of Life at Sea Convention (SOLAS)[158]. The SOLAS covers a wide range of matters ranging from construction standards to operational rules to security measures. It sets forth specific provisions about the safety of navigation and rescue obligations. The other relevant IMO Convention is the 1979 International Convention on Maritime Search and Rescue (SAR Convention)[159]. In May 2004, in the wake of the *Tampa* incident[160] and the initiatives that it fuelled[161], the SAR and SOLAS Conventions were amended to impose for the first time an obligation on States to "cooperate and coordinate" to ensure that ships' masters are allowed to disembark rescued persons to a place safety. This obligation applies irrespective of the nationality or status of those upon the ship, and with minimal disruption to the ship's planned itinerary[162].

158. See International Convention for the Safety of Life at Sea, adopted 1 November 1974, entered into force 25 May 1980 (1184 *UNTS*, No. 278).

159. See International Convention on Maritime Search and Rescue, adopted 27 April 1979, entered into force 22 June 1985 (1405 *UNTS*, No. 23489).

160. See the relevant discussion in C. M. Bostock, "The International Legal Obligation Owed to the Asylum-Seekers on the M.V. *Tampa*", 14 *International Journal of Refugee Law* (2002), 279.

161. See *inter alia* IMO Assembly Resolution on the Review of Safety Measures and Procedures for the Treatment of Persons Rescued at Sea, 22nd session, Agenda Item No. 8, IMO Assembly Res. A.920(22), November 2001, and UNHCR, "Note on International Protection", 53rd session, UN doc.A/AC.96/965 (11 September 2002).

162. See IMO, MSC Res 153 (78), MSC Doc. 78/26.Add.1, Annex 5 (20 May 2004) with regard to the amendments to SOLAS and IMO, MSC Res. 155 (78) with regard to amendments to SAR Convention. Both amendments entered into force on 1 July 2006; see further information at http://www.imo.org/OurWork/Facilitation/IllegalMigrants/Pages/Default.aspx.

This obligation of the State parties to SOLAS and the SAR Convention to provide "a place of safety" as soon as reasonably practicable does not necessarily mean that the State responsible for the SAR region is obliged to disembark the survivors in its own area. In other words, on the face of the provisions in question, there is no residual obligation of the coastal State to allow disembarkation on its own territory when it has not been possible to do so anywhere else [163]. This has rightly been criticized as the most notable shortcoming of the relevant treaty regime [164].

C. Other instruments countering the trafficking of human beings at sea

Firstly, reference should be made to the Smuggling Protocol adopted in 2000. In general, the Smuggling Protocol is designed to fight cross-border crimes by obliging signatories to adopt national legislative measures, to open information channels and to promote co-operation in enforcement of international law. As far as the boarding provision of the Smuggling Protocol is concerned, it should be noted that it is modelled upon Article 17 of the Vienna Convention. *In casu*, the relevant measures are to be enforced against a vessel suspected of being engaged in the smuggling of migrants and may include measures against masters or crews involved in the smuggling. However, since measures are to be enforced against a vessel, measures under the Protocol may not be undertaken against stowaways, a situation in which the vessel as a unit is not engaged in the illicit activity. The right to visit as such of a foreign-flagged vessel is stipulated in Article 8 (2) as follows:

> "A State Party that has reasonable grounds to suspect that a vessel exercising freedom of navigation in accordance with international law and flying the flag or displaying the marks of registry of another State Party is engaged in the smuggling of migrants by sea may so notify the flag State, request confirmation of registry and, if confirmed, request authorisation from the flag State to take appropriate measures with regard to that vessel. The flag State may authorise the requesting State, *inter alia: (a)* To board the vessel; *(b)* To search the vessel; and *(c)* If evidence is found that the vessel is engaged in the smuggling of migrants by sea, to take appropriate measures with respect to the vessel and persons and cargo on board, as authorized by the flag State."

163. For a contrary opinion see S. Trevisanut, "Search and Rescue Operations in the Mediterranean: Factor of Cooperation or Conflict?", 25 *IJMCL* (2010), 523, 530.

164. See also Coppens, Chapter 10, *infra*.

Obviously, under this provision, any action against a foreign vessel on the high seas must be based on the express flag State authorization. Neither tacit consent, nor simply the consent of the master of the vessel, is sufficient to trigger Article 8 (2) of the Protocol.

There has recently been a number of bilateral agreements concerning the suppression of illegal migration, which provide for, among others, the right to board vessels on the high seas. It is a truism that the majority of these agreements have been concluded by the United States. What historically propelled the US action and led to the conclusion of the first agreement of this type was the Haitian exodus[165]. Following an Executive Order by President Reagan initiating the Haitian Migrant Interdiction Operation, the United States concluded a bilateral agreement with Haiti on 23 September 1981, in the form of an Exchange of Letters relating to the Establishment of a Cooperative Program of Interdiction and Selective Return of Certain Haitian Migrants and Vessels[166]. This agreement is not the only one which the United States has concluded in the broader Caribbean area. After a certain period of extended interdiction operations on unstable legal ground, it reached an agreement with Cuba, namely the United States-Cuba Joint Communiqué on Migration (9 September 1994). It enunciated *inter alia* that

> "The two governments will take effective measures in every way they possibly can to oppose and prevent the use of violence by any persons seeking to reach, or who arrive in, the US from Cuba by forcible diversions of aircraft and vessels."[167]

Besides Cuba, the United States has similar agreements with the Dominican Republic (May 2003)[168], Bahamas (2004)[169] and Ecuador[170].

165. From the abundant academic literature on the Haitian interception policy and its legal repercussions, see, *inter alia*, B Frelick, "Haitian Boat Interdiction and Return", 26 *Cornell Journal of International Law* (1993), 675; D. Martin, "Interdiction, Intervention and the New Frontiers of Refugee Law", 33 *Virginia Journal of International Law* (1993), 473.

166. See 33 UST (1981), 3559.

167. See also the Cuba-United States Joint Statement on the Normalization of Migration, Building on the Agreement of 9 September 1994, 2 May 1995, 35 *ILM* (1995), 327.

168. See Agreement between the Government of the United States of America and the Government of the Dominican Republic concerning Maritime Migration Law Enforcement, signed at Washington 20 May 2003; entered into force 20 May 2003. *TIAS* 03-520, 2003 *UST LEXIS* 32.

169. See Agreement between the Government of the United States of America and the Government of the Bahamas concerning cooperation in Maritime Law Enforcement, signed at Nassau 29 June 2004; entered into force 29 June 2004.

170. See Ecuador-United States operational procedures for boarding and inspecting vessels suspected of illicit traffic in narcotic drugs and psychotropic substances and of smuggling migrants by sea, signed at Quito, 30 August 2006.

However, such migration interdiction agreements are found also in the European milieu and more specifically in the Mediterranean Sea. For example, Italy has been very active in seeking co-operation with other neighbouring countries in order to tackle illicit immigration[171]. First, in the mid-1990s, when Italy was faced with a major influx of immigrants from Albania, it concluded an agreement with Albania with an Exchange of Notes of 25 March 1997 for the control and suppression of clandestine migration by sea[172]. The most notable partnership of Italy in this regard, however, was with Libya. First, on 29 December 2007, Italy and Libya signed a bilateral co-operation agreement in Tripoli on the fight against clandestine immigration. On the same date the two countries signed an additional Protocol setting out the operational and technical arrangements for implementation of the said Agreement. On 4 February 2009 Italy and Libya signed an Additional Protocol in Tripoli, intended to strengthen bilateral co-operation in the fight against clandestine immigration. That Protocol partially amended the agreement of 29 December 2007, in particular through the inclusion of a new article, which provided for joint patrols. On 30 August 2008 in Benghazi, Italy and Libya signed a Treaty on Friendship, Partnership and Cooperation[173].

This series of agreements served as the legal background for Italy's controversial "push-back operations". In nine push-back operations between 6 May and 6 November 2009, a total of 834 migrants intercepted in international waters were collectively and indiscriminately shipped to Libya by Italian border authorities, while 23 people were returned to Algeria[174]. Some of those people were the applicants in the *Hirsi* case before the ECtHR (2012)[175].

---

171. On the Italian practice vis-à-vis immigration in general see A. Di Pascale, "Migration Control at Sea: The Italian Case", in B. Ryan and V. Mitsilegas (eds.), *Extraterritorial Immigration Control: Legal Challenges*, Leiden, Martinus Nijhoff, 2010, pp. 281-310.

172. For academic commentary see T. Scovazzi, "Le Norme di Diritto Internazionale sull'Immigrazione Illegale via Mare con Particolare Riferimento ai Rapporti tra Albania e Italia", in A. de Guttry and F. Pagani, *La Crisi Albanese del 1997*, Milan, Angeli, 1999, p. 239.

173. On these agreements see ECHR, *Hirsi Jama a.o.* v. *Italy* (Appl. No. 27765/09), Grand Chamber Judgment of 23 February 2012 case, paras. 19-20.

174. *Submission by the Office of the United Nations High Commissioner for Refugees in the Case of Hirsi and Others* v. *Ital,* App. No. 27765/09 (ECtHR), 3. See also V. Moreno-Lax, "Seeking Asylum in the Mediterranean: Against a Fragmentary Reading of EU Member States' Obligations Accruing at Sea", 23 *International Journal of Refugee Law* (2011), 174, 185, and M. Giuffré, "State Responsibility beyond Borders: What Legal Basis for Italy's Push-backs to Libya? 24", *International Journal of Refugee Law* (2012), 692-734.

175. See *supra* footnote 173.

Paragraph 4 **Piracy and Armed Robbery at Sea**

A. Introduction

The crime of piracy remains at the centre of international concern, particularly in view of its surge off the coast of Somalia and more recently in the Gulf of Guinea[176]. According to the International Maritime Organization (IMO), in the first eight months of 2012 there were 84 attacks against ships in the waters off the coast of Somalia, resulting in the hijacking of 13 ships. The majority of attacks leading to vessels being hijacked during 2012 took place in the western Indian Ocean.

As of 31 August 2012, 224 people and 17 vessels (including three fishing vessels and eight dhows) were being held hostage. This compares with 378 people and 18 vessels (including 4 fishing vessels, 1 dhow and 1 yacht) held at the end of August 2011[177].

This extraordinary growth in piracy in the region has attracted unprecedented media coverage which has subsequently led to a multipronged international response. The international community has responded with a series of initiatives, such as the deployment of naval operations (EUNAVFOR *Operation Atalanta*, NATO *Operation Ocean Shield* and CTF 151) or the adoption of Security Council resolutions, *inter alia,* authorizing, in accordance with Somalia's consent, the entry into territorial waters and territory to suppress piracy. Additionally in 2008, the Combined Task Force established a maritime security patrol area (MSPA) in international waters off the Somali coast, which was followed by a Shared Awareness and Deconfliction process (SHADE) among States with naval assets in the Gulf[178]. Finally, the IMO has adopted Recommendations for Flag States, who, in an increasing number of cases, employ private armed guards to augment shipboard security arrangements when transiting the area of the Gulf of Aden and West Indian Ocean[179].

---

176. See the Report of the International Expert Group on Piracy off the Somali Coast commissioned by the Special Representative of the Secretary-General of the United Nations to Somalia, at p. 15; available at http://www.imcsnet.org/imcs/docs/somalia_piracy_intl_experts_report_consolidated.pdf.

177. IMO source. For an updated list of cases of piracy and armed robbery, see at http://gisis.imo.org/Public/PAR/Default.aspx.

178. See further information at D. Guilfoyle, "Combating Piracy: Executive Measures on the High Seas", 53 *Japanese Yearbook of International Law* (2011), 149, at 155.

179. See MSC 1/Circ 1406 (23 May 2011). On the use of private armed guards see C. Spearin, "Private Military and Security Companies v. International Naval Endeavours v. Somali Pirates", 10 *Journal of International Criminal Justice* (2012), 823-837, and Williams, Chapter 9, *infra*.

B. The law of the sea and piracy

Piracy *jure gentum* has traditionally been described as "every unauthorized act of violence by a private vessel on the open sea with the intent to plunder *(animo furandi)*"[180]. This broad definition was narrowed by the conventional definitions of the 1958 Geneva Convention on the High Seas and LOSC, which should be considered as declaratory of customary international law[181]. Article 101 of LOSC defines piracy as consisting of any of the following acts:

> "[a]ny illegal acts of violence or detention, or any act of depredation, committed for private ends by the crew or passengers of a private ship . ; . and directed: *(a)* on the high seas, against another ship . . . *(b)* against a ship, aircraft, persons or property in a place outside the jurisdiction of any State . . .".

It is true that the most controversial issue concerning the definition of piracy *jure gentium* is the requirement for "private ends". It has been already discussed that the most convincing interpretation of this requirement is that it means piracy "without due authority"[182].

As far as the suppression of piracy is concerned, it has customarily been recognized and codified that those on board a pirate vessel may be arrested by the seizing vessel. These individuals may be subsequently tried by any State and are subject to penalties imposed by that State's laws (Article 105, LOSC)[183]. Throughout the past several hundred years, the legitimacy of universal jurisdiction over piracy has been recognized by jurists and scholars of every major nation[184].

Nevertheless, it is evident that the most remarkable and controversial issue since the initiation of the counter-piracy campaign off the coast of Somalia in 2008, has been the assertion of jurisdiction over suspected pirates in the region. The prosecutions of suspected pirates still mark low in comparison with the number of attacks[185].

---

180. L. Oppenheim, "Disputes, War and Neutrality", in H. Lauterpacht (ed.), *International Law: A Treatise*, 8th ed., 1955, p. 608. The qualification *jure gentium* serves as the distinguishing trait between piracy under international law and piracy under national law.

181. On the provisions of LOSC concerning piracy see Nordquist, *Commentary*, 182. On piracy in general see H. Dubner, *The Law of International Sea Piracy*, 2nd ed., The Hague, Martinus Nijhoff, 1988; A. Rubin, *The Law of Piracy*, 2nd ed., New York, Transnational, 1998.

182. See *supra* footnote 82 and accompanying text.

183. "The courts of the State which carried out the seizure may decide upon the penalties to be imposed, and may also determine the action to be taken with regard to the ships, aircraft or property, subject to the rights of third parties acting in good faith", Article 105, LOSC.

184. See, e.g., A. Van Zwanenberg, "Interference with Ships on the High Seas", 10 *ICLQ* (1961), 785, at 805.

185. See also Grymaneli, Chapter 5, *infra*.

With regard to the assertion of the latter, suffice it to refer to an empirical study completed by E. Kontorovich and S. Art who state,

> "of all clear cases of piracy punishable under universal jurisdiction, international prosecution occurred in no more than 1.47 percent. This figure includes the unprecedented international response to the Somali piracy surge that began in 2008 and accounts for the majority of prosecutions. Prior to 2008, nations invoked universal jurisdiction, a doctrine that arose precisely to deal with piracy, in a negligible fraction of cases (just 0.53 percent, a total of four cases)."[186]

It is readily apparent that the dominant approach has been to avoid capturing pirates in the first instance, or, alternatively releasing them without charge or transferring them to a third State. The latter option has been the most common solution: States such as the United States[187] and the United Kingdom[188] and the European Union[189] have opted for entering into Memoranda of Understanding (MoU) with countries in the region (for example Kenya, Seychelles, Tanzania and Mauritius) to transfer the suspects to the latter States. Nonetheless, the transfer of

186. E. Kontorovich and S. Art, "An Empirical Examination of Universal Jurisdiction over Piracy", 104 *AJIL* (2010), 436, 436. Also Professor Rubin has shown in his authoritative history of piracy law that very few criminal prosecutions for piracy can be found that depended on universal jurisdiction. He enumerates fewer than five cases in the past 300 years; see A. Rubin, *The Law of Piracy*, 2nd ed., NY, Transnational Publishers Inc., 1998, at pp. 302, 348.

187. See, e.g., Memorandum of Understanding between the United States of America and the Republic of the Seychelles concerning the conditions of transfer of suspected pirates and armed robbers and seized property in the western Indian Ocean, the Gulf of Aden, and the Red Sea, signed at Victoria 14 July 2010.

188. Reportedly, the United Kingdom has signed relevant agreements with Kenya, Seychelles, Tanzania and more recently with Mauritius. See, e.g., "Republic of Kenya and the United Kingdom Sign A Memorandum of Understanding on Piracy along the Coast of Somalia", available at http://www.mfa.go.ke/mfacms/index.php?option=com_content&task=view&id=305&Itemid=62, and "Signing of Piracy Agreement with Mauritius" (8 June 2012); available at http://www.number10.gov.uk/news/piracy-agreement-mauritius/.

189. See Exchange of Letters between the European Union and the Government of Kenya on the conditions and modalities for the transfer of persons suspected of having committed acts of piracy (6 March 2009); Exchange of Letters between the European Union and the Republic of Seychelles on the Conditions and Modalities for the Transfer of Suspected Pirates and Armed Robbers (2 December 2009) and Agreement between the European Union and the Republic of Mauritius on the Conditions and Modalities for the Transfer of Suspected Pirates and Associate Seized Property from the European-led Naval Force to the Republic of Mauritius and on the Conditions of Suspected Pirates after Transfer (14 July 2011). The text of the agreements and all relevant information are available at http://www.consilium.europa.eu/eeas/security-defence/eu-operations/eunavfor-somalia/legal-basis.aspx?lang=en.

piracy suspects to regional States remains complicated largely due to the lack of requisite capacity in the region, which, rightly, has been at the centre of the focus of the international community lately[190].

In close interplay with the problems in asserting jurisdiction over the suspected pirates in the region are human rights considerations. Both in the relevant Security Council resolutions and in academic literature[191], it is stressed that prosecutions must be "in accordance with international human rights law". For example, in the resolution 2020 (2011), the Council

> "*[c]alls upon* all States to criminalize piracy under their domestic law and to favourably consider the prosecution of suspected, and imprisonment of convicted, pirates apprehended off the coast of Somalia, and their facilitators and financiers ashore, consistent with applicable international law including *international human rights law*"[192].

C. Armed robbery at sea

From the definition of piracy as outlined above, it is evident that acts of violence that occur in the territorial or in the internal waters of the coastal State fall beyond the ambit of the international regulation of piracy *jure gentium*. This raises significant problems, since the majority of relevant incidents in the beginning of the twenty-first century occurred in territorial waters or ports of States, while the ships were at anchor or berthed. Therefore acts of piracy committed, for example, in the territorial waters of States littoral to Malacca Straits[193], as well as in the territorial sea of Somalia, cannot be designated as piracy *jure gentium*. In view of this, the international community, and in particular, the IMO referred to the crime of "armed robbery against ships" as:

---

190. On the exercise of domestic criminal jurisdiction over piracy, see Grymaneli, Chapter 5, *infra*. See further information, UNODC Counter-Piracy Programme Brochure, Issue 8 (February 2012); available at http://www.unodc.org/documents/easternafrica//piracy/20120206-UNODC_Brochure_Issue_8.1.pdf.

191. See in general S. Piedimonte Bodini, "Fighting Maritime Piracy under the European Convention on Human Rights", 22 *European Journal of International Law* (2011), 829, D. Guilfoyle, "Counter-piracy Law Enforcement and Human Rights", 59 *International & Comparative Law Quarterly* (2010), 141, C. Laly-Chevalier, "Lutte conre le piraterie maritime et droits de l'homme", 42 *Revue belge de droit international* (2009), 5.

192. SC res. 2020 (2011); para. 16 (emphasis added). See also Batsalas, Chapter 11, *infra*.

193. On the attacks in the Malacca Straits see *inter alia* J. S. Burnett, *Dangerous Waters: Modern Piracy and Terror on the High Seas*, NY, Plume, 2003, p. 9.

> "any unlawful act of violence or detention or any act of depredation or threat thereof, other than an act of piracy, directed against a ship or against persons or property on board such a ship, within a state's jurisdiction over such offences"[194].

This crime reflects what has been acknowledged as piracy in many national jurisdictions (i.e. acts of piracy within territorial waters)[195]. Despite this, it is highly unlikely that this expansive notion of piracy within territorial jurisdiction has entered the corpus of international customary law. Moreover, this provision does not fall under the scope of Article 105 of LOSC (i.e. attracting universal jurisdiction). Hence, each coastal State must enact relevant legislation with regard to armed robbery within its waters[196]. In regard to cases of armed robbery at sea within Somali territorial waters, third States would have prescriptive jurisdiction only if the vessel attacked had their flag (principle of vessel registration) or had its nationals involved in the offence (principle of active or passive personality).

Paragraph 5 **Illegal Fishing**

A. Introduction

One of the most long-standing and recurrent illicit activity at sea is indubitably illegal fishing, which is currently considered as part of the called "illegal, unreported, unregulated (IUU) fishing"[197]. In more detail, "illegal fishing" includes all fishing activities conducted in contravention of national and international laws, as well as agreed regional fisheries management and conservation measures[198]. Such fishing may include fishing beyond allowable catch limits, the

194. IMO, Code of Practice for the Investigation of the Crimes of Piracy and Armed Robbery against Ships, adopted 29 November 2001, Res A.922(22), Art. 2 (2), http://www.pmaesa.org/Maritime/Res%20A.922(22).doc. Cf. also Article 1 of the Regional Cooperation Agreement on Combating Piracy and Armed Robbery against Ships in Asia (28 April 2005), *ILM* (2005), 829.

195. See also Abdoul, Chapter 7, *infra*.

196. See further *ibid*.

197. See 2005 Rome Declaration on Illegal, Unreported and Unregulated Fishing adopted by the FAO Ministerial Meeting on Fisheries, Rome, 12 March 2005, available at ftp://ftp.fao.org/fi/document/ministerial/2005/iuu/declaration.pdf. See also Closing the Net: Stopping Illiegal Fishing on the High Seas, Final Report of the Ministerially-led Task Force on IUU Fishing on the High Seas, 2006, available at www.high-seas.org, and M. Palma *et al.*, *Promoting Sustainable Fisheries: The International Legal and Policy Framework to Combat Illegal, Unreported and Unregulated Fishing*, Leiden, Martinus Nijhoff, 2010, p. 245 (hereinafter, Palma, *Fisheries*).

198. See para. 3.1 of the IPOA-IUU.

taking of juvenile fish, the taking of prohibited fish species, fishing during closed seasons or fishing in closed areas[199].

Combating illegal fishing has been one of the main issues on the international fisheries agenda for the past decade, as it has been recognized as a major threat to fisheries conservation and marine biodiversity[200]. It is reported that "in case of fisheries, more than 75 per cent of the world's fish stocks are reported as already fully exploited or overexploited and increasing numbers of marine species are considered threatened or endangered"[201].

Numbers regarding IUU fishing, including illegal fishing, are telling: "the 2008 estimates for the total value of IUU losses worldwide are between USD10 and 23 billion annually"[202].

The international community has endeavoured to address this particular problem either globally by adopting multilateral instruments, such as the UN Fish Stocks Agreement (1995) and the FAO Compliance Agreement (1993)[203], or regionally by the action of an array of regional fisheries management organisations (RFMOs)[204]. To this end, joint enforcement operations and inspection schemes have been extensively employed both in areas under national jurisdiction and on the high seas[205].

---

199. Cf. Article 62 of LOSC and FAO Code of Conduct for Responsible Fisheries, adopted at the 28th session of the FAO Conference, Rome, Italy, 31 October 1995, para. 8.2.2 (hereinafter, FAO Code of Conduct).

200. See T. Lobach, "Combating IUU Fishing: Interaction of Global and Regional Initiatives", in D. Vidas (ed.), *Law, Technology and Science for Oceans in Globalisation: IUU Fishing, Oil Pollution, Bioprospecting, Outer Continental Shelf*, Leiden, Martinus Nijhoff, 2010, pp. 109, 109.

201. R. Rayfuse, "Moving beyond the Tragedy of Global Commons: The Grotian Legacy and the Future of Sustainable Management of the Biodiversity of the High Seas", in D. Leary and B. Pisupati (eds.), *The Future of International Environmental Law*, Tokyo, United Nations University Press, 2010, pp. 201, 204.

202. K. Gjerde, "High Seas Fisheries Governance: Prospects and Challenges in the 21st Century", in D. Vidas and J. Schei (eds.), *The World Ocean in Globalisation: Climate Change, Sustainable Fisheries, Biodiversity, Shipping, Regional Issues*, Leiden, Martinus Nijhoff, 2011, pp. 221, 224.

203. Agreement to Promote Compliance with International Conservation and Management Measures by Fishing Vessels on the High Seas (1994), 2221 *UNTS* 91. The FAO Compliance Agreement was approved on 24 November 1993 by Resolution 15/93 of the Twenty-Seventh Session of the FAO Conference and entered in force on 24 April 2003.

204. See, e.g., M Lodge, "Developing a Model for Improved Governance by Regional Fisheries Management Organizations", in D. Vidas (ed.), *Law, Technology and Science for Oceans in Globalisation: IUU Fishing, Oil Pollution, Bioprospecting, Outer Continental Shelf*, Leiden, Martinus Nijhoff, 2010, pp. 157-174.

205. See *inter alia* R. Rayfuse, *Non-Flag State Enforcement in High Seas Fisheries*, Leiden, Brill Academic Publishers, 2004.

B. Illegal fishing and the law of the sea

The regulation of illegal fishing in zones of national sovereignty and jurisdiction has already been discussed previously. As far as the high seas is concerned, LOSC devotes Articles 116-120 to the regulation of high seas fisheries[206]. Flag States have the primary responsibility to exercise enforcement jurisdiction over their vessels for unlawful fishing activities wherever they occur. In addition, Article 117 refers to States taking measures for their "respective nationals as may be necessary for the conservation of the living resources of the high seas". This provision affords the legal basis for States to take action against their nationals who engage in IUU fishing even if the national is on a vessel flagged to another State[207].

As regards enforcement on the high seas, LOSC falls short of providing for interception powers against foreign-flagged vessels on the high seas. The only ground under LOSC that may be invoked in order to board and inspect a fishing vessel on the high seas is the statelessness of vessels (Article 110 (1) *(d)* of LOSC)[208]. Besides this, there must be a treaty granting such powers to contracting States, such as the Straddling Stocks Agreement. This lacuna under the LOSC became evident in the famous *Estai* case, that is, the dispute between Canada and Spain before the ICJ concerning fishing immediately outside Canada's EEZ. Canada sought to extend its enforcement powers to these vessels on the basis, *inter alia*, of an ecological emergency, whereas Spain argued that Canada had to respect the principle of exclusive flag State jurisdiction on the high seas. At the end, the Court held that it lacked jurisdiction to resolve the dispute and thus the merits of the case were never discussed[209].

The global treaty that allows for enforcement action against foreign vessels on the high seas is the 1995 Straddling Stocks Agreement[210]. In general, the Agreement establishes a general framework and principles

206. See in general E. Hey, "The Fisheries Provisions of the LOS Convention", in E. Hey (ed.), *Developments in International Fisheries Law*, The Hague, Kluwer Law International, 1999, p. 20.

207. See Guilfoyle, *supra* footnote 60, at 101.

208. See *inter alia* T. McDorman, "Stateless Fishing Vessels, International Law and the UN High Seas Fisheries Conference", 25 *Journal of Maritime Law and Commerce* (1994), 531.

209. *Fisheries Jurisdiction* case *(Spain* v. *Canada)*, Preliminary Objections, *ICJ Reports 1998*, p. 432. For commentary see R. Churchill, in 12 *LJIL (*1999), 597-611.

210. See also M. Hayashi, "The 1995 Agreement on the Conservation and Management of Straddling and Highly Migratory Fish Stocks: Significance for the Law of the Sea Convention", 29 *Ocean & Coastal Management* (1995), 51-69.

and rules within which particular straddling and highly migratory fish stocks may be better managed at the regional level. One of the most significant aspects is the emphasis on co-operation among States to conserve and manage these stocks through appropriate regional or subregional fisheries management organizations and arrangements[211]. Co-operation in the conservation and management of resources on the high seas is not only an obligation of RFMO members but it is also extended to non-members of or non-participants in such organizations. Article 8 (3) stipulates that States fishing for these stocks on the high seas may choose not to join in the respective RFMO, yet they are obliged not to undermine the conservation and management measures adopted by the latter organization. In addition, under Article 17 (1), non-member States of RFMOs are not discharged from the obligation to co-operate in the conservation and management of such fish stocks.

C. Regional fisheries management organizations

The most advanced and efficient initiative to manage fisheries on the high seas has been the establishment of regional fisheries management organizations (RFMOs)[212]. Such organizations have the competence to prescribe fishery conservation and management measures, including total allowable catches (TACs) for some fish stocks, as well as to take various steps to promote compliance with these measures[213]. These enforcement mechanisms applicable between the contracting States include what may be characterized as more traditional maritime enforcement measures, such as intercepting, boarding, inspecting and potentially arresting a vessel.

To provide an example, the North Pacific Anadromous Fish Commission, which was established in 1993 with a treaty between Japan, the United States, Canada and Russia[214], aims to prevent directed fishing for certain salmon species within the management area. The said Convention sets forth a reciprocal boarding and inspection scheme: duly authorized officials of any State party may board any other party's fishing vessel upon reasonable suspicion that it is in violation of the Convention

---

211. Article 8 of Fish Stocks Agreement.

212. On RFMOs in general see *inter alia* R. Barston, "The Law of the Sea and Regional Fisheries Organisations", 14 *IJMCL* (1999), 333; T. Henriksen *et al., Law and Politics in Ocean Governance: The UN Fish Stocks Agreement and Regional Fisheries Management Regimes*, Leiden, Martinus Nijhoff, 2006.

213. For a list of the principal RFMOs, see A. Sydnes, "Regional Fishery Organizations: How and Why Organizational Diversity Matters", 32 *Ocean Development & International Law* (2001), 349, 353.

214. See Convention for the Conservation of Anadromous Stocks in the North Pacific Ocean, *TIAS* 11465.

and inspect the vessel and question persons aboard. The inspecting State may arrest a person or the vessel should it reasonably believe that it has breached the Convention, and conduct further investigations if necessary. However, only the flag State may try violations and impose penalties upon the delinquent vessel[215].

Paragraph 6 **Pollution of Maritime Environment**

A. Introduction

> "Each year, up to 810,000 tons of oily waste is intentionally and illegally dumped into the world's oceans by commercial vessels. As a consequence, seabird populations are reduced, the habitats for slow-moving shellfish such as clams, oysters, and mussels are poisoned, and fish — if not killed by the harmful toxins of the oil — lose the ability to reproduce, reproduce deformed offspring, or upon ingestion of the oil, create even more toxic substances. Separately, mammals, reptiles, and amphibians whose natural habitats are either in or close to coastal waters either suffocate to death from oil ingestion or die from eating wildlife previously poisoned by oily waste."[216]

This short paragraph aptly describes the threat to the marine environment and to the biodiversity of the global ecosystem posed by the illegal dumping of oil. Vessel-source pollution is responsible for some 12 per cent of marine pollution. Thus it is subject to strict international regulation. A significant amount of this pollution is due to oil bunkering. It is reported that

> "to reduce the chances of getting caught, vessels most often illegally discharge their oily waste outside of any port, flag, or coastal state's territorial seas, along regular shipping routes or in an area of recent oil accidents at nighttime"[217].

B. Maritime pollution and the law of the sea

The legal regime for preventing vessel-source pollution is aptly described in Part XII on the "Protection and Preservation of the

215. See *op. cit. supra* footnote 214, Article 5 (2).

216. B. S. Gullo, "The Illegal Discharge of Oil on the High Seas: The US Coast Guard's Ongoing Battle against Vessel Polluters and a New Approach toward Establishing Environmental Compliance", 209 *Military Review* (2011), 122.

217. See OECD Report, "Cost Savings Stemming from Non-Compliance with International Environmental Regulations in the Maritime Sector" (2003), at p. 47.

Marine Environment" of LOSC[218]. Besides the LOSC, vessel-source pollution is mainly governed by conventions concluded under the auspices of the International Maritime Organization (IMO). First and the most relevant is obviously MARPOL 1973/78, which mainly addresses the prevention of pollution[219]. Another relevant IMO Convention is the International Convention on Oil Pollution Preparedness, Response and Co-operation, 1990, which covers the response in case of pollution from ships[220].

SECTION 4 **CONCLUDING REMARKS**

As aptly demonstrated in the above analysis, combating crimes at sea poses numerous challenges, both to States and international organizations. This is because organized crime at sea is a multifaceted problem, involving many criminal activities and many practical difficulties both on the international place as well as in the domestic setting. Challenges may arise when conducting enforcement operations at sea. Such operations may involve multinational forces with no specific mandate or knowledge of how to tackle sensitive issues relevant to evidence collection, witnesses' testimonies or human rights. In addition, the problem of the necessary legal basis for the interdiction operation looms large in many occasions.

Also, challenges are observed firstly in relation to the establishment of jurisdiction over transnational organized crimes at sea and secondly in ensuring efficient co-operation amongst various State authorities. This may be addressed by co-ordination between competent international organizations and by the development of more Mutual Legal Assistance (MLA) and extradition agreements. The ratification of existing multilateral treaties concerning criminal activities at sea and the harmonization of domestic legislation is imperative in the fight against crime at sea.

All these issues were addressed during the 2012 Centre for Studies and Research of the Hague Academy of International Law and the products of the meticulous research of the participants are to be found in the following chapters.

---

218. See also Gahlen, Chapter 3, *infra*.

219. International Convention for the Prevention of Pollution from Ships, 2 November 1973, 1983 *UNTS* 184 (entered into force 2 October 1983) and Protocol of 1978 Relating to the International Convention for the Prevention of Pollution from Ships, 17 February 1978, 1983 *UNTS* 62 (entered into force 2 October 1983).

220. International Convention on Oil Pollution Preparedness, Response and Co-operation (OPRC): Adoption: 30 November 1990; entry into force: 13 May 1995.

2 La criminalité en mer : l'approche du droit international

Kimberley N. Trapp *

SECTION 1 INTRODUCTION

Les limites dont la « poliçabilité » des biens communs maritimes souffre ont été exploitées par les criminels depuis des siècles. En conséquence, le défi qu'amener les auteurs de crimes en mer devant la justice représente — en raison de leur existence transnationale et des limites de compétences des Etats — est un problème de longue date auquel la communauté internationale tente de répondre. Avec la sophistication constante de l'organisation des crimes transnationaux et la globalisation qui dépend largement du transport maritime, la suppression de la criminalité en mer se profile encore davantage comme une priorité pour la communauté internationale. La réponse à ce phénomène a pris la forme d'une augmentation extraordinaire dans la conclusion d'arrangements coopératifs, *ad hoc*, bilatéraux, multilatéraux, régionaux et globaux. Ces arrangements ont tous l'objectif de faire face à l'utilisation (abusive) de l'espace maritime à des fins criminelles. Les Etats ont approché les actes criminels en mer sous deux angles : d'un côté, en les considérant comme l'expression d'un phénomène criminel, ils ont imposé des obligations relevant du droit pénal pour la mise en application et la coopération entre les Etats ; de l'autre, en traitant ces actes comme un problème sécuritaire, ils ont riposté — par l'intermédiaire des canaux du Conseil de sécurité et des accords de coopération — avec des pouvoirs d'exécution qu'ils n'auraient pas en temps normal, sans ces autorisations. Ces arrangements coopératifs — dont nombre forment le sujet de chapitres dans cet ouvrage — sont une source de droit international en eux-mêmes, mais ils existent à l'intérieur, et en dépendent largement, du cadre général du droit international, tout en étant influencés par certains domaines spécialisés de ce droit (par exemple le droit pénal international).

* Directrice de la section de langue française du Centre. Lecturer in Public International Law, Faculty of Laws, UCL. (k.trapp@ucl.ac.uk.) Par cette note, l'auteur tient à exprimer sa gratitude à Solène Guggisberg pour son aide dans la préparation de ce texte.

Ainsi, au fil de ce volume se retrouve un thème commun, à savoir l'interaction entre les régimes de droit international ; les limites entre ces régimes applicables aux opérations de lutte contre les actes criminels en mer ont perdu de leur clarté, en particulier dans la mesure où les criminels qui exploitent les difficultés de mise en application du droit en mer ont sophistiqué leurs méthodes. Quoi qu'il en soit, l'analyse légale des questions soulevées par la criminalité en mer requiert une distinction soigneuse entre les différents régimes légaux et les problèmes qui peuvent surgir au sein de chacun d'entre eux. Ce chapitre introductif fournit un cadre analytique à la problématique de la criminalité maritime (trame que les contributions suivantes enrichissent), avec un accent particulier marqué pour les questions de compétence et de responsabilité.

SECTION 2 CADRE GÉNÉRAL : LE DROIT INTERNATIONAL ET LES CRIMES EN MER

Paragraphe 1 La « juridiction »/« compétence » sous toutes ses formes

En droit international général, le terme « juridiction » ou « compétence »[1] fait référence au pouvoir qu'a un Etat afin de réguler la conduite de certaines personnes (naturelles et légales)[2]. Il est généralement accepté qu'il existe au moins deux sortes de compétences : la compétence prescriptive se rapporte au pouvoir d'un Etat de rendre son droit applicable envers certaines personnes (compétence législative)[3] tandis que la compétence d'exécution correspond au pouvoir qu'un Etat a de prendre des mesures exécutives dans la mise en application des lois adoptées (il s'agit par exemple du pouvoir d'arrêter et de détenir des individus avant un jugement et de les emprisonner à sa suite)[4]. Le pou-

1. En anglais, « compétence » se traduit par « jurisdiction », ce qui donne régulièrement lieu à des confusions, en partie en raison des différentes significations rattachées au mot *jurisdiction*. Pour cette raison, le terme *compétence* est préferé à celui de *juridiction* en français (sauf lorsqu'il s'agit de la « juridiction » exclusive de l'Etat de pavillon en haute mer dans les termes utilisés à l'article 92 de la CNUDM) — mais les confusions de terminologie seront examinées plus loin sous le titre C.

2. Crawford, *Brownlie's Principles of Public International Law*, OUP, 2012, p. 456.

3. La « compétence legislative » est aussi appelée la « compétence normative » (voir *Affaire du navire « SAIGA » (n° 2) (Saint-Vincent-et-les-Grenadines c. Guinée)*, arrêt du 1er juillet 1999, Tribunal international du droit de la mer, par. 76). Aux fins du présent chapitre, étant donné l'accent sur l'adoption de cadres législatifs, « compétence législative » sera préférée.

4. Certains commentateurs argumentent sur l'existence d'une troisième forme de compétence, à savoir la compétence adjudicative ou judiciaire, qui fait référence au pouvoir d'un Etat d'intenter une action en justice (en application des

voir d'un Etat de criminaliser la conduite de certaines personnes n'équivaut pas nécessairement à un pouvoir de mettre en application ces lois — en particulier lorsque les personnes en question se trouvent au-delà des limites territoriales de l'Etat qui a exercé sa compétence législative[5]. En conséquence, les différentes bases de compétence — dans la mesure où elles sont pertinentes pour la suppression des crimes en mer — sont étudiées ci-après de manière séparée. L'analyse des questions de compétence envers les crimes en mer est rendue ardue non seulement par la localisation physique des conduites ou des actions réglementées, mais aussi par le droit spécifique qui entoure la juridiction maritime, en particulier tel que développé dans la CNUDM[6], qui reconnaissent que des questions et des intérêts distinctifs sont soulevés dans le contexte maritime.

A. *La compétence législative*

i) *Territorialité*

En droit international général, l'Etat a une compétence législative pleine eu égard aux personnes se trouvant et conduites se déroulant *à l'intérieur de son territoire*. Les seules limites à cette compétence absolue sont celles qui découlent du droit international[7] (par exemple les droits humains, qui requièrent que cet exercice de compétence législative adhère au principe de légalité).

La compétence législative pleine est une conséquence de la nature absolue de la souveraineté territoriale en droit international classique. Néanmoins, dans le cadre maritime, cet absolutisme est en conflit direct avec un autre principe de droit international classique, à savoir celui de *mare liberum*, dont le principe de la liberté de navigation découle[8]. Afin

---

lois adoptées). D'autres commentateurs considèrent que cette compétence est la manifestation de la compétence législative vu que les décisions judiciaires sont sources de droit (dans les systèmes de *common law*) ou représentent la mise en pratique de la compétence législative (Crawford, *supra* note 2, p. 456). En ce qui concerne les crimes en mer (par rapport auxquels les questions d'immunités ne sont pas applicables, mis à part les cas de crimes de guerre), la compétence adjudicative se rattache à l'exercice de la compétence législative et ne sera donc pas traitée séparément dans ce chapitre.

5. Voir O'Keefe, «Universal Jurisdiction; Clarifying the Basic Concept», *Journal of International Criminal Justice*, vol. 2 (2004) p. 735.

6. Nations Unies, *Recueil des traités*, vol. 1833 («CNUDM»).

7. Voir Shaw, *International Law*, 6e éd., CUP, 2008, p. 650.

8. Voir Feenstra, dir. publ., *Hugo Grotius Mare Liberum 1609-2009: Original Latin Text and English Translation*, Kluwer Academic Publishers, 2009. Pour plus de détails, voir Papastavridis, «The Right of Visit on the High Seas in a Theoretical Perspective: *Mare Liberum* v. *Mare Clausum* Revisited», *Leiden Journal of International Law*, vol. 24 (2011), pp. 45-69.

de permettre un équilibre entre les intérêts opposés des Etats côtiers et ceux de la libre navigation, la CNUDM organise les zones maritimes en un éventail échelonné de degrés de souveraineté. Plus on se trouve proche de la terre et plus les intérêts de l'Etat côtier sont directement en jeu, plus la CNUDM traite l'espace maritime comme un territoire où l'Etat côtier bénéficie d'une compétence législative complète ; réciproquement, plus on se situe loin de la côte et moins les intérêts de l'Etat côtier sont impliqués, plus la CNUDM protège la liberté de navigation. Plusieurs chapitres de cet ouvrage s'intéressent à ce dégradé de compétences, en évaluant à quel point l'équilibre atteint permet de supprimer efficacement la criminalité en mer.

En ce qui concerne les eaux intérieures — en d'autres termes « les eaux situées en deçà de la ligne de base de la mer territoriale »[9] — et les ports, la CNUDM ne modifie en rien la compétence pleine de l'Etat côtier. Le droit pénal national est applicable dans sa totalité aux agissements des personnes à bord d'un navire étranger dans les eaux intérieures ou en port (même si une compétence législative parallèle n'est pas à exclure en la forme du droit de l'Etat pavillonnaire, qui peut aussi s'appliquer de manière extraterritoriale, tel qu'il sera discuté plus loin).

Cependant, lorsqu'on s'éloigne de la frontière terrestre de l'Etat côtier, l'intérêt opposé de la liberté de navigation a pour effet de nuancer l'absolue souveraineté territoriale de cet Etat (ainsi que sa compétence législative pleine, qui en est une illustration). Les règles relatives au passage inoffensif à travers la mer territoriale[10] représentent l'écart le plus important face à la compétence territoriale pleine. L'article 21 de la CNUDM limite l'étendue du pouvoir dont l'Etat côtier bénéficie afin de règlementer le passage de navires étrangers à travers ses eaux territoriales[11]. Cet article utilise le passage inoffensif comme point de départ

---

9. Article 8, paragraphe 1, de la CNUDM.

10. L'article 3 de la CNUDM définit la mer territoriale comme « 12 milles marins mesurés à partir de lignes de base établies conformément à la Convention ». Dans ce chapitre, mer territoriale et eaux territoriales ont la même signification.

11. Selon l'article 21 de la CNUDM :

> « 1. L'Etat côtier peut adopter, en conformité avec les dispositions de la Convention et les autres règles du droit international, des lois et règlements *relatifs au passage inoffensif dans sa mer territoriale*, qui peuvent porter sur les questions suivantes :
>
> *a)* sécurité de la navigation et régulation du trafic maritime ;
> *b)* protection des équipements et systèmes d'aide à la navigation et des autres équipements ou installations ;
> *c)* protection des câbles et des pipelines ;
> *d)* conservation des ressources biologiques de la mer ;
> *e)* prévention des infractions aux lois et règlements de l'Etat côtier relatifs à la pêche ;

— un droit dont, d'après une interprétation large, découle une relative liberté pour les navires dans leurs rapports avec les règlements de l'Etat côtier. Depuis ce point de départ, l'article 21 reconnaît une sphère d'intérêts à l'Etat côtier et lui *permet* (d'une manière exhaustive) d'exercer sa compétence législative à l'égard de ces questions. Cependant, même dans les cas d'un tel exercice autorisé de compétence *relative* au passage inoffensif, la CNUDM crée un plafond de régulation : les Etats côtiers ne sont pas autorisés à « imposer aux navires étrangers des obligations ayant pour effet d'empêcher ou de restreindre l'exercice du droit de passage inoffensif de ces navires »[12].

Il faut reconnaître que l'article 21 ne restreint pas l'applicabilité du droit pénal traditionnel (par exemple) envers les navires étrangers, dans la mesure où ce droit n'est pas « relatif au passage inoffensif »[13]. Il convient également de noter que la liste des compétences de l'Etat côtier selon l'article 21 est étendue. Néanmoins, même pour les chapitres de compétence reconnus dans le premier paragraphe de cet article, une limitation d'importance s'impose : les lois et règlements ne peuvent s'appliquer à la conception, à la construction ou à l'armement des navires étrangers, à moins qu'ils ne donnent effet à des règles ou à des normes internationales généralement acceptées[14]. Cette exception se caractérise par un équilibre entre l'intérêt véritable qu'un Etat peut avoir de réguler la sécurité des navires qui traversent ses eaux territoriales et les intérêts de la liberté de navigation (qui serait mise à mal si les navires devaient respecter les différentes lois des Etats dont ils traversent les eaux territoriales). La recherche d'un tel équilibre n'est pas sans conséquence, en particulier en ce qui concerne la compétence de l'Etat côtier de réguler la pollution accidentelle causée par des navires étrangers qui passent à travers ses eaux territoriales[15].

Lorsque les navires étrangers soit ne sont pas *de passage* à travers les eaux territoriales[16] ou que leur passage n'est pas inoffen-

---

f) préservation de l'environnement de l'Etat côtier et prévention, réduction et maîtrise de sa pollution ;
g) recherche scientifique marine et levés hydrographiques ;
h) prévention des infractions aux lois et règlements douaniers, fiscaux, sanitaires ou d'immigration de l'Etat côtier. » (L'italique est de nous.)

12. Article 24, paragraphe 1, lettre *a)*, de la CNUDM.

13. Déterminer si un Etat peut mettre en application son droit pénal (par voie d'un exercice de compétence d'exécution) à bord d'un navire qui utilise son droit de passage inoffensif est cependant une autre question (discutée ci-après).

14. Article 21, paragraphe 2, de la CNUDM.

15. Voir *infra* Gahlen, chapitre 3.

16. Le passage doit être « continu et rapide », mais peut comprendre l'arrêt et le mouillage

« s'ils constituent des incidents ordinaires de navigation ou s'imposent par suite d'un cas de force majeure ou de détresse ou dans le but de porter

sif[17], l'Etat côtier récupère sa pleine compétence de légiférer. En ce qui concerne certaines formes de criminalité en mer, la capacité de l'Etat côtier de réguler le passage non inoffensif est essentielle dans la lutte contre l'impunité. Par exemple, le vol à main armée en mer — un sujet d'intérêt relativement nouveau en droit international[18] — est clairement une exception au passage inoffensif (dans la mesure où il s'agit d'une «activité sans rapport direct avec le passage» qui «porte ... atteinte à la paix, au bon ordre ou à la sécurité de l'Etat côtier»)[19], et est ainsi soumis entièrement au droit pénal de l'Etat côtier. De manière similaire, selon l'article 19, paragraphe 2, point i), de la CNUDM, les Etats côtiers ont une compétence législative pleine eu égard aux activités de pêche dans leurs eaux territoriales — activités auxquelles peuvent être liées des sanctions pénales[20]. La pollution intentionnée et sérieuse causée par des navires étrangers en mer territoriale tombe aussi sous le coup du droit pénal de l'Etat côtier[21].

La plupart des questions problématiques liées à la lutte contre la criminalité en mer se situent autour de la distinction entre le passage inoffensif et le passage non inoffensif. Entres autres exemples, dans la lutte

---

secours à des personnes, des navires ou des aéronefs en danger ou en détresse» (Article 18, paragraphe 2, de la CNUDM).

17. Selon l'article 19, paragraphe 2, de la CNUDM:

«Le passage d'un navire étranger est considéré comme portant atteinte à la paix, au bon ordre ou à la sécurité de l'Etat côtier si, dans la mer territoriale, ce navire se livre à l'une quelconque des activités suivantes:

a) menace ou emploi de la force contre la souveraineté, l'intégrité territoriale ou l'indépendance politique de l'Etat côtier ou de toute autre manière contraire aux principes du droit international énoncés dans la Charte des Nations Unies;
b) exercice ou manœuvre avec armes de tout type;
c) collecte de renseignements au détriment de la défense ou de la sécurité de l'Etat côtier;
d) propagande visant à nuire à la défense ou à la sécurité de l'Etat côtier;
e) lancement, appontage ou embarquement d'aéronefs;
f) lancement, appontage ou embarquement d'engins militaires;
g) embarquement ou débarquement de marchandises, de fonds ou de personnes en contravention aux lois et règlements douaniers, fiscaux, sanitaires ou d'immigration de l'Etat côtier;
h) pollution délibérée et grave, en violation de la Convention;
i) pêche;
j) recherches ou levés;
k) perturbation du fonctionnement de tout système de communication ou de tout autre équipement ou installation de l'Etat côtier;
l) toute autre activité sans rapport direct avec le passage.»

18. Voir *infra* Abdoul, chapitre 7.
19. Article 19 de la CNUDM.
20. Voir *infra* Oanta, chapitre 4.
21. Voir *infra* Gahlen, chapitre 3.

contre le trafic de migrants[22], le droit pénal de l'Etat côtier peut s'appliquer à un navire engagé dans un tel trafic qui l'a pris comme destination — cela est justifié par le fait que le navire en question n'exerce pas son droit de passage inoffensif et est par là même soumis à la compétence législative pleine de l'Etat côtier. Mais lorsque le navire est utilisé pour le trafic de migrants *à travers* les eaux territoriales d'un Etat côtier, sa conduite ne tombe pas sous le coup de la compétence législative de cet Etat (et moins encore sous sa compétence d'exécution, comme cela sera discuté ci-après), pour la simple raison que le navire n'a aucune intention de « débarque[r] de[s] personnes en contravention aux lois et règlements d'immigration de l'Etat côtier »[23] et que son passage reste ainsi inoffensif. Dans l'exercice d'équilibrage entre la liberté de navigation et la souveraineté de l'Etat côtier, les Etats se sont pourvus d'une marge de manœuvre afin de protéger leurs propres intérêts. Néanmoins, la CNUDM n'envisage pas l'exercice de la compétence législative dans l'intérêt de la communauté internationale dans son ensemble, pour des objectifs de politique publique internationale (ce qui inclurait certainement le trafic de migrants, qu'ils soient destinés à être débarqués dans l'Etat côtier ou non), ou même pour le maintien de la paix et de la sécurité internationales.

Une problématique similaire surgit avec le transport d'armes de destruction massive (ADM), transport qui fait l'objet de plusieurs résolutions du Conseil de sécurité agissant dans le cadre du chapitre VII de la Charte des Nations Unies[24]. Cette problématique se trouve relativement élevée dans la liste des priorités de la communauté internationale dans sa lutte contre la criminalité en mer. Alors que la

> « menace ou emploi de la force contre la souveraineté, l'intégrité territoriale ou l'indépendance politique de l'Etat côtier ou de toute autre manière contraire aux principes du droit international énoncés dans la Charte des Nations Unies »

rendrait le passage d'un navire non inoffensif et donc le soumettrait au droit pénal de l'Etat côtier, la prolifération en tant que telle (sans aucune intention d'utiliser les armes ou de les introduire dans l'Etat côtier) pourrait ne pas atteindre le niveau requis pas l'article 19, paragraphe 2, lettre *a)*, de la CNUDM[25]. Cela est particulièrement vrai dans la mesure

22. Voir *infra* Guggisberg, chapitre 6.
23. Article 19, paragraphe 2, lettre *g)* de la CNUDM.
24. Voir par exemple la résolution 1540 (2004) du Conseil de sécurité. Sur la criminalisation des ADM et ses liens avec les conventions contre le terrorisme et le traité de non prolifération, voir *infra* Cherief, chapitre 13.
25. Voir l'argument de Guilfoyle sur la signification de l'article 19, paragraphe 2, lettre *a)*, de la CNUDM, *Shipping Interdiction and the Law of the Sea*, CUP, 2009, pp. 241-242.

où les résolutions du Conseil sur les ADM sont adressées à la prolifération causée par des acteurs non étatiques, qui ne sont pas liés par l'interdiction de l'utilisation de la force telle que développée dans la Charte. Néanmoins, puisque le Conseil de sécurité a obligé les Etats à criminaliser le transport et le transfert d'ADM[26], il est très difficile de voir comment cette conduite — même si elle n'a pas pour but l'Etat côtier — peut être perçue comme inoffensive.

En 1982, lorsque la CNUDM a été adoptée, la guerre froide faisait rage et le Conseil de sécurité était dans une impasse. Les menaces à la «paix et la sécurité internationales» (que le Conseil est chargé de maintenir)[27] étaient aussi sans doute plus limitées que dans ce nouveau siècle. Dans un tel contexte historique, il n'est pas surprenant que les Etats qui ont codifié et progressivement développé les exceptions au passage inoffensif n'aient pas envisagé d'inclure des activités qui ne touchent pas les intérêts directs de l'Etat côtier, mais qui impliquent la paix et la sécurité internationales, pour le maintien desquelles une réaction de l'Etat côtier pourrait être requise. Cependant, si la CNUDM a vraiment l'ambition de servir de «Constitution pour les océans», elle ne peut être excessivement limitée par la situation géopolitique du milieu des années quatre-vingt. En effet, le droit international général fournit aux Etats et aux cours un éventail d'outils destinés à rafraîchir les traités, leur permettant ainsi de les adapter au contexte contemporain (tout en respectant soigneusement l'objet et le but du traité), mais sans devoir faire recours aux lourdes contraintes liées à une modification formelle d'un traité[28]. Par exemple, la Cour internationale de Justice (CIJ) a fait appel à l'article 31, paragraphe 3, alinéa *c)*, de la CVDT afin de moderniser des traités à travers un processus d'interprétation[29]. L'article 19, paragraphe 2, lettre *b)*, de la CNUDM contient une exception fourre-tout au passage inoffensif («toute autre activité sans rapport direct avec le passage») qui pourrait bien servir de base à une interprétation liant cette exception à «toute règle pertinente de droit international applicable dans les relations entre les parties»[30], comme les résolutions du Conseil de sécurité. Cela aurait pour conséquences que toute conduite que le Conseil a demandé aux Etats de réprimer (par exemple la prolifération d'ADM) rendrait le

26. Résolution 1540 (2004) du Conseil de sécurité, par. 2.

27. Article 25, paragraphe 1, de la Charte des Nations Unies, 26 juin 1945, Nations Unies, *Recueil des traités*, vol. 1, p. xvi).

28. Voir les règles d'interprétation des traités, telles qu'exposées dans les articles 31 à 33 de la Convention de Vienne sur le droit des traités, Nations Unies, *Recueil des traités des Nations Unies*, vol. 1155, p. 331 (ci-après: «CVDT»).

29. Voir *Plates-formes pétrolières (République islamique d'Iran c. Etats-Unis d'Amérique)*, arrêt, *CIJ Recueil 2003*, p. 16, par. 31-45.

30. Article 31, paragraphe 3, lettre *c)*, de la CVDT.

passage non inoffensif et donc le soumettrait au droit pénal de l'Etat côtier.

ii) *La compétence extraterritoriale*

Au-delà de la mer territoriale — dans la zone contiguë (qui peut s'étendre jusqu'à 24 milles marins depuis les lignes de base[31]), la zone économique exclusive (qui peut s'étendre quant à elle jusqu'à 200 milles marins des lignes de base de l'Etat côtier[32]) et bien sûr en haute mer[33] — la CNUDM s'intéresse principalement à la compétence d'exécution des Etats. Leur compétence législative est quant à elle déterminée par les règles générales de droit international en matière de compétence extraterritoriale.

Comme nous le développerons ci-après, lorsque la CNUDM aborde l'étendue de la compétence législative, elle le fait d'une manière qui illustre (plutôt qu'elle n'en diffère) les bases de compétence législative extraterritoriale qui sont fournies en droit international général.

En droit international général, les Etats peuvent réguler, dans certaines circonstances, la conduite de personnes qui se trouvent au-delà de leur territoire (et de leur mer territoriale). En 1927, la Cour permanente de Justice internationale a semblé conclure, de manière controversée, que la compétence législative est quasiment sans limite, même lorsqu'elle est exercée de manière extraterritoriale — et que les seules exceptions à ce plein pouvoir découlent d'interdictions particulières[34]. L'approche moderne la plus largement acceptée se base sur le postulat inverse[35] et s'apparente plus à la démarche suivie dans le contexte du droit de la mer: un balancement d'intérêts contraires est fait et il est requis des Etats qu'ils aient un lien ou un intérêt substantiel envers des personnes ou des conduites qu'ils souhaitent soumettre à leur droit[36]. En

31. Article 33, paragraphe 2, de la CNUDM.
32. Article 57, de la CNUDM.
33. Article 86, de la CNUDM.
34. *Affaire du Lotus* (1927), *CPIJ série A n° 10*, p. 19:

> «Loin de défendre d'une manière générale aux Etats d'étendre leurs lois et leur juridiction à des personnes, des biens et des actes hors du territoire, il leur laisse, à cet égard, une large liberté, qui n'est limitée que dans quelques cas par des règles prohibitives; pour les autres cas, chaque Etat reste libre d'adopter les principes qu'il juge les meilleurs et les plus convenables.»

35. Voir Mills, *Confluence of Public and Private International Law*, CUP, 2009, p. 225; Shaw, *supra* note 7, p. 656; *Mandat d'arrêt du 11 avril 2000 (République démocratique du Congo c. Belgique)*, arrêt, *CIJ Recueil 2002*, p. 3, opinion individuelle commune de Mme Higgins et de MM. Kooijmans et Buergenthal, juges.
36. Voir par exemple Mann, «The Doctrine of Jurisdiction in International Law», *Recueil des cours*, tome 111 (1964), pp. 43-51.

l'absence d'un lien ou d'un intérêt substantiel, l'application extraterritoriale du droit pénal d'un Etat s'apparente à de l'ingérence entre Etats, ce que le droit international général, qui défend le principe de non-intervention[37], regarde d'un mauvais œil.

Le droit international reconnaît un certain nombre de bases (qui se chevauchent souvent) sur lesquelles un Etat peut exercer sa compétence législative extraterritoriale[38] — chacune illustrant une connexion ou un intérêt réel avec la personne et/ou la conduite : i) le principe de nationalité (la conduite de ses nationaux à l'étranger) ; ii) le principe de personnalité passive (la conduite de tiers à l'étranger lorsque celle-ci cause du tort à des nationaux) ; iii) le principe de protection (la conduite de non-nationaux, à l'étranger, lorsqu'elle a un effet sur les intérêts sécuritaires de l'Etat) ; iv) la doctrine des effets (dans sa forme la plus étendue, elle est la base de compétence législative extraterritoriale la moins bien acceptée, mais également celle sur laquelle certains Etats comptent pour criminaliser la conduite de non-nationaux à l'étranger, lorsque cette conduite a un effet sur l'Etat — mais l'effet n'a pas besoin de toucher des intérêts sécuritaires essentiels) ; et finalement v) la compétence universelle (les crimes internationaux et crimes basés sur des traités[39] « committed abroad by persons who, at the time of commission, are non-resident aliens, where such offences are not deemed to constitute threats to the fundamental interests of the prescribing state or ... to give rise to effects within its territory »[40]). Cette dernière base de compétence législative ne prend pas sa source sur une quelconque connexion entre l'Etat légiférant et les personnes dont la conduite est criminalisée. Il s'agit plutôt de l'intérêt réel que tout Etat peut avoir de donner corps aux politiques publiques internationales[41].

En règle générale, la CNUDM n'empêche pas les Etats d'exercer leur

---

37. Voir Déclaration des Nations Unies sur les relations amicales entre Etats, (Nations Unies, résolution 2625 (1970)), qui est considérée comme une expression du droit international coutumier par la Cour internationale de Justice dans sa décision sur le fond *Activités militaires et paramilitaires au Nicaragua et contre celui-ci (Nicaragua c. Etats-Unis d'Amérique)*, arrêt, *CIJ Recueil 1986*, p. 14, par. 202.

38. Voir généralement « Restatement of the Law Third, Foreign Relations Law of the United States », adopté par l'American Law Institute le 14 mai 1986, par. 402-404.

39. Les crimes selon le droit international, ou « crimes internationaux » se limitent selon la majorité des avis au génocide, aux crimes de guerre et aux crimes contre l'humanité. La responsabilité pénale individuelle est liée à ces crimes par le droit international coutumier. Ils doivent être distingués des « crimes conventionnels » qui font l'objet de traités de mise en application du droit pénal (un certain nombre d'entre eux sont examinés dans cet ouvrage). *Infra* notes 103 et 104.

40. O'Keefe (2004), *supra* note 5, p. 745.

41. Crawford (2012), *supra* note 2, p. 467.

compétence législative extraterritoriale sur les bases présentées ci-dessus et parfois clarifie même leur droit de le faire, bien que celui-ci soit soumis à certaines limites. Par exemple, l'article 211, paragraphe 5, de la CNUDM permet aux Etats «[d']adopter pour leur zone économique exclusive des lois et règlements visant à prévenir, réduire et maîtriser la pollution par les navires». Malgré la présence de cette règle permissive dans la CNUDM, un tel exercice de compétence législative serait de toute manière possible selon le principe territorial (sur une base objective, dans la mesure où une partie du délit prend place dans le territoire de l'Etat) ou selon la doctrine des effets (puisque la pollution dans la ZEE peut avoir des effets, certes non liés à la sécurité, mais néanmoins dévastateurs pour l'Etat côtier). La CNUDM restreint toutefois la compétence législative de l'Etat côtier au sujet de la pollution: de telles lois ne doivent pas être adoptées d'une manière qui crée des effets allant au-delà des «règles et normes internationales généralement acceptées établies par l'intermédiaire de l'organisation internationale compétente ou d'une conférence diplomatique générale»[42].

Alors que les Etats peuvent être autorisés à considérer leurs lois nationales comme applicables dans des zones se situant au-delà de leur mer territoriale (sur la base des principes présentés ci-dessus), la liberté de navigation demeure, naturellement, une priorité. Elle est protégée par des restrictions relatives à la compétence d'exécution (comme cela sera discuté plus loin). En conséquence, les Etats sont libres de criminaliser extraterritorialement certaines conduites, et sont même fréquemment, par le biais du droit international des traités, dans l'obligation de le faire, alors qu'ils peuvent ne jamais être en position de mettre en application ces règles de droit pénal. Devoir criminaliser extraterritorialement certaines conduites n'est cependant pas sans but: si jamais un criminel se trouve sous leur compétence d'exécution, cela assure que les Etats ont ainsi un cadre législatif approprié[43].

Nombre de traités internationaux relatifs à la mise en application du droit pénal et qui s'adressent à la criminalité en mer[44] obligent les Etats à criminaliser sur une base extraterritoriale certaines conduites en mer[45].

42. Article 211, paragraphe 5, de la CNUDM. Sur le résultat de l'exercice d'équilibrage entre les intérêts des Etats côtiers et la liberté de navigation dans la ZEE, voir *infra* Gahlen, chapitre 3.

43. Voir *infra*, présente section, paragraphe 2, titre B, point ii).

44. *Infra* note 104 et texte s'y référant.

45. Un exemple typique, adopté à la suite de l'incident de l'*Achille Lauro* est la Convention pour la répression d'actes illicites contre la sécurité maritime, Nations Unies, *Recueil des traités*, vol. 1678 (1988), p. 201 (entrée en vigueur le 1er mars 1992) (ci-après: «SUA»). Pour plus de détails sur la nature des obligations de mise en application du droit pénal en matière de criminalité maritime, voir *infra*, présente section, paragraphe 2, lettre A, point ii).

La base de compétence la plus commune dans ces traités est une variation des principes de nationalité et de personnalité passive — exigeant ainsi des Etats la criminalisation de conduites se déroulant à bord[46] des navires battant leur pavillon ou ayant lieu à l'encontre de ceux-ci[47].

En raison de criminalisations sur de telles bases, un exercice de compétences législatives concurrentes ou chevauchantes survient souvent, puisque les Etats doivent également criminaliser la conduite de leurs nationaux[48] (qui peuvent bien logiquement travailler sur un navire battant le pavillon d'un autre Etat), et ont le droit d'établir leur compétence sur la base du principe de protection — lorsque le crime «est commi[s] dans le but de contraindre [un] Etat à accomplir un acte quelconque ou à s'en abstenir»[49]. A cet égard, le droit international général ne fournit pas à un groupe d'Etats particuliers une priorité dans l'exécution de son droit pénal[50].

L'élément décisif finit souvent par être d'une nature très pratique, à savoir que l'exercice de compétence revient généralement à l'Etat qui a exercé sa compétence d'exécution et qui, par là même, a les criminels sous sa garde. Comme les Etats ont régulièrement une compétence d'exécution exclusive envers leurs navires[51], l'Etat pavillonnaire (ou tout autre Etat qui a reçu l'autorisation de celui-ci) détient les criminels et est donc de fait dans une position lui permettant d'assurer la mise en application de son droit pénal extraterritorial.

B. La compétence d'exécution

La compétence d'exécution est généralement perçue comme le pouvoir de prendre des mesures de type exécutif afin d'appliquer les règles de conduite en vigueur. Dans le contexte maritime, l'exercice de cette compétence peut être divisé en deux catégories distinctes: d'un côté, arrêter un navire, monter à bord et le fouiller

46. Voir par exemple l'article 6, paragraphe 1, lettre *a)*, de la SUA.

47. *Ibid.* Voir aussi l'article 15, paragraphe 1, lettre *a)*, de la Convention des Nations Unies contre la criminalité transnationale organisée 2000, Nations Unies, *Recueil des traités*, vol. 2225, p. 209 (ci-après «Convention contre la criminalité transnationale organisée»).

48. Voir par exemple l'article 6, paragraphe 1, lettre *c)*, de la SUA. L'article 15, paragraphe 2, lettre *b)*, de la Convention contre la criminalité transnationale organisée demande l'établissement d'une telle juridiction, mais sur une base permissive plutôt qu'obligatoire.

49. Voir par exemple l'article 6, paragraphe 2, lettre *c)*, de la SUA.

50. L'article 11, paragraphe 5, de la SUA requiert cependant des Etats qu'ils prennent en compte les intérêts de l'Etat pavillonnaire lorsqu'ils se décident entre plusieurs demandes d'extradition.

51. *Infra* note 65 et le texte s'y référant.

(« visite ») et, de l'autre, arrêter les membres d'équipage et saisir le navire (« arrestation » ou « confiscation »)[52].

En droit international général, l'exercice de la compétence d'exécution est principalement territorial. La maxime de la CPJI dans l'affaire du *Lotus* reste d'actualité :

> « Or, la limitation primordiale qu'impose le droit international à l'Etat est celle d'exclure — sauf l'existence d'une règle permissive contraire — tout exercice de sa puissance sur le territoire d'un autre Etat. Dans ce sens, la juridiction est certainement territoriale ; elle ne pourrait être exercée hors du territoire, sinon en vertu d'une règle permissive découlant du droit international coutumier ou d'une convention. »[53]

La « règle permissive » à laquelle la CPJI fait référence prend plus souvent qu'à son tour la forme du consentement de l'Etat — ce qui signifie qu'un Etat peut exercer son pouvoir d'exécution du droit sur le territoire d'un autre Etat avec l'accord de ce dernier. Exceptionnellement, le besoin de consentement peut être évité par le Conseil de sécurité lorsqu'il agit dans le cadre de ses pouvoirs découlant du chapitre VII et par l'invocation de l'article 103 de la Charte des Nations Unies — cette situation consiste toutefois encore en l'utilisation d'une « règle permissive » pour autant que la compétence d'exécution extraterritoriale soit concernée.

Déterminer si cette règle générale de droit international s'applique à l'identique aux espaces maritimes, et en particulier à l'intérieur de la mer territoriale d'un Etat, reste une question ouverte. A certains égards, la CNUDM ne modifie pas la nature pleine de la compétence d'exécution (à la fois pour les visites et pour les arrestations et confiscations) au sein des eaux territoriales d'un Etat. Par exemple, selon l'article 27, paragraphe 2, de la CNUDM, un Etat peut librement exercer cette compétence dans sa mer territoriale à l'encontre de navires qui quittent ses eaux intérieures. En ce qui concerne les navires qui ne font que traverser les eaux territoriales, toutefois, la relation que la CNUDM entretient avec la nature pleine de la compétence d'exécution à l'intérieur d'un Etat est plus ambiguë. L'article 27, paragraphe 1, semble particulièrement enclin à demander aux Etats de faire preuve de retenue dans leur exercice de la compétence d'exécution[54], sauf :

---

52. Voir Papastavridis, *The Interception of Vessels on the High Seas : Contemporary Challenges to the Legal Order of the Oceans*, Hart, 2013, pp. 51-53. Voir aussi Guilfoyle, *supra* note 25, p. 9.

53. Affaire du *Lotus* (1927), *CPJI série A n° 10*, pp. 18-19.

54. Article 27, paragraphe 1, de la CNUDM :

« L'Etat côtier *ne devrait pas* exercer sa juridiction pénale à bord d'un

«*a)* si les conséquences de l'infraction s'étendent à l'Etat côtier;
b) si l'infraction est de nature à troubler la paix du pays ou l'ordre dans la mer territoriale;
c) si l'assistance des autorités locales a été demandée par le capitaine du navire ou par un agent diplomatique ou un fonctionnaire consulaire de l'Etat de pavillon; ou
d) si ces mesures sont nécessaires pour la répression du trafic illicite des stupéfiants ou des substances psychotropes.»

Le débat fait (académiquement) rage dans la littérature contemporaine pour savoir si l'article 27 interdit aux Etats d'exercer leur compétence d'exécution dans leurs eaux territoriales dans les cas non prévus au paragraphe 1 ou si cet article n'a qu'une valeur indicative[55]. Dans le contexte de la criminalité en mer, cette polémique n'a probablement pas d'applicabilité pratique. En effet, même si l'on considère que l'article 27, paragraphe 1, constitue une interdiction générale de l'exercice de la compétence d'exécution dans les eaux territoriales, sauf dans les circonstances énumérées, ces circonstances sont néanmoins formulées de manière très large et peuvent englober les crimes en mer examinés dans cet ouvrage. Soit «les conséquences de l'infraction s'étendent à l'Etat côtier», par exemple dans les cas de pollution[56], de trafic de drogue, de traite d'êtres humains, de trafic de migrants[57] ou de prolifération d'ADM[58] lorsqu'elles sont destinées aux côtes de l'Etat littoral, soit le crime tombe dans une catégorie de problèmes internationaux plus généraux (qui n'affectent pas particulièrement l'Etat côtier) et pourrait être qualifié sur cette base comme troublant «l'ordre dans la mer territoriale» selon l'article 27, paragraphe 1, lettre *b)*, de la CNUDM. Ce deuxième cas de figure serait certainement pertinent lorsque la criminalité rend les eaux territoriales dangereuses (comme dans la situation de vol à main armée en mer[59]) ou lorsque l'activité en question est sujette à des résolutions du Conseil de sécurité dans le cadre du chapitre VII de la Charte (par exemple en ce qui concerne la prolifération d'ADM).

Il est en effet implicitement reconnu dans les résolutions du Conseil

---

navire étranger passant dans la mer territoriale pour y procéder à une arrestation ou à l'exécution d'actes d'instruction à la suite d'une infraction pénale commise à bord pendant le passage, sauf dans les cas suivants» (l'italique est de nous).

55. Voir Guilfoyle, *supra* note 25, p. 11. Pour plus de détails, voir *infra* Guggisberg, chapitre 6; Gahlen, chapitre 3, et Cherief, chapitre 13, sur les implications du débat relatif respectivement au trafic de migrants, à la pollution maritime et à la prolifération d'ADM.
56. Voir *infra* Gahlen, chapitre 3.
57. Voir *infra* Guggisberg, chapitre 6.
58. Voir *infra* Cherief, chapitre 13.
59. Voir *infra* Abdoul, chapitre 7.

sur les ADM que la conduite visée met en danger la paix et la sécurité internationales et que la coopération est nécessaire à sa suppression. Comme il a été dit plus haut, les possibilités d'interprétation offertes par l'article 31, paragraphe 3, lettre *c)*, de la CVDT permettent aux provisions de la CNUDM de s'adapter aux besoins du monde moderne. Les menaces à la paix et à la sécurité internationales qui prennent la forme de l'usage (souvent abusif) des espaces maritimes sont certainement un défi pour le bon ordre de ces zones, y compris dans les eaux territoriales. Comme la prolifération est un crime continu (à savoir qu'il est en train d'être commis tant que les ADM sont à bord), elle ne tomberait pas dans l'interdiction absolue d'exercer sa compétence d'exécution contenue à l'article 27, paragraphe 5, de la CNUDM. Selon cet article en effet,

> «l'Etat côtier ne peut prendre aucune mesure à bord d'un navire étranger qui passe dans la mer territoriale en vue de procéder à une arrestation ou à des actes d'instruction judiciaire à la suite d'une infraction pénale commise avant l'entrée du navire dans la mer territoriale si le navire, en provenance d'un port étranger, ne fait que passer dans la mer territoriale sans entrer dans les eaux intérieures.» [60]

Les crimes en mer qui font l'objet de conventions de mise en application du droit pénal international (par exemple le trafic de migrants et la traite de personnes, les crimes contre la sécurité de la navigation et la prolifération d'ADM) [61] peuvent être d'une manière similaire considérés comme «de nature à troubler l'ordre dans la mer territoriale». Cela est particulièrement vrai dans la mesure où ces conventions font partie du contexte dans lequel la CNUDM doit être interprétée (selon l'article 31, paragraphe 3, lettre *c)*, de la CVDT). Face à la globalisation croissante, «l'ordre dans la mer territoriale» ne peut plus être vu seulement à travers le prisme national, mais doit plutôt refléter la nature de biens communs des espaces maritimes. Dans la mesure où nombre des conventions qui s'intéressent aux crimes en mer les qualifient de «préoccup[ant] gravement la communauté internationale dans son ensemble» [62], «port[ant] gravement préjudice aux Etats concernés» [63] et «min[ant] la confiance

60. Même si l'interdiction de l'article 27, paragraphe 5, de la CNUDM était applicable, l'article 103 de la Charte des Nations Unies permettrait de résoudre le conflit entre cette interdiction et l'obligation se trouvant dans des résolutions du Conseil de sécurité de coopérer dans la répression de certains crimes en mer.

61. *Infra* note 104.

62. SUA, préambule.

63. Protocole contre le trafic illicite de migrants par terre, air et mer 2000, Nations Unies, *Recueil des traités*, vol. 2241, p. 519 (ci-après «Protocole contre le trafic illicite de migrants»), préambule.

des peuples du monde dans la sécurité de la navigation maritime»[64], il est difficile de voir comment leur perpétration pourrait ne pas menacer le bon ordre des eaux territoriales (et bien évidemment aussi des zones plus au large). Il convient en particulier de noter que l'absence d'exercice d'une compétence d'exécution dans un tel cas crée pour des navires qui ont déjà commis une activité criminalisée ou qui sont en train de l'entreprendre un refuge dans les eaux territoriales. Dans ces circonstances, l'infraction, tout comme la création d'une telle zone d'impunité, «est de nature à troubler l'ordre dans la mer territoriale».

Même si l'on accepte que les Etats côtiers bénéficient d'une compétence d'exécution pleine dans leurs eaux territoriales face aux crimes en mer — en accord avec le droit international général, mais grâce à des mécanismes interprétatifs découlant de l'article 31, paragraphe 3, lettre *c)*, de la CVDT — il faut garder à l'esprit que la grande majorité des espaces maritimes se situe au-delà de la compétence des Etats. Une mise en application efficace du droit pénal dans ces zones de biens communs requiert par conséquent une autre base légale de compétence. Selon l'article 92, paragraphe 1, de la CNUDM, l'Etat pavillonnaire a la «juridiction exclusive en haute mer» envers les navires battant son pavillon[65]. Au-delà de la mer territoriale[66], les Etats ne peuvent donc pas exercer leur compétence d'exécution à l'encontre de navires étrangers à moins *a)* que la CNUDM ne le prévoie); *b)* que l'Etat pavillonnaire ou côtier ait donné son accord ou *c)* que le Conseil de sécurité, agissant dans le cadre du chapitre VII d'une manière qui appelle les pouvoirs hiérarchiques de l'article 103 de la Charte de Nations Unies, ait autorisé une telle action.

i) *A moins que la CNUDM ne le prévoie*

La CNUDM prévoit un certain nombre d'exceptions à l'exclusivité de la juridiction (compétence d'exécution) de l'Etat pavillonnaire au-delà des eaux territoriales de l'Etat côtier. Tout d'abord, le droit de poursuite chaude consiste dans:

---

64. SUA, préambule.

65. Cette «juridiction exclusive» réfère uniquement à la compétence d'exécution, vue qu'une compétence législative parallèle n'est pas à exclure en la forme du droit de l'Etat de nationalité à criminaliser les comportements de ses ressortissants, même en haute mer à bord des navires battant pavillon étranger. Selon l'article 58, paragraphe 2, de la CNUDM, la juridiction exclusive de l'État pavillonnaire s'applique également à la ZEE, sauf quand il en est prévu différemment dans la partie V de la CNUDM.

66. Cette règle est plus nuancée en ce qui concerne la zone contiguë et à la ZEE: les Etats pavillonnaires ont une juridiction exclusive par rapport aux sujets que la CNUDM n'attribue pas à la juridiction de l'Etat côtier. En tant que telles, ces zones sont examinées ci-dessous sous le point «i) A moins que la CNUDM ne le prévoie».

> «The right of a State to pursue foreign ships which have offended its law within its national jurisdiction was well-established in the nineteenth century, although the derivation of the right is obscure.»[67]

Quelles que soient ses sources, ce droit est fermement implanté dans la CNUDM: la poursuite d'un navire battant le pavillon d'un autre Etat

> «peut être engagée si les autorités compétentes de l'Etat côtier ont de sérieuses raisons de penser que ce navire a contrevenu aux lois et règlements de cet Etat. Cette poursuite doit commencer lorsque le navire étranger ou une de ses embarcations se trouve dans les eaux intérieures, dans les eaux archipélagiques, dans la mer territoriale.»[68]

Ce droit de poursuite chaude est particulièrement pertinent ici en ce qui concerne la suppression du vol à main armée en mer, dans les cas où le navire en question fait ensuite route vers la haute mer, ou dans les cas où l'Etat côtier a «de sérieuses raisons de penser» que des activités liées au trafic de migrants ou à la prolifération maritime ont eu lieu et que le navire incriminé prend le chemin du large.

Quant à la zone contiguë, la CNUDM permet à l'Etat côtier d'exercer le

> «contrôle nécessaire en vue de ... prévenir les infractions à ses lois et règlements douaniers, fiscaux, sanitaires ou d'immigration sur son territoire ou dans sa mer territoriale [et de] réprimer les infractions à ces mêmes lois et règlements commises sur son territoire ou dans sa mer territoriale»[69].

Ainsi, l'Etat côtier peut exercer sa compétence d'exécution envers les navires étrangers se situant dans sa zone contiguë, sans l'accord de l'Etat pavillonnaire, en réponse, par exemple, à un trafic de migrants qui s'est déjà produit dans ses eaux territoriales, ou (de manière plus débattue) en réponse à une tentative de trafic de migrants[70]. Les mêmes remarques pourraient être faites pour les cas de pollution intentionnelle dans les eaux territoriales, qui rendraient le passage non inoffensif et donc le soumettraient à la compétence législative de l'Etat côtier[71]. L'Etat côtier a aussi le droit de poursuite chaude contre les navires étran-

67. O'Connell, *The International Law of the Sea*, Clarendon Press, 1982, p. 1076.
68. Article 111, paragraphe 1, de la CNUDM.
69. Article 33, paragraphe 1, lettres *a)* et *b)*, de la CNUDM.
70. Voir *infra* Guggisberg, chapitre 6.
71. *Supra* note 21 et texte s'y référant.

gers qui quittent sa zone contiguë, s'il a une bonne raison de croire que le navire a violé les lois et règlements applicables dans cette zone[72].

Au sein de la ZEE, la CNUDM autorise l'Etat à utiliser sa compétence d'exécution à l'encontre des navires étrangers, sans l'accord de l'Etat pavillonnaire, en ce qui concerne les sujets sur lesquels il bénéfice de droits souverains. D'une pertinence particulière au vu des crimes en mer examinés dans ce volume, les Etats côtiers peuvent exercer leur compétence d'exécution envers les navires étrangers dans leur ZEE en réponse à des violations du droit de la pêche[73]. Cette exception au principe d'exclusivité de la juridiction exclusive de l'Etat pavillonnaire est néanmoins sujette à bon nombre de limites, dont l'obligation de notifier l'Etat pavillonnaire (au lieu du traditionnel consentement préalable) et celle de libérer promptement les navires et les membres d'équipage arrêtés contre versement d'une caution ou d'une garantie raisonnable. En ce qui concerne la répression de la criminalité en mer, la compétence d'exécution accordée aux Etats côtiers en matière de pêche est plutôt limitée:

> «Les sanctions prévues par l'Etat côtier pour les infractions aux lois et règlements en matière de pêche dans la zone économique exclusive ne peuvent comprendre l'emprisonnement, à moins que les Etats concernés n'en conviennent autrement, ni aucun autre châtiment corporel.»[74]

En conséquence, sans l'accord de l'Etat pavillonnaire et probablement aussi celui de l'Etat de nationalité de chaque membre d'équipage détenu (puisque chacun de ces Etats constitue un «Etat concerné»), les sanctions pénales vont être limitées à des amendes. En haute mer, deux exceptions bien connues à la juridiction exclusive de l'Etat pavillonnaire existent et permettent *à la fois la visite et l'arrestation*: la piraterie[75] et

72. La poursuite doit être continue (sans interruption) et un ordre d'arrêt doit avoir été donné correctement au navire soumis à la poursuite (article 111 de la CNUDM).

73. Voir *infra* Oanta, chapitre 4. Le droit de poursuite chaude s'applique aussi aux violations des lois et règlements de pêche dans la ZEE (article 111 de la CNUDM).

74. Article 73, paragraphe 3, de la CNUDM.

75. Article 105 de la CNUDM:

> «Tout Etat peut, en haute mer ou en tout autre lieu ne relevant de la juridiction d'aucun Etat, saisir un navire ou un aéronef pirate, ou un navire ou un aéronef capturé à la suite d'un acte de piraterie et aux mains de pirates, et appréhender les personnes et saisir les biens se trouvant à bord. Les tribunaux de l'Etat qui a opéré la saisie peuvent se prononcer sur les peines à infliger, ainsi que sur les mesures à prendre en ce qui concerne le navire, l'aéronef ou les biens, réserve faite des tiers de bonne foi.»

L'article 110 de la CNUDM prévoit un droit de visite dans les cas où ils y a des soupçons raisonnables de piraterie.

les émissions non autorisées[76]. La compétence d'exécution dans les cas de piraterie est établie sur une base universelle, à savoir que *tout Etat* peut s'emparer d'un navire pirate et arrêter les personnes à bord[77]. L'existence d'une compétence d'exécution opérant de manière universelle souligne, voire renforce, le charactère lui-même universel de la compétence législative en ce qui concerne les actes de pirateries[78]. En ce qui concerne les émissions non autorisées, l'étendue légale de la compétence de l'Etat non pavillonnaire dépend de la nature de la compétence exercée. Pour le droit de visite, l'article 110 de la CNUDM autorise tous les Etats à exercer une telle compétence d'exécution si des soupçons raisonnables existent qu'une telle activité prend place. Quant au droit d'arrêter le navire ou son équipage, la compétence d'exécution résulte (bien qu'elle en soit évidemment indépendante) d'un exercice de compétence législative extraterritoriale autorisé par le droit international général. Emettre de manière non autorisée *n*'est *pas* un crime international de compétence universelle — en réalité, la compétence législative extraterritoriale aura besoin d'être exercée sur une des bases de compétence acceptées en droit international général (telles qu'elles ont été discutées plus haut[79]).

L'Etat pavillonnaire du navire émetteur (principe de nationalité); l'Etat d'immatriculation de l'installation (personnalité passive); l'Etat dont la personne responsable de l'émission est ressortissante (principe de nationalité); tout Etat où les émissions peuvent être captées (doctrine des effets) et tout Etat dont les radiocommunications autorisées sont brouillées par ces émissions (doctrine des effets), tous sont habilités par la CNUDM à arrêter un navire étranger ou son équipage en haute mer si le navire est engagé dans des émissions non autorisées[80]. Il est implicitement compris dans cette délégation de compétences d'exécution (et de compétence judiciaire, dans la mesure où l'article 109, paragraphe 3, de la CNUDM envisage des poursuites devant les tribunaux nationaux) que la compétence législative aura été exercée sur une des bases extraterritoriales énumérées entre parenthèses ci-dessus. La CNUDM, à travers cette reconnaissance implicite que les émissions non autorisées de type extraterritorial auront été criminalisées en droit national, ne se distancie en aucune manière des bases de droit international général relatives à l'exercice de la compétence législative. Elle clarifie plutôt la permissi-

76. Articles 109 et 110 de la CNUDM.
77. Voir *infra* Grymaneli, chapitre 5.
78. *Mandat d'arrêt du 11 avril 2000 (République démocratique du Congo c. Belgique)*, arrêt, *CIJ Recueil 2002*, p. 3, opinion individuelle commune de Mme Higgins et de MM. Kooijmans et Buergenthal, juges, par. 39.
79. Voir *supra*, présente section, paragraphe 1, titre A, point ii).
80. Article 109 de la CNUDM.

bilité d'un tel exercice dans les cas controversés (en particulier lorsque la compétence législative se base sur la doctrine des effets).

La CNUDM fournit également une exception à l'exclusivité de la juridiction de l'Etat pavillonnaire, exception certes plus limitée mais qu'il convient néanmoins de relever, dans les cas d'esclavage. Selon l'article 110, les navires gouvernementaux des Etats non pavillonnaires ont le droit de monter à bord d'un navire s'ils ont des raisons suffisantes de suspecter qu'il se livre au commerce d'esclaves. Ce droit de visite limité (il s'agit d'un des aspects de la compétence d'exécution) n'englobe pas, selon la CNUDM, un droit de confiscation ou d'arrestation, pour lequel l'autorisation de l'Etat pavillonnaire doit être recherchée.

ii) *Avec l'accord de l'Etat pavillonnaire ou de l'Etat territorial*

Plusieurs des conventions liées à la mise en application du droit pénal qui sont examinées dans cet ouvrage fournissent des cadres au sein desquels le consentement de l'Etat pavillonnaire peut être recherché [81]. Dans les cas où aucun régime conventionnel prévoyant ce type de procédure n'existe, l'accord de l'Etat pavillonnaire est à rechercher d'une manière *ad hoc* [82], ce qui va souvent de pair avec des difficultés pratiques, dont des délais dans les réponses aux demandes de consentement. Ces difficultés compromettent très naturellement les efforts dans la lutte contre l'impunité liée à certains crimes en mer. Elles reflètent également l'importance, encore aujourd'hui, de la liberté de navigation (telle que protégée par la juridiction exclusive de l'Etat pavillonnaire), même lorsque celle-ci s'oppose à des priorités relatives au maintien de l'ordre public des océans.

Afin de répondre aux défis posés par la mise en application du droit pénal dans le contexte maritime et sur une base extraterritoriale, les Etats ont développé des arrangements coopératifs innovatifs. Il convient particulièrement de noter les accords de *shiprider*, qui seront discutés dans ce volume [83].

Les accords *shiprider* (qui s'intègrent dans des accords plus généraux ayant pour objet la coopération étatique afin de mettre un terme aux crimes en mer) prévoient qu'un agent d'un Etat partie (le *shiprider*) embarque sur le navire de l'autre Etat partie. La compétence d'exécution de l'Etat qui visite et arrête est exercée sur une base extraterritoriale, avec l'accord du *shiprider* — qui vient de l'Etat ayant le droit d'exercer

81. Voir *infra*, présente section, paragraphe 2, titre B, point ii).
82. Voir *infra* note 150 pour une discussion sur les complications qui apparaissent en matière de droits humains lorsqu'une autorisation d'exercice de compétence d'exécution est donnée de manière *ad hoc*.
83. Voir *infra* Tesfalidet, chapitre 16.

sa compétence d'exécution (et donc d'autoriser un autre Etat à en bénéficier), soit parce que le navire en question est dans ses eaux territoriales, soit que, en haute mer, le navire inspecté batte son pavillon.

iii) *Avec l'autorisation du Conseil de sécurité*

Le Conseil de sécurité a adopté une série de résolutions dans le cadre du chapitre VII de la Charte eu égard à deux formes de criminalité en mer : la piraterie et la prolifération d'ADM. En ce qui concerne la piraterie, les résolutions du Conseil servent de soutien à une mise en application efficace du droit pénal — bien qu'elles ne modifient pas le régime de compétence applicable discuté ci-dessus. En particulier, il convient de relever que la résolution-cadre du Conseil prévoyant la coopération dans la suppression de la piraterie vers la côte somalienne *décide*

> « que, pour une période de six mois à compter de l'adoption de la présente résolution, les Etats qui coopèrent avec le Gouvernement fédéral de transition à la lutte contre la piraterie et les vols à main armée au large des côtes somaliennes et dont le Gouvernement fédéral de transition aura préalablement communiqué les noms au Secrétaire général sont autorisés :
>
> *a)* à entrer dans les eaux territoriales de la Somalie afin de réprimer les actes de piraterie et les vols à main armée en mer, d'une manière conforme à l'action autorisée en haute mer en cas de piraterie en application du droit international applicable ;
>
> *b)* à utiliser, dans les eaux territoriales de la Somalie, d'une manière conforme à l'action autorisée en haute mer en cas de piraterie en application du droit international applicable, tous moyens nécessaires pour réprimer les actes de piraterie et les vols à main armée ;
>
> ... et affirme en outre que la présente autorisation n'a été donnée qu'à la suite de la réception de la lettre datée du 27 février 2008 adressée au Président du Conseil de sécurité par le Représentant permanent de la République somalienne auprès de l'Organisation des Nations Unies et transmettant l'accord du Gouvernement fédéral de transition »[84].

---

84. Conseil de sécurité, résolution 1816 (2008), par. 7, 9. Les renouvellements de l'autorisation dans la résolution 1816 (2008) mettent en avant « que les présentes autorisations n'ont été reconduites qu'à la suite de la réception des lettres datées des 2 et 6 novembre 2009, par lesquelles le Gouvernement fédéral de transition a signifié son accord ». Voir aussi Conseil de sécurité, résolution 1897 (2009), par. 8 ; résolution 2020 (2011), par. 10.

Contrairement aux apparences, cette résolution n'*autorise* pas un Etat étranger à exercer sa compétence d'exécution à l'intérieur des *eaux territoriales somaliennes* — ce qui contreviendrait à la souveraineté de la Somalie sur ses eaux territoriales. Ce que la résolution 1816 (2008) du Conseil de sécurité reconnaît (et confirme) est un droit de poursuite chaude inversée (en d'autres termes la poursuite d'un navire pirate depuis la haute mer jusque dans les eaux territoriales somaliennes), *avec l'accord du gouvernement somalien*. Un tel droit existe, que le Conseil le prévoie ou non dans une résolution dans le cadre du chapitre VII. Cela ne signifie pas pour autant que les résolutions du Conseil sur la piraterie soient sans utilité. Elles forment un point central pour les efforts coopératifs en vue de supprimer la piraterie dans la région, et les efforts internationaux pour se débarrasser de la piraterie (dans le cadre de la CNUDM et du droit international coutumier) ont augmenté de manière significative après que le Conseil de sécurité a porté son attention sur ce problème.

De manière similaire, dans le cadre des ADM, le Conseil n'a pas modifié le régime juridique discuté ci-dessus. Alors qu'il a requis des Etats qu'ils exercent leur compétence législative

> « interdisant à tout acteur non étatique de fabriquer, se procurer, mettre au point, posséder, transporter, transférer ou d'utiliser des armes nucléaires, chimiques ou biologiques ou leurs vecteurs, en particulier à des fins terroristes, réprimant toutes les tentatives de l'une quelconque de ces activités, le fait d'y participer en tant que complice et le fait d'y fournir assistance ou de la financer » [85],

rien dans cette autorisation ne suggère une application autre que territoriale [86]. De plus, le Conseil de sécurité n'a pas permis aux Etats d'exercer leur compétence d'exécution d'une quelconque manière qui serait inconsistante avec la CNUDM ou avec leurs obligations internationales de droit coutumier. En particulier, la résolution 1540

> « *[d]emande* à tous les Etats, comme autre moyen de contrer cette menace, d'agir de concert, avec l'aval de leurs autorités judiciaires, *dans le respect … du droit international*, pour empêcher le trafic des armes nucléaires, chimiques ou biologiques, de leurs vecteurs et des éléments connexes » [87].

---

85. Conseil de sécurité, résolution 1540 (2004), par. 2.
86. La criminalisation du transport d'ADM à travers les eaux territoriales respecterait les obligations de la CNUDM liées au passage inoffensif. *Supra* note 24 et texte s'y référant.
87. Conseil de sécurité, résolution 1540 (2004), par. 10. (L'italique est de nous.)

En conséquence, les Etats peuvent mettre en application leur droit national (criminalisant la prolifération d'ADM en mer) à l'encontre des navires étrangers dans leur mer territoriale[88], mais, en haute mer, cette mise en application doit être conditionnée au consentement de l'Etat pavillonnaire.

Le Conseil de sécurité pourrait évidemment outrepasser la compétence d'exécution exclusive de l'Etat côtier ou de l'Etat pavillonnaire, respectivement dans les eaux territoriales et en haute mer, par l'adoption d'une résolution dans le cadre du chapitre VII. Une telle résolution pourrait (par exemple) imposer une obligation ou offrir un droit aux Etats d'exercer leur compétence d'exécution à l'encontre des navires pirates dans les eaux territoriales somaliennes ou envers les navires étrangers raisonnablement suspectés de prolifération en haute mer (dans les deux cas sans consentement de l'Etat pertinent). Cela résoudrait la question des obligations divergentes en droit de la mer et en droit coutumier international, sous le couvert de l'article 103 de la Charte de Nations Unies[89]. Le fait que le Conseil de sécurité n'ait rien fait de tel illustre non seulement la capacité des règles de droit international général (dont les accords coopératifs qui fournissent des cadres pour obtenir le consentement des Etats pavillonnaires) à répondre, si ce n'est à tous, du moins à certains des défis découlant d'une criminalité maritime en hausse, mais aussi la priorité que les Etats continuent à accorder à la souveraineté territoriale et à la liberté de navigation.

C. Les différentes significations de «juridiction»

Un dernier point sur la «compétence» où la «juridiction» mérite d'être examiné et est particulièrement pertinent en ce qui concerne la responsabilité de l'Etat (discutée plus loin). La juridiction est un terme régulièrement sujet à confusion, en partie en raison des différentes significations attachées à ce mot, particulièrement en anglais[90]. La «juridiction» présentée ci-dessus consiste dans la compétence d'un Etat de réguler des personnes et des conduites. Un autre sens existe cependant, différent, mais pas pour autant complètement détaché du concept de juridiction en droit international général: il s'agit du concept de «juridiction» dont découlent les obligations en droits humains. L'applicabilité de toutes (ou presque toutes) les obligations des droits

88. *Supra* note 60 et texte s'y référant.

89. Voir Cour européenne des droits de l'homme (grande chambre), *Al Jedda c. Royaume-Uni* (requête n° 27021/08), 7 juillet 2010, par. 102.

90. Voir Milanovic, «From Compromise to Principle: Clarifying the Concept of State Jurisdiction in Human Rights Treaties», *Human Rights Law Review*, vol. 8 (2008), p. 411.

humains aux niveaux international et régional dépend de la présence de la personne en question (celle dont les droits ont été supposément violés) sous la juridiction de l'Etat défendeur[91].

Bien que les cours de droits humains ne soient pas étrangères à considérer les différentes conceptions de juridiction de manière collective[92], il semble généralement accepté qu'aucune bonne raison n'existe pour restreindre au seul territoire d'un Etat la «juridiction» qui sert de déclencheur aux obligations de droits humains (limitation qui se justifierait par le fait que leur compétence juridictionnelle d'exécution ne s'applique généralement pas au-delà de cet espace géographique). Cela est particulièrement vrai dans le contexte moderne où les Etats agissent souvent de manière extraterritoriale[93]. En lieu et place d'une telle interprétation restrictive, la «juridiction» qui occasionne les obligations de droits humains devrait être déterminée par le contrôle d'un Etat par rapport à certaines personnes et par sa capacité d'action. Un tel système de création d'obligations requiert probablement différents degrés de «juridiction» dans le contexte des droits humains, selon le droit en question. Par exemple, les droits qui donnent lieu à des obligations négatives (tels que le droit à la vie, qui force l'Etat à *se retenir* de tuer de manière arbitraire) peuvent être déclenchés dès qu'une personne est sous le contrôle physique d'agents de l'Etat, où que ce contrôle s'exerce (un modèle personnel de juridiction)[94]. Quant aux droits qui donnent naissance à des

91. Voir par exemple l'article 1 de la Convention européenne des droits de l'homme, Nations Unies, *Recueil des traités*, vol. 213, p. 223 (ci-après «CEDH»): «Les Hautes Parties contractantes reconnaissent à toute personne relevant de leur juridiction les droits et libertés définis au titre I de la présente Convention.»

92. Il est bien connu que la Cour européenne des droits de l'homme a assimilé la «juridiction» en tant que déclencheur de l'applicabilité des obligations de fond de droits humains, et la «juridiction» selon le droit international général, dans sa décision largement critiquée *Banković et autres c. la Belgique* (requête n° 52207/99), 12 décembre 2001, par. 59-61 :

> «En ce qui concerne le «sens ordinaire» des termes pertinents figurant dans l'article 1 de la Convention, la Cour considère que, du point de vue du droit international public, la compétence juridictionnelle d'un Etat est principalement territoriale. Si le droit international n'exclut pas un exercice extraterritorial de sa juridiction par un Etat, les éléments ordinairement cités pour fonder pareil exercice (nationalité, pavillon, relations diplomatiques et consulaires, effet, protection, personnalité passive et universalité, notamment) sont en règle générale définis et limités par les droits territoriaux souverains des autres Etats concernés [citations omises]. ... La Cour estime-t-elle que l'article 1 de la Convention doit passer pour refléter cette conception ordinaire et essentiellement territoriale de la juridiction des Etats, les autres titres de juridiction étant exceptionnels et nécessitant chaque fois une justification spéciale, fonction des circonstances de l'espèce...»

93. Voir Milanovic, *supra* note 90.

94. Voir par exemple Comité des droits de l'homme, *Lopez Burgos* v. *Uruguay* (comm. n° 52/1979), «Views of 29 July 1981», par. 12.3.

obligations positives (tels que le droit accessoire d'être protégé contre les violations de droits humains), ils demandent plus que le contrôle envers la personne à protéger. Ils sont déclenchés par un contrôle effectif du territoire ou tout du moins l'exercice de l'autorité gouvernementale sur ce territoire, afin que les mécanismes de mise en application du droit puissent être développés et appliqués (un modèle territorial de juridiction)[95].

Même la Cour européenne des droits de l'homme accepte désormais que la «juridiction» en tant qu'élément déclencheur de l'applicabilité des obligations de la Convention européenne des droits de l'homme et la compétence juridictionnelle d'exécution sont deux concepts différents[96]. Il est important, néanmoins, de comprendre la relation entre ces deux concepts, si indépendants soient-ils. Généralement, lorsqu'un Etat exerce *légalement* sa compétence d'exécution (soit sur son propre territoire ou dans sa mer territoriale, soit avec le consentement de l'Etat territorial ou pavillonnaire), il sera également touché par la «juridiction» en matière de droits humains, du moins en ce qui concerne ses obligations négatives. Cela dit, ces deux types de juridiction ne coïncident pas nécessairement. Même lorsqu'un Etat exerce sa compétence d'exécution *de manière illicite* (par exemple en arrêtant un navire battant un pavillon étranger ainsi que son équipage sans l'autorisation de l'Etat pavillonnaire), il peut malgré tout avoir «juridiction» en termes d'obligations de droits humains (par exemple si les personnes en question sont sous son contrôle).

Ainsi, la relation entre la compétence juridictionnelle d'exécution et la juridiction relative aux droits humains est comparable à la relation entre le *jus ad bellum* (droit international relatif à l'utilisation de la force entre Etats) et le *jus in bello* (règles régissant la conduite des hostilités). Le *jus ad bellum* réglemente la licéité de l'usage de la force — en d'autres termes détermine quand un Etat peut utiliser la force dans un territoire étranger. De manière similaire, les règles de compétence d'exécution dictent la licéité d'une action exécutive. De son côté, le *jus in bello* réglemente le mode d'opération des conflits armés. L'applicabilité du *jus in bello* ne dépend en rien de la légalité de l'usage de la force, mais est simplement déterminée par le fait que la force est utilisée. De manière

95. Voir par exemple Cour européenne des droits de l'homme (grande chambre), affaire *Loizidou c. Turquie (exceptions preliminaires)* (requête n° 15318/89), 23 mars 1995, par. 62-64.

96. La Cour a de plus accepté que les droits de la CEDH pourraient être «fractionnés et adaptés», de manière que les obligations négatives puissent être déclenchées par une forme de juridiction, alors les obligations positives dépendraient de l'autre (Cour européenne des droits de l'homme (grande chambre)), *Affaire Al-Skeini et autres c. Royaume-Uni* (requête n° 55721/07), 7 juillet 2011, par. 137.

similaire, la «juridiction» en tant que déclencheur des obligations de droits humains réglemente le mode d'exercice du pouvoir d'exécution. Les droits humains s'appliquent dès qu'un tel pouvoir est exercé, que les opérations d'exécution respectent ou non les limites de compétence juridictionnelles pertinentes qui découlent du droit international général et du droit de la mer.

Paragraphe 2 **La responsabilité dans toutes ses formes**

En liaison avec les questions de compétences discutées ci-dessus, la gamme des régimes légaux applicables implique également un éventail de modes de responsabilité. Cette section introduit la responsabilité pénale individuelle, la responsabilité de l'Etat ainsi que les mesures adoptées par le Conseil de sécurité en application de la Charte des Nations Unies (y compris les actions coercitives); chacun de ces thèmes est examiné dans cet ouvrage (à la fois individuellement et en relation avec les interactions qui surgissent entre les régimes).

A. La responsabilité pénale individuelle

Le thème du Centre de recherche de 2012 de l'Académie de La Haye se concentre sur le paradigme de l'exécution du droit pénal dans le cadre maritime. Les règles de droit international qui ont pour but d'assurer que la responsabilité pénale individuelle pour les crimes en mer soit appliquée sont donc étudiées en détail dans les chapitres suivants. Cette section présente le cadre au sein duquel ces règles opèrent — en mettant en exergue, lorsque cela est pertinent, l'utilisation des règles de droit international relatives aux compétences législative et d'exécution présentées ci-dessus.

i) *Des questions purement nationales*

Le vol à main armée en mer est un problème relativement nouveau en tant que sujet de préoccupation pour la communauté internationale dans sa lutte contre la criminalité en mer[97]. Selon sa définition, l'*actus reus* du vol à main armée en mer prend place dans les eaux territoriales d'un Etat[98] et l'Etat côtier a donc une base de compétence à la fois pour prescrire et pour agir (ce qui inclut un pouvoir de poursuite chaude au-delà

97. Voir *infra* Abdoul, chapitre 7.
98. *Recueil de règles pratiques pour la conduite des enquêtes sur les délits de piraterie et de vol à main armée à l'encontre des navires*, Organisation maritime internationale, résolution A.922 (22), 29 novembre 2001, par. 2.2.

des eaux territoriales)[99]. Cela est le cas même lorsque le navire utilisé pour commettre le crime bat le pavillon d'un autre Etat, puisque les vols à main armée dans la mer territoriale sont de nature à «troubler l'ordre dans la mer territoriale»[100] — ils sont donc soumis au droit d'exécution du droit pénal de l'Etat côtier[101]. En conséquence, les vols à main armée en mer ne posent pas de problèmes majeurs en termes de compétence et ils ne font pas l'objet d'arrangements coopératifs internationaux (bien qu'ils fassent l'objet d'un certain nombre de résolutions du Conseil de sécurité et de l'OMI)[102].

En ce qui concerne les autres crimes en mer examinés dans ce volume, qui ont tous une composante transnationale non négligeable, les Etats ont néanmoins une compétence législative pleine pour criminaliser, dans leurs territoires, toute conduite qui sert de préparation à ces crimes ainsi qu'une compétence d'exécution pleine pour arrêter et mettre en détention les personnes se trouvant sur leurs territoires et qui sont engagées dans de telles activités. Alors que cet exercice purement national de compétence ne fait pas l'objet de commentaires relatifs à la suppression de la criminalité en mer, il peut certainement jouer un rôle important dans la lutte contre l'impunité. En effet, la criminalité maritime, que ce soit sous son volet du trafic de migrants, de la prolifération d'ADM ou de la piraterie, nécessite des travaux préparatoires qui se déroulent régulièrement dans les ports et territoires soumis à la compétence de l'Etat côtier.

Il est cependant peu probable que les Etats adoptent des cadres législatifs qui imposent une responsabilité de complicité eu égard aux crimes sur lesquels ils n'auront pas de compétence (parce que ces crimes sont commis hors de leurs eaux territoriales, par exemple). En conséquence, le cadre conventionnel discuté ci-après, qui prévoit un exercice de compétence législative sur une base universelle envers un certain nombre de crimes en mer, est un outil important dans la lutte contre l'impunité.

ii) *Le droit international exigeant l'exercice de la compétence pénale nationale*

La communauté internationale a depuis déjà longtemps fait face à la criminalité maritime à travers l'adoption de traités qui ont pour but d'assurer la responsabilité individuelle des criminels[103]. Dans le

99. *Supra* notes 68 et 72.
100. Article 27, paragraphe 1, lettre *b)*, de la CNUDM.
101. *Supra* note 55 et texte s'y référant.
102. Voir *infra* Abdoul, chapitre 7.
103. Voir par exemple la convention relative à l'esclavage (1926), Société des Nations, *Recueil des traités*, vol. 60, p. 253 (entrée en vigueur le 9 mars 1927),

contexte moderne, la CNUDM a été la première de nombreuses conventions multilatérales à imposer aux Etats des obligations de mise en application du droit pénal en ce qui concerne les crimes en mer. Par exemple, l'article 99 de la CNUDM exige de

> «[t]out Etat [qu'il] pren[ne] des mesures efficaces pour prévenir et réprimer le transport d'esclaves par les navires autorisés à battre son pavillon et pour prévenir l'usurpation de son pavillon à cette fin».

Afin d'être en mesure de punir le commerce d'esclave sur ses navires, l'Etat doit au préalable avoir criminalisé cette conduite (soit parce qu'une partie du crime est commise sur son territoire ou sur une base extraterritoriale telle que le principe de nationalité).

A la suite de la CNUDM, mais à l'intérieur et dans le respect du cadre de droit de la mer qu'elle crée, les Etats ont négocié une série de traités de mise en application du droit pénal, dont le but spécifique est de s'assurer qu'aucune impunité ne subsiste pour les crimes qui mettent en danger la sécurité et le bon ordre des biens communs maritimes. Les conventions internationales pertinentes et leurs protocoles s'intéressent aux crimes contre la sécurité de la navigation en mer, l'usage et la prolifération d'ADM dans le contexte maritime, le trafic de migrants et les prises d'otages (dont celles commises en mer) et exigent des Etats parties qu'ils i) criminalisent dans leur droit national les manifestations de la criminalité maritime visées par l'instrument en question (notamment sur une base universelle); ii) coopèrent dans la prévention de ces crimes en mer, et iii) agissent pour s'assurer que les criminels présumés soient tenus pour responsables de leurs crimes[104] (à travers une obligation de les juger ou de les extrader[105]).

---

qui exige des Etats qu'ils criminalisent le commerce des esclaves (art. 6) et les forcent

> «à prendre toutes mesures utiles en vue de prévenir et réprimer l'embarquement, le débarquement et le transport des esclaves dans leurs eaux territoriales, ainsi que, en général, sur tous les navires abordant leurs pavillons respectifs» (art. 3).

Pour plus de détails, voir la convention supplémentaire relative à l'abolition de l'esclavage, de la traite des esclaves et des institutions et pratiques analogues à l'esclavage, Nations Unies, *Recueil des traités*, vol. 266, p. 3.

104. SUA, Protocole de 2005 relatif à la Convention pour la répression d'actes illicites contre la sécurité de la navigation maritime, OMI, doc. LEG/CONF.15/21 (2005) (ci-après «Protocole SUA 2005»); Convention internationale contre la prise d'otages, Nations Unies, *Recueil des Traités*, vol. 1316, p. 212 (ci-après «Convention contre la prise d'otages»); Convention contre la criminalité transnationale organisée; Protocole contre le trafic illicite de migrants.

105. Cette obligation est communément désignée par l'expression abrégée «extrader ou poursuivre» ou, en latin, *aut dedere, aut judicare*. Alors que la version française ne reflète pas exactement la manière dont cette obligation est formulée dans les traités examinés — qui n'exigent pas une mise en examen,

En ce qui concerne l'obligation de criminaliser les crimes en mer en question, les Etats doivent criminaliser la conduite à bord des navires sur lesquels ils ont des pouvoirs d'exécution (par exemple dans leur mer territoriale[106] ou à bord d'un navire battant leur pavillon qui se trouve en haute mer[107]) *ainsi qu'*à l'encontre de ceux sur lesquels ils n'ont pas de pouvoirs d'exécution immédiats (par exemple par rapport à la conduite de nationaux, même s'ils se trouvent sur des navires étrangers[108], à la conduite de navires étrangers dirigée contre un navire battant son propre pavillon en haute mer[109], ou à la conduite de ses propres navires, même lorsqu'ils se trouvent dans les eaux territoriales d'un autre Etat[110]). Cela permet qu'en cas de changement de circonstances (par exemple si le navire criminel entre dans les eaux territoriales ou si les criminels montent à bord d'un navire battant son propre pavillon) l'Etat qui a déjà exercé sa compétence législative se trouve en mesure d'appliquer son droit pénal national.

---

mais seulement la remise de l'affaire aux autorités compétentes pour intenter des poursuites (*infra* note 134 et la discussion ci-dessous), le terme «judicare» en latin est suffisamment large pour couvrir toute sorte d'enquête visant à déterminer si une procédure judiciaire doit être engagée ou non. Voir Bassiouni and Wise, *Aut Dedere Aut Judicare : The Duty to Extradite or Prosecute in International Law*, Dordrecht, Martinus Nijhoff Publishers, 1995, p. 4.

106. La criminalisation d'une conduite en mer territoriale est un exercice de compétence législative basée sur le principe de territorialité (voir par exemple l'article 6, paragraphe 1, lettre *b)*, de la SUA), et si le navire incriminé reste dans les eaux territoriales, l'Etat côtier peut aussi avoir une compétence d'exécution (voir *infra*, présente section, paragraphe 2, titre B).

107. La criminalisation d'une conduite à bord d'un navire battant le pavillon de l'Etat est un exercice de compétence législative basée sur le principe de nationalité (voir par exemple l'article 6, paragraphe 1, lettre *a)*, de la SUA) et, si les personnes incriminées restent à bord de ce navire, l'Etat pavillonnaire a aussi une compétence d'exécution en haute mer (*supra* note 65).

108. La criminalisation d'une conduite de nationaux est un exercice de compétence législative basée sur le principe de nationalité (voir par exemple l'article 6, paragraphe 1, lettre *c)*, de la SUA) et, si le national incriminé est à bord d'un navire battant le pavillon d'un autre Etat, l'Etat de nationalité n'aura pas de compétence d'exécution immédiate (en raison de la juridiction exclusive de l'Etat pavillonnaire) (*supra* note 65).

109. La criminalisation d'une conduite commise contre un navire battant le pavillon de l'Etat est un exercice de compétence législative basée sur le principe de personnalité passive (voir par exemple l'article 6, paragraphe 1, lettre *a)*, de la SUA) et, si les personnes incriminées restent à bord du navire battant un pavillon étranger, l'Etat pavillonnaire du navire victime n'aura pas de compétence d'exécution immédiate (en raison de la juridiction exclusive de l'Etat pavillonnaire) (*supra* note 65).

110. La criminalisation d'une conduite à bord d'un navire battant le pavillon de l'Etat est un exercice de compétence législative basée sur le principe de nationalité (voir par exemple l'article 6, paragraphe 1, lettre *a)*, de la SUA), mais un Etat pavillonnaire n'a pas de compétence de mise en application — même envers ses propres navires — dans les eaux territoriales d'un autre Etat (voir *infra*, présente section, paragraphe 2, titre B).

Il est également possible qu'une personne ayant commis un crime en mer, crime avec lequel un Etat n'a aucun lien [111], entre dans un territoire soumis à la compétence nationale de celui-ci ou monte, en haute mer, à bord d'un navire battant son pavillon. Ces deux cas de figure expliquent en partie pourquoi une obligation conventionnelle d'établir une compétence législative universelle face à certains crimes en mer est requise par ces traités. La SUA [112], le Protocole SUA 2005 [113], la Convention contre la prise d'otages [114] et dans une moindre mesure la Convention contre la criminalité transnationale organisée [115] (qui s'applique *mutadis mutandis* au Protocole contre le trafic illicite de migrants) exigent des Etats qu'ils criminalisent sur une base universelle les actes visés. Dans l'hypothèse où le criminel est sur le territoire d'un Etat ou à bord d'un navire soumis à sa compétence d'exécution, l'obligation que cet Etat a d'établir sa compétence législative universelle soutient l'obligation *aut dedere, aut judicare* qui se trouve également dans certaines conventions de mise en application du droit pénal discutées dans cet ouvrage [116]. A moins que l'Etat sous le contrôle duquel les criminels présumés se trouvent n'ait exercé sa compétence législative universelle, il ne sera pas en mesure de remplir son obligation de poursuivre ces personnes, à moins de les extrader (cela est tout au moins vrai lorsqu'il n'a pas d'autre base de compétence législative utilisable, par exemple car le crime n'a pas été commis par un national, contre un national, sur un navire battant son pavillon ou à l'encontre d'un tel navire).

---

111. Par exemple, le criminel présumé n'est pas un national, les victimes ne sont pas des nationaux et le crime n'est pas commis dans les eaux territoriales de cet Etat, sur un navire battant son pavillon ou à son encontre.

112. Article 6, paragraphe 4, de la SUA.

113. *Ibid.*

114. Article 5, paragraphe 2, de la Convention contre la prise d'otage.

115. Voir article 15, paragraphe 3, de la Convention contre la criminalité transnationale organisée qui exige seulement l'établissement de la compétence universelle dans les cas où l'Etat dans le territoire duquel le criminel présumé se trouve n'extrade pas ce dernier « au seul motif qu'il est l'un de ses ressortissants ». Dans tous les autres cas de figure, l'établissement de la compétence universelle (qui permet aux Etats d'être en mesure de poursuivre un criminel présumé qui se trouve sur leur territoire s'ils refusent l'extradition pour d'*autres* raisons que la nationalité de la personne en question) est permis mais pas obligatoire. Article 15, paragraphe 4, de la Convention contre la criminalité transnationale organisée. Pour une discussion en profondeur sur les obligations de mise en application du droit pénal imposées par la Convention contre la criminalité transnationale organisée, voir *infra* Guggisberg, chapitre 6.

116. Voir l'article 10 de la SUA. Selon la Convention contre la criminalité transnationale organisée (et donc selon le Protocole contre le trafic illicite de migrants auquel la convention-cadre s'applique), l'obligation *aut dedere, aut judicare* s'applique seulement dans les cas où le criminel présumé est un national de l'Etat dans lequel il ou elle se trouve. Article 16, paragraphe 1, de la Convention contre la criminalité transnationale organisée.

En plus de la compétence universelle et de l'obligation *aut dedere, aut judicare*[117], les conventions de mise en application du droit pénal qui s'intéressent aux crimes en mer tentent de combattre l'impunité en faisant face aux difficultés liées à la juridiction exclusive de l'Etat pavillonnaire en haute mer. En raison de cette juridiction exclusive, ces régimes de mise en application du droit pénal sont souvent inapplicables en haute mer, à moins qu'un navire criminel ne rencontre un navire gouvernemental battant le même pavillon que lui (ou que les circonstances changent, comme cela a été décrit ci-dessus). Afin de minimiser l'impact de la juridiction exclusive de l'Etat pavillonnaire sur leur efficacité, nombre des conventions citées prévoient des procédures-cadres grâce auxquelles les Etats non pavillonnaires peuvent exercer leur compétence d'exécution. La SUA, le premier traité de mise en application du droit pénal à s'intéresser aux crimes en mer, ne modifie en rien la répartition des compétences juridictionnelles telles que définies par la CNUDM[118]. Le Protocole SUA 2005 (qui exige des Etats la criminalisation de la prolifération d'ADM) et le Protocole contre le trafic illicite de migrants (combiné à la Convention contre la criminalité transnationale organisée), quant à eux, créent un cadre au sein duquel le consentement de l'Etat pavillonnaire pour la compétence d'exécution peut être demandé et reçu[119].

iii) *Les crimes internationaux à proprement parler*

Les conventions de mise en application du droit pénal présentées ci-dessus et leurs obligations *aut dedere, aut judicare* ont été décrites comme n'appartenant pas à la catégorie de la compétence universelle à proprement parler[120]. Selon le droit international coutumier (en addition au droit conventionnel), certains crimes en mer sont des crimes internationaux en tant que tels et font l'objet de compétence universelle : le droit international coutumier s'intéresse à la fois à la conduite des acteurs non étatiques actifs dans les crimes en mer (par son applicabilité

117. Pour une discussion en détail sur l'obligation *aut dedere, aut judicare* dans le contexte des crimes en mer, voir *infra* Cheah, chapitre 8.

118. Selon l'article 9 de la SUA :

> « Aucune disposition de la présente Convention n'affecte de quelque façon que ce soit les règles du droit international concernant l'exercice de la compétence des Etats en matière d'enquête ou d'exécution à bord des navires qui ne battent pas leur pavillon. »

119. Voir l'article 8 *bis* du Protocole SUA 2005 et l'article 8, paragraphe 2, du Protocole contre le trafic illicite de migrants.

120. Voir *Mandat d'arrêt du 11 avril 2000 (République démocratique du Congo c. Belgique)*, arrêt, *CIJ Recueil 2002*, p. 3, opinion individuelle commune de Mme Higgins et de MM. Kooijmans et Buergenthal, juges, par. 42.

à la piraterie par exemple) et aux conduites des acteurs étatiques (par l'intermédiaire du droit international humanitaire qui peut être pertinent dans les situations de conflits armés en mer).

En ce qui concerne la piraterie, le droit international coutumier relatif à sa criminalisation et à sa sanction sur une base universelle est codifié à l'article 105 de la CNUDM [121]. Le langage de cet article est permissif, tout comme celui des résolutions du Conseil de sécurité qui s'attaquent à la suppression de la piraterie au large des côtes somaliennes [122]. En conséquence, les Etats ne sont pas obligés d'adopter des cadres légaux de droit pénal pour la suppression de la piraterie sur une base universelle, ce qui a visiblement un impact sur la disponibilité de lieux de procès [123]. Quant aux crimes de guerre en mer, l'exercice de la compétence législative universelle est permissive, mais l'Etat de nationalité dont dépend le criminel de guerre présumé est obligé de réprimer de tels crimes [124].

B. La responsabilité étatique

Le droit international général de la responsabilité étatique [125] est certes applicable à la criminalité en mer, mais d'une manière dérivée : le droit international relatif aux crimes en mer se charge principalement de réglementer la conduite d'acteurs privés et ne s'intéresse qu'indirectement aux activités des Etats, en cela que les Etats sont les

121. « Tout Etat peut, en haute mer ou en tout autre lieu ne relevant de la juridiction d'aucun Etat, saisir un navire ou un aéronef pirate, ou un navire ou un aéronef capturé à la suite d'un acte de piraterie et aux mains de pirates, et appréhender les personnes et saisir les biens se trouvant à bord. Les tribunaux de l'Etat qui a opéré la saisie peuvent se prononcer sur les peines à infliger, ainsi que sur les mesures à prendre en ce qui concerne le navire, l'aéronef ou les biens, réserve faite des tiers de bonne foi. »

122. *Supra* note 84 et texte s'y référant.

123. Voir *infra* Grymaneli, chapitre 5.

124. Voir *infra* Sergis, chapitre 14.

125. A la différence de la responsabilité pénale individuelle, la responsabilité de l'Etat n'est pas de nature punitive (pas plus qu'elle n'est de nature civile d'ailleurs)). Voir H. Kelsen, « Théorie du droit international public », *Recueil des cours*, tome 84 (1953), p. 87. La responsabilité de l'Etat est « purely and simply international » (J. R. Crawford, *First Report on State Responsibility, Addendum 1*, Nations Unies, doc. A/CN.4/490.Add.1 (1998), p. 9, par. 60. Voir aussi *Application de la convention pour la prévention et la répression du crime de génocide (Bosnie-Herzégovine c. Serbie-et-Monténégro)*, arrêt, *CIJ Recueil 2007*, p. 43, par. 65-66 ; J. R. Crawford, « The System of International Responsibility », *The Law of International Responsibility* (Crawford, Pellet *et al.*, dir. publ., Oxford University Press, 2010, pp. 17, 22, et son but est restoratif : en rétablissant la relation légale qui existait avant la commission de l'acte illicite entre l'Etat fautif et l'Etat lésé. Pour une discussion en profondeur du régime de la responsabilité de l'Etat dans son application à la criminalité en mer, voir *infra* Neri, chapitre 15.

moyens par lesquels les conduites privées sont régulées[126]. Par exemple, la responsabilité d'un Etat peut être invoquée si un Etat faillit à remplir correctement ses obligations de mise en application du droit pénal envers les crimes en mer. Dans ce cas, le régime de la responsabilité étatique agit comme soutien à l'objectif plus général qui est de mettre un terme à l'impunité dont bénéficie la criminalité maritime. Cependant, lorsque la responsabilité étatique est invoquée à l'encontre d'un Etat pour une violation du droit international commise *au cours de ses opérations d'exécution*, une telle invocation risque plutôt d'avoir un effet négatif sur les efforts visant à en finir avec cette impunité.

Que les Etats puissent être tenus responsables pour un exercice excessif de leur compétence d'exécution, ou pour des violations de droits humains commises au cours d'un tel exercice de compétence, pourrait en effet dissuader les Etats d'agir pour réprimer la criminalité maritime. Cela sera particulièrement le cas si des limitations à cette compétence (par exemple celles imposées par l'article 27 de la CNUDM dans les eaux territoriales) sont interprétées sans intégrer le cadre plus général du droit international et en particulier la suppression de la criminalité maritime. Une autre situation hautement problématique est liée aux droits humains, en particulier s'ils sont interprétés d'une manière qui manque de prendre suffisamment en compte les défis liés à l'environnement maritime et les différences fondamentales entre les opérations d'interdiction maritime et les opérations de police sur la terre ferme[127]. La simple existence de certaines obligations de droits humains, néanmoins, peut avoir pour résultat que les Etats seront plus prudents dans leur exercice de la compétence d'exécution — par exemple que les obligations liées à l'asile (comme l'analyse de chaque demande individuellement) soient déclenchées par des opérations d'interdiction maritime pourrait bien dissuader les Etats de participer à des opérations d'exécution, sauf si leurs intérêts sécuritaires ou pécuniaires propres sont en jeu[128].

i) *Les obligations de mise en application du droit pénal*

La responsabilité d'un Etat pour un acte international illicite peut découler de son échec à mettre en place les nécessaires cadres de mise

126. L'exception principale a trait à la réglementation des crimes de guerre en mer, cas dans lequel la conduite des acteurs étatiques est soumise à une régulation directe. Voir *infra* Sergis, chapitre 14, pour une discussion sur les crimes de guerre en mer.

127. Voir *infra* Batsalas, chapitre 11.

128. Pour une discussion sur l'impact des obligations de non-refoulement sur la lutte contre le trafic de migrants, voir *infra* Guggisberg, chapitre 6. Pour une évaluation de l'effet de telles obligations sur les opérations d'exécution par les Etats, voir *infra* Batsalas, chapitre 11, et Montas, chapitre 12.

en application du droit pénal ou à réprimer efficacement les crimes en mer[129]. Il convient à cet égard de noter que le simple fait qu'un Etat soit habilité à exercer une compétence d'exécution en vertu du droit international ne crée en rien une obligation d'exercer cette compétence. En l'absence d'une obligation conventionnelle explicite, la compétence d'exécution est un droit d'arrêter et de détenir dans le but de supprimer la criminalité en mer.

En conséquence de cette brèche dans les règles primaires de droit international coutumier relatives à la criminalité maritime, les traités pertinents imposent l'obligation suivante aux Etats :

> « [l]'Etat Partie sur le territoire duquel l'auteur ou l'auteur présumé de l'infraction est découvert est tenu, s'il ne l'extrade pas, de soumettre l'affaire, sans retard et sans aucune exception, que l'infraction ait été ou non commise sur son territoire, à ses autorités compétentes pour l'exercice de l'action pénale... »[130]

Cette obligation est formulée en termes très généraux. Lorsqu'une demande d'extradition est introduite, rien dans cette version du principe *aut dedere, aut judicare* ne force l'Etat receveur de cette demande à y faire suite[131]. Cela est particulièrement clair dans la mesure où l'extradition est soumise aux conditions prévues par la loi de l'Etat aux mains duquel les criminels présumés se trouvent[132]. De telles conditions peuvent inclure des restrictions à l'encontre de l'extradition de nationaux, et doivent en tout cas inclure un certain degré de certitude que l'Etat potentiel de destination ne torturera pas le criminel présumé[133]. Un Etat qui reçoit une demande en ce sens peut extrader la personne concernée, mais n'est jamais obligé de le faire ; le langage des conventions de mise en application du droit pénal reconnaissent toute l'étendue des pouvoirs discrétionnaires de l'Etat à cet égard.

Cependant, lorsqu'un Etat refuse d'extrader, pour quelque raison que ce soit, il se retrouve dans la même situation qu'un Etat de détention auquel aucune demande d'extradition n'a été faite, à savoir qu'il est

---

129. Pour plus de détails, voir *infra* Neri, chapitre 15.

130. Voir par exemple l'article 10 de la SUA.

131. Voir *Questions d'interprétation et d'application de la convention de Montréal de 1971 résultant de l'incident aérien de Lockerbie (Jamahiriya arabe libyenne c. Royaume-Uni)*, mesures conservatoires, ordonnance du 14 avril 1992, *CIJ Recueil 1992*, p. 3, déclaration commune de MM. Evensen, Tarassov, Guillaume et Aguilar Mawdsley, par. 3.

132. Voir par exemple l'article 11, paragraphes 2 et 3, de la SUA.

133. Il est interdit aux Etats d'expulser, de refouler ou d'extrader une personne vers un autre Etat où il y a des motifs sérieux de croire qu'elle risque d'être soumise à la torture. Voir par exemple l'article 3 de la Convention contre la torture et autres peines ou traitements cruels, inhumains ou dégradants, 10 décembre 1984, Nations Unies, *Recueil des traités*, vol. 1465, p. 85.

dans l'obligation de soumettre le cas en question aux autorités compétentes afin d'entamer des poursuites. Il est néanmoins vrai que même cette obligation n'est pas très contraignante. Tout ce que l'obligation *aut dedere, aut judicare* exige est que les Etats soumettent un cas d'espèce à leurs autorités compétentes, s'ils refusent de faire suite à une demande d'extradition. Les autorités compétentes doivent prendre leurs décisions de la même manière qu'elles le feraient dans le cas de tout autre délit grave. Tout au moins, cela présuppose une intention d'appliquer de bonne foi et efficacement les obligations de mise en application du droit pénal ; bien qu'une issue potentielle demeure le refus de poursuivre une affaire, il est important qu'elle ne se base que sur des raisons objectives (par exemple, en cas d'insuffisance de preuves)[134]. Souffrir d'un manque de preuves est un problème particulièrement pertinent dans le contexte maritime en raison de la nature transnationale des conduites en question et du fait qu'il s'agit de crimes organisés, rendant la présence de témoins volontaires improbable. De ces problèmes découle le besoin d'arrangements coopératifs d'assistance légale mutuelle — arrangements qui ne sont pas du tout aussi nombreux et/ou développés qu'ils le devraient pour permettre de lutter efficacement contre la criminalité en mer[135].

En formulant l'obligation de soumettre un cas à des poursuites en des termes qui s'adaptent à la pratique générale de l'Etat de détention, une marge de manœuvre est certainement fournie aux autorités compétentes, leur permettant de refuser de poursuivre tout en respectant l'obligation *aut dedere, aut judicare*[136]. Puisque les Etats ne sont pas obligés, dans les traités analysés ci-dessus, de répondre positivement à une demande d'extradition, la liberté laissée aux Etats dans les questions de procédure judiciaire mine potentiellement le but de « zéro impunité » poursuivi par l'obligation *aut dedere, aut judicare*.

ii) *Les modalités de la mise en application du droit pénal*

La responsabilité étatique peut aussi découler de la *manière par laquelle* les Etats remplissent leurs responsabilités internationales relatives au cadre de mise en application du droit pénal.

a) *Compétence excessive*

Les Etats peuvent être tenus responsables pour un acte internationalement illicite lorsqu'ils exercent leur compétence au-delà des limites

134. Trapp, *State Responsibility for International Terrorism*, Oxford University Press, 2011, partie 3.2.1.

135. Voir *infra* Cheah, chapitre 8.

136. Voir Kolb, « The Exercise of Criminal Jurisdiction over International Terrorists », dans Bianchi, dir. publ., *Enforcing International Law Norms Against Terrorism*, Oxford, Hart Publishing, 2004, pp. 227, 261.

imposées par le droit international[137]. Une telle responsabilité est généralement déclenchée dans les cas d'un excès de compétence d'exécution, par exemple lorsqu'un Etat côtier visite ou arrête un navire étranger et l'équipage dans sa zone contiguë ou sa ZEE dans des circonstances autres que celles autorisées par la CNUDM, lorsqu'un navire gouvernemental visite et arrête un navire étranger et l'équipage en haute mer (sans le consentement de l'Etat pavillonnaire) alors que ce navire ne commet pas de piraterie ou d'émissions non autorisées, lorsqu'un navire gouvernemental visite un navire étranger en haute mer sans de raisons suffisantes pour soupçonner une implication dans le commerce d'esclaves, ou lorsqu'un navire gouvernemental exerce un pouvoir d'exécution dans le cas d'autres crimes en mer (par exemple le trafic de drogues ou le terrorisme maritime) sans le consentement de l'Etat pavillonnaire[138].

Dans de tels cas, pour autant que les voies de recours internes disponibles et efficaces aient été épuisées et que les conditions en matière de nationalité de la réclamation soient respectées[139], les règles générales de la responsabilité étatique exigeraient la réparation intégrale pour le dommage causé par l'acte internationalement illicite (réparation qui peut prendre la forme de restitution, de compensation et/ou de satisfaction)[140]. La CNUDM prévoit également des réparations dans de tels cas, bien que les articles en question ne fassent qu'illustrer les règles générales de la responsabilité étatique, telle qu'elle s'appliquerait au cas d'espèce. Par exemple, l'article 106 de la CNUDM convient que:

> «lorsque la saisie d'un navire ou aéronef suspect de piraterie a été effectuée sans motif suffisant, l'Etat qui y a procédé est responsable vis-à-vis de l'Etat dont le navire ou l'aéronef a la nationalité de toute perte ou de tout dommage causé de ce fait».

La demande de dommages est soumise à la règle de nationalité des plaintes et rien dans le langage de l'article 106 ne suggère que la CNUDM se distancie de la condition d'épuisement des voies de remèdes internes.

---

137. Pour une discussion sur les décisions judiciaires relatives à la responsabilité pour un excès de juridiction, voir *infra* Neri, chapitre 15.

138. En ce qui concerne le trafic de drogues, le terrorisme maritime, le trafic de migrants et les autres crimes maritimes soumis à des traités de mise en application du droit pénal, le traité pertinent prévoit une procédure-cadre pour obtenir l'accord de l'Etat pavillonnaire. Voir présente section, paragraphe 2, titre B, lettres *a)* et *b)* ci-dessus.

139. Article 44 du Projet d'articles sur la responsabilité de l'Etat pour fait internationalement illicite, avec commentaires, dans *Rapport de la Commission du droit international sur les travaux de sa cinquante-troisième session*, Nations Unies, doc. A/56/10 (2001), p. 31 (ci-après «Projet d'articles sur la responsabilité de la CDI»).

140. Article 34 du Projet d'articles sur la responsabilité de la CDI.

En ce qui concerne un excès dans la compétence d'exécution (sous la forme de visite) lorsque les soupçons de piraterie, de transport d'esclaves ou d'émissions non autorisées se révèlent dénués de fondement, la CNUDM prévoit cependant que la compensation pour les pertes ou les dommages doit être payée directement au navire visité [141]. Cela nécessite que les Etats exerçant leur compétence d'exécution en haute mer aient un mécanisme au niveau national grâce auquel les navires visités peuvent obtenir compensation de la part de l'Etat visitant — en l'absence d'un tel mécanisme, l'Etat visitant risque en effet de voir sa responsabilité étatique invoquée, pour la simple raison qu'il ne respecte pas ses obligations de compensation développées à l'article 110 de la CNUDM.

Plus complexes sont les questions liées à la responsabilité étatique dans les cas d'un excès dans la compétence législative. Alors que le principe du *Lotus* (tout est permis à moins que cela ne soit interdit) [142] n'est plus considéré comme correct (et ne l'a peut-être jamais été) [143], les limites précises de la compétence législative (par exemple le statut en droit coutumier de la compétence universelle et les confins de la doctrine des effets) sont encore contestées en pratique [144]. Ces aspects controversés peuvent être pertinents en ce qui concerne les crimes en mer et l'exercice par un Etat de sa compétence législative en accord avec ses obligations découlant des traités de mise en application du droit pénal. Les crimes en mer qui font l'objet de tels textes conventionnels (les crimes contre la sécurité de la navigation maritime, le transport ou l'usage d'ADM à bord ou contre des navires, le trafic de migrants) ne sont pas des crimes internationaux à proprement parler et ne tombent donc pas sous le coup d'une compétence universelle en droit international général. Il en résulte ainsi que l'exercice de la compétence universelle par un Etat partie à ces conventions sera légal à l'égard des autres Etats parties, mais pourrait bien être considéré un excès de compétence par un Etat tiers dont les nationaux sont visés. Cette conclusion ne peut être valable que si le principe du *Lotus* a en effet été renversé (de telle manière que tout exercice de compétence législative est interdit sauf s'il est autorisé par l'une des bases de compétences reconnues). Il ne fait dans tous les cas pas de doute que certains tribunaux nationaux considèrent que la compétence universelle ne peut pas être exercée à l'encontre de personnes dont l'Etat de nationalité n'est pas partie au traité obli-

141. Article 110, paragraphe 3, de la CNUDM. Voir P. Wendel, *State Responsibility for Interferences with the Freedom of Navigation in Public International Law* (Berlin, Springer, 2007), pp. 113-115. Pour plus de détails, voir *infra* Neri, chapitre 15.

142. *Supra* note 34 et le texte s'y référant.

143. *Supra* note 35.

144. Voir Crawford, *supra* note 2, pp. 477-478.

geant les Etats à criminaliser sur une base universelle la conduite reprochée[145].

b) *Les obligations de droits humains*

Les Etats peuvent aussi être tenus responsables pour une violation des obligations de droits humains applicables lors d'une opération d'exécution du droit en mer. Les droits à la vie, à la liberté, à la sécurité de la personne, et le droit de ne pas être soumis à la torture ou à d'autres formes de traitements cruels sont les droits les plus visiblement pertinents lors de telles opérations[146]. La responsabilité pour la violation de l'un d'eux exige à la fois que la conduite soit attribuable à l'Etat[147] et que les personnes en question soient sous la «juridiction» de l'Etat qui exerce sa compétence d'exécution, dans le sens (par exemple) de l'article 1 de la CEDH. Alors que souvent l'attribution et la «juridiction» vont de pair, il est important qu'elles restent analytiquement distinctes[148]. Les clauses de juridiction (tel l'article 1 de la CEDH) sont liées à l'émergence de l'obligation de l'Etat — la juridiction est un critère seuil qui détermine quand un Etat s'expose à des obligations sous le traité. Comme présenté à l'article 2 des articles de la Commission du droit international sur la responsabilité étatique,

> «[i]l y a fait internationalement illicite de l'Etat lorsqu'un comportement consistant en une action ou une omission: *a)* est attribuable à l'Etat en vertu du droit international; et *b)* constitue une violation d'une obligation internationale de l'Etat».

La notion de juridiction dans les traités de droits humains est une question qui concerne l'article 2, lettre *b)*: une obligation existe-t-elle (de telle manière que la conduite en question pourrait en être une violation), et non pas l'article 2, lettre *a)*: est-ce que cette conduite-là peut être attribuée à un Etat.

Dans l'hypothèse où les droits humains s'appliquent, la responsabilité d'un Etat pour la violation de droits humains lors d'une opération

145. Voir *infra* Grymaneli, chapitre 5, qui examine l'application par les Etats-Unis d'Amérique de la législation adoptée en accord avec les obligations relatives aux poursuites judiciaires contre les pirates, obligations contenues dans la Convention contre la prise d'otages.

146. Voir *infra* Montas, chapitre 12.

147. Sur l'attribution en général et sur les défis liés à certaines méthodes de répression des crimes en mer (par exemple l'utilisation de gardes armés privés à bord de navires marchands et les opérations multilatérales de mise en application) en particulier, voir *infra* Neri, chapitre 15. Voir aussi Williams, chapitre 9.

148. Voir Cour européenne des droits de l'homme (grande chambre), *Catan et autres c. Moldavie et Russie* (requêtes n°s 43370/04, 8252/05 et 18454/06), 19 octobre 2012, par. 115.

maritime peut dépendre de la légalité de cette opération en vertu du droit international général. Dans l'affaire *Medvedyev c. France*[149], le Cambodge avait consenti dans une note diplomatique que la France exerce sa compétence d'exécution envers ses navires (afin de combattre le trafic de drogues). Alors que la Cour a fait quelques remarques factuelles quant à la portée et au contenu précis, le point à relever est que la Cour a considéré que la licéité, selon le droit international général, de l'exercise de compétence d'exécution sur le navire *Cambodge* par la France, est un facteur pertinent afin de déterminer si les restrictions de liberté subies par l'équipage étaient «prescrites par la loi» selon l'article 5 de la CEDH[150]. Alors que la licéité ou non de l'exercice en mer de la compétence d'exécution ne devrait pas être liée à l'*existence* d'obligations de droits humains[151], l'affaire *Medvedyev* suggère que l'illicéité peut être liée à une évaluation du comportement étatique et de sa conformité (or non) avec *la substance* des droits humains[152]. La décision de la Cour a créé une synergie entre la substance des obligations de droits humains et le droit international général relatif à la compétence, diminuant ainsi les risques de fragmentation.

C. Des mesures d'exécution imposées par le Conseil de sécurité

Comme cela a été développé plus haut, une nouvelle forme de mise en application du droit pénal a été imposée aux Etats, forme dont la source est la législation du Conseil de sécurité dans le cadre du chapitre VII de la Charte. Le Conseil a abordé en particulier la menace à la paix et à la sécurité internationales émanant des possibles proliférations d'ADM par des acteurs non étatiques. Il a ainsi obligé les Etats à criminaliser le transport et le transfert d'ADM et à créer des cadres nationaux efficaces dans le but de superviser et de sécuriser leur production, leur utilisation, leur stockage ou leur transport[153]. Alors que la «législation du Conseil de sécurité» a initialement été perçue comme un exercice controversé des pouvoirs du chapitre VII, la plupart des

149. Cour européenne des droits de l'homme (grande chambre), *Affaire Medvedyev et autres c. France* (requête n° 3394/03), arrêt du 29 mars 2010. Pour des commentaires, voir Papastavridis, «ECHR: *Medvedyev* v. *France*», *International and Comparative Law Quarterly*, vol. 59 (2010), pp. 867-882.

150. *Affaire Medvedyev et autres c. France*, par. 100. Voir *infra* Batsalas, chapitre 11.

151. Voir *infra*, titre C.

152. Pour une analyse de la violation de droits substantifs qui est occasionnée par la lutte contre la criminalité en mer, voir *infra* Montas, chapitre 12.

153. Voir Conseil de sécurité, résolution 1540 (2004), par. 2-3. Pour plus de détails, voir *infra* Cherief, chapitre 13.

Etats se sont conformés aux obligations de transmissions d'informations qui leur ont été imposées — particulièrement en ce qui concerne le Comité 1540 et ses efforts pour supprimer la prolifération d'ADM par la mer.

En raison de l'implication du Conseil de sécurité, le système de responsabilité (« accountability ») du chapitre VII pourrait bien servir à la suppression des activités criminelles en mer. L'échec des Etats dans leur lutte contre la prolifération d'ADM, telle que formulée dans la résolution 1540 (2004) du Conseil de sécurité, pourrait bien résulter dans une menace pour la paix et la sécurité internationales, menace à laquelle le Conseil pourrait répondre sous le chapitre VII de la Charte des Nations Unies. Le but et les limites des mesures sous le chapitre VII seraient en tout cas définies par un paradigme sécuritaire plutôt que des questions de responsabilité légale : le cadre du chapitre VII se différencie légalement et conceptuellement de la responsabilité étatique. En effet, le but des interventions entreprises en son sein est de « maintenir ou rétablir la paix et la sécurité internationales »[154], ce qui doit être distingué du but de la responsabilité étatique qui vise à rétablir la relation légale qui existait entre l'Etat fautif et l'Etat lésé avant la commission de l'acte illicite. Quant au champ de conduites auxquelles le chapitre VII peut répondre, il n'est pas limité comme celui de la responsabilité étatique qui n'existe que dans les cas de violations des obligations internationales. Il n'empêche que la responsabilité dans le cadre du chapitre VII peut aller de pair avec la responsabilité étatique pour lutter contre la prolifération des ADM, pour autant que l'Etat en question soit *aussi* partie au Protocole SUA 2005 et une violation des obligations selon ce protocole coïncide avec une violation des obligations du chapitre VII qui engendrerait une menace pour la paix et la sécurité internationales.

SECTION 3 **CONCLUSION**

Comme l'analyse ci-dessus le démontre, la suppression de la criminalité en mer suscite nombre de questions intéressantes concernant l'application du droit international général, en particulier celui relatif à l'interprétation des traités (et la possibilité d'utiliser la CVDT pour moderniser la CNUDM, de manière à la rendre pertinente face aux défis du XXIe siècle). Les limitations de compétences et les interactions entre le droit international général, le droit pénal international, les droits humains et le cadre constitutionnel fourni par la

154. Article 39 de la Charte des Nations Unies.

CNUDM sont d'autres problématiques soulevées par un tel sujet transversal. Ces thématiques ont été dressées avec succès lors du programme de 2012 du Centre d'étude et de recherche de l'Académie de droit international de La Haye. Les chapitres qui suivent rassemblent les résultats des recherches studieuses des participants.

PREMIÈRE PARTIE

PART I

La répression

Suppression

3 La compétence nationale en matière de pollution marine

Sarah Fiona Gahlen *

SECTION 1 INTRODUCTION

Il est regrettable, mais néanmoins établi, que les efforts des Etats dans le domaine de la protection de l'environnement marin sont renforcés, et même souvent déclenchés, par des événements catastrophiques. Cette tendance est certainement perceptible dans les régimes internationaux destinés à régler la responsabilité civile pour les incidents maritimes ; les régimes existants ont été développés à travers les réponses fournies à un bon nombre d'accidents désastreux, du *Torrey Canyon* en 1969 jusqu'au *Prestige* en 2002 [1].

Il semble que le développement en matière de législation criminelle soit similaire. Les premiers efforts visant à établir des standards pour les décharges de polluants et les sanctions pour des violations de ces règles sont visibles dans la convention OILPOL de 1954 [2], qui obligeait les Etats parties à soumettre les infractions contre les standards de décharge à des sanctions appropriées. La convention MARPOL 73/78 [3], successeur de la convention OILPOL et dont la portée et le champ d'application sont plus étendus, emploie la même stratégie, en introduisant un système de normes techniques ainsi que des standards de recherche. Elle astreint également les Etats parties à soumettre les violations de ces normes à des sanctions assez sévères pour en garantir le respect. Si certains auteurs ont observé que la criminalisation des acteurs maritimes

---

* Candidate au doctorat à l'International Max Planck Research School for Maritime Affairs, Hambourg. Titulaire d'une maîtrise en droit international et européen, Université de Rouen, et d'un LL.M. en droit commercial, King's College, Londres.

1. Voir l'exposé détaillé par Colin M. De la Rue et Charles B. Anderson, *Shipping and the Environment : Law and Practice*, 2ᵉ éd., Informa Law, 2009, pp. 7 ss.

2. International Convention for the Prevention of Pollution of the Sea by Oil, 1954, Nations Unies, *Recueil des traités*, vol. 237, p. 3 (ci-après, OILPOL).

3. International Convention for the Prevention of Pollution by Ships, 1973, as modified by the 1978 Protocol, Nations Unies, *Recueil des traités*, vol. 1340, pp. 61 et 184 (ci-après, MARPOL).

pour des pollutions de l'environnement marin est un phénomène plutôt récent[4], il semble que cette tendance est due à un changement de mentalité des Etats côtiers en ce qui concerne la mise en application renforcée des normes existantes. Mais on peut aussi constater une tendance croissante des Etats côtiers — et de l'Union européenne — à défendre leur intérêt dans un environnement marin propre par des moyens du droit pénal. Cette étude va porter, d'un côté, sur le pouvoir de législation des Etats côtiers, compte tenu des difficultés du droit international dans ce domaine (section 2). De l'autre, sur la législation en matière criminelle qui exige un système de mise en application et un pouvoir de police grâce auquel les infractions peuvent être poursuivies et sanctionnées. Ici encore, les mers sont un domaine spécial, difficile à contrôler et présentant des problèmes de fait et de droit qui ne se posent pas dans un environnement terrestre. Vu le rôle du droit pénal, qui, normalement, exige une législation claire et sans ambiguïté et une procédure précise et élaborée afin de garantir les droits de l'accusé, la mise en œuvre de la législation criminelle face à la pollution marine n'est pas facile (section 3).

SECTION 2 LA COMPÉTENCE NATIONALE EN MATIÈRE CRIMINELLE FACE À LA POLLUTION MARINE DANS LE CADRE DU DROIT INTERNATIONAL

Les mers, même les eaux territoriales, sont un domaine où les intérêts des Etats côtiers se heurtent aux intérêts du transport maritime ; il est régi par le droit international. Les limites dans lesquelles les Etats côtiers peuvent légiférer en matière criminelle et prévoir des sanctions pour des infractions qui ont eu lieu sur la mer ne sont pas toujours très claires. Il semble que beaucoup d'Etats invoquent des droits dont la portée n'a jamais été déterminée, et que beaucoup d'Etats légifèrent, apparemment, sans trop prendre en compte le droit international public sous-jacent. Cette étude va, dans un premier temps, analyser le droit de la mer et les compétences qu'il confère généralement aux Etats côtiers en matière criminelle (paragraphe 1). Dans ce cadre légal, les Etats ont plusieurs possibilités pour atteindre leurs buts, en faisant valoir différents dispositifs normatifs internationaux. Dans un second temps, seront examinés de plus près ces cadres législatifs, telle la convention MARPOL, et leurs relations avec les lois nationales (paragraphe 2).

4. Philipp Wendel, *State Responsibility for Interferences with the Freedom of Navigation in Public International Law* (2007), p. 48.

Paragraphe 1 **Des limites dans le droit de la mer**

Le droit de la mer, tel qu'il est en vigueur aujourd'hui, est généralement considéré comme codifié dans la Convention des Nations Unies sur le droit de la mer (CNUDM), conclue à Montego Bay (Jamaïque) le 10 décembre 1982. La «constitution des océans» est un instrument de compromis, qui concilie des intérêts variés; il est ainsi sujet à des interprétations très différentes.

De plus, la Convention a été négociée à une époque où beaucoup d'accords internationaux dans le domaine du droit maritime existaient déjà, non seulement en matière de sécurité maritime, de responsabilité civile pour la pollution marine, mais aussi dans le domaine de la protection de l'environnement. Ainsi, la CNUDM s'appuie sur des accords préexistants et se réfère à des standards déjà établis. En ce qui concerne la compétence des Etats côtiers d'adopter des règles et des normes nationales applicables dans les eaux adjacentes à leurs côtes, le système de la CNUDM fait des différences selon les zones dont il s'agit.

A. Les eaux intérieures

Dans les eaux intérieures[5], les Etats jouissent, selon les articles 2 et 8 de la CNUDM, d'une souveraineté qui ne se distingue pas de la souveraineté qu'ils exercent sur leur territoire terrestre[6]. Les Etats côtiers peuvent alors légiférer librement, sans tenir compte des intérêts d'autres Etats concernant la navigation à travers ces zones.

Ainsi, les navires battant pavillon étranger et qui entrent dans ces eaux seront, théoriquement, soumis à la juridiction de l'Etat côtier. L'Etat côtier peut, généralement, mettre en application toute disposition nationale, y compris les normes de droit pénal, contre les personnes qui se trouvent sur un navire dans le port. Dans ce conflit possible entre la souveraineté de l'Etat du pavillon et celle de l'Etat côtier, surtout sur des navires se trouvant dans les ports, ce dernier n'invoquera ses propres lois que dans l'hypothèse où le comportement incriminé a des répercussions sur ses intérêts[7]. Néanmoins, nul n'empêche les Etats portuaires de

5. Il s'agit de toutes les eaux qui se trouvent du côté terrestre des lignes de base, à savoir les estuaires, les ports et toutes les eaux qui peuvent être considérées comme étant en-deçà du littoral de l'Etat (CNUDM, art. 8).

6. R. R. Churchill et A. V. Lowe, *The Law of the Sea* (3e éd., Juris Pub., Manchester University Press, 1999), p. 65; Ho-Sam Bang, «Is Port State Control an Effective Means to Combat Vessel-Source Pollution? An Empirical Survey of the Practical Exercise by Port States of Their powers of Control», *The International Journal of Marine and Coastal Law*, n° 23, p. 720.

7. R. R. Churchill et A. V. Lowe, *op. cit. supra* note 6, pp. 66 ss.; Ho-Sam Bang, «Port State Jurisdiction and Article 218 of the UN Convention on the Law of the Sea», *Journal of Maritime Law and Commerce* (2009), n° 40, p. 295.

faire valoir leurs lois dans leurs ports[8], et les problèmes qui se présentent alors sont ceux qui se posent toujours dans les cas de mise en œuvre du droit pénal transnational.

Quant à la compétence juridictionnelle pour des cas de pollution marine, les Etats portuaires, selon l'article 218 de la CNUDM, disposent d'un pouvoir assez étendu pour contrôler les navires se trouvant volontairement dans leurs ports. Ces pouvoirs plus étendus pour l'Etat portuaire ont été créés car le contrôle dans le port, une fois que le navire y est volontairement entré et y reste pour un certain temps, est une entrave moins grande à la libre navigation que celle d'interrompre un navire de passage[9].

Les pouvoirs de l'Etat portuaire peuvent être différenciés : le contrôle *(Port State Control)* d'un côté et la juridiction de l'autre. Le premier vise à garantir que tous les navires se conforment aux standards internationaux avant qu'ils ne quittent le port. Le contrôle a seulement pour objectif de vérifier que la condition du navire corresponde aux normes internationales en vigueur, et non de punir ou de poursuivre le propriétaire ou l'équipage pour les vices découverts. Il n'y a ainsi pas de compétence juridictionnelle pénale dans le cadre du *Port State Control*[10].

En revanche, la juridiction de l'Etat du port *(Port State Jurisdiction)* recouvre des actions dans l'Etat du port, le plus souvent pour des infractions qui ont été commises avant l'escale du navire. Dans le cadre de la juridiction sur ces infractions, l'Etat du port doit ainsi se référer à la zone maritime dans laquelle l'infraction a eu lieu et au régime légal qui s'y applique[11]. Vu les pouvoirs conférés par l'article 218 de la CNUDM, l'Etat du port jouit d'un rôle assez important dans la mise en œuvre de la législation, mais il n'applique pas de dispositions nationales.

Néanmoins, le pouvoir de l'Etat du port est affaibli par le fait que sa compétence en matière de mise en œuvre des dispositions est assujettie au droit de l'article 228 de la CNUDM de l'Etat du pavillon (voir *infra*).

B. La mer territoriale

Bien que les Etats jouissent, dans leur mer territoriale, d'une « souveraineté », selon l'article 2, paragraphes 1 et 2, de la CNUDM,

8. R. R. Churchill et A. V. Lowe, *op. cit. supra* note 6, pp. 66 ; Erik J. Molenaar, « Port State Jurisdiction : Toward Comprehensive, Mandatory and Global Coverage », *Ocean Development and International Law* (2007), n° 38, p. 228.

9. J. P. A. Bernhardt, « A Schematic Analysis of Vessel-Source Pollution : Prescriptive and Enforcement Regimes in the Law of the Sea Conference », *Virginia Journal of International Law* (1980), n° 20, p. 290.

10. Ho-Sam Bang, « Is Port State Control an Effective Means to Combat Vessel-Source Pollution ? An Empirical Survey of the Practical Exercise by Port States of Their powers of Control », *op. cit. supra* note 6, p. 717.

11. Ho-Sam Bang, « Port State Jurisdiction and Article 218 of the UN Convention on the Law of the Sea », *op. cit. supra* note 7, p. 292.

la Convention précise que cette souveraineté n'est pas absolue, en désignant dans l'article 2, paragraphe 3 de la CNUDM que les pouvoirs de l'Etat côtier ne s'exercent que dans les conditions prévues par la CNUDM elle-même et dans le respect des autres règles du droit international. L'une de ces restrictions se trouve dans l'article 27 de la CNUDM, selon lequel l'Etat côtier ne devrait pas exercer sa juridiction pénale à bord d'un navire étranger, sauf si les conséquences de l'infraction s'étendent à l'Etat côtier (CNUDM, art. 27, par. 1, al. *a)*). C'est le cas dans toutes les infractions de pollution marine perceptible, même minime ; ainsi, l'exercice de la juridiction pénale est généralement accordé à l'Etat côtier.

Les Etats côtiers ont, selon l'article 21, paragraphe 1, de la CNUDM le droit d'adopter, « en conformité avec les dispositions de la Convention et les autres règles du droit international, des lois et règlements relatifs au passage inoffensif » dans leur mer territoriale, qui peuvent porter sur un nombre de domaines, entre autres la « préservation de l'environnement de l'Etat côtier et prévention, réduction et maîtrise de sa pollution ». Ainsi, l'Etat côtier peut dicter des normes pénales pour la protection de l'environnement marin.

La compétence de l'article 21, paragraphe 1, de la CNUDM est en premier temps restreinte par son article 21, paragraphe 2, qui énonce que l'Etat ne peut pas édicter de lois et règlements relatifs à la conception, à la construction et à l'armement des navires étrangers, sauf s'ils donnent effet à des « règles ou des normes internationales généralement acceptées ». L'article 21, paragraphe 1, de la CNUDM sert à garantir les intérêts des Etats en faveur de la liberté de la navigation : La conception, la construction et l'armement des navires (« CCA ») sont des données que l'équipage du navire ne peut pas changer en route [12]. Ainsi, si chaque Etat demandait l'adhésion à des standards différents dans ces domaines, la libre navigation serait beaucoup restreinte. La CNUDM garantit donc la libre navigation et renforce en même temps les standards internationaux de conception, de construction et d'armement [13]. Pour les navires, ce sont des standards minimaux auxquels ils doivent adhérer.

12. Alan E. Boyle, « Marine Pollution under the Law of the Sea Convention », *The American Journal of International Law*, 1985, vol. 79, p. 360 ; Erik J. Molenaar, *op. cit. supra* note 8, p. 230. Daniel Bodansky, « Protecting the Marine Environment from Vessel-Source Pollution : UNCLOS III and Beyond », *Ecology Law Quarterly*, 1991, n° 18, p. 750 (note de bas de page 152), indique quand même que quelques standards de rejet peuvent demander un équipement spécial, ce qui peut être consideré comme ayant une répercussion sur les standards CCA.

13. Bernard Oxman, « The Duty to Respect Generally Accepted International Standards », *New York University Journal of International Law and Policy*, 1991, n° 24, p. 113.

Néanmoins, pour les Etats côtiers, ces «règles et normes internationales généralement acceptées» (ci-après «RNIGA») sont des standards maximaux — ils ne peuvent pas demander aux navires de remplir des conditions au-delà de ce que les RNIGA prévoient. Le succès de cette stratégie dépend néanmoins d'une même compréhension de la notion des RNIGA. Le système a aussi été employé dans la CNUDM — le problème des RNIGA et l'interprétation de ce qui en fait partie seront abordés dans cette étude dans un autre contexte (voir *infra*). De toute façon, les standards posés par les conventions MARPOL et SOLAS[14], conventions antérieures à la CNUDM, font partie des RNIGA.

Pour le moment, il suffit de constater que l'article 21, paragraphe 2, de la CNUDM s'oppose à ce que l'équipage ou l'armateur d'un navire soient soumis à des peines pénales pour ne pas avoir adhéré à des normes de construction, de conception ou d'armement unilatéralement adoptées par l'Etat côtier. L'article 21, paragraphe 2, de la CNUDM pose donc une limite à la compétence législative des Etats dans leurs eaux territoriales, mais cela ne concerne que les CCA.

On peut alors conclure que, pour toute disposition autre que les CCA, les Etats sont libres dans leur législation[15], surtout en ce qui concerne les interdictions ayant trait aux comportements des équipages et armateurs dans la mer territoriale. Il est en effet parfaitement possible pour les navires de suivre des règles de conduite différentes dans différentes mers territoriales[16], tant que ces règles sont dûment publiées[17]. Les Etats côtiers sont alors libres d'imposer des sanctions pénales pour les actes de pollution dans leur mer territoriale. Néanmoins, cette différenciation entre les caractéristiques du navire immuables et le comportement de l'équipage pose un problème considérable dans le domaine de la pollution accidentelle ou négligente. Tandis que, dans les cas de pollution délibérée, il y a un comportement qu'on peut reprocher à l'équipage, une décision consciente qui n'a rien à voir avec la condition du bateau, tel n'est pas le cas lors des incidents de pollution accidentelle. Dans les situations où l'on reproche au capitaine ou à l'équipage du navire d'avoir agi avec négligence, ce sont plutôt des manques de maintenance

14. International Convention for the Safety of Life at Sea, 1974, Nations Unies, *Recueil des traités*, vol. 1184, p. 3.

15. J. P. A. Bernhardt, *op. cit. supra* note 9, p. 277; Doris König, «The EU Directive on Ship-Source Pollution and on the Introduction of Penalties for Infringements: Development or Breach of International Law?», dans Tafsir M. Ndiaye et Rüdiger Wolfrum (dir. publ.), *Law of the Sea, Environmental Law and Settlement of Disputes*, Martinus Nijhoff, 2007, p. 772.

16. J. P. A. Bernhardt, *op. cit. supra* note 9, p. 268; Erik J. Molenaar, *op. cit. supra* note 8, p. 230.

17. Cela incombe aux Etats selon l'article 21, paragraphe 3, de la CNUDM; voir aussi Doris König, *op. cit. supra* note 15, p. 773.

dont ils sont accusés. Il s'agit donc de reproches tenant à la condition du navire et aux CCA, envers lesquels la compétence législative de l'Etat côtier est limitée par l'adhésion aux RNIGA[18]. Il est vrai que le plus souvent cela ne pose pas de problèmes, car les Etats ont apparemment tendance à définir la limite entre un accident et un comportement répréhensible par la voie des RNIGA — surtout les standards de MARPOL et SOLAS — et de reprocher aux responsables la violation de ces normes internationales. Néanmoins, déterminer si les Etats ont le droit d'infliger des sanctions pénales aux personnes responsables dépend beaucoup de l'origine des pollutions accidentelles.

Même pour les dispositions nationales qui ne sont pas relatives aux CCA, la CNUDM, dans un désir de concilier les intérêts des Etats côtiers avec les exigences de la libre navigation, pose une limite : selon l'article 211, paragraphe 4, de la CNUDM, qui fait allusion à l'ensemble des règles concernant la compétence législative de l'Etat côtier, et selon l'article 24, paragraphe 1, de la CNUDM, l'Etat côtier ne peut pas, par la voie de lois ou de règlements nationaux, empêcher ou restreindre le droit de libre passage inoffensif des navires.

Ce droit au passage inoffensif, clé de voûte du régime légal de la mer territoriale, n'est pas facile à concilier avec les compétences pénales des Etats côtiers. La notion est indirectement définie à l'article 19, paragraphe 2, de la CNUDM, qui énonce des circonstances dans lesquelles un bateau ne peut plus être considéré en passage inoffensif[19], dont la « pollution grave et délibérée ». Littéralement, la disposition stipule qu'un navire qui pollue les mers territoriales accidentellement, ou dans un cadre qui ne peut pas être considéré comme « grave », est toujours en passage inoffensif, avec des compétences d'intervention de l'Etat côtier probablement très réduites. Il est parfois argumenté que l'article 19, paragraphe 2, de la CNUDM peut être lu comme ayant des effets hors de sa portée littérale, à savoir que la liste énoncée n'est pas

18. Agustín Blanco-Bazán, « Marine Pollution and Its Scapegoats : The Fragile Legitimacy of A European Directive and A European Judgment », dans Mielle Bultermann *et al.* (dir. publ.), *Views of European Law from the Mountain : Liber Amicorum Piet Jan Slot*, Kluwer Law International, 2009, p. 240. Dans sa conclusion, il soutient que le régime de MARPOL, y compris l'exception d'avarie (voir *infra*, paragraphe 2, titre A, point i)), s'applique dans la mer territoriale.

19. Article 19 de la CNUDM :

> « 1. Le passage est inoffensif aussi longtemps qu'il ne porte pas atteinte à la paix, au bon ordre ou à la sécurité de l'Etat côtier. Il doit s'effectuer en conformité avec les dispositions de la Convention et les autres règles du droit international. 2. Le passage d'un navire étranger est considéré comme portant atteinte à la paix, au bon ordre ou à la sécurité de l'Etat côtier si, dans la mer territoriale, ce navire se livre à l'une quelconque des activités suivantes : ... *h)* pollution délibérée et grave en violation de la Convention... »

exhaustive et qu'il peut y avoir d'autres circonstances, non mentionnées, qui rendent un passage offensif[20]. Il y a, en effet, de très bons arguments pour soutenir que la liste n'est pas exhaustive en tant que telle, notamment parce que l'article 19, paragraphe 1, de la CNUDM n'ajouterait rien à la portée de l'article 19, paragraphe 2, de la CNUDM, ce dernier énonçant déjà toutes les circonstances dans lesquelles le passage n'est plus inoffensif. En outre, le sous-paragraphe de l'article 19, paragraphe 2, alinéa *l)*, de la CNUDM, faisant allusion à « toute autre activité sans rapport direct avec le passage » indique qu'il y a des cas non mentionnés[21]. Néanmoins, il semble difficile d'y inclure une pollution accidentelle ou légère. Si le texte de l'article 19, paragraphe 2, de la CNUDM était destiné à couvrir toute forme de pollution, l'allusion au caractère « grave et délibéré » serait dépourvue de tout sens. Il ne semble pas que l'on puisse interpréter cet article comme susceptible de couvrir les circonstances mentionnées aux alinéas *a)* à *l)*, mais en allant au-delà des qualifications énoncées.

Il est vrai que la portée de l'article 19, paragraphe 2, de la CNUDM est alors très réduite, les cas de « pollution grave et délibérée, en violation de la Convention » étant assez rares. Les pollutions graves sont normalement les conséquences d'accidents et par conséquent ne sont pas délibérées, et les pollutions délibérées sont le plus souvent de caractère opérationnel et ne peuvent pas, normalement, être considérées comme graves[22]. Les deux critères de « grave » et « délibéré » sont cumulatifs. Ainsi, les législations nationales d'un bon nombre d'Etats qui ne visent qu'un des deux critères[23] pour rendre un passage offensif sont suscep-

20. Voir, à titre d'exemple, Bernhardt, *op. cit. supra* note 9, p. 277 ; Wolfgang Vitzthum et Gerhard Hafner, *Handbuch des Seerechts*, Beck, 2006, p. 124, considérant la liste de l'article 19, paragraphe 2, de la CNUDM comme exhaustive, tandis que Churchill et Lowe, *op. cit. supra* note 6, p. 85, et König, *op. cit. supra* note 15, pp. 779 ss., inclinent vers l'opinion contraire.

21. Kari Hakapää et Erik J Molenaar, « Innocent Passage — Past and Present », *Marine Policy*, 1999, n° 23, p. 132.

22. Boyle, *op. cit. supra* note 12, p. 359 ; Alan K-J Tan, *Vessel-Source Marine Pollution : The Law and Politics of International Regulation*, Cambridge University Press, 2006, p. 207.

23. Par exemple, la Pologne (Act concerning the Maritime Areas of the Polish Republic and the Maritime Administration, art. 9 (8)) ou la Croatie qui s'appuie alternativement sur les deux critères (Maritime Code art., 24 (8)). Voir traductions des législations, UN LOS Department Database, http://www.un.org/Depts/los/LEGISLATIONANDTREATIES/index.htm (consulté le 13 octobre 2012) ; voir également Hakapää et Molenaar, *op. cit. supra* note 21, pp. 139 ss. ; William K. Agyebeng, « Theory in Search of Practice : The Right of Innocent Passage in the Territorial Sea », *Cornell International Law Journal*, 2006, n° 39, p. 394 ; Julio Jorge Urbina, « Prevención y control de la contaminación causada por buques en el mar territorial : Competencias del Estado ribereño y contribución de las organizaciones internacionales », *Revista española de derecho internacional*, 2008, n° 60, p. 77 pour plus de détails.

tibles d'inconventionnalité[24]. Il est vrai que la signification du terme «grave» est très ouverte à l'interprétation dans toutes les hypothèses[25]. Certaines législations, par exemple, considèrent que la pollution rend un passage offensif dès qu'elle présente un risque ou un dommage aux intérêts du littoral[26]. Ce critère pourrait servir pour déterminer si la pollution est «grave» selon le sens de l'article 19, alinéa *h)*, de la CNUDM. Cependant, afin d'être compatible avec la disposition, la législation nationale devrait aussi remplir le critère d'intention pour rendre le passage offensif.

Selon la CNUDM, les navires qui polluent les mers territoriales accidentellement sont toujours en passage inoffensif — pourvu qu'ils puissent être considérés «en passage». Il semble clair qu'un bateau réduit à l'état d'épave, qui ne pourra pas continuer son voyage, n'est plus en «passage» tel que défini par l'article 18 de la CNUDM. Parfois, il pourrait être très difficile de faire la différence entre un arrêt ou un mouillage imposé par un cas de force majeure ou de détresse et une condition qui ne permet plus de continuer le passage.

Il s'agit de savoir si un Etat côtier peut exercer sa juridiction pénale sur un navire pollueur en passage inoffensif, dans la mesure où les conséquences de l'infraction s'étendent à l'Etat côtier, selon l'article 27 de la CNUDM. A première vue, l'exercice de cette juridiction ne semble pas être très conciliable avec le droit du navire de poursuivre son passage inoffensif[27]. Néanmoins, il a été considéré déjà très tôt après la conclusion de la Convention[28] que la mise en œuvre des dispositions nationales de l'Etat côtier ne peut pas être, comme telle, une entrave au droit de passage inoffensif[29]. Pourtant, de nombreux Etats prévoient, dans leur législation nationale, la mise en application de leurs normes

24. Hakapää et Molenaar, *op. cit. supra* note 21, p. 144.
25. Agyebeng, *op. cit. supra* note 23, p. 388.
26. Voir la législation du Belize (Maritime Areas Act 1992, art. 11, par. 1, al. *g)*), des Bahamas (Act 37 of 1993 respecting the territorial sea, archipelagic waters, internal waters and the exclusive economic zone, art. 5, par. 2, al. *f)*). Voir traductions des législations, UN LOS Department Database, http://www.un.org/Depts/los/LEGISLATIONANDTREATIES/index.htm (consulté le 13 octobre 2012); voir également Jorge Urbina, *op. cit. supra* note 23, p. 77.
27. Michel Morin, «Note TGI Brest, 27 janvier 1995», *Droit maritime français*, 1995, n° 47, p. 918; Thomas A. Mensah, «Sovereign Rights in Legislation of Member States under UNCLOS and MARPOL», 8th Cadwallader Memorial Lecture, Londres, 4 octobre 2005, http://www.shippinglbc.com/content/uploads/documents/8_cad.pdf (consulté le 13 octobre 2012); Jorge Urbina, *op. cit. supra* note 23, p. 74.
28. Boyle, *op. cit. supra* note 12, p. 359.
29. König, *op. cit. supra* note 15, p. 781; Alan K.-J. Tan, «The EU Ship-Source Pollution Directive and Recent Expansions of Coastal State Jurisdiction», dans Davor Vidas (dir. publ.), *Law, Technology and Science for Oceans in Globalisation*, Martinus Nijhoff, 2010, p. 296.

nationales même envers des navires considérés comme en passage inoffensif[30].

Cette pratique est confirmée par les dispositions de mise en application. Tandis qu'il paraît étrange d'avoir recours à la compétence procédurale des Etats côtiers de poursuivre des infractions pour savoir si la CNUDM leur permet d'exercer sa juridiction sur des bateaux se trouvant en passage inoffensif dans leurs eaux, l'article 220, paragraphe 2, de la CNUDM[31] donne des compétences considérables à l'Etat côtier envers les navires soupçonnés de violations. L'article fait, quant aux infractions qui ont eu lieu dans les mers territoriales, explicitement allusion aux règles nationales que l'Etat côtier a adoptées en conformité avec la Convention, c'est-à-dire dans le cadre du passage inoffensif. La disposition ne présuppose pas que les navires soumis au pouvoir de l'Etat côtier doivent avoir perdu le droit au passage inoffensif avant que l'Etat côtier puisse intervenir et commencer une action contre les contrevenants[32].

C. La zone économique exclusive (ZEE)

Le concept légal de la zone économique exclusive (ZEE) a été codifié pour la première fois dans la CNUDM. Dans cette zone qui s'étend jusqu'à 200 milles marins en partant des lignes de base (CNUDM, art. 57), l'Etat côtier a des droits relatifs à l'usage des ressources naturelles dans la mer et le sous-sol marin, mais ses droits souverains sont beaucoup plus restreints que dans la mer territoriale. En ce qui concerne la pollution des mers due à l'immersion[33], la CNUDM y

30. Voir la liste énoncée par Hakapää et Molenaar, *op. cit. supra* note 21, pp. 140 ss.

31. Article 220, paragraphe 2, de la CNUDM :

> « Lorsqu'un Etat a de sérieuses raisons de penser qu'un navire naviguant dans sa mer a enfreint, lors de son passage, des lois et règlements qu'il a adoptés en conformité de la Convention ou des règles et normes internationales applicables visant à prévenir, réduire et maîtriser la pollution par des navires, il peut procéder, sans préjudice de l'application des dispositions pertinentes de la section 3 de la partie II, à l'inspection matérielle du navire pour établir l'infraction et, lorsque les éléments de preuve le justifient, intenter une action et notamment ordonner l'immobilisation du navire conformément à son droit interne, sous réserve de la section 7. »

32. Hakapää et Molenaar, *op. cit. supra* note 21, p. 136.

33. « Immersion », dans ce contexte, ne désigne que les déchets terrestres apportés en mer. Les déchets produits par les navires au cours de leur voyage sont visés par MARPOL, annexe V. Voir David L. VanderZwaag et Anne Daniel, « International Law and Ocean Dumping : Steering a Precautionary Course Aboard the 1996 Protocol, but Still an Unfinished Voyage », dans Aldo E. Chircop, Ted L. McDorman et Susan Rolston (dir. publ.), *The Future of Ocean Regime-building : Essays in tribute to Douglas M. Johnston*, Martinus Nijhoff Publishers, 2009, p. 524 ; et Louise de La Fayette, « The Sound Management of

fait allusion dans son article 20 en se référant à des accords internationaux, à savoir la convention de Londres de 1972 sur la prévention de la pollution des mers résultant de l'immersion de déchets et le protocole de 1996[34]. Il est intéressant de souligner que, généralement, l'immersion de déchets transportés de la terre à la mer pour les couler au large se déroule sous le contrôle des autorités étatiques. Les substances dont on se débarrasse de cette manière sont, généralement, des armes chimiques[35] et des substances radioactives[36], traitées sous un contrôle étatique. Ainsi, la criminalisation des responsables pour des actions illicites dans ce cadre n'est peut-être pas perçue comme nécessaire.

Quant à la pollution par les installations d'exploration et d'exploitation du sous-sol marin, il n'existe pas de convention internationale concernant la responsabilité pour les pollutions potentielles. L'article 208 de la CNUDM, néanmoins, astreint les Etats parties à adopter des lois et des règlements, afin de prévenir, réduire et maîtriser la pollution de l'environnement marin. L'article contient une allusion aux règles internationales, stipulant que les Etats ne peuvent pas légiférer en deçà de leurs standards, mais, étant donné le vide juridique au plan international, la disposition n'a pas beaucoup de pertinence. Quelques Etats, dont les Etats-Unis, sanctionnent les violations de normes nationales qui provoquent une pollution marine par hydrocarbures, causée par les plates-formes de forage et d'autres installations d'exploration et d'exploitation. Il semble d'ailleurs que cela soit en accord avec le droit de la mer. L'exploitation des ressources du sous-sol marin, dans la ZEE, incombe clairement à l'Etat côtier; ainsi, il n' y a pas de conflit possible entre les intérêts de celui-ci et les intérêts d'une autre partie.

C'est dans le domaine de la pollution par les navires que le règlement par les Etats côtiers est problématique. Vu la souveraineté réduite de l'Etat côtier quant à l'usage de la ZEE aux fins de navigation, l'Etat ne peut soumettre les navires battant pavillon étranger à sa juridiction que dans des circonstances spéciales. Néanmoins, la CNUDM reconnaît le besoin des Etats de protéger l'environnement marin dans leurs ZEE, et

---

Wastes Generated at Sea: MARPOL, not BASEL», *Environmental Policy and Law*, 2009, n° 39, pp. 207 ss. quant aux champs d'application des conventions respectives.

34. Nations Unies, *Recueil des traités*, vol. 1046, p. 120. Voir VanderZwaag et Daniel, *op. cit. supra* note 33, p. 519, pour plus d'information sur la convention.

35. Voir Joshua Newman et Dawn Verdugo, «Building Awareness of Sea-dumped Chemical Weapons», *Disarmament Forum*, 2010, n° 2, p. 45, pour plus de détails.

36. Voir Edward L. Miles, «Sea Dumping of Low-Level Radioactive Waste, 1964 to 1982», dans Edward L. Miles *et al.* (dir. publ.), *Environmental Regime Effectiveness* (MIT Press 2002), p. 87 ss.

les articles 56, alinéa *b)*, 58, paragraphe 3, et 211, paragraphe 5, de la CNUDM autorisent l'Etat — et l'obligent en même temps — à adopter des lois et des règlements qui «soient conformes et donnent effet aux règles et normes internationales généralement acceptées établies par l'intermédiaire de l'organisation internationale compétente ou d'une conférence diplomatique générale». A nouveau, la CNUDM fait allusion aux RNIGA, pour l'ensemble des règles et normes à adopter par les Etats dans leur ZEE. La protection de l'environnement marin dans cette zone est pleinement soumise à l'accord international[37]. L'Etat n'a généralement pas le droit de légiférer unilatéralement[38].

Reste à déterminer quelles sont les «règles et normes internationales généralement acceptées et établies par l'intermédiaire de l'organisation internationale compétente». La disposition de la CNUDM est aujourd'hui[39] considérée comme faisant référence à l'OMI[40] et aux conventions MARPOL[41] et SOLAS[42], antérieures à la CNUDM, et qui avaient déjà établi un certain cadre de normes et de standards techniques pour les navires avant la négociation de la Convention de Montego Bay. S'il y a d'autres normes qui font partie des RNIGA, quelles sont-elles? Un autre problème se pose: celui des Etats qui ont ratifié la CNUDM, mais qui ne sont pas parties à MARPOL.

Il faut noter que l'allusion aux normes «généralement acceptées» a une connotation liée à un accord international, auquel la majorité des Etats sont parties. Cela est valable pour MARPOL et SOLAS[43]. Néan-

37. Christian Tomuschat, «Obligations Arising for States Without or Against Their Will», *Recueil des cours* (1993), vol. 241, p. 349; Tan, *Vessel-Source Marine Pollution*, *op. cit. supra* note 22, p. 180; Alan K.-J. Tan, «The EU Ship-Source Pollution Directive and Coastal State Jurisdiction over Ships», *Lloyd's Maritime and Commercial Law Quarterly*, 2010, p. 476.

38. Il faut aussi mentionner les exceptions à cette règle. Selon l'article 211, paragraphe 6, de la CNUDM, les Etats ont la possibilité de désigner, en accord avec l'OMI, dans leurs ZEE des zones particulièrement vulnérables à la pollution marine, dans lesquelles s'appliqueront des provisions de protection environnementale au-delà des standards des RNIGA. En outre, les Etats riverains des zones recouvertes par les glaces ont le droit d'adopter des lois et règlements non discriminatoires, mais plus sévères pour lutter contre la pollution marine dans ces zones.

39. Voir Boyle, *op. cit. supra* note 12, p. 361, expliquant que ce fait n'était pas explicitement reconnu lors des négociations.

40. Il n'y avait pas accord universel entre les Etats négociateurs sur ce point, voir Bernhardt, *op. cit. supra* note 9, p. 274.

41. Boyle, *op. cit. supra* note 12, p. 354.

42. Veronica Frank, «Consequences of the «Prestige» Sinking for European and International Law», *International Journal of Marine and Coastal Law*, 2005, n° 20, p. 8.

43. Les ratifications par des Etats des conventions et leurs protocoles respectifs correspondent à environ 90 pour cent du tonnage maritime global; voir http://www.imo.org/About/Conventions/StatusOfConventions/Documents/status-x.xls (consulté le 13 octobre 2012).

moins, certains Etats ne sont pas partie à ces instruments et n'ont jamais consenti à ce cadre technique. Imposer ces dispositions, par la voie des RNIGA, aux navires battant le pavillon de ces Etats pourrait être perçu comme une atteinte grave à leur souveraineté[44] et un déni des principes bien établis du droit international[45], notamment les articles 34 et 35 de la Convention de Vienne sur le droit des traités[46], selon lesquels les Etats tiers à des traités ne sont liés par leurs dispositions que s'ils y ont explicitement consenti. Cependant, les termes de la disposition de la CNUDM ne présupposent pas un accord mondial total[47], et le système des RNIGA repose sur le fait que ces standards sont quelque peu flous et susceptibles de changement à tout moment, tant qu'il y a un accord étendu pour la plupart des Etats[48]. Le système des RNIGA est tellement inhérent à la CNUDM que tous les Etats contractants doivent être conscients de l'applicabilité de ces normes internationales, même s'ils n'ont pas ratifié les conventions sous-jacentes, et qu'ils ont ainsi indirectement consenti à être liés par les RNIGA[49].

Une autre question se pose quant à leur portée. Même s'il est maintenant bien établi que les dispositions de MARPOL et SOLAS font partie, ou sont le noyau des RNIGA, il reste à déterminer s'il y a d'autres lois et règles qu'il faut prendre en compte. Il a été argumenté que les RNIGA ne peuvent pas seulement consister dans les règles de deux — ou d'un nombre supérieur — conventions, vu que les négociateurs de la CNUDM auraient alors eu recours à d'autres termes pour exprimer l'inclusion de MARPOL et SOLAS dans la CNUDM[50], et il a été soutenu que d'autres principes et dispositions pourraient être invoqués[51]. Néanmoins, il semble que dans le domaine du droit pénal, où les Etats désirent soumettre un certain comportement à des peines criminelles, une compétence qui n'est pas clairement définie peut poser de graves problèmes.

44. Boyle, *op. cit. supra* note 12, p. 356.

45. Gwendoline Gonsaeles, « Of Mice and Men : Some Observations on the EU Approach towards Seafarers Liability for Marine Pollution », dans Kristiaan Bernauw et Wouter Den Haerynck (dir. publ.), *Free on Board : Liber amicorum Marc A. Huybrechts*, Intersentia, 2011, p. 325.

46. Nations Unies, *Recueil des traités*, n° 1155, p. 33.

47. Tomuschat, *op. cit. supra* note 37, p. 351.

48. Boyle, *op. cit. supra* note 12, p. 356 ; Christopher P. Mooradian, « Protecting « Sovereign Rights » : The Case for Increased Coastal State Jurisdiction over Vessel-Source Pollution in the Exclusive Economic Zone », *Boston University Law Review*, 2002, n° 82, p. 779.

49. Gonsaeles, *op. cit. supra* note 45, p. 326.

50. Erik Franckx, « Marine Environment Jurisditional Issues : Coastal States », dans Myron H. Nordquist, John N. Moore et Said Mahmoudi (dir. publ.), *The Stockholm Declaration and Law of the Marine Environment*, Nijhoff, 2003, p. 291.

51. A titre d'exemple, des conventions pas encore entrées en vigueur, voir Oxman, *op. cit. supra* note 13, p. 141, ou des standards régionaux, hypothèse qui est critiquée par Bernhardt, *op. cit. supra* note 9, p. 289.

La convention MARPOL, selon son article 4, prévoit des sanctions pour les comportements interdits par ses règles, et astreint les Etats parties à poursuivre et sanctionner ces violations, tout en exigeant que les sanctions soient d'une rigueur suffisante et égale (MARPOL, art. 4 (4)). La Convention ne contient pas de règles plus détaillées quant à la procédure et les sanctions à imposer, respectant que le droit pénal est au fond un aspect de la souveraineté des Etats[52].

Il n'en est pas de même en ce qui concerne les comportements incriminés. L'article 4 de MARPOL fait référence à «toute violation des dispositions de la présente Convention» et aux dispositions des annexes. Celles-ci contiennent des standards techniques bien définis, dans le but d'établir clairement les comportements à sanctionner. MARPOL est une convention unique et intégrale[53]. La Convention reconnaît aussi la nécessité de permettre aux navires des décharges dites «opérationnelles», dont la portée et les conséquences nocives sont considérées négligeables par rapport au bénéfice économique pour la navigation.

Compte tenu des circonstances et des cas directement visés par MARPOL, la Convention et ses règles couvre toute la législation possible dans ces cas. Une réglementation qui va au-delà des standards visés et viole ainsi les permissions et les exemptions de MARPOL est contraire à la Convention et, à travers les RNIGA, à la CNUDM[54].

Il n'en est pas de même pour les situations qui ne sont pas visées par MARPOL, à savoir les circonstances explicitement exclues du champ d'application de la Convention, telles l'immersion et les pollutions qui résultent de l'exploitation et l'exploration des ressources des fonds des mers (MARPOL, art. 2 (3 *a*)). De plus, en ce qui concerne la pollution par des navires — qui tombe dans le champ d'application de la Convention —, il peut y avoir des circonstances qui ne sont pas considérées par la Convention et qui restent non réglées. Cette étude va (paragraphe 2) analyser quelques questions qui se sont récemment posées quant à l'applicabilité de MARPOL.

En ce qui concerne la mise en application des règles et des lois par les Etats dans leurs ZEE, la CNUDM contient un régime assez élaboré, qui tient compte du principe général selon lequel l'Etat du pavillon devrait veiller à ce que les navires battant son pavillon adhèrent aux lois et règlements en vigueur. Selon les articles 220 à 223 de la CNUDM, l'Etat côtier ne dispose, pour des infractions qui ont eu lieu dans sa ZEE, que

52. Proshanto K. Mukherjee, «The Penal Law of Ship-Source Marine Pollution: Selected Issues in Perspective», dans Tafsir M. Ndiaye et Rüdiger Wolfrum (dir. publ.), *Law of the Sea, Environmental Law and Settlement of Disputes*, Martinus Nijhoff, 2007, p. 478.

53. *Ibid*., p. 466.

54. Mooradian, *op. cit. supra* note 48, p. 797.

de droits échelonnés, selon la gravité de la pollution et du degré de soupçon qu'il a envers le navire. Pour les infractions simples, les pouvoirs de l'Etat côtier se limitent à la demande d'informations au bateau (CNUDM, art. 220 (3)) qui doivent servir non pas à poursuivre les responsables, mais uniquement à établir l'existence d'une infraction. C'est seulement dans l'hypothèse d'une pollution grave, endommageant ou menaçant les ressources littorales de l'Etat côtier que ce dernier a le droit d'entamer des poursuites incluant l'immobilisation du navire. Ici encore, les dispositions de la CNUDM par rapport à la mise en application des règles sont révélatrices du pouvoir législatif accordé aux Etats côtiers. Considérant que la CNUDM favorise les Etats du pavillon, les seules règles qui peuvent être en vigueur dans la ZEE sont de caractère international, car un Etat du pavillon ne poursuivra pas les responsables sur son propre navire pour des infractions émanant d'une législation étrangère unilatérale.

D. La haute mer

Le fait que la haute mer est « le patrimoine commun de l'humanité entière » et n'est pas assujettie à la souveraineté d'un Etat quelconque est l'un des principes les mieux établis dans l'ensemble du droit de la mer[55]. En haute mer, les navires sont soumis aux seuls pouvoirs de l'Etat dont ils battent le pavillon (CNUDM, art. 92 (1)), et la compétence pénale envers le capitaine ou les membres de l'équipage pour les incidents de navigation incombe aux Etats dont ils ont la nationalité et à l'Etat du pavillon (CNUDM, art. 97).

Ces principes du droit de la mer n'ont néanmoins pas empêché quelques Etats d'étendre leurs pouvoirs à des interventions en haute mer sur différents fondements de compétence. Un Etat peut, notamment se prévaloir de droits non-territoriaux pour intervenir auprès d'un navire battant pavillon étranger et qui présente une menace pour les intérêts de l'Etat côtier. Selon l'article 221 de la CNUDM[56], qui concerne les mesures en cas d'accident maritime qui met en danger les intérêts de l'Etat côtier, cela est généralement admis comme une codification du droit à la défense légitime *(necessity)*[57]. Néanmoins, ce droit à la défense légitime permet seulement aux Etats de prendre des mesures

55. Cet ancien principe n'a jamais été mis en cause pendant les négociations de la CNUDM ; voir Boyle, *op. cit. supra* note 12, p. 358.

56. Voir également la Convention de Bruxelles de 1969 sur l'intervention en haute mer.

57. Voir Aage T. Falkanger, *Maritime Casualties and Intervention : Coastal State Measures when Casualties Pose the Threat of Pollution*, Fagbokforlaget, 2011, pp. 65 ss., pour plus de détails.

afin de protéger leur littoral ou les intérêts connexes, par conséquent, d'intervenir pour atténuer les conséquences mêmes des accidents. Le droit pénal, en général, ne remédie pas aux conséquences du fait incriminé, et le commencement de procédures pénales n'a pas, normalement, de répercussion sur le dommage. Il est alors presque impensable qu'un Etat côtier puisse exercer une juridiction pénale sur un bateau en haute mer pour des effets survenus sur ses côtes[58].

E. La suspension des poursuites suite à l'engagement de poursuites par l'Etat du pavillon

Selon l'article 228 de la CNUDM[59], l'engagement de poursuites par l'Etat du pavillon va, généralement, mettre fin aux procédures par l'Etat côtier. Ainsi, la compétence de l'Etat du pavillon pour toutes les infractions hors de la mer territoriale d'un Etat est très renforcée, et la disposition est souvent invoquée par des accusés comme privant les cours de l'Etat côtier de compétence.

L'article 228 de la CNUDM connaît deux exceptions, qui sont, d'une part, le dommage grave causé à l'Etat côtier et, de l'autre, l'omission répétée de l'Etat du pavillon de mettre en application les normes internationales à l'égard de ses navires. Tandis que le manque de volonté de certains Etats d'appliquer les normes internationales sur les bateaux battant leur pavillon est souvent déploré[60], il semble qu'aucune autorité

58. Mais, dans ce sens, Pierre Bonassies, « Compatibilité de la loi du 5 juillet 1983 avec la Convention MARPOL », *Droit maritime français*, 2010, n° 62, p. 896.

59. Article 228 de la CNUDM :

> « 1. Lorsque des poursuites ont été engagées par un Etat en vue de réprimer une infraction aux lois et règlements applicables ou aux règles et normes internationales visant à prévenir, réduire et maîtriser la pollution par les navires, commise au-delà de sa mer territoriale par un navire étranger, ces poursuites sont suspendues dès lors que l'Etat du pavillon a lui-même engagé des poursuites du chef de la même infraction, dans les six mois suivant l'introduction de la première action, à moins que celle-ci ne porte sur un cas de dommage grave causé à l'Etat côtier ou que l'Etat du pavillon en question ait à plusieurs reprises manqué à son obligation d'assurer l'application effective des règles et normes internationales en vigueur à la suite d'infractions commises par ses navires. L'Etat du pavillon qui a demandé la suspension des poursuites conformément au présent article remet en temps voulu au premier Etat un dossier complet de l'affaire et les minutes du procès. Lorsque les tribunaux de l'Etat du pavillon ont rendu leur jugement, il est mis fin aux poursuites. Après règlement des frais de procédure, toute caution ou autre garantie financière déposée à l'occasion de ces poursuites est restituée par l'Etat côtier. »

60. Voir, à titre d'exemple, Elizabeth R. DeSombre, *Flagging Standards: Globalization and Environmental Safety and Labor Regulations at Sea* (MIT Press, 2006), relatif au problème des « pavillons de complaisance », et Jean-

étatique n'ait jamais mis en avant qu'un autre Etat omettait en permanence de remplir ses obligations de contrôle des normes internationales[61]. Cela est sans doute le cas parce qu'il s'agirait d'un affront politique[62]. En revanche, l'hypothèse du «dommage grave» causé à l'Etat côtier vient de faire l'objet, pour la première fois, d'une décision récente de la Cour de cassation française, dans l'arrêt final de l'affaire de l'*Erika*. Ce naufrage d'un pétrolier battant pavillon maltais dans la ZEE française a donné lieu à des poursuites criminelles envers les responsables du navire, notamment l'affréteur et les propriétaires, pour avoir causé une pollution dramatique du littoral français. Les décisions des premières instances, condamnant les accusés à des peines criminelles, ont déclenché de nombreuses discussions quant à l'applicabilité de la convention MARPOL — et au sein de la législation française — aux pollutions accidentelles dans la ZEE (voir *infra*). Dans sa décision finale du 25 septembre 2012[63], la Cour de cassation a invoqué l'article 228 de la CNUDM afin de confirmer la compétence de la Cour de soumettre les accusés à une loi nationale qui n'était pas tout à fait en accord avec les dispositions de la convention MARPOL[64]. Tandis qu'il s'agissait, en l'espèce, clairement d'une pollution «grave», le naufrage ayant causé la pollution de plusieurs centaines de kilomètres de côte, il ne semble pas que la Cour de cassation ait fait bon usage de la disposition. L'article 228 de la CNUDM, en faisant allusion aux «poursuites» de la pollution,

---

Pierre Cot, «A propos de l'article 228 de la convention de Montego Bay: compétence de l'Etat du pavillon et compétence de l'Etat côtier en matière de répression des infractions pour pollution illicite», dans Rafael Casado Raigón et Giuseppe Cataldi (dir. publ.), *Mélanges de droit de la mer offerts à Daniel Vignes: l'évolution et l'état actuel du droit international de la mer*, 2009, Bruylant, p. 189, quant à la défaillance fréquente des Etats du pavillon de commencer des poursuites, d'un point de vue français.

61. Il est possible de faire des recoupements avec l'article 17, paragraphe 1, alinéa *b)*, du Statut de la Cour pénale internationale (CPI) (Nations Unies, *Recueil des traités*, vol. 2187, p. 3), qui déclare une affaire irrecevable si un Etat ayant compétence en l'espèce ne l'a pas poursuivie suite à un manque de volonté ou à l'incapabilité de mener véritablement à bien l'affaire, hypothèses qui n'ont pas encore été retenues; voir Sharon A. Williams et William A. Schabas, «Art. 17», dans Otto Triffterer (dir. publ.), *Commentary on the Rome Statute of the International Criminal Court*, 2e éd., 2008, et C. H. Beck, pp. 616 ss., pour plus de détails. Voir Kaveri Vaid, «What Counts as «State Action» under Article 17 of the Rome Statute?: Applying the ICC's Complementary Test to Non-Criminal Investigations by the United States into War Crimes in Afghanistan», *International Law and Politics*, 2012, n° 44, pp. 596 ss., pour une considération des cas potentiels en Afghanistan.

62. Patrick O'Connell et Ivan A. Shearer, *The International Law of the Sea*, Clarendon Press, 1984, p. 994.

63. *«Erika» — Décision finale*, 2012, Cour de cassation, France, http://www.courdecassation.fr/IMG///Crim_arret3439_20120925.pdf (consulté le 13 octobre 2012).

64. *Ibid.*, p. 107.

souligne la compétence juridictionnelle d'un Etat et le pouvoir d'entamer des procédures devant ses cours. Il ne s'agit pas de la compétence législative d'un Etat et du pouvoir d'édicter des lois nationales ayant force contraignante au-delà de sa mer territoriale. La France aurait pu invoquer la disposition et la gravité des dommages afin de confirmer sa compétence juridictionnelle si un autre Etat avait exprimé la volonté d'engager des poursuites — ce qui n'était pas le cas en l'espèce, Malte en tant qu'Etat du pavillon n'ayant jamais fait usage de sa juridiction sur l'*Erika*. Contrairement à ce que la Cour de cassation fait comprendre en citant la disposition dans le contexte de la compétence législative, l'article 228 de la CNUDM confère uniquement un pouvoir de juridiction à l'Etat côtier et non pas une compétence de mettre en œuvre des lois nationales dont la compatibilité avec les RNIGA est pour le moins discutable.

Dans la mesure où l'article 228 de la CNUDM a fait l'objet de décisions de tribunaux nationaux dans des cas d'un vrai conflit de compétence entre l'Etat du pavillon et l'Etat côtier, les cours de ce dernier ont souvent essayé de contourner la disposition. Ainsi, des tribunaux nationaux français ont refusé dans les premières instances de mettre fin à des procédures[65], au motif que les amendes prononcées par les tribunaux des Etats du pavillon n'étaient pas assez sévères, mais cette interprétation de l'article 228 de la CNUDM a été rejetée en cassation[66]. Les termes de l'article 228 de la CNUDM sont assez clairs pour déterminer que cette disposition n'offre pas aux autorités nationales de l'Etat côtier le pouvoir de procéder à une analyse des procédures menées dans l'Etat du pavillon[67] et des sanctions infligées afin de juger si elles ont une valeur dissuasive suffisante. L'Etat côtier est lié par le fait que des procédures ont été effectuées dans l'Etat du pavillon et ne peut se prévaloir du pouvoir de mettre à l'écart ces procédures que si l'Etat du pavillon manque à plusieurs reprises à son devoir d'imposer des sanctions contraignantes[68] — mais la valeur dissuasive d'une sanction reste de toute façon très discutable (voir *infra*, section 3, paragraphe 2).

Dans d'autres cas, les cours ont essayé de montrer que les procédures menées dans les Etats du pavillon visaient d'autres infractions. Ainsi, un

65. Voir Cot, *op. cit. supra* note 60, pp. 189 ss., pour plus de détails.
66. *Trans Arctic et Fast Independence*, 2009, Cour de cassation (France), *Droit maritime français*, n° 61, p. 717.
67. Les articles 17 et 18 du Statut de la CPI, au contraire, confèrent clairement une compétence de révision au fond des procédures nationales aux procureurs de la CPI. Voir Michael A. Newton, « The Complementarity Conundrum: Are We Watching Evolution or Evisceration ? », *Santa Clara Journal of International Law*, 2008, n° 8, p. 136.
68. Pierre Bonassies, « Observations, Cour de cassation, 05 mai 2009 », *Droit maritime français*, 2009, n° 61, p. 723.

tribunal français a jugé que les autorités de l'Etat du pavillon avaient traité l'affaire comme étant un cas de pollution accidentelle, alors qu'il s'agissait assez clairement d'un rejet délibéré. Cette argumentation a été rejetée en appel[69], vu que les procédures concernaient les mêmes actes. Le fait que les accusés risquent d'être frappés de deux procédures pour le même acte et sanctionnés deux fois a aussi été avancé comme un moyen de défense par des suspects dans des procédures aux Etats-Unis[70]. Les décisions citées, donnant la primauté à la juridiction de l'Etat du pavillon, évitent ainsi la violation du principe de *double jeopardy* ou *ne bis in idem* sur le plan international[71]. Pourtant une telle solution peut paraître peu satisfaisante dans le cas où l'Etat du pavillon est très laxiste. En l'espèce, les tribunaux américains avaient contourné le problème en poursuivant non pas la pollution, mais les manquements aux obligations d'information, délit clairement différent (voir *infra*).

Paragraphe 2 **La relation entre les lois nationales et les règlements internationaux**

Pour les dispositions concernant les CCA dans les eaux territoriales et pour toute disposition relative à la lutte contre la pollution dans la ZEE, la législation des Etats côtiers doit se conformer aux « règles et normes internationales généralement acceptées ».

Néanmoins, une tendance marquée et croissante parmi les Etats côtiers de légiférer hors ou à proximité des confins de ces compétences a été constatée[72]. C'est surtout en matière de pollution par les hydrocarbures que cette volonté législative se manifeste, les hydrocarbures étant les polluants les plus perceptibles et les plus répandus — se trouvant à bord de chaque navire —, mais les mêmes problèmes se posent pour les autres polluants, comme les produits chimiques. Assez souvent, les textes législatifs ne font pas de différence entre les infractions commises en mer territoriale et dans la ZEE, sans tenir compte des différents régimes applicables, et de nombreux Etats ont essayé de soumettre des pollutions

69. *Vytautas — Appel*, 2011, Cour d'appel de Rennes, *Droit maritime français*, n° 63, p. 560.

70. Shaun Gehan, « United States *v.* Royal Caribbean Cruises, Ltd.: Use of Federal « False Statements Act » to Extend Jurisdiction over Polluting Incidents into Territorial Seas of Foreign States », *Ocean and Coastal Law Journal*, 2001, n° 7, p. 176, énonce un cas dans lequel l'Etat du pavillon avait mis fin à ses procédures après une enquête sommaire.

71. Voir Linda E. Carter, « The Principle of Complementarity and the International Criminal Court: The Role of *Ne Bis in Idem* », *Santa Clara Journal of International Law*, 2010, n° 8, p. 165, pour un énoncé de ce problème sous le statut de la CPJ.

72. Mooradian, *op. cit. supra* note 48, pp. 798 ss.

accidentelles à des sanctions pénales, souvent dans le cas d'accidents maritimes catastrophiques. Et ce ne sont pas seulement les Etats qui poussent les limites de leur compétence législative dans ce domaine. Avec la directive 2005/35/EC relative à la pollution par des bateaux, l'introduction de sanctions criminelles pour des violations et la décision-cadre correspondante 2005/667/JAI, annulée ensuite par la Cour de justice de l'Union européenne, l'Union européenne s'est aussi lancée dans la réglementation pénale de la pollution marine, législation qui a suscité beaucoup de critiques, en particulier parce qu'elle dépasserait les limites de compétence de l'Union européenne envers ses Etats membres[73] et serait contraire au droit international de la mer.

Néanmoins, il reste à rappeler que toutes ces projets de législation ne sont pas automatiquement contraires au régime instauré par la CNUDM. Premièrement, dans les systèmes des conventions internationales comme MARPOL et SOLAS, parfaitement incorporées dans la CNUDM, il peut y avoir des lacunes, à savoir des cas simplement non envisagés par la Convention. Comme il a été énoncé *supra*, il faut alors analyser la portée exacte de la Convention, afin de savoir si elle règle la situation indirectement ou sous-entend qu'elle doit être traitée d'une certaine manière, ou si cette hypothèse se trouve hors du champ d'application de la Convention. Dans ce dernier cas, cette lacune peut être comblée par une autre règle qui peut être considérée comme faisant partie des RNIGA.

A. Le rôle de MARPOL

La convention MARPOL est un accord international assez complet sur la prévention de la pollution par les navires. Selon son article 4, les Etats parties doivent sanctionner toute violation de ses dispositions par des peines qui doivent être suffisamment sévères pour décourager le comportement incriminé. Dans ses six annexes, MARPOL stipule des standards techniques et des contraintes pour la prévention de la pollution par les hydrocarbures (annexe I), par les substances liquides nocives transportées en vrac (annexe II), par les substances nuisibles

73. Ce premier point n'est pas l'objet de cette étude. Pour une analyse de la directive et la décision-cadre du point de vue du droit européen, voir Martin Hedemann-Robinson, « The EU and Environmental Crime: The Impact of the ECJ's Judgment on Framework Decision 2005/667 on Ship-Source Pollution », *Journal of Environmental Law*, 2008, n° 20, pp. 286 ss.; Iliana Christodoulou-Varotsi, « Recent Developments in the EC Legal Framework on Ship-Source Pollution: The Ambivalence of the EC's Penal Approach », *Annuaire de droit maritime et océanique*, 2008, n° 26, pp. 224 ss.; E. Symeonidou-Kastanidou, « Ship-Source Marine Pollution: The ECJ Judgments and their Impact on Criminal Law », *European Journal of Crime, Criminal Law and Criminal Justice*, 2009, n° 17, p. 335.

transportées par mer dans des emballages ou véhicules (annexe III), par les eaux usées des navires (annexe IV), par les ordures des navires (annexe V) et la pollution de l'air par les navires (annexe VI). Les règles de l'annexe I de MARPOL, en question ici, ont été renumerotées par une résolution en 2004[74]; cette étude adopte la nouvelle numérotation, suivie systématiquement par l'ancienne.

Les standards techniques exigés par MARPOL sont généralement clairs et mesurables, mais certains problèmes se posent si les Etats utilisent la convention comme base pour des dispositions de droit pénal. MARPOL ne donne pas de réponse concrète quant aux personnes qui peuvent être tenues responsables pour des actes de pollution, quant au degré de négligence ou dol nécessaires, ou quant à la question de savoir si les Etats peuvent poursuivre des infractions dites «documentaires» qui ont un lien direct avec la pollution. Ces questions, les plus urgentes quant à l'interprétation des dispositions MARPOL, sont donc examinées dans cette section.

i) *Le sanctionnement pénal des pollutions accidentelles par les hydrocarbures dans la ZEE*

La convention MARPOL, dans la règle 34 (ancienne règle 9) de l'annexe I, énonce le principe de l'interdiction totale du rejet des hydrocarbures, mais stipule aussi des exceptions à cette règle. Les exceptions visées dans la règle 15 (ancienne règle 10) s'appliquent à des décharges dites «opérationnelles», qui, généralement, sont permises si le bateau est en route et ne rejette qu'une quantité totale d'hydrocarbures qui est, notamment, calculée en fonction de la teneur de l'effluent, de manière à ce que les rejets ne causent pas une pollution visible de la mer[75]. Dans les règles 1.11, 15 et 34 (ancienne règle 10), le volume autorisé de ces décharges opérationnelles est encore plus limité dans des zones spéciales où la mer est censée être plus vulnérable.

Outre l'exception pour les décharges opérationnelles, il existe des exceptions pour des décharges «extraordinaires» dans la règle 4 de l'annexe I (ancienne règle 11)[76]. Selon cette disposition, les règles 15 et 34,

74. Résolution MEPC.117 (52) (annexe I révisée de MARPOL 73/78) adoptée le 15 octobre 2004 et entrée en vigueur le 1er janvier 2007, www.imo.org/KnowledgeCentre (consulté le 13 octobre 2012).

75. Richard A. Udell, «United States Criminal Enforcement of Deliberate Vessel Pollution: A Document-Based Approach to MARPOL», dans Davor Vidas (dir. publ.), *Law, Technology and Science for Oceans in Globalisation*, Martinus Nijhoff, 2010, p. 277.

76. Règle 4 (ancienne règle 11) de l'annexe I de MARPOL:

> «Exceptions. Les règles 15 et 34 (anciennes règles 9 et 10) de la présente annexe ne s'appliquent pas: 1. Au rejet à la mer d'hydrocarbures ou de

à savoir, l'interdiction des rejets, ne s'appliquent pas aux rejets qui sont effectués afin d'assurer la sécurité d'un navire ou le sauvetage de vies humaines en mer (règle 4.1 de l'annexe I). Evidemment, cette disposition vise des rejets déliberés, mais effectués dans une situation d'urgence, afin d'alléger le bateau. Un rejet délibéré est également autorisé dans la règle 4.3, qui s'applique au déversement de substances approuvées afin de lutter contre une pollution déjà survenue.

Quant aux rejets accidentels, la règle 4.2.1 stipule que les règles 15 et 34 ne s'appliquent pas aux rejets survenus à la suite d'une avarie, à condition que toutes les précautions raisonnables aient été prises pour empêcher ou réduire ce rejet après l'avarie ou la découverte du rejet — exception d'avarie. Il faut souligner que la «condition» de la règle 4.2.1 ne vise que les efforts à fournir après le rejet accidentel et non pas les efforts de l'empêcher[77].

Il existe une dérogation à cette exception d'avarie dans la règle 4.2.2: si le propriétaire ou le capitaine ont agi soit avec l'intention de provoquer un dommage, soit témérairement et avec conscience qu'un dommage pourrait en résulter, les règles 15 et 34 s'appliquent de nouveau. Cette dérogation à l'exception a causé beaucoup d'incertitude dans l'interprétation de la disposition. C'est pourquoi pour mieux comprendre le système MARPOL, il est important de rappeler que, généralement, l'interdiction des rejets ne s'applique pas aux avaries[78], tant que toutes les précautions ont été prises après l'avarie pour en atténuer les conséquences[79]. Il est néanmoins assez difficile de déterminer quelles sont ces précautions, vu qu'une interprétation très stricte pourrait réduire la

---

mélanges d'hydrocarbures effectué par un navire pour assurer sa propre sécurité ou celle d'un autre navire, ou sauver des vies humaines en mer; 2. Au rejet à la mer d'hydrocarbures ou de mélanges d'hydrocarbures provenant d'une avarie survenue à un navire ou à son équipement: 2.1. à condition que toutes les précautions raisonnables aient été prises après l'avarie ou la découverte du rejet pour empêcher ou réduire ce rejet, et sauf si le propriétaire ou le capitaine a agi soit avec l'intention de provoquer un dommage, soit témérairement et avec conscience qu'un dommage en résulterait probablement; 2.2. Au rejet à la mer de substances contenant des hydrocarbures approuvées par l'Autorité, lorsque ces substances sont utilisées pour lutter contre un cas particulier de pollution afin de réduire les dommages dus à cette pollution. Tout rejet de cette nature est soumis à l'approbation du Gouvernement, quel qu'il soit, dans les limites de la juridiction duquel il est prévu de l'effectuer.»

77. Epaminondas Embiricos, «Acting As an Advocate for the Industry» (8th Cadwallader Memorial Lecture, London, 4 octobre 2005) 35, http://www.shippinglbc.com/content/uploads/documents/8_cad.pdf (consulté le 13 octobre 2012)

78. Mensah, *op. cit. supra* note 27, p. 25; Marc A. Huybrechts, «De criminalisatie van kapitein en scheepsbemanning in geval van olieverontreiniging: Een brug te ver?», dans Filiep Deruyck *et al.* (dir. publ.), *De wet voorbij: liber amicorum Luc Huybrechts*, Intersentia, 2009, p. 187.

79. *Embiricos*, *op. cit. supra* note 77, p. 32.

signification de l'exception de l'avarie à néant. Ainsi, la Cour d'appel française, dans l'affaire de l'*Erika*, a reproché à l'affréteur et au propriétaire du navire de n'avoir pas averti les autorités françaises à temps quand le navire faisait face aux premières difficultés et de ne pas avoir pris la décision de dérouter le navire vers le port le plus proche, argumentation qui a été confirmée par la Cour de cassation[80]. Dans la mesure où la condition pourrait être utilisée pour juger des décisions prises dans une situation de détresse a posteriori, le raisonnement des cours françaises semble aller à l'encontre des termes de la disposition, faisant allusion aux précautions «raisonnables». La disposition n'exige pas que les personnes en question aient agi d'une manière complètement irréprochable après l'avarie. La condition ne devrait entrer en jeu que dans les hypothèses où la conduite des personnes en question ne peut plus être considérée comme «raisonnable» — un terme qui se prête à l'interprétation.

Considérant la dérogation dans la règle 4.2.2, selon laquelle les rejets dans les avaries sont interdits, les limites en sont ici plus restrictives: il faut que soit le propriétaire soit le capitaine aient agi avec l'intention de provoquer un dommage ou bien, témérairement et avec conscience, qu'un dommage en résulterait probablement. Toutes les autres hypothèses ne sont pas visées dans la dérogation à l'exception, et l'exception générale s'applique: les avaries ne font pas l'objet de l'interdiction des règles 15 et 34[81]. Cette interprétation est strictement fondée sur les termes mêmes de la convention, moyen d'interprétation primordial des traités internationaux selon l'article 31, paragraphe 1, de la Convention de Vienne de 1969 sur le droit des traités et la jurisprudence des cours internationales[82].

Cependant, cette interprétation ne fait pas l'unanimité. Comme, dans son préambule, MARPOL s'applique à toute forme de pollution causée par les navires, il ne semble pas acceptable d'exclure les accidents de son champ d'application. Considérant que le préambule de la convention reconnaît les rejets de substances nuisibles, accidentelles et délibérées, comme une source de pollution importante, ce raisonnement est compréhensible, et souligne le principe d'interprétation intégrale des traités internationaux[83]. Telle a été l'argumentation de la Cour d'appel de Paris dans l'affaire de l'*Erika*, qui a été confirmée par la Cour de cassation[84].

80. *Erika — Décision finale*, *op. cit. supra* note 63, p. 107.

81. Embiricos, *op. cit. supra* note 77, p. 36; Luc Grellet, «Observations CJCE 3 juin 2008», *Droit maritime français*, 2008, nº 60, p. 906.

82. Oliver Dörr et Kirsten Schmalenbach, *Vienna Convention on the Law of Treaties: A Commentary*, Springer-Verlag 2012, pp. 522 et 542.

83. *Ibid.*, p. 561, pour un énoncé du principe.

84. *Erika — Décision finale*, *op. cit. supra* note 63, p. 107.

La Cour d'appel n'a simplement pas accepté que les accidents soient exclus du champ d'application de MARPOL[85], bien que la cour en première instance ait indiqué la portée de la règle 4.2 (ancienne règle 11 *b)*) de l'annexe I et envisagé que la convention ne couvrait pas les rejets accidentels. En effet, il semble que toute interprétation de MARPOL qui veut fonder une compétence criminelle sur la règle 4.2.2 va à l'encontre des termes de cette règle, limite absolue de l'interprétation. Le Tribunal correctionnel de Paris, jugeant en première instance le naufrage de l'*Erika* en droit pénal, a trouvé un autre fondement conventionnel, et ce directement dans la CNUDM[86] — interprétation douteuse compte tenu du fait que la CNUDM renvoie explicitement aux RNIGA[87].

Il est clair que cette interprétation de MARPOL n'est guère conciliable avec la tendance actuelle des Etats côtiers de s'appuyer sur le droit pénal afin de réglementer les accidents maritimes. Il est peut-être important de rappeler que les pollutions accidentelles ne sont pas visées par MARPOL au premier chef. Les dispositions de la Convention sont en effet majoritairement consacrées à la pollution opérationnelle et délibérée[88], circonstances où il est parfaitement possible d'attacher des sanctions pénales uniquement au fait qu'il y ait eu pollution. MARPOL est une convention technique qui définit les infractions selon des limites absolues sans accorder d'importance à la préméditation des responsables. Elle s'applique à tous les rejets, dès qu'il y a un rejet, et définit si le rejet est permis selon les limites absolues. C'est dans ce sens que l'exception dans la règle 4.2.2 de l'annexe I doit être entendue : si elle n'existait pas, les Etats seraient contraints, selon l'article 4 de MARPOL, de poursuivre les personnes présumées responsables d'une décharge accidentelle, indépendamment de toute autre circonstance, pour avoir largement dépassé les limites dans lesquelles les décharges opérationnelles sont admises. En raison de l'exception dans la règle 4.2, les rejets accidentels sont complètement retirés du système d'interdiction et de permission de MARPOL.

Dans son champ d'application — le règlement de la pollution —, les accidents en mer ne sont pas des « violations des dispositions de la présente Convention » et un Etat côtier donné ne peut pas fonder sur MARPOL une sanction pénale pour une pollution accidentelle qui n'est

---

85. *Erika — Appel*, 2010, Cour d'appel de Paris, *Droit maritime français*, n° 62, pp. 862 ss.

86. *Erika*, 2008, Tribunal de grande instance de Paris, *Annuaire de droit maritime et océanique*, n° 26, p. 704.

87. Grellet, *op. cit. supra* note 81, pp. 906 ss.

88. Stephen J. Darmody, « The Oil Pollution Act's Criminal Penalties : On a Collision Course with the Law of the Sea », *Boston College Environmental Affairs Law Review*, 1993, n° 21, p. 102.

pas causée intentionnellement ou témérairement dans sa ZEE. Tandis qu'il est impossible d'intenter une action contre les responsables d'un navire pour le fait d'avoir causé un rejet d'hydrocarbures, il est possible d'intenter une action contre les personnes responsables du mauvais entretien d'un bateau, pour avoir manqué à des obligations de sécurité ou pour une faute nautique[89] — tant que ces règles et obligations reflètent des règles et normes internationales généralement acceptées que l'Etat côtier peut appliquer dans sa ZEE (voir *infra*). Il ne semble pas nécessaire de procéder à une interprétation de MARPOL quant à son efficacité[90], d'autant plus qu'il existe d'autres normes internationales qui définissent mieux la responsabilité pour les navires au-dessous des normes.

ii) *Le degré de dol nécessaire pour un sanctionnement des rejets accidentels*

En ce qui concerne la dérogation de l'exception qui est énoncée dans la règle 4.2.2 de l'annexe I de MARPOL, la convention ne sanctionne les rejets survenus suite à une avarie que dans l'hypothèse où le propriétaire ou le capitaine ont agi soit avec l'intention de provoquer un dommage, soit témérairement et avec conscience qu'un dommage en résulterait probablement. Ainsi, les éléments constitutifs de cette dérogation ne sont pas souvent remplis. Le sens du degré de dol décrit est, semble-t-il, bien établi en droit international public[91], contenant clairement un élément de préméditation équivalant presque à l'intention.

Dans la directive 2005/35/EC (art. 4), ont été incriminés comme infractions les rejets des polluants s'ils ont été commis intentionnellement, témérairement ou à la suite d'une négligence grave (*serious negligence* dans la version anglaise). Etant donné que la directive s'applique, selon son article 3, paragraphe 1, à toutes les zones maritimes des eaux intérieures des Etats membres jusqu'à la haute mer, la disposition a été gravement critiquée car elle dépasse le standard de protection que MARPOL prévoit comme la norme internationale[92]. Ainsi, la directive a

89. Olagunju G. Anthony, « Criminalization of Seafarers for Accidental Discharge of Oil: Is there Justification in International Law for Criminal Sanction for Negligent or Accidental Pollution of the Sea? », *Journal of Maritime Law and Commerce*, 2006, n° 37, p. 238.

90. Voir Dörr et Schmalenbach, *op. cit. supra* note 82, p. 527, pour un énoncé du principe.

91. Symeonidou-Kastanidou, *op. cit. supra* note 73, p. 354; Blanco-Bazán, *op. cit. supra* note 18, p. 242; Bernard Vanheule, « Penalties against Ship-Source Pollution », dans Kristiaan Bernauw et Wouter Den Haerynck (dir. publ.), *Free on Board: Liber amicorum Marc A. Huybrechts*, Intersentia, 2011, p. 697.

92. Symeonidou-Kastanidou, *op. cit. supra* note 73, p. 354; Tan, « The EU Ship-Source Pollution Directive and Coastal State Jurisdiction over Ships », *op. cit. supra* note 37, p. 476.

finalement été l'objet d'un arrêt de la CJE (cas C-308/06)[93]. La Cour ne s'est pas prononcée sur la compatibilité de la directive avec la CNUDM[94], en soutenant que le requérant ne pouvait pas se prévaloir de la Convention parce qu'elle ne conférait pas des droits aux particuliers[95]. Cette approche rejette clairement certaines dispositions, comme l'article 230 de la CNUDM[96], et pose des problèmes aux niveaux légal[97] et diplomatique[98]. Quant à sa contradiction possible avec MARPOL, la Cour a maintenu[99] que l'Union européenne, n'étant pas partie à MARPOL, n'est pas liée par ses dispositions[100], bien que la directive 2005/35/EC fasse allusion à la Convention à plusieurs reprises[101]. Dans la version modifiée de la directive, qui a été amendée par la directive 2009/123/EC, l'allusion à la « négligence grave » existe toujours.

A la première lecture, on note que la directive, dans sa désignation des degrés du dol, va au-delà de ce que MARPOL dans la règle 4.2.2 de l'annexe I prévoit. Si l'on considère que la description des degrés de négligence (« intentionnellement, témérairement, à la suite d'une négligence grave ») n'est pas redondante, il faut noter que la directive contient trois degrés de négligence, tandis que MARPOL n'en nomme que deux, le second se composant d'un élément de fait (« témérairement ») et d'un élément de dol (« avec la conscience qu'un dommage en résulterait probablement »)[102]. En outre, le degré de « négligence grave »

93. *Intertanko*, 2008, C-308/06, Cour de justice de l'Union européenne, *Recueil de la jurisprudence*, vol. I p. 04057.

94. *Ibid.*, point 64.

95. Voir Annie Cudennec, « La politique communautaire de préservation du milieu marin : quelle place pour le droit international ? », dans Rafael Casado Raigón et Giuseppe Cataldi (dir. publ.), *Mélanges de droit de la mer offerts à Daniel Vignes : l'évolution et l'état actuel du droit international de la mer*, Bruylant, 2009, pp. 213 ss., sur le raisonnement de la Cour basé sur la notion de l'effet direct.

96. Blanco-Bazán, *op. cit. supra* note 18, pp. 243 ss.; Bernard Vanheule, « Criminal Sanctions in Reaction to Ship-source Pollution », dans Norman A. Martínez Gutiérrez (dir. publ.), *Serving the Rule of International Maritime Law : Essays in Honour of Professor David Joseph Attard*, Routledge, 2011, p. 68.

97. Grellet, *op. cit. supra* note 81, pp. 911 et 912 ; Cudennec, *op. cit. supra* note 95, p. 214 ; voir également Huybrechts, *op. cit. supra* note 78, pp. 188 et 196, sur la contradiction avec la jurisprudence antérieure relative au traité GATT.

98. Vanheule, « Criminal Sanctions in Reaction to Ship-source Pollution », *op. cit. supra* note 96, p. 73.

99. *Intertanko*, *op. cit. supra* note 93, points 49 et 50.

100. Voir Cudennec, *op. cit. supra* note 95, pp. 217 ss., pour un résumé du raisonnement.

101. Huybrechts, *op. cit. supra* note 78, p. 197 ; Blanco-Bazán, *op. cit. supra* note 18, p. 238.

102. Mukherjee, « The Penal Law of Ship-Source Marine Pollution : Selected Issues in Perspective », *op. cit. supra* note 52, p. 493.

est un concept complètement nouveau, n'ayant pas de précédent ni dans le droit européen ni dans le droit international public[103].

Dans un arrêt de la CJE, le cas C-308/06, la Cour a essayé de définir la notion de « négligence grave » ; selon elle le terme « grave » s'applique à la négligence et non pas aux conséquences. Il semble néanmoins que la « négligence grave » couvre aussi des situations dans lesquelles on ne peut pas reprocher aux responsables d'avoir agi avec la conscience de la probabilité du dommage.

Cela englobe beaucoup plus de situations que le cas prévu par MARPOL d'« action téméraire », où le responsable doit avoir une conscience marquée de ce que son comportement est négligent et du dommage probable.

Il faut rappeler qu'en droit criminel le sanctionnement d'un comportement négligent plutôt que prémédité va toujours poser des problèmes. C'est avec raison qu'en général, le droit pénal ne s'applique que dans l'hypothèse où les accusés agissent avec dol[104], et que les infractions négligentes sont généralement plus restreintes et bien définies, faisant allusion à un comportement incriminé et non pas seulement à la conséquence grave.

iii) *Les personnes visées comme potentiellement responsables*

MARPOL restreint, selon ses détracteurs, le groupe de personnes tenues responsables pour des rejets d'hydrocarbures aux propriétaires de bateaux et à leurs capitaines[105], probablement parce que la dérogation de l'exception, dans la règle 4.2.2, ne vise que le comportement intentionnel ou téméraire de ces deux groupes de personnes. En outre, dans les avaries « normales », celles qui ne sont pas causées par le dol qualifié de la règle 4.2.2, les propriétaires et les capitaines sont exemptés de

103. Embiricos, *op. cit. supra* note 77, p. 34; Mukherjee, « The Penal Law of Ship-Source Marine Pollution: Selected Issues in Perspective », *op. cit. supra* note 52, p. 493.

104. Aleka Mandaraka-Sheppard, « Address and Welcome », 8th Cadwallader Memorial Lecture, Londres, 4 octobre 2005, p. 2, http://www.shippinglbc.com/content/uploads/documents/8_cad.pdf (consulté le 13 octobre 2012); Vanheule, « Criminal Sanctions in Reaction to Ship-Source Pollution », *op. cit. supra* note 96, p. 72.

105. Darmody, *op. cit. supra* note 88, p. 135, se réfère plutôt à la CNUDM; Fotis Karamitsos, « On the European Directive 2005/35/EC », 8th Cadwallader Memorial Lecture, Londres, 4 octobre 2005, p. 19, http://www.shippinglbc.com/content/uploads/documents/8_cad.pdf (consulté le 13 octobre 2012); Grellet, *op. cit. supra* note 81, p. 901; Tullio Treves, « Jurisdiction over Vessels in the Areas of Pollution and Fisheries: General Report », dans Erik Franckx et Philippe Gautier (dir. publ.), *The Exercise of Jurisdiction over Vessels: New Developments in the Fields of Pollution, Fisheries, Crimes at Sea and Trafficking of Weapons of Mass Destruction*, Bruylant, 2010, p. 23.

responsabilité, alors que ce bénéfice n'est pas accordé à d'autres personnes[106].

Néanmoins, dans le système de la règle, de l'exception et de la dérogation à l'exception, l'identité des contrevenants potentiels n'est pas claire[107]. L'article 4 de MARPOL astreint les Etats parties à sanctionner les infractions aux dispositions de la Convention ; les règles 1, 15, 34, 38 de l'annexe I interdisent les décharges autres que les décharges opérationnelles ; et la règle 4.2 énonce l'exception de l'avarie, sauf dans les cas où le propriétaire, le capitaine ou les membres de l'équipage ont agi intentionnellement ou témérairement (dérogation à l'exception). Les termes de la Convention qui mentionnent ces trois groupes se réfèrent non pas à leur responsabilité, mais à leur comportement[108]. Les avaries sont de nouveau soumises à l'interdiction de la règle si ces groupes de personnes ont un comportement répréhensible, mais il n'est pas question de leur pénalisation ou de leur non-pénalisation.

Dans ce système, les Etats visent la criminalisation de toute personne qui peut être considérée comme responsable d'actes de pollution. Néanmoins, il s'agit ici non pas d'une « lacune réglementaire »[109], mais d'une large compétence, à savoir un droit et une obligation de poursuivre toute personne à qui on peut reprocher un tel comportement répréhensible.

Il a été argumenté que de comprendre l'exception comme générale porterait atteinte au régime entier de MARPOL, en disculpant son auteur de toute responsabilité dans les avaries ordinaires[110]. Il faut rappeler que la réglementation des avaries n'est pas le premier objectif de MARPOL (voir *supra*), la Convention s'attachant plutôt à la poursuite des pollutions délibérées où les responsables ont le choix d'agir ou non. Elle ne vise que les accidents dans lesquels il y a un élément d'intention ou d'action téméraire équivalant presque à une intention.

Dans l'hypothèse d'une avarie qualifiée, la dérogation à l'exception (règle 4.2.2), la pollution est de nouveau soumise à l'interdiction générale des règles 1, 15, 34 et 38 et au pouvoir de sanctionnement des Etats, énoncé dans l'article 4 MARPOL. Etant donné la portée de l'article 4 et

106. Frank, *op. cit. supra* note 42, p. 47 ; Tan, « The EU Ship-Source Pollution Directive and Coastal State Jurisdiction over Ships », *op. cit. supra* note 37, p. 470.

107. Mensah, *op. cit. supra* note 27, p. 26 ; Bonassies, « Compatibilité de la loi du 5 juillet 1983 avec la Convention MARPOL », *op. cit. supra* note 58, p. 894 ; Vanheule, « Criminal Sanctions in Reaction to Ship-Source Pollution », *op. cit. supra* note 96, p. 67. C'était également le point de vue des tribunaux français dans l'affaire *Erika*, *Erika — Appel*, *op. cit. supra* note 85, p. 863 ; *Erika — Décision finale*, *op. cit. supra* note 63, p. 107.

108. Mensah, *op. cit. supra* note 27, p. 26.

109. Dans ce sens, voir Karamitsos, *op. cit. supra* note 105, p. 18.

110. Tan, « The EU Ship-Source Pollution Directive and Coastal State Jurisdiction over Ships », *op. cit. supra* note 37, p. 473.

le fait qu'il laisse l'identification des personnes ciblées à la discrétion de l'Etat, non seulement le propriétaire, le capitaine ou les membres de l'équipage, mais aussi toute autre personne, pourraient être accusés de la pollution. En outre, dans l'hypothèse d'une avarie « ordinaire », exempte d'intention ou d'action téméraire, aucun individu ne peut être accusé de la pollution d'après MARPOL. Dans ce type d'avarie, la pollution peut avoir plusieurs raisons ou plusieurs causes, et peut être attribuée à plusieurs auteurs, tandis que, dans l'hypothèse de la pollution délibérée ou causée intentionnellement, il n'y a qu'une seule cause : l'intention et la libre décision du coupable de commettre l'infraction, de telle sorte qu'on peut punir la pollution comme telle.

Indépendamment du comportement de ces personnes, on peut argumenter que le comportement intentionnel ou téméraire de l'armateur, de l'affréteur, de la société de classification ou de tout autre acteur devrait déclencher une responsabilité pénale, même dans le cas d'une avarie où un tel comportement ne peut pas être reproché à l'équipage[111]. Il est vrai que ce serait désirable, mais tel n'est pas l'objectif de MARPOL. Encore une fois, MARPOL vise la pénalisation des pollutions en partant de la pollution elle-même, et non pas en partant d'un comportement donné. La plupart des avaries sont exclues du champ d'application de MARPOL, et ce avec raison. La responsabilité de la société de classification ou de l'armateur, ou bien des compagnies de sauvetage, ne se réfère pas à la pollution elle-même, mais à la mauvaise classification ou au mauvais équipement du navire, et la responsabilité des compagnies de sauvetage est généralement engagée pour avoir commis des fautes dans le sauvetage du navire, donc dans une prestation de services. MARPOL n'offre pas tous les instruments nécessaires pour savoir si ces obligations ont été bien ou mal accomplies, et la présence ou la gravité de la pollution ne sont pas un indice suffisant pour en juger.

Si les Etats désirent criminaliser des comportements qui mènent à des accidents de mer, tels que la gestion d'un navire en condition déplorable, l'emploi d'équipages mal formés ou des fautes nautiques, c'est à partir de ces comportements-là que des dispositions à l'encontre de ces violations doivent être mises en place. Une analyse en sera effectuée plus loin.

iv) *Le sanctionnement des infractions dites « documentaires »*

Selon les règles de MARPOL, tout navire auquel la convention s'applique doit posséder un registre des hydrocarbures qui listera tous les rejets effectués en route, opérationnels et accidentels. L'obligation de

111. Tan, *op. cit. supra* note 110, p. 474.

tenir un rapport doit être considérée comme aussi importante que les dispositions liées aux décharges dans la Convention[112]. Toute omission d'un rejet quelconque dans le registre ou toute donnée erronée sont considérées comme une violation des dispositions de la Convention et sont susceptibles d'être sanctionnées selon l'article 4 MARPOL.

S'il est difficile de prouver et de sanctionner un acte de pollution, il existe des situations dans lesquelles il peut être facile de prouver une infraction à MARPOL en inspectant le registre d'hydrocarbures, par exemple. Les entrées erronées ou manquantes peuvent, d'un côté, être détectées en calculant le volume des eaux usées qui devrait se trouver sur le bateau, sauf si elles ont été déchargées en mer[113]. De l'autre, les autorités des Etats côtiers qui inspectent souvent les registres d'hydrocarbures d'un navire après avoir observé une décharge en mer peuvent poursuivre l'équipage pour l'absence d'une entrée correspondante[114].

La poursuite des infractions «documentaires» plutôt que celle de la pollution comme telle est surtout exercée aux Etats-Unis, bien que cette possibilité existe aussi dans le droit d'autres Etats[115]. Les Etats-Unis, qui ne sont pas parties à la CNUDM, estiment que bon nombre des dispositions de la Convention relèvent du droit international coutumier et se considèrent liés par ces principes. En revanche, ils ont ratifié la convention MARPOL et ont incorporé ses dispositions dans leur droit interne. Dans les cas qui ont fait l'objet de procédures en justice, les autorités américaines se sont fondées sur des dispositions de droit pénal général, condamnant le délit de fausses déclarations envers des autorités comme celles des gardes-côtes et la falsification de registres officiels[116], et parfois le délit de cacher un acte criminel. Elles se sont aussi directement appuyées sur les dispositions de protection environnementale, fondées sur la convention MARPOL. Dans les cas cités, les autorités américaines ont poursuivi des infractions qui ont eu lieu en haute mer, dans la ZEE d'un autre Etat[117] ou dans un lieu inconnu. Quelques cas

112. Udell, *op. cit. supra* note 75, p. 271.

113. Stefan W. Douvier, *MARPOL — Umweltschutz auf dem Meer : Bestandsaufnahme und Ausblick*, Salzwasser-Verlag, 2005, p. 202, fait référence aux pratiques des autorités allemandes.

114. Andrew W. Homer, «Red Sky at Morning: The Horizon for Corporations, Crew Members and Corporate Officers as the United States Continues Aggressive Criminal Prosecution of Intentional Pollution from Ships», *Tulane Maritime Law Journal*, 2007, nº 32, p. 157, cite un cas devant les cours des Etats-Unis.

115. Voir Udell, *op. cit. supra* note 75, p. 286, et Molenaar, *op. cit. supra* note 8 p. 243, cite les provisions nationales respectives.

116. Udell, *op. cit. supra* note 75, p. 281 ; voir Homer, *op. cit. supra* note 114, p. 155, pour plus de détails.

117. Gehan, *op. cit. supra* note 70, p. 168, présente le premier de ces cas aux Etats-Unis.

ont été sanctionnés par des peines d'emprisonnement, sanction inconciliable avec l'article 230 de la CNUDM.

Les compagnies maritimes et les membres d'équipage mis en accusation soutiennent souvent que les Etats portuaires ou côtiers ne peuvent se prévaloir de la compétence de poursuivre de telles infractions dans l'hypothèse où le rejet a eu lieu au-delà des eaux de l'Etat côtier. En revanche, il a été retenu dans la jurisprudence américaine que la présentation de rapports falsifiés avait eu lieu dans le port et, par conséquent, dans une zone soumise à la souveraineté de l'Etat côtier [118], et que, même dans l'hypothèse d'omission d'entrées, la violation devait être considérée comme ayant eu lieu dans le port, étant donné que l'équipage du navire pouvait toujours ajouter des entrées omises au port avant de montrer le registre aux autorités [119]. Une argumentation comparable a été soutenue par les cours allemandes [120].

En invoquant des dispositions du droit pénal général comme la présentation de rapports falsifiés ou la fraude aux autorités, qui ne sont pas liées à des délits maritimes, les Etats côtiers sortent clairement du système de la CNUDM et de MARPOL, et ne sont plus liés par des dispositions comme l'article 230 de la CNUDM. Ces dispositions du droit pénal général ne cherchent pas à protéger l'environnement marin, mais visent à protéger le travail des autorités étatiques [121]. Ainsi, dans ces procédures, des questions quant à la compétence des Etats de poursuivre sur le plan criminel des nationaux d'autres Etats peuvent se poser, dans la mesure où la falsification du registre d'hydrocarbures par exemple, ne porte généralement pas atteinte aux intérêts de l'Etat côtier [122] si les décharges ont eu lieu hors des eaux territoriales. Les cours américaines, néanmoins, considèrent que la présentation de rapports falsifiés aux autorités porte atteinte aux intérêts de l'Etat et déclenche par conséquent la compétence juridictionnelle, même si les falsifications concernent des rejets que les Etats-Unis n'auraient pas pu poursuivre sans la demande de l'Etat du pavillon ou de l'Etat concerné par la pollution. Il s'ensuit une situation un peu paradoxale où l'équipage n'aurait pas été poursuivi

118. R. M. Underhill, « False Statement Act as Applied to Marine Pollution », *University of San Francisco Maritime Law Journal*, 2002, n° 15, pp. 281 et 284.

119. Voir Udell, *op. cit. supra* note 75, pp. 284 ss., et Homer, *op. cit. supra* note 114, pp. 156 ss., pour un résumé géneral des cas.

120. Douvier, *op. cit. supra* note 113, pp. 201 ss.

121. Benedict S. Gullo, « The Illegal Discharge of Oil on the High Seas : The US Coast Guard's Ongoing Battle against Vessel Polluters and a New Approach toward Establishing Environmental Compliance », *Military Law Review*, 2011, n° 209, p. 145.

122. Mais dans ce sens, Gehan, *op. cit. supra* note 70, p. 174, maintient que le registre falsifié peut mener à ce que le bateau soit examiné plus vite et échappe à des sanctions qui pourraient bénéficier à l'Etat du port.

s'il avait bien noté tous les rejets illégaux au-delà des eaux américaines avant de présenter le registre aux autorités des Etats-Unis [123].

Si, par ailleurs, les Etats côtiers fondent leur compétence sur MARPOL, de telles questions ne se posent pas, étant donné que MARPOL oblige tous les Etats parties à poursuivre et sanctionner les violations à la Convention. Néanmoins, si les Etats côtiers ou portuaires se servent des dispositions MARPOL, ils doivent respecter les dispositions procédurales et s'en tenir aux sanctions de la CNUDM, étant donné que la compétence de poursuivre des délits documentaires sous MARPOL n'est conférée qu'afin de protéger l'environnement marin dans la ZEE selon les articles 58 et 56 de la CNUDM, et cela, dans les conditions étroites du droit de la mer. Ainsi, pour les procédures criminelles qui sont fondées sur les dispositions de MARPOL, les cours nationales ne peuvent infliger que des peines monétaires, sauf s'il s'agit d'actes délibérés et graves de pollution dans les mers territoriales (CNUDM, art. 230 (2)). Même si l'on considère que la violation de MARPOL consiste en la fausse documentation de rejets et est ainsi commise dans le port, il semble qu'il s'agisse toujours d'un «cas d'infraction aux lois et règlements ... visant à prévenir, réduire et maîtriser la pollution du milieu marin, ... commise par des navires étrangers au-delà de la mer territoriale» selon l'article 230, paragraphe 1, de la CNUDM. Il est vrai que les termes de l'article se réfèrent, dans leur sens littéral, à la violation de la disposition environnementale, et non pas à la pollution. Néanmoins, il serait étrange qu'un Etat, selon l'article 230, paragraphe 1, de la CNUDM, soit empêché d'infliger une peine d'emprisonnement pour un rejet dans sa ZEE, mais puisse le faire pour un manquement de documentation du même acte de pollution.

B. A côté de MARPOL: des RNIGA relatives à la pollution marine à mettre en œuvre par les Etats côtiers?

Dans la première section de ce chapitre, il est démontré que MARPOL contient des limites importantes quant à la compétence des Etats côtiers de soumettre les actes de pollution à des sanctions pénales. Néanmoins, MARPOL ne présente pas un système unique de RNIGA qui peut s'appliquer à la pollution marine. En matière de pollution accidentelle, l'inapplicabilité de MARPOL ne signifie pas nécessairement qu'il est impossible d'engager la responsabilité criminelle des auteurs des accidents, mais la responsabilité est à chercher dans des faits

123. Nicolas H. Berg, «Bringing It All Back Home: The Fifth and Second Circuits Allow Domestic Prosecutions for Oil Record Book Violations on Foreign-Flagged Vessels», *Tulane Maritime Law Journal*, 2009, n° 34, p. 277.

autres que la seule pollution. Il est important qu'il existe une responsabilité criminelle potentielle pour les pollutions accidentelles, mais elle ne peut pas être trouvée dans MARPOL. De nombreux accidents sont dus à des manquements dans l'entretien ou dans la gestion du navire — les Etats côtiers peuvent-ils fonder une responsabilité pénale sur l'infraction à des dispositions de construction, de conception et d'armement?

Il est évident que MARPOL ne couvre pas les dispositions relatives aux CCA, alors que, la plupart du temps, c'est la violation de ces standards qui provoque l'accident ou contribue à ses conséquences. Dans de nombreux accidents, le bateau n'est pas toujours conforme aux standards en vigueur. Parfois, dans des cas comme celui de l'*Erika*, il y a des falsifications de documents par des responsables [124] et, dans cette affaire, la responsabilité pénale de la société de classification pour une inspection insuffisante a été établie [125]. Il est cependant vrai que la sécurité maritime n'est pas garantie même si tous les navires répondent aux standards établis par des conventions comme SOLAS, la convention de 1978 sur les normes de formation des gens de mer, de délivrance de brevets et de veille (STCW) [126] ou les standards d'armement de MARPOL [127]. Néanmoins, des standards à un niveau donné afin d'établir une responsabilité, notamment une responsabilité pénale, sont indispensables.

Selon certains auteurs, le contrôle de ces standards de construction, de conception et d'armement incombe non pas aux Etats côtiers, mais aux Etats du pavillon [128]. Ainsi, ce n'est pas aux Etats côtiers d'avoir une stratégie pour établir la responsabilité pénale des coupables. Dans l'hypothèse du passage normal de navires à travers une ZEE, il peut être déjà difficile pour l'Etat côtier de surveiller le passage du navire comme tel, et, normalement, il n'a pas intérêt à utiliser les droits réduits qui lui sont conférés par l'article 220, paragraphe 3, de la CNUDM et à demander des renseignements au bateau. Dans l'hypothèse où la violation d'un standard CCA a provoqué une pollution et où l'article 220, paragraphes 5 et 6, de la CNUDM permet à l'Etat côtier de procéder à une inspection matérielle du bateau pour établir le soupçon, et, dans l'hypothèse d'une pollution grave, causant des « dommages importants » au littoral de l'Etat côtier, ce dernier ne se voit pas empêché d'intenter une action contre les responsables et, cela, en droit pénal aussi. Il est vrai que ce droit de l'Etat côtier est assujetti au droit de l'Etat du

124. *Erika*, *op. cit. supra* note 86, p. 709.

125. *Ibid.*, pp. 711 ss.

126. International Convention on Standards of Training, Certification and Watchkeeping for Seafarers, Nations Unies, *Recueil des traités*, vol. 1361, p. 2.

127. Voir Frank, *op. cit. supra* note 42, p. 8, pour qui le *Prestige*, avant son naufrage, adhérait à tous les standards internationaux en vigueur.

128. *Ibid.*, p. 14.

pavillon selon l'article 228 de la CNUDM, mais ce droit doit être d'abord utilisé par l'Etat du pavillon. L'Etat côtier peut toujours se prévaloir de l'exception du « dommage grave » causé à ses côtes.

L'article 1, alinéa *a)*, de la convention SOLAS astreint les gouvernements parties à faire prévaloir les dispositions de la Convention et l'article 1, alinéa *b)*, précise que les Etats peuvent adopter « toute loi, régulation, ordre ou régulation et ... prendre toute autre mesure nécessaire » afin de donner plein effet à la Convention. Il paraît évident que les Etats peuvent ainsi se servir des lois criminelles afin d'encourager le respect des dispositions de la Convention.

Il paraît évident que les violations des standards CCA peuvent être plus difficiles à prouver que le seul fait qu'il y a eu pollution. Néanmoins, dans l'hypothèse d'accidents maritimes graves, il y a, selon les dispositions des conventions MARPOL (art. 12) et SOLAS, une obligation de mener une enquête afin de découvrir les causes de l'accident. Il devrait, normalement, être possible de déterminer les causes de l'accident et de savoir si le désastre a été la conséquence d'une violation des standards en vigueur. De plus, il devrait être possible de déterminer les responsables et d'établir si le fait ou l'omission étaient la cause d'un ordre donné par le propriétaire ou s'ils sont à reprocher à l'équipage ou au capitaine.

Même s'il existe des difficultés pratiques dans la mise en œuvre de la responsabilité pénale pour la violation des CCA ayant causé un accident, il semble que, de toute façon, le sanctionnement de ces violations est beaucoup plus juste et adapté à la situation que de fonder des sanctions pénales sur les dispositions MARPOL, qui ne sont pas destinées à s'appliquer aux pollutions accidentelles.

SECTION 3 LA MISE EN ŒUVRE DE LA COMPÉTENCE NATIONALE EN MATIÈRE CRIMINELLE

L'engagement de procédures criminelles est souvent considéré comme plus à même de décourager les contrevenants potentiels que des actions en droit civil pour la compensation du dommage, cela en raison de la stigmatisation d'une condamnation au pénal [129]. Les organes de l'Union européenne, en donnant les raisons qui les ont conduits à promulguer la directive 2005/35/CE, ont maintenu que les régimes de responsabilité civile n'étaient pas suffisants pour encourager

129. David M. Uhlmann, « After the Spill Is Gone : The Gulf of Mexico, Environmental Crime and the Criminal Law », *Michigan Law Review*, 2011, n° 109, p. 1443.

les intéressés du transport maritime à se comporter conformément à la convention MARPOL[130].

Il faut noter, pourtant, que le droit pénal est le moyen le plus drastique dont disposent les Etats et, en plus, un domaine souvent considéré comme formant le noyau de souveraineté nationale. Ainsi, les dispositions matérielles et procédurales sont très différentes dans les Etats membres de l'Union européenne[131], sans parler de ce problème sur un plan global.

Généralement, le droit pénal demande que les faits de l'affaire soient établis avec un degré de certitude plus élevé qu'en droit civil, car il s'agit non pas de trouver une solution équitable entre deux particuliers, mais de soumettre l'accusé à une sanction étatique. Pour les actes de pollution commis dans le milieu marin, l'enquête et la collecte de preuves peuvent être un défi pour toute autorité étatique côtière[132].

Dans la seconde partie de cette étude, il convient d'analyser d'abord les difficultés qui sont particulières à la mise en œuvre de la responsabilité pénale pour la pollution marine (paragraphe 1). Ensuite, l'analyse va se centrer sur la question de savoir si les procédures pénales telles qu'elles sont conduites aujourd'hui présentent une réponse appropriée à la pollution marine, si le système est juste et efficace et quelles sont les alternatives qu'on pourrait envisager pour décourager la pollution marine à l'échelle la plus grande possible (paragraphe 2).

Paragraphe 1 **Difficultés d'enquête et de mise en œuvre de la responsabilité pénale**

L'investigation d'infractions de pollution en mer doit faire face non seulement à tous les problèmes qui se présentent pendant les investigations des crimes environnementaux terrestres, mais aussi aux difficultés émanant du caractère mobile et international de la navigation. Afin de découvrir la pollution illégale en mer, les Etats côtiers doivent disposer de capacités pour surveiller leurs côtes et les navires ciblés. Il faut souligner que, dans un grand nombre d'Etats, la pollution marine peut ne pas ou insuffisamment être poursuivie. Les normes internationales applicables posent quelques problèmes s'il s'agit d'établir la préméditation des responsables. Concernant les sanctions, il existe aussi un problème quant à la portée de l'article 230 de la CNUDM pour les procédures nationales.

---

130. Directive 2005/35/CE, 7e considérant.

131. Hedemann-Robinson, *op. cit. supra* note 73, p. 290 ; Symeonidou-Kastanidou, *op. cit. supra* note 73, p. 349, indique que même le concept du droit pénal varie entre les Etats membres.

132. Mukherjee, « The Penal Law of Ship-Source Marine Pollution : Selected Issues in Perspective », *op. cit. supra* note 52, p. 470.

Cette section de l'étude porte sur les pollutions volontaires, car elles sont, par définition, plus susceptibles d'être cachées aux autorités des Etats côtiers et portuaires, alors que les pollutions accidentelles sont normalement trop importantes pour échapper à l'attention. Néanmoins, dans certains cas, quand les équipages de navires cachent des avaries ayant causé des pollutions [133], les problèmes d'investigation ressemblent beaucoup aux difficultés des cas de pollution délibérée.

A. *Les moyens d'investigation*

Sur la base des dispositions de la CNUDM, les Etats du port peuvent enquêter s'ils soupçonnent un cas de rejet dans leurs eaux territoriales ou leurs ZEE et ils peuvent faire de même pour toute infraction dans un autre lieu si elle risque de mettre en danger leurs côtes ou si l'Etat concerné le demande. En général, les moyens d'investigation des Etats côtiers sont réduits et varient selon le degré de pollution, la certitude d'une infraction et en fonction de la zone dans laquelle elle est susceptible d'être survenue. En vertu de l'article 220, paragraphe 2, de la CNUDM, l'inspection matérielle n'est permise que pour des infractions dans la mer territoriale ou, selon l'article 220, paragraphe 5 dela CNUDM, pour des infractions qui risquent de causer une «pollution notable». L'Etat doit avoir de «sérieuses raisons» de soupçonner ces infractions dans les deux hypothèses.

Ce n'est que si l'Etat côtier a des «preuves manifestes» de rejets dans la ZEE qui ont causé ou risquent de causer des «dommages importants» au littoral que l'Etat peut procéder à une action qui inclut l'immobilisation du navire (CNUDM, art. 220 (6)). Dans tous les autres cas, notamment de rejets mineurs dans la ZEE, les plus fréquents en pratique, l'Etat côtier ne peut que demander des renseignements au bateau (CNUDM, art. 220 (3)), afin de soumettre le cas à une investigation par les autorités du prochain port.

i) *Les mesures et la surveillance en mer*

Les Etats côtiers privilégient la surveillance des navires en mer, afin d'observer des pollutions illicites. La limite pour les décharges permises selon MARPOL en fonction du pourcentage réduit d'hydrocarbures dans le mélange rejeté est calculée selon la visibilité du rejet — il est scientifiquement établi qu'un rejet permis selon les dispositions de la convention ne peut pas être perceptible [134]. C'est pourquoi les autorités doivent

133. L'incident du *M/S Freja Jutlandic* au port de Baltimore, mentionné par Homer, *op. cit. supra* note 114, p. 163.

134. Cheng-Pang Wang, «A Review of the Enforcement Regime for Vessel-Source Oil Pollution Control», *Ocean Development and International Law*,

être alertées dès qu'une nappe de pétrole apparaît autour d'un bateau. Néanmoins, les observations et les surveillances de pollutions illicites dépendent beaucoup du temps et des conditions climatiques dans les régions [135]. Grâce à des techniques de surveillance spéciales [136], il est également possible d'observer des rejets illicites dans la nuit, mais l'utilisation d'images satellitaires n'est pas encore partout retenue [137]. En plus, la surveillance de zones maritimes réparties entre plusieurs Etats présuppose pour être efficace une certaine coopération [138].

Même si, dans certains cas, les autorités ont considéré une seule photo aérienne comme preuve principale suffisante [139], sa valeur est assez douteuse. La nappe peut par exemple être causée par un autre navire [140], ou il peut s'agir d'un phénomène autre que la pollution. Pour exclure toutes ces possibilités, l'Etat côtier doit disposer, au-delà de moyens de surveillance aérienne, de forces en mer pour faire des prélèvements dans le sillage du navire et les comparer avec les hydrocarbures utilisés sur le navire. La valeur contraignante de l'échantillon comme preuve peut être douteuse dans les cas — les plus fréquents — où les polluants sont des mélanges d'hydrocarbures [141]. En effet, les analyses des prélèvements peuvent mettre en question des faisceaux d'indices autrement bien établis [142].

En outre, la comparaison entre les prélèvements et les hydrocarbures à bord ne peut s'effectuer que quand le navire s'arrête assez longtemps pour embarquer un représentant de l'autorité de l'Etat côtier qui procé-

1986, n° 16, p. 319; Udell, *op. cit. supra* note 75, p. 277; voir aussi la documentation pour la mise en place de l'Accord de Bonn de 1983 relatif à la coopération en matière de lutte contre la pollution en mer du Nord, http://www.bonnagreement.org/fr/html/manuel_FEPO/chapter1_introduction.htm (consulté le 13 octobre 2012).

135. Jean-Loup Velut, «Protection de l'environnement et lutte contre les activités illicites: de l'évolution de la norme juridique à l'action en mer: l'exemple de la Méditerranée (1)», *Droit maritime français*, 2011, n° 63, p. 519.

136. Udell, *op. cit. supra* note 75, p. 277; Gullo, *op. cit. supra* note 121, p. 153.

137. Griselda Capaldo, «Innovative Tools for Preventing Marine Pollution from Ships», dans Jack W. Harris (dir. publ.), *Maritime Law: Issues, Challenges and Implications*, Nova Science, 2011, p. 57; Velut, *op. cit. supra* note 135, p. 520.

138. En Méditerranée, on constate les premiers efforts visant à accepter les preuves trouvées par des agents d'autres Etats.

139. *Traquair*, 1995, Tribunal de grande instance de Brest, *Droit maritime français*, n° 47, p. 913; la pratique est critiquée par Patrick Simon, «La pénalisation du droit est-elle efficace en matière de pollution marine?», *Droit maritime français*, 2004, n° 56, p. 167.

140. *Ibid.*, p. 168.

141. Christophe Marques, «La répression des rejets illicites d'hydrocarbures: 1983-2003: 20 ans d'évolution législative et jurisprudentielle», *Droit maritime français*, 2004, n° 56, p. 321.

142. Velut, *op. cit. supra* note 135, p. 520.

dera à une inspection sommaire du bateau. Une telle visite n'est pas permise sur des bateaux en passage dans la ZEE, sauf si la pollution est « notable » (CNUDM, art. 220 (5)). En outre, comme le rejet peut avoir été causé par un accident ou un mauvais fonctionnement de l'équipement, la pollution devrait être exclue du champ d'applicabilité de la convention MARPOL. Cette possibilité peut seulement être exclue par une inspection au cours de laquelle l'équipement du bateau est sérieusement examiné, par un contrôle du registre des hydrocarbures et par des interrogatoires des membres de l'équipage [143], ce qui n'est également possible que dans les eaux territoriales de l'Etat côtier ou s'il agit d'une pollution au moins « notable » (CNUDM, art. 220 (2) et (5)).

Peut-être est-ce pour cette raison que quelques cours nationales acceptent des photos comme preuves suffisantes de la présence physique d'hydrocarbures dans la mer, même s'il existe aussi des cas dans la jurisprudence française, dans lesquels les accusés ont été acquittés suite à des ambiguïtés dans l'interprétation de la photo [144]. Néanmoins, il y a un risque d'accusations et de fausses condamnations si les tribunaux nationaux se contentent d'observations comme preuves uniques.

ii) *Les inspections portuaires et en mer*

Les inspections du navire, de l'équipement et des registres d'hydrocarbures peuvent fournir les preuves les plus convaincantes, surtout en ce qui concerne les pollutions illicites délibérées.

Tous les navires doivent, selon les dispositions de MARPOL, posséder l'équipement nécessaire pour que toutes les décharges d'hydrocarbures restent sous les seuils prévus par la Convention. Le mélange d'eau et d'hydrocarbures, qui émane des machines du navire et s'accumule, est généralement passé à travers un Oily Water Seperator (OWS) qui sépare l'eau des hydrocarbures [145] jusqu'à ce que la densité d'hydrocarbures ne dépasse plus les limites posées par MARPOL. L'eau est alors rejetée en mer, tandis que les hydrocarbures sont retenus ; ils seront rejetés plus tard dans des dispositifs appropriés, dans un port, ou bien incinérés en route, en accord avec les dispositions applicables à la pollution de l'air. Généralement, il n'est pas possible de décharger des quantités d'hydrocarbures plus importantes ou plus denses par des voies normales et les équipages des navires se servent de tuyaux additionnels pour contourner l'équipement. Si l'équipage démonte ces installations avant le contrôle, les représentants des autorités maritimes peuvent en détecter certains indices, tels que la présence d'une installation illicite ou des traces

143. Udell, *op. cit. supra* note 75, p. 277.
144. Marques, *op. cit. supra* note 141, p. 322.
145. Voir Gullo, *op. cit. supra* note 121, p. 130, pour plus de détails.

d'huile autour de l'OWS et ses vannes ou dans les tuyaux situés vers la dernière vanne avant que le contenu ne soit déchargé[146]. En outre, les violations des lois sur la protection de l'environnement marin sont souvent détectées car l'équipage du navire est incapable de faire fonctionner l'équipement comme l'OWS[147], ou car l'équipement est manifestement en panne ou inopérable[148].

Un examen aussi minutieux prend du temps et ne peut pas s'effectuer quand le navire est en route. La plupart de ces visites se font dans le cadre du contrôle portuaire. Un Etat côtier ne peut pas contrôler un navire en passage, en particulier si celui-ci se trouve au-delà des eaux territoriales et si la pollution causée n'est pas «notable». Même pour les navires qui se trouvent dans les eaux territoriales et qui sont soupçonnés d'actes de pollution illicite, les autorités étatiques doivent intercepter le navire assez vite avant qu'il ne sorte de cette zone[149]. Dès qu'il entre dans la ZEE, et même pour des actes de pollution qui ont eu lieu dans la mer territoriale, le régime de l'article 220, paragraphe 3, de la CNUDM s'applique: les pouvoirs des Etats se réduisent à la demande de renseignements afin d'opérer des mesures du contrôle portuaire dans le prochain port d'escale. Ce délai avant que le navire n'arrive au port permet généralement à l'équipage de cacher les traces de leurs actes illicites.

iii) *Les informateurs et le «whistle-blowing»*

Beaucoup d'infractions contre les dispositions de la convention MARPOL et les lois nationales correspondantes n'auraient jamais été découvertes si certaines juridictions n'encourageaient pas des individus impliqués dans des actions illicites à en informer les autorités[150]. C'est surtout aux Etats-Unis que des informateurs peuvent obtenir des sommes considérables pour certaines confessions — jusqu'à la moitié de la peine pécuniaire pour les délits de pollution marine[151]. Il va sans dire que les informateurs ne seront pas poursuivis pour le comportement incriminé, même s'ils y ont activement participé.

Les témoignages de tels «whistle-blowers» et leurs répercussions sur les investigations de crimes commis dans des sociétés font l'objet de bien de discussions[152]. Les gens de mer qui se confient aux autorités portuaires et témoignent contre leurs employeurs courent le risque de

146. Udell, *op. cit. supra* note 75, p. 278.
147. *Ibid.*; Gullo, *op. cit. supra* note 121, p. 153.
148. *Ibid.*, pp. 152 et 154.
149. Udell, *op. cit. supra* note 75, p. 274.
150. *Ibid.*, p. 280 (note de bas de page 20), pour la liste des seuls cas américains.
151. *Ibid.*, p. 279.
152 Voir Anthony, *op. cit. supra* note 89, p. 237; Homer, *op. cit. supra* note 114, p. 172, maintient un point de vue assez critique.

vivre des conditions abusives à bord du navire[153], de perdre leur travail[154], de se trouver détenu à l'étranger sans l'assistance de leur employeur pendant le procès et de ne plus trouver de travail dans leur profession, une fois stigmatisés comme «traître»[155]. Seule une récompense généreuse peut les encourager à donner des informations aux autorités.

En outre, le montant des récompenses accordées aux informateurs dans les cas cités peut facilement encourager des employés à fournir des informations fausses ou exagérées[156]. Il en est de même avec le bénéfice de ne pas être poursuivi, surtout dans les cas où il y a déjà un soupçon et où les membres de l'équipage sentent la nécessité de s'offrir comme témoins[157]. Les membres de l'équipage qui hésitent à s'adresser aux autorités portuaires seront alors ceux qui seront accusés de violations, tout comme les membres de l'équipage qui n'étaient pas au courant des actes illicites[158]. En plus, les poursuites aux Etats-Unis ont montré que de nombreux gens de mer, surtout dans les échelons les moins qualifiés, ont tendance à ne jamais mettre en cause les ordres[159], et ne sont peut-être même pas conscients de l'illégalité d'un ordre.

Encourager des informateurs est un moyen efficace d'obtenir des témoignages substantiels contre les pollueurs, mais il faut s'en servir avec prudence. Les informations obtenues ne doivent pas être les seules preuves dans une investigation de pollution maritime, mais cela vaut probablement pour le «whistle-blowing» dans tous les domaines de droit pénal.

B. Le degré de preuve exigé et l'établissement de l'élément psychologique

En général, les procédures de droit pénal demandent un degré de certitude plus élevé dans l'établissement des faits que les procédures civiles. Surtout en ce qui concerne la préméditation, il faut généralement que la preuve en soit établie, afin de protéger l'accusé contre des procédures injustes[160].

Pour les rejets d'hydrocarbures en mer, la convention MARPOL offre l'exception d'avarie de la règle 4.2 (ancienne règle 11) de l'annexe I. Rien n'empêche l'équipage d'un navire chargé d'un rejet illicite de

153. Cette crainte a été exprimée dans des procédures américaines récentes; voir Udell, *op. cit. supra* note 75, p. 279.
154. Anthony, *op. cit. supra* note 89, p. 236.
155. Udell, *op. cit. supra* note 75, p. 273.
156. Gullo, *op. cit. supra* note 121, p. 162.
157. Homer, *op. cit. supra* note 114, p. 167.
158. Anthony, *op. cit. supra* note 89, p. 237.
159. Udell, *op. cit. supra* note 75, p. 273.
160. Mukherjee, «The Penal Law of Ship-Source Marine Pollution: Selected Issues in Perspective», *op. cit. supra* note 52, p. 481.

plaider que la décharge a été le résultat d'un mauvais fonctionnement du système de filtrage ou d'une autre avarie mineure. Dans la plupart des systèmes juridiques, c'est un des principes du droit pénal que la preuve de l'infraction doit être apportée par l'accusation et que le bénéfice de la présomption d'innocence est accordé à l'accusé, qui devrait donc être acquitté s'il n'est pas établi que sa défense d'avarie n'est pas vraie. Qu'une avarie ou un mauvais fonctionnement n'ait pas eu lieu est extrêmement difficile à prouver.

Cependant, il a été maintenu en doctrine [161] et aussi dans la juridiction nationale française [162] que la convention MARPOL ou les lois nationales la mettant en œuvre traitent l'exception d'avarie comme une défense qui doit être alléguée et prouvée par l'accusé, et que la charge de la preuve pour l'avarie est ainsi inversée [163]. Dans les cas cités, le capitaine avait allégué que le rejet observé par la surveillance aérienne était involontaire et avait été causé par une vanne qui s'était légèrement ouverte suite à de simples vibrations. Les cours françaises ont rejeté cette défense en soutenant que la décharge observée était trop importante pour émaner du conduit décrit, que le rejet n'avait pas été inscrit dans le registre d'hydrocarbures [164] et que la décharge avait cessé dès que l'avion de surveillance avait été aperçu par l'équipage du navire fautif [165].

En ce qui concerne la dernière allégation, il est impossible de savoir s'il s'agissait d'une coïncidence extraordinaire ou non [166]. Tout équipage d'un navire peut facilement plaider qu'il a seulement remarqué le rejet involontaire quand il a compris que son bâtiment présentait un intérêt particulier pour la surveillance aérienne et, afin de renforcer l'allégation, ajouter une entrée correspondante dans le registre d'hydrocarbures. En outre, comme certaines autorités nationales se dirigent vers une véritable présomption de culpabilité pour tous les rejets observés, il paraît difficile pour tous les navires d'échapper à la charge.

Il reste à souligner qu'il paraît assez compliqué d'apporter la preuve d'une pollution préméditée en mer, et que les cours devront souvent avoir recours à des présomptions de mauvaise foi ou des faisceaux d'indices afin d'établir le côté psychologique de l'infraction [167]. Leur

161. Mukherjee, *op. cit. supra* note 160, pp. 491 ss., où il fait aussi une distinction entre la preuve pour l'avarie comme telle et la preuve que des précautions raisonnables ont été prises après l'avarie (règle 11 *b)* i) de l'annexe I de MARPOL).

162. *Traquair*, *op. cit. supra* note 139 ; *Traquair — Appel* 1996, cour d'appel de Rennes, *Droit maritime français*, n° 49, p. 100.

163. Raymond Leost, « Observations CA Rennes, 19 septembre 1996 », *Droit maritime français*, n° 49, p. 108.

164. *Traquair —Appel*, *op. cit. supra* note 162, p. 103.

165. *Traquair*, *op. cit. supra* note 139, p. 915.

166. Morin, *op. cit. supra* note 27, p. 916.

167. Marques, *op. cit. supra* note 141, p. 313.

tâche devient d'autant plus difficile s'il s'agit d'attribuer le comportement incriminé à un individu donné à bord. Les personnes visées seront le plus souvent le capitaine ou l'ingénieur en chef, ayant recours à la présomption que tous les événements à bord se passent sous leur autorité [168].

C. Les sanctions

La convention MARPOL, dans son article 4, paragraphe 4, impose aux Etats contractants de soumettre les infractions à la Convention à des sanctions suffisamment sévères pour décourager toute infraction et d'une sévérité égale sans égard au lieu de l'infraction. Etant donné que dans les pays européens, des différences marquées existent quant aux montants des amendes infligées [169], il ne semble pas que cet objectif ait été atteint depuis l'entrée en vigueur de MARPOL. L'Union européenne a instauré des niveaux de peines à peu près uniformes par la décision-cadre 2005/667/JAI mais, après l'annulation de celle-ci par la CJE, cette question est de nouveau laissée à la libre appréciation des Etats membres. Le niveau des peines pécuniaires dépend beaucoup des standards de vie dans les pays qui légifèrent et les méthodes de calcul [170] ainsi que les facteurs à prendre en considération sont aussi très différents. Dans le même pays et pour la même infraction, le niveau des peines peut également varier considérablement [171].

Les seules peines pécuniaires n'ont pas toujours un effet dissuasif suffisant [172] en comparaison avec la menace de l'incarcération [173], vu la force économique des entreprises dans le secteur pétrolier, par exemple, et souvent même les peines infligés à des employés seront payés par les entreprises.

---

168. Homer, *op. cit. supra* note 114, p. 167, fait allusion aux délits documentaires.

169. Karamitsos, *op. cit. supra* note 105, p. 21.

170. Ingo E. Fromm, « Urteilsanmerkung EuGH, Urt. v. 23.10.2007 », 2008, Zeitschrift für Internationale Strafrechtsdogmatik, p. 176, se réfère à la méthode des taux journaliers en Allemagne, calculés en fonction des revenus du condamné.

171. Voir le cas du *Traquair* précité où l'amende a été augmentée de 30 000 à 250 000 francs en deuxième instance, *Traquair — Appel*, *op. cit. supra* note 162, p. 104.

172. Günter Heine, « Marine (Oil) Pollution : Prevention and Protection by Criminal Law — International Perspectives, Corporate and/or Individual Criminal Liability », dans Michael G. Faure et James Hu (dir. publ.), *Prevention and Compensation of Marine Pollution Damage : Recent Developments in Europe, China and the US*, Kluwer Law International 2006, p. 47, fait référence à des sources allemandes et à la possibilité d'assurance contre les amendes ; Berg, *op. cit. supra* note 123, p. 277.

173. Darmody, *op. cit. supra* note 88, p. 118 ; Uhlmann, *op. cit. supra* note 129, p. 1443.

Comme il a été énoncé plus haut, le droit de la mer restreint le pouvoir des Etats de sanctionner les infractions à des normes environnementales par l'article 230, paragraphe 1, de la CNUDM, et déclare clairement que les peines autres que pécuniaires ne peuvent être infligées que pour des actes délibérés et graves, commis dans la mer territoriale, hypothèse qui n'est certainement pas fréquente. Le seuil de la « gravité » au sens de l'article 230 de la CNUDM est très difficile à déterminer, mais il semble qu'il pourrait être dépassé dans les hypothèses de pollution réitérée — bien qu'il paraît peu probable qu'un navire se livre à de tels actes à moins de 12 milles nautiques de la côte d'un Etat.

De nombreux Etats ont, malheureusement, violé cette disposition du droit de la mer, en attribuant des peines de prison pour des accidents maritimes [174] et en condamnant effectivement des capitaines de navires naufragés à des peines de prison [175]. Sans oublier les détentions provisoires, qui, sans être des peines au sens propre du terme, sont normalement perçues comme des peines d'incarcération pour les détenus [176], même si elles sont des mesures procédurales et non punitives [177].

i) *Sanctions envers des personnes légales*

En Europe, la plupart des Etats membres de l'Union européenne connaissent la responsabilité pénale des entreprises [178], tandis que le concept est strictement rejeté dans d'autres Etats comme l'Allemagne [179]. La question de savoir si le fait de sanctionner pénalement des personnes légales est une réponse appropriée à des crimes typiquement commis dans le cadre des grandes corporations est d'un grand intérêt dans le domaine du droit environnemental [180]. Cela est également valable pour

174. Voir Proshanto K. Mukherjee, « Criminalisation and Unfair Treatment: the Seafarer's Perspective », *Journal of International Maritime Law*, pp. 334 ss., qui fait référence à une étude du Comité maritime international; et Olivia Murray, « Fair Treatment of Seafarers — International Law and Practice », *The Journal of International Maritime Law*, 2012, n° 18, p. 159, qui souligne que les sanctions sont souvent basées sur des provisions qui ciblent non pas la pollution marine, mais un autre comportement, et cela qu'à l'occasion d'une grave marée noire.

175. Voir les études de cas enoncés par Anthony, *op. cit. supra* note 89, pp. 220 ss., et Murray, *op. cit. supra* note 174, pp. 155 ss.

176. Blanco-Bazán, *op. cit. supra* note 18, p. 236.

177. Voir aussi Mukherjee, « Criminalisation and Unfair Treatment: The Seafarer's Perspective », *op. cit. supra* note 174, p. 331, qui critique la pratique de fixer des cautions à des montants outranciers.

178. Heine, *op. cit. supra* note 172, p. 51.

179. Ingo E. Fromm, « Auf dem Weg zur strafrechtlichen Verantwortlichkeit von Unternehmen/Unternehmensvereinigungen in Europa? », *Zeitschrift für Internationale Strafrechtsdogmatik*, 2007, pp. 279.

180. Uhlmann, *op. cit. supra* note 129, p. 1439.

la pollution marine par les navires, vu l'organisation hiérarchique de la gestion des navires et la responsabilité du capitaine envers son employeur[181]. Il est très probable que la décision de se débarrasser de certaines substances de manière illicite a été prise, au fond, par la direction de l'entreprise[182] et potentiellement, de manière indirecte, en offrant des récompenses à l'équipage pour une réduction substantielle des frais de port ou de maintenance[183].

En ciblant les corporations et les voies par lesquelles les actions illicites sont encouragées[184], on sanctionne la corporation en la privant d'une partie du gain qu'elle a obtenu en violant les dispositions environnementales. En outre, surtout aux Etats-Unis, les personnes légales peuvent non seulement être punies par des peines pécuniaires, mais aussi être condamnées à des mesures plus matérielles, par exemple l'établissement d'un plan d'observation des normes environnementales, dont la mise en œuvre va être contrôlée par les autorités judiciaires[185]. Parfois, des corporations ont été condamnées à ne plus recevoir l'attribution de contrats gouvernementaux[186]. Dans la mesure où les autorités effectuent réellement le contrôle, ces stratégies, très efficaces pour augmenter la conscience environnementale des corporations, sont peut-être plus favorables que les peines pécuniaires[187]. Il en est de même avec la condamnation à investir dans des projets de protection environnementale[188]. Néanmoins, de telles sanctions ne sont pas des peines pécuniaires dans le sens de l'article 230 de la CNUDM: elles ne peuvent être infligées que pour des violations ayant eu lieu dans les mers territoriales ou pour des infractions graves et délibérées. Quant à savoir si l'obligation de gérer tel plan ou tel programme fait partie de la peine pécuniaire et peut être considérée comme une condition pour l'infliction ou l'aggravation de l'amende, la réponse va dépendre de la manière dont les lois nationales traitent cette condamnation. De toute façon, les limites de l'article 230 de la CNUDM s'opposent à la création de peines extraordinaires ou compliquées, ce qui est peut-être regrettable dans certains cas, mais, ainsi, l'article 230 de la CNUDM agit comme une disposition protectrice

---

181. Anthony, *op. cit. supra* note 89, p. 236; Morin, *op. cit. supra* note 27, p. 917.
182. Marques, *op. cit. supra* note 141, p. 310.
183. Gullo, *op. cit. supra* note 121, p. 132; Udell, *op. cit. supra* note 75, p. 273; Homer, *op. cit. supra* note 114, p. 152.
184. Heine, *op. cit. supra* note 172, p. 50.
185. Udell, *op. cit. supra* note 75, pp. 286 ss.
186. Uhlmann, *op. cit. supra* note 129, p. 1451, par rapport aux infractions qui ont lieu lors de l'exploitation du sol sous-marin.
187. Udell, *op. cit. supra* note 75, p. 276.
188. Ces peines sont fréquentes aux Etats-Unis, voir *ibid.*, p. 287, mais aussi, suite à l'admission de parties civiles dans les procédures, en France, voir Marques, *op. cit. supra* note 141, pp. 314 ss.

contre l'infliction d'obligations qui sont trop difficiles ou même impossibles à remplir.

En même temps, sanctionner des personnes légales est susceptible de présenter des problèmes sur un plan sociétal. Dans certains cas, des entreprises avaient tendance à rendre coupables leurs employés afin d'éviter que la société ne soit tenue responsable[189]. Cette tendance est peut-être moins marquée dans les enquêtes qui ne visent que des individus, et où l'entreprise comme un tout ne risque pas d'être condamnée «faute de mieux» si les individus responsables ne sont pas identifiés. A part la dimension humaine des cas précités et l'injustice manifeste d'ainsi rendre responsable un individu, de telles «pertes» d'employés seront facilement considérées comme un coût des affaires par les entreprises. Ainsi, elles ne seront pas découragées de commettre des infractions contre des normes environnementales.

ii) *Sanctions civiles et procédures administratives*

A part les sanctions pénales, les Etats peuvent aussi se servir de sanctions plus administratives qui visent à réparer le dommage et à empêcher le comportement incriminé dans le futur. Ces sanctions se distinguent des sanctions pénales dans leurs objectifs: il s'agit non pas de stigmatiser le comportement, mais de demander la réparation du dommage causé à la société. C'est dans ce cadre que s'inscrivent les «sanctions civiles», des peines infligées par l'Etat mais destinées à être utilisées pour le rétablissement de l'environnement marin[190].

Une sanction administrative d'un caractère assez différent a été récemment créée par les autorités des Etats-Unis, à savoir le bannissement d'un navire fautif des ports du pays. Après avoir établi des violations des dispositions environnementales, les gardes-côtes américains ont banni le navire de tous les ports du pays pendant une période de trois ans[191]. Même si les charges contre les responsables du navire ont depuis été levées[192], la décision d'une telle mesure d'exclusion afin de décourager les violations des normes environnementales est certainement un développement intéressant. Premièrement, du point de vue du droit de la mer, les navires n'ont généralement pas un droit absolu d'accès aux ports[193], et un tel bannissement n'est alors pas contraire au droit de la

189. Homer, *op. cit. supra* note 114, pp. 171 et 173.

190. Voir Marques, *op. cit. supra* note 141, p. 314, qui énonce une telle classification des sanctions civiles en droit français.

191. Le cas est présenté en détail par Gullo, *op. cit. supra* note 121, pp. 164 ss.

192. Voir le communiqué de presse de l'armateur, http://www.docstoc.com/docs/52137445/USCG-ALLEGATION-CONCERNING-VIOLATION-OF-MARPOL-REGULATION-BY-MT (consulté le 13 octobre 2012).

193. Voir la Convention de Genève de 1923 sur le régime international des ports maritimes (Société des Nations, *Recueil des traités*, vol. 58, p. 285), article 3

mer tant qu'il n'est pas infligé d'une manière qui pourrait être considérée comme discriminatoire[194]. Le bannissement présente l'avantage d'être une sanction rapide et simple qui est d'un effet économique directement perceptible par les personnes ou les entités qui bénéficient de la gestion du navire[195], tandis que l'équipage est beaucoup moins affecté que dans une procédure pénale[196]. En même temps, le bannissement conduit à une stigmatisation du navire — et probablement de ses gestionnaires — comparable à celle d'une condamnation criminelle. Il s'agit néanmoins d'une mesure très drastique, susceptible de réduire à néant la valeur d'un navire qui n'est peut-être pas touché par des vices inhérents.

Le rôle des sanctions administratives dans le système de MARPOL reste encore à être déterminé. L'étendue des termes de l'article 4 de MARPOL permet facilement aux Etats contractants de non pas seulement se servir du droit pénal, mais d'appliquer aussi des mesures dissuasives émanant du droit administratif. Sortir du cadre des peines criminelles peut présenter l'avantage d'échapper au caractère assez strict de la procédure pénale, mais peut s'avérer d'une valeur douteuse et peut-être injuste.

Paragraphe 2 **Les sanctions pénales : une réponse appropriée à la pollution marine ?**

La discussion sur le sanctionnement criminel des actes de pollution marine trouve, au premier chef, sa source dans des pollutions graves qui sont le plus souvent le résultat d'accidents désastreux. Ce fait est avéré pour la législation européenne précitée, qui a été inspirée par les marées noires causées par les naufrages du *Prestige* et de l'*Erika*, et le Oil Pollution Act 1990 des Etats-Unis qui est la conséquence directe de l'accident catastrophique de l'*Exxon Valdez*[197]. Dans la mesure où les dommages causés dépassaient de loin toutes les réparations possibles matérielles et financières, il n'est peut-être pas trop surprenant que les législateurs ont eu recours au droit pénal, le moyen le plus contraignant dont les Etats disposent pour mettre la pollution au ban de la société, dans un but fort probable de calmer l'opinion

---

du statut annexé, et, à titre d'exposé sommaire, Louise de La Fayette, « Access to Ports in International Law », *International Journal of Marine and Coastal Law*, 1996, n° 11, p. 1.

194. Voir Churchill et Lowe, *op. cit. supra* note 6, p. 63 ; Molenaar, *op. cit. supra* note 8, p. 228 par rapport aux conditions générales d'entrée dans les ports.

195. Gullo, *op. cit. supra* note 121, p. 169.

196. *Ibid.*, p. 173.

197. Darmody, *op. cit. supra* note 88, p. 110.

publique. La législation et la pratique des Etats côtiers sont ainsi souvent critiquées, car injustes envers les gens de mer. En même temps, il paraît douteux que les objectifs poursuivis puissent vraiment être atteints de cette manière[198].

A. La criminalisation des pollutions marines et la dimension humaine

Ce n'est pas pour rien que l'article 230 de la CNUDM rappelle aux Etats contractants les droits généraux des accusés de la pollution marine. Tandis que l'article a une portée générale et s'applique, selon ses termes, à tous les contrevenants et pas seulement aux gens de mer, dans la plupart des cas, ce sont les membres de l'équipage et les capitaines des navires qui sont accusés par les Etats côtiers, pour la simple raison qu'ils sont présents et attirent les premiers l'attention des autorités. Il faut peut-être rappeler que les procédures criminelles contre les gens de mer sont, compte tenu de leur dimension internationale, souvent très compliquées[199]. De plus, rester disponible pour les autorités d'un Etat donné correspond à une entrave à toute activité professionnelle. Les barrières de la langue et les différences culturelles sont susceptibles d'aggraver encore la situation[200].

De plus, suite à des actes de pollution, accidentels et délibérés, il y a souvent une forte pression de l'opinion publique pour condamner les personnes présumées coupables[201], alors que les faits sont souvent difficiles à comprendre, voire impossibles pour des non-professionnels[202]. Le danger existe que des accusés soient, pour des raisons politiques nationales[203], jugés non pas selon la gravité des fautes, mais selon leurs conséquences catastrophiques[204]. Ainsi, dans les cas de naufrage et de pollution accidentelle par exemple, des gens de mer ont été parfois détenus pendant de longues périodes sans que les autorités étatiques n'aient produit de preuves suffisantes pour certifier une faute professionnelle. Il semble aussi que les cas dans lesquels des membres d'équipage ont été

198. Murray, *op. cit. supra* note 174, p. 151.

199. A noter qu'on assiste, en France, à une spécialisation croissante des tribunaux ; voir Marques, *op. cit. supra* note 141, pp. 316 ss.

200. Ainsi, l'accusé britannique, dans l'affaire *Traquair*, avait évoqué que ses propos pendant l'inspection du navire avaient été mal traduits par l'équipe de recherche française (*Traquair — Appel*, *op. cit. supra* note 162, p. 101).

201. Mukherjee, « Criminalisation and Unfair Treatment: The Seafarer's Perspective », *op. cit. supra* note 174, p. 329 ; Murray, *op. cit. supra* note 174, p. 151.

202. Marques, *op. cit. supra* note 141, p. 316 ; Heine, *op. cit. supra* note 172, p. 51.

203. Murray, *op. cit. supra* note 174, p. 158.

204. Uhlmann, *op. cit. supra* note 129, p. 1460.

arrêtés dans le but d'inciter le propriétaire du navire à assumer une responsabilité pour un accident ne sont pas rares[205].

Dans un accident de mer, les personnes concernées subissent souvent une situation compliquée, suite à la perte du bateau qui est leur lieu de travail et de vie à la fois, et aussi suite à la perte de collègues et d'amis. C'est pourquoi il est d'autant plus grave de les astreindre à assister à de longues procédures dans un pays étranger s'il n'y a pas de preuves claires d'un comportement fautif qui justifierait ces mesures.

B. Des finalités atteintes ?

Le droit pénal en matière de protection de l'environnement a, en général, deux objectifs[206], à savoir punir les coupables, afin d'interférer avec le comportement de l'accusé pour qu'il ne puisse pas jouir des avantages que son infraction lui a conférés, et décourager de tels comportements dans le futur, en stigmatisant le fait incriminé pour dissuader les criminels potentiels. Dans le but d'analyser si ces finalités peuvent être atteintes en matière de pénalisation de la pollution marine, il faut clairement distinguer la pollution accidentelle, qui était peut-être prévisible mais certainement pas intentionnelle, de la pollution délibérée.

i) *Châtiment*

Le caractère punitif du droit pénal, le rétablissement de la paix légale, est souvent perçu comme l'objectif le plus important dans ce domaine de droit. Quand il s'agit d'interférer avec le comportement incriminé de la personne qui s'est rendue coupable, la punition du condamné est facile à justifier. En matière de violations délibérées des normes environnementales, le mobile le plus fréquent des infractions est certainement un intérêt financier[207]. En se livrant à des décharges illicites, les équipages gestionnaires des navires obtiennent des avantages financiers importants, en n'utilisant pas les installations des ports et en gagnant du temps. Il est essentiel d'annuler ces avantages, en condamnant les coupables à des amendes qui atteignent au moins le montant des sommes

205. Mukherjee, « Criminalisation and Unfair Treatment : The Seafarer's Perspective », *op. cit. supra* note 174, p. 328, se refère aux cas du *Tasman Spirit* et du *Prestige* ; Edgar Gold, « Fair Treatment of Seafarers in the Event of a Maritime Accident : New International Guidelines », dans Tafsir M. Ndiaye et Rüdiger Wolfrum (dir. publ.), *Law of the Sea, Environmental Law and Settlement of Disputes*, Martinus Nijhoff, 2007, p. 413 ; Huybrechts, *op. cit. supra* note 78, p. 201 ; Murray, *op. cit. supra* note 174, p. 151.

206. Uhlmann, *op. cit. supra* note 129, p. 1449 ; Darmody, *op. cit. supra* note 88, p. 118.

207. Udell, *op. cit. supra* note 75, p. 272.

économisées. En plus, par des amendes infligées aux contrevenants, le droit pénal corrige aussi l'avantage qu'ils ont gagné sur leurs concurrents en évitant les coûts causés par l'observation des normes environnementales[208]. Néanmoins, cette stratégie ne peut être entièrement efficace que si seuls les responsables subissent la conséquence de la sanction financière, et non pas la corporation ou une autre entité qui percevrait le désavantage financier comme le «coût des affaires». Les autorités étatiques doivent aussi estimer la portée des pollutions illicites, même non découvertes, et juger exactement les coûts évités. Le danger que les peines infligées restent dérisoires en comparaison aux avantages de la pollution illicite explique peut-être pourquoi les cours nationales infligent des amendes très importantes, y compris pour des infractions plutôt mineures. Il faut tout de même remarquer que les pollutions volontaires peuvent avoir des mobiles qui ne sont pas uniquement financiers, telle l'absence d'installations de réception des effluents dans les ports[209], qui obligent les équipages à s'en débarrasser illicitement.

Quant aux peines autres que pécuniaires, elles ne sont concernées par le droit de la mer que pour les infractions graves et délibérées dans la mer territoriale. Dans tous les cas, les mêmes difficultés s'appliquent aux peines de prison — il faut que l'individu soit vraiment coupable et pas non pas seulement le bouc émissaire pour une décision qui avait été prise collectivement[210].

En matière de pollution accidentelle, la punition criminelle des responsables est plus difficile à justifier. Les accidents sont, par nature, involontaires et tout ce qu'on peut reprocher aux responsables sont les faits qui ont causé la catastrophe et qui sont, généralement, multiples[211] et provoqués par des auteurs différents. Il paraît ainsi assez difficile de cibler la personne responsable pour un fait ou une omission, et ce sont les omissions dans la maintenance du bateau ou le non-respect des normes de sécurité qui devraient être reprochés aux responsables et non pas la pollution comme telle[212]. Malheureusement, la poursuite criminelle des accidents maritimes dans la plupart des Etats côtiers dépend beaucoup des dommages qui ont été causés, et moins de la gravité des faits ou des omissions concernant la sûreté maritime[213]. De telles infractions ne sont jamais poursuivies au pénal tant qu'elles ne causent pas d'accident, tandis que l'équipage et le capitaine d'un navire naufragé

208. Udell, *op. cit. supra* note 75, p. 276.
209. Gullo, *op. cit. supra* note 121, p. 129.
210. Anthony, *op. cit. supra* note 89, p. 240.
211. Gold, *op. cit. supra* note 205, p. 412; Murray, *op. cit. supra* note 174, p. 152.
212. Uhlmann, *op. cit. supra* note 129, pp. 1420 et 1454.
213. *Ibid.*, p. 1443, faisant allusion à des études menées aux Etats-Unis.

risquent d'être poursuivis pour le seul fait de pollution. Que MARPOL exclue les pollutions accidentelles de son champ d'application et cède la place à d'autres règles et normes internationales devrait être un signe clair de la difficulté de pénaliser les avaries.

Contrairement aux pollutions volontaires, les accidents ne bénéficient à personne. Il n'y a là aucun avantage économique pour les responsables, avantage qu'il faudrait leur ôter. Si leur comportement leur a donné des avantages financiers, ces profits sont liés au non-respect des standards techniques et des normes de sûreté maritime, commis de façon délibérée, et c'est pour l'infraction de ces normes qu'ils devraient être punis.

ii) *La valeur dissuasive*

La dissuasion des contrevenants potentiels est certainement un but du droit pénal, mais déclarer que des peines plus sévères mènent automatiquement à une diminution de la pollution est discutable[214]. Premièrement, il paraît clair que les peines n'ont de valeur dissuasive que si elles sont mises en œuvre avec un certain degré de certitude, ce qui présuppose des contrôles très minutieux et une surveillance étendue. Les observations des autorités françaises dans la nouvelle zone de protection écologique (ZPE) en Méditerranée indiquent une diminution des constats de pollution[215], tandis que dans les zones où il y a de graves problèmes de compétence et où la poursuite devient improbable, comme le canal de Corse, les pollutions ne cessent pas[216]. Ainsi, plus de contrôles et une coopération plus étroite des autorités étatiques pourraient peut-être aider à décourager les délits de pollution sans qu'il ne soit nécessaire d'aggraver les peines.

Deuxièmement, pour que les dispositions pénales puissent avoir une valeur dissuasive, il faut absolument que les normes soient certaines, et qu'il soit possible de prévoir si un acte représente une pollution répréhensible. Dans le domaine des pollutions délibérées, la convention MARPOL énonce clairement l'équipement nécessaire et les exceptions à la règle absolue de l'interdiction de la pollution. Malheureusement, il n'en est pas de même dans le domaine des accidents. Il y a de graves incertitudes quant au caractère pénal d'un comportement donné et il semble que beaucoup d'autorités nationales se soient contentées de constater qu'il y avait des omissions dans la maintenance du bateau afin de poursuivre le

---

214. Voir Roland Hefendehl, « Europäischer Umweltschutz: Demokratiespritze für Europa oder Brüsseler Putsch ? », 2006, *Zeitschrift für Internationale Strafrechtsdogmatik*, pp. 161 et 166, qui exprime de sérieux doutes.
215. Velut, *op. cit. supra* note 135, p. 519.
216. *Ibid.*

capitaine ou l'ingénieur en chef, tenus responsables du navire comme un tout. Ainsi, la poursuite des accidents ne peut pas manifestement décourager des comportements qui mènent à des accidents.

L'instrumentalisation de MARPOL afin de pénaliser la pollution involontaire porte atteinte à la sécurité juridique et paraît gravement injuste pour les équipages et capitaines, menacés de procédures pénales devant une cour à l'étranger. Afin de vraiment remédier aux dommages causés, il semble que le droit civil est beaucoup mieux placé pour compenser les dommages que des peines pécuniaires versées à des tiers.

SECTION 4 **CONCLUSION**

Le droit pénal est un moyen beaucoup plus compliqué pour réglementer la pollution marine qu'il n'y paraît. Premièrement, il se heurte à des limites importantes dans le droit de la mer et la portée des normes internationales décisives n'est établie que pour les pollutions délibérées. Deuxièmement, la mise en application des normes est coûteuse et difficile et une investigation sommaire risque de porter atteinte aux droits des accusés. Il est ainsi surprenant que les Etats côtiers prêtent tant d'attention à la poursuite criminelle des actes de pollution en mer et favorisent le droit pénal par rapport à d'autres moyens comme les sanctions civiles ou le droit administratif afin de lutter contre la pollution marine.

En matière de pollution accidentelle, le droit pénal est souvent utilisé afin de démontrer une volonté générale de cibler les responsables, en tenant compte non pas des causes des accidents mais de leurs conséquences graves. Ce développement paraît assez inquiétant, notamment dans la mesure où beaucoup de législations nationales dépassent les limites posées par le droit de la mer, en ce qui concerne les dispositions matérielles tout comme les dispositions procédurales et surtout dans le domaine des sanctions. Il faut reconnaître les conséquences catastrophiques des accidents maritimes graves, qui ne sont parfois que très sommairement soulagées par les régimes de responsabilité civile, et les craintes et la colère de la population littorale face à des marées noires répétées. Il faut sensibiliser les responsables du transport maritime à l'importance des règles et des normes relatives à la sûreté maritime et les punir pour leur non-respect, et cette approche doit être également adoptée dans les cas où les faits ou les omissions n'ont pas encore eu de conséquences dramatiques.

L'objectif de la protection de l'environnement marin serait beaucoup mieux servi si les Etats procédaient à une meilleure coopération des services de surveillance et de contrôle dans les ports, sans aggraver nécessairement les peines déjà prévues. Il paraît aussi possible de récompenser les propriétaires par des bénéfices financiers pour leur gestion responsable des navires[217]. Il serait néanmoins souhaitable d'unifier les niveaux des sanctions pécuniaires afin d'éviter que les équipages des navires se livrent consciemment à la pollution dans des juridictions plus laxistes. Pour les infractions délibérées, répétées ou non, la poursuite criminelle telle que prévue dans la convention MARPOL est certainement une réponse appropriée, mais on ne peut que rappeler aux Etats qu'ils ne doivent pas sortir du cadre de leur propre procédure pénale et qu'ils ne doivent pas adapter leurs standards des droits de l'accusé aux particularités des enquêtes en mer.

217. Capaldo, *op. cit. supra* note 137, pp. 56 ss., énonce le concept du «Green Award Flag», concours organisé par le Ministère du transport néerlandais.

4 Illegal Fishing as a Criminal Act at Sea

Gabriela A. Oanta *

SECTION 1 INTRODUCTION[1]

Nowadays, nobody questions the fact that illegal fishing, as part of Illegal, Unreported and Unregulated (IUU) fishing, constitutes one of the most serious threats for the public order of the oceans. Its consequences are extremely damaging and encompass a broad range of very varied sectors. Indeed, illegal fishing represents not merely an environmental problem, failing as it does to respect the rules on conservation and management of living marine resources. This type of fishing also entails significant economic consequences worldwide, leading to the impoverishment both of those operators who do respect the marine environment, whose profits are harmed by the criminal activities of illegal fishing[2], and of local traditional fishing communities, and even of coastal States. Moreover, illegal fishing diminishes the ability of millions of people who depend on the state of marine resources to feed themselves. We must not overlook the fact that the seas make up 90 per cent of the habitat of life on Earth, and that over 140 countries are carrying on some kind of activity related to marine fishing.

These illegal fishing activities are taking place at a moment when the world's fishing stocks are rapidly diminishing, as reported by the Food

* PhD Lecturer in Public International Law and International Relations, and Academic Coordinator of the "University Master in Law: European Union Studies" at the University of A Coruña (Spain). Bachelor of Art in Law in Bucharest (Romania) and LL.M and PhD from A Coruña (Spain).

1. This research has been carried out with the support of the Hague Academy of International Law, "Campus do Mar" Centre of International Excellence Mobility Scholarship (University of Vigo, Spain) and also within the research project "The United Nations Convention for the Law of the Sea Face to the Challenges in the International Society: Proposals for Development and Revision" (DER2010-21732) financed by the Ministry of Science and Innovation from Spain for the period 1 January 2011-31 December 2013. E-mail: gabriela.oanta@udc.es.

2. For an analysis of the significant losses caused by illegal fishing worldwide, see D. J. Agnew, J. Pearce, G. Pramod, T. Peatman, R. Watson, J. R. Beddington and T. J. Pitcher, "Estimating the Worldwide Extent of Illegal Fishing", *Plos One*, 4 (2009), No. 2, pp. 1-8.

and Agriculture Organization of the United Nations (FAO), which estimates that, currently, 85 per cent of the world's fishing stocks are either over-exploited, exhausted or recovering from depletion, while just 3 per cent are under-exploited and 12 per cent moderately exploited. Nevertheless, in the case of the ten most fished species in the world, representing 30 per cent of global fishing catches, the data are even more worrisome: most of these fish stocks are fully exploited[3]. But this situation does not come as surprise; bearing in mind that the world's fishing fleet is up to 250 per cent larger than is needed for sustainable fishing practices[4].

Illegal fishing, as part of IUU fishing, is primarily responsible for this difficult situation that the seas currently face[5]. It is not known exactly how much fish is caught in this way; there is merely data indicating that it makes up a significant percentage of the total volume of fish caught annually. Certain data, such as those used by FAO, the Organisation for Economic Co-operation and Development (OECD) and the European Union, reveal that IUU fishing constitutes between 15 per cent and 30 per cent of the total volume of annual fishing catches worldwide. This would mean that between 11 and 26 million tonnes of fishery products caught annually are the result of IUU fishing.

The economic agents involved in these fishing activities pursue them in fishing areas where it is difficult to carry out thorough checks (for example, remote high seas areas), or where the capacities of the national authorities are not enough to deter them, especially in maritime waters of developing countries. It is first and foremost these countries that have to pay a price too high, due to the devastating consequences of IUU fishing on their fisheries. Thus, in the Exclusive Economic Zones (EEZs) of West African countries, where abundant fishing stocks are to be found, it is estimated, for example, that 40 per cent more is caught than is actually registered officially[6]. It must be added that these catches

---

3. Data available in "The State of World Fisheries and Aquaculture 2010", FAO, Rome, 2010, p. 8; "The State of World Fisheries and Aquaculture 2012", FAO, Rome, 2012, p. 13.

4. In this regard, see H. Tuerk, "The Waning Freedom of the Seas", in R. Casado Raigon and G. Cataldi (eds.), *L'évolution et l'état actuel du droit international de la mer. Mélanges de droit de la mer offerts à Daniel Vignes*, Bruylant, Brussels, 2009, pp. 933-934.

5. For an analysis of the disastrous consequences of illegal fishing on marine resources, see H. N. Scheiber, "Economic Uses of the Oceans and the Impacts on Marine Environments: Past Trends and Challenges Ahead", in D. Vidas and P. J. Schei (eds.), *The World Ocean in Globalisation: Climate Change, Sustainable Fisheries, Biodiversity, Shipping, Regional Issues*, Martinus Nijhoff Publishers, Leiden/Boston, 2011, pp. 82-85.

6. Data available in "Policy Brief — Illegal, Unreported and Unregulated Fishing", *MRAG*, 8 (2009), p. 1; "Record of the 1st Meeting of the Stop Illegal

are mixed together with those made legally, making it even harder to trace these activities[7].

The proliferation of illegal fishing activities can be largely explained by the dynamics of international fishing relations. The transformations in the fishing world, above all from the second half of the twentieth century on, have not been halted by the signing of the United Nations Convention on the Law of the Sea in 1982 (UNCLOS)[8]. The problems posed by this type of fishing go beyond the provisions of this *Magna Carta of the Sea* regarding the international fishing regime.

Also, the dynamics of international fishing relations brings into question some of the institutions and mechanisms provided for in this Convention.

At the same time, this very practice does no more than develop new patterns of illegal fishing. Amongst them, suffice it to mention: fishing without a licence, fishing out of season, using forbidden fishing gear, failure to respect fishing quotas. It is by these means that those who practise this kind of fishing are attempting to avoid detection. Often, they fish in areas where monitoring, control and surveillance are insufficient.

This entails that a part of fishing is carried out by vessels registered in the coastal States themselves, especially in the form of captures undeclared or declared in an unsatisfactory way, and, also, that foreign fishing vessels act without the permission of the coastal State, that is,

---

Fishing Working Group. Gaborone, Botswana 11-12 March 2010", *Stop Illegal Fishing*; available at http://www.stopillegalfishing.com. See also T. M; Ndiaye, "Illegal, Unreported and Unregulated Fishing: Responses in General and West Africa", *Chinese Journal of International Law*, 10 (2011), No. 2, pp. 374-378.

7. For example, this holds true in the waters under Guinean sovereignty or jurisdiction where illegal fishing has been pursued for several years. This is an area where there is practically no control over fishing activities, due, basically, to the lack of economic resources. Thus, it is reckoned that over the period 2009-2010, there were approximately 1,300 illegal fishing boats in the area, of which only 58 were arrested. The loss for Guinea is estimated up to $100 million per annum. See in this regard T. M. Ndiaye, "Illegal, Unreported and . . .", *op. cit.*, pp. 376-377. Other States from the same geographical area, such as Nigeria or Ghana, also are very affected by illegal fishing. In this regard, see A. Eyiwunmi Falaye, "Illegal Unreported Unregulated (IUU) Fishing in West Africa (Nigeria & Ghana)", Marine Resources Assessment Group Ltd. (MRAG), London, January 2008.

8. See amongst others L. Caflisch, "La Convention des Nations Unies sur le droit de la mer adoptée le 30 avril 1982", *Schweizerisches Jahrbuch für internationales Recht*, 39 (1983), pp. 39-104; J. A. De Yturriga Barberán, *Ámbitos de soberanía en la Convención de las Naciones Unidas sobre el Derecho del mar: una perspectiva española*, Ministerio de Asuntos Exteriores (Secretaría General Técnica), Madrid, 1993; L.-A. Duvic-Paoli, *La Convention des Nations Unies sur le droit de la mer: instruments de régulation des relations internationales par le droit*, Harmattan, Paris, 2012.

engaging in unauthorized fishing, or fishing activities which violate the conditions of access set by the coastal State[9].

On the other hand, it must be said that such criminal fishing activities, unforeseen by UNCLOS, are not subject to any national or international legal regulation, or at least they have not been until recently. This has enabled a large number of vessels to devote their activity to illegal fishing. The diversity of these marine activities as well as the very provisions contained in UNCLOS relating to the flag State and the coastal State, the port State, and, in particular, those relating to fishing, should make us reflect on the complex legal framework currently in force regarding fishing. It is as if the international community were attempting to combat illegal fishing without being aware, or wishing to be aware, that, at present, there is no international authority with powers of control and police of fishing as a whole. It seems also as forgetting that most of this type of fishing is carried out on high seas or in EEZs of failed States or States which do not have sufficient means to deal with the marine fishing stocks found in waters under their sovereignty or jurisdiction.

Evidently, a real turning point in this matter was the adoption, in the year 2001, of FAO's International Plan of Action to prevent, deter and eliminate Illegal, Unreported and Unregulated Fishing (IPOA-IUU). It actually comprises the *ratione materiae* scope of illegal fishing activities. While it lacks any binding effect as such, its provisions have been adopted in several legal texts drawn up at both regional (by the Regional Fisheries Management Organizations and the European Union) and national levels.

This legal framework has progressed significantly with the Agreement on Port State Measures to Prevent, Deter and Eliminate Illegal, Unreported and Unregulated Fishing, adopted on 22 November 2009 within the FAO framework (2009 Agreement on Port State Measures). This Agreement once come into force, will be the first legally binding text, of international scope, and specific to the area of the fight against illegal fishing. Its primary aim is to prevent illegally obtained fishing catches from entering the markets along and across the world by way of a myriad of existing ports. Suffice it to say, for example, that under this Agreement, foreign fishing vessels wishing to enter a port must previously have applied for an entry permit. In this sense, port States will regularly inspect, those fishing vessels that fail to comply with regulations will be denied access to use port facilities or certain port services, and database will be set up that can be shared by all interested parties.

9. "Stopping Illegal, Unreported and Unregulated (IUU) Fishing", FAO, Rome, 2002, p. 3; M. H. Nordquist *et al.* (ed.), *United Nations Convention on the Law of the Sea 1982. A Commentary*, Vols. I-VI, Center for Oceans Law and Policy, Martinus Nijhoff Publishers, Dordrecht/Boston/London.

It is a trite knowledge that illegal fishing is a global phenomenon. It is found in all seas, and currently it constitutes one of the greatest challenges to the existing international fisheries law. Thus, it is a widespread and complex phenomenon in which a large number of actors and situations take part. This makes its prevention and eradication more difficult. As it has been stressed many times, an effective fight against illegal fishing must tackle not only fishing activities themselves, but also operations taking place before and after the act of fishing itself. Such operations could be: ranging from the organizational details of the ship's ownership, registration and obtaining a flag, the activities strictly related to fishing, including supply at sea and transfer of fish, the transfer of fish to specially prepared reefers or to cargo ships, their arrival at ports, the fish landing, the transhipment of fish, its processing and its marketing in the State or in the States of final destination [10]. On the other hand, the legal instruments to combat these illegal activities are found not only in international law of the sea. This is also due to the fact that the recipient States of the respective regulations are not exclusively the traditional States concerned (flag, coastal and port States), but also the market State and the State of nationality of the fishing crews.

In recent years, this complex situation has also been recognized by various international organizations. Moreover, it is evident that as the international community has begun to work on the prevention and suppression of illegal fishing, the criminal networks involved in this type of fishing have changed their *modus operandi*, to the extent that they have become integrated in transnational organized criminal networks. This is in accordance with what the United Nations Secretary-General stated when he warned, in his Annual Report on "Oceans and the Law of the Sea" (10 March 2008), that illegal fishing "has also been associated with organized crime and other illicit activities" [11]. This new scenario has

10. On the various phases of the chain of illegal fishing operations, see D. G. M., Miller, "Occupying the High Ground: Technology and the War on IUU Fishing", in D. Vidas (ed.), *Law, Technology and Science for Oceans in Globalization. IUU Fishing, Oil Pollution, Bioprospecting, Outer Continental Shelf*, Martinus Nijhoff Publishers, Leiden/Boston, 2010, pp. 82-87; D. Vidas, "IUU Fishing or IUU Operations? Some Observations on Diagnosis and Current Treatment", in D. D. Caron and H. N. Scheiber (eds.), *Bringing New Law to Ocean Waters*, Martinus Nijhoff Publishers, Leiden/Boston, 2010, pp. 127-130.

11. Such as, for example, activities aimed at avoiding detection, bribery, corruption, and armed resistance to operations of surveillance and deterrence. See "Oceans and the Law of the Sea. Report of the Secretary-General", A/63/63, 10.3.2008, point 100, p. 30. Also see "Closing the Net: Stopping Illegal Fishing on the High Seas", 2006, available at www.high-seas.org; J. Swan, "Ocean and Fisheries Law: Port State Measures to Combat IUU Fishing: International and Regional Developments", *Sustainable Development Law and Policy*, 38 (2006) No. 7, p. 38.

been acknowledged by the United Nations Office on Drugs and Crime, too, in its report presented in Vienna in 2011, "Transnational Organized Crime in the Fishing Industry"[12]. It has been reiterated also by the European Parliament and INTERPOL.

Besides the international regulations, both of *hard law* and *soft law,* that set out the rights, duties and responsibilities of the States involved in the prevention and suppression of illegal fishing (flag State, coastal State, port State, market State and the State of the nationality of the fishing crews involved in illegal fishing), there is also a series of provisions concerning the competences of these States to apply these rules. These provisions reflect the common principles governing the assertion of jurisdiction in the international law of the sea[13].

The present chapter will be divided further into three main sections: in Section 2, we will address the issue of what is understood by "IUU fishing" and how far illegal as part of IUU fishing constitutes a criminal activity at sea. We will devote Section 3 to a study of the normative framework currently existing in this field. And in Section 4 we address the enforcement jurisdiction of States over the prevention and suppression of illegal fishing.

SECTION 2 **DEFINITION OF ILLEGAL FISHING AS A CRIMINAL ACT AT SEA**

The inclusion of illegal fishing in the international agenda is, to a great extent, due to the initiatives of the Regional Fisheries Management Organizations (RFMOs). In 1997, illegal fishing was included in the seventh session of the Standing Commission on Observation and Inspection of the Canberra Convention on the Conservation of Antarctic Marine Living Resources (CCAMLR) in relation with the stocks of deep-sea cod[14]. Henceforth, this type of fishing was

12. "Transnational Organized Crime in the Fishing Industry", United Nations Office on Drugs and Crime, Vienna, 2011.

13. B. Simma and A. T. Müller, "Exercise and Limits of Jurisdiction", in J. Crawford and M. Koskenniemi (eds.), *The Cambridge Companion to International Law*, Cambridge University Press, Cambridge, 2012, pp. 134-157.

14. In this regard, see G. Andreone, "Illegal, Unreported, Unregulated Fishing", in G. Tamburelli (ed.), *The Antarctic Legal System and Environmental Issues*, Istituto di Studi Giuridici Internazionali, Giuffrè Editore, Milan, 2006, pp. 121-123. For an analysis of the international evolution of IUU fishing, see K. Bray, "Illegal, Unreported and Unregulated Fishing", in M. H. Nordquist and J. N. Moore (eds.), *Current Fisheries Issues and the Food and Agriculture Organization of the United States*, Martinus Nijhoff Publishers, The Hague, 2000, pp. 115-135; J. M. Sobrino Heredia and A. Rey Aneiros, "Plan de Acción Internacional para prevenir, desalentar y eliminar la pesca ilegal, no declarada y no reglamentada", *Revista Española de Derecho Internacional*, LIV (2002), No. 1, pp. 481-487.

regulated by these RFMOs. At the same time, FAO has discussed many of the measures at successive meetings of its Committee on Fisheries (COFI), while later they have been provided for in different international legal instruments.

For its part, from 1999 onwards, the United Nations General Assembly has given serious consideration to the issue of illegal fishing in frequent resolutions, stressing how it has turned into "a serious threat to fish stocks and marine habitats and ecosystems, to the detriment of sustainable fisheries as well as the food security and the economies of many States, particularly developing States" [15]. And in its latest resolutions, it has paid particular attention to marine issues.

On the other hand, specific reference must be made to the IPOA-IUU, adopted in 2001. Its purpose is to assist FAO Members and other interested parties to become familiar with the legal tools already in force in this matter [16], and also to propose which of these it was appropriate to use in each case, as well as to offer a range of alternative solutions in order to apply them in the struggle against illegal fishing [17]. In the opinion of the author, one of its main achievements is certainly the consensus regarding the meaning of "illegal, unreported and unregulated fishing". Nevertheless, as it has been noted by Judge Treves [18], this conceptual definition, apart from shedding some light on the range of meaning of each of its elements, is not very relevant in practice, as the three types of criminal fishing tend to act in conjunction. These definitions try to include all the possible manifestations of this type of criminal act;

15. Resolution adopted by the General Assembly "Sustainable fisheries, including through the 1995 Agreement for the Implementation of the Provisions of the United Nations Convention on the Law of the Sea of 10 December 1982 relating to the Conservation and Management of Straddling Fish Stocks and Highly Migratory Fish Stocks, and related instruments", A/RES/66/68, 28.3.2012. See, above all, Preamble and points 43-60.

16. See *inter alia* the 1995 Agreement for the Implementation of the Provisions of the United Nations Convention on the Law of the Sea of 10 December 1982 relating to the Conservation and Management of Straddling Fish Stocks and Highly Migratory Fish Stocks; the 1993 Agreement to Promote Compliance with International Conservation and Management Measures by Fishing Vessels on the High Seas; the 1995 Code of Conduct for Responsible Fisheries; and the Agreements adopted in the Cancun Declaration of 1992, the Rio Declaration on Environment and Development, also of 1992, in particular Agenda 21, Chapter 17, and other international statements and instruments related to responsible fishery.

17. In this regard, see "Aplicación del Plan de Acción Internacional para prevenir, desalentar y eliminar la pesca ilegal, no declarada y no reglamentada", FAO, Rome, 2002, p. xiii.

18. T. Treves, "La pesca ilegal, no declarada y no reglamentada: Estado del pabellón, Estado costero y Estado del puerto", in J. Pueyo Losa and J. Jorge Urbina (eds.), *La cooperación internacional en la ordenación de los mares y océanos*, Iustel, Madrid, 2009, p. 138.

further, they have later been gathered together in other legal instruments adopted at international, regional and national level[19].

By virtue of paragraph 3.1 of IPOA-IUU, by *illegal fishing* it is understood all those fishing activities

> "3.1.1. conducted by national or foreign vessels in waters under the jurisdiction of a State, without the permission of that State, or in contravention of its laws and regulations;
>
> 3.1.2. conducted by vessels flying the flag of States that are partied to a relevant regional fisheries management organization but operate in contravention of the conservation and management measures adopted by that organization and by which the States are bound, or relevant provisions of the applicable international law; or
>
> 3.1.3. in violation of national laws or international obligations, including those undertaken by cooperating States to a relevant regional fisheries management organization".

In paragraph 3.2. of IPOA-IUU it stipulates that *unreported fishing* is made up of those fishing activities

> "3.2.1. which have not been reported, or have been misreported, to the relevant national authority, in contravention of national laws and regulations; or
>
> 3.2.2. undertaken in the area of competence of a relevant RFMO which have not been reported or have been misreported, in contravention of the reporting procedures of that organization".

Meanwhile, in paragraph 3.3. of IPOA-IUU, reference is made to *unregulated fishing*, which is constituted by those fishing activities performed

> "3.3.1. in the area of application of a relevant RFMO that are conducted by vessels without nationality, or by those flying a flag of a State not party to that organization, or by a fishing entity, in a manner that is not consistent with or contravenes the conservation and management measures of that organization; or
>
> 3.3.2. in areas or for fish stocks in relation to which there are no applicable conservation or management measures and where such fishing activities are conducted in a manner inconsistent with State

---

19. This is what has happened, for example, in the case of the 2009 Agreement on Port State Measures (see Article 1 *(e)*), and Council Regulation (EC) No. 1005/2008 of 29 September 2008, establishing a Community System to Prevent, Deter and Eliminate Illegal, Unreported and Unregulated Fishing, Amending Regulations (EEC) No. 2847/93, (EC) No. 1936/2001 and (EC) No. 601/2004 and Repealing Regulations (EC) No. 1093/94 and (EC) No. 1447/1999, *OJ* L 286, 29.10.2008, p. 1 (see Article 2).

responsibilities for the conservation of living marine resources under international law".

For present purposes, *illegal fishing* is understood as those activities performed by foreign persons or vessels, regardless of their flag, which contravene the fishing regulations of a coastal State in waters under its jurisdiction or which contravene fishing conservation and management measures established by an RFMO on the high seas; by *unreported fishing,* it is understood those activities that go unreported or are reported misleadingly to the competent national authority or the relevant RFMO; and by *unregulated fishing* it is understood those activities performed either by vessels without nationality or flying the flag of a State which is not part of a certain RFMO, contravening the conservation and management measures of the said Organization, or in a manner incompatible with the responsibility of the State established by international law in relation to the conservation of living fishing resources.

Likewise, it should be stressed that not all forms of IUU fishing can be designated as criminal acts at sea and nor does every form of criminal act fall under the heading of illegal fishing, according to the definition of IUU fishing[20]. Paragraph 3 (4) of IPOA-IUU leaves open the door to the possibility that "certain unregulated fishing may take place in a manner which is not in violation of applicable international law". That is to say, unregulated fishing may be considered a criminal act if, and only if, it is proven that it has been in violation of general international law[21]. Inevitably, if the fishing is carried out on the high seas where an RFMO has competences of conservation and management, those States which are not members of this Organization will be performing unregulated fishing according to the provisions of IPOA-IUU. Such fishing will also be illegal in the case of a violation of international law, if the conservation measures adopted by the State concerned are identical to those applicable by the RFMO in question[22].

It is worth pointing out in this regard that only the minority of the international doctrine[23] argues that unregulated fishing should also be

20. See "Informe sobre la adaptación del Ordenamiento jurídico español a las nuevas exigencias internacionales y de Derecho comunitario europeo relacionadas con la lucha contra la pesca ilegal, no declarada y no reglamentada (pesca INDNR)", Consejo de Estado de España, No. E 2/2007, July 2009, p. 43.

21. It has thus been indicated, also, by a part of the doctrine: G. Andreone, *op. cit.*, pp. 125-126; T. Treves, "La pesca ilegal, no . . .", *op. cit,*, p. 138.

22. This is a hypothesis suggested by authors like Prof. Gemma Andreone. See G. Andreone, *op. cit.*, p. 126.

23. See R. Rayfuse, "Non-Flag State Enforcement and Protection of the Marine Environment: Responding to IUU Fishing", in M. H. Nordquist, T. T. B. Koh and J. N. Moore (eds.), *Freedom of Seas, Passage Rights and the 1982 Law of the Sea Convention*, Martinus Nijhoff Publishers, Leiden/Boston, 2009, p. 582.

considered illegal, due to the fact that the rules governing the conservation and management of living marine resources on the high seas are binding and, thus, have *erga omnes* obligations. Accordingly, regulations governing the conservation of fishing stocks adopted by a RFMO would be, likewise, binding on all the States which are not parties to the said Organization, under Articles 117[24] and 118[25] of UNCLOS. Undoubtedly, this is not free of controversy. It is the view of the present author that the regulations of an RFMO cannot really constitute conventional obligations for all the States in the international community, since by virtue of the well-known principle of the relative effect of treaties *(res inter alios acta)*, such a rule can create neither obligations nor rights for a third party State without its consent.

SECTION 3 INTERNATIONAL LEGAL FRAMEWORK FOR THE PREVENTION AND SUPPRESSION OF ILLEGAL FISHING

The international community, RFMOs, the European Union and States have embarked on a series of initiatives to address the problem of illegal fishing. The first fruits have been borne in the spirit rather than in the letter of UNCLOS. But it has been chiefly since the 1990s when the greatest regulatory effort has been made in this matter, above all in the FAO framework. To this end, efforts have been made to complement the UNCLOS provisions; strengthen the regime established in the field of fisheries; clarify the field of application of co-operation between States in the case of shared, straddling and migratory fish stocks; and regulate the management of fisheries on the high seas, including the regime of monitoring, control and surveillance applicable[26].

---

24. Article 117, UNCLOS, refers to the duty of the States to adopt measures for the conservation of living resources of the high seas in relation to their own nationals:

> "All States have the duty to take, or to cooperate with other States in taking, such measures for their respective nationals as may be necessary for the conservation of the living resources of the high seas."

25. Under Article 118, UNCLOS, the States bear an obligation of conduct, which is to co-operate in the conservation and management of living resources:

> "States shall cooperate with each other in the conservation and management of living resources in the areas of the high seas. States whose nationals exploit identical living resources, or different living resources in the same area, shall enter into negotiations with a view to taking the measures necessary for the conservation of the living resources concerned. They shall, as appropriate, cooperate to establish subregional or regional fisheries organizations to this end."

26. In this regard, see D. M. Sodik, "Post-LOSC Legal Instruments . . .", *op. cit.*, pp. 71-72.

Indeed, at present, there are different legal instruments which, depending on their nature and scope, can be divided into two major groups: binding (para. 1) and non-binding (para. 2). In the following paragraphs of the present chapter, we will focus on the survey of the current international legal action for the prevention and suppression of illegal fishing. Particular emphasis will be placed upon the rights, obligations and responsibilities belonging to the different States which may intervene at certain stages of the chain of criminal fishing — that is to say, the flag State, the coastal State, the port State, the market State, and the State of nationality of those fishermen involved in illegal fishing.

Paragraph 1 **Binding International Instruments for the Prevention and Suppression of Illegal Fishing**

The current international legal framework governing the phenomenon of illegal fishing is made up of three international treaties, namely: UNCLOS, the 1993 FAO Agreement to Promote Compliance with International Conservation and Management Measures by Vessels Fishing on the High Seas (commonly known as the 1993 FAO Compliance Agreement); and the 1995 Agreement for the Implementation of the Provisions of the United Nations Convention on the Law of the Sea of 10 December 1982 relating to the Conservation and Management of Straddling Fish Stocks and Highly Migratory Fish Stocks (commonly known as the 1995 New York Agreement).

The Montego Bay Convention contains provisions relating to fisheries in the different marine areas. These provisions attempt to strike a balance among the interest of navigation, the interest for the conservation, management and exploitation of resources, and the interest in protecting the marine ecosystem. Hence, it is considered that in the first of these cases, protection has to be afforded by the flag State, in the second by the coastal State, while, in the third, responsibility would fall either on the coastal State in marine areas under its sovereignty or jurisdiction, or on the flag State in the other marine areas of interest for fisheries[27].

Meanwhile, the remaining two binding legal instruments seek to complement UNCLOS, as far as fishing and the responsibilities of the flag States of fishing vessels are concerned. In fact, the 1993 Compliance Agreement, which has been in force since 24 April 2003, and to which

27. In this regard, see T. Treves, "Jurisdiction over Vessels in the Areas of Pollution and Fisheries: General Report", in E. Franckx and P. Gautier (eds.), *The Exercise of Jurisdiction over Vessels: New Developments in the Fields of Pollution, Fisheries, Crimes at Sea and Trafficking of Weapons of Mass Destruction*, Bruylant, Brussels, 2010, pp. 9-10.

38 countries and the European Union are parties[28], defines and gives substance to the responsibility of the flag State of a vessel engaging in fishing on the high seas, paying special attention to the question of flags of convenience. The 1995 New York Agreement, which came into force on 11 December 2001 and currently includes 77 countries plus the European Union as parties[29], aims to develop, define and reinforce the obligations of States to co-operate in order to conserve and manage fishing on the high seas, but only as far as straddling and highly migratory fish stocks are concerned. This has been explicit in the context of the RFMOs, introducing, broadly speaking, a new regime in the field of access to resources and control. This situation draws attention to the unsatisfactory reality of the problems caused by the practice of flags of convenience.

A. The role of the coastal State

Under Article 21 (1) *(d)* and *(e)* of UNCLOS, the coastal State has legal competence in its territorial waters for "the conservation of the living resources of the sea", as well as for "the prevention of infringement of the fisheries laws and regulations". And in the EEZs, the coastal State enjoys "sovereign rights for the purpose

28. This treaty was adopted by the FAO via Resolution 15/93 of the 27th session of the FAO Conference, held in November 1993, and began to form an integral part of the FAO Code of Conduct on Responsible Fisheries at the same time it was adopted by this international organization in 1995. See G. Moore, "The FAO Compliance Agreement", in M. H. Nordquist and J. Norton Moore (eds.), *Current Fisheries Issues and the Food and Agriculture Organization of the United Nations*, Martinus Nijhoff Publishers, The Hague, 2000, pp. 77-91; D. M. Warner-Kramer and K. Canty, "Stateless Fishing Vessels: The Current International Regime and a New Approach", *Ocean and Coastal Law Journal*, 5 (2000), No. 2, p. 232.

29. The 1995 New York Agreement was signed on 8 September 1995 (UN doc. A/CONF.164/37) and came into force on 11 December 2001, and, as had been scheduled in its articles, has been the subject of two international amendment conferences: (1) 22-26 May 2006; (2) 24-28 May 2010. See, amongst others D. Freestone, "Implementing the Law of the Sea Convention, the FAO Compliance Agreement and the UN Fish Stocks Agreement: A View from the World Bank", in M. H. Nordquist and J. Norton Moore (eds.), *Current Fisheries Issues and the Food and Agriculture Organization of the United Nations*, Martinus Nijhoff Publishers, The Hague, 2000, pp. 167-182; B. Kunoy, "Conservation and Management of Shared Fish Stocks and the Applicable International Trade Regime", *German Yearbook of International Law*, 54 (2011), pp. 421-458; E. J. Molenaar, "Non-Participation in the Fish Stocks Agreement: Status and Reasons", *International Journal of Marine and Coastal Law*, 26 (2011), pp. 195-234; G. Vigneron, "Compliance and International Environmental Agreements: A Case Study of the 1995 United Nations Straddling Fish Stocks Agreement", *Georgetown International Environmental Law Review*, 10 (1998) No. 2, pp. 581-623.

of exploring and exploiting, conserving and managing the natural resources, whether living or non-living, of the waters superjacent to the seabed". But these States must take into account the rights and obligations of other States provided for by UNCLOS. It must be stressed that Article 58, UNCLOS, ensures freedom of navigation for all States, whether coastal or landlocked, although Articles 88-115 of this Convention regarding high seas will be applied insofar as they are not incompatible with the provisions relating to the EEZ.

The position of the coastal States in respect of fisheries is strengthened by the provisions of Article 297 (2) *(a)* and (3) *(a)* of UNCLOS, by which the coastal State "shall not be obliged to accept the submission to such settlement" in Part XV

> "relating to its sovereign rights with respect to the living resources in the exclusive economic zone or their exercise, including its discretionary powers for determining the allowable catch, its harvesting capacity, the allocation of surpluses to other States and the terms and conditions established in its conservation and management laws and regulations"[30].

It is true that even though the coastal States have the same competences when dealing with illegal fishing, not all of them have the same capability to address this problem. Therefore, in this context, a deep fracture exists as to the coastal States' role in the fight against illegal fishing. It must be recalled that more that 90 per cent of the world's fishing catches are in waters controlled by coastal States, that an important part of this fishing is carried out in these same waters, and that most of this fishing is performed by vessels registered in these same States. In other cases, foreign vessels fish without the coastal State's permission (that is, illegally) or transgress the conditions of access imposed by the coastal State. However, it is submitted that illegal fishing in these waters is not so much due to the absence of a legal framework to regulate these activities as to the lack of means on control and enforce this regulation by many countries, especially underdeveloped ones[31].

---

30. For a commentary of this matter, see T. Treves, "Jurisdiction over Vessels in . . .", *op. cit.*, p. 2.

31. Regarding this problem, certain proposals have been put forward which could contribute to the suppression of illegal fishing, among which are the following: the acceptance as an evidence in a court of the electronic information obtained by satellite monitoring systems; the introduction of a system of civil penalties (lower standards of proof, faster decision-making procedures); the indirect limitation of freedom of navigation, via the establishment of the obligation to inform of entry and exit; or the definition of certain transition zones as an exception, in these cases, to the principle of freedom of navigation in EEZs.

B. The role of the flag State

The premise on which any analysis of the position of flag States must be based, with regard to fisheries, is that current international regulations grant them wide-ranging competences on the high seas. In fact, these States enjoy both freedom of navigation (Articles 87 (1) *(a)* and 90 of UNCLOS) and freedom to fish on the high seas (Articles 87 (1) *(e)* and 116 of UNCLOS). And, at the same time, they have exclusive competence over administrative, technical and social matters regarding all fishing vessels flying their flag (Article 94 (1) of UNCLOS)[32].

But these competences are not unlimited. By virtue of Article 117, UNCLOS, the flag State is obliged "to take, or to cooperate with other States in taking such measures for their respective nationals as may be necessary for the conservation of the living resources of the high seas". This is a duty already provided for in the 1958 Geneva Convention on the High Seas (Article 1 (2))[33]. Its content coincides with that of Article 118, UNCLOS, according to which the flag State has the possibility to co-operate with the other States "in the conservation and management of living resources in the areas of high seas"[34], and even that of setting up "subregional or regional fisheries organizations to this end". With the passage of time, this co-operation has borne fruit in three different ways[35]: the first of them, via bilateral agreements between neighbouring States regarding joint management of the fish stocks they share[36]; secondly, the RFMOs set up within the FAO framework[37]; and thirdly, those RFMOs set up by means of an international treaty, but outside the FAO framework[38].

32. In this regard, see T. Treves, "La pesca ilegal . . .", *op. cit.*, p. 143.

33. "All States have the duty to adopt or to cooperate with other States in adopting such measures for their respective nationals as may be necessary for the conservation of the living resources of the high seas."

34. To this we might add Article 119, UNCLOS, dealing with the conservation of living resources on the high seas.

35. D. Freestone, "Fisheries, Commissions and Organizations", in R. Wolfrum (ed.), *The Max Planck Encyclopedia of Public International Law*, Vol. IV, Oxford University Press, Oxford, 2012, p. 59.

36. We are referring to two such organizations created by Canada and the United States, namely: the International Pacific Halibut Commission (IPHC) and the Pacific Salmon Commission (PSC).

37. For example, amongst others: the Indian Ocean Tuna Commission (IOTC), the General Fisheries Commission for the Mediterranean (GFCM), the Asia-Pacific Fisheries Commission (APFIC), the Regional Commission for Fisheries (RECOFI), the South West Indian Ocean Fisheries Commission (SWIOFC), and so on.

38. Suffice to mention now the following: North-East Atlantic Fisheries Commission (NEAFC), the Northwest Atlantic Fisheries Organization (NAFO), the South-East Atlantic Fisheries Organization (SEAFO), and so on.

These UNCLOS provisions were complemented some years later with the 1993 FAO Compliance Agreement and the 1995 New York Agreement.

Thus, the 1993 FAO Compliance Agreement, after it had established that its provisions would be applied "to all fishing vessels that are used or intended for fishing on the high seas" (Article II (1)), seeks to define and give substance to the responsibility for the flag State of a fishing vessel performing its activities on the high seas (Article III (I) *(a)*), when it lays down that

> "[e]ach Party shall take such measures as may be necessary to ensure that fishing vessels entitled to fly its flag do not engage in any activity that undermines the effectiveness of international conservation and management measures".

It is argued that this treaty pays also special attention to the problem of flags of convenience, when it stipulates that

> "[e]ach Party shall, for the purpose of this Agreement, maintain a record of fishing vessels entitled to fly its flag and authorized to be used for fishing on the high seas, and shall take such measures as may be necessary to ensure that all such fishing vessel are entered in that record" (Article IV).

For its part, the 1995 New York Agreement considers that this obligation borne by the States needs to be expressed especially by the conduct of the RFMOs, and broadly introduces a new regime with regard to access to resources and controls. Thus, in accordance with Article 8 (4), it is laid down that the only States that will enjoy access to fishery measures whose conservation and management are the responsibility of an RFMO are Member States of the RFMO in question, or those who are participants in it, or those who agree "to apply the conservation and management measures established by such organization or arrangement". Furthermore, by virtue of Article 8 (3), these States are under

> "the duty to cooperate by becoming members of such organization or participants in such arrangement, or by agreeing to apply the conservation and management measures established by such organization or arrangement. States having a real interest in the fisheries concerned may become members of such organization or participants in such arrangement".

This regime is completed by the provisions of Article 17 of the 1995 New York Agreement: in its first paragraph, it is laid down that the obligation to co-operate in this field exists also for non-members of an

RFMO[39]. And as for the control framework is concerned, Article 18 (1) of this Agreement stipulates that

> "[a] State whose vessels fish on the high seas shall take such measures as may be necessary to ensure that vessels flying its flag comply with subregional and regional conservation and management measures and that such vessels do not engage in any activity which undermines the effectiveness of such measures".

However, it is currently observed that certain States are in no condition to, or do not wish to, exercise an effective control over those fishing vessels flying their flag. It is beyond doubt that there is a dangerous, general correlation between illegal fishing and flags of convenience. According to the relevant rules of international law, the flag State is obliged to exercise "its jurisdiction effectively" over ships which fly its flag (Articles 92 (1) and 94 of UNCLOS, Article 18 of 1995 New York Agreement), in such a way that these vessels shall respect the sovereign rights of coastal States over those fisheries stocks in their EEZ, and shall comply with those obligations imposed on fishery on the high seas by international law, and, in some of their zones, by rules proceeding from the RFMOs. Also, it falls exclusively upon each State to determine the necessary prerequisites in order to grant its nationality to the vessels (1958 Geneva Convention on the High Seas, Article 5, and Article 91 (1), UNCLOS).

Nevertheless, it is very frequently observed that certain countries are in no condition to exercise jurisdiction effectively, as there is no real relationship between themselves and the vessels flying their flags, a *genuine link* (in Spanish, *relación auténtica*; in French, *lien substantiel*), as required by Article 91 (2), UNCLOS. This situation is encouraged by those countries which have adopted systems of open registers[40], favour-

39. For a detailed analysis of the role of the different RFMOs in relation with the management of fisheries on the high seas, see K. Bangert, "Fisheries Agreements", in R. Wolfrum (ed.), *The Max Planck Encyclopedia of Public International Law*, Vol. IV, Oxford University Press, Oxford, 2012, pp. 59-62; D. Freestone, "Fisheries, High Seas", in R. Wolfrum (ed.), *The Max Planck Encyclopedia of Public International Law*, Vol. IV, Oxford University Press, Oxford, 2012, pp. 71-73; D. Guilfoyle, *Shipping Interdiction and the Law of the Sea*, Cambridge University Press, Cambridge, 2009, pp. 116-160.

40. In our view, the issue of countries that practise open registers offers some very illustrative data on the complexity of activities at sea. For instance, Mongolia, the world's largest land-locked country, due to the fact that it adopted the system of open registers in 2003, currently has over 250 vessels flying its flag. This situation seems to be favoured by North Korea's decision to introduce very strict controls over vessels flying its flag, which encouraged Japan to decide to register its ships in Mongolia. See A. Syrigos, "Developments on the Interdiction of Vessels on the High Seas", in A. Strati, M. Gavouneli and N. Skourtos (eds.), *Unresolved Issues and New Challenges to the Law of the Sea: Time before and Time After*, Martinus Nijhoff Publishers, Leiden, 2006, p. 153.

ing the existence of numerous vessels which sail and engage in their fishing activities under flags of convenience[41], making most international provisions aimed at ensuring long-term conservation and sustainable use of fish stocks practically devoid of substance[42].

In short, it is clear from UNCLOS, the 1993 FAO Compliance Agreement[43] and the 1995 New York Agreement[44] that the flag State has a duty to exercise effective control over fishing vessels that fly its flag, as well as over any vessels that serve as auxiliaries to them, and ensure that the activities of such vessels do not lessen the effectiveness of conservation and management measures adopted in accordance with international law and approved at national, regional, sub-regional or global level. It is submitted that compliance with this duty would inevitably lead to the elimination of illegal fishing. However, it could hardly be complied with by a State which does not demand that the vessels having its nationality should have a real and effective link with it, keeping open registers and favouring flags of convenience. This scenario has led certain shipowners and operators to register their vessels in certain countries offering significant benefits, generally of a fiscal or administrative nature, or related to industrial relations[45]. But for the purpose of tacking this type of fishing, it is perhaps not so much that some States grant this type of

41. J. M. Sobrino Heredia, "Pabellones de conveniencia y pesca ilegal", in J. Branco De Sampaio, F. Mayor Zaragoza and M. Oreja Aguirre, *Soberanía del Estado y Derecho Internacional. Libro Homenaje al Prof. J. A. Carrillo Salcedo*, Universidad de Sevilla, Secretariado de Publicaciones [etc.], Seville, 2005, pp. 1331-1348.

42. A more thorough study of the issue of flags of convenience and their relationship with illegal fishing can be found in M. Gianni, "IUU Fishing and the Cost to Flag of Convenience Countries", in *Fish Piracy: Combating Illegal Unreported and Unregulated Fishing*, OECD, Paris, 2004, pp. 285-288; M. Gianni and W. Simpson, *How Flags of Convenience Provide Cover for Illegal, Unreported and Unregulated Fishing*, Australian Department of Agriculture, Fisheries and Forestry, International Transport Workers' Federation, and WWF International, 2005; D. Warner-Kramer, "Control Begins at Home: Tackling Flags of Convenience and IUU Fishing", *Golden Gate University Law Review*, 34 (2004) No. 3, pp. 497-529.

43. Article III. Flag State Responsibility.

44. Articles 21 and 22. The exclusive jurisdiction of the flag State on the high seas is enshrined in this treaty.

45. This has frequently produced a situation where economic benefits are obtained at the cost of the ship's safety, human lives, and exploitation, and has facilitated numerous cases of maritime fraud and tax evasion. For a wider analysis of these matters, see E. Andrews-Chouicha (ed.), *Pourquoi la pêche pirate perdure : les resorts économiques de la pêche illégale, non déclarée et non réglementée*, OCDE, Paris, 2005; P. Bender and G. Lugten, "Taxing Illegal Fishing: A Proposal for Using Taxation Law to Reduce Profiteering from IUU Fishing Offences", *International Journal of Marine and Coastal Law*, 22 (2007), No. 4, pp. 517-544; U. R. Sumaila, J. Alder and H. Keith, "Global Scope and Economics of Illegal Fishing", *Marine Policy*, 30 (2006), No. 6, pp. 696-703.

facilities as that, once flags are granted to ships, States should exercise their jurisdiction and a real effective control over them. At present, there are many fishing vessels that fly a *flag of non-compliance*, that is, of a State that, even though it may belong to an RFMO, and therefore its flag cannot be considered a flag of convenience, fails to comply with its duty regarding the control of the vessels flying its flag[46].

It is submitted that without a real and co-ordinated fight against the significant economic benefits provided by illegal fishing to certain participants in international fishing, it is hard to see how this global scourge can be eradicated. On the other hand, we believe that the genuine link could serve as a support in order to demand to the flag State to fulfil its duties in accordance with the international law regarding all ships flying its flag. This idea may be developed along three lines of reasoning in an attempt to reach an explanation of what a genuine link may mean from the perspective of the suppression of illegal fishing[47].

(i) *First argument (a non-formalistic solution)*

It is a truism that international law of the sea recognizes exclusive competences for each State in the question of granting nationality to a vessel, allowing it a great deal of freedom when determining the criteria which led it to grant the right to fly its flag[48]. In the light of UNCLOS and the jurisprudence of the International Tribunal for the Law of the Sea (ITLOS), the flag State is responsible for the damage caused by a vessel of its nationality. In this sense, Article 18 of the 1995 New York Agreement requires certain conduct from the flag States of vessels that sail the high seas[49]. Thus, otherwise, the absence of such conduct would allow us to deduce the existence of a purely formal relationship and the absence of an authentic one.

46. This is the case, for example, of Equatorial Guinea or Panama, which are members of the International Commission for the Conservation of Atlantic Tunas (ICCAT). The concept of "flags of non-compliance" was first used by the CCAMLR in 2002. See, for example, the Resolution (ROI/XXI) or the Conservation Measure 10-07 (2006), available at www.ccamlr.org.

47. For a deeper study of these three possible solutions in order to identify the genuine link, see J. M. Sobrino Heredia, "Pabellones de conveniencia . . .", *op. cit.*, pp. 1341-1345.

48. International jurisprudence speaks clearly in this respect; we could cite the example of the sentence of the Permanent Court of Arbitration, 8 August 1905, *Boutres de Mascate* case, RSA XI, p. 97. In this regard, see F. V. Wodié, "La haute mer", in M. Bedjaoui, *Droit international. Bilan et perspectives*, Vol. 2, Paris, 1991, pp. 952-953.

49. For example, the granting of fishing licences, the authorization, different controls and prohibition of fishing in certain areas, the national register of fishing vessels, systems of periodical reports from vessels, verification of catches of certain species, and so on.

From this point of view, it would be possible to argue that Article 5 of the 1958 Geneva Convention on High Seas and Article 91, UNCLOS, should be read in the light of the development of international law, in the sense that granting nationality to a vessel is conditional on the existence of a genuine relationship. This is an obligation that falls on the flag State and which must be complied with in good faith. It is an obligation that not only interests the flag State but all coastal States and the whole of the international community, precisely due to the risks of contamination and destruction of the marine ecosystem, which may be entailed by ships' navigation and the effects of their fishing activities on fishing resources (above all long-term conservation and the sustainable exploitation of fishing stocks). In this sense, it is not enough merely to comply with the administrative formalities of registration and licensing, but also that this genuine link should in fact exist. These would be two cumulative conditions, so that the other States could disregard the nationality of the vessel's flag State when non-compliance took place.

But also, the development of the international law of the sea sets out certain limits for the freedom of flag States, when it introduces the concept of *genuine link*. This concept incorporates the idea of effectiveness of the nationality, in the same line as the sentence given by the International Court of Justice on 6 April 1955, in the *Nottebohm* case, in the sense that requires an effective nationality as a condition for opposing third party States[50]. Besides, as ITLOS states in the *Saiga 2* case, Article 91, UNCLOS, attempts to ensure that flag States respect their obligations more effectively, not the establishment of criteria which might be invoked by other States in order to contest the validity of vessels' registration in a flag State[51].

(ii) *Second argument (a formalistic solution)*

The competence to grant a vessel the right to fly its flag, whether via registry or registration, is accorded exclusively to each State, as evident from Article 5 of the 1958 Geneva Convention on the High Seas and Article 91, UNCLOS. These provisions set forth that there must be a *genuine link* between the flag State and the vessels of its nationality. Besides, Article 94 (1) of the latter legal text adds that all States must exercise their jurisdiction and control over those vessels flying their flags in an effective way, in administrative, technical and social matters.

50. *Nottebohm*, *ICJ Reports 1955*. Amongst the doctrine referred to this case in relation with the Law of the Sea, R. D. Sloane, "Breaking the Genuine Link: The Contemporary International Legal Regulation of Nationality", *Harvard International Law Journal*, Vol. 50, No. 1, 2009, pp. 1-60.

51. *ITLOS Saiga 2 (Saint Vicent and the Grenadines* v. *Guinea)*, Case No. 2, 1 July 1999, point 83.

And Article 94 (6) of UNCLOS specifies that

> "[a] State which has clear grounds to believe that proper jurisdiction and control with respect to a ship have not been exercised may report the facts to the flag State. Upon receiving such a report, the flag State shall investigate the matter and, if appropriate, take any action necessary to remedy the situation."

It is readily apparent from Article 5 of the 1958 Geneva Convention on the High Seas and from Articles 91 and 94 of UNCLOS, that the absence of effective jurisdiction does not allow to disregard the nationality but rather, on the contrary, compels to refer to it. In relation to this, it must be stressed that the European Union Court of Justice, in the *Poulsen* case, has ruled in the sense that it is for the State to establish the conditions necessary to obtain its registration or to have access to its registry, and it is also for it to control the existence of a genuine link when nationality is granted[52].

International law is not interested in the elements of socio-economic linkage existing between the vessel and a certain national legal order. But it is concerned with whether the flag State can ensure in real terms the enforcement jurisdiction and control over the vessel registered in its registry. This formalistic solution is based on the characteristics which the international jurisprudence attributes to the genuine link. Hence, it can be concluded that, even though there exists no more than a formal genuine link, this produces an obligation for the flag State with regard to both third-party States and the international community — which in some cases can be an *erga omnes* obligation — due to the fishery activities of the vessels flying its flag.

(iii) *Third argument (mixed solution)*

This mixed solution is premised upon the combination of the flag State obligation to ensure effective jurisdiction and control over the vessel flying its flag and the effectiveness of the genuine link (obligation of due diligence). Given that a merely "formal" link means that it is impossible, more than likely, for the State to comply with its obligations. Hence, practically from the moment when the State grants its nationality to a vessel heedless of whether a genuine link exists, it could be argued that it is already beginning to fail to comply with the obligations imposed on it by the international law regarding the conservation and management of marine living resources and the environment protection.

---

52. European Court of Justice, *Poulsen* case, 24 November 1992, C-286/90, *ECR* 1992, p. I-6019, points 14-16.

But, ultimately, what could make up a genuine link within the framework of the fight against illegal fishing? As is well known, the flag is the external manifestation of the link existing between a vessel and the State. This link is the nationality, which is a manifestation of the State's sovereignty. Then, granting of the nationality to a vessel is an act of sovereignty and it falls upon the State to establish the conditions as it wishes. The attribution of the nationality means, on the one hand, that national legal norms of a State will be applied to that vessel and, on the other hand, that the State has the obligation to control that vessel's activity, with the possibility that such obligation may result in international responsibility. Formally, apart from some historically based exception or one derived from the existence of international organizations, nationality and flag coincide: as a vessel has a nationality and, thus, it may fly that State's flag. The nationality and its external expression, the flag, are a significant factor of legal certainty.

Therefore it seems necessary that they should express the existence of a genuine link in an effective relationship. But what makes up this link? In our view, in the case of the nationality of physical persons this legal link includes the existence of a pre-existing and effective real relationship (see the *Nottebohm* case), so that its absence results in the loss of international effects of such nationality. And in the case of vessels' nationality, this link gives rise to a State's obligation to ensure the international inviolability of the vessel, imposing on it the respect for its safety, labour, fisheries, environmental, etc. norms. Hence, the absence of a genuine link does not result in the loss of its international effects, and does not impede its effects against third countries. It means the responsibility of the State which has failed to observe its obligations of surveillance and control regarding fisheries, and, moreover, has failed to comply with the obligation of due diligence, registering a vessel in its registry heedless of the existence of a genuine link with it.

From this point of view, the genuine link that should exist between a State and a vessel to which it has granted its flag could be the capacity of that State to exercise an effective control over that vessel's activities, and work diligently to this end. If this control does not exist, it is illusory to speak of a genuine link. The definition thus proposed of the genuine link would distance it from the traditional economic and internal view, whereas it would approach that of international responsibility (the breach of a behaviour obligation). It is argued that it would be of greater benefit from the point of view of the fight against illegal fishing, as it would seem more effective and conclusive to act repeatedly against a State with open registry because it fails to control its vessels that are involved in illegal fishing, than to act against the ship and consider it stateless because it lacks such a genuine link.

C. The role of the port State

Unlike the coastal State and the flag State, which have specific regulations in the three binding international legal instruments concerning fisheries, no specific legislative competences are recognized to the port State, though it does possess executive and judicial competences in this field. Until very recently, the emphasis in international regulations concerning fisheries had been on the role of coastal and flag States, respectively. It was even the case, on occasions, that some of the provisions regarding coastal States' competences were applied to port States by virtue of the internal national legislation of the State concerned. The International Court of Justice aligned itself with this opinion in the case of *Military and Paramilitary Activities in and against Nicaragua*, when it ruled that the coastal State had the right to regulate access to its ports in virtue of the sovereignty it exercises in these areas[53].

It is argued that, in this way, a very significant aspect was ignored that is strictly related to fishing engaged in EEZs or on the high seas. In the last few decades, the changes in international fishing relations have brought to light the need to establish a specific legal framework for the port State that would enable it to adopt effective measures for the prevention and suppression of illegal fishing. These measures, which currently have no binding effect, would cover, by analogy, the provisions of Article 218, UNCLOS, whereby the port State's right of control over the protection of the environment is recognized, as we will discuss further in Section 4.

This shift of direction is largely due to the work carried out by FAO, which in the last ten years has spared no effort in drawing the attention of the international community to the importance of the port State in the fight against illegal fishing. As has been already stressed, the flag State is often in no condition to, or has no wish to, control the fishing activities of the vessels flying its flag. Thus, for example, Article 23 (1) of the 1995 New York Agreement provides that the port State has not only the right but also the duty, to adopt measures in accordance with international law, with the aim of promoting "the effectiveness of subregional, regional and global conservation and management measures". But this would be possible if the port State, by doing so, shall not discriminate against the vessels of any State "in form or in fact". For its

53. "It is also by virtue of its sovereignty that the coastal State may regulate access to its ports". *ICJ Reports 1986*, p. 111, para. 213. For an analysis of these issues, see R. Casado Raigón, "El Acuerdo de la FAO de 2009 sobre medidas del Estado rector del puerto destinadas a prevenir, desalentar y eliminar la pesca ilegal, no declarada y no reglamentada", *Noticias de la Unión Europea*, No. 326, 2012, pp. 4-5.

part, in the Review Conference of the 1995 New York Agreement in May 2010, many delegations recognized the importance of the adoption of the 2009 Agreement on Port State Measures, and considered it "as a major development in combating" illegal fishing[54].

Paragraph 2 Non-Binding Instruments in the Field of Fisheries

Along with these new trends in international fisheries law, which tend towards the introduction of a greater degree of responsibility in fishing activities, the work has been on-going in recent years within the framework of the United Nations on the implementation of a scheme with a universal scope, in which concrete measures in the fight against IUU fishing, including illegal fishing, would be defined. As a result of this work, IPOA-IUU was approved by consensus in COFI in March 2001. Its adoption has represented a watershed in the legal regulation of the problem of IUU fishing on an international scale[55]. Even though, at first sight, it is not legally binding, this does not signify, by any means, that IPOA-IUU is bereft of any legal effectiveness. On several occasions it refers to the UNCLOS provisions or it states that it is according to other relevant rules of international law[56]. This interna-

54. "Report of the resumed Review Conference on the Agreement for the Implementation of the Provisions of the United Nations Convention on the Law of the Sea of 10 December 1982 relating to the Conservation and Management of Straddling Fish Stocks and Highly Migratory Fish Stocks. Prepared by the President of the Conference", A/CONF.210/2010/7, 27 July 2010, point 97.

55. IPOA-IUU was implemented within the framework of the provisions of Article 2 *(d)* of the FAO Code of Conduct for Responsible Fisheries. Its rulings are interpreted and applied in the light of Articles 1 (1), 1 (2), 3 (1) and 3 (2) of this same legal instrument. This international text was ratified on 23 June 2001 by the FAO Council in its 120th period of sessions. For an analysis of IPOA-IUU, see R. J. Baird, *Aspects of Illegal, Undeclarated and Unregulated Fishing in the Southern Ocean*, Springer, Dordrecht, 2006, especially pp. 14-19 and 99-105 ; D. J. Doulman, "FAO Action to Combat IUU Fishing : Scope of Initiatives and Constraints on Implementation", in D. Vidas (ed.), *Law, Technology and Science for Oceans in Globalisation. IUU Fishing, Oil Pollution, Bioprospecting, Outer Continental Shelf*, Martinus Nijhoff Publishers, Leiden/Boston, 2010, pp. 134-136 ; W. Edeson, *op. cit.*, pp. 603-623 ; J. M. Sobrino Heredia, "La reforma de la Política Pesquera Común y la pesca ilegal, no declarada y no reglamentada", *Noticias de la Unión Europea*, 277 (2008), pp. 81-84.

56. For example, the 1995 New York Agreement, the 1993 FAO Compliance Agreement, the Code of Conduct for Responsible Fishing mentioned above, or what was agreed on in the 1992 Cancun Declaration, the 1992 Rio Declaration on Environment and Development, especially Chapter 17 of Programme 21, and also in other declarations and international instruments related to this problem. For more details, see W. Edeson, "The International Plan of Action on Illegal Unreported and Unregulated Fishing : The Legal Context of a Non-Legally Binding Instrument", *The International Journal of Marine and Coastal Law*, 16 (2001), No. 4, pp. 612-617.

tional text defines what is understood by IUU fishing, and proposes different measures to combat and eliminate this type of fishing, specifically for each of the five possible categories of States that can intervene at a particular point in the fishing chain. These are measures that are distinguished depending on the role that the States have to play in the global fight against illegal fishing.

Since the implementation of the 2001 IPOA-IUU, some concrete actions have been proposed by various States and the European Union, affected by these fishing activities, and in particular, those that strengthen the content of the responsibilities that could be derived in general for all the States, and specifically for coastal States, port States, flag States, and, more recently, for market States and State whose nationality those fishermen involved in illegal fishing have. And the 2009 Agreement on the Port State Measures could not be clearer, noting in the Preamble that the measures to address this type of fishing

> "should build on the primary responsibility of flag States and use all available jurisdiction in accordance with international law, including port State measures, coastal State measures, market related measures and measures to ensure that nationals do not support or engage in"

illegal fishing.

Moreover, different measures have been adopted by the different parties involved in the fight against illegal fishing. This comprehensive body of *soft law* norms certainly invites discussion. In this regard, special attention will be paid to the provisions of the 2009 Agreement on the Port State Measures, as it is the only international text of these characteristics that has the possibility to be binding at international level in the future, and, from that moment on, to be applicable to all ports[57]. And, there will be the possibility to see whether any role is granted to the market State and also to the State whose nationality the fishermen who are involved in illegal fishing have.

As far as IPOA-IUU is concerned, the measures laid down for the fight against illegal fishing can be grouped together under the following headings: in the first place, general measures to strengthen and broaden the scope of monitoring, control and surveillance, as well as to penalize non-compliance; secondly, concrete measures to improve and increase flag States' control; thirdly, parallel measures to enhance the trans-

57. Article 3 (5) of the 2009 Agreement on Port States Measures stipulates that

> "[a]s this Agreement is global in scope and applies to all ports, the Parties shall encourage all other entities to apply measures consistent with its provisions. Those that may not otherwise become Parties to this Agreement may express their commitment to act consistently with its provisions".

parency of markets and hamper the commercialization and profitability of illegal fishing; and lastly, we could speak in general of other measures to combat illegal fishing.

Many of these measures have also been set out in the Model Scheme on Port State Measures to Combat IUU Fishing adopted in 2005 (2005 Model Scheme). This is a voluntary fishing instrument which, to a great extent, follows the basic approach of regional schemes or mechanisms of measures of port State control — the so-called Memoranda of Understanding (MoU) — which will be addressed in Section 4 of this chapter, and which were already in being in the field of the prevention of marine pollution, though it is true that in this particular case they are applied to the fight against illegal fishing[58]. The main aim of the 2005 Model Scheme is that of facilitating the application of effective measures on the part of the port State to prevent, discourage and eliminate illegal fishing, not exclusively from a unilateral or national point of view, as has occurred up to now, but by means of a co-ordinated, harmonized approach of consultation and co-operation between several port State schemes. What is being sought is that there should be surveillance as to whether ships voluntarily entering ports comply with the pertinent measures of fishing conservation and management.

RFMOs have played a great role in the consolidation of this international legal framework, at both normative and operational levels. Indeed, most of them have already taken steps in this field, among which the following are some of the most outstanding: establishing important programmes of control and inspection; the adoption of measures of control by the port State; ships' obligation to fit vessel monitoring systems (VMS); registration of catches, regulation of fishing gear; listing of vessels authorized to fish and of vessels considered involved in illegal fishing activities; trade measures applicable to States which do not respect those measures in force, and so on. It suffices to mention the case of the "ship-rider" agreement signed in 1993 within the framework of the North Pacific Anadromous Fish Commission (NPAFC) by the United States (which is a member of this RFMO) with China (a State which is not part of this Organization), or the "ship-rider" agreement signed between Australia and France in 2007 within the framework of

58. The 2005 Model Scheme was drawn up in September 2004 on the occasion of a technical consultation meeting, and was adopted the following year by the FAO Committee on Fisheries. For a further development of these issues, see D. J. Doulman, "FAO Action to . . .", *op. cit.*, pp. 136-138; T. Lobach, "Combating IUU Fishing: Interaction of Global and Regional Initiatives", in D. Vidas (ed.), *Law, Technology and Science for Oceans in Globalisation. IUU Fishing, Oil Pollution, Bioprospecting, Outer Continental Shelf*, Martinus Nijhoff Publishers, Leiden/Boston, 2010, pp. 113-117.

the CCAMLR Convention, and the importation schemes for fishery products adopted by different RFMOs, the North-East Atlantic Fisheries Commission (NEAFC), the South East Atlantic Fisheries Organization (SEAFO) or the Western and Central Pacific Fisheries Commission (WCPFC)[59].

There are, also, measures dealing either with the fisheries products marketing, by means of which the RFMOs have attempted to curtail the access of such products to the markets, or which have sought to establish checks and other measures intended to prevent fish caught by illegal fishing from being unloaded in ports. All of them are measures that the RFMOs are trying to apply, above all, to non-member States of these organizations. But, as the problems of illegal fishing have not been eliminated, quite the opposite, in recent years the RFMOs have attempted to diversify the measures adopted in this matter, and their efforts have been directed towards measures that market States could bring in, as well as those of the fishermen's national States, in the same direction as the efforts made by the international community in this field[60].

The international instrument elaborated to have the greatest prominence in this field, that is, the 2009 Agreement on Port State Measures[61], is a legal text that, due to its binding nature, when it eventually comes into force, will be a watershed in the legal approach to these problems. At present, only four States or regional economic integration organizations have ratified, accepted, approved or acceded to it[62], while it

59. In this regard, see D. Guilfoyle, *Shipping Interdiction and . . ., op. cit.*, especially pp. 119-120, 125-128, 145-146 and 156-158.

60. For a deeper analysis of RFMO practices carried out in relation to the different measures of combatting illegal fishing, see, amongst others, D. S. Calley, *Market Denial and International Fisheries Regulation. The Targeted and Effective Use of Trade Measures against the Flag of Convenience Fishing Industry*, Martinus Nijhoff Publishers, Leiden/Boston, 2012, pp. 103-160; D. Guilfoyle, *Shipping Interdiction and . . ., op. cit.*, pp. 116-160; D. Warner-Kramer, *op. cit.*, pp. 510-522.

61. See J. Broweleit, "The Draft 2009 FAO Legally-Binding Port State Measures Agreement: An Evaluation of its Potential to Combat Illegal, Unreported and Unregulated Fishing", *Antarctic and Southern Oceans Law and Policy*, Occasional Papers, University of Tasmania, 13 (2009), pp. 21-45; J. Harrison, *Making the Law of the Sea: A Study in the Development of International Law*, Cambridge University Press, Cambirdge, 2011, pp. 221-224; M. Morin, "L'Accord FAO sur les mesures de contrôle des navires par l'Etat du port", *Annuaire de droit maritime et océanique*, 28 (2010), pp. 393-410; X. Pons Rafols, "La Unión Europea y el Acuerdo de la FAO sobre las medidas del Estado rector del puerto destinadas a prevenir, desalentar y eliminar la pesca ilegal, no declarada y no reglamentada", *Revista General de Derecho Europeo*, 27 (2012), pp. 1-48.

62. So far, only Norway has ratified it, the European Union has approved it, Myanmar and Sri Lanka have acceded to it. However, there are many more signatories. So, besides Norway and the European Union, another 8 States signed it on 22 November 2009, that is, the same day when it was adopted (these

needs 25 of such instruments of these characteristics in order for it to come into force[63], though there are hopes that other countries will soon take this step forward[64].

By virtue of this Agreement, States enjoy the sovereign prerogative to make decisions concerning which foreign ships may enter their ports. At the same time, it sets a *global minimum standard* about actions that must be taken against those vessels that engage in or support the activities of illegal fishing. States and international organizations can adopt more restrictive measures in this field, as long as these are in accordance with international law. Some of the key provisions include: the prohibition of known or suspected illegal fishing vessels or support ships to enter a port or use port facilities; the standardization of requirements of information from vessels that seek to enter ports; improvements in information-sharing, including verification of authorization to fish, between the flag State and the port State; designation of those ports that allow unloading; the establishment of specific functions for the flag States in co-operation with port States; standardization of ship inspections and training of inspectors, and recognition of the necessity to assist developing countries in order for them to apply this instrument.

Together with the significant role ascribed by the international law of the sea to the port State in this field, a new participant has joined these relations; we are referring to the *market State of the fishery products*. In fact, in the respective international texts, it is generally proposed to establish internationally agreed trade measures in order to prevent the commercialization of catches obtained by illegal fishing. These are exceptional and never unilaterally applied which must be interpreted and applied in consistency with the principles, rights and obligations established by the World Trade Organization[65]. Furthermore, these trade

were: Angola, Brazil, Chile, the United States of America, Indonesia, Iceland, Samoa and Uruguay); and another 13 States have done so subsequently (Australia, Benin, Canada, Russia, France, Gabon, Ghana, Kenya, Mozambique, New Zealand, Peru, Sierra Leone, and Turkey). See http://www.fao.org.

63. Article 29 of the 2009 Agreement on Port State Measures lays down:

> "1. This Agreement shall enter into force thirty days after the date of deposit with the Depositary of the twenty-fifth instrument of ratification, acceptance, approval or accession in accordance with Article 26 or 27.
>
> 2. For each signatory which ratifies, accepts or approves this Agreement after its entry into force, this Agreement shall enter into force thirty days after the date of the deposit of its instrument of ratification, acceptance or approval."

64. "Recent Major Developments with Regard to Combating Illegal, Unreported and Unregulated (IUU) Fishing", FAO, Committee on Fisheries, 13th ed., Rome, COFI/2012/8, 9-13 July 2012; available at www.fao.org.

65. As is well known, it is forbidden for States to apply unilaterally rules hampering trade for reasons of protection of the environment, for example. We

measures should take into consideration the principles of equity, transparency and non-discrimination.

Undoubtedly, the most effective way to put an end to this lucrative business is to eliminate the incentive for crime, making it extremely difficult, if not impossible, to commercialize products of this type of fishery with significant economic benefits. As the European Commission points out, this is far from easy, international trade in fisheries products has grown considerably as part of economic globalization, and this has provided illegal operators with many lucrative new opportunities. In order to disguise the illegal origin of catches, they usually follow complex routes before reaching the final market, including transhipments on the high seas, landings in *ports of convenience* and processing in a country which is different from both the flag and the market States [66]. Therefore, the transnational nature of the phenomenon of illegal fishing requires the adoption of an integrated approach to address these activities throughout the whole supply chain "from the net to the supermarket" [67]. On this issue, it will be necessary to pay more attention to the commercial side of illegal fishing so as to ensure that those products that reach the markets have been caught in compliance with relevant management and conservation rules.

In relation to this issue, it is interesting to note that Point 11 (1) (11) of the Code of Conduct for Responsible Fisheries establishes that

> "[t]he States should ensure that international and domestic trade in fish and fishery products accords with sound conservation and management practices, improving the identification of the origin of fish and fishery products traded".

---

need only point out, for now, the trade differences existing in the framework of the World Trade Organization: *United States — Measures concerning the Importation, Marketing and Sale of Tuna and Tuna Products*, WT/DS381; *United States — Import Prohibition of Certain Shrimp and Shrim Products*, WT/DS58 and WT/DS61. For an analysis of these issues, see D. S. Calley, *op. cit.*, pp. 207-228; X. Pons Rafols, "Implicaciones jurídicas y prácticas de la nueva normativa europea para prevenir, desalentar y eliminar la pesca ilegal, no declarada y no reglamentada", FAO Legislative Study No. 85, November 2010; www.fao.org/legal/prs-ol/paper-e.htm.

66. COM(2007) 601 final: *Communication from the Commission to the European Parliament, the Council, the European Economic and Social Committee and the Committee of the Regions on a new strategy for the Community to prevent, deter and eliminate Illegal, Unreported and Unregulated fishing*, Brussels, 17.10.2007, p. 3.

67. On this issue, see M. Borit and P. Olsen, "Evaluation Framework for Regulatory Requirements Related to Data Recording and Traceability Designed to Prevent Illegal, Unreported and Unregulated Fishing", *Marine Policy*, 36 (2012), pp. 96-102; B. Le Gallic, "The Use of Trade Measures against Illicit Fishing: Economic and Legal Considerations", *Ecological Economics*, 64 (2008), pp. 858-866.

One way in which to improve this identification would be to establish a comprehensive system of traceability enabling us to identify fishery products throughout all stages of extraction, transport, storage, importation, processing, distribution, sale or supply to the final consumer[68]. Moreover, when uncertainty persists, the precautionary principle should be taken into account, aimed, at the international level, at ensuring that the measures of conservation and management of fishery resources should be applied to the highest possible degree; such measures should be proportionate and temporary, and should not restrain trade any more than is required in order to reach the objective of preventing illegal fishing[69].

At the Review Conference of the 1995 New York Agreement, held in May 2010, several delegations stressed the need for the RFMOs to reinforce measures of control throughout the chain of commercialization, among other measures by means of the adoption of catch documentation schemes. Within this context, it seems to be urgent that these organizations draw up a harmonized system of certification of fishing catches, which should be required on landing, transhipment, importation or exportation. In a similar vein, Council Regulation (EC) No. 1005/2008, adopted by the European Union, contains the principle according to which fishery products proceeding from illegal fishing cannot be imported into the European Union. And at the same time, it is intended that only those fishery products accompanied by a catch certificate can be imported[70]. This certificate must be validated by the flag State of the

68. Regarding the role of the principle of traceability in the fight against illegal fishing, see T. Treves, "La pesca ilegal, no . . .", *op. cit.*, p. 140. For example, at the EU level all Member States are obliged to control in their territory the Common Fisheries Policy rules in all aspects of the chains of production, processing, distribution and commercialization of fisheries products and aquaculture, from capture or harvesting down to retail level, including transport. See Council Regulation (EC) No. 1224/2009 of 20 November 2009 establishing a Community control system for ensuring compliance with the rules of the common fisheries policy, amending Regulations (EC) No. 847/96, (EC) No. 2371/2002, (EC) No. 811/2004, (EC) No. 768/2005, (EC) No. 2115/2005, (EC) No. 2166/2005, (EC) No. 388/2006, (EC) No. 509/2007, (EC) No. 676/2007, (EC) No. 1098/2007, (EC) No. 1300/2008, (EC) No. 1342/2008, and repealing Regulations (EEC) No. 2847/93, (EC) No. 1627/94 and (EC) No. 1966/2006, *OJ* 343, 22.12.2009, p. 1, Articles 56-70.

69. Regarding the precautionary principle and its consequences for fisheries, see O. Schram Stokke, "International Fisheries Politics. From Sustainability to Precaution", in S. Andreson, E. Lerum Boasson and G. Honneland (eds.), *International Agreements. An Introduction*, Routledge, New York/Leiden, 2012, pp. 97-116.

70. Council Regulation (EC) No. 1005/2008 of 29 September 2008 establishing a Community System to Prevent, Deter and Eliminate Illegal, Unreported and Unregulated Fishing, Amending Regulations (EEC) No 2847/93, (EC) No. 1936/2001 and (EC) No. 601/2004 and Repealing Regulations (EC) No. 1093/94 and (EC) No. 1447/1999, *OJ* L 286, 29.10.2008, p. 1. See, espe-

vessel or vessels that have made the catches from which the fishery products were obtained, and gather together those data required by the pertinent regulations. It is also possible that the flag State agrees with the certificate being established, validated or presented electronically or substituted by electronic traceability systems which would guarantee the same level of control as would that of the authorities. It is argued that the fact that a catch certificate is required will allow fishing products to be monitored from the ship to the point of sale to the consumer. This certification regime is complemented with a series of detailed technical provisions.

All of these tools for the fight against illegal fishing have been strengthened by the recognition of the active personality principle, whereby a State will have jurisdiction to control the fishing activities engaged in by its nationals abroad. Such jurisdiction will be complementary to the competences of the flag State[71]. Hence, where the *State of fishermen's nationality* is concerned, national legislations (for example, the Spanish legislation, via Royal Decree 1134/2002), or the European Union's legislation (see the Regulation (EC) No. 1005/2008) are concerned with the situation in which nationals who are on board third State vessels find themselves, and also the question of how to make them comply, independently of the obligations of the flag State of vessel in which they may find themselves, with the regulations applicable to fight against illegal fishing[72]. For example, in Spain the offender will be pursued only in those cases where flag States fail to exercise the power to impose penalties inherent in its jurisdiction. It will be understood to be so when three months have passed since official notification of the infringement was sent, reliably attested, or when there has been no response to such notification, or when necessary steps have not been taken to sanction. Meanwhile, by expressly providing the responsibilities of the State of fishermen's nationality, the Regulation (EC) No. 1005/2008 tries to avoid that all nationals of the Member States participate or support illegal fishing activities[73].

---

cially, Article 12. Specifically, validation of the said catch certificate needs to be authorized by a public authority of the flag State with competence in this field, which must do this in accordance with the model indicated in Annex II of this Regulation.

71. In this regard, D. König, "Flags of Convenience", in R. Wolfrum (ed.), *The Max Planck Encyclopedia of Public International Law*, Oxford University Press, Oxford, 2012, p. 123.

72. D. Erceg, "Deterring IUU Fishing through State Control over Nationals", *Marine Policy*, 30 (2006), pp. 173-179.

73. Thus, with regard to the nationals of the Member States, it rules that they will be subject to the following obligations: they shall not assist illegal fishing (Article 39 (1)); they shall neither support nor engage in illegal fishing (Article 39 (1)); it is forbidden to export and sell fishing vessels to operators

Paragraph 3 New Challenges in the Fight against Illegal Fishing

Since the United Nations Secretary-General stated in his Annual Report on "Oceans and the Law of the Sea", presented on 10 March 2008, that "a link has been established between some IUU fishing activities, organized crime and other criminal activities"[74]; different international organizations and organisms have expressed themselves in the same direction, such as the United Nations Office on Drugs and Crime (UNODC)[75], the European Parliament[76] and INTERPOL[77]. This position has already been made clear in the doctrine[78]. It has even been considered that illegal as part of IUU fishing is an international environmental crime[79], and thus a crime against living marine resources,

---

who participate in the exploitation, management or ownership of those fishing vessels included in the EU list as illegal fishing vessels (Article 40 (2)).

74. For example, such activities as seek to avoid detection, bribery and corruption and armed resistance to surveillance and law enforcement. See "Oceans and the Law of the Sea. Report of the Secretary-General", A/63/63, 10.3.2008, point 100, pp. 31-32. See also, "Closing the Net: Stopping Illegal Fishing on the High Seas", Final report of the Ministerially Task Force on IUU Fishing on the High Seas, 2006 (www.high-seas.org); J. Swan, "Ocean and Fisheries Law: Port State Measures to Combat IUU Fishing: International and Regional Developments", *Sustainable Development Law and Policy*, 38 (2006), No. 7, p. 38.

75. "Transnational Organized Crime . . .", *doc. cit.*

76. It is one of the seven institutions of the European Union. See "Resolution of the European Parliament on Combating Illegal Fishing at the Global Level — the Role of the EU", A7-0362/2011, 17 November 2011.

77. "Combating the Problem of Transnational Organized Crime Committed at Sea. The Commission on Crime Prevention and Criminal Justice", Resolution 20/5, E/2011/30, E/CN.15/2011/21. Above all, the Preamble and point 9 should be consulted. In recent years, INTERPOL has begun to consider illegal fishing as a transnational crime which needs to be combatted. On this issue, during the Conference held in Bangkok in February 2012 a Fishing Crimes Workgroup (FCWG) was set up, which will focus specifically on crimes committed in relation to fishing, above all in the West African coastal States. In the conference held in Lyon from 26 to 28 February 2013, the SCALE Project has been launched, by means of which INTERPOL will attempt to identify, combat and eliminate crimes in the field of fishing and thus improve the exchange of information between countries about actions to be taken with regard to fishing.

78. See, amongst others, K. M. Anderson and R. Mccusker, "Crime in the Australian Fishing Industry: Key Issues", *Trends & Issues in Crime and Criminal Justice*, April 2005; B. Wilson, "Submersibles and Transnational Criminal Organizations", *Ocean and Coastal Law Journal*, 17 (2011).

79. See K. M. Anderson and R. Mccusker, *op. cit.*; F. Comte, "Environmental Crime and the Police in Europe: A Panorama and Possible Paths for Future Action", *European Environmental Law Review*, 15 (2006), pp. 190-231; B. Robinson, "The Nature of Environmental Crime", in N. Gunningham, S. Mckillop and J. Norberry, *Environmental Crime : Proceedings of a Conference Held 1-3 September 1993, Hobart*, Australian Institute of Criminology, Canberra, ACT, 1995, pp. 1-8.

and, likewise, a new threat to a State's maritime security, together with piracy, armed robbery, illegal trafficking in conventional weapons and weapons of mass destruction, trafficking in drugs and persons, etc.[80]

It should be pointed out in this regard that by environmental crimes it is understood those criminal activities that could have a negative impact on the environment. These are crimes that, due to their special characteristics, can be distinguished from traditional forms of criminal activities, are relatively easy to commit, and in which most criminals pursue economic benefits. Moreover, the damage caused to the environment is hard to identify and, even more so, to quantify[81]. According to the UNODC[82], environmental crimes may consist either in natural resource crime[83] or else in pollution crimes[84]. Its economic impact is very great, and it is reckoned to be one of the most profitable forms of illicit activities that currently exist, with a turnover of between $20,000 million and $40,000 million annually[85]. Among the most significant causes to be found in the origin of the appearance of environmental crimes we could mention, among many others: the gap between the costs occasioned by the activity and the value of the illegal products, the failure of regulation and the application of the regulatory framework in place in these fields, the liberalization in trade, which has meant that frontier controls are harder to enforce, the implication in multilateral environmental agreements of developing countries, which lack the necessary resources to comply with commitments undertaken in the international arena, etc.[86]

With respect to illegal fishing, apart from being understood as an

80. N. Klein, *Maritime Security and the Law of the Sea*, Oxford University Press, Oxford, 2011, pp. 301-327.

81. F. Comte, *op. cit.*, pp. 190-196.

82. "Transnational Organized Crime . . .", *doc. cit.*, pp. 95-96.

83. Namely, illicit trafficking in natural resources when such resources are gathered, transported or commercialized breaching regulations in force in the matter.

84. Such as, illicit trafficking in substances which harm the ozone layer and hazardous waste products, together with the intentionally illegal transportation or dumping of hazardous waste products, etc.

85. Data available in "Environmental Crime", Crime Profile Series, Australian Government, 2011, p. 1; "Environmental Crime. A Threat to Our Future", Environmental Investigation Agency, 2008, p. 2. See also D. Brack, "Combatting International Environmental Crime", in R. White (ed.), *Environmental Crime: A Reader*, Cullompton, Willan, 2009, p. 492.

86. In this regard, D. Brack, *op. cit.*, pp. 485-492. See also H.-J. Albrecht, "The Extent of Organized Environmental Crime: A European Perspective", in F. Comte and L. Krämer (eds.), *Environmental Crime in Europe: Rules of Sanctions*, Europa Law Publishing, Groningen, 2004, pp. 88-92; M. Srinivasan, S. Raja Pandian and A. Enoch, "International Crimes: Cyber Crime, Crimes against Cultural Heritage, Environmental Crimes, and Money Laundering", in S. Kethineni (ed.), *Comparative and International Policing, Justice and Transnational Crime*, Carolina Academic Press, Durham, 2010, pp. 395-398.

international crime against living marine resources, in some parts of the world it is also considered a new manifestation of transnational organized crime[87]. Activities would include the illegal fishing of some marine species where it is reckoned that organized criminal groups could be involved transnationally, or crimes committed by different transnational fishing operators against living marine resources, such as could be the case of, for example, the toothfish[88]. Here are included a whole range of activities which could fit perfectly well in the list of those dealt with in Article 3 (2) of the United Nations Convention against Transnational Crime[89]. Even though, we consider that nowadays it would be hard to invoke the provisions of this legal instrument for the field of illegal fishing, given that its scope refers either to crimes which States parties should adopt in their domestic legal system when they are intentionally committed, or to serious offences, that is to say, those conducts which constitute "an offence punishable by a maximum deprivation of liberty of at least four years, or a more serious penalty"[90].

Moreover, it must not be forgotten that one of the greatest problems that the international community currently faces, unlike other environmental crimes[91], is the lack of a treaty of universal scope focusing

---

87. Regarding an analysis of the scope of the transnational organized crime, see F. G. Madsen, *Transnational Organized Crime*, Routledge, London, 2009, pp. 46-50; T. Obokota, *Transnational Organized Crime in International Law*, Hart Publishing, Oxford/Portland, 2010, pp. 1-80; C. D. Ram, *Meeting the Challenge of Crime in the Global Village: An Assessment of the Role and Future of the United Nations Commission on Crime, Prevention and Criminal Justice*, Publication Series No. 73, Helsinki, 2012, pp. 24-52.

88. See "Transnational Organized Crime . . .", *doc. cit.*, pp. 98-109. Regarding illegal fishing which affects the Patagonian toothfish, see C. C. Joyner and L. Aylesworth, "Managing IUU Fishing in the Southern Ocean: Rethinking the Plight of the Patagonian Toothfish", *Ocean Yearbook*, Vol. 22, pp. 249-290; L. Little and M. A. Orellana, "Can CITES Play a Role in Solving the Problem of IUU Fishing?: The Trouble with Patagonian Toothfish", *Colombia Journal of International Environmental Law*, No. 22, 2005, pp. 21-122.

89. The United Nations Convention against Organized Transnational Crime was open for signature on 12 December 2000 in Palermo (Italy), and came into force on 29 September 2003. So far, 147 States have signed it and 173 have ratified it; see: http://www.unodc.org/unodc/en/treaties/CTOC/signatures.html. By virtue of Article 3 (2) it is ruled that a transnational offence will be one that:

> "*(a)* is committed in more than one State; *(b)* is committed in one State but a substantial part of its preparation, planning, directing or control takes place in another State; *(c)* it is committed in one State, but involves an organized criminal group that engages in criminal activities in more than one State; or *(d)* it is committed in one State but has substantial effects in another State".

90. Article 2 *(b)* of the United Nations Convention against Transnational Organized Crime. See also Article 3.

91. For example, in the case of those species of flora and fauna in danger of extinction, the Convention on International Trade in Endangered Species

specifically on the problem of illegal fishing as a whole. This undoubtedly hampers the work of protecting the marine environment, which is greatly harmed by criminal fishing activities. To this we must add the multiplicity of sanctions that could be applied to illegal fishing, but which vary from one country's domestic legal order to another: there are differences as to the nature of the competent bodies with the power to sanction an activity of these characteristics or as to those persons who can be considered responsible, the penalties applicable are different and even the elements that constitute an offence vary[92].

On the other hand, it should be mentioned that the European Union has had a great opportunity to criminalize illegal fishing conduct. Finally, it opted to typify as serious offences: (1) illegal fishing activities engaged in by fishing vessels in violation of measures of conservation and management applicable in the area where such activities have taken place: (2) trade activities directly related to illegal fishing; the falsification of documents referring to fishing activities or the use of such false or invalid documents[93]. In relation to this, it is worth pointing out that in a judgment passed immediately after the publication of the proposed new Framework Regulation in the fight against illegal fishing, in the *Commission/Council* case, the EU Court of Justice had made it clear that on the issue of pollution from vessels, the conduct of nationals or vessels flying the flag of a Member State could be criminalized, within the limits of its existing case-law. But, in all events, the decision as to the type and degree of penal sanctions that must be applied will not fall within the EU's competence[94], as it is the national authorities who will

of Wild Fauna and Flora (CITES, Washington, 1973) exists; as for ozone-depleting substances, in 1987 the Montreal Protocol was adopted, relating precisely to ozone-depleting substances; and with regard to hazardous waste the Basle Convention was adopted on the control of cross-border transport hazardous waste and its elimination (1989). See F. Comte, *op. cit.*, pp. 191-192.

92. M. Wallström, "Introductory Speech on Environmental Crime", in F. Comte and L. Krämer (eds.), *Environmental Crime in Europe: Rules of Sanctions*, Europa Law Publishing, Groningen, 2004, pp. 53-55. For example, Article 334 of the Spanish Criminal Code stipulates an imprisonment sentence of four months to two years or an eight to twenty-four months fine, and, at any case, a disqualification for the exercise of the right to hunt or fish for length of two to four years. See J. A. Ramos Vázquez, "Article 334", in P. Faraldo Cabana (ed.) and L. M. Puente Aba (co-ed.), *Ordenación del territorio, patrimonio histórico y medio ambiente en el Código Penal y la legislación especial*, Tirant lo Blanch, Valencia, 2011, pp. 397-411.

93. Regulation (EC) No. 1005/2008, *doc. cit.*, Articles 3 and 42 (1).

94. ECJ Judgment of 23 October 2007, *Commission/Council*, C-440/07, *ECJ* 2007, p. I-9097, point 71. See M. Sobrido Prieto, "Competencia penal para la represión de la contaminación de buques. Comentario a la sentencia del TJCE de 23 de octubre de 2007 (Comisión c. Consejo, C-440/05)", *Revista General de Derecho Europeo*, No. 16, 2008, p. 14. See also "Informe sobre la adaptación del Ordenamiento . . .", *doc. cit.*, p. 29.

punish infringements of the EU law committed by natural and legal persons[95].

SECTION 4 THE ENFORCEMENT JURISDICTION IN THE INTERNATIONAL LAW OF THE SEA FOR THE PREVENTION AND SUPPRESSION OF ILLEGAL FISHING

It is clear that UNCLOS is a watershed in the artificial compartmentalization of the physical unity that is the marine environment, creating a series of areas in which the States will not always enjoy sovereignty or exercise jurisdiction[96]. As is well known, the State has competence to manage its own territory, and, from the law of the sea perspective, it exercises a series of rights and responsibilities in the marine domain, varying according to whether it is a coastal State, a flag State or a port State. In other words, each State may have access to a certain jurisdiction in matters concerning the sea, and even land-locked States will enjoy rights and responsibilities relating to the sea.

Fundamentally, by "jurisdiction" is understood "the extent of each state's right to regulate conduct or the consequences of events"[97]. And, observing the development of contemporary international law, it describes, likewise, "the limits of the legal competence of a State or other regulatory authority (such as the European Community) to make, apply, and enforce rules of conduct upon persons"[98]. UNCLOS provisions on fisheries distinguish between, on the one hand, legislative jurisdiction (as we have seen in detail in the previous part of this study), and, on the other hand, enforcement jurisdiction[99]. In the words of Rüdiger Wolfrum, enforcement jurisdiction covers "all the actions taken by States or other entities to induce or compel States to comply" with their rules and regulations adopted in conformity with obligations existing in the international law of the sea, being "the reaction to an identified

95. Regulation (EC) No. 1005/2008, *doc. cit.*, Article 44.

96. Regarding an analysis of the compartmentalization of seas in the UNCLOS, see J. L. Meseguer Sánchez, *Los espacios marítimos en el nuevo Derecho del mar*, Marcial Pons, Madrid/Barcelona, 1999; J. M. Sobrino Heredia and G. A. Oanta, "Control y vigilancia de las fronteras en los diferentes espacios marítimos", *Anuario da Facultade de Dereito da Universidade da Coruña*, 14 (2010), pp. 767-780.

97. R. Jennings and A. Watts (eds.), *Oppenheim's International Law*, 9th ed., Longman, London, 1992-1996, p. 456.

98. V. Lowe, "Jurisdiction", in M. D. Evans, *International Law*, Oxford University Press, Oxford, 2003, p. 329.

99. For a deeper analysis of jurisdiction in the fisheries sector, see T. Treves, "Jurisdiction over Vessels in . . .", *op. cit.*, pp. 1-28.

non-compliance"[100]. Therefore, even though a State or any other subject of international law has jurisdiction to apply the UNCLOS provisions, it will not always have jurisdiction to enforce compliance or to compel other States to respect these rules[101].

There are two overriding principles of international jurisdiction that have substantiated States' actions in relation to fishing in the different areas of the sea. In the first place, there is the *principle of territoriality*, whereby a State is competent to penalize, in accordance with its domestic legal order, acts committed within its territory *(locus regit actum)*, whatever the nationality of the author of the wrongful act. In this context, the legal concept of "territory" comprises both the territory in a geographical sense and those vessels or aircraft flying the flag of a State which are found in an area where the sovereignty of another State does not exist. Under the law of the sea, this principle constitutes "the single most important basis for States to assert jurisdiction"[102].

However, bearing in mind the development of the international community, several exceptions are accepted to this principle[103]. Such is the case, among others, of the "personal or nationality principle", which enables that a criminal rule of a State can be applied to acts committed by its nationals abroad, even though it has a limited character, as it cannot be applied to all the crimes committed by its nationals. As regards this point, it is worth mentioning that Article 117, UNCLOS, rules that it is the duty of all States either to adopt those measures referring to its own nationals, whom it esteems "necessary for the conservation of the living resources of the high sea" or "to cooperate with other States in taking such measures". With reference to this Article, the European Union lays down in its secondary law referring to the Common Fisheries Policy that illegal activities performed by European citizens will be pursued also in waters not under the sovereignty or jurisdiction of its Member States, as well as against any other activity in support of illegal fishing[104]. At the

100. R. Wolfrum, "Means of Ensuring Compliance with and Enforcement of International Environmental Law", *Recueil des cours*, 272 (1998), p. 30.

101. H. Caminos, "Enforcement Jurisdiction under the United Nations Convention on the Law of the Sea. An Overview", in H. P. Hestermeyer, D. König, N. Matz-Lück, V. Röben, A. Seibert-Fohr, P-T. Stoll and S. Vöneky (eds.), *Coexistence, Cooperation and Solidarity. Liber Amicorum Rüdiger Wolfrum*, Vol. 1, Martinus Nijhoff Publishers, Leiden/Boston, 2012, p. 738.

102. B. Simma and A. T. Müller, *op. cit.*, p. 141.

103. For example, in Spanish criminal legislation three exceptions are accepted to the principle of territoriality of criminal law, that is: the principle of personality, the real or protective principle, and the principle of universal justice. See F. Muñoz Conde and M. García Arán, *Derecho Penal. Parte General*, Tirant lo Blanch, Valencia, 2007, pp. 155-160.

104. This is the active personality principle, whereby the States possess jurisdiction to know of the criminal acts committed by its nationals outside

same time, Member States are obliged to co-operate with third-party States in order to identify those of their nationals who support or are engaged in this type of fishing [105]. Moreover, in the EU system, it is provided that an illegal fishing vessel will be considered one that is proven to be infringing the measures of conservation and management applicable to the area where fishing activities have been engaged in.

To these situations it must be added the case of the absence of nationality of the fishing vessel according with the international law of the sea provisions [106]. It must be remembered that Article 92 (2), UNCLOS lays down that

> "[a] ship which sails under the flags of two or more States, using them according to convenience, may not claim any of the nationalities in question with respect to any other State, and may be assimilated to a ship without nationality".

Moreover, by virtue of Article 110 (1) *(d)* UNCLOS, a warship has the right of visit on the high seas over a vessel not flying its flag if "there is reasonable ground for suspecting that . . . the ship is without nationality". This UNCLOS provision is specifically relevant in the new international fishing scenario, being seen as a way to counter threats such as, among others, the transnational organized crime at sea [107].

On the other hand, it is worth recalling that States have different types of jurisdiction depending on the maritime zone involved, and that this will be reduced the further it is from the territory, understood in the sense of the mainland. This is, then, jurisdiction that is understood differently whether it covers marine areas under the sovereignty or the jurisdiction of a State or marine areas beyond national jurisdiction of a State.

In the field of fisheries, it is well known that UNCLOS grants a major

---

that State's territory. For further analysis of these questions, see I. Bantekas, "Criminal Jurisdiction of States under International Law", in R. Wolfrum (ed.), *The Max Planck Encyclopedia of Public International Law*, Vol. IV, Oxford University Press, Oxford, 2012.

105. Thus, the Member States will be able to impose penalties amounting to at least five times the value of the fishery products obtained, and eight times that value in the event of repeated infringements within a five-year period. And in order to calculate the cost of the damage caused by illegal fishing, the Member States will take into account the harm caused to fishing stocks and the marine ecosystem. See Council Regulation (EC) No. 2371/2002 of 20 December 2002 on the conservation and sustainable exploitation of fisheries resources under the Common Fisheries Policy, *OJ* L 358, 31.12.2002, p. 59, Article 1; Regulation (EC) No. 1005/2008, *doc. cit.*, Articles 39-40.

106. Regulation (EC) No. 1005/2008, *doc. cit.*, Article 3 (1) *(1)*.

107. In this regard, see E. Papastavridis, "The Right of Visit on the High Seas in a Theoretical Perspective: *Mare Liberum* versus *Mare Clausum* Revisited", *Leiden Journal of International Law*, 24 (2011) 1, pp. 45-69.

role to the coastal States[108]. In our view, the most important problems that coastal States face with regard to illegal fishing are related to enforcement jurisdiction in the EEZs. As was pointed out previously, the majority of illegal fishing on a global scale occurs in EEZs, above all those of developing nations with lengthy oceanic coastlines. In relation to this, Article 73, UNCLOS, rules in paragraph 1 that coastal States will have sovereignty in their EEZs for the exploration, exploitation, conservation and management of fishing resources. Furthermore, paragraphs 2, 3 and 4 of this article list the limits of enforcement jurisdiction of the coastal States; these are that (1) arrested vessels and their crews must be released as soon as possible once a reasonable bond or other guarantee has been fixed; (2) unless otherwise agreed between the interested States, the penalties fixed by the coastal State cannot be imprisonment; (3) in the event of arrest or detention of a fishing vessel, the coastal State must inform the flag State as soon as possible about the conducts, measures and penalties imposed.

Furthermore, Article 292, UNCLOS, sets forth the obligatory jurisdiction for coastal States regarding the prompt release of ships and their crews. Thus, if a coastal State fails to respect the provisions of Article 73 (2), UNCLOS, the dispute arising will be referred to a court or a tribunal chosen by the two parties, or to the ITLOS. The application for release may only be presented before the court or the tribunal by the flag State or in its name (Article 292 (2), UNCLOS). It will be dealt with as soon as the court or the tribunal receiving news of such release or liberation (Article 292 (3), UNCLOS). The bond will be fixed by the court or the tribunal and the coastal State will comply promptly with such a decision (Article 292 (4), UNCLOS). Undoubtedly, this obligatory jurisdiction will be, for the coastal States, in the words of ITLOS Judge, Professor Treves,

> "*a contrario* from Article 298, paragraph 1 *(b)*, of the 1982 Convention by virtue of which states may declare, if they so decide, that compulsory jurisdiction under Part XV of the 1982 Convention is excluded with respect to disputes relating to fisheries enforcement activities"[109].

Likewise, it is worth pointing out that the prompt release of vessels seized and their crews constitutes the limit of coastal States' enforcement jurisdiction, to which the greatest attention has been paid on the part of ITLOS. Of the 20 cases brought before this Tribunal up to now,

---

108. For example, see Articles 2 (1), 56 (1), 77 (1) and 220 of UNCLOS. In this regard, see H. Caminos, "Enforcement Jurisdiction under . . .", *op. cit.*, pp. 738-756.

109. T. Treves, "Jurisdiction over Vessels . . .", *op. cit.*, p. 7.

eight refer precisely to this matter[110], of which seven relate to IUU fishing activities performed in the EEZ of some State forming part of UNCLOS — the *Camouco* case[111], the *Monte Confurco* case[112], the *Grand Prince* case[113], the *Volga* case[114], the *Juno Trader* case[115], the *Hoshinmaru* case[116], and the *Tominmaru* case[117]. In the present author's view, ITLOS has thus far wasted the opportunities offered by each of these cases to expressly declare itself on the subject of illegal fishing, though numerous allegations have been presented by States involved in these cases, in which reference has been made to this type of criminal fishing activity. Nonetheless, so far the Tribunal has gone no further than to use UNCLOS provisions simply to curb actions by coastal States with regard to enforcement jurisdiction in their respective EEZs.

This stance of ITLOS regarding illegal fishing can be changed substantially in the near future, as on 28 March 2013, the Sub-Regional Fisheries Commission submitted to this Tribunal a request for an Advisory Opinion[118]. Two of the questions raised by this RFMO in this occasion refer specifically to the enforcement jurisdiction of the coastal States in the fight against illegal fishing. On the one hand, the ITLOS is requested to rule on the rights and obligations of the coastal State in ensuring the sustainable management of shared stocks and stocks of

---

110. For an overall view of the issue of the prompt release of fishing vessels and their crews, see, amongst others, J. Akl, "Jurisprudence of the International Tribunal for the Law of the Sea in Prompt Release Proceedings", in H. P. Hestermeyer, D. König, N. Matz-Lück, V. Röben, A. Seibert-Fohr, P-T. Stoll and S. Vöneky (eds.), *Coexistence, Cooperation and Solidarity. Liber Amicorum Rüdiger Wolfrum*, Vol. 1, Martinus Nijhoff Publishers, Leiden/Boston, 2012, pp. 1591-1614; T. A. Mensah, "The Tribunal and the Prompt Release of Vessels", *International Journal of Marine and Coastal Law*, 22 (2007), No. 3, pp. 425-449; D. Rothwell and T. Stephens, "Illegal Southern Ocean Fishing and Prompt Release: Balancing Coastal and Flag State Rights and Interests", *International and Comparative Law Quarterly*, 53 (2004), pp. 171-187.

111. *"Camouco" (Panama* v. *France), Prompt Release, Judgment, ITLOS Reports 2000*, p. 10.

112. *"Monte Confurco" (Seychelles* v. *France), Prompt Release, Judgment, ITLOS Reports 2000*, p. 86.

113. *"Grand Prince" (Belize* v. *France), Prompt Release, Judgment, ITLOS Reports 2001*, p. 17.

114. *"Volga" (Russian Federation* v. *Australia), Prompt Release, Judgment, ITLOS Reports 2002*, p. 10.

115. *"Juno Trader" (Saint Vincent and the Grenadines* v. *Guinea-Bissau), Prompt Release, Judgment, ITLOS Reports 2004*, p. 17.

116. *"Hoshinmaru" (Japan* v. *Russian Federation), Prompt Release, Judgment, ITLOS Reports 2005-2007*, p. 12.

117. *"Tomimaru" (Japan* v. *Russian Federation), Prompt Release, Judgment, ITLOS Reports 2005-2007*, p. 74.

118. See ITLOS Case No. 21. For more details, see "The International Tribunal for the Law of the Sea Receives a Request for an Advisory Opinion from the Sub-Regional Fisheries Commission", Press Release, ITLOS/Press 190, 28 March 2013.

common interest, especially the small pelagic species and tuna. And, on the other hand, the Tribunal will have to express its position in relation to the possibility for a State or international agency to be held liable for the violation of the fisheries legislation of the coastal State by the vessel which received a fishing licence within the framework of an international agreement with the flag State or with an international agency[119].

Besides the territorial waters and the EEZ, enforcement questions may arise in other sea areas not under the sovereignty or jurisdiction of any States, without there being any resulting vacuum of jurisdiction[120]. Reference is made to to the high sea, where, among others, the freedom to fishery exists (Article 87 (1) *(e)*) and where the principle of the flag States exclusive jurisdiction operates over those vessels flying their flags (Article 92 (1), UNCLOS)[121]. The high seas is an area where illegal fishing also occurs due to the enormous complexity that the conservation and management of the marine living resources mean, and where the enforcement jurisdiction belongs, in principle, to the flag State. The flag State competence in this field is a personal competence, based on nationality, as we have already analysed in other parts of this chapter. In this context, the existence of States with open registers for the licensing of fishing vessels favours the existence of flags of convenience.

However, the Montego Bay Convention allows several exceptions to the flag State exclusive jurisdiction[122], such as the right of visit under Article 110, UNCLOS, and the right of hot pursuit stipulated by Article 111, UNCLOS. Thus, by virtue of Article 110, UNCLOS, warships and other duly authorized ships "being on government service" have the right to visit on the high seas those ships which are suspected on a "reasonable ground" to be engaged in activities such as piracy,

119. The Sub-Regional Fisheries Commission also asked the Tribunal on the following two matters: (1) the obligations of the flag State in cases where IUU fishing activities are conducted within the EEZ of third party States; (2) to what extent the flag State shall be held liable for IUU fishing activities conducted by vessels sailing under its flag.

120. As it was expressed rightly by the doctrine. In this regard, see D. Momtaz, "La haute mer", in R.-J. Dupuy and D. Vignes, *Traité du nouveau droit de la mer*, Economica et Bruylant, Paris, 1985, p. 353; B. Simma and A. T. Müller, *op. cit.*, p. 138.

121. For an overview of the problem of jurisdiction on the high seas, and a specific approach to enforcement jurisdiction on the high seas referring to the particular case of the Mediterranean Sea, see E. Papastavridis, "Enforcement Jurisdiction in the Mediterranean Sea: Illicit Activities and the Rule of Law on the High Seas", *International Journal of Marine and Coastal Law*, 25 (2010), pp. 576-599.

122. On this issue, see, amongst others, H. Caminos, *op. cit.*, pp. 769-772; A. L. Kolodkin, V. N. Gutsuliak and I. V. Bobrova, *The World Ocean: International Legal Regime*, Eleven International Publishing, The Hague, 2008, pp. 144-169.

slave trade, unauthorized broadcasting, to be a ship without nationality or to be suspected of having the same nationality as the warships and the other duly authorized ships[123].

The right to hot pursuit is especially relevant to the problems dealt with in this chapter. Thus, Article 111, UNCLOS, provides that the coastal State has enforcement jurisdiction regarding the vessel which does not fly its flag, when it has sufficient evidence to believe that the said vessel has breached its national rules. This is an exception to the principle of the flag State exclusive jurisdiction on the high seas, but it is also a limitation to the freedom of navigation on the high seas[124]. The coastal State will only be able to have this jurisdiction insofar as the infringements have been committed in a maritime area where it has jurisdiction[125]. This rule derives from the quasi-territorial principle of law of the coastal State, unlike other exceptions to the primacy of flag State's jurisdiction on the high sea, such as piracy or slave trade, which stem from the principle of universality[126].

The UNCLOS provisions in this field have been complemented by other legal instruments adopted subsequently at the international level, to which we have already referred in the Second Part of this study. By means of these instruments further constraints have been placed upon the flag States' exclusive jurisdiction on the high seas. Thus, the 1995 New York Agreement stands out, providing, as it does, for the possibility of an RFMO-authorized inspector going on board and also inspecting vessels flying the flag of a Member or non-Member State of the said Organization, to thus ensure compliance with the conservation and management measures of these fishing stocks. It is submitted that this is

123. But there is an exception in the case of those ships which enjoy immunity (foreign warships and certain government vessels). For an overview of the problem of the right of visit on the high seas, see, amongst others, E. Papastavridis, "The Right of Visit on . . .", *op. cit.*, pp. 45-69; D. Rothwell and T. Stephens, *The International Law of the Sea*, Hart Publishing, Oxford and Portland, 2010, p. 166.

124. Regarding the right of hot pursuit, see N. M; Poulantzas, *The Right of Hot Pursuit in International Law*, 2nd ed., Martinus Nijhoff Publishers, The Hague/London/New York, 2002, pp. 39-268; D. Rothwell and T. Stephens, *op. cit.*, pp. 166-167; R. Walker, "International Law of the Sea: Applying the Doctrine of Hot Pursuit in the 21st Century", *Auckland University Law Review*, 17 (2011), pp. 194-218.

125. UNCLOS has extended the provisions of the 1958 Geneva Convention regarding the right of hot pursuit, laying down that they can also be applied for infringements committed in EEZs and in archipelagic waters. In this regard, see I. A. Shearer, "Problems of Jurisdiction and Law Enforcement against Delinquent Vessels", *International and Comparative Law Quarterly*, 35 (1986), p. 445.

126. E. J. Molenaar, "Multilateral Hot Pursuit and Illegal Fishing in the Southern Ocean: The Pursuits of the Viarsa 1 and the South Tomi", *International Journal of Marine and Coastal Law*, 19 (2004), No. 1, p. 28.

a controversial issue because this Agreement is a conventional rule and, by permitting another State, which is not the fishing vessel's flag State, to intervene unilaterally on the high seas seems to be ignoring the well-known principle of international law *"res inter alios acta"* [127].

In fact, Article 21 (1) of the 1995 New York Agreement rules that

> "[i]n any high seas area covered by a subregional or regional fisheries management organization or arrangement, a State Party which is a member of such organization or a participant in such arrangement may, through its duly authorized inspectors, board and inspect, in accordance with paragraph 2, fishing vessels flying the flag of another State Party to this Agreement, whether or not such State Party is also a member of the organization or a participant in the arrangement, for the purpose of ensuring compliance with conservation and management measures for straddling fish stocks and highly migratory fish stocks established by that organization or arrangement".

In short, a State which is a member of an RFMO, but is not the flag State of a fishing vessel engaged in fishing activities in that part of the high seas regulated by the said Organization, can have enforcement jurisdiction over the said vessel that either flies the flag of another State or flies the flag of a State which is not a part of the RFMO. This has been interpreted by a part of the doctrine as a refined version of the *mare clausum* [128]. It is submitted that the provisions of the 1995 New York Agreement should not be understood as a panacea for the problem of illegal fishing as, despite the fact that this international treaty entered into force several years ago, there is no evidence yet that the phenomenon of illegal fishing has diminished, neither has it been ratified by all the States with interests in the field of fisheries [129].

For its part, the European Union has adopted, by way of Council

---

127. See J. A. De Yturriaga, *The International Regime of Fisheries. From UNCLOS 1982 to the Presential Sea*, Martinus Nijhoff Publishers, The Hague/London/New York, 1997, p. 224.

128. In this regard, see H. Tuerk, "The Waning Freedom of the Seas", in R. Casado Raigón and G. Cataldi (eds.), *L'évolution et l'Etat actuel du droit international de la mer. Mélanges de droit de la mer offerts à Daniel Vignes*, Bruylant, Brussels, 2009, p. 933. See also M. Gorina-Ysern, "World Ocean Public Trust: High Seas Fisheries after Grotius — Towards a New Ocean Ethos?", *Golden Gate University Law Review*, 34 (2004), p. 684. With reference to the famous controversy between *mare liberum* and *mare clausum*, examined in the light of the developments in the present-day international law of the sea, although this doctrinal work focuses more on the study of visiting rights stipulated in Article 110, UNCLOS, see E. Papastavridis, "The Right of Visit on . . .", *op. cit.*, pp. 45-54.

129. On this issue, see the information regarding the 1995 New York Agreement contained in the Section 3 of this chapter.

Regulation (EC) No. 1224/2009[130], a fairly complex system of control of activities in the field of its Common Fisheries Policy. This system establishes, among other things, that the EU Member States can control fishing activities performed by those vessels flying their flag on the high seas or in the internal waters of third-party countries[131]. In this way, the activities of European nationals performed on board vessels flying the flags of third States would be excluded, and these would come within the provisions of Regulation (EC) No. 1005/2008[132], regarding the EU system to fight against illegal fishing. All these aspects confirm the consensus among the EU Member States regarding the application of the personality principle in the control of this policy, which had already been set out in the Regulation (EC) No. 1005/2008[133].

The use of force on the high seas by a Member State of an RFMO against a fishing vessel flying the flag of a third State constitutes another controversial issue regarding States' enforcement jurisdiction in their fight against illegal fishing. A minor part of the doctrine[134] considers it to be a legitimate measure to ensure that fishing vessels of a third State do not engage in IUU fishing activities. On the one hand, it is considered that both an RFMO Member State and a third State have enforcement jurisdiction on the high seas because there is a duty of all States to co-operate in the conservation and management of resources. In this regard, it is considered that the obligation to co-operate in this matter provided by Article 118, UNCLOS, derives from *jus cogens*, which thus creates *erga omnes* obligations for all the States of the international community.

On the other hand, it is considered that Articles 20-22 of the 1995 New York Agreement would allow the use of force in international fishing relations by States not being flag States. These would start to act when the flag State of the fishing vessel fails to co-operate, as would be the case, for example, of States with flags of convenience, or non-compliant States. This approach would also be endorsed by the constitutive treaties of several RFMOs and their respective legal frameworks adopted by virtue of their competences of conservation and management, as well as by bilateral treaties, as is the case of the ship-rider

130. Regulation (EC) No. 1224/2009, *doc. cit.*

131. *Ibid.*, Article 5 (2).

132. Regulation (EC) No. 1005/2008, *doc. cit.*

133. A. Rey Aneiros, "Compleja reforma integral del sistema de control de la Política Pesquera Común", *Revista General de Derecho Europeo*, 23 (2011), pp. 8-9.

134. Above all, we are referring to the opinion of Professor Rosemary Gail Rayfuse. On this issue see R. G. Rayfuse, *Non-Flag State Enforcement in High Seas Fisheries*, Martinus Nijhoff Publishers, Leiden/Boston, 2004, and "Non-Flag State Enforcement and Protection of the . . .", *op. cit.*

agreements[135]. Thus, Article 22 (1) *(f)* of this international treaty, in relation with the basic procedures for boarding and inspection pursuant to Article 21 referred to subregional and regional co-operation for the purpose of implementation, lays down that

> "The inspecting State shall ensure that its duly authorized inspectors: . . . avoid the use of force except when and to the degree necessary to ensure the safety of the inspectors and where the inspectors are obstructed in the execution of their duties. The degree of force used shall not exceed that reasonably required in the circumstances."

As is well known, Article 49 of the 2001 ILC Articles on the Responsibility of States for Internationally Wrongful Acts[136] contemplates that in certain circumstances a State may adopt countermeasures against another State which is responsible for an intentionally wrongful act that has harmed it, in order to uphold their rights, recognized by the international law, and in order to induce that State to comply with the obligations derived from responsibility for the wrongful act committed. But it must be taken into account that the said State, in the words of James Crawford,

> "acts at its peril, if its view of the question of wrongfulness turns out not to be well founded. A State which resorts to countermeasures based on its unilateral assessment of the situation does so at its own risk and may incur responsibility for its own wrongful conduct in the event of an incorrect assessment. In this respect there is no difference between countermeasures and other circumstances precluding wrongfulness."[137]

An obligation of this type could be, for example, the duty of the flag State to co-operate in ensuring the conservation of highly migratory species, provided by Article 64, UNCLOS[138].

135. R. G. Rayfuse, *Non-Flag State Enforcement in High . . .", op. cit.*, pp. 327-350, and "Non-Flag State Enforcement and Protection of the . . .", *op. cit.*, pp. 592-595. On the enforcement jurisdiction under the shiprider agreements, see D. Guilfoyle, *Shipping Interdiction and . . ., op. cit.*, pp. 119-120; D. R. Rothwell, "Law Enforcement in Antarctica", in A. D. Hemmings, D. R. Rothwell and K. N. Scott (eds.), *Antarctic Security in the Twenty-First Century. Legal and Policy Perspectives*, Routledge, London and New York, 2012, pp. 140-141.

136. ILC Articles on State Responsibility, as adopted by the ILC at its fifty-third session in 2001.

137. J. Crawford, *The International Law Commission's Articles on State Responsibility. Introduction, Text and Commentaries*, Cambridge University Press, Cambridge, 2002, p. 285.

138. In this regard, P. Gautier, "Comments on Flag State's Responsibility, Enforcement Measures against IUU Fishing Activities, and the Settlement of

It is submitted that it would be a serious mistake to consider countermeasures as a universal panacea for the absence of sufficient mechanisms to fight against illegal fishing in the existing legal framework. It is true that Article 42 of the 2001 ILC Articles on the Responsibility of States for Internationally Wrongful Acts allows an injured State "to invoke the responsibility of another State if the obligation breached is owed to (a) that State individually or *(b)* a group of States including that State, or the international community as a whole"[139]. And Article 48 of the 2001 ILC Articles on the Responsibility of States for Internationally Wrongful Acts refers to the invocation of responsibility by States "other than an injured State" acting in the collective interest.

But taking into account all the characteristics of illegal fishing it is quite impossible to identify which State is injured in the case of high seas fisheries or to consider that the breach of the obligation "is of such a character as radically to change the position of all the other States to which the obligation is owed with respect to the further performance of the obligation"[140]. This would be possible regarding fishing only if there are obligations *erga omnes partes* or obligations *erga omnes*. In our view, it is very difficult to uphold this argument. Nevertheless, this scenario is different in the case of the RFMO measures, as the fishing obligations breached are easier to be identified. The challenge here is to demonstrate that an individual State has breached an obligation regarding the respect of a common resource[141].

Another issue is the use of force. Undoubtedly, enforcement jurisdiction could consist of the detention of a vessel, and such application could involve the use of force, to some extent[142]. The international law of the sea allows this, but, in our view, only in those maritime areas where the State which employs force has jurisdiction. It is the view of the present author that a completely different situation exists with regard

---

Disputes", in E. Franckx and P. Gautier (eds.), *The Exercise of Jurisdiction over Vessels: New Developments in the Fields of Pollution, Fisheries, Crimes at Sea and Trafficking of Weapons of Mass Destruction*, Bruylant, Brussels, 2010, pp. 85-86.

139. For an analysis of Article 42 of the 2001 ILC's Articles on the Responsibility of States for Internationally Wrongful Acts, see J. Crawford, *op. cit.*, pp. 304-309.

140. ILC Articles on State Responsibility, Article 42 *(b)* (ii). In this regard, see: J. Crawford, *op. cit.*, pp. 259-260; D. Guilfoyle, *Shipping Interdiction and . . ., op. cit.*, pp. 164-165.

141. In accord seems to be Guilfoyle. See D. Guilfoyle, "Interdicting Vessels to Enforce the . . .", *op. cit.*, p. 166.

142. The Permanent Court of Arbitration has declared on this issue in the *Guyana/Suriname* case of 17 September 2007, in relation to Article 287 and Annexe VII of UNCLOS. See point 445. For further development, see P. Gautier, "Comments on Flag State's Responsibility . . .", *op. cit.*, pp. 86-90.

to the high seas, where the principle of exclusive flag State jurisdiction exists, and where, therefore, the threat or use of force is prohibited[143].

The focus of the analysis will shift now to the issue of the possible enforcement jurisdiction by the port State in the field of illegal fishing. It is worth reiterating that UNCLOS is silent on this issue, though it is true that, in accordance with general international law, a State can impose conditions for the entry into its ports of vessels that do not comply with certain requisites[144]. To our knowledge, this will be subjected to very prominent changes once the 2009 Agreement on Port State Measures comes into force. This Agreement will affect the practices followed by States during the coming decades in the establishment of regional regimes concerning port State controls — the so-called Memorandums of Understanding (MoUs)[145]. Actually, the FAO Agreement mentioned above does not have the same legal standing as the MoUs: the former is a multilateral international treaty, containing the rights, obligations and responsibilities of the States in relation to the ports of all the States of the international community, and which, once it comes into force, will have highly significant repercussions for international fishing relations affected by illegal fishing; on the other hand, the MoUs are administrative agreements adopted between the maritime authorities of the States involved, are in accordance with the UNCLOS provisions, they have no binding legal force, and they do not create legal rights and obligations for the States adopting them[146].

---

143. For an analysis of the countermeasures that a State can adopt in the marine environment, and its relationship with the use of force in international fishing relations, see, amongst others, D. Guilfoyle, *Shipping Interdiction and . . ., op. cit.*, pp. 160-169, and "Interdicting Vessels to Enforce the Common Interest: Maritime Countermeasures and the Use of Force", *International and Comparative Law Quarterly*, 56 (2007), pp. 69-82.

144. Article 218, UNCLOS. Also see T. Treves, "Jurisdiction over Vessels . . .", *op. cit.*, p. 7.

145. I.e. Memorandum of Understanding.

146. At present, nine agreements of this nature exist, covering practically all the seas, namely: the Paris MoU (for Europe and North Atlantic, 1982); the Tokyo MoU (for Asia and Pacific, 1993); the Viña del Mar MoU (for Latin America, 1992); the Caribe MoU (for Caribbean, 1996); the Abuja MoU (for West and Central Africa, 1998); the Black Sea MoU (for the Black Sea region, 2000); the Mediterranean MoU (for the Mediterranean area, 1997); the Indian Ocean MoU (for the Indian Ocean, 1998); the Riyadh MoU (for the Persian Gulf region, 2005). From the doctrine, suffice to mention, amongst others, R. Churchill, "Compliance Mechanism in the International Law of the Sea: From the Individual to the Collective", in H. P. Hestermeyer, D. König, N. Matz-Lück, V. Röben, A. Seibert-Fohr, P-T. Stoll and S. Vöneky (eds.), *Coexistence, Cooperation and Solidarity. Liber Amicorum Rüdiger Wolfrum*, Vol. 1, Martinus Nijhoff Publishers, Leiden/Boston, 2012, pp. 792-797; D. König, "The Enforcement of the International Law of the Sea by Coastal and Port State", *Heidelberg Journal of International Law*, 62 (2002), pp. 7-10; R. Rayfuse, "The Anthropocene, Autopoiesis and the Disingenuousness of the Genuine Link:

The case of the 2009 Agreement on Port State Measures is clearly different. From the moment it comes into force all port States will apply its provisions to all vessels which do not fly its flag and which request entry to or which are in its ports (Article 3 (1)). It contains minimum standards for the port States' measures, for example, in relation to the information that has to be supplied before entry to ports (Article 8 (1)); for ship inspection by the RFMOs, FAO or other means (Article 12 (2)); the respect of the inspectors' functions during inspections (Article 13 (1)); and for the results of inspections that need to be included in the written report containing the results of each of the inspections carried out (Article 14 (1)). These minimum standards will be complemented with more binding measures adopted both at the regional and national level.

With regard to this, the example of the European Union merits attention; the European Union has adopted several Regulations referring to the fight against illegal fishing and has shaped an extremely restrictive framework, based on port State controls, applied to all landings of sea products from non-Member countries. Indeed, conditions of access have been provided for fishing vessels from non-Member States calling at the ports of Member States with the aim of preventing, deterring and eliminating illegal fishing, and likewise the *modus operandi* of the inspections which will be performed in those ports designated to that end by Member States [147]. Moreover, the European has set up an early warning system which informs the States, where appropriate, when doubts exist as to compliance with conservation and management measures by fishing vessels or the fishing products of certain third States [148].

SECTION 5 **CONCLUDING REMARKS**

Illegal fishing, as part of IUU fishing, constitutes one of the greatest challenges which international fisheries law faces. Its effects are felt directly and in a negative way in the conservation and management of living resources. Likewise, it affects maritime security and represents unfair competition with responsible operators within the fishing sector. In short, illegal fishing is a real and serious threat to the sustainable management of living resources at the global level.

In some cases, these illicit fishery activities are integrated within

Addressing Enforcement Gaps in the Legal Regime for Areas beyond National Jurisdiction", in E. J. Molenaar and A. G. Oude Elferink (eds.), *The International Legal Regime of Areas beyond National Jurisdiction: Current and Future Developments*, Martinus Nijhoff Publishers, Leiden/Boston, 2010, pp. 181-182.

147. Regulation (EC) No. 1005/2008, *doc. cit.*, Articles 4-11.

148. *Ibid.*, Articles 23 and 24.

transnational organized criminal networks, which, in certain societies and countries, corrode the social fabric, increase levels of corruption and encourage the violation of human rights. Moreover, such activities represent a serious danger for marine biodiversity and fragile marine ecosystems.

In order to tackle the proliferation of these fishing activities, since the last decade of the twentieth century, different legal instruments, varying in scope, have been created. It is suffice to mention, amongst others, the IPOA-IUU (2001) and, more recently, the Agreement on Port States Measures (2009). In this short period of time a significant legal development has taken place, going from simply a programming and incentive instrument to a legally binding text, once it comes into force. This legal framework has been developed at RFMO, EU and national level and aims to strengthen the contents of flag State, port State and coastal State responsibility. At the same time, it contemplates a series of commercial and market measures that aim to hamper these odious and harmful fishing practices.

It is precisely the need to tackle these criminal fishing practices that makes it necessary for flag States to exercise as effectively as possible their jurisdiction over the vessels flying their flag. In order for this to happen, it is essential that there is a genuine link between the States and the vessels flying their flag. As we have pointed out throughout this chapter, these requirements do not exist in the case of vessels with flags of convenience. We believe that, in order to fight against illegal fishing, it is urgent both to define the flag State's responsibilities and to introduce mechanisms that will enable verification of whether such responsibilities are being shouldered appropriately. In our view, this would be possible by means of an effective system of registration (regulation and control of fishing vessels in the national register of each State), as well as fishing authorization (the exercise of a fishery to be subject to authorization).

In this context, the traceability of all business operations of the fishing sector can be seen as the key to guarantee that importers, transhippers, clients, consumers, suppliers of materials, banks, insurance companies and other service suppliers in the field of fishing refrain from maintaining commercial relations with vessels involved in illegal fishing. These mechanisms should be complemented by the introduction into national legislations of provisions whereby, on the one hand, fish trade or fish products from illegal fishing should be an offence and, on the other hand, proportionate, transparent and non-discriminatory trade sanctions should be established. Undoubtedly, this would reflect the present global scenario of fisheries relations. As Bruno Simma and Andreas Th. Müller so eloquently state, "[t]he world of international law has become more differentiated and colourful also in terms of actors and beneficiaries" [149].

It is worth pointing out in this regard that the contemporary dimensions of the criminal acts at sea justify a change of course regarding the primacy of the flag State jurisdiction and the freedom of navigation. States cannot be indifferent to these new realities. Hence, we consider that it is not anymore possible to apply the classical rule according to which the flag State is responsible for the fight against criminal acts committed on high seas, and the coastal State is responsible for the fight against criminal acts committed in the different marine areas under its sovereignty or jurisdiction. Moreover, although all States are aware of this fact, none of them seem to be willing to change the rules of the game when they make decisions.

It is submitted that the main problem nowadays in the fight against illegal fishing is not so much the lack of sufficient legal instruments with pertinent provisions as the lack of will to apply the existing legal framework at the international, regional and national level. In short, all of these are legal instruments — many of them very recent ones — and actions which enable us to fight against illegal fishing and, hence, to improve the welfare of the fishing communities worldwide, to establish a fair trade for fish products, and to achieve sustainability of fishery resources and a better management and control of global fisheries.

149. B. Simma and A. T. Müller, *op. cit.*, p. 156.

5 La compétence des tribunaux internes en matière de piraterie

Aikaterini Grymaneli *

SECTION 1 INTRODUCTION

Phénomène que l'on croyait obsolète et que l'on se contentait d'aborder plutôt sous un angle littéraire et artistique non sans un certain romantisme, la piraterie est depuis quelques années de retour. Les incidents se multiplient malgré la réaction de la communauté internationale, notamment au large des côtes somaliennes et plus récemment dans le golfe de Guinée. Selon le rapport annuel pour l'année 2011 de l'Organisation maritime internationale (OMI), cinq cent quarante-quatre (544) incidents de piraterie et de vols à main armée (y compris les simples tentatives) lui ont été signalés, quatre cent quatre-vingt-cinq (485) actes ayant été dénombrés en 2010, ce qui représentait une augmentation de presque 20 % par rapport à 2009 [1].

L'une des raisons principales du relatif échec de la lutte contre la piraterie est sans doute le manque de volonté de la part des Etats d'exercer effectivement et pleinement leur pouvoir juridictionnel, c'est-à-dire au degré le plus élevé qui leur est reconnu par le droit international, représenté par la compétence universelle [2]. En effet, par sa résolution 2077 adoptée le 21 novembre 2012, le Conseil de sécurité, après s'être déclaré « une nouvelle fois inquiet que des personnes soupçonnées de piraterie soient libérées sans avoir été jugées » et « résolu à faire en sorte que les pirates soient amenés à répondre de leurs actes », a

> « [d]emand[é] à tous les Etats d'ériger la piraterie en infraction dans leur droit interne et d'envisager favorablement de poursuivre

* Master 2 recherche en droit international public, Université Paris II (Panthéon-Assas).

1. Rapports annuels 2011, MSC.4/Circ.180, et 2010, MSC.4/Circ.169. Les rapports peuvent être consultés sur le site internet de l'OMI: http://www.imo.org/OurWork/Security/SecDocs/Pages/Maritime-Security.aspx.

2. Pour la distinction entre les termes « pouvoir » et « compétence », voir l'analyse de J. Combacau, « Conclusions générales », dans SFDI, *Les compétences de l'Etat en droit international*, Colloque de Rennes 2005, Paris, Pedone, 2006, notamment pp. 304-309.

> les personnes soupçonnées de piraterie qui ont été appréhendées au large des côtes somaliennes ainsi que celles qui ont facilité ou financé leurs actes et d'incarcérer celles qui ont été reconnues coupables, dans le respect du droit international, y compris du droit international des droits de l'homme».

Incitation réitérée dans maintes résolutions[3] depuis que le Conseil de sécurité s'est saisi de la question de la piraterie au large des côtes somaliennes visant à mettre fin à la pratique dite de «catch and release» suivie par les Etats qui se sont lancés dans la lutte contre la piraterie dans la région[4]. L'Assemblée générale de son côté, dans sa résolution 66/231 *Les océans et le droit de la mer* et en dehors du contexte restreint de la piraterie somalienne, a

> «[e]ngag[é] les Etats à veiller à l'application effective du droit international applicable à la lutte contre la piraterie tel que le consacre la Convention, et les (a) invit(és) à prendre des mesures dans le cadre de leur législation interne pour faciliter, dans le respect du droit international, la capture et la poursuite des personnes soupçonnées d'avoir commis des actes de piraterie, ou d'avoir financé ou facilité de tels actes, en tenant compte des autres instruments pertinents compatibles avec la Convention…»[5].

Cette faille relevée principalement à propos des incidents de piraterie

---

3. S/RES/1851 (2008) du 16 décembre 2008, S/RES/1897 (2009) du 30 novembre 2009, S/RES/1918 (2010) du 27 avril 2010, S/RES/1976 (2011) du 11 avril 2011, S/RES/2015 (2011) du 24 octobre 2011 et S/RES/2020 (2011) du 22 novembre 2011.

4. Dans sa dernière résolution S/RES/2077 (2012), le Conseil de sécurité

> «not[ait] avec préoccupation que le manque de moyens et l'absence de législation interne permettant de détenir et poursuivre les pirates présumés après leur capture ont empêché de mener une action internationale plus vigoureuse contre les pirates agissant au large des côtes somaliennes et, trop souvent, contraint à libérer des pirates sans les avoir traduits en justice alors même que les éléments à charge étaient suffisants pour justifier des poursuites».

La résolution fut adoptée suite au rapport du Secrétaire général au Conseil de sécurité (S/2012/783 du 22 octobre 2012), selon lequel 1186 personnes soupçonnées d'actes de piraterie avaient été traduites en justice ou étaient en attente de jugement dans les vingt Etats suivants: Allemagne, Belgique, Comores, Emirats arabes unis, Espagne, Etats-Unis, France, Inde, Japon, Kenya, Madagascar, Malaisie, Maldives, Oman, Pays-Bas, République de Corée, Seychelles, Somalie (Puntland, Somaliland et Centre-Sud), République-Unie de Tanzanie et Yémen.

Sur le tableau ci-contre figure l'état des poursuites, de 2006 jusqu'au 30 septembre 2012.

5. A/RES/66/231, *Les océans et le droit de la mer*, distribution générale du 5 avril 2012, par. 85.

au large des côtes somaliennes vaut d'autant plus pour les autres régions du monde qui ne sont pas couvertes par les résolutions du Conseil de sécurité incitant les Etats à contribuer à la répression de ladite infraction.

La présente étude se propose de clarifier les contours du champ dans lequel les Etats peuvent exercer leur pouvoir juridictionnel en matière de piraterie et d'examiner dans quelle mesure ce pouvoir est exercé dans la pratique afin de démontrer pourquoi ce phénomène n'a toujours pas été mis en échec — loin s'en faut.

Pays	*Nombre de détenus*	*Notes*
Allemagne	10	
Belgique	2	1 condamné
Comores	6	
Emirats arabes unis	10	
Espagne	8	2 condamnés
Etats-Unis d'Amérique	28	17 condamnés
France	18	5 condamnés
Inde	119	
Japon	4	
Kenya	137	74 condamnés, 17 acquittés, 10 peines exécutées
Madagascar	12	
Malaisie	7	
Maldives	41	En attente de déportation en l'absence de loi permettant d'engager des poursuites
Oman	32	25 condamnés
Pays-Bas	29	10 condamnés
République de Corée	5	5 condamnés
République-Unie de Tanzanie	12	6 condamnés
Seychelles	105	83 condamnés, 2 retournés au Puntland
Somalie		
« Puntland »	290	Environ 240 condamnés
« Somaliland »	35	35 condamnés (76 ultérieurement remis en liberté)
« Centre-sud »	18	L'état des poursuites n'est pas clair
Yémen	123	123 condamnés, 6 acquittés

Si la Convention de Montego Bay sur le droit de la mer est la source principale du régime de la répression de la piraterie, elle n'est pas la seule applicable en la matière: les Etats peuvent (ou doivent) s'appuyer sur d'autres conventions, comme celle pour la répression d'actes illicites contre la sécurité de la navigation maritime de 1988 ou celle contre la prise d'otages de 1979 (section 2). Certes les sources de droit international prévoient jusqu'où peut aller l'action des Etats dans la poursuite des pirates présumés, mais il n'en reste pas moins que les Etats les traduisent en justice en vertu de leur droit interne. Il convient donc d'étudier comment les Etats ont incorporé le droit international dans leur droit interne et comment ils l'interprètent (section 3).

SECTION 2 LES SOURCES DU DROIT INTERNATIONAL APPLICABLE EN MATIÈRE DE PIRATERIE

La Convention de Montego Bay de 1982, reflétant le droit international général applicable en la matière, sert de point de référence pour la définition de l'infraction et le régime de sa répression (paragraphe 1). Une fois les éléments constitutifs de la piraterie précisés, il convient d'étudier les autres conventions internationales qui lui sont applicables (paragraphe 2).

Paragraphe 1 Définition de la piraterie

A. La définition de la piraterie en vertu du droit international général

Diverses définitions de la piraterie — certaines étroites, d'autres larges — ont été proposées par la doctrine avant l'apparition de textes internationaux recueillant un certain consensus autour de la notion et de ses éléments constitutifs[6].

Il convient de s'entendre sur le concept actuel de piraterie et pour ce

6. Pour une définition assez large, voir J. Basdevant, *Dictionnaire de la terminologie du droit international*, Sirey, Paris, 1960, p. 452:

> «Brigandage maritime. Fait de courir les mers sans commission d'aucun Etat en commettant à des fins privées des actes de violence contre les personnes et les biens, mettant en danger la sécurité générale, considéré, en conséquence, comme un crime du droit des gens dont la répression appartient à tout Etat, quel que soit le pavillon arboré par le pirate.»

Pour un recueil de définitions doctrinales, voir Harvard Law School, *Research in International Law — Drafts of Conventions Prepared for the Codification of International Law. IV. Piracy*, Cambridge, Massachusetts, 1932, pp. 769-784.

faire on va s'appuyer sur la définition contenue dans la Convention des Nations Unies sur le droit de la mer signée à Montego Bay le 10 décembre 1982 (ci-après CNUDM), qui reprend quasiment mot à mot celle de la Convention de Genève de 1958 sur la haute mer[7] — elle-même appuyée largement sur le Harvard Draft Convention on Piracy de 1932[8] — et qui est largement admise comme codifiant des règles coutumières en la matière[9].

La CNUDM, dans ses articles 100 à 107, expose le cadre juridique de la lutte contre la piraterie.

Selon l'article 101,

> « on entend par piraterie l'un quelconque des actes suivants :
>
> *a)* tout acte illicite de violence ou de détention ou toute déprédation commis par l'équipage ou des passagers d'un navire ou d'un aéronef privé, agissant à des fins privées, et dirigé :
>
> i) contre un autre navire ou aéronef, ou contre des personnes ou des biens à leur bord, en haute mer ;
>
> ii) contre un navire ou aéronef, des personnes ou des biens, dans un lieu ne relevant de la juridiction d'aucun Etat ;
>
> *b)* tout acte de participation volontaire à l'utilisation d'un navire ou d'un aéronef, lorsque son auteur a connaissance de faits dont il découle que ce navire ou aéronef est un navire ou aéronef pirate ;
> *c)* tout acte ayant pour but d'inciter à commettre les actes définis aux lettres *a)* ou *b)*, ou commis dans l'intention de les faciliter ».

7. Convention sur la haute mer, conclue à Genève le 29 avril 1958. Entrée en vigueur le 30 septembre 1962, *RTNU*, vol. 450, p. 82, art. 15.

8. Harvard Law School, *Research in International Law — Drafts of Conventions…*, *op. cit.*, pp. 739-1013.

9. Toutes les résolutions du Conseil de sécurité affirment que « le droit international, tel qu'édicté dans la Convention des Nations Unies sur le droit de la mer, en date du 10 décembre 1982, définit le cadre juridique de la lutte contre la piraterie en mer ». Sur le plan doctrinal, voir D. Guilfoyle, « Prosecuting Somali Pirates : A Critical Evaluation of the Options », *Journal of International Criminal Justice (JICJ)*, n° 10, 2012, p. 771 ; J. Combacau et S. Sur, *Droit international public*, Montchrestien, Paris, 2010, p. 461 ; I. Shearer, « Piracy », *Max Planck Encyclopedia of Public International Law*, version électronique mise à jour en octobre 2010 ; T. Treves, « Piracy, Law of the Sea, and Use of Force : Developments off the Coast of Somalia », *European Journal of International Law (EJIL)*, n° 20, 2009, p. 401 ; M. H. Nordquist (dir. publ.), *United Nations Convention on the Law of the Sea 1982 : A Commentary*, vol. III, Martinus Nijhoff Publishers, La Haye/Londres/Boston, 1995, p. 197 ; R.-J. Dupuy et D. Vignes, *Traité du nouveau droit de la mer*, Economica, Bruylant, 1985, pp. 368-369 ; voir néanmoins l'aphorisme de Rubin qui affirme que les règles conventionnelles sur la piraterie sont « incomprehensible and therefore codify nothing » (A. P. Rubin, *The Law of Piracy*, New York, Transnational Publishers, 1997, pp. 373 et 393) ; pour une position plus nuancée, voir L. Lucchini et M. Voelckel, *Droit de la mer*, vol. 2, Pédone, Paris, 1996, pp. 159-160.

On ne va pas s'attarder sur tous les problèmes que posent les ambiguïtés des termes employés par cet article, qui ont fait d'ailleurs l'objet de maintes analyses doctrinales[10]. Une chose est certaine : les actes commis peuvent présenter des caractères tellement singuliers que l'on ne peut pas toujours les qualifier avec certitude d'actes de piraterie. Les ambiguïtés se reflètent dans la transposition de la définition *jure gentium* en droit interne : tous les Etats n'entendent pas de la même manière le terme piraterie, ce qui donne des jurisprudences divergentes[11] (section 3, paragraphe 1).

Pour résumer, on requiert un/des acte(s) de violence ou de détention ou une déprédation commis en haute mer (ou dans un lieu ne relevant de la juridiction d'aucun Etat) à des fins privées par l'équipage ou des passagers d'un navire privé et dirigés contre un autre navire ou contre des personnes ou des biens à son bord.

Sont ainsi exclus de la piraterie *jure gentium* les actes commis dans la mer territoriale ou les eaux intérieures, même s'ils sont matériellement identiques à ceux commis en haute mer. En matière de piraterie, la zone économique exclusive est assimilée à la haute mer selon l'article 58 de la CNUDM et compte tenu de la raison d'être de la juridiction de l'Etat côtier sur cette zone qui se limite aux fins d'exploration, d'exploitation, de conservation et de gestion des ressources naturelles. Qu'il soit clair : il ne peut être question de piraterie que si les actes sont commis dans un espace en dehors de la juridiction nationale d'un Etat quelconque.

La condition des « deux navires » ne demande pas plus de précisions. L'adoption de la Convention pour la répression d'actes illicites contre la sécurité de la sécurité maritime (SUA) de 1988 (paragraphe 2) s'explique, notamment, par le fait justement que la CNUDM ne couvrait pas les cas de mutinerie ou de détournement de navire « de l'intérieur ».

Quant à la condition relative à la commission d'actes « à des fins privées », la question de savoir si ceux commis dans un but politique rentrent dans la notion de piraterie fut longtemps très controversée et continue de l'être. Si la CNUDM exige que l'acte ait été commis à des fins « privées » (et avant elle, la Convention de Genève pour des buts « personnels », or les deux instruments emploient l'expression « private ends »

10. A titre indicatif, voir J. L. Jesus, « Protection of Foreign Ships against Piracy and Terrorism at Sea : Legal Aspects », *International Journal of Marine and Constal Law (IJMCL)*, 2003, vol. 18, n° 3, pp. 375-381 ; L. Lucchini et M. Voelckel, *Droit de la mer, op. cit.*, pp. 153-174 ; M. Halberstam, « Terrorism on the High Seas : The Achille Lauro, Piracy and the IMO Convention on Maritime Safety », *American Journal of International Law (AJIL)*, 1988, n° 82, pp. 276-290.

11. Voir M. Gardner, « Piracy Prosecutions in National Courts », *JICJ*, n° 10, 2012, p. 798.

en version anglaise, ce qui nous conduit à tenir les termes pour interchangeables[12]), cela ne veut pas dire qu'il doive nécessairement avoir été commis *animo furandi*. Alors que, selon certains auteurs, l'expression exclut tout acte commis à des fins politiques, d'autres, trouvant cette approche très extensive, soutiennent que ce n'est pas la motivation qui compte mais l'endossement étatique du comportement[13]. Ainsi ne seraient commis à des fins privées que les actes qui ne recueillent pas l'approbation étatique. Cette interprétation semble plus fidèle à l'historique de l'adoption de ladite disposition. Selon le commentaire du Harvard Draft Convention, la condition des «fins privées» a été ajoutée afin d'exclure les actes des belligérants contre le gouvernement qu'ils cherchaient à renverser, le commentaire de la Convention de Genève ne nous éclairant guère plus en la matière[14].

B. Des définitions extensives?

i) *OMI*

L'OMI, agence spécialisée des Nations Unies, se contente de renvoyer à la définition contenue dans la CNUDM et opère la distinction entre la piraterie et les vols à main armée en mer, distinction officialisée dans le Code de conduite adopté le 29 novembre 2001 par son assemblée et intitulé *Code of Practice for the Investigation of the Crimes of Piracy and Armed Robbery against Ships*[15]. Le vol à main armée y est défini comme «any unlawful act of violence or detention or any act of depredation, or threat thereof, other than an act of piracy, directed against a

---

12. Voir J. Verhoeven, *Droit international public*, Larcier, Bruxelles, 2000, p. 568, qui cite la décision de la Cour de cassation belge du 19 décembre 1986 (*Pas*., 1987, 1, 497) relative aux actes de violence commis par Greenpeace pour s'opposer à l'immersion de déchets en haute mer. Voir République des Seychelles C. Dahir, SCSC 86, du 26 juillet 2010.

13. En ce sens D. Guilfoyle, *Treaty Jurisdiction over Pirates: A Compilation of Legal Texts with Introductory Notes*, par. 11, http://ucl.academia.edu/DouglasGuilfoyle/Papers/116803/Treaty_Jurisdiction_over_Pirates_A_Compilation_of_Legal_Texts_with_Introductory_Notes; D. Guilfoyle, *Shipping Interdiction and the Law of the Sea,* Cambridge University Press, 2009, p. 36; R. Geiss et A. Petrig, *Piracy and Armed Robbery at Sea: The Legal Framework for Counter-piracy Operations in Somalia and the Gulf of Aden*, Oxford University Press, 2011, p. 61; la législation japonaise, voir A. Kanehara, «Japanese Legal Regime Combating Piracy-Act on Punishment of and Measures against Acts of Piracy», *Japanese Yearbook of International Law*, 2010, n° 53, p. 478.

14. Harvard Law School, *Research in International Law — Drafts of Conventions..., op. cit.*, pp. 798 et 857; *Annuaire de la Commission de droit international*, 1955, vol. 1, p. 40; R. Geiss et A. Petrig, *Piracy and Armed Robbery at Sea..., op. cit.*, p. 61.

15. Résolution A.922(22), révoquée par la résolution A.1025(26) adoptée le 2 décembre 2009, qui maintient la distinction.

ship or against persons or property on board such a ship, within a State's jurisdiction over such offences»[16].

La définition de la piraterie contenue dans la CNUDM n'est donc pas remise en cause. Le vol à main armée est une infraction à part qui vient combler certaines lacunes, puisque, avec son introduction, sont désormais couverts les actes qui ont lieu dans un espace relevant de la juridiction d'un Etat sans que la condition des deux navires ne soit requise.

ii) *BMI*

Le Bureau maritime international (BMI), division interne de la Chambre de commerce internationale, qui recense les incidents de piraterie et de vol à main armée en mer, adopte lui aussi la définition de la piraterie de la CNUDM ainsi que la définition du vol à main armée en mer donnée par l'OMI dans sa résolution A.1025(26)[17]. Il ne semble pas pour autant tirer des conséquences de cette distinction, mélangeant dans ses rapports les incidents ayant eu lieu dans des espaces internationaux et dans des espaces sous juridiction nationale, ce qui paraît assez compréhensible vu que son objectif est de dresser des statistiques afin de prévenir l'industrie *shipping* sur les dangers que courent les navires[18].

iii) *Conseil de sécurité*

Le Conseil de sécurité, dans ses résolutions relatives à la «piraterie» somalienne, endosse quant à lui la distinction entre piraterie et vols à main armée dans l'optique d'établir un cadre complet pour la lutte contre des actes portant atteinte à la sécurité maritime dans la région. Il ne ressort pas clairement des formules employées si la distinction tient au lieu de commission de l'infraction. Il convient d'interpréter la phrase «des actes de piraterie et des vols à main armée commis dans les eaux

16. La résolution A.1025(26) remplace «within a State's jurisdiction» par «within a State's internal waters, archipelagic waters and territorial sea» et ajoute «any act of inciting or of intentionally facilitating an act described above».

17. Voir rapport annuel du BMI pour 2011.

18. Voir D. Chang, «Piracy Laws and the Effective Prosecution of Pirates», *Boston College ILR,* n° 33, 2010, pp. 276-277:

> «For statistical purposes, the IMB adopts a broad definition of piracy that includes actual and attempted attacks both when the ship is at anchor or at sea. Thus, the IMB defines «piracy and armed robbery» as «an act of boarding or attempting to board any ship with the apparent intent to commit theft or any other crime and with the apparent intent or capability to use force in the furtherance of that act». The IMB's expansive definition affects the number of attacks that the IMB will track. Since this definition differs from the UNCLOS and SUA definitions of piracy, not every incident reported to IMB would be considered formal piracy under international law.»

territoriales de la Somalie et en haute mer»[19], qui a été remplacée par la suite par la phrase «piraterie et vols à main armée en mer au large des côtes somaliennes»[20], conjointement avec celle répétée dans chaque résolution et réaffirmant que le cadre juridique de la lutte contre ces infractions est celui fixé par la Convention de Montego Bay. Etant donné que celle-ci donne une définition stricte de la piraterie la réservant aux actes commis en haute mer, les vols à main armée, eux, doivent avoir lieu dans les eaux territoriales de la Somalie. L'intérêt de la distinction réside dans les pouvoirs accordés aux Etats. Ainsi, non seulement les Etats peuvent pénétrer dans la mer territoriale afin de continuer la poursuite qui a commencé en haute mer (poursuite chaude inversée), mais ils peuvent également réprimer en mer territoriale des actes de vol à main armée commis en mer territoriale.

Paragraphe 2 **Autres conventions susceptibles d'application en matière de piraterie**

A. La Convention pour la répression d'actes illicites contre la sécurité de la navigation maritime (SUA)[21]

L'arsenal juridique traditionnellement axé sur la CNUDM se voit enrichi par la convention connue sous le sigle SUA, conçue après le détournement du paquebot italien *Achille Lauro* en 1985 par un groupe «terroriste» palestinien, cas auquel les dispositions de la CNUDM relatives à la piraterie n'étaient pas applicables étant donné que l'incident n'impliquait pas deux navires[22]. La convention vise sans distinction tous les actes de violence envers les navires ayant lieu dans les espaces maritimes au-delà de la juridiction nationale d'un Etat sans tenir compte des finalités poursuivies. Son article 3, paragraphe 1, établit que

«commet une infraction pénale, toute personne qui, illicitement et

---

19. S/RES/1816 (2008), par. 3, et S/RES/1846, par. 17.

20. La phrase « piraterie et vols à main armée commis en mer » a été reprise dans les récentes résolutions concernant le golfe de Guinée (S/RES/2018 (2011), S/RES/2039 (2012)).

21. Conclue à Rome le 10 mars 1988, *RTNU*, 1992, vol. 1678; cent soixante Etats parties à la Convention et vingt-deux au Protocole de 2005 selon l'OMI: http://www.imo.org/About/Conventions/StatusOfConventions/Documents/Status%20-%202012.pdf (version du 30 septembre 2012).

22. L'incident a par ailleurs ranimé le débat autour de la notion des «fins privées» de l'article 101 de la CNUDM puisque les auteurs des actes avaient détourné le navire et pris les passagers en otages dans le but d'exercer une pression sur Israël afin d'obtenir la libération de cinquante Palestiniens prisonniers. Voir J.-P. Pancracio, «L'affaire de l'*Achille Lauro* et le droit international», *AFDI*, n° 31, 1985, pp. 221-236; M. Halberstam, «Terrorism on the High Seas...», *op. cit.*, pp. 269-310.

> intentionnellement *a)* s'empare d'un navire ou en exerce le contrôle par violence ou menace de violence; *b)* ou accomplit un acte de violence à l'encontre d'une personne se trouvant à bord d'un navire, si cet acte est de nature à compromettre la sécurité de la navigation du navire; *c)* ou détruit un navire ou cause à un navire ou à sa cargaison des dommages qui sont de nature à compromettre la sécurité de la navigation du navire; *d)* ou place ou fait placer sur un navire, par quelque moyen que ce soit, un dispositif ou une substance propre à détruire le navire ou à causer au navire ou à sa cargaison des dommages qui compromettent ou sont de nature à compromettre la sécurité de la navigation du navire... ».

On constate que la convention ne fait pas référence à la piraterie expressément, or certains actes peuvent constituer à la fois la piraterie et une infraction sous la convention SUA. Ainsi en est-il d'un acte de violence dans le but de s'emparer d'un navire et en exercer le contrôle, ou des actes de violence à l'encontre des personnes à bord, lorsque ceux-ci compromettent la sécurité de la navigation dudit navire et qu'ils impliquent deux navires.

Ce champ d'application *ratione materiae* de la convention en fait un outil supplémentaire dans la lutte contre la piraterie, ce que confirment le Code de conduite de l'OMI[23] ainsi que les résolutions du Conseil de sécurité sur la piraterie somalienne[24]. Cela étant, la convention a été peu utilisée dans la pratique en matière de piraterie. A notre connaissance, seules les juridictions des Etats-Unis et des Pays-Bas ont poursuivi et condamné des pirates somaliens sur la base de la convention SUA. Cela est peut-être dû au fait qu'après tout la SUA est un instrument simplement complémentaire par rapport à la Convention de Montego Bay, qui, malgré ses quelques ambiguïtés, fournit le cadre juridique principal et

23. Voir l'article 3, paragraphe 2, du *Code of Practice for the Investigation of Crimes of Piracy and Armed Robbery against Ships*, résolution A.1025 (26): «States are encouraged to implement the provisions of UNCLOS, the Convention for the Suppression of Unlawful Acts Against the Safety of Navigation, 1988, and the Protocol for the Suppression of Unlawful Acts against the Safety of Fixed Platforms Located on the Continental Shelf, 1988.»

24. Voir, par exemple, S/RES/1846 (2008), par. 15: «exhorte les Etats parties à ladite Convention à s'acquitter pleinement des obligations que celle-ci leur impose»; S/RES/1851 (2008), par. 5: «encourage également tous les Etats... qui luttent contre la piraterie et les vols à main armée au large des côtes somaliennes ... à appliquer la Convention pour la répression d'actes illicites contre la sécurité de la navigation maritime»; S/RES/1897(2009), par 14, S/RES/1950 (2010), par. 19, et S/RES/2020 (2011), par. 23: «exhorte les Etats parties à la Convention (ndlr: «de Montego Bay») et à la Convention pour la répression d'actes illicites contre la sécurité de la navigation maritime à s'acquitter pleinement des obligations que leur imposent en la matière lesdites conventions».

suffisant pour la lutte contre la piraterie. D'ailleurs, celle-ci confère aux Etats le maximum de compétences pour y faire face — dont la possibilité de saisir en haute mer des navires battant pavillon étranger, d'appréhender des pirates présumés qui ne sont pas leurs nationaux et d'étendre leur pouvoir juridictionnel à leur égard (compétence universelle, section 3, paragraphe 2) et cela sans les y obliger. En revanche, la convention SUA énonce une obligation expresse d'ériger en infraction dans leurs droits internes les actes prévus dans l'article 3 et prévoit l'exercice du pouvoir juridictionnel sur la base des titres classiques, grosso modo de type territorial ou personnel. S'y ajoute une obligation d'exercer ce pouvoir dès que l'individu se trouve sur leur territoire à défaut de l'extrader vers un autre Etat partie qui le réclamerait (obligation *aut dedere aut judicare*, section 3, paragraphe 2). Cette dernière paraît assez contraignante aux Etats qui préfèrent jouir d'une certaine discrétion à propos des suites à donner à l'arrestation des auteurs présumés des actes en cause. Une autre explication pour la non-invocation de la SUA pourrait être trouvée dans le fait que celle-ci exige que l'auteur présumé des actes se trouve sur leur territoire, ce qui n'est pas d'habitude le cas : les navires d'Etat appréhendent des navires et arrêtent des personnes en haute mer, loin du territoire de l'Etat auquel ils appartiennent, ce qui veut dire que l'auteur ne « se trouve pas sur le territoire », à moins que l'on considère que le navire capteur est une portion du territoire de son Etat, ce qui n'est plus soutenu aujourd'hui. D'aucuns proposent, afin de sortir de cette impasse, une interprétation large de cette condition qui consisterait à considérer qu'il suffit que la personne arrêtée soit sous la juridiction de l'Etat, ce qui sera le cas dès le moment de l'arrestation[25] ; or on comprend bien que l'on se trouve ici devant l'hypothèse très rare selon laquelle les Etats témoigneraient d'une volonté de poursuivre et chercheraient un fondement juridique à leur action. Les Etats-Unis ont surmonté cet obstacle dans l'arrêt *Etats-Unis c. Shi* de 2008 avec une argumentation selon laquelle « later found » sur le territoire ne veut pas forcément dire « volontairement » ; suivant cette jurisprudence, on pourrait considérer qu'il suffirait que les navires de guerre ayant effectué l'arrestation amènent le suspect sur le territoire de leur Etat[26].

Enfin, le fait que la convention a été conçue principalement comme

25. Voir R. Geiss et A. Petrig, *Piracy and Armed Robbery at Sea…, op. cit.*, p. 164.

26. United States Court of Appeals for the Ninth Circuit, *United States c. Shi*, nº 06-10389 D.C. et nº CR-02-00116-1-HG, 24 avril 2008 : « [10] We are persuaded by this analysis, and conclude that the requirement that a defendant be « later found » does not contain the implicit requirement that the defendant's arrival in the United States be voluntary. »

un instrument de lutte contre le terrorisme joue un rôle dissuasif quant à son invocation pour lutter contre la piraterie[27].

B. La Convention internationale contre la prise d'otages[28]

La Convention internationale contre la prise d'otages définit l'infraction de prise d'otages comme les actes commis par « quiconque s'empare d'une personne (ci-après dénommée « otage »), ou la détient et menace de la tuer, de la blesser ou de continuer à la détenir afin de contraindre une tierce partie, à savoir un Etat, une organisation internationale intergouvernementale, une personne physique ou morale ou un groupe de personnes, à accomplir un acte quelconque ou à s'en abstenir en tant que condition explicite ou implicite de la libération de l'otage » (art.1(1)). Constituent également des infractions aux fins de cette convention la tentative de commission et la complicité à la commission d'un acte de prise d'otages (art.1(2)). On y reconnait le *modus operandi* des pirates somaliens qui s'emparent des navires, tiennent les passagers ou l'équipage en otage et réclament des rançons contre leur libération. La convention, ne contenant pas de limitations territoriales, peut s'appliquer à des actes commis en haute mer. En effet, son article 5 prévoit que

> « tout Etat partie prend les mesures nécessaires pour établir sa compétence aux fins de connaître des infractions prévues à l'article premier, qui sont commises : *a)* sur son territoire ou à bord d'un navire ou d'un aéronef immatriculé dans ledit Etat ; *b)* par l'un quelconque de ses ressortissants, ou, si cet Etat le juge approprié, par les apatrides qui ont leur résidence habituelle sur son territoire ; *c)* pour le contraindre à accomplir un acte quelconque ou à s'en abstenir ; ou *d)* à l'encontre d'un otage qui est ressortissant de cet Etat lorsque ce dernier le juge approprié ».

---

27. Voir J.-P. Pancracio, *Droit international de la mer*, Dalloz, Paris, 2010, p. 447 :

> « du point de vue de la définition de la piraterie ... elle apporte plus de confusion que d'éclaircissement ... Au regard de la lutte contre la piraterie maritime, la convention de 1988 apparaît peu efficiente parce que trop marquée par le contexte de la lutte contre le terrorisme ».

Voir aussi M. Halberstam, « Terrorist Acts against and on Board Ships », *Israel Yearbook on Human Rights*, 1989, n° 19, pp. 331-342 ; C. C. Joyner, « Suppression of Terrorism on the High Seas : The 1988 IMO Convention on the Safety of Maritime Navigation », *Israel Yearbook on Human Rights*, 1989, n° 19, pp. 343-369.

28. Adoptée par l'Assemblée générale des Nations Unies le 17 décembre 1979, *RTNU*, 1983, vol. 1316, p. 205 ; http://treaties.un.org/pages/ViewDetails.aspx?src=TREATY&mtdsg_no=XVIII-5&chapter=18&lang=fr (cent soixante-dix Etats parties, dernière visite le 30 octobre 12).

La convention est intéressante, d'une part, par cette panoplie de bases de compétence qu'elle offre — certaines obligatoires, d'autres facultatives — d'autre part, par l'inclusion d'une obligation de poursuivre ou d'extrader, tout comme la convention SUA. Il est étonnant, à cet égard, que le Conseil de sécurité n'exhorte pas expressément les Etats à l'utiliser, bien qu'il condamne les prises d'otages et souligne la nécessité de poursuivre les pirates présumés pour prise d'otages[29]. On pourrait supposer que sa formulation qui la rapproche des conventions antiterroristes la rend moins susceptible d'invocation dans le contexte de la piraterie somalienne.

C. La Convention des Nations Unies contre la criminalité transnationale organisée[30]

La convention couvre *inter alia* le blanchiment du produit du crime (art. 6), la corruption (art. 8), l'entrave au bon fonctionnement de la justice (art. 23), ainsi que des infractions graves définies comme des actes constituant des infractions passibles d'une peine privative de liberté dont le maximum ne doit pas être inférieur à quatre ans ou d'une peine plus lourde (art. 2). Les Etats parties sont là encore invités à conférer le caractère d'infraction pénale, lorsque commis intentionnellement, i) au fait de s'entendre avec une ou plusieurs personnes en vue de commettre une infraction grave à une fin liée directement ou indirectement à l'obtention d'un avantage financier ou autre avantage matériel et, lorsque le droit interne l'exige, impliquant un acte commis par un des participants en vertu de cette entente ou impliquant un groupe criminel organisé; ii) à la participation active d'une personne ayant connaissance

29. La résolution S/RES/2020 (2011)

> «constat[e] que les pirates se tournent de plus en plus vers les enlèvements et la prise d'otages et que ces activités les aident à se procurer des fonds pour acheter des armes, attirer de nouvelles recrues et poursuivre leurs opérations, mettant ainsi en danger la sûreté et la sécurité de civils innocents et portant atteinte à la liberté du commerce; réaffirm[e] la condamnation que suscitent dans la communauté internationale les enlèvements et les prises d'otages, y compris ceux qui sont réprimés par la Convention internationale contre la prise d'otages; condamn[e] fermement la pratique persistante de la prise d'otages par des pirates présumés opérant au large des côtes somaliennes; se déclar[e] gravement préoccupé par les conditions inhumaines dans lesquelles les otages sont retenus en captivité; conscient des répercussions sur la vie de leur famille; demand[e] la libération immédiate de tous les otages et constat[e] l'importance de la coopération entre Etats Membres concernant la question de la prise d'otages, ainsi que la nécessité de poursuivre les pirates présumés pour prise d'otages...».

30. Adoptée par l'Assemblée générale des Nations Unies, résolution 55/25, du 15 novembre 2000.

soit du but et de l'activité criminelle générale d'un groupe criminel organisé soit de son intention de commettre les infractions en question: a. aux activités criminelles du groupe criminel organisé; b. à d'autres activités du groupe criminel organisé lorsque cette personne sait que sa participation contribuera à la réalisation du but criminel susmentionné (art. 5).

La condition de transnationalité est satisfaite lorsque l'infraction est commise: *a)* dans plus d'un Etat; *b)* dans un Etat mais qu'une partie substantielle de sa préparation, de sa planification, de sa conduite ou de son contrôle a lieu dans un autre Etat; *c)* dans un Etat mais implique un groupe criminel organisé qui se livre à des activités criminelles dans plus d'un Etat; *d)* dans un Etat mais a des effets substantiels dans un autre Etat (art. 3). Enfin, la condition du «groupe criminel organisé» est remplie lorsqu'on est en présence d'un groupe structuré de trois personnes ou plus existant depuis un certain temps et agissant de concert dans le but de commettre une ou plusieurs infractions graves ou infractions établies conformément à la présente convention, pour en tirer, directement ou indirectement, un avantage financier ou un autre avantage matériel (art. 2).

La convention peut s'appliquer dans le contexte de la piraterie dans la mesure où les actes de piraterie — actes de violence, prises d'otages — peuvent être considérés comme des «infractions graves». Quant à l'élément transnational, le problème qui se pose est si la commission en haute mer peut rentrer dans le champ d'application de la convention. Une interprétation combinée des articles 15.1.*b)* qui prévoit que «chaque Etat Partie adopte les mesures nécessaires pour établir sa compétence à l'égard des infractions établies conformément aux articles 5, 6, 8 et 23 ... lorsque l'infraction est commise à bord d'un navire qui bat son pavillon ... au moment où ladite infraction est commise» et 3, ci-dessus exposé, permet d'admettre l'application de la convention aux actes commis à bord d'un navire d'un Etat partie — celui-ci se trouvant dans un espace ne relevant pas de la juridiction nationale d'un Etat — et préparés ou planifiés sur le territoire d'un autre Etat.

La convention s'inscrit dans le même cadre que celles précitées eu égard aux bases de compétence qu'elle prévoit et de l'inclusion de la clause *aut dedere aut judicare*.

Si le Conseil de sécurité ne la mentionne pas *expressis verbis* dans ses résolutions, il «*considère* qu'il faut prendre des mesures d'enquête et de poursuite non seulement contre les pirates présumés capturés en mer, mais aussi contre quiconque incite à la commission d'un acte de piraterie ou la facilite intentionnellement, y compris les cerveaux des réseaux criminels de piraterie qui planifient, organisent, facilitent ou financent les attaques perpétrées par des pirates ou en tirent profit illicitement» ou «*prie instamment* tous les Etats de prendre les mesures voulues dans le cadre de leur droit interne en vigueur pour empêcher le financement illicite d'actes de piraterie et le blanchiment des produits qui en sont tirés»[31], ce qui renvoie implicitement aux infractions couvertes par cette convention.

SECTION 3 POUVOIR JURIDICTIONNEL DES ÉTATS EN MATIÈRE DE PIRATERIE

Si le droit international général reconnaît aux Etats la compétence universelle en la matière, il n'en reste pas moins que cette compétence a un caractère facultatif, lacune qui peut être comblée par l'application d'autres conventions qui prévoient des obligations concrètes pour les Etats parties (paragraphe 2). Que la compétence soit facultative ou obligatoire, le pouvoir juridictionnel des Etats ne peut être exercé que si ceux-ci ont préalablement incriminé la piraterie dans leur droit interne (paragraphe 1).

Paragraphe 1 La piraterie, entre droit international et droit interne

A. De la nécessité d'ériger la piraterie en crime dans le droit interne

On a répété *ad nauseam* que la piraterie est le plus ancien exemple d'application du principe de compétence universelle, réservée normalement aux crimes internationaux les plus graves, tels que les crimes de guerre, les crimes contre l'humanité ou le génocide. La piraterie est-elle toutefois vraiment un crime international[32]? Il est utile de noter que la Commission du droit international ne l'a pas incluse dans son projet de Code des crimes contre la paix et la sécurité de l'humanité de 1954[33] et que, depuis, elle n'a jamais été inscrite dans la liste

31. S/RES/2020 (2011), par. 17.

32. Voir définition dans J. Salmon, *Dictionnaire de droit international public*, Bruylant, Bruxelles, 2001, p. 289: «crime ou délit du droit des gens», expression doctrinale vieillie couvrant des violations de normes fondamentales du droit des gens.

33. *Annuaire de la Commission du droit international*, 1951, vol. II, p. 134, par. 52 *a)*:

> «The Commission first considered the meaning of the term «offences against the peace and security of mankind», contained in resolution 177 (II). The view of the Commission was that the meaning of this term should be limited to offences which contain a political element and which endanger

des crimes dont la poursuite a été prise en charge par la justice pénale internationale[34].

Selon les rédacteurs du Harvard Draft Convention on Piracy, la piraterie n'est pas un crime du droit des gens. Elle est simplement

> «the basis of an extraordinary jurisdiction in every state to seize and to prosecute and punish persons, and to seize and dispose of property, for factual offences which are committed outside the territorial and other ordinary jurisdiction of the prosecuting state and which do not involve attacks on its peculiar interests»[35].

Ainsi le projet d'article 14, paragraphe 2, dispose-t-il que «subject to the provisions of this convention, the law of the state which exercises such jurisdiction defines the crime, governs the procedure and prescribes the penalty»[36]. Il est ainsi évident que cela revient aux Etats souhaitant réprimer des actes de piraterie au sens du droit international d'incorporer le crime dans leurs droits internes, de le définir, d'en prévoir la procédure des poursuites et les peines à infliger[37].

> or disturb the maintenance of international peace and security. For these reasons, the draft code does not deal with questions concerning conflicts of legislation and jurisdiction in international criminal matters; nor does it include such matters as piracy, traffic in dangerous drugs, traffic in women and children, slavery, counterfeiting currency, damage to submarine cables, etc.»

34. Voir les crimes contenus dans le Statut de Rome de la Cour pénale internationale, adopté le 17 juillet 1998, *RTNU*, vol. 2187, n° 38544, pp. 3 ss., art. 5-8.

35. Harvard Law School, *Research in International Law — Drafts of Conventions…*, *op. cit.*, p. 760.

36. En ce sens, R. Geiss et A. Petrig, *Piracy and Armed Robbery at Sea…*, *op. cit.*, pp. 139-143.

37. Voir V. Pella, «La répression de la piraterie», *RCADI*, 1926, vol. 15, p. 181:

> «Il faut soigneusement séparer l'incrimination des actes de piraterie, considérée en elle-même, et l'universalité de la répression qui en est une conséquence. Quant à l'incrimination en elle-même, elle trouve son fondement dans la législation des différents Etats et non dans la coutume internationale. En effet, la grande majorité des Etats prévoient et punissent les actes de piraterie du droit commun, par leurs codes pénaux ou par des lois spéciales.»

En ce sens, voir aussi la décision *In Re Piracy Jure Gentium*, [1934] A.C. 586 (P.C. 1934) (UK):

> «with regard to crimes as defined by international law, that law has no means of trying or punishing them. The recognition of international crimes as constituting domestic crimes, and the trial and punishment of criminals are left to the municipal courts of each country.»

Dans une opinion *R* v. *Jones (Appellant)*, [2006] UKHL 16, le House of Lords a dit que (par. 28)

> «when it is sought to give domestic effect to crimes established in customary international law, the practice is to legislate. Examples may be found

Si la piraterie telle que conçue par la Convention de Montego Bay ne s'apparente pas aux autres infractions qui constituent sans doute des crimes internationaux[38], cela ne veut pas pour autant dire que ce n'est pas un crime du droit des gens. Simplement, sans incrimination de ladite activité dans les droits internes, la poursuite des auteurs est impossible. Inversement, si elle n'avait pas été érigée en infraction par le droit international d'abord, les Etats n'auraient pas pu étendre leur pouvoir juridictionnel à des actes avec lesquels rien ne les lie. Incrimination par le droit international et incrimination par le droit interne se trouvent ainsi étroitement liées[39]. Certes les législations nationales peuvent employer le terme «piraterie» comme bon leur semble, c'est-à-dire pour des actes qui ne correspondent pas à la notion de piraterie *jure gentium*, comme ils l'ont déjà fait à propos d'actes de violence et de déprédations perpétrés dans des espaces sous leur juridiction nationale[40], mais cela ne change

---

in the Geneva Conventions Act 1957 and the Geneva Conventions (Amendment) Act 1995, dealing with breaches of the Geneva Conventions of 1949 and the Additional Protocols of 1977; the Genocide Act 1969, giving effect to the Genocide Convention of 1948; the Criminal Justice Act 1988, s 134, giving effect to the Torture Convention of 1984; the War Crimes Act 1991, giving jurisdiction to try war crimes committed abroad by foreign nationals; the Merchant Shipping and Maritime Security Act 1997, s 26, giving effect to provisions of the United Nations Convention on the Law of the Sea 1982 relating to piracy... (par. 29) it is for those representing the people of the country in Parliament, not the executive and not the judges, to decide what conduct should be treated as lying so far outside the bounds of what is acceptable in our society as to attract criminal penalties.»

38. Voir, par exemple, les formules différentes employées par la Convention sur la prévention et la répression du génocide ou les dispositions du Statut de la Cour pénale internationale faisant référence aux crimes soumis à sa compétence.

39. On serait tenté d'affirmer avec P. Fauchille, *Traité de droit international public*, vol. 1, Rousseau et Cie, Paris, 1922, p. 87 (n° 483 (52)), que «la piraterie est considérée comme un crime du droit des gens. Cela ne signifie pas que c'est un crime qui n'est pas spécial à chaque pays et que répriment toutes les nations...»; voir opinion dissidente du juge Moore, jointe à l'arrêt de la CPJI du 7 septembre 1927 en l'affaire *Lotus*, série A, n° 10, p. 70: «Bien qu'il y ait des législations qui en prévoient la répression, elle est une infraction au droit des gens.»

40. Voir J. L. Brierly, *The Law of Nations: An Introduction to the International Law of Peace*, Oxford Clarendon Press, 1928, p. 154:

> «Any state may bring in pirates for trial by its own courts, on the grounds that they are «*hostes humani generis*». This applies only to persons who are pirates at international law, and acts may be piratical at municipal law, which are not so at international law; for example, in English criminal law, it is piracy to engage in slave trading.»

Voir les dispositions de la section 69 du code pénal de Kenya en vigueur de 1967 à 2009, lorsqu'elle a été remplacée par le Kenyan Merchant Shipping Act, entré en vigueur le 1er septembre 2009, selon lesquelles «any person who, in territorial waters or upon the high seas, commits any act of piracy *jure gentium* is guilty of the offence of piracy»; voir A. Kanehara, «Japanese Legal Regime

rien au fait qu'ils ne peuvent pas étendre la compétence universelle exceptionnelle à des actes qui ne sont pas constitutifs de piraterie au sens du droit international.

La question de savoir si les Etats peuvent entamer des poursuites à l'encontre des pirates présumés sans avoir adopté une législation mettant en œuvre la Convention de Montego Bay ou le droit international général n'est pas des moindres. Pella avait envisagé cette hypothèse dans son cours à l'Académie de La Haye en 1930 et a rejeté comme totalement inacceptable l'idée que le fondement de l'incrimination et des poursuites qui s'ensuivent se trouve uniquement dans la coutume internationale[41]. Se fondant sur les principes fondamentaux du droit pénal, tel le *nullum crimen nulla poena sine lege*, il soutient que nulle poursuite ne saurait être engagée si le droit interne ne prévoit pas le crime de piraterie. On se trouve ici clairement face au problème classique du droit international

---

Combating Piracy», *op. cit.*, pp. 469-489, qui présente la nouvelle législation japonaise du 24 juin 2009, selon laquelle

> «the term «acts of piracy» as used in this Act shall mean acts falling under any of the following items committed for private ends on the high seas (including exclusive economic zone prescribed in the United Nations Convention on the Law of the Sea) or *territorial sea* as well as *internal waters* of Japan...».

Selon le Parliamentary Secretary for Land, Infrastructure, Transport and Tourism, la raison pour laquelle le champ territorial d'application de l'acte s'étend également aux eaux territoriales est que, s'il n'en avait pas été ainsi, les auteurs des actes qui matériellement s'apparentent à la piraterie dans ses eaux seraient soumis aux dispositions et aux peines du code pénal qui sont moins sévères, ce qui constituerait une injustice.

> «A statute may make any offense piracy, committed within the jurisdiction of the nation passing the statute, and such offense will be punishable by that nation. But piracy, under the law of nations, which alone is punishable by all nations, can only consist in an act which is an offense against all. No particular nation can increase or diminish the list of offenses thus punishable.» (The Chapman, 5 F. Cas. 471, 474 (D.C. Cal. 1864), cité dans *United States* v. *Dire*, 680 F.3d, 454.)

41. V. Pella, « La répression de la piraterie », *op. cit.*, p. 180:

> «Nul fait ne saurait être aujourd'hui puni s'il n'a pas été préalablement prévu par une loi déterminant les éléments constitutifs de l'infraction en fixant la peine. Il faut de plus que cette loi ait déterminé le domaine de son application, soit par rapport au lieu où l'infraction a été commise, soit par rapport aux personnes qui l'ont perpétrée. Ce principe apparaît en droit pénal comme un impératif catégorique, comme une garantie extrêmement puissante contre l'abus et l'arbitraire dans l'exercice de la répression.»

Et p. 183:

> «Pour qu'(un navire de guerre) puisse déférer les pirates à ses tribunaux, il est nécessaire que la législation de l'Etat auquel appartient le navire de guerre capteur ait prévu elle-même la piraterie comme une infraction susceptible de répression, même quand elle a été commise en dehors du domaine de son application territoriale.»

qui consiste à opposer monisme et dualisme. Il convient de rappeler à cet égard que les dispositions de la Convention de Montego Bay sont dépourvues d'effet direct[42].

Quoi qu'il en soit, la pratique des Etats, qui, après avoir capturé des pirates en haute mer, ne voient d'autre option que de les remettre en liberté faute des lois internes prévoyant l'incrimination du comportement en cause, confirme la nécessité d'ériger la piraterie en infraction dans le droit interne et cela dans des termes suffisamment précis pour que la condition de *nullum crimen nulla poena sine lege stricta* soit respectée[43] (B). Aux antipodes de ces Etats, il en est d'autres qui n'ont pas érigé la piraterie en tant que telle en infraction dans leur droit interne, mais qui affirment que les éléments constitutifs de piraterie *jure gentium* peuvent tomber sous le coup des infractions comme les blessures volontaires, l'homicide volontaire, l'enlèvement, la séquestration arbitraire, le vol qualifié, le vol avec violence, etc. Ces législations soit contiennent une clause de compétence universelle selon laquelle celle-ci sera exercée dès lors que le droit international le permet[44], soit n'en contiennent pas, ce qui signifie que des poursuites pourront éventuellement être engagées simplement en vertu des bases de compétence classiques.

Finalement, c'est parce que l'introduction de l'infraction en droit interne est nécessaire que le Conseil de sécurité ne cesse d'inviter les Etats à le faire. Si la Convention de Montego Bay ou le droit international général suffisaient, il se contenterait d'inciter à l'engagement de poursuites[45]. C'est dans ce même contexte que l'OMI, dans son Code de conduite, encourage les Etats à établir une législation nationale leur permettant d'appréhender, poursuivre ou encore recevoir ou extrader des pirates présumés[46].

---

42. Voir CJCE, 3 juin 2008, aff. C-308/06, *Intertanko*, point 64: «Dans ces circonstances, il convient de constater que la Convention de Montego Bay ne met pas en place des règles destinées à s'appliquer directement et immédiatement aux particuliers...»

43. C'est notamment le cas de la Russie qui participe activement aux opérations de surveillance au large des côtes somaliennes, mais qui a systématiquement libéré les personnes capturées. Voir commentaire de cette pratique dans J. A. Roach, «General Problematic Issues on Exercise of Jurisdiction over Modern Instances of Piracy», dans C. R. Symmons (dir. publ.), *Selected Contemporary Issues in the Law of the Sea*, Nijhoff, Leyde, 2011, pp. 120-121.

44. Voir la législation chinoise, la lettre du Secrétaire général adressée au Président du Conseil de sécurité, S/2012/177, *op. cit.*, pp. 13-15; voir aussi exemples tirés de la jurisprudence chinoise dans K. Zou, «New Developments in the International Law of Piracy», *Chinese Journal of International Law*, n° 8, 2009, pp. 341-344.

45. Voir note 2.

46. Code of Practice for the Investigation of Crimes of Piracy and Armed Robbery against Ships, résolution A.1025 (26), *op. cit.*, art. 3.1:

> «States are recommended to take such measures as may be necessary to

B. Problèmes liés à la nécessité d'ériger la piraterie en infraction en droit interne

i) *Les ambiguïtés de la définition reflétées dans des législations variables et une jurisprudence incohérente*

Si la définition de la piraterie fournie par la CNUDM laisse subsister des doutes quant aux éléments constitutifs précis de l'infraction, cela n'est pas sans conséquences pour les législations internes censées l'incorporer en leur sein. En effet, il est des Etats qui reprennent telle quelle la définition contenue dans la CNUDM — soit ils reprennent mot à mot son article 101[47], soit ils se contentent d'incriminer la piraterie *jure gentium* sans plus[48]. Les ambiguïtés relevées ci-dessus sortent plutôt renforcées que dissipées, les Etats interprétant différemment les divers éléments de cette même définition. Certes, la plus sérieuse concerne les actes commis dans un but politique, or le problème n'a pas été posé dans la pratique récemment, puisque les actes de violence commis à l'époque actuelle poursuivent un but purement lucratif, notamment dans le contexte de la «piraterie» somalienne[49]. La lutte contre la piraterie somalienne s'intensifiant, les tribunaux internes se trouvent confrontés à des questions jamais posées auparavant. C'est notamment le cas des infractions connexes. Les résolutions du Conseil de sécurité mettent de plus en plus l'accent sur une répression qui ne se limite pas aux personnes effectuant les attaques contre les navires, mais qui s'étend

establish their jurisdiction over the offences of piracy and armed robbery against ships, including adjustment of their legislation, if necessary, to enable those States to apprehend and prosecute persons committing such offences. States are furthermore encouraged to take the necessary national legislative, judicial and law enforcement actions as to be able to receive, prosecute or extradite any pirates or suspected pirates and armed robbers arrested by warships or military aircraft or other ships or aircraft clearly marked and identifiable as being on government service. States should take into consideration appropriate penalties when drafting legislation on piracy.»

47. Ainsi les législations française, belge, kenyane, mauricienne.

48. Voir, par exemple, la législation des Etats-Unis (18 USC, par. 1651: «Whoever on the high seas commits the crime of piracy as defined by the law of nations, and is afterwards brought into or found in the United States, shall be imprisoned for life.»)

49. Il convient de noter toutefois que, lors de l'adoption de la nouvelle législation japonaise, il a été précisé que les actes de violence contre les navires de pavillon japonais dans un but de protestation «écologique» — et donc politique au sens large du terme — ne seront pas poursuivis sur la base des dispositions relatives à la piraterie. En l'affaire *République des Seychelles c. Dahir*, 2010, SCSC 86 (26 juillet 2010), la Cour suprême des Seychelles a estimé qu'il ne faut pas confondre terrorisme et piraterie (par. 37), http://www.saflii.org/sc/cases/SCSC/2010/81.html.

aux «cerveaux», à ceux qui facilitent ou financent la commission de ces actes ou profitent du produit obtenu suite à la commission de ces actes[50]. Emblématique à cet égard est la décision de la District Court of Columbia en l'affaire *Etats-Unis c. Ali* du 13 juillet 2012[51], où la cour a dû se prononcer sur les poursuites entamées contre un Somalien pour conspiration aux fins de commettre des actes de piraterie et pour avoir facilité la commission d'actes de piraterie. Concernant le premier chef d'accusation, la cour est d'avis que la définition de la piraterie *jure gentium* ne comprend pas la conspiration et que, par conséquent, la compétence universelle des Etats ne s'y étend pas. Pour ce qui est des actes allégués ayant pour but de faciliter la commission d'actes de piraterie[52], la cour fournit une interprétation intéressante de la disposition de l'article 101, alinéa *c)*, de la CNUDM et de celle qui l'incorpore dans le droit américain. Elle estime que la compétence universelle attribuée par le droit international ne peut s'étendre à des actes qui n'ont pas eu lieu en haute mer, autrement dit que les actes ayant pour but de faciliter ceux de piraterie doivent eux aussi avoir eu lieu en haute mer, comme les actes de piraterie proprement dits pour qu'un Etat puisse y étendre sa compétence universelle. Le Congrès, en ne prévoyant pas expressément que les actes d'«aiding and abetting» puissent être couverts par la compétence universelle où qu'ils aient eu lieu, n'a pas exprimé une volonté d'aller à l'encontre du droit international, qui ne reconnaît pas aux Etats de compétence prescriptive pour des actes ayant lieu sur le territoire d'un autre Etat. La cour n'envisage pas une interprétation grammaticale des dispositions de l'article 101 de la CNUDM qui ne contient pas la condition du *locus delicti commissi* pour les infractions des alinéas *b)* et *c)*, soit la participation et l'incitation, contrairement aux actes de piraterie tels que décrits dans l'alinéa *a)*, mais repose sur l'économie générale de l'article. Selon cette interprétation, les trois types d'actes prévus par l'article 101 sont des actes de piraterie proprement dite, les uns et les autres devant se produire en haute mer. Or, il n'est pas très réaliste d'attendre que les «cerveaux» derrière les attaques, ceux qui incitent à la commission des actes de piraterie, se rendent eux aussi en haute mer, qu'ils se trouvent eux aussi à bord du navire attaquant, bien au contraire. Une interprétation téléologique de ces dispositions visant à lutter contre

---

50. Voir note 31.

51. Il s'agit de la première affaire d'exercice de compétence universelle, c'est-à-dire dans laquelle il n'y a absolument aucun lien entre les faits et les Etats-Unis, depuis deux cents ans.

52. La cour considère les termes «aiding and abetting» de la législation américaine et «acte ayant pour but d'inciter à commettre les actes définis aux lettres *a)* ou *b)*, ou commis dans l'intention de les faciliter» de l'article 101 de la CNUDM, comme équivalents.

la piraterie à tous ses stades permet de soutenir que ceux qui participent à la commission des actes de piraterie d'une façon quelconque peuvent se trouver dans n'importe quel lieu [53].

ii) Nullum crimen nulla poena sine lege stricta

Lorsqu'il s'agit d'incorporer dans le droit interne une infraction définie par le droit international coutumier, caractérisé par une certaine souplesse, les juridictions d'un Etat qui s'est contenté de renvoyer à la piraterie *jure gentium* peuvent être confrontées à des questions de droit intertemporel. Comment l'évolution d'une définition peut-elle être intégrée dans un texte de droit interne qui reste figé ? Il faut noter que la plupart des législations internes qui ont érigé la piraterie *jure gentium* en infraction ont gardé ce simple renvoi à la définition internationale sans avoir apporté plus de précisions par la suite [54]. Or, une disposition de droit interne qui renvoie à la définition de l'infraction par le droit international général doit-elle être interprétée conformément à celle-ci, valable à l'époque de l'adoption de celle-là ou conformément à son contenu à l'époque de la commission des actes ? La question s'est posée à plusieurs reprises devant les juridictions des Etats-Unis dont les dispositions relatives à la piraterie remontent à 1816. Les tribunaux ont adopté des positions divergentes à ce propos. Dans un arrêt *Etats-Unis c. Said*, la District Court in Norfolk [55] a interprété la disposition 18 USC, paragraphe 1651, comme se limitant à des actes de vol en mer et pour ce faire elle s'est appuyée sur le célèbre précédent que constitue la décision de la Cour suprême de 1820 *Etats-Unis c. Smith*, une décision qui, selon son analyse, fournissait une définition qui recueillait un consensus indubitable. Néanmoins, la Cour reconnaît que les actes des accusés, qui consistaient dans cette affaire en une simple attaque violente lancée d'un navire contre un autre sans vol, pourraient tomber sous le coup de la

53. L'hypothèse n'est pas envisagée dans la bibliographie. Certains commentaires ont été publiés sur la toile suite à la publication de la décision en question. Ainsi D. Guilfoyle, « Committing Piracy on Dry Land : Liability for Facilitating Piracy », http://www.ejiltalk.org/committing-piracy-on-dry-land-liability-for-facilitating-piracy/ ; E. Kontorovich, « About Today's Piracy Decision », http://www.volokh.com/2012/07/13/from-prof-eugene-kontorovich-about-todays-piracy-decision/ ; voir aussi R. L. Philips, « Pirate Accessory Liability — Developing a Modern Legal Regime Governing Incitement and Intentional Facilitation of Maritime Piracy », http://papers.ssrn.com/sol3/papers.cfm?abstract_id=2158023.

54. Avec la notable exception du Kenya qui, avec son nouveau Merchant Shipping Act de 2009, a remplacé la référence à la piraterie *jure gentium* avec des précisions sur les éléments constitutifs de la piraterie la rapprochant ainsi de la définition de la CNUDM.

55. *United States c. Said*, 17 août 2010, 757 F. Supp. 2d 554 (E.D. Va. 2010) (Jackson, J.).

définition de l'article 101 de la CNUDM, or elle lui nie une autorité coutumière à la lumière de certains doutes exprimés par certains commentateurs[56]. Certes, cette démarche montre que la Cour ne rejette pas la prise en compte de l'évolution du droit coutumier et, par conséquent, l'inclusion des nouveaux éléments à la définition de la piraterie, mais il convient de noter également que son analyse commence par le postulat qu'une disposition doit être interprétée selon le sens ordinaire des termes au moment de son entrée en vigueur, toute autre approche risquant de la rendre inconstitutionnellement vague et ainsi contraire au principe du procès équitable[57]. Le débat fut tranché d'une manière plus claire dans une décision du 23 mai 2012 *Etats-Unis c. Dire* de la Court of Appeals for the Fourth District[58], qui confirme la thèse adoptée dans une décision dite *Hasan I*[59]. La Cour s'est prononcée en faveur d'une lecture évolutive de la définition de la piraterie. A travers une étude minutieuse des sources du droit international, elle a conclu que la définition de l'article 101 de la CNUDM reflète le droit international coutumier valable à l'époque de la commission des faits — définition plus large que celle admise dans la décision *Smith* — qui couvre les actes de violence sans exiger l'accomplissement d'un vol[60].

56. *United States c. Said*, 17 août 2010, 757 F. Supp. 2d 554 (E.D. Va. 2010) (Jackson, J.), pp. 563-564.

57. «If the definition of piracy [were adopted] from the debatable international sources whose promulgations evolve over time, defendants in United States courts would be required to constantly guess whether their conduct is proscribed by par. 1651[,] render[ing] the statute unconstitutionally vague.» *Ibid.*, p. 566.

58. Voir http://www.ca4.uscourts.gov/Opinions/Published/114310.P.pdf.

59. *United States c. Hasan (Hasan I)*, 747 F. Supp. 2d 599, 603 (E.D. Va. 2010).

60. «We are constrained to agree with the district court that paragraph 1651 incorporates a definition of piracy that changes with advancements in the law of nations. We also agree with the district court that the definition of piracy under the law of nations, at the time of the defendants' attack on the *USS Nicholas* and continuing today, had for decades encompassed their violent conduct. That definition, spelled out in the UNCLOS, as well as the High Seas Convention before it, has only been reaffirmed in recent years as nations around the world have banded together to combat the escalating scourge of piracy. For example, in November 2011, the United Nations Security Council adopted Resolution 2020, recalling a series of prior resolutions approved between 2008 and 2011 «concerning the situation in Somalia»; expressing «grave concern [about] the ongoing threat that piracy and armed robbery at sea against vessels pose»; and emphasizing «the need for a comprehensive response by the international community to repress piracy and armed robbery at sea and tackle its underlying causes». Of the utmost significance, Resolution 2020 reaffirmed «that international law, as reflected in the [UNCLOS], sets out the legal framework applicable to combating piracy and armed robbery at sea». Because the district court correctly applied the UNCLOS definition of piracy as customary international law, we reject the defendants' challenge to their Count One piracy convictions, as well as their mandatory life sentence.» (*United States c. Dire*, *op. cit.*, pp. 41-42, http://www.ca4.uscourts.gov/Opinions/Published/114310.P.pdf.)

Le problème théorique évoqué par les décisions ci-dessus est celui du principe *nullum crimen nulla poena sine lege*. Celui-ci exige notamment que la loi pénale soit stricte, qu'elle définisse l'infraction avec suffisamment de précision, qu'elle soit prévisible et accessible[61]. Si une infraction est définie par renvoi au droit coutumier, les individus peuvent en effet se trouver dans l'incertitude concernant la légalité de leurs actes. Néanmoins, le propre même de la coutume est le large appui sur une certaine pratique, la constance de la pratique suivie par les Etats de sorte que le degré nécessaire de prévisibilité et d'accessibilité peut être considéré comme acquis. En matière de piraterie en particulier, les choses paraissent plus simples eu égard à la transcription de la règle dans une convention largement ratifiée comme la CNUDM, d'autant plus que cette dernière reprend, et réaffirme donc, la définition de la Convention sur la haute mer de 1958, qui se trouve ainsi cristallisée à l'époque actuelle. Avec l'ampleur qu'a prise la lutte contre la piraterie somalienne, il est difficile pour les individus — notamment les Somaliens — de soutenir qu'ils n'ont pas été suffisamment prévenus quant au contenu des actes de piraterie[62].

Paragraphe 2 La compétence universelle en matière de piraterie

A. Raison d'être de la compétence universelle en matière de piraterie

La compétence dite universelle intervient lorsque font défaut les liens de rattachement qui sont mis au premier plan et qui expriment l'autorité de l'Etat sur le sujet (lien territorial-lien personnel). La compétence universelle exprime un rattachement qui a trait à un élément matériel, à l'objet que l'Etat vise à régir. En matière de piraterie, c'est justement la menace contre la sécurité de la navigation dans un espace commun qui concerne potentiellement tous les Etats qui justifie que n'importe quel Etat se charge de la répression de l'activité. Cela étant dit, d'autres justifications ont été invoquées, telles la perte de nationalité et la gravité du crime.

i) *Perte de nationalité*

La thèse fut défendue un temps que le pirate est un criminel vagabond qui défie les règles de l'humanité tout entière et qui par ce fait cesse

61. Voir J. Nilsson, « The Principle *Nullum Crimen Sine Lege* », dans O. Olusanya (dir. publ.), *Rethinking International Criminal Law: The Substantive Part*, Europa Law Publishing, 2007, pp. 35-64 ; M. Gardner, « Piracy prosecutions… », *op. cit.*, pp. 818-819.

62. En ce sens, M. Gardner, « Piracy Prosecutions… », *op. cit.*, pp. 819-820.

d'être le national d'un Etat. S'il en est ainsi, la compétence basée sur la nationalité active ne joue plus et, puisque la compétence territoriale n'est pas applicable non plus, les actes étant commis par définition en haute mer, la compétence universelle paraît comme une solution acceptable afin d'éviter que les pirates échappent à la justice[63]. Le droit international ne confirme pas cette idée. Il ne prévoit pas de perte «automatique» de nationalité. Par ailleurs, la CNUDM laisse dans son article 104, qui certes ne traite pas directement des pirates, mais on ne voit pas pourquoi il en irait autrement pour les personnes physiques, la conservation ou la perte de la nationalité d'un navire au choix des Etats.

Il semble plutôt que le pirate ne puisse pas compter sur le «privilège» de la soumission à la seule juridiction de son Etat de nationalité et non pas qu'il n'y soit plus soumis.

ii) *Atrocité du crime*

Traditionnellement, on associe compétence universelle et atrocité du crime. Ainsi les juges Higgins, Kooijmans et Buergenthal, dans leur opinion individuelle commune jointe à l'arrêt du *Mandat d'arrêt*, affirment-ils qu'«[i]l est également nécessaire que la compétence pénale universelle ne soit exercée qu'à l'égard des crimes considérés comme les plus odieux par la communauté internationale. La piraterie est l'exemple classique...»[64] Or, il est difficile de comparer en termes de gravité la piraterie avec des crimes comme le génocide ou les crimes contre l'humanité[65]. Par ailleurs, certains invoquent la pratique du «privateering»

63. Voir Harvard Law School, *Research in International Law — Drafts of Conventions..., op. cit.*, pp. 825-828.

64. CIJ, 14 février 2002, *Mandat d'arrêt du 11 avril 2000 (République démocratique du Congo c. Belgique), CIJ Recueil 2002*, p. 81.

65. Ainsi V. Lowe, «Jurisdiction», dans M. D. Evans (dir. publ.), *International Law*, Oxford University Press, 3e éd., 2010, p. 326:

> «some crimes are regarded as so heinous that every State has a legitimate interest in their repression. That is the traditional explanation of universal jurisdiction. But given that the first, and one of the most firmly established, of the instances of crimes covered by the universality principle is piracy, one may wonder if the traditional explanation is entirely satisfactory. It is probably more accurate to say that there are two strands running together to make up the universality principle. One is the strand that is indeed made up of heinous crimes, such as genocide, crimes against humanity, and serious war crimes, all of which are subject to universal jurisdiction. The second is crimes that are serious, and which might otherwise go unpunished. Piracy ... may involve relatively minor uses of force; and not every act of piracy can properly be described as heinous ... the justification for universal jurisdiction over pirates is not so much that piracy is inherently heinous, and on a par with genocide and war crimes, as the fact that because pirates operate on the high seas it is very easy for them to evade the jurisdiction of any State that might have jurisdiction over them on some other basis, unless any State that happens to have them within its jurisdiction is entitled to try them.»

en temps de guerre pour neutraliser cet argument. Le «privateering» consistait à la commission des mêmes actes *ratione materiae* mais avec une autorisation des Etats qui procuraient des lettres de marque. Si les actes de piraterie étaient d'une telle atrocité qui justifierait la compétence universelle, comment a-t-on pu supporter dans le même ordre juridique un comportement matériellement identique ?[66]

iii) Locus delicti commissi

Il nous semble que ce qui explique le mieux la compétence universelle dans la poursuite des pirates est la commission des actes dans un espace ne relevant de la juridiction d'aucun Etat et dans lequel tout Etat a intérêt à voir ses navires naviguer en toute sécurité. Par ailleurs, on ne peut compter exclusivement sur l'Etat de nationalité des auteurs des actes qui peut ne s'intéresser guère à leur poursuite en justice ou même ne pas être au courant des actes perpétrés en haute mer[67]. Le Conseil de sécurité, quant à lui, invoque à la fois l'inaction du gouvernement somalien et la menace que constitue la piraterie pour la sécurité des voies maritimes[68].

B. Une compétence universelle facultative ?

i) *Compétence universelle facultative en vertu de la Convention de Montego Bay*

L'article 105 est plus que clair lorsqu'il prévoit qu'un Etat *peut* en haute mer saisir un navire pirate, appréhender les personnes et saisir les biens se trouvant à bord et que ses tribunaux *peuvent* se prononcer sur les peines à infliger, ainsi que sur les mesures à prendre en ce qui concerne le navire ou les biens. Il s'agit clairement d'une règle permissive qui n'oblige point les Etats à adopter une législation y afférente[69].

66. E. Kontorovich, «The Piracy Analogy: Modern Universal Jurisdiction's Hollow Foundation», *Harvard International Law Journal*, 2004, n° 45, pp. 222-223.
67. Voir R. Geiss et A. Petrig, *Piracy and Armed Robbery at Sea…, op. cit.*, p. 147.
68. Voir, par exemple, S/RES/1851 et S/RES/1816.
69. Voir J. L. Jesus, «Foreword», *American University Law Review*, 2010, vol. 59, p. 1214: «the fundamental nature of the international law governing piracy at sea … does not impose on States any obligation to prosecute and punish the offenders or to dispose of seized property», et p. 1216: «UNCLOS does not impose on States an obligation to criminalize under their domestic legislation acts that constitute piracy under international law»; B. Stern, «A propos de la compétence universelle», dans E. Yakpo et T. Boumedra (dir. publ.), *Liber Amicorum Judge Mohammed Bedjaoui*, La Haye, Kluwer Law

Il en va de même, à notre sens, de l'engagement de poursuites dans le cas où un Etat se serait déjà doté d'une législation. Il s'agit là encore d'un pouvoir discrétionnaire.

Cela dit, tous les auteurs lisent cette disposition conjointement avec celle de l'article 100 qui énonce une obligation générale de coopération dans la répression de la piraterie[70]. Le commentaire de l'article 38 de la Convention 1958 précise que:

> «un Etat qui, tout en ayant l'occasion de prendre des mesures contre les pirates, négligerait de le faire, violerait un devoir que le droit international lui impose... Il va cependant de soi qu'il faut laisser à l'Etat une certaine latitude quant au choix des mesures qu'il devra prendre à cet effet dans chaque cas d'espèce.»

Le contenu des obligations qui incombent aux Etats en la matière paraît assez vague. Déduire de ces dispositions une obligation d'ériger la piraterie en infraction en droit interne et de poursuivre en justice serait aller trop loin[71]. Quoi qu'il en soit, on voit mal comment les Etats qui n'adoptent pas de législation anti-piraterie ou qui ne poursuivent pas verraient leur responsabilité internationale engagée[72].

International, 1999, p. 738: «lorsqu'un Etat a une compétence universelle, il s'agit en principe, sauf indication contraire, d'une *compétence universelle permissive* ou facultative. Il en va ainsi dans tous les cas où la compétence universelle résulte d'une règle de droit international coutumier: par exemple, la compétence universelle en matière de piraterie...»; A. Roach, «General Problematic Issues on Exercise of Jurisdiction over Modern Instances of Piracy», dans C. Symmons, *Selected Contemporary Issues..., op. cit.*, p. 121.

70. «Tous les Etats coopèrent dans toute la mesure du possible à la répression de la piraterie en haute mer ou en tout autre lieu ne relevant de la juridiction d'aucun Etat» (art. 100) et «Tous les Etats doivent coopérer dans toute la mesure du possible à la répression de la piraterie en haute mer ou dans tout autre endroit en relevant de la juridiction d'aucun Etat» (Convention de 1958, art. 38).

71. Voir R. Wolfrum, «Fighting Terrorism at Sea: Options and Limitations under International Law», dans M. H. Nordquist *et al.* (dir. publ.), *Legal Challenges in Maritime Security*, Martinus Nijhoff, Leyde/Boston, 2008: «reading articles 100 et 107 together, it can be argued that states may not lightly decline to intervene against acts of piracy» (p. 9) et que

> «coastal states which do not engage in the suppression of piracy, or whose authorities are accomplices to such crimes, can be held internationally liable for damage to affected ships. We may ask why in the past no case has been brought against states in whose territorial waters pirates have operated for failure in the suppression of piracy, and why no ship owner has thus far approached its national government for diplomatic protection vis-à-vis these states.» (P. 11.)

72. Pour une discussion plus détaillée de la question, voir K. Saiful, «Is There an International Obligation to Prosecute Pirates?», *Netherlands International Law Review*, n° 58, 2011, pp. 387-407.

Les choses se compliquent avec l'implication du Conseil de sécurité dans la lutte contre la piraterie somalienne. Dans ses résolutions, il se déclare préoccupé que «de nombreuses personnes soupçonnées de piraterie soient libérées sans avoir été jugées», «demande» aux Etats d'ériger la piraterie en infraction dans leur droit interne et d'«envisager favorablement» de poursuivre les personnes soupçonnées de piraterie qui ont été appréhendées au large des côtes somaliennes[73]. L'adoption des résolutions sous le Chapitre VII est devenue la règle[74], mais est-ce à dire que le Conseil de sécurité a créé une nouvelle obligation qui irait plus loin que la CNUDM ? Cela est fort douteux. On ne va pas s'attarder ici sur la problématique du pouvoir législatif du Conseil de sécurité ; la réponse nous semble se trouver ailleurs. Certes, selon l'article 25 de la Charte, les Etats sont obligés de suivre les décisions du Conseil de sécurité, mais il se peut que celles-ci contiennent de simples recommandations et les formules concernant les poursuites des pirates semblent être exhortatoires. Quoi qu'il en soit, il faut toujours garder à l'esprit l'idée que, si le Conseil de sécurité s'est mobilisé, ce n'était que dans le contexte de la piraterie somalienne et que son action n'a changé en rien l'état du droit international applicable en la matière[75]. D'ailleurs, c'est non pas la piraterie en tant que telle qui constitue une menace contre la paix et la sécurité internationales, mais la situation particulière dans laquelle se trouve la Somalie.

Les choix législatifs des Etats confirment le caractère facultatif de la compétence universelle. Un relativement grand nombre d'Etats qui incriminent la piraterie ont adopté le principe de compétence universelle (ainsi les Pays-Bas, les Etats-Unis, la Grèce, le Japon, le Kenya...), mais ne l'ont appliquée que très marginalement. A part les Etats de la région (essentiellement le Kenya, les Seychelles, la Tanzanie et les Maldives), qui ont répondu positivement à l'invitation du Conseil de sécurité, et les Etats-Unis qui en règle générale n'hésitent pas à exercer leur compétence extraterritoriale, la plupart des Etats n'entament des poursuites que lorsque l'affaire présente un *nexus* avec eux. C'est notamment le cas des Etats européens qui participent aux patrouilles dans la région au large de la Somalie. Ainsi, le peu d'affaires jugées devant les juridictions des Pays-Bas concernaient uniquement des attaques contre des navires battant le pavillon du pays. Dans la décision *«Cygnus»*[76] du 17 juin 2010, la

73. Voir S/RES/1950 (2010) et S/RES/2020 (2011).

74. Voir S/RES/1918 (2010), qui n'a pas été adoptée sous le Chapitre VII.

75. Le Conseil de sécurité le répète dans toutes ses résolutions. Voir, par exemple, la toute dernière S/RES/2077(2012), par. 13: «souligne en particulier que la présente résolution ne saurait être regardée comme établissant un droit international coutumier...».

76. *International Law Reports*, n° 145, pp. 491-515.

District Court de Rotterdam, après avoir analysé les dispositions du droit interne néerlandais et affirmé que celles-ci prévoient l'exercice de la compétence universelle en matière de piraterie en conformité avec le droit international, examine l'opportunité de l'engagement de poursuites pour des actes ne présentant aucun lien avec les Pays-Bas[77]. En l'espèce, il s'agissait d'une attaque contre un navire battant pavillon des Antilles néerlandaises, ainsi l'intérêt des Pays-Bas était indiscutable. Inversement, le Danemark, dont les navires de guerre ont effectué l'arraisonnement du navire pirate et l'arrestation des personnes à bord, en a immédiatement prévenu les autorités néerlandaises dans la perspective d'un éventuel transfert des suspects et n'a pas entamé des poursuites lui-même en l'absence de tout lien avec l'affaire. Pareille «stratégie» dans la première affaire de piraterie devant les juridictions allemandes, jugée le 19 octobre 2012[78]: une frégate néerlandaise a capturé des pirates présumés ayant lancé une attaque contre un navire allemand avec des personnes de nationalité allemande à bord et les a transférés par la suite en Allemagne qui avait un intérêt particulier à les poursuivre.

D'autres ont relativisé cette compétence universelle de principe en ajoutant qu'ils l'exerceront uniquement à défaut d'entente avec un autre

---

77. *International Law Reports*, n° 145, p. 495:

> «Cases of piracy could occur whereby the Netherlands is not involved in any manner whatsoever, and in which a prosecution of the suspects involved would for this reason not be plausible and would seem undesirable. In cases like these, however, the jurisdiction of the Netherlands would be an issue open to debate, but it could very well be that proceedings in this country would be deemed non-admissible as being contrary to the principles of good rules of procedure because there is no reasonable interest therein. The option of prosecution is therefore not a matter of jurisdiction but of opportunity.»

Voir pareille disposition dans la legislation belge: Loi relative à la lutte contre la piraterie maritime et modifiant le Code judiciaire du 30 décembre 2009, par. 4:

> «Le procureur fédéral juge de l'opportunité des poursuites en tenant compte des circonstances concrètes de l'affaire. Pour autant que cette juridiction présente les qualités d'indépendance, d'impartialité et d'équité, tel que cela peut notamment ressortir des engagements internationaux pertinents liant la Belgique et l'Etat de cette juridiction, il peut décider que, dans l'intérêt d'une bonne administration de la justice et dans le respect des obligations internationales de la Belgique, cette affaire devrait être portée: soit devant la juridiction de l'Etat du pavillon du navire contre lequel les faits ont été commis; soit devant la juridiction de l'Etat dont l'auteur est ressortissant ou du lieu où il peut être trouvé; soit devant la juridiction d'un Etat tiers et ce dès lors que les conditions de ce transfert ont été arrêtées avec cet Etat d'une manière conforme au droit international applicable.»

78. Urteil im sog. «Piratenprozess» vor dem Landgericht Hamburg — Angeklagte zu mehrjährigen Freiheits — und Jugendstrafen verurteilt, 19 octobre 2012, http://justiz.hamburg.de/oberlandesgericht/3658808/pressemeldung-2012-10-19-olg-01.html.

Etat qui aurait établi sa compétence. C'est le cas de la France dont la nouvelle loi sur la piraterie dispose dans son article 5 que :

> « à défaut d'entente avec les autorités d'un autre Etat pour l'exercice par celui-ci de sa compétence juridictionnelle, les auteurs et complices des infractions mentionnées au II de l'article 1er et commises hors du territoire de la République peuvent être poursuivis et jugés par les juridictions françaises lorsqu'ils ont été appréhendés par les agents mentionnés à l'article 4 »[79].

Autrement dit, les autorités françaises vont d'abord chercher à transférer les personnes capturées par les navires français à un Etat qui entretient un lien avec l'affaire et ne vont entamer des poursuites qu'en dernier ressort.

L'hésitation à exercer la compétence universelle se reflète par ailleurs dans les décisions des juridictions kényanes inférieures : malgré l'engagement international de l'Etat pris en bloc de recevoir aux fins de poursuites des personnes arrêtées par les Etats surveillant les eaux de la région, les tribunaux interprètent systématiquement les dispositions du chapitre 3 du code pénal comme excluant l'exercice de leur compétence à l'égard d'actes commis en dehors du territoire kényan vidant ainsi de sens toute référence à la piraterie *jure gentium* au sein du chapitre 8. Le 18 octobre 2012, la cour d'appel de Nairobi a renversé ce précédent dans une décision *In re Mohamud Mohamed Hashi and others*[80], en soulignant que les deux chapitres sont autonomes : le premier se réfère à l'exercice de la compétence territoriale des tribunaux, le second, intitulé « Offences affecting Relations with Foreign States and External Tranquility », concerne la compétence extraterritoriale. Le conflit entre les deux est par conséquent exclu. Il s'agit d'une décision-phare qui va permettre au Kenya de remplir le rôle qu'il a assumé dans le cadre de la lutte contre la piraterie dans la région.

ii) *Compétence en vertu des autres conventions*

a) *Une compétence obligatoire mais non universelle ou quasi universelle*

La Convention SUA — et il en va de même des conventions précitées qui portent sur d'autres formes de criminalité[81] — oblige les Etats

79. Loi 2011-13 du 5 janvier 2011 relative à la lutte contre la piraterie et à l'exercice des pouvoirs de police de l'Etat en mer.

80. Voir le site http://piracylaw.files.wordpress.com/2012/10/kenya-hashi-appeal-opinion.pdf.

81. Article 2 de la Convention internationale contre la prise d'otages ; articles 5-8 de la Convention des Nations Unies contre la criminalité transnationale organisée.

parties à ériger en infraction dans leur droit interne les infractions qu'elle vise: son article 5 prévoit en effet que «tout Etat partie réprime les infractions prévues à l'article 3 par des peines appropriées».

A l'instar d'autres conventions à vocation «antiterroriste», telle la Convention pour la répression de la capture illicite d'aéronefs de 1970[82] et la Convention pour la répression d'actes illicites dirigés contre la sécurité de l'aviation civile de 1971[83], elle prévoit dans son article 6 les bases de compétence suivantes: personnalité active, territorialité, pavillon, personnalité passive et principe de protection[84].

La Convention SUA s'appuie donc sur les bases de compétence classiques du droit international sans aller jusqu'à établir la compétence universelle[85]. Néanmoins, la disposition du paragraphe 4[86] oblige les Etats à établir leur compétence dans le cas où l'auteur présumé de l'infraction se trouve sur leur territoire et où ils ne l'extradent pas vers un autre Etat qui aurait établi sa compétence conformément à la convention, ce qui permet aux Etats d'entamer des poursuites sans aucun *nexus* avec l'incident[87]. Certains ont qualifié cette compétence de «quasi universelle» ou d'«universelle territoriale»[88].

---

82. Art. 4.

83. Art. 5.

84. Pour une présentation rapide, voir J. Salmon, *Dictionnaire…, op. cit.*, pp. 210-213; pour une présentation détaillée, voir V. Lowe, «Jurisdiction», *op. cit.*, pp. 315-327; plus précisément pour la Convention SUA, voir R. Geiss et A. Petrig, *Piracy and Armed Robbery at Sea…, op. cit.*, pp. 156-163.

85. Voir aussi l'article 5 de la Convention internationale contre la prise d'otages et l'article 15 de la Convention des Nations Unies contre la criminalité transnationale organisée.

86. Voir aussi l'article 8, paragraphe 1, de la Convention internationale contre la prise d'otages et l'article 15, paragraphe 3, de la Convention des Nations Unies contre la criminalité transnationale organisée.

87. D. Guilfoyle, «Combating Piracy: Executive Measures on the High Seas», *Japanese Yearbook of International Law*, n° 53, 2010, p. 166; voir législation américaine qui prévoit comme une base de compétence à part la présence de l'auteur présumé de l'acte sur le territoire du pays.

88. Pour une discussion plus détaillée de la question, voir B. Stern, «A propos de la compétence universelle…», *op. cit.*, pp. 738-739:

> «dans de nombreux cas, telle la piraterie aérienne, la préoccupation des Etats est extrême, du fait que les actes peuvent porter atteinte à n'importe qui dans le monde, ainsi les Etats décident-ils de créer une compétence universelle obligatoire. Le juge Guillaume parle plus justement de compétence «obligatoire, mais subsidiaire», pour bien rappeler qu'elle n'est en réalité obligatoire qu'à défaut d'extradition. En effet, lorsqu'on parle de compétence universelle obligatoire, on se réfère en général au principe *aut dedere aut judicare*.»

Voir V. Lowe, «Jurisdiction», *op. cit.*, p. 328; M. N. Shaw, *International Law*, Cambridge University Press, 6e éd., 2008, p. 674, qui cite l'opinion des juges Higgins, Kooijmans, Buergenthal, jointe à l'arrêt du *Mandat d'arrêt*, selon laquelle la situation créée par ce type de traités peut être qualifiée de «obliga-

b) L'apport de la clause aut dedere aut judicare

C'est justement l'ajout de la clause *aut dedere aut judicare* et sa formulation particulière qui permettent de dire que ces conventions prévoient une compétence quasi universelle. Pour s'en tenir à la Convention SUA, ses articles 6, paragraphe 4, et 10, paragraphe 1 [89], se prêtent à des interprétations divergentes quant au contenu exact des obligations qui incombent aux Etats sur le territoire desquels se retrouve l'auteur présumé de l'infraction. Selon la première interprétation, la demande d'extradition n'est pas un prérequis pour la naissance de l'obligation de poursuivre. Une seule obligation incombe à l'Etat: de soumettre l'affaire à ses autorités compétentes pour l'exercice de l'action pénale. L'extradition est simplement un autre moyen pour s'acquitter de son obligation primaire. Selon la deuxième interprétation, l'obligation naît une fois qu'une demande d'extradition lui a été adressée et tant qu'il n'a pas refusé d'extrader il n'a pas d'obligation de poursuivre. La première nous paraît plus fidèle à la lettre de la convention et en parfait accord avec la disposition de l'article 7 qui prévoit une enquête préliminaire et la prise des mesures nécessaires «afin d'assurer la présence de l'individu pendant le délai nécessaire à l'engagement de poursuites pénales ou d'une procédure d'extradition». C'est par ailleurs la thèse qu'a retenue la Cour internationale de justice le 20 juillet 2012 en l'affaire *Questions concernant l'obligation de poursuivre ou d'extrader (Belgique c. Sénégal)* (par. 94) s'agissant d'une obligation semblable contenue dans la Convention contre la torture:

> «La Cour considère que le paragraphe 1 de l'article 7 impose à l'Etat concerné l'obligation de soumettre l'affaire à ses autorités compétentes pour l'exercice de l'action pénale, indépendamment de l'existence, au préalable, d'une demande d'extradition à l'encontre du suspect. C'est pour cela que le paragraphe 2 de l'article 6 oblige l'Etat à procéder immédiatement à une enquête préliminaire, aussitôt que le suspect se trouve sur son territoire. L'obligation de saisine des autorités compétentes, en vertu du paragraphe 1 de l'article 7, peut déboucher ou non sur l'engagement de

---

tory territorial jurisdiction over persons» ou «jurisdiction to establish a territorial jurisdiction over persons for extraterritorial events»; R. O'Keefe, «Universal Jurisdiction: Clarifying the Basic Concept», *Journal of International Criminal Justice*, n° 2, 2004, pp. 735-760.

89. «L'Etat Partie sur le territoire duquel l'auteur ou l'auteur présumé de l'infraction est découvert est tenu, dans les cas où l'article 6 s'applique, s'il ne l'extrade pas, de soumettre l'affaire, sans retard et sans aucune exception, que l'infraction ait été ou non commise sur son territoire, à ses autorités compétentes pour l'exercice de l'action pénale selon une procédure conforme à la législation de cet Etat...»

poursuites en fonction de l'appréciation par celles-ci des éléments de preuve à leur disposition, relatifs aux charges qui pèsent sur le suspect.

Par. 95. En revanche, si l'Etat sur le territoire duquel se trouve le suspect est saisi d'une demande d'extradition dans l'un des cas prévus par les dispositions de la convention, il peut se libérer de son obligation de poursuivre en faisant droit à la demande d'extradition. Il en résulte que le choix entre l'extradition ou l'engagement des poursuites, en vertu de la convention, ne revient pas à mettre les deux éléments de l'alternative sur le même plan. En effet, l'extradition est une option offerte par la convention à l'Etat, alors que la poursuite est une obligation internationale, prévue par la convention, dont la violation engage la responsabilité de l'Etat pour fait illicite.»[90]

c) Compétence quasi universelle inter partes*?*

Ce type de conventions présente un problème du point de vue des effets susceptibles de se produire à l'égard des Etats tiers. On peut envisager l'éventualité de la commission d'un acte incriminé par la convention SUA par un national d'un Etat non partie et l'établissement de la compétence de la part d'un Etat partie conformément à la convention, par exemple sur la base de la nationalité des victimes. D'aucuns estiment que des poursuites dans un tel cas ne peuvent être entamées, à moins qu'il puisse être prouvé que le droit international coutumier interdit les actes en question et soumet leurs auteurs à des sanctions[91], ce qui

---

90. Seule la Convention des Nations Unies sur la criminalité transnationale organisée exige *expressis verbis* la demande d'extradition comme condition de l'obligation de poursuivre:

> «Un Etat Partie sur le territoire duquel se trouve l'auteur présumé de l'infraction, s'il n'extrade pas cette personne au titre d'une infraction à laquelle s'applique le présent article au seul motif qu'elle est l'un de ses ressortissants, est tenu, *à la demande de l'Etat Partie requérant l'extradition*, de soumettre l'affaire sans retard excessif à ses autorités compétentes aux fins de poursuites.» (Art. 16, par. 10.) (Les italiques sont de moi.)

91. J. J. Paust, «Extradition of the *Achille Lauro* Hostage-Takers: Navigating the Hazards», *Vanderbilt Journal of Transnational Law*, n° 20, 1987, p. 254:

> «Universal jurisdiction by treaty under the Hostages Convention, or jurisdiction under article 5(d) thereof, which adopts the victim or passive personality theory, is highly suspect with regard to defendants who are not nationals of a signatory to the Hostages Convention. A basis under international law (i.e., the universality principle) can exist, however, which permits the United States to use whatever statutory basis for prosecution it finds convenient.»

Selon M. Halberstam, «Terrorism on the high seas...», *op. cit.*, pp. 271-272,

n'est pas difficile à prouver à propos de la piraterie. Les choses se compliquent lorsqu'un Etat entame des poursuites non pour l'infraction de piraterie, mais pour la prise d'otages ou l'entrave au trafic maritime, sur la base donc de dispositions transposant les infractions prévues par les conventions SUA et contre la prise d'otages. Ainsi, la District Court de Columbia a refusé d'appliquer la Convention contre la prise d'otages dans l'affaire *Etats-Unis c. Ali*, où il s'agissait d'un Somalien par la suite retrouvé sur le territoire américain, étant donné que la Somalie n'était pas partie à ladite convention. La cour a notamment précisé que, si cette convention visait à la répression universelle des infractions qu'elle prévoyait, elle n'a créé en aucun cas une compétence universelle, ni une compétence universelle conventionnelle *(treaty-based universal jurisdiction)*, et elle ne lie que les Etats parties. Plus concrètement, elle a mis en place une compétence *aut dedere aut punire* de nature purement contractuelle. Il nous semble en effet que les nationaux d'un Etat ne peuvent être soumis au pouvoir d'un autre Etat sur la base d'une convention que seul le dernier aurait ratifiée. Un tel exercice du pouvoir juridictionnel serait excessif et constituerait un fait internationalement illicite à l'égard de l'Etat tiers.

d) Absence de hiérarchisation entre les diverses bases de compétence

Les conventions qui prévoient cet ensemble des bases de compétence ne prennent pas la peine d'exprimer une préférence à l'égard de l'un ou l'autre juge, contrairement à ce que peut laisser penser la distinction entre compétence primaire obligatoire (SUA, art 6, par. 1) et compétence primaire optionnelle (SUA, art. 6, par. 2). Est-ce à dire que tous les juges sont au même point légitimes pour connaître d'une affaire donnée[92] ? La question manque éventuellement d'intérêt pratique étant

envisageant l'hypothèse de la commission d'un acte terroriste par un national d'un Etat non-partie sur le territoire d'un Etat non-partie, la compétence universelle au regard du terrorisme est déjà reconnue par le droit international coutumier. Elle évoque également la vaste ratification de ce genre de traités, ce qui peut engendrer une nouvelle coutume, ainsi que la multiplication des législations internes incriminant tous ces comportements qui se trouvent à la base du terrorisme (détournement de véhicules, prise d'otages...).

92. Voir J. Verhoeven, «Remarques critiques sur les lois du 16 juin 1993 et du 10 février 1999», dans J. Wouters et H. Panken (dir. publ.), *De genocidewet in internationaal perspectief*, Gent, Larcier, 2002, p. 188:

> «En matière pénale comme en matière civile, tout *«forum»* n'est pas nécessairement *«conveniens»*. Les conventions, dans l'ensemble récemment conclues, qui imposent une obligation de punir ou d'extrader *(aut dedere, aut punire)* se sont certes refusées à établir quelque compétence préférentielle au profit de l'un ou l'autre juge, par exemple du lieu de l'infraction, pour ce qui concerne la répression des infractions qu'elles visent, contrairement à ce qui est implicitement admis, par exemple, dans la

donné que les différents Etats dont les intérêts sont en cause dans une même affaire de piraterie ne s'empressent pas de la revendiquer. Néanmoins, il se peut qu'un accusé remette en cause l'opportunité de sa comparution devant les juridictions d'un Etat donné. La question s'est posée récemment devant les tribunaux des Etats-Unis et a été examinée sous l'angle du principe de *due process*[93]. Il s'agissait de la première affaire devant les juridictions américaines qui portait sur cette convention[94]. Pour la cour d'appel, le principe du procès équitable ne va pas forcément de pair avec l'existence d'un lien avec l'Etat qui poursuit. L'universalité de la répression visée par cette convention est l'élément qui la distingue des autres conventions pour lesquelles un *nexus* est requis. On peut supposer que la cour a opté pour cette position en l'absence de manifestation de volonté de poursuivre de la part des autres Etats qui auraient pu exercer leur compétence (Etat de nationalité de l'auteur et des victimes, Etat du pavillon). Une fois l'auteur retrouvé sur leur territoire, les Etats-Unis n'avaient d'autre option que de poursuivre. On ne peut être sûr que la solution aurait été différente dans le cas où les autres Etats impliqués auraient revendiqué l'affaire, étant donné que la cour a énoncé le principe général selon lequel la convention de par sa nature n'exige pas de lien avec l'Etat sur le territoire duquel se trouve l'auteur de l'infraction.

C. Une compétence universelle limitée ?

i) *Poursuites par l'Etat capteur et par un Etat entretenant un lien avec l'incident*

La rédaction plutôt claire de l'article 105 de la CNUDM semble réserver le droit d'engager des poursuites à l'égard des pirates présumés à l'Etat dont les navires de guerre ont opéré la saisie et l'arrestation. Or, la

convention du 9 décembre 1948 sur le génocide. Leurs dispositions témoignent de la volonté des Etats contractants d'éradiquer le plus rapidement possible certains phénomènes de violence particulièrement dommageables pour les rapports internationaux, comme il en va notamment de la piraterie aérienne. Elles ne confirment pas que la politique de principe de la communauté internationale soit de laisser chacun libre en principe de punir qui il veut, quand bien même le droit dit positif ne le lui interdit pas. Même dans l'application de ces conventions, il ne manquerait d'ailleurs pas d'arguments pour soutenir que l'extradition doit être préférée à la punition lorsqu'elle permet d'attraire la personne présumée responsable d'un crime devant son juge (plus) « naturel »... »

93. *Etats-Unis c. Shi*, 525 F.3d 709, 129 S.Ct. 324 (2008) (appel), 24 avril 2008.

94. Voir E. Kontorovich, « International Decisions: *United States* v. *Shi* », *AJIL*, 2009, n° 103, pp. 734-740.

plupart des auteurs interprètent cette disposition assez librement soutenant que ce serait aller à l'encontre de la *ratio* de la règle codifiée par cet article que d'exclure que d'autres Etats puissent le faire. La disposition ne fait qu'incorporer la règle de droit international coutumier qui consiste à mettre à la disposition des Etats une base de compétence supplémentaire : la compétence universelle[95]. Il est légitime de penser que l'article 105 fait référence à l'Etat «capteur» parce que c'est l'Etat le plus directement concerné par les suites potentielles de l'arrestation effectuée (ainsi que le sort du navire et des biens saisis) ; c'est à lui de voir ce qu'il va faire des personnes arrêtées, du navire et des biens saisis, et c'est justement à cet Etat qu'est accordé le droit de s'en occuper par la suite en exerçant son pouvoir juridictionnel. Par ailleurs, en l'absence de cette disposition, l'Etat capteur n'aurait aucun fondement pour entamer des poursuites.

L'article 105 n'exclut point l'invocation des autres titres de compétence largement admis en droit international. Ainsi, l'Etat de nationalité de l'auteur des actes, des victimes, l'Etat du pavillon du navire victime peuvent également engager des poursuites. Pourrait-il être interprété comme introduisant une règle de conflits de normes ? La question continue de faire l'objet d'un débat doctrinal[96], mais il nous semble que la disposition affirme ce qui va de soi : que c'est à la discrétion de l'Etat capteur de décider du sort des personnes arrêtées (et du navire et des biens saisis), d'exercer son pouvoir juridictionnel ou de transférer les suspects à un autre Etat qui justifierait son intérêt appuyé sur les titres de compétence classiques[97]. Ainsi la nouvelle loi française sur la pirate-

95. D. Guilfoyle, «Treaty jurisdiction...», *op. cit.*, par. 18-19 ; I. Brownlie, *Principles of Public International Law*, 7e éd., Oxford University Press, 2008, p. 229 ; L. Lucchini et M. Voelckel, *Droit de la mer, op. cit.*, p. 182 ; Harvard Law School, *Research in International Law — Drafts of conventions..., op. cit.*, pp. 852-856 ; CIJ, *Mandat d'arrêt du 11 avril 2000 (République démocratique du Congo c. Belgique), CIJ Recueil 2002*, p. 3 (président Guillaume (opinion individuelle), par. 5, et juges Higgins, Kooijmans and Buergenthal (opinion individuelle commune), par. 61) ; E. Kontorovich, «International Decisions...», *op. cit.*, p. 739.

96. En ce sens, C. Touret, *La piraterie au vingtième siècle : piraterie maritime et aérienne,* LGDJ, Paris, 1992, p. 158 : «L'article 105 fait primer la compétence de l'Etat capteur sur celle de l'Etat du pavillon du navire ou celle de l'Etat national des pirates» ; R. Geiss et A. Petrig, *Piracy and Armed Robbery at sea..., op. cit.* p. 151.

97. Ainsi D. Guilfoyle, «Treaty Jurisdiction...», *op. cit.*,

> «The general international law of jurisdiction provides no rule of priority between competing potential jurisdictions. It is sometimes suggested that before proceeding to exercise universal jurisdiction the prosecuting State should, for example, offer the suspect for prosecution to the State where the offence was committed or to their State of nationality. Such suggestions are at best de *lege ferenda*. While they might be sensible as a matter of policy,

rie, qui introduit ce que certains ont appelé une compétence « quasi universelle », prévoit la possibilité pour les tribunaux français de poursuivre des présumés pirates « à défaut d'entente avec les autorités d'un autre Etat pour l'exercice par celui-ci de sa compétence juridictionnelle »[98]. Evidemment, c'est dans ce contexte que la coopération internationale prend toute sa valeur[99].

ii) *Transfèrement à un Etat tiers*

Qu'un Etat autre que l'Etat capteur puisse exercer sa compétence grâce à un lien de rattachement qu'il entretient avec l'incident en cause est tout à fait compréhensible. La pratique la plus controversée est celle du transfert des personnes appréhendées vers des pays tiers auxquels l'incident est totalement étranger. A notre connaissance, la pratique a fait son apparition dans le cadre de la lutte contre la piraterie au large des côtes somaliennes. Des Etats participant à des patrouilles dans la région avec leurs forces navales qui ne sont pas prêts à amener les personnes capturées devant leurs juridictions internes ont opté pour la conclusion d'accords avec des Etats de la région, à commencer par les Etats-Unis

---

they are not binding as a matter of law. » (Par. 20.) « Nothing in Article 105, however, affects the right of a State with custody of a suspected criminal to either prosecute that person (if they have jurisdiction at international law) or transfer them to another State for prosecution (subject to applicable human rights law. » (Par. 21.)

98. Loi précitée, art. 5.

99. L'OMI en a tenu compte et ainsi retrouve-t-on dans le Code de conduite, *op. cit.*, sous le chapeau « Agreements or arrangements for investigations », un rappel de l'article 100 de la CNUDM ainsi qu'un encouragement adressé aux Etats à « cooperate to the fullest possible extent in the investigation of acts or attempted acts of piracy and to enter into bilateral or multilateral agreements with other interested States such as the flag State or the coastal State so as to facilitate such investigations and the *prosecution* of the perpetrators ». Sous le chapeau « Overall management/other liaison/cooperation », la responsabilité principale du déroulement des enquêtes devrait être assumée par l'Etat du pavillon, mais cela ne lui accorde en aucun cas une priorité en matière d'exercice de poursuites :

> « In cases of piracy, the flag State of the ship should take lead responsibility, ... In all cases it should be recognized that other States will have legitimate interests, and therefore liaison and cooperation between them is vital to a successful investigation and apprehension of the perpetrator. Le Code de Djibouti prévoit quant à lui dans son article 6 que « the Participants recognize that multiple States, including the flag State, State of suspected origin of the perpetrators, the State of nationality of persons on bord the ship, and the State of ownership of cargo may have legitimate interests in cases arising pursuant to articles 4 and 5. Therefore, the Participants intend to liaise and cooperate with such States and stakeholders, and to coordinate such activities with each other to facilitate the rescue, interdiction, investigation and *prosecution*. » (Les italiques sont de moi.)

qui ont signé un Memorandum of Understanding (MOU) avec le Kenya le 16 janvier 2009. Le même pays africain a conclu des accords avec le Royaume-Uni, l'Union européenne, la Chine, le Danemark et le Canada. Il est intéressant de noter que le premier procès de pirates somaliens au Kenya, *République c. Hassan Mohamud Ahmed,* qui a eu lieu en 2006, est intervenu suite à un transfèrement de la part des Etats-Unis bien avant la conclusion d'un MOU entre les deux Etats et avant les résolutions du Conseil de sécurité incitant les Etats à conclure des accords en vue de transfèrement de suspects [100]. Ce premier procès a abouti à la condamnation des accusés sur la base de la section 69(1) du Code pénal — révoquée en 2009 — qui incriminait la piraterie *jure gentium* [101].

Le transfert des personnes arrêtées aux fins de jugement à l'Etat dont les forces navales ont effectué l'arrestation posant de nombreux problèmes pratiques, les accords avec des pays de la région se sont multipliés. Ainsi, après le Kenya, les Etats qui effectuent des activités de patrouille ont conclu des accords avec les Seychelles [102], la République de Maurice [103] et la Tanzanie [104].

Le transfèrement peut être défini comme la remise d'une personne par l'Etat détenteur à un autre Etat souhaitant la poursuivre en justice ou, dans le cas où la personne serait déjà jugée et condamnée, à un Etat qui

100. Voir, par exemple, S/RES/1976 (2011), par. 20: «Le Conseil de sécurité demande aux Etats, à l'Organisation des Nations Unies contre la drogue et le crime et aux organisations régionales d'envisager d'adopter des mesures conformes aux règles du droit international des droits de l'homme applicable pour faciliter le transfèrement de pirates présumés en vue de leur jugement et celui de pirates condamnés en vue de leur emprisonnement, notamment dans le cadre d'accords de transfèrement ou d'arrangements prévus à cet effet, et salue les efforts déployés jusqu'ici par le Groupe de contact à cet égard.»

101. *Republic c. Hassan Mohamud Ahmed*, Crim. n° 434 de 2006 (Chief Magis. Ct. Nov. 1, 2006) (Jaden Acting Sr. Principal Mag.), *Hassan M. Ahmed c. Republic*, Crim. App. n°s 198, 199, 201, 203, 204, 205, 206 et 207 et 208 (High Ct. May 12, 2009) (Azangalala, J.). Pour un commentaire, voir J. T. Gathii, «Kenya's Piracy Prosecutions», *AJIL*, 2010, n° 104, pp. 416-436.

102. Voir la lettre du Secrétaire général adressée au Président du Conseil de sécurité, datée du 26 mars 2012, avec en annexe une compilation des informations reçues des Etats Membres sur les mesures qu'ils ont prises pour ériger la piraterie en infraction dans leur droit interne et pour faciliter les poursuites contre les personnes soupçonnées de piraterie au large des côtes somaliennes et incarcérer celles qui ont été reconnues coupables (S/2012/177, pp. 6 et 18).

103. *Ibid.*, pp. 65-76; «Accord entre l'Union européenne et la République de Maurice relatif aux conditions de transfert, de la force navale placée sous la direction de l'Union européenne à la République de Maurice, des personnes suspectées d'actes de piraterie et des biens associés saisis, et aux conditions des personnes suspectées d'actes de piraterie après leur transfert», *JOUE* L 254/3, 30/9/2011.

104. Voir lien https://www.gov.uk/government/news/uk-signs-agreement-with-mauritius-to-transfer-suspected-pirates-for-prosecution?view=News&id=773845482.

accepte de se charger de l'exécution de la peine[105]. La Convention de Montego Bay n'en disant mot, on peut le considérer comme toléré ou en tout cas comme non exclu[106]. Certains critiquent la pratique sur la base de la lettre seule de l'article 105 de la CNUDM qui dispose que «les tribunaux de l'Etat qui a opéré la saisie peuvent se prononcer sur les peines à infliger, ainsi que sur les mesures à prendre en ce qui concerne le navire, l'aéronef ou les biens, réserve faite des tiers de bonne foi». Néanmoins, il ne faut pas oublier le commentaire du Harvard Draft Convention on Piracy selon lequel «a state which has lawful custody of a person suspected of piracy may prosecute and punish that person». A notre sens, n'importe quel Etat sous le contrôle duquel se trouve l'auteur présumé peut entamer des poursuites, peu importe que ce contrôle ait été obtenu suite à un transfert. De toute façon, les transferts se multipliant, on peut affirmer être en présence d'une «pratique ultérieurement suivie dans l'application du traité par laquelle est établi l'accord des parties à l'égard de l'interprétation du traité»[107].

Tout autre chose est la problématique de la garantie des droits de l'homme dans l'Etat de destination[108]. Les Etats qui ont négocié avec les Etats de la région ont insisté sur l'inclusion d'un certain nombre de droits qui devraient être respectés par les derniers, tels les droits de la défense, le droit à un procès équitable, l'interdiction de la torture, des peines ou traitements inhumains et dégradants, l'interdiction de la peine de mort[109]. Qui plus est, le transfèrement à un Etat de la région peut être considéré comme une solution au problème des détentions à bord d'une extrêmement longue durée, susceptible d'être considérée comme une violation des droits des détenus[110].

Le renouveau de la piraterie maritime est venu secouer quelques certitudes concernant le régime juridique de la lutte contre cette activité aux

105. Voir J.-C. Martin, «La répression des actes de piraterie maritime: développements récents en matière de poursuites et détention des pirates somaliens», *AFDI*, n° 56, 2010, p. 510, citant la Convention sur le transfèrement des personnes condamnées adoptée en 1983 au sein du Conseil de l'Europe. Pour une présentation détaillée, voir R. Geiss et A. Petrig, *Piracy and Armed Robbery at Sea…, op. cit.*, pp. 186-220.

106. Les choses sont moins ambiguës en ce qui concerne la Convention SUA qui prévoit un encadrement relativement détaillé de la remise de l'auteur présumé entre les mains d'un autre Etat partie: voir art. 6, par. 1, art. 11 et art. 8, qui permet la remise à un autre Etat partie par le capitaine d'un navire.

107. Convention de Vienne sur le droit des traités, signée à Vienne le 23 mai 1969, entrée en vigueur le 27 janvier 1980, *RTNU*, 1969, vol. 1155, p. 134, art. 31, par. 3, al. *b)*.

108. Voir chapitre 6, Guggisberg.

109. Voir Accord entre l'Union européenne et la République de Maurice, *op. cit.*, art. 4.

110. Voir l'arrêt rendu par la Grande Chambre de la CEDH le 29 mars 2010 dans l'affaire *Medvedyev et autres c. France* (requête 3394/03).

origines très lointaines. On a beau affirmer le statut coutumier des normes internationales en la matière, les efforts déployés par les Etats, les nouvelles formes de coopération, l'intensification de la répression qui s'étend depuis peu aux infractions connexes, ainsi que la coexistence de divers outils juridiques, soulèvent de nouvelles questions. Une fois de plus, ce sont les juridictions internes qui sont appelées à y répondre de manière à ce que le régime de la lutte contre la piraterie obtienne la cohérence qui convient à un régime relatif à une activité menaçant la sécurité maritime dans les eaux internationales. On en est encore loin...

6 Le trafic illicite de migrants en mer

Solène Guggisberg *

SECTION 1 INTRODUCTION

Paragraphe 1 Problématique

L'usage par les migrants des transports maritimes afin d'atteindre leur destination est une réalité qui fait régulièrement l'actualité, et cela depuis des décennies — on se souviendra des *boat people* dans les années soixante-dix, de l'épisode du *MV Tampa* aux alentours de l'Australie, mais aussi des meurtrières années 2011 et 2013 en Méditerranée. Ce phénomène, où, fuyant un pays et/ou attirées par les promesses d'une vie plus facile ailleurs, des personnes tentent leur chance souvent sur des embarcations de fortune, touche tous les continents. En effet, que ce soit en Méditerranée, dans les Caraïbes, vers la Corne de l'Afrique ou en Océanie, la réalité est la même, avec des migrants déterminés à entrer dans un pays, de manière irrégulière s'il le faut, souvent via des réseaux de trafiquants qui ne placent pas la sécurité de « leurs clients » en haut de la liste de leurs priorités, et faisant face à des autorités nationales farouchement décidées à éviter cette immigration illégale [1].

Le trafic de migrants par la mer n'existe évidemment pas en vase clos ; les personnes engagées dans cette activité, tant les passeurs que les migrants, les routes et probablement les aspects financiers font partie de la famille plus large des activités illicites transnationales [2]. Cependant, il est utile ici de se concentrer sur les activités en mer, qui soulèvent

---

* Doctorante à la Bucerius Law School, chercheuse associée à l'International Max Planck Research School for Maritime Affairs, Hambourg.

1. Office des Nations Unies contre la drogue et le crime (UNODC), « Issue Paper — Smuggling of Migrants by Sea » (Vienne, 2011), pp. 9-19 ; « The Interception and Rescue at Sea of Asylum Seekers, Refugees and Irregular Migrants », *Report of the Committee on Migration, Refugees and Population*, doc. 12628, 1er juin 2011 (Parliamentary Assembly/ Council of Europe), pp. 7-9.

2. UNODC, « Issue Paper — Smuggling of Migrants by Sea », *op. cit. supra* note 1, p. 9.

suffisamment de questions légales et de besoins de clarifications. Les trajets par mer de migrants, bien que ceux-ci ne représentent pas les chemins les plus répandus, sont en grande partie aux mains de groupes criminels, sont ceux qui causent le plus de morts[3] et, souvent, ceux qui ciblent les migrants les plus démunis. En effet, les transports par avion sont financièrement inaccessibles à ces derniers[4] et nombre de routes migratoires plus sûres sont aujourd'hui fermées[5]. Il est néanmoins vrai que les conséquences terrestres des actions en mer, en particulier les obligations de protection internationale, conditionnent en négatif la mise en pratique du droit en mer et de la lutte contre la criminalité transnationale organisée.

Afin de faire face à ces flux migratoires considérés comme indésirables et participant en de nombreux cas à la criminalité organisée, les Etats ont adopté des instruments criminalisant certaines activités en mer, à savoir le trafic de migrants et la traite de personnes. Cependant, les réponses à fournir à ce trafic en mer sont complexes, ce qui est illustré par l'enchevêtrement théorique et pratique des cadres légaux applicables. Ces questions se situent en effet à la croisée entre le droit de la mer, les mesures contre la criminalité transnationale organisée et les règles de droits humains, en particulier le droit des réfugiés. Les cadres légaux de la première catégorie définissent les droits et les obligations des Etats dans les différentes zones maritimes. Celui de la seconde tente de juguler le trafic illicite de migrants par terre, mer et air sous l'angle de la criminalisation du trafic en tant qu'activité criminelle transnationale. Quant à la troisième catégorie, elle regroupe les règles relatives à la protection minimale que les différents Etats doivent octroyer aux migrants, que ces derniers désirent ou non demander l'asile.

3. L'actualité de 2011 en Afrique du Nord a fait de la Méditerranée une zone de passage très prisée et, tragiquement, dramatique pour beaucoup. Il semble que, avec environ 1500 morts, cela soit une des années les plus meurtrières pour les migrants en mer dans la région, mais 2013, avec ses nombreux drames près de Lampedusa, s'approche de ce triste record. Certains épisodes ont particulièrement marqué les mémoires, tel que celui du « left-to-die » boat, où une embarcation en détresse a été laissée à la dérive au vu et au su des autorités et de divers navires, résultant dans la mort de 63 des 72 personnes à bord (Parliamentary Assembly, « Lives Lost in the Mediterranean Sea : Who Is Responsible ? », Strasbourg, 2012, http://assembly.coe.int/CommitteeDocs/2012/20120329_mig_RPT.EN.pdf).

4. UNODC, « Issue Paper — Smuggling of Migrants by Sea », *op. cit. supra* note 1, pp. 11-12 ; D. Guilfoyle, *Shipping Interdiction and the Law of the Sea*, Cambridge University Press, 2009, pp. 182-183.

5. Par exemple, en raison du contrôle efficace exercé sur le détroit de Gibraltar, la route « choisie » pour atteindre l'Espagne depuis l'Afrique du Nord s'est déplacée vers les îles Canaries, un voyage dangereux d'une dizaine de jours (*ibid.*, pp. 216-217) ; voir également L. A. Nessel, « Externalized Borders and the Invisible Refugee », *Columbia Human Rights Law Review*, n° 40, 2009, pp. 650-652.

Cette étude va donc examiner, avec un accent sur la criminalisation, la cohérence du régime entre les compétences de prescription et celles d'action et l'utilité pratique, compte tenu des intérêts des Etats, d'une approche pénale dans la lutte contre le trafic et la migration irrégulière. Pour ce faire, après avoir mentionné les droits et les obligations pertinents (section 2), il convient de clarifier pour chaque zone maritime, autant que l'état de la *lex lata* qui a évolué dans la dernière décennie le permet, les droits et les obligations des Etats d'agir envers les navires soupçonnés de trafic de migrants, les droits et les obligations des Etats envers les personnes interceptées en mer, qu'elles soient des trafiquants ou des migrants, en matière de compétence pénale et de droits humains (section 3) avant de conclure sur la cohérence du régime et l'utilité de l'approche pénale (section 4). Un tel point de situation est en effet profitable, car il permet d'examiner les améliorations apportées par les derniers développements dans le droit applicable, en particulier le Protocole contre le trafic de migrants et la jurisprudence récente.

Paragraphe 2 **Différenciations**

Les personnes qui se trouvent sur un bateau dans un but migratoire appartiennent souvent à des catégories diverses. Un premier groupe de personnes, qui sont l'objet principal de cette étude, comprend les trafiquants. Régulièrement, ils se trouvent sur les bateaux qu'ils dirigent, mais il arrive aussi que des navires de personnes trafiquées n'aient aucun organisateur à bord[6]. Ces personnes font partie de réseaux criminels transnationaux et sont visées par le cadre légal de la lutte contre la criminalité transnationale organisée.

Quant aux migrants eux-mêmes, une catégorisation utile ici, même si compliquée à mettre en pratique, est de savoir sous quelles conditions ils se trouvent sur le bateau. Sur certains navires, des migrants ont embarqué sans que le capitaine ne soit au courant; les clandestins sont soumis à un régime particulier, qui ne fait pas l'objet d'une analyse dans cette étude. En effet, ils ne tombent pas sous le coup de la criminalité transnationale organisée, ils ne font pas, en général, l'objet de trafic et leur débarquement est une question à part[7]. Sur les bateaux uniquement utilisés

6. UNODC, «Issue Paper — Smuggling of Migrants by Sea», *op. cit. supra* note 1, p. 46.

7. Un clandestin est défini comme:

> «a person who is secreted on a ship or a cargo which is subsequently loaded on the ship, without the consent of the shipowner or the master or any other responsible person, and who is detected on board the ship after it has departed from a port, or in the cargo while unloading it in the port of arrival, and is reported as a stowaway by the master to the appropriate authorities»

pour le transfert de migrants se trouvent parfois des personnes que nous qualifierons d'indépendantes, à savoir qu'elles ont organisé elles-mêmes le trajet, sans les services de passeurs — à nouveau, elles sont au-dehors du champ d'analyse de cette étude car elles ne répondent pas aux critères de personnes trafiquées.

D'autres, probablement bien plus nombreuses, payent le passage à des réseaux de criminels qui agissent en vue d'un bénéfice financier. Ce qui est appelé ici trafic de migrants est combattu dans le Protocole contre le trafic illicite de migrants par terre, air et mer[8]. Cet instrument, lié à la Convention des Nations Unies contre la criminalité transnationale organisée[9], vise les actions permettant l'entrée illégale de personnes dans un pays, actions entreprises dans le but d'un avantage financier ou matériel[10]. Finalement, certaines personnes qui se trouvent sur les navires n'ont ni contrôle sur leur voyage ni sur leur futur dans le pays de destination[11]; il s'agit des victimes de la traite. Cette activité criminelle est caractérisée dans le Protocole visant à prévenir, réprimer et punir la traite des personnes, en particulier des femmes et des enfants[12] comme englobant différentes actions, dont le transport, entreprises par divers moyens, dont la menace, les contraintes ou l'abus d'une situation de vulnérabilité, à des fins d'exploitation. L'exploitation inclut de manière non exhaustive le travail forcé, l'esclavage ou des pratiques similaires et l'exploitation sexuelle[13]. Le consentement à l'exploitation ne change pas la qualification

---

> (International Maritime Organization, «Revised Guidelines on the Prevention of Access by Stowaways and the Allocation of Responsibility to Seek Successful Resolution of Stowaway Cases», 9 septembre 2011, Res. Fal. 11(37) 2.1);

voir également S. Trevisanut, «The Principle of Non-Refoulement at Sea and the Effectiveness of Asylum Protection», dans A. von Bogdandy et R. Wolfrum (dir. publ.), *Max Planck Yearbook of United Nations Law*, Brill, 2008, p. 228.

8. Protocole contre le trafic illicite de migrants par terre, air et mer, Nations Unies, *Recueil des traités*, 2000, vol. 2241, p. 519.

9. Convention des Nations Unies contre la criminalité transnationale organisée, Nations Unies, *Recueil des traités*, 2000, vol. 2225, p. 209.

10. Protocole contre le trafic illicite de migrants par terre, air et mer, *op. cit. supra* note 8, art. 3(a).

11. E. Papastavridis, «Interception of Human Beings on the High Seas: A Contemporary Analysis under International Law», *Syracuse Journal of International Law and Commerce*, nº 36, 2008-2009, p. 157.

12. Protocole visant à prévenir, réprimer et punir la traite des personnes, en particulier des femmes et des enfants, Nations Unies, *Recueil des traités*, 2000, vol. 2237, p. 319.

13. *Ibid.*, art. 3(a). Que les victimes de la traite de personnes en vue d'une exploitation sexuelle ou autre soient considérées comme des esclaves modernes est une possibilité, mais cette discussion va au-delà du présent article (voir, par exemple, Papastavridis, *op. cit. supra* note 11, pp. 163-178; T. Obokata, «The Legal Framework concerning the Smuggling of Migrants at Sea under the UN Protocol on the Smuggling of Migrants by Land, Sea and Air», dans B. Ryan et V. Mitsilegas (dir. publ.), *Extraterritorial Immigration Control: Legal Chal-*

de traite[14]. Ces deux dernières catégories — trafic et traite — sont régulièrement imbriquées, du moins partiellement[15]. Il est en effet admis, même dans les instruments spécialisés, que la frontière entre trafic et traite n'est pas facile à tracer[16]. Par exemple, le Protocole contre le trafic illicite de migrants mentionne une circonstance aggravante pour les auteurs de trafic, à savoir le «traitement inhumain ou dégradant de ces migrants, y compris pour l'exploitation»[17].

Lorsque l'on garde en mémoire qu'une des composantes de la traite de personnes est le but d'exploitation, l'on peut facilement voir les chevauchements. Cependant, la traite inclut un élément de contrôle sur les personnes; là où les migrants objets de trafic ont choisi d'entreprendre cette activité, les victimes de la traite sont forcées ou trompées.

Une autre différence majeure est le but exploitatif de la traite après le voyage également, ce que le trafic de migrants ne comporte pas nécessairement[18].

Malgré les chevauchements, il est important de prendre en compte l'existence de deux régimes légaux différenciés par une terminologie qui prête elle aussi à confusion: en français, le trafic de migrants équivaut au «smuggling» anglais, mais la traite d'êtres humains se traduit par «trafficking».

Dans tous les cas, les migrants ont en général un aspect en commun, à savoir qu'ils désirent entrer dans un pays dont ils n'ont pas la nationalité et cela sans les documents requis par les services d'immigration de ce pays. Une différenciation d'importance ici est la raison qui a poussé ces migrants à quitter leur pays et à tenter l'entrée dans un autre Etat de manière irrégulière. En effet, ceux qui poursuivent un but économique ne sont généralement pas reconnus comme ayant besoin d'une protection internationale, alors que ceux qui ont quitté leur pays en raison de per-

---

lenges (Immigration and Asylum Law and Policy in Europe), Martinus Nijhoff Publishers, 2010, p. 160; P. Mallia, *Migrant Smuggling By Sea: Combating a Current Threat to Maritime Security through the Creation of a Cooperative Framework*, Martinus Nijhoff Publishers, 2010, p. 67). Sur les formes contemporaines d'esclavage, voir, par exemple, D. Weissbrodt, «Slavery», dans R. Wolfrum (dir. publ.), *The Max Planck Encyclopedia of Public International Law*, Oxford University Press, 2008, par. 8-22.

14. Protocole visant à prévenir, réprimer et punir la traite des personnes, en particulier des femmes et des enfants, *op. cit. supra* note 12, art. 3(b).

15. Papastavridis, *op. cit. supra* note 11, pp. 157-158.

16. Obokata, *op. cit. supra* note 13, p. 153; Guilfoyle, *op. cit. supra* note 4, pp. 180-181.

17. Protocole contre le trafic illicite de migrants par terre, air et mer, *op. cit. supra* note 8, art. 6(3)(b).

18. Obokata, *op. cit. supra* note 13, pp. 152-153; UNODC, «Manuel de formation de base sur les enquêtes et les poursuites relatives au trafic illicite de migrants; Module 1: concepts et catégories du trafic illicite de migrants et des actes connexes», New York, 2011, pp. 5-12.

sécutions pour des motifs de race, de religion, de nationalité, d'appartenance à un certain groupe social ou d'opinions politiques devraient pouvoir se prévaloir du statut de réfugiés. Le phénomène de migration est régulièrement de nature mixte, à savoir que des migrants économiques et des demandeurs d'asile voyagent dans les mêmes conditions et souvent en parallèle.

SECTION 2 **DROITS ET OBLIGATIONS PERTINENTS**

Paragraphe 1 **Interceptions**

Le droit d'interception varie selon l'Etat en question et la zone maritime dans laquelle le bateau appréhendé se trouve. La théorie de la compétence de mise en application et d'exécution, selon laquelle un Etat ne peut pas prendre des mesures sur le territoire d'un autre Etat sans l'accord de celui-ci[19], est utile à garder à l'esprit, mais n'est pas totalement adéquate pour les questions maritimes, cela pour deux raisons. Premièrement, les espaces maritimes sont gouvernés par des règles propres avec le principe de la juridiction du pavillon en haute mer et la souveraineté limitée par un droit de passage inoffensif en mer territoriale. Ainsi un Etat peut agir hors de son territoire envers les navires battant son pavillon et l'Etat côtier doit exercer une certaine retenue face aux navires traversant sa mer territoriale. Deuxièmement, même dans les exceptions qui ouvrent les champs d'action des Etats envers les navires, l'interception n'est pas à considérer comme une exécution dans son ensemble. En effet, il s'agit à la fois d'un droit de visite, de fouille et, si l'autorisation est donnée, de prise de contrôle sur le navire et ses occupants[20]. Ces actions de police peuvent permettre l'application du droit national et une compétence de mise en application, mais ne représentent qu'une étape préliminaire de contrôle.

Seuls les navires de guerre ou dûment habilités et identifiables comme étant au service de l'Etat peuvent mener une interception. Une interception est entreprise soit par un Etat soit par plusieurs Etats en collaboration, parfois à travers un organisme supranational, tel que l'Agence européenne pour la gestion de la coopération opérationnelle aux frontières extérieures des Etats membres de l'Union européenne (Frontex)[21].

19. I. Brownlie, *Principles of Public International Law*, Oxford University Press, 7e éd., 2008, p. 309; R. O'Keefe, «Universal Jurisdiction: Clarifying the Basic Concept», *International Criminal Justice*, n° 2, 2004, p. 740.

20. Guilfoyle, *op. cit. supra* note 4, p. 9.

21. Frontex a été instituée par le «Règlement (CE) n° 2007/2004 du Conseil du 26 octobre 2004 portant création d'une Agence européenne pour la gestion de la coopération opérationnelle aux frontières extérieures des Etats membres de l'Union européenne», *JO L 349 du 25 novembre 2004*, pp. 1-11.

Le terme interception — qui est synonyme d'interdiction en mer — a été défini par l'UNHCR en 2000 comme englobant l'interception, l'interdiction maritime et en général les mesures physiques prises de manière extraterritoriale pour éviter l'entrée de migrants non désirés sur le territoire national[22]. Une interception contient donc une interférence avec les navires, et peut prendre la forme d'une visite, d'une inspection, d'une arrestation et/ou d'une destruction du navire[23], ainsi que des actions de «push-back» lors desquelles ces navires sont empêchés d'entrer ou celles de «tow-back» où ils sont ramenés de force dans une autre zone maritime[24]. Les buts de l'interception sont de contrôler certains flux migratoires, d'éviter l'entrée de migrants sans papiers dans le territoire national[25] et de combattre le trafic illicite de migrants, ainsi que la traite de personnes.

Des exemples d'interception sont les activités des gardes-côtes américains dans les Caraïbes, en particulier par rapport aux migrants haïtiens, cubains et dominicains[26], de l'Italie en Méditerranée et dans les eaux territoriales libyenne et albanaise[27], et celles de Frontex en Afrique de l'Ouest et en Méditerranée. Un exemple d'opération coordonnée par Frontex avec la participation, entre autres pays, de l'Espagne, de l'Italie et du Luxembourg est en effet la série d'opérations *Hera* qui se sont déroulées depuis 2006 dans les zones côtières d'Afrique de l'Ouest, avec pour but d'éviter que les navires de migrants n'atteignent les îles Canaries[28].

---

22. B. Miltner, «Irregular Maritime Migration: Refugee Protection Issues in Rescue and Interception», *Fordham International Law Journal*, n° 30, 2007, p. 79; Agence des Nations Unies pour les réfugiés (UNHCR), *Interception of Asylum-Seekers and Refugees: the International Framework and Recommendations for a Comprehensive Approach*, 2000, EC/50/SC/CRP.17, par. 10. Une autre définition de l'UNHCR en 2003 de l'interception englobe la prévention de l'embarquement, de la suite du voyage une fois commencé et la prise de contrôle des navires suspectés de transporter des personnes en contravention des règles nationales et internationales du droit de la mer (UNHCR, *Conclusion on Protection Safeguards in Interception Measures*, n° 97, LIV, 10 octobre 2003).

23. Miltner, *op. cit. supra* note 22, p. 84.

24. *Ibid.*, p. 84; cela a par exemple été la pratique australienne, voir Guilfoyle, *op. cit. supra* note 4, pp. 206-208.

25. Miltner, *op. cit. supra* note 22, pp. 84-85.

26. Nessel, *op. cit. supra* note 5, pp. 638-643; A. Brouwer et J. Kumin, «Interception and Asylum: When Migration Control and Human Rights Collide», *Refuge*, n° 21, 2003, p. 8.

27. E. T. Bulgherini, «Il traffico via mare di clandestini», dans U. Leanza (dir. publ.), *Studi in onore di Umberto Leanza III*, Editoriale Scientifica, 2008, p. 1841.

28. I. L. Delgado, «España y la lucha contra el tráfico ilícito de inmigrantes por mar», dans J. Pueyo Losa et J. J. Urbina (dir. publ.), *La cooperación internacional en la ordenación de los mares y océanos,* El Papel de las Organizaciones Internacionales en el Derecho del Mar: tendencias revisionistas y consecuencias para España, 13 novembre 2008; Santiago de Compostela, Iustel, 2009, pp. 419-424.

Paragraphe 2 Droits et obligations pertinents envers les personnes à bord

Un certain nombre de règles sont applicables au trafic de migrants, règles qui lient les Etats parties aux instruments pertinents, à la fois dans le but de les autoriser ou même les obliger à criminaliser certaines actions et dans celui d'assurer le respect des droits humains dont bénéficient les personnes trafiquées. Ainsi, le cadre légal place les Etats dans une position centrale entre les criminels et les victimes.

A. Criminalisation du trafic de migrants

Le principe du *Lotus*[29], selon lequel, en matière de juridiction législative, tout ce qui n'est pas interdit est permis, ouvre, s'il est accepté comme valide, le champ des possibles à l'infini[30]; dans le cas étudié ici, dans la mesure où aucune règle n'interdit aux Etats de légiférer sur ce qui se passe en haute mer, le trafic de migrants pourrait être criminalisé par tout Etat qui le désire. Cependant, l'interprétation du *Lotus* est sujette à des critiques presque unanimes[31] et il semble qu'aujourd'hui le principe inverse représente la norme, à savoir qu'en matière de pouvoirs législatifs tout ce qui n'est pas autorisé est interdit et que seulement certains liens entre les actes visés et un Etat sont acceptés en droit international[32]. Les titres de juridiction traditionnels qui permettent d'intenter une action criminelle sont le principe territorial, de nationalité, protectif et universel[33].

Le Protocole contre le trafic illicite de migrants requiert de ses Etats

---

29. 1927, PCIJ, *Série A, n°10*.

30. Cette interprétation est contredite par V. Lowe et C. Staker, «Jurisdiction», dans M. D. Evans (dir. publ.), *International Law*, Oxford University Press, 3e éd., 2010, p. 319, mais les opinions de ces auteurs concordent avec la conclusion générale qui considère que le poids de prouver une compétence légale revient à l'Etat qui désire exercer sa juridiction, et non pas à celui qui la remet en question.

31. La Cour internationale de Justice (CIJ) considère que des limites à cette liberté existent (*Compétence en matière de pêcheries* et *Nottenbohm*), tel que rappelé dans Brownlie, *op. cit. supra* note 19, p. 303 et notes 24-26; B. H. Oxman, «Jurisdiction of States», dans R. Wolfrum (dir. publ.), *The Max Planck Encyclopedia of Public International Law*, Oxford University Press 2008, par. 10; Lowe et Staker, *op. cit. supra* note 30, p. 319. Une différence doit être faite de toute manière entre la compétence législative, la compétence adjudicative et la compétence de mise en application (enforcement).

32. B. Simma et A. T. Müller, «Exercise and limits of jurisdiction», dans J. Crawford et M. Koskenniemi (dir. publ.), *The Cambridge Companion to International Law*, Cambridge University Press, 2012, p. 137.

33. A. Bennett, «That Sinking Feeling: Stateless Ships, Universal Jurisdiction, and the Drug Trafficking Vessel Interdiction Act», *The Yale Journal of International Law*, n° 37, 2012, <http://www.yjil.org/docs/pub/37-2-bennett-that-sinking-feeling.pdf>, p. 436.

parties qu'ils confèrent à certaines actions le caractère d'infraction pénale. Ainsi, le trafic illicite de migrants est défini comme « le fait d'assurer, afin d'en tirer, directement ou indirectement, un avantage financier ou un autre avantage matériel, l'entrée illégale dans un Etat partie d'une personne qui n'est ni un ressortissant ni un résident permanent de cet Etat »[34]. Cet acte, ainsi que la fabrication ou la procuration d'un document d'identité ou de voyage frauduleux et le fait de permettre à une personne entrée illégalement de demeurer dans l'Etat, actes commis de manière intentionnelle et dans le but d'un avantage financier ou d'un autre avantage matériel, doivent ainsi être criminalisés[35]. La tentative d'accomplir de tels actes, de s'en rendre complice ou de les organiser sont également à criminaliser si le droit national le permet[36]. Mettre en danger la vie ou la sécurité des migrants ou risquer de le faire, ou les traiter de manière inhumaine ou dégradante sont des circonstances aggravantes[37].

La criminalisation du trafic de migrants peut se faire sur la base d'une loi spéciale, mais aussi, dans certains cas où de telles provisions n'existent pas en droit interne ou s'il est impossible de prouver le trafic, à travers d'autres infractions, telles que la fraude de documents ou l'entrée clandestine[38]. Les Etats-Unis, par exemple, n'ont pas adopté de loi spécifique, mais utilisent une loi contre la facilitation de l'immigration illégale[39].

Les Etats parties au Protocole peuvent prendre des mesures plus strictes et prévoir des définitions plus générales dans leur droit interne afin de combattre la criminalité transnationale organisée[40]. Ainsi par exemple, les Pays-Bas criminalisent le trafic de migrants, qui est défini sans référence au gain financier ou autre gain matériel[41] — cela peut être vu comme problématique, dans la mesure où cette condition vise à éviter la criminalisation des actes bénévoles ou de membres d'une même famille[42]. De plus, l'exigence du *mens rea*, prévue comme « inten-

34. Protocole contre le trafic illicite de migrants par terre, air et mer, *op. cit. supra* note 8, art. 3(a).
35. *Ibid.*, art. 6(1)(a)(b)(c).
36. *Ibid.*, art. 6(2)(a)(b)(c).
37. *Ibid.*, art. 6(3)(a)(b).
38. UNODC, « Manuel de formation de base sur les enquêtes et les poursuites relatives au trafic illicite de migrants. Module 7 : questions législatives », New York, 2011, p. 7.
39. *Bringing In and Harboring Certain Aliens*, 8 USC, par. 1324.
40. Convention des Nations Unies contre la criminalité transnationale organisée, *op. cit. supra* note 9, art. 34(3).
41. Code pénal néerlandais (art. 197(a)) tel que présenté dans UNODC, « Manuel de formation de base sur les enquêtes et les poursuites relatives au trafic illicite de migrants », *op. cit. supra* note 38, pp. 2-3.
42. UNODC, « Travaux préparatoires des négociations en vue de l'élaboration de la Convention des Nations Unies contre la criminalité transnationale organisée et des Protocoles s'y rapportant », New York, 2008, p. 493 ; Rapport du

tionnel» par le Protocole, peut également être remplie par un critère moindre, tel que l'imprudence ou la négligence[43]. Finalement, d'autres circonstances aggravantes sont envisageables, comme aux Etats-Unis où une loi considère le manque d'obéissance envers les gardes-côtes comme un tel facteur[44].

Il convient de préciser que le crime de trafic n'est commis, selon la définition du Protocole, qu'après l'entrée illégale dans un Etat partie, ce qui limite son applicabilité, en mer, aux eaux territoriales et intérieures. Cependant, l'un des crimes dits accessoires, à savoir la tentative d'entrée illégale peut servir en haute mer. Une limitation supplémentaire à noter est que la criminalisation du trafic de migrants selon le Protocole ne s'applique qu'aux infractions de «nature transnationale et [lors]qu'un groupe criminel organisé y est impliqué»[45]. Finalement, la criminalisation vise seulement les trafiquants, et non les migrants eux-mêmes, et lie uniquement les Etats parties au Protocole[46].

Le Protocole affirme en effet que «[l]es migrants ne deviennent pas passibles de poursuites pénales en vertu du présent Protocole du fait qu'ils ont été l'objet» de tels actes[47]. L'inclusion de cette disposition démontre la volonté des Etats de différencier les auteurs de l'action criminelle — les trafiquants — de ses objets — les migrants. Cependant, il est aussi admis que les Etats peuvent prendre des mesures contre une personne qui agit d'une manière qui contrevient au droit interne[48]; aucune immunité n'est donc fournie[49]. Il convient de noter que, pour de

Comité spécial sur l'élaboration d'une convention contre la criminalité transnationale organisée sur les travaux de ses première à onzième sessions — Notes interprétatives pour les documents officiels (travaux préparatoires) des négociations sur la Convention des Nations Unies contre la criminalité transnationale organisée, 2000, A/55/383/Add.1 (Assemblée générale des Nations Unies), par. 88.

43. UNODC, «Manuel de formation de base sur les enquêtes et les poursuites relatives au trafic illicite de migrants», *op. cit. supra* note 38, p. 10. Dans le cas de la Nouvelle-Zélande, l'imprudence suffit, Crimes Act 1961 (art. 98C), tel que présenté dans UNODC, «Loi type contre le trafic illicite de migrants», New York, 2011, p. 34.

44. Criminal Sanctions for Failure to Heave to, Obstruction of Boarding, or Providing False Information, USA 18 USC, par. 2237, tel que présenté dans B. W. Robinson, «Smuggled Masses: The Need for a Maritime Alien Smuggling Law Enforcement Act», *Army Lawyer*, n° 447, 2010, p. 40.

45. Protocole contre le trafic illicite de migrants par terre, air et mer, *op. cit. supra* note 8, art. 4. Cependant, il est intéressant de noter l'interprétation surprenante de l'UNODC, selon laquelle une lecture de l'article 4 du Protocole avec l'article 34(2) de la Convention signifie qu'il n'y a pas de besoin d'un lien avec la criminalité organisée (UNODC, «Loi type contre le trafic illicite de migrants», *op. cit. supra* note 43, p. 7).

46. Papastavridis, *op. cit. supra* note 11, p. 163.

47. Protocole contre le trafic illicite de migrants par terre, air et mer, *op. cit. supra* note 8, art. 5.

48. *Ibid.*, art. 6(4).

49. Mallia, *op. cit. supra* note 13, p. 118.

nombreux Etats, l'entrée irrégulière sur leur territoire constitue un crime passible d'amende ou de prison[50].

Un autre crime est celui de la traite et/ou de l'esclavage. En effet, le Protocole contre la traite, alors qu'il n'a pas pour objet direct le transport en mer, inclut des provisions pertinentes, dans la mesure où la traite est comprise, comme entre autres agissements, le transport

> «par la menace de recours ou le recours à la force ou à d'autres formes de contrainte, par enlèvement, fraude, tromperie, abus d'autorité ou d'une situation de vulnérabilité, ou par l'offre ou l'acceptation de paiements ou d'avantages pour obtenir le consentement d'une personne ayant autorité sur une autre aux fins d'exploitation»[51].

Cet instrument requiert de ses Etats parties qu'ils confèrent aux actes décrits comme la traite de personnes le caractère d'infraction pénale et cela sur la base de l'article 15 de la Convention[52]. Ainsi, les bases de compétence examinées ci-dessous pour le trafic s'appliquent de manière similaire pour la traite. Quant à l'esclavage au sens propre du terme, les Etats pavillonnaires doivent prendre, selon la Convention des Nations Unies sur le droit de la mer (CNUDM), «des mesures efficaces pour prévenir et réprimer le transport d'esclaves»[53] par leurs navires, ce qui limite la criminalisation aux actes de ses propres navires.

Dans la CNUDM, référence est faite aux esclaves, qui sont automatiquement considérés comme libres dès qu'ils montent sur un autre bateau, mais aucune autre conséquence pour les victimes n'est mentionnée. De même, aucune disposition clarifiant les mesures qui pourraient être prises contre les victimes de la traite qui sont en situation irrégulière d'immigration ne se trouve dans le Protocole de Palerme. Vu que les mesures envers ces personnes sont protectrices par nature[54], il n'est pas envisageable que d'être victime de la traite puisse être criminalisé. Cependant, aucune obligation claire quant aux possibilités pour les lois migratoires pertinentes de s'appliquer n'est incluse dans cet instrument;

50. Commissioner for Human Rights, «Criminalisation of Migration in Europe: Human Rights Implications», Strasbourg, 2010, <https://wcd.coe.int/ViewDoc.jsp?id=1579605#P121_19294>; Royaume-Uni, Immigration Act 1971, section 24, tel que présenté dans M. V. McCreight, «Smuggling of Migrants, Trafficking in Human Beings and Irregular Migration on a Comparative Perspective», *European Law Journal*, nº 12, 2006, p. 122; Improper Entry by Alien, USA 8 USC, par. 1325.

51. Protocole visant à prévenir, réprimer et punir la traite des personnes, en particulier des femmes et des enfants, *op. cit. supra* note 12, art. 3(a).

52. *Ibid.*, art. 5(1).

53. CNUDM, Nations Unies, *Recueil des traités*, vol. 1833, p. 3, art. 99.

54. Protocole visant à prévenir, réprimer et punir la traite des personnes, en particulier des femmes et des enfants, *op. cit. supra* note 12, art. 6-7.

en effet, la formulation « chaque Etat partie envisage d'adopter des mesures législatives ou d'autres mesures appropriées qui permettent aux victimes de la traite des personnes de rester sur son territoire »[55] ne crée pas de réelle obligation.

Si plusieurs juridictions existent en parallèle, soit parce que l'activité criminelle a eu lieu dans plusieurs pays, soit parce que plusieurs Etats ont des titres de compétence divers mais valables, il convient que ces Etats collaborent et examinent à la fois les lois de chaque pays, l'endroit où l'accusé et/ou les témoins potentiels se trouvent, etc.[56].

B. Obligations envers les migrants[57]

i) *Non-refoulement*

Les Etats de destination des migrations n'ont pas l'obligation de permettre l'entrée des personnes irrégulières sur leur territoire et les personnes persécutées ne bénéficient pas non plus d'un droit à l'asile[58]. Ces Etats ont en effet, en vertu de leur souveraineté territoriale, le droit d'exercer un contrôle sur l'entrée, le séjour et la potentielle expulsion

55. *Op. cit. supra* note 12, art. 7(1).

56. UNODC, « Manuel de formation de base sur les enquêtes et les poursuites relatives au trafic illicite de migrants », *op. cit. supra* note 38, p. 14.

57. D'autres droits sont en jeu lors d'opérations d'interception ou de secours, tels que l'interdiction de détention arbitraire. Il semble que des migrants sous le contrôle effectif d'autorités étatiques à bord d'un navire, sans liberté de partir ou de participer dans la prise de décision les concernant, sont sous le coup d'une détention. Le Judge North de la Federal Court of Australia a considéré que les passagers du *Tampa* étaient détenus de manière arbitraire, tel que présenté dans Trevisanut, *op. cit. supra* note 7, pp. 229-230; I. Khan, « Trading in Human Misery: A Human Rights Perspective on the *Tampa* Incident », *Pacific Rim Law and Policy Journal*, n° 12, 2003, pp. 15-16. L'applicabilité des règles de droits humains en haute mer n'est probablement pas seulement limitée au non-refoulement (« The Interception and Rescue at Sea of Asylum Seekers, Refugees and Irregular Migrants », *op. cit. supra* note 1, p. 12, par. 34). Cependant, selon certains avis, les droits humains applicables diffèrent selon le niveau d'attachement entre le migrant et l'Etat (T. Gammeltoft-Hansen, « The Refugee, the Sovereign and the Sea: European Union Interdiction Policies », dans R. Adler-Nissen et T. Gammeltoft-Hansen (dir. publ.), *Sovereignty Games: The Instrumentalization of State Sovereignty in Europe and Beyond*, Palgrave, 2008, p. 177). Des droits procéduraux sont applicables à tous, y compris aux trafiquants présumés (UNODC, « Manuel de formation de base sur les enquêtes et les poursuites relatives au trafic illicite de migrants. Module 9: droits de l'homme », New York, 2011, pp. 11-12).

58. Selon les travaux préparatoires, il est évident que les Etats n'ont pas voulu que l'article 14 de la Déclaration universelle des droits de l'homme 1948 (Assemblée générale des Nations Unies) représente un droit d'asile. Voir C. M. J. Bostock, « The International Legal Obligations Owed to the Asylum Seekers on the MV *Tampa* », *International Journal of Refugee Law*, n° 14, 2002, p. 283.

des non-nationaux. Cependant, de manière explicite ou implicite, les traités relatifs aux droits humains, en particulier les conventions relatives aux réfugiés, incluent une clause selon laquelle une personne ne peut être refoulée si elle encourt certains risques en cas de retour. Ainsi, alors que le principe de non-refoulement ne crée pas de droit à recevoir l'asile, il circonscrit ce que les Etats peuvent entreprendre de manière légale[59].

Cette obligation de non-refoulement se trouve dans la Convention sur le statut des réfugiés[60], dans la Convention contre la torture[61], dans le Protocole contre le trafic illicite de migrants[62], dans des conventions régionales[63], et, de manière implicite, dans d'autres instruments de droits humains[64].

L'on débat encore pour déterminer si cette obligation, qui est considérée comme une pierre angulaire du système de protection des réfugiés,

59. G. S. Goodwin-Gill, «The Right to Seek Asylum: Interception at Sea and the Principle of Non-Refoulement», *International Journal of Refugee Law*, nº 23, 2011, pp. 443 et 444; R. Barnes, «Refugee Law at Sea», *International and Comparative Law Quarterly*, nº 53, 2004, p. 70.

60. Convention relative au statut des réfugiés, Nations Unies, *Recueil des traités*, vol. 189, p. 137, art. 33(1).

61. Convention contre la torture et autres peines ou traitements cruels, inhumains ou dégradants, Nations Unies, *Recueil des traités*, vol. 1465, p. 85, art. 3.

62. Protocole contre le trafic illicite de migrants par terre, air et mer, *op. cit. supra* note 8, art. 19(1).

63. La Convention de l'OUA régissant les aspects propres aux problèmes des réfugiés en Afrique, Nations Unies, *Recueil des traités*, vol. 1001, p. 53, art. 2(3); Convention américaine relative aux droits de l'homme, Nations Unies, *Recueil des traités*, vol. 1144, p. 183, art. 22(8).

64. Pacte international relatif aux droits civils et politiques, Nations Unies, *Recueil des traités*, vol. 999, p. 187, art. 2 et 7, tels qu'interprétés par le Comité des droits de l'homme (CDH); «La nature de l'obligation juridique générale imposée aux Etats parties au Pacte», *Observation générale*, nº 31, 29 mars 2004, par. 12; *G. T. c. Australie*, 1997, 706/1996, par. 8.1-8.2. OHCHR, «General Comment concerning Prohibition of Torture and Cruel Treatment or Punishment», 1992, *General Comment*, nº 20, par. 9; Convention européenne des droits de l'homme, Nations Unies, *Recueil des traités*, vol. 213, p. 221, art. 3, tel qu'interprété pour l'extradition dans *Soering c. Royaume-Uni*, 1989, 14038/88, par. 88 et 91; pour l'extradition et *Cruz Varas et autres c. Suède*, 1991, 15576/89, par. 69-70; *Hilal c. Royaume-Uni*, 2001, 45276/99, par. 59; *Salah Sheekh c. Pays-Bas*, 2007, 1948/04, par. 135; *Hirsi Jamaa et autres c. Italie*, 2012, 27765/09, par. 81 et 113-114, par rapport aux expulsions. Ce dernier cas a opposé un groupe de migrants somaliens et érythréens dont les bateaux ont été interceptés en haute mer mais dans la zone SAR maltaise, par les gardes-côtes et la garde des finances italiens. Ces migrants ont été transférés sur des navires militaires italiens qui les ont ramenés, sans leur annoncer la destination du trajet, en Libye, le pays où ils avaient embarqué. Ils ont été remis aux autorités libyennes. Ils ont saisi la CEDH, car, selon eux, l'Italie a violé non seulement son obligation de les protéger contre la torture, les traitements inhumains et dégradants qu'ils risquaient de subir après leur retour en Libye — et ensuite probablement en Somalie et en Ethiopie —, mais aussi l'interdiction d'expulser des étrangers de manière collective.

est entrée dans le droit coutumier international[65], ou a même atteint le statut de *jus cogens*[66].

Selon le traité en question, l'application *ratione personae* et *ratione materiae* varie. Alors que le non-refoulement vise toutes les personnes dans les conventions de droits humains[67], il n'est obligatoire qu'envers les réfugiés — et les demandeurs d'asile[68] — dans les conventions relatives aux réfugiés. Le principe de non-refoulement a donc deux champs d'application qui se superposent en partie. Applicable envers tous existe une interdiction de refouler les personnes qui seraient à risque d'être torturées ou soumises à des traitements ou des punitions cruels, inhumains ou dégradants. Pour certaines personnes qui ne font pas face à ces risques mais qui sont demandeuses d'asile, le rejet, retour ou expulsion est interdit si cela a pour conséquence une menace de persécution, une menace pour la vie ou la liberté pour des raisons de race, nationalité, religion, statut social ou opinions politiques[69]. Dans ce second cas, il y a des limites au non-refoulement, à savoir qu'une per-

65. Sont en faveur: Bostock, *op. cit. supra* note 58, p. 289; Trevisanut, *op. cit. supra* note 7, p. 215; E. Lauterpacht et D. Bethlehem, «The Scope and Content of the Principle of Non-Refoulement: Opinion», 2001, <http://www.unhcr.org/419c75ce4.html>, p. 149, par. 216; Papastavridis, *op. cit. supra* note 11, p. 216.

66. B. Miltner, «Human Security and Protection from Refoulement in the Maritime Context», dans A. Edwards et C. Ferstman (dir. publ.), *Human Security and Non-Citizens: Law, Policy and International Affairs*, Cambridge University Press, 2010, p. 201; Goodwin-Gill, *op. cit. supra* note 59, p. 444, considère que cette obligation appartient au droit coutumier mais ne se prononce pas sur le *jus cogens*. En faveur de l'entrée du principe de non-refoulement dans le *jus cogens*, voir «Report of UNHCR to ECOSOC (1985): UN Doc E/1985/62», 1985, par. 22-23; UNHCR, General Executive Committee Conclusion n° 25 (XXXIII) 1982, al. *b)*; Cartagena Declaration on Refugees, Colloquium on the International Protection of Refugees in Central America, Mexico and Panama, 1984, par. III(5); A. Orakhelashvili, *Peremptory Norms in International Law*, Oxford University Press, 2006, p. 55; Trevisanut, *op. cit. supra* note 7, p. 215; J. Allain, «The *Jus Cogens* Nature of Non-Refoulement», *International Journal of Refugee Law*, n° 13, 2001, p. 533.

67. Papastavridis, *op. cit. supra* note 11, p. 225.

68. Cette interprétation ouverte de «réfugiés» permet d'éviter qu'un individu ne soit refoulé avant d'avoir vu son statut reconnu par un Etat. En effet, si quelqu'un remplit les conditions de l'article premier (Convention relative au statut des réfugiés, *op. cit. supra* note 60, art. IA(2)), il ou elle est un réfugié *de facto*, même si cela n'a pas encore été reconnu. L'UNHCR a également donc clarifié cela (General Executive Committee Conclusion n° 25, *op. cit. supra* note 66, par. 28); J. C. Hathaway, *The Rights of Refugees under International Law*, Cambridge University Press, 2005, pp. 303-304; Goodwin-Gill, *op. cit. supra* note 59, p. 444; Miltner, *op. cit. supra* note 66, p. 203; M. Crock, «In the Wake of the *Tampa*: Conflicting Visions of International Refugee Law in the Management of Refugee Flows», *Pacific Rim Law and Policy Journal*, n° 12, 2003, pp. 49 et 57; Lauterpacht et Bethlehem, *op. cit. supra* note 65, pp. 115-118, par. 88-98.

69. Lauterpacht et Bethlehem, *op. cit. supra* note 65, p. 163, par. 253.

sonne ne doit pas bénéficier de la protection accordée aux réfugiés s'il y a de forts soupçons qu'elle ait commis des actes la rendant indigne de ce statut (*inter alia* un crime contre la paix, un crime de guerre ou un crime contre l'humanité) ou si elle représente un danger pour la sécurité du pays ou la communauté (dans ce cas, sur la base d'une condamnation définitive) du pays où elle se trouve[70]. Alors que le Protocole contre le trafic illicite de migrants ne fait, en matière de non-refoulement, référence explicitement qu'aux instruments relatifs aux réfugiés, les obligations découlant des droits humains doivent aussi être respectées en raison de la mention du respect dû au droit international[71]. La loi type telle que développée par l'UNODC fait de plus une référence explicite au non-refoulement sur la base de traités de droits humains[72].

Il est également interdit de renvoyer une personne dans un pays où elle risque d'être refoulée. Ainsi, une protection existe contre le refoulement en chaîne ou refoulement indirect[73]. Cela a été rappelé, par rapport au non-refoulement lié à la torture, par la CEDH lorsqu'elle a affirmé que « le renvoi indirect d'un étranger dans un pays intermédiaire n'enlève rien à la responsabilité de l'Etat contractant expulsant de veiller à ce que l'intéressé ne se trouve pas exposé, du fait de son expulsion, à des traitements contraires à l'article 3 de la Convention »[74].

En pratique, l'Etat doit examiner si les conséquences prévisibles d'un retour sont d'exposer une personne à un dommage sérieux[75]. Il lui est donc nécessaire de déterminer le statut de cette personne et ses besoins de protection internationale. Un examen de la demande d'asile[76] ou tout du moins des risques prévisibles encourus est nécessaire[77], sur la base des circonstances personnelles du migrant et de la situation dans son

---

70. Convention relative au statut des réfugiés, *op. cit. supra* note 60, art. 33(2).

71. Protocole contre le trafic illicite de migrants par terre, air et mer, *op. cit. supra* note 8, art. 19. Evidemment, les obligations sur la base des traités ne s'appliquent qu'envers les Etats parties, mais il est bon de noter que la plupart des obligations pertinentes forment du droit coutumier (Mallia, *op. cit. supra* note 13, p. 120).

72 UNODC, « Loi type contre le trafic illicite de migrants », *op. cit. supra* note 43, p. 18.

73. Lauterpacht et Bethlehem, *op. cit. supra* note 65, pp. 122-123, par. 115-121.

74. *Salah Sheekh c. Pays-Bas*, *op. cit. supra* note 64, par. 141.

75. Goodwin-Gill, *op. cit. supra* note 59, p. 444.

76. R. Barnes, « The International Law of the Sea and Migration Control », dans B. Ryan et V. Mitsilegas (dir. publ.), *Extraterritorial Immigration Control : Legal Challenges*, Immigration and Asylum Law and Policy in Europe, vol. 21, Martinus Nijhoff Publishers, 2010, pp. 116-117.

77. V. Moreno-Lax, « Seeking Asylum in the Mediterranean : Against a Fragmentary Reading of EU Member States' Obligations Accruing at Sea », *International Journal of Refugee Law*, n° 23, 2011, p. 15 (n. 246-254 et texte s'y rapportant).

pays de nationalité ou de résidence[78]. Que cela nécessite une procédure complète de détermination du statut de réfugié (DSR)[79] ou qu'un screening initial suffise est sujet à débat. Il semblerait approprié que, pour tous les cas difficiles, ou ceux où un doute subsiste — en pratique, ce cas de figure touche la majorité des examens en raison de la complexité des décisions —, une DSR prenne place[80]. Cette procédure requiert l'accès à des conseils légaux[81], une période de temps suffisante pour préparer son cas, la présence de professionnels spécialisés, une interview, une décision écrite qui fournit les raisons de la décision et l'existence d'un appel/d'une possibilité de réexamen des décisions négatives[82].

L'accès à un recours effectif est jugé nécessaire par la CEDH avant l'application de la mesure d'éloignement et semble difficile à mettre en pratique sur un navire[83]. Dans le cas *Hirsi Jamaa c. Italie*, le gouvernement lui-même a admis «que de telles procédures n'étaient pas envisageables à bord des navires militaires sur lesquels on a fait embarquer les requérants. Le personnel à bord ne comptait d'ailleurs ni interprètes ni conseils juridiques.»[84] Ainsi, la DSR et le traitement des demandes de protection internationale doivent au maximum être gérés à terre, vu que c'est seulement là que les garanties procédurales et une procédure équitable et efficace sont accessibles[85]. Entreprendre un tel examen à bord d'un navire comporte de plus un risque majeur d'injustice, en raison de

78. Khan, *op. cit. supra* note 57, p. 15; C. Bailliet, «The *Tampa* Case and Its Impact on Burden Sharing at Sea», *Human Rights Quarterly*, n° 25, 2003, p. 743; *Vilvarajah et autres c. Royaume-Uni*, 13163/87, 13164/87, 13165/87, 13447/87, 13448/87, par. 108.

79. Papastavridis, *op. cit. supra* note 11, pp. 217 et 223.

80. UNHCR, «Maritime Interception Operations and the Processing of International Protection Claims: Legal Standards and Policy Considerations with respect to Extraterritorial Processing: Protection Policy Paper», 2010, p. 5, par. 16, et p. 15, par. 55, <http://www.unhcr.org/refworld/pdfid/4cd12d3a2.pdf>.

81. Khan, *op. cit. supra* note 57, pp. 15-16. Le non-respect de cette obligation a été critiqué par le juge North, tel que présenté par Bailliet, *op. cit. supra* note 78, p. 743.

82. UNHCR, «Maritime Interception Operations and the Processing of International Protection Claims: Legal Standards and Policy Considerations with respect to Extraterritorial Processing», *op. cit. supra* note 80, p. 6, par. 19-20, et p. 15, par. 55-58; UNHCR, «Handbook on Procedures and Criteria for Determining Refugee Status under the 1951 Convention and the 1967 Protocol relating to the Status of Refugees», Genève, 1992; Moreno-Lax, *op. cit. supra* note 77, p. 16 (n. 268-270 et texte s'y rapportant).

83. *Hirsi Jamaa et autres c. Italie*, *op. cit. supra* note 64, par. 197-198, 202 et 205.

84. *Ibid.*, par. 197-198.

85. UNHCR, «Maritime Interception Operations and the Processing of International Protection Claims: Legal Standards and Policy Considerations with respect to Extraterritorial Processing», *op. cit. supra* note 80, pp. 2 et 15, par. 55; *MSS c. Belgique et Grèce*, 2011, 30696/09, par. 286 et 293.

la fatigue et du stress liés à l'intervention[86]. Finalement, le statut du migrant dépend de la situation dans son Etat de nationalité ou de résidence. A cet égard, l'Etat sous le contrôle duquel il se trouve doit déterminer non seulement l'existence d'une législation interne pertinente, la ratification de traités internationaux, des assurances de l'Etat de réception[87], mais aussi et surtout prendre en compte la situation réelle[88]. De telles informations, dont l'Etat est censé avoir connaissance, ne sont pas nécessairement accessibles à bord.

Dans les cas où l'Etat interceptant décide de ne pas accorder luimême l'asile sur son territoire, mais que la personne en question bénéficie d'une protection internationale, il doit trouver un pays de destination sûr[89]. Pour ce faire, un examen positif du système d'asile ou de protection de l'Etat tiers est nécessaire et incombe à l'Etat qui désire amener les migrants dans un pays tiers[90]. Ainsi, tout transfert de responsabilité de l'Etat interceptant à un autre Etat doit être fait sur la base d'assurances formelles et de preuves concrètes que le niveau de protection sera respecté[91]. Cela inclut au minimum la ratification des conventions pertinentes, l'existence d'un système d'asile[92] et l'application pratique des protections pertinentes[93]. Ainsi, la pratique australienne d'envoyer des

---

86. J. L. Jacobson, « At-Sea Interception of Alien Migrants : International Law Issues », *Willamette Law Review*, n° 28, 1991-1992, p. 816 ; Bailliet, *op. cit. supra* note 78, p. 759.

87. Sur les assurances diplomatiques dans les cas d'expulsion de réfugiés, voir C. Wouters, « Reconciling National Security and Non-Refoulement : Exceptions, Exclusion, and Diplomatic Assurances », dans A. M. de Salinas Frías, K. L. H. Samuel et N. D. White (dir. publ.), *Counter-terrorism : International Law and Practice*, Oxford University Press, 2012, pp. 588-592.

88. *Chahal c. Royaume-Uni*, 1996, 22414/93, par. 105, et *Saadi c. Italie*, 2008, 37201/06, par. 147-148.

89. M. Tondini, « The Legality of Intercepting Boat People under Search and Rescue and Border Control Operations — with Reference to Recent Italian Interventions in the Mediterranean Sea and the ECtHR Decision in the *Hirsi* Case », *The Journal of International Maritime Law*, n° 18, 2012, p. 66 ; Lauterpacht et Bethlehem, *op. cit. supra* note 65, p. 113, par. 76.

90. *Hirsi Jamaa et autres c. Italie*, *op. cit. supra* note 64, par. 133 et 157.

91. UNHCR, « Maritime Interception Operations and the Processing of International Protection Claims : Legal Standards and Policy Considerations with respect to Extraterritorial Processing », *op. cit. supra* note 80, p. 10, par. 34-35.

92. *Ibid.*, p. 11, par. 38 ; *High Court of Australia Plaintiff M70/2011 c. Minister for Immigration and Citizenship ; Plaintiff M106/2011 c. Minister for Immigration and Citizenship*, 2011, HCA 32, 31 août 2011 (Refugee Swap Deal case), par. 135.

93. Les assurances diplomatiques ne sont pas à considérer comme suffisantes si elles ne semblent pas refléter la réalité (*MSS c. Belgique et Grèce*, *op. cit. supra* note 85, par. 354). Il est reconnu comme nécessaire, en général, de prendre en compte l'application pratique des règles pertinentes de droits humains dans le pays de destination prévu sur la base d'informations largement accessibles comme des rapports de l'UNHCR (*NS (C-411/10) c. Secretary of State for the Home Department et M. E. et autres (C-493/10) c. Refugee Applications Com-*

demandeurs d'asile à Nauru et de tenter de les renvoyer en Indonésie est probablement illégale, vu que ces Etats ne sont pas parties à la Convention de 1951[94].

ii) *Interdiction de l'expulsion collective*

Dans les systèmes régionaux du Conseil de l'Europe et des Amériques, les expulsions collectives de non-nationaux sont interdites[95]. Cela a été interprété par la Commission européenne des droits de l'homme comme «toute mesure de l'autorité compétente contraignant des étrangers, en tant que groupe, à quitter un pays sauf dans les cas où une telle mesure est prise à l'issue et sur la base d'un examen raisonnable et objectif de la situation particulière de chacun des étrangers qui forment le groupe»[96].

Dans l'arrêt *Hirsi Jamaa*, la CEDH a pour la première fois statué sur la question de l'expulsion collective. Que les interceptions de type «push-back», voir «tow-back», puissent être considérées comme des expulsions collectives, et donc interdites si la situation individuelle des migrants n'est pas examinée, ouvre des horizons nouveaux pour la protection de ces personnes. En effet, l'interdiction d'expulsions collectives clarifie et renforce l'obligation d'examen en bonne et due forme du statut de chaque individu[97]. «Le but de l'article 4 du Protocole n° 4 est d'éviter que les Etats puissent éloigner un certain nombre d'étrangers sans examiner leur situation personnelle et, par conséquent, sans leur permettre d'exposer leurs arguments s'opposant à la mesure prise par l'autorité compétente.»[98] Cette analyse peut aussi avoir, dans le futur, une implication plus étendue que l'espace européen, vu que la même interdiction existe dans le pacte de San José à l'article 22(9).

---

missioner et Minister for Justice, Equality and Law Reform, 21 décembre 2011 (Cour de Justice de l'UE), par. 91 et 106) ou sur celles des observateurs de droits humains non gouvernementaux (*Hirsi Jamaa et autres c. Italie*, *op. cit. supra* note 64, par. 118 et 123).

94. Bailliet, *op. cit. supra* note 78, p. 769; Bostock, *op. cit. supra* note 58, pp. 290-291.

95. Convention européenne des droits de l'homme, *op. cit. supra* note 64, protocole 4, art. 4(2); Convention américaine relative aux droits de l'homme, *op. cit. supra* note 63, art. 22(9).

96. *Henning Becker c. Danemark*, 1975, 7011/75 256.

97. Il est vrai que chaque cas doit toujours être examiné de manière individuelle (UNHCR, *The Problem of Manifestly Unfounded or Abusive Applications for Refugee Status or Asylum*, 20 octobre 1983, Executive Committee Conclusion n° 30 (XXXIV), par. (e)(i)); J. A. Hessbruegge, «European Court of Human Rights Protects Migrants Against «Push Back» Operations on the High Seas», 17 avril 2012, par. 16(14), <http://www.asil.org/insights120417.cfm>; Lauterpacht and Bethlehem, *op. cit. supra* note 65, pp. 118-119, par. 100-102.

98. *Hirsi Jamaa et autres c. Italie* (n. 64), par. 177.

En pratique donc, si une décision de retour dans le pays de départ devait être prise, elle doit être basée sur un examen individuel, à la fois car c'est ainsi que la détermination du statut doit se dérouler[99] et parce que les expulsions collectives sont interdites.

iii) *Droit de quitter son propre pays et liberté de mouvement*

Un droit de quitter son propre pays existe dans les droits humains, de même que la liberté de mouvement[100]. Ces droits impliquent probablement des limitations aux pouvoirs d'interception des Etats.

En premier lieu, des opérations d'interception par l'Etat côtier (ou un autre Etat agissant dans cette zone) de vaisseaux qui tentent de quitter la mer territoriale pourraient équivaloir à une violation du droit de quitter son pays[101]. Il est aussi intéressant de noter que, d'après le CDH, les violations de ce droit sont potentiellement commises non seulement par les Etats dont on cherche à partir — ou qui les soutiennent par des opérations jointes dans la mer territoriale —, mais également par les Etats de destination[102].

Quant au trajet, on peut se demander comment considérer sous l'angle des droits humains les interceptions en haute mer, y compris par les navires de l'Etat pavillonnaire. Il semblerait que, par une opération d'interception en haute mer, la liberté de mouvement des individus à bord soit mise à mal. En effet, toute personne bénéficie de la liberté de mouvement et de quitter un pays, qu'il soit celui dont elle a la nationalité ou non[103]. En haute mer, toute opération qui vise à repousser un navire dans une direction particulière ou à le ramener dans les eaux territoriales d'où

99. Moreno-Lax, *op. cit. supra* note 77, p. 15 (n. 254 et texte s'y rapportant).

100. Pacte international relatif aux droits civils et politiques, *op. cit. supra* note 64, art. 12(2); Convention européenne des droits de l'homme, *op. cit. supra* note 64, protocole 4, art. 2(2); Charte africaine des droits de l'homme et des peuples 1981, Nations Unies, *Recueil des traités*, vol. 1520, p. 217, art. 12(2); Déclaration universelle des droits de l'homme, *op. cit. supra* note 58, art. 13(2); Convention américaine relative aux droits de l'homme, *op. cit. supra* note 63, art. 22(7).

101. P. García Andrade, «Extraterritorial Strategies to Tackle Irregular Immigration by Sea: A Spanish Perspective», dans B. Ryan et V. Mitsilegas (dir. publ.), *Extraterritorial Immigration Control: Legal Challenges*, Immigration and Asylum Law and Policy in Europe, vol. 21, Martinus Nijhoff Publishers, 2010, p. 321.

102. E. Papastavridis, «Fortress Europe» and FRONTEX: within or without International Law?», *Nordic Journal of International Law*, n° 79, 2010, p. 109. Le CDH a conclu dans ses observations sur l'Autriche que certaines mesures localisées avant la frontière peuvent déclencher des violations de l'article 12(2) (CDH, Observations finales du Comité des droits de l'homme: Autriche CCPR/C/79/Add.103, 19 novembre 1998, par. 11); Brouwer et Kumin, *op. cit. supra* note 26, pp. 16-17.

103. Goodwin-Gill, *op. cit. supra* note 59, p. 443.

il est parti risque de violer ces droits. Cependant, dans la mesure où l'Etat pavillonnaire est celui par qui la liberté de navigation en haute mer existe pour les navires battant son pavillon, il a probablement le droit de restreindre l'usage de ses navires.

Il semble que, lors d'interceptions, les personnes à bord doivent être consultées quant au choix de destination alternative. Le CDH a en effet exprimé que le droit de quitter son pays inclut le droit de choisir sa destination[104]. Alors que cela ne donne pas le droit d'entrée dans un pays, cela signifie au moins que la personne interceptée a le droit de choisir sa destination alternative[105]. Dans le cas du *MV Tampa*, le projet d'envoyer les migrants en Nouvelle-Zélande et à Nauru a été développé sans les consulter[106], ce qui a donc violé leur liberté de mouvement.

SECTION 3 APPROCHE ZONALE

Parallèlement à la question du champ d'action légal ouvert aux différents Etats pour intercepter des navires et des personnes, il est important de clarifier à la fois les possibilités pour les différents Etats engagés d'appliquer des sanctions pénales et les droits humains dont les migrants bénéficient.

Paragraphe 1 Mer territoriale

A. Interception

Un Etat côtier bénéficie dans ses eaux territoriales, qui s'étendent jusqu'à un maximum de douze mille marins[107], d'une souveraineté légèrement réduite comparée à celle exercée sur terre. Elle est en effet limitée par les provisions de la CNUDM et les autres règles de droit international[108]. La règle pertinente de droit de la mer est celle du droit au passage inoffensif, dont jouissent, à part dans des cas particuliers, les navires de tous les Etats[109]. Ainsi, un passage continu et expéditif, parallèlement aux côtes, en direction ou en provenance d'un port est autorisé.

Cependant, le passage n'est pas considéré comme inoffensif s'il nuit

104. CDH, General Comment, n° 27: Freedom of movement (art. 12), 2 novembre 1999, par. 8.
105. Brouwer et Kumin, *op. cit. supra* note 26, p. 17.
106. Opinion du juge North, telle que présentée par Bailliet, *op. cit. supra* note 78, p. 743.
107. CNUDM, *op. cit. supra* note 53, art. 3.
108. *Ibid.*, art. 2(3).
109. *Ibid.*, art. 17.

à la paix, au bon ordre ou à la sécurité de l'Etat côtier, par exemple si le navire s'engage dans le débarquement de personnes en violation des lois et des règlements liés à l'immigration [110]. L'Etat côtier a le droit de prendre dans ses eaux territoriales les mesures nécessaires pour éviter tout passage non inoffensif [111]. Ainsi il peut certainement inspecter un navire, le repousser [112] et probablement même en prendre le contrôle.

On peut néanmoins se demander si de transporter des personnes qui désirent demander l'asile suffit à rendre le passage non inoffensif [113]. Vu que l'Etat côtier peut prendre des mesures contre l'immigration clandestine, mais doit le faire dans le respect du droit international applicable [114], des obligations de droits humains, tel le non-refoulement, s'appliquent à ses actions [115]. Il est donc probable que des demandeurs d'asile ne puissent pas être traités de la même manière que des migrants économiques. De plus, il n'est pas clair s'il suffit pour un navire d'avoir des personnes sans document valable à bord pour que le passage cesse d'être inoffensif ou s'il faut une action de débarquement. Le pouvoir discrétionnaire de l'Etat côtier est probablement large, puisqu'il peut intervenir afin de prévenir une violation, mais les mesures doivent être nécessaires au but escompté. En particulier, les passages dits latéraux [116], où un navire traverse la mer territoriale sans aucune intention de débarquement, ne devraient pas pouvoir être considérés comme non inoffensifs.

B. Compétence pour criminaliser

L'Etat côtier a le droit d'adopter des règles de droit pénal par rapport à des comportements qui se déroulent dans sa mer territoriale, et peut les appliquer envers les navires qui y circulent, pour autant que cela soit en accord avec la CNUDM. En effet, alors que le territoire national comprend la mer territoriale [117] et que le principe de

110. CNUDM, *op. cit. supra* note 53, art. 19(1) et 19(2)(g).
111. *Ibid.*, art. 25(1).
112. Mallia, *op. cit. supra* note 13, p. 51.
113. M. Pallis, «Obligations of States towards Asylum Seekers at Sea: Interactions and Conflict between Legal Regimes», *International Journal of Refugee Law*, n° 14, 2002, p. 356; Moreno-Lax, *op. cit. supra* note 77, p. 7 (n. 110-113 et texte s'y rapportant); G. S. Goodwin-Gill et J. McAdam, *The Refugee in International Law*, Oxford University Press, 3e éd., 2007, pp. 274-275.
114. CNUDM, *op. cit. supra* note 53, art. 21(1)(h).
115. *Ibid.*, art. 2(3); Miltner, *op. cit. supra* note 22, p. 101; Mallia, *op. cit. supra* note 13, p. 52.
116. Passage latéral (par opposition au passage d'entrée ou de sortie), voir G. Gidel, *Le droit international public de la mer*, Chateauroux, 1932-1934, p. 204, et sa catégorisation des trois genres de passage.
117. UNODC, «Loi type contre le trafic illicite de migrants», *op. cit. supra* note 43, pp. 22-23.

juridiction territoriale s'applique par conséquent aux actes commis dans cette zone[118], le droit de la mer restreint cette capacité afin de promouvoir une navigation fluide.

Selon la CNUDM, l'Etat côtier a le droit d'adopter «en conformité avec les dispositions de la Convention et les autres règles du droit international» des règles relatives au passage inoffensif, en vue entre autres finalités de prévenir les violations de ses règles liées à l'immigration[119]. Il semble donc avoir une compétence pour légiférer contre le trafic de migrants et l'entrée illégale de migrants sur son territoire. Ainsi, si le passage d'un navire n'est plus inoffensif, il tombe sous le coup d'application du droit national. De plus, on avance que le trafic de migrants nuit à la sécurité et la stabilité de l'Etat côtier de destination, en particulier si ces arrivées sont régulières[120]. Cependant, le passage latéral, sans volonté manifeste de débarquement, est un passage inoffensif et, ainsi, ne devrait pas être assujetti aux lois migratoires de l'Etat côtier[121].

Il convient de noter que

> «[l']Etat côtier ne devrait pas exercer sa juridiction pénale à bord d'un navire étranger passant dans la mer territoriale pour y procéder à une arrestation ou à l'exécution d'actes d'instruction à la suite d'une infraction pénale commise à bord pendant le passage, sauf ... si les conséquences de l'infraction s'étendent à l'Etat côtier»[122].

Alors que cet article semble limiter l'usage d'une compétence en matière pénale face aux comportements à bord d'un navire en mer territoriale, il faut noter l'utilisation de «devrait» et non pas de «doit» — cette limitation ne constitue donc pas du droit dur[123]. De plus, les conséquences du trafic et de l'entrée illicite de migrants s'étendent à l'Etat côtier lorsqu'il est la destination de ce trafic, ce qui correspond à l'exception susmentionnée[124].

Finalement, comme les Etats ont adopté le Protocole contre le trafic illicite de migrants qui requiert la criminalisation du trafic de migrants, il semblerait qu'une volonté internationale existe pour permettre aux Etats de criminaliser ce comportement. La responsabilité pénale des

118. Lowe et Staker, *op. cit. supra* note 30, p. 320.
119. CNUDM, *op. cit. supra* note 53, art. 21(1)(h).
120. Mallia, *op. cit. supra* note 13, p. 46.
121. Ce point de vue n'est pas partagé par Mallia, selon qui être dans la mer territoriale en violation des lois migratoires implique à la fois une violation du droit national — ce qui ne fait pas de doute — et la non-innocence du passage, qui permet l'application du droit national face aux personnes impliquées (*ibid.*, p. 48).
122. CNUDM, *op. cit. supra* note 53, art. 27(1)(a).
123. Mallia, *op. cit. supra* note 13, p. 49.
124. *Ibid.*, p. 51.

migrants n'est pas engagée selon le Protocole[125], mais cet instrument rappelle la possibilité en droit national de faire de l'entrée irrégulière dans un Etat une infraction et de prendre des mesures sur cette base[126].

Selon la Convention contre la criminalité transnationale organisée, qui s'applique *mutatis mutandis* au Protocole, chaque Etat partie « adopte les mesures nécessaires pour établir sa compétence ... [l]orsque l'infraction est commise sur son territoire »[127]. Ainsi, vu que la commission du crime implique l'entrée illégale dans le territoire de l'Etat côtier, une compétence basée sur cet instrument existe. Pour les Etats parties au Protocole et à la Convention, une obligation de criminaliser le trafic sur leur territoire s'impose, alors que, pour les Etats qui n'y sont pas parties, une compétence basée sur la territorialité objective est envisageable. Ce principe permet à un Etat d'appliquer sa compétence pénale pour des actes dont au moins une partie principale — par exemple ses conséquences — s'est déroulée sur le territoire national[128].

En conclusion, des bases de compétence existent en mer territoriale pour criminaliser l'entrée illégale dans la mer territoriale si ce n'est pas seulement à des fins de passage inoffensif, mais en vue d'un débarquement et pour criminaliser le trafic de migrants, que la commission du crime ait lieu afin d'amener les migrants à terre ou non. Si un Etat a adopté des dispositions pertinentes dans son droit interne, il peut donc engager des poursuites envers les trafiquants et, le cas échéant, contre les migrants. Il faut noter que, comme certains d'entre eux sont des demandeurs d'asile, ils ne devraient pas être soumis à des sanctions pénales en raison de leur entrée illégale dans le pays[129]. Certains Etats ont néanmoins une application souple de cette règle, criminalisent l'entrée illégale sans distinction et/ou placent les demandeurs d'asile en détention[130].

---

125. Protocole contre le trafic illicite de migrants par terre, air et mer, *op. cit. supra* note 8, art. 5.

126. *Ibid.*, art. 6(4).

127. Convention des Nations Unies contre la criminalité transnationale organisée, *op. cit. supra* note 9, art. 15(1).

128. Brownlie, *op. cit. supra* note 19, p. 301 ; Oxman, *op. cit. supra* note 31, par. 23 ; I. Bantekas, « Criminal Jurisdiction of States under International Law », dans R. Wolfrum (dir. publ.), *The Max Planck Encyclopedia of Public International Law*, Oxford University Press, 2008, par. 5.

129. Convention relative au statut des réfugiés, *op. cit. supra* note 60, art. 31 :

> « Les Etats contractants n'appliqueront pas de sanctions pénales, du fait de leur entrée ou de leur séjour irréguliers, aux réfugiés qui, arrivant directement du territoire où leur vie ou leur liberté était menacée au sens prévu par l'article premier, entrent ou se trouvent sur leur territoire sans autorisation, sous la réserve qu'ils se présentent sans délai aux autorités et leur exposent des raisons reconnues valables de leur entrée ou présence irrégulières. » (Voir Miltner, *op. cit. supra* note 22, p. 103.)

130. En pratique, environ deux tiers des Etats appliquent parfois ou toujours des sanctions envers les demandeurs d'asile et les sanctions pénales dans ce cadre

C. Applicabilité des droits humains

Il semble relativement bien accepté — mais pas de manière unanime[131] — que l'application des obligations de droits humains s'étend à la mer territoriale[132]. En effet, la Convention de Vienne sur le droit des traités dit clairement que, à part si volonté explicite du contraire, «un traité lie chacune des parties à l'égard de l'ensemble de son territoire»[133]. Le droit national ne peut pas servir comme justification à une violation du droit international. Ainsi, la pratique d'excision territoriale australienne, selon laquelle certaines îles ne représentent pas le territoire national à des fins migratoires[134], a été largement critiquée comme non conforme au droit international[135].

Certains commentateurs s'interrogent sur la définition à donner à l'entrée sur le territoire, pour savoir si cela signifie la terre ferme seulement ou également la mer territoriale[136]. Cette question est importante par rapport aux demandes d'asile et certaines obligations qui en découlent, mais n'est pas pertinente pour le non-refoulement. En effet, alors qu'aucun pays n'a l'obligation de recevoir les demandeurs d'asile, l'obligation de protection liée au non-refoulement s'applique lorsque les demandeurs d'asile sont dans la mer territoriale[137].

---

doivent être comprises de manière large, incluant la détention (G. S. Goodwin-Gill, «Article 31 of the 1951 Convention relating to the Status of Refugees: Non-Penalization, Detention and Protection» *Background Paper for the Global Consultations on International Protection in the Context of the Fiftieth Anniversary of the 1951 Convention*, 2001, pp. 206-214 et 219, <http://www.unhcr.org/419c778d4.html>); UNHCR, «Détention des réfugiés et des personnes en quête d'asile», *Conclusion générale*, n° 44 (XXVII), 13 octobre 1986; Khan, *op. cit. supra* note 57, p. 15; Bostock, *op. cit. supra* note 58, pp. 291-292. A Malte, l'entrée irrégulière a pour conséquence une sanction administrative, et non pas pénale, mais qui comprend la détention jusqu'au rapatriement (N. de Blouw, «Drowning Policies: A Proposal to Modify the Dublin Agreement and Reduce Human Rights Abuses in the Mediterranean», *California Western International Law Journal*, n° 40, 2009-2010, pp. 348-349.)

131. Trevisanut, *op. cit. supra* note 7, p. 222; Barnes, *op. cit. supra* note 76, pp. 121-122.

132. Khan, *op. cit. supra* note 57, pp. 14-15; Barnes, *op. cit. supra* note 59, p. 69; *Minister for Immigration and Multicultural Affairs c. Khawar* [2002] HCA 14, par. 42; P. Mathew, «International Association of Refugee Law Judges Conference: Address — Legal Issues concerning Interception», *Georgetown Immigration Law Journal*, n° 17, 2002-2003, p. 235.

133. Convention de Vienne sur le droit des traités, Nations Unies, *Recueil des traités*, vol. 1155, p. 331, art. 29.

134. Migration Act 1958, par. 5, et Migration Amendement (Excision from Migration Zone) Act of 2001, tels que présentés dans Bailliet, *op. cit. supra* note 78, p. 746; Bostock, *op. cit. supra* note 58, p. 280; Crock, *op. cit. supra* note 68, p. 54.

135. Bostock, *op. cit. supra* note 58, p. 300.

136. Miltner, *op. cit. supra* note 22, pp. 93-94.

137. Mallia, *op. cit. supra* note 13, p. 50.

Paragraphe 2 **Zone contiguë**

A. Interception

Dans la zone contiguë, qui peut s'étendre jusqu'à vingt-quatre mille marins suite à une déclaration de l'Etat côtier, celui-ci est également autorisé à exercer le contrôle nécessaire pour prévenir ou sanctionner des violations de ses lois et règlements liés à l'immigration[138]. En ce qui concerne les navires quittant la mer territoriale après avoir commis un acte contrevenant aux lois de l'Etat côtier, ce dernier peut en prendre le contrôle afin de punir de telles violations.

Pour les navires qui se dirigent vers la mer territoriale, la situation légale est moins claire. En effet, comme la zone contiguë constitue la haute mer et que la CNUDM précise que le contrôle doit être nécessaire, une certaine proportionnalité entre la volonté de l'Etat côtier d'éviter une immigration illégale et la liberté de navigation doit s'appliquer[139]. Ainsi, il semble probable que l'Etat côtier ne soit autorisé à intercepter un navire que s'il montre l'intention d'entrer dans la mer territoriale en violation du droit national lié à l'immigration — et pas seulement celle de vouloir exercer son droit de passage inoffensif en mer territoriale. Il convient néanmoins d'admettre que cette différenciation est basée sur la perception, par l'Etat côtier, des intentions du navire approchant, ce qui ne fournit pas de critères tangibles afin d'examiner la légalité d'une interception et laisse donc une large marge de manœuvre à cet Etat. L'Etat côtier peut dans tous les cas repousser un navire au-delà de sa zone contiguë afin d'éviter une telle violation — à la condition que cela ne consiste pas en du refoulement[140]. Pour les navires en simple transit dans la zone contiguë, l'Etat côtier ne peut pas intervenir[141].

B. Compétence pour criminaliser

Le contrôle nécessaire que l'Etat côtier peut exercer afin de « prévenir ... et réprimer les infractions à ses lois et règlements ... d'immigration sur son territoire ou dans sa mer territoriale »[142] n'équivaut pas automatiquement à une juridiction, mais il semble accepté que cela puisse servir de base légale à des poursuites pénales contre la

138. CNUDM, *op. cit. supra* note 53, art. 33.

139. Moreno-Lax, *op. cit. supra* note 77, p. 7 (n. 105 et texte s'y rapportant).

140. D. R. Rothwell et T. Stephens, *The International Law of the Sea*, Hart Publishing, 2010, p. 80; Pallis, *op. cit. supra* note 113, pp. 353-354.

141. A part peut-être dans les cas d'un navire-mère qui permet à des navires plus petits de commettre une violation des règles migratoires dans la mer territoriale. Voir Guilfoyle, *op. cit. supra* note 4, p. 13.

142. CNUDM, *op. cit. supra* note 53, art. 33(1).

violation des lois et des règlements de l'Etat côtier dans les domaines mentionnés [143].

L'étendue de ce droit, tout comme celui d'intercepter les navires, fait néanmoins débat. En effet, pour certains, seule la prévention, et non pas la punition, est pertinente envers les navires se dirigeant vers la mer territoriale; pour qu'une punition puisse être appliquée, il faudrait en effet que le navire ait violé le droit national et donc que l'Etat côtier ait la compétence de légiférer par rapport aux actions prenant place dans la zone contiguë elle-même [144]. Un autre courant de doctrine considère que tant que l'action en question a un lien avec la mer territoriale — par exemple en représentant une tentative d'entrer en violation des lois migratoires dans la mer territoriale —, elle peut être régulée par l'Etat côtier [145].

Selon cette seconde opinion, l'Etat côtier est autorisé à criminaliser la tentative d'entrer dans la mer territoriale en violation des règles d'immigration, ce qui ferait un parallèle intéressant avec la possibilité de criminaliser la tentative de trafic. Ainsi, si le navire de migrants se dirige vers la mer territoriale, seule une tentative d'entrée irrégulière peut être reprochée aux personnes à bord, alors que si le navire revient de la mer territoriale, le délit est potentiellement consommé.

Quant au trafic lui-même, le Protocole prévoit que sa tentative soit criminalisée [146]; le crime peut donc déjà commencer hors des frontières. L'Etat interceptant peut adopter des mesures envers ses nationaux s'ils sont les auteurs de ce crime, envers des étrangers si le crime touche ses nationaux et/ou quand son instigateur est sur son territoire [147]. Ainsi, si aucune des deux premières bases de compétence n'existe, l'Etat côtier peut probablement ramener le navire à terre et appliquer la juridiction quasi universelle basée sur la présence sur le territoire national.

En conclusion, dans sa zone contiguë, l'Etat côtier peut criminaliser la tentative de violation ou la violation des lois d'immigration, ce qui vise les migrants eux-mêmes et la tentative de trafic, commise par ses nationaux, contre ses nationaux ou en général; dans ce dernier cas de

---

143. Simma et Müller, *op. cit. supra* note 32, p. 138.

144. G. Fitzmaurice, «Some Results of the Geneva Convention on the Law of the Sea», *International and Comparative Law Quarterly*, n° 8, 1969, p. 113, tel que présenté dans Mallia, *op. cit. supra* note 13, pp. 56-57.

145. S. Oda, «The Concept of the Contiguous Zone», *International and Comparative Law Quarterly*, n° 11, 1962, p. 133, et D. P. O'Connell, *The International Law of the Sea*, Clarendon Press, 1984, pp. 1058-1059, tels que présentés dans Mallia, *op. cit. supra* note 13, p. 57; pour la pratique des Etats, voir *ibid.*, p. 60 (n. 60).

146. Protocole contre le trafic illicite de migrants par terre, air et mer, *op. cit. supra* note 8, art. 6(2)(a).

147. Convention des Nations Unies contre la criminalité transnationale organisée, *op. cit. supra* note 9, art. 15.

figure, des mesures peuvent être prises lorsque l'auteur du trafic est sur le territoire de l'Etat côtier.

C. Applicabilité des droits humains

Comme la zone contiguë fait partie de la haute mer, la discussion ci-dessous est pertinente pour les deux sections.

Paragraphe 3 **Haute mer**

A. Interception

Le régime de la haute mer s'applique, pour les questions qui nous intéressent ici, dans toutes les zones au-delà de la mer territoriale et de sa zone contiguë, à savoir dès vingt-quatre milles marins[148]. Ce régime est caractérisé par les libertés de la haute mer, dont la liberté de navigation[149]. Les navires sont donc soumis exclusivement aux contrôles et à la juridiction de leur Etat pavillonnaire[150], sauf exceptions incluses dans la CNUDM ou « dans les cas où l'intervention procède de pouvoirs conférés par traité »[151].

Les cas particuliers dans lesquels le navire de guerre d'un Etat tiers peut arraisonner un bateau en haute mer comprennent donc l'autorisation explicite d'une telle intervention en vertu d'un traité[152]. Pendant des décennies, les Etats-Unis ont combattu l'immigration irrégulière en provenance d'Haïti. Pour ce faire, un échange de notes permettait entre 1981 et 1994 aux navires des gardes-côtes américains d'intercepter en haute mer les navires utilisés pour le transport de migrants[153]. Cet accord bilatéral autorisait les autorités américaines à exercer un droit de visite sur les navires haïtiens, un droit de fouille et, après avoir informé Haïti, un droit de renvoyer les personnes suspectées de tenter d'entrer aux Etats-Unis, même si la violation n'avait pas encore eu lieu[154]. Ce

148. La zone économique exclusive qui s'étend de douze à deux cents milles marins au maximum est une zone fonctionnelle qui n'est pas pertinente pour les questions de liberté de navigation et d'immigration. En effet, le régime de la zone économique exclusive n'a pas d'implication ici vu que la liberté de navigation s'y applique (CNUDM, *op. cit. supra* note 53, art. 57-58(1)).

149. *Ibid.*, art. 87.

150. *Ibid.*, art. 92(1).

151. *Ibid.*, art. 110.

152. *Ibid.*, art. 110(1).

153. « Agreement to Stop Clandestine Migration of Residents of Haiti to the United States », *International Legal Materials*, n° 20, 1981, p. 1198, tel que présenté dans Guilfoyle, *op. cit. supra* note 4, p. 189. Voir également Jacobson, *op. cit. supra* note 86, pp. 815-816.

154. Exchange of Letters, relating to the Establishment of a Cooperative Program of Interdiction and Selective Return of Certain Haitian Migrants and

traité a été dénoncé par Haïti lors du retour au pouvoir du président Aristide et les Etats-Unis n'ont en conséquence plus le droit d'aborder des navires haïtiens en haute mer. Un autre traité, encore en vigueur, avec la République dominicaine, autorise les Etats-Unis à aborder, fouiller et même arrêter, en attendant les instructions de l'Etat pavillonnaire, les navires dominicains en haute mer, lorsqu'ils sont suspectés de trafic de migrants[155].

Un autre exemple est celui du Protocole contre le trafic illicite de migrants qui reconnaît l'existence et l'utilité des interceptions maritimes[156] afin de contrôler les frontières[157]. Il prévoit que, si un Etat non pavillonnaire soupçonne avec des bases raisonnables — plus qu'un soupçon pur, mais moins que des preuves[158] — un navire qui exerce sa liberté de navigation — donc en haute mer[159] — d'être engagé dans le trafic de migrants, il doit en référer à l'Etat pavillonnaire et demander une autorisation d'arraisonnement et de visite[160]. Toute mesure supplémentaire dépend à nouveau de l'autorisation de l'Etat pavillonnaire[161]. Dans le cas d'un Etat tiers agissant en haute mer avec l'accord de l'Etat pavillonnaire donné dans le cadre du Protocole, l'Etat interceptant peut probablement prendre toutes les mesures acceptées ou requises par l'Etat pavillonnaire. L'autorisation *ad hoc* d'un Etat pavillonnaire non partie au Protocole peut faire débat, vu qu'un tel type d'exception n'est pas envisagé par la CNUDM et qu'une telle autorisation n'est pas prévisible pour les personnes à bord du navire[162].

Une possibilité supplémentaire existe si le bateau est sans nationalité, ou soupçonné de l'être[163]. L'étendue du droit de visite sur de tels navires est discutée[164]. Selon certaines lois nationales et certains commen-

---

Vessels, 33 U.S.T. 3559, 23 septembre 1981, tel que présenté dans Papastavridis, *op. cit. supra* note 11, p. 179.

155. Agreement between the Government of the United States of America and the Government of the Dominican Republic concerning Cooperation in Maritime Migration Law Enforcement 2003, KAV 6187, art. 8, tel que présenté dans Guilfoyle, *op. cit. supra* note 4, p. 196.

156. Miltner, *op. cit. supra* note 66, p. 200.

157. Miltner, *op. cit. supra* note 22, p. 105.

158. X. Hinrichs, « Measures against Smuggling of Migrants at Sea : A Law of the Sea Related Perspective », *Revue belge de droit international*, n° 36, 2003, p. 434 ; Papastavridis, *op. cit. supra* note 11, p. 191.

159. Hinrichs, *op. cit. supra* note 158, pp. 435-437.

160. Protocole contre le trafic illicite de migrants par terre, air et mer, *op. cit. supra* note 8, art. 8(2).

161. *Ibid.*

162. Cela est sujet à une discussion poussée en référence à la possibilité d'appliquer des sanctions pénales. Voir *op. cit. infra* note 190, *Medvedyev c. France* (et texte qui s'y rapporte).

163. CNUDM, *op. cit. supra* note 53, art. 110(1)(d).

164. Guilfoyle, *op. cit. supra* note 4, p. 17.

tateurs, un navire sans nationalité peut être complètement soumis à la juridiction de l'Etat pavillonnaire du navire visitant et par conséquent être arrêté[165]. Pour la majorité cependant, ce droit se limite à vérifier les documents du navire et, probablement dans des circonstances où les soupçons d'activités illicites sont très forts, à fouiller le navire[166]. Pour qu'une arrestation soit possible, un lien supplémentaire est nécessaire[167]. Il semble dans tous les cas que l'absence de nationalité soit la justification la plus fréquemment utilisée pour arraisonner un navire avec des migrants à bord[168]. Le Protocole contre le trafic illicite de migrants réitère le droit pour un Etat tiers d'arraisonner et de visiter un navire sans nationalité soupçonné d'être engagé dans le trafic. Les mesures qui peuvent découler d'une telle visite ne sont cependant pas limpides: «Si les soupçons [que le navire se livre au trafic illicite de migrants et qu'il est sans nationalité] sont confirmés par des preuves, cet Etat Partie prend les mesures appropriées conformément au droit interne et au droit international pertinents.»[169] Il est donc soumis à une obligation de prendre des mesures[170], mais leur nature n'est pas clarifiée.

Un autre cas de figure est celui où un bateau se livre au commerce d'esclave. L'esclavage est traditionnellement défini comme «l'état ou condition d'un individu sur lequel s'exercent les attributs du droit de propriété ou certains d'entre eux»[171]. Si les victimes de la traite de personnes, par exemple celles qui sont victimes d'un trafic en vue d'une exploitation sexuelle, sont considérées comme des esclaves modernes

---

165. *Naim Molvan c. Attorney-General for Palestine*, *The Asya*, [1948] AC 351, tel que présenté par Mallia, *op. cit. supra* note 13, p. 69; Guilfoyle, *op. cit. supra* note 4, p. 17 (n. 51). Cela est, par exemple, la pratique des Etats-Unis (*US Commander Handbook*, 2007, par. 3.112.3; *US c. Marino-Garcia*, [1982] 679 F.2d 1373; J. E. Kramek, «Bilateral Maritime Counter-Drug and Immigrant Interdiction Agreements: Is This the World of the Future?», *University of Miami Inter-American Law Review*, nº 31, 2000, p. 127); de l'Italie (*Pamuk e Altri*, Tribunale di Crotone, 27 septembre 2001, *Rivista di Diritto Internazionale*, nº 84, 2001, p. 1155, tel que mentionné dans Papastavridis, *op. cit. supra* note 11 (n. 68); Moreno-Lax, *op. cit. supra* note 77 (n. 77)); de la Norvège (Bennett, *op. cit. supra* note 33, p. 444). García Andrade, *op. cit. supra* note 101, p. 315, considère qu'un Etat tiers a le droit d'intercepter les navires sans nationalité.

166. CNUDM, *op. cit. supra* note 53, art. 110(2); Papastavridis, *op. cit. supra* note 11, pp. 153-154.

167. R. R Churchill et A. V. Lowe, *The Law of the Sea*, Manchester University Press, 1999, p. 214; Guilfoyle, *op. cit. supra* note 4, p. 17; Mallia, *op. cit. supra* note 13, p. 69.

168. Papastavridis, *op. cit. supra* note 11, p. 159.

169. Protocole contre le trafic illicite de migrants par terre, air et mer, *op. cit. supra* note 8, art. 8(7).

170. Mallia, *op. cit. supra* note 13, p. 126.

171. Convention relative à l'esclavage 1926, Société des Nations, *Recueil des traités*, vol. 60, p. 253, art. 1.

alors un arraisonnement est possible pour un navire d'un Etat non pavillonnaire[172]. Un droit de visite est en effet envisagé dans la CNUDM envers les navires battant un autre pavillon[173]. Cependant, au-delà de la vérification des titres et, si les soupçons continuent à sembler fondés, d'un examen à bord, aucune action supplémentaire n'est permise sans l'autorisation de l'Etat pavillonnaire. Ainsi, selon la CNUDM, le droit de visite dans le cas de navires soupçonnés d'esclavage n'inclut pas un droit d'arrestation ou de prise de contrôle du navire. Dans la mesure où aucune provision sur l'interdiction maritime ne se trouve dans le Protocole contre la traite, le cadre légal n'est pas modifié par cet instrument[174].

Finalement, si des violations du droit de l'Etat côtier ont pris place dans la mer territoriale, cet Etat est autorisé à utiliser son droit de poursuite qui peut l'amener à poursuivre le bateau, légitimement, en haute mer, et à en prendre contrôle[175]. En effet, il s'agit de la continuation, dans des eaux internationales, d'une application de la juridiction nationale telle qu'exercée dans les eaux territoriales[176]. Ce droit n'inclut pas des actions préventives qui auraient lieu avant que le navire «poursuivi» n'entre dans la zone contiguë ou les eaux territoriales[177]. Cependant, selon la doctrine de la présence constructive, si un bateau-mère placé en haute mer sert de base permettant à d'autres navires de se rendre dans les eaux territoriales pour y commettre des infractions, le navire-mère peut être poursuivi et arrêté[178].

Alors que les Etats tentent de contrôler tout ce qu'ils considèrent comme touchant leurs intérêts, beaucoup de liens entre la volonté de contrôle des Etats et certaines situations ne sont pas acceptés par le droit international[179], en particulier par rapport à la compétence d'application du droit. Par exemple, par désir d'assurer un ordre minimal en haute mer, certains argumentent que lorsqu'un Etat pavillonnaire ne veut ou ne peut pas exercer son autorité, d'autres Etats peuvent agir[180]; alors que cet état de fait serait peut-être désirable, il ne trouve pas de base dans le droit positif.

De même, les tentatives de certains Etats d'inclure les questions de

---

172. Papastavridis, *op. cit. supra* note 11, pp. 176-177.
173. CNUDM, *op. cit. supra* note 53, art. 110(1)(b).
174. Sur le trafic, voir note 13 et texte s'y rapportant.
175. CNUDM, *op. cit. supra* note 53, art. 111.
176. Mallia, *op. cit. supra* note 13, p. 64.
177. Mathew, *op. cit. supra* note 132, p. 226.
178. Mallia, *op. cit. supra* note 13, p. 65; B. Gilmore, «Hot Pursuit and Constructive Presence in Canadian Law Enforcement», *Marine Policy*, n° 12, 1988, p. 109.
179. Simma et Müller, *op. cit. supra* note 32, p. 137.
180. Mallia, *op. cit. supra* note 13, pp. 72-73.

sécurité nationale comme justification légitime de visites en haute mer sont globalement considérées comme illicites[181].

B. Compétence pour criminaliser

Il convient tout d'abord de préciser que seul le trafic (et par là-même la traite) peut être criminalisé en haute mer. En effet, les migrants eux-mêmes ne commettent aucun acte illicite en se trouvant sur un navire en haute mer sans document valable pour entrer dans un Etat[182].

Si un Etat agit contre un navire de son pavillon, il a pleine compétence pour juger les actions des trafiquants à bord. En effet, «[c]haque Etat Partie adopte les mesures nécessaires pour établir sa compétence ... [l]orsque l'infraction est commise à bord d'un navire qui bat son pavillon»[183]. Ainsi, il ne s'agit pas seulement d'une possibilité d'établir sa compétence, mais d'une obligation de légiférer.

Après une poursuite chaude, il est possible pour l'Etat interceptant d'intenter une action contre les trafiquants arrêtés en haute mer en raison d'une infraction commise en mer territoriale[184]. En effet, tant que la poursuite a commencé en mer territoriale et a été ininterrompue, le navire intercepté est considéré comme s'il avait été arrêté dans la mer territoriale. La base de compétence se trouve à la fois dans le droit de la mer traditionnel et dans la lutte contre la criminalité transnationale organisée. En effet, l'infraction est commise sur le territoire de l'Etat partie, qui doit donc adopter des mesures pour établir sa compétence[185]. Il est aussi possible que le navire-mère, localisé en haute mer, soit arrêté[186]. La criminalisation de ses actions est envisageable sur la base de la présence constructive et/ou du principe territorial objectif.

Dans le cas d'un navire au service de l'Etat agissant en haute mer

---

181. En effet, le principe de protection selon lequel certains actes peuvent tellement nuire au pouvoir gouvernemental d'un Etat que ce dernier a la compétence de combattre de telles actions où qu'elles se produisent semble peu convaincant dans les problèmes migratoires, même s'ils touchent un grand nombre d'individus. De plus, il s'agit d'un principe applicable pour la compétence législative seulement (Simma et Müller, *op. cit. supra* note 32, pp. 143-144). Voir également Papastavridis, *op. cit. supra* note 11, pp. 194-197; Miltner, *op. cit. supra* note 22, p. 104.

182. Papastavridis, *op. cit. supra* note 102, pp. 84-85; Pallis, *op. cit. supra* note 113, p. 352. Il vaut la peine de noter, néanmoins, que les cours italiennes en ont jugé autrement dans le cas du *Pamuk*, tel que présenté dans Papastavridis, *op. cit. supra* note 11, p. 163, et qu'un raisonnement basé sur une compétence de protection peut être développé.

183. Convention des Nations Unies contre la criminalité transnationale organisée, *op. cit. supra* note 9, art. 15(1)(b).

184. Mallia, *op. cit. supra* note 13, p. 64.

185. Convention des Nations Unies contre la criminalité transnationale organisée, *op. cit. supra* note 9, art. 15(1)(a).

186. CNUDM, *op. cit. supra* note 53, art. 111.

envers un navire d'un Etat tiers, toute mesure d'interception et de prise de contrôle est basée sur le consentement de l'Etat pavillonnaire. Si l'Etat interceptant reçoit l'autorisation de ramener le navire au port et d'intenter des poursuites contre les trafiquants, il le peut. Une action en justice est bien sûr uniquement envisageable s'il a adopté les lois nécessaires pour être compétent de manière quasi universelle. Il n'est cependant sous aucune obligation d'avoir adopté de telles lois[187]. Il lui est également possible d'établir sa compétence envers les trafiquants s'ils sont ses ressortissants ou si les victimes du trafic le sont[188]. Néanmoins, en pratique, il faudra une autorisation de l'Etat pavillonnaire afin de pouvoir exercer un contrôle effectif à des buts judiciaires sur le navire et ses occupants, et il conviendra de ramener ce navire sur la terre ferme afin de poursuivre les trafiquants. Dans ce dernier cas, la base de compétence selon laquelle un Etat peut intenter une action contre un trafiquant s'il se trouve sur son territoire s'applique également[189].

Il est important que les Etats s'engagent de manière prévisible dans la lutte contre le trafic de migrants, par exemple en ratifiant le Protocole pertinent. En effet, dans le cas *Medvedyev c. France*, la CEDH s'est prononcée sur la possibilité d'amener devant un tribunal français un trafiquant de drogue pratiquant son trafic sur un navire battant le pavillon d'un Etat non partie aux conventions relatives à la lutte internationale contre le trafic de drogue. Elle a considéré que même une autorisation explicite de l'Etat pavillonnaire n'est pas suffisante pour autoriser un Etat tiers à intercepter le navire car cela viole le principe de prévisibilité[190]. De plus, le droit interne ne doit pas s'opposer à la compétence exclusive de l'Etat pavillonnaire et donc, en raison du manque de lien entre la France et les trafiquants, l'application de la loi française n'est pas souhaitable[191]. En cela, dans la lutte contre le trafic de migrants, la ratification du Protocole par l'Etat pavillonnaire rend envisageable qu'il donne son accord à un Etat tiers pour agir en haute mer. Il convient de noter que le point de vue de la CEDH n'est pas partagé par tous et qu'une lecture de l'article 20 des articles sur la responsabilité des Etats laisse penser qu'un consentement préalable à un acte illicite par l'Etat potentiellement lésé rend ce comportement licite[192]. Néanmoins, ces

---

187. Convention des Nations Unies contre la criminalité transnationale organisée, *op. cit. supra* note 9, art. 15(4).

188. *Ibid.*, art. 15(2)(a)(b).

189. *Ibid.*, art. 15(4).

190. CEDH, *Medvedyev et autres c. France*, 2010, 3394/03, par. 100.

191. *Ibid.*, par. 91.

192. Commission du droit international, «Projet d'articles sur la responsabilité de l'Etat pour fait internationalement illicite», 2001, *Documents officiels de l'Assemblée générale*, cinquante-sixième session, supplément n° 10 (A/56/10), art. 20; avis partagé par Papastavridis, *op. cit. supra* note 11, p. 198.

deux opinions sont probablement conciliables si l'on garde en tête que l'article 20 évite que l'intervention ne viole les droits de l'Etat pavillonnaire, mais n'a aucune incidence sur les droits individuels des personnes à bord.

Dans le cas des navires sans nationalité, les mesures possibles à la suite d'une visite sont débattues. Si la juridiction nationale prévoit qu'un navire sans pavillon équivaut, en matière de compétence, à un navire de leur pavillon, une obligation existe d'établir sa compétence envers les actes de trafic[193]. Dans les autres cas de figure, il est également possible pour un Etat interceptant d'établir sa compétence de la même manière que pour les autres navires tiers; il lui faut une loi permettant d'agir contre les navires sans nationalité tout comme envers ceux des autres Etats parties au Protocole[194]. Cependant, la question de l'autorisation de prendre sous son contrôle le navire et ses occupants reste irrésolue en théorie[195], avec le relatif consensus doctrinal qu'un lien supplémentaire[196] ou une autre base de compétence est nécessaire[197]. Il convient de noter qu'un tel lien était prévu dans une version préliminaire du Protocole, faisant référence à la nationalité des trafiquants et au fait que le navire avait sans aucun doute pour destination la côte de l'Etat intervenant[198]. En pratique, les Etats risquent rarement de se trouver face à une contestation d'un autre Etat[199]: aucun Etat pavillonnaire n'existe et il est peu probable

193. Convention des Nations Unies contre la criminalité transnationale organisée, *op. cit. supra* note 9, art. 15(1)(b).

194. UNODC, «Loi type contre le trafic illicite de migrants», *op. cit. supra* note 43, p. 87.

195. Selon certains (Mathew, *op. cit. supra* note 132, pp. 224-225; Barnes, *op. cit. supra* note 76, p. 133; Papastavridis, *op. cit. supra* note 11, pp. 161-162; Churchill et Lowe, *op. cit. supra* note 167, pp. 213-214), il est peu probable que l'Etat interceptant bénéficie après l'exercice du droit de visite du droit d'exercer sa juridiction par rapport aux personnes sur le navire, vu que rien de tel n'est inclus dans la CNUDM, alors que, pour les navires engagés dans des activités de piraterie, le droit universel de le saisir et d'appréhender les personnes à bord est explicité (CNUDM, *op. cit. supra* note 53, art. 105). Selon d'autres, ces navires sont sans protection et peuvent donc être considérés comme assimilés au pavillon du navire interceptant (O'Connell, *op. cit. supra* note 145, pp. 755-756) et aucun Etat ne peut légitimement faire objection à cette compétence (*Naim Molvan c. Attorney-General for Palestine*, *op. cit. supra* note 165, pp. 369-370). Sur la pratique américaine de lutte contre le trafic de drogue, voir *US c. Caicedo* (47 F.3d 370, 372 (9th Circ. 1995)); *US c. Marino-Garcia* (679, F.2d 1373, 1382 (11th Circ. 1982)); *US c. Bravo* 489 F3d 1, par. 17; A. W. Anderson, «Jurisdiction over Stateless Vessels on the High Seas: An Appraisal under Domestic and International Law», *Journal of Maritime Law and Commerce*, n° 13, 1982, p. 323.

196. Pour de tels liens, voir par exemple «Draft Convention on Jurisdiction with respect to Crime: Harvard Research in International Law», *Supp. American Journal of International Law*, 1935, p. 439.

197. Brownlie, *op. cit. supra* note 19, p. 311.

198. Article F du projet italien de 1997 tel que présenté dans Mallia, *op. cit. supra* note 13, p. 114.

199. O'Connell, *op. cit. supra* note 145, vol. II, p. 755.

que les Etats de nationalité des migrants, qui sont souvent des réfugiés et donc sans la protection de leur pays, ou des trafiquants ne réagissent.

Alors que certaines actions peuvent être criminalisées en droit interne, sans lien particulier avec cet Etat, selon le principe d'universalité[200], celui-ci n'est pas applicable au trafic de migrants. Deux logiques sous-tendent ce principe: le besoin de juger des crimes particulièrement odieux qui mettent en danger la communauté internationale dans son ensemble et le fait que certains crimes risqueraient autrement de rester impunis[201], par exemple la piraterie[202]. Il semblerait judicieux d'utiliser un raisonnement similaire à ce dernier pour combattre le trafic de migrants en particulier sur les navires sans nationalité. En effet, selon les travaux préparatoires de la CNUDM, le principe de la compétence quasi exclusive de l'Etat pavillonnaire a été inclus, en addition au concept de liberté de navigation, car l'absence d'autorité sur les navires en haute mer amènerait le chaos[203]. Mais, en droit positif, l'absence de pavillon ne déclenche pas de compétence universelle. La tendance des Etats-Unis, dans le cadre de la lutte contre le trafic de drogue, de rendre le fait d'être à bord d'un navire sans nationalité un crime universel contrevient donc probablement au droit international[204].

Un lien entre l'Etat interceptant et les trafiquants est celui de la nationalité. Le principe de nationalité s'applique en effet envers les nationaux qui ont commis un crime et, de manière beaucoup moins consensuelle en général, lorsque les victimes sont des nationaux de l'Etat qui désire appliquer son droit[205]. Si les trafiquants et/ou les victimes sont des nationaux, le lien de nationalité peut être pertinent. Alors que, pour des crimes commis sur le territoire d'un autre Etat, cette base de compétence risque de créer un chevauchement, elle peut être très utile pour les actes criminels dans les zones sans juridiction nationale[206].

Le lien supplémentaire peut aussi être trouvé dans le principe de protection, ou dans le principe territorial objectif[207]. Selon le principe de

200. O'Keefe, *op. cit. supra* note 19, p. 745.

201. Lowe et Staker, *op. cit. supra* note 30, pp. 326-327; Simma et Müller, *op. cit. supra* note 32, pp. 144-145.

202. C. Kreß, «International Criminal Law», dans R. Wolfrum (dir. publ.), *The Max Planck Encyclopedia of Public International Law*, Oxford University Press, 2008, par. 9.

203. Report of the International Law Commission covering the work of its Eighth Session (A/3159), art. 29, *ILC Yearbook 1956*, vol II, p. 279, par. 3.

204. Bennett, *op. cit. supra* note 33, p. 445; *Drug Trafficking Vessel Interdiction Act of 2008*, Pub. L. n° 110-407, 18 USC, par. 2285 (West 2011).

205. Simma et Müller, *op. cit. supra* note 32, pp. 142-143; Lowe et Staker, *op. cit. supra* note 30, p. 330.

206. Brownlie, *op. cit. supra* note 19, pp. 303-304.

207. Papastavridis, *op. cit. supra* note 11, p. 162; Mathew, *op. cit. supra* note 132, p. 225.

protection, les Etats ont la possibilité d'exercer leur juridiction sur des actes commis à l'étranger par des non-nationaux, si ces actes mettent en danger des intérêts essentiels de l'Etat ou sa sécurité[208]. Alors que l'application typique de ce principe se réfère au trafic de drogue[209], l'immigration illégale est également considérée par certains Etats comme une menace capable de compromettre la sécurité nationale[210]. Cependant, on peut se demander si cette dernière activité touche vraiment des intérêts tellement cruciaux pour l'existence de l'Etat[211]. En effet, l'application de ces principes est critiquable en raison du niveau relatif de menace que des migrants représentent pour un pays et du manque d'effet clair sur le territoire[212].

C. Applicabilité des droits humains

Sur la haute mer, la question de l'applicabilité des droits humains est complexe et doit être déterminée pour chaque traité. Dans les cadres légaux du Pacte international relatif aux droits civils et politiques et de la Convention européenne des droits de l'homme, les Etats ont clairement des obligations envers toutes les personnes sur leur territoire et sous leur juridiction[213]. Ainsi, les personnes interceptées en haute mer qui se trouvent en conséquence sous le contrôle *de jure* ou/et *de facto* des autorités d'un Etat partie à l'une de ces conventions bénéfi-

---

208. Brownlie, *op. cit. supra* note 19, pp. 304-305; Lowe et Staker, *op. cit. supra* note 30, pp. 325-326; «Draft Convention on Jurisdiction with respect to Crime: Harvard Research in International Law», *op. cit. supra* note 196, art. 7; Bennett, *op. cit. supra* note 33, p. 436; O'Keefe, *op. cit. supra* note 19, p. 739; Oxman, *op. cit. supra* note 31, par. 27; Bantekas, *op. cit. supra* note 128, par. 20.

209. Par exemple, les Etats-Unis considèrent le trafic de drogue comme déclenchant le principe de protection (1986 Maritime Drug Law Enforcement Act; *US c. Gonzalez*, 776 F.2d 931 (1985); *US c. Biermann*, 678 F. Supp. 1437 (1988); *US c. Marino Garcia* 679 F. 2d 1373 (1982)). Voir Lowe et Staker, *op. cit. supra* note 30, p. 326; Mathew, *op. cit. supra* note 132, p. 225; Churchill et Lowe, *op. cit. supra* note 167, p. 139.

210. Voir, par exemple, *US c. Pizzarusso*, 388 F.2d 8 (1968) et *US c. Williams*, 464 F.2d 599 (2nd Circ 1972), tels que mentionnés par M. Davies, «Obligations and Implications for Ships Encountering Persons in Need of Assistance at Sea», *Pacific Rim Law and Policy Journal*, n° 12, 2003, p. 123 (n. 71).

211. Simma et Müller, *op. cit. supra* note 32, p. 144. Certains considèrent que si, voir par exemple Bantekas, *op. cit. supra* note 128, p. 20. Cela dépend en tout cas des situations particulières; il est, par exemple, vrai que l'arrivée de milliers de demandeurs d'asile à Malte peut créer une situation de crise (N. de Blouw, *op. cit. supra* note 130, pp. 344-346).

212. Papastavridis, *op. cit. supra* note 11, pp. 195-196.

213. Pacte international relatif aux droits civils et politiques, *op. cit. supra* note 64, art. 2(1); Convention européenne des droits de l'homme, *op. cit. supra* note 64, art. 1.

cient du non-refoulement, des divers droits humains applicables et, dans les cas pertinents, de l'interdiction d'expulsion collective[214].

De plus, des interprétations qui font autorité ont réitéré le champ d'applicabilité de ces instruments. Le CDH n'a laissé aucun doute quant à l'extraterritorialité des obligations: «un Etat partie doit respecter et garantir à quiconque se trouve sous son pouvoir ou son contrôle effectif les droits reconnus dans le Pacte même s'il ne se trouve pas sur son territoire»[215].

De plus, par rapport au non-refoulement, il est dit que

> «l'obligation que fait l'article 2 aux États parties de respecter et garantir à toutes les personnes se trouvant sur leur territoire et à toutes les personnes soumises à leur contrôle les droits énoncés dans le Pacte entraîne l'obligation de ne pas extrader, déplacer, expulser quelqu'un ou le transférer par d'autres moyens de leur territoire»[216].

Cette interprétation a été endossée par la CIJ dans son arrêt sur les conséquences légales du mur palestinien[217]. La CEDH a clarifié, une nouvelle fois, dans l'arrêt *Hirsi Jamaa*, que les obligations des Etats parties à la Convention s'appliquent de manière extraterritoriale[218]: le niveau de contrôle détermine les obligations. La CEDH a également examiné l'interdiction de l'expulsion collective des étrangers, qui est considérée comme applicable de manière extraterritoriale[219].

Quant à l'obligation de non-refoulement des réfugiés, la Convention sur le statut des réfugiés reste silencieuse sur la question, mais l'opinion générale veut que cette obligation soit applicable, comme celle des autres instruments, de manière extraterritoriale[220]. En effet, nulle référence n'est faite dans le paragraphe 1 de l'article 33 au territoire de l'Etat potentiellement refouleur. Que plusieurs verbes soient utilisés conjointement (expulser ou refouler) signifie que ces actions diffèrent; là où expulser signifie clairement «pousser hors de», probablement du

---

214. G. Andreone et G. Cataldi, «Regards sur les évolutions du droit de la mer en Méditerranée», *Annuaire français de droit international*, nº 56, 2010, p. 31.

215. La nature de l'obligation juridique générale imposée aux Etats parties au Pacte, *Observation générale*, nº 31, *op. cit. supra* note 64, par. 10.

216. *Ibid.*, par. 12.

217. CIJ, *Conséquences juridiques de l'édification d'un mur dans le territoire palestinien occupé, avis consultatif*, *CIJ Recueil 2004*, p. 136, par. 109; Barnes, *op. cit. supra* note 76, p. 112.

218. *Hirsi Jamaa et autres c. Italie, op. cit. supra* note 64, par. 75; *Bankovic et autres c. Belgique et 16 autres Etats contractants* (2001), 52207/99, par. 73.

219. *Hirsi Jamaa et autres c. Italie*, *op. cit. supra* note 64, par. 178.

220. Miltner, *op. cit. supra* note 66, p. 206; Brouwer et Kumin, *op. cit. supra* note 26, pp. 13-14.

territoire, refouler n'a de sens que si ce terme englobe le rejet avant l'entrée sur le territoire. De plus, il est clairement dit que l'interdiction est d'expulser ou de refouler «de quelque manière que ce soit», une terminologie ouverte s'il en est. Finalement, la Convention perdrait son sens si les Etats étaient capables d'éviter leurs obligations simplement en déterritorialisant leurs actions[221]. Cela est l'interprétation suivie par l'UNHCR[222] et la Commission interaméricaine des droits de l'homme[223], mais pas par la Cour suprême des Etats-Unis.

En effet, dans l'arrêt *Sale*, la Cour Suprême des Etats-Unis a conclu que l'interdiction de non-refoulement incluse dans la Convention relative au statut des réfugiés ne s'applique pas de manière extraterritoriale[224]. Selon la base argumentaire utilisée, il serait illogique que le paragraphe 1 de l'article 33 s'applique au-delà des frontières, alors que le paragraphe 2 est limité au territoire: «dangerous aliens on the high seas would be entitled to the benefits of 33.1 while those residing in the country that sought to expel them would not»[225]. De plus, la Cour suprême a fait appel aux travaux préparatoires, en particulier aux déclarations suisse et néerlandaise contre l'application extraterritoriale[226].

Il convient également de noter que l'UNHCR dans une conclusion du Comité exécutif reste silencieuse quant à l'application extraterritoriale des obligations de droits humains[227]. Alors que cet «oubli» a été critiqué comme relevant l'Etat intervenant de ses obligations par exemple en haute mer[228], le texte pris dans son ensemble et certaines déclarations plus récentes telles que présentées ci-dessus soutiennent une lecture ouverte du paragraphe 1.

---

221. Miltner, *op. cit. supra* note 22, p. 95.

222. UNHCR, Non-refoulement, Executive Committee, Conclusion n° 6 (XXVIII), 1977, par. c.

223. Respectivement, UNHCR, Avis consultatif sur l'application extra-territoriale des obligations de non-refoulement en vertu de la Convention de 1951 relative au statut des réfugiés et de son Protocole de 1967 (2007) <http://www.unhcr.org/refworld/docid/45f17a1a4.html> et *The Haitian Center for Human Rights c. US*, Case 10.675, Report n° 51/96, OEA/Ser.L./V/II.95 doc. 7 (1997) (Inter-American Court of Human Rights), par. 183-188, concluant que les interdictions et les rapatriements forcés de certains Haïtiens représentent une violation de la Déclaration américaine des droits de l'homme, en particulier le droit à la vie, liberté, sécurité, égalité devant les cours, et le droit de demander et recevoir l'asile.

224. US Supreme Court, *Sale c. Haitian Centers Council*, 509 US 155 (1993).

225. *Ibid.*, pp. 23-27.

226. US Supreme Court, *Sale c. Haitian Centers Council, American Society of International Law*, 1994, vol. 88, pp. 121-122; Goodwin-Gill and McAdam, *op. cit. supra* note 113, pp. 206 et 247.

227. Conclusion on Protection Safeguards in Interception Measures, n° 97 (LIV), *op. cit. supra* note 22.

228. Miltner, *op. cit. supra* note 22, pp. 120 et 122-123.

A part cette opinion et cet oubli critiqué[229], la plupart des voix concordent pour considérer l'obligation de non-refoulement comme applicable de manière extraterritoriale, à savoir qu'elle s'applique aux actions entreprises par les Etats, où que ce soit — en haute mer également[230] — par rapport à ceux qui sont sous leur contrôle effectif[231]. En effet, la responsabilité d'un Etat est engagée par l'exercice de sa juridiction, que cela soit à l'intérieur ou à l'extérieur du territoire national[232]. Cette vision de l'application extraterritoriale du non-refoulement peut éviter que les Etats, afin de se décharger de leurs obligations internationales, ne s'engagent dans des opérations en haute mer[233]. La loi type contre le trafic illicite de migrants, telle que développée par l'UNODC, prévoit que le non-refoulement doit être applicable aux rejets à la frontière et aux interceptions extraterritoriales[234].

On est cependant obligé d'admettre que, en pratique, beaucoup d'Etats tentent, avec succès, de contourner cette obligation. Les Etats-Unis illustrent très bien cette tendance: les gardes-côtes reconnaissent, en tout cas implicitement, les bénéfices des interceptions en haute mer, car les migrants peuvent être renvoyés plus facilement dans leur pays[235]. L'Australie a également une pratique qui se base sur une compréhension exclusivement territoriale de la juridiction, ce qui lui évite de devoir respecter le non-refoulement au-delà de ses frontières. Les activités de l'Union européenne de contrôles extraterritoriaux ne sont pas moins préoccupantes[236].

Paragraphe 4 **Mer territoriale d'un autre Etat**

A. Interception

Sans accord de l'Etat côtier, un Etat tiers ne peut intervenir dans les eaux territoriales et appliquer ses règles migratoires ou

229. Voir l'opinion dissidente de Justice Blackum dans *Sale c. Haitian Centers Council, op. cit. supra* note 224; UN High Commissioner for Refugees Responds to US Supreme Court Decision dans *Sale c. Haitian Centers Council, International Legal Materials*, n° 32, 1993, p. 1215; G. S Goodwin-Gill, «The Haitian *Refoulement* Case: A Comment», *International Journal of Refugee Law*, n° 6, 1994, p. 103; Moreno-Lax, *op. cit. supra* note 77, p. 12 (n. 204-205 et texte s'y rapportant); Miltner, *op. cit. supra* note 22, pp. 122-123.

230. Lauterpacht et Bethlehem, *op. cit. supra* note 65, p. 111, par. 67, et pp. 159-160, par. 242; Goodwin-Gill, *op. cit. supra* note 59, p. 444; Goodwin-Gill et McAdam, *op. cit. supra* note 113, p. 248.

231. Bostock, *op. cit. supra* note 58, p. 287; Lauterpacht et Bethlehem, *op. cit. supra* note 65, p. 111, par. 67.

232. Jacobson, *op. cit. supra* note 86, p. 814.

233. Hessbruegge, *op. cit. supra* note 97.

234. UNODC, «Loi type contre le trafic illicite de migrants», *op. cit. supra* note 43, p. 18.

235. Miltner, *op. cit. supra* note 22, pp. 120-121.

236. Nessel, *op. cit. supra* note 5, pp. 631 et 645.

même des règles internationales telles que l'interdiction du trafic de migrants ou de la traite d'êtres humains. La Convention contre les activités criminelles transnationales déclare explicitement que les mesures prises afin d'exécuter les obligations de cette Convention doivent être appliquées «d'une manière compatible avec les principes de l'égalité souveraine et de l'intégrité territoriale des Etats»[237]. Le droit de poursuite chaude s'arrête également dès qu'un navire entre dans les eaux territoriales d'un autre Etat que celui engagé dans la poursuite.

Dans la mesure où un Etat tiers a conclu un accord avec l'Etat côtier et sous réserve du respect des modalités de cet accord, des interventions sont possibles. En général, de tels traités autorisent l'Etat tiers à déployer certains de ses navires dans les eaux territoriales, avec ou sans la présence à bord d'un officier de l'Etat côtier pour permettre l'application du droit national, un «ship-rider». Les accords entre les Etats-Unis et la République dominicaine ou entre l'Italie et l'Albanie envisagent les deux cas de figure[238]. L'Italie a reçu une autorisation globale de demander des informations, d'aborder et d'inspecter, d'ordonner un retour au port de départ et, si le navire ne se conforme pas à de tels ordres, d'accompagner le navire jusqu'à un port italien, de détenir puis de rapatrier les non-nationaux[239]. Un autre exemple est celui des accords entre l'Espagne et la Mauritanie, le Cap-Vert, le Sénégal, la Gambie, la Guinée et la Guinée-Bissau. Dans la mesure où ces traités ne sont pas rendus publics, il est difficile de savoir ce qu'ils autorisent exactement[240]. C'est probablement sur cette base contractuelle que les opérations *Hera* de Frontex ont pris place dans les eaux territoriales de ces pays, mais ces traités n'incluaient pas les autres Etats européens qui ont participé à ces opérations[241].

On peut néanmoins s'interroger sur la légalité de telles autorisations. En effet, si l'Etat côtier est un Etat de départ, non seulement le navire bénéficie de la liberté de navigation, mais, de plus, les personnes à bord ont le droit de quitter tout pays, y compris le leur[242]. Lorsque l'Etat côtier est un Etat de transit, comme les Bahamas en partance de Cuba[243], le passage latéral est inoffensif et il semble donc que le navire doive ne

237. Convention des Nations Unies contre la criminalité transnationale organisée, *op. cit. supra* note 9, art. 4(1).
238. Guilfoyle, *op. cit. supra* note 4, p. 196; Papastavridis, *op. cit. supra* note 11, p. 181; Robinson, *op. cit. supra* note 44, p. 27.
239. Guilfoyle, *op. cit. supra* note 4, pp. 210-211.
240. García Andrade, *op. cit. supra* note 101, pp. 319-320; Papastavridis, *op. cit. supra* note 11, pp. 182-183.
241. Papastavridis, *op. cit. supra* note 102, pp. 88-90.
242. Voir, *supra* notes 100-106, et texte s'y rapportant.
243. UNODC, «Issue Paper — Smuggling of Migrants by Sea», *op. cit. supra* note 1, p. 17.

pas être intercepté. Cette analyse n'a cependant pas de réalité pratique. En effet, que ce soit dans les eaux territoriales des Etats de départ ou de transit, les exemples ci-dessus montrent que des Etats tiers reçoivent l'autorisation d'intervenir, bien que cela soit probablement en violation du droit international.

B. Compétence pour criminaliser

Il semble difficile d'envisager la criminalisation du trafic lui-même dans la mer territoriale de départ. En effet, cette action n'a pas encore eu lieu vu qu'aucune tentative d'entrée n'a pris place. De plus, les migrants, qu'ils soient nationaux de l'Etat de départ ou non devraient bénéficier du droit de quitter tout pays. Un Etat peut néanmoins, en vertu de la CNUDM, appliquer ses lois contre le passage inoffensif, qui inclut « l'embarquement ... de personnes en contravention aux lois et règlements ... d'immigration »[244].

S'il s'agit de la mer territoriale d'un autre Etat que celui de départ, l'Etat intervenant ne peut agir qu'avec l'autorisation de l'Etat côtier. Ainsi, s'il y est autorisé et qu'un acte de trafic a eu lieu, par exemple lors d'un transit, il peut probablement amener à terre — sur son territoire ou celui de l'Etat côtier — un navire de migrants objets de trafic, et les responsables peuvent être poursuivis. Quant aux migrants, ils sont entrés dans la mer territoriale de l'Etat côtier de manière irrégulière et sont donc susceptibles des conséquences prévues à cet effet dans cet Etat.

C. Applicabilité des droits humains

La question de l'applicabilité *ratione loci* prend une tournure particulièrement intéressante dans les cas d'interception dans la mer territoriale de l'Etat de départ ; en effet, le réfugié n'a pas encore traversé une frontière internationale et ne peut donc pas bénéficier de la protection liée à son statut[245]. Cependant, certains réfugiés ne se trouvent déjà plus dans leur Etat de départ et se soustraient à cette situation kafkaïenne. Pour les personnes qui craignent des persécutions et qui fuient directement leur pays — et donc s'y trouvent encore —, la situation est plus complexe ; elles ne bénéficient pas *de jure* du principe de non-refoulement, si elles sont interceptées par des navires de leur Etat. Lauterpacht et Bethlehem, mettant l'accent sur le risque de persécution

244. CNUDM, *op. cit. supra* note 53, art. 19(2)(h).
245. Gammeltoft-Hansen, *op. cit. supra* note 57, p. 184 ; Papastavridis, *op. cit. supra* note 102, pp. 104-105 ; Moreno-Lax, *op. cit. supra* note 77, p. 13 (n. 216 et texte s'y rapportant).

et non pas sur la géographie, suggèrent que le principe de non-refoulement s'applique également lorsque le réfugié est encore dans son propre pays[246]. Dans tous les cas, l'obligation de non-refoulement basée sur les droits humains ne souffre pas de limitation géographique[247].

On peut se demander si les Etats tiers qui financent ou sont actifs dans ces interceptions en mer territoriale de l'Etat de départ ne violent pas leur obligation d'appliquer de bonne foi leurs obligations internationales[248]. Ces Etats s'engagent en effet dans des activités qui leur permettent d'éviter leur obligation de non-refoulement. Cela a été discuté par la CEDH et une question similaire, à savoir le refus de fournir un visa, ce qui empêche *de facto* la personne d'entrer dans le pays tiers et de demander l'asile, a été traitée par la House of Lords. Les cours respectives ont conclu que les méthodes employées ne violaient pas le droit de quitter son pays et/ou de demander l'asile, mais avaient pour but d'éviter l'entrée dans un pays donné[249]. De manière plus générale, de telles mesures, même bilatérales ont été critiquées, car de nature à empêcher de quitter son pays et d'accéder à la protection internationale[250]. La CEDH, dans un autre arrêt, a considéré que la possibilité de quitter le pays peut devenir purement théorique si aucun Etat avec un niveau de protection similaire à celui de l'Etat dans lequel les demandeurs d'asile cherchent refuge n'est prêt à les laisser entrer[251]. De plus, il est défendable qu'une personne interceptée dans la mer territoriale de son Etat par le navire d'un Etat tiers, sous la juridiction duquel elle tombe en pratique, puisse se réclamer du principe de non-refoulement; le retour sur le territoire de l'Etat côtier entraînerait en effet un transfert, si ce n'est entre pays du moins entre juridictions[252].

L'applicabilité des obligations de droits humains de l'Etat intervenant, lorsqu'il agit dans les eaux territoriales d'un Etat tiers, est discutable. En effet, alors que les agents d'un Etat sont en action, ils se trouvent néanmoins sur le territoire d'un autre Etat. On peut se demander quel Etat est responsable en matière des droits humains. En effet, l'Etat côtier a

246. Lauterpacht et Bethlehem, *op. cit. supra* note 65, p. 122, par. 113-114.

247. Papastavridis, *op. cit. supra* note 102, p. 105; Moreno-Lax, *op. cit. supra* note 77, p. 13 (n. 216 et texte s'y rapportant).

248. C. Brolan, «An Analysis of the Human Smuggling Trade and the Protocol against the Smuggling of Migrants by Land, Air and Sea (2000) from a Refugee Protection Perspective», *International Journal of Refugee Law*, n° 14, 2002, p. 575.

249. Nessel, *op. cit. supra* note 5, pp. 673-675; CEDH, *Xhavara et autres c. Italie et Albanie* (2001) 39473/98; House of Lords, *Regina (European Roma Rights Center) c. Immigration Officer at Prague Airport* (2005) 2 A.C. 1 (2004) U.K.HL 55.

250. Nessel, *op. cit. supra* note 5, pp. 675-677.

251. CEDH, *Amuur c. France* (1996) 19776/92, par. 48.

252. García Andrade, *op. cit. supra* note 101, p. 322.

juridiction sous le titre de territorialité, la seule juridiction rappelée par l'UNHCR[253], mais l'Etat pavillonnaire exerce son contrôle sur les migrants. En général, il semble que ces questions sont considérées directement dans les accords entre ces Etats. Sinon, dans les cas d'opérations Frontex, la règle par défaut est la responsabilité de l'Etat côtier[254]. Finalement, si rien n'est prévu, et/ou en cas d'opérations jointes, les règles d'attribution sont à appliquer[255]. Mais les Etats ne devraient pas pouvoir se prévaloir de la non-applicabilité de leurs obligations juste parce qu'ils agissent au-delà de leur territoire. La jurisprudence illustre bien cette ambiguïté. Alors que le CDH a déterminé, dans *López Burgos*, que l'arrestation et les mauvais traitements du plaignant, par des forces de sécurité uruguayennes en Argentine, engageaient la responsabilité de l'Uruguay, la CEDH semble considérer que la responsabilité extraterritoriale des Etats s'impose seulement lorsqu'ils contrôlent totalement un individu[256]. Selon un tel raisonnement, les Etats interceptants qui arrêtent des navires et y montent sont de toute façon responsables, mais ceux qui ne font que les escorter vers la haute mer ne le sont pas[257].

SECTION 4 CONCLUSION — EFFICACITÉ DU RÉGIME DE LA CRIMINALISATION DU TRAFIC EN MER

Paragraphe 1 Cohérence juridique

Dans sa propre mer territoriale, l'Etat dont les migrants tentent de partir peut probablement intercepter les navires selon le droit de la mer, mais contrevient au droit de chacun de quitter un pays, dont le sien. Le droit de la mer et les droits humains sont donc potentiellement contradictoires. L'application du non-refoulement est probablement limitée à sa composante de droits humains. Des poursuites pénales

253. Conclusion on Protection Safeguards in Interception Measures, nº 97 (LIV), *op. cit. supra* note 22.

254. Papastavridis, *op. cit. supra* note 11, p. 186; selon les Guidelines de Frontex (2010), un débarquement devrait avoir lieu dans le pays de départ, le pays traversé ou le pays responsable de la zone SAR (Andreone et Cataldi, *op. cit. supra* note 214, p. 32; The Interception and Rescue at Sea of Asylum Seekers, Refugees and Irregular Migrants, *op. cit. supra* note 1, pp. 16-17, par. 52).

255. Papastavridis, *op. cit. supra* note 11, p. 185.

256. *Sergio Euben Lopez Burgos c. Uruguay*, Communication R 12/52 (6 juin 1979), UN Doc. Supp. nº 40 (A/36/40); *Bankovic et autres c. Belgique et 16 autres Etats contractants, op. cit. supra* note 218, tel que présenté dans Gammeltoft-Hansen, *op. cit. supra* note 57, pp. 184-185.

257. Gammeltoft-Hansen, *op. cit. supra* note 57, p. 185.

peuvent être engagées contre les trafiquants, sur la base de certains actes accessoires, mais pas sur la base du trafic par mer lui-même. En effet, il n'a pas encore eu lieu et sa tentative ne peut pas être prouvée.

Si la mer territoriale d'un Etat sert de transit, il n'est pas possible à l'Etat côtier d'intercepter le navire, sauf avec l'autorisation de l'Etat pavillonnaire ; en effet, il s'agit de passage inoffensif. Cependant, il est dans l'obligation de criminaliser le trafic de migrants lorsque le trafic se déroule sur son territoire. Une dissonance entre le manque de droit d'appréhender et l'obligation de criminaliser existe donc. Cela semble peu logique que, selon une convention internationale, l'Etat côtier doive se retenir d'intervenir alors qu'il est dans l'obligation, selon un autre instrument, de pénaliser un certain comportement. Il est clair que l'Etat de transit n'aura en général pas envie de prendre le contrôle sur le navire en question, en raison des obligations de droits humains qui en découlent.

Quant à un Etat dont la mer territoriale est celle de destination, il peut agir contre les navires de migrants qui s'y trouvent. En effet, le passage n'est plus inoffensif. La criminalisation des trafiquants est obligatoire pour les Etats parties au Protocole et celle des migrants, possible. Ainsi, par rapport aux activités dans sa propre mer territoriale, le Protocole n'apporte rien quant aux interceptions, mais crée des bases de compétence pour la criminalisation.

Dans la mer territoriale d'un autre Etat, l'Etat interceptant doit avoir l'autorisation de l'Etat côtier d'agir et, selon les dispositions de l'accord, les points ci-dessus s'appliquent. Des questions complexes de détermination des responsabilités sont soulevées, qui vont au-delà de la présente étude.

Dans sa zone contiguë, l'Etat côtier peut intercepter un navire qui se dirige vers la mer territoriale ou qui en provient dans la mesure où cela est lié à un comportement contrevenant au droit national lié à l'immigration. Il est possible à l'Etat côtier, mais pas obligatoire, de criminaliser la tentative de trafic, ainsi que la tentative d'entrée irrégulière. On peut se demander s'il est logique que le droit d'interception semble plus large en zone contiguë qu'en mer territoriale, vu qu'il s'agit ici de prévenir et réprimer l'entrée irrégulière et non pas seulement la tentative de débarquement.

En haute mer, après une interception, seul l'Etat pavillonnaire face à son propre navire et seul l'Etat côtier face à un navire intercepté à la suite d'une poursuite chaude doivent avoir une base juridictionnelle pour poursuivre respectivement la tentative de trafic et le trafic commis sur un navire battant son pavillon ou dans la mer territoriale. Dans les autres cas de figure où un navire de migrants est intercepté par un navire non pavillonnaire — ce qui présuppose, sauf en cas de poursuite chaude, l'autorisation de l'Etat pavillonnaire car le régime d'interception n'est pas modifié par le Protocole — l'Etat interceptant peut, sur la base de l'autorisation explicite de l'Etat pavillonnaire, ramener les trafiquants à terre et ensuite intenter une poursuite pénale à leur égard. Une compétence quasi universelle non obligatoire est prévue envers les personnes sur le territoire d'un Etat partie. Une compétence sur la base de la nationalité de l'auteur ou de la victime du crime existe, mais ne semble pas utile dans le cas d'une interception maritime — la compétence basée sur la localisation du trafiquant suffit. La criminalisation vise seulement les trafiquants, et non pas les migrants qui n'ont encore violé aucune loi. Les navires interceptés sans pavillon sont dans une situation où une autorisation de l'Etat pavillonnaire serait peut-être, *stricto sensu*, nécessaire mais n'a aucune applicabilité pratique; un lien supplémentaire est considéré comme suffisant.

En résumé, le Protocole contre le trafic illicite de migrants est une pierre à l'édifice contre la criminalité organisée, mais ne change pas de manière majeure le cadre légal applicable aux migrants en mer. Il sert de base pour la conclusion d'accords généraux ou *ad hoc* entre Etats dans leurs interventions en mer. En particulier pour les autorisations *ad hoc*, la participation à ce régime de l'Etat pavillonnaire du navire utilisé par les migrants fournit une prévisibilité nécessaire, selon la CEDH, pour rendre une interception par un Etat tiers légale. Cependant, cet instrument ne change pas le besoin d'une autorisation supplémentaire pour de telles opérations. A cet égard, il ne fait que répéter le droit existant et ne crée pas une compétence universelle permettant de prendre le contrôle des trafiquants. Il inclut le respect des droits humains, dont le principe de non-refoulement dans ses garanties.

Cet instrument fournit un cadre utile pour la criminalisation de certaines activités et de leurs auteurs[258]. Ainsi, les Etats parties — mais non pas les Etats non parties — ont la possibilité d'étendre leurs bases de compétence de manière quasi universelle envers les trafiquants[259]. Les seuls cas où une obligation de criminaliser existe sont celles concernant les activités commises sur son territoire et sur les navires battant son pavillon. La juridiction quasi universelle prévue par le Protocole et la Convention est positive car elle permet aux Etats qui le désirent d'adopter des règles dans leur droit national afin de criminaliser le trafic de migrants, et cela sans risque d'outrepasser leurs limites de compétence.

Néanmoins, les manques d'obligation de criminaliser les actes de

258. Obokata, *op. cit. supra* note 13, pp. 153 et 156.

259. O'Keefe, *op. cit. supra* note 19, p. 746, avec référence à R. Higgins, *Problems and Process: International Law and How We Use It*, Oxford University Press, 1994, pp. 63-65.

manière universelle et de juger ou d'extrader affaiblissent le régime car une large latitude est laissée aux Etats, sans pour autant qu'ils n'aient de vrai intérêt à agir. Il convient également de noter que le Protocole souffre d'un manque de clarté à l'égard du cadre d'action autour du trafic. Alors que l'agissement qui est criminalisée, le trafic, comprend une entrée illégale dans un pays — et il est vrai, la tentative d'entrée —, les dispositions sur le trafic en mer se réfèrent à une situation où la liberté de navigation s'applique, donc en haute mer. Bien qu'il soit possible de réconcilier les deux aspects, ce document ne reflète pas les particularités maritimes avec précision.

Paragraphe 2 **Utilité et faisabilité**

L'Etat du navire interceptant voit sa responsabilité face aux migrants engagée, en matière de non-refoulement et, lorsque cette règle est applicable, en matière d'interdiction d'expulsion collective. Ainsi, que cela soit dans sa mer territoriale, en haute mer et, probablement même, dans les eaux territoriales d'un autre Etat, il doit examiner le statut et les besoins de protection des personnes sous son contrôle effectif. Alors que seul le régime luttant contre la traite encourage l'Etat à prendre des mesures protectrices et d'accueil sur son territoire[260], à court terme, les obligations de respecter le non-refoulement sont similaires dans le cas de la lutte contre le trafic[261].

En pratique donc, de nombreuses obligations envers les migrants incombent aux Etats. Cela s'applique aussi aux activités extraterritoriales et, probablement, quel que soit le nom qui leur est donné. En effet, la CEDH a rappelé dans son arrêt *Hirsi Jamaa* que les Etats sont liés par leurs obligations lorsqu'ils exercent leur juridiction *de facto* ou *de jure*. Dans la mesure où des migrants de statuts différents voyagent côte à côte, il semble qu'en général une détermination de leurs besoins de protection s'impose et qu'elle nécessite des garanties procédurales qu'on ne trouve qu'à terre. Au vu de ces lourdes responsabilités en matière de droits humains, on peut douter d'une volonté active des Etats de chasser les trafiquants en mer. En effet, pour chaque trafiquant potentiellement arrêté et inculpé, un certain nombre de migrants, souvent demandeurs d'asile, se retrouvent sous le contrôle de l'Etat interceptant et donc sous sa responsabilité. De plus, alors que cet état de fait découle de toute interception en mer, des obligations supplémentaires découlent

260. Protocole visant à prévenir, réprimer et punir la traite des personnes, en particulier des femmes et des enfants, *op. cit. supra* note 12, art. 6 et 7(1).

261. Protocole contre le trafic illicite de migrants par terre, air et mer, *op. cit. supra* note 8, art. 19(1); protocole visant à prévenir, réprimer et punir la traite des personnes, en particulier des femmes et des enfants, *op. cit. supra* note 12, art. 14(1).

de l'arrivée sur le territoire national: l'Etat se retrouve alors sous l'obligation d'examiner formellement les demandes d'asile.

Ainsi, la criminalisation, bien que possible dans de nombreux cas, engage des ressources étatiques importantes pour une utilité discutable. Certaines difficultés se laissent en effet entrevoir. Tout d'abord, les trafiquants en mer sont en général des petites mains dans l'organisation criminelle. En effet, il s'agit d'une des étapes les plus dangereuses et les organisateurs et les chefs du trafic sont basés à terre. Les trafiquants, ou passeurs, sont parfois même des pêcheurs locaux[262]. Ainsi, la criminalisation, bien qu'elle puisse avoir un effet dissuasif, n'a aucune chance de porter un coup important aux réseaux de criminalité organisée. Il est aussi probable qu'il sera facile de remplacer une ou plusieurs personnes emprisonnées[263]. De plus, le critère de criminalité organisée fait que beaucoup de cas de trafic de migrants risquent de tomber en dehors du Protocole[264].

De plus, pour qu'une action en justice puisse avoir lieu, il ne suffit pas que l'Etat interceptant ait le droit d'agir contre les migrants et que le crime de trafic de migrants existe en droit interne. Il faut aussi que l'Etat ait identifié le trafiquant et soit en possession de preuves ou de témoignages. Cela est hautement problématique. Il semble que les trafiquants demandent aux migrants de se taire et ne pas les identifier en cas d'interception. Un avantage substantiel leur est proposé, à savoir une deuxième chance après le retour dans le pays d'embarquement[265]. Sans témoignage, il est en général très difficile de différencier un migrant d'un trafiquant à bord. Sur certains navires ne se trouve aucun trafiquant[266]. De plus, réunir les preuves de l'avantage financier, de l'illégalité de l'entrée et de l'intention du trafiquant peut être complexe, surtout dans la mesure où les Etats ne veulent pas des migrants sur leur sol[267]. Cependant, certaines lois nationales peuvent faciliter l'obtention de preuves, par exemple le fait qu'en coopérant les migrants bénéficient d'une chance de ne pas être expulsés[268].

262. UNODC, «Issue Paper — Smuggling of Migrants by Sea», *op. cit. supra* note 1, p. 21; UNODC, «Transnational Organized Crime in the Fishing Industry: Focus on: Trafficking in Persons, Smuggling of Migrants and Illicit Drugs Trafficking», Vienne, 2011, p. 74.

263. UNODC, «Manuel de formation de base sur les enquêtes et les poursuites relatives au trafic illicite de migrants», *op. cit. supra* note 18, p. 24.

264. Papastavridis, *op. cit. supra* note 11, p. 188.

265. UNODC, «Issue Paper — Smuggling of Migrants by Sea», *op. cit. supra* note 1, pp. 31-32.

266. *Ibid.*, p. 46.

267. Robinson, *op. cit. supra* note 44, p. 36.

268. Loi organique 8/2000 du 22 décembre 2000, art. 59, Espagne, tel que présentée dans UNODC, «Loi type contre le trafic illicite de migrants», *op. cit. supra* note 43, p. 68.

Néanmoins, d'après une publication de l'UNODC, l'application de peines sévères a eu un impact important sur les routes utilisées et a augmenté la sécurité des migrants en mer, dans la mesure où certaines actions ou omissions (par exemple, de fournir des gilets de sauvetage) sont entrées dans la loi[269]. Seul le futur permettra de juger si la criminalisation de telles actions permet vraiment de diminuer le trafic de migrants. Il semble toutefois que, pour l'instant, les peines encourues par les trafiquants ne soient pas suffisamment lourdes[270] pour exercer un véritable effet de dissuasion[271]. De manière contraire, les peines contre les migrants semblent, elles, être en hausse[272]. On peut se demander si le problème n'est pas approché sous le mauvais angle; en effet, certains affirment que l'augmentation du trafic de migrants est due aux pratiques migratoires de plus en plus restrictives[273].

A cet égard, finalement, la criminalisation des trafiquants ne résout pas la question plus générale de la migration irrégulière, qui continuera de se pratiquer par les routes qui restent ouvertes, tant que les facteurs «push/pull» ne seront pas résolus. Ainsi, une telle approche ne semble pas vraiment utile face à l'un des buts énoncés dans le Protocole, à savoir la lutte contre la migration irrégulière, qui de plus sort du cadre de la criminalité transnationale organisée. Le transport par mer n'est qu'une partie d'un voyage généralement plus long et cette étape n'est probablement pas la plus adéquate pour combattre son aspect criminel. L'adoption du Protocole démontre ainsi la volonté des Etats de combattre le trafic de migrants, mais pas nécessairement leur capacité à prendre des mesures adaptées et coûteuses.

En conclusion, il semble que les mécanismes légaux existent pour les Etats qui désirent combattre le trafic de migrants, mais qu'ils ne changent rien au droit de la mer applicable qui encadre de manière restrictive les possibilités, pour les navires d'Etat, d'intercepter des bateaux en mer.

Au vu des obligations en matière de droits humains qui risquent de leur incomber suite à une interception, il est peu probable que les Etats choisissent cette route et partent à la chasse au trafiquant. En effet, pour chaque trafiquant mineur potentiel qui est arrêté et ramené à terre afin de baser une compétence, des dizaines de migrants viennent aussi.

---

269. UNODC, «Issue Paper — Smuggling of Migrants by Sea», *op. cit. supra* note 1, p. 45.

270. Par exemple, en comparaison avec le trafic de drogue, voir Robinson, *op. cit. supra* note 44, pp. 25 et 36, au sujet du Maritime Drug Law Enforcement Act, 46 USC, par. 70501-70507 (2006).

271. Robinson, *op. cit. supra* note 44, p. 26.

272. *Ibid.*, p. 38.

273. Brolan, *op. cit. supra* note 248, pp. 576-577.

L'aspect humain est une différence majeure avec la lutte contre le trafic de drogue[274]. Cependant, au moins, avec cette possibilité de criminaliser le trafic de migrants, si les Etats interceptant des navires respectent leurs obligations envers les réfugiés potentiels, en les ramenant à terre dans un lieu sûr, ils ont les bases de compétence législative afin de poursuivre les trafiquants.

274. Mallia, *op. cit. supra* note 13, p. 14.

7 Le vol à main armée en mer

Nasser Abdoul*

SECTION 1 INTRODUCTION

La mer. Cette étendue d'eau salée qui entoure les continents est un don providentiel offert à l'humanité tout entière. Car, non seulement elle constitue en elle-même une ressource et regorge d'innombrables richesses, mais aussi et surtout son utilité pour le transport et les échanges commerciaux entre les différentes nations reste plus que jamais patente. Cette situation originelle et primitive ne pouvait perdurer en raison de la volonté manifestée par certains Etats à vouloir contrôler la mer[1] et donc finalement à y interdire le passage de certains navires[2].

Réagissant énergiquement à cette attitude unilatéraliste, hégémoniste et inique, Hugo Grotius[3] formula le principe de *Mare liberum*[4], principe selon lequel la mer est un territoire international et que toutes les nations étaient libres de l'utiliser tant pour la navigation en général que pour le commerce maritime en particulier. Bien qu'ayant fait l'objet d'une riposte de la part du célèbre juriste et humaniste anglais John Selden dans son *Mare clausum*[5], cette thèse allait poser les jalons de ce qui allait devenir le droit de la mer.

Considéré aujourd'hui comme la plus ancienne branche du Droit international et issu essentiellement des règles coutumières, le droit de la mer délimite les espaces maritimes et détermine en même temps les

---

* Docteur en droit international de l'Université de Douala (Cameroun). Diplômé de l'Académie internationale de droit constitutionnel (2007). Enseignant chercheur à l'ISS, Université de Maroua (Cameroun).

1. C'est le cas de l'Angleterre qui avait proclamé sa souveraineté sur les mers entourant les îles Britanniques.

2. C'est dans cet ordre d'idées qu'un amiral de la Compagnie anglaise des Indes orientales avait saisi un bateau portugais.

3. Célèbre juriste hollandais et considéré comme le père fondateur du droit international.

4. Hugo Grotius, traduit par Antoine de Courtin et Claude Monet, *Mare liberum — De la liberté des mers*, Presses universitaires de Caen, 1990.

5. John Selden, *Mare clausum*, Meighen, 1636. Ouvrage disponible en version électronique (http://gallica.bnf.fr/ark :/12148/bpt6k93841b.r=mare+clausum.langEN).

droits et les devoirs des Etats dans ces espaces[6]; reprenant ainsi le principe de la liberté des mers tel que consacré par Grotius au XVIIe siècle. Mais il a fallu attendre la conférence de Genève de 1958 pour assister à la codification des règles relatives au régime des mers[7]. L'issue de cette première conférence des Nations Unies portant sur le droit de la mer aboutit à la conclusion de quatre conventions internationales, à savoir la convention sur le plateau continental[8], la convention sur la haute mer[9], la convention sur la mer territoriale et la zone contiguë[10] et, enfin, la convention sur la pêche et la conservation des ressources biologiques[11].

Cette avancée historique allait très vite être remise en cause par de nouveaux événements ayant interféré sur la configuration mondiale du point de vue de la géopolitique notamment. Il s'agissait précisément de la décolonisation et dont la principale conséquence était la naissance d'une pléthore d'Etats ayant accédé à la souveraineté internationale et devenus membres de l'Organisation des Nations Unies. Ces jeunes Etats, soutenus par un certain nombre d'autres Etats en voie de développement, n'entendaient pas se soumettre aux règles sur lesquelles ils n'avaient pas exprimé leur consentement[12]; faisant ainsi allusion aux quatre conventions de Genève de 1958. Leurs revendications, de plus en plus soutenues et de surcroît justifiées, allaient être prises en compte lors de la troisième conférence des Nations Unies sur le droit de la mer entamée en 1973; enclenchant ainsi un long processus qui allait aboutir à l'élaboration laborieuse d'une convention internationale et dont l'intitulé est révélateur à plus d'un titre[13].

Cette convention, signée le 10 décembre 1982 à Montego Bay, en Jamaïque[14], est un exemple sans précédent dans le monde; ce qui lui a valu la qualification de «Constitution pour les océans»[15]. Car, «jamais dans les annales du droit international une convention n'avait été signée par 119 pays dès le premier jour où elle était ouverte à la signature»[16]. Non seulement elle a permis de résoudre les problèmes jadis liés à la

6. Il s'agit d'un régime relatif à l'exploitation des ressources maritimes, la protection du milieu marin et surtout de la navigation.
7. Jusque-là coutumières, parce qu'issues essentiellement de la pratique des Etats en la matière.
8. *Recueil des traités des Nations Unies*, vol. 499, p. 311.
9. *Ibid.*, vol. 450, p. 82.
10. *Ibid.*, vol. 516, p. 205.
11. *Ibid.*, vol. 559, p. 285.
12. Voir, en ce sens, le principe du consensualisme en droit international.
13. Convention des Nations Unies sur le droit de la mer.
14. Elle est entrée en vigueur le 16 novembre 1994.
15. Tommy Thon-Bee Koh, Président de la troisième conférence des Nations Unies sur le droit la mer, déclaration disponible sur http://www.un.org/Depts/los/convention_agreements/texts/koh_french.pdf (consultée le 30 août 2012).
16. *Ibid.*

délimitation des mers en précisant un certain nombre de notions apparues dans le droit coutumier telles que la mer territoriale, la zone économique exclusive ou le plateau continental, mais aussi elle a clairement défini les principes généraux régissant l'exploitation des ressources maritimes. En outre, l'un des apports fondamentaux de la convention de Montego Bay est la création du Tribunal international du droit de la mer, compétent pour connaître des litiges liés à ce domaine [17].

Ainsi, si le succès de la convention des Nations Unies sur le droit de la mer ne fait aucun doute quant à la résolution des problèmes inhérents aux revendications concurrentielles de territoire maritime, ses rédacteurs avaient pourtant laissé de côté les questions inhérentes à la criminalité maritime à l'instar du trafic de drogue, du trafic des migrants, du terrorisme maritime ou même de la piraterie. S'il est vrai que cette dernière reste régie par les articles 100 à 111 de la convention de Montego Bay, il est tout aussi vrai que les rédacteurs de ladite convention avaient «largement perçu la piraterie maritime comme un phénomène dépassé du XVIIIe siècle» [18].

Cependant, à côté de ces fléaux qui portent sérieusement atteinte à la sécurité et à la sûreté maritimes, une nouvelle forme de criminalité maritime est apparue mettant ainsi en exergue les limites du droit de la mer, ou à tout le moins l'obsolescence de certaines de ses dispositions. Les vols à main armée commis en mer sont exemplatifs à cet égard, car traduisant parfaitement une nouvelle forme de criminalité maritime et laissant transparaître ainsi un vide juridique. D'ailleurs, c'est là que réside toute la difficulté du droit à cerner les nouveaux concepts [19].

En effet, le vol à main armée en mer est un concept apparu récemment dans le vocabulaire juridique international. Sorti des fonts baptismaux par la résolution A.545(13) [20] de l'Organisation maritime internationale en date du 17 novembre 1983, ce concept restera privé de sens pendant presque deux décennies. Il a fallu attendre jusqu'en 2001 pour que la résolution A.922(22) du même organe en donne une première définition plutôt alambiquée. Les résolutions précédentes y relatives, notamment les résolutions 683(17) et 738(18), ne se sont contentées que de trouver un intitulé convenable [21].

---

17. Ce tribunal siège à Hambourg, en Allemagne.

18. Voir avant-propos de l'ouvrage sur *La piraterie maritime*, Berlin, Duncker & Humblot, 2010.

19. Problème d'adaptation du droit aux nouveaux enjeux.

20. La résolution A.545(13) est intitulée «Mesures à prendre pour prévenir la piraterie et les vols à main armée à l'encontre des navires».

21. Résolution A.683(17) du 6 novembre 1991 sur la «Prévention et répression des actes de piraterie et des vols à main armée à l'encontre des navires» et résolution A.738(18) du 4 novembre 1993 sur les «Mesures destinées à prévenir et à réprimer la piraterie et le vol à main armée à l'encontre des navires».

Le concept de vol à main armée en mer sera finalement défini aux termes de la résolution A.922(22) comme

> «tout acte illicite de violence ou de détention ou toute déprédation, ou menace de déprédation, autre qu'un acte de piraterie, commis contre un navire, ou contre des personnes ou des biens à son bord, dans une zone relevant de la juridiction d'un Etat compétent pour connaître de tels délits»[22].

Cette première définition révélera très vite ses limites et sera reprise pour être complétée par l'Accord régional de coopération sur la lutte contre la piraterie et l'attaque armée contre les navires en Asie, connu sous le sigle anglais de ReCAAP[23]. Elle sera modifiée lors de la réunion sous-régionale sur les actes de piraterie et les vols à main armée à l'encontre des navires dans la région de l'océan Indien occidental, du golfe d'Aden et de la mer Rouge, qui s'est tenue à Dar es-Salaam du 14 au 18 avril 2008. L'expression «à des fins privées» sera ajoutée à cette définition. De même, la formulation «dans les eaux intérieures, les eaux archipélagiques et la mer territoriale» figurant dans les résolutions précédentes remplace l'expression «dans une zone relevant de la juridiction d'un Etat». Cette nouvelle formulation tient compte du fait que la définition du vol à main armée contre les navires ne devrait pas s'appliquer aux actes commis au-delà de la mer territoriale.

Le Code de conduite concernant la répression des actes de piraterie et des vols à main armée à l'encontre des navires dans l'océan Indien occidental et le golfe d'Aden[24], annexé à la résolution 1025(26), redéfinit le «vol à main armée contre les navires» comme:

> «1. Tout acte illicite de violence ou de détention ou toute déprédation, ou menace de déprédation, autre qu'un acte de piraterie, commis à des fins privées contre un navire, ou contre des personnes ou des biens à son bord, dans les eaux intérieures, les eaux archipélagiques ou la mer territoriale d'un Etat;
>
> 2. tout acte ayant pour but d'inciter à commettre un acte défini ci-dessus ou commis dans l'intention de le faciliter.»

Ainsi, après avoir trouvé une définition qui sied à cette nouvelle forme de criminalité maritime, il reste donc à préciser son cadre juri-

22. Paragraphe 2.2 du «Recueil de règles pratiques pour la conduite des enquêtes sur les délits de piraterie et de vol à main armée à l'encontre des navires», adopté par la résolution A.922(22) du 29 novembre 2001.

23. Regional Cooperation Agreement on Combating Piracy and Armed Robbery against Ships in Asia.

24. Ce document est beaucoup plus connu sous l'appellation de Code de Djibouti.

dique. La question que l'on se pose ici est celle du droit applicable à l'infraction de vol à main armée en mer. Plus précisément, s'agit-il du droit international ou des droits internes ? Telles sont les interrogations auxquelles se sont attelées l'Organisation des Nations Unies (ONU), l'Organisation maritime internationale (OMI) et d'autres organisations régionales à l'instar de l'Union européenne (UE).

A la lecture des multiples textes juridiques adoptés à cet effet[25], l'on se rend compte que les deux ordres juridiques que sont notamment le droit international et les droits nationaux sont invoqués en vue de prévenir et de lutter contre les actes de piraterie et de vol à main armée en mer. Toutefois, en raison de l'imprécision et de l'inadéquation du droit international en matière de vol à main armée contre les navires (section 2), il convient de rechercher la solution juridique dans les droits internes (section 3).

SECTION 2 **L'IMPRÉCISION DU DROIT INTERNATIONAL EN MATIÈRE DE VOL À MAIN ARMÉE EN MER**

Sur le plan formel, le droit international public est constitué, aux termes de l'article 38 du Statut de la Cour internationale de Justice, des sources qualifiées aujourd'hui de classiques (paragraphe 1) et auxquelles il convient d'ajouter de nouvelles sources (paragraphe 2).

Paragraphe 1 **L'inadéquation des sources classiques**

Le vol à main armée en mer est un phénomène récent. Cependant, son caractère récent est plus manifeste au niveau de son énonciation et de sa qualification qu'au niveau de sa commission. Pendant longtemps, le vol à main armée commis contre les navires était assimilé à la piraterie. C'est ce qui explique l'inadéquation du droit international à cet acte. Cette inadéquation est perceptible tant sur le plan conventionnel (A) que sur les autres sources du droit international (B).

A. Les conventions internationales et le vol à main armée en mer

Le droit international est constitué principalement des conventions internationales. Celles-ci, qu'elles soient générales ou spéciales, établissent des « règles expressément reconnues par les Etats »[26].

25. Résolutions du Conseil de sécurité, de l'Assemblée générale de l'ONU ou de l'OMI ; directives de l'UE sur la piraterie et les vols à main armée.
26. Article 38 du Statut de la Cour internationale de Justice.

La question qui se pose ici est celle de savoir s'il existe une ou des conventions internationales dont l'objet ou même une disposition porte sur le vol à main armée. En l'absence d'une telle convention, la réponse doit être recherchée dans les conventions internationales qui régissent les différentes formes de criminalité. Il s'agit principalement de la convention sur le droit de la mer (i)) et de la convention pour la répression des actes illicites contre la navigation (ii)).

i) *La convention sur le droit de la mer*

Dans la convention de Montego Bay du 10 décembre 1982 sur le droit de la mer, on ne trouve aucune disposition réservée au vol à main armée commis en mer. Toutefois, en raison de la similitude qui existe entre vol à main armée contre les navires et piraterie[27], il y a lieu d'évoquer ici les contours de la piraterie maritime telle que prévue par ladite convention[28]. Cette convention qui, en réalité, reprend les dispositions de la convention de Genève de 1958 sur la haute mer[29] définit la piraterie comme:

> «*a)* tout acte illicite de violence ou de détention ou toute déprédation commis par l'équipage ou des passagers d'un navire ou d'un aéronef privé, agissant à des fins privées, et dirigé:
> i) contre un autre navire ou aéronef, ou contre des personnes ou des biens à leur bord, en haute mer;
> ii) contre un navire ou aéronef, des personnes ou des biens, dans un lieu ne relevant de la juridiction d'aucun Etat;
>
> *b)* tout acte de participation volontaire à l'utilisation d'un navire ou d'un aéronef, lorsque son auteur a connaissance de faits dont il découle que ce navire ou aéronef est un navire ou aéronef pirate;
>
> *c)* tout acte ayant pour but d'inciter à commettre les actes définis aux lettres *a)* ou *b)*, ou commis dans l'intention de les faciliter»[30].

A la lecture de cette disposition, l'on constate que la piraterie et le vol à main armée ont les mêmes éléments constitutifs du point de vue délictuel[31]. Cependant, la différence réside au niveau du lieu de leur commission; ce qui justifie la différence du régime juridique applicable. Pour la piraterie, il s'agit de «la haute mer» ou d'une «zone ne relevant de

27. Les deux infractions sont constituées des mêmes éléments matériels.
28. Voir notamment les articles 100 à 107, 110 et 111 de la convention de Montego Bay, qui régissent la piraterie.
29. Articles 14 à 23 relatifs à la piraterie.
30. Article 101 de la convention sur le droit de la mer.
31. Pour la définition du vol à main armée, voir *supra*.

la juridiction d'aucun Etat»[32]. Pour le vol à main armée contre les navires, il s'agissait d'une «zone relevant de la juridiction d'un Etat compétent pour connaître de tels délits»[33] avant d'être substituée par «les eaux intérieures, les eaux archipélagiques ou la mer territoriale d'un Etat»[34].

Au-delà de cette différence substantielle, il en est une autre qui n'est pas moins fondamentale. Il s'agit en l'occurrence du nombre de navires en cause. Pour la piraterie, l'article 101 de la convention de Montego Bay exige la présence d'au moins deux navires; ce qui n'est pas le cas pour le vol à main armée en mer. Celui-ci peut être commis contre un navire sans qu'il y ait besoin qu'il soit commis à partir d'un autre navire. Peu importe donc le moyen utilisé par les brigands (voleurs) pour atteindre leur cible[35].

La convention sur le droit de la mer n'évoquant ni implicitement ni explicitement le vol à main armée contre les navires, il convient de rechercher ce délit dans d'autres conventions internationales, telle celle réprimant les actes illicites contre la navigation maritime.

ii) *La convention pour la répression d'actes illicites contre la sécurité de la navigation maritime (SUA)*

La convention pour la répression d'actes illicites contre la sécurité de la navigation maritime a été conclue à Rome le 10 mars 1988. A l'instar de la convention sur le droit de la mer, cette convention ne fait pas allusion au vol à main armée commis contre les navires. Toutefois, eu égard à son objet et à son champ d'application très étendu, il convient de voir dans quelle mesure certaines de ses dispositions pourront être applicables aux actes de vol à main armée en mer. La convention SUA vise tout acte illicite de violence commis contre un navire ou une personne se trouvant à son bord[36]. Or, l'acte de violence commis en mer n'est pas sans rappeler la piraterie[37] ou le vol à main armée[38].

32. Paragraphe 2.2 de la résolution A.92(22) du 29 novembre 2001 portant adoption du «Recueil de règles pratiques pour la conduite des enquêtes sur les délits de piraterie et de vol à main armée à l'encontre des navires».

33. Paragraphe 2.2 du «Recueil de règles pratiques pour la conduite des enquêtes sur les délits de piraterie et de vol à main armée à l'encontre des navires», adopté par la résolution A.922(22) de l'OMI du 29 novembre 2001.

34. Paragraphe 2.2, alinéas 1 et 2, de la résolution A.1025(26) de l'OMI du 2 décembre 2009.

35. Ainsi, les voleurs peuvent utiliser des simples pirogues à pagaies, des pirogues à moteurs (skiffs) ou un navire pour commettre leur forfait. On peut même évoquer la nage quand il s'agit d'une courte distance (pour les navires se trouvant à quai par exemple).

36. Voir article 3, alinéa 1, paragraphes *a)* à *g)*, de la convention.

37. Article 15 de la convention sur la haute mer et article 101 de la convention sur le droit de la mer.

38. Résolution 2025(26) ayant adopté le Code de conduite de Djibouti.

Dès lors, le vol à main armée contre les navires en tant qu'acte de violence, de détention ou de déprédation est un acte illicite commis contre la sécurité de la navigation maritime en général et tomberait sous le coup des infractions prévues aux alinéas 1 et 2 de l'article 3 de la convention SUA. La convention SUA étant très générale quant à la formulation de son objet[39], elle a l'avantage de couvrir, à défaut de toutes les infractions commises en mer, du moins un grand nombre d'entre elles, y compris le vol à main armée. Mais, en même temps, sa généralité peut être source d'incertitude juridique dans la mesure où elle ne mentionne pas explicitement le vol à main armée. D'ailleurs, c'est ce que l'on remarque après un examen des autres sources classiques du droit international public.

B. La méconnaissance du vol à main armée par les autres sources classiques

Outre les conventions internationales, l'article 38 du Statut de la Cour internationale de Justice énumère comme sources du droit international la coutume internationale «comme preuve d'une pratique générale, acceptée comme étant le droit»[40], «les principes généraux de droit reconnus par les nations civilisées»[41], les décisions judiciaires et la doctrine des publicistes les plus qualifiés des différentes nations[42]. Dès lors, il importe de savoir si le vol à main armée commis contre les navires est prévu par l'une quelconque de ces sources sus évoquées. Les principes généraux de droit, la doctrine[43] tout comme

39. La convention porte sur «la répression des actes illicites contre la sécurité de la navigation maritime». Il s'agit ainsi de tous les actes, quels qu'ils soient, qui peuvent revêtir un caractère illicite ou qui sont qualifiés comme tels relativement à la sécurité de la navigation maritime.

40. Article 38, alinéa 1 *b)*, du Statut de la Cour internationale de Justice.

41. Article 38, alinéa 1 *c)*, du Statut de la Cour internationale de Justice.

42. L'article 38 sus-évoqué précise que la jurisprudence et la doctrine constituent des «moyens auxiliaires de détermination des règles de droit». Voir alinéa 1 *d)* du même article.

43. Il convient de rappeler ici que, en matière de vol à main armée en mer, la doctrine reste extrêmement pauvre. Aucun ouvrage, ni article, n'a porté à ce jour sur ce sujet. Il n'en existe que des évocations ponctuelles traitées en complément de la piraterie. Voir, entre autres contributions, R. Geiss et A. Petrig, *Piracy and Armed Robbery at Sea: The Legal Framework for Counter-Piracy Operations in Somalia and the Gulf of Aden*, Oxford University Press, 2011; S. Bateman, «Piracy and Armed Robbery against Ships in Indonesian Waters», dans Robert Cribb et Michele Ford (dir. publ.), *Indonesia beyond the Water's Edge: Managing an Archipelagic State, Singapore, Institute of Southeast Asian Studies (ISEAS)*, 2009, pp. 117-133; E. Frécon, «Piracy and Armed Robbery at Sea along the Malacca Straits: Initial Impressions from Fieldwork in the Riau Islands», dans Graham Gerard Ong-Webb (dir. publ.), *Piracy, Maritime Terrorism and Securing the Malacca Straits, Singapore: ISEAS*, Institute of Southeast

l'équité[44], ne seront pas analysés dans le cadre de cette réflexion en raison du faible rôle et de la place résiduelle qu'ils occupent comparativement aux autres sources. Seules la coutume et la jurisprudence internationales seront examinées relativement à la problématique du vol à main armée contre les navires.

i) *La coutume internationale*

En droit international comme en droit interne, la coutume est une règle de droit non écrite. Son existence exige la réunion de deux éléments, l'un matériel consistant en la répétition concordante d'actes et/ou de comportements des Etats dans les relations internationales[45] et l'autre psychologique traduisant le sentiment d'être lié par la pratique répétée des actes et/ou comportements[46], c'est-à-dire d'obéir à une règle de droit. C'est ce que résume l'alinéa 1 *b)* de l'article 38 du Statut de la Cour internationale de Justice en parlant de « pratique générale acceptée comme étant le droit ».

Cependant, a-t-on déjà observé des comportements des Etats ou même des organisations intergouvernementales reconnaissant et consacrant l'existence d'une règle de droit (coutumière) en matière de vol à main armée contre les navires ? Sans doute pas, pour la simple raison que la notion de vol à main armée en mer est une notion récente. Et à l'instar de tout concept nouveau, la criminalisation du vol à main armée en mer ne saurait (pour l'instant) constituer une règle coutumière car il nécessite une pratique concordante dans la durée et dans l'espace[47].

ii) *La jurisprudence internationale*

Les décisions judiciaires internationales sur le vol à main armée en mer sont tout aussi inexistantes que la coutume internationale dans ce domaine. Ici, le fait est que la jurisprudence internationale en tant que « moyen auxiliaire de détermination des règles de droit »[48] ne procède que d'un litige opposant les Etats et soumis à une juridiction judiciaire[49]

Asian Studies, 2006, pp. 68-83 ; W. Heintschel von Heinegg, « Repressing Piracy and Armed Robbery at Sea : Towards a New International Legal Regime », *Israel Yearbook on Human Rights*, n° 40, 2010, pp. 219-241 ss.

44. Voir à ce sujet l'article 38, alinéa 2, du Statut de la Cour internationale de Justice.

45. Le *consuetudo*.

46. L'*opinio juris sive necessitatis*.

47. A moins qu'il ne s'agisse d'une coutume sauvage dont le sentiment d'être lié précède toujours la pratique et ne nécessitant pas la durée pour sa consécration.

48. Alinéa 1 *d)* de l'article 38 précité.

49. Notamment la Cour internationale de Justice, la Cour pénale internationale ou le Tribunal international du droit de la mer selon le cas.

ou arbitrale[50] saisie en vue de rendre une décision ayant force obligatoire à l'égard des parties. Or, à ce jour, aucun litige de ce genre n'a été soumis à une juridiction internationale. D'ailleurs, il est même difficile d'assister à une situation où un litige opposerait deux ou plusieurs Etats en matière de vol à main armée ; à moins que ce ne soit le fait de l'Etat lui-même.

Car, aucun Etat ne soutiendrait l'action des voleurs ou pirates, fussent-ils ses ressortissants.

Par ailleurs, dans le cadre de sa compétence consultative, la Cour internationale de Justice est amenée souvent à rendre un avis consultatif quand une organisation internationale compétente venait à la saisir d'une question juridique relative au vol à main armée commis contre les navires.

Malheureusement, il n'en a rien été à ce jour, quoique l'OMI, l'Assemblée générale et le Conseil de sécurité des Nations Unies se montrent particulièrement préoccupés par les questions de piraterie et de vols à main armée en mer[51].

Finalement, les sources classiques du droit international telles que mentionnées à l'article 38, alinéas 1 et 2, du Statut de la Cour internationale de Justice ne font aucunement référence au concept de vol à main armée en mer.

C'est la raison pour laquelle il convient de le rechercher dans les sources dites nouvelles.

Paragraphe 2 **L'éveil de nouvelles sources du droit international concernant le vol à main armée en mer**

Les sources nouvelles du droit international public sont constituées essentiellement des actes unilatéraux des principaux acteurs de la société internationale que sont les Etats et les organisations internationales intergouvernementales. Les Etats n'ayant pas encore adopté des actes unilatéraux en matière de vol à main armée en mer, seuls seront examinés ici les actes unilatéraux des organisations internationales et particulièrement les résolutions des organes principaux de l'ONU d'une part (A) et celles adoptées dans le cadre de l'OMI d'autre part (B).

50. Cour permanente d'arbitrage ou tribunal arbitral constitué à cet effet.

51. Voir à ce sujet les activités des organes de l'OMI et particulièrement les résolutions du Comité de sécurité maritime (MSC1./Circ.1404, MSC1./Circ. 1334...) et celles du Conseil de sécurité sur les actes de piraterie et de vol à main armée en mer (résolution 2039 du 29 février 2012, résolution 2018 du 31 octobre 2011...).

A. Les résolutions des principaux organes de l'ONU relatives aux vols à main armée

Depuis la recrudescence des actes de violence, de déprédation et de prise d'otages en mer dans certaines régions du monde[52], l'ONU a connu une activité intense tant au niveau du Conseil de sécurité qu'au niveau de l'Assemblée générale.

Sur le fondement du chapitre VII de la Charte des Nations Unies, le Conseil de sécurité a été amené à la suite de la résurgence de la piraterie à adopter un certain nombre de résolutions qui font la place belle au vol à main armée en mer[53]. En moins de quatre années seulement[54], le Conseil de sécurité des Nations Unies a adopté une dizaine de résolutions relatives « à la piraterie et au vol à main armée en mer ». Parmi ces différentes résolutions, quatre ont été adoptées en 2008[55], une en 2009[56], deux en 2010[57], trois en 2011[58] et une en 2012[59].

De même, l'Assemblée générale des Nations Unies a eu à se prononcer, à la suite du Conseil de sécurité, sur les questions relatives à la piraterie et au vol à main armée en mer. A travers notamment les résolutions 64/71[60] et 66/231[61], l'Assemblée générale des Nations Unies a reconnu et affirmé la différence qui existe entre piraterie et vol à main armée en mer lorsqu'elle énumère « la piraterie, les vols à main armée commis en mer, la contrebande, les actes terroristes contre des navires, des installations au large et d'autres intérêts maritimes » comme activités qui compromettent la sûreté et la sécurité de la navigation maritime[62] ou qui constituent des menaces à celles-ci[63].

Toutes ces résolutions portent sur les actes de piraterie et les vols à main armée commis contre les navires. Leur quintessence réside dans le fait qu'elles autorisent les Etats :

> « *a)* A entrer dans les eaux territoriales ... afin de réprimer les actes de piraterie et les vols à main armée en mer, d'une manière

52. Il s'agit principalement de l'océan Indien occidental, du golfe d'Aden, du détroit de Malacca, des côtes somaliennes et du golfe de Guinée.
53. Quasiment toutes les références à la piraterie sont immédiatement suivies du concept de « vols à main armée en mer ».
54. Précisément entre 2008 et 2012.
55. S/RES/1816 (2008) du 2 juin, S/RES/1838 (2008) du 7 octobre, S/RES/1846 (2008) du 2 décembre et S/RES/1851 (2008) du 16 décembre.
56. S/RES/1897 (2009) du 30 novembre.
57. S/RES/1918 (2010) du 27 avril et S/RES/1950 (2010) du 23 novembre.
58. S/RES/1976 (2011) du 11 avril, S/RES/2015 (2011) du 24 octobre, S/RES/2018 (2011) du 31 octobre et S/RES/2020 (2011) du 22 novembre.
59. S/RES/2039 (2012) du 29 février.
60. A/RES/64/71 du 12 mars 2010.
61. A/RES/66/231 du 5 avril 2012.
62. Préambule (par. 20) de la résolution A/RES/64/71 du 12 mars 2010.
63. Préambule (par. 21) de la résolution A/RES/66/231 du 5 avril 2012.

conforme à l'action autorisée en haute mer en cas de piraterie en application du droit international applicable; *b)* A utiliser, dans les eaux territoriales ..., d'une manière conforme à l'action autorisée en haute mer en cas de piraterie en application du droit international applicable, tous moyens nécessaires pour réprimer les actes de piraterie et les vols à main armée.»

Toutefois, le Conseil de sécurité des Nations Unies affirme par ailleurs que les dispositions des différentes résolutions relatives aux actes de vol à main armée (et de piraterie) s'appliquent à la seule situation de la Somalie[64] et n'affectent pas les droits, obligations ou responsabilités des Etats dérivant du droit international. De même, ces différentes résolutions qui établissent des mesures destinées à prévenir les actes de vol à main armée (et de piraterie) ne sauraient être regardées comme établissant un droit international coutumier en la matière[65]. Ainsi, à côté de ces activités de l'Assemblée générale et du Conseil de sécurité des Nations Unies sur les actes de piraterie et de vol à main armée en mer, il convient de rappeler celles de l'OMI qui joue un rôle de premier plan dans ce domaine.

B. Les résolutions de l'OMI en matière de vol à main armée en mer

S'il y a une institution qui a joué et qui joue encore un rôle prépondérant en matière de vol à main armée en mer, c'est bien l'OMI. C'est elle qui a mis au grand jour le concept de vol à main armée en mer[66]. Deux de ses organes, à savoir l'Assemblée et le Comité pour la sécurité maritime, sont particulièrement actifs dans ce domaine.

Sur le fondement de l'article 15 *j)* de la convention portant création de l'OMI, l'Assemblée de cette organisation est compétente pour adopter des règles et des directives concernant la sécurité maritime, la prévention de la pollution des mers par les navires et la lutte contre cette pollution. Le vol à main armée contre les navires constituant une

---

64. En raison notamment de la défaillance de cet Etat et de son incapacité à contrôler son territoire maritime et terrestre servant ainsi de refuge aux pilleurs des navires.

65. Paragraphe 10 de la résolution 2020 du 22 novembre 2011, paragraphe 8 de la résolution 1950 du 23 novembre 2010, Préambule (par. 4) de la résolution 1918 du 23 avril 2010, paragraphe 8 de la résolution 1897 du 30 novembre 2009, paragraphe 10 de la résolution 1851 du 16 décembre 2008, paragraphe 7 de la résolution 1838 du 7 octobre 2008 et paragraphe 9 de la résolution 1816 du 6 novembre 2008.

66. Voir *supra*.

menace à la sécurité maritime, l'Assemblée de l'OMI a eu à adopter un certain nombre de résolutions y relatives[67].

Le Comité pour la sécurité maritime a pour sa part adopté des textes à caractère juridique (quoique non contraignants) en rapport avec la prévention et/ou la répression du vol à main armée perpétré à l'encontre des navires. Parmi ces textes, on peut citer les innombrables circulaires dont les plus récentes sont les circulaires MSC.1/Circ.1333[68], MSC.1/Circ.1334[69], MSC.1/Circ.1335[70], MSC.1/Circ.1339[71] et MSC.1/Circ.1404[72]. Toutes ces circulaires du Comité pour la sécurité maritime traitent du vol à main armée (ainsi que des actes de piraterie) au large des côtes somaliennes et dans le golfe de Guinée. A côté de ces nombreuses circulaires, il y a évidemment la résolution MSC.305(87) du 17 mai 2010 portant sur les «Directives relatives aux procédures opérationnelles pour la diffusion des renseignements sur la sécurité maritime qui concernent les actes de piraterie et les opérations de lutte contre la piraterie»[73].

Cependant, on peut douter de la valeur juridique opérationnelle et contraignante de tous ces textes adoptés par l'OMI dans le cadre de la prévention et de la répression des actes de vol à main armée contre les navires. Pour autant, ils n'en restent pas moins des actes juridiques destinés à fixer les principes directeurs ou l'établissement des codes de bonne conduite en matière de vol à main armée en mer. En outre, ces textes servent de source d'inspiration à l'endroit des Etats. Dès lors, tous ces actes unilatéraux de l'OMI (résolutions et circulaires), qu'ils émanent de l'Assemblée ou du Comité pour la sécurité maritime, relèveraient de la «soft law».

Les résolutions du Conseil de sécurité des Nations Unies[74] sont dou-

67. A.545(13), A.683(17), A.738(18) 1993, A.922(22) 2001, A.1002(25), A.1025(26), A.1026(26), A.1044(27).

68. Du 26 juin 2009 sur les «Recommandations aux gouvernements concernant la prévention et la répression des actes de piraterie et de vol à main armée à l'encontre des navires».

69. Du 23 juin 2009 sur les «Principes directeurs destinés aux propriétaires, aux exploitants, aux capitaines et aux équipages des navires concernant la prévention et la répression des actes de piraterie et de vols à main armée à l'encontre des navires».

70. Du 29 septembre 2009 sur les «Meilleures pratiques de gestion pour décourager la piraterie dans le golfe d'Aden et au large des côtes somaliennes, élaborées par le secteur maritime».

71. Du 14 septembre 2011 sur les «Best Management Practices for Protection against Somalia based Piracy».

72. Du 23 mai 2011 sur le «Guideline to Assist in the Investigation of the Crime of Piracy and Armed Robbery against Ships».

73. Même si cette résolution ne mentionne pas explicitement le vol à main armée dans son intitulé, elle le traite quand même dans son dispositif.

74. Sur la valeur juridique des résolutions du Conseil de sécurité des Nations Unies, voir M.-P. Lanfranchi, «La valeur juridique en France des résolutions du Conseil de sécurité», *Annuaire français de droit international (AFDI)*, vol. 43,

blement limitatives dans le temps[75] et dans l'espace[76], en même temps que le droit conventionnel et le droit coutumier restent muets sur les questions du vol à main armée contre les navires. D'où la nécessité de rechercher un cadre juridique adapté et efficace.

SECTION 3 LA QUÊTE D'UN CADRE JURIDIQUE ADAPTÉ AUX ACTES DE VOL À MAIN ARMÉE EN MER

Constatant un vide juridique au niveau international en ce qui concerne les actes de vol à main armée commis contre les navires, la communauté internationale s'est évertuée à rechercher des solutions dans les différents ordres juridiques nationaux. La prégnance des droits nationaux quant à la lutte contre les vols à main armée contre les navires (paragraphe 1) doit cependant tenir compte des dispositions du droit international pertinentes en la matière (paragraphe 2).

Paragraphe 1 **La prégnance des droits nationaux dans la prévention et la répression des actes de vol à main armée contre les navires**

Ce qui caractérise le vol à main armée contre les navires et le distingue de la piraterie, c'est principalement son lieu de commission. Le vol à main armée est un délit commis dans une zone relevant de la compétence d'un Etat territorialement compétent pour connaître un tel délit[77] ou plus exactement un délit commis dans les eaux intérieures, les eaux archipélagiques et la mer territoriale d'un Etat[78]. De ce fait, il incombe à l'Etat côtier de prendre toutes les mesures en vue de prévenir et de réprimer les actes de vol à main armée contre les navires. Ces mesures devront alors procéder de la mise en place d'un dispositif juridique efficace (A) qui doit lui-même tenir compte des dispositions du droit international relatives à la considération de la personne humaine (B).

1997, pp. 31-57. Voir également dans ce sens et dans le même *Annuaire*, M. Virally, « La valeur juridique des recommandations des organisations internationales », vol. 2, 1956, pp. 66-96.

75. Une période de six mois au début, puis de douze mois renouvelables en accord avec l'autorisation du Gouvernement fédéral de transition somalien, exprimée par lettre datée du 27 février 2008 et adressée au Président du Conseil de sécurité, puis réitérée dans des lettres ultérieures.

76. La Somalie au départ et toute la région du golfe d'Aden par la suite.

77. Paragraphe 2.2 de l'annexe de la résolution A.922 de l'OMI du 29 novembre 2001. Voir également *supra*.

78. Paragraphe 2.2, alinéa 1, de l'annexe de la résolution A.1025(26) de l'OMI du 2 décembre 2009.

A. La mise en place d'un dispositif juridique efficace en vue de prévenir et de réprimer les actes de vol à main armée contre les navires

Sur le fondement du principe de souveraineté, les Etats sont libres d'organiser et de gérer leurs affaires internes comme il leur semble bon. Toutefois, ils doivent veiller à ce que les activités menés sur leurs territoires ne soient pas préjudiciables aux autres Etats[79]. Dès lors, et en tant que garant de l'ordre et de la sécurité au niveau national, un Etat est amené à mettre en place un dispositif juridique à cet effet. Dans cet ordre d'idées, l'on assiste généralement à l'élaboration de législations et de réglementations nationales là où il n'en existe pas[80]. Cette élaboration a pour but d'ériger en infraction les actes ou les comportements qui troublent l'ordre public, ou qui portent atteinte à la sécurité des personnes et des biens. Les actes de vol à main armée contre les navires rentrent dans cette catégorie.

Mais, aussi surprenant que cela puisse paraître, nombre d'Etats, sinon quasiment tous, ne disposent (pour le moment) ni de lois ni de règlements en vue de prévenir et de réprimer les actes de vol à main armée contre les navires[81] se trouvant dans leurs eaux intérieures, leurs eaux archipélagiques ou leur mer territoriale. Pourtant, les mêmes actes commis sur la terre ferme sont réprimés à travers des dispositions à caractère pénal. C'est la raison pour laquelle le Conseil de sécurité des Nations Unies

> «note avec préoccupation que le manque de moyens et l'absence de législation interne permettant de détenir et poursuivre les pirates présumés après leur capture ont empêché de mener une action internationale plus vigoureuse contre les pirates agissant au large des côtes ... et, dans certains cas, contraint à libérer les pirates sans les avoir traduits en justice, alors même que les éléments à charge étaient suffisants pour justifier des poursuites»[82]

---

79. Voir à ce sujet l'affaire du *Détroit de Corfou (Royaume-Uni de Grande-Bretagne et d'Irlande du Nord c. Albanie)*, CIJ, arrêt du 9 avril 1949, p. 22. Voir également dans le même sens le principe 21 de la Déclaration de Stockholm de 1972 et le principe 2 de la Déclaration de Rio de 1992 sur l'utilisation non dommageable du territoire.

80. L'élaboration de la législation et de la réglementation doit toujours être faite en conformité avec les dispositions de la Constitution, en tant que norme suprême dans l'ordre juridique étatique. Dans le cas contraire, elles peuvent être annulées devant la juridiction compétente en matière constitutionnelle.

81. Qu'il s'agisse de leurs propres navires ou des navires battant pavillon étranger qui se trouveraient dans les eaux relevant de la compétence de l'Etat côtier.

82. Paragraphe 8 (préambule) de la résolution 1897 du 30 novembre 2009 du Conseil de sécurité des Nations Unies.

ou encore que «le droit interne de certains Etats n'érige pas la piraterie en infraction ou ne contient pas les dispositions de procédure nécessaires pour engager efficacement des poursuites pénales contre les personnes soupçonnées de piraterie»[83].

S'il est vrai que les résolutions du Conseil de sécurité des Nations Unies ne parlent que de la piraterie, il est tout aussi vrai qu'elles renvoient implicitement aux actes de vol à main armée en mer; eu égard à la carence de législations dans ce domaine. C'est ce qui a amené le Conseil de sécurité[84] à encourager vivement les Etats côtiers à

> «ériger en infraction le fait de s'emparer d'un navire ou d'en exercer le contrôle par violence ou menace de violence ou toute autre forme d'intimidation, à établir leur compétence à l'égard de ces infractions, et à accepter la remise des personnes responsables ou soupçonnées de tels actes»[85].

La prévention et la répression du vol à main armée contre les navires incombe ainsi aux Etats qui disposent des eaux intérieures, des eaux archipélagiques et d'une mer territoriale dont la largeur peut s'étendre jusqu'à douze milles marins mesurés à partir des lignes de base établies conformément à la convention sur le droit de la mer[86]. Ainsi, tout Etat côtier devrait adopter des lois devant ériger en infraction les actes de vol à main armée commis contre les navires se trouvant dans les eaux relevant de sa compétence territoriale[87].

B. La compétence juridictionnelle de l'Etat côtier en matière de vol à main armée contre les navires

Tenant toujours compte des résolutions du Conseil de sécurité des Nations Unies sur les actes de piraterie et de vol à main armée contre les navires, tout Etat côtier devrait établir sa compétence juridictionnelle sur ses eaux intérieures, ses eaux archipélagiques ainsi que sur sa mer territoriale. C'est parce que ces trois zones font partie du territoire maritime de l'Etat dont les côtes en sont adjacentes que celui-ci est normalement tenu de veiller à ce que l'ordre et la sécurité y règnent au même titre que sur son territoire terrestre ou aérien[88].

---

83. Paragraphe 14 (préambule) de la résolution 1918 (2010) du Conseil de sécurité des Nations Unies.

84. Tout comme l'Organisation maritime internationale.

85. Paragraphe 8 de la résolution 1897 du 30 novembre 2009 du Conseil de sécurité des Nations Unies.

86. Voir les articles 3 et 4 de la convention du 10 décembre 1982 sur le droit de la mer.

87. Pour la compétence personnelle, la convention sur le droit de la mer règle le problème en instituant la loi du pavillon.

88. Voir *supra* note 79.

Cependant, après avoir incriminé les actes de vol à main armée contre les navires dans leur différent ordre juridique[89], c'est-à-dire après avoir pris des lois et des règlements y relatifs, les Etats côtiers doivent établir la compétence de leur juridiction au niveau interne. En principe, dans chaque Etat, il devra être défini la procédure, ainsi que les autorités compétentes pour constater et réprimer les infractions[90]. Certes, il s'agira des autorités judiciaires et tous ceux qui leur prêtent secours et assistance dans l'accomplissement de leur mission, à savoir rendre justice[91]. Dès lors, les Etats côtiers seront en mesure de poursuivre et d'arrêter les auteurs d'actes de vol à main armée contre les navires. S'il s'agit d'un navire battant pavillon de l'Etat sur le territoire duquel le vol a été commis, il n'y aura pas de difficultés à faire arrêter et condamner les voleurs dans la mesure où la procédure relève entièrement de la compétence exclusive dudit Etat. Par contre, s'il s'agit d'un navire étranger, la question semble être plus complexe en raison notamment d'une éventuelle concurrence de compétences entre l'Etat côtier et l'Etat du pavillon.

En effet, la convention de Montego Bay reconnaît aux navires de tous les Etats, avec ou sans littoral, le droit de passage inoffensif dans la mer territoriale[92]. C'est ce droit de passage inoffensif qui se trouve à la base d'une compétence concurrentielle entre l'Etat côtier d'une part et l'Etat du pavillon d'autre part. En pareille circonstance, c'est-à-dire au cas où un vol à main armée venait à être commis contre un navire étranger, le principe posé à l'article 27, alinéa 1, donne compétence à l'Etat du pavillon[93]. Toutefois (et c'est là que la concurrence intervient), l'Etat côtier dispose également d'une compétence pour intervenir sur le navire étranger en vue de réprimer, conformément à son droit interne, toutes les formes d'infractions commises à bord, y compris le vol à main armée. Cette compétence repose sur un double fondement. Tout d'abord, l'Etat côtier n'est habilité à intervenir sur un navire étranger que si celui-ci, qui se trouve dans la mer territoriale, est parti de ses eaux intérieures[94]. Ensuite (ce qui constitue une exception au principe posé à l'article 27, alinéa 1, ci-dessus), l'Etat côtier peut intervenir sur un navire étranger si les conséquences de l'infraction s'étendent sur l'Etat côtier[95] ou si l'in-

---

89. Par une loi ou à travers les dispositions du Code pénal.
90. Objet des Codes sur le droit pénal et la procédure pénale.
91. Les agents et les officiers de police judiciaire notamment.
92. Voir article 17 de la convention de Montego Bay.
93. Article 27, alinéa 1: «L'Etat côtier ne devrait pas exercer sa juridiction pénale à bord d'un navire étranger passant dans la mer territoriale pour y procéder à une arrestation ou à l'exécution d'actes d'instruction à la suite d'une infraction pénale commise à bord pendant le passage...»
94. Article 27, alinéa 2, de la convention de Montego Bay.
95. Article 27, alinéa 1 *a)*, de la convention de Montego Bay.

fraction est de nature à troubler la paix du pays ou l'ordre de la mer territoriale[96] ou, enfin, si le capitaine du navire ou les autorités diplomatiques ou consulaires de l'Etat du pavillon en font la demande[97].

Ainsi, l'existence de lois définissant de façon assez large l'infraction de vol à main armée en mer ainsi que la détermination précise des autorités compétentes et disposées pour agir en vue de prévenir et réprimer une telle infraction constitueront une étape importante à la lutte contre cette forme de criminalité maritime. D'ailleurs, c'est ce qui ressort en filigrane de la résolution 1897 quand elle énonce « que les Etats doivent ériger la piraterie en infraction dans leur droit interne et envisager favorablement de poursuivre s'il y a lieu les pirates présumés, dans le respect du droit international »[98]. Le respect du droit international par les droits internes dans la répression du vol à main armée contre les navires est un aspect important qu'il ne faudra guère négliger.

Paragraphe 2 **Le respect du droit international en matière de lutte contre les actes de vol à main armée contre les navires**

L'incrimination des actes de vol à main armée contre les navires dans les droits internes entraîne comme conséquence l'établissement des règles relatives à la poursuite des voleurs[99], à leur arrestation et, éventuellement, leur condamnation. Tout cela doit être fait en tenant compte des considérations liées au respect de la dignité et de la vie des auteurs d'actes de vol à main armée contre les navires. La préservation de la vie des hommes et le respect de leur dignité sont généralement prévus par des règles juridiques internationales se rapportant soit au domaine des droits de l'homme (A), soit à celui du droit humanitaire (B).

A. Le respect des droits de l'homme en matière de répression du vol à main armée contre les navires

Les droits de l'homme visent généralement à la reconnaissance et au respect de la dignité de la personne humaine. Ils s'appliquent à tout être humain, quelles que soient sa nationalité, sa religion, son origine ethnique ou sociale. De même, ces droits qui revêtent un caractère fondamental sont reconnus et applicables à des individus,

96. Article 27, alinéa 1 *b)*, de la convention de Montego Bay.
97. Article 27, alinéa 1 *c)*, de la convention de Montego Bay.
98. Paragraphe 8 de la résolution 1897 du 30 novembre 2009 du Conseil de sécurité des Nations Unies.
99. Pilleurs des navires ou preneurs d'otages dans les navires.

quels que soient les forfaits qu'ils ont commis ou qu'ils commettent dans une société donnée. Leur importance et leur universalité sont tellement affirmées que l'on ne peut renoncer à leur bénéfice, ni en être privé.

Les droits de l'homme sont universels parce que tous les êtres humains ont des droits fondamentaux que l'on ne peut nier sous peine de nier l'humanité elle-même. Partout et en tout temps, l'on doit respecter l'intégrité de la personne humaine. Dès lors, les êtres humains ont le droit à des conditions de vie satisfaisantes[100]; en même temps, ils ne doivent pas être torturés, tués, mutilés ou être réduits en esclavage sous prétexte d'avoir commis un crime, fût-il grave.

Plusieurs textes juridiques consacrent les différents droits reconnus à l'endroit de la personne humaine. Et c'est ainsi que, sur le plan universel, l'on peut citer, entre autres instruments juridiques, la déclaration universelle des droits de l'homme adoptée par l'Assemblée générale des Nations Unies[101], les deux pactes internationaux relatifs d'une part aux droits civils et politiques et d'autre part aux droits économiques, sociaux et culturels de 1966, la convention contre la torture et autres peines ou traitements cruels, inhumains ou dégradants de 1984...

Ces instruments juridiques internationaux à caractère universel doivent être complétés par des conventions régionales relatives aux droits de l'homme. Il s'agit notamment de la convention européenne des droits de l'homme de 1950, de la convention américaine relative aux droits de l'homme de 1969 ou encore de la charte africaine des droits de l'homme et des peuples de 1981. Tous ces textes juridiques de portée universelle ou régionale proclament un certain nombre de droits qui s'imposent aux Etats et auxquels ceux-ci ne peuvent déroger. C'est le cas notamment du droit à la vie, de l'interdiction de la torture, du recours à des peines et traitements inhumains ou dégradants, de l'esclavage, de la servitude...

Cependant, le vol à main armée commis contre les navires, parce qu'il constitue un acte de violence donnant parfois lieu à des prises d'otages, fait partie de ces types d'infractions qui mériteraient la qualification de crime grave. Toutefois, autant les victimes sont des êtres humains, autant les délinquants (pilleurs de navires ou preneurs d'otages en l'espèce) le sont et mériteraient tout le respect inhérent à la personne humaine quant aux conditions de leur détention ou le sort qui leur sera réservé à la suite de leur arrestation.

Dès lors, les Etats doivent tenir compte des aspects inhérents à la protection des droits de l'homme dans leur législation relative à la préven-

100. Accès au soin, droit à l'éducation, à la culture...
101. Elle a été adoptée le 10 décembre 1948.

tion et à la répression des actes de vol à main armée contre les navires se trouvant dans leurs eaux intérieures, leurs eaux archipélagiques ou leur mer territoriale. Cela emporte comme conséquence que les Etats sont tenus de respecter les droits de l'homme en toutes circonstances, c'est-à-dire même en période de trouble ou de conflit armé.

B. La conformité au droit international humanitaire des mesures de répression

A l'instar du droit international des droits de l'homme, le droit international humanitaire vise à protéger la personne humaine dans un contexte particulier.

> «Par droit international humanitaire, il faut entendre l'ensemble des principes, des usages et des règles qui obligent actuellement les nations envers elles-mêmes et envers les autres nations afin de tenir compte, en tout temps, du respect qui est dû à la personne humaine.» [102]

L'évocation du droit international humanitaire en matière de vol à main armée contre les navires peut a priori être surprenante. Car, le lien qu'on peut trouver entre ces deux domaines ne semble pas évident. Pourtant, le droit international humanitaire a toute sa place dans la problématique liée à la considération ou même à la protection de la personne humaine. A ce sujet, deux raisons peuvent justifier l'exigence de la conformité des législations nationales relatives à la répression d'infraction de vol à main armée contre les navires au droit international humanitaire.

Tout d'abord, il convient de rappeler ici que le droit international humanitaire est complémentaire au droit international des droits de l'homme. Ces deux disciplines visent à protéger la vie et la dignité de la personne humaine. Alors que les droits de l'homme sont conçus pour s'appliquer dans les situations de paix, le droit humanitaire s'applique dans les situations de conflit armé. Les règles qu'il consacre imposent des obligations à toutes les parties à un conflit et sont contenues pour l'essentiel dans les quatre conventions de Genève du 12 août 1949 [103] et leurs protocoles additionnels [104].

---

102. M. H. Coursier, «Evolution du droit international humanitaire», *Recueil des cours*, tome 99 (1960), pp. 357-466.

103. La première convention s'applique aux blessés et malades dans les forces armées en campagne, la deuxième aux blessés, malades et naufragés des forces armées sur mer, la troisième se rapporte aux prisonniers de guerre et enfin la quatrième s'applique aux personnes civiles en temps de guerre.

104. Deux protocoles avaient été adoptés en 1977 sur la protection des victimes des conflits armés internationaux et non internationaux, auxquels il faut ajouter le protocole de 2005 sur la question des emblèmes.

C'est surtout le Protocole II relatif à la protection des victimes des conflits armés non internationaux qui est visé ici. Car, l'infraction de vol à main armée, telle qu'elle ressort de la définition de la résolution A.2025(26) de l'OMI, relèverait de la compétence exclusive de l'Etat côtier. Et donc, en période de conflit armé interne, les règles du droit humanitaire s'appliqueraient. Or, à l'observation, l'on se rend compte que les pilleurs de navires et les preneurs d'otages dans les eaux relevant de la compétence d'un Etat côtier[105] sont plus actifs dans les Etats qui connaissent une situation de conflit armé interne ou dont le gouvernement n'est plus à mesure d'assurer l'ordre, la stabilité et la sécurité des personnes et des biens. Dans ce dernier cas, on parle d'Etat défaillant.

De nos jours, nombre d'Etats connaissent des situations telles qu'ils n'arrivent pas à contrôler la totalité de leur territoire. Les pirates et les voleurs ont très vite compris l'avantage que leur procure cette situation surtout lorsqu'il s'agit d'un Etat côtier. La Somalie est aujourd'hui le prototype d'Etat côtier défaillant à la merci des criminels des mers[106]. Ainsi, tout Etat qui se trouverait dans la situation actuelle de la Somalie ou plus concrètement dans une situation de paix ou de conflit armé doit « faire en sorte que les personnes qui se livrent à la piraterie et aux vols à main armée en mer soient poursuivies et, en cas de condamnation, punies en tenant dûment compte des règles et principes généralement reconnus du droit international »[107], lesquels règles et principes font référence aux droits de l'homme et au droit humanitaire.

SECTION 4 **CONCLUSION**

Au regard des événements qui se déroulent dans les différentes eaux internationales et internes depuis quelques années et que certains auteurs qualifient de résurgence de la piraterie, il y a lieu de rallonger la liste des infractions caractérisant la criminalité en mer. A côté de la piraterie de type classique, du trafic des stupéfiants, du trafic illicite des migrants clandestins, du terrorisme en mer, il existe une autre forme de criminalité nouvelle à l'apparence mais dont les manifestations ne diffèrent guère de la piraterie telle que définie à l'article 101 de la

105. Certains commettent leurs forfaits ailleurs (haute mer ou mer territoriale d'un autre Etat) et utilisent le territoire de l'Etat défaillant comme lieu de refuge.

106. La situation de la Somalie a retenu l'attention particulière du Conseil de sécurité des Nations Unies qui a adopté plusieurs résolutions portant sur les actes de piraterie et de vol à main armée au large des côtes somaliennes.

107. Paragraphe 16 du préambule de la résolution 2039 du 29 février 2012.

convention sur le droit de la mer. Il s'agit en l'occurrence du vol à main armée contre les navires.

La ressemblance entre le vol à main armée contre les navires et la piraterie est tellement patente que quasiment tous les auteurs qui se sont intéressés à la piraterie ou au vol à main armée en mer ont considéré globalement ces deux types d'infractions et finissent toujours par les confondre dans l'analyse qu'ils en font. Peut-être que certains auteurs se basent sur la flagrance des éléments matériels de leur commission [108], peut-être que d'autres sont influencés par la linéarité ou la complémentarité qui existe entre les deux infractions [109], peut-être enfin que d'autres se sont basés sur les nombreuses résolutions du Conseil de sécurité sur les actes de piraterie qui font la tragique confusion en

> «*réaffirmant* que le droit international, tel que consacré dans la Convention des Nations Unies sur le droit de la mer du 10 décembre 1982, en particulier ses articles 100, 101 et 105, définit le cadre juridique de la lutte contre la piraterie et le vol à main armée en mer, parmi d'autres activités maritimes» [110];

toujours est-il que l'infraction de piraterie reste distincte de celle de vol à main armée, quoique commis contre un navire.

Certes, sur le plan pratique, la distinction entre piraterie et vol à main armée en mer ne tient qu'à un fil: le lieu de leur commission. Pour la piraterie, il s'agit de la haute mer ou d'un espace maritime ne relevant de la juridiction d'aucun Etat [111], tandis que, pour le vol à main armée, il s'agit du même acte commis dans une zone relevant de la compétence de la juridiction d'un Etat. Il s'agit plus précisément des eaux intérieures, des eaux archipélagiques et de la mer territoriale. Toutefois, sur le plan juridique, cette légère différence définitionnelle emporte des conséquences importantes quant à la mise œuvre de ces deux concepts. Cela signifie en d'autres termes que les auteurs d'acte de violence, de

108. Dans les deux cas (piraterie et vol à main armée), ce sont des actes de violence, de détention ou de déprédation commis à des fins privées contre un navire, son équipage, les personnes ou les biens se trouvant à son bord. Voir, pour la piraterie, article 101 de la convention sur le droit de la mer; pour le vol à main armée, résolution A.2025(26) de l'OMI.

109. Les pilleurs de navire utilisent indistinctement les espaces maritimes internationaux et sous juridiction étatique. Généralement, ils quittent la haute mer vers la mer territoriale ou les eaux intérieures des Etats, ou vont d'une mer territoriale vers une autre mer territoriale moins gardée et leur servant de refuge.

110. Paragraphe 4 du préambule de la résolution 2039 du 29 février 2012, paragraphe 6 du préambule de la résolution 2018 du 31 octobre 2011, paragraphe 6 du préambule de la résolution 2015 du 24 octobre 2011, paragraphe 8 du préambule de la résolution 1976 du 11 avril 2011 et paragraphe 3 du préambule de la résolution 1918 du 27 avril 2010.

111. Article 15 de la convention sur la haute mer de 1958 et article 101 de la convention sur le droit de la mer du 10 décembre 1982.

détention ou de déprédation commis à des fins privées contre un navire (contre son équipage, des personnes ou des biens se trouvant à son bord) ne seront pas régis par les mêmes règles de droit.

Si l'auteur d'un tel acte a attaqué le navire en haute mer ou dans une zone internationale, il commet un acte de piraterie telle que réglementée par les dispositions pertinentes du droit international, et notamment la convention sur le droit de la mer[112]. Si, en revanche, l'auteur d'un tel acte a agi contre un navire se trouvant dans une zone sous juridiction d'un Etat (eaux intérieures, eaux archipélagiques et mer territoriale), il commet un acte de vol à main armée qui n'est régi — pour l'instant — par aucune disposition du droit international, ni sur le plan conventionnel ni même sur le plan coutumier.

Cette situation de non-réglementation du vol à main armée en mer, qui semble à bien des égards normale parce qu'elle relève essentiellement des droits nationaux, a amené la doctrine à la suite de la communauté internationale à assimiler les actes de vol à main armée contre les navires aux actes de piraterie. Le Conseil de sécurité des Nations Unies, dont les nombreuses résolutions y relatives constituent aujourd'hui le fondement juridique en matière de prévention et de répression du vol à main armée en mer, crée un quiproquo en affirmant et «*réaffirmant* que … la Convention des Nations Unies sur le droit de la mer du 10 décembre 1982, en particulier ses articles 100, 101 et 105, définit le cadre juridique de la lutte contre … le vol à main armée en mer, parmi d'autres activités maritimes»[113].

Or, les dispositions de la convention sur le droit de la mer ne définissent, ni dans la lettre ni même dans l'esprit, le cadre juridique du vol à main armée en mer. De même, la convention pour la répression d'actes illicites contre la sécurité de la navigation maritime tout comme celle relative à la prise d'otages ou au terrorisme en mer ne semblent y faire allusion. Est-ce à dire pour autant qu'il existe un vide juridique en matière de vol à main armée en mer? La réponse ne saurait être affirmative que si les cadres juridiques nationaux restent silencieux sur cette question.

Le vol à main armée en mer est par définition une infraction commise dans une zone relevant de la compétence juridictionnelle d'un Etat côtier. Par conséquent, il ne peut être régi que par les droits internes des Etats. C'est la raison pour laquelle le Conseil de sécurité des Nations Unies, se rendant finalement compte de cette réalité,

> «*prie instamment* les Etats … de mettre en œuvre des stratégies

112. Articles 101 à 111 de la convention de Montego Bay du 10 décembre 1982.
113. Paragraphe 5 de la résolution 2039 précitée.

nationales de sécurité maritime, notamment pour ce qui est de mettre en place un cadre juridique visant à interdire, prévenir et réprimer les actes de piraterie et les vols à main armée en mer, ainsi que de poursuivre les auteurs de ces crimes et de punir quiconque en est reconnu coupable»[114].

Ce qu'il convient de retenir en dernière analyse, c'est que le vol à main armée en mer est distinct de la piraterie et que les deux sont régis par deux ordres juridiques distincts[115]. Celle-ci est commise dans une zone ne relevant de la compétence d'aucune juridiction nationale[116] et reste encadrée par le droit international, en particulier la convention sur le droit de la mer, tandis que celui-là est commis dans une zone relevant de la compétence juridictionnelle des Etats[117] et relèveraient en principe des ordres juridiques nationaux. Au-delà de la distinction, au-delà même de la répartition des compétences dans les différents ordres juridiques, la coopération semble plus que jamais nécessaire pour combler tout vide juridique ou toute défaillance quant à la prévention et la répression des actes de vol à main armée en mer ou encore pour venir en aide aux Etats côtiers défaillants, véritable refuge des pilleurs de navires et matrice des voleurs de cargaisons.

114. Point 5 de la résolution 2039.
115. Ou devraient être régis.
116. Haute mer et espace international.
117. Eaux intérieures, eaux archipélagiques et mer territoriale.

8 Extradition and Mutual Legal Assistance in the Prosecution of Serious Maritime Crimes: A Comparative and Critical Analysis of Applicable Legal Frameworks

Cheah Wui Ling *

SECTION 1 INTRODUCTION

Despite the international community's condemnation of piracy and other serious maritime crimes, pirates or maritime criminals are often released by law enforcement agencies after being relieved of their illicit cargo or vessel. This may be because these pirates or maritime criminals were apprehended before they had committed any serious harm to particular persons. In addition, the law enforcement agencies may belong to a State that is located far away. Significant resources and political will may be needed to transport the apprehended criminals back to the apprehending State for trial. The State concerned must have the legal framework and capacity to conduct such trials. These demands explain why it may be more convenient for law enforcement authorities to release pirates or maritime criminals after confiscating or destroying their arms, ships, or ill-gotten goods. This practice has, however, most recently been condemned by the UN Security Council in the context of Somali piracy. The Council has insisted on the investigation and prosecution of apprehended suspects[1]. States have indeed demonstrated an increased political will to prosecute suspected pirates, as reflected in a rise in the number of prosecutions and suspects held for prosecution[2]. The Contact Group on Piracy off the Coast of Somalia, which was established pursuant to Security Council resolution 1851 (2008) has put

* Assistant Professor, Faculty of Law of the National University of Singapore (NUS). Research Fellow, NUS Centre of International Law. Qualified lawyer, called to the New York Bar. Diploma in arbitration, Queen Mary, University of London. LL.B and LL.M, National University of Singapore, LL.M, Harvard. Diploma from the Academy of European Law (EUI).

1. SC res. 1897 (2009), preamble.
2. S-G Report, SC res. 1950 (2010), para. 58.

substantial focus on developing frameworks and strategies to ensure the prosecution of pirates[3].

Facilitating and ensuring the prosecution of pirates and maritime criminals is not easy due to the many cross-border elements involved. These crimes usually involve perpetrators and victims of different nationalities. They take place on the high seas or across different territorial seas. This is because general international law recognizes a variety of jurisdictional grounds based on which a State may prescribe acts as crimes under its domestic laws[4]. General international law, however, does not obligate States to exercise their jurisdictional powers, though this may be required by specific treaties that a State is party to[5]. The case could be that no competent State would be willing to exercise jurisdiction over the suspected persons. General international law also prohibits States from impinging on the territorial sovereignty of another State, a situation which may arise when a State is seeking to enforce its jurisdictional powers over accused or evidence located in another State's territory[6]. One may therefore be faced with a situation where a State willing to investigate or prosecute does not have custody of the accused or the necessary evidence, while the State in whose territory the accused or evidence is located is not willing to investigate or prosecute. The former State is nevertheless prevented from obtaining the accused or evidence by entering the latter State's territory without its consent, as that would infringe the latter's territorial sovereignty.

One possible answer to this conundrum is to enhance and strengthen the modalities of interstate co-operation, such as extradition and mutual legal assistance. This will enable States willing to prosecute to do so with the co-operation of other States that have custody of the accused or evidence. Cross-border co-operation will facilitate the transfer of accused persons, the questioning of witnesses, and the exchange of evidence. Efficient interstate co-operation mechanisms will secure the "procedural continuity" necessary for effective prosecution from the crime's commission to the prosecution and punishment of those involved[7].

This chapter ascertains and assesses the extent to which existing legal

3. This work has been largely undertaken by Working Group 2 of the CGPCS, S-G Report, SC res. 1950 (2010), para. 22.

4. James Crawford, *Brownlie's Principles of Public International Law*, 8th ed., OUP, 2012, pp. 457-471.

5. Examples of these treaties include those incorporating *aut dedere aut judicare* provisions requiring State Parties to establish jurisdiction over the offence when the accused is present in its territory and it fails to extradite the accused to any of the other States having jurisdiction over the case pursuant to the treaty. Crawford, *op. cit.*, at pp. 469-471.

6. Crawford, *op. cit.*, p. 479.

7. Report of the Special Adviser to the Secretary-General, para. 44.

frameworks, at the regional and international level, facilitate interstate co-operation and enable the effective prosecution of maritime criminals. There has been a proliferation of regional and international initiatives to combat piracy and serious maritime crimes, particularly in danger zones, like Somalia. However, none of these initiatives have particularly focused on extradition or mutual legal assistance. While interstate co-operation may be facilitated informally at the investigatory stage, more formal legal arrangements, such as extradition and mutual legal assistance, are necessary when a case is being prepared for trial. The UN Secretary-General has recognized the need "to expand and formalize the mechanism for investigative and prosecutorial purposes" in the context of addressing piracy off the coast of Somalia[8]. The international community's response to serious maritime crimes, such as piracy and maritime terrorism, has thus far focused on the development of policing-type enforcement powers, such as interdiction, hot-pursuit, and the seizure of ships[9]. Less attention has been paid to assessing and strengthening interstate co-operation at the formal and legal level. Such co-operation is nevertheless essential to the successful prosecution and trial of maritime criminals. It is necessary to examine the extent to which existing and applicable international legal instruments provide for such co-operation.

In terms of the types of frameworks examined, this chapter focuses on treaties rather than "softer" versions of international law. As mentioned above, this chapter aims to address a real-life problem faced by practitioners in the prosecution of piracy and serious maritime crime. For practitioners, treaties have the advantage of being comparatively clear and certain as compared to other "softer" versions of international law. This chapter will first examine treaties of a general nature, before turning to those that are crime and context-specific. General legal frameworks, such as the United Nations Convention on the Law of the Sea (UNCLOS), are usually pitched at a more abstract level due to the need to obtain a broad level of consensus. Frameworks that address narrower subject matters are usually more comprehensive, elaborating on and adjusting the default positions set out in more general legal frameworks. By proceeding from more general frameworks to more specific frameworks, this chapter explains why each of these are potentially applicable

8. S-G Report, SC res. 1950 (2010), para. 50.

9. Cutting-edge scholarly works in the area of serious maritime crimes have also focused on policing-type enforcement power. See, for example, Douglas Guilfoyle, *Shipping Interdiction and the Law of the Sea*, CUP, 2009; Natalie Klein, *Maritime Security and the Law of the Sea*, OUP, 2011; Efthymios Papastavridis, *The Interception of Vessels on the High Seas: Contemporary Challenges to the Legal Order of the Oceans*, Oxford, Hart Publishing, 2013.

and how they particularize general default positions articulated in UNCLOS. In doing so, this chapter also compares the advantages and disadvantages afforded by these different legal frameworks in relation to interstate co-operation matters. The various treaties may, at first sight, appear to be unrelated to the type of piracy and serious maritime crimes that we commonly encounter today. Some, such as the 2000 UN Convention against Transnational Organized Crime (2000 UNTOC), the UN drug trafficking conventions, and the 2003 UN Convention against Corruption (2003 CAC), may appear more applicable to crimes occurring on land than that at sea. However, they are as applicable to crimes at sea as to crimes on land. Some, like the 1988 Convention for the Prevention of Unlawful Acts against the Safety of Maritime Navigation (1988 SUA) or the 1999 Terrorism Financing Convention (1999 TFC), are sometimes misunderstood as only applicable to typical terrorist crimes or crimes with a terrorist motive. As further explained in my chapter, the relevant treaty provisions do not impose such a motive requirement. Rather, they focus on certain harmful acts committed rather than the objectives underlying the acts. There is no legal obstacle to applying these treaties to piracy or serious maritime crimes if other treaty requirements are met.

A careful appreciation of the acts targeted by these treaties and when they apply is necessary to appreciate the scope and potential of these treaties. Individually, these treaties may not capture the essence of the maritime crime under consideration due to their focus on different acts. For example, the TFC focuses on illegal financing and the 2000 UNTOC focuses on organized crime. But because contemporary maritime crimes often include varied elements, these treaties could be of relevance[10]. States Parties will then be able to benefit from the treaty's provisions on interstate co-operation. The Section 2 of this chapter is devoted to UNCLOS, specifically to its relevance to questions of interstate co-operation in criminal matters. The Sections 3 and 4 explore crime-specific treaties applicable to serious maritime crimes. The Section 5 examines regional and locale-specific frameworks adopted by the international community. An example of the latter would be action undertaken with respect to acts of piracy and armed robbery occurring off the coast of Somalia. This chapter concludes that there is a need for policy-makers and practitioners to be more aware of the different interstate co-operation provisions in these frameworks, specifically how they intersect and complement one another. Interstate co-operation can be pursued based

10. Full and accurate labelling of the crime may still be a concern, particularly at the domestic level, though this at present lies beyond the scope of this chapter which focuses on interstate co-operation.

on existing legal frameworks if they are interpreted and applied in a way that maximizes their potential application to concrete situations.

SECTION 2 THE LEGAL FRAMEWORK OF UNCLOS: INTERPRETING UNCLOS PROVISIONS IN FAVOUR OF INTERSTATE CO-OPERATION

UNCLOS is the primary universal treaty governing the oceans and addresses a wide variety of topics, such as the delimitation of maritime boundaries, the jurisdictional powers and duties of States, the settlement of disputes, and maritime scientific research[11]. While none of the 320 articles of UNCLOS addresses expressly interstate co-operation in criminal matters, the treaty remains an important starting point for a number of reasons. Firstly, it sets out what jurisdictional rights and duties each State has in each maritime zone. Secondly, it specifically singles out, and requires States to take certain action in response to, a number of offences, such as piracy and drug trafficking. Once again, these UNCLOS provisions that deal with jurisdiction allocation and specific offences do not expressly require or mention extradition, mutual legal assistance, or other modalities of interstate co-operation. While such co-operation is not explicitly mentioned or required by these provisions, this chapter proposes that they should nevertheless be interpreted in favour of interstate co-operation.

Article 31 of the Vienna Convention on the Law of Treaties (VCLT), which is widely accepted to reflect customary international law, requires treaty provisions to be interpreted "in good faith" and "in accordance with the ordinary meaning to be given to the terms of the treaty in their context and in the light of its object and purpose"[12]. Treaty provisions are to be understood against the context and objectives of the treaty as a whole. In its preamble, UNCLOS declares the treaty's objective as establishing "a legal order for the seas and oceans". This, among its other substantive goals, is to "promote the peaceful uses of the seas and oceans"[13]. Furthermore, the "codification and progressive development of law" undertaken by UNCLOS is intended to "contribute to the strengthening of peace, security, cooperation and friendly relations among all nations"[14]. UNCLOS further states that its legal order aims to further the "peaceful" use of seas and oceans and the strengthening of interstate relations. One of the main objectives of UNCLOS is therefore

11. UNCLOS contains 320 articles and 9 annexes.
12. Art. 31, Vienna Convention on the Law of Treaties.
13. UNCLOS, preamble.
14. *Ibid.*

to establish a legal order that facilitates collective and inclusive use of the seas. It expressly recognizes the spirit of "mutual understanding and cooperation" in which it was concluded[15]. These objectives and the context of UNCLOS favour an interpretative approach that promotes rather than undermines interstate co-operation. Treaty provisions should thus be interpreted in a manner that creates positive conditions for interstate co-operation.

As mentioned above, UNCLOS sets out the jurisdictional rights and duties of particular States in each maritime zone. By specifying how jurisdictional powers are distributed and identifying which States are entitled or required to exercise these powers, it does place the cornerstone on which interstate co-operation should take place. In principle, it is the flag State that has primary jurisdictional powers over the ship concerned. However, UNCLOS also recognizes that under certain circumstances and depending on the *locus delicti*, law enforcement powers may be concurrently exercised by States other than the flag State[16]. For example, Article 27 of UNCLOS identifies a number of instances when the coastal State may exercise criminal jurisdiction over a ship passing through its territorial sea, namely, "if the consequences of the crime extend to the coastal State", "if the crime is of a kind to disturb the peace of the country or the good order of the territorial sea", "if the assistance of the local authorities has been requested by the master of the ship or by a diplomatic agent or consular officer of the flag State", or "if such measures are necessary for the suppression of illicit traffic in narcotic drugs or psychotropic substances"[17]. In line with the treaty's objective of securing the collective objective of a public order on the seas, it may be argued that Article 27 should be generously interpreted so as to ensure maximum law enforcement within territorial waters[18]. Such a recognition of concurrent jurisdiction is necessary as the flag State may not be in a position, despite all good faith efforts, to police its flag ship at all times throughout the ship's journey, while the coastal State may be in a better position to do so. However, UNCLOS does not expressly address a case in which both the flag State and coastal State may wish to exercise its jurisdiction over the ship in an Article 27 scenario.

The need for jurisdictional co-ordination is better anticipated by UNCLOS when dealing with maritime casualties or navigation incidents on the high seas. Specifically, Article 94 (7) states that the flag State has

---

15. UNCLOS, preamble.
16. For a concise overview of State jurisdiction over ships and aircraft, see Crawford, *op. cit.*, pp. 464-466.
17. UNCLOS, Art. 27.
18. Klein, *op. cit.*, p. 77.

a duty to hold an inquiry into every "maritime casualty or incident of navigation on the high seas involving a ship flying its flag" when this causes "loss of life or serious injury to nationals of another State or serious damage to ships or installations of another State or to the marine environment"[19]. The provision goes on to note that "the flag State and the other State shall cooperate in the conduct of any inquiry held by that other State" in these matters[20]. This duty to co-operate is stated in mandatory terms. However, when it comes to "penal or disciplinary proceedings" instituted against the "master or of any other person in the service of the ship", as opposed to an "inquiry", Article 97 (1) states that jurisdiction may only be exercised by the judicial or administrative authorities of the flag State or the State of the offender's nationality, without expressly indicating how jurisdiction may be co-ordinated[21]. It may be argued, however, that the duty to co-operate which applies in an inquiry, which would usually precede any "penal or disciplinary" proceeding against an individual, should continue to apply when "penal or disciplinary proceedings" are initiated. Failure to co-operate or co-ordinate jurisdictional problems would otherwise give rise to complications, especially since Article 97 (3) states that no order for the ship's arrest or detention, "even as a measure of investigation", is to be given by any authorities other than that of the flag State's[22].

UNCLOS dedicates a number of provisions to certain crimes, namely piracy, slave-trading, drug trafficking, and unauthorized broadcasting. It sets out the definitions of these offences and the rights or obligations of States Parties with respect to each of the offences. As this chapter focuses on the topic of interstate co-operation, it will not go into the debates surrounding the definitions of these offences. However, it should be noted that the UNCLOS definition of piracy, which refers to "any illegal acts of violence or detention, or any act of depredation" committed "for private ends" and "on the high seas" against "another ship or aircraft", has been criticized as being too narrow for contemporary purposes[23]. It, however, continues to be widely accepted as reflecting customary international law.

Another point to note is that the various provisions on piracy, the transport of slaves, and the traffic of drugs, and unauthorized broadcasting fall under Part VII of UNCLOS entitled "High Seas". As entitled, Part VII's provisions largely focus on addressing the concerns and jurisdictional powers of States on the high seas. However, unless explicitly

19. UNCLOS, Art. 94 (7).
20. UNCLOS, Art. 94 (7).
21. UNCLOS, Art. 97 (1).
22. UNCLOS, Art. 97 (3).
23. Reference to chapter on piracy in same compilation.

stated, the treaty provisions in Part VII should not be restrictively interpreted to limit their application to the high seas. For example, Article 99 calls on States to take effective measures to "prevent and punish" the transport of slaves on ships authorized to fly their flags. This obligation of flag States applies to the transport of slaves wherever they take place and not only when they take place on the high seas. Neither does this provision require that such measures be limited only to that on the high seas. In contrast, Article 108 calls on States to co-operate to suppress drug trafficking "on the high seas" as "contrary to international conventions".

It should be noted that none of the crime-specific provisions in Part VII expressly obligate States to criminalize, prosecute, or co-operate in the prosecution of the crime concerned. However, these provisions do recognize — to varying degrees — general duties of co-operation, which would arguably include interstate co-operation. Article 99 deals with the transport of slaves and calls on States that they "shall take effective measures to prevent and punish the transport of slaves" on ships flying its flag[24]. This duty to "prevent" and "punish" however applies only to the flag State. Article 99 does not specifically mention interstate co-operation measures, but it may be argued that, depending on the case, such measures may be necessary to enable the flag State to "prevent" and "punish" the offender concerned. A good faith textual interpretation or the principle of effective treaty interpretation would impose on requested States a duty to, at the very least, diligently consider and attempt to meet requests for interstate co-operation.

Similar to Article 99, Article 108 and Article 109 of UNCLOS recognize a mandatory obligation of States to "cooperate" in the "suppression" of "illicit traffic in narcotic drugs and psychotropic substances" and "unauthorized broadcasting from the high seas" respectively[25]. The wording of Article 100, which relates to piracy, differs slightly from that of Articles 99, 108 and 109. Article 100 states that all States "shall cooperate to the fullest possible extent in the repression of piracy on the high seas or in any other place outside the jurisdiction of any State"[26]. The duties of States to co-operate in Articles 99, 100, 108 and 109 are all expressed in mandatory terms. However, with respect to Article 100 on piracy, States are only required to perform this duty "to the fullest possible extent"[27]. Scholars have observed that this phrase should not be interpreted to sanction lower levels of action or co-operation with

24. UNCLOS, Art. 99.
25. UNCLOS, Arts. 108 and 109.
26. UNCLOS, Art. 100.
27. UNCLOS, Arts 108 and 109.

respect to Article 100[28]. Rather the Article 100 phrase "to the fullest possible extent" should be interpreted consistent with the objective of UNCLOS to secure the legal order of the oceans. States should be required to do their best to co-operate with each other or, at the very least, to take the reasonable steps required for such co-operation.

Unlike Article 99 of UNCLOS which expressly calls for the punishment of those involved in slave trading, the UNCLOS provisions on piracy, drug-trafficking and illegal broadcasting do not explicitly obligate States to criminalize these offences or prosecute them. However, their treaty provisions assume or anticipate such prosecution. An argument may be made that these provisions should be broadly interpreted to support the interstate co-operation that is necessary for the effective prosecution of these crimes. In relation to piracy, Article 105 recognizes that the "courts" of the State that seized a pirate ship or aircraft "may decide upon the penalties to be imposed". By referring to the imposition of a penalty, Article 105 implicitly assumes the application of, at the very least, a judicial process. Indeed, this provision, along with Article 100 of UNCLOS, was referred to by the Dutch District Court of Rotterdam in a recent case. The court held that these provisions authorized the detention of Somali pirates, who had attacked a ship flying the flag of the Netherlands Antilles on the high seas, by the Danish authorities prior to the transfer of the said pirates to the Netherlands for trial[29].

Article 108, which relates to drug trafficking, calls on States to co-operate in the suppression of drug trafficking that is "contrary to international conventions". The various UN drug conventions in turn foresee prosecution. Article 109, which addresses the offence of unauthorized broadcasting, lists the different courts before which an accused may be tried and the right of States to arrest an accused. It recognizes a range of possible judicial forums: the courts of the flag State, the State of registry of the installation, the nationality State, the State where the transmissions can be received, or any State where authorized radio communication is suffering interference. By providing for multiple forums of prosecution, this treaty provision implicitly recognizes the need for interstate co-operation to facilitate co-ordination between interested States.

28. Special Adviser's Report to the Secretary-General (2011), para. 49. Roach observes that the history of the wording of Article 100 appears to go against finding a mandatory duty to act, the failure of which may result in liability. Despite this, he observes that "it would seem better to urge all states to ensure that they fulfil their duty to cooperate, and to point out that an obvious way to do so is to enact or modernize national laws criminalizing piracy", p. 406.

29. District Court of Rotterdam, Judgment of 17 June 2010, LJN: BM8116, 10/600012-09, reported in Netherlands Country Report, p. 18. For an English translation of the decision, see http://www.unicri.it/maritime_piracy/docs/Netherlands_2010_Crim_No_10_6000_12_09%20Judgment.pdf.

SECTION 3 UNIVERSAL *AUT DEDERE AUT JUDICARE* TREATIES: MANDATING INTERSTATE CO-OPERATION AND LIMITING STATE DISCRETION

While UNCLOS remains instrumental for interstate co-operation in piracy and serious maritime crimes, there is a need to look to other international instruments for express and more detailed provisions on interstate co-operation. As observed by Roach, there is a variety of such instruments applicable to serious maritime crimes, and a better appreciation of the applicability of widely ratified "criminal law treaties" to serious acts of piracy would enable better enforcement and co-ordination of action among States[30]. Due to the serious and multi-faceted nature of contemporary piracy, such acts would also fall within the scope of these different criminal law treaties. These criminal law treaties target specific offences. What these treaties have in common is that they set out clear definitions of the offence, require States Parties to criminalize the offence concerned, and identify States that have the obligation or right to exercise jurisdiction over the offence. These treaties also provide for extradition and mutual legal assistance to varying degrees. This section considers the interstate co-operation provided for in a number of universal *aut dedere aut judicare* treaties, all of which contain what is commonly known as an "extradite or prosecute" clause[31]. Such *aut dedere aut judicare* clauses are commonly included in the UN conventions against terrorism. These are in fact a list of "sectoral" treaties that deal with crimes commonly associated with terrorism[32]. Because of this, there is often the understandable misconception that these treaties only apply to crimes committed with a terrorist purpose.

---

30. Scholars have pointed out the potential of using these universal instruments. Specifically, Roach, in 2010, observed the applicability of the SUA Convention, the Hostages Convention, the Financing Convention, and UNTOC to the Somalia piracy situation, pp. 406, 408. J. Ashley Roach, "Countering Piracy off Somalia: International Law and International Institutions" (2010) 104:3 *American Journal of International Law* 397.

31. Indeed, the text of the treaties do not use this phrase of "prosecute of extradite". For example, this clause as expressed in Article 8 of the 1979 Hostages Convention states:

> "The State Party in the territory of which the alleged offender is found shall, if it does not extradite him, be obliged, without exception whatsoever and whether or not the offence was committed in its territory, to submit the case to its competent authorities for the purpose of prosecution, through proceedings in accordance with the laws of that State. Those authorities shall take their decision in the same manner as in the case of any ordinary offence of a grave nature under the law of that State."

32. Crawford, *op. cit.*, pp. 469-471.

However, as explained below, this is not the case. Rather, the treaties focus on the specific acts committed and the accused person's state of mind with respect to the act concerned. The majority of these treaties do not refer to the ultimate objective or purpose for which the acts were committed. Indeed, these treaties were each adopted to address a particular type of crime, such as hostage-taking and bombing. These crimes are often committed by terrorists and, indeed, the treaty may have been enacted in response to a terrorist act. But they are not necessarily the sole province of terrorists, as demonstrated by the hostage-taking practices of pirates or maritime criminals. These treaties should not be avoided simply because the crime concerned was not committed by terrorists or with the political objective that typically accompanies terrorist acts.

These *aut dedere aut judicare* treaties deal with crimes of a particular magnitude and may not apply to maritime crimes of a less serious nature. They would however apply to maritime crimes of a serious nature, such as the type of piracy prevalent in the Gulf of Aden which involves the taking of captured crew as "human shields" and for ransom purposes[33]. An *aut dedere aut judicare* treaty specifically relevant in this context would be the 1988 SUA. The latter was concluded in direct response to terrorist hijacking of the *MS Achille Lauro* that resulted in the death of an innocent passenger[34]. This particular historical background of the 1988 SUA has often resulted in it being perceived as a "counter-terrorism" treaty. While the preamble of the 1988 SUA does expressly condemn "international terrorism" alongside "unlawful acts against the safety of maritime navigation", Article 3 of the treaty defines the treaty's targeted offence in terms of acts that "endanger the safe navigation of a ship". The preamble's reference to "international terrorism" is a recognition of the treaty's historical background, but cannot be said to introduce an additional "terrorist purpose" or "political objective" element into Article 3's offence definition.

Another applicable *aut dedere aut judicare* treaty in light of the hostage-taking practices of pirates would be the 1979 International Convention against the Taking of Hostages (the 1979 Hostages Convention). Similar to the 1988 SUA, the 1979 Hostages Convention does not make reference to any terrorist or political objective in its Article 1 definition of hostage-taking. According to Article 1of the 1979 Hostages Convention, it applies to acts of hostage-taking done in order "to compel a third

33. SG-Report, SC res. 1950 (2010), paras. 7, 9-10.

34. Christopher C. Joyner, "Suppression of Terrorism on the High Seas: The 1988 IMO Convention on the Safety of Maritime Navigation" (1989) 19 *Israel Yearbook on Human Rights* 341.

party, namely, a State, an international intergovernmental organization, a natural or juridical person, or a group of persons" to do or not to do something. This does not need to target a State or State-like entity; it may also target "a natural or juridical person, or a group of persons". By including non-State private entities, it implicitly accepts that the compulsion by hostage-takers may be undertaken for private ends, such as commercial profit.

Article 2 of the 1999 Terrorism Financing Convention (1999 TFC) identifies the criminal acts which fall within the scope of the treaty. It states that a financing offence is committed if a person "by any means, directly or indirectly, unlawfully and wilfully, provides or collects funds with the intention that they should be used or in the knowledge that they are to be used" for certain specified acts. These financed acts are set out in two limbs of Article 2: *(a)* those falling within the scope of treaties listed in the 1999 TFC's annex, or *(b)* any act

> "intended to cause death or serious bodily injury to a civilian, or to any other person not taking an active part in the hostilities in a situation of armed conflict, when the purpose of such act, by its nature or context, is to intimidate a population, or to compel a government or an international organization to do or to abstain from doing any act".

The second limb of Article 2 therefore refers to activities done with the purpose "to intimidate a population" or "to compel a government or an international organization to do or abstain from doing any act". Most acts of piracy would not fall within this definition. However, it is often overlooked that the first limb of Article 2 refers to treaties listed in its annex. This annex includes the 1979 Hostages Convention and the 1988 SUA. In other words, the 1999 TFC could apply to acts that finance the taking of hostages and the endangerment of maritime navigation, as defined in the 1979 Hostages Convention and the 1988 SUA respectively.

These *aut dedere aut judicare* treaties share a common feature in that they make some forms of interstate co-operation mandatory in certain situations for their member States, rather than leaving these to the State's discretion. For example, certain obligations are imposed on the custodial State regardless of whether it has jurisdictional interest in the matter. First, the custodial State is required to take steps to ensure the accused person's presence "for such time as necessary to enable any criminal or extradition proceedings to be instituted". The State is also required to "make a preliminary inquiry into the facts"[35]. Secondly, if

35. SUA, Art. 7 (2); 1979 Hostages Convention, Art. 6 (1). Note that the 1999 Financing Convention has a similarly worded provision, Art. 9 (2).

the custodial State decides not to extradite the accused, the said State is "obliged" to submit the case without delay to its authorities for prosecutorial purposes and any decision taken should be made "in the same manner as in the case of any other offence of a grave nature under the law of that State"[36]. The custodial State will have to choose between extraditing the accused and trying the accused under its own legal system. In implementing these treaty obligations at the domestic level, States Parties would need to ensure that they have appropriate domestic legislation in place that would enable them to undertake such prosecutions, even if no jurisdictional link to the State exists, if they choose not to extradite the individual concerned.

These treaties also aim to ensure that the offences concerned are recognized as extraditable offences in other treaties separately concluded by the States Parties. The offences are to be considered "as extraditable offences in any extradition treaty" existing and to be concluded between States Parties[37]. For States with domestic legal systems that require a treaty as a basis for extradition, the State "may at its option" consider the *aut dedere aut judicare* treaty concerned as a legal basis for extradition[38]. For States that do not make extradition conditional upon a treaty, they are to recognize these offences as "extraditable offences" between themselves, "subject to the conditions provided by the law of the requested State"[39]. In order for extradition to be effective, separately concluded extradition treaties and domestic extradition laws need to be complete and adequate. One potential problem arises when extradition treaties concluded by a State Party or the State's domestic extradition law identifies extraditable offences according to the applicable years of imprisonment instead of types of crime. The treaty offence may not be subject to a level of imprisonment that is sufficiently high in the State Party's domestic legal system to qualify as an extraditable offence, particularly when involving more peripheral forms of liability. This has been identified as a problem of Japan's domestic law on extradition. Specifically, the intimidation offence criminalized under the 1988 SUA is not subject to a term of imprisonment under Japanese law that is sufficiently high to qualify it as an extraditable offence under Japanese law[40]. For extradition purposes, these offences are to be treated "as if

36. SUA, Art. 10 (1); 1979 Hostages Convention, Art. 8 (1); 1999 Financing Convention, Art. 10 (1).

37. SUA, Art.11 (1); 1979 Hostages Convention, Art. 10 (1); 1999 Financing Convention, Art. 11 (1).

38. SUA, Art. 11 (2); 1979 Hostages Convention, Art. 10 (2); 1999 Financing Convention, Art. 11 (3).

39. SUA, Art. 11 (1); 1979 Hostages Convention, Art. 10 (1); 1999 Financing Convention, Art. 11 (2).

40. Japan Country Report, 2011 CIL Workshop, p. 23.

they had been committed not only in the place in which they occurred but also in a place within the jurisdiction of the State Party requesting extradition"[41].

A custodial State Party may be faced with competing requests from a number of States Parties seeking to exercise jurisdictional powers over the case. As mentioned above, this is due to the numerous bases of jurisdiction recognized in general international law. Furthermore, the *aut dedere aut judicare* treaties specifically require certain States Parties to exercise jurisdiction over the case: the territorial State, the ship flying the flag of the State, the State in which the aircraft is registered (the 1979 Hostages Convention), the State which is being compelled to do or abstain from doing an act (1979 Hostages Convention), and the State of which the accused is a national. The *aut dedere aut judicare* treaties address this possibility by providing for some level of information exchange between the States concerned. For example, Article 11 (5) of the 1988 SUA provides that a requested State "shall" in choosing which State to extradite the offender to "pay due regard to the interests and responsibilities of the State Party whose flag the ship was flying" at the time the crime was committed[42]. It is proposed that this may be interpreted as giving some level of preference to the flag State's request for extradition. States Parties that have taken custody of an accused are also required to "immediately notify" other States Parties that have established jurisdiction according to the treaty and, if considered "advisable", "any other interested States Parties"[43]. These treaties also impose a general obligation on States Parties to co-operate with each other by recognizing that States Parties "shall afford one another the greatest measure of assistance in connection with criminal proceedings" including "assistance in obtaining evidence at their disposal necessary for these proceedings"[44].

These *aut dedere aut judicare* treaties limit the grounds on which States Parties may deny a State's request for interstate co-operation. Questions and decisions on whether or not to comply with requests for extradition and mutual legal assistance were traditionally understood as falling within the discretion of requested States. The *aut dedere aut judicare* treaties circumscribe the discretion of member States to a certain extent, such as by expressly prohibiting the denial of cooperation requests on the ground that the offence concerned is a political offence or fiscal offence[45]. However, these treaties also expressly state that

41. SUA, Art. 11 (4); 1970 Hostages Convention, Art. 10 (4).
42. SUA, Art. 11 (5).
43. 1999 Financing Convention, Art. 9 (6).
44. SUA, Art. 12 (1); 1979 Hostages Convention, Art. 11 (1).
45. 1999 Financing Convention, Arts. 13 and 14.

nothing in the treaty should be interpreted as imposing an obligation to extradite or offer mutual legal assistance if the requested State has "substantial grounds" for believing that the request for co-operation is made

> "for the purpose of prosecuting or punishing a person on account of that person's race, religion, nationality, ethnic origin or political opinion or that compliance with that request would cause prejudice to that person's position for any of these reasons"[46].

Taken together, these provisions regulate, to a certain degree, the traditional discretion of States regarding interstate co-operation in criminal matters.

The 1988 SUA is particularly noteworthy because it addresses a number of co-operation issues that are encountered at sea. For example, it deals with the dilemma that a ship's master faces when he has an offender on board his ship in the middle of a journey. Article 8 (1) recognizes that a ship's master "may deliver to the authorities of any other State Party" a person "who he has reasonable grounds to believe has committed" an offence recognized by the 1988 SUA[47]. The State Party is required to accept the delivery unless it "has grounds to consider" the 1988 SUA does not apply[48]. However the receiving State may subsequently "request the flag State to accept delivery of the person". The flag State is obligated to "consider" this request[49].

SECTION 4 THE UN TRANSNATIONAL ORGANIZED CRIME TREATY REGIME: ACHIEVING CONCEPTUAL AND PROCEDURAL CLARITY AND REGULATING STATE DISCRETION IN INTERSTATE CO-OPERATION

The *aut dedere aut judicare* treaties discussed above go a significant way to facilitating interstate co-operation by mandating interstate co-operation under certain circumstances and limiting State discretion in co-operation matters; however, they do not elaborate on how such co-operation should take place or the procedure that should be followed. Another potentially applicable treaty regime is the 2000 UNTOC and its Protocols[50]. Modern-day piracy attacks usually involve

46. 1999 Financing Convention, Art. 15.
47. SUA, Art. 8 (1).
48. SUA, Art. 8 (3).
49. SUA, Art. 8 (5).
50. Protocol to Prevent, Suppress and Punish Trafficking in Persons, Especially Women and Children, supplementing the United Nations Convention

several persons and a degree of co-ordination between them. The 2000 UNTOC applies to a number of offences: participation in an organized criminal group, money laundering, corruption, obstruction of justice, and the residual category of "serious crime" if this "serious crime" is transnational and involves an organized criminal group. The potential of the 2000 UNTOC lies in its broad definition of offences. For example, Article 5 sets out two definitions of participation in an organised criminal group; one focusing on agreement, and the other focusing on conduct. The 2000 UNTOC defines organized criminal group as any "structured group of three or more persons" that exists for a period of time and acts in concern to commit a UNTOC offence. The offence should be committed for "a financial or other material benefit", whether directly or indirectly[51]. A similarly broad definition is applied to the offence of "serious crime". "Serious crime" is defined as referring to offences punishable by a maximum sentence of at least four years by a State party[52].

By targeting a range of offences, such as corruption and money laundering, the 2000 UNTOC enables the prosecution of individuals benefiting at different levels from the proceeds of piracy and serious maritime crime. The UNTOC Protocols, which build on UNTOC's framework, address additional offences: the trafficking in persons, migrant smuggling, and firearm trafficking. Another relevant treaty is the 2003 CAC. By following the money and targeting the broader ramifications of an offence, these treaties go beyond immediate perpetrators and enable the prosecution of those higher up in the chain of command. Such a broader approach is necessary for the effective and long-term suppression of piracy and serious maritime offences. UNTOC States Parties are required to criminalize the various offences targeted by the treaty, and they are obligated to exercise their jurisdiction over them if the crime is committed on its territory or on board a flag Ship or aircraft registered in the State during the time of the offence[53].

What is most relevant for the purposes of this chapter is the detailed interstate co-operation regime established by the 2000 UNTOC, particularly in the area of mutual legal assistance. Article 3 sets out the treaty's scope by stating that the 2000 UNTOC's provisions, unless as stated otherwise, apply to offences established by the treaty but only when the

against Transnational Organized Crime; Protocol against the Smuggling of Migrants by Land, Sea and Air, supplementing the United Nations Convention against Transnational Organized Crime; Protocol against the Illicit Manufacturing and Trafficking in Firearms, Their Parts and Components and Ammunition, supplementing the United Nations Convention against Transnational Organized Crime.

51. UNTOC, Art. 2 *(a)*.
52. UNTOC, Art. 2 *(b)*.
53. UNTOC, Art. 34 (1).

offences are "transnational in nature" and involve an organised criminal group". This "transnational" nature is defined broadly and deemed to exist if the offence it committed in more than on State; has a substantial part of its preparation, planning, direction or control in another State; involving an organized criminal group that engages in criminal activity in more than one State; or has substantial effects in another State[54]. This express requirement of the transnational element and involvement of an organized armed group is because UNTOC States Parties are not required to include these elements when criminalizing UNTOC offences[55]. For example, the definition of money laundering in the 2000 UNTOC does not include these elements. The definition of the offence of participating in an organized criminal group does not include a transnational element. However, it should be noted that Article 3, which requires a transnational element and involvement of an organized armed group for the 2000 UNTOC to apply, itself states that these elements are required "except as otherwise stated herein". It is therefore important to scrutinize the individual UNTOC provisions on interstate co-operation to see if they explicitly exempt any or both of these elements. For example, Article 16 (1) on extradition does not require transnationality as long as the offence is a crime in the requesting and requested State, satisfying the principle of dual criminality.

In comparison to earlier criminal law treaties and the *aut dedere aut judicare* treaties mentioned above, the 2000 UNTOC recognizes more modalities of interstate co-operation and elaborates on each modality with greater comprehensiveness. However, it should also be noted that in comparison to the *aut dedere aut judicare* treaties, the 2000 UNTOC imposes a lower level of obligation to co-operate or enforce jurisdiction on its States Parties. There is more room for the exercise of State discretion. For example, the *aut dedere aut judicare* treaties considered in the section above require a custodial State to exercise jurisdiction over the offender if it chooses not to extradite the individual concerned. The 2000 UNTOC only requires the custodial State to do so only if its refusal to extradite the offender was made on the sole ground that the person concerned was a national of the custodial State, thereby implicitly recognizing that extradition may be refused on non-nationality grounds[56]. States Parties to the 2000 UNTOC are also obligated to recognize the relevant offences as "extraditable offences"[57]. For States

54. UNTOC, Art. 3 (2).
55. If this was required, it would narrow the scope of domestic criminalization. Neil Boister, *An Introduction to Transnational Criminal Law*, OUP, 2012, p. 84.
56. CAC, Art. 42 (3); UNTOC, Art. 16 (10).
57. UNTOC, Art. 16; CAC, Art. 44.

that make extradition conditional on the existence of a treaty, the transnational crime treaty "may" be considered as a basis, and they commit, "where appropriate", to conclude extradition treaties to make the said offences extraditable[58]. This obligation, for States that make extradition conditional upon a treaty, is less strict compared to that imposed by counter-terrorism treaties[59].

The 2000 UNTOC and its Protocols do seek to limit or regulate the way States Parties exercise their discretion in interstate co-operation matters. Like the *aut dedere aut judicare* treaties considered above, they explicitly recognize certain grounds on which States may not refuse requests for extradition or mutual legal assistance. For example, the 2000 UNTOC notes that extradition may not be refused solely because the offence is considered to also involve "fiscal matters"[60]. It also prohibits States Parties from declining requests for mutual legal assistance on grounds of "bank secrecy"[61]. It sets out the grounds on which a request for mutual legal assistance may be refused[62]. Some of these grounds are relatively broad. For example, a request may be refused if a requested State decides that compliance is "likely" to adversely affect its "sovereignty", "security", "*ordre public*", or "other essential interests"[63]. While the broad nature of these categories enables States Parties to retain a significant measure of interpretive discretion, the word "likely" may be interpreted as imposing a limit to the State discretion exercised. Specifically, there needs to be a certain degree of probability that the refusing State's sovereignty, security, *order public,* or essential interests are affected before it is entitled to refuse a request. The 2000 UNTOC also seeks to guide or regulate the remaining discretion of its States Parties by requiring them to "endeavour" to exercise their discretionary powers under domestic laws with the aim to "maximize the effectiveness of law enforcement measures" and "the need to deter the commission of such offences"[64].

The 2000 UNTOC also contains various provisions that perform an important "soft" regulatory function by clarifying the principles and pro-

---

58. Cf. 1999 Financing Convention, Art. 11.
59. For example, Article 11 (1) of the 1999 Financing Convention requires that the relevant offences "shall be deemed to be included as extraditable offences in any extradition treaty existing between any of the States Parties before the entry into force of this Convention". Further, "States Parties undertake to include such offences as extraditable offences in every extraditable treaty to be subsequently concluded between them."
60. UNTOC, Art. 16 (14).
61. UNTOC, Art. 18 (9).
62. UNTOC, Art. 21.
63. UNTOC, Art. 21 *(a)*.
64. UNTOC, Art. 11 (2).

cedure related to interstate co-operation. While there is yet to be a universal convention that deals with extradition or mutual legal assistance in general, there is a corpus of principles commonly accepted to apply in matters of interstate co-operation, such as the principle of double criminality, the principle of speciality, and the political offence exception [65]. There remains, however, much debate about the exact content and scope of these principles. Their interpretation and application has differed from State to State. For example, different countries have developed different interpretations of the political offence exception [66]. The 2000 UNTOC broadens the common ground between States by clarifying some principles on extradition and mutual legal assistance. Article 18 (2) of the 2000 UNTOC defines the principle of dual criminality which may serve as a ground for denying co-operation [67]. It states that such dual criminality arises when the underlying conduct is criminalized under the laws of the requesting and the requested State, regardless of whether it is placed in the same category or if the same terminology is used. It also defines the scope of this principle, noting that States may still choose to undertake co-operative action in cases of dual criminality when this "does not involve coercive action" [68].

Apart from clarifying the principles applicable to interstate co-operation in criminal matters, the 2000 UNTOC also sets out the procedure to be followed in extradition and mutual legal assistance matters. For example, the 2000 UNTOC expressly details what should be included in a request for mutual legal assistance [69]. Numerous provisions require consultation and information exchange between requesting and requested States. This reduces the chance of the said request being denied for lack of information and also reduces the time required to process extradition or mutual legal assistance requests. Furthermore, to ensure the timely treatment of requests, a requesting State has the right to make "reasonable requests" to the requested State regarding the status of its request [70]. The requested State in turn is required to consider as fully as possible any deadlines put forward by a requesting State, and

65. Crawford, *op. cit.*, p. 482.
66. Michael R. Littenberg, "Comment: The Political Offence Exception: A Historical Analysis and Model for the Future" (1990) 64 *Tulane Law Review* 1196. As observed by Littenberg, Swiss courts have developed a "three-pronged test" that requires an act to be politically motivated, proportionate to the objective, and occur incidentally to a struggle for political power. UK courts have adopted a "political character" test, while US courts have developed different versions of an "incidence" test over time.
67. CAC, Art. 43 (2).
68. CAC, Art. 46 (9) *(b)*.
69. UNTOC, Art. 18 (15).
70. UNTOC, Art. 18 (24).

should respond to reasonable requests made by a requesting State on the processing status. The requested State, "where appropriate", is to provide the requesting State with "ample opportunity" to present its case and provide necessary information[71]. While these provisions are not phrased in absolute mandatory terms, the use of terms such as "reasonable" and "appropriate" should be interpreted as requiring the State concerned to demonstrate that it made a good faith attempt to meet the request for co-operation, one that can be objectively explained if necessary. Such an interpretation would be in line with the 2000 UNTOC's objectives of securing more effective interstate co-operation by promoting trust and confidence between States.

The creation and preservation of trust between States is fundamental to interstate co-operation. This is particularly so in the area of information exchange where any leak or improper use of the information concern may undermine ongoing investigations, impinge on the rights of the individuals concerned, or threaten security interests. The 2000 UNTOC requires information-receiving States to observe confidentiality requirements and respect any restrictions imposed by the information-transmitting State on the information concerned[72]. Requesting States are also required to use the information received only for the purposes stated in the request, unless prior consent is obtained from the requested State[73]. In addition, Article 18 (23) of the 2000 UNTOC requires States Parties to provide reasons when rejecting any request for mutual legal assistance. This requirement to provide reasons is phrased in obligatory terms. Such a reason-giving obligation secures a certain degree of transparency in decision-making, which preserves confidence and trust between States Parties. It also helps the requesting State to understand, in objective terms, why its request has been denied. The requesting State is then in a position to evaluate its request and decide if any further information may be provided to the requested State that will enable the latter to accede to its request.

SECTION 5 CONTEXTUAL APPROACHES: REGIONAL AND LOCALE-SPECIFIC ARRANGEMENTS

So far, this chapter has considered treaties that are intended to be universal in terms of State membership and geographical application. In this section, we will consider regional or locale-specific arrangements that address themselves to specific regional groupings of

71. CAC, Art. 44 (17); UNTOC, Art. 16.
72. CAC, Art 46 (5); UNTOC, Art. 18 (5).
73. UNTOC, Art. 18 (19).

States or particular geographical areas. The universal treaties considered above in fact anticipate or call on States Parties to enter into additional arrangements. As mentioned earlier, the *aut dedere aut judicare* treaties require States Parties, for which extradition is conditional on the existence of a treaty, to treat treaty offences as extraditable in any extradition treaty existing between States Parties and in future extradition treaties to be concluded. Article 16 (17) of the 2000 UNTOC states that States Parties "shall seek to conclude bilateral and multilateral agreements or arrangements to carry out or to enhance the effectiveness of extradition". For mutual legal assistance, the 2000 UNTOC imposes a more qualified obligation: States Parties "shall consider, as may be necessary, the possibility of concluding bilateral or multilateral agreements or arrangements" that will enhance UNTOC provisions on mutual legal assistance. Indeed, the 2000 UNTOC foresees States Parties attempting to conclude further agreements among themselves to give effect to different types of interstate co-operation, such as the relocation of witnesses and the use of special investigative techniques[74].

Additional agreements are necessary because these universal treaties are unable to set out obligations and rights at a high level of detail. Interstate co-operation modalities, such as extradition and mutual legal assistance, involve complicated issues of procedure that differ according to a State's domestic legal system[75]. Treaties concluded on the basis of universal membership are therefore only able to secure consensus at a relatively general level. Furthermore, such co-operation often involves a requested State's investment of resources and time in proceedings that occur outside a requested State's jurisdiction. States are reluctant to commit themselves to detailed or comprehensive obligations which they may not be able to fulfil or control. Extradition and mutual legal assistance also have the potential to substantially impact domestic criminal justice processes and the fundamental rights of individuals involved. States are therefore more willing to enter into more detailed arrangements with States with which they have a certain level of political trust. This is why more detailed arrangements are concluded at the regional or bilateral level, between States with common interests or a familiarity with each other's legal systems. States sharing a common legal tradition may also have a better understanding of each other's legal systems. For example, the London Scheme of Extradition is an informal non-binding instrument that applies to Commonwealth countries which come from

74. UNTOC, Art. 24 (3) and Art. 20 (2).

75. Boister notes that while States are gradually "reducing state-based prerogatives that provide obstacles to extradition", States remain "notoriously sceptical of extradition." Boister, *op. cit.*, p. 234.

different regions but which have been influenced by the British common law tradition[76]. Regional arrangements are particularly comprehensive and developed in the European Union, with its European Arrest Warrant and the Eurojust system[77].

Regional instruments may also consolidate and incorporate more updated understandings about co-operation at the regional level. One interesting example is the 2007 ASEAN Convention on Counter-terrorism (ACCT). The ACCT's innovation lies in its identification of substantive offences by reference to a list of treaties, which are also commonly referred to as the UN counter-terrorism treaties[78]. It is contingent upon a member State, which is not a member of any of the listed treaties, to declare that the particular universal instrument is not to be included. The extradition and mutual legal assistance obligations listed in the ACCT are more detailed and stricter compared to that in the listed treaties, and commits its members to a level of closer co-operation. For example, a number of the older listed treaties do not have a fair treatment obligation, but the ACCT has such a fair treatment provision in its main text. ASEAN States will need to adhere to the fair treatment provision stated in the ASEAN Convention when co-operating with respect to a listed treaty's offence, even if the said listed treaty does not have a fair treatment provision in its text[79]. Also, not all of the listed treaties expressly reject the application of the political offence exception[80]. The ACCT explicitly states that none of the offences defined in the listed universal counter-terrorism treaties are to be considered as political offences in matters of extradition and mutual legal assistance undertaken pursuant to the convention[81]. In this manner, the ASEAN Convention effectively "updates" or applies more comprehensive co-operation obligations to offences criminalized by a range of older and newer treaties.

In addition to more detailed regional approaches, the international community has recognized the need to take additional measures above and beyond what would apply in normal circumstances to deal with urgent problems of crime and security in certain areas of the world, specifically off the coast of Somalia. These measures are designed to be temporary and foresee the return to more normal conditions in the future. The Security Council has passed a number of resolutions aimed

76. Unlike treaties, this scheme is not binding.

77. See generally, Mark Mackarel, "The European Arrest Warrant — the Early Years: Implementing and Using the Warrant" (2007) *European Journal of Crime, Criminal Law and Criminal Justice* 37.

78. ASEAN Convention, Art. I.

79. ASEAN Convention, Art. VIII (1).

80. Both the 1988 SUA and the 1979 Hostages Convention do not expressly deny application of the political offence exception.

81. ASEAN Convention, Art. XIV.

at strengthening international and regional co-operation in law enforcement measures against "piracy" and "armed robbery" occurring off the coast of Somalia[82]. These resolutions empower third States to go beyond what is authorized under the UNCLOS regime and undertake law enforcement measures within Somalia's territorial sea. However, as many commentators have noted, these resolutions require the consent of Somalia, are limited to the specific example of Somalia, are not intended to create or change existing law, and therefore are not that revolutionary in nature[83]. Some States involved in these law enforcement activities have prosecuted seized pirates before their national courts, but some are unable to due to a lack or inappropriateness of domestic law[84]. However, many of these States have also concluded transfer agreements with other States that have agreed to receive and try seized pirates. Regional prosecution centres have been established so far in Kenya, the Seychelles and Mauritius[85].

Due to the many arrangements that have developed to facilitate the arrest and prosecution of pirates off the coast of Somalia, there may be different States involved in policing, arresting the accused, interviewing the victims, gathering the evidence, and trying the accused, and a corresponding need for close interstate co-operation. Accused persons may also wish, or be expected, to serve out their sentence back in the State of origin as opposed to the State that prosecuted them. Indeed the UNDOC has worked with the Government of Somalia to establish prisons in Somalia for this purpose[86]. The need for interstate co-operation has been recognized by the UN Security Council in its various resolutions. In resolution 1897 (2009), the Security Council called upon all States with jurisdiction over the offence, "in particular flag, port, and coastal States, States of the nationality of victims and perpetrators" and "other States with relevant jurisdiction" "to render assistance by, among other actions, providing disposition and logistics assistance with respect to the persons under their jurisdiction and control, such as victims and witnesses and persons detained"[87]. The practice of concluding shiprider agreements has developed in partial response to this problem. In resolution 1851 (2008), the UN Security Council invited all States and regional organizations engaged in the combating of piracy off the coast of Somalia to

82. The first of these resolutions was SC res. 1816 (2008). Other subsequent resolutions include: SC res. 1897 (2009), SC res. 1976 (2011), SC res. 2020 (2011), SC res. 2015 (2011).

83. Papastavridis, *op. cit.*, p. 180.

84. *Ibid.*, 183.

85. *Ibid.*, 183.

86. For an update of UNODC's work in this area see http://www.unodc.org/easternafrica/en/piracy/index.html.

87. SC res. 1897 (2009), para. 12.

conclude shiprider agreements with States willing to take custody of pirates to enable investigation and prosecution of the latter[88]. Such agreements are subject to the advance consent of the Somali Government.

The potential of applying existing universal treaties to the Somalia situation needs to be borne in mind. As explained in the various sections of this chapter, these treaties contain a range of provisions on interstate co-operation and wide grounds of jurisdiction. As observed by Roach, the potential of applying different legal frameworks to serious maritime crimes has not been fully appreciated[89]. The UN Security Council has in fact recognized the potential applicability of many of these instruments in its various resolutions. For example, in 2011, the UN Security Council again referred to SUA's applicability as well as that of the 1979 Hostages Convention[90]. The UN Security Council has also recognized the transnational organized nature of Somalia piracy. This hints at the potential applicability of UNTOC. In resolution 1976 (2011) and resolution 2020 (2011) the Security Council noted the importance of dealing with the financial aspect of Somali piracy, calling for "the need to investigate and prosecute those who illicitly finance, plan, organise or unlawfully profit from pirate attacks off Somalia" and "the laundering of its proceeds"[91]. This in turn highlights the important role that the TFC could play.

SECTION 6 CONCLUSION: MAXIMIZING THE POTENTIAL OF MULTIPLE FRAMEWORKS TO STRENGTHEN INTERSTATE CO-OPERATION

At first sight, the treaties most applicable to serious crimes at sea, such as UNCLOS and the 1988 SUA, do not appear to have sufficiently robust or detailed provisions governing interstate co-operation in criminal matters. This does not mean that there is a normative gap or lacuna. There is a need to examine the variety of potentially applicable normative frameworks, such as that established by transnational crime treaties, so as to fully realize their cross-cutting potential in facilitating interstate co-operation with respect to serious crimes at sea. However, these different frameworks each have their strengths and

88. Papastavridis, *op. cit.*, p. 188.
89. Roach, *op. cit.*, pp. 408-409.
90. SC res. 2020 (2011), preamble, para. 23.
91. SC res. 1976 (2011), para. 5; SC res. 2020 (2011), para. 17. See also SC res. 2015 (2011), para. 17.

weaknesses. For example, the maritime security and anti-terrorism treaties impose more absolute obligations to co-operate as compared to corresponding provisions of transnational crime treaties. The latter in turn contain more detailed provisions on the procedure to be followed when undertaking such co-operation. By understanding the similarities and differences between these treaties, States can select which ones best fit their needs in a particular case with a view to enhancing interstate co-operation. In addition, the international community has also adopted context-specific frameworks, such as that applicable to piracy and armed robbery occurring off the coast of Somalia. There may be scope for the development of such context-specific approaches, particularly on a regional level. The Somalia framework may be seen as particularly invasive, and while it is unlikely that it will be replicated at a general or universal level, some aspects may be relevant at the regional level where there is a higher level of mutual interest among States in preventing and repressing serious maritime crimes in their waters. Such enhanced levels of regional co-operation makes sense as while the geographical scope of maritime crimes has increased due to technological advances, many of these crimes still occur at the regional as opposed to global level.

The normative landscape governing interstate co-operation in furtherance of the prosecution of serious maritime crimes is therefore varied but substantial. However, to realize the potential of existing legal frameworks, there is a need to encourage their widespread ratification and effective implementation at the domestic level. This is particularly so for countries subscribing to the monist model of international law by which international treaties are only given effect at the domestic level if they are implemented through domestic legislation. In February 2010, the *Asta* tugboat which flew the Singapore flag was hijacked in Malaysian territorial seas by Indonesian pirates[92]. The tugboat and the offenders were later located and arrested in the Philippines. Though the Philippines authorities arrested the offenders, the prosecutor-in-charge noted that he did not have sufficient resources to undertake prosecution, particularly with respect to the bringing in of foreign witnesses from Malaysia and Indonesia[93]. In such a situation, where the custodial State does not have sufficient resources to bring a prosecution, the State may decide to extradite the accused persons to another State with links to the case, in this case Malaysia, Indonesia, or Singapore. Unfortunately, though the 1988 SUA framework could potentially apply, both Malaysia and Indonesia have not yet ratified this treaty. The Philippines has not yet implemented domestic legislation. It would not be able to extradite

92. Beckman and Palakrishnan, *op. cit.*, p. 12.
93. Philippines Country Report, 2011 CIL Workshop.

to Singapore, the remaining State with links in the matter and which has ratified the 1988 SUA[94].

The full potential of these various instruments should also be maximized at the implementation and institutional level. At the practical implementation level, the potential applicability of multiple legal frameworks is often overlooked due to institutional arrangements. At the domestic level, responsibility over individual treaties is divided and separately assigned to different governmental departments. At the international level, treaties is negotiated, deposited, and monitored under the auspices of different international organizations, such as the IMO or the United Nations. A lack of co-ordination or co-operation between different governmental departments or international organizations may result in the overlooking of a potentially applicable treaty or legal framework[95]. Practical guidelines should be established to assist practitioners in their day-to-day work. Officials should be able to quickly identify the most applicable framework that will facilitate the required interstate co-operation. In some cases, this may be as simple as referring to UNCLOS. In others, it may require reference to two or more treaties, including regional and bilateral agreements. As the international community increasingly emphasizes the pursuit of individual accountability and punishment for serious maritime crimes, such as piracy, quick and efficient interstate co-operation will become ever more important.

94. For the ratification status of SUA, please see ratification table, in *Piracy and International Maritime Crimes in ASEAN: Prospects for Cooperation*, Edward Eelgar Publishing Ltd., 2012. Also see Philippines Country Report, p. 21.

95. 2011 CIL Workshop Report, para. 68.2.

DEUXIÈME PARTIE

PART II

La prévention

Prevention

9 Private Armed Guards in the Fight against Piracy

Eniola Williams *

SECTION 1 INTRODUCTION

Contracting the services of Private Armed Guards (PAG) on board merchant vessels in High Risk Areas (HRA) and the use of firearms where occasion demands is currently engaging the affairs of States. A major area of contention is the lack of uniformity or settled law, resulting in multiplicity of regimes, practices and divergent opinions. To this end, this chapter seeks to examine current trends, views and positions held by parties, flag and port States, the International Maritime Organization (IMO), the International Chamber of Shipping (ICS), the Baltic and International Maritime Council (BIMCO), insurers and other stakeholders towards arriving at an acceptable legal basis for the use of armed guards on board vessels. In addition, this chapter will attempt to proffer answers to research questions, which include *inter alia*: Under what laws are the Private Armed Guards currently operating? Who takes responsibility during piracy attack, particularly for the just or unjustified use of firearms on board? What happens when armed guards capture pirates — who should they hand them over to since they are private concerns? Who takes responsibility when a guard shoots a person on board? What is the precise status of such PAG on board the vessel? What are the attendant risks to the master, crew or passengers on vessels with armed guards? What are the likely legal and administrative requirements for the reception of merchant vessels at ports with armed guards? Is the disposal of weapons at sea or use of floating armories as a means of storing weapons permissible under international law? The chapter further considers other related arrangements where Governments still retain monopoly of security under the socalled Vessel Protection Detach-

* Bachelor of Laws (LL.B), University of Lagos, Akoka, Nigeria (1985), Barrister at Law (BL) (1986), Masters Degree in International Maritime Law (LLM) (1998), IMO International Maritime Law Institute, Malta (IMLI). Assistant General Manager, Legal, Nigerian Ports Authority. Currently research candidate at IMLI.

ment and Shipriders Agreement. Incidents bordering on fatal shootings and consequential legal actions instituted are also dealt with along with national practices. The conclusion presents a summation of issues, emerging trends, recommendations and the way forward.

Paragraph 1 **Threat to Maritime Security/Global Response**

The continuous threat posed to international shipping, notably off the coast of Somalia, Gulf of Aden (GOA), South China Sea, Gulf of Guinea, Arabian Sea, Indian Ocean and Malacca Straits, has attracted a series of international intervention and industry-induced solutions. The International Maritime Organization (IMO) received reports of 198 incidents between January and June 2012 in these areas[1]. The attacks were noted to be more sophisticated than traditional modes of operation with the pirates firing automatic weapons and rocket propelled grenades at merchant vessels while attempting to board or hijack them.

The world maritime community has orchestrated a response to this problem, which has brought about a plethora of logistical and legal challenges[2]. For example, the United Nations has been called upon to intervene, in respect of incidents off the coast of Somalia/Gulf of Aden[3]. It is reported that "since the crisis off the coast of Somalia began to escalate in 2008, more than 3,000 seafarers have so far been kidnapped and held ransom, enduring months of appalling conditions"[4].

The effect has been high level co-operation between States, particularly in the detachment of naval troops to patrol these areas now designated as High Risk Areas (HRA). Consequently, naval and State ships have continued to protect the shipping lanes particularly for vessels delivering humanitarian aid under the World Food Programme (WFP). In addition, the co-operation has facilitated global protection of international trade and suppression of piracy by interdicting pirate ships and escorting susceptible merchant vessels out of the HRA.

The international shipping community on its part, in collaboration with other relevant bodies, notably the UN Contact Group on Piracy has put in place Best Management Practices (BMPs)[5] aimed at assisting

1. IMO Global Integrated Shipping Information Systems (GISIS), http://gisis.imo.org/Secretariat/Default.aspx (accessed on 30 October 2012).

2. G. Rodden and J. Walsh, "The Legal Issues of Private Armed Security on Commercial Ships", *The Federal Lawyer*, Vol. 58, No. 4, May 2001, at 30

3. Series of resolutions have been passed by the UN Security Council. Resolution 1816 authorizes foreign forces to enter into the Somali territorial sea, others include 1838, 1846, 1851.

4. International Maritime Organization (IMO), *Piracy in the Indian Ocean*, World Maritime Day 2011 publication.

5. The latest version is the BMP4, "Best Management Practices for Protection against Somalia Based Piracy (Version 4, August 2011) Suggested Planning and

ships to avoid, deter or delay piracy attacks in the HRA[6]. BMP is strongly recommended to be applied throughout the HRA.

With the magnitude of violence being recorded in the Gulf of Guinea and its designation as HRA, plans are under way by the Economic Community of West African States (ECOWAS) to jointly combat the violence aimed at looting goods on board. Positive steps taken include joint sea patrols, launched by the Federal Government of Nigeria and Benin Republic, with the backing of France. The IMO and the Maritime Organization of West and Central Africa (MOWCA) are also holding consultations, with a view to establishing coast-guard functions, Maritime Domain Awareness and other logistic requirements in the area. The Round Table of international shipping associations (BIMCO, ICS, INTERCARGO and INTERTANKO) recently developed a set of Interim Guidelines for Owners, Operators and Masters for protection against piracy and armed robbery in the Gulf of Guinea region[7]. The guidelines, though stand-alone in nature, are to be read in conjunction with the BMP4.

With respect to the applicable law, there is no comprehensive legal framework on the issue of Private Armed Guards for maritime operations or regulation of carriage of arms on board merchant vessels. This position makes it imperative to establish a legal basis upon which armed guards are currently deployed on vessels. It is noteworthy that all the guidelines issued by IMO to date are not mandatory. The Law of the Sea Convention (UNCLOS), however, gives direction in respect of activities permitted in different maritime zones, which shall be accordingly examined.

Paragraph 2 **The Observed Gaps in Past Initiatives**

Although there has been some remarkable global response to piracy by way of anti-piracy actions through naval patrols by the European Union Naval Force (EU NAVFOR), North Atlantic Treaty Organization (NATO) and the Combined Maritime Force (CMF) off the coast of Somalia and the application of Best Management Practices, some gaps still exist in attaining the desired level of security. Geo-

---

Operational Practices for Ship Operators, and Masters of Ships Transiting the High Risk Area", available at http//www.liscr/portals/o/BMP4.pdf (accessed on 18 October 2012).

6. BMP4, item 2.4, "The High Risk Area defines itself by where pirate activity/and or attacks have taken place. For the purpose of BMP the High Risk Area is an area bounded by the Suez and the Strait of Homuz . . ."

7. New Interim Anti-Piracy Guidelines for Gulf of Guinea, available at http :// www.shipping.nato.int/Pages/Guidelines-for-Gulf-of-Guinea.aspx (accessed on 28 March 2013).

graphical factors, such as the vast nature of coastlines, also limit the effectiveness of the patrols of the international navies, coupled with the reduction in most countries' defence budgets are mostly responsible for this development.

It has also been observed that as international navies are shrinking, the volume of trade by sea, on the other hand, is increasing. For example, the International Maritime Bureau (IMB) report for the first half of 2012 reflects that "Somali pirates continue to attack vessels in the northern Somali coast in the Gulf of Aden and the southern Red Sea in the Bab El Mandeb TSS despite the presence of warships"[8]. Most attacks were said to involve the use of highly sophisticated weapons, which is of great concern to the merchant navy fleet, as this poses serious threats not only to seafarers but also to the ship, cargo and environment. Spearing notes that, "the effective handling of Somali pirates has been an ephemeral and problematic task. Despite the international naval presence, the incidence of Somali piracy has increased."[9]

The world's insatiable demand for oil and gas draws prospectors to untapped reserves, much of which lie offshore. The limited natural resources will be underscored as the global population increases, stressing the vulnerability of the world's ports, as supply chain nodes. Against this backdrop, maritime crime will become very lucrative[10].

Paragraph 3 **Emergence of the Solution of Private Armed Guards**

Arising from the need for enhanced shipboard security, the current trend is a growing demand for the use of private armed guards. This development has been attributed largely to the perceived failure of Governments in their duty to offer the expected degree of protection to international shipping to correspond with the upsurge of the menace of unlawful acts at sea, notably piracy on strategic international routes. The limited effect navies have had so far precipitated a call by the United States to international commercial shippers to rely upon Private Security Companies[11].

---

8. ICC, International Maritime Bureau, Piracy and Armed Robbery against Ships. Report of 1 January-30 June 2012, p. 23.

9. C. Spearing, "A Private Security Solution to Somali Piracy: The U.S calls for Private Security Engagement and the Implications for Canada", https://www.Usnwc.edu/getattachment/C6f939ef-5695-4ed8-bfoa-14, at p. 56, accessed on 13 August 2012. (Naval War College Review, Autumn 2010, Vol. 63, No. 4.)

10. UK House of Commons Foreign Affairs Committee (Piracy off the Coast of Somalia submitted by the Security Association for the Maritime Industry (SAMI). http://www.publications.parliament.uk/, accessed 23 August 2012.

11. C. Spearing, *supra* footnote 9, p. 56.

The shipping community received this development with mixed feelings: on the positive side, these companies accord protection to vessels travelling in dangerous waters. The seas are much too vast for warships to protect all merchant vessels [12]. The private armed guard initiative has consequently evolved as a mitigating factor in the face of the observed threats. Based on reluctance to accept additional cost and liability associated with self-protection, commercial shipping associations and trade unions have been more adamant in the past on their position that keeping the sea lanes safe is the exclusive job of States. However, in February 2011, this position was reviewed when the International Chamber of Shipping (ICS) Chairman declared a change in its stance and acknowledged that "arming ships is a necessary alternative . . ." [13].

Rinehard referred to the view expressed by Peverett [14] that the armed maritime security providers "seem to be working, as there has been no successful attack on a vessel that has been carrying private armed security" [15]. As regards hijackings by Somali pirates, Cook stated that "no ship with armed guards on board has been hijacked by Somali pirates" [16].

It has also been expressed that "there is now a general acceptance of armed guards across the industry, although some flag states are still not permitting" [17]. This can be further corroborated by the action of States in allowing arms on board commercial vessels pursuant to relevant legislative amendments. In any case, a positive effect of this is that the navy (military) remains as the "preserve of the State" [18].

According to Hoeger, "[h]aving armed guards is cheaper than the extra fuel required to detour around pirate areas or to go fast enough to outrun them" [19]. Despite the surrounding controversies the deployment

12. C. Spearing, *supra* footnote 9, p. 61.

13. C. Berube and P. Cullen, Editors' Introduction, "The Emergence of Private Maritime security", in C. Berube and P. Cullen (eds.), *Maritime Private Security: Market Responses to Piracy, Terrorism and Waterborne Security Risks in the 21st Century*, London, Routledge, 2012, pp. 51-64.

14. T. Peverett, Head of Maritime Security, International Maritime Organization.

15. B. Rinehard, "Armed Guards on Merchant Vessels", https:www.cimicweb.org., accessed on 1 July 2012.

16. Michelle Wiese Bockmann and Alan Katz, "Shooting to Kill Pirates Risks Black Water Moment", views expressed by Peter Cook, Chairman, Security Association for the Maritime Industry, http://www.bloomberg.com/news/2012-05-08/shooting-to-kill-pirates-risks-blackwater-moment.html, accessed on 14 August 2012.

17. "Piracy — Issues Arising from the Use of Armed Guards", http://www.skuld.com/upload/News%20and%20Publications/Publications/Piracy/Ince-Pirates-issues-arising-from-the-use-of-armed-guards.pdf, pg4, accessed on 3 August 2012.

18. C. Spearing, *supra* footnote 9, p. 62.

19. *Supra* footnote 16: views expressed by R. Hoeger.

of PAG on commercial vessels is gaining ground. For example, warning shots fired by armed guards on board the *Maersk Alabama* foiled a pirate attack against the vessel[20].

In summary, pirate activities remain a challenge, which cannot be completely remedied through conventional approaches. Having PAG on board reduces the vulnerability of vessels to attacks and serves as a preventive measure in comparison to the high costs associated with post-hijacking efforts such as negotiators' fees, ransom payments, rescue attempts and the need to transit longer routes via the Cape of Good Hope[21]. Theodore describes armed security guards on merchant ships as a necessary evil and argues that if pirates know that there are armed guards on board that acts as a deterrent[22].

Be that as it may, PAG are not to be viewed as substitutes, but a complementary solution to multinational naval coalition and similar initiatives. Ship-owners should keep all options open in order to deter piracy attacks and defend their crews and vessels. The BMP4 contains, *inter alia*, provisions on crew safety, particularly safe muster point or citadel, freeboard, speed, sea state, planning and conduct expected prior to and during a typical pirate attack. It does not, however, recommend or endorse the general use of armed guards as this is considered as a matter for individual ship operators to decide following their own voyage risk assessment and approval of the respective flag States.

Paragraph 4 **Terminology**

The use of private security companies as service providers is considered not to be entirely new to the shipping industry as observed by Harrelson[23]; for years, private security companies provided services ranging from consulting on preventive measures to post attack services. It is further noted however that "the use of PAG varies from company to company". The need for definitions and distinctions becomes imperative due to the different nature of contracts which under certain circumstances involve the Government. Consequently, for the purposes of consistency and convenience, the following defined terms will be used throughout this paper.

20. The *Maersk Alabama* attacked previously on two occasions was targeted again by pirates on 9 March 2011; the attack was successfully repelled.

21. Source: "The American Club", Mutual Protection and Indemnity Club domiciled in the United States of America.

22. *The Nation*, 25 March 2010.

23. J. Harrelson, "Blackbead Meets Blackwater: An Analysis of International Conventions that Address Piracy and the Use of Private Security Companies to Protect the Shipping Industry", *American University International Law Review* 25 (2010), No. 2, p. 297

Paragraph 5 Definitions and Distinctions

A. Private Armed Guards/Privately Contracted Armed Security Personnel

Private Armed Guards (PAG) are individuals on contract with Private Maritime Security Companies (PMSC), who serve as guards on board vessels. IMO adopts the term "Privately Contracted Armed Security Personnel" (PCASP) and regards them as employees of PMSC[24]. A number of PAG are "former members of the military and are highly trained in the proper handling of weapons and use of force during a crisis"[25]. For the purposes of this chapter, the terms PAG and PCASP are used interchangeably and denote the same meaning.

B. Private Maritime Security Companies

These are security companies specifically for maritime domain, who enter into contracts directly with the shipping companies without any government involvement. IMO defines the PMSC as private contractors employed to provide security personnel, both armed and unarmed on board for protection against piracy. There are other private security companies who address land based issues and operate with or without government involvement. Mineau presents a catalogue of major Private Security Companies[26].

C. Escort vessels

This is an arrangement whereby PAG are not on board the merchant vessel but are in a smaller vessel engaged to lead the bigger vessel into or out of the HRA. The arrangement has been viewed as an effective way to remove shipboard threat through the use of escort platforms including ships, helicopters and small boats to provide a secure perimeter[27]. Experts consider the practice of convoying and escorting merchant vessels as an effective means of navigating in HRA.

---

24. MSC.1/1405.Rev.1.
25. G. Rodden and J. Walsh, "The Legal Issues of Private Armed Security on Commercial Ships", *The Federal Lawyer*, Vol. 58, No. 4, May 2001.
26. M. Mineau, "Pirates, Blackwater and Maritime Security: The Rise of Private Navies in Response to Modern Piracy", *Journal of International Business and Law* 9 (2010), No. 1, pp. 63-78.
27. C. G. Berube, "Anti-Piracy Escorts in the Gulf of Aden: Problems and Prospects", in C. Berube and P. Cullen (eds.), *Maritime Private Security: Market Responses to Piracy, Terrorism and Waterborne Security Risks in the 21st Century*, London, Routledge, 2012, pp. 74-85.

The escort vessel may be approached and visited since it cannot enjoy immunity, being neither a warship nor a ship used only on government service and cannot exercise a right of visit. The escort ship does not possess the status of a commissioned vessel, which can be used for pirate hunting. Berube observes further that this concept is not necessarily new; historically, the use of armed escort vessels was apparent throughout most of the age of sail particularly in the form of privateers which were legitimate, State-sponsored security who might be issued letters of marquee to attack enemy commerce[28].

D. Vessel Protection Detachment

This term refers to small military teams deployed on civilian merchant vessel. In discussing this model Ronzitti highlights the fact that it is a similar but completely different phenomenon involving the detachment of armed soldiers on board[29]. The legal basis for the arrangement lies in international[30] and national[31] instruments. Vessel Protection Detachments (VPDs) are included within the scheme of EU NAVFOR, "Operation Atlanta". Additionally, it involves uniformed personnel under regular discipline and thus differs from PAG. Armed teams are stationed on land in the Gulf of Aden region.

VPD teams are not only to resist and defend ships from pirates, but also to deter and intervene in order to bring an end to acts of piracy, including powers of arrest and seizure of assets under pirate control. The EU anti-piracy task force has organized a system of VPD for helping ships under piratical attack. Occasionally, navies provide an escort for a fee; for instance, the Yemeni navy provides escort services in the Gulf of Aden and charges up to US$55,000 per ship. The EU anti-piracy task force has also organized a system of VPD for helping ships under piratical attack. Pirate hunting should, however, be excluded since the merchant ship cannot qualify as a warship or a duly authorized vessel on government service, even though it has a VPD on board[32]. Hence, there is no room for the application of Article 110 of UNCLOS.

The presence of VPD requires an agreement between the State to which the armed team belongs and the flag State of the merchant ship

28. Letters of Marquee were outlawed by the Treaty of Paris of 1856.

29. N. Ronzitti, "The Use of Private Contractors in the Fight against Piracy: Policy Options", in F. Francioni and N. Ronzitti (eds.), *War by Contract, Human Rights, Humanitarian Law and Private Contractors*, Oxford University Press, 2011, pp. 37-51.

30. Article 92, UNCLOS.

31. Article 97 (1) of the Constitution of the Netherlands serves as the legal basis for VPDS on board vessels registered under its flag.

32. Please see definition of warship, Article 29, UNCLOS.

requesting the service. Declarations, which serve as a form of indemnity to the navies, are often signed.

E. Shiprider

This operates by an agreement in which a law enforcement officer embarks on a vessel, usually a government warship, sailing a national flag different from the nationality of the shiprider. The purpose is to enlarge the powers of the vessel by embarking on board a law enforcement officer with due authorization to perform certain acts which may involve entry into territorial waters of the State, sending the shiprider or boarding and seizing a vessel flying the flag of that State or direct enforcement of its national laws.

The contracts are mainly on the protection of the marine environment, prevention of illegal trafficking of weapons, piracy and illegal migration. The shiprider arrangement also addresses issues of jurisdiction on probable areas of concurrence.

Paragraph 6 **Scope**

This chapter will be confined to private maritime security arrangement. Hence, only PAG and Private Security Escorts will be examined. It will also seek to examine the main controversies and complexities in the use of PAG through the lens of the UNCLOS and industry regulations, with particular focus on IMO guidelines. Through a critical analysis of the complex subject of PAG, this chapter will make recommendations to the maritime world on the main issues in the use of PAG and consequential use of force on board merchant vessels. The legal and regulatory framework with regard to the use of PAG and the obligations incumbent on flag States, ship-owners, PMSC and PAGs will be also addressed here.

SECTION 2 **THE GENERAL LEGAL FRAMEWORK OF PAG**

Paragraph 1 **Legal and Regulatory Framework**

The movement of vessels with PAG on board is subject to regulations, which are international, regional or national in nature. To date, there is no international regulatory framework of a binding nature that comprehensively addresses the subject and no uniformity of laws on armed non-state actors at sea at the national level. Consequently, States have taken different initiatives and measures. It has been observed that there is an array of standards created since 2009 which suggest good practice for private security teams, but none is legally binding[33]. Similarly, Cullen has expressed the view that "regulating maritime security companies is a very grey area"[34]. This section examines the relevant international treaty regimes as well as soft-law instruments; reference is also made to national laws and regulations.

A. The Law of the Sea Convention

There are no explicit provisions on PAG or escort vessels in the Law of the Sea Convention (UNCLOS). However, the right of coastal States to legislate on safety of navigation[35] as well as of the flag State to regulate the safety of its vessels[36] is beyond any doubt. It is submitted that these provisions afford the requisite legal basis for States to enact legislations as they deem necessary towards enhancing shipboard security. Other relevant provisions having impact on the subject are discussed under relevant sections.

B. IMO Convention/Resolution/Guidelines

Presently, there is no international convention by IMO on this subject. Attempts are however being made to establish a nexus between the International Ship and Port Security Facility Code (ISPS Code), which provides for private sector participation in managing maritime security risks, and PAG. The IMO, in collaboration with key stakeholders through its Maritime Safety Committee (MSC), has produced guidelines respectively to ship-owners, ship operators and ship masters, and made recommendations to flag, port and coastal States which are neither legally binding nor certifiable standards[37] on the use of PCASP.

---

33. *The Economist*, "Laws and Guns Armed Guards on Ships Deter Pirates. But Who Says They Are Legal?", http://www.economist.com/node/21552553, accessed on 29 August 2012.

34. P. Cullen, "Private Guards Kill Somali Pirates for First Time", http://www.foxnews.com/world/2010/03/24/private-guards-kill-Somali-pirate-time, accessed on 1 July 2012.

35. Article 21 (1) *(a)*, United Nations Convention on the Law of the Sea, 1982.

36. *Ibid.*, Articles 92 and 94.

37. MSC.1/Circ.1405 — Interim Guidance to Shipowners, Ship Operator and Shipmasters on the Use of Privately Contracted Armed Security Personnel on Board Ships in the High Risk Area. MSC.1/Circ.1406 — Interim Recommendations for Flag States Regarding the Use of Privately Contracted Armed Security Personnel on Board Ships in the High Risk Area. MSC.1/Circ.1408 — Interim Recommendations for Port and Coastal States Regarding the Use of Privately Contracted Armed Security Personnel on Board Ships in the High Risk Area.

In Circular MSC.1/Circ.1405.Rev.1, IMO notes

> "[T]he increased threat to commercial shipping by Somalia-based pirates has led to extended use of armed guards and a marked expansion in the number of firms offering armed maritime security services for vessels transiting the HRA. The Organization, whilst not endorsing the use of privately contracted armed security personnel (PCASP), understands that shipping companies may find it difficult to identify reliable, professional private providers of armed security."

The decision on the employment of PCASP on board ships is a complex one for a ship-owner. The absence of applicable regulation and industry self-regulation coupled with complex legal requirements governing legitimate transport, carriage and use of firearms gives cause for concern. IMO notes further

> "this situation is further complicated by the rapid growth in the number of PMSC and doubts about the capabilities and maturity of some of these companies. Significant competence and quality variations are present across the spectrum of contractors offering services."[38]

The following issues are all addressed in circular MSC.1/Circ.1405. Rev.1.

Risk assessment, PMSC Selection Criteria, PMSC Background Information, Selection and Vetting of PMSC, Training of PCASP, Service Provision considerations (Insurance, ship-owners insurance cover, PMSC insurance cover), PCASP Team Size, Composition and Equipment Command and Control of On-board Security Team — including relationship with the Master, Management of Firearms and Ammunition from Embarkation to Disembarkation, Rules for the Use of Force, Reporting and Record Keeping Categorization of PCASP, Reporting within HRA, Familiarization for Master and the crew.

A special segment of the MSC discussed the possible approaches, which the international community can adopt on issues related to the deployment of PCASP on board ships and the carriage of arms on board ships in HRA[39]. The outcome was MSC.1/Circ.1443, the Interim Guidance on "Private Maritime Security Companies Providing Privately Contracted Armed Security Personnel on Board Ships in the High Risk

38. MSC.89/WP.6, Annex 3, p. 2.

39. Session convened by the IMO Secretary-General, Koji Sekimizu, to discuss policy matters related to arms on board ships in the piracy high risk area, requested a working group to develop the Interim Guidance. MSC 90th session, 16 to 25 May 2012.

Areas"[40] coupled with MSC.1/Circ.1446 to prevent and mitigate Somali-based piracy. MSC.1/Circ.1443 makes provision, *inter alia*, for PMSC professional certification, company requirement, applicable law, insurance, PCASP composition and equipment, command and control, management of firearms, use of force and record keeping.

The Facilitation Committee (FAL) has also issued questionnaires on information on port and coastal State requirements on the subject[41]. These initiatives are in recognition of the growing demand and placement of armed guards on board vessels and the need for a degree of regulation.

Quite recently, the IMO has assigned the International Standards Organization (ISO) the task to develop the first global standards for PMSC which should be based on IMO MSC.1/Circ.1443. Accordingly, ISO with the liaison and participation of IMO, has developed the only published International Standards dealing with armed guards on ships referred to as ISO/PAS 28007:2012, "Ships and Marine Technology — Guidelines for Private Maritime Security Companies (PMSC)", providing privately contracted armed security personnel (PCASP) on board ships (and pro forma contract). The document is presumed to have received the support of many stakeholders, including the UN Contact Group on Piracy off the Coast of Somalia[42].

In the determination of the applicable law on PAG, numerous international conventions, regional arrangements and domestic law have a bearing, including human rights law.

MSC.1/1443 specifically makes reference to two other documents, i.e.

> "The Montreux Document on Pertinent International Legal Obligations and Good Practices for States related to Operations of Private Military and Security Companies during Armed Conflict[43], and the International Code of Conduct for Private Security Service Providers (ICoC)."[44]

These documents are not directly relevant to the situation of piracy and armed robbery in the maritime domain and do not provide sufficient guidance for PMSC.

The Montreux Document restates rules of international law and provides a set of good practices for States. The ICoC, on its part, addresses

40. Circular of 25 May 2012.
41. MSC-FAL./CIRC.2 of 22/09/2011.
42. Fighting Piracy — ISO Guidelines for Armed Maritime Guards, http://www.iso.org/iso/home/news_index/news_archive/news.htm?refid=Ref1717, accessed on 28 March 2013.
43. http://www.eisf.eu/resources/item/?d=2051.
44. The ICoC sets forth a set of principles for private security companies.

the private security industry and identifies a set of principles and processes for private security service providers on the support for the rule of law and respect for human rights. However, it is elaborated in the context of self-regulation and directed at land-based security companies only.

C. The UN Draft Convention

The UN Draft Convention (Regulation, Oversight and Monitoring of Private Military and Security Companies) may also be considered as a related document when it will come into force. The Draft Convention has been the result of the legitimate concerns about the great dangers involved in the delegation or outsourcing of inherently governmental functions[45].

In contemplation of the fact that important gaps remain in the national and international legal regimes applicable to private military and security companies, the duty of every State to exercise its criminal jurisdiction over those responsible for international crimes is of significance. Emphasis is placed on the responsibility to protect all persons, whether civilians or military personnel, from abuses of their human rights by the actions or omissions of non- State actors including the private military and security companies[46].

Noteworthy are the provisions on State responsibility contained in Article 4 (1) and (2) which provide respectively that:

> "[E]ach State Party bears civil and criminal responsibility for the use of force under national and international law, whether the use of force occurs within its territory or outside its borders"

and that

> "[E]ach State party bears responsibility for the military and security activities of private entities registered or operating under their jurisdiction, whether or not these entities are contracted by the State."

---

45. The final draft of the proposed convention for distribution is dated 13 July 2009, available at http://www.mgimo.ru/files/121626/draft.pdf, accessed on 19 January 2013.

46. The draft defines Private Military and/or Security Company (PMSC) as a corporate entity that provides on a compensatory basis military and/or security services, including investigation services by physical persons and/or legal entities. Military services refer to specialized services related to military actions including strategic planning, intelligence, investigation, land, sea or air reconnaissance etc., while Security services refer to armed guarding or protection of buildings, installations, property and people etc.

In addition, the companies are obliged to take cognizance of and to observe the norms of international humanitarian law and human rights law as well as relevant domestic law.

D. BIMCO GUARDCON contract for employment of security guards

The BIMCO GUARDCON contract for the employment of security guards on vessels (GUARDCON) was developed for the benefit of the wider shipping community. It is a product of a working group comprising ship-owners, property underwriters, insurance groups, Protection & Indemnity (P&I) clubs, maritime lawyers, representatives of security companies and other ship-owners and Maritime Insurance Associations. The intention is to harmonize the terms of engagement of PMSC as well as to simplify the processes for vetting and approval of contracts by members and their P&I clubs. It also constitutes a recommendation by BIMCO for the use of PAG on board vessels[47]. In this regard, PAG are only to be considered for placement on board a vessel after a risk assessment has been carried out with the master being involved in the decision-making process.

GUARDCON represents a positive attempt at creating uniformity in standards of the employment of security guards on vessels. Key issues addressed by GUARDCON by way of standards, which the PMSCs must adhere to, include: insurance, permits and licences to legally transfer weapons, knock-for-knock principle (liability and indemnity), masters' responsibility for the safe navigation and overall command of the vessel.

E. National legislation and guidelines

At the national level, States that allow PAG must set out an adequate regulatory framework. This can be construed from the duty of "due diligence" imposed to minimize risks to foreign nationals and States in respect of dangerous activities within their jurisdiction. Consequently, States that allow PAG are expected to make open declarations with necessary supportive legislation and guidelines[48]. The United Kingdom has issued an Interim Guidance to UK-flagged ships. In the United States, Club Guidance is in place via American Club Circular

47. BIMCO Circular 5/12, published on 28 March 2012.

48. D. Guilfoyle, "Shooting Fishermen Mistaken for Pirates: Jurisdiction, Immunity and State Responsibility", http://www.ejiltalk.org/shooting-fishermen-mistaken-for-pirates-jurisdiction-immunity-and-state-responsibility, accessed on 19 January 2013.

No. 18/11 of 3 June 2011, while the Liberian Bureau of Maritime Affairs developed similar guidance[49]. India is an example of a country that has amended its national laws to reflect its current position. Further considerations are given to this under "Use of Force by Private Armed Guards — Regulation by National Law" (Section 3, para. 2, *infra*).

Paragraph 2 The Relevant Stakeholders and Their Obligations under International Law

A. Flag States

The law of the flag State is of paramount importance for the employment of PAG on board merchant vessels. This is in line with the provisions of Article 94 (1) of UNCLOS which states that "every State shall effectively exercise its jurisdiction and control in administrative, technical and social matters over ships flying its flag". To this end, the flag State is expected to issue explicit regulations with respect to licences/permits required for the carriage of arms and use of weapons on board its vessels, set rules of engagement/rules for the use of force and provide written consent to the ship-owners. The position of IMO, as stated in its Circular, is that "the decision to allow PCASP, on board ships is the prerogative of flag States and not all flag States may allow their use"[50]. Therefore, the responsibility to allow and regulate further the deployment of PCASP falls upon the flag States.

B. Ship-owner

The ship-owner is vested with the responsibility of operating the vessel safely with the required degree of care for the crew and co-ordinate effective training between master, crew, and security company personnel, particularly the proper designation of roles and responsibilities.

As regards vessels with PAG on board, the main operational factors are safety, security, legal compliance and competence[51]. The ship-owner is therefore expected to act in due diligence and undertake some prelimi-

49. The Republic of Liberia, Bureau of Maritime Affairs, Maritime Security Advisory: Interim Guidance on the Use of Privately Contracted Armed Security Personnel on Board Ships in High Risk Area, htpp://www.liscr.com/liscr/portals/0/securityAdvisory_03/2011.

50. MSC.1/Circ.1443, Annex, p. 1, para. 1.2.

51. Darren Dixon, Oxberry Risk Strategies, "What to Expect Operationally When Armed Guards Are Used on Board", paper presented at 4th Maritime Piracy & Security Summit 30-31 January 2013, London.

nary steps by way of conducting detailed risk assessment in the selection of the PMSC that will deploy the PAG. In the discharge of this obligation, it is expected that the PAG to be deployed must be trained, intimately familiar with BMP and carry only licensed weapons on board. Furthermore, the ship-owner bears the duty to enquire if the respective flag State allows PAG on their vessels as well as to enquire of the related issues of licences or permits requirements for the carriage and use of weapons and rules of engagement.

In addressing the question of "how does a commercial ship owner choose an appropriate private security firm" Hook responds that

> "there are many domestic and international companies that offer armed and unarmed security services, and they have an equally broad range of experience, skills and abilities. While this is a good start, there are still a number of issues that confront a commercial operator in this process, particularly in the due diligence required to access private security reliability, quality of training and consistency of performance . . ."[52]

It is noted that a number of companies lacking required expertise have come on stage, which suggest compromise on standards. In the words of Ramachandran[53],

> "[a] number of maritime companies have jumped into the fray, but the quality of manpower employed by many of these companies is questionable. There have been reports of inadequate professional expertise, sloppy behavior and failure to follow safety regulations. What is more worrisome is the absence of standards or appropriate regulations to reign in security companies or clear guidelines on the use of force, particularly lethal force, on when to use the force and how much."

The ship-owner must also provide the P&I club with the flag State's written consent and should verify that PMSC maintain insurance cover for themselves, their personnel and third-party liability cover and ensure that the PMSC terms of engagement do not prejudice or potentially prejudice the ship-owner's insurance cover. It is therefore strongly recommended that ship-owners consult with their insurers prior to con-

---

52. G. E. Van Hook, "Private Security at Sea; A Customers Perspective", in C. Berube and P. Cullen (eds.), *Maritime Private Security: Market Responses to Piracy, Terrorism and Waterborne Security Risks in the 21st Century*, London, Routledge, 2012, pp. 65-73.

53. U. Ramachandran, "Armed Men on Board Merchant Ships — Boon or Bane?", http://www.thehindubusinessline.com/industry-and-economy/logistics/armed-men-on-board-merchant-ships-boon-or-bane/article3342539.ece, accessed on 29 September 2012.

tracting with and embarking PAG to assess the potential impact on their insurance cover, particularly as it relates to armed engagements and liability insurance held by the PMSC. Consequently, effective liaison with the master and crew which includes overview of vessel defence strategy, realistic review of threat and risk assessment and weapons safety brief have been identified as critical success factors[54]. Understanding of the national laws of the country, where the security company employing PAG is based, as well as the insurance cover is also important.

C. Master

The master is endowed upon with the overall responsibility of the vessel particularly safe passage of vessel, with authority to take any step to avoid threats to passage or danger to crew[55] and comply with BMPs while navigating through HRA. For the example, in the *Maersk Alabama* case[56], the master's judgment to take the vessel through a particular route was erroneous.

Where PAG are on board the vessel, the question of who is responsible in the event of a piracy attack is much debated. This is based on the expertise that can only be demonstrated by PAG when the use of force becomes imminent. Under GUARDCON contract, the master has the authority to order the cease-fire. However, the authority to use of force is retained by the PAG. This position is not shared by the IMO.

D. Private Maritime Security Company

It is the duty of the employers of PAG to seek the approval for their deployment, firstly, from the competent authorities in countries where PMSC is registered and, secondly, from the authorities in countries in which operations are conducted, including those in which PAG may transit (MSC.1/Circ.1443). Awareness and understanding of applicable laws of flag, port and coastal States with respect to the transport, carriage, storage and use of firearms, security related equipment and the use of force are also required. In addition, the PMSC should possess a policy governing command and control of PAG on board; it should ensure that PAG are fully aware of them and the team manages firearms and ammunition in a responsible manner at all times.

---

54. Darren Dixon, Oxberry Risk Strategies, *supra* footnote 51.
55. Regulation 8, The International Ship and Port Facility Security Code (ISPS Code) implemented through Chapter X1-2 of the International Convention for Safety of Life at Sea.
56. *Supra*, footnote 20.

E. Privately Armed Guards/Private Contracted Armed Security Personnel

In the discharge of their obligations, it is of utmost importance that all steps taken by PAG are consistent with its role, which is exclusively the protection of life of persons on board and the ship from armed pirate attack. All reasonable steps must be taken to avoid the use of force; however, if force is eventually used, it should be used as part of a graduated response plan, including strict implementation of the BMP. In general, the use of force in excess of what is strictly necessary and reasonable in the circumstances must be avoided and care taken to minimize damage/injury and to respect and preserve human life. It is envisaged that firearms would only be used against persons in self-defence or in defence of others.

The need for PAG to have a complete understanding of, and fully comply with, the applicable laws governing the use of force cannot therefore be over-emphasized.

Based on the variety of high-risk tasks committed to PAG including convoy duties and close protection of individuals at risk of suffering harm, concerns have been raised about their mental health which may have commercial implications with research currently underway to determine the mental health of PAG[57].

In order to accommodate the presence of PAG on board, they are often listed as "supernumeraries", which is preferable to listing them as passengers which creates problems on terms of employment and carriage of weapons[58]. Such designation alleviates the concerns raised by some ports on the status of non-crew on the ship. As a measure of comfort, seafarers have expressed the appeal for PAG aboard ships especially in HRA[59].

The numerous controversies surrounding the use of PAG have made the Contact Group on Piracy off the Coast of Somalia to view it as "more legally challenging than VPDs"[60]. Rinehard rightly points out that "the use of PAG remains controversial and several aspects have to be considered, including legal aspects"[61].

---

57. L. McMahon, "A New Frame of Mind for Armed Guards", *Lloyd's List*, 31 May 2012.
58. BIMCO GUARDCON, "Explanatory Notes".
59. M. Garfinkle, "The Psychological Impact of Piracy on Seafarers", The Seamen's Church Institute, 2012.
60. Communiqué of the Eleventh Plenary Session of the Contact Group on Piracy off the Coast of Somalia, 29 March 2012, http://www.thecgpcs.org/plenary.do;jsessioid=7UgnMnFBHbHOavdRDL8NmfcjifC2ckgaQ7NOSqgNkp11S1sG1e51ZyYM7VuwD11XF?action=plenarySub&seq=20,para(5c).
61. B. Rinehard, *supra* footnote 15.

F. Insurance

The presence of PAG on board does have consequences on insurance cover. IMO calls upon the PMSC to hold and maintain public and employers' liability insurance cover to an appropriate level required by the ship-owner and personal accident, medical expenses, hospitalization and repatriation insurance. PAG, who carry and use the firearms, are to be insured for accidents, injury and damage arising from the use of firearms and liability for any claim that might arise from the carriage and/or negligent or intentional misuse of arms.

Conversely, PAG on board vessels may have a positive impact on insurance premiums. Reportedly, the growing trend among kidnap and ransom insurers is to demand the presence of armed guards on vessels transiting the Gulf of Aden and the Indian Ocean as a condition for providing cover, while others give substantial discounts to ship-owners with PAG on board in HRA. The IMO invites PSCs to note the impact that deployment of PAG may have on ship-owner's property and liability insurance cover.

The BIMCO GUARDCON has been recognized as a guide to minimum standards for P&I Clubs facing the challenge of identifying an appropriate provider. It prescribes four-man security on board comprising three supports and a team leader. A compromise on this has far-reaching consequences as

> "[a]ny company that agrees to reduce manning levels on transit to less than four risks invalidating its insurance cover — as well as risking the lives of crew on board if its remaining staff prove unable to deter a pirate attack"[62].

Other factors that may negate insurance cover include the use of other personnel to double as security team members referred to as "weapon guardians", engaged to monitor the use and location of hired weapons, or the use of staff with language barrier[63].

SECTION 3 OPERATION OF PRIVATE ARMED GUARDS UNDER INTERNATIONAL AND NATIONAL LAWS

Paragraph 1 Jurisdiction

Private security operations are not as complicated on land as they are in the maritime environment in ways typically not

62. L. McMahon, PMSC, "cost-cutting tactics could invalidate insurance." Views expressed by T. Jakobsson, in *Lloyd's List*, No. 60, 17 October 2012.
63. *Ibid.*

encountered by their counterparts on land[64]. Security operatives on land have defined operational zones mostly confined to a single State. However, for maritime operatives it is necessary to cross over different jurisdictions with differing legal systems and laws. PAG are therefore often subjected to the overlapping jurisdictions of both the flag State as well as the littoral State whose territorial waters they are traversing. The maritime zones that vessels with PAG on board transit are the following.

A. High seas

Under UNCLOS, a vessel on the high seas is subject to the exclusive jurisdiction of the flag State[65]; this entails that PAG fall under the general criminal jurisdiction of the flag State. For example, in the *Almezaan* incident, which involved a Panama-flagged merchant vessel attacked by pirates off the Somalia coast, the death of one of the assailants by PAG would attract the flag State criminal jurisdiction and concurrent jurisdiction of other States involved.

B. Internal waters/port

By virtue of its sovereignty, the coastal State is entitled to regulate and prescribe conditions for access to its ports[66]. By entering foreign ports and internal waters, ships put themselves within the territorial sovereignty of the coastal State. Accordingly, that State is entitled to enforce its laws against the ship and those on board, subject to the normal rules relating to sovereign and diplomatic immunities which arise chiefly in the case of State-owned ships[67]. It is pertinent to mention that States do not however exercise jurisdiction over the internal affairs of ships in its ports as this remains under the control of the flag States.

With respect to the reception of vessels with PAG on board into port, the legal and administrative requirements in this respect are still unclear. It is for the coastal State to set forth conditions on admission of ships with PAG to its internal waters or port and request information in that connection.

In contemplation of the fact that the facilitation of the movement of

64. C. G. Berube and P. Cullen, "The Future of Private Security at Sea", in C. Berube and P. Cullen (eds.), *Maritime Private Security: Market Responses to Piracy, Terrorism and Waterborne Security Risks in the 21st Century*, London, Routledge, 2012, at pp. 139-149.

65. Article 92, UNCLOS.

66. Article 25 (2), UNCLOS.

67. R. R. Churchill and A. V. Lowe, *The Law of the Sea*, 3rd ed., Manchester University Press, 1999, p. 54.

PAG should be subject to national legislation of port and coastal States, the IMO developed recommendations to coastal and port States on aspects related to the embarkation, disembarkation and carriage of PCASP and of firearms and security related equipment, for use by PCASP on ships entering, transiting or leaving their territorial sea(s)[68]. The Guidelines encourage Governments in developing such policies to take the following factors into consideration: embarkation (requirements regarding notification of firearms and security related equipment proposed for embarkation); disembarkation (requirements relating to pre-arrival notification of ships carrying PCASP, firearms and security related equipment); vessel calling (requirements regarding the notification of PCASP, firearms and security related equipment retained on board).

The varying legal regimes encountered by PAG when transiting from port to port highlights the need for harmonization of the laws regarding the admission of vessels into their ports which must be respected by foreign vessels. As a way out of these conflicting legal regimes, some private companies have reportedly stored guns aboard floating armories on the high seas while some have disposed of weapons at sea[69]. The legality of floating armories in international law is unclear and recently highlighted as "one pressing and ongoing regulatory problem . . ."[70].

A number of vessels have been chartered to act as floating armories as a reaction to the increase in regulation and cost of moving weapons in and out of littoral States[71]. Hook, on his part, posits that except the PMSC secure transit licence rights at multiple voyage points, for their escort ships, security personnel and weapons, their ability to provide escort services is severely hampered. Some companies have attempted to avoid this complication by using ships that can store weapons and permit transfer at sea[72]. It has been concluded that "[d]espite the legal grey area that surrounds floating armories, they may be permitted if private maritime security companies can prove they fulfill licensing requirements" and, in addition, "that no international law specifically

68. MSC.1/1408 drawn up to address the concerns of port and coastal States with respect to the presence of PCASP and of firearms and security-related equipment for use by PCASP.

69. G. Manchuk, "Armed Guards, Marine Insurance, and the Implied Warranty of Legality", *U.S.F. Maritime Law Journal*, Vol. 24, No. 2, pp. 309-373, at p. 313, "since AK-47s are inexpensive, a provider could readily dump them overboard before it entered the territorial waters of a state that prohibited them".

70. View expressed by S. Askins, in L. McMahon, "Consistent Global Standards for Guards Hard to Achieve", *Lloyd's List*, 11 October 2012.

71. "Piracy — Issues Arising from the Use of Armed Guards", *supra* footnote 17.

72. Van Hook, *supra* footnote 52.

prohibit PMSC storing weapons offshore"[73]. The issue of the UN arms embargo on Somalia requires clarification in relation to the deployment of PAG.

C. Territorial waters/contiguous zones

Under international law, States exercise sovereignty over their territorial sea[74], subject to the right of innocent passage, in respect of which States may adopt laws and regulations relating to the said innocent passage through the territorial sea[75]. UNCLOS, however, precludes such laws and regulations from applying to the design, construction, manning or equipment of foreign ships. The question that arises here is whether the deployment of PAG on board vessels can be seen as manning of the vessel, which is exempted from the legislative powers of a State. In the view of the author, manning in relation to this subject will be viewed from the broader perspective of security.

It is observed that an increased number of attacks on vessels are now being recorded in the territorial waters of some States with a high degree of violence; however, this would not qualify as piracy as defined under UNCLOS[76]. It is pertinent to state that hunting pirates entering the territorial sea from the high seas or taking any police action against armed robbers is forbidden in foreign territorial seas unless authorized by the coastal State.

Maintaining law and order within territorial waters is an activity reserved for the coastal State and cannot be performed by foreign States unless the territorial sovereign consents.

Article 27, UNCLOS, imposes a limitation on the criminal jurisdiction of the coastal States. As such, this jurisdiction should not be exercised on board a foreign ship passing through the territorial sea either to arrest any person or to conduct any investigation in connection with any crime committed on board the ship except in circumstances listed in the convention[77].

Arguably, a coastal State may regard the death of a fisherman or pirate as a result of defensive action taken by a merchant ship as an exceptional circumstance. This may subject the ship to confiscation.

---

73. *World Maritime News*, "Gulf of Aden: Armed Guards Use Floating Armories", http//worldmaritimenews.com.
74. Article 2, UNCLOS.
75. Article 21 contains provisions on laws and regulations of a coastal State regarding innocent passage.
76. Article 101, UNCLOS. Such incidents are covered by the Convention for the Suppression of Unlawful Acts of Violence against the Safety of Maritime Navigation (SUA), 1988, and its 2005 Protocol.
77. See Article 27 (1) *(a)* to *(d)*.

D. Innocent passage

Special reference must be made to the right of innocent passage, which is granted to ships of all States navigating through the territorial sea. In relation to PAG, this right has generated a lot of controversy with a number of questions being raised. Ronzitti puts forward the following:

> "Are merchant vessels with security teams on board whether PMSCs or VPDs, entitled to innocent passage through the territorial sea of foreign states and to transit passage through international straits? Does the same solution apply to merchant vessels escorted by PMSCs or are escorting vessels required to abandon the escort before entering the territorial sea or at the embouchure of an international strait? Does a carrying armed team on board constitute a violation of the rules of innocent passage?"[78].

Ronzitti submits that the question may be answered in the negative as long as weapons are stored on board and the ship is not carrying out "any exercise or practice with weapons of any kind", an activity which is forbidden under Article 19 (2) *(a)* of UNCLOS. It is further submitted that while it may be within the rights of coastal States to prohibit ships from entering their ports with weapons on board they cannot prohibit the presence of weapons on board during passage, placing reliance on Article 21 of UNCLOS, which does not prohibit arms on board during passage. This position may not be flawed considering the fact that warships with heavy ammunitions are granted the right of innocent passage *(argumentum ad majore ad minus)*. The concerns raised with respect to PAG with weapons on board in my view is predicated on the fact that placement in this circumstance is on board merchant vessels with possibility of arms proliferation; this may be far-fetched as the passage must be expeditious.

Another school of thought, however, avers that the passage of vessels with armed escorts may indeed be denied. Whilst it is recognized that Article 17 of UNCLOS grants to ships of all States the right of innocent passage through the territorial sea, the passage rights to be enjoyed will only remain innocent "so long as it is not prejudicial to the peace, good order, or security of the coastal State"[79]. Article 19 (2) *(a)* and *(b)* mentions prejudicial circumstances as including, *inter alia*: any threat or use of force against the sovereignty, territorial integrity or the political independence of the coastal State and any exercise or practice with weapons of any kind, respectively. The combined effect of the foregoing pro-

78. N. Ronzitti, *supra* footnote 29.
79. Article 19 (1).

visions will be that States have the authority to pass laws to prevent vessels from entering territorial waters if the vessel poses a threat to the peace and order of the State. Fedeli, therefore, submits that "[h]eavily armed security guards aboard a vessel could legitimately pose a threat to the safety and of a State"[80].

Liss expresses the view that "while UNCLOS does not address the employment of armed guards/escort vessels specifically, its regulations may however give some insights"[81]. UNCLOS regulations are open to interpretations permitting some observers to see the above as principally allowing armed PMSC personnel, with others seeing armed guard (particularly when heavily armed) on board vessels and certainly armed escort vessels as breaching the condition of innocence and transit passage as defined above, if the guards do not comply with laws of (or have permission from) the States in whose waters they are operating. Arguably, most Governments would most likely interpret the UNCLOS regulations as not allowing armed personnel on board vessels in national waters.

E. Straits used for international navigation

For straits used for international navigation, UNCLOS includes specific regulations relating to transit passage. All ships enjoy the right of transit passage which shall not be impeded except in circumstances provided[82]. Article 38 defines "transit passage" as the exercise of the freedom of navigation for the purpose of continuous and expeditious transit of the straits. The Strait of Malacca had witnessed a number of armed robbery incidents upon which the Dutch Ship-owners Association sought government protection through provision of naval protection to vessels transiting the straits. The request was however stepped down based on the finding that large parts of the straits formed part of the territorial waters of the coastal States.

The Strait of Malacca is crucially important for the Malaysian and Indonesian Governments. These States have demonstrated strong reactions to unauthorized PMSC, thus requiring strict compliance with extant regulations. Singapore may also be involved, depending on the route of the vessel[83].

80. T. Fedeli, "The Rights and Liabilities of Private Actors, Pirates, Masters and Crew", One Earth Future Foundation Working Paper, July 2010, http// www.onearthfuture.org, accessed on 22 August 2012.

81. C. Liss, "Commercial Anti-Piracy Escorts in Malacca Strait", in C. Berube and P. Cullen (eds.), *Maritime Private Security: Market Responses to Piracy, Terrorism and Waterborne Security Risks in the 21st Century*, London, Routledge, 2012, pp. 51-64.

82. Article 38, UNCLOS.

83. C. Liss, *supra* footnote 81.

Paragraph 2 Use of Force by Private Armed Guards — Regulation by National Law

The use of force by PAG is subject to multiple national laws: the laws of the flag State of the vessel with PAG concerned on board, the laws of the flag State of the vessel against which force was used, the laws of the State of nationality of the victim and of the PAG respectively. Resorting to force, particularly lethal, must after all be considered a measure of last resort, as there are other non-violent means of repelling attacks[84].

IMO Circulars and virtually all industry guidelines have included provisions on the use of force. The need for clear rules concerning the use of force (RUF) has been reiterated by experts. Titahena and Sumser-Lupson observe that

> "one of the complications therefore is that there is no current uniform system that can be adopted by a security system. Therefore, because each flag state and indeed security companies are likely to have their own RUF it is likely that problems posed by this issue will arise in the near future."[85]

Thus,

> "If a Private Security Company uses force resulting in the death, or injury of crew and pirates, multiple states could assert jurisdiction over issues concerning the use of force. Legal standards and authorities differ from country to country and countries have different standards for judging whether their use of force was necessary or proportional."[86]

Concerns have also been raised about the safety of crew members when force is being used. They are seen as more likely to suffer the negative consequences of having armed guard on vessels. The pirates claim to have no desire to hurt the crew members, however potentials of violence escalating is very high during exchange of fire between them and PAG. The crew members are considered as

> "currently safer being taken hostage rather than being caught in a gun battle, the dangers to the crew members may therefore out-

84. Ships are known to have used non-lethal means in the face of piracy attacks which include, sonic weapons, high pressure water cannons, blinding strobe lights, foam, chemicals that can burn the eyes for about 45 minutes.

85. J. Titahena and K. Sumser-Lupson, *Privately Contracted Armed Security Personnel (PCASP) on Ships in High Risk Areas, Impacts, Concerns and Challenges*.

86. Rodden and Walsh, *supra* footnote 25, p. 32.

> weigh the potential deterrent effect of putting armed guards on vessels"[87].

Suffice to say that IMO does not permit arming crew on merchant vessels.

Paragraph 3 **Arrest of Pirates**

When PAG foil a pirate attack and successfully capture/arrest the pirates, the question arises as to the appropriate party to hand them over to since PAG are private concerns with no capability under international law to hold them in custody. No express provision is contained in UNCLOS on the capture of pirates by private concerns[88]. The call to pay closer attention to what happens with captured pirates was reiterated by Kraska and Wilson[89]; they argue that the greatest challenge is not the capturing of the pirates but the detention and prosecution which stem from the numerous nationalities involved.

Harrelson notes that the

> "UN Security council passed numerous temporary resolutions. The most current resolution extends the authority of co-operating states to enter and capture pirates in areas normally considered Somalia's sovereign territory"[90].

He further notes that the United States has agreed to turn captured pirates over to Kenya for detention and prosecution. These types of agreements are currently necessary "because no country including the U.S, has been willing to hold the (captured) pirates". He proceeds to observe that "similar agreements exist between other countries: however there is no uniformity among the various agreements due to different political climates and practical issues". Another international partnership, the Contact Group on Piracy off the Coast of Somalia, has as its main goal to "examine practical options for strengthening the ability of countries willing to detain and prosecute suspected pirates".

Noteworthy is the fact that some pirates have been treated on a "catch and release basis" which involves the return of pirates to Somali beaches based on issues of jurisdiction and lack of social infrastructure to prosecute the pirates in Somalia[91]. PAG are to observe the norms of international humanitarian law and human right law in this area.

---

87. J. Harrelson, *supra* footnote 23, p. 311.
88. Articles 105 and 107 recognizes only government vessels as able to seize pirates, pirate ships and property on board.
89. J. Kraska and B. Wilson, "Fighting Pirates. The Pen and the Sword", *World Policy Journal*, 25 (4), pp. 41-52.
90. Harrelson, *supra* footnote 23, pp. 289-290.
91. J. Kraska and B. Wilson, "Fighting Pirates. The Pen and the Sword", *World Policy Journal*, 25 (4), pp. 41-52.

It is safe to conclude therefore that where pirates are in the hands of PAG they should be handed over to the master of the vessel, who will in turn use the same principles as if PAG were not on board. Thereafter, the registry or flag of the attacked vessel, the State of nationality of any of the victims, the nationality of the on-scene warship, and coastal and port States in some instances all have a valid basis for asserting jurisdiction, provided that they have asserted the necessary legislative jurisdiction by enacting adequate national laws[92]. The US Municipality Statute provides that "whoever commits the crime of piracy as defined by the law of nations and afterwards brought into the U.S shall be imprisoned for life"[93]. It is equally possible to prosecute a pirate in English court as piracy is an offence under its statute laws[94]. The Joint Cyprus Shipowners Association (JCSA) strongly advocates that individual States must amend their national legislation in order to provide for PAG and allow for arrest, prosecution and sentencing of pirates in fast track procedure.

In conclusion, Ronzitti expresses the view that

> "arming vessels and hiring contractors for pirate hunting is legally possible if the vessel is on government service, authorised to chase Pirates, and the hiring government bears the international responsibility".

Paragraph 4 **Case Law/Incidents**

A. The Almezaan

Reportedly,

> "private security guards on board a UAE-owned cargo ship registered in Panama shot dead a pirate attempting to hijack the vessel off the coast of Somalia. The incident is the first in which a hijacker was killed by private contractors . . ."[95].

The Spanish frigate *ESPS Navara* forces aboard the warship took custody of the pirate's body and sank the larger boat while six others were

92. BBC News "What to do with a captured pirate", http//www.bbc.co.uk/news/world–africa-11813168, accessed on 19 January 2013.
93. 18 USC, § 1651-Sec.1651, Piracy under Law of Nations, http://www.us-code.vlex.com/vid/sec-piracy-under-law-nations-19190482, full text 18 USC, Chapter 81.
94. S.26, Merchant Shipping and Maritime Security Act, 1997.
95. See article by Loveday Morris, "Pirate Shot Dead in Attack on UAE Ship", *The National*, http:thenational.ae/news/uae-news/pirate-shot-dead-in-attack-on-uae-ship, accessed on 9 October 2012.

arrested but subsequently released by the EU NAVFOR because the captain declined to identify them for the purposes of legal action. According to Fox News,

> "The killing raises questions over who has jurisdiction over a growing army of armed guards on merchant ships flying flags from many nations. . . . Legal experts said there is no consensus on who is responsible for investigating the incident, and there are several possibilities: Panama, whose flag the Almezaan flies, the United Arab Emirates, where the ship's owners are based; or the nations which the security contractors come from . . ."

B. MV Enrica Lexie

This incident involved the shooting and killing of two unarmed Indian fishermen by Italian naval guards, which mistook them for pirates. While the focus of this chapter is not on naval guards, this incident is being referred to as a means of highlighting and drawing a distinction on the effect of the action of the navy and PAG.

According to reports[96], India claims that the fishing boat, *St. Antony*, carrying 11 unarmed crew reported being fired upon at 1500 hrs, 2 or 3 nautical miles off the coast of India. Of the 11 fishermen two were shot. India claims that 20 shots were fired by the two Italian marines without any warning shots fired by the marines, who took the fishing boat to be a pirate vessel.

Italy, on the other hand, claims that at 1600 hrs, while navigating 33 nautical miles off the Indian coast, a 12-metre boat with six armed men was spotted approaching the Italian tanker. It kept nearing even after the soldiers showed their guns at which point they opened fire into the air and the water and the boat turned away without anyone being hit. *Enrica Lexie* immediately reported the incident to authorities in Rome. Italy says that satellite data confirms that the ship was 33 nautical miles off the Indian coast, whereas India says it was 2-3 nautical miles off the Indian coast. The two Italian marines were charged with murder under the Indian penal code (IPC) with Italy commencing its national investigation into the incident. India is considered as having a tangible advantage being in custody of the marines.

This incident involves significant legal questions concerning jurisdiction, State responsibility and immunities. It has been stated that

96. *MV Enrica Lexie* off Kochi. Source: Aijaz Rahi/Associated Press, "The Enrica Lexie Incident and International Law: Some Preliminary Thoughts", http://ilcurry.wordpress.com/2012/02/27/the-enrica-lexie-incident-and-international-law-some-preliminary-thoughts, accessed on 8 October 2012.

> "ever since the Indian authorities detained the ship, and instituted murder charges against the guards, a diplomatic row has arisen with Italy insisting that India does not have jurisdiction to try the crew of an Italian ship sailing beyond India's territorial waters. On the other hand, Indian authorities insist that the perpetrators will face Indian Law as the victims were fishermen on board an Indian fishing vessel."[97]

Pursuant to India's position on jurisdiction and immunity for the Italian guards, it has been suggested that State immunity is not lost in fatal injury cases and likely to be upheld in cases of genuine mistake[98]. Be that as it may, Italy has reversed its earlier position as demonstrated by its decision to send the marines back to India for trial based on the assurance by India to protect their fundamental human rights[99].

C. Maersk Alabama

A member of the crew of the US flagged container ship *Maersk Alabama* filed a lawsuit against Maersk Line Ltd. and the company that supplied the crew following a pirate attack at sea on April 2009 in the Gulf of Aden[100]. He alleged that Maersk was negligent and that the *Maersk Alabama* was unseaworthy by sending him to a pirate infested zone rather than taking another safer route, which led to his injury.

It is reported that

> "on April 8, 2009, the U.S. flagged container ship *Maersk Alabama* was attacked by pirates in the Gulf of Aden. Four pirates armed with assault rifles boarded the cargo ship and attempted to take over the vessel and its 21 crew members. The majority of the ship's crew locked themselves in the ships steering room and remained there for nearly twelve hours . . ."[101]

The question for the court was whether the *Maersk Alabama* was an

97. U. Ramanchandran, *supra* footnote 53.
98. See post of Guilfoyle and Messineo at http://www.ejiltalk.org., accessed on 19 January 2013.
99. See post of K. S. Harisankar, http://www.ejiltalk.org/jurisdictional-and-immunity-issues-in-the-story-of-enrica-lexie-a-case-of-shoot-scoot-turns-around, accessed on 1 April 2013.
100. Law-suit (case 2009-26129) filed on behalf of Richard Hicks, a steward on board *Maersk Alabama* in the 270th Judicial Court in Houston, Harris County, Texas.
101. Darren Frieman, "Liability Lessons from Maersk Alabama", http:www.maritime-executive.com/article/2009-06-18-liability-lessons-maersk-alab, accessed on 8 October 2012.

unsafe work place because she was ordered to pass through waters that were infested with armed criminals who happen to be modern-day pirates[102]. This case emphasizes the ship-owner's obligations in this regard.

Paragraph 5 National Practices

The use of PAG on board vessels is gradually accepted by States and the international community. The International Chamber of Shipping (ICS) in conjunction with the European Shipowners Association (ECSA) compiled rules and policies of several flag States which reveals the position of these States on the matter[103]. These can be categorized as follows: States that allow, expressly prohibit, VPD option, States in consultation with a view to allowing or maintaining status quo.

The United Kingdom now allows PAG on United Kingdom flagged vessels and has issued interim guidelines; the United States, for its part, allows under the principle of self-defence, Greece has also recently passed a law allowing PAG, while Qatar has approved a proposal by the Interior Ministry to allow ships with armed guards on board to enter into the Middle East nation's territorial waters.

It is noted that a number of countries are in the process of enacting legislation in support of PAG (Norway/Germany). Poland, for its part, has expressed no legal disposition to place armed guards, private or State, on merchant ships due to registration of almost all ocean-going vessels under third country flags.

Japan and the Netherlands are major maritime nations that are yet to allow PAG on board vessels. Nigeria also belongs to this category; however, discussions are ongoing at the highest level in Nigeria with a view to determining if the time has come for a policy reversal with legislative backing in line with current realities.

As noted earlier, the positive effect of the activities of the international navies in the Gulf of Aden has caused a dispersal of piracy to the Gulf of Guinea and off the coast of Nigeria, a factor that becomes relevant in government decision-making on the matter.

Provisions relating to the carriage of arms are contained in a number of laws which include the Constitution of the Federal Republic of Nigeria,

102. M. Schuler, "Maersk Alabama Crew Member Files Lawsuit against Ship Owner — Legal Principles behind the Claim", http:gcaptain.com/Maersk-alabama-crew-member-files/ accessed on 8/10/2012.

103. International Chamber of Shipping, Circular MLC(12)20/IC(12)05, Flag State Rules and Requirements on Arms and Private Armed Guards on Board Vessels: Updated ICS/ECSA, Table.

the Armed Forces Act of Nigeria and related statutes. Under these laws, the possession of any form of firearm within Nigerian territory by any persons other than those expressly permitted is illegal[104]. A breach of any of these laws may attract penalties ranging from a fine to up to 10 years' imprisonment or both. The carriage of firearms by unauthorized persons have recently been viewed much more seriously amidst the land-based security challenges and escalating incidents of attack on vessels around the geographical area. The Federal Government of Nigeria would take a dim view of anyone caught with firearms, whether on land or within Nigerian territorial waters.

Without prejudice to whatever the laws of the flag State may provide, it is settled international law that the coastal State would continue to enjoy full territorial sovereignty over its geographical zone. As amply demonstrated, Nigerian law will frown at unauthorized persons carrying firearms within the country's territory, whether on land or water. It is also settled law that by entering foreign ports and other internal waters, ships put themselves within the territorial sovereignty of the coastal States[105]. Where a ship-owner requires escort within territorial waters, the ship-owner must contract with the Nigerian Government[106].

It is pertinent to mention that private security provides a critical component of offshore oil and gas security in the Gulf of Guinea. The success of the Private Security Companies in providing this service relies on the selection of qualified maritime security professionals who understand the complexity of the threat, and design and deliver a security solution grounded in maritime offshore operations in the Gulf of Guinea[107].

The Netherlands is one of the notable States that have opted for the "so-called VPD model" along with Belgium, Estonia, France, Italy and the United States. This option is a reflection of maintaining government monopoly on the use of force. The domestic framework for implementation rests on each State taking into cognizance their respective circumstances.

The VPD model was adopted by the Netherlands as a national measure

---

104. Nigerian Navy or men of the Nigerian police (Marine Division) are entitled to carry firearms on board any vessel. This is clearly borne out by the provisions of the Nigerian Navy Act (1990), the Armed Forces Act (2004) and the Police Act (2004).

105. Unpublished Legal Opinion by Femi Atoyebi, Senior Advocate of Nigeria, Femi Atoyebi & Co. Solicitors, No. 26, Keffi, Lagos, Nigeria.

106. T. Fedeli, *supra* footnote 80.

107. R. Hawkes, "Securing the Offshore Oil Industry in the Gulf of Guinea", in C. Berube and P. Cullen (eds.), *Maritime Private Security Market Responses to Piracy, Terrorism and Waterborne Security Risks in the 21st Century*, London, Routledge, 2012, pp. 65-73 at pp. 139-149.

to protect ships flying its flag. The Government also posits that under certain circumstances, the protection of individual maritime transport was its responsibility. A daily charge is however imposed for the provision of the security team. This has generated a lot of controversy and viewed as discriminatory against the practice in other European Union countries who do not request such payment. It is argued that there can be no legal basis for the payment based on the fact that security of the Dutch merchant fleet is a defence task force and a constitutional duty[108].

The French practice is to embark armed teams belonging to the French State (Equipes de Protection Embarquées) protecting ships traversing the Gulf of Aden and also on board trawlers with the French flag stationed in the Seychelles. To this end, a Status of Force Agreement (SOFA) has been negotiated by France with the Seychelles for the protection of fishing vessels in sea areas plagued by pirates. The service is free of charge and is provided only for French flagged ships[109]. The Chinese and Russian navies are offering VPD services that have been accepted by a number of ships.

The position of Egypt with respect to the Suez Canal is considered unique as presented below:

> "In August 2011, the Egyptian Ministry of Defence announced a prohibition on the carriage of armed guards, weapons and ammunition on vessels in transit in the Suez and Egyptian waters. The position was reviewed and replaced with a requirement that vessels carrying armed guards, weapons or ammunition must submit to the Suez Canal Authority in advance or transit a letter endorsed by the flag State with the following: name of the vessels and owners, quantity and description of weapons and ammunition on board, number of armed guards on board, identity of the armed guards' employer, and confirmation that the weapons will not be used while the vessel is in Egyptian territorial waters."[110]

Owners are advised to check with local agents prior to entering the Suez Canal or Egyptian territorial waters to ensure that they are able to meet the requirements as set by the Government.

---

108. Geert Jan Knoops, "Waarblijven die privéebewakers?" (Where Are Those Private Escorts?), http://digitaleeditie.nrc.nl/digitaleeditie/NH/2012/7/2012o817-/arivle6-image.h .5-9-2012.

109. N. Ronzitti, *supra* footnote 29.

110. SKULD, National Regulations on the Use of Armed Guards, https://extranet.skuld.com/Insight/Piracy/Armed-Guards/National-regulations-on-the-use-of-armed-guards accessed on 19 October 2012.

SECTION 4 STATE RESPONSIBILITY AND LIABILITY ISSUES

Paragraph 1 State Responsibility

The issue of State responsibility arising out of the operation of PAG is of primary significance in the current discourse. Primarily, no governmental element can attach to a private contract upon which PAG arrangement rests in the light of Article 5 of ILC Articles on the Responsibility of States for Internationally Wrongful Acts (2001). It is not envisaged that any duty will be imposed on the flag State of the vessel on which PAG is deployed.

This fact can be appreciated from the cases referred to above (The *Almezaan* and *Enrica Lexie*) where the issue of State responsibility was immediately brought to the fore based on the involvement of the Italian marines. According to Papastavridis,

> "the only basis for attribution of such acts to the flag state seems to be article 5 of ILC Articles on State Responsibility, namely the conduct of persons or entities exercising elements of governmental authority. This would depend upon each state's domestic legislation authorizing the use of PAGs. However, it appears difficult to find legislation, which would explicitly empower such persons with governmental authority . . ."[111]

The draft UN Convention[112] seeks to impose responsibility on States for the activities of Private Security Companies registered in their jurisdiction, whether or not these entities are contracted by the State[113].

A question that has also arisen for determination is whether Article 94 of UNCLOS imposes liability on the flag State that allows the use of PAG on its vessels. This certainly invites further research in the future.

Paragraph 2 Liability Issues under International and National Legislation

A. Rules for the use of force

The Rules on the Use of Force (RUF) refer to standards set for the use of force either in legislations or guidelines. Potential

111. A. Papastavridis, Responses for "Shooting fishermen mistaken for pirates, jurisdiction, immunity and state responsibility", by D. Guilfoyle, http://www.ejiltalk.org/shooting-fishermen-mistaken-for-pirates-jurisdiction-immunity-and-state-responsibility, 12 March 2012, accessed on 29 August 2012.

112. See footnote 45, *supra*, UN Convention on Regulation Oversight and Monitoring.

113. See Article 4 (2).

liability may arise should PAG not comply with the law or laid-down standards.

A key question to address is who takes responsibility for the just or unjustified use of firearms on board? The authority of the master on board a vessel has long been established; Article 34 (1) of SOLAS states that,

> "[T]he owner, Charterer, the Company operating the ship as defined in Regulation IX/1 or any other person shall not prevent or restrict the Master of the ship from taking or executing any decision which, in the master's professional judgment is necessary for the safety of life at sea and protection of the marine environment."

Under the International Ship and Port Facility Security Code (ISPS Code)[114], the master of a ship has the ultimate responsibility for the safety and security of the ship at all times. PMSC are expected to have policy and procedures governing command and control of PAG on board, with a clear statement recognizing that at all times the master remains in command and is the overriding authority, and agreed procedure in the event that the master is unavailable.

Manchuk explained the reason why common law gives the master unbridled authority to lawfully compel others to obey by citing the statement of Judge Ware in *Bangs* v. *Little*[115], in which he proposed that

> "[t]he service in which [the master] is employed is one of uncommon peril, not only requiring great skill, but often demanding great promptitude of decision and action, and admitting not time of delay for deliberation, reasoning, or expostulation. Upon him the obligation is imposed to meet and provide for these emergencies, and if there is not an instantaneous obedience to his orders, it may involve the loss of the ship and all who are in it. The law, therefore, vests him with the absolute power of command, and clothes him with all the authority which is necessary to enforce the most prompt obedience to his orders."

The presence of PAG on board should therefore not impact on the authority ordinarily exercisable by the master. This position should be maintained irrespective of a situation whereby the master may need to abide by expert security provided by PAG on board, given that they are the security expert on board. The prior consent of the master to assume control of the incident situation must, nevertheless, be obtained. There-

114. The ISPS Code is an amendment to the Safety of Life at Sea (SOLAS) Convention (1974/1988) which came into force in 2004.

115. G. Manchuk, *supra* footnote 69, p. 371.

after, the master shall — subject to his overriding authority — respect the instructions of the PAG and shall reassume the authority granted upon cessation of the incident[116]. The masters' authority will be displaced whenever force can be used without the masters' prior approval which can be regarded as a breach on the part of PAG.

Titahena affirms[117] that RUF should be attached to the contract and discussed in detail with the master and crew and these should also be endorsed by the flag State, whose laws would govern the use of force in deterring or preventing any criminal act.

India, for example, has issued Guidelines on Deployment of Armed Security Guards on Merchant Ships[118]. This provides *inter alia* complete understanding of the rules for the use of force as agreed between shipowner, PMSC and the master and fully complies with them together with a detailed graduated response plan to a pirate attack as part of its team's operational procedures.

All responsible steps must be taken to avoid the use of force and where the same is to be applied; it should be in a manner consistent with applicable law. In no case should the use of force exceed what is strictly necessary and in all cases should be proportionate to the severity of threat and actual situation at the material point in time. PMSC should require that their personnel not use firearms against persons except in self-defence or in defence of others against the imminent threat of death or serious injury, or to prevent the preparation of a particularly serious crime involving grave threat to life.

The right of self-defence in this circumstance is deemed to override the master's authority. IMO emphasizes the need for clear definition of roles, documented command and control structure on the use of force.

Norway has adopted new regulations to govern the use of armed guards on ships, the IMO guidelines provides the basis for the Norwegian rules[119]. The rules applicable to Norwegian registered ships and drilling units sets out when force can be used in self-defence[120], which

116. G. Manchuk, *supra* footnote 69, p. 367.

117. J. Titahena, *supra* footnote 85, p. 8, this is in agreement with the views expressed by Askins (2011), *Shipping Piracy — Issues arising from the Use of Armed Guards*, Ince & Co., International Law Firm, London, United Kingdom.

118. Pursuant to some sections in its existing law (S. 86, "Transit and Transshipment of Stores", 77 — Declaration by Owner of Baggage, and 80 — Temporary Detention of Baggage of Customs Act, 1962, and Section 45A of the Indian Arms Act, 1959.

119. Rules adopted on 1 July 2001, through amendments to the existing Security Regulations for Ships, 2004, and the weapons Regulations, 2009, and entered into force immediately.

120. Rein Wikborg, "New Regulations Govern Use of Armed Guards on Ships", International Law Office, Shipping and Transport, Norway.

is generally permitted under the criminal code and now endorsed in safety regulation. Force, which must be proportionate, can only be used when there is a direct, imminent, substantial and unavoidable threat.

The master must approve each instance of a carrying arms or the actual use of force, which must be respected by all persons on board including PAG. It is expected, where possible, that attackers should be warned through light and sound signals, as well as warning shots, before firing any direct shots.

The US Coast Guard Authorization Act[121] removes liability for monetary damages for injury or death caused by the use of force to defend a United States-flagged vessel against an act of piracy from owners, operators or individuals who use or authorize such force. The use of force must be in accordance with the standard rules of self-defence for the immunity to apply. It has been observed that the UK Interim Guidance requires critical details on application of force and answers on what is permissible, especially if PAG on board United Kingdom-flagged vessel can open fire at a fast approaching skiff.

From the customers' perspective, Hook notes that most US companies abide by Rules of Engagement (ROE). This framework is closely aligned with the US Coast Guard's Port Security Advisory (PSA) programme which discusses the use of force and closely follows established law for self-defence, the defence of others and the vessel. Under such laws, deadly force may only be used in self-defence or defence of others when an individual has a reasonable belief the person or persons to whom the deadly force would be directed possesses an "imminent danger of death or great bodily harm". In other words, the objective when using deadly force is defence of life and not the vessel[122].

In conclusion, the need for set and clear guidance on the RUF cannot be over-emphasized. This is because the moment of monitoring an impending attack would not be a time for questions of legality to be uppermost in the minds of the master and PAG.

In this regard, it is advocated[123] that ship masters be guided so they become "comfortable, confident and cognizant in the use of force from their vessel".

---

121. US Coast Guard Authorization Act of 2010, Section 912, Use of Force against Piracy, Chapter 81 of Title 46 is amended by adding a new Section 8107.

122. G. E. Van Hook, "Private Security at Sea ; A Customers Perspective", in C. Berube and P. Cullen (eds.), *Maritime Private Security : Market Responses to Piracy, Terrorism and Waterbourne Securiy Risks in the 21st Century*, London, Routledge, 2012, pp. 65-73.

123. Security Association for the Maritime Industry (SAMI), http://www.seasecurity.org/mediacentre/force-is-the-issue, accessed on 30 January 2013.

Paragraph 3 **Criminal and Civil Actions for Breach by Private Armed Guards**

The prohibition of the use of potentially deadly force, save for self-defence and proportionate application of force by PAG, implies that there would be consequences for a breach or non-compliance, which may extend to the master and the ship-owner.

In the event that the crew or guards on board the vessel exceed their right of self-defence by using excess force, the person along with the master may face criminal prosecution. Further, under the Norwegian rules of criminal liability, the ship-owner can also be subjected to prosecution. Cook notes that there are many fears and concerns for masters today as they wrestle with issues of criminalization, which should be recognized[124].

According to Fedeli,

> "If private security personnel were to egregiously kill unarmed civilians on the high seas, it would be defined as piracy under international law, and any state would have jurisdiction to prosecute. Armed private guards who perpetrate acts of violence on the high seas do meet the requirements for being declared pirates under UNCLOS."[125]

He further observed that

> "Innocent fishermen killed or injured at sea might also seek civil damages against private security guards personally and against private security companies generally, under the theory of *respondeat superior* sea."[126]

The question of who bears the cost of reparation when a guard shoots has also been raised. It is the view of the author that this should be covered by insurance. The exposure to liability claims and criminal charges influenced the global call for a proposal to amend SOLAS to give a limited degree of transactional immunity to "any person who in good faith injures a putative pirate to protect the lives aboard"[127]. GUARDCON under the "knock-for-knock" principle embraces the mutual allocation of risk approach where each party is responsible for loss, damage to, and death of and injury to any of its own property without recourse to the other party.

---

124. *Op. cit. supra* footnote 123.
125. T. Fedeli, *supra* footnote 80.
126. *Ibid.*
127. J. Carter, "Call for Changes to SOLAS to Suppress Piracy at Sea", http://www.marinelink.com/news/changes-combat-piracy338392.aspx, accessed on 23 August 2012.

SECTION 5 CONCLUSION

The deployment of PAG on board vessels, though gaining wider acceptability, is still being approached with great caution, largely due to the legal and regulatory complexities involved. As it stands, there has been no valid endorsement or proposal for institutionalization by the IMO and other major players. While the selling point for the PAG arrangement remains that no vessel with PAG on board has ever been hijacked, the reality is that it lacks the capacity to solve the piracy problem. This is because the arrangement has not been designed to address the root cause of piracy. The possibility of mistaken identity of innocent fishermen for pirates and egregious conduct by PAG have generated public outcry and regarded as condemnable [128]. In addition, the potential escalation of violence, possibility of explosion when inflammable cargo is on board and consequent environmental damage are equally worrisome.

Paragraph 1 Emerging Trend/Recommendations/the Way Forward

The above concerns coupled with other challenges suggest that concerted efforts of all players are still required. It is recommended that all ongoing initiatives on the suppression of piracy should be sustained. Regional co-operation resulting in the Djibouti Code of Conduct for East Africa should be mirrored for the West African region in view of the upsurge in violence and attacks on vessels at the Gulf of Guinea.

With specific reference to PAG, it is recommended that maritime strategy, which will fast track the proposed global standards for PMSC/PAG with robust legislations at the national level, be adopted as a matter of urgency; this is without prejudice to current efforts. It is further proposed that with effective standardization and international certification akin to the seafarer, the quality of PAGS can be guaranteed.

Considerations can also be given to the under listed proposals as a way forward and future research:

- Adoption of an international convention providing a required legal/regulatory framework.
- PAG to act under licences and supervision by Government; this may be a form of reactivation of outlawed Letters of Marques.

---

128. Th. T. Richard, "Reconstructing the Letter of Marque: Utilizing Private Security Provider against Piracy", *Public Contract Law Journal*, 39, No. 3, pp. 411-464.

- Refine and adopt the Montreux Document for the maritime environment. Collaborations with local authorities for embarking and paying for shipriders from the local coast-guards or naval forces during transits through their waters is appropriate noting the multitude of laws PAGs are subjected to[129].
- Proposal for a robust legal framework for African ports that play host to vessels.

129. M. Tempest, "Legal Considerations for Private Naval Company Armed Anti-Piracy Escorts", in C. Berube and P. Cullen (eds.), *Maritime Private Security: Market Responses to Piracy, Terrorism and Waterbourne Securiy Risks in the 21st Century*, London, Routledge, 2012, pp. 139-149.

TROISIÈME PARTIE

PART III

La protection et la sécurité

Protection and Security

10 Search and Rescue

Jasmine Coppens *

SECTION 1 INTRODUCTION

The Arab Spring recently highlighted the problem of migrants at sea and the shortcomings of the international legal framework. Indeed, due to the social uprisings in Tunisia and Libya, thousands of people tried to reach Europe by sea. This is a dangerous journey, as these asylum-seekers often travel in unseaworthy vessels. As a result of the Arab Spring, it is estimated more than 1,500 people drowned or went missing while attempting to cross the Mediterranean to reach Europe in 2011 [1]. In 2012, UNHCR also expressed its concerns on the loss of life in maritime incidents in the Caribbean among people trying to escape — often in unseaworthy vessels — difficult conditions in Haiti following the 2010 earthquake [2]. For example, in summer 2012, several persons lost their lives in Bahamian and US waters while trying to reach the shores of Florida. US Coast Guard data show that as of December 2011 over 900 people have been found on boats in rescue operations including some 652 Haitians, 146 Cubans and 111 people from the Dominican Republic [3].

These events are a reminder of the extremes that people in difficult situations sometimes resort to. Although no firm statistics exist, it is estimated that, as a result, hundreds of deaths occur yearly [4]. The inter-

* Master in Law as well as Master in Maritime Sciences. Post-doctoral Researcher at the Maritime Institute of Ghent University, Belgium. PhD, "Migrants at Sea: A Legal Analysis of a Maritime Safety and Security Problem".

1. UNHCR, "Mediterranean Takes Record as Most Deadly Stretch of Water for Refugees and Migrants in 2011", Briefing Note (31 January 2012), available online: http://www.unhcr.org/4f27e01f9.html.
2. UNHCR, "More People are Risking Lives in the Caribbean to Reach Safety", Statement (13 July 2012), available online: http://www.unhcr.org/refworld/docid/50001c5a2.html.
3. US Coast Guard, "US Coast Guard Maritime Migrant Interdictions", available online: http://www.uscg.mil/hq/cg5/cg531/AMIO/FlowStats/currentstats.asp.
4. UNHCR, "More People are Risking Lives in the Caribbean to Reach Safety", Statement (13 July 2012), available online: http://www.unhcr.org/refworld/docid/50001c5a2.html.

national community is aware that this problem has to be tackled as soon as possible in order to prevent further loss of life. This chapter will first deal with the search and rescue obligations of flag States and their shipmasters as well as those of coastal States. Secondly, the regional initiative for the Mediterranean Basin will be discussed. Finally, we will discuss State responsibility as well as criminal sanctions for shipmasters where international obligations are not being met.

SECTION 2 **SEARCH AND RESCUE**

Paragraph 1 **The Duty to Render Assistance**

The moral obligation to render assistance to persons in peril or lost at sea is one of the oldest and most deep-rooted maritime traditions. The early maritime law was concerned with the preservation of maritime property, rather than with the protection of seafarers[5]. However, by the mid-nineteenth century, one in five British mariners died at sea. Among sailors, mortality was higher than in any other occupation. Between 1861 and 1870, as many as 5,826 ships were wrecked off the British coast with the loss of 8,105 lives[6]. In 1880, the legal obligation of rendering assistance at sea was recognized in the *Scaramanga* v. *Stamp* case, where it was decided:

> "To all who have trust themselves to the sea it is of the utmost importance that the promptings of humanity in this respect should not be checked or interfered with by prudential considerations which may result to a ship or cargo from the rendering of needed aid."

In 1897, the Comité Maritime International (CMI) held its first international conference in Brussels to advance issues regarding collisions and salvage, as well as the duty to render assistance at sea. As a result, the Brussels Convention on Salvage was signed on 23 September 1910[7]. In 1989, the International Maritime Organization (IMO) concluded the International Convention on Salvage, which replaced the 1910 Brussels

---

5. Edgar Gold, Aldo E. Chircop and Hugh M. Kindred, *Maritime Law*, Toronto, Irwin Law, 2003, pp. 193-195.

6. See Nicolette Jones, *The Plimsoll Sensation : The Great Campaign to Save Lives at Sea*, London, Little Brown, 2006.

7. International Convention for the Unification of Certain Rules of Law related to Assistance and Salvage at Sea and Protocol of Signature (adopted 23 September 1910, entered into force 1 March 1913), 4 *UKTS* 6677.

Convention[8]. The provisions in these conventions expressly articulate an unqualified duty to render assistance to "persons" or to "any person" "in distress" or "in danger of being lost at sea"[9]. Article 10 of the 1989 Salvage Convention stipulates:

> "(1) Every master is bound, so far as he can do so without serious danger to his vessel and persons thereon, to render assistance to any person in danger of being lost at sea.
>
> (2) The States Parties shall adopt the measures necessary to enforce the duty set out in paragraph 1.
>
> (3) The owner of the vessel shall incur no liability for a breach of the duty of the master under paragraph 1."

Also, the 1982 Law of the Sea Convention (LOSC)[10] contains a similar provision.

Nowadays, it is a legal obligation for shipmasters and States under customary international law, as well as under Articles 58 (2) and 98 (1), LOSC, to render assistance to persons in danger of being lost and to proceed with all possible speed to the rescue of persons in distress. Article 98 (1), LOSC, states:

> "Every State shall require the master of a ship flying its flag, in so far as he can do so without serious danger to the ship, the crew or the passengers: *(a)* to render assistance to any person found at sea in danger of being lost; *(b)* to proceed with all possible speed to the rescue of persons in distress, if informed of their need of assistance, in so far as such action may reasonably be expected of him; *(c)* after a collision, to render assistance to the other ship, its crew and its passengers and, where possible, to inform the other ship of the name of his own ship, its port of registry and the nearest port at which it will call."

Although the LOSC only mentions this duty in the exclusive eco-

---

8. International Convention on Salvage (adopted 28 April 1989, entered into force 14 July 1996), 1953 *UNTS* 194 (1989 Salvage Convention). Article 10 stipulates:

> "(1) Every master is bound, so far as he can do so without serious danger to his vessel and persons thereon, to render assistance to any person in danger of being lost at sea. (2) The States Parties shall adopt the measures necessary to enforce the duty set out in paragraph 1. (3) The owner of the vessel shall incur no liability for a breach of the duty of the master under paragraph 1."

9. Sophie Cacciaguidi-Fahy, "The Law of the Sea and Human Rights", 9 *Panoptica* 1 (2007), 6.

10. United Nations Convention on the Law of the Sea (adopted 10 December 1982, entered into force 16 November 1994), 1833 *UNTS* 3 (LOSC).

nomic zone (EEZ) and on the high seas, a State cannot rely on its sovereign powers to disregard this obligation in its territorial sea[11]. Indeed, Article 18 (2), LOSC, stipulates that — for the purpose of rendering assistance to persons, ships or aircraft in danger or distress — passage may include stopping and anchoring. Furthermore, the provision in Article 98 (1), LOSC, mentions "any person found at sea" and not "any person found on the high seas". As assistance must be given to "any" person[12], the obligation applies regardless of the persons' nationality or status or the circumstances in which they are found[13]. Therefore, migrants cannot be excluded from this obligation.

First of all, there is a duty to render assistance to persons in danger of being lost. There is a variety of acts that may constitute assistance, for example to tow the vessel to safety, extricate a grounded vessel, fight a fire aboard a ship, provide food and supplies, embark crewmen aboard to replace the tired or the missing, secure aid or assistance from other nearby ships, or simply stand by to provide navigational advice[14]. Secondly, there is an obligation to proceed with all possible speed to the rescue of persons in distress. However, the LOSC does not mention what "distress" is. In the case of *The Eleanor*, it was submitted that distress must entail urgency, but that "there need not be immediate physical necessity"[15].

The decision on the *Kate A. Hoff* established that it is not required for the vessel to be "dashed against the rocks" before a claim of distress can be invoked[16].

In the *Rainbow Warrior* case, the tribunal took a broader view of the circumstances justifying a plea of distress, accepting that a serious

11. MSC, "Review of Safety Measures and Procedures for the Treatment of Persons Rescued at Sea", IMO Doc. MSC 76/22/8 (31 July 2002), Annex, "Report-Record of Decisions on the United Nations Inter-Agency Meeting on the Treatment of Persons Rescued at Sea", para. 6; Richard A. Barnes, "Refugee Law at Sea", 53 *International and Comparative Law Quarterly* 47 (2004), 50-52.

12. LOSC, Art. 98 (1).

13. International Convention for the Safety of Life at Sea (adopted 1 November 1974, entered into force 25 May 1980) 1184 *UNTS* 278 (SOLAS Convention), Chapter V, Regulation 33, para. 1.

14. Martin J. Norris, *The Law of Salvage*, Mount Kisco NY, Baker/Voorhis, 1958, pp. 15-31; Ina H. Wildeboer, *The Brussels Salvage Convention: Its Unifying Effect in England, Germany, Belgium, and The Netherlands*, Leiden, A.W. Sijthoff, 1965, p. 95; Frederick J. Kenney and Vasilios Tasikas, "The Tampa Incident: IMO Perspectives and Responses on the Treatment of Persons Rescued at Sea", 12 *Pacific Rim Law & Policy Journal* 143 (2003), 151-152.

15. *The Eleanor Case*, Edw. 135 (1809), 135.

16. General Claims Commission United States and Mexico, *Kate A. Hoff* v. *The United Mexican States*, 2 April 1929, 4 *UNRIAA* 444 (1929), reprinted in 23 *American Journal of International Law* 860 (1929).

health risk would suffice[17]. Finally, the International Law Commission (ILC) — founded in 1948 and promoting the progressive development of international law and its codification — confirmed that a situation of distress "may at most include a situation of serious danger, but not necessarily one that jeopardizes the very existence of the person concerned"[18].

The actual distress phase is defined by the 1979 International Convention on Maritime Search and Rescue (SAR Convention)[19] — a treaty monitored by the IMO that imputes multi-State co-ordination of search and rescue systems — as: "A situation wherein there is reasonable certainty that a person, a vessel or other craft is threatened by grave and imminent danger and requires immediate assistance."[20] When exactly a situation is identified as requiring immediate assistance can be different according to which State is handling the situation. For some States the vessel must really be on the point of sinking[21]. However, the ILC stated that — although a situation of distress may at most include a situation of serious danger — it is not necessarily one that jeopardizes the life of the persons concerned[22]. In contrast, for other States it is sufficient for the vessel to be unseaworthy[23].

---

17. Arbitral Award, Case concerning the difference between New Zealand and France concerning the interpretation or application of two agreements concluded on 9 July 1986 between the two States and which related to the problems arising from the *Rainbow Warrior* affair, *New Zealand* v. *France*, 30 April 1990, 10 *UNRIAA* 215 (1990), para. 79.

18. ILC, *Yearbook of the International Law Commission*, New York, ILC, 1973, Vol. II, p. 134, para. 4, available online: http://untreaty.un.org/ilc/publications/yearbooks/Ybkvolumes%28e%29/ILC_1973_v2_e.pdf.

19. International Convention on Maritime Search and Rescue (adopted 27 April 1979, entered into force 22 June 1985), 405 *UNTS* 97 (SAR Convention).

20. SAR Convention, Annex, Chapter 1, para. 1.3.13.

21. European Commission Proposal for a Council Decision of 27 November 2007 supplementing the Schengen Borders Code as regards the surveillance of the sea external borders in the context of the operational cooperation coordinated by the European Agency for the Management of Operational Cooperation at the External Borders, COM(2009)658 final, Explanatory Memorandum, para. 2.

22. ILC, *Yearbook of the International Law Commission*, New York, ILC, 1979, Vol. II, Part II, p. 135, para. 10, available online: http://untreaty.un.org/ilc/publications/yearbooks/Ybkvolumes%28e%29/ILC_1979_v2_p2_e.pdf. Although this definition was given during the discussions on the concept of "distress" as one of the grounds for excluding wrongfulness with regard to the Draft Articles on State Responsibility, the definition is often being used to describe the situation of distress of persons at sea. See, for example, Richard A. Barnes, "Refugee Law at Sea", 53 *International and Comparative Law Quarterly* 47 (2004), 60.

23. European Commission Proposal for a Council Decision of 27 November 2007 supplementing the Schengen Borders Code as regards the surveillance of the sea external borders in the context of the operational cooperation coor-

Moreno-Lax even suggests that unseaworthiness *per se* entails distress[24].

Council Decision 2010/252/EU[25] adopted additional guidelines that must be respected by European Member States during search and rescue situations at sea when operating within a FRONTEX joint operation at sea. When deciding whether a vessel is in distress or not, search and rescue units should take all relevant elements into account, in particular:

> "*(a)* the existence of a request for assistance; *(b)* the seaworthiness of the ship and the likelihood that the ship will not reach its final destination; *(c)* the number of passengers in relation to the type of ship (overloading); *(d)* the availability of necessary supplies (fuel, water, food, etc.) to reach a shore; *(e)* the presence of qualified crew and command of the ship; *(f)* the availability of safety, navigation and communication equipment; *(g)* the presence of passengers in urgent need of medical assistance; *(h)* the presence of deceased passengers; *(i)* the presence of pregnant women or children; and *(j)* the weather and sea conditions."[26]

Although the European Court of Justice (ECJ) annulled Council Decision 2010/252, and thus also the guidelines therein, the effects of the Council Decision have to be maintained until a new act can be adopted in accordance with ordinary legislative procedures[27].

According to these guidelines, although unseaworthiness is certainly an element to take into consideration when assessing the situation, it does not automatically imply a distress situation. Indeed, every situation is different and whether persons at sea are in distress or not will dependent on the specific circumstances. Therefore, an assessment can only be

---

dinated by the European Agency for the Management of Operational Cooperation at the External Borders, COM(2009)658 final, Explanatory Memorandum, para. 2.

24. Violeta Moreno-Lax, "Seeking Asylum in the Mediterranean: Against a Fragmentary Reading of EU Member States' Obligations Accruing at Sea", 23 *International Journal of Refugee Law* 174 (2011), 195. See also Efthymios Papastavridis, *The Interception of Vessels on the High Seas*, Oxford, Hart Publishing, 2013, p. 295.

25. Council Decision (EU) No. 2010/252 of 26 April 2010 supplementing the Schengen Borders Code as regards the surveillance of the sea external borders in the context of the operational cooperation coordinated by the European Agency for the Management of Operational Cooperation at the External Borders, *OJ* L 111/20 of 4 May 2010.

26. *Ibid.*, Annex, Part II, para. 1.3.

27. ECJ, *European Parliament* v. *Council of the European Union*, 17 April 2012, Opinion of Advocate General Mengozzi, Case C-355/10 (2012), and ECJ, *European Parliament* v. *Council of the European Union*, 5 September 2012, Case C-355/10 (2012).

made on a case-by-case basis. Although the definition of distress is quite vague, this allows shipmasters and States to take all relevant elements into account. States' margin of appreciation to decide whether persons are in distress is regarded as being essential. However, one element that is indisputable is that the existence of an emergency should not be exclusively dependent on or determined by an actual request for assistance[28].

Paragraph 2 **The Obligation to Co-operate**

Coastal States shall establish adequate and effective search and rescue (SAR) services (for example, through the creation of a Rescue Co-ordination Centre or RCC) and, where circumstances so require, co-operate with neighbouring States for this purpose[29]. The basic elements for a search and rescue service are a legal framework, the assignment of a responsible authority, the organization of available resources, communication facilities, co-ordination and operational functions and processes to improve the service including planning, domestic and international co-operative relationships and training[30]. In the SAR Convention, rescue is described as "an operation to retrieve persons in distress, provide for their initial medical or other needs, and deliver them to a place of safety"[31].

Until the adoption of the SAR Convention, there was actually no international system covering search and rescue operations. Consequently, in some areas there was a well-established organization able to provide assistance promptly and efficiently, in others there was nothing at all. The SAR Convention thus aims at developing an international search and rescue plan. As a result, no matter where an accident occurs, the rescue of persons in distress at sea will be co-ordinated by a search and rescue organization and — when necessary — by co-operation between neighbouring search and rescue organizations[32]. Basically, the world's oceans are divided into 13 search and rescue areas, in each of which the countries concerned have delimited search and rescue regions

28. Council Decision (EU) No. 2010/252 of 26 April 2010 supplementing the Schengen Borders Code as regards the surveillance of the sea external borders in the context of the operational cooperation coordinated by the European Agency for the Management of Operational Cooperation at the External Borders, *OJ* L 111/20 of 4 May 2010, Annex, Part II, para. 1.4.
29. LOSC, Art. 98 (2); SAR Convention, Annex, Chapter 2, para. 2.1.1.
30. SAR Convention, Annex, Chapter 2, para. 2.1.2.
31. SAR Convention, Annex, Chapter 1, para. 1.3.2.
32. IMO, "Search and Rescue", available online: http://www.imo.org/OurWork/Safety/RadioCommunicationsAndSearchAndRescue/SearchAndRescue/Pages/Default.aspx.

for which they are responsible[33]. States must ensure that sufficient Search and Rescue Regions (SRR) are established within each sea area. These regions should be contiguous and — as far as practicable — not overlap[34]. Each SRR shall be established by agreement among parties concerned[35]. The delimitation of SRRs is not related to and shall not prejudice the delimitation of any boundary between States[36]. Parties are required to ensure the closest practicable co-ordination between maritime and aeronautical services[37]. The International Aeronautical and Maritime Search and Rescue Manual (IAMSAR Manual) — which was jointly published by IMO and the International Civil Aviation Organization (ICAO) — provides guidelines for a common aviation and maritime approach to organizing and providing search and rescue services[38].

According to Article 98 (2), LOSC, where circumstances so require, coastal States have to cooperate with neighbouring States. What exactly is "co-operation"? The LOSC contains many undertakings to co-operate in a great variety of contexts. As a result of the principle *pacta sunt servanda*, a duty of co-operation created by the LOSC would actually require a Party to act co-operatively in respect of all Parties or a prescribed category of such Parties, as directed by the particular provision[39]. "Co-operation" derives from the Latin verb *cooperari*, which means working or acting together or jointly, or uniting to produce an effect. Therefore, the duty to co-operate implies action. This action could for example exist of entering into negotiations in good faith at the request of any interested party, the creation at national level of institutions designed to foster international co-operation or the conclusion of bilateral, regional or global agreements. As a result, the refusal to respond to a request to negotiate for example could amount to a breach of the obligation and as a result justify appropriate remedial action[40].

33. IMO, "SAR Convention", available online: http://www.imo.org/OurWork/Safety/RadioCommunicationsAndSearchAndRescue/SearchAndRescue/Pages/SARConvention.aspx.
34. SAR Convention, Annex, Chapter 2, para. 2.1.3.
35. SAR Convention, Annex, Chapter 2, para. 2.1.4.
36. SAR Convention, Annex, Chapter 2, para. 2.1.7.
37. SAR Convention, Annex, Chapter 2, para. 2.4.
38. IMO/ICAO, "International Aeronautical and Maritime Search and Rescue Manual", London/Montreal (2003). For an extensive discussion on the IMO-ICAO search and rescue regions and the IAMSAR Manual see Isavella Maria Vasilogeorgi, "Delimitation of IMO-ICAO Search and Rescue Regions — A Case of Jurisdictional Compilation and Complication", 36 *Annals of Air and Space Law* (2011), 251-278.
39. VCLT, Preamble and Arts. 26, 27 and 31 (1).
40. Christopher W. Pinto, "The Duty of Co-operation and the United Nations Convention on the Law of the Sea", in Adriaan Bos and Hugo Siblesz (eds.), *Realism in Law-Making — Essays on International Law in Honour of Willem Riphagen*, Dordrecht, Martinus Nijhoff Publishers, 1986, p. 145.

Nevertheless, the obligation to co-operate is an obligation of conduct, not an obligation of result. Taking countermeasures for instance would therefore prove to be difficult. In the *Gabčíkovo-Nagymaros Project* case, the ICJ accepted that countermeasures may justify otherwise unlawful conduct "taken in response to a previous international wrongful act of another State and . . . directed against that State"[41]. However, certain conditions have to be met. It is for example not very likely that there will be an actual injured State[42]. While discussing the obligation to co-operate in suppressing piracy, Guilfoyle notes:

> "While a duty to cooperate to the fullest possible extent may seem a strong obligation, the international community has not agreed that it has any specific minimum content. Identifying a breach of a duty to cooperate is notoriously difficult."[43]

It is thus clear that a number of loopholes seriously impair the effectiveness of the duty to co-operate[44]. First of all, in public international law there is no general customary law-based obligation for States to co-operate. Therefore, duties to co-operate are treaty-based and as such the co-operative relationship is being artificially created. Secondly, provisions on co-operative conduct are often not manifestly demonstrably based on reciprocity or mutuality of benefit. Thirdly, the wording of the obligation leaves it unclear as to the specific conduct required in fulfilment of that obligation. Therefore, the proof of such a breach would be very difficult. Fourthly, treaties that include an obligation of co-operation often include a level of discretion. For example, Article 98 (2), LOSC, asks coastal States to co-operate "where circumstances so

41. ICJ, *Gabčíkovo-Nagymaros Project (Hungary/Slovakia)*, 25 September 1997, *ICJ Reports 1997*, 55-56.

42. For a discussion on the concepts "countermeasures" and "injured State", see Denis Alland, "The Definition of Countermeasures", in James Crawford, Alain Pellet and Simon Olleson (eds.), *The Law of International Responsibility*, Oxford, Oxford University Press, 2010, pp. 1127-1136; Giorgio Gaja, "The Concept of an Injured State", in James Crawford, Alain Pellet et Simon Olleson (eds.), *The Law of International Responsibility*, Oxford, Oxford University Press, 2010, pp. 941-948.

43 Douglas Guilfoyle, "The Challenges in Fighting Piracy", in Bibi van Ginkel et Frans-Paul van der Putten (eds.), *The International Response to Somali Piracy*, Leiden, Martinus Nijhoff Publishers, 2010, p. 130.

44. Jost Delbrück, "The International Obligation to Cooperate — An Empty Shell or a Hard Law Principle of International Law? — A Critical Look at a Much Debated Paradigm of Modern International Law", in Holger P. Hestermeyer *et al.* (eds.), *Coexistence, Cooperation and Solidarity — Liber Amicorum Rüdiger Wolfrum*, Leiden, Martinus Nijhoff Publishers, 2012, pp. 13-14; Christopher W. Pinto, "The Duty of Co-operation and the United Nations Convention on the Law of the Sea", in Adriaan Bos and Hugo Siblesz (eds.), *Realism in Law-Making — Essays on International Law in Honour of Willem Riphagen*, Dordrecht, Martinus Nijhoff Publishers, 1986, pp. 1337-1338.

require". Lastly, the effectiveness of a co-operation duty can also be impaired by non-cooperation. A particular problem is unilateral actions by States. For example, powerful States may turn to unilateralism when they decide that they may achieve their foreign policy goals by unilateral action rather than co-operation. As the international system is based upon sovereign equality of States, the system is in fact characterized by gross inequalities in power that are a structural obstacle to co-operation and thus encourages powerful States "to go it alone"[45]. On the one hand, there is a growing number of obligations to co-operate in international law. On the other hand, there exists an unsatisfactory degree of implementation of these duties because of non-compliance[46].

In April 2009, the Panamanian flagged Turkish ship *M/V Pinar E* rescued 142 African migrants off the coast of Lampedusa. The ship and the rescued migrants were the subject of an ensuing stand-off between Italy and Malta regarding who would receive the migrants. While Malta insisted that the *M/V Pinar E* would take the migrants to Lampedusa because it was the nearest port to where the stricken boats were found, Italy maintained that the persons were rescued in the Maltese SRR and thus fell under Malta's responsibility. Although Italy eventually agreed to allow disembarkation in Sicily, the decision was made exclusively in consideration of the painful humanitarian emergency aboard the cargo ship. Italy made clear that its acceptance of the migrants must not in any way be understood as a precedent nor as recognition of Malta's reasons for refusing them[47]. This is one of the many incidents that highlight the lack of co-operation and co-ordination between the SAR services of these two States.

As already mentioned, the SAR Convention aims to create an international system for co-ordinating rescue operations and therefore States parties are invited to conclude SAR agreements with neighbouring States to regulate and co-ordinate SAR operations and services in the

45. Christoph H. Schreuer, "State Sovereignty and the Duty of States to Cooperate — Two Incompatible Notions?", in Jost Delbrück (ed.), *International Law of Cooperation and State Sovereignty: Proceedings of an International Symposium of the Kiel Walther Schücking Institute of International Law*, Berlin, Duncker & Humblot, 2002, p. 177.

46. Jost Delbrück, "The International Obligation to Cooperate — An Empty Shell or a Hard Law Principle of International Law? — A Critical Look at a Much Debated Paradigm of Modern International Law", in Holger P. Hestermeyer *et al.* (eds.) *Coexistence, Cooperation and Solidarity — Liber Amicorum Rüdiger Wolfrum*, Leiden, Martinus Nijhoff Publishers, 2012, p. 15.

47. BBC, "Italy Takes in Stranded Migrants" (20 April 2009), available online: http://news.bbc.co.uk/2/hi/europe/8007379.stm; *Times of Malta*, "Migrants Standoff: PM Insists Malta Did Its Duty" (20 April 2009), available online: http://www.timesofmalta.com/articles/view/20090420/local/migrants-standoff-pm-insists-malta-did-its-duty.253648.

agreed maritime zone[48]. Such agreements do not only technically and operatively implement the obligation laid down in Article 98 (2), LOSC, they also diminish the risk of non-rescue incidents. In addition, they can offer an economic advantage to the extent that the contracting parties can share costs arising from organizing and carrying out SAR operations[49]. For the moment, several States in the Mediterranean have, for example, unilaterally declared an SRR. However, there is no regional agreement yet on the co-ordination among them[50]. At the time of writing, a Regional Memorandum of Understanding for the Mediterranean on Disembarkation is being drafted (as discussed in Section 3). Co-ordinating SAR operations will also be part of this agreement.

In 2004, Australia and Indonesia did conclude such an agreement. These countries designated their RCCs for the agreed SAR region and defined the modalities by which the RCCs should interact, exchange information and execute cross-border SAR operations. During these operations, the rescue unit of one State can enter the territorial sea of the other State after a notification. In order to determine the RCC that will be responsible for carrying out a certain operation, the area where the vessel is located will be decisive. The RCC responsible for this area organizes the operation. In case the exact location is unknown, the RCC that received the distress call is responsible[51].

Although Australia and Indonesia disagree on several other points of their maritime policies, this agreement has definitely become an important tool for operational co-operation between the two States, thus enhancing the efficiency of SAR services and the safety of life at sea[52]. Nevertheless, there may be negative consequences resulting from such an agreement.

When an SAR operation occurs in the zone under Indonesian competence, people will be disembarked in this country.

However, asylum seekers often prefer Australia instead of Indonesia. For example, in October 2009, the *Ocean Viking* wanted to bring some

48. SAR Convention, Chapter 3.

49. Seline Trevisanut, "Search and Rescue Operations in the Mediterranean: Factor for Cooperation or Conflict?", 25 *International Journal of Marine & Coastal Law* 523 (2010), 528-529.

50. See Seline Trevisanut, "Search and Rescue Operations in the Mediterranean: Factor of Cooperation or Conflict?", 25 *International Journal of Marine & Coastal Law* 523 (2010), 523-542.

51. Arrangement between Australia and Indonesia for the co-ordination of search and rescue services (adopted 5 April 2004), IMO Doc. SAR.6/Circ.22 (13 April 2004), Annex, available online: http://www.imo.org/blast/blastDataHelper.asp?data_id=9310&filename=22.pdf.

52. Seline Trevisanut, "Search and Rescue Operations in the Mediterranean: Factor for Cooperation or Conflict?", 25 *International Journal of Marine & Coastal Law* 523 (2010), 539.

rescued Sri Lankan Tamil asylum seekers to Indonesia[53]. However, these people refused to disembark in this country[54].

Paragraph 3 **Place of Safety**

Rescue implies that persons in distress have to be delivered to a place of safety[55]. The IMO Guidelines on the Treatment of Persons Rescued at Sea state that a place of safety can be defined as a location where rescue operations are considered to terminate, where the survivors' safety or life is no longer threatened, basic human needs (such as food, shelter and medical needs) can be met and transportation arrangements can be made for the survivors' next or final destination[56]. Disembarkation of asylum-seekers recovered at sea, in territories where their lives and freedom would be threatened, must be avoided[57] in order to prevent the violation of the *non-refoulement* principle[58]. Also, Council Decision 2010/252/EU[59] stated that the *non-refoulement* principle should be respected[60].

The Government responsible for the SRR in which survivors were

53. Tamil are an ethnic group native to the north-eastern region of Sri Lanka.

54. Donald R. Rothwell, "Howard's Way Still Figures Large in Asylum-Seeker Policy", *The Australian* (10 November 2009), available online: http://www.theaustralian.com.au/news/opinion/howards-way-still-figures-large-in-asylum-seeker-policy/story-e6frg6zo-1225795886606.

55. SAR Convention, Annex, Chapter 1, para. 1.3.2.

56. MSC, "Guidelines on the Treatment of Persons Rescued at Sea", MSC Resolution 167 (78) (20 May 2004), para. 6.12.

57. *Ibid.*, para. 6.17.

58. Convention relating to the Status of Refugees (adopted 28 July 1951, entered into force 22 April 1954), 189 *UNTS* 137 (Refugee Convention). Article 33 of the Refugee Convention states that:

> "No Contracting State shall expel or return ('refouler') a refugee in any manner whatsoever to the frontiers of territories where his life or freedom would be threatened on account of his race, religion, nationality, membership of a particular social group or political opinion."

This principle is not only applicable to refugees but also to all asylum-seekers. See for example, Daniel Bethlehem and Elihu Lauterpacht, "The Scope and Content of the Principle of Non-Refoulement: Opinion", in Erika Feller, Volker Türk and Frances Nicholson (eds.), *Refugee Protection in International Law: UNHCR's Global Consultations on International Protection*, Cambridge, Cambridge University Press, 2003, pp. 116-118; UNHCR, "The Protection of Asylum-Seekers and Refugees Rescued at Sea", in Alexander T. Aleinikoff and Vincent Chetail (eds.), *Migration and International Legal Norms*, The Hague, Asser Press, 2003.

59. Council Decision (EU) No. 2010/252 of 26 April 2010 supplementing the Schengen Borders Code as regards the surveillance of the sea external borders in the context of the operational cooperation coordinated by the European Agency for the Management of Operational Cooperation at the External Borders, *OJ* L 111/20 of 4 May 2010.

60. *Ibid.*, Preamble, para. 10.

recovered will be responsible for providing a place of safety or ensuring that such a place of safety is provided[61]. Although an assisting ship may only serve as a temporary place of safety[62], there is no actual duty for States to disembark the persons rescued[63]. Both the International Convention on Safety of Life at Sea (SOLAS Convention) and SAR Convention state that States must arrange for the disembarkation of persons rescued at sea as soon as reasonably practicable[64]. In other words, a State can refuse disembarkation onto its own territory or make this dependent on certain conditions[65].

Ironically, the "place of safety"-provision often hinders that migrants are being brought to a safe place in an efficient way. By lacking a clear disembarkation duty, persons rescued at sea can spend weeks on the rescuing ship before a State allows them to go ashore[66]. On 11 July 2011, the *Almirante Juan de Borbón* — a Spanish frigate participating in NATO *Operation Unified Protector* — rescued 114 migrants from drowning in the Mediterranean. After the vessel had left Libya, the engine broke down and the persons on board drifted around for two days without food or water. When the warship was informed about their condition, they provided immediate assistance. On 13 July 2011, a man and his pregnant wife were brought to Malta for medical treatment. Spain agreed to receive a 10-month-old baby. However, neither Spain nor Italy nor Malta wanted to accept disembarkation onto their territory. Malta stated that NATO was responsible for the problem. Eventually, the migrants were transferred to Tunisia on 16 July 2011[67]. As some of the asylum-

61 MSC, "Guidelines on the Treatment of Persons Rescued at Sea", MSC Resolution 167(78) (20 May 2004), para. 2.5.

62. *Ibid.*, para. 6.13.

63. See, for example, Killian S. O'Brian, "Refugees on the High Seas: International Refugee Law Solutions to a Law of the Sea Problem", 3 *Goettingen Journal of International Law* 715 (2011), 723-725.

64. SOLAS Convention, Chapter V, Regulation 33; SAR Convention, Chapter 3, para. 3.1.9.

65. Guy S. Goodwin-Gill, *The Refugee in International Law*, Oxford, Clarendon Press, 2nd ed., 1996, p. 157.

66. See Jasmine Coppens and Eduard Somers, "Towards New Rules on Disembarkation of Persons Rescued at Sea?", 25 *International Journal of Marine & Coastal Law* 377 (2010), 377-404.

67. Migrants at Sea, "Italy and Malta Turn Back NATO Ship Carrying 100 Rescued Migrants" (14 July 2011), available online: http://migrantsatsea.wordpress.com/2011/07/14/italy-and-malta-turn-back-nato-ship-carrying-100-rescued-migrants/; Migrants at Sea, "Malta Says the 111 Rescued Migrants Aboard Spanish Frigate Are NATO's Problem, Not Malta's Problem" (15 July 2011), available online: http://migrantsatsea.wordpress.com/2011/07/15/malta-says-the-111-rescued-migrants-aboard-spanish-frigate-are-nato%E2%80%99s-problem-not-malta%E2%80%99s-problem/; Migrants at Sea, "NATO Transfers Rescued Migrants to Tunisia" (16 July 2011), available online: http://migrantsatsea.wordpress.com/2011/07/16/nato-transfers-rescued-migrants-to-tunisia/.

seekers were of Tunisian origin and due to the political situation in that country, this was a violation of the *non-refoulement* principle.

Moreover, by making the Government of the SRR in which survivors were recovered responsible for providing a place of safety or ensuring that such a place of safety is provided, migrants in distress at sea are sometimes being ignored or brought to the SRR of another State. Indeed, States know that they will not only be responsible for providing assistance, but also for the place of safety. In March 2011, a boat carrying 72 migrants spent 16 days drifting in the Mediterranean after it had left Tripoli to reach Italy. Migrants stated that several ships and even a NATO aircraft carrier ignored pleas for help. The out-of-fuel ship eventually washed up on a western Libyan beach. Only 11 people survived while the others had died of thirst and starvation at sea[68]. There are even testimonies of asylum-seekers that the Greek coast-guard for example tows people into the Turkish SRR[69].

Although recent international and European soft law initiatives do focus on a real disembarkation duty, they also put too much burden on the coastal States. Indeed, the 2009 IMO Guidelines on Principles Relating to Administrative Procedures for Disembarking Persons Rescued at Sea mention that if disembarkation from the rescuing ship cannot be arranged swiftly elsewhere, the Government responsible for the SRR should accept the disembarkation[70]. EU Council Decision 2010/252, supplementing the Schengen Borders Code, spells out guidelines for sea border operations co-ordinated by Frontex. As regards the surveillance of the sea external borders, the guidelines try to impose a layered duty to disembark[71]. The operational plan, used during a joint operation at sea, should spell out the modalities for the disembarkation of the per-

68. *The Guardian*, "Aircraft carrier left us to die, say migrants" (8 May 2011), available online: http://www.guardian.co.uk/world/2011/may/08/nato-ship-libyan-migrants. See also Efthymios Papastavridis, "Rescuing 'Boat People' in the Mediterranean Sea: The Responsibility of States under the Law of the Sea", *EJIL: Talk!* (31 May 2011), available online: http://www.ejiltalk.org/author/epapastavridis/; Seline,Trevisanut, "Aircraft carrier left us to die, say migrants", *EJIL: Talk!* (31 May 2011), available online: http://www.ejiltalk.org/author/strevisanut/.

69. ECRE, "What Price Does a Refugee Pay to Reach Europe?" (10 February 2009), pp. 6-7, available online: http://www.ecre.org/resources/ECRE_actions/1313.

70. FAL, "Principles Relating to Administrative Procedures for Disembarking Persons Rescued at Sea", *IMO Doc*. FAL 35/Circ.194 (22 January 2009), para. 2.3.

71. Council Decision (EU) No. 2010/252 of 26 April 2010 supplementing the Schengen Borders Code as regards the surveillance of the sea external borders in the context of the operational cooperation coordinated by the European Agency for the Management of Operational Cooperation at the External Borders, *OJ* L 111/20 of 4 May 2010.

sons rescued. Unless otherwise specified in the operational plan, priority should be given to disembarkation in the third country from where the ship carrying the persons departed or through the territorial waters or search and rescue region of which that ship transited and if this is not possible, priority should be given to disembarkation in the host Member State unless it is necessary to act otherwise to ensure the safety of these persons. This means that the mission's host country carries the ultimate responsibility. Malta strongly opposes these guidelines and as a result stopped hosting Frontex operations.

After the adoption of the EU Council Decision 2010/252, the Dutch Government also declared that — within a FRONTEX operation — The Netherlands will not be responsible for handling the asylum applications of rescued persons made on board a Dutch ship[72]. The Netherlands considers the inclusion of a provision in the operational plan — stating that the host State will be responsible for dealing with asylum claims — a condition to participate in a FRONTEX operation. On the one hand, this approach could be considered as quite reasonable, as the Dutch navy operates far away from its territory. Therefore, the migrants' disembarkation in the intervening State's territory would simply be unfeasible. On the other hand, putting the disembarkation burden primarily on the host State's shoulders seems a somewhat opportunistic way of avoiding any further problems arising from the transfer of migrants[73].

Without any prior agreements on burden-sharing between States, the life of many migrants is being jeopardized. It is estimated that for every 100 people safely landing after a dangerous journey in the Mediterranean, 5 people drown without leaving any trace[74]. However, some States fear that clarifying obligations and solving the problem through burden-sharing would produce an enormous pull factor, thus encouraging migrants to come to Europe by sea[75].

---

72. Letter from the Dutch Minister of Justice E. M. H. Hirsch Ballin, to the President of the House of Representatives, Kamerstuk 21501-28 No. 61 (3 September 2010), available online: https://zoek.officielebekendmakingen.nl/kst-21501-28-61.html.

73. Matteo Tondini, "The Legality of Intercepting Boat People under Search and Rescue and Border Control Operations with Reference to Recent Italian Interventions in the Mediterranean Sea and the ECtHR Decision in the Hirsi Case", 18 *Journal of International Maritime Law* 59 (2012), 65-66.

74. LEG, "Report of the Legal Committee on the work of its ninety-eighth session", IMO Doc. LEG 98/14 (18 April 2011), Annex 9.

75. European Union Committee of the House of Lords, "FRONTEX: The EU External Borders Agency", 9th Report of Session 2007-08 (5 March 2008), para. 115, available online: http://www.publications.parliament.uk/pa/ld200708/ldselect/ldeucom/60/60.pdf. See also Violeta Moreno-Lax, "Seeking Asylum in the Mediterranean: Against a Fragmentary Reading of EU Member States' Obligations Accruing at Sea", 23 *International Journal of Refugee Law* 174 (2011), 176.

SECTION 3 REGIONAL MEMORANDUM OF UNDERSTANDING FOR THE MEDITERRANEAN ON DISEMBARKATION

Paragraph 1 From an International to a Regional Approach

At the meeting of the IMO Sub-Committee on Radiocommunications and Search and Rescue (COMSAR) in March 2010, the United States stated that the discussions between Mediterranean countries concerning rescue and disembarkation of migrants at sea is based on a regional problem requiring a regional solution. However, Italy, Malta and Spain expressed their disappointment that other countries seemingly did not recognize that the problem was much wider than simply a regional one. Indeed, other parts of the world are also confronted with similar difficulties and, even more importantly, ships of all flags are currently involved in the resulting rescue operations. Therefore, the IMO Secretary-General proposed to first develop a pilot project for a regional solution in the Mediterranean. Secondly, if this project works, it could be applied in other parts of the world[76].

One of the primary concerns of the IMO is the integrity of the search and rescue and, consequentially, the safety of life at sea regime[77]. Therefore, the IMO wants to prevent incidents — which cause loss of life at sea — from recurring[78]. COMSAR launched the idea of developing a pilot project for a regional solution in the Mediterranean in March 2010. On the one hand, the system of rescuing migrants in the Mediterranean Basin has to be improved. On the other hand, these persons also have to be disembarked at a place of safety in accordance with the SAR and SOLAS Conventions[79]. If the project works, it could be extended to other parts of the world experiencing similar situations[80].

Meanwhile, the IMO is even waiting to take steps on the international level — for example amending the Facilitation Convention[81] — until the results of this Regional Agreement are ready[82]. In May 2010 the IMO

76. COMSAR, "Report to the Maritime Safety Committee", IMO Doc. COMSAR 14/17 (22 March 2010), paras. 10.1-10.26.

77. MSC, "Report of the Maritime Saftey Committee on Its Eighty-Seventh Session", IMO Doc. MSC 87/26 (25 May 2010), para. 14.18.

78. LEG, "Report of the Legal Committee on the Work of Its Ninety-Eighth Session", IMO Doc. LEG 98/14 (18 April 2011), para. 13.25.

79. *Ibid.*

80. COMSAR, "Report to the Maritime Safety Committee", IMO Doc. COMSAR 14/17 (22 March 2010), paras. 10.1-10.26.

81. Convention on Facilitation of International Maritime Traffic (adopted 9 April 1965, entered into force 5 March 1967), 591 *UNTS* 265 (FAL Convention).

82. COMSAR, "Report to the Maritime Safety Committee", IMO Doc. COMSAR 15/16 (25 March 2011), para. 10.3.

Secretary-General made his good offices available to take this matter forward for informal consultations with a group of interested parties[83]. A first draft of the Terms of Reference for such a consultation group was established by the IMO Secretariat in co-operation with interested parties, including Italy, Malta and Spain[84].

A first meeting of the consultation group was held under the auspices of, and chaired by, the IMO Secretary-General on 28 July 2010. It was attended by representatives from Italy, Malta, Spain and the IMO Secretariat. The meeting had agreed upon the Terms of Reference for the group and it finalized a list of issues to be discussed in the development of a Regional Agreement on concerted procedures relating to the disembarkation of persons rescued at sea. The IMO Secretariat prepared a draft for this Regional Agreement which was tabled for the parties concerned to consider and to comment[85]. However, since not sufficient progress could be made, the delegations of Italy, Malta and Spain requested an extension of the target completion date to 2012[86]. Indeed, due to the non-availability of delegations a second meeting had to be postponed[87].

Italy requested that the consultation group of interested parties should be extended to the other relevant regional institutions, for instance the European Union, in order to avoid the stalling of future consultations due to non-availability of delegations[88].

In 2011, States however realized that the situation in the Mediterranean region had deteriorated over the following months after the first meeting. The need for precipitating the proceedings was evident, as a consequence of a wave of social uprising affecting the northern part of the African continent, thus resulting in a massive migration by sea towards Europe[89]. In March 2011, NATO warships as well as aircraft started patrolling the approaches to Libyan territorial waters as part of *Operation Unified Protector*.

As called for in United Nations Security Council resolution 1973[90], their purpose is to reduce the flow of arms, related material and mercenaries to Libya. This operation was part of the broad international effort

83. MSC, "Report of the Maritime Saftey Committee on Its Eighty-Seventh Session", IMO Doc. MSC 87/26 (25 May 2010), para. 14.18.
84. *Ibid.*, para. 14.20.
85. COMSAR, "Report to the Maritime Safety Committee", IMO Doc. COMSAR 15/16 (25 March 2011), para. 10.4.
86. *Ibid.*, para. 10.5.
87. *Ibid.*, paras. 10.4.4 and 10.6.
88. *Ibid.*, para. 10.6.
89. *Ibid.*, para. 10.6.
90. UNSC, "Resolution 1973 (2011)", UN doc. S/RES/1973 (17 March 2011), available online: http://www.un.org/Docs/sc/unsc_resolutions11.htm.

to protect civilians in Libya from the violence committed by the Ghaddafi regime[91].

On 6 April 2011, a second meeting — again under the auspices of and chaired by the IMO Secretary-General — was held pursuant to this debate. It was attended by representatives from Italy, Spain and the IMO Secretariat[92]. Exactly on that day, over 250 migrants were lost after their vessel capsized in the Mediterranean Sea, which proved again to the meeting how urgent this matter was[93]. The Terms of Reference were reviewed and accepted[94]. It was concluded that the development of the Regional Agreement was to:

> "(1) establish and strengthen co-operation among Parties to enable them to cope with incidents involving persons rescued at sea; (2) establish a system of communication between the countries in the region to exchange information on the movement of persons by sea; (3) ensure the safety of persons rescued at sea, pending a decision as to the place where such persons will be safely delivered, taking into account the prevailing weather and other conditions, including the safety of the delivering ships and the capacity of the places where they are delivered to provide care as may be necessary under the circumstances; (4) arrange that delivery of persons takes place without undue delays to the rescuing ships which should be allowed to promptly proceed to their destination once the delivery operation is over; and (5) promote co-operation for the delivery of persons rescued at sea to a port of a place of safety"[95].

In addition, the meeting prepared the draft text for the Regional Agreement which should be used as a basis for consideration at a future meeting[96]. They agreed that the group should be expanded to include other interested parties concerned in the region, such as relevant regional and international organizations[97]. Malta stated that it was unable to attend the second meeting and that it not completely agreed with the outcome of that meeting. While they had no difficulties with the essence of the Terms of Reference, the text needed to be revised in

91. NATO, "Operation Unified Protector — Factsheet" (25 March 2011), available online: http://www.nato.int/nato_static/assets/pdf/pdf_2011_03/20110325_110325-unified-protector-factsheet.pdf.
92. MSC, "Measures to Protect the Safety of Persons Rescued at Sea", IMO Doc. MSC 89/INF.23 (12 April 2011), para. 4.
93. *Ibid.*, para. 5.
94. *Ibid.*, para. 6.
95. *Ibid.*, Annex.
96. *Ibid.*, para. 7.
97. *Ibid.*, para. 8.

the interest of clarity and consistency. Moreover, Malta had reservations on both the expansion of the consultation group and the draft text of the Regional Agreement. The country therefore proposed another meeting to discuss all these issues [98].

The third meeting of the consultation group was held on 15 June 2011. The meeting further developed the Terms of Reference and discussed a draft Regional Agreement on concerted procedures relating to the disembarkation of persons rescued at sea. Next to this, it was agreed that the consultation group — Italy, Spain and Malta — should be expanded [99].

As a first expansion step, all Mediterranean countries were invited through Circular Letter No. 3203 of 18 August 2011 [100]. This regional meeting was being held back-to-back with the celebrations of the World Maritime Day parallel event in Rome on 12 October 2011 attended by 10 Member States in the Mediterranean. The ultimate goal here was the development of a Regional Agreement in the form of a Memorandum of Understanding (MoU) on concerted procedures relating to the disembarkation of persons rescued at sea [101].

At COMSAR 16, it was considered beneficial — in order to make significant progress towards finalizing the draft Regional MoU — to hold informal consultations among interested parties to agree on some of the more contentious issues and associated draft texts before organizing the next regional formal meeting. Accordingly, informal consultations were held at IMO Headquarters on 21 February 2012. Some of the most contentious aspects were discussed and agreements reached on sensitive subjects and the draft text of the Regional MoU was improved accordingly [102].

However, after some discussion, taking into account that the work on this matter was still in progress, COMSAR decided to invite the

98. MSC, "Report of the Maritime Safety Committee on Its Eighty-Ninth Session", IMO Doc. MSC 89/25 (27 May 2011), para. 13.15.

99. FAL, "Formalities Connected with the Arrival, Stay and Departure of Persons — Measures to Protect the Safety of Persons Rescued at Sea", IMO Doc. FAL 37/6/1 (1 July 2011), para. 10.

100. IMO, "Meeting on a Regional Memorandum of Understanding on Concerted Procedures Relating to the Disembarkation of Persons Rescued at Sea, in Rome (Italy) on 12 October 2011", Circular Letter No. 3203 (18 August 2011); IMO, "Meeting on a Regional Memorandum of Understanding on Concerted Procedures Relating to the Disembarkation of Persons Rescued at Sea, in Rome (Italy) on 12 October 2011", Circular Letter No. 3203/Add/1 (16 September 2011).

101. FAL, "Address of the Secretary-General at the Opening of the Thirty-Seventh Session of the Facilitation Committee", IMO Doc. FAL 37/INF.5 (5 September 2011), pp. 3-4.

102. COMSAR, "Report to the Maritime Safety Committee", IMO Doc. COMSAR 16/17 (23 March 2012), para. 10.3.

Maritime Safety Committee (MSC) to extend the target completion year to 2013[103]. MSC agreed to postpone the deadline to 2013[104].

A MoU is a well-accepted type of legal instrument in international law and practice and it is being identified as "an informal but nevertheless legal agreement" between two or more parties[105]. Whether this MoU is meant to be binding is not clear at the moment. However, a soft law agreement would not necessarily be a negative factor. Hard and soft law are used as alternatives or they can interact in complementary ways. Legal positivists tend to favour hard law as it refers to legal obligations of a formally binding nature, while soft law refers to those that are not formally binding but may nonetheless lead to binding hard law. Rationalists, in contrast, contend that hard and soft law have distinct attributes that States choose for different contexts and thus they can build upon each other. Lastly, constructivists maintain that State interests are formed through socialization processes of interstate interaction which hard and soft law can facilitate. Therefore, constructivists often favour soft law instruments for their capacity to generate shared norms and a sense of common purpose and identity, without the constraints raised by concerns over potential litigation[106].

Regardless of their views about the strengths and weaknesses of hard and soft law, all three schools examine how hard and soft law can serve as mutually supporting complements to each other[107]. Moreover, soft law can sometimes be more effective than hard law. Effectiveness goes beyond looking at implementation or compliance to determine whether an international norm —whatever its source in domestic or international law — achieves its policy objective[108]. A rule is deemed effective when it led to certain behaviour which may or may not meet the legal standard of compliance[109]. The development of a soft law framework has been

103. *Op. cit. supra* footnote 102, para. 10.4.

104. MSC, "Revised biennial agenda of the COMSAR Sub-Committee for the 2012-2013 biennium and provisional agenda for COMSAR 17 — Note by the Secretariat", IMO Doc. MSC 90/25/Add. 1 (5 April 2012), Annex 1, para. 5.1.2.2.

105. Arnold D. McNair, *The Law of Treaties*, Oxford, Clarendon Press, 1961, p. 15; Duncan B. Hollis, *The Oxford Guide to Treaties*, Oxford, Oxford University Press, 2012, pp. 46 *et seq.* See also ICJ, *Maritime Delimitation and Territorial Questions between Qatar and Bahrain* (*Qatar* v. *Bahrain)*, 1 July 1994, *ICJ Reports 1994*, p. 112, para. 27, on what constitutes a binding agreement.

106. Gregory C. Shaffer and Mark A. Pollack, "Hard vs. Soft Law: Alternatives, Complements, and Antagonists in International Governance", 94 *Minnesota Law Review* 706 (2010), 707-708.

107. *Ibid.*

108. Jose E. Alvarez, "Why Nations Behave", 19 *Michigan Journal of International Law* 303 (1998), 305.

109. Compliance as a concept merely identifies a conformity between a legal rule and behaviour. However, it does not draw a causal linkage between these

successfully applied to address gaps in international law in the past[110]. Barnes states that — consistent with the general trend towards the use of soft law instruments — new legal initiatives concerning migrants at sea are most likely to take the form of non-binding measures[111].

Paragraph 2 From an Interagency to a Maritime Approach

During the meetings, it was stressed that the development of a Regional Agreement should be restricted to purely maritime matters, in view of IMO's primary concern for the integrity of the search and rescue regime[112]. Although the competences of the IMO only extend to the search and rescue part at sea and to the provision of a place of safety afterwards[113], it is definitely a shift in view towards the issue. Indeed, William O'Neil — the former IMO Secretary-General — already stated in 2001 that the implementation of measures for safety at sea would not suffice since the problem of migrants at sea is not only a maritime issue. In a situation involving asylum-seekers, certain principles of refugee law and human rights must be respected[114]. As a result, an Interagency Group was set up in July 2002 to deal with the problem

two. For example, compliance may occur without implementing legislation. On the other hand, it is also possible that a State may not be in compliance with international law, even with implementing legislation in place. See Kal Raustiala, "Compliance & Effectiveness in International Regulatory Cooperation", 32 *Case Western Reserve Journal of International Law* (2000), 398; Jose E. Alvarez, "Why Nations Behave", 19 *Michigan Journal of International Law* 303 (1998), 305.

110. Betts illustrates this by giving the example of the soft law framework for IDP's. Alexander Betts, "Towards a 'Soft Law' Framework for the Protection of Vulnerable Irregular Migrants", 22 *International Journal of Refugee Law* 209 (2010), 224-225.

111. Richard A. Barnes, "The International Law of the Sea and Migration Control", in Bernard Ryan and Valsamis Mitsilegas (eds.), *Extraterritorial Immigration Control*, Leiden, Martinus Nijhoff Publishers, 2010, pp. 113-114.

112. MSC, "Measures to Protect the Safety of Persons Rescued at Sea", IMO Doc. MSC 89/INF.23 (12 April 2011), para. 9; Hartmut Hesse, "Persons Rescued at Sea", Presentation by the Senior Deputy Director, IMO Maritime Safety Division at the Expert Meeting on Refugee and Asylum Seekers in Distress at Sea (8-10 November 2011), available online: http://www.unhcr.org/4ef3061c9.html.

113. Convention on the International Maritime Organization (adopted 6 March 1948, entered into force 17 March 1958), 289 *UNTS* 48 (IMO Convention), Arts. 1 and 15 *(j)*; Convention on Facilitation of International Maritime Traffic (adopted 9 April 1965, entered into force 5 March 1967), 591 *UNTS* 265 (FAL Convention); SOLAS Convention; SAR Convention.

114. William O'Neil, Speech at the IMO Headquarters London (19 November 2001); available online: http://www.imo.org/Newsroom/mainframe.asp?topic_id=82&doc_id=1703.

of migrants at sea[115]. The IMO, the United Nations High Commissioner for Refugees (UNHCR), the United Nations Division for Ocean Affairs and the Law of the Sea (UNDOALOS), the United Nations Office on Drugs and Crime (UNODC), the United Nations Office of the High Commissioner for Human Rights (OHCHR) and the International Organization for Migration (IOM) are all participating in this Interagency Group. Therefore, it is quite remarkable that agencies such as the UNHCR or the IOM are not yet being involved in drafting the MoU too. Although this will probably happen during future meetings, when also countries outside the region are invited[116], it is strange that this is not the case for the moment. Even when they are invited, their role will definitely be limited since the agreement will be restricted to purely maritime matters.

It is clear that past developments did not occur in the isolation of particular fields of law, but with a considerable degree of co-operation between international organizations and experts from across a number of fields. This integrated approach must thus continue[117]. The International Tribunal for the Law of the Sea affirmed in the *M/V Saiga* case that considerations of humanity must apply to the Law of the Sea as they do in other areas of international law[118]. As Treves correctly stated:

> "[t]he Law of the Sea and the law of human rights are not separate planets rotating in different orbits. Instead, they meet in many situations. Rules of the Law of the Sea are sometimes inspired by human rights considerations and may or must be interpreted in light of such considerations."[119]

Even the IMO itself recognizes this. In April 2011, the IMO stated that the problem is not entirely in IMO's hands, as political developments — due to the Arab Spring — had exacerbated the situation beyond its competence[120].

115. MSC, "Review of Safety Measures and Procedures for the Treatment of Persons Rescued at Sea", IMO Doc. MSC 76/22/8 (31 July 2002), Annex, "Report-Record of Decisions on the United Nations Inter-Agency Meeting on the Treatment of Persons Rescued at Sea".

116. LEG, "Report of the Legal Committee on the Work of Its Ninety-Eighth Session", IMO Doc. LEG 98/14 (18 April 2011), para. 13.25.

117. Richard A. Barnes, "The International Law of the Sea and Migration Control", in Bernard Ryan and Valsamis Mitsilegas (eds.), *Extraterritorial Immigration Control*, Leiden, Martinus Nijhoff Publishers, 2010, p. 149.

118. ITLOS, *The M/V Saiga* case (No. 2), *Saint Vincent and the Grenadines* v. *Guinea*, 1 July 1999, *ITLOS Reports* (1999), para. 155, available online: http://www.itlos.org/fileadmin/itlos/documents/cases/case_no_2/merits/Judgment.01.07.99.E.pdf.

119. Tullio Treves, "Human Rights and the Law of the Sea", 28 *Berkeley Journal of International Law* 1 (2010), 12.

120. LEG, "Report of the Legal Committee on the Work of Its Ninety-Eighth Session", IMO Doc. LEG 98/14 (18 April 2011), para. 13.25.

At the end of 2011, the UNHCR developed a Draft Model Framework for co-operation following rescue at sea operations. This framework contains principles of burden and responsibility-sharing among States during and after rescue[121]. It could be complementary or supplementary to the regional MoU. The Model Framework could be added by *Standard Operating Procedures for Shipmasters* (SOPs) when faced with distress at sea situations involving undocumented migrants, refugees and asylum-seekers. SOPs could provide guidance as regards the appropriate procedures to be followed and they could be incorporated into "industry best practice" guidance to be developed in conjunction with the International Chamber of Shipping (ICS), to ensure that humanitarian and protection concerns are taken into account.

They could *inter alia* include contact points for relevant authorities (i.e. Maritime Rescue Co-ordination Centres) in specific countries, a list of potential places of safety for disembarkation, as may be designated by Governments for their respective Search and Rescue Region (SRR), along with relevant criteria that may assist to make a determination in any particular case, advice on information that shipmasters may be able to collect about rescued persons and recommendations on proper management of the human remains and handling of data on deceased persons[122].

Paragraph 3 **Malta and the Regional Agreement**

A. Malta: a distinct view on migrants at sea

Malta is a small island of only 316 km^2. Nevertheless, in some ways Malta has a bigger stake in the Mediterranean than most of the other coastal States. It is an island State with an important fishing industry, a high level of tourism and marine-related industries such as shipbuilding and ship repairs. Therefore, Malta is clearly one of the Mediterranean's most sea-dependent States. As a result, maritime affairs — especially those of a political kind — are followed keenly by the

121. UNHCR, "Refugees and Asylum-Seekers in Distress at Sea — How Best to Respond?", Background paper (8-10 November 2011), available online: http://www.unhcr.org/4ec1436c9.html. The Model Framework is based on and further develops the UNHCR's 10 Point Plan of Action on Refugee Protection and International Migration. See UNHCR, "Refugees and Asylum-Seekers in Distress at Sea — How Best to Respond?", Summary Conclusions (8-10 November 2011), available online: http://www.unhcr.org/4ede2ae99.html, para. 13.

122. UNHCR, "Refugees and Asylum-Seekers in Distress at Sea — How Best to Respond?", Summary Conclusions (8-10 November 2011), available online: http://www.unhcr.org/4ede2ae99.html, paras. 17-19.

Maltese people[123]. Due to its population density, the island feels under pressure from migrants arriving by boat across the Mediterranean[124]. Malta is party to the 1982 LOSC[125] and it is thus bound by the legal obligations therein. Although Malta acceded to the 1974 SOLAS Convention on 8 August 1986 and to the 1979 SAR Convention on 24 September 2002[126], it has not yet signed the 2004 SOLAS and SAR Amendments. On 22 December 2005, the IMO received a communication from the Ministry of Foreign Affairs of Malta declaring that Malta "is not yet in a position to accept these amendments"[127]. The Armed Forces of Malta (AFM) deals with the search and rescue operations. The Department of Civil Aviation (DCA) operates jointly with the AFM in the event of an aeronautical incident[128]. Although there is certain discretion in deciding when a person is in distress or not, the AFM is being accused of not fulfilling its duty, by for example only helping persons who are actually requesting assistance[129].

In 2001, COMSAR/Circ.27 invited States to submit all details concerning the current availability of their SAR services as well as the exact co-ordinates of their SRR[130]. Malta submitted this information on 30 September 2005[131]. Although Malta is only as small as 316 km^2, it claimed a maritime SRR that coincides with the Malta Aeronautical SRR and the Malta Flight Information Region (FIR)[132]. Since the coun-

123. Gerald H. Blake, "Coastal State Sovereignty in the Mediterranean Sea: The Case of Malta", 41 *GeoJournal* 173 (1997), 173.

124. Silja Klepp, "A Double Bind: Malta and the Rescue of Unwanted Migrants at Sea, A Legal Anthropological Perspective on the Humanitarian Law of the Sea", 23 *International Journal of Refugee Law* 538 (2011), 545.

125. Malta accessed the Convention on 26 June 1996.

126. IMO, "Status of multilateral conventions and instruments in respect of which the International Maritime Organization or its Secretary-General performs depositary or other functions", available online: http://www.imo.org/About/Conventions/StatusOfConventions/Documents/Status%20-%202011.pdf.

127. IMO, "Status of multilateral conventions and instruments in respect of which the International Maritime Organization or its Secretary-General performs depositary or other functions", available online: http://www.imo.org/About/Conventions/StatusOfConventions/Documents/Status%20-%202011.pdf.

128. COMSAR, "Matters concerning Search and Rescue Including Those Related to the 1979 SAR Conference and the Introduction of the GMDSS", IMO Doc. COMSAR 5/INF. 2 (17 April 2000), para. 52.

129. Silja Klepp, "A Double Bind: Malta and the Rescue of Unwanted Migrants at Sea, A Legal Anthropological Perspective on the Humanitarian Law of the Sea", 23 *International Journal of Refugee Law* 538 (2011), 551-554.

130. COMSAR, "Data Format for a New Combined SAR.2 and SAR.3 Circular concerning Information on the Current Availability of SAR Services", IMO Doc. COMSAR/Circ.27 (12 October 2001), para. 4.

131. IMO, "Global SAR Plan Containing Information on the Current Availability of SAR Services", IMO Doc. SAR.8/Circ.1/Corr.3 (20 October 2005), Annex 2, p. 25.

132. *Ibid.*, Annex 2, p. 25.

try "inherited" an enormous Flight Identification Region (FIR) from Great Britain, Malta is now responsible for a region that amounts to 250,000 km². Towards the west, the Maltese SRR almost reaches the territorial waters of Tunisia. Towards the east, it nearly stretches to Crete. Moreover, towards the north, Malta claimed partly the same area as Italy did. This is reflected on the map which was attached to SAR.8/Circ.3[133]. For example, the Italian island of Lampedusa is both part of the Maltese and the Italian SRR. Migrants coming from the north African coast and crossing the Mediterranean to reach Italy have to pass through the Maltese SRR.

Although Italy is pressing Malta to give up part of this vast area, this is definitely not an option for the Maltese Government. One of the reasons is that this area is connected to the lucrative income the island derives from its Flight Information Region (FIR), as the size of the latter is bound to the SRR. Malta earns millions of euros a year from air traffic control charges on aircraft using the area. Next to this, there are rumours that Malta thinks the SRR could be an asset when delimiting its continental shelf[134]. Indeed, Malta's maritime boundary system is only partially delimited[135] and there are strong indications of oil and gas resources in the areas between Tunisia and Malta on the one hand and Sicily and Malta on the other hand[136]. However, the SAR Convention is very clear on this issue. It states that the delimitation of SRR is not related to and shall not prejudice the delimitation of any boundary between States[137].

Is Malta actually able to operate this unilateral declared SRR? First of all, the unilateral declaration of the Maltese SRR is subject to the principle of good faith. This principle creates a need to ensure compliance with unilateral commitments[138]. The SAR Convention only asks States

133. *Op. cit. supra* footnote 131, Annex 4, p. 7.

134. *Times of Malta*, "Shrinking Malta's search and rescue area is 'not an option' — Italy applying pressure directly and indirectly" (26 April 2009), available online: http://www.timesofmalta.com/articles/view/20090426/local/shrinking-maltas-search-and-rescue-area-is-not-an-option.254380.

135. See, for example, Gerald H. Blake, "Coastal State Sovereignty in the Mediterranean Sea: The Case of Malta", 41 *GeoJournal* 173 (1997), 173-180.

136. See, for example, Umberto Leanza, "The Delimitation of the Continental Shelf of the Mediterranean Sea", 8 *International Journal of Marine & Coastal Law* 373, 373-395.

137. International Convention on Maritime Search and Rescue (adopted 27 April 1979, entered into force 22 June 1985), 405 *UNTS* 97 (SAR Convention), Annex, Chapter 2, para. 2.1.7.

138. ILC, "Ninth Report on Unilateral Acts of States", UN doc. A/CN.4/569/Add.1 (6 April 2006), para. 12, available online: http://untreaty.un.org/ilc/documentation/english/a_cn4_569_add1.pdf; ILC, "Guiding Principles Applicable to Unilateral Declarations of States Capable of Creating Legal Obligations", UN doc. A/61/10 (9 September 2006), p. 368, para. 1, available online: http://

to co-ordinate search and rescue services in the area under their responsibility. Thus, there is no obligation for States to do this individually as they can act in co-operation with other States [139].

For example, on 6 April 2011, Malta informed the Italian Maritime Rescue Co-ordination Centre of the presence of a boat in distress, 45 miles from the Italian island of Lampedusa. As Maltese patrol boats were temporarily unavailable, Italian search and rescue assets were shipped to the area. The boat — which had departed from the Libyan port of Zuara — carried some 300 persons who had been fleeing the north coast of Africa in search of a better life. Normally, the type of vessel was only capable of holding a maximum of 40 people. Moreover, the engine was severely damaged, which made it impossible to manœuvre the boat. Over 250 migrants were lost after their vessel capsized due to flooding. Eventually, only 52 persons could be saved by the Italian Coast-Guard [140]. The fact that Italy was asked to deal with the rescue does not mean that Malta did not live up to its obligations under the SAR Convention. However, is the Maltese co-ordination efficient enough when 250 migrants are lost? Moreover, due to an overlap of the Maltese and the Italian SRR, there can be a delay in deciding who is responsible, thus jeopardizing the lives of migrants in distress. Although the SAR Convention mentions that overlaps have to be avoided as far as practicable [141], it also states that SRRs be established by agreement among parties [142]. This is not the case up until today.

According to Malta there is a safe place in terms of search and rescue and there is a safe place in terms of humanitarian law [143]. As Malta did not sign the 2004 SOLAS and SAR Amendments and as it does not accept the 2004 IMO Guidelines on the Treatment of Persons Rescued at Sea, it does not recognize the link between the two concepts which was established in these instruments. Next to this, the country does not accept any link between responsibility for the search and rescue and responsibility for providing a place of safety or ensuring that such a place of safety is provided. Nevertheless, due to the 2012 ECtHR judg-

www.un.org/Docs/journal/asp/ws.asp?m=A/61/10. The declaration can be regarded as a unilateral act *stricto sensu* as it is not part of a treaty relationship. Although the declaration was made during a meeting within the IMO (the depositary of the SAR Convention), it was not officially registered by the Secretary-General in the context of the SAR Convention.

139. SAR Convention, Annex, Chapter 2.

140. LEG, "Report of the Legal Committee on the Work of Its Ninety-Eighth Session", IMO Doc. LEG 98/14 (18 April 2011), para. 13.25 and Annex 9.

141. SAR Convention, Annex, Chapter 2, para. 2.1.3.

142. SAR Convention, Annex, Chapter 2, para. 2.1.4.

143. Silja Klepp, "A Double Bind: Malta and the Rescue of Unwanted Migrants at Sea, A Legal Anthropological Perspective on the Humanitarian Law of the Sea", 23 *International Journal of Refugee Law* 538 (2011), 549.

ment in the case *Hirsi Jamaa and Others* v. *Italy*, the principle of *non-refoulement* will be applicable when a State has continuous and exclusive control over persons[144].

It is however understandable that Malta wants to divide the two concepts as the country is situated at the frontline of European border controls. The Dublin II Regulation is regarded as unfavourable for Malta as the Member State responsible for an asylum claim will be the State through which the asylum-seeker first entered the European Union. Therefore, the country considers burden-sharing a crucial element[145]. De Blouw believes that the modification of the Dublin Regulation is the first and most important step to eradicating human rights abuses in Southern Europe as this could lessen the immigration burden on coastal Mediterranean Member States[146]. To help Malta to cope with the migration problem, EUREMA (European Relocation Malta) — a pilot project for intra-European Union re-allocation of beneficiaries of protection from Malta — was launched in July 2009. It was co-funded by the European Union under the European Refugee Fund (ERF) and supported by IOM and UNHCR. Its objectives are the implementation of the principle of solidarity among States, the identification of resettlement solutions for people in need and the improvement of the situation for those who remain in Malta. Nevertheless, this project is not a solution to the negative impact of the Dublin II Regulation[147].

B. Malta and the regional MoU: a mutual impact

Why did the IMO suddenly shift towards a purely maritime approach? One of the reasons could be that they definitely wanted Malta to be part of the agreement. As Malta does not accept a link between the maritime and the humanitarian elements of the problem, the country could have restraints due to the fact that the agreement could contain similar provisions as incorporated in the 2004 SOLAS and SAR Amendments and the IMO Guidelines on the Treatment of Persons Rescued at Sea. It was indeed remarkable that Malta was absent during

144. ECtHR, *Hirsi Jamaa and Others* v. *Italy*, 23 February 2012, Appl. No. 27765/09 (2012).

145. Silja Klepp, "A Double Bind: Malta and the Rescue of Unwanted Migrants at Sea, A Legal Anthropological Perspective on the Humanitarian Law of the Sea", 23 *International Journal of Refugee Law* 538 (2011), 546.

146. Nicholas De Blouw, "Drowning Policies: A Proposal to Modify the Dublin Agreement and Reduce Human Rights Abuses in the Mediterranean", 40 *California Western International Law Journal* 335 (2010), 368.

147. UNHCR, "EUREMA (2010-2011) — A Pilot Project for Intra-EU Re-allocation of Beneficiaries of Protection from Malta", Presentation at the Expert Meeting on Refugee and Asylum Seekers in Distress at Sea, Djibouti (8-10 November 2011), available online: http://www.unhcr.org/4ef338859.html.

the second meeting of the consultation group in April 2011. The problem is that if Malta is not willing to negotiate or decides not to be part of the MoU, simply there could not be an efficient agreement. Since Malta has an enormous SRR, it is of utmost importance that this country is being included. In that way, an issue that could be dealt with in the agreement is the co-ordination between the several SRRs in the Mediterranean.

Next to this, an essential element of the agreement has to be a system of burden-sharing, especially if other countries want Malta to co-operate. However, a few problems arise in this respect. Firstly, some European States fear that clarifying obligations and solving the problem through burden-sharing would produce an enormous pull factor, thus encouraging migrants to come to Europe by sea[148]. Secondly, the United States of America has begun to play a small yet important role in resettling refugees from Malta in order to reduce the burden for this country[149]. Yet, since this agreement is a regional one, this kind of burden-sharing cannot be included. Thirdly, burden-sharing clearly goes beyond a purely maritime approach.

On the one hand, the Regional Agreement is positive for Malta, since a system of burden-sharing could be established. On the other hand, Malta could be obliged to accept certain provisions in the 2004 SOLAS and SAR Amendments and the IMO Guidelines on the Treatment of Persons Rescued at Sea. Moreover, due to the agreement Malta could be forced to give up part of its SRR. Therefore, it seems that it would be better for Malta to decide not to negotiate or to be part of this agreement as the negative consequences outweigh the positive ones. This is merely a rational choice.

Paragraph 4 **Conclusion**

The Arab Spring highlighted once more the problem of migrants at sea. Due to the increased loss of life in the Mediterranean in 2011, the negotiations on the Draft Regional Agreement on concerted procedures relating to the disembarkation of persons rescued at sea in the Mediterranean Basin were speeded up. Malta has an important role

148. European Union Committee of the House of Lords, "FRONTEX: The EU External Borders Agency", 9th Report of Session 2007-2008 (5 March 2008), para. 115, available online: http://www.publications.parliament.uk/pa/ld200708/ldselect/ldeucom/60/60.pdf. See also Violeta Moreno-Lax, "Seeking Asylum in the Mediterranean: Against a Fragmentary Reading of EU Member States' Obligations Accruing at Sea", 23 *International Journal of Refugee Law* 174 (2011), 176.

149. Alexander Betts, "Towards a 'Soft Law' Framework for the Protection of Vulnerable Irregular Migrants", 22 *International Journal of Refugee Law* 209 (2010), 235.

in this agreement due to its enormous SRR. One of the problems that should be tackled is the co-ordination between the several SRRs in the Mediterranean. Also, a system of burden-sharing has to be part of the agreement. When the Regional Agreement could meet part of the concerns Malta has, it could even go further than purely maritime matters and thus include provisions on human rights and humanitarian law.

On the one hand the draft MoU contains certain elements that are negative for Malta, such as the provision that the primary responsibility rests with the Government responsible for respective SRR. Also a definition of what constitutes a distress phase is incorporated into the MoU. On the other hand the draft MoU is positive for Malta as it takes into consideration the respective capacities of a State when providing a place of safety and the particular circumstances of the case. Next to this, a place of safety may be outside the SRR (next or nearest port). Finally, States have to co-operate in providing a suitable place of safety, taking into account relevant factors, risks and circumstances, particularly when the number of survivors exceeds the capacity of the responsible State for SRR.

SECTION 4 STATE RESPONSIBILITY

Paragraph 1 State Responsibility of Flag States and Coastal States

First of all, the flag State — whose flag the vessel in distress is flying — can be responsible. Indeed, under the law of the sea, there is an obligation of every State to exercise its jurisdiction and control over ships flying its flag. According to Article 94 (3), LOSC, "[e]very State shall take such measures for ships flying its flag as are necessary to ensure safety at sea with regard, *inter alia*, to: *(a)* the construction, equipment and seaworthiness of ships". Therefore, with regard to migrants at sea, it is deemed critical that flag States exercise effective jurisdiction and control over their vessels in order to ensure strict compliance with safety standards set out in relevant international instruments. Unseaworthy vessels should not be permitted to sail[150]. The situation, wherein a State permits unseaworthy vessels carrying migrants

150. UNHCR, "The Treatment of Persons Rescued at Sea: Conclusions and Recommendations from Recent Meetings and Expert Round Tables Convened by the Office of the United Nations High Commissioner for Refugees — Report of the Office of the United Nations High Commissioner for Refugees,", UN doc. A/AC.259/17 (11 April 2008), para. 11, available online: http://www.un.org/Depts/los/consultative_process/consultative_process.htm.

to fly its flag, will raise questions of international responsibility of that State. Nevertheless, this State is not in this capacity subject to the obligation of Article 98, LOSC, which only refers to the flag States in the vicinity of the vessel in distress[151].

Under the law of State responsibility, every internationally wrongful act of a State — consisting of an action or omission — entails the international responsibility of that State. An act is internationally wrongful when the conduct is attributable to the State under international law and when it constitutes a breach of an international obligation of the State[152]. The failure of a vessel to provide assistance to persons in distress at sea can be attributable to its flag State in two cases: (1) when the vessel is a warship or other duly designated State vessel and (2) when the vessel is private and the shipmaster is acting on the instructions of — or under the direction or control of — the flag State[153]. In the first case, the shipmaster — with which the pertinent duty to provide assistance lies — is a *de jure* organ of the flag State. His conduct will be attributable to the flag State pursuant to Article 4, ILC Articles. In the second case, should the flag State instruct the shipmaster to turn a blind eye to persons in distress at sea, this omission would be attributable to the flag State according to Article 8, ILC Articles. However, it must be stressed that flag States — which enact a duty of assistance in their domestic legislation and exercise disciplinary control and jurisdiction over potential infringements of this duty in accordance with their legislation — should be considered to meet their obligations under Article 98 (1), LOSC[154].

There is a third — although unlikely — possibility that the conduct of a private vessel will be attributable to the flag State, namely when the vessel is private and the shipmaster is empowered by the law to exercise elements of governmental authority. In this case, the conduct shall be considered an act of the State, provided that the person or entity is acting in that capacity in the particular instance[155]. Whether the shipmaster will be empowered to exercise "elements of governmental authority"

151. Efthymios Papastavridis, "Rescuing Migrants at Sea: The Responsibility of States under International Law", Working Paper Series Social Science Research Network (27 September 2011), pp. 16-17, available online: http://papers.ssrn.com/sol3/papers.cfm?abstract_id=1934352.
152. ILC, "Draft Articles on Responsibility of States for Internationally Wrongful Acts" (adopted 9 August 2001), UN doc. A/56/10 (24 October 2001), Supp. No. 10, Arts. 1-2, available online: http://untreaty.un.org/ilc/texts/instruments/english/draft%20articles/9_6_2001.pdf (ILC Draft Articles).
153. Efthymios Papastavridis, "Rescuing Migrants at Sea: The Responsibility of States under International Law", Working Paper Series Social Science Research Network (27 September 2011), pp. 17-18, available online: http://papers.ssrn.com/sol3/papers.cfm?abstract_id=1934352.
154. *Ibid.*, p. 19.
155. ILC Draft Articles, Art. 5.

and to what extent, will be a matter of internal law. Shipmasters often enjoy certain public powers, for example the power to arrest and to board a vessel. When there would exist a similar delegation of governmental authority with respect to search and rescue at sea in the national law, it would be difficult to contest the attribution of the conduct to the flag State[156]. What is being regarded as "governmental" depends on the particular society, its history and traditions. Not only the content of the powers will be important, but also the way they are conferred on an entity, the purposes for which they are to be exercised and the extent to which the entity is accountable to Government for their exercise. Article 5, ILC Articles, does not cover situations where internal law confers powers upon or authorizes conduct by citizens or residents generally[157]. Therefore, it is a very narrow category. Moreover, rendering assistance can be regarded as a humanitarian duty, rather than a governmental activity[158].

The obligations for coastal States under Article 98 (2), LOSC, as well as under the SAR and SOLAS Conventions are to promote the establishment, operation and maintenance of an adequate and effective search and rescue service, where circumstances so require co-operate with neighbouring States for this purpose and to ensure that a place of safety is provided. The conduct of a Rescue Co-ordination Centre (RCC) will always be attributed to its coastal States, as the RCC administrators are necessarily *de jure* organs of the State[159]. Although an RCC can be operated either unilaterally by personnel of a single military service (e.g. an Air Force or a Navy) or either by a single civilian service (e.g. a national police force or a coast-guard), it will always be regarded as a State organ. Article 4 (1), ILC Articles, reads:

> "The conduct of any State organ shall be considered an act of that State under international law, whether the organ exercises legislative, executive, judicial or any other functions, whatever position it holds in the organization of the State, and whatever its character as an organ of the central Government or of a territorial unit of the State."

---

156. Efthymios Papastavridis, "Rescuing Migrants at Sea: The Responsibility of States under International Law", Working Paper Series Social Science Research Network (27 September 2011), 18, available online: http://papers.ssrn.com/sol3/papers.cfm?abstract_id=1934352.

157. ILC, "Draft Articles on Responsibility of States for Internationally Wrongful Acts, with Commentaries", 43, available online: http://untreaty.un.org/ilc/texts/instruments/english/commentaries/9_6_2001.pdf.

158. Efthymios Papastavridis, "Rescuing Migrants at Sea: The Responsibility of States under International Law", Working Paper Series Social Science Research Network (27 September 2011), p. 18, available online: http://papers.ssrn.com/sol3/papers.cfm?abstract_id=1934352.

159. *Ibid.*, p. 19.

The fact that the State is responsible for the conduct of its own organs — acting in that capacity — has long been recognized in international judicial decisions. One of the earliest sources of this principle was Umpire Lieber's statement in the *Moses* case, a decision of a Mexico-United States Mixed Claims Commission:

> "An officer or person in authority represents *pro tanto* his government, which in an international sense is the aggregate of all officers and men in authority." [160]

The International Court of Justice (ICJ) has also confirmed this rule. In its Advisory Opinion on *Difference Relating to Immunity from Legal Process of a Special Rapporteur of the Commission on Human Rights*, it said that according to a well-established rule of international law, the conduct of any organ of a State must be regarded as an act of that State. This rule is of a customary character [161].

The words of Article 98 (2), LOSC, indicate that coastal States shall promote — not provide — a certain level of search and rescue services. Indeed, search and rescue services have to be "adequate and effective". However, it is not always clear what "adequate and effective" means. Moen gives the example of the recent Arctic luxury eco-tourism. Cruise ships — ice-breaking vessels that need no escort to navigate — now take advantage of ice-free conditions during the summer months to sail from Iceland to Alaska through the Northwest Passage. Nevertheless, travelling along the Northwest Passage still imposes serious risks, making the potential for a humanitarian disaster real. Canada should therefore adapt its search and rescue services in order to adequately and effectively deal with these new risks [162]. It can be concluded that coastal States are under an obligation of conduct, not an obligation of result [163]. For States Parties to the 2004 SAR and SOLAS Amendments, there is an additional obligation to ensure that a place of safety is being provided for the persons rescued at sea. Whether this requirement will be met, will have to be decided on a case-by-case basis.

160. John Bassett Moore, *History and Digest of the International Arbitrations to Which the United States Has Been a Party*, Washington D.C., Government Printing Office, 1871, Vol. III, p. 3129.

161. ICJ, *Difference Relating to Immunity from Legal Process of a Special Rapporteur of the Commission on Human Rights*, Advisory Opinion, 29 April 1999, *ICJ Reports 1999*, p. 62, para. 62.

162. Amy E. Moen, "For Those in Peril on the Sea: Search and Rescue under the Law of the Sea Convention", 24 *Ocean Yearbook* 377 (2010), 377-410.

163. Efthymios Papastavridis, "Rescuing Migrants at Sea: The Responsibility of States under International Law", Working Paper Series Social Science Research Network (27 September 2011), 20, available online: http://papers.ssrn.com/sol3/papers.cfm?abstract_id=1934352.

According to Article 98 (2), LOSC, coastal States also have to co-operate where appropriate. But in practice, this is not also the case. On 9 November 2011, 44 people — mostly sub-Saharans — were rescued by the Italian navy ship *Foscari* after two days of sending out distress calls from a satellite phone in the Mediterranean Sea. The delay in rescuing the boat led to huge risks to the lives of the persons in distress. Risks for example included drowning, dehydration and exposure. After the rescue, the migrants were transported to Sicily, not to Lampedusa or Malta which were the two closest ports. UNHCR spokesman Adrian Edwards stated that UNHCR was grateful that the Italian navy took this initiative despite the fact that the boat was in Maltese SRR[164]. In response, the Armed Forces of Malta (AFM) and the Maltese SAR authorities both rejected what they characterized as the "impression conveyed" by the UNHCR spokesperson that Maltese SAR authorities abdicated from their responsibilities and did not co-operate with the relevant Italian authorities. The AFM statement — as reported by the newspaper *Times of Malta* — outlines in detail the Maltese response to the distress call from the migrant boat. The AFM said that the decision for the *Foscari* to take the rescued migrants to an Italian port in Sicily was the result of Italian insistence that Lampedusa does not represent a place of safety for the disembarkation of migrants. According to Malta, Lampedusa did represent the nearest place of safety under the relevant legal regime applicable with the Malta SRR. Therefore, the persons should have been disembarked there[165].

Could Malta be responsible for not co-operating? First of all, as was mentioned in Section 2, paragraph 2, of this chapter, it will be difficult to establish a breach of the duty to co-operate. Second, there are migrant boats that refuse to be rescued by Malta, because they want to go to Italy. For example, on 9 July 2012, a boat — reportedly carrying 50 Eritreans and Somalis — was at sea. They refused to be rescued by Maltese military forces. UNHCR reported that over 1,000 people on 14 boats have arrived in Malta from Libya so far in 2012. Two other boats were intercepted by Maltese authorities. It is striking that the majority elected not to be rescued and continued to Italy[166].

---

164. UNHCR, "UNHCR Thanks Italian Navy for Rescuing Boat in Distress Packed with Refugees from Libya", Briefing Notes (11 November 2011), available online: http://www.unhcr.org/4ebd29809.html.

165. *Times of Malta*, "UNHCR Comments Give the Wrong Impression — AFM" (14 November 2011), available online: http://www.timesofmalta.com/articles/view/20111114/local/unhcr-comments-give-the-wrong-impression-afm.393791.

166. UNHCR, "One Survivor, 54 Die at Sea Attempting the Voyage to Italy from Libya", Press Release (10 July 2012), available online: http://www.unhcr.org/4ffc59e89.html.

Paragraph 2 An Example: The Left-to-Die Boat

A recent incident that gave rise to a discussion on responsibility for failing to meet search and rescue obligations involved a disabled boat filled with migrants fleeing Libya. It was left to drift for two weeks in the Mediterranean before finally landing back in Libya on 10 April 2011. The boat ran into trouble not long after its departure from Tripoli. Despite several distress calls as well as sightings by survivors of a military helicopter and a warship, the boat received no help. It is almost certain that the helicopter must have come from a ship[167]. The warship was of an off-white or light grey colour and the boat was close enough for them to see people on board wearing different coloured military uniforms. However, none of the survivors could remember seeing the ship's flag[168]. The situation on board the boat when they encountered the ship was very different to the situation when they encountered the helicopter. Indeed, when the ship came across them, many persons had already died and there was no food and water. In an attempt to approach the ship, the migrants jumped into the sea and started pushing their boat in its direction. They even held up the dead babies and the sick women as well as the empty fuel tanks. However, no assistance was provided and after a short while, the military vessel sailed away[169]. It should have been clear that the survivors and the boat were in distress and that the situation required immediate rescue. As a result, in these circumstances there was a clear failure to intervene[170]. Ultimately, 63 persons — including 20 women and two babies — out of the 72 passengers died. As of 24 March 2011 — two days before the migrant boat left Tripoli — NATO and France, Great Britain, Italy, Spain, the United States, and Canada all had warships patrolling NATO's Maritime Surveillance Area, to enforce the arms embargo on Libya[171].

But the question is which military vessel ignored the calls for assistance? According to the fact-finding PACE report of Tineke Strik of 29 March 2012, at least two vessels involved in NATO's operations were in the boat's vicinity when the distress call was sent, namely the Spanish frigate *Méndez Núñez* (11 miles away) and the Italian *ITS*

167. PACE, "Lives Lost in the Mediterranean Sea: Who is Responsible?", Report of the Committee on Migration, Refugees and Displaced Persons (29 March 2012), Explanatory Memorandum, para. 138, available online: http://assembly.coe.int/CommitteeDocs/2012/20120329_mig_RPT.EN.pdf.

168. *Ibid.*, Explanatory Memorandum, paras. 41-43.

169. *Ibid.*, Explanatory Memorandum, para. 43.

170. *Ibid.*, Explanatory Memorandum, para. 99.

171. FIDH, "NATO: Clarify Response to Deaths at Sea" (26 March 2012), available online: http://www.fidh.org/IMG/article_PDF/article_a11532.pdf.

Borsini (37 miles away)[172]. Tineke Strik met with NATO officials in Brussels on 28 November 2011[173]. She also requested written information from NATO and from the ministers of defence of countries involved in NATO operations with vessels with aircraft and/or helicopter-carrying facilities (Canada, France, Greece, Italy, Romania, Spain, Turkey, the United Kingdom and the United States)[174]. However, NATO stated:

> "In all cases, NATO warships did everything they could to respond to distress calls and provide help when necessary. In addition, through coordination with national authorities, NATO has indirectly facilitated the rescue of many hundreds more. Commanders of warships under NATO command were, and remain, fully aware of their obligations under the International Law and Law of the Sea and responded appropriately."[175]

As — at that time — all vessels in the area were under NATO command, the vessel must have been under the command of NATO, whatever its nationality was. As a result, according to Ms Strik, NATO must take responsibility for the ships ignoring the calls for assistance from the "left-to-die boat"[176]. The report of Tineke Strik was adopted by the PACE Committee on Migration, Refugees and Displaced Persons. It demanded that NATO would conduct an enquiry into the incident. Next to this, national parliaments of the States concerned should also carry out inquiries[177].

On 11 April 2012, three NGOs — La Fédération internationale des

172. PACE, "Lives Lost in the Mediterranean Sea: Who is Responsible?", Report of the Committee on Migration, Refugees and Displaced Persons (29 March 2012), Draft Resolution, para. 8, available online: http://assembly.coe.int/CommitteeDocs/2012/20120329_mig_RPT.EN.pdf.

173. *Ibid.*, Explanatory Memorandum, para. 8.

174. *Ibid.*, Explanatory Memorandum, para. 10.

175. Stephen Evans, "Letter from Mr Stephen Evans, Assistant Secretary General for Operations of NATO, to Ms Strik, Rapporteur of the Committee on Migrations, Refugees and Displaced Persons" (27 March 2012), available online: http://assembly.coe.int/CommitteeDocs/2012/20120329_mig_LET.APENDIX.EN.pdf. See also Richard Froh, "Letter from Mr Richard Froh, Deputy Assistant Secretary General, Operations Directorate of NATO, to Ms Strik, Rapporteur of the Committee on Migrations, Refugees and Displaced Persons" (8 February 2012), available online: http://assembly.coe.int/CommitteeDocs/2012/20120329_mig_RPT.APENDIX.EN.pdf.

176. PACE, "Lives Lost in the Mediterranean Sea: Who is Responsible?", Report of the Committee on Migration, Refugees and Displaced Persons (29 March 2012), Explanatory Memorandum para. 148, available online: http://assembly.coe.int/CommitteeDocs/2012/20120329_mig_RPT.EN.pdf.

177. PACE, "PACE Committee Finds a 'Catalogue of Failures' that Led to Deaths of 63 People Fleeing Libyan Conflict by Sea", Press Statement (29 March 2012), available online: http://assembly.coe.int/ASP/NewsManager/EMB_NewsManagerView.asp?ID=7567&L=2.

ligues des droits de l'homme (FIDH), Groupe d'information et de soutien des immigrés (GISTI) and Migreurop — held a press conference to announce the filing of a legal complaint against the French military with the Procureur de la République du Tribunal de Grande Instance de Paris, alleging that military forces failed to render assistance to a migrant boat within the NATO military zone during *Operation Unified Protector*[178]. FIDH, GISTI and Migreurop concluded that the French military must have had knowledge of the distress situation, based upon three reasons:

> "(1) Compte tenu de la connaissance de la présence et de la localisation (33° 45 mn de latitude nord et 13° 05 mn de longitude est) de ce bateau par un avion de reconnaissance français le 27 mars à 14h55. (2) Compte tenu de la présence de l'armée française dans le périmètre de 50 milles nautiques, à partir de la localisation de l'embarcation, lors de la diffusion du message de détresse le 27 mars à 20h54 (18h54 GMT) par les garde-côtes italiens. (3) Compte tenu de l'importante présence de l'armée française dans le périmètre de la diffusion du message Hydrolant en date du 28 mars 2011 à 06h06 et de sa diffusion durant les dix jours suivants toutes les quatre heures."[179]

Indeed, information provided by the Rome MRCC indicates a sighting of a boat full of migrants by a French aircraft on 27 March 2011. According to the French sighting, the boat was a rubber dinghy, had about 50 persons on board and was under propulsion. A photograph taken by the aircraft was provided to Ms Strik by the Rome MRCC, showing distinctly a blue boat packed with people and steadily moving ahead. The boat in the picture was identified as the boat in question by two of the survivors[180]. According to information provided by the French military, no such event occurred off the Libyan shores during the NATO operations. The French Minister of Defence stated that the French vessel *Meuse* encountered a vessel carrying migrants on 28 March 2011, approximately 12 nautical miles south of Malta. However, this could not have been the boat in question. The Minister went on to say that all other French assets were operating in the Gulf of Sidra. Therefore, they were not in the area of concern. NATO's written reply

---

178. FIDH, GISTI and Migreurop, "Plainte Contre X" (11 April 2012), available online: http://www.gisti.org/IMG/pdf/plainte_2012-04_c-armee-francaise.pdf.

179. *Ibid.*, p. 18.

180. PACE, "Lives Lost in the Mediterranean Sea: Who is Responsible?", Report of the Committee on Migration, Refugees and Displaced Persons (29 March 2012), Explanatory Memorandum, paras. 85-87, available online: http://assembly.coe.int/CommitteeDocs/2012/20120329_mig_RPT.EN.pdf.

was that "based on a review of existing records in NATO operational headquarters, there is no record of any aircraft or ship under NATO command having seen or made contact with the small boat in question". These responses fail to provide any concrete answers as to the identity of the French aircraft that took a picture of the boat[181].

One of the problems is the isolated nature of the ocean. Therefore, it is difficult to prove a failure of search and rescue obligations. Nevertheless, satellite images for example could provide for proof. The European Union Satellite Centre (EUSC) gathers a great deal of data and pictures across the globe[182]. In the light of the PACE fact finding report "Lives Lost in the Mediterranean Sea: Who is Responsible?", Tineke Strik asked EUSC for satellite images. However, EUSC replied that the Centre did not have archived products available for the indicated area and the indicated time frame. It continued stating that — considering that the area of interest coincided with the area of NATO *Operation Unified Protector* — the envisaged investigation could involve classified "NATO confidential" information. Nevertheless, EUSC admitted that access to satellite imagery of the area would have been an invaluable tool to identify the location of ships as military vessels are certainly large enough to be spotted and possibly identified from such data[183]. This identification could lead to States being hold responsible.

Paragraph 3 **Unmanned Aerial Vehicles: A Solution?**

In July 2012, the Armed Forces of Malta (AFM) expressed interest in benefiting from a European Union-sponsored project involving the deployment of "drones" — Unmanned Aerial Vehicles (UAVs) — to assist in migrant patrols at sea. While the AFM is fully involved in the development of the system, it is however not yet participating in the testing of such drones[184]. FRONTEX's Research and Development Unit is currently engaged in a study to identify more cost-efficient and operational-effective solutions for aerial border surveillance, in particular Unmanned Aircraft Systems (UASs) with Optional Piloted Vehicles

181. *Op. cit. supra* footnote 180, Explanatory Memorandum, paras. 90-91.

182. For information on the European Union Satellite Centre see http://www.eusc.europa.eu/.

183. PACE, "Lives Lost in the Mediterranean Sea: Who is Responsible?", Report of the Committee on Migration, Refugees and Displaced Persons (29 March 2012), Explanatory Memorandum, paras. 141-143, available online: http://assembly.coe.int/CommitteeDocs/2012/20120329_mig_RPT.EN.pdf.

184. *Malta Today*, "AFM 'Interested' in EU-sponsored Drones for Migrant Surveillance at Sea" (29 July 2012), available online: http://www.maltatoday.com.mt/en/newsdetails/news/national/AFM-interested-in-EU-sponsored-drones-for-migrant-surveillance-at-sea-20120728.

(OPVs) that could be used during joint operations at sea[185]. The United States is already using "Predator drones" to monitor land and sea borders. However, serious questions have been raised about the effectiveness of surveillance drones operating over the sea as — until now — the drones have had limited success in for example spotting drug runners in the open ocean[186].

The use of drones for land and sea border surveillance is contemplated by in the EU Commission's proposal on the establishment of the European Border Surveillance System (EUROSUR)[187]. The main purpose of EUROSUR is to improve the situational awareness and reaction capability at the external borders of the Member States of the European Union[188]. The planned surveillance of the Mediterranean — using UAVs, satellites and shipboard monitoring systems — could aid in the rescue of refugees shipwrecked on the open seas[189]. However, EUROSUR could cover up a lack of substance. For example, maritime rescue services are not part of EUROSUR and border guards do not share information with them[190]. Moreover, EUROSUR should be adapted to meet certain need of asylum-seekers. For example, the exchange of personal data with third countries should be prohibited, as this exchange may jeopardize both the safety and protection of asylum-seekers and refugees, and their data protection rights[191].

185. FRONTEX, "Programme of Work 2012" (2012), p. 105, available online: http://www.frontex.europa.eu/assets/About_Frontex/Governance_documents/Work_programme/2012/frontex_pow_2012.pdf.

186. *Los Angeles Times*, "U.S. Plans More Drone Flights over Caribbean" (23 June 2012), available online: http://articles.latimes.com/2012/jun/23/nation/la-na-drugs-caribbean-20120623.

187. European Commission Proposal of 12 December 2011 for a Regulation of the European Parliament and of the Council Establishing the European Border Surveillance System (EUROSUR), COM(2011)873 final. This proposal is currently being considered by the European Parliament.

188. European Commission Proposal of 12 December 2011 for a Regulation of the European Parliament and of the Council Establishing the European Border Surveillance System (EUROSUR), COM(2011)873 final, Article 1.

189. Human Rights Watch, "Hidden Emergency — Migrant Deaths in the Mediterranean" (August 2012), p. 11, available online: http://www.hrw.org/sites/default/files/related_material/2012_EU_Hidden%20Emergency.pdf.

190. Ben Hayes and Mathias Vermeulen, "Borderline — The EU's New Border Surveillance Initiatives", Heinrich Böll Foundation (June 2012), pp. 74-76, available online: http://www.statewatch.org/news/2012/jun/borderline.pdf.

191. LIBE, Draft Report on the Proposal for a Regulation of the European Parliament and of the Council establishing the European Border Surveillance System (EUROSUR) by Rapporteur Jan Mulder, COD (2011) 0427; Meijers Committee — Dutch Standing committee of experts in international immigration, refugee and criminal law, "Note on the Proposal for a Regulation Establishing the European Border Surveillance" (12 September 2012), available online: http://www.statewatch.org/news/2012/sep/eu-meijers-cttee-eurosur.pdf?.

SECTION 5 SANCTIONS FOR THE MASTER AND THE SHIP-OWNER

Paragraph 1 Shipmaster

When the 1989 Salvage Convention added Article 10 (2), it placed the obligation to give effect to the duty to render assistance on the States, rather than on masters[192]. Indeed, although Article 10 (1) says that every master is bound — so far as he can do so without serious danger to his vessel and persons thereon — to render assistance to any person in danger of being lost at sea, paragraph 2 says: "The States Parties shall adopt the measures necessary to enforce the duty set out in paragraph 1."

Also other multinational instruments do not directly obligate masters to render assistance. At first sight the treaties refer to the masters of ships and they appear to create obligations for them. However, the binding element is on States parties[193]. Also, Article 98 (1), LOSC, says "Every State shall require the master of a ship flying its flag . . . to render assistance". Indeed, international law seldom imposes obligation directly on individuals[194].

Article 2 of the 1989 Salvage Convention provides that States must bring judicial and arbitral proceedings regarding a breach of the duty to render assistance. Despite the fact that the duty to render assistance has been widely accepted, sometimes it still remains unenforced against masters[195]. There are several reasons for this. First of all, failures to render assistance are rarely reported, as a survivor of a disaster at sea would have to be able to somehow identify a vessel whose master had failed to render assistance[196]. Second, an action against a master requires that he is subject to the enforcing State's jurisdiction[197]. It may be possible for States other than the flag State to assert criminal jurisdiction due to failure by a shipmaster to assist persons in need of assistance on

192. Arthur Alan Severance, "The Duty to Render Assistance in the Satellite Age", 36 *California Western International Law Journal* 377 (2006), 382.

193. Martin Davies, "Obligations and Implications for Ships Encountering Persons in Need of Assistance at Sea", 12 *Pacific Rim Law & Policy Journal* 109 (2003), 109-143, 128; Arthur Alan Severance, "The Duty to Render Assistance in the Satellite Age", 36 *California Western International Law Journal* 377 (2006), 384.

194. Robert Jennings and Arthur Watts (eds.), *Oppenheim's International Law*, Harlow, Longman, 9th ed., 1992, paras. 374-375.

195. Patrick J. Long, "The Good Samaritan and Admiralty: A Parable of a Statute Lost at Sea", 48 *Buffalo Law Review* 591 (2000), 627.

196. *Ibid.*, 610.

197. Daniel P. O'Connell (ed. by Ivan A. Shearer), *The International Law of the Sea*, Oxford, Clarendon Press, 1982/1984, Vol. II, p. 907.

the high seas[198]. Third, many States — such as flags of convenience — are either unable or unwilling to enforce the duty[199]. Moreover, even otherwise responsible flag States are unwilling to enforce the duty. For example, in the case *Korpi* v. *United States*, the Court held that as a matter of law "[a] private party has no affirmative duty to rescue a vessel or person in distress"[200]. Last, as the master has a discretionary power to decide whether or not to provide assistance, as well as what kind of assistance to give, it is difficult to actually prove a breach of the duty he has.

Article 16 (1) of the 1989 Salvage Convention says:

> "1. No remuneration is due from persons whose lives are saved, but nothing in this article shall affect the provisions of national law on this subject.
>
> 2. A salvor of human life, who has taken part in the services rendered on the occasion of the accident giving rise to salvage, is entitled to a fair share of the payment awarded to the salvor for salving the vessel or other property or preventing or minimizing damage to the environment."

Therefore, States do not need to grant masters the right to a reward unless their national laws provide otherwise. Nevertheless, this could be an incentive to fulfil the legal duty to assist. However, one has to be careful that this does not amount to the act of smuggling. Smuggling is the explicit and mutually beneficial arrangement between two parties involving illegal entry (crossing borders without complying with the necessary requirements for legal entry into the receiving State) into a given country[201].

It has been suggested that the Global Maritime Distress and Safety System (GMDSS) could be used to assist in the enforcement of the duty to render assistance[202]. The GMDSS is said to be "the biggest change to maritime communications since the invention of radio"[203]. The basic concept of this system is that search and rescue authorities ashore, as

---

198. Martin Davies, "Obligations and Implications for Ships Encountering Persons in Need of Assistance at Sea", 12 *Pacific Rim Law & Policy Journal* 109 (2003), 109-143.

199. Richard A. Barnes, "Refugee Law at Sea", 53 *International and Comparative Law Quarterly* 47 (2004), 51.

200. *Korpi* v. *United States*, 961 F. Supp. 1346, N.D. Cal. (1997).

201. Smuggling Protocol, Arts. 3 *(a)* and 3 *(b)*.

202. Arthur Alan Severance, "The Duty to Render Assistance in the Satellite Age", 36 *California Western International Law Journal* 377 (2006), 398-399.

203. IMO, "SOLAS 1974 — A Brief History", available online: http://www.imo.org/KnowledgeCentre/ReferencesAndArchives/HistoryofSOLAS/Documents/SOLAS%201974%20-%20Brief%20History%20-%20List%20of%20amendments%20to%20date%20and%20how%20to%20find%20them.html.

well as ships in the vicinity, will be alerted in the event of an emergency. Therefore, it helps shipmasters and States to fulfil their duty to provide search and rescue services. The GMDSS makes use of the satellite communications provided by Inmarsat as well as terrestrial radio. The equipment required by ships varies according to the sea area in which they operate. For example, ships travelling to the high seas must carry more communications equipment than those which remain within reach of specified shore-based radio facilities. In addition to distress communications, the GMDSS also provides for the dissemination of general maritime safety information[204].

Paragraph 2 **Ship-owner**

Could a ship-owner be liable for damages to a stranger in peril on the high seas to whom the shipmaster has failed to give aid? In the case *Warschauer* v. *Lloyd Sabaudo* (1934)[205], the plaintiff Warschauer — a United States citizen — brought an action against an Italian corporation which owned and operated the steamship *Conte Biancamano*. The complaint alleged that on the afternoon of 31 October 1931, the plaintiff and a companion were adrift on the high seas in a disabled motorboat. They had no gasoline and no food and when the defendant's operating personnel of the *Conte Biancamano* observed the distress signals, they refused to heed them or to stop and take the plaintiff aboard. In the case at hand, they could have done so without peril to themselves or their vessel. Although Warschauer was rescued by the coast-guard two days later, he had suffered permanent physical injuries due to the exposure and deprivations to which he was subjected by the failure of the defendant's steamship to render assistance. Therefore, Warschauer demanded damages for the pain and subsequently incurred medical expenses. This situation involved no personal dereliction by the ship-owner. Such dereliction was that of the master. Only by applying the doctrine of *respondeat superior* it could be imputed to the ship owner.

The Court referred to Article 11 of the 1910 Salvage Convention that the owner of the vessel incurs no liablity by reason of contravention of the master's obligation to render assistance. The applicant in this case

204. 1988 Amendments Relating to the International Convention for the Safety of Life at Sea, 1974 (adopted 11 November 1988, entered into force 1 February 1992), Resolutions SOLAS/CONF.1 and SOLAS/CONF.2.

205. *Warschauer* v. *Lloyd Sabaudo, S.A.*, 71 F. 2d 146, 2d Cir., cert. denied, 293 US 610 (1934), as published in Louis B. Sohn and John E. Noyes, *Cases and Materials on the Law of the Sea*, Ardsley, Transnational Publishers, 2004, pp. 94-97.

held that this provision only referred to the criminal liability of the owner. However, the Court decided that such an interpretation would seem most unlikely. It said that:

> "Unless it was intended to cover civil liability, no reason is apparent for mentioning the owner's exemption from liability. It is almost inconceivable that criminal responsibility should be imputed to an owner who had not directed the dereliction of his agent. . . . A penal statute is construed to apply only to the class of persons to whom it specifically refers."[206]

Therefore, if the 1910 Salvage Convention only refers to the master's duty, breach of which is to be enforced by the criminal law, there would have been no need to express the owner's exemption from responsibility. However, if the master's liability can be civil as well as criminal, then the provision referring to the owner serves a purpose as it clearly relieves him from civil liability.

This is confirmed by the 1989 Salvage Convention. Indeed, although Article 10 (1) of the 1989 Salvage Convention requires that every master is bound — so far as he can do so without serious danger to his vessel and persons thereon — to render assistance to any person in danger of being lost at sea, paragraph 3 continues: "The owner of a vessel incurs no liability by reason of contravention of the above position."

Paragraph 3 **When the Rescuer Becomes a Smuggler**

As States are reluctant to accept rescued migrants onto their territory, the rescuer is sometimes being assimilated with a smuggler. In 2000, the Smuggling Protocol was attached to the United Nations Convention against Transnational Organized Crime (UNTOC) in 2000[207]. While there is no express reference to distress situations at sea, Article 7, Smuggling Protocol, mentions that States have to co-operate in accordance with the international law of the sea[208]. Next to this Article 8, Smuggling Protocol, stipulates that — although measures such as boarding are not allowed without the express authorization of

---

206. *Warschauer* v. *Lloyd Sabaudo, S.A.*, 71 F. 2d 146, 2d Cir., cert. denied, 293 US 610 (1934), as published in Louis B. Sohn, and John E. Noyes, *Cases and Materials on the Law of the Sea*, Ardsley, Transnational Publishers, 2004, p. 95.

207. United Nations Convention against Transnational Organised Crime (adopted 15 November 2000, entered into force 29 September 2003), 2225 *UNTS* 209 (UNTOC).

208. Smuggling Protocol, Art. 7.

the flag State — States can take measures necessary to relieve imminent danger to the lives of persons[209]. Lastly, Article 19 (1), Smuggling Protocol, states that nothing in the Protocol shall affect the other rights, obligations and responsibilities of States and individuals under international law.

In 2009, a Sicilian court acquitted three Germans from *Cap Anamur* — a humanitarian non-profit organization that has its headquarters in Cologne — of criminal charges that they aided illegal migration by bringing a boatload of African migrants they rescued at sea to shore in Sicily in 2004. The former *Cap Anamur* president, as well as the ship's captain and first officer faced several years in prison[210]. However, the Smuggling Protocol entered into force for Italy on 2 August 2006 — 2 years after the *Cap Anamur* incident[211]. Nevertheless, in 2007 there was a similar case when two Tunisian fishing boat captains rescued 44 migrants and brought them to Lampedusa despite being ordered by the Italian authorities not to enter the port. The migrant boat — which had departed from Libya — had been at sea for three days and was carrying asylum-seekers from Eritrea, Ethiopia and Sudan. Most of the migrants were seriously ill. The two captains as well as their crew members were arrested and criminally charged with facilitating illegal immigration. Eventually, they were acquitted by the Court of Agrigento of these charges in November 2009[212].

A smuggler is someone who obtains, directly or indirectly, a financial or other material benefit. Although this should be understood broadly — to include, for example, crimes in which the predominant motivation may be sexual gratification, such as the receipt or trade of materials by

---

209. Smuggling Protocol, Art. 8 (5).

210. *The Malta Independent*, "Cap Anamur Crew Acquitted of Aiding Illegal Migration" (11 October 2009), available online: http://www.independent.com.mt/news.asp?newsitemid=95465.

211. UNODC, "Status of UNTOC", available online: http://www.unodc.org/unodc/en/treaties/CTOC/countrylist.html. In Italian law there does exist a specific exemption from criminal liability in the event humanitarian aid and assistance is given to persons in need. See di Alessia Pascale, "Migration Control at Sea: The Italian Case", in Bernard Ryan and Valsamis Mitsilegas (eds.), *Extraterritorial Immigration Control*, Leiden, Martinus Nijhoff Publishers, 2010, p. 301.

212. Migrants at Sea, "Italian Appeals Court Acquits Two Tunisian Fishing Boat Captains Who Rescued Migrants in 2007" (29 September 2011), available online: http://migrantsatsea.wordpress.com/2011/09/29/italian-appeals-court-acquits-2-tunisian-fishing-boat-captains-who-rescued-migrants-in-2007/. However, it must be noted that the two captains were convicted in 2009 of charges of resisting a public officer and committing violence against a warship in connection with their refusal to turn their boats around and not enter the port. In 2011, the Court of Appeal of Palermo formally acquitted them, bringing the case to an end after 4 years.

members of child pornography rings, the trading of children by members of paedophile rings or cost-sharing among ring members[213] — the reference to "a financial or other material benefit" as an element of the definition was especially included in order to emphasize that the intention was to only include the activities of organized criminal groups acting for profit, but to exclude the activities of those who provided support to migrants for humanitarian reasons or on the basis of close family ties. It was not the intention of the Protocol to criminalize the activities of family members or support groups such as religious or non-governmental organizations[214].

However, the reasoning of the decision which validated the initial arrest of the captain and officials of *Cap Anamur* does contain a reference to the notion of profit: according to the court they actually wanted to get the greatest media coverage and publicity in favour of the organization[215]. *Cap Anamur* became well known in the 1980s for helping Vietnamese boat people — fleeing for the communist regime — in the South China Sea. The committee "Ein Schiff für Vietnam" ("A boat for Vietnam") chartered a cargo ship — *Cap Anamur* — which rescued more than 10,000 boat persons[216]. Rumours therefore suggest that the *Cap Anamur* activists staged a stunt in 2004 to attract news media attention[217].

In the 2007 case concerning two Tunisian fishing boats, neither net nor fish were found on the fishing boat by Italian authorities[218]. The UN General Assembly already noted in its resolution 64/72 on sustainable fisheries of 4 December 2009 that it had concerns about possible connections between international organized crime and illegal fishing in certain regions of the world[219]. A 2011 UNODC study on transnational

213. UNGA, "Report of the Ad Hoc Committee on the Elaboration of a Convention against Transnational Organized Crime on the Work of Its First to Eleventh Sessions, Interpretative Notes for the Official Records *(travaux préparatoires)* of the Negotiation of the Protocol against Smuggling of Migrants by Land, Sea and Air, supplementing the United Nations Convention against Transnational Organized Crime", UN doc. A/55/383.Add.1 (3 November 2000), para. 3.

214. *Ibid*., para. 88.

215. Tribunale di Agrigento, *Cap Anamur Case*, Ordinanza 16 luglio 2004, Decision of the Court of Agrigento (16 July 2004), available online: http://www.tribunale.agrigento.it.

216. Cap Anamur, "Über uns", available online: http://www.cap-anamur.org/service/%C3%BCber-uns.

217. *The Malta Independent*, "Cap Anamur Crew Acquitted of Aiding Illegal Migration" (11 October 2009), available online: http://www.independent.com.mt/news.asp?newsitemid=95465.

218. Alessia di Pascale, "Migration Control at Sea: The Italian Case", in Bernard Ryan and Valsamis Mitsilegas (eds.), *Extraterritorial Immigration Control*, Leiden, Martinus Nijhoff Publishers, 2010, p. 304.

219. UNGA, "Sustainable fisheries, including through the 1995 Agreement for the Implementation of the Provisions of the United Nations Convention on the Law of the Sea of 10 December 1982 relating to the Conservation and

organized crime in the fishing industry found that there are indeed fishing vessels that are involved in smuggling of migrants, illicit traffic in drugs (primarily cocaine), illicit traffic in weapons and acts of terrorism. Fishing vessels are being used as mother ships, as supply vessels for other vessels engaged in criminal activities or simply as cover for clandestine activities at sea and in ports. Although fishers are often recruited by organized criminal groups due to their skills and knowledge of the sea, they seldom seem to be regarded as the masterminds behind organized criminal activities involving the fishing industry or fishing vessels. Therefore, it is unfortunate that fishermen — rather than more centrally placed persons in the criminal networks — are likely to be targeted when criminal activities involving fishing vessels or the fishing industry are investigated and prosecuted, particularly in light of the possibility that some of these fishers may be victims of human trafficking[220]. There are no available comprehensive data on the extent to which fishers are involved in smuggling of migrants at sea across the Mediterranean. The IMO biannual reports made by Italy, Greece and Turkey suggest that relatively few fishing vessels are used for smuggling of migrants at sea into Italy and Greece compared to the use of amongst others inflatable boats and smaller engine powered plastic, wooden or fibreglass boats[221]. Therefore, there seems to be very little basis upon which to claim that fishers are involved in an organized manner in migrant smuggling into Europe[222].

We can conclude that — although every flag State must require the master of a ship flying its flag to proceed with all possible speed to the rescue of persons in distress when informed of their need of assistance[223] — the fear of criminalization by those who go to the rescue of boats carrying migrants is one of the reasons why commercial vessels fail to go to the rescue of boats in distress. This was confirmed by a 2012 report of the Parliamentary Assembly of the Council of Europe (PACE)[224].

Management of Straddling Fish Stocks and Highly Migratory Fish Stocks, and related instruments", UN doc. A/RES/64/72 (4 December 2009), para. 61.

220. UNODC, "Transnational Organized Crime in the Fishing Industry — Focus on: Trafficking in Persons, Smuggling of Migrants and Illicit Drugs Trafficking", Issue Paper (2011), p. 4, available online: http://www.unodc.org/documents/human-trafficking/Issue_Paper_-_TOC_in_the_Fishing_Industry.pdf.

221. MSC, "Unsafe Practices Associated with the Trafficking or Transport of Migrants by Sea", Biannual Reports, available online: www.imo.org.

222. UNODC, "Transnational Organized Crime in the Fishing Industry — Focus on: Trafficking in Persons, Smuggling of Migrants and Illicit Drugs Trafficking", Issue Paper (2011), p. 60, available online: http://www.unodc.org/documents/human-trafficking/Issue_Paper_-_TOC_in_the_Fishing_Industry.pdf.

223. LOSC, Art. 98 (1).

224. PACE launched an enquiry in 2011 to investigate why over 1,000 migrants had died or perished in the Mediterranean Sea while trying to reach

SECTION 6 CONCLUSION

Although it is a legal obligation for shipmasters and States under customary international law as well as under the LOSC to render assistance to persons in danger of being lost and to proceed with all possible speed to the rescue of persons in distress, there is no comparable duty to disembark these persons. As a result, rescued asylum-seekers can spend weeks on a ship before going ashore. Shipmasters are therefore reluctant to rescue migrants at sea. At the fourth meeting of the Interagency Group in June 2008, involving IMO, UNDOALOS, UNHCR, OHCHR, ILO and IOM, the participants stated: "If States fail to meet their obligations, then masters of ships cannot fulfil their duties either."[225] Therefore it is deemed crucial to solve the disembarkation problem.

Recent international and European soft law initiatives do focus on a real disembarkation duty. However, they also put too much burden on the coastal States. Indeed, the 2009 IMO Guidelines on Principles Relating to Administrative Procedures for Disembarking Persons Rescued at Sea mention that if disembarkation from the rescuing ship cannot be arranged swiftly elsewhere, the Government responsible for the SRR should accept the disembarkation[226]. Similarly, Council Decision 2010/252/EU[227] states in its Guidelines that regarding disembarkation, priority should be given to the third country from where the ship carrying the persons departed or through the territorial waters or SRR of which that ship transited. If this is not possible, priority should be given to disembarkation in the Member State hosting the surveillance operation at sea[228]. Without any prior agreements on burden-sharing between States, the life of many migrants is being jeopardized. It is estimated that for every 100 people safely landing after a dangerous journey in the

European soil from North Africa. See PACE, "Lives Lost in the Mediterranean Sea: Who is Responsible?", Report of the Committee on Migration, Refugees and Displaced Persons (29 March 2012), para. 13.4, available online: http://assembly.coe.int/CommitteeDocs/2012/20120329_mig_RPT.EN.pdf.

225. UNGA, "Report on the Work of the United Nations Open-ended Informal Consultative Process on Oceans and the Law of the Sea at Its Ninth Meeting", UN doc. A/63/174 (25 July 2008), para. 100, available online: http://www.un.org/Depts/los/consultative_process/consultative_process.htm.

226. FAL, "Principles Relating to Administrative Procedures for Disembarking Persons Rescued at Sea". IMO Doc. FAL 35/Circ.194 (22 January 2009), para. 2.3.

227. Council Decision (EU) No. 2010/252 of 26 April 2010 supplementing the Schengen Borders Code as regards the surveillance of the sea external borders in the context of the operational cooperation coordinated by the European Agency for the Management of Operational Cooperation at the External Borders, *OJ* L 111/20 of 4 May 2010.

228. *Ibid.*, Annex, Part II, para. 2.1.

Mediterranean, 5 people drown without leaving any trace[229]. However, some States fear that clarifying obligations and solving the problem through burden-sharing would produce an enormous pull factor, thus encouraging migrants to come to Europe by sea[230].

The Arab Spring highlighted once more the problem of migrants at sea. Due to the increased loss of life in the Mediterranean in 2011, the negotiations on the Draft Regional Agreement on concerted procedures relating to the disembarkation of persons rescued at sea in the Mediterranean Basin were speeded up. Malta has an important role in this agreement due to its enormous SRR. One of the problems that should be tackled is the co-ordination between the several SRRs in the Mediterranean. Also, a system of burden-sharing has to be part of the agreement. When the Regional Agreement could meet part of the concerns Malta has, it could even go further than purely maritime matters and thus include provisions on human rights and humanitarian law.

229. LEG, "Report of the Legal Committee on the Work of Its Ninety-Eighth Session", IMO Doc. LEG 98/14 (18 April 2011), Annex 9.

230. European Union Committee of the House of Lords, "FRONTEX: The EU External Borders Agency", 9th Report of Session 2007-2008 (5 March 2008), para. 115, available online: http://www.publications.parliament.uk/pa/ld200708/ldselect/ldeucom/60/60.pdf. See also Violeta Moreno-Lax, "Seeking Asylum in the Mediterranean: Against a Fragmentary Reading of EU Member States' Obligations Accruing at Sea", 23 *International Journal of Refugee Law* 174 (2011), 176.

11 Maritime Interdiction and Human Rights

Dimitrios Batsalas *

SECTION 1 INTRODUCTION

In the course of this article, I will examine the relationship, or, more precisely, the interaction between human rights law and Maritime Interdiction Operations (hereafter MIOs)[1]. This examination will be structured in two broad steps. First, I will try to present the conditions under which a MIO is permissible under human rights law. That will include an overview of all phases of the operations, including the periods before and after the actual operation but only to the extent that there is a strong connection with the operation itself. The intention is to identify what would reasonably be expected from a human rights point of view in order for a MIO to be in full compliance with the relevant law. Then, after examining when MIOs are permissible and when they are not, I will try to elaborate on the idea that although it is undisputed that human rights obligations continue to regulate the conduct of States towards people within their jurisdiction, either in or outside their territory, a somehow different approach should be adopted in the evaluation of these obligations in the fight against criminal activity at sea. This could prove beneficial for the protection of the rights of the captured suspects as it would encourage States to uphold their human rights obligations, rather than consider them as an unbearable burden, in which case they might seek ways to escape them altogether. It is then proposed that the distance between the *modus operandi* of a MIO and the obligations imposed by human rights law cannot be covered only by the adap-

* LLM (Warwick), LLB (Democritus University of Thrace). Teaching and Research Assistant at the Democritus University of Thrace (2009-2012). Attorney-at-Law (Member of Naousa Bar, Greece).

1. Maritime interdiction is "one particular tool of maritime law enforcement [that involves] stopping and searching a vessel at sea, and potentially seizing cargo and arresting persons aboard". D. Guilfoyle, "Maritime Interdiction of Weapons of Mass Destruction", 12 *Journal of Conflict and Security Law* 1 (2007), pp. 1-2.

tation of the *modus operandi* of the naval forces but also, at a certainly lesser extent, by the adaptation of the obligations imposed by the law.

* * *

It is a truism that throughout the centuries, the sea has been a very prosperous area for criminal activity, mainly because of the practical obstacles it presents to law enforcement operations. Recently, criminal activity at sea has seen a rapid increase[2], which persuaded States to assign more resources in policing the seas and combating maritime crime. That said, quite often crime at sea remains unreported for reasons that relate to interests of ship-owners, ship masters and even flag States[3]. In any case, it is important to consider how these policing, law enforcement operations affect the protection of human rights of targeted suspects.

SECTION 2 CONDITIONS OF PERMISSIBILITY

This section will be devoted to the analysis of the conditions under which a State carries out a MIO in conformity with its human rights obligations. To do that, it is necessary, first, to identify the legal framework, then, to address questions of applicability and attribution and, finally, to examine the relevant rights and the possible ways they may be protected during a MIO. While clearly distinct, those steps are closely interrelated because the identification of the law substantially defines the conditions of applicability and the scope of protection of the relevant rights. Equally, on a practical level, it is often the case that the right in need of protection might also guide us as to the applicable law; and the conditions establishing the applicability might define the relevant law. These issues will be presented in the following order: what is the law (Section 2, paragraph 1), is it applicable (Section 2, paragraph 2), and the scope of protection (Section 2, paragraph 3).

Paragraph 1 The Legal Framework

An initial observation is that the relevant legal framework consists of numerous legal regimes; of course, not all of these

2. See L. M. Diaz and B. H. Dubner, "On the Evolution of the Law of International Sea Piracy: How Property Trumped Human Rights, the Environment and the Sovereign Rights of States in the Areas of the Creation and Enforcement of Jurisdiction", 13 *Barry Law Review* 175 (2009).

3. B. H. Dubner, "Human Rights and Environmental Disaster — Two Problems that Defy the 'Norms' of the International Law of Sea Piracy", 23 *Syracuse J. Int'l L. and Com.* 1 (1997), at p. 23.

regimes are applicable in every case. For example, in a given case of a MIO and only with respect to its effects on human rights, relevant law might include the 1982 Law of the Sea Convention[4], SOLAS[5], SUA[6], UN Security Council resolutions, soft law regulating the MIOs[7], the UN Charter, the UN Declaration of Human Rights[8], the two international human rights Covenants[9], regional human rights Conventions, the Refugee Convention[10], the Convention against Torture,[11] customary human rights law. There is also discussion of whether international humanitarian law ("IHL") and, in particular, Geneva Convention III and Geneva Convention IV is relevant in some cases of counter piracy operations[12], with some scholars suggesting that IHL applies[13], while others disagree[14].

Due to the spatial confinements of the present chapter not all of the above will be examined. An elimination process must take place and the criteria for this elimination can be no other than considerations of practical realities. To begin with, a first restriction is the international ele-

4. United Nations Convention on the Law of the Sea, 1982. See http://www.un.org/Depts/los/ convention_agreements/texts/unclos/unclos_e.pdf.

5. International Convention for the Safety of Life at Sea, 1974. See http://www.imo.org/about/conventions/listofconventions/pages/international-convention-for-the-safety-of-life-at-sea-%28solas%29,-1974.aspx.

6. Convention for the Suppression of Unlawful Acts against the Safety of Maritime Navigation, 1988. See http://treaties.un.org/doc/db/Terrorism/Conv8-english.pdf.

7. This soft law might emanate from widely recognized and applied guidelines for the conduct of MIOs; for instance the NATO guidelines or the EUNAVFOR guidelines.

8. See https://www.un.org/en/documents/udhr/.

9. International Covenant on Civil and Political Rights, 1966, see http://treaties.un.org/doc/ Publication/UNTS/Volume%20999/volume-999-I-14668-English.pdf. Also, the International Covenant on Economic, Social and Cultural Rights, 1966, see http://www.ohchr.org/EN/ProfessionalInterest/Pages/ CESCR.aspx.

10. Convention Relating to the Status of Refugees, 1951. See http://treaties.un.org/doc/Publication/ UNTS/Volume%20189/volume-189-I-2545-English.pdf.

11. Convention against Torture and Other Cruel, Inhuman or Degrading Treatment or Punishment, 1984. See http://www.ohchr.org/EN/Professional Interest/Pages/CAT.aspx.

12. For a general discussion on the issue, see M. Odello and G. L. Beruto (eds.), *Non-State Actors and International Humanitarian Law. Organised Armed Groups: A Challenge for the 21st Century*, Milan, FrancoAngeli, 2010.

13. See M. H. Passman, "Protections Afforded to Captured Pirates under the Law of War and International Law", 33 *Tul. Mar. LJ* 1 (2008), at p. 4. Also, E. Kontorovich, "A Guantanamo on the Sea: The Difficulties of Prosecuting Pirates and Terrorists", 98:1 *Cal. L. Rev.* 243 (2010), at p. 263; available at http://scholarship.law.berkeley.edu/cgi/viewcontent.cgi?article=1108&context=californialawreview.

14. For a view negating the application of IHL in cases of piracy, see T. Neumann and T. R. Salomon, "Kein Krieg vor Somalia", 24 *Humanitäres Völkerrecht* 165 (2011).

ment of the MIO. Thus, there will be no discussion of the operations of a State against a ship of its own flag or its own nationals. Secondly, the chapter will focus on systematic naval operations that include MIOs and take place in specific parts of the oceans and from specific interdicting naval forces. Thirdly, the question of the applicability or the potential application of IHL to an MIO will not be addressed. Although there is no doubt that some basic human rights are protected by IHL, for the purposes of this chapter it is submitted that it is a clearly distinct area of law and it should be discussed elsewhere. This restriction also indicates that interdictions against private ships or boats will not be examined. Finally, this chapter will be based on practice. It is not meant to be only a theoretical approach; hence, incidents that have been reported or cases that have reached the courts will be canvassed.

Paragraph 2 **Questions of Applicability**

The first step in applying human rights law to a specific situation is to ascertain whether the persons concerned are under the jurisdiction of a State. If the latter exercises no jurisdiction, it cannot enforce its laws and, of course, it cannot be held liable for any breach of human rights law. Since, as mentioned above, this chapter deals with MIOs that have an international character, the examination of the establishment of jurisdiction will mostly concern instances occurring outside the territorial waters of a State.

A. Extraterritorial application

Although there have been arguments favouring the idea that areas beyond the boundaries of a State are in a legal vacuum, i.e. the norms of ICCPR or the ECHR do not apply [15], it should be underscored that States cannot escape their human rights obligations simply by acting extraterritorially [16].

15. The US position on Guantanamo or the UK position regarding the occupation of Iraq are examples of this approach. On these issues, the "legal vacuum" argument has been presented by H. H. Koh, "Rights to Remember", *Economist*, 30/10/2003, at p. 24 (available online at http://www.economist.com/node/2173160); Priest and Gellman, "Stress and Duress: Tactics Used on Terrorism Suspects Held in Secret Overseas Facilities", *Washington Post*, 26/12/2002 (available online at http://www.commondreams.org/headlines02/1226-03.htm); D. Van Natta Jr., "Questioning Terror Suspects in a Dark and Surreal World", *New York Times*, 09/03/2003.

16. R. Wilde, "Legal 'Black Hole'? Extraterritorial State Action and International Treaty Law on Civil and Political Rights", 26 *Michigan Journal of International Law* 739 (2004-2005), p. 805. Also, R. Wilde, "Extraterritorial Application of International Human Rights Law", in P. Eden and T. O'Donnell (eds.),

As far as the ICCPR is concerned[17], the HRC has held that jurisdiction is not restricted by territoriality. In its General Comment No. 31, the HRC reaffirms the extraterritorial application of the ICCPR when it concludes that "[any] State Party must respect and ensure the rights laid down in the Covenant to anyone within the power or effective control of that State Party, even if not situated within the territory of the State Party"[18].

The ECtHR in *Medvedyev* v. *France* reiterated the Bankovic proposition that the extraterritorial application of the ECHR is exceptional[19]. According to the interpretation of the Court, two tests are to determine whether the ECHR's protection should be extended to cover extraterritorial conduct. First, when the State exercises effective control over a foreign territory and secondly, when an individual comes under the authority and control of State agents acting outside the territory of the State.

In *Medvedyev*, the Court correctly found that the boarding of the *Winner* constituted an exercise of jurisdiction of a kind that should engage the protection of the ECHR. However, although the result is not problematic, the reasoning of the Court is not so clear. Guilfoyle suggests it is possible that the Court did not want to address the "thorny" issue of the exact test underlying the extraterritorial application of the Convention; an unwillingness that delivers a judgment based on a "wanting and odd" reasoning[20].

A joint evaluation of *Bankovic, Öcalan*[21], *Issa*[22], *Al-Skeini*[23], *and Medvedyev,* leads to certain conclusions. Although the Court is unwilling

September 11, 2001 : A Turning Point in International and Domestic Law ?, New York, Transnational Publishers, 2005, pp. 255-334.

17. See also D. Guilfoyle, *Shipping Interdiction and the Law of the Sea*, Cambridge, University Press, 2009. Guilfoyle submits that "[ICCPR] standards are prima facie applicable to the extraterritorial conduct of State organs, at least where those organs exercise 'effective control of an area outside . . . national territory'" (p. 268).

18. Human Rights Committee, General Comment No. 31, at para. 13.

19. *Bankovic and Others* v. *Belgium and Others*, Admissibility Decision, 12.12.2001, para. 71.

20. D. Guilfoyle, "Current Legal Developments. European Court of Human Rights: Medvedyev and Others v. France", 25 *Int. J. Marine and Coastal Law* 437 (2010), at p. 439. On the other hand, Bodini (S. P. Bodini, "Fighting Maritime Piracy under the European Convention on Human Rights", *European Journal of International Law* (2011), at p. 10) identifies the test, suggesting that the Court used the "authority and control" test. He supports this proposition by a reference to in paragraph 67 of the Judgment, where the Court said that since France "exercised full and exclusive control over the Winner and its crew . . ." then the applicants were under French jurisdiction.

21. Case of *Öcalan* v. *Turkey*, Grand Chamber Judgment of 12.5.2005.

22. *Issa and Others* v. *Turkey*, Judgment of 16.11.2004.

23. *Al-Skeini and Others* v. *The United Kingdom*, Grand Chamber Judgment of 7.7.2011.

to overrule Bankovic, it did not stick to its "legal space" argument[24]. It seems that it turns to an approach that evaluates the level of "physical power and control over the person"[25].

After the *Medvedyev* judgment, coercive law enforcement jurisdiction over a foreign vessel on the high seas will probably render this vessel and its crew under the protective umbrella of the ECHR[26], although a simple boarding that stays clear of further actions, such as those envisaged under Article 105 UNCLOS concerning piracy, will not trigger the application of the ECHR[27]. However, not all the questions about this issue have such a firm answer. For instance, it is not at all clear whether a warship firing from distance or a fighter jet bombing a pirate vessel would establish jurisdiction and engage the application of the ECHR. *Bankovic* and possibly *Medvedyev* would probably point to a negative answer, although *Pad and Others* v. *Turkey*[28] might point the other way. In the latter case, fire discharged by gunship helicopters on a group of people inside Iranian territory was an act establishing extraterritorial jurisdiction. This seems more convincing as a guide in the aforementioned situations, since it is not really a matter of a "cause and effect" notion of jurisdiction as in *Bankovic*[29]. Pirate vessels are not an accidental target or a collateral damage of an attack; they are the targets of the military attacks, so bombing or firing at them will bring them under the control of the military. However, Bodini suggests that there should be a further qualification in this case, namely that the military capacity of the suspected criminals is not capable of opposing the State's capacity[30],

24. On the "legal space" argument and how it should be dismissed, see R. Wilde, "The 'Legal Space' or 'Espace juridique' of the European Convention on Human Rights: Is It Relevant to Extraterritorial State Action?", *European Human Rights Law Review* (2005), pp. 115-124.

25. Al-Skeini, *supra* footnote 23, para. 136.

26. Guilfoyle, *supra* footnote 20, at p. 439.

27. D. Guilfoyle, "Counter Piracy Law Enforcement and Human Rights", 59 *ICLQ* 141 (2010), at p. 155.

28. *Pad and Others* v. *Turkey*, Admissibility Decision of 28.6.2007.

29. The *Bankovic* test has not escaped criticism, which is further justified by the ECtHR's own later jurisprudence. See for instance Scheinin who submits that "in Bankovic the ECtHR made a methodological mistake by not addressing the issue of extraterritorial effect under a 'control-entails-responsibility' approach" (M. Scheinin, "Extraterritorial Effect of the ICCPR", in F. Coomans *et al.* (eds.), *Extraterritorial Application of Human Rights*, Antwerp, Intersentia, 2004, p. 73, at p. 80). See also Lawson, who emphatically maintains that "the Court got it all wrong" (R. Lawson, "Life after Bankovic: On the Extraterritorial Application of the ECHR", in F. Coomans *et al.* (eds), *Extraterritorial Application of Human Rights*, Antwerp, Intersentia, 2004, p. 83, at p. 85) and he refers to the ILC who said, in 1975, that the conduct of organs of State A in the territory of State B without the consent of State B "is and remains an act of the State to which the organ belongs" (ILC, *Yearbook*, 1975, Vol. II, p. 83).

30. Bodini, *supra* footnote 20, at p. 10.

presumably because otherwise it would be hard to support that the suspected criminals are brought under the control of the State. In any event, the human rights obligations that are triggered are those which are relevant to the situation of the individuals [31] and to the extent of the control that the State establishes over them [32].

B. Operations under international organizations

The establishment of jurisdiction faces another challenge when States conduct their operations under the umbrella of an international organization [33]. That could be the case where a UN Security Council resolution imposes on States the conduct of MIOs, or where such operations are performed under the command of the European Union, NATO or other international or regional organizations. Thus, warships operating under EU NAVFOR might fall outside the reach of the ECHR, since, at the time of writing, the European Union is not yet a party to the Convention [34]; or an interpretation of a Security Council resolution that would require the operation of a maritime interdiction would also fall outside the protection of the ECHR, since the ECtHR has judged that it cannot review the legality of a Security Council resolution. This notwithstanding, when States operate under the umbrella of an international organization, they cannot escape their human rights obligation, unless the relevant international organization effectively controls the disposition of the victims; even in this case, a State may be bound to take positive steps to ensure that the international organization's mission will be compatible with the relevant human rights law [35].

There is a legitimate fear that should be expressed at this point, namely that an operation under the mandate of an international organization could provide an effective means of escaping human rights obli-

31. Al-Skeini, *supra* footnote 23, at para. 137. The Court, in a decision strongly contrasting its previous *Bankovic* judgment, seems to understand the rights under the Convention as able to be "divided and tailored".

32. Lawson, *supra* footnote 29, at p. 120.

33. See how Milanovic and Papic criticize the stance of the ECtHR in its *Behrami and Saramati* admissibility decision with respect to the Court's application of the international law of State responsibility and the doctrines of attribution. M. Milanovic and T. Papic, "As Bad as It Gets: The European Court of Human Rights's Behrami and Saramati Decision and General International Law", 58 *ICLQ* 267 (2009).

34. Cf. the recent conclusion of the Accession Agreement of the European Union to the ECHR; see Fifth Negotiating Meeting between the CCDH *Ad Hoc* Negotiation Group and the European Commission on the Accession of the European Union to the European Convention on Human Rights; Final Report (4 April 2013); available at http://www.coe.int/t/dghl/standardsetting/hrpolicy/accession/ Meeting_reports/47_1%282013%29008_final_report_EN.pdf.

35. Guilfoyle, *supra* footnote 27, at pp. 168-169.

gations. However, it is not certain that an umbrella of such a nature could result in such a situation. For example, the HRC has stated that its application reaches beyond the territory of a State Party to

> "those within the power or effective control of the forces of [the] State Party . . . regardless of the circumstances in which such power or effective control was obtained, such as forces constituting a national contingent of a State Party assigned to an international peace-keeping or peace-enforcement operation"[36].

Furthermore, as the ECHR has affirmed in the *Al-Jedda* case, the UN Security Council should be presumed as not intending to impose an obligation on Member States to breach human rights[37].

On the other hand, it is quite extreme to suggest that States are operating through international organizations in order to avoid the obligations imposed on them by various human rights regimes[38]. That could only be a possibility if human rights obligations were such or interpreted in a way that would render the conduct of an efficient and successful interdiction operation totally impossible. This, however, does not seem to be the case and more often than not the requirements of the various human rights regimes can be fulfilled without extreme burdens to the operational necessities of a maritime interdiction operation.

C. *Private security companies*

Another issue that is problematic is the use of private security companies in order to combat crime at sea. So far, it has appeared as a means adopted by ship-owners in order to protect their ship, cargo and crew from pirates. However, it is possible that in the future private security companies could be used by States as patrolling forces against crime at sea, since such companies have already been used for analogous purposes on land[39].

---

36. HRC, *supra* footnote 18, at para. 10.
37. *Al-Jedda* v. *The United Kingdom*, Grand Chamber Judgment of 7.7.2011.
38. Cf. also Article 61 of the ILC Draft Articles on the Responsibility of International Organizations which sets out that

> "A State member of an international organization incurs international responsibility if, by taking advantage of the fact that the organization has competence in relation to the subject-matter of one of the State's international obligations, it circumvents that obligation by causing the organization to commit an act that, if committed by the State, would have constituted a breach of the obligation."

39. See J. Harrelson, "Blackbeard Meets Blackwater: An Analysis of International Conventions that Address Piracy and the Use of Private Security Companies to Protect the Shipping Industry", 25 *Am. U. Int'l L. Rev.* 283 (2009-2010).

SECTION 3 MARITIME INTERDICTION OPERATIONS AS A THREAT TO HUMAN RIGHTS

It is reasonable to presume that human rights can be affected or threatened not only during a maritime interdiction, but also immediately before or after the actual interdiction. Therefore, at this point, it would be appropriate to split this examination in three distinct parts: the phase immediately before the interdiction, the phase of the actual interdiction and the phase immediately after. In this context, it should be noted that the meaning of "immediately" does not have a fixed meaning and refers to the acts that occur prior to or after the interdiction and are by their nature so closely connected to that operation that they can be examined as parts of it.

Paragraph 1 Prior to the Interdiction

It is certain that before an interdiction operation actually starts, which we shall, for present purposes, identify as the point of the boarding of the vessel, there is a series of prior actions on the part of the intercepting powers.

It is expected that warships operating in regions with, for example, heavy piratical activity will have a preventive function which will not be restricted only to the extent that their mere presence should discourage potential pirates from committing their planned crimes. They will probably look for information about imminent threats using all means available to them in order to retrieve such information. Therefore, it is probably safe to say that all vessels sailing inside and around the areas of operation of those warships will be subject to radar, photo, audio and video monitoring; "radio and cellular phone communications, maybe e-mails . . . are probably being intercepted [right now]"[40].

Those actions are clear interferences with the right to respect for private life, which is protected under Article 8 of the ECHR. They could be permissible under ECHR if they are in accordance with the law, pursue specific legitimate aims (found in Article 8 (2), ECHR) and are necessary in a democratic society. The qualification "necessary in a democratic society" could be met, for instance, when the monitoring of vessels takes place in maritime zones with strong piratical activity[41]. Further, the interception of communications should also be authorized and conducted under the supervision of a judge or another authority,

40. Bodini, *supra* footnote 20, at p. 4.
41. *Ibid.*, p. 5.

independent from the executive that is responsible for or ordered the interdiction[42].

However, there is another issue that should be considered here, namely the establishment of jurisdiction. As mentioned above, there can be no obligations, hence no infringement of a right, unless the protection of the ECHR is engaged through the establishment of jurisdiction. It is difficult to assert that a warship establishes effective control over a region by its mere presence in it. That said, it is a fact that the warship quite possibly is equipped with advanced electronic means which give the ability to intercept, jam, record or filter the communications of the vessels as well as to monitor with great detail, in an audio or visual format, their "targets". This would seem enough to regard that the vessels are for these purposes under the effective control of the warship. The test applied here would probably be the effective control over the territory. The warship, operating its advanced electronic or other technological equipment, has the capacity to interfere with communications or access audio and visual signals projected from the vessel. Within the actual range of operation of this equipment the warship is exercising effective control.

Paragraph 2 **During the Interdiction**

The actual operation of a maritime interdiction could be a peaceful process where the boarding forces face no resistance from the vessel and they do not resort to violence (necessary or otherwise). However, it is unfortunately not rare for an interdiction operation to turn violent. The warship receives and returns fire and loss of life is not unlikely.

For instance, during the boarding of the *Winner* in the *Medvedyev* case, one suspect was injured and later died. Curiously enough, the family of the victim did not bring a claim for a violation of the right to life before the Court and it is not known how the Court would have evaluated the specific circumstances. However, it is safe to say that there may be instances where the interference with the right to life will be in breach of human rights obligations.

First, although the use of force in law-enforcement operations is not prohibited[43], lethal force must be subject to extreme scrutiny[44] and

42. See for instance, *Klass and Others* v. *Germany*, Judgment of 6.9.1978, at para. 56; *Kennedy* v. *United Kingdom*, Judgment of 18.5.2010, at para. 169; *Dumitru Popescu* v. *Romania (No. 2)*, Judgment of 26.4.2007, at para. 71.

43. A. V. Lowe, "National Security and the Law of the Sea", 17 *Thesaurus Acroasium* (1991), p. 162.

44. *McCann and Others* v. *United Kingdom*, Judgment of 27.9.1995.

justified only when it is absolutely necessary[45]. A question that arises is whether a military vessel can open fire against a suspected private vessel in order to stop it. In answering this question, it makes a big difference whether we are considering opening fire against a suspected vessel found at sea or if the vessel in question is carrying a group of armed criminals that are shooting at the warship involved. In the former case, opening fire to stop the vessel would not be allowed.

Further, whenever an interdiction operation takes place in order to resolve a hostage-taking situation, it can be presumed that the Court would address this case in an analogous fashion to *Andronicou and Constantinou* v. *Cyprus*[46], In such a case, the operation will not constitute violation of Article 2, ECHR, if it is carried out by specially trained forces and if the conduct of each individual participating officer does not include force used recklessly or beyond what is necessary.

Apart from the right to life, excessive violence during the interdiction might lead to a violation of the prohibition of torture or other inhuman or degrading treatment or punishment, found in Article 3 of the ECHR. This article introduces an absolute right, which guarantees that a person shall not be subject to inhuman or degrading treatment, irrespective of the victim's conduct[47]. It is true that the Court has shown a greater disposition to characterize State conduct as torture, instead of inhuman or degrading treatment, and based this shift on the "living instrument" interpretation tool[48], Therefore, violence that is severe and does not lead to death will be considered under the provisions of this article.

Paragraph 3 **After the Boarding**

When the boarding is completed and the naval forces have gained control over the private vessel and the people on board, there is a series of human rights that become relevant and whose protec-

45. This is an approach that can be agreed by both human rights lawyers and international law of the use of force specialists. Indeed, the prohibition of use of force operates as *lex generalis* and the conditions under which the use of force is permitted, albeit "in extreme moderation and in strict accordance with the requirements of necessity and proportionality" (E. Papastavridis, "European Convention of Human Rights and the Law of the Sea: The Strasbourg Court in Unchartered Waters?", in M. Fitzmaurice and P. Merkouris (eds.), *The Interpretation and Application of the European Convention of Human Rights: Legal and Practical Implications*, Leiden, Martinus Nijhoff Pub., 2013, at pp. 117-146) are the *lex specialis*. For an example of this approach see *M/V "SAIGA"* (No. 2), ITLOS Judgment of 1.7.1999, para. 155.

46. *Andronicou and Constantinou* v. *Cyprus*, Judgment of 9.10.1997.

47. *Chahal* v. *United Kingdom* (1997), Grand Chamber Judgment of 15.11.1996.

48. *Selmouni* v. *France*, Grand Chamber Judgment of 28.7.1999, at para. 101.

tion may be violated. As already pointed out, in most cases of interdiction at sea "the legal issue at stake is not how to board the vessel but what to do with the illicit cargo, the vessel and the persons on board"[49].

To begin with, if the naval forces have boarded a vessel out of suspicion of a criminal act, then the suspected criminals have either been killed during the boarding operation or they are alive and in this case they either remain under the custody of the boarding forces or have been released and allowed to leave the vessel. The first scenario has been examined under the previous paragraph; under this paragraph we shall examine the two other scenarios.

A. Right to liberty and security of person

In case that the suspected criminals remain in the custody of boarding forces, there is a first clear infringement of their rights in the form of a violation of their right to liberty and security of person. Questions about the legality of authority to detain arise also within this context.

Article 5 (1) *(c)* provides that a deprivation of personal liberty shall be justified if it is in accordance with a procedure prescribed by law and if it is a result of a lawful arrest or detention effected for the purpose of bringing that person before the competent legal authority due to reasonable suspicion of having committed an offence or when it is reasonably considered necessary to prevent that person committing an offence or fleeing after having done so. Therefore, the primary consideration is whether the procedure that leads to the arrest or detention is prescribed by law.

In *Medvedyev* case, the Court examined whether the French naval forces were entitled to board the *Winner* and arrest and detain the crew suspected of criminal conduct. The basis on which France ordered the boarding was a diplomatic note exchanged between Cambodia and France, by which Cambodia expressed its consent that France could "intercept, inspect and take legal action" against the ship. The Court was willing to find that the boarding of the *Winner* by the French forces was a procedure "prescribed by law" if *(a)* there was a clear legal authority for this action either in French law or in international law and *(b)* if that law satisfied a quality of foreseeability, in the sense that those to whom the law applies should be able to predict this application[50].

---

49. E. Papastavridis, "Enforcement Jurisdiction in the Mediterranean Sea: Illicit Activities and the Rule of Law on the High Seas", 25 *The International Journal of Marine and Coastal Law* 543 (2010), at p. 549.

50. *Medvedyev* v. *France*, Grand Chamber Judgment of 29.3.2010, at paras. 82-103. See also Guilfoyle, *supra* footnote 20, at p. 439 and E. Papastavridis, "ECHR, *Medvedyev v. France*", 59 *International and Comparative Law Quarterly* (2010), pp. 867-882.

In examining the relevant law, the Court made the following observations: French law could not serve as the basis for the boarding of the *Winner* since its provisions could not apply to the specific circumstances of this boarding. The then French law regarding interdiction of drug trafficking provided only for consensual interdictions against ships flying a flag of a State party to the UN Narcotics Convention, 1988; however, Cambodia was not a party to that Convention, neither was it a party to the UN Convention on the Law of the Sea. Therefore, a textual interpretation of the domestic law could not allow the boarding of the *Winner*. In other words, this procedure was not prescribed by French law.

This raises a question as to whether appropriate and complete French law would satisfy the Court as a sufficient legal basis to apprehend and prosecute the crew of the *Winner.* This should be the case, since those suspects would have been apprehended and prosecuted as prescribed by law. However, although those circumstances would prima facie meet the requirements of the Convention, it is apt to question how the relevant and appropriate French legislation might enhance the element of "foreseeability" that the Court has advanced. Is it reasonable to expect the crew of a Cambodian ship to be familiar with French criminal legislation or even more with domestic legislation of every other State that might conduct interdiction operations? If this is unreasonable, as indeed it appears to be, there is no reason for the Court to examine whether there is appropriate domestic legislation, because even if there were such legislation it would by no means satisfy the "foreseeability" criterion as used by the Court. On the other hand, since the Court sought for appropriate domestic legislation in order for the interference to be "prescribed by law", it should not use the "foreseeability" test as it has, either with respect to domestic law or, especially, when it examined the relevant international law.

The other option was to seek a legal basis for the interdiction in international law. The only available international law in this case was the diplomatic notes exchanged between Cambodia and France. The European Court accepted that the note was a treaty for purposes of international law and a satisfactory basis for the boarding of the ship[51], but found it difficult to consider the same about the legality of the detention of the crew[52], since the wording "to intercept, inspect and take legal action [against the ship]" was considered as of not sufficient clarity. It should be pointed out that under the law of the sea, the interception of the *Winner* was legal pursuant to the exchange of diplomatic notes[53].

51. *Medvedyev*, *supra* footnote 50, at para. 96.
52. *Ibid.*, para. 99.
53. Papastavridis, *supra* footnote 50, at p. 874.

However, since each adjudicating body can have a different perspective, it is possible that they will understand the same rules differently[54].

Nevertheless, the Court went further and said that it did not really make a difference whether the provision of the diplomatic note for legal action "against the ship" included the crew or not, since even if it expressly did so, it would still fail to pass the test of foreseeability. According to the Court, a diplomatic note exchanged between the two countries shortly before the actual interdiction would never give a practical ability to the members of the crew to predict that they were subject to the application of French law[55]. That condition could only be met if the basis for the detention were a formal multilateral or bilateral treaty[56].

Another important question is raised by this statement of the Court. If the basis of detention and prosecution is a formal multilateral treaty, the Court seems satisfied that the conditions posed by the Convention are met. However, even in this case, the effects of a multilateral treaty do not bind its signatories before ratification[57]. Therefore, what is suggested is that the crew of a ship involved in the conduct described as illegal in the multilateral treaty is required to know in which of the signatories the treaty has acquired binding force through ratifications, in order to "foresee" that they could be brought, according to this treaty, under the jurisdiction of that State, which can apprehend and prosecute them. Such a requirement is not reasonable.

In reading the *Medvedyev* decision, very contradictory conclusions can be drawn. On the one hand, it may be supposed that a treaty such as the 1982 UN Convention on the Law of the Sea could satisfy the requirements set out by the Court[58]. At least as far as piracy is con-

54. T. Treves, "Human Rights and the Law of the Sea", 28 *Berkeley Journal of International Law* 1 (2010), at p. 12 (http://scholarship.law.berkeley.edu/cgi/viewcontent.cgi?article=1375&context=bjil, last access 19/4/2013).

55. It would have some merit to consider how the Court in its *Öcalan* Judgment (*supra* footnote 21, at paras. 83-99) recognized an informal agreement absent of a formal extradition treaty as a sufficient legal basis to pass the threshold of the "prescribed by law" test and enough to secure compatibility with Article 5 (1). See also how *Öcalan* is invoked by Vasseur (in A. Vasseur, "Légalité de l'arrestation, du transfèrement et du jugement en France des 6 preneurs d'otages du navire 'le Ponant'", *Sentinelle*, No. 145, 20.8.2008, available at <http://sentinelle-droit-international.fr/bulletins/a2008/20080420_bull 145/sentinelle_145.htm#securitemer1>) in order to submit that French behaviour in the incident of the "Ponant" was also lawful under the ECHR.

56. *Medvedyev*, *supra* footnote 50, at para. 100.

57. Of course, there are international agreements that create binding effects without ratification, but here it is used as an example the most common way in which multilateral treaties of this nature enter into force.

58. It is noteworthy to remember the *Women on Waves* case, in which the Court recognized the UNCLOS as a sufficient legal basis for the actions of a State assessed under the ECHR. See *Women on Waves and Others* v. *Portugal*, Judgment of 3.2.2009, at para. 48.

cerned, the 1982 Convention could be considered clear and detailed enough to pass both the tests of a process that is thoroughly prescribed by law[59] and the one of foreseeability[60]. On the other hand, we should not ignore the partially dissenting opinion of Judges Tulkens *et al.*, in which the eight judges argue that in cases of a maritime interdiction operation ECHR should be applied strictly. This partially dissenting opinion echoes the decision of the Court in First Instance, where instead of the test of foreseeability that was employed by the Grand Chamber, France was found in violation of its ECHR obligations because of a failure of the relevant law to "regulate the conditions of deprivation of liberty on board ship, and in particular the possibility for the persons concerned to contact a lawyer or a family member".

Further, the Court in 2008 also commented on the failure of the applied law to place the detention of the crew under the supervision of a judicial authority[61]. This becomes even more important if we take into account the fact that the Grand Chamber decision does not mention the foreseeability as the only test that France failed; it is just one test that France failed and there was no need for the Grand Chamber to examine whether more conditions had to be tested. Therefore, even the UNCLOS provisions for piracy might not be considered as a sufficient legal basis for the detention of captured pirates, in the absence of other procedural guarantees. Finally, it is worth mentioning that the ECtHR seems to completely ignore the customary character of the universal jurisdiction over pirates as a potential legal basis[62].

A different approach is found in the dissenting opinion of Judges Costa *et al.* who assert that cases, like the one under examination, should be dealt with certain realism, since an interdiction operation

59. Interestingly enough, Passman finds a quasi right to a trial in UNCLOS in Article 105 of the Convention (where it reads "the courts of the State . . . may decide upon the penalties to be imposed"). Passman, *supra* footnote 13, at p. 17. See also the *Samanyolu* case in the Netherlands (2010), in which the Court used Article 105 of UNCLOS as the "law" in terms of Article 5 of ECHR; LJN: BM8116, Rotterdam District Court, 10/600012-09 (17-6-2010); a summary in English is available at http://www.unicri.it/topics/piracy/database/Netherlands_2010_Crim_No_10_6000_12_09%20Judgment.pdf.

60. Bodini, *supra* footnote 20, p. 3.

61. Case of *Medvedyev* v. *France*, (Fifth Section), Judgment of 10.7.2008, at para. 61.

62. See for instance the decision on the US case *United States* v. *Smith*, 18 US (5 Wheat.) 153 (1820) (available online at http://supreme.justia.com/cases/federal/us/18/153/case.html). In p. 161, the decision recognizes as part of common law that piracy is punished as an offence "against the law of nations . . . as an offence against the universal law of society". See also E. D. Dickinson, "Is the Crime of Piracy Obsolete?", 38 *Harvard Law Review* 334 (1925) who suggests that universal jurisdiction over pirates was accepted since the early seventeenth century (in pp. 335-339).

taking place on the high seas cannot be viewed under the same lens as instances of infringements that occur within the territory of a State. The seven judges maintained that their preference in favour of a "realistic" application of the ECHR in such cases does not bend or circumvent the Convention. They held that the qualification for foreseeability is there in order that a person might predict that a certain conduct would fall under the provisions of a certain law. In their view, the crew obviously knew that their conduct could result in criminal punishment. They did not operate on an assumption that their conduct was legal. Therefore, the obvious knowledge of the illegality of their conduct was sufficient for the fulfilment of the foreseeability requirement.

Secondly, the interpretation of a diplomatic note governed by international law cannot be as strict as the interpretation of a domestic statute. The practical necessities of dealing with drug smuggling, the natural consequence that the authorities will in most cases be given a very narrow window of time to react in order to prevent or suppress this illegal conduct, mean that it is not possible for the communications between the authorities of two countries to be as sophisticated in their articulation as domestic statutes that are being drafted and redrafted over a significant period of time. Therefore, in such cases, an interpretation that will not stick so much to the actual wording of the agreement and will go further into examining the intention of the parties might be more appropriate. Thirdly, the judges mentioned that it was somehow artificial to hold that the diplomatic note sufficiently authorized the detention of the ship but not the detention of the crew, since it is not possible to dissociate the crew from the ship itself.

It seems that this issue is not definitively settled. The tight balance between the Judges of the Grand Chamber (with 8 judges pushing for a strict application of the treaty law and 7 judges calling for a realistic consideration of the very exceptional circumstances) makes it difficult to extract any concrete conclusions. In a future case, with a different composition of the Court, it is just as possible that the ruling will point in the other direction.

For the time being, however, it might be the case that if the suspects were given some of the procedural guarantees, as they were in *Rigopoulos*, such as to promptly inform family members, to give them access to a lawyer, or to put the whole process under the supervision of a judicial authority, the Court might have been more inclined to conclude that the law prescribing the interdiction was adequate.

B. Other procedural guarantees

Another right that could be infringed in situations of detention is the right to be informed promptly, in a language that the suspects can understand, of the reasons of their arrest and of any charges against them. Again, in this case there can be an interpretation that strictly follows the law of the Treaty and one that approaches the issue with "certain realism" considering the specific circumstances. The first would suggest that in areas where criminality at sea is a daily phenomenon and the conduct of interdiction operations intense, it is necessary that an interpreter is present, who could communicate this information in the languages or the dialects of the wider region. It is true that from this assertion can stem many practical difficulties, if not impossibilities. Certainly, the most piratical attacks in the Gulf of Aden are attributed to Somali pirates from the area of Galmudug and it could be suggested that for warships operating in that region an interpreter familiar with the dialect of Galmudug might resolve a big problem. However, this will certainly lead to other problems, involving the requirement from the boarding forces to find out, before they proceed in any enforcement actions, whether the suspects actually are Somalis or not. On the other hand, it stands to reason to submit that it is impossible that on board every ship performing interdiction operations we will have interpreters familiar with all the regional languages and dialects.

Another obligation incumbent upon States is to ensure that a suspect that is arrested will be promptly brought before a competent judicial authority. Normally, a delay of a few days would render the detention unlawful. However, in *Medvedyev* case, the Court, following its judgment on *Rigopoulos*, held that delays in bringing the suspects before a judicial authority, if materially impossible to avoid, do not violate Article 5 (3). Moreover, the Court examined and rejected the argument that alternative means of transport could reduce the period of detention after the arrest; the eight-judge partly dissenting opinion also raises this issue[63]. However, in cases less straightforward than *Rigopoulos* and *Medvedyev*, it is not as clear whether Article 5 (3) would be violated if the delay in bringing the captured suspects before a Court was not the result of a lengthy journey to the port but of a lengthy negotiation between States unwilling to prosecute.

Such an example is the case of a Danish warship, *Absalon,* which captured suspected pirates and held them on board while Denmark and the Netherlands were negotiating the transfer of the captured pirates to Dutch custody. In this case, the captured pirates remained on board for over a month, which is a period long enough to result in a violation of Article 5 (3). As far as the identification of the "competent" judicial authority is concerned, the District Court of Rotterdam held that the

63. Judges *Tulkens et al.*, partly dissenting opinion, *Medvedyev* case, *supra* footnote 50.

judicial authority must be independent from the executive, must hear itself the individual brought before it and must be able to examine the legality of the arrest and must have the jurisdiction to order the release of the suspect if it finds no reasons to justify the detention[64].

The right to an attorney while in custody is another occasion where the considerations of the "certain realism" approach advanced by the seven-judge dissenting opinion in *Medvedyev* should be seriously taken into account. The right to an attorney should not be considered outside the special circumstances of the reality of a military interdiction operation at sea[65]. It should be agreed that the presence of a lawyer that would undertake to protect the interests of captured suspects aboard all vessels that engage in interdiction operations is impractical and probably impossible. Moreover, although easier to achieve, the option to give the captured suspects the possibility to contact lawyers of their choosing over the phone would create doubts as to the effectiveness of such practice.

Therefore, although the right to an attorney while in custody is crucial, as both the ECtHR and the US Supreme Court have held[66], it would be easier to resolve this problematic situation by accepting that access to a lawyer during custody after the arrest is difficult for every capturing State to accommodate, hence access to an attorney will be granted as soon as possible after the warship calls at a port. However, such a lack of legal counsel must be compensated and the best possible way is to hold all statements made by the captured suspects inadmissible as evidence or confession. Moreover, the personnel taking place in interdiction operations should inform the suspects of their rights to disclose no information during their presence aboard the vessel.

Relevant to the above is the issue of admissibility of evidence, which could also arise in situations of interdiction. First of all, during an interdiction operation or, better, after its successful outcome, the collection of evidence is carried out by personnel of the naval forces, who are non-experienced staff, unlike the trained criminal investigators who carry out such tasks within the territory of the State[67]. Secondly, the tactical success of such operations will almost certainly come first in the minds of the interdicting forces and probably no considerations of the long-term

64. The last two are the procedural and substantive requirements posed under Article 5 (3), as identified in *Schiesser* v. *Switzerland*, Judgment of 4.12.1979, at paras. 24-38.

65. The "exceptional circumstances" in *Medvedyev* could easily be the test justifying a less strict application of the right to legal assistance.

66. See for the USSC *Miranda* v. *Arizona*, 384 US 436 (1966) and for the ECtHR *Salduz* v. *Turkey*, Grand Chamber Judgment of 27.11.2008.

67. Bodini, *supra* footnote 20, p. 8.

effects with respect to the trial of the suspects will guide their mode of conduct. Therefore, an issue as to the quality of evidence is a problem that must be addressed. However, in any case, it should go without saying that evidence collected under the use or threat of torture will not be acceptable as rendering the proceedings as a whole unfair[68].

C. *Right to property*

Property rights can come into play since as a result of an interdiction operation the interdicted vessels (and whatever goods are on those vessels) could be destroyed, abandoned or formally confiscated. All these actions would be considered interferences with property rights[69]. UN Security Council resolutions (e.g. 1846, 1851, and 1897) permit States to interfere with property rights by seizing and disposing of equipment that could be used in piracy activities[70]. Moreover, the fight against the said criminal acts would probably be considered as a cause in accordance with the general interest which would justify such interferences. However, the requirement of proportionality is relevant and whenever the interference with property is more severe than what is necessary for the protection of the general interest, the interference will not be lawful.

D. Non-refoulement

Another very important set of questions regarding the protection of the human rights of detainees is the one addressing the issues of the obligation of *non-refoulement*[71]. In *Soering* v. *United Kingdom* the ECtHR held that extradition is contrary to Article 3, ECHR, if it exposes an individual "to a real risk of treatment going beyond the threshold set by Article 3"[72]. The obligation is very strong and cannot be derogated from even by national security interests. In fact, as the Court has already decided, the activities of the individual (the detainee), no matter how undesirable or dangerous they might have been, cannot be a material consideration when a State explores its possible courses of action or when examining the fulfilment of the *non-refoulement* obligation of a State[73]. The principle applies to maritime

68. *Gäfgen* v. *Germany*, Grand Chamber Judgment of 1.6.2010.
69. Bodini, *supra* footnote 20, p. 9.
70. Res. 1851 at para. 2, res. 1846 at para. 9, res. 1897 at para. 3.
71. On the principle of *non-refoulement*, see Sir E. Lauterpacht and D. Bethlehem, "The Scope and Content of the Principle of Non-Refoulement: Opinion", in E. Feller *et al*. (eds.), *Refugee Protection in International Law* (2001).
72. *Soering* v. *UK*, Judgment of 7.7.1989, at para. 111.
73. *Chahal* v. *United Kingdom*, *supra* footnote 47, at para. 80.

operations on the high seas and it is a fundamental component of the human rights implications that such operations entail[74]. It also applies even if the deportation to an "unsafe"[75] territory is likely to occur from the State where the individual is deported in the first place (chain *refoulement*)[76]. So, when Belgium transferred an Afghan asylum-seeker back to Greece, it was found in breach of its obligations of *non-refoulement*, because Greece was likely to deport him to Afghanistan without examining the merits of his case[77].

Moreover, interdiction resulting in a transfer of the captured individuals to the country of departure, which triggers the *non-refoulement* obligation, should be distinguished from an interdiction that constitutes a denial of entry to the territorial waters[78]. However, even a mere denial of entry and towing ships back to the high seas may result in *refoulement* or "refugees in orbit"[79], which in itself may amount to a violation of human rights[80].

It should also be stressed that whether a State is safe or unsafe for someone to be deported to is a question that cannot be answered in absolute terms. Let us take as an example piracy off the coast of Somalia:

74. See the case of *Hirsi Jamaa and Others* v. *Italy*, Judgment of 23.2.2012, paras. 113-158, where the Court held that the obligation of *non-refoulement* was breached on a double count (since there was a risk of inhuman treatment in Libya and a risk that Libya would arbitrarily deport the individuals to Eritrea, where there was a risk of inhuman treatment, is grave). Also, see generally G. Goodwin-Gill, "The Right to Seek Asylum: Interception at Sea and the Principle of Non-Refoulement", 23 *International Journal of Refugee Law* 443 (2011); E. Papastavridis, "Interception of Human Beings on the High Seas: A Contemporary Analysis under International Law", 36 *Syracuse Journal of International Law and Commerce* 145 (2009).

75. On the concept of the "safe third country" and the legal framework under which this should be assessed, see M.-T. Gil-Baso, "The Practice of Mediterranean States in the Context of the European Union's Justice and Home Affairs External Dimension. The Safe Third Country Concept Revisited", 18 *International Journal of Refugee Law* 571 (2006).

76. Article 33 of the Refugee Convention prohibits the *refoulement* "in any matter whatsoever". The obligation of *non-refoulement* is thus both an obligation of conduct and an obligation of result. See P. Mathew, "Legal Issues concerning Interception", 17 *Geo. Immigr. LJ* 221 (2002), at p. 229. It should also be noted that the status of "refugee" exists as soon as an individual fulfils the criteria contained in the Refugee Convention. Therefore, the recognition of this status by a State is simply declaratory: see M. Pallis, "Obligations of States towards Asylum Seekers at Sea: Interactions and Conflicts between Legal Regimes", 14 *Int'l J. Refugee L.* 329 (2002), at p. 363.

77. *M.S.S.* v. *Belgium and Greece*, Grand Chamber Judgment of 21.1.2011, paras. 344 *et seq.*

78. G. S. Goodwin-Gill, "The Refugee in International Law", 2nd ed., Oxford, University Press, 1996.

79. G. Melander, *Refugees in Orbit*, International University Exchange Fund, Geneva, 1978.

80. L. A. See Nessel, "Externalized Borders and the Invisible Refugee", 40 *Columbia Human Rights Law Review* 625 (2008-2009).

even though the latter has been found as an unsafe country by the ECtHR[81], there should be some further deliberation on this, since it is one thing to consider Somalia as an unsafe country for the average individual to be deported to, and a totally different thing to examine whether Somalia is an unsafe country for the average captured pirate. In certain areas of Somalia, a deported pirate might well be returning to a safe and familiar environment[82].

In an effort to override their *non-refoulement* obligation, States have tried to obtain assurances from third countries where they seek to deport or extradite individuals that these countries will not treat the individuals deported in ways contrary to international human rights standards. As a general rule, but probably not without exceptions, diplomatic assurances should not of themselves be considered able to exclude the responsibility of the deporting State.

In several cases international human rights-protection organs have opined against the adequacy of such assurances to guarantee the protection of the individual's rights[83].

However, some States seem to endorse this practice, despite the strong arguments against it. Some of them express the view that they use this practice only in limited circumstances, when the deportation is actually the only viable option. For instance, the United Kingdom has entered arrangements for assurances with Jordan, Libya, Lebanon and Algeria[84]. It is, of course, a matter of appreciation whether deportation would be the only viable solution as well as under which circumstances all other options are non-viable. However, it is important to notice also that States *per* this option view the deportation with assurances as a means to safeguard human rights rather than avoiding their obligations[85]. On the other hand, despite the positive reaction that such a declaration might trigger, we should try to ascertain why deportation with assurances is a means to safeguard human rights. It is true that assurances will increase the protection of the rights of the deportees. However, it is not against the "plain" deportation that we should weigh

81. *Salah Sheekh* v. *Netherlands*, Judgment of 11.1.2007.

82. See ECtHR, *Sufi and Elmi* v. *United Kingdom*, Judgment of 28.6.2011, where membership in majority clan (and protection which results therefrom) counts as an element in deciding whether *non-refoulement* obligations would be breached by deportation.

83. See for instance *Agiza* v. *Sweden* before the UN Committee against Torture. But see ECtHR case of *Othman (Aby Qatada)* v. *The United Kingdom*, Judgment of 17.1.2012, in which the Court accepts assurances *re* Article 3 risk (although holds that there is an Article 6 *non-refoulement* obligation because torture evidence might be in Jordan.

84. K. Jones, "Deportations with Assurances: Addressing Key Criticisms", 57 *ICLQ* 183 (2008), at p. 184.

85. *Ibid.*, p. 185.

the efficiency of the deportation with assurances; we should weigh it against the other options, such as keeping the suspects in the arresting State, especially if it is a party to the ECHR. Weighed against this option, a deportation, even with assurances, to a country with a bad record of human rights protection can hardly convince that it serves as a means of safeguarding human rights.

Nevertheless, it is true that many times a State tries to get adequate assurances from a third State, in order to proceed to the deportation. In any case, the reliability of assurances must be assessed on the facts of each particular case.

Sometimes assurances can reduce the risk of a breach of the prohibition of torture to a level below the threshold that would engage the *non-refoulement* principle [86].

Lastly, it should be noted that the principle of *non-refoulement* should apply also in cases where the individuals have been intercepted before exiting the territorial waters of the State of departure and therefore have not acquired the status of refugees. However, the intercepting State is still under the obligation not to transfer them to a territory where they would face a risk of torture or other cruel or inhuman treatment [87].

SECTION 4 **SHOULD HR BE PERCEIVED AS A THREAT TO MIOs?**

The wide spectrum of human rights obligations involved in a Maritime Interdiction Operation has led to the formulation of an idea that human rights law limits the ability of international forces to combat crime at sea [88]. It is true that States are not always willing to prosecute criminals they apprehend at sea, because of the fear of breaching human rights law [89].

This has led to a situation where "a culture of impunity reigns

86. *Mamatkulov and Askarov* v. *Turkey*, Grand Chamber Judgment of 4.2.2005. Also SIAC, *Y* v. *SSHD* (Case No. 7) at p. 390.

87. A. Klug and T. Howe, "The Concept of State Jurisdiction and the Applicability of the Non-Refoulement Principle to Extraterritorial Interception Measures", in R. Ryan and V. Mitsilegas (eds.), *Extraterritorial Immigration Control*, The Hague, Brill, 2010, p. 69, at p. 94.

88. P. J. Pham, "Anti-Piracy, Adrift", 18 *Journal of International Security Affairs* (2010), online at http://www.securityaffairs.org/issues/2010/18/pham.php.

89. S. De Bont, "Murky Waters: Prosecuting Pirates and Upholding Human Rights Law", 7 *Journal of International Law and International Relations* 104 (2011), at p. 106. Apart from scholars, this proposition is also supported by numbers: a great majority of apprehended criminals at sea are released instead of prosecuted.

whereby nations are not holding pirates accountable for the violent crimes they commit"[90].

More specifically, States involved in interdictions fear that captured suspects will claim asylum the moment they find themselves within the jurisdiction of the interdicting State, either by boarding a flagged warship or by being transferred within the territory of the State[91]. However, despite the potentially widespread intention of captured sea criminals to seek asylum, it is highly unlikely that such a status can be actually granted. The 1951 UN Refugee Convention[92] in Article 1 *(f)* makes it clear that individuals who have committed a serious crime outside the jurisdiction of the country of refuge are not entitled to refugee status. Furthermore, it is much easier for States to prove their compliance with the *non-refoulement* principle even in cases where they transfer captured criminals back to their State of departure, since it is probably unlikely that those criminals could show that they would be tortured or treated inhumanely if returned[93]. On the other hand, the fear of asylum claims is not the only problem relating to the future of captured criminals after they have been tried and served their sentences.

The most problematic issue is the *non-refoulement* obligation that precludes States from returning individuals to countries where they might face risk of torture, inhuman or degrading treatment or even a denial of other important human rights, such as the right to a fair trial[94], in cases where there is a "flagrant denial of a fair trial" in the receiving State[95]. The principle of *non-refoulement*, found in several human rights treaties[96], poses a significant obstacle with political and economic implications for the countries that wish to get involved in interdiction operations. If a State that apprehends and captures sea criminals is by this action unable

90. Y. M. Dutton, "Pirates and Impunity: Is the Threat of Asylum Claims a Reason to Allow Pirates to Escape Justice?", 34 *Fordham Int'l LJ* 236 (2010-2011), at p. 236.

91. See for instance B. Waterfield, "Somali Pirates Embrace Capture as Route to Europe", *The Telegraph* (UK), 19 May 2009, found online at http://www.telegraph.co.uk/news/worldnews/ piracy/5350183/Somali-pirates-embrace-capture-as-route-to-Europe.html. This article includes the example of two of a group of captured pirates who have gone on trial in the Netherlands and have declared their intention to stay as residents.

92. Convention relating to the Status of Refugees, 28 July 1951, 189 *UNTS* 150.

93. Dutton, *supra* footnote 90, at pp. 292-293.

94. *Soering* v. *The United Kingdom*, *supra* footnote 72, para. 113.

95. We should not forget though that the threshold for a violation of Article 6, ECHR, is high, described as a "flagrant denial" of a fair trial. In *Mamatkulov* (*supra* footnote 86), the dissenting opinion of Judges Bratza, Bonello and Hedigan implies that "flagrant" mean a breach so fundamental as to amount to a nullification or destruction of the very essence of the right.

96. CAT Article 3 (1), ICCPR Article 7, ECHR Article 3, ACHR Article 5 (2), are the most notable examples.

to deport those criminals after their capture, or trial, or the end of their sentence, it will be unwilling to proceed to any form of criminal enforcement, which is already the case.

The problem grows because of the non-derogable nature of the principle, which has been upheld by several courts and committees that have applied carious international treaties [97]. This principle applies regardless of the circumstances under which the individual has been brought within the jurisdiction of the State. Therefore, it applies "wherever [the State] exercises its jurisdiction . . . even when operating outside its territory" [98].

States have tried to overcome this obstacle by returning captured criminals to safe third countries, or to countries from which they have obtained assurances that the deported criminals will not face risk of torture or other inhuman or degrading treatment. The issues that arise are first to find third countries willing to accept captured suspects, to establish that a third country is "safe" and to define the type and extent of assurances that are necessary in order to pass the threshold of the obligation of *non-refoulement*.

As to the first issue, there are means to persuade a third country to accept captured criminals, put them on trial and imprison them if a court decides so. For instance, the example of Kenya is illuminating. Interdicting States have agreed to provide the necessary funding to improve Kenya's justice system and prisons and Kenya, in return, agreed to receive captured suspects, put them on trial and imprison them. Such agreements may prove very beneficial for both sides since the interdicting States do not have to bear the operational, financial or political burden of dealing with captured criminals, and, on the other hand, receiving third countries have the opportunity to welcome significant funding that helps improve their judicial or penitentiary systems [99].

When it comes to deporting with assurances, the ECtHR has held that assurances or accession to treaties do not suffice in themselves and that what matters is the practical application of such assurances and whether they can provide an actual guarantee that the deported individual would be protected from any violation of his fundamental rights [100]. Although a

97. See for instance the HRC, "CCPR General Comment No. 29: Article 4: Derogations during a State of Emergency", *UNGAOR*, 72nd Session, UN doc. CCPR/C/21/Rev.1/Add.11 (2001) at para. 11. Also, ECtHR Decisions *Chahal* (*supra* footnote 47) and *Saadi* v. *Italy*, Grand Chamber Judgment of 28.2.2008.

98. European Committee for the Prevention of Torture and Inhuman or Degrading Treatment or Punishment, "Report to the Italian Government", 27-31 July 2009, CPT/Inf (2010), at para. 49.

99. Notably, a Kenyan official has described the agreement as "a blessing in disguise". See T. McConnell, "Kenyan Courts on Legal Front Line in Battle to Stop Somali Pirates", *The Sunday Times*, 10.12.2009.

100. *Saadi* v. *Italy*, *supra* footnote 97, at para. 147.

bad record of human rights violations makes it hard to accept that diplomatic assurances are an adequate guarantee for the capturing State to deport the suspects, while at the same time upholding its international obligations, this bad record does not pose an absolute prohibition of such a transfer of suspects to these countries. Whether this transfer shall be prohibited depends on the merits of each individual case and especially on whether the deporting States have managed to establish adequate judicial mechanisms for reviewing the assurances agreements and have ensured that they will be able to monitor effectively the status of the deported individuals over time[101].

If a wider approach based on the "realistic evaluation" is adopted, it is suggested that the level of protection which States accord to individuals extraterritorially cannot be the same with that accorded to individuals within the States' boundaries.

The reason is that it would be impossible for States to accord beyond their territory the rights and freedoms set out in human rights law to a level analogous to the protection those rights enjoy within the State's boundaries. In these cases, the level of protection, the argument goes, should depend on the extent of control that the State exercises over the individual[102].

Finally, apart from operational obstacles that human rights law may pose to interdiction operations, or apart from the problems regarding the future of the captured criminals inside the capturing State, there is another consideration, namely the direct and indirect costs involved. Trials in Western European or North American States tend to be seriously expensive as compared to trials in other parts of the world[103]. Moreover, the costs of maintaining convicted criminals in prisons are equally high as are the costs to find, transfer and support witnesses and evidence.

Finally, during the time that a suspect is transferred from the point of his arrest to the port of the country that will receive him, the warship that transfers him cannot participate in operations, which means that another warship should take its place, a solution that places further costs on the naval forces.

---

101. Committee against Torture, "Conclusions and Recommendations of the Committee against Torture: United States of America" 36th Session, UN doc. CAT/C/USA/CO/2, 2006, para. 21. See also the *Qatada* Judgment, *supra* footnote 83, where the public nature of the case meant that Jordan was more likely to abide by its assurances.

102. Lawson, *supra* footnote 29, at p. 105.

103. One Earth Future, in "The Economic Cost of Maritime Piracy" (working paper of December 2010, found at http://oneearthfuture.org/images/imagefiles/Cost%20of% 20Piracy%20Final% 20Report.pdf), has estimated that trials in North America cost six times more than trials in East Africa (at p. 19).

SECTION 5 CONCLUSIONS

There is no doubt that the ECtHR's decision in the *Medvedyev* case drastically affected the contemporary discourse over the fight against crimes on the high seas[104]. Security operations, such as FRONTEX, do not have excuses for disregarding human rights[105]. It is therefore important to set out clear guidelines towards the compatibility of interdiction operations with human rights law.

A suggestion could be to include some of the crimes at sea within the jurisdiction of the International Criminal Court (ICC)[106]. Such an initiative would eliminate doubts as to the fair trial guarantees of future apprehended suspects. However, hundreds of piracy or drug trafficking cases would probably become an unbearable burden for the ICC.

Another suggestion is for the UN Security Council to adopt resolutions that explicitly authorize interdictions and enforcement powers with respect to those criminal acts at sea that are most suitable to be regulated by a Security Council resolution, such as piracy, WMD proliferation etc.[107] This would enable States that are willing to undertake the prosecution of the suspects and guarantee that they would operate lawfully.

Notwithstanding the means to achieve it, there needs to be a clear framework that sets out the rules regulating law enforcement over crimes at sea which must be in accordance with applicable human rights law[108]. Harmonization and clarification of rules with regard to identifying suspect vessels, dealing with seized cargo, rules of engagement are

104. Papastavridis, *supra* footnote 49, at p. 555.

105. See for instance De Blow who criticized FRONTEX whose policies rather aim to prevent immigrants from entering the European Union than protecting their human rights. See M. De Blouw, "Drowning Policies: A Proposal to Modify the Dublin Agreement and Reduce Human Rights Abuses in the Mediterranean", 40 *California Western International Law Journal* 335 (2009-2010), at p. 343. On the other hand, FRONTEX now tries to accommodate human rights considerations in their operational framework. Very recently, on 27 September 2012, the FRONTEX Management Board designated the first FRONTEX Fundamental Rights Officer. Although the effectiveness of this new office remains to be seen in practice, it is however an example that should be followed, in principle, by all operating forces.

106. Y. M. Dutton, "Bringing Pirates to Justice: A Case for Including Piracy within the Jurisdiction of the International Criminal Court", 11 *Chi. J. Int'l L.* 201 (2010).

107. M. A. Becker, "The Shifting Public Order of the Oceans: Freedom of Navigation and the Interdiction of Ships at Sea", 46 *Harvard International Law Journal* 131 (2005), at p. 219.

108. E. Andersen, B. Brockman-Have and P. Geoff, "Suppressing Maritime Piracy: Exploring the Options in International Law", 2009. Found online at http://acuns.org/wp-content/uploads/2012/06/SuppressingMaritimePiracy ExploringOptionsIntlLaw.pdf, at p. 14.

necessary. This is further reiterated by the European Union, which in Recommendation 840 proposes to each State to determine a framework of rules regulating the detention of suspected pirates, the means of monitoring the detention, as well as other matters. Similar recommendations were proposed by the Special Adviser to the United Nations Secretary-General, Jack Lang, who suggested the development of a legal framework compatible with human rights law and the operational constraints[109]. Regarding Somali piracy, he has also suggested the creation of three specialized courts and three prisons (two in Somalia, and a third that will still be Somali but outside the territory of Somalia). What seems to be clear now is that the situation where intercepting States handed suspects over to Kenya was not the ideal solution to the problem of prosecution[110].

However, a significant international assistance, either in the form of resources or in the form of technical assistance, to encourage prosecution, trials and enforcement of the penalties in the region where such crimes occur or the country of origin of the suspects would be preferable, at more than one level[111]. First, it would strengthen local justice systems and, secondly, it has the advantage that nothing new needs to be created, since national courts will apply national laws under clear rules, triggering no questions of legality or compatibility with human rights norms.

Another solution is for States to include laws in their penal legislation that will criminalize piracy or any other significant crime at sea (such as drug trafficking or slave trade), giving a legal basis to prosecute in those instances that a State wishes to prosecute captured criminals in its domestic courts.

On the other hand, courts should not interpret human rights obligations when combating crime on the high seas in the same strict way that they do when evaluating a State conduct within its borders. It should be recognized that the circumstances pertaining to a high seas operation are very challenging, very different to what the State faces when operating on its territory and the resources are far less in numbers and less effective in nature. In this case, an approach close to the "certain realism" doctrine proposed by the dissenting opinion in *Medvedyev* would be far more beneficial, since it guarantees the best possible protection of

109. UNSC, Report of the Special Adviser to the Secretary-General on Legal Issues Related to Piracy off the Coast of Somalia, S/2011/30 (2011).

110. C. Kreß, "Die modern Piraterie, das Strafrecht und die Menchenrechte Gedanken aus Anlass der deutschen Mitwirkung and der Seeoperation ATALANTA", in D. Weingärtner (ed.) "Die Bundeswehr als Armee im Einsatz: Entwicklungen im nationalen und internationalen Recht", Baden-Baden, Nomos, 2010, p. 95, at p. 121.

111. Guilfoyle, *supra* footnote 27, at p. 169.

human rights while at the same time encourages States to seek prosecution of criminals. Courts applying human rights law, when assessing the legal basis of an intercepting State to board and take further enforcement action against the cargo or the crew, should not ignore the reality that even a lawful interdiction "would be pointless without the exercise of further enforcement measures regarding the illicit cargo and the alleged offenders"[112].

No matter how ambiguous it may seem to States, upholding their human rights obligations while fighting crime at sea should not deter them from prosecuting captured suspects. It is clear that so far the political will of the States operating on the high seas is more focused on deterrence rather than criminal enforcement, but the importance of criminal prosecution as a major deterrent of future crime should not be overlooked[113]. In the end, what is important is to understand that in cases of maritime interdiction human rights law should not operate as a real threat to the human rights of the individuals concerned. If the law is unreasonably strict, it will discourage States from embracing it and lead either to impunity of criminals or to State operations entirely outside the ambit of human rights law, covert operations and questionable human rights standards. It is true that only a few and relatively easy adjustments could render prosecution in accordance with human rights law possible.

112. Papastavridis, *supra* footnote 49, at p. 572.
113. Dutton, *supra* footnote 90, at p. 253.

12

La lutte contre la criminalité en mer à l'épreuve de la Cour européenne des droits de l'homme

Arnaud Montas *

SECTION 1 INTRODUCTION

Longtemps le juge n'a connu du droit pénal maritime que les infractions au droit de la pêche, où la criminalité restait de faible intensité ; à l'inverse, le juge réservait son approche de la criminalité grave, à l'étude, devenue largement théorique, des textes sur la traite maritime des esclaves et sur la piraterie en haute mer inspirés par les Anglais au début du XIXe siècle.

Avec l'adoption des conventions des Nations Unies de Montego Bay en 1982 sur le droit de la mer[1] et de Vienne en 1988 sur les trafics de stupéfiants[2], le droit pénal maritime a commencé un retour en force illustré par la floraison depuis lors ininterrompue de lois pénales de fond et de forme visant à réprimer des formes de criminalité aussi diverses et inquiétantes que le trafic international de stupéfiants, la traite des êtres humains ou encore les pollutions marines. Aujourd'hui, chacune de ces préoccupations reçoit des réponses normatives progressivement affinées au gré de la transposition des conventions dans les droits nationaux, mais aussi de faits divers majeurs, qui rappellent à chacun que la mer est un environnement privilégié pour la criminalité moderne.

Comme toute activité de puissance publique, aussi légitime soit-elle, la lutte étatique contre la criminalité en mer est limitée par le nécessaire respect des droits de l'homme en général et des droits fondamentaux des prévenus et autres suspects, en particulier. En Europe, ce contrôle de la

* Docteur en droit privé de l'Université de Nantes. Maître de conférences en droit privé et en sciences criminelles, faculté de droit de l'Université de Bretagne-Occidentale. Chercheur à l'UMR Amure, Institut universitaire européen de la mer.

1. Convention des Nations Unies sur le droit de la mer, Montego Bay, 10 décembre 1982, *Recueil des traités*, vol. 1833, n° 31363 (ci-après « CNUDM »).

2. Convention des Nations Unies contre le trafic illicite de stupéfiants et substances psychotropes, Vienne, 20 décembre 1988, *Recueil des traités*, vol. 1582, n° 27627.

conformité aux droits de l'homme de l'action de l'Etat en mer relève de la compétence de la Cour européenne des droits de l'homme.

Instituée dès 1959 par la Convention de sauvegarde des droits de l'homme et des libertés fondamentales, usuellement appelée Convention européenne des droits de l'homme, la Cour est chargée de veiller au respect de la Convention par les états signataires: dès lors, et après épuisement des voies de recours internes, elle peut être saisie par toute personne s'estimant victime d'une violation de la Convention. Signée dans le cadre du Conseil de l'Europe en 1950 et entrée en vigueur en 1953, la Convention a pour fonction, comme son nom l'indique, de protéger les droits de l'homme et les libertés fondamentales en permettant un contrôle judiciaire du respect de ces droits.

Plus précisément, la Cour est compétente pour traiter les recours portés contre un Etat membre qui a ratifié la Convention et ses Protocoles, mais qui ne respecterait pas les droits et libertés qui y sont reconnus. La portée des arrêts de la Cour dépend du type de décision qu'elle rend. Certaines de ses décisions se bornent à constater une violation des droits et libertés qu'elle protège. De ce point de vue, ses arrêts sont essentiellement déclaratoires et se bornent à déclarer l'existence ou l'absence d'une violation de la Convention. Pour expliquer cela, il faut ici rappeler la compétence supra-étatique et subsidiaire de la Cour, qui l'empêche d'abroger les lois et les décisions à l'origine de la violation. Ses arrêts ont une portée simplement individuelle. De la même manière, elles ne valent pas titre exécutoire en droit interne, même si la Cour se reconnaît compétente pour surveiller l'exécution de ses arrêts, à la demande d'un requérant individuel. D'autres arrêts accordent au plaignant une satisfaction équitable. De nature pécuniaire, elle est accordée à la victime «lorsque le droit interne de l'Etat mis en cause est impuissant à faire disparaître complètement la violation constatée». L'indemnité ainsi allouée, à la charge de l'Etat coupable d'une violation des droits, correspond aux frais et dépens exposés, ainsi qu'au préjudice matériel et moral de la victime.

De manière générale, si la jurisprudence qu'elle construit progressivement est prise en compte par la doctrine juridique, une autre retombée très concrète de son activité est la modification d'une législation interne à la suite d'une condamnation.

Pour relever les défis contemporains de la lutte contre la criminalité en mer, la mise en place de normes internationales opérationnelles et le développement des réseaux de coopération, de même que l'enrichissement rapide de la jurisprudence de la Cour qui en découle, permettent d'envisager progressivement une meilleure réponse judiciaire à la criminalité en mer, en cohérence avec les réponses diplomatiques, militaires ou autres. Les aspects judiciaires de la lutte contre la criminalité en mer connaissent une expansion récente mais continue. En la matière, on sait que l'action de l'Etat en mer est fondée, d'une part, sur les instruments internationaux et, d'autre part, sur leur introduction en droit interne. Tout est donc question d'équilibre entre les obligations imposées aux Etats par leurs engagements conventionnels et le nécessaire respect des droits et libertés fondamentales tel qu'exigé par la Convention.

A l'examen, il apparaît que l'œuvre jurisprudentielle de la Cour en matière de contrôle de la légalité de la lutte contre la criminalité en mer se manifeste à travers une double préoccupation reposant sur la distinction entre les droits (dits) substantiels d'un côté (section 2) et les droits procéduraux de l'autre (section 3).

SECTION 2 LA COUR EUROPÉENNE DES DROITS DE L'HOMME ET LES ATTEINTES AUX DROITS SUBSTANTIELS DANS LA LUTTE CONTRE LA CRIMINALITÉ EN MER

Depuis l'adoption de grandes conventions internationales dans les années quatre-vingt et la normalisation accélérée du droit maritime international, l'action pénale des Etats a fait un bond en avant, de sorte que chaque activité illicite entreprise en mer reçoit désormais une réponse juridique et souvent judiciaire. Cependant, la lutte contre la criminalité en mer n'est pas inconditionnelle et n'autorise pas les Etats à porter atteinte aux droits substantiels que la Convention, parmi d'autres instruments, garantit.

Constituant la base des droits subjectifs, les droits dits « substantiels » (ou matériels), sont des règles de fond régissant un domaine particulier du droit, par opposition aux droits procéduraux qui déterminent la manière dont les sujets de droit peuvent précisément les faire valoir[3]. De ce point de vue, c'est naturellement que le texte de la Convention est étroitement lié à la jurisprudence de la Cour, dont les arrêts expliquent et interprètent le contenu.

Au titre des droits substantiels prévus par la Convention, son article 3 interdit de manière inconditionnelle la torture et les traitements inhumains et dégradants, et ce en toutes circonstances. Dans le même sens, les Etats ont également l'obligation de mettre en place des mécanismes de prévention et de répression sanctionnant les traitements qui lui sont contraires, ainsi que de mener des enquêtes approfondies sur toute allégation de torture ou de mauvais traitement. En matière de criminalité en mer, la Cour a déjà appliqué cette disposition à la lutte contre les migrations clandestines par voie maritime (paragraphe 1).

3. Voir section 3.

L'article 10 de la Convention protège quant à lui la liberté d'expression, fondement essentiel d'une société démocratique. Est notamment protégé le droit pour un navire pacifique d'entrer dans les eaux territoriales d'un autre pour y exprimer des positions critiques à l'endroit de l'Etat côtier (paragraphe 2).

Enfin, dans une autre optique, la lutte des Etats contre la criminalité en mer ne leur permet pas de porter abusivement atteinte au droit de propriété de l'armateur d'un navire suspecté de transporter des armes interdites; la jurisprudence de la Cour en atteste (paragraphe 3).

Paragraphe 1 **L'interdiction de la torture et des peines ou traitements inhumains ou dégradants (art. 3)**

En droit positif, complétant la Convention des Nations Unies contre la criminalité transnationale organisée[4], le protocole de Palerme[5], adopté le 15 novembre 2000 et entré en vigueur en 2004, a pour objet la lutte contre le trafic illicite de migrants[6]. Il oblige à cette fin les Etats parties à ériger en infraction pénale les actes constitutifs de ce trafic, condition première de l'amélioration de la coopération judiciaire pénale entre les Etats parties[7]. Si le protocole ne mentionne pas le rôle du juge national, celui-ci intervient dans son application et veille au respect des dispositions du droit national sur la sanction de l'aide à l'entrée et aux séjours irréguliers.

Appliqué à la criminalité en mer, où la règle de l'accord préalable de l'Etat de pavillon est maintenue pour arraisonner et visiter un navire étranger, il est important de préciser que, n'ayant pas pénétré sur le territoire d'un Etat partie, les migrants ne peuvent être juridiquement qua-

---

4. Convention des Nations Unies contre la criminalité transnationale organisée, New York, 15 novembre 2000, *Recueil des traités*, vol. 2225, nº 39574.

5. Protocole contre le trafic illicite de migrants par terre, mer et air, additionnel à la Convention des Nations Unies contre la criminalité transnationale organisée, Nations Unies, *Recueil des traités*, vol. 2241, p. 519.

6. F. Sánchez, «Tráfica ilegal de personas y cooperacíon marítima internacional», dans J. Pueyo Losa et J.-J. Urbina (dir. publ.), *La cooperación internacional en la ordenación de los mares y océanos*, Madrid, Iustel, 2009, pp. 363-396. M. Abad Castelos, «Measures Taken by International Organizations to Combat Illicit Human Trafficking and Transnational Organized Crime», dans J.-M. Sobrino Heredia, *Sûreté maritime et violence en mer*, Bruxelles, Bruylant, 2011, pp. 47-68. P. Mallia, *Migrant Smuggling by Sea: Combating a Current Threat to Maritime Security through the Creation of a Cooperative Framework*, Leyde, Nijhoff, 2010. United Nations Office on Drugs and Crime, *Smuggling of Migrants by Sea*, Vienne, UNODC, 2011.

7. Les migrants victimes de ces trafics doivent le plus souvent être secourus en mer car ils peuvent être qualifiés de personnes en détresse au sens de la convention SAR («Search and Rescue»), signée à Hambourg en 1979 et entrée en vigueur en 1985 (chapitre X: Obligation de porter secours).

lifiés d'immigrants clandestins. De ce point de vue, en vertu de l'article 5 du Protocole, «Les migrants ne deviennent pas passibles de poursuites pénales ... du fait qu'ils ont été l'objet [de trafic]». En conséquence, seuls les trafiquants (les «passeurs») sont en l'espèce auteurs d'infraction et donc susceptibles d'être condamnés en cas de non-respect du droit interne, le Protocole ne consacrant en la matière aucune immunité.

Ces politiques pénales, fondées sur des intérêts légitimes des Etats, ne doivent cependant pas leur permettre d'adopter des comportements contraires aux dispositions de la Convention en général et de son article 3 en particulier.

Pour reprendre l'expression de la Cour, l'article 3, qui déclare que «Nul ne peut être soumis à la torture ni à des peines ou traitements inhumains ou dégradants»[8], «consacre l'une des valeurs les plus fondamentales d'une société démocratique». La Cour, de façon permanente et répétée, a toujours traité cette disposition par référence à l'article 2 («Droit à la vie»)[9], comme l'un des droits les plus fondamentaux protégés par la Convention, dont le but est d'assurer la dignité et l'intégrité physique de la personne. Ce caractère inconditionnel de l'article 3 a des répercussions extraterritoriales puisque chacun doit être protégé contre les mauvais traitements qu'il pourrait subir ou risquer de subir au-delà du territoire de l'Etat membre[10].

Cet article, qui ne supporte aucune dérogation ou restriction légale[11], est énoncé en termes absolus et sans réserve; il ne comporte pas, notam-

---

8. U. Erdal et H. Bakirci, «Article 3 of the European Convention on Human Rights, a Practicitioner's Handbook», Organisation mondiale contre la torture (OMCT), Genève, 2006. A. Reidy, «L'interdiction de la torture, Un guide sur la mise en œuvre de l'article 3 de la Convention européenne des droits de l'homme», *Précis sur les droits de l'homme*, n° 6, Editions du Conseil de l'Europe, 2006. H. Fourteau, *L'application de l'article 3 de la CEDH dans le droit interne des Etats membres*, LGDJ, 2006.

9. F. Tulkens, «Le droit à la vie et le champ des obligations des Etats dans la jurisprudence récente de la Cour européenne des droits de l'homme», *Mélanges Cohen-Jonathan*, Bruylant, 2004, pp. 1605 ss. F. Przetacznik, «The Right of Life As a Basic Human Right», *Revue des droits de l'homme*, 1976, pp. 585 ss.

10. Sur la question de savoir si les Etats contractants ont normalement l'obligation d'appliquer la Convention seulement sur leur propre territoire, voir CEDH, 7 juillet 2011, *Al-Skeini et autres c. Royaume-Uni*, requête n° 55721/07: au sens de l'article 1 de la Convention européenne des droits de l'homme («obligation de respecter les droits de l'Homme»), ce n'est que dans des circonstances exceptionnelles qu'un acte extraterritorial relève de la juridiction d'un Etat contractant. L'une de ces exceptions consacrées par la jurisprudence de la Cour est la situation où un Etat contractant assume à titre extraterritorial des prérogatives de puissance publique sur le territoire d'un autre Etat, sur lequel il exerce un contrôle effectif.

11. L'article 15, qui admet un certain nombre de dérogations à la Convention européenne des droits de l'homme en cas d'état d'urgence, n'en admet cependant aucune concernant l'article 3.

ment, de deuxième paragraphe précisant les circonstances dans lesquelles il est acceptable d'infliger une torture ou des peines ou traitements inhumains ou dégradants. De même, ses termes signifient qu'il ne peut jamais y avoir, en vertu de la Convention ou du droit international, de justification pour des actes qui enfreignent l'article. En d'autres termes, aucun facteur ne saurait être invoqué par un système juridique national comme une justification valable pour recourir à un comportement interdit. Notamment, la Cour rappelle que la conduite de la victime ne saurait en aucune façon être considérée comme un motif acceptable pour recourir à ce type de comportement : ainsi en matière de lutte contre le crime organisé en général et contre les migrations clandestines par voie maritime en particulier[12].

Un certain nombre d'affaires portent sur l'application de l'article 3 dans des cas d'expulsion[13]. Aux termes de la jurisprudence constante de la Cour, l'expulsion d'un individu vers un pays où il peut être soumis à un traitement qui viole l'article 3 engage, au titre de la Convention, la responsabilité de l'Etat qui y procède. A la suite de l'arrêt *Soering c. Royaume-Uni* du 7 juillet 1989[14], plusieurs affaires sont venues consolider le principe voulant qu'en présence de motifs sérieux et avérés de croire que l'intéressé, si on le livre à l'Etat requérant, y courra un risque réel d'être soumis à la torture ou à des peines ou traitements inhumains ou dégradants, la responsabilité de l'Etat qui expulse sera engagée à raison d'un acte exposant autrui à des traitements prohibés. Il apparaît donc essentiel d'examiner avec rigueur toute allégation selon laquelle une expulsion dans un pays tiers exposerait une personne à un traitement interdit par l'article 3. Notamment, un arrêt du 29 juillet 2010, *Shchukin et autres c. Chypre*[15], admet une violation de l'article pour absence d'enquête effective des autorités chypriotes, suite aux allégations de mauvais traitements subis par un membre de l'équipage d'un navire ukrainien, au

---

12. R. Barnes, « The International Law of the Sea and Migration Control », dans B. Ryan et V. Mitsilegas (dir. publ.), *Extraterritorial Immigration Control : Legal Challenges*, Leyde, Nijhoff, 2010, pp. 103-149. X. Hinrichs, « Measures against Smuggling of Migrants at Sea : A Law of the Sea Related Perspective », *Revue belge de droit international*, vol. 36 (2003), n° 2, pp. 413-451. A. Fornerod, « L'article 3 de la Convention européenne des droits de l'homme et l'éloignement forcé des étrangers : illustrations récentes », *Revue trimestrielle des droits de l'homme*, 2010, pp. 315 ss.

13. Par exemple, CEDH, 30 octobre 1991, *Vilvarajah et autres c. Royaume-Uni*, requête n° 13163/87, 4 février 2005 ; *Mamatkulov et Askarov c. Turquie*, requêtes n° 46827/99 et 46951/99.

14. Requête n° 14038/88. W. Ganshof Van Der Meersch, « L'extradition et la Convention européenne des droits de l'homme. L'affaire *Soering* », *RTDH*, 1990, pp. 5-24. F. Sudre, « Extradition et peine de mort : l'arrêt *Soering* du 7 juillet 1989 », *Revue générale de droit international public (RGDIP)*, 1990, pp. 103-121.

15. Requête n° 14030/03.

cours de son expulsion suite à la faillite du propriétaire du navire *Primexpress Island*. Le fait de ne pas donner de suite appropriée aux allégations de violation peut dès lors constituer, en soi, une violation par les autorités judiciaires de l'article 3.

Outre l'obligation *prima facie* qui est celle des autorités judiciaires de ne pas commettre elles-mêmes d'actes prohibés, ces autorités ont aussi l'obligation d'enquêter sur les allégations de violation de l'article 3. Cette interdiction impose donc une extrême vigilance aux autorités judiciaires et les expose au risque d'aggraver les violations de l'article 3 et de commettre des violations distinctes du fait de leurs propres actes. Toute violation étant un manquement grave à la garantie des droits fondamentaux, les enquêtes sur les allégations de violation doivent respecter des normes strictes: elles doivent ainsi être exhaustives, efficaces et propres à identifier et punir les auteurs des violations. Pour déterminer si les éléments de preuves indiquent une violation de l'article et ainsi rompre l'engrenage de l'impunité, la Cour doit être convaincue que les allégations sont prouvées «au-delà de tout doute raisonnable».

En matière de lutte contre la criminalité en mer, un arrêt frappant du 23 février 2012, *Hirsi Jamaa et autres c. Italie*[16], traite du refoulement de migrants en Libye sans examen du risque qu'ils invoquaient d'être exposés à un risque de mauvais traitements.

Les requérants sont onze ressortissants somaliens et treize ressortissants érythréens, qui font partie d'un groupe d'environ deux cents personnes qui, en 2009, quittèrent la Libye à bord de trois embarcations dans le but de rejoindre les côtes italiennes. En mai 2009, alors que les embarcations se trouvent à l'intérieur de la zone maritime de recherche et de sauvetage relevant de la compétence de Malte, elles sont approchées par des navires d'Etat italiens. Les occupants sont transférés sur les navires militaires et reconduits vers la Libye. Arrivés au port de Tripoli, les migrants sont livrés aux autorités libyennes. Les requérants s'y opposèrent mais furent obligés par la force à quitter les navires italiens. Deux des requérants sont décédés dans des circonstances inconnues après les faits litigieux. Le Gouvernement italien expliqua que les opérations d'interception des embarcations en haute mer et de renvoi des migrants faisaient suite à l'entrée en vigueur, en février 2009, d'accords bilatéraux conclus avec la Libye. Entre juin et octobre 2009, quatorze des requérants ont cependant obtenu le statut de réfugié auprès du bureau du Haut Commissariat des réfugiés de Tripoli.

Saisie de ces faits, la Cour rappelle le principe de droit international, transcrit dans le code italien de la navigation, selon lequel un navire en haute mer est soumis à la juridiction exclusive définie par son pavillon.

16. Requête n° 27765/09.

De leur montée à bord jusqu'à leur remise aux autorités libyennes, les requérants se sont trouvés sous le contrôle continu et exclusif, en droit et en fait, des autorités italiennes. Par conséquent, les faits dont découlent les violations alléguées relevaient de la juridiction de l'Italie au sens de l'article 1 de la Convention. La Cour, bien que consciente de la pression sur les Etats que représente le flot de migrants par voie maritime, rappelle que cette situation ne les exonère pas de leur obligation de ne pas éloigner une personne risquant de subir des traitements prohibés par l'article 3 dans le pays de destination. Notant la dégradation de la situation en Libye à compter d'avril 2010, la Cour se réfère à la seule situation à l'époque des faits. A cet égard, elle note que les migrants irréguliers et demandeurs d'asile étaient systématiquement arrêtés et détenus dans des conditions inhumaines, évoquant notamment des cas de torture. Le Gouvernement italien a maintenu que la Libye était un lieu sûr pour les migrants et que ce pays respecterait ses engagements internationaux en matière d'asile et de protection des réfugiés. La Cour souligne que l'existence de textes internes et la ratification de traités internationaux ne suffisent pas toujours à assurer une protection adaptée contre le risque de mauvais traitements lorsque des sources fiables font état de pratiques contraires à la Convention. Cette réalité en Libye étant notoire, les autorités italiennes savaient ou devaient savoir au moment d'éloigner les requérants qu'ils y seraient exposés à des traitements interdits, le fait que les requérants n'aient pas expressément demandé l'asile ne dégageant en rien l'Italie de ses responsabilités. La Cour rappelle les obligations des Etats en matière de réfugiés, dont le «principe de non-refoulement» que consacre aussi la Charte des droits fondamentaux de l'Union européenne proclamée à Nice le 7 décembre 2000[17].

La Cour conclut que le transfert des requérants vers la Libye par les autorités italiennes les ont exposés, en connaissance de cause, à des traitements contraires à l'article 3 de la Convention.

Au-delà du refoulement des migrants maritimes clandestins, la lutte contre la criminalité en mer trouve aussi ses limites dans le sort réservé par les Etats contractants aux migrants appréhendés par les autorités administratives ou judiciaires des Etats signataires. De ce point de vue, le droit positif distingue entre les migrants clandestins qui ont fait l'objet d'un trafic et dont le comportement ne saurait être criminalisé pour cette raison (Protocole, art. 5) et les autres, dès lors susceptibles de faire l'objet de mesures coercitives dans les Etats signataires.

Ainsi, l'arrêt *A. A. c. Grèce*[18] du 22 juillet 2010 a admis qu'un

---

17. *Journal officiel des Communautés européennes (JOCE)*, du 18 décembre 2000, C 364/1.

18. Requête n° 12186/08.

migrant, demandeur d'asile, a été retenu illégalement et dans des conditions sordides dans un centre de rétention en Grèce, en contradiction avec l'article 3. Le requérant, A. A., est un ressortissant palestinien résidant en Grèce. Fuyant le camp de réfugiés où il vivait au Liban, il arriva dans les eaux territoriales grecques où il fut appréhendé par la gendarmerie maritime alors que l'embarcation qu'il occupait était en train de sombrer. Les autorités de police le placèrent en détention provisoire, puis le procureur ordonna son renvoi dans son pays d'origine. Dans cette affaire, la Cour rappelle que le droit des Etats de placer en détention des demandeurs d'asile en vertu de leur «droit indéniable de contrôler … l'entrée et le séjour des étrangers sur leur territoire» doit s'exercer en conformité avec les dispositions de la Convention. En l'occurrence, les allégations du requérant concernant l'état du centre où il a été détenu sont corroborées par plusieurs rapports concordants d'organisations internationales et d'organisations non gouvernementales faisant état des éléments suivants: surpopulation carcérale, exiguïté et saleté extrêmes, toilettes mixtes délabrées, salle de bains baignant dans un centimètre d'eau, hospitalisation impossible, système d'égout défectueux, odeurs nauséabondes, problèmes dermatologiques transmissibles, violences lors des arrestations. Pour la Cour, le fait que le requérant ait séjourné durant trois mois dans ces conditions constitue un traitement dégradant contraire à l'article 3 tant en raison des conditions de vie prévalant dans le centre de détention, ayant entraîné à l'encontre du requérant un traitement dégradant, qu'en raison du manque de diligence des autorités pour lui apporter une assistance médicale appropriée.

Paragraphe 2 **La liberté d'expression (art. 10)**

Si le droit international permet aux Etats, dans la limite du droit de passage inoffensif tel que prévu aux articles 17 et suivants de la Convention des Nations Unies sur le droit de la mer (CNUDM)[19], de prévenir toute forme de délinquance susceptible d'être commise dans ses eaux territoriales, il ne les autorise cependant pas à procéder au mépris des libertés civiles garanties par la Convention: ainsi de la liberté d'expression, garantie par son article 10[20].

19. Voir notamment l'article 21, al. *h)*, de la CNUDM permettant à l'Etat côtier d'adopter, en conformité avec les dispositions de la Convention et les autres règles du droit international, des lois et règlements relatifs au passage inoffensif dans sa mer territoriale, qui peuvent porter sur la prévention des infractions à ses lois et règlements … d'immigration.

20. Article 10 («Liberté d'expression»):

> «1. Toute personne a droit à la liberté d'expression. Ce droit comprend la liberté d'opinion et la liberté de recevoir ou de communiquer des informa-

L'article 10 se compose de deux paragraphes : le premier identifie trois éléments du droit à la liberté d'expression : la liberté d'opinion ; la liberté de recevoir des informations et des idées ; enfin la liberté de communiquer des informations et des idées[21]. Quelle que soit l'expression, ou le mode d'expression en cause, le second accorde cependant aux Etats le pouvoir de s'ingérer dans l'exercice de la liberté d'expression à la réunion de trois conditions : l'ingérence doit être prévue par la loi ; elle doit viser à protéger l'un des intérêts ou des valeurs suivants : sécurité nationale, intégrité territoriale, sûreté publique, défense de l'ordre et prévention du crime, protection de la santé ou de la morale, protection de la réputation ou des droits d'autrui, prévention de la divulgation d'informations confidentielles et garantie de l'autorité et de l'impartialité du pouvoir judiciaire ; elle doit enfin être nécessaire dans une société démocratique. La liste des motifs légitimes de restriction étant exhaustive, les autorités nationales ne peuvent pas invoquer un motif n'y figurant pas. Par conséquent, lorsqu'ils sont appelés à appliquer une disposition légale susceptible de porter atteinte à la liberté d'expression, les tribunaux nationaux doivent identifier la valeur ou l'intérêt protégé par ladite disposition et vérifier qu'il figure bien dans l'énumération du paragraphe 2.

Bien que l'article 10 ne la mentionne pas explicitement, la Cour a élaboré une jurisprudence abondante énonçant un ensemble de principes qui confèrent à la presse un statut spécial dans l'exercice des libertés garanties[22], notamment lorsque des questions d'intérêt public sont concernées.

Indispensable pour garantir un régime démocratique, la liberté d'expression est un droit en soi, en même temps qu'un élément d'autres

---

tions ou des idées sans qu'il puisse y avoir ingérence d'autorités publiques et sans considération de frontière.

Le présent article n'empêche pas les Etats de soumettre les entreprises de radiodiffusion, de cinéma ou de télévision à un régime d'autorisations.

2. L'exercice de ces libertés comportant des devoirs et des responsabilités peut être soumis à certaines formalités, conditions, restrictions ou sanctions prévues par la loi, qui constituent des mesures nécessaires, dans une société démocratique, à la sécurité nationale, à l'intégrité territoriale ou à la sûreté publique, à la défense de l'ordre et à la prévention du crime, à la protection de la santé ou de la morale, à la protection de la réputation ou des droits d'autrui, pour empêcher la divulgation d'informations confidentielles ou pour garantir l'autorité et l'impartialité du pouvoir judiciaire. »

21. J.-P. Costa, « La liberté d'expression selon la jurisprudence de la Cour européenne des droits de l'homme », *RTDH*, 2002, pp. 671 ss. A. Spielmann, « La liberté d'expression et ses limites », *Annales de droit luxembourgeois*, 1991, pp. 272 ss.

22. Voir notamment CEDH, 7 décembre 1976, *Handyside c. Royaume-Uni*, requête n° 5493/72 ; CEDH, 26 avril 1979, *Sunday Times c. Royaume-Uni*, requête n° 6538/74 ; CEDH, 31 janvier 1986, *Barthold c. Allemagne*, requête n° 8734/79.

droits protégés par la Convention (cas de la liberté de réunion). Elle peut parfois entrer en conflit avec certains autres droits énoncés par l'instrument: droit à un procès équitable, droit au respect de la vie privée, liberté de conscience et de religion, etc. Dans cette hypothèse de collision de droits protégés, il appartiendra aux juges de Strasbourg de déterminer l'importance respective et l'équilibre des droits concernés.

Par principe, la protection accordée par l'article 10 s'étend à toute expression, quels que soient son contenu et la forme de sa diffusion, à la condition qu'elle ne serve pas à favoriser l'altération des autres droits et libertés reconnus par la Convention.

Dans l'arrêt du 20 mai 1999 rendu dans l'affaire *Bladet Tromso et Stensaas c. Norvège*[23], la Cour rappelle que la lutte contre certaines formes de criminalité en mer ne saurait porter atteinte à la liberté de la presse, considérée comme découlant de la liberté d'expression[24]. Plus précisément, la Cour condamne un Etat pour avoir sanctionné un organe de presse relayant une forme particulière de criminalité en mer: la chasse illégale. En 1992, une société de presse et son éditeur furent ainsi condamnés pour diffamation par un tribunal norvégien. Le journal avait publié plusieurs articles sur la chasse au phoque ainsi qu'un rapport officiel, mais secret, faisant référence à une série de violations de la réglementation relative à cette chasse maritime. Ces documents faisaient un certain nombre d'allégations à l'encontre de cinq membres d'équipage d'un navire de chasse au phoque, tenus responsables de pratiques illicites d'abattage. Le tribunal considérant «nulles et dépourvues de fondement» certaines des affirmations litigieuses de l'article et du rapport, le journal et son éditeur furent condamnés à verser des dommages-intérêts aux demandeurs. Pour la Cour, cette condamnation constitue une violation de l'article 10 de la Convention. Selon ses juges, certaines allégations des articles étaient «relativement sérieuses», mais le possible effet défavorable des déclarations litigieuses sur la réputation ou les droits de chacun des chasseurs de phoque était atténué par plusieurs facteurs; la Cour a en particulier estimé que «la critique ne constituait pas (en l'espèce) une attaque dirigée contre l'ensemble des membres d'équipage ni contre l'un d'eux en particulier».

Dans un arrêt du 3 février 2009, *Women On Waves et autres c. Portugal*[25], la Cour contrôle cette fois la conformité à la Convention du

23. Requête nº 21980/93.

24. G. Malinverni, «Freedom of Information in the European Convention on Human Rights and in the International Covenant on Civil and Political Rights», *Human Rights Law Journal*, 1983, pp. 446 ss. J.-M. Larralde, «L'article 10 de la Convention européenne des droits de l'homme et la liberté de la presse», *RTDH*, 2007, pp. 39 ss.

25. Requête nº 31276/05.

refus des autorités portugaises de laisser entrer dans leurs eaux territoriales un navire associatif affrété en vue d'œuvrer pour la dépénalisation de l'interruption volontaire de grossesse. Outre l'article 10, l'affaire concernait la liberté de circulation, telle que prévue à l'article 2 du Protocole n° 4[26].

Les trois associations requérantes ont pour but notamment de promouvoir le débat sur les droits reproductifs. En 2004, la société Women on Waves affréta le navire *Borndiep* à destination du Portugal. Des rencontres sur la prévention des maladies sexuellement transmissibles, le planning familial et la dépénalisation de l'interruption volontaire de grossesse devaient se tenir à bord. L'entrée du navire dans les eaux territoriales portugaises fut interdite par arrêté ministériel et empêchée par un navire de guerre. La demande faite par les sociétés requérantes aux tribunaux portugais d'autoriser son entrée fut rejetée car jugée dépourvue d'utilité dans la mesure où le navire avait déjà quitté les eaux portugaises.

En l'espèce, c'est non pas un espace privé ou un bien appartenant au domaine public qui était en cause, mais la mer territoriale de l'Etat défendeur, qui est un espace public et ouvert de par sa nature même. Par ailleurs, même si la CNUDM (art. 17 et suivants) permet à chaque Etat partie, dans les limites du droit de passage inoffensif, de prévenir toute atteinte à ses droits dans sa mer territoriale, cette restriction doit être fondée en droit et s'appuyer sur un intérêt légitime.

Or, empêcher l'expression d'idées contraires à celles de l'Etat côtier ne participe pas de la lutte contre la criminalité en mer et ne saurait dès lors être légitimée par la Cour. Par ailleurs, l'espèce interpelle sur le terrain des obligations négatives découlant de la Convention, où la marge d'appréciation des Etats est plus étroite. De même, aucun indice suffisamment sérieux et permettant de penser que les requérantes avaient l'intention de violer de manière délibérée la législation portugaise de l'époque en matière de droits de la femme ne peut être décelé dans les

---

26. P. Jean, «Le contenu de la liberté de circulation», dans F. Flory *et al.* (dir. publ.), *La liberté de circulation des personnes en droit international*, Economica, 1988. Protocole n° 4 (art. 2): «Liberté de circulation»:

> «1. Quiconque se trouve régulièrement sur le territoire d'un Etat a le droit d'y circuler librement et d'y choisir librement sa résidence.
>
> 2 Toute personne est libre de quitter n'importe quel pays, y compris le sien.
>
> 3. L'exercice de ces droits ne peut faire l'objet d'autres restrictions que celles qui, prévues par la loi, constituent des mesures nécessaires, dans une société démocratique, à la sécurité nationale, à la sûreté publique, au maintien de l'ordre public, à la prévention des infractions pénales, à la protection de la santé ou de la morale, ou à la protection des droits et libertés d'autrui.
>
> 4. Les droits reconnus au paragraphe 1 peuvent également, dans certaines zones déterminées, faire l'objet de restrictions qui, prévues par la loi, sont justifiées par l'intérêt public dans une société démocratique.»

faits de la cause. Dès lors, la Cour décide que la liberté d'exprimer des opinions au cours d'une réunion ne saurait subir de limitation dans la mesure où les requérants n'ont pas commis d'acte répréhensible à cette occasion. En l'espèce, l'Etat disposait assurément d'autres moyens pour atteindre les buts légitimes de la défense de l'ordre et de la protection de la santé que le recours à une interdiction totale d'entrée du *Borndiep* dans ses eaux territoriales, qui plus est moyennant l'envoi d'un bâtiment de guerre contre un navire civil. Par une mesure aussi radicale, l'ingérence en question ne répondait donc pas à un «besoin social impérieux» et ne saurait passer pour «nécessaire dans une société démocratique».

Pour toutes ces raisons, c'est à l'unanimité que la Cour admet en l'espèce une violation de l'article 10 de la Convention.

Paragraphe 3 **La protection de la propriété (Protocole n° 1, art. 1)**

L'article 1 du Protocole n° 1 à la Convention garantit la protection de la propriété et dispose à cette fin que

> «Toute personne physique ou morale a droit au respect de ses biens. Nul ne peut être privé de sa propriété que pour cause d'utilité publique et dans les conditions prévues par la loi et les principes généraux du droit international. Les dispositions précédentes ne portent pas atteinte au droit que possèdent les Etats de mettre en vigueur les lois qu'ils jugent nécessaires pour réglementer l'usage des biens conformément à l'intérêt général ou pour assurer le paiement des impôts ou d'autres contributions ou des amendes.»[27]

S'il apparaît à la lecture de cette disposition que l'Etat bénéficie d'une grande marge d'appréciation dans la mise en œuvre de ce droit et par conséquent dans les ingérences qui pourraient lui être opposées, il ne s'ensuit cependant pas que la Cour n'a aucun rôle à jouer pour en déterminer la légitimité.

Elle l'a d'ailleurs fait observer le 21 février 1986 dans l'affaire *James et autres c. Royaume-Uni*[28]: Si la Cour admet qu'elle ne saurait subs-

27. IDHAE (collectif), *La protection du droit de propriété par la Cour européenne des droits de l'homme*, Bruylant, 2005. R. Libchaber, «La propriété, droit fondamental», dans R. Cabrillac, M.-A. Frison-Roche et Th. Revet (dir. publ.), *Libertés et droits fondamentaux*, 18e éd., Dalloz, 2012, pp. 879 ss. F. Sudre, *La protection du droit de propriété par la Cour européenne des droits de l'homme*, 1998, pp. 71 ss.

28. Requête n° 8793/79. CDE 1998, p. 479 (obs. G. Cohen-Jonathan); AFDI, 1987, p. 239 (obs. V. Coussirat-Coustère); JDI, 1997, p. 722 (obs. P. Rolland et P. Tavernier). C. Russo, «L'applicabilité aux nationaux des principes généraux du droit international visés à l'article 1er du Protocole n° 1», *Protecting Human Rights: the European Dimension. Protection européenne des droits de l'homme: la dimension européenne*, Cologne, Carl Heymans, 1988, pp. 547-554.

tituer sa propre appréciation à celle des autorités nationales, elle estime cependant que son rôle est de «contrôler les mesures litigieuses et, à cette fin, d'étudier les faits à la lumière desquels lesdites autorités ont agi». Ces dernières années, la Cour a ainsi pu considérer qu'un Etat avait dépassé les limites acceptables de sa marge d'appréciation et porté atteinte au droit de propriété tel que garanti par la Convention[29].

La lutte contre la criminalité en mer n'échappe pas à ce constat, ainsi qu'en témoignent plusieurs affaires récentes dont certaines ont fait grand bruit.

En matière de transport maritime d'explosifs tout d'abord. Dans l'arrêt *Compagnie de navigation de la République islamique d'Iran c. Turquie* rendu le 13 décembre 2007[30], la société requérante avait affrété le navire *Cape Maleas*, appartenant à un chypriote. La charte-partie fut complétée par un addendum disposant que la société requérante pouvait charger 2500 mètres cubes de marchandises appartenant à la catégorie «Classe 1 — explosifs» prévue par le Code maritime international des marchandises dangereuses[31].

La société demanda que le navire rallie le port de Burgas (Bulgarie) et commença le chargement de marchandises supplémentaires, parmi lesquelles des armes, des munitions et des pièces de rechange de nature militaire relevant de la catégorie IMCO 1.

Le manifeste de cargaison (la liste et le type des marchandises transportées) et les connaissements indiquaient que le chargement d'armes consistait en «équipements spéciaux» et que le port de déchargement était le port syrien de Tartous. Le navire quitta le port de Burgas avec l'ordre de rallier le port de Setúbal, au Portugal, pour y charger d'autres marchandises. Pour s'y rendre, en octobre 1991, le navire était sur le point de s'engager dans le Bosphore, arborant le pavillon international signalant qu'il transportait des marchandises dangereuses. Les autorités turques pensèrent que le chargement d'armes était destiné à Chypre, d'où il entrerait en contrebande en Turquie. Les gardes-côtes turcs montèrent à bord du navire et le capturèrent. Les parties à l'affaire partirent par la suite du principe que la capture du navire s'était produite dans les détroits, zone régie par la Convention de Montreux du 20 juillet 1936 sur le régime des détroits turcs[32].

Les autorités turques découvrirent le chargement d'armes et interrogè-

29. Voir notamment CEDH, 23 septembre 1982, *Sporrong et Lonroth c. Suède*, requête n°s 7151/75 et 7152/75. CEDH, 28 septembre 1995, *Scollo c. Italie*, requête n° 19133/91.
30. Requête n° 40998/98.
31. Code maritime international des marchandises dangereuses, OMI, résolution A716(17) (http://www.imo.org/Publications/IMDGCode/Pages/Default.aspx).
32. Société des Nations, *Recueil des traités*, vol. CLXXIII, p. 229.

rent le capitaine. Le capitaine, le second et l'opérateur radio du navire furent placés en garde à vue par les autorités turques.

La société requérante allègue que la saisie par les autorités turques du navire et de sa cargaison est constitutive d'une mesure injustifiée de réglementation de l'usage des biens au sens de l'article 1 du Protocole n° 1. Sur le fond, la Cour rappelle que cet article contient trois normes distinctes : la première énonce le principe du respect de la propriété ; la deuxième vise la privation de propriété et la soumet à certaines conditions ; quant à la troisième, elle reconnaît aux Etats le droit de réglementer l'usage des biens conformément à l'intérêt général, en mettant en vigueur les lois qu'ils jugent nécessaires pour atteindre ce but. Elle considère qu'il n'y a eu en l'espèce ni confiscation ni saisie puisque la société requérante a recouvré la possession du chargement après une immobilisation temporaire du navire. Etait donc en jeu la réglementation de l'usage de biens.

Dès lors, c'est le second alinéa de l'article 1 qui trouve à s'appliquer et en vertu duquel il convient de déterminer si l'atteinte au droit de propriété de la société requérante était compatible avec le droit que possèdent les Etats « de mettre en vigueur les lois qu'ils jugent nécessaires pour réglementer l'usage des biens conformément à l'intérêt général ».

Rappelant qu'il doit exister un rapport raisonnable de proportionnalité entre le but visé par un Etat et les moyens qu'il emploie à cette fin, la Cour rappelle qu'une mesure d'ingérence doit ménager un juste équilibre entre les exigences de l'intérêt général et les impératifs liés à la sauvegarde des droits fondamentaux. En tout état de cause, pour apprécier la proportionnalité de l'ingérence, la Cour doit examiner le degré de protection offert contre l'arbitraire par les procédures mises en œuvre en l'espèce et déterminer si une absence d'indemnisation se justifie sur le terrain de l'article 1 du Protocole n° 1. En l'occurrence, la capture du navire se fondait sur la crainte des autorités qu'il ne soit impliqué dans de la contrebande internationale d'armes : cette crainte a été rapidement dissipée.

Les autorités de poursuite ont quant à elle rappelé l'état de guerre subsistant entre la Turquie et Chypre, et la non-jouissance par le navire de la liberté de passage dans les détroits au sens de l'article 5 de la Convention de Montreux : cette affirmation a elle aussi été démentie.

C'est pourquoi la Cour estime que l'immobilisation du navire et de son chargement était arbitraire, rien ne permettant de soupçonner une contrebande d'armes ni n'habilitant à saisir le navire à raison de l'existence d'un état de guerre entre la Turquie et Chypre. Dès lors, la violation de l'article 1 du Protocole n°1 est caractérisée.

De manière générale, cette décision participe, certes indirectement, de la lutte contre la prolifération des armes de destruction massive, tout particulièrement par voie maritime. Du point de vue de la Cour, il s'agit ici de renforcer, à titre préventif, le régime de non-prolifération par l'universalisation et la mise en œuvre intégrale des traités et des accords internationaux pertinents.

SECTION 3 LA COUR EUROPÉENNE DES DROITS DE L'HOMME ET LES ATTEINTES AUX DROITS PROCÉDURAUX DANS LA LUTTE CONTRE LA CRIMINALITÉ EN MER

A côté des droits purement substantiels conférés aux individus, des garanties exclusivement procédurales, formelles, leur sont également reconnues par la Convention.

Ici s'exprime une véritable collaboration entre les droits, l'effectivité des droits substantiels ne pouvant se concevoir sans l'assurance du respect des droits procéduraux.

En matière de lutte contre la criminalité en mer, c'est la jurisprudence de la Cour qui, par une interprétation constructive, a permis d'encadrer l'action des Etats signataires dans le sens du respect strict de l'ensemble des droits procéduraux que la Convention garantit.

Ainsi, son article 5 permet notamment de contrôler les conditions de régularité d'une détention et, par conséquent, de protéger les personnes contre des arrestations et des détentions arbitraires.

Les Etats sont également tenus de fournir aux détenus un certain nombre de garanties procédurales; toute personne arrêtée doit notamment être informée dans le plus court délai des raisons de son arrestation et doit être aussitôt traduite devant un juge ou libérée en attendant son procès.

Par ailleurs, toute personne victime d'une arrestation ou d'une détention contraires aux droits garantis par l'article 5 a droit à une réparation (paragraphe 1).

Par ailleurs, une place doit être accordée à l'interdiction des expulsions collectives (Protocole n° 4, art. 4).

Au sens de la Cour, une expulsion collective est une mesure contraignant des étrangers, en tant que groupe, à quitter leur pays, sauf dans les cas où une telle mesure est prise à l'issue et sur la base d'un examen raisonnable et objectif de la situation particulière de chacun des étrangers qui forment le groupe.

En matière maritime, cette disposition concerne notamment le refoulement de migrants (paragraphe 2).

Paragraphe 1 Le droit à la liberté et à la sûreté (art. 5)[33]

Au titre des droits procéduraux garantis par la Convention, l'article 5, paragraphe 3, englobe plusieurs garanties essentielles pour faire de la privation de liberté l'exception et pour assurer le contrôle judiciaire des arrestations et des détentions[34]. L'obligation qu'énonce cet article comprend trois éléments : la qualité de la personne exerçant le contrôle ; le rôle de l'autorité judiciaire chargée de mettre un terme à la détention ; enfin, le délai dans lequel le contrôle doit s'exercer. La lutte contre la criminalité en mer regorge de décisions en la matière.

En réponse aux marées noires successivement provoquées par le *Torrey Canyon*, l'*Amoco Cadiz*, l'*Exxon Valdez*, l'*Erika* ou le *Prestige*, la prise de conscience de la communauté internationale va entraîner l'émergence progressive d'une réglementation conventionnelle exigeante, constitutive d'un corpus juridique conséquent en matière de lutte contre les pollutions marines[35]. En droit international comme au niveau interne, l'action du droit positif est marquée par une approche systématique et évolutive de la lutte contre la pollution par les hydrocarbures ; en matière civile, la reconnaissance du préjudice écologique par les juridictions françaises dans l'affaire *Erika* est à ce titre remarquable. De portée et d'autorité différentes, les conventions MARPOL de 1973[36] et

33. Extrait de l'article 5 :

> « Toute personne a droit à la liberté et à la sûreté. Nul ne peut être privé de sa liberté, sauf dans les cas suivants et selon les voies légales : *(a)* s'il est détenu régulièrement après condamnation par un tribunal compétent ; *(b)* s'il a fait l'objet d'une arrestation ou d'une détention régulières pour insoumission à une ordonnance rendue, conformément à la loi, par un tribunal ou en vue de garantir l'exécution d'une obligation prescrite par la loi ; *(c)* s'il a été arrêté et détenu en vue d'être conduit devant l'autorité judiciaire compétente, lorsqu'il y a des raisons plausibles de soupçonner qu'il a commis une infraction ou qu'il y a des motifs raisonnables de croire à la nécessité de l'empêcher de commettre une infraction ou de s'enfuir après l'accomplissement de celle-ci ; *(d)* s'il s'agit de la détention régulière d'un mineur, décidée pour son éducation surveillée ou de sa détention régulière, afin de le traduire devant l'autorité compétente ; *(e)* s'il s'agit de la détention régulière d'une personne susceptible de propager une maladie contagieuse, d'un aliéné, d'un alcoolique, d'un toxicomane ou d'un vagabond ; *(f)* s'il s'agit de l'arrestation ou de la détention régulières d'une personne pour l'empêcher de pénétrer irrégulièrement dans le territoire, ou contre laquelle une procédure d'expulsion ou d'extradition est en cours. »

34. B. Belda, *Les droits de l'homme des personnes privées de liberté*, contribution à l'étude du pouvoir normatif de la Cour européenne des droits de l'homme, coll. « Droit de la CEDH », Bruylant, 2010. M. Delmas-Marty, *Libertés et sûreté dans un monde dangereux*, Le Seuil, 2010.

35. Voir notamment l'annexe 1 de la Convention internationale pour la prévention de la pollution par les navires (dite « MARPOL »), Londres, 2 novembre 1973, puis Protocole modificatif du 17 février 1978, *Recueil des traités*, vol. 1790, annexe A, n° 22484.

36. Voir *supra*.

de Montego Bay constituent le socle international de la prévention des dommages de pollution. D'autres instruments complètent le dispositif international. Les règles de responsabilité pénale et civile qui organisent la sanction des auteurs de pollution marine et l'indemnisation de leurs victimes sont riches et donnent corps à un dispositif juridique contraignant assez impressionnant, notamment mis en œuvre dans le cadre de la convention CLC 1969[37]. Cependant cet arsenal juridique ne saurait permettre aux Etats de mettre en mouvement des textes ou des décisions qui méconnaîtraient les droits fondamentaux en général et le droit à la liberté et à la sûreté en particulier.

Notamment, dans l'arrêt du 28 septembre 2010, *Mangouras c. Espagne*[38], la Cour s'interroge, dans une affaire de répression de la pollution marine[39], sur la garantie assurant la comparution à l'audience d'un capitaine de navire et sur le montant de la caution fixée à son encontre.

Le requérant, de nationalité grecque, était en 2002 le capitaine du navire *Prestige* qui, alors qu'il naviguait près des côtes espagnoles, déversa dans l'océan Atlantique 70 000 tonnes du fuel qu'il transportait dans ses cuves en raison de l'ouverture d'une voie d'eau dans la coque du bateau. La perte de la cargaison provoqua une catastrophe écologique dont les effets sur la faune et la flore marines se prolongèrent durant plusieurs mois et se propagèrent jusqu'aux côtes françaises. Une enquête pénale fut ouverte et le juge d'instruction ordonna le placement du requérant en détention provisoire, avec libération subordonnée au versement d'une caution de 3 000 000 d'euros. L'accent fut mis sur l'attitude du requérant, qui pouvait donner matière à l'existence d'un délit contre les ressources naturelles et l'environnement, ainsi que d'un délit de désobéissance aux autorités administratives. La gravité de ces délits présumés et la nationalité étrangère du requérant justifiaient, de l'avis du juge, le montant élevé de la caution. Le requérant sollicita sa remise en liberté et l'abaissement de la caution à 60 000 euros. Tant son recours *de reforma* que son appel furent rejetés.

Sur le fondement de l'article 5, paragraphe 3, la Cour rappelle qu'une caution ne peut être exigée qu'aussi longtemps que prévalent des raisons justifiant la détention de l'intéressé, et que les autorités doivent consacrer autant de soin à fixer un cautionnement approprié qu'à décider si le maintien en détention d'une personne accusée demeure ou non indispensable. En outre, si son montant doit être apprécié par rapport à l'inté-

37. Convention sur la responsabilité civile pour les dommages dus à la pollution par les hydrocarbures, Bruxelles, 29 novembre 1969, *Recueil des traités*, vol. 973, n° 14097.

38. Requête n° 12050/04.

39. A. Boyle et M. Anderson, *Human Rights Approaches to Environmental Protection*, Oxford, Clarendon Press, 1996.

ressé et à ses ressources, il n'est toutefois pas toujours déraisonnable de prendre également en compte le préjudice imputé. Si en l'espèce le montant de la caution dépassait les ressources personnelles du requérant, les juridictions nationales entendaient prendre en compte, outre sa situation personnelle, la gravité du délit dont il était accusé.

La Cour doit dès lors examiner si pareille approche est conforme à l'article 5, paragraphe 3. Sur ce point, elle estime que de nouvelles réalités doivent être prises en compte dans l'interprétation des exigences de cet article, à savoir la préoccupation croissante à l'égard des délits contre l'environnement, ainsi qu'une tendance à recourir au droit pénal comme moyen de mise en œuvre des obligations environnementales imposées par le droit international et le droit européen. Rappelant qu'un niveau croissant de protection des droits de l'homme implique une fermeté accrue envers les atteintes aux valeurs fondamentales des sociétés démocratiques, elle considère qu'il n'est pas exclu que le milieu professionnel de l'activité en cause soit pris en considération pour déterminer le montant de la caution. Ainsi, la Cour estime ici que les tribunaux espagnols ont suffisamment tenu compte de la situation personnelle du requérant, en particulier de son statut d'employé de l'armateur, de ses liens professionnels avec les personnes appelées à servir de cautions, de sa nationalité et de son domicile ainsi que de son absence d'attaches en Espagne et de son âge, enfin — et surtout —, de la gravité des infractions en cause et de l'ampleur du préjudice imputé au requérant. Pour ces raisons, elle conclut à la non-violation de l'article 5, paragraphe 3.

En matière de lutte contre le trafic de stupéfiants, de nombreux Etats tirent profit de la Convention de Vienne du 20 décembre 1988, précitée[40], dont l'article 17 constitue la clé de voûte de la coopération entre Etats, déjà mentionnée à l'article 108 de la CNUDM. Si l'accord de l'Etat de pavillon pour arraisonner un navire suspecté de se livrer à un tel trafic est nécessaire et doit être formulé par la voie diplomatique, l'autorité judiciaire peut intervenir en aval de l'opération si l'Etat de pavillon renonce à sa compétence juridictionnelle.

Concernant la zone des Caraïbes l'accord dit « de San Jose »[41], adopté

---

40. Convention des Nations Unies contre le trafic illicite de stupéfiants et de substances psychotropes, Vienne, 20 décembre 1988, *Recueil des traités*, vol. 1582, p. 95.

41. Accord concernant la coopération en vue de la répression du trafic illicite maritime et aérien de stupéfiants et de substances psychotropes dans la région des Caraïbes, signé à San José le 10 avril 2003. Son apport principal réside dans les possibilités d'intervention ouvertes dans les eaux territoriales des Etats parties sur les navires soupçonnés de trafic de stupéfiants. Il renforce le dispositif de coopération mis en place par les différents Etats de la région, au premier rang desquels les Etats-Unis. Son champ d'application géographique, la région des Caraïbes, y est défini comme suit: « le Golfe du Mexique, la mer des Caraïbes et

en 2003 et entré en vigueur en 2008, constitue l'instrument international de coopération multilatérale le plus abouti. Selon cet accord et parmi les options offertes par son article 12.1, un Etat partie à l'accord doit toujours demander l'accord d'un autre pour arraisonner un navire se trouvant dans ses eaux territoriales. En revanche, un silence de quatre heures des autorités vaut autorisation pour arraisonner un navire se trouvant en haute mer.

Cette Convention ne néglige cependant pas le rôle de l'autorité judiciaire, les Etats parties ayant l'obligation d'établir leur compétence juridictionnelle à l'égard notamment des infractions commises dans leur mer territoriale. Sauf renonciation, c'est l'Etat de pavillon qui est compétent si le navire a été arraisonné en haute mer.

Ainsi, son arrêt «Medvedyev et autres c. France», rendu le 29 mars 2010[42], constitue une excellente illustration de ces questionnements. Les requérants, ressortissants ukrainiens, roumains, grecs et chiliens, étaient membres de l'équipage du *Winner*, cargo battant pavillon cambodgien. Dans le cadre de la coopération internationale contre le trafic de stupéfiants[43], les autorités françaises apprirent que ce navire était susceptible de transporter d'importantes quantités de drogue. Le Cambodge donna son accord à l'intervention des autorités françaises, qui procédèrent, le 13 juin 2002, à son interception en haute mer puis à son détournement vers Brest. Les requérants, placés sous le contrôle des forces militaires françaises, furent privés de leur liberté durant toute la traversée. Leur situation après l'arraisonnement constituait bien une privation de liberté au sens de l'article 5 de la Convention européenne des droits de l'homme. Après leur arrivée en France, les requérants furent placés en garde à vue le 26 juin 2002.

A noter que la Grande Chambre de la Cour européenne des droits de l'homme appelle les Etats à adapter la règle cardinale de la compétence de l'Etat du pavillon (le Cambodge en l'espèce) en haute mer à la lutte contre les stupéfiants. D'après la Cour,

> «au regard tant de la gravité que de l'ampleur du problème posé

---

l'océan Atlantique à l'ouest du méridien de longitude 45 degrés ouest, au nord de la latitude 0 (Equateur) et au sud de la latitude 30 degrés nord, à l'exception de la mer territoriale des Etats non parties au présent accord».

42. Requête n° 3394/03.

43. E. Errigo et I. Marinelli, «Il traffico internazionale via mare di armi e stupefacenti: profili giuridice e poteri degli stati», dans G. Reale (dir. publ.), *Il contrasto alle attività illecite in mare*, Naples, Edizioni Scientifiche Italiane, 2011, pp. 189-220. F. Schamp, «Commerce maritime illégal et criminalité: le commerce de la drogue», dans L. Le Hard (dir. publ.), *Criminalité et trafics maritimes: des enjeux politiques aux conséquences juridiques*, Namur, Presses universitaires de Namur, 2008, pp. 75-79. United Nations Office on Drugs and Crime, *Transnational Organized Crime in the Fishing Industry*, Vienne, UNODC, 2011.

> par le trafic de stupéfiants, une évolution du droit international public qui consacrerait le principe selon lequel tous les Etats auraient compétence par exception à la règle de l'Etat du pavillon constituerait une avancée significative dans la lutte contre cette activité illicite. Cela permettrait d'aligner le droit international relatif au trafic de stupéfiants sur ce qui existe déjà depuis longtemps en matière de piraterie.»

En l'espèce, dès lors que le Cambodge n'est pas partie à cette Convention, la CNUDM ne saurait fonder l'intervention des autorités françaises. Ainsi, dès lors que le *Winner* ne battait pas pavillon français et qu'aucun membre d'équipage n'était de nationalité française, la loi française n'avait normalement pas vocation à s'appliquer.

Cependant l'accord donné par le Cambodge pour l'intervention des autorités françaises, sous la forme d'une note verbale, constitue une source de droit international susceptible d'être qualifiée d'accord lorsqu'elle constate un consentement des autorités concernées. En l'espèce, si la note verbale constatait l'accord des autorités cambodgiennes pour l'interception du *Winner*, il n'est pas établi que la privation de liberté des membres de l'équipage avait fait l'objet d'un accord interétatique susceptible de représenter un droit «clairement défini» au sens de la jurisprudence de la Cour. La Cour estime, à la lumière du but et de l'objet de l'article 5, paragraphe 1, de la Convention, que la privation de liberté subie par les requérants, à partir de l'arraisonnement jusqu'à l'arrivée du navire à Brest, n'était pas régulière faute de base légale ayant les qualités requises pour satisfaire au principe général de sécurité juridique.

Sur le terrain de l'article 5, paragraphe 3, cette fois, il est acquis qu'une personne peut être privée de sa liberté dans trois cas: lorsqu'elle est soupçonnée d'avoir commis une infraction; lorsqu'il est nécessaire de l'empêcher d'en commettre une ou lorsqu'elle risque de s'enfuir après la commission de celle-ci. Cette mesure privative de liberté ne sera considérée comme compatible avec l'article 5, paragraphe 1, alinéa *c)*, que si elle est prise dans le but d'intenter des poursuites pénales contre l'intéressé. Telle est la conséquence du lien indissoluble entre les articles 5, paragraphe 5, alinéa *c)*, et 5, paragraphe 3, de la Convention: si le premier autorise la privation de liberté, le second prévoit que la personne concernée doit être «aussitôt traduite devant un juge ou un autre magistrat habilité par la loi à exercer des fonctions judiciaires et a le droit d'être jugée dans un délai raisonnable, ou libérée pendant la procédure».

Dans cet arrêt, la Cour reproche précisément à la France son absence de cadre légal pour les conditions de privation de liberté à bord des navires ainsi que le défaut d'intervention d'autorités judiciaires indépendantes. La simple information du procureur de la République a de ce point de vue été considérée comme une garantie insuffisante, ce magistrat ne bénéficiant pas de l'indépendance requise à l'égard de l'exécutif et ne pouvant dès lors être qualifié de «magistrat habilité par la loi à exercer des fonctions judiciaires» au sens de l'article 5, paragraphe 3.

En droit français, c'est à la suite de cette affaire que la loi du 5 janvier 2011 est venue corriger les lacunes de la loi de 1994 sur l'action de l'Etat en mer afin d'encadrer la période pendant laquelle la personne retenue à bord d'un navire fait l'objet de mesures restrictives ou privatives de liberté. Ainsi, avant l'expiration d'un délai de quarante-huit heures à compter de la mise en œuvre de ces mesures, le juge des libertés et de la détention, saisi par le procureur de la République, statue sur la prolongation éventuelle de ces mesures pour une durée maximale de cent vingt heures à compter de l'expiration du délai précédent, durée renouvelable. En outre, il peut solliciter du procureur de la République «tout élément de nature à apprécier la situation matérielle et l'état de santé de la personne qui fait l'objet d'une mesure de restriction ou de privation de liberté», ordonner un nouvel examen de santé et communiquer avec la personne. Il s'agit là d'une nouvelle intervention du juge national dans l'application du droit international.

En matière d'éloignement des migrants par voie maritime, l'arrêt *A. A. c. Grèce* du 22 juillet 2010[44] admet qu'un demandeur d'asile, migrant maritime, a été retenu illégalement et dans des conditions sordides dans un centre de rétention en Grèce[45]. Déjà évoqué à propos de l'article 3, cet arrêt posait également question concernant l'article 5 de la Convention européenne des droits de l'homme et les droits à la liberté et à la sûreté qu'il consacre. Pour mémoire, le requérant est un ressortissant palestinien résidant en Grèce. Fuyant le camp de réfugiés où il vivait au Liban, il fut placé en détention provisoire puis renvoyé vers son pays d'origine. Il dénonçait des conditions de détention sordides au centre de Samos. Ayant atteint la limite légale de détention de trois mois il fut enfin libéré. Par ailleurs, sa demande d'asile fut rejetée au motif qu'il n'avait pas prouvé le risque de poursuites à son égard dans son pays pour des raisons liées à la religion, la nationalité ou les convictions politiques.

La Cour relève que le requérant n'étant en possession d'aucun document d'identité, la mesure d'arrestation apparaissant dès lors nécessaire

44. Requête n° 12186/08.

45. L. Marzano, «La protection offerte par la Convention européenne des droits de l'homme aux demandeurs d'asile et aux réfugiés», *Revue universelle des droits de l'homme (RUDH)*, 2002, pp. 176 ss.

et raisonnable. La suspension de sa procédure d'expulsion ne pouvait, en vertu du droit grec, s'étendre automatiquement à sa détention. Or, précise la Cour, l'article 5, paragraphe 1, n'exige pas seulement qu'une privation de liberté respecte le droit national, mais qu'elle soit en outre conforme à la protection de l'individu contre l'arbitraire. Ainsi, une telle mesure peut être régulière selon la législation interne tout en étant arbitraire, donc contraire à la Convention. La Cour relève également que ce n'est qu'à la troisième tentative du requérant que sa demande d'asile a été enregistrée alors même que, en vertu de la loi, la procédure de renvoi devait être suspendue à partir de l'enregistrement de la demande d'asile. Or, en dépit de cette règle, le requérant a été maintenu en détention. Ainsi, au moins à partir de la date à laquelle sa demande d'asile a été enregistrée, et jusqu'à cette date, il a été privé de liberté sans base légale. En l'absence d'autres motifs sérieux pouvant justifier sa prolongation, la Cour considère que la détention du requérant postérieure à l'enregistrement de sa demande d'asile, qui plus est dans des conditions contraires à l'article 3, n'était pas nécessaire aux fins de l'objectif poursuivi. Elle conclut à la violation de l'article 5, paragraphe 1.

Paragraphe 2 **L'interdiction des expulsions collectives (Protocole nº 4, art. 4)**

Au sens de la Cour, «expulsion collective» désigne toute mesure contraignant des étrangers, en tant que groupe, à quitter leur pays, sauf dans les cas où une telle mesure est prise à l'issue et sur la base d'un examen raisonnable et objectif de la situation particulière de chacun des étrangers qui forment le groupe.

Déjà évoquée, l'affaire *Hirsi Jamaa et autres c. Italie* du 23 février 2012 concernait un groupe de migrants en provenance de Libye, arrêtés en mer puis reconduits en Libye par les autorités italiennes. Pour rappel, la Cour a considéré que les requérants relevaient de la juridiction de l'Italie au sens de l'article 1 de la Convention européenne des droits de l'homme car ils s'étaient trouvés sous le contrôle continu et exclusif, en droit et en fait, des autorités italiennes de leur montée à bord des navires militaires jusqu'à leur remise aux autorités libyennes.

Les notions de juridiction et d'expulsion sont étroitement liées au territoire national. Toutefois, là où la Cour reconnaît, comme en l'espèce, qu'un Etat a pu exceptionnellement exercer sa juridiction en dehors de son territoire national, il n'en demeure pas moins que l'exercice par un Etat d'une juridiction extraterritoriale peut être qualifiée d'expulsion collective. Par ailleurs, précise la Cour, la spécificité du contexte maritime ne saurait avoir pour effet de consacrer un espace de non-droit au sein duquel les individus ne relèveraient d'aucun régime juridique susceptible de leur accorder le bénéfice des droits et garanties prévus par la Convention. De ce point de vue, l'article 4 du Protocole n° 4 est ici applicable.

La Cour, pour la première fois dans cette espèce, est appelée à examiner l'applicabilité de cet article à un cas d'éloignement d'étrangers vers un Etat tiers effectué en dehors du territoire national, de sorte à déterminer si le transfert des requérants vers la Libye était susceptible de constituer une expulsion collective au sens de l'article considéré. Pour ce faire, la Cour observe tout d'abord que ni le texte de la Convention, ni ses travaux préparatoires ne s'opposent à une application extraterritoriale de l'article 4. Or, pour la Cour, en limiter l'application aux expulsions collectives effectuées à partir du territoire d'un Etat signataire priverait les migrants qui ne seraient pas parvenus à atteindre un Etat d'un examen de leur situation personnelle avant expulsion, au contraire des migrants par voie terrestre.

Au fond, il n'est pas contesté que le transfert des requérants en Libye a eu lieu sans examen des situations individuelles; aucune procédure d'identification n'a été menée par les autorités italiennes qui ont simplement embarqué puis débarqué les requérants en Libye. En ce sens, l'éloignement des requérants pris comme «groupe» a eu en l'espèce un caractère collectif contraire à l'article 4 du Protocole n° 4[46].

La Cour a également conclu à la double violation de l'article 13 («Droit à un recours effectif»)[47] combiné avec l'article 3 et de l'article 13 combiné avec l'article 4 du Protocole n° 4, les requérants n'ayant pas obtenu un examen rigoureux de leurs griefs par une autorité compétente. En l'espèce, les requérants alléguaient n'avoir reçu aucune information de la part des militaires italiens, qui leur auraient fait croire qu'ils étaient dirigés vers l'Italie et ne les auraient pas renseignés sur la procédure à suivre pour empêcher leur renvoi en Libye. Cette version des faits, si elle est contestée par le Gouvernement, est corroborée par de nombreux témoignages auxquels la Cour attache un poids particulier.

---

46. J.-Y. Carlier, «L'expulsion collective d'étrangers», dans Ch. Lambert et Ch. Pettiti (dir. publ.), *Les mesures relatives aux étrangers à l'épreuve de la Convention européenne des droits de l'homme*, Bruylant, 2003, pp. 11 ss. F. Julien-Laferrière, «L'éloignement du territoire», dans H. Fulchiron (dir. publ.), *Les étrangers et la Convention européenne de sauvegarde des droits de l'homme et des libertés fondamentales*, LGDJ, 1999, pp. 229 ss. D. Lochak, «Article 4 (Prot. n° 4)», dans L.-E. Pettiti, E. Decaux et P.-H. Imbert (dir. publ.), *La Convention européenne des droits de l'homme*, 2e éd., 1999, pp. 1057 ss.

47. Article 13 («Droit à un recours effectif»):

> «Toute personne dont les droits et libertés reconnus dans la présente Convention ont été violés, a droit à l'octroi d'un recours effectif devant une instance nationale, alors même que la violation aurait été commise par des personnes agissant dans l'exercice de leurs fonctions officielles.»

Elle réitère ici l'importance de garantir aux personnes concernées par une mesure d'éloignement, mesure dont les conséquences sont potentiellement irréversibles, le droit d'obtenir des informations suffisantes leur permettant d'avoir un accès effectif aux procédures et d'étayer leurs griefs. Les requérants ont ainsi été privés de toute voie de recours qui leur eût permis de soumettre à une autorité compétente leurs griefs tirés des articles 3 de la Convention et 4 du Protocole n° 4, et d'obtenir un contrôle attentif et rigoureux de leurs demandes avant que la mesure d'éloignement ne soit mise à exécution.

SECTION 4 **CONCLUSION**

Si la mise en place de normes internationales et internes opérationnelles tout comme le développement des réseaux de coopération permettent d'envisager une meilleure réponse judiciaire à la criminalité en mer, l'enrichissement constant de la jurisprudence de la Cour européenne des droits de l'homme permet d'exercer un contrôle a posteriori des décisions jurisprudentielles internes en particulier et des politiques pénales des Etats signataires en général, en cohérence avec les droits substantiels et procéduraux que la Convention européenne des droits de l'homme consacre et organise.

Il n'est pas question ici de suggérer que l'action de la Cour européenne des droits de l'homme viendrait ralentir ou freiner toute réponse pénale à la criminalité en mer; bien au contraire, en s'assurant de leur conformité aux garanties fondamentales que la Convention européenne des droits de l'homme a mis en mouvement depuis 1950, la jurisprudence de la Cour participe activement et de manière convaincante à la lutte contre les activités criminelles en mer, considérées au sens large.

S'assurer de la cohérence de politiques pénales avec le respect des droits de l'homme n'est pas assurément un acte de censure, mais un acte d'accompagnement et, mieux, de consolidation.

QUATRIÈME PARTIE

PART IV

Pénalisation internationale

International Criminalization

13 La pénalisation de la prolifération maritime des armes de destruction massive

Hamza Cherief*

SECTION 1 INTRODUCTION

La non-prolifération des armes nucléaires désigne la volonté d'empêcher «la dissémination de matières, de technologies et de savoir-faire permettant de fabriquer une arme nucléaire»[1]. Elle constitue, sans doute, la façade la plus médiatique des politiques de non-prolifération dont l'objet dépasse toutefois les seules armes atomiques. Les armes chimiques et bactériologiques sont également visées par ces politiques, de même que leurs vecteurs, notamment missiliers, et le matériel nécessaire à leur fabrication, leur entretien et leur fonctionnement. Le concept d'armes de destruction massive (ADM) recouvre à la fois les armes nucléaires, les armes chimiques et les armes bactériologiques (biologiques). Comme le souligne Serge Sur, la définition de la notion d'ADM demeure problématique. Ces dernières sont davantage «nommées» que définies[2], et la liste établie n'est pas exempte de critiques. «Sans doutes les armes radiologiques ou les moyens de modification de l'environnement à des fins hostiles pourraient facilement être inclus», écrit ainsi Jean Salmon, «alors que les armes chimiques ne sont probablement pas nécessairement des armes de destructions massives.»[3] Le

* Docteur en droit international public. Chercheur associé au Centre de recherche en droit et en science politique (CREDESPO), Université de Bourgogne. Chercheur associé (2008-2011) pour le projet «Priv-War» de la Commission européenne. Assistant-ingénieur au Centre de recherche sur le droit des marchés et des investissements internationaux (CREDIMI), Université de Bourgogne.

1. M.-H. Labbe, «La non-prolifération nucléaire», dans T. de Montbrial et J. Klein (dir. publ.), *Dictionnaire de stratégie*, Paris, PUF, 2007, p. 370. La contre-prolifération désignerait, pour sa part, «l'ensemble des moyens actifs (embargo, coercition, etc.) que certaines puissances nucléaires, notamment les Etats-Unis, entendent utiliser pour lutter contre la prolifération». J. Salmon, *Dictionnaire de droit international public*, Bruxelles, Bruylant, 2001, p. 750.

2. S. Sur, «La résolution 1540 du Conseil de sécurité (28 avril 2004): entre la prolifération des armes de destruction massive, le terrorisme et les acteurs non étatiques», *RGDIP*, 2004, p. 870.

3. J. Salmon, *op. cit.*, p. 84.

concept d'ADM n'est donc pas univoque. Il recouvre un ensemble d'armes distinctes, tant par leur nature et par leurs effets[4] que par leurs implications juridiques et stratégiques.

Les armes chimiques «consistent en agents létaux incapacitants ou irritants» et se «caractérisent par le fait qu'elles n'affectent que la matière vivante: hommes, animaux ou plantes»[5]. L'état du droit positif applicable à ces armes a été unifié et lissé par la Convention de Paris du 13 janvier 1993 sur l'interdiction de la mise au point, de la fabrication, du stockage et de l'emploi des armes chimiques et sur leur destruction. Outre que leur interdiction est une règle coutumière, applicable dans les conflits armés internationaux et non internationaux, la Convention de Paris souligne, à son article premier, que «chaque Etat partie ... s'engage à ne jamais, en aucune circonstance ..., employer d'armes chimiques». Le caractère absolu de cette interdiction est renforcé par le fait que l'article 22 de la Convention exclut toute forme de réserve. Les Etats ratifiant la Convention de Paris ne peuvent donc, à l'inverse de ce que permettent les dispositions du Protocole de Genève concernant la prohibition d'emploi à la guerre de gaz asphyxiants, toxiques ou similaires et de moyens bactériologiques du 17 juin 1925, «recourir à l'arme chimique en second, c'est à dire riposter avec des armes chimiques contre un adversaire qui en utiliserait en premier»[6].

Les armes bactériologiques ne portent également atteinte qu'à la matière vivante et «sont constituées d'organismes vivants susceptibles de se reproduire et de libérer des toxines attaquant les hommes, les plantes et les animaux»[7]. L'interdiction d'employer des armes bactériologiques est d'origine coutumière, elle s'applique tant aux conflits internationaux qu'aux conflits non internationaux. Elle est renforcée par la Convention de Londres, Moscou et Washington du 10 avril 1972 sur l'interdiction de la mise au point, de la fabrication et du stockage des armes bactériologiques (biologiques) ou à toxines et sur leur destruction. Les armes bactériologiques sont très rarement employées et ce, malgré l'existence avérée de programmes de fabrication d'armes biologiques en URSS et en Irak dans les années soixante-dix et quatre-vingt. De la

4. «Bien que [les armes chimiques et biologiques] soient différentes des armes nucléaires par leur nature et leurs effets, elles leur sont associées dans l'appellation «armes de destruction massive», écrit ainsi Hauman Yaakoubi («Armes chimiques et biologiques», dans T. de Montbrial et J. Klein, *op. cit.*, p. 49).

5. E. David, *Principes de droit des conflits armés*, Bruxelles, Bruylant, 2008, 4e éd., p. 374, par. 2.157.

6. E. David, *op. cit.*, p. 376, par. 2.160. Si le texte de 1993, à la différence de celui de 1925, interdit la mise au point, la fabrication, la détention, le transfert ou l'emploi d'armes chimiques, l'articulation des deux textes ne va pas sans soulever un certain nombre de difficultés.

7. *Ibid.*, p. 383, par. 2.176.

même manière, si le régime syrien a été fortement soupçonné de recourir à une arme chimique le 23 décembre 2012 dans la ville de Homs[8], les condamnations se sont fait entendre y compris parmi ses soutiens. Les protestations du Gouvernement russe en témoignent.

Les armes nucléaires désignent, de manière générale, «tout dispositif susceptible de libérer de l'énergie nucléaire d'une façon incontrôlée et qui possède un ensemble de caractéristiques propres à l'emploi à des fins belliqueuses»[9]. Pour la Cour internationale de Justice (CIJ),

> «les armes nucléaires sont des engins explosifs dont l'énergie procède de la fusion ou de la fission de l'atome. Par sa nature même, ce processus ... libère non seulement d'énormes quantités de chaleur et d'énergie, mais aussi un rayonnement puissant et prolongé.»[10]

En matière nucléaire, les objectifs de non-prolifération sont plus complexes et davantage conflictuels que pour les armes chimiques ou bactériologiques. La non-prolifération des armes nucléaires correspond, sans aucun doute, à une volonté de protéger la paix et la sécurité internationales en réduisant les possibilités d'usage d'armes au très fort potentiel de destruction. Toutefois, comme le rappelle Gérard Chaliand, la non-prolifération «vise [également] à retarder le plus possible la sanctuarisation des puissances moyennes, surtout quand elles sont hostiles ... Pour le plus puissant, il s'agit de conserver la capacité de contraindre le faible.»[11] Elle est, en d'autres termes, traversée et modelée par des affrontements stratégiques intenses et la recherche d'intérêts aussi multiples que contradictoires. Ceux-ci sont d'autant plus violents que l'enjeu nucléaire, de par le pouvoir de destruction des armes concernées, est réellement vital pour les Etats et pour les peuples.

L'expression de ces intérêts stratégiques est favorisée par les ambiguïtés qui caractérisent le cadre juridique au sein duquel s'inscrivent les stratégies de dissuasion nucléaire[12]. La CIJ n'a, en effet, pas pu se prononcer clairement sur la légalité de ces dernières dans son avis consul-

---

8. «Soupçons d'emploi d'une arme chimique à Homs en Syrie» (lefigaro.fr, 19 janvier 2013).

9. J. Salmon, *op. cit.*, p. 87.

10. CIJ, 8 juillet 1996, *Licéité de la menace ou de l'emploi d'armes nucléaires*, avis consultatif, par. 35.

11. G. Chaliand, «La guerre psychologique est perdue», dans G. Chaliand (dir. publ.), *Guérillas. Du Vietnam à l'Irak*, Paris, Hachette, 2008, p. 583.

12. La dissuasion nucléaire désigne une pratique stratégique dont le but est

> «de détourner un candidat-agresseur d'agir militairement en le menaçant de représailles nucléaires calculées de telle sorte que leurs effets physiques probables constituent, à ses yeux, un risque inacceptable eu égard aux finalités politiques motivant son initiative» (G. Chaliand et A. Blin, *Dictionnaire de stratégie militaire*, Paris, Perrin, 1998, p. 181).

tatif rendu, le 8 juillet 1996, sur la *Licéité de la menace ou de l'emploi d'armes nucléaires*. Si, pour la Cour,

> «il ressort … que la menace ou l'emploi d'armes nucléaires serait généralement contraire aux règles du droit international applicable dans les conflits armés, et spécialement aux principes et règles du droit humanitaire, [elle ne peut] au vu de l'état actuel du droit international, ainsi que des éléments de fait dont elle dispose, … conclure de façon définitive que la menace ou l'emploi d'armes nucléaires serait licite ou illicite dans une circonstance extrême de légitime défense dans laquelle la survie même d'un Etat serait en cause.» [13]

La position ambiguë de la Cour affermit le cadre stratégique au sein duquel la dissuasion nucléaire est inscrite. La CIJ consacre et explicite en effet le consensus sans lequel aucune stratégie de dissuasion n'est envisageable: la guerre nucléaire est irrationnelle et doit être évitée. Ainsi que le note le général Lucien Poirier, «la crédibilité de la [stratégie de dissuasion] suppose le consensus au moins implicite des adversaires-partenaires sur la règle incontournable, l'axiome qui la fonde — l'irrationalité politique de la guerre nucléaire paroxystique» [14]. Or, la Cour confirme ce fait en reconnaissant que l'emploi de l'arme nucléaire viole les règles du droit international public en général et celles du droit international humanitaire en particulier. Dans le même temps, elle consolide la structure des rapports impliqués par une stratégie de dissuasion. Outre qu'elle refuse de se prononcer sur la légalité des stratégies de dissuasion, alors même qu'elle considère que l'emploi de l'arme atomique est «généralement» contraire aux règles du droit international, les imprécisions de sa décision préservent les espaces d'ambiguïté nécessaires à une pratique optimale de la dissuasion nucléaire [15]. Qui décidera

13. CIJ, *Licéité de la menace ou de l'emploi d'armes nucléaires, op. cit.*, par. 105, al. 2. Cette solution s'explique, notamment, par le fait que la Cour ne pouvait «ignorer la pratique dénommée «politique de dissuasion» à laquelle une partie appréciable de la communauté internationale a adhéré pendant des années» (*ibid.*, par. 96).

14. L. Poirier, *Stratégie théorique*, Paris, Economica, 1997, p. 271.

15. L'efficacité de la dissuasion nucléaire repose, en effet, largement sur la perception qu'en aura l'agresseur potentiel. Cette perception dépendra, dans une large mesure, de l'image que lui renverra le dissuadeur. Pour cette raison, la dissuasion repose sur un rapport complexe de certitudes et d'ambiguïtés. Le dissuadeur tiendra, en effet, à entretenir un flou sur le moment critique d'emploi de l'arme nucléaire dont il aura soin de dissimuler les caractéristiques essentielles. Cette incertitude doit pousser l'agresseur potentiel à un surcroît de prudence. Ce facteur d'ambiguïté ne doit pas être trop excessif pour ne pas qu'il y ait une incompréhension totale. Néanmoins, il doit être suffisant afin que l'agresseur, tout en sachant que le dissuadeur possède les moyens de le frapper de manière efficace, ne puisse déterminer avec certitude le moment réel du déclenchement

de la gravité d'une agression mettant en cause la « survie de l'Etat » ? Que signifie, du point de vue juridique, la « survie de l'Etat » ?

A ce titre, les difficultés à établir l'emploi d'armes nucléaires, dans le cadre de stratégies de dissuasion, comme fait internationalement illicite susceptible d'engager la responsabilité internationale de l'Etat, tranchent avec la consécration progressive de la prolifération des armes de destruction massive en infraction du droit international pénal. Les normes du droit international ont, en effet, établi les fondements nécessaires à l'émergence d'une nouvelle infraction internationale, l'infraction de prolifération. La résolution 1540, adoptée par le Conseil de sécurité le 28 avril 2004, se donne ainsi pour objectif de prévenir « la prolifération des armes nucléaires, chimiques et biologiques et de leurs vecteurs » que le Conseil assimile à « une menace pour la paix et la sécurité internationales ». Pour ce faire, le Conseil de sécurité impose notamment aux Etats d'« adopter et appliquer, conformément à leurs procédures internes, une législation appropriée et efficace interdisant ... de fabriquer, se procurer, mettre au point, posséder, transporter, transférer ou d'utiliser des armes nucléaires, chimiques ou biologiques ou leurs vecteurs ». Il s'agit donc, pour les Etats, d'assurer dans leurs ordres juridiques respectifs la répression de l'infraction de prolifération d'ADM définie par le droit international.

La mise en place d'un cadre, général, de lutte contre la prolifération des ADM par le Conseil de sécurité s'est accompagnée de l'élaboration d'un ensemble normatif prenant en compte la dimension spécifiquement maritime de cette prolifération. Il s'agissait alors, pour le droit international, d'affiner la répression et de « saisir » une activité, la prolifération, dans un contexte particulier, celui des espaces maritimes. Lieu de passage, ces espaces sont en effet, par leur immensité et l'intensité de l'activité commerciale qui les caractérise, propices au fleurissement de toutes sortes de trafic. L'émergence de la prolifération maritime au sein des préoccupations juridiques et stratégiques constitue, pour la doctrine, l'une des conséquences directes des actes terroristes du 11 septembre 2001. Ainsi que le rappelle T. L. McDorman, « the events of September 11, 2001 have led to significant attention being given to terrorism in international law, and this has included terrorism involving commercial vessels »[16]. En réalité, cette émergence paraît découler de la conjonction

du feu nucléaire. C'est dans ce délicat équilibre que réside toute la dangerosité du « jeu » de la dissuasion nucléaire. Ce dernier a été, paradoxalement, consacré par les règles du droit international public.

16. T. L. McDorman, « Maritime Terrorism and the International Law of Boarding of Vessels at Sea : A Brief Assessment of the New Developments », dans D. D. Cameron et H. N. Scheiber (dir. publ.), *The Ocean in the Nuclear Age. Legacies and Risk*, Leyde, Martinus Nijhoff Publishers, 2010, p. 239.

des événements du 11 septembre 2001 et de l'arraisonnement du *So San* et, un an plus tard, du *BBC China*.

Le *So San*, navire civil battant pavillon cambodgien, mais dont l'équipage était nord-coréen, a été intercepté le 9 décembre 2002 par la frégate espagnole *Navarra* dans le cadre de l'opération Enduring Freedom transportant quinze missiles Scud ainsi que des produits chimiques [17] en provenance de la Corée du Nord et à destination du Yémen. En octobre 2003, le navire cargo *BBC China*, navire sous pavillon allemand, est intercepté alors qu'il transportait des éléments de centrifugeuses, susceptibles de servir à l'enrichissement de l'uranium, en provenance de Malaisie et à destination de la Libye. L'arraisonnement de ces deux navires a vraisemblablement conduit à l'élaboration du protocole du 14 octobre 2005 (ci-après le protocole de 2005) à la Convention pour la répression d'actes illicites contre la sécurité de la navigation maritime du 10 mars 1988 (ci-après la Convention de 1988), dont les dispositions viennent consacrer la prise en compte de la dimension maritime de la prolifération des ADM. L'épisode du *So San* ainsi que celui du *BBC China* ont mis en lumière non seulement l'existence d'une prolifération par voie marine, mais également l'implication des navires civils dans ces comportements proliférants. De la même manière, la découverte, en 2003, du réseau dirigé par le docteur Abdul Qader Khan, réseau privé proposant « principalement à ses clients des solutions complètes dans le domaine de l'enrichissement de l'uranium » [18], a eu pour conséquence d'attirer l'attention des Etats sur le rôle joué par des acteurs non étatiques dans le domaine de la prolifération des ADM [19].

Le protocole de 2005, qui est entré en vigueur en 2010, reste d'une applicabilité très limitée. Aucune puissance nucléaire n'a, en particulier, ratifié ce texte. La lutte contre la prolifération maritime des ADM est, en conséquence, également encadrée par les dispositions de la résolution 1540 et par les règles classiques du droit de la mer avec lesquelles elles sont susceptibles d'entrer en contradiction. Tant la résolution 1540 que le protocole de 2005 constituent un prolongement novateur du système établi par le Traité sur la non-prolifération des armes nucléaires (TNP) du 1er juillet 1968. A la différence du TNP, ces deux textes visent, en effet, non pas le comportement des Etats, mais celui des « acteurs non

17. D. Guilfoyle, « The Proliferation Security Initiative: Interdicting Vessels in International Waters to Prevent the Spread of Weapons of Mass Destruction ? », *Melbourn University Law Review*, 2005, pp. 735-736.

18. Rapport relatif à la lutte contre la prolifération des armes de destruction massive et de leurs vecteurs par M. Michel Voisin, Assemblée nationale, 28 septembre 2010, p. 14.

19. « La découverte de l'étendue du réseau de Khan a constitué un choc pour la communauté internationale ... Perçu comme un facteur de paix, le commerce international devenait le terreau favorable des proliférations. » (*Ibid.*, p. 15.)

étatiques», en ce qui concerne la résolution 1540, et celui des «personnes» pour le protocole de 2005. A ce titre, il convient de préciser le champ d'application des textes assurant la pénalisation de la prolifération maritime des armes de destruction massive, tant du point de vue *rationae personae* que du point de vue *rationae materiae* (section 2).

Outre cette différence tenant au champ d'application, les textes assurant la pénalisation de la prolifération maritime des ADM se distinguent du TNP par leur objet particulier. La non-prolifération se rattache traditionnellement au désarmement, lequel désigne un «processus visant ... à une diminution du niveau d'armement existant»[20]. Cependant la résolution 1540 et le protocole de 2005 constituent des textes de droit international pénal incriminant les comportements proliférants. Ce faisant, ils déplacent les tensions classiques qui caractérisent les grandes conventions de désarmement en matière de procédure de contrôle[21] sur le terrain de la coopération pénale, c'est-à-dire sur celui de l'établissement de la compétence des Etats vis-à-vis des auteurs de l'infraction de prolifération (section 3).

Les enjeux stratégiques propres à l'arme nucléaire vont peser lourdement sur la mise en œuvre des textes incriminant la prolifération maritime des ADM, limitant ainsi leur effectivité. Les discussions et les négociations qui ont précédé l'adoption de la résolution 1540 «font apparaître que les Etats se sont surtout attachés aux armes nucléaires»[22].

A ce titre, les équivoques qui caractérisent la lutte contre la prolifération étatique des armes nucléaires caractérisent également le régime juridique de la lutte contre la prolifération maritime des ADM (section 4).

«Derrière les acteurs non étatiques, relève Serge Sur, ce sont les Etats qui sont visés»[23] et, plus précisément, la capacité à accéder au feu nucléaire que ces mêmes Etats entendent conserver.

---

20. J. Salmon, *op. cit.*, p. 237.

21. Serge Sur reconnaît ainsi que, en matière de désarmement, la «question du contrôle international anciennement et généralement posée ... revêt ... une acuité et des caractéristiques particulières». Il en reconnaît les limites intrinsèques: «des procédures internationales aussi intrusives soient-elles, conduites à l'encontre d'instances étatiques dont l'opacité en matière d'activités de sécurité et de défense est la règle, ne sauraient tout mettre à jour» (S. Sur, «Vérification en matière de désarmement», *Recueil des cours*, tome 293 (1998), pp. 35 et 101). Les procédures de vérifications en matière de désarmement peuvent, par ailleurs, être la source de tensions diplomatiques considérables. Le cas de la crise nucléaire iranienne en témoigne.

22. S. Sur, «La résolution 1540 du Conseil de sécurité (28 avril 2004)», *op. cit.*, p. 871.

23. *Ibid.*, p. 870.

SECTION 2 LE CHAMP D'APPLICATION DES NORMES RELATIVES À LA PROLIFÉRATION MARITIME DES ARMES DE DESTRUCTION MASSIVE

Le processus de pénalisation de la prolifération des ADM se structure autour d'une double extension du concept de prolifération consacrée par le droit international. Le concept de prolifération, qui visait d'abord les armes nucléaires, s'est progressivement étendu à la « prolifération des armes bactériologiques, biologiques, chimiques, voire des missiles »[24]. A la faveur de cette première extension, ce concept a, d'autre part, progressivement évolué *rationae personae*. Il a ainsi progressivement inclus les comportements des acteurs non étatiques à la faveur du développement du cadre juridique de la lutte contre le terrorisme (paragraphe 1). Du point de vue *rationae materiae*, la lutte contre la prolifération des armes de destruction massive dépasse le strict cadre de la lutte contre le terrorisme et vise à incriminer les comportements proliférants en tant que tels (paragraphe 2). Cette double extension, portée initialement par la résolution 1540 du Conseil de sécurité, caractérise également le protocole de 2005. Elle concerne donc l'ensemble du régime juridique applicable à la lutte contre la prolifération maritime des ADM.

Paragraphe 1 Le champ d'application *rationae personae* de la lutte contre la prolifération maritime des armes de destruction massive

La prolifération d'armes de destruction massive désigne initialement la prolifération étatique. L'architecture normative de la lutte contre la prolifération nucléaire, dont le TNP constitue la clé de voûte, établit une série d'obligations qui pèsent exclusivement sur les Etats. De manière très caractéristique, l'article premier du TNP souligne que « tout Etat doté d'armes nucléaires qui est partie au Traité s'engage ... à n'aider, n'encourager ni inciter d'aucune façon un Etat non doté d'armes nucléaires, quel qu'il soit, à fabriquer ou acquérir de quelque autre manière des armes nucléaires ». La non-prolifération, dans sa dimension nucléaire, est donc traditionnellement rapportée à la figure étatique.

Il convient de relever que le lien avec les acteurs non étatiques a été établi nettement plus tôt en ce qui concerne les armes chimiques[25], sans être toutefois adossé au concept de prolifération.

---

24. J. Salmon, *op. cit.*, p. 892.

25. La Convention de Paris sur l'interdiction des armes chimiques impose ainsi aux Etats d'incriminer les actes prohibés par la Convention : mettre au point, fabriquer, acquérir, stocker, transférer, employer des armes chimiques ou

La résolution 1540 constitue, de ce point de vue, une innovation eu égard aux instruments internationaux de lutte contre la prolifération des armes nucléaires[26]. Traduisant en termes juridiques l'orientation initiée dès 1999 par le concept stratégique de l'OTAN[27], elle associe le phénomène de la prolifération des ADM aux acteurs non étatiques. La résolution 1540 souligne ainsi que les « Etats doivent s'abstenir d'apporter un appui, quelle qu'en soit la forme, à des acteurs non étatiques » et « doivent prendre et appliquer » des dispositions juridiques « interdisant à tout acteur non étatique » les comportements proliférants. Par acteurs non étatiques, la résolution 1540 semble désigner toute « personne ou entité qui, n'agissant pas sous l'autorité légale d'un Etat, mène des activités tombant sous le coup de la présente résolution »[28]. Le lien entre prolifération des ADM et acteurs non étatiques a été opéré par le Conseil de sécurité à la faveur de l'élaboration du cadre juridique de la lutte contre le terrorisme.

La cristallisation d'un corps de règles juridiques visant à criminaliser la prolifération d'ADM émanant d'acteurs non étatiques trouve d'abord son origine dans les attentats du 11 septembre 2001. Ces derniers ne constituent, certes, pas une rupture stratégique au sens où ils n'ont pas entraîné « de redistribution de la puissance au sein du système international »[29]. Toutefois, leur portée psychologique a été sans commune mesure avec cette moindre importance sur le plan stratégique. Ils ont, en particulier, eu pour effet de placer le terrorisme au centre des préoccu-

---

favoriser ces comportements. Cela s'est traduit par l'apparition, dans les ordres juridiques internes des Etats, d'incriminations correspondant aux comportements prohibés par la Convention. Ces dispositions se caractérisent par la mise en œuvre d'une compétence limitée. Les Etats ne peuvent, en effet, réprimer les faits que lorsqu'ils sont commis par des personnes se trouvant sous leur juridiction, soit par des personnes physiques possédant la nationalité de ces Etats lorsqu'elles se trouvent à l'étranger.

26. Cette analyse est confirmée par Daniel H. Joyner pour qui

> « at the international level there is no substantive restriction on private parties, including business entities as well as other non-state actors, engaging in any of these activities. The utility of Resolution 1540 in addressing this non-state actor gap in the non-proliferation treaties and regimes system was noted by numerous states, particularly in the context of international effort to combat the phenomenon of terrorism. » (D. H. Joyner, « The Security Council As Legal Hegemon », *Georgetown Journal of International Law*, 2012, vol. 43, p. 228.)

27. Sur ce point, voir D. Momtaz, « Le pavillon en temps de crise. Le pavillon dans l'engrenage de la lutte contre la prolifération des armes de destruction massive », *Le pavillon : actes écrits du colloque organisé les 2 et 3 mars 2007*, Paris, Pedone, 2008, p. 29.

28. S. Sur, « La résolution 1540 du Conseil de sécurité (28 avril 2004) », *op. cit.*, p. 869.

29. A. Baconnet, « 1989, dernière rupture du système international », www.diploweb.com, 1er novembre 2010.

pations de la société internationale. Le processus de pénalisation de la prolifération des ADM, initiée par la résolution 1540, correspond notamment à une volonté de prévenir l'acquisition de ces armes par des organisations terroristes. Ainsi, la résolution 1540 témoigne du fait que le Conseil de sécurité est «gravement préoccupé par la menace du terrorisme et par le risque de voir des acteurs non étatiques ... se procurer des armes nucléaires, chimiques ou biologiques ou leurs vecteurs, en mettre au point, se livrer à leur trafic ou en faire usage».

Cette extension, sur le plan du droit, de la notion de prolifération aux acteurs non étatiques dans le cadre de la lutte contre le terrorisme a été consacrée par deux conventions. En premier lieu, la Convention internationale pour la répression des actes de terrorisme nucléaire du 14 septembre 2005 incrimine, en tant qu'acte de terrorisme, la «prolifération violente». Constitue en effet une infraction au sens de la Convention le fait pour toute personne d'«exiger illicitement et intentionnellement la remise de matières ou engins radioactifs ou d'installations nucléaires en recourant à la menace, dans des circonstances qui la rendent crédible, ou à l'emploi de la force». La formulation large de l'article 2, paragraphe 2 *b)*, permet d'incriminer un tel comportement commis à l'encontre d'un Etat ou d'individus. Le champ d'application de la Convention n'exclut a priori pas les comportements terroristes commis en milieu maritime, mais elle ne s'attache pas spécifiquement à les prendre en compte. Le fait d'intercepter un navire afin de s'approprier, par la contrainte, «matières ou engins radioactifs ou installations nucléaires» est donc susceptible de constituer un acte de terrorisme au sens de l'article 2, paragraphe 2 *b)*, sous réserve que cette intervention ne soit pas couverte par les termes du paragraphe 2 de l'article 4[30]. Il s'agit alors d'assimiler une forme bien spécifique de prolifération maritime, forme impliquant un acte de prédation violent, au terrorisme.

30. Aux fins de l'article 4 ne seront pas considérés comme des actes de terrorisme

> «les activités des forces armées en période de conflit armé, au sens donné à ces termes en droit international humanitaire, qui sont régies par ce droit, ne sont pas régies par la présente Convention, et les activités accomplies par les forces armées d'un Etat dans l'exercice de leurs fonctions officielles, en tant qu'elles sont régies par d'autres règles de droit international, ne sont pas régies non plus par la présente Convention» (art. 4, par. 2).

De manière plus générale, l'article 4, paragraphe 1, précise qu'«aucune disposition de la présente Convention ne modifie les autres droits, obligations et responsabilités qui découlent pour les Etats et les individus du droit international, en particulier des buts et principes de la Charte des Nations Unies et du droit international humanitaire». Ainsi, l'interception d'un navire lors d'une opération de lutte contre la prolifération ou de lutte contre le terrorisme n'est pas susceptible d'être qualifiée d'acte de terrorisme pour autant qu'elle soit régie par les règles du droit international applicables en la matière.

En second lieu, le protocole de 2005 se rattache, dès son préambule, au cadre de la lutte contre le terrorisme en l'inscrivant, cette fois, dans une dimension spécifiquement maritime eu égard à l'objet du protocole. Les Etats parties reconnaissent ainsi que « les actes terroristes constituent une menace pour la paix et la sécurité internationales » et inscrivent le protocole dans la continuité des résolutions 49/60 du 9 décembre 1994 et 51/210 du 16 janvier 1997 de l'Assemblée générale des Nations Unies (AGNU) condamnant le recours au terrorisme et réaffirmant la nécessité de lutter contre ce dernier. Le protocole de 2005 rappelle en outre que « la résolution 1540 (2004) du Conseil de sécurité des Nations Unies ... reconnaît qu'il est nécessaire que tous les Etats prennent d'urgence des mesures effectives supplémentaires pour empêcher la prolifération des armes nucléaires, chimiques et biologiques et de leurs vecteurs ». Tout comme la Convention internationale pour la répression des actes de terrorisme nucléaire, le protocole de 2005 ne vise pas les Etats. Aux termes de l'article 4, paragraphe 5, ce sont les « personnes » qui sont susceptibles de commettre une infraction. A la différence de la résolution 1540, ces deux textes concernent les « personnes » et non pas les « acteurs non étatiques ». Ainsi, tant le protocole de 2005 que la Convention internationale pour la répression des actes de terrorisme nucléaire sont susceptibles d'inclure les individus en tant qu'agents de l'Etat. La notion de « personne » semble, en effet, a priori plus large que celle d'« acteur non étatique » qui exclut tout lien avec l'Etat.

Bien que le terrorisme ait servi de catalyseur à la solidification du lien entre prolifération et acteurs non étatiques, la lutte contre la prolifération maritime des ADM ne se limite pas à la lutte contre le terrorisme.

Paragraphe 2 **Le champ d'application *rationae materiae* de la lutte contre la prolifération maritime des armes de destruction massive**

Si elle accorde une place importante au terrorisme, la résolution 1540 ne limite pas la lutte contre la prolifération maritime des ADM à cette seule activité. En réalité, elle prohibe une prolifération qui peut servir « en particulier » à des fins terroristes. La lutte contre la prolifération des ADM, notamment dans le cadre de sa dimension maritime, ne s'épuise donc pas dans la lutte contre le terrorisme[31]. De fait, sur le

31. Déplorant que « seuls les actes motivés par une intention terroriste sont érigés en infraction », le Comité 1540 souligne dans son rapport 2011 que la résolution 1540 (2004) ne vise pas les seuls actes inspirés par une intention terroriste » (Rapport du Comité 1540, Conseil de sécurité, 12 septembre 2011, par. 35). Le Comité 1540 a été créé par la résolution 1540 (2004). Il a pour mission de « aider le Conseil de sécurité à contrôler l'application de la résolution en

plan stratégique, le terrorisme se caractérise par un emploi extrêmement limité d'ADM. Les attentats du 11 septembre 2001 sont une action terroriste «conventionnelle», au sens où elle n'implique pas l'utilisation d'armes nucléaires, chimiques ou bactériologiques. En réalité, deux actions terroristes émanant d'acteurs non étatiques utilisant des armes chimiques et bactériologiques sont principalement à relever. Il s'agit, en premier lieu, de l'attentat au gaz sarin dans le métro de Tokyo par Aum Shinirikyô, le 20 mars 1995, et, en second lieu, de la dissémination du *bacillus anthracis* en octobre 2011 aux Etats-Unis. Sur le plan stratégique, ces deux actions d'ampleur très limitée se caractérisent par une portée nulle[32].

Le protocole de 2005 incrimine pour sa part deux types distincts de comportements qu'il convient de séparer strictement. L'article 4, paragraphe 5, incrimine le fait de viser ou d'«utiliser un navire» comme instrument d'un acte terroriste impliquant des ADM, ou «d'une manière qui provoque la mort ou des dommages corporels ou matériels graves» (à l'article 4, paragraphe 5, la Convention de 1988 ajoute un article 3*bis*, paragraphe 1, alinéa *a)* i) et iii)). Il incrimine également le fait de transporter des armes de destruction massive destinées à une action terroriste (à l'aricle 4, paragraphe 5, la Convention de 1988 ajoute un article 3*bis*, paragraphe 1, alinéa *b)* i)). Ce faisant, le protocole de 2005 incrimine bien deux catégories particulières d'actions. La première catégorie désigne l'action terroriste proprement dite. Cette dernière, envisagée par l'article 3*bis*, paragraphe 1, alinéa *a)* i), consiste à utiliser «contre ou à bord d'un navire, ou déverser à partir d'un navire, des explosifs, des matières radioactives ou des armes BCN, d'une manière qui provoque ou risque de provoquer la mort ou des dommages corporels ou matériels graves». Elle peut également, aux termes de l'article 3*bis*, paragraphe 1, alinéa *a)* iii), consister à utiliser le navire lui-même comme instrument d'exécution de l'acte terroriste. Les Black Sea Tigers, branche maritime du mouvement Liberation Tigers of Tamil Eleam, ont ainsi effectué le 10 juillet 1990 le premier attentat-suicide réussi de l'histoire maritime[33].

---

examinant les mesures pertinentes prises par tous les Etats Membres de l'Organisation des Nations Unies, à organiser de nombreuses activités d'information, à resserrer la coopération avec d'autres organes antiterroristes créés par le Conseil ainsi qu'avec des organisations intergouvernementales œuvrant aux échelons mondial, régional et sous-régional et à la rendre avantageuse pour toutes les parties, à créer des outils facilitant l'assistance et favorisant la transparence, et à renforcer ses échanges avec les différents Etats.» (Rapport du Comité 1540, 8 juillet 2008, p. 2.)

32. Cependant, l'attaque au gaz sarin organisée dans le métro de Tokyo s'est soldée par douze morts et cinq mille blessés.

33. H. Eudeline, «Renaissance et évolution du terrorisme maritime», *Diplomatie-Les grands dossiers*, 2012, n° 10, p. 35.

La seconde catégorie, visée par l'article 3*bis*, paragraphe 1, alinéa *b)* i) de la Convention de 1988 issu de l'article 4, paragraphe 5, du protocole de 2005, renvoie à l'utilisation d'un navire en tant que moyen de transport d'armes de destruction massive proprement dites, ou du matériel qui s'y rapporte[34], «en sachant que ceux-ci sont destinés» à un acte de terrorisme ou à la menace d'un acte de terrorisme. Le protocole incrimine alors deux types de comportements proliférants. Il incrimine, d'une part, une prolifération qui est intimement et intrinsèquement rattachée au terrorisme. Le texte vise alors non pas les armes nucléaires, mais les explosifs et la matière radioactive, à l'exclusion des armes chimiques et bactériologiques. Il incrimine, d'autre part, les comportements proliférants en tant que tels, pour eux-mêmes, comportements étendus à tout le spectre des armes de destruction massive. Ainsi, l'article 3*bis*, paragraphe 1, alinéa *b)* ii) créé par l'article 4, paragraphe 5, du protocole de 2005 incrimine le fait de transporter à bord d'un navire «toute arme BCN, en sachant qu'il s'agit d'une arme BCN» au sens de la Convention et toute matière brute ou

> «produits fissiles spéciaux, équipements ou matières ... en sachant que des matières, produits ou équipements sont destinés à une activité explosive nucléaire ou à toute autre activité nucléaire non soumise à des garanties en vertu d'un accord de garanties généralisées de l'AIEA».

Or, l'article 3*bis*, paragraphe 1, alinéa *b)* i) visait pour sa part exclusivement les «explosifs» et «les matières radioactives», sans rattacher ces dernières à la catégorie des produits destinés «à une activité explosive nucléaire ou à toute autre activité nucléaire». Le protocole de 2005 relie donc directement ces explosifs et ces matières radioactives à une menace terroriste qui apparaît, en quelque sorte, plus immédiate. Le texte précise, en effet, qu'ils sont destinés à un acte terroriste où à la menace d'un acte terroriste. Lorsqu'il s'agit d'envisager la prolifération d'ADM, rapportée au terrorisme nucléaire, le protocole établit donc une distinction entre les bombes sales, c'est-à-dire des bombes contenant de la matière radioactive mais n'entraînant aucune réaction de fission ou de fusion, et les armes proprement dites. Les explosifs et les matières nucléaires sont d'un maniement plus aisé que les armes nucléaires. La prolifération de ces dernières est donc prohibée mais dans une optique temporelle plus lointaine, celui de la dissémination des ADM. Son rattachement au terrorisme n'est pas exclu, il est tout simplement éventuel. Sur ce point, le protocole de 2005 entend prohiber la prolifération de manière générale et pas uniquement au nom de la lutte contre le terrorisme.

34. T. L. McDorman, *op. cit.*, p. 239.

La résolution 1540 et le protocole de 2005 se caractérisent, en réalité, par l'imbrication de la lutte contre le terrorisme au sein d'un ensemble juridique élargi aux objectifs de non-prolifération en tant que tels. La résolution 1540, le protocole de 2005 et la Convention internationale pour la répression des actes de terrorisme nucléaire apparaissent, dès lors, comme une série d'instruments venant compléter l'ensemble normatif encadrant la non-prolifération étatique. Elles en constitueraient en quelque sorte le prolongement à un niveau différent, le niveau infra-étatique. Le protocole de 2005 s'attache de manière plus spécifique à une prolifération qui utiliserait les voies marines. Cependant, bien qu'entré en vigueur en 2010, le protocole de 2005 souffre d'un manque de ratifications qui entravent largement son effectivité et son efficacité.

Au 31 mai 2012, aucune puissance nucléaire n'avait ratifié le protocole additionnel.

Les Etats-Unis, la France et le Royaume-Uni ont certes signé ce texte, mais cette signature ne vaut pas ratification. La Chine, la Fédération de Russie n'ont, quant à elles, pas signé ce texte pas plus que la République islamique d'Iran qui est, il est vrai, identifiée, dans le cadre de l'Initiative de sécurité contre la prolifération (ISP)[35] en tant qu'Etat «of proliferation concern».

En dehors des puissances nucléaires «légitimes», c'est-à-dire reconnues par le TNP, l'Inde, le Pakistan, Israël ou encore la Corée du Nord n'ont pas signé le texte du protocole. En raison de l'applicabilité limitée du texte de 2005, la lutte contre la prolifération maritime des ADM reste soumise au cadre général établi par la résolution 1540 et par les règles du droit de la mer.

Ce cadre juridique complexe soulève un certains nombre de difficultés, particulièrement en ce qui concerne l'établissement de la compétence pénale des Etats.

35. L'ISP, proposée par les Etats-Unis en 2003, a pour but de lutter contre le trafic d'armes de destruction massive (ADM), de leurs vecteurs et de leurs éléments constitutifs, à destination ou en provenance d'Etats comme d'acteurs non étatiques, qui suscitent des préoccupations en matière de prolifération. L'ISP ne dispose pas de structure permanente mais vise à permettre aux Etats qui le souhaitent de coordonner leurs efforts pour lutter contre la prolifération, notamment maritime, des ADM. L'arraisonnement du *BBC China* constitue, à ce jour, l'exemple de coopération réussie dans le cadre de l'ISP le plus connu. C'est grâce à l'action conjuguée des Etats-Unis et de la Grande Bretagne, mais également de l'Allemagne qui a autorisé l'arraisonnement de ce navire battant son pavillon et de l'Italie qui a ouvert l'un de ses ports pour permettre le déchargement des marchandises, que les éléments de centrifugeuse ont pu être interceptés. Les consentements de l'Allemagne et de l'Italie ne valaient que pour la situation particulière du *BBC China* illustrant parfaitement le caractère informel et souvent *ad hoc* des actions menées dans le cadre de l'ISP.

SECTION 3 LE CADRE LÉGAL DE LA LUTTE CONTRE LA PROLIFÉRATION MARITIME DES ARMES DE DESTRUCTION MASSIVE

L'un des principaux enjeux de la mise en place du cadre normatif de la lutte contre la prolifération des ADM demeure, sans aucun doute, la mise en œuvre de mécanismes de vérification visant à assurer l'absence effective de prolifération. Dans le cadre de négociations précédant l'adoption de la résolution 1540, la France avait notamment plaidé pour la mise en place d'un corps d'inspecteurs internationaux[36]. La résolution 1540, bien que contraignante, n'établit toutefois aucun mécanisme de contrôle internationalisé. Elle oblige, en revanche, les Etats à établir un cadre juridique qui se décompose en deux volets. D'une part, un volet pénal qui enjoint aux Etats d'incriminer la prolifération des armes nucléaires par les acteurs non étatiques dans leur droit interne. D'autre part, un volet administratif visant à donner à l'Etat les moyens juridiques de mettre en œuvre les incriminations qu'ils auront incluses dans leurs droits.

Les Etats seront, en particulier, tenus de

> « prendre et appliquer des mesures efficaces afin de mettre en place des dispositifs internes de contrôle destinés à prévenir la prolifération des armes nucléaires, chimiques ou biologiques ou de leurs vecteurs, y compris en mettant en place des dispositifs de contrôle appropriés pour les éléments connexes ».

En l'absence d'un organe international d'inspection, sur le modèle classique des procédures de désarmement, la pénalisation de la prolifération des armes de destruction massive implique d'accorder une place toute particulière à l'établissement de la compétence des Etats à l'égard des auteurs de l'infraction de prolifération. Dans la mesure où les Etats se conforment aux obligations découlant de la résolution 1540 et du protocole de 2005, ils sont tenus d'incorporer dans leur droit interne des dispositions incriminant la prolifération des armes de destruction massive. Dans le cadre de la criminalité maritime, l'établissement de la compétence pénale des Etats hors du territoire soumis à leur souveraineté se traduit par la contradiction entre les objectifs de la lutte contre cette criminalité et le respect du principe général de liberté de navigation[37].

---

36. S. Sur, « La résolution 1540 du Conseil de sécurité (28 avril 2004) », *op. cit.*, p. 873.

37. B. H. Oxman, « Crimes at Sea and Trafficking of Weapons of Mass Destruction : General Report », dans E. Francx et P. Gautier (dir. publ.), *The Exercise of Jurisdiction over Vessels : New Development in the Fields of Pollution, Fisheries, Crimes at Sea and Trafficking of Weapons of Mass Destruction*, Bruxelles, Bruylant, 2010, pp. 133 ss.

Il convient alors d'établir une distinction entre l'établissement de la compétence pénale de l'Etat sur des navires battant son pavillon (paragraphe 1) d'une part et sur des navires battant un pavillon étranger, d'autre part. Dans ce dernier cas, il est alors nécessaire d'établir à nouveau une distinction entre l'établissement de la compétence de l'Etat en haute-mer (paragraphe 2) ou, au contraire, dans les eaux soumises à sa souveraineté (paragraphe 3).

Paragraphe 1 **La compétence pénale de l'Etat sur les navires battant son propre pavillon**

Le premier cas de figure ne soulève aucune difficulté sérieuse en termes de compétence pénale et ce, que le navire se trouve dans les eaux soumises à la souveraineté de l'Etat du pavillon ou en haute mer. Le Statement of Interdiction Principles, adopté dans le cadre de l'ISP, demande ainsi aux Etats de, « at their own initiative, or at the request and good cause shown by another state, to take action to board and search any vessel flying their flag in their internal waters or territorial seas, or areas beyond the territorial seas of any other state » (par. 4, al. *b)*). De la même manière, l'article 9 de la Convention pour la répression des actes de terrorisme nucléaire impose aux Etats de prendre les mesures nécessaires afin d'établir sa compétence lorsqu'une « infraction est commise à bord d'un navire battant son pavillon ou d'un aéronef immatriculé conformément à sa législation au moment où l'infraction a été commise ». Cette disposition peut s'avérer décisive en matière de prolifération des ADM dans le cadre des dispositions prévues à l'article 2, paragraphe 2, alinéa *b)*, incriminant la « prolifération violente ».

Le principal enjeu réside dans la transposition en droit interne[38], par les Etats, des dispositions incriminant la prolifération des armes de destruction massive, en accord avec la résolution 1540. Or, la création d'infractions ayant pour objet la prolifération des ADM ne va pas sans rencontrer un certain nombre d'obstacles. Les rapports du comité 1540 soulignent ainsi que, jusqu'en 2011, l'adoption, par les Etats, de textes incriminant la prolifération des armes de destruction massive demeurait globalement inégale. Certains Etats n'incriminent pas les comportements prohibés par la résolution ou le font de manière sélective. Globalement, le Comité souligne que « les interdictions concernant les armes nucléaires, chimiques et biologiques et leurs vecteurs résultant du para-

38. Ou la ratification du protocole de 2005 qui incrimine lui-même les comportements mais impose aux Etats, à son article 5, de réprimer les infractions prévues par le protocole « par des peines appropriées qui prennent en considération la nature grave de ces infractions ».

graphe 2 de la résolution ne sont pas nécessairement toutes consacrées par une législation spéciale»[39].

L'absence de pénalisation de la prolifération des ADM constitue, à n'en pas douter, une violation des obligations de l'Etat aux fins de la résolution 1540. L'établissement du Comité 1540 semble néanmoins orienter le régime juridique vers davantage de consensualisme. Le Conseil de sécurité paraît également privilégier une voie pédagogique, ainsi qu'en témoignent les rapports du Comité. Il s'agit «d'expliquer» aux Etats le sens et la portée de la résolution 1540 afin de les amener, de manière progressive, à traduire dans leurs ordres juridiques respectifs les dispositions de la résolution 1540. Le Comité prend note, en particulier, que «les Etats ont … consenti des efforts remarquables pour appliquer la résolution», et entend «redoubler d'efforts pour aider à titre prioritaire les Etats qui ne l'ont pas encore fait à rendre compte de la mise en œuvre de la résolution»[40].

Les enjeux sont plus complexes lorsque le navire à l'égard duquel l'Etat entend établir sa compétence arbore un pavillon étranger. Le régime juridique diffère alors selon que le navire se situe en haute mer ou dans les eaux soumises à la souveraineté de l'Etat.

Paragraphe 2 **La compétence pénale de l'Etat sur un navire battant pavillon étranger en haute mer**

La recherche d'un fondement juridique à la compétence pénale de l'Etat au titre de la mise en œuvre de l'infraction de prolifération, lorsqu'il s'agit d'arraisonner un navire battant pavillon étranger et suspecté de transporter des ADM ou le matériel afférent, est particulièrement complexe. Cette problématique a concentré l'essentiel des débats en doctrine. Ainsi, B. H. Oxman souligne-t-il que la question «of boarding a ship, or compelling it to proceed to a designated port, without express flag state consent … has captured the imagination of lawyers»[41]. La résolution 1540 n'établit expressément aucun mécanisme permettant de fonder l'arraisonnement d'un navire battant pavillon étranger.

Elle paraît, au contraire, laisser aux Etats le soin de fixer par voie conventionnelle les modalités concrètes d'une éventuelle coopération pénale en la matière. Elle s'aligne, à cet égard, sur le cadre non contraignant promu par l'ISP dont la mise en œuvre repose avant tout sur la

39. Rapport du Comité 1540, créé par la résolution 1540 (2004), 12 septembre 2011, *op. cit.*, par. 35.
40. *Ibid.*, par. 21.
41. B. H. Oxman, *op. cit.*, p. 147.

coopération bilatérale entre Etats ayant adhéré à cette initiative. Ce faisant, elle écarte résolument toute initiative unilatérale et tout dépassement des souverainetés étatiques. Les Etats impliqués dans l'ISP entendent ainsi autoriser réciproquement l'arraisonnement des navires battant leur pavillon s'ils sont suspectés de transporter des armes de destruction massive ou du matériel qui leur est lié. Le Statement of Interdiction Principles formalise cette structure qui sous-tend le cadre juridique établi par la résolution 1540.

Il souligne à son paragraphe 4, alinéa *c)*, que les Etats devraient

> «seriously consider providing consent under the appropriate circumstances to the boarding and searching of its own flag vessels by other states, and to the seizure of such WMD-related cargoes in such vessels that may be identified by such states».

La logique de l'ISP peut, sur ce point être transposée à celle de la résolution 1540. Un tel consentement peut intervenir au cas par cas, sur une base *ad hoc*, comme ce fut le cas pour le navire *BBC China*[42]. Il peut également prendre la forme d'accords bilatéraux, ou accords de shipboarding, établissant une compétence pénale en matière de lutte contre la prolifération des ADM pour les navires du pavillon des Etats signataires. Les Etats-Unis ont ainsi conclu une série d'accords bilatéraux avec les Etat «holding the largest shipping registries, and hence having the greatest number of flag vessels under their control and exclusive jurisdiction»[43].

Ces accords s'appliquent à la haute mer. Ils se rattachent en conséquence aux interventions procédant de pouvoirs conférés par traité évoquées par l'article 110 de la Convention des Nations Unies sur le droit de la mer (CNUDM) du 10 décembre 1982. Si la résolution 1540 ne modifie pas, par elle-même, le texte de l'article 110, ces accords permettent aux Etats, sur une base bilatérale, d'étendre, dans des domaines sectorialisés, les exceptions à la compétence exclusive de l'Etat du pavillon dans les eaux internationales. Aux termes de l'article 110, l'arraisonnement de navires étrangers ne peut légalement intervenir qu'en cas de soupçon de piraterie, de trafic d'esclaves, d'émissions non autorisées ou de doute sur la nationalité du navire.

Sur ce point, l'un des enjeux majeurs du protocole de 2005 est, précisément, de mettre en place un corps de règle permanent et universel assurant une meilleure coopération en matière pénale. Toutefois, bien que le protocole prévoie un mécanisme d'acceptation préalable, au

42. L'arraisonnement de ce navire n'a été rendu possible que par le consentement donné par le Gouvernement allemand.
43. N. Klein, *Maritime Security and Law of the Sea*, Oxford University Press, 2011, p. 184.

moment du dépôt des instruments de ratification, c'est bien sur le consentement donné au cas par cas par l'Etat du pavillon que repose le protocole ainsi qu'en témoigne le régime établi par l'article 8 *bis*, paragraphe 5[44]. Ce fait est confirmé par Nathalie Klein pour qui «this structure underlines that permission to board requires express flag state authorization and that tacit and advance authorizations to board are only optional»[45]. Lorsque, en revanche, se pose la question de l'établissement de la compétence de l'Etat sur les navires battant pavillon étranger dans les eaux soumis à sa souveraineté, la coopération pénale fait place à l'opposition des deux souverainetés: celle de l'Etat côtier et celle de l'Etat du pavillon.

Paragraphe 3 **La compétence de l'Etat sur les navires battant pavillon étranger dans les eaux soumises à sa souveraineté**

L'Etat côtier peut, certes, intervenir sur un navire situé sur son port ou ses eaux intérieures dans la mesure où sa compétence territoriale prime celle de l'Etat du pavillon. De la même manière, lorsque le navire quitte les eaux intérieures, «l'Etat côtier est en droit de prendre toutes les mesures prévues par son droit interne en vue de procéder à des arrestations ou à des actes d'instruction»[46]. C'est ce qui ressort de l'article 27, paragraphe 2, de la CNUDM. Toutefois, lorsque le navire ne fait que traverser la mer territoriale, l'exercice de la juridiction pénale à bord est cette fois encadrée par la CNUDM. En cas de passage latéral, les droits souverains de l'Etat sont conditionnés par le droit d'un navire étranger d'exercer son libre droit de passage innocent excluant toute intervention de la part de l'Etat côtier. Il y a là un prolongement de la tension entre les objectifs de lutte contre les comportements proliférants et le respect du principe de la liberté de navigation.

Il convient, à cet égard, d'établir une distinction entre la prolifération des ADM qui s'inscrit dans le cadre du terrorisme et la lutte contre la prolifération pour elle-même. Dans le premier cas, si l'Etat côtier est susceptible d'être visé par un acte terroriste avec des armes ou des maté-

44. L'alinéa *b)* précise que, lorsqu'il existe des «raisons sérieuses de soupçonner que le navire ou une personne à bord du navire a été, est ou est sur le point d'être impliqué dans la commission d'une infraction» incriminée par le protocole, «la Partie requérante demande à ... [l'Etat du pavillon] l'autorisation d'arraisonner le navire».

45. N. Klein, *op. cit.*, p. 178.

46. P. Gautier, «Quelques observations sur le soi-disant caractère inadapté du droit international face aux actes de la criminalité en mer», dans L. Le Hardy De Beaulieu (dir. publ.), *Criminalité et trafic maritimes: des enjeux politiques aux conséquences juridiques*, Namur, PUN, p. 64.

riels qui transitent par sa mer territoriale, il dispose de moyens juridiques plus solides pour intervenir et arraisonner un navire battant pavillon étranger. L'utilisation d'une arme nucléaire par un mouvement terroriste pourrait permettre à l'Etat de considérer que le passage n'est plus inoffensif. Constitutif d'une « menace ou [d'un] emploi de la force contre la souveraineté, l'intégrité territoriale ou l'indépendance politique de l'Etat côtier ou de toute autre manière contraire aux principes du droit international énoncés dans la Charte des Nations » au titre de l'article 19, paragraphe 2 *a)*, de la CNUDM, le passage du navire serait à même de justifier, sur le plan du droit, son arraisonnement.

Dans tous les cas, si la menace se révèle être de moindre intensité, l'article 27, paragraphe 1 *a)*, de la CNUDM fournit un autre fondement juridique susceptible de permettre à l'Etat d'arraisonner un navire battant pavillon étranger dans sa mer territoriale. L'Etat peut, en effet, établir

> « sa juridiction pénale à bord d'un navire étranger passant dans la mer territoriale pour y procéder à une arrestation ou à l'exécution d'actes d'instruction à la suite d'une infraction pénale commise à bord pendant le passage ... si les conséquences de l'infraction s'étendent à l'Etat côtier ».

Dans le cadre d'un comportement proliférant, constitutif d'une infraction, conduisant à un acte terroriste sur le territoire de l'Etat côtier, les dispositions de l'article 27 trouveraient pleinement à s'appliquer[47].

La situation est quelque peu différente lorsque le matériel en transit dans la mer territoriale ne conduit pas à une action terroriste sur le territoire de l'Etat côtier ou n'a aucun rapport avec un quelconque projet d'acte terroriste. Dans ce dernier cas, il s'agit d'un comportement proliférant incriminé pour lui-même. A cet égard, le trafic d'ADM ne constitue pas une activité susceptible de justifier qu'il soit porté atteinte, par exception, au principe de libre passage inoffensif. Sur ce point, certains Etats, tels que la France, ont intégré dans leur droit interne un ensemble de dispositions visant à lutter contre la prolifération des ADM qui soulèvent un certain nombre de difficultés. En droit français, c'est notamment l'objet de la loi n° 2011-266 du 14 mars 2011 relative à la lutte contre la prolifération des armes de destruction massive et de leurs vecteurs.

L'infraction de prolifération a été consacrée par les articles L 1333-13-1 et s. du Code de la défense pour les matières nucléaires, et par les

47. On peut se reporter, sur ce point, à l'article 421-1, paragraphe 4, du Code pénal français pour lequel la prolifération des ADM est assimilable à un acte terroriste lorsqu'elle est commise « intentionnellement en relation avec une entreprise individuelle ou collective ayant pour but de troubler gravement l'ordre public par l'intimidation ou la terreur ».

articles L 2341-1 et s. et L 2342-1 et s. du même code en ce qui concerne respectivement les armes biologiques et chimiques. Du strict point de vue de la prolifération maritime des ADM, l'article 61 du Code des douanes, dans sa rédaction issue de l'article 14 de la loi nº 2011-266, soulève quelques difficultés d'interprétation. L'article 61 permet aux agents des douanes d'immobiliser les biens «à double usage civil et militaire non communautaires» dans le cadre de la lutte contre le transport illicite de tels biens. Très clairement, il s'agit

> «de combler un vide juridique en permettant aux agents des douanes d'adopter des mesures conservatoires permettant d'immobiliser des biens à double usage en transit. Par ailleurs, cet amendement vise à donner aux agents une base juridique pour rechercher et constater un délit douanier en cas de transit illégal. Enfin, il vise à favoriser l'échange spontané d'informations entre les services concernés.»[48]

Cet article peut-il s'appliquer à un navire en transit dans la mer territoriale de l'Etat français? L'étendue de l'application de ce texte reste peu claire. S'il venait à permettre aux agents des douanes françaises d'immobiliser un navire battant pavillon étranger, cela étendrait sensiblement les possibilités ouvertes par les dispositions de la CNUDM. Ces dernières ne concernent, ainsi qu'en témoigne l'article 19, que l'embarquement ou le débarquement de «fonds ou de personnes en contravention aux lois et règlements douaniers, fiscaux, sanitaires ou d'immigration de l'Etat côtier» et non pas le transport proprement dit. Or le législateur français entend appliquer sa législation au «transit» d'ADM ou de produits en relevant.

Eu égard aux dispositions de la CNUDM, les atteintes au principe de libre passage inoffensif visent à assurer la sécurité de l'Etat côtier. En d'autres termes, il se donne pour objectif de permettre à l'Etat côtier d'intervenir dans sa mer territoriale afin de prévenir toute action susceptible de porter «atteinte à la paix, au bon ordre ou à la sécurité (art. 19, par. 1). Or, le sens du texte du code des douanes n'est pas, en lui-même, d'assurer la protection de l'Etat français mais de lui permettre de «renforcer l'efficacité et la cohérence de la législation française afin qu'elle ait un caractère dissuasif pour toute personne qui souhaiterait accomplir un acte favorisant la prolifération d'ADM»[49]. Il existe donc un hiatus entre l'objectif limité de la CNUDM, à savoir la protection de la sécurité de l'Etat côtier, et l'objet de la lutte contre la prolifération des ADM qui constitue une menace contre la paix et la sécurité internationales.

---

48. Rapport relatif à la lutte contre la prolifération des armes de destruction massive et de leurs vecteurs par M. Michel Voisin, *op. cit.*, p. 43.

49. *Ibid.*, p. 16.

Est-il envisageable, au titre de la préservation de la paix et de la sécurité, de dépasser les compétences dévolues à l'Etat dans le cadre de la CNUDM ? Deux raisonnements peuvent à cet égard être tenus. On peut, en premier lieu, considérer que la protection de la sécurité de l'Etat côtier s'inscrit dans le cadre de la protection de la paix et de la sécurité internationales. En d'autres termes, l'article 19 de la CNUDM a pour objet, en permettant à l'Etat de se défendre contre toute action illicite, de participer au maintien de la paix et de la sécurité internationales. Dès lors, en se protégeant, l'Etat protège ces dernières. En conséquence, l'extension de la compétence de l'Etat français se conformerait aux dispositions de la CNUDM dans la mesure où l'article 19 ne viserait qu'à autoriser un type particulier de protection sans pour autant limiter *in abstracto* les capacités de l'Etat à porter atteinte au droit de passage inoffensif. D'application limitée, l'article 19 n'aurait ainsi pas de caractère limitatif. Le paragraphe 1 de l'article 19 est susceptible de renforcer une telle interprétation. Ce dernier précise en effet que le passage inoffensif doit s'entendre de tout passage qui, non seulement « ne porte pas atteinte à la paix, au bon ordre où à la sécurité de l'Etat côtier » mais doit en plus s'effectuer « en conformité avec les dispositions de la [CNUDM] et les autres règles du droit international ».

Le fondement juridique de l'extension de la compétence de l'Etat français serait alors à rechercher dans les résolutions du Conseil de sécurité et, plus particulièrement, dans le cadre de la résolution 1540 qui appartiendrait à ces « autres règles du droit international ». A cet égard, la Commission de la défense nationale a pu, sans ambiguïté, réinscrire les dispositions du projet de loi dans le cadre des obligations pesant sur le France eu égard aux dispositions de la résolution 1540.

> « Le projet de loi, écrit Michel Voisin, a donc pour origine une obligation [qui] résulte de la résolution n° 1540 précitée, qui enjoint aux Etats d'améliorer leurs outils juridiques pour prendre en compte les formes multiples des modes de prolifération. »[50]

Une telle interprétation qui réinscrirait la CNUDM dans un ensemble normatif plus large dont elle constituerait une dimension particulière modifierait sans aucun doute son texte. Cependant, une telle interprétation n'est pas nécessairement conforme à l'économie générale de la CNUDM. Ainsi que le soulignent René-Jean Dupuy et David Vignes, « l'intention innovatrice de la Convention de 1982 se manifeste dans le fait que la longue liste de l'article 19, paragraphe 2, se présente comme exhaustive »[51].

50. *Op. cit. supra* note 48, p. 6.
51. R.-J. Dupuy et D. Vignes, *Traité du nouveau droit de la mer*, Bruxelles, Bruylant, 1985, p. 756.

Il est donc également possible de considérer que le même article 19 constitue l'expression du droit coutumier et entend précisément limiter les atteintes qu'il est possible de porter au droit de libre passage inoffensif. En d'autres termes, l'article 19 devra faire l'objet d'une interprétation stricte, son champ d'application étant nécessairement limitatif. Il ne tolérerait pas d'autres atteintes que celles qui sont strictement énoncées dans le cadre de l'article 19, paragraphe 2, et uniquement dans le but d'assurer, à l'Etat côtier, une protection contre une menace le visant immédiatement. Le caractère inoffensif du passage ne dépendrait pas, en dernière analyse, de la licéité des objets transportés mais de leur rapport à l'ordre public de l'Etat côtier. Ce dernier ne disposerait pas d'autres compétences lui permettant d'étendre sensiblement les atteintes à la liberté de transit et ne disposerait en particulier pas de compétences particulières en matière de protection contre la paix et la sécurité internationales. A ce titre, l'extension de la compétence de l'Etat français entrerait en contradiction avec celles de l'article 19, paragraphes 1 et 2, de la CNUDM. Or, dans la mesure où la loi adoptée par l'Etat français est fondée sur les dispositions de la résolution 1540, il y aurait donc une contradiction entre cette dernière et le texte de la CNUDM[52].

L'article 103 de la Charte des Nations Unies a précisément pour objet de dépasser ce type de conflits susceptibles de survenir entre les obligations internationales pesant sur les Etats de la société internationale. Aux termes de ce dernier, « en cas de conflit entre les obligations des Membres des Nations Unies en vertu de la présente Charte et leurs obligations en vertu de tout autre accord international, les premières prévaudront ». Une lecture simple des dispositions de l'article 103 impliquerait donc de faire primer les dispositions de la résolution 1540 sur celles de

52. Le dernier point de l'article 19, paragraphe 2, alinéa *l)*, ne paraît pas, en particulier, de nature à inclure le trafic d'ADM comme exception à la protection du passage inoffensif. Dans le cas d'un navire en transit, le trafic ne constitue pas une activité qui n'a « aucun rapport » avec le passage mais est, au contraire, intimement liée au passage lui-même. Il ne s'agit pas, dans ce cas précis, d'effectuer une opération particulière à l'occasion du passage dans la mer territoriale mais bien de purement et simplement la traverser. Le caractère illégal du trafic, notamment eu égard aux dispositions de la résolution 1540, découle alors de la qualité intrinsèque des objets transportés par le navire. De ce fait, il est délicat d'affirmer que le trafic d'ADM est sans rapport avec « le passage » que l'article 18, paragraphe 1, définit de manière strictement technique. Pour cet article, en effet, « on entend par « passage » le fait de naviguer dans la mer territoriale aux fins de la traverser » ou de se « rendre dans les eaux intérieures ou les quitter ». Dans le cas d'un navire en transit, le transport d'ADM est en rapport avec le passage puisqu'il s'agit pour le navire de simplement passer par la mer territoriale d'un Etat. Or, les dispositions de l'article 19 ne visent pas de manière particulière un type de cargaison mais les activités du navire rapportées au passage : c'est donc la conformité de l'activité vis-à-vis de la notion juridique de passage qui est en jeu pour l'article 19, paragraphe 2, alinéa *l)*.

la CNUDM. Au nom de la préservation de la paix et de la sécurité internationales, et dans la mesure où ils s'appuient sur les dispositions de la résolution 1540 du Conseil de sécurité, les Etats seraient autorisés à étendre le champ des atteintes portées au principe du libre passage inoffensif au-delà des exceptions prévues par l'article 19 de la CNUDM.

Cependant, dans le même temps, la Cour de justice des Communautés européennes (CJCE), devenue aujourd'hui la Cour de justice de l'Union européenne (CJUE), a modéré, ne serait-ce que par les conséquences de sa décision, la portée de l'article 103 de la Charte des Nations Unies. Dans l'affaire *Kadi et Al Barakaat International Foundation*, elle n'a ainsi pas hésité à établir un contrôle de proportionnalité entre les buts recherchés par un règlement européen visant à mettre en œuvre les dispositions d'une résolution du Conseil de sécurité et les atteintes portées aux libertés individuelles. Ainsi, après avoir souligné que

> « les mesures restrictives prévues par le règlement litigieux contribuent à la mise en œuvre, au niveau de la Communauté, des mesures restrictives décidées par le Conseil de sécurité à l'encontre d'Oussama ben Laden, du réseau Al-Qaida, des Taliban ainsi que des autres personnes, groupes, entreprises et entités qui leur sont associés »[53].

Or, pour la Cour,

> « au regard d'un objectif d'intérêt général aussi fondamental pour la communauté internationale que la lutte par tous les moyens, conformément à la Charte des Nations Unies, contre les menaces à l'égard de la paix et de la sécurité internationales que font peser les actes de terrorisme, le gel des fonds, avoirs financiers et autres ressources économiques des personnes identifiées par le Conseil de sécurité ou le comité des sanctions comme étant associées à Oussama ben Laden, au réseau Al-Qaida et aux Taliban ne saurait, en soi, passer pour inadéquat ou disproportionné »[54].

Il n'y aurait donc pas, si l'on se situe dans un cadre d'interprétation impliquant une contradiction entre la CNUDM et la résolution 1540, de supériorité de principe de cette dernière sur d'autres textes du droit international. Conformément à la jurisprudence de la CJCE, il y aurait lieu d'établir un examen sur l'équilibre réalisé par la résolution 1540

53. CJCE, Grande Chambre, *Yassin Abdullah Kadi et Al Barakaat International Foundation c. Conseil de l'Union européenne, Commission des Communautés européennes, Royaume-Uni de Grande-Bretagne et d'Irlande du Nord*, 3 septembre 2008, par. 362.
54. *Ibid.*, par. 363.

entre les objectifs poursuivis et les atteintes substantielles qui sont portées au principe du libre passage inoffensif mais, également, à la souveraineté de l'Etat dont le navire bat pavillon. Même si la Cour ne mentionne pas l'article 103, elle en atténue la rigueur. L'extension des pouvoirs normatifs que le Conseil de sécurité peut s'octroyer semble ainsi se traduire par un abaissement de la portée de l'article 103, lequel n'était, a priori, pas établi pour encadrer un Conseil de sécurité dont les résolutions tendent à posséder une portée normative de plus en plus contraignante et de plus en plus étendue. En d'autres termes, la portée de l'article 103 de la Charte évoluerait en même temps que les résolutions du Conseil de sécurité se modifieraient. Cet article ne serait, en effet, plus à même de rendre compte de l'équilibre nouvellement établi en faveur des résolutions du Conseil, nouvel équilibre dont la résolution 1540 constituerait précisément un exemple. Pour Daniel H. Joyner, cette résolution ne vise, en particulier, pas à s'appliquer à une situation précise, *ad hoc*. Au contraire, elle tend à imposer « a broad set of obligation upon all UN member states, which were purposed in changing permanently the structure and content of national legal systems »[55].

Or, pour l'auteur, il s'agit clairement d'une extension des pouvoirs du Conseil de sécurité dépassant l'esprit et la lettre de la Charte. Il insiste notamment sur le fait qu'il n'existe aucune « justification for going around the Charter system and assuming a lawmaking authority which was never intended to be exercised by the Council under the Charter »[56]. L'arrêt *Kadi et Al Barakaat International Foundation* semble, sur ce point, prendre en compte, afin d'en limiter les conséquences, l'évolution qui marque les résolutions du Conseil de sécurité. Comment peut-on interpréter autrement la position de la CJCE lorsque celle-ci se plaît à souligner que

> « le Tribunal a commis une erreur de droit en jugeant, aux points 212 à 231 de l'arrêt attaqué *Kadi* ainsi que 263 à 282 de l'arrêt attaqué *Yusuf et Al Barakaat*, qu'il découle des principes régissant l'articulation des rapports entre l'ordre juridique international issu des Nations Unies et l'ordre juridique communautaire que le règlement litigieux, dès lors qu'il vise à mettre en œuvre une résolution adoptée par le Conseil de sécurité au titre du chapitre VII de la Charte des Nations Unies ne laissant aucune marge à cet effet, doit bénéficier d'une immunité juridictionnelle quant à sa légalité interne sauf pour ce qui concerne sa compatibilité avec les normes relevant du *jus cogens* » ?[57]

55. D. H. Joyner, *op. cit.*, p. 231.
56. *Ibid.*, p. 237.
57. CJCE, 3 septembre 2008, *op. cit.*, par. 327.

Les difficultés rencontrées dans le cadre de la lutte contre la prolifération maritime des ADM résident principalement dans la volonté des Etats de limiter au maximum la compétence des Etats étrangers sur les navires battant leur propre pavillon. Cette limite peut être constatée dans la volonté de privilégier une approche bilatérale, mais également dans la difficile application du protocole de 2005. Ces difficultés sont la conséquence des équivoques de la lutte contre la prolifération maritime des ADM, équivoques qui trouvent leur source dans les mécanismes visant à assurer la non-prolifération des armes nucléaires.

SECTION 4 LES ÉQUIVOQUES DE LA PÉNALISATION DE LA PROLIFÉRATION MARITIME DES ARMES NUCLÉAIRES

Le cadre juridique visant à assurer la répression de l'infraction de prolifération se caractérise par un certain nombre de lacunes. Au niveau du droit interne, les Etats sont davantage réticents à transposer l'incrimination de la prolifération des armes nucléaires et biologiques que celle concernant les armes chimiques. Dans son rapport de 2011, le Comité 1540 souligne en particulier qu'« il ressort que les Etats ont adopté davantage de mesures contre les armes chimiques que contre les armes nucléaires ou biologiques, mais peu de mesures pour interdire le transport des armes chimiques »[58]. A l'occasion de l'Examen de l'état d'avancement de la mise en œuvre de la résolution 1540 (2004) pour 2012 du 27 décembre 2012, le Comité 1540 a d'ailleurs rappellé que le Conseil de sécurité avait constaté que « l'application intégrale de la résolution 1540 (2004) par tous les Etats était une œuvre de longue haleine »[59].

Au niveau du droit international, les lacunes sont perceptibles tant au niveau du cadre général qu'au niveau des règles concernant la dimension spécifiquement maritime de la lutte contre la prolifération des armes de destruction massive. Au niveau général, la résolution 1540 ne définit pas et n'assure pas par elle-même la mise en place du cadre juridique visant à prohiber les comportements proliférants émanant d'acteurs non étatiques. Elle ne dépasse pas les souverainetés étatiques au sens où elle ne constitue pas un instrument juridique susceptible de permettre à un Etat d'établir sa compétence sur un navire battant pavillon

58. Rapport du Comité du Conseil de sécurité créé par la résolution 1540 (2004), *op. cit.*, par. 38.

59. Examen de l'état d'avancement de la mise en œuvre de la résolution 1540 (2004) pour 2012, Comité 1540, Conseil de sécurité, 28 décembre 2012, n° S/2012/963, p. 2.

d'un autre Etat. Au niveau des textes traitant spécifiquement de la dimension maritime de la prolifération des ADM, la doctrine perçoit la volonté affichée par les Etats de s'inscrire dans une démarche coopérative, démarche qui caractérise tant le régime du protocole de 2005 que les accords bilatéraux de *ship-boarding*, comme un facteur d'affaiblissement du régime juridique visant à assurer la répression des comportements proliférants.

Pour la doctrine, « these weaknesses exist because of what appears to amount to undue deference being accorded to the traditional paradigm emphasizing freedom of navigation and exclusive jurisdiction of flag states on the high seas » [60]. Pour Douglas Guilfoyle, « one difference between WMD interdiction, and a more established field such as narcotics interdiction, is the undoubted underlying illegality of drug trafficking ... The « criminalisation » of trade in WMD is less obviously complete. » [61] Cet argument est cependant à nuancer. Seules les armes nucléaires utilisées dans le cadre d'une stratégie de dissuasion nucléaire ne font pas l'objet d'une condamnation absolument établie. En réalité, les limites inhérentes aux mécanismes de répression de la prolifération maritime des ADM trouvent également leur origine dans les équivoques traditionnelles de la lutte contre la prolifération nucléaire au niveau étatique. En matière nucléaire du moins, il demeure particulièrement délicat de détacher la prolifération étatique et celle émanant des acteurs non étatiques.

A ce titre,

> « bien que [le docteur Abdul Qader Kahn] ait présenté ses activités comme indépendantes de l'Etat, il est irréaliste d'envisager qu'il les ait développées sans l'accord tacite des autorités de son pays, dont il a servi un temps les objectifs stratégiques. Son laboratoire de recherche, Kahuta (KRL: Kahuta research laboratories), était en effet étroitement intégré dans le réseau pakistanais de production d'armes nucléaires, supervisé par la Pakistan Atomic Energy Commission. Il est notamment impossible que des relations entre le réseau Khan et la Corée du Nord se soient établies sans l'approbation du gouvernement d'Islamabad. » [62]

Il semble donc cohérent de voir les tensions animant la prolifération des armes nucléaires au niveau étatique se répercuter au niveau de l'ensemble des textes susceptibles de s'appliquer à la lutte contre la prolifération maritime des ADM et, plus particulièrement, la résolution 1540 et le

60. N. Klein, *op. cit.*, p. 191.

61. D. Guilfoyle, « Maritime Interdiction of Weapons of Mass Destruction », *Journal of Conflict and Security Law*, 2007, p. 2.

62. Rapport relatif à la lutte contre la prolifération des armes de destruction massive et de leurs vecteurs par M. Michel Voisin, *op. cit.*, p. 13.

protocole de 2005. Il convient donc d'identifier, dans un premier temps, les équivoques propres aux mécanismes de non-prolifération des armes nucléaires au niveau étatique (paragraphe 1). Il s'agira, dans un second de temps, d'analyser dans quelle mesure ces équivoques pèsent sur les textes assurant la pénalisation de la prolifération maritime des ADM par les acteurs non étatiques. Ces textes tendent, en effet, à orienter cette dernière vers la préservation, par les cinq puissances nucléaires reconnues par le TNP, de leur avantage stratégique en matière nucléaire (paragraphe 2). Le cadre juridique de la lutte contre la prolifération maritime des ADM apparaît alors comme une tentative d'étendre, hors du TNP, les obligations de non-prolifération pesant sur les Etats (paragraphe 3).

Paragraphe 1 **Le régime juridique de la lutte contre la prolifération étatique, la notion de situation objective conventionnelle**

La doctrine du droit international utilise le concept de situation objective quand un nombre restreint d'Etats tentent d'établir «un véritable droit objectif, de vrais statuts politiques dont les effets se font sentir en dehors même du cercle des parties contractantes»[63]. Comme le soulignent Patrick Daillier et Alain Pellet,

> «l'effet *erga omnes* de telles conventions repose sur la volonté et la capacité des Etats parties d'en garantir le respect par les autres Etats ... L'ancienneté des situations établies, mais aussi leur conformité aux principes de droit international prédominants à chaque époque, conditionne le maintien de telles conventions.»[64]

Le maintien de toute situation objective repose, en fin de compte, sur le consentement, tacite la plupart du temps, des Etats[65]. En matière nucléaire, en revanche, les Etats expriment ce dernier de manière formalisée à l'intérieur de traités, et notamment à l'intérieur du TNP, alors qu'une situation objective traditionnelle se caractérise par le consentement donné par des Etats à un traité auquel ils ne sont pas parties. Dans ce dernier cas, le maintien de la situation est nettement plus fragilisé car ce consentement ne repose que sur le bon vouloir des Etats tiers, plus ou moins orienté par les capacités de contrainte dont disposent les Etats fondant cette situation. La situation ici objectivée désigne la supériorité

63. P. Daillier, M. Forteau et A. Pellet, *Droit international public*, Paris, LGDJ, 8e éd., 2009, p. 273, par. 161.
64. *Ibid.*.
65. P.-M. Dupuy, *Droit international public*, Paris, Dalloz, 7e éd., 2004, pp. 321-322, par. 290.

stratégique impliquée par la détention de l'arme nucléaire, qui se traduit par la sanctuarisation du territoire national au moyen d'une stratégie de dissuasion. Le TNP consacre, en effet, la possession par les cinq membres permanents du Conseil de sécurité de l'arme atomique et interdit, dans le même temps, à tout Etat partie au TNP d'acquérir ou de chercher à acquérir une telle arme (art. II).

En raison du réseau de normes internationales soutenant ce rapport stratégique déséquilibré, et de la formalisation initiale du consentement des Etats «tiers» à la situation, c'est-à-dire ne disposant pas d'armes nucléaires, mais parties au TNP, on peut considérer qu'il y a instauration d'une situation objective «conventionnalisée». L'ensemble des traités concernés, dont le TNP est la pierre angulaire[66], a, en effet, pour conséquence la solidification de l'avantage acquis par les Etats possédant l'arme nucléaire. Le déséquilibre stratégique établi concerne, d'une part, les relations entre Etats possédant l'arme nucléaire et Etats ne possédant pas une telle arme, distinction qui fonde le régime instauré par le TNP. Il s'entend, d'autre part, de la distinction entre les puissances possédant l'arme nucléaire dans le cadre du TNP et celles possédant une telle arme en dehors de ce traité. Ces dernières voient alors leur statut de puissances nucléaires toléré mais très fortement critiqué sur le plan de la légitimité.

Dans le cadre de la pénalisation de la prolifération maritime des ADM, la conventionnalisation de la situation objective initiale se traduit par la reproduction, au sein des normes du droit international établissant le cadre répressif des activités proliférantes, d'un régime discriminatoire établi au profit des puissances nucléaires reconnues par le TNP. Le caractère discriminatoire de ce régime découle de l'absence de règles prohibant, en droit international général, l'acquisition d'armes nucléaires et leur utilisation dans le cadre de stratégies de dissuasion nucléaire. L'originalité en la matière tient au fait que ce rapport discriminatoire est formalisé par le consentement des Etats auxquels ce rapport s'impose. Il est vrai que le régime juridique applicable à la prolifération des ADM au niveau infra-étatique repose également sur une résolution du Conseil de sécurité.

Il n'y a cependant pas à proprement parler de dépassement de la logique de conventionnalisation du simple fait que la résolution 1540 soit la principale norme initiatrice du processus de pénalisation de la prolifération des ADM. Certes, l'adoption de cette résolution instille une dimension unilatérale dans l'établissement de ce régime discriminatoire.

---

66. Il convient d'y inclure également l'ensemble des traités créant les zones exemptes d'armes nucléaires. Sur ce point, voir H. Cherief, «Les équivoques de la lutte contre la prolifération nucléaire», www.diploweb.com, 30 janvier 2011.

Toutefois, le consensualisme reste à la base du corps de règle établi, d'autant que le protocole de 2005 et la Convention internationale pour la répression des actes de terrorisme nucléaire sont des normes d'origine conventionnelle. Le maintien de l'avantage stratégique des puissances nucléaires n'est pas imposé aux Etats. L'enjeu, pour les puissances nucléaires reconnues par le TNP est, au contraire, de maintenir le caractère conventionnalisé de la situation objective, condition même de sa solidité et de sa pérennité[67].

Paragraphe 2 **Le maintien de l'avantage stratégique des puissances nucléaires «légitimes» dans le cadre de la lutte contre la prolifération maritime des ADM**

Les enjeux stratégiques impliqués par la possession de l'arme nucléaire sont clairement présents à l'esprit des Etats impliqués dans la lutte contre la prolifération maritime des armes de destruction massive par les acteurs non étatiques. Elle influence la structuration des instruments juridiques visant ces derniers en pesant sur les négociations préalables à l'adoption d'actes internationaux, conventionnels ou non, et en déterminant le contenu de ces actes. Ce contenu traduit des préoccupations diverses dont l'expression varie en fonction de la position stratégique des Etats: possèdent-ils ou non l'arme nucléaire et la possèdent-ils dans ou en dehors du cadre juridique du TNP? Elles varient également en fonction de l'objet et de la nature de l'instrument juridique considéré: s'agit-il de prohiber la prolifération en elle-même ou dans le cadre de la lutte contre le terrorisme international, s'agit-il d'une résolution du Conseil de sécurité ou d'un instrument conventionnel?

Du point de vue des Etats dotés de l'arme nucléaire, il apparaissait nécessaire de s'assurer que les textes adoptés au titre de la lutte contre la prolifération des ADM et du terrorisme ne réduisent pas leur marge de manœuvre dans le cadre des politiques de dissuasion nucléaire. L'article 4, paragraphe 4, de la Convention internationale pour la répression des actes de terrorisme nucléaire relève de cette logique. Il rappelle que «la présente Convention n'aborde ni ne saurait être interprétée comme abordant en aucune façon la question de la licéité de l'emploi ou de la menace de l'emploi des armes nucléaires par des Etats». Cette clause de sauvegarde doit être lue au bénéfice des cinq puissances nucléaires reconnues par le TNP, mais également des puissances dotées de l'arme nucléaire situées en dehors de ce dernier. La structure même des stra-

67. Il est significatif que la résolution 1718 adoptée par le Conseil de sécurité le 14 octobre 2006 «exige ... que la République populaire démocratique de Corée revienne au Traité sur la non-prolifération des armes nucléaires et aux garanties de l'Agence internationale de l'énergie atomique (AIEA)».

tégies de dissuasion aurait permis d'assimiler ces dernières à des actes de terrorisme, quand bien même il s'agirait d'un terrorisme étatique. La définition même de la dissuasion nucléaire[68] implique de peser sur la capacité décisionnelle d'un Etat en lui inspirant la terreur par la menace de représailles nucléaires, donc potentiellement apocalyptiques. La clause de l'article 4, paragraphe 4, rend cette assimilation juridiquement impossible. Ce faisant, elle permet d'étendre les possibilités de ratification de la Convention sur le terrorisme nucléaire tout en pérennisant les stratégies de dissuasion nucléaire des Etats. Cela permet ainsi de renforcer l'effectivité de la lutte contre le terrorisme sans remettre en cause l'avantage stratégique fondamental que procure la possession d'une arme nucléaire.

La résolution 1540, tout en s'inscrivant dans la même démarche, est plus ambiguë dans son contenu. Elle souligne, en particulier, qu'aucune « des obligations énoncées dans la présente résolution ne doit être interprétée d'une manière qui la mette en contradiction avec les droits et obligations des Etats parties au Traité sur la non-prolifération des armes nucléaires ». Deux lectures sont alors possibles. D'une part, la résolution protège le droit des puissances nucléaires à posséder l'arme dans le cadre de stratégies de dissuasion. Ce droit leur est reconnu par le TNP. D'autre part, il reproduit le régime discriminatoire établi par le TNP dans la mesure où les puissances dotées de l'arme nucléaire en dehors du TNP ne jouissent pas d'une protection identique. Elles disposent pourtant, au titre du droit international général, d'un droit équivalant à posséder une arme nucléaire dans le cadre d'une stratégie de dissuasion. Plus exactement, aucune règle du droit international général ne vient prohiber l'acquisition par ces Etats d'armes nucléaires dans le but de disposer des moyens matériels de la dissuasion nucléaire.

Le protocole de 2005 paraît, sur ce point, avoir tenté de « gommer » les défauts de la résolution 1540. La généralité de la formulation de l'article 3 permet en effet d'envisager que soit également protégé le droit des Etats situé hors du TNP à acquérir et posséder l'arme nucléaire dans un seul but dissuasif. L'article 3, paragraphe 2, du protocole de 2005 souligne ainsi que

> « la présente Convention ne s'applique pas aux activités des forces armées en période de conflit armé, au sens donné à ces termes en droit international humanitaire, qui sont régies par ce droit, ni aux activités menées par les forces armées d'un Etat dans l'exercice de leurs fonctions officielles, en tant qu'elles sont régies par d'autres règles de droit international ».

---

68. Voir *supra*, note 12.

Cependant, deux points viennent largement réduire la portée éventuelle de ces dispositions.

En premier lieu, la protection dont sont susceptibles de jouir les puissances nucléaires en dehors du TNP n'est garantie que dans la mesure où les activités menées par les forces armées d'un Etat « dans l'exercice de leurs fonctions officielles ... sont régies par d'autres règles de droit international ». Or, précisément, il n'existe pas à proprement parler de régime juridique existant en dehors du TNP qui serait susceptible de s'appliquer à ces puissances. Ainsi, la CIJ, dans son avis sur la *Licéité de l'emploi ou de la menace de l'emploi d'armes nucléaires* se borne-t-elle à considérer que l'interdiction ou la menace de l'emploi ou l'emploi d'armes nucléaires ne sont pas, de manière générale et absolue, prohibées par le droit international. En revanche, elle ne dit rien, sur le plan du droit coutumier, de l'acquisition des armes nucléaires. De cette sorte, il apparaît que, s'il existe une interdiction faite aux Etats d'acquérir de telles armes, il n'existe, en revanche, pas à proprement parler de régime juridique qui s'y applique.

En second lieu, et il s'agit là d'un argument décisif, les dispositions de l'article 3 du protocole de 2005 doivent être lues à la lumière de celles de l'article 4, selon lesquelles

> « ne constitue pas une infraction au sens de la Convention le fait de transporter des biens ou matières visés au par. 1 *b)* iii) ou, dans la mesure où ils ont un rapport avec une arme nucléaire ou autre dispositif explosif nucléaire, au par. 1 *b)* iv), si ces biens ou matières sont transportés à destination ou en provenance du territoire d'un Etat Partie au Traité sur la non-prolifération des armes nucléaires ou sous son contrôle ».

La portée de l'article 3 est en quelque sorte précisée par le contenu de l'article 4. Ce dernier réduit la protection effective du transport de matériel nucléaire aux seules relations interétatiques qui s'inscrivent dans le cadre du TNP. Tout transport d'armes, ou de matériel, nucléaires qui ne relèverait pas de ce cadre juridique spécifique ne serait pas susceptible d'échapper aux dispositions du protocole de 2005.

Le protocole de 2005 et la résolution 1540 retranscrivent donc, dans le corps même des instruments assurant la lutte contre la prolifération des armes de destruction massive des acteurs non étatiques, la structure discriminatoire du régime de la non-prolifération étatique. Ils consacrent, en premier lieu, la distinction entre Etats dotés et Etats non dotés de l'arme nucléaire, distinction qui fonde le régime du TNP. Ils favorisent, en second lieu, les Etats dotés de l'arme nucléaire et reconnus comme tels par le TNP en leur accordant un surcroît de protection dont ne bénéficient pas les Etats situés en dehors du TNP.

Paragraphe 3 L'extension en dehors du TNP des obligations de non-prolifération pesant sur les Etats dans le cadre de la lutte contre la prolifération maritime des ADM

Les considérations stratégiques étaient quelque peu différentes du point de vue des Etats non dotés de l'arme nucléaire. Ces derniers ont craint de voir leurs obligations découlant du TNP renforcées de manière unilatérale, dans le cadre de la résolution 1540. A été soulevée la question de l'imposition aux Etats de la volonté des membres du Conseil de sécurité, et notamment des cinq puissances nucléaires disposant chacune d'un droit de veto. Les Etats possédant l'arme nucléaire, mais en dehors du TNP, se sont retrouvés dans une situation plus ambiguë. D'un côté, leurs intérêts ont pu coïncider avec ceux des puissances nucléaires reconnues par le TNP. L'article 4, paragraphe 4, de la Convention internationale pour la répression des actes de terrorisme nucléaire en témoigne. D'un autre côté, la reproduction de la structure du TNP au cœur même des instruments de lutte contre la prolifération venant d'acteurs non étatiques a fait craindre à ces Etats de voir les dispositions du TNP s'étendre au-delà du champ conventionnel d'application du traité. Leur situation ne différait guère en ce sens des Etats non dotés de l'arme nucléaire, mais parties au TNP.

La démarche consensuelle adoptée, tant dans le cadre de la résolution 1540 que dans celui du protocole de 2005, et reposant avant tout sur la coopération interétatique, témoigne d'une volonté d'apaiser ces craintes. On doit, sur ce point, relever un remarquable revirement dans l'attitude des Etats-Unis qui se sont rapidement détournés de l'approche unilatérale. L'approche bilatérale interdit, en principe, toute extension unilatérale du régime conventionnel de la non-prolifération étatique et permet aux Etats de contrôler le champ de la lutte contre la prolifération en s'assurant qu'elle reste circonscrite aux acteurs non étatiques. Aucune intervention ne peut se faire sur le navire d'un Etat si ce dernier ne donne pas son consentement, du moins dans le cadre des eaux internationales. De ce point de vue, l'extension des compétences de l'Etat côtier sur les navires en transit dans les eaux territoriales constituerait une rupture dans l'économie générale du cadre juridique de la lutte contre la prolifération des acteurs non étatiques. Quelle que soit la solidité de son assise juridique, si le droit français opte pour une extension de la compétence de l'Etat français à l'égard des navires battant pavillon étranger en transit dans sa mer territoriale, il instituera un mécanisme d'intervention unilatérale. Or, cet unilatéralisme trancherait nettement avec la contexture du cadre juridique applicable à la lutte contre la non-prolifération.

Pour autant, les Etats non dotés de même que les puissances nucléaires en dehors du TNP se trouvent nécessairement contraints par le maillage normatif dont la résolution 1540 constitue le point d'ancrage[69]. Que penser d'un Etat qui refuserait de donner son consentement à une interception alors qu'il serait établit que le navire battant son pavillon transporte des ADM ? Une telle position constituerait, à n'en pas douter, un manquement aux obligations internationales de l'Etat, notamment au titre de la résolution 1540. Cette dernière prévoit, en effet, que

> «tous les Etats doivent s'abstenir d'apporter un appui, quelle qu'en soit la forme, à des acteurs non étatiques qui tenteraient de mettre au point, de se procurer, de fabriquer, de posséder, de transporter, de transférer ou d'utiliser des armes nucléaires, chimiques ou biologiques ou leurs vecteurs».

Certes, les dispositions du protocole de 2005 permettent aux Etats de refuser les demandes émanant d'autres Etats: l'article 8, paragraphe 2, prévoit de rajouter à la Convention pour la répression d'actes illicites contre la sécurité de la navigation maritime un article 8 *bis*, paragraphe 5 *c)* iv), qui permet notamment aux Etats de refuser «d'autoriser un arraisonnement ou une fouille». Toutefois, ces dispositions ne sont pas reprises par le texte de la résolution 1540 qui ne consacre, en conséquence, pas de mesures à même de nuancer les obligations pesant sur les Etats en matière de lutte contre la prolifération. Dans la mesure où l'Etat, dûment informé, persisterait à refuser à un Etat étranger le droit d'arraisonner ledit navire, cela pourrait être assimilé à un appui apporté à la prolifération d'ADM, indépendamment de l'objectif poursuivi par les acteurs non étatiques proliférants. Il serait donc en mesure de voir sa responsabilité internationale engagée.

Bien plus, les actions contre la prolifération des armes nucléaires, qu'elles tendent à empêcher les comportements proliférants pour eux-mêmes ou réinscrits dans le cadre d'actions terroristes, sont susceptibles de fonder des actions qui seront perçues *in fine* comme ayant pour but de prévenir l'émergence de nouvelles puissances nucléaires. Dans la

---

69. Serge Sur mentionne ainsi «l'effet matriciel» de la résolution 1540:

> «L'effet matriciel est en définitive le plus important, mais aussi le plus problématique, car il implique un effet indirect. Il s'agit d'obliger les Etats à prendre une série de mesures internes dans différents registres (par. 2 et 3). Mesures législatives interdisant aux acteurs non étatiques de se livrer aux activités prohibées, «en particulier à des fins terroristes» et de réprimer ces tentatives (par. 2); mesures administratives pour «mettre en place des dispositifs intérieurs de contrôle destinés à prévenir la prolifération» des ADM, mesures dont le contenu technique est détaillé au paragraphe 3. Ce dédoublement du processus normatif est inévitable, dès lors que les résolutions du Conseil n'ont pas d'effet direct en droit interne, mais doivent être mises en application par des procédures et règles internes.» (S. Sur, «La résolution 1540 du Conseil de sécurité (28 avril 2004)», *op. cit.*, p. 867.)

mesure où le transport d'armes nucléaires ne fait l'objet d'aucune protection particulière de la part des textes du droit international, quand il implique deux ou plusieurs Etats entre lesquels les dispositions du TNP ne trouvent pas à s'appliquer, le simple fait de transporter ces armes peut être assimilé à un comportement proliférant prohibé. Cette possibilité est de nature à affaiblir l'intensité de la coopération interétatique. Cette dernière sera nécessairement inhibée par les tensions stratégiques opposant les puissances nucléaires établies dans le cadre du TNP et celles qui, en dehors du TNP, souhaitent accéder au rang de puissance nucléaire ou améliorer le potentiel de leur arsenal nucléaire.

Ainsi dans la mesure où le transport de matériel ou d'armes nucléaires par des acteurs non étatiques est interdit, le simple fait pour une puissance nucléaire en dehors du TNP de chercher à obtenir du matériel afin d'améliorer son armement est susceptible d'être empêché en raison de son assimilation à un comportement proliférant prohibé. Le seul moyen pour ce type d'Etats de protéger l'intégrité de leurs stratégies de dissuasion est alors de prévenir toute action d'Etats étrangers contre les navires portant leur propre pavillon ou le pavillon d'un Etat allié susceptible de leur fournir le matériel adéquat. Il ne s'agit pas, ici, de déplorer ou d'acquiescer à de telles pratiques. Il est simplement possible de constater que ces enjeux stratégiques sous-jacents ne sont pas de nature à permettre l'établissement d'un cadre juridique effectif assurant l'optimisation de la lutte contre les comportements proliférants. Bien plus, les conséquences des implications stratégiques pourtant propres aux seules armes nucléaires sont susceptibles d'impacter directement la lutte contre la prolifération d'armes bactériologiques et chimiques. Les Etats pourront, en effet, se montrer réticents à se lancer dans une coopération effective en matière de prolifération d'armes chimiques et biologiques s'ils y voient un prétexte susceptible de permettre à d'autres Etats d'empêcher l'acquisition du matériel propre à leur permettre d'accéder au feu nucléaire. L'enjeu est loin d'être négligeable. Ainsi que le soulignent Gérard Chaliand et Arnaud Blin, « l'usage de telles armes par des groupes terroristes ..., bien que très rare jusqu'à présent, pourrait se développer dans l'avenir »[70].

N'eût-il pas été plus pertinent de détacher la lutte contre la prolifération visant spécifiquement les armes nucléaires de celle concernant les armes bactériologiques et chimiques. La probabilité d'une action terroriste impliquant l'usage d'armes nucléaires est possible mais demeure autrement plus hypothétique que celle impliquant l'usage d'armes bactériologiques et chimiques. Il existe, en effet, un hiatus entre la puissance des ADM, en particulier l'arme nucléaire, et la logique propre au terro-

70. G. Chaliand et A. Blin, *op. cit.*, p. 32.

risme. Le terrorisme insurrectionnel, sur le plan stratégique, « vise à faire basculer une situation asymétrique en la faveur de son élément faible, c'est-à-dire le terroriste (ou bien son commanditaire) »[71]. Sa caractéristique principale est de « produire des effets psychologiques qui sont inversement proportionnels aux moyens physiques employés »[72]. L'emploi d'armes de destruction massive extrait le mouvement terroriste de ce rapport asymétrique et le fait basculer vers un affrontement plus classique, distinct de l'action terroriste et se rapprochant du conflit armé[73].

A la faveur d'une conception globalisante, le concept d'ADM a été élaboré sans tenir compte des implications stratégiques propres à chaque type d'arme qu'il recouvre. Les conséquences juridiques de ces lacunes initiales sont de nature à menacer la paix et la sécurité internationales en minant l'efficacité du cadre juridique applicable. En abaissant l'efficacité des mécanismes juridiques, l'effectivité de la lutte contre la prolifération des ADM se trouve nécessairement affectée. La difficile traduction dans le droit interne de certains Etats des infractions établies au niveau international en matière de lutte contre la prolifération ne permet pas d'établir une incrimination continue et uniforme des comportements proliférants au niveau international. Surtout, les ambiguïtés du cadre normatif en matière nucléaire impactent négativement la lutte contre la prolifération des armes chimiques et biologiques par contamination: les relations bilatérales n'offrent, en effet, pas les garanties d'un cadre efficace de lutte contre le terrorisme ou contre les comportements proliférants qui ne sont pas distingués en fonction de leur objet. Les modalités d'intervention et d'arraisonnement étant identiques pour les armes chimiques, biologiques et nucléaires, les blocages que sont susceptibles d'entraîner les dernières rejailliront nécessairement sur les deux premiers types d'arme.

Ignorant tout bonnement les implications stratégiques du concept d'ADM, la doctrine du droit international tend parfois à tenir ce dernier responsable des obstacles que rencontre la lutte contre les comportements proliférants, en particulier dans sa dimension maritime. « L'état actuel du droit de la mer ne permettrait pas, aux yeux de certains, une lutte efficace contre de tels méfaits. »[74] Cependant, plutôt que de s'attacher au concept d'ADM et à la faiblesse des conceptions juridiques et straté-

---

71. A. Baconnet, « Les limites du terrorisme islamiste », *Revue Défense nationale*, p. 52.

72. A. Blin, « Vers un terrorisme de destruction massive ? », *Questions internationales*, n° 13, août-septembre 2005, p. 75.

73. Voir sur ce point le Rapport d'information fait au nom de la commission des affaires étrangères, de la défense et des forces armées sur le désarmement, la non-prolifération nucléaires et la sécurité de la France, par Jean-Pierre Chevènement, Sénat, 24 février 2010, pp. 132 ss.

74. P. Gautier, *op. cit.*, p. 53.

giques propres à la matière, la doctrine tente avec plus ou moins de succès de tordre à l'extrême la réalité pour la forcer à s'accommoder de concepts juridiques impropres à saisir la réalité qu'on leur soumet. Ainsi, la lutte contre le terrorisme ayant été assimilée à un conflit armé au sens juridique du terme, elle pourrait justifier, aux yeux de certains auteurs, l'extension à la lutte contre la prolifération des ADM de certaines pratiques consacrées par le droit des conflits armés susceptibles de permettre aux Etats d'arraisonner des navires en haute mer[75]. C'est oublier un peu rapidement que la relative stabilité normative de l'ordre juridique international est également un facteur de paix et de sécurité internationales.

75. D. Guilfoyle, «The Proliferation Security Initiative: Interdicting Vessels in International Waters to Prevent the Spread of Weapons of Mass Destruction?», *op. cit.*, pp. 744 ss.

14 War Crimes during Armed Conflicts at Sea

Panagiotis Sergis*

SECTION 1 INTRODUCTION

Despite the fact that individual criminal responsibility for serious violations of international humanitarian law is nowadays firmly established, especially after the "revolution" of the 1990s with the establishment of the International Criminal Tribunal for the former Yugoslavia (ICTY), the International Criminal Tribunal for Rwanda (ICTR) and subsequently, the International Criminal Court (ICC), it is not the same with war crimes during armed conflict at sea. Someone interested in the case-law regarding such crimes has to go as far back as the Nuremberg trials in order to find a case regarding the conduct of hostilities at sea. The absence of criminal proceedings seems to go hand with hand with the fact that the legal regulation of naval warfare has hardly been a priority for the international community. As Roach observes "[t]here is virtually no modern treaty law governing the use of force in naval warfare"[1]. If it were not for the San Remo Manual, it would be easy to conclude that international humanitarian law regarding naval warfare had been frozen in the interwar period.

The absence of serious interest in naval warfare may be due to the simple fact that major naval powers are not anymore conducting warfare operations; or at least, that is what they claim. Naval warfare is squeezed between action in "self-defence" and "law enforcement operations". On the one hand, the relation between *jus ad bellum* and *jus in bello* in the context of naval operations is not well defined, with self-defence serving as a panacea for military action, displacing regulation of

*HN, Hellenic Naval Academy (1995). Served as the Legal Advisor to the first Force Commander of the European Union operation, "Atalanta" (2008-2009). Law degree, University of Athens (2002), LLMs from the UoL (2004) and LSE (2005) and MSc in International Relations from the Panteion University, Athens (2008).

1. J. Ashley Roach, "Legal Aspects of Modern Submarine Warfare", 6 *Max Planck YB UNL* (2002), 367, at 368.

the conduct of hostilities[2]. A perfect example where *jus ad bellum* has almost replaced the traditional *jus in bello* as a source of justification can be found in the context of the belligerent right of visit[3]. On the other hand, modern naval operations are primarily focused on the enforcement of public order at sea. Navies' modern role is to conduct Maritime Interdiction Operations (MIOs), fighting, for example, piracy, combating drug-trafficking, dealing with migrant smuggling and enforcing Security Council resolutions. Only when the fleets are performing their traditional activity, war-fighting, does the issue of war crimes, and their subsequent penal repression, arise.

The criminalization of the commitment of certain war-time acts has proved to be a very complicated process, in which the "role of national or international courts [has been] conspicuously crucial"[4]. The courts have to give precise content to the customary rules and to clarify treaties in order to reach the legal precision that is required by criminal law. This extraordinary role of the tribunals has instigated the criticism of judicial activism and "judge-made" law. Others observe, paraphrasing Clausewitz, that "it is hard to avoid thinking that law is also the continuation of war by other means"[5]. The latter remark, despite the fact that it is strongly reminiscent of the cliché of "victor's justice", implies that there are also other interests served with the personification of responsibility for atrocities during armed conflicts. In any case, there are compelling reasons for the perpetrators of war crimes to face justice. In spite of the catharsis resulting from the criminal proceedings, naval warfare seems to remain immune from the hegemonic aspiration of international criminal law to punish war criminals.

---

2. As A. V. Lowe argues

> "in essence, there appear to be two almost entirely distinct bodies of law and principle — the traditional laws of war and neutrality, and 'Charter' rules on self-defence — which may be used as criteria of legality, neither of which is clearly established in international law to the exclusion of the other" (A. V. Lowe, "Self-defence at Sea", in W. E. Butler (ed.), *The Non-Use of Force in International Law*, Kluwer Academic Publishers, Dordrecht, 1989, p. 185, at p. 199).

3. As Papastavridis observes "[t]here are abundant examples of conflicts where the belligerent right of visit has been employed under the guise of self-defence, while very few where it has been invoked *eo nomine*"; E. Papastavridis, *The Interception of Vessels on the High Seas: Contemporary Challenges to the Legal Order of the Oceans*, Oxford, Hart Publishing, 2013, at p. 100.

4. Antonio Cassese, *International Criminal Law*, Oxford University Press, Oxford, 2003, at p. 21.

5. David Kennedy, "Lawfare and Warfare", in J. Crawford and M. Koskenniemi (eds.), *The Cambridge Companion to International Law*, Cambridge University Press, Cambridge, p. 158, at p. 161.

The aim of this chapter is to highlight the shortcomings of the concept of "war crimes" in naval warfare. The main obstacles, which prevent the criminalization process, are firstly the difficulty of accepting the existence of an "armed conflict" in the maritime milieu, secondly the underdevelopment of the law regulating naval warfare, and finally the intrinsic limitations in the symbiotic relationship between International Criminal Law (ICL) and International Humanitarian Law (IHL). They both negatively affect the legal evaluation of real-time operations, as will become evident later from the analysis of the *Mavi Marmara* incident in 2010.

SECTION 2 **EXISTENCE OF AN "ARMED CONFLICT"**

War crimes can only exist in the context of an armed conflict. A prerequisite for the applicability of international humanitarian law, and subsequently for individual criminal responsibility for its violation, is the existence of an armed conflict, whether international or non-international[6]. The determination of its existence is a rather perplexing issue especially in the maritime environment.

What is an "armed conflict" is not defined in the Geneva Conventions, in which the term acquired for first time legal significance[7], or in any other instrument of international humanitarian law. The "omission . . . was apparently deliberate, since it was hoped that this term would continue to be purely factual and not become laden with legal technicalities as did the definition of war"[8],

The ICTY in the *Tadić* case dealt with the existence of an "armed conflict" both of an international and a non-international character, and created a precedence which was generally followed in the jurisprudence of the international criminal courts during the last two decades. According to the Appeals Chamber of the Tribunal "an armed conflict exists whenever there is a resort to armed force between States or protracted armed violence between governmental authorities and organized armed

6. The criminalization of atrocities in non-international armed conflicts was not accepted until the establishment of ICTY and ICTR in the 1990s and their subsequent jurisprudence. Moreover, as Meron observes, it was asserted that "the normative customary law rules applicable in non-international armed conflicts do not encompass the criminal element of war crimes". For more details see Theodor Meron, "International Criminalization of Internal Atrocities" 89 *Am. J. Int'l L.* (1995), 554, at 559.

7. The introduction of the term served the purpose of the applicability of international humanitarian law without the existence of a formal state of war.

8. Christopher Greenwood, "Scope of Application of Humanitarian Law", in Dieter Fleck (ed.), *The Handbook of Humanitarian Law in Armed Conflicts*, Oxford University Press, Oxford, 1995, p. 39, at p. 42.

groups or between such groups within a State"[9]. The decision seems to treat differently international and non-international armed conflicts. Whereas any armed confrontation between two States does suffice for the former, as regards the latter two cumulative criteria must be met: that of organization and more significantly that of a minimum intensity. But subsequently, in the same paragraph of the judgment, the Appeals Champers changes direction significantly, and takes a different approach, by applying the intensity criterion both to international and non-international armed conflicts:

> "Applying the foregoing concept of armed conflicts to this case, we hold that the alleged crimes were committed in the context of an armed conflict . . . These hostilities exceed the intensity requirements applicable to both international and internal armed conflicts. There has been protracted, large-scale violence between the armed forces of different States and between governmental forces and organized insurgent groups."[10]

Unfortunately, this confusion is intensified by the different approaches found in legal scholarship.

The ICRC, the organization which is generally regarded as the "guardian" of the Geneva Conventions, accepts a very low threshold regarding the existence of an international armed conflict:

> "A State can always pretend, when it commits a hostile act against another State, that it is not making war, but merely *engaging in a 'police action'*, or acting in legitimate self-defence. The expression 'armed conflict' makes such arguments less easy. Any difference arising between two States and leading to the intervention of armed forces is an armed conflict . . ."[11]

The International Law Association (ILA) in its Final Report on the Meaning of Armed Conflict in International Law takes a diametrically different approach:

---

9. *Prosecutor* v. *Tadić*, Case No. IT-94-1-T, Decision on Defence Motion for Interlocutory Appeal on Jurisdiction, 2 October 1995, para. 70.

10. *Ibid.*

11. Jean S. Pictet (ed.), *The Geneva Conventions of 12 August 1949 Commentary — Volume I*, International Committee of the Red Cross, Geneva, 1952, at 32 (emphasis added). The ICRC remains constant in this position. In an opinion paper titled "How is the Term 'Armed Conflict' Defined in International Humanitarian Law?" of March 2008, published in ICRC website (http://www.icrc.org/eng/assets/files/other/opinion-paper-armed-conflict.pdf, visited 4 September 2012), it is stated that "An IAC occurs when one or more States have recourse to armed force against another State, regardless of the reasons or the intensity of this confrontation" and confirms this view with reference to the Pictet's Commentary mentioned above.

> "As a matter of customary international law a situation of armed conflict depends on the satisfaction of two essential minimum criteria, namely: a. the existence of organized armed groups [and] b. engaged in fighting of some intensity."[12]

The first requirement obviously exists in an international armed conflict, being a confrontation between armed forces of different States. The criterion of a minimum intensity is the one that creates the major difference with the ICRC's approach.

This view, requiring a rather high threshold to qualify a clash as an armed conflict, was not left unchallenged by ICRC, which explicitly mentioned political considerations as a reason for raising the threshold for admitting the existence of an armed conflict:

> "[T]he absence of a requirement of threshold of intensity for the triggering of an IAC should be maintained because it helps avoid potential legal and political controversies about whether the threshold has been reached based on the specific facts of given situation . . . The fact that a state does not, for political or other reasons, explicitly refer to the existence of an IAC in a particular situation does not prevent its being legally classified as such."[13]

On the other hand, the ICRC's approach is evidently fraught with policy considerations. The very low threshold accepted by the organization aims at the encouragement of the wider possible applicability of international humanitarian law, so as O'Connell argues "the ICRC position is based on policy rather than, perhaps, its view of what the Conventions require as a matter of law"[14].

The question of the threshold, above which an international armed conflict does exist, is of great significance in the context of the operations at sea. The issue is more acute in trying to distinguish between law enforcement operations at sea and naval warfare. As has been mentioned in the Introduction, most navies are engaged nowadays in the former

12. International Law Association, The Hague Conference (2010) — Use of Force, "Final Report on the Meaning of Armed Conflict in International Law", at p. 32 (available in ILA website http://www.ila-hq.org/en/committees/index.cfm/cid/1022, visited 28 August 2012).

13. 31st International Conference of Red Cross and Red Crescent, *International Humanitarian Law and the Challenges of Contemporary Armed Conflicts*, Geneva, Switzerland, 28 November-1 December 2011, at P. 7 (available in ICRC website http://www.icrc.org/eng/assets/files/red-cross-crescent-movement/31st-international-conference/31-int-conference-ihl-challenges-report-11-5-1-2-en.pdf, visited 5 September 2012).

14. Mary Ellen O'Connell, "Defining Armed Conflict", 13 *J. Conflict and Security Law* (2008), 393, at 397). It is significant to underscore that O'Connell was the Chairperson of the ILA Committee that drafted the Report mentioned *supra* footnote 12.

rather than the latter[15]. But in many instances it is very difficult to draw a line between law enforcement and military operations, especially in the case where the "police action" is conducted against a "violator", which is a foreign State's naval vessel.

This is a frequent phenomenon, since most of the maritime space has not been delimited. In sharp contrast with what is occurring on land, where the territorial jurisdictional allocation is firmly established and undisputed[16], numerous maritime boundaries are contested. The expansion of coastal States' jurisdiction after the World War II has significantly contributed to this result, creating the need for a great number of delimitations of maritime zones between opposing or adjacent States, affected by treaty or judicial decision.

The determination of the existence of an armed conflict is significant for defining the legal paradigm that is applicable in each situation[17]. There are no easy answers to the problem. To paraphrase Kwast, on the one hand, if a low threshold for the application of international humanitarian law is accepted, this might lead *jus in bello* to cover minor incidents that occur worldwide every day. On the other hand, if the concept of "police force" is defined too broadly, it might create a large and dangerous gap in the applicability of a very serious branch of international law[18].

It is difficult to extrapolate clear-cut answers from State practice in the maritime milieu. Although States were in most cases unwilling to

---

15. Many international relations analysts believe that this trend is going to continue in the years to come. Ollivant, for example, referring to the US Navy predicts that "the most likely future involves the Navy more or less peaceably patrolling the seas" (Douglas A. Ollivant, "Go Army, Beat Navy. Forget Ships and Drones. The Future of War Is Still on Land", 28 September 2012, available in Foreign Policy website, http://www.foreignpolicy.com/articles/2012/09/28/go_army_beat_navy, visited 1st October 2012).

16. Or in the case of dispute, there is at least a State which has a *de facto* control of the territory.

17. The two paradigms are not mutually exclusive but may overlap.

> "[A] wide range of activities occurring in situations of armed conflict are governed exclusively by the law enforcement paradigm, such as the exercise of administrative, disciplinary, and judicial authority over occupied territory, the civilian population and persons deprived of their liberty". (Nils Melzer, "Conceptual Distinction and Overlaps between Law Enforcement and the Conduct of Hostilities", in Terry Gill and Dieter Fleck (eds.), *Handbook of the International Law of Military Operations*, Oxford University Press, Oxford, p. 33, at p. 37).

This coexistence is possible only one way: law enforcement operations to take place during armed conflict or occupation. The reverse is not conceivable.

18. Patricia Jimenez Kwast, "Maritime Law Enforcement and the Use of Force", 13 *J. Conflict and Security Law* (2008), 49, at 59. The article examines the relationship of law enforcement operations with Article 2 (4), UN Charter, in the light of the *Guyana/Suriname* Award.

accept that they were engaged in armed conflict, they were eager to demand the protection accorded by international humanitarian law to the victims of these minor engagements. For example, when the Iranians in 2007 detained the crew of a British naval unit, allegedly within Iranian territorial waters, although none of the parties in the engagement invoked the existence of an armed conflict, the spokesperson for the British Prime Minister claimed that the appearance of the sailors on the Iranian television was in violation of the Third Geneva Convention[19].

The blurring of the lines between "police action" and armed conflict exists also in situations where the application of the law enforcement paradigm seems straightforward, because these do not involve confrontation between naval units of various States. In the context of the anti-piracy operations taking place at the Horn of Africa, although it is generally accepted that the pirates are criminals and not combatants[20], the Detention Standard Operating Procedure (SOP) of the European Naval Operation "EUNAVFOR Atalanta", stipulates that the ICRC should be informed when suspects are detained by EUNAVFOR Units, and should be granted access to them while they are detained[21]. Moreover, the UN Security Council, in resolution 1851, while authorizing land-operations on Somali soil for the first time, embraced the possibility that international humanitarian law could be applicable in the context of anti-piracy operations. Although the reference to that body of law is maybe made out of the desire of the Council to emphasize the caution under which such operations should be conducted, only two legal explanations seem possible regarding the applicability of international humanitarian law:

> "On the one hand, third states co-operating with the TFG in Somalia — as Resolution 1851 explicitly requests — could become parties to the existing conflict there simply by collaborating with an entity that is already party to an ongoing non-international armed conflict. On the other hand, Resolution 1851 could be

19. Matthew B. Stannard, "What Law Did Tehran Break? Capture of British Sailors a Gray Area in Application of Geneva Conventions", San Francisco Chronicle, 1 April 2007, available in http://www.sfgate.com/news/article/What-law-did-Tehran-break-Capture-of-British-2576880.php, visited 1 September 2012.

20. Douglas Guilfoyle, "The Laws of War and the Fight against Somali Piracy: Combatants or Criminals", 11 *Melb. J. Int'l L.* (2010), 141, at 142.

21. SOP Legal 001 dated 26 March 2009 (on file with the author). Although the provision in the SOP regarding the ICRC is maybe driven by political considerations, the involvement of the principal organization ensuring humanitarian protection and assistance for victims of war and armed violence highlights the absence of a sharp distinction between the concept of armed conflict on the one hand, and the law enforcement operations on the other.

read in such a way that the counterpiracy operations in and of themselves — independently of the ongoing conflict in Somalia — could eventually reach the threshold of a non-international armed conflict, thereby triggering the application of IHL."[22]

In another rather different approach, it is submitted that the distinction to be drawn should not be between law enforcement operations and situations of armed conflict but between low intensity hostilities and full-scale war[23]. The quest of a different legal regime applicable to limited hostilities creates a rupture in the armed conflict paradigm and virtually integrates law intensity conflicts within the law enforcement paradigm, highlighting the blurring of the lines between the two paradigms.

Regarding the existence of a non-international armed conflict, there is a general agreement about the requirements of the organization of the rival groups and intensity of the fighting, as they were set by the *Tadić* Appeals Champers judgment[24]. But there is a need to distinguish between internal armed conflicts and cases of lesser violence. *Jus in bello interno* is not applicable in cases of "internal disturbances and tensions, such as riots, isolated and sporadic acts of violence and other acts of a similar nature, as not being armed conflicts"[25]. Although it is rather

22. Robin Geiss, "Armed Violence in Fragile States: Low — Intensity Conflicts, Spillover Conflicts, and Sporadic Law Enforcement Operations by Third Parties", 91 *International Review of the Red Cross Number 873* (2009), 127, at 140.

23. This is the approach of O'Connell, one of the most eminent experts in the law of naval warfare. For example, in assessing how international law affects naval planning, he observes, equating law enforcement action with restricted warfare, that "[i]n conditions of limited hostilities, or 'police actions' — which are the most likely naval operations of the immediate future — the situation clearly depends on the restrictions which the international community has succeeded in building into the exercise of seapower" (D. P. O'Connell, "International Law and Contemporary Naval Operations", 44 *Brit. YB Int'l L.* (1970), 19, at 59).

24. *Supra* footnote 9.

25. Protocol Additional to the Geneva Conventions of 12 August 1949, and relating to the Protection of Victims of Non-International Armed Conflicts (Protocol II), 8 June 1977, Article 1 (2). This provision is repeated verbatim in the ICC Statute, Articles 8 (2) *(d)* and 8 (2) *(f)*. In the same Article 8 (2) *(f)*, it is added that the provision regarding war crimes during internal armed conflicts "applies to armed conflicts that take place in the territory of a State when there is protracted armed conflict between governmental authorities and organized armed groups or between such groups". The influence of the "*Tadić* formula" in the wording of this provision is apparent. For an analysis of this provision and the significance of the distinction between "protracted armed violence" of the *Tadić* decision and "protracted armed conflict" of Article 8 (2) *(f)* of the ICC Statute see Anthony Cullen, "The Parameters of Internal Armed Conflict in International Humanitarian Law", 12 *U. Miami Int'l & Comp. L. Rev.* (2004), 189, at 206.

difficult nowadays to envisage an internal armed conflict with a dominant naval dimension, because of the peculiarities of naval warfare, the issue is far from theoretical, as the *Mavi Marmara* incident has clearly illustrated.

In view of the present author, it would be more apt to adopt another approach, i.e. to focus on the mode of the conduct of the opposing forces in relation to human rights law and especially the right to life as the decisive criterion for determining whether an armed conflict exists, international or non-international[26]. The difference between a law enforcement operation and an armed conflict lies in the *modus operandi* of the fighting forces. In the context of police actions, Governments tend to use minimum force in order to arrest the suspected criminals, while respecting their right to life. On the other hand, during armed conflicts the need to overwhelm the adversary gives more latitude in the use of force, allowing for casualties even among the civilians, if they are not disproportionate to the concrete and direct military advantage anticipated. It is always a possibility that a limited law enforcement action escalates in a situation of an armed conflict. Real life situations are usually not crystal clear and grey areas should be expected. This notwithstanding, the actual behaviour of the adversaries is the best indicator of which paradigm, the law enforcement or the armed conflict, is relevant. But even in cases where the application of the latter is straightforward, another hindrance arises: that of law regulating the conduct of naval warfare.

SECTION 3 **REGULATING THE NAVAL WARFARE**

Developing law regulating the execution of naval warfare has not been the first priority of the international community especially after World War II. On the one hand, there has not been a feeling of urgency in the need to clarify and develop the legal framework of naval warfare. On the other, it would have been meaningless to adopt legal rules without the consent of the major naval powers. The demise of the significance of the humanitarian law concerning naval warfare is reflected in the writings of the international law scholars. Whereas the older books treat in a balanced manner the law of the sea during peacetime and the law of naval warfare, the more contemporary writings almost ignore the latter[27]. The underdevelopment of this branch of inter-

26. Arne Willy Dahl and Magnus Sandbu, "The Threshold of Armed Conflict", 45 *The Military Law and the Law of War Review* (2006), 369, at 374.

27. William J. Fenrick, "Legal Aspects of Targeting in the Law of Naval Warfare", 29 *Can. YB Int'l L.* (1991), 238, at 238.

national humanitarian law is at odds with the overdevelopment of the law governing land warfare. Although the idea that all forms of warfare must be subject to the same body of law is gaining acceptance[28], the current development of international humanitarian law leaves much to be desired in order to reach this ideal concept.

The basic treaty law regulating naval warfare is limited to the following: (i) the dated VII, VIII, IX, XI and XIII Hague Conventions of 1907, which, although they set out the basic principles in this regard, they have not incorporated the technological, political and legal developments of the last century; (ii) the Geneva Convention II of 1949[29] and (iii) the Procès-verbal of 6 November 1936 relating to the Rules of Submarine Warfare set forth in Part IV of the Treaty of London of 22 April 1930.

The Diplomatic Conference that led to the adoption of the two 1977 Additional Protocols to the 1949 Geneva Conventions decided not to address the regulation of naval warfare[30]. The unfortunate consequence is that "there is still no comprehensive treaty governing naval warfare"[31].

That being the case, the law of naval warfare is mainly of a customary nature. Many treaty instruments, like the London Declaration of 1909, are regarded to be declaratory of existing customary law. The major problem regarding the customary humanitarian law is the difficulty of finding evidence of custom in an armed conflict, especially in the maritime environment[32]. Moreover, there always exists a possibility to

28. Emmanuel Roucounas, "Some Issues Relating to War Crimes in Air and Sea Warfare", in Yoram Dinstein and Mala Tabory (eds.), *War Crimes in International Law*, Martinus Nijhoff, Leiden, 1996, p. 275.

29. These above-mentioned conventions deal with the following issues:

(a) Hague Convention VII: The Conversion of Merchant Ships into War-Ships.
(b) Hague Convention VIII: The Laying of Automatic Submarine Contact Mines.
(c) Hague Convention IX: Bombardment by Naval Forces in Time of War.
(d) Hague Convention XI: Certain Restrictions with Regard to the Exercise of the Right of Capture in Naval War.
(e) Hague Convention XIII: The Rights and Duties of Neutral Powers in Naval War.
(f) Geneva Convention II: For the Amelioration of the Condition of Wounded, Sick and Shipwrecked Members of Armed Forces at Sea.

30. Ashley Roach, *supra* footnote 1, at 384.

31. Ashley Roach, "The Law of Naval Warfare at the Turn of Two Centuries", 94 *Am. J. Int'l L.* (2000), 64, at 65.

32. Various reasons contribute to this effect, for example the exceptional circumstances under which humanitarian law is applicable and the prohibitive nature of its norms. See Sonja Boelaert-Suominen, "Grave Breaches, Universal Jurisdiction and Internal Armed Conflict: Is Customary Law Moving Towards a Uniform Enforcement Mechanism for All Armed Conflicts?", 5 *J. Conflict & Sec. L.* (2000), 63, at 66.

accept norms as customary law, ignoring the absence of concrete State practice, in order to enhance the applicability of the noble and humanizing principles of *jus in bello*. In humanitarian law "the 'ought' merges with the 'is', the *lex ferenda* is confused with the *lex lata*"[33]. In any case, without judicial decisions clarifying its content, international law of armed conflict remains in an amorphous status, rendering it almost impossible to reach a common understanding of its exact contours. In this context, it is rather regrettable that authors of the recent study of the ICRC regarding the customary humanitarian law "decided not to research customary law applicable to naval warfare"[34].

It is rather exaggerative yet true that the word chaos has been frequently used to describe the condition of the law of naval warfare[35]. This has a profound impact on criminalization of violations of the law. As Ronzitti avers,

> "[t]he crisis of the law of naval warfare has rendered less certain the content of the rules by which belligerents are to abide . . . In effect, a theory of crimes of war . . . cannot be properly elaborated, unless there is a common agreement on the content of the rules and the importance of the values they embody"[36].

In order to fill this regulatory gap, a group of specialists in international law and naval experts drafted the renowned 1994 San Remo Manual[37], which purports to provide a contemporary restatement of international humanitarian law regulating naval warfare, including some provisions which might be considered to be a progressive development of it. The Manual was met with widespread acceptance and has strongly influenced many national manuals on the law of armed conflict. Still, its extensive reliance on Additional Protocol I has been severely criticized as reflecting a less rigorous approach to customary international

33. Theodor Meron, "The Geneva Conventions as Customary Law", 81 *Am. J. Int'l L.* (1987), 348, at 361. For the problem of judge-made law, see *infra*.

34. Jean-Marie Henckaerts and Louise Doswald-Beck, *Customary International Humanitarian Law – Volume I: Rules*, Cambridge University Press, Cambridge, 2005, at p. xxx. The rationale behind this decision is that the law of naval warfare was the subject of a major restatement, namely the San Remo Manual. This position is not easily defendable, taking into account that there are serious reservations regarding the Manual's approach to customary international law (see *infra*).

35. Emmanuel Roucounas, *supra* footnote 28, at p. 279.

36. Natalino Ronzitti, "The Crisis of the Traditional Law Regulating International Armed Conflicts at Sea and the Need for Its Revision", in N. Ronzitti (ed.), *The Law of Naval Warfare*, Kluwer Academic Publishers, Dordrecht, 1988, p. 1, at p. 2.

37. For the Manual and its Explanation see Louise Doswald-Beck (ed.), *San Remo Manual on International Law Applicable to Armed Conflicts at Sea*, Cambridge University Press, Cambridge, 2005.

law[38]. In any case, the San Remo Manual is a non-binding instrument and its impact on the planning and execution of naval operations remains to be proven.

The equivocal status of the law of naval warfare is perfectly illustrated by the example of the ambiguities related to the application of the principle of distinction, in the context of naval warfare.

The principle of distinction, which is characterized by the International Court of Justice as cardinal, fundamental and intransgressible[39], is an excellent example illustrating the problems of the law of naval warfare. In accordance with the principle

> "the Parties to the conflict shall at all times distinguish between the civilian population and combatants and between civilian objects and military objectives and accordingly shall direct their operations only against military objectives"[40].

It could be expected that in the maritime environment, where naval vessels can easily be distinguished from merchant ships, the application of the principle of distinction would have been straightforward. Unfortunately, in the context of naval warfare the application of the principle is much more difficult than in land warfare.

Instrumental for the application of the principle of distinction is the definition of the military objective. According to the definition given in the Additional Protocol I, military objectives

> "are limited to those objects which by their nature, location, purpose or use make an effective contribution to military action and whose total or partial destruction, capture or neutralization, in the circumstances ruling at the time, offers a definite military advantage"[41].

This definition is widely accepted and many international law experts regard it as reflecting customary law[42]. The main problem is that this definition is not applicable in the context of naval warfare. Or to be more accurate, it applies only "to all attacks from the sea . . . against objectives on land but do not otherwise affect the rules of international

38. Jane Gilliland Dalton, "A Comparison between the San Remo Manual and the U.S. Navy's Commander's Handbook", 36 *IYHR* (2006), 71, at 76.

39. *Legality of the Threat or Use of Nuclear Weapons*, Advisory Opinion of 8 July 1996, *ICJ Reports 1996*, p. 26, at p. 257, paras. 78-79.

40. Protocol Additional to the Geneva Conventions of 12 August 1949, and relating to the Protection of Victims of International Armed Conflicts (Protocol I), 8 June 1977, Article 48.

41. *Ibid.*, Article 52 (2).

42. Theodor Meron, *Human Rights and Humanitarian Norms as Customary Law*, Clarendon Press, Oxford, 1989, at p. 64.

law applicable in armed conflict at sea or in the air"[43]. The San Remo Manual, after extensive debate[44], adopted the definition of Additional Protocol I, incorporating into the law of naval warfare the developments of regulation in the context of land warfare, despite the fact that the Protocol is not applicable as such in the conflicts at sea. Obviously, this is not the final word on the issue and the perplexing question concerning which objects cannot be lawfully attacked at sea has yet to be solved.

The economic dimension of naval warfare, namely the vital contribution of merchant ships to the war effort of the belligerents, has made it difficult to articulate a comprehensive approach regarding which merchant ships are civilian objects and thus immune from attack. The United States, for example, a major naval power indeed, adopts a wider approach concerning military objectives: for an object to qualify as a military objective, it does not need to make an effective contribution to military action. It suffices just to "effectively contribute to the enemy's war-fighting or war-sustaining capability"[45]. Some naval experts and international law scholars subscribe to the same view. For example, Fenrick argues that

> "[t]he primary legal criterion for determining whether or not a merchant vessel is a legitimate military objective should be a functional one based on the task the merchant vessel is employed on at the time the targeting decision is made"[46].

This legal approach was used in order to legitimize the indiscriminate Iraqi attacks during the first Gulf War, or the Gulf Tanker War, in sharp contrast with the evaluation of the Iranian attacks. This approach to the identification of the military objective in naval warfare, which Politakis calls the "functional approach"[47], is too vague and ill-defined, placing almost no restriction on the destruction of merchant ships simply because they are engaged in the enemy's commerce. The widening of the scope of the notion of military objective, giving a *carte blanche* to the targeting of merchant vessels, is situated in the apologetic extreme of the spectrum of international law[48], and can hardly promote a compre-

43. *Supra* footnote 40, Article 49 (3).
44. *Supra* footnote 37, Article 40, at p. 114.
45. Department of the Navy, *The Commander's Handbook on the Law of Naval Operations (NWP 1-14M)*, July 2007, at p. 8-1.
46. W. J. Fenrick, "Legal Aspects of Targeting in the Law of Naval Warfare", 29 *Can. YB Int'l L.* (1991), 238, at 274.
47. George Politakis, *Modern Aspects of the Laws of Naval Warfare and Maritime Neutrality*, Kegan Paul International, London, 1998, at p. 632.
48. For the oscillation of international law between apology and utopia see Martti Koskenniemi, *From Apology to Utopia: The Structure of International Legal Argument*, Lakimiesliiton Kustannus, Finnish Lawyers' Publishing Company, Helsinki, 1989.

hensive approach of the notion of military objectives in all types of warfare. These definitional ambiguities are not, however, the only obstacle for the regulation of targeting during war at sea.

A unique feature of war at sea is the capacity for arming merchant vessels and the latitude of the permissible ruses of war. These characteristics of naval warfare give a further blow to the principle of distinction. The experience of the two World Wars illustrates the lawlessness that can ensue from their effects. So long as the enemies' merchant marines are armed[49], a thorny question arises: at which point can a vessel be considered as participating in the hostilities and thus lawfully attacked? In accordance with the traditional approach the decisive criterion was the type of armament. Defensive armament could not alter the legal status of the enemy merchant vessels as civilian objects[50]. The merchant ships liable to seizure could defend themselves and even seize the attacking warship[51]. But without an attack, a merchant vessel of a belligerent could not participate in the hostilities.

With the gradual evolution of weaponry systems, it became obvious that it was difficult to draw a line between defensive and offensive armament. That is why the "concept of defensively armed merchant vessels is an anachronism"[52]. The San Remo Manual focuses on the ability of the armament of the merchant vessel to inflict damage on a warship. Thus, only deflective systems are allowed and individual weapons exclusively for the defence of personnel[53]. It seems that the modern approach to the armament of merchant ships allows only for

49. Converting merchant ships into warships is not addressed here. It suffices, for the purposes of this chapter, to underline that the issue remains a controversial one, especially as regards when and where the conversion can be effected and if the converted into warship merchant vessel can be reconverted again before the cessation of the hostilities. For more see Yoram Dinstein, "The Laws of War at Sea", 10 *IYHR* (1980), 38, at 58.

50. Lassa Oppenheim and Hersh Lauterpacht, *International Law: A Treatise*, 7th ed., Longmans, London, 1955, at p. 468.

51. *Ibid.*, at p. 266.

52. W. J. Fenrick, "Introductory Report — Military Objectives in the Law of Naval Warfare", in H. G. Von Heinegg (ed.), *The Military Objective and the Principle of Distinction in the Law of Naval Warfare – Report, Commentaries and Proceedings of the Round Table of Experts on International Humanitarian law Applicable to Armed Conflicts at Sea, Ruhr-Universität Bochum, 10-14 November 1989*, Universitätsverlag Dr. N. Brockmeyer, Bochum, 1991, at p. 42.

53. *Supra* footnote 37, Article 60, at p. 150. This is the approach taken by the drafters of the UK Manual on the Law of Armed Conflict. On the contrary the US Commander's *Handbook on the Law of Naval Operations*, allows for attack even in case of very light armament exclusively for defensive purposes. For more see Natalino Ronzitti, "Naval Warfare", in R. Wolfrum, *The Max Planck Encyclopedia of Public International Law*, Vol. VII, Oxford University Press, Oxford, 2012, at p. 559.

"soft kill" defensive weapon systems, such as chaffs flares and decoys, whereas the "hard kill" systems, physically interacting with the target, is doubtful if they meet the requirements of the Manual. If the Manual's approach is adhered to, it will work against the assumption of armed merchant marine, which resulted in unrestricted warfare during the World Wars. Besides the arming of merchant vessels, the permissible ruses of war in the context of naval warfare enhance the difficulty to distinguish between civilian objects and military objectives.

Using ruses of war is a permissible method of warfare in both the land and the naval context, and should be distinguished from perfidious acts, that is, acts specifically planned to invite the confidence of the adversary in order to betray it subsequently, which are prohibited. It is not generally easy to distinguish between permissible ruses and prohibited perfidy. The issue is more controversial in the context of naval warfare[54]. The old rule of allowing the use of false flag during armed conflicts at sea is still applicable, as it is clearly stipulated in the relevant articles of Additional Protocol I[55]. Moreover, law of naval warfare allows the disguise of warships as merchant vessels, compromising in a very serious aspect the application of the distinction principle. The only requirement for the warship is to reveal her true identity only just before launching the attack, thus at a time when the disguise is useless. The important issue, in the view of the present writer, is not whether the false flag rule is sanctioned or just tolerated. In any case, modern weapons reduce the operational value of flying a false flag. The vital issue is that the anachronistic view that naval warfare is not subject to the same rules as warfare on land is perpetuated. Another aspect of the same approach regards the usage of exclusion zones during armed conflicts at sea, which creates more problems in applying the principle of distinction.

The wide adoption of war zones during armed conflict at sea and the "rights" claimed by the belligerents inside such zones is a reality difficult to reconcile with international humanitarian law. The free-fire policy within the zones is in sharp contrast with the principle of distinction. Scholars have expressed a wide variety of approaches regarding their legality covering the whole spectrum of positions: from absolute condemnation to whole-hearted approval. Some scholars argue that regarding this issue "the law is in a state of flux and because the perceived legitimacy or illegitimacy of particular uses of exclusion zones will

---

54. For an operational approach of the delineation between ruses and perfidy at sea see Mary Hall, "False Colors and Dummy Ships: The use of Ruse in Naval Warfare", XLII *Naval War College Review Number 3* (1989), 52.

55. *Supra* footnote 40, Articles 39 (3) and 37 (1) *(d)*.

depend to a considerable extent on the context of the conflict in which they are used"[56]. Others propose the, difficult to define, criterion of reasonableness to access the legality of the zones[57].

Even the San Remo Manual does not take a clear-cut position perpetuating the existence of "grey area" in this aspect. Although the drafters of the Manual seemingly adopted a firm stance against the use of such zones, they later compromised their position by acknowledging the fact that parties to the conflict "might be more likely to do certain things in a zone than outside of a zone, particularly if the zone is created for defensive purposes"[58].

For present purposes, the most interesting justification for the employment of fire-at-sight zones is based on the UN Charter. *Jus ad bellum* is used to legitimize the adoption of the zones, displacing *jus in bello*. This was readily illustrated by the legal arguments used to justify the adoption of the British Total Exclusion Zone (TEZ) during the Falklands Conflict. This zone was proclaimed as a free-fire zone, based on the right of self-defence in accordance with Article 51 of UN Charter:

> "The legality of the TEZ avoided the necessity for determining whether any ship or aircraft in the area in fact presented an immediate threat to the task force . . . All unauthorized ships and aircraft in the zone were deemed to be threatening and so liable to attack in self-defence."[59]

The UN Charter is used in order to offer legitimacy in practices of dubious legality, if not patently unlawful under humanitarian law, actually rendering the distinction principle simply a euphemism[60]. More interestingly, when in the context of the same conflict the British submarine *Conqueror* sank the Argentinean warship *General Belgrano* outside the TEZ, traditional *jus in bello* arguments were put forward for justification, *Belgrano* being a lawful military target[61].

---

56. W. J. Fenrick, "The Exclusion Zone Devise in the Law of Naval Warfare", 24 *Can. YB Int'l L.* (1986), 91, at 124.

57. For an excellent criticism of this approach and a general analysis of reasonableness in international law see George Politakis, *supra* footnote 47, at p. 145.

58. *Supra* footnote 37, at p. 181. For an effort to mitigate the effects of this "gray area", see Fausto Pocar, "Missile Warfare and Exclusion Zones in Naval Warfare", 28 *IYHR* (1998), 215, at 223.

59. R. R. Churchill and A. V. Lowe, *The Law of the Sea*, Manchester University Press, Manchester, 1999, at p. 424.

60. For this trend see *supra* footnote 2.

61. See for example Wolff Heintschell Von Heinegg, "War Zones", in R. Wolfrum, *supra* footnote 53, Vol. X, at p. 768. This flip-flop approach or forum shopping seems to accommodate a more "realistic" approach to international law and the dictates of power politics.

The difficulties concerning the application of the principle of distinction are characteristic of the current development of the international humanitarian law regulating naval warfare. This situation is even more perplexing in situations of non-international armed conflicts (NIAC) at sea.

Although States were unwilling to subject International Armed Conflicts (IACs) and Non-International Armed Conflicts (NIACs) to the same, treaty-based legal regime, the tendency during the last 20 years[62] is to bridge the regulatory gap of NIACs through customary international law. It is observed that there exists a widespread tendency to apply the rules regulating IACs to NIACs, by the acceptance of the existence of customary law. This convergence, which is driven by judicial decisions[63], is reflected in the ICRC study regarding customary international humanitarian law[64]. Out of the 161 identified customary rules, 142 rules are equally applicable in both IACs and NIACs[65]. The extent to which this convergence is relevant to armed conflicts at sea was not addressed in the ICRC study[66], because of the drafting of the San Remo Manual. But the latter leaves also the question open:

> "[A]lthough the provisions of this Manual are primarily meant to apply to international armed conflict at sea, this has intentionally not been expressly indicated . . . in order not to dissuade the implementation of these rules in non-international armed conflicts involving naval operations."[67]

As a result, it is unfortunate that the international humanitarian law governing NIACs at sea remains rather obscure. In more detail, the wording of the drafters of the San Remo Manual ("not to dissuade the implementation") is disquieting as regards the legal obligation to apply

62. Earlier, States were unwilling to accept the existence of customary law regulating NIACs. For example, during the negotiations that resulted in the Additional Protocol II "[i]t was apparently felt that the regulation of non-international armed conflicts was too recent a matter for state practice to have sufficiently developed in this field" (Commentary to the Additional Protocol II, published at ICRC website, http://www.icrc.org/ihl.nsf/COM/475-760002?OpenDocument, visited 5 September 2012).

63. The issue identified *supra* regarding the pressure enforced by the humanitarian principles in the customary law norm creating procedure is enhanced in the context of NIACs, due to the minimal treaty law regulation of such conflicts. For the issue of judge-made law see *infra*.

64. See *supra* footnote 34.

65. Emily Crawford, "Blurring the Lines between International and Non-International Armed Conflicts — The Evolution of Customary International Law Applicable in Internal Armed Conflicts", 15 *Australian International Law Journal* (2008), 29, at 53.

66. See *supra* footnote 34.

67. See *supra* footnote 37, at p. 73.

the rules of the Manual during NIACs *in toto*. According to the traditional approach, in the case of "recognized belligerency"[68] or "wars of national liberation"[69] the full body of law of naval warfare is applicable. On the one hand, the applicability in NIACs of the rules of IACs regulating the methods and means of warfare, the special protection of persons and objects, the target discrimination and the measures short of attack against the ships of the conflicting parties do not raise serious legal questions. On the other hand, there are divergent views regarding the rights of the belligerents against the vessels of third States in the context of NIACs on the high seas[70].

Some scholars argue that in the context of NIACs no party to the conflict has the right to interfere with third parties' ships on the high seas[71]. There is, however, a contrary view that there should be no difference between IACs and NIACs on the actions that may be adopted against vessels flying the flag of a neutral State[72]. Between these two extremes, there seems to be a more pragmatic view which links the existence of belligerent rights against neutral vessels on the high seas with the intensity of the conflict[73]. It is doubtful whether such a schism between the law regulating limited and unrestricted armed conflicts can be accepted. The drafters of the San Remo Manual have not endorsed the notion of limited warfare, even though elements of this concept can be found in the articles and the commentary describing the relation between armed conflicts and the law of self-defence, especially the impact of the con-

68. It is doubtful whether the belligerency doctrine has survived in contemporary international law. "The doctrine has declined to the point where recognition of belligerency is almost unknown today" according to the UK Manual (UK MOD, *The Joint Service Manual of the Law of Armed Conflict (JSP 383)*, 2004, at p. 384, para. 15.1.2). Despite this fact, the doctrine has served as a starting point for the idea that internal conflicts are not immune from international law. See Anthony Cullen, *The Concept of Non-International Armed Conflict in International Humanitarian Law*, Cambridge University Press, Cambridge, 2010, at p. 23.

69. As a consequence of Article 1 (4) of Additional Protocol I.

70. For the existence of such a right within the territorial sea, see Wolff Heintschell Von Heinegg, "The Legality of MIOs within the Framework of Operation Enduring Freedom", in W. P. Heere (ed.), *Terrorism and the Military*, TMC Asser Press, The Hague, 2003, p. 43, at p. 46. For a more reluctant acceptance see Natalino Ronzitti, *supra* footnote 36, at p. 12.

71. Natalino Ronzitti, *supra* footnote 36, at p. 12.

72. Daniel Benoliel, Israel, "Turkey and the Gaza Blockade", 33 *U. Pa. J. Int'l L.* (2011-2012), 615, at 642, and James Kraska, "Rule Selection in the Case of Israel's Naval Blockade of Gaza: Law of Naval Warfare or Law of the Sea?", in M. N. Schmitt *et al.* (eds.), 13 *Yearbook of International Humanitarian Law* (2010), TMC Asser Press, The Hague, 2011, p. 367, at p. 392.

73. D. P. O'Connell introduced the concept of limited warfare, which is subject to different laws insulating high seas from belligerent acts. (See, for example, D. P. O'Connell, *The Influence of Law on Sea Power*, Manchester University Press, Manchester, 1975, at p. 114 and also *supra* footnote 23).

cepts of necessity and proportionality on a tactical level[74]. In any case, there are occasions of high intensity NIACs during which the international community acquiesced in belligerent measures against neutral shipping on the high seas, such as the blockades during the US Civil War and the Israel-Hezbollah conflict of 2006. As it is observed "[t]he right of states to implement measures against neutral vessels in NIACs is thus at best an unsettled question"[75].

The law governing IACs and NIACs at sea has many "gray areas". Without the clarification of the applicable law, it is difficult to elaborate a coherent theory of war crimes at sea. On the other hand, the experience of the 1990s with the establishment of the ICTY, the ICTR and finally the ICC clearly shows that the judicial oversight of the conduct of hostilities sheds light on the obscurities surrounding the applicable law. The ambition of the rule of law to regulate every aspect of human life is clearly illustrated in the symbiotic relationship between international criminal law and international humanitarian law.

SECTION 4 **CRIMINALIZATION OF VIOLATIONS OF IHL**

The relationship between IHL and ICL is twofold: on the one hand, IHL provides the substantive rules for ICL regarding war crimes. On the other, not only is ICL one of the most effective means to implement IHL, but also the jurisprudence of national and international tribunals has contributed to the clarification of the rules of IHL and even their development[76]. As of today, the relationship between IHL and ICL is best characterized as synthesis between the two branches of international law[77].

Which rules of IHL create individual criminal responsibility is not a straightforward issue. Not every violation of the laws of war amounts to

74. See *supra* footnote 37, at p. 75.

75. Douglas Guilfoyle, "The *Mavi Marmara* Incident and Blockade in Armed Conflict", 81 *BYIL* (2011), 171, at 193.

76. For an analysis of the two-way relationship see Marco Sassoli, "Humanitarian Law and International Criminal Law", in Antonio Cassese (ed.), *The Oxford Companion to International Criminal Law*, Oxford University Press, Oxford, 2002, p. 111.

77. This relationship today embraces human rights law too. The need for the cross-reference between human rights law and humanitarian law is analysed by Christopher Greenwood, "Human Rights and Humanitarian Law — Conflict or Convergence", 43 *Case W. Res. J. Int'l L.* (2010-2011), 491, at 505. For an analysis of the different phases of the relationship between ICL and IHL see Hans-Peter Gasser, "The Changing Relationship between International Criminal Law, Human Rights Law and Humanitarian Law", in Jose Doria *et al.* (eds.), *The Legal Regime of the ICC: Essays in the Honor of Prof. I. P. Blishchenco*, Koninklijke Brill, Leiden, 2009, p. 1111.

a war crime, as it was, erroneously, contended in the past[78]. War crimes are violations of the laws and customs applicable in armed conflict, to which international law attaches individual criminal responsibility. As Abi-Saab clarifies,

> "[I]n fact, for a violation of a rule *jus in bello* to produce the special legal effect of entailing the criminal responsibility of the individual who commits it, one should prove not only the existence of the violated rule in international law, but also the parallel existence of a secondary rule, usually a customary one, ascribing to the former rule this special legal effect in case of violation."[79]

This secondary rule is the decisive criterion of whether to accept a war crime and not of how "grave" or "serious" the violation of international humanitarian law is, as it is generally accepted. Following the same reasoning and trying to distinguish between the original technical concept of "grave breaches" and "war crimes", Oberg emphasizes that "war crimes consist of secondary rules of international criminal law that attach criminal sanctions to breaches of primary rules of international humanitarian law"[80]. In any case, the courts have a unique role either in identifying the existence of the secondary rule or in defining which violations are serious, and thus creating individual criminal responsibility.

The courts' role is not limited to the determination of the existence of the secondary rule criminalizing the violation. The judiciary, especially of the ICTY and ICTR, had an unparalleled impact on the development of IHL. The definition of "armed conflict", the expansion of the concept of "protected persons" based not on nationality but on ethnicity, the establishment of individual criminal responsibility for violations of IHL during internal conflicts, the incorporation of war crimes not previously elaborated in IHL, and finally the clarification of the content of existing crimes can be enumerated as the significant contributions of the international tribunals to the advancement of IHL.

The above-mentioned impact upon IHL would have been impossible without the display of remarkable judicial creativity. The extent of the judicial dynamism has led some commentators to even speak about the

78. For criticism of this thesis see Yoram Dinstein, *The Conduct of Hostilities under the Law of International Armed Conflict*, Cambridge University Press, Cambridge, 2004, at p. 229.

79. Georges Abi-Saab, "The Concept of 'War crimes'", in Sienho Yee and Wang Tieya (eds.), *International Law in the Post-Cold War World*, Routledge, London, 2001, p. 99, at p. 112.

80. Marko Divac Oberg, "The Absorption of Grave Breaches into War Crimes Law", 91 *International Review of the Red Cross Number 873* (2009), 163, at 166.

"reinvention" of war crimes by the international criminal tribunals. "There is little doubt that the judicial creativity . . . in the area of war crimes has amounted to judicial law-making"[81]. The "vehicle" to achieve the development of IHL was customary law.

It is beyond the scope of the present work to analyse the formulation of customary law in public international law. Just for a brief analysis, two are the classical elements of the customary norm, the objective one, namely State practice, and the subjective one, that is, *opinio juris sive necessitatis*. Regarding the first element, it is accepted that the State practice needs not to be absolutely uniform[82]. Another crucial issue regarding the objective element is how much time is needed to elapse for the practice to acquire customary status. As the ICJ has held, extensive practice can lead to the formation of a customary rule, even in a short period of time[83]. The subjective element, that the States act in a certain way because they believe they have a legal obligation to do so, is very difficult to discern. The motives of State action could be just political, without any legal connotation. Therefore, the ICJ's basic way to assert the subjective element was to base *opinio juris* on extensive State practice[84]. In just a minority of cases, the Court adopted a strict approach requiring specific proof of the *opinio juris*[85], and then only to deny the existence of a customary rule[86].

The most practical way to determine whether a specific practice is performed out of legal obligation is the official pronouncement of one State's opinion regarding what the content of the law is. This is why the

81. Shane Darcy, "The Reinvention of War Crimes by the International Criminal Tribunals", in S. Darcy and J. Powderly (eds.), *Judicial Creativity at the International Criminal Tribunals*, Oxford University Press, Oxford, 2010, p. 106, at p. 127.

82. "State practice, including that of States whose interests are specially affected, should [be] both extensive and virtually uniform." (*North Sea Continental Shelf* cases, Judgment of 20 February 1969, *ICJ Reports 1969*, at p. 43, para. 74).

83. "Passage of only a short period of time is not necessarily, or of itself, a bar to the formation of a new rule of customary international law." *(Ibid.)*

84. As Kirgis analyses the two elements of custom are in equilibrium. When one element is scarce, it can be substituted by the other, if the existence of it is in abundance (Frederic Kirgis, "Custom on a Sliding Scale", 81 *Am. J. Int'l L.* (1987), 146, at 147).

85. Ian Brownlie, *Principles of Public International Law*, Oxford University Press, Oxford, 2008, at p. 8.

86. In this way the Court found a way to escape from the paradox identified by Thirlway regarding international customary law: "[H]ow can a practice develop into a customary rule if States have to believe that a rule already exists before their acts of practice can be significant for the creation of the rule?" (Hugh Thirlway, "The Sources of International Law", in Malcolm D. Evans (ed.), *International Law*, Oxford University Press, Oxford, 2010, p. 95, at p. 102).

military manuals are cited by Brownlie as material sources of custom[87]. But he does not leave this statement unqualified. He adds that "[o]bviously the value of these sources varies and much depends on the circumstances"[88]. There are many caveats regarding the value of the manuals as evidence of customary international law. As is observed, "we should at the very least be extremely cautious about how we approach military manuals as a source, or as an expression of a source, of customary international law"[89]. Leaving aside the issues related to the issuing authority and its purpose, there are conflicting views regarding the elements of customary international law, both the objective and the subjective one, as reflected in the manual.

The International Tribunal for the former Yugoslavia (ICTY) cited military manuals as *indicia* of States' practice, taking into account the difficulties related with ascertaining it in the theatre of military operations[90]. This is also the position taken by the drafters of the ICRC study on customary international law[91] and of the San Remo Manual[92]. On the contrary, there is the view that manuals represent the subjective element of customary law[93]. Others take a more balanced approach by avoiding clarifying which element of customary law is illuminated by military manuals[94]. The issue is actually one of appraising the significance of battlefield actions on the one hand, and official statements on the other, in determining State practice. Although the former may have preponderance in shaping State practice[95], this does not exclude the possibility

87. "A material source of law is simply the place . . . in which the terms of the rule are set out . . . In identifying a material source no account need be taken of the legal authority of the textual instrument." (*Ibid*, at p. 96.) Other important functions of military manuals are firstly the dissemination of IHL and secondly its development as part of the "international lawmaking process" (W. Michael Reisman and William K. Leitzau, "Moving International Law from Theory to Practice: The Role of Military Manuals in Effectuating the Law of Armed Conflict", in Horace W. Robertson, *The Law of Naval Operations*, International Law Studies, Naval War College, Newport Rhode Island, 1991, p. 1.

88. See *supra* footnote 85, at p. 6.

89. David Turns, "Military Manuals and the Customary Law of Armed Conflict", in Nobuo Hayashi (ed.), *National Military Manuals on the Law of Armed Conflict*, FICHL Publication Series No. 2, Oslo, 2010, p. 65, at p. 67.

90. See *supra* footnote 9, para. 99.

91. See *supra* footnote 34, at p. xxxii.

92. See *supra* footnote 37, at p. 67.

93. See for example Kalshoven, referring to the US Commander's Handbook on the Law of Naval Operations (Frits Kalshoven, *Reflections on the Law of War*, Martinus Nijhoff Publishers, Leiden, 2007, at p. 536.

94. "At the highest level, national manuals provide evidence of state practice and *opinio juris* in relation to the states by whom they are issued." (Charles Garraway, "Military Manuals, Operational Law and the Regulatory Framework of Armed Forces", *supra* footnote 89, p. 45, at p. 46).

95. W. Hays Parks, "The ICRC Customary Law Study: A Preliminary Assessment", *ASIL Proceedings 2005*, p. 208, at p. 210.

of asserting the objective element from the national military manuals. In any case, the whole issue bolsters the thesis that the two elements of customary international law are closely intertwined, giving to the judiciary latitude in shaping it.

The plasticity of international customary law was an essential precondition to the judicial creativity regarding IHL. The thorniest question is whether the judiciary has gone beyond the allowable limits, if any, during administering justice for alleged war crimes. On the one hand, judicial law-making can hardly be reconciled with legal positivism. On the other, common law legal systems are familiar with this judicial dynamism, which has been held to be compatible with the European Convention on Human Rights.

As far as the methodology of the tribunals is concerned, suffice it to mention that, in the context of IHL, it has not been easy to discern the classical elements of the customary norm. There were "efforts to anchor this normative process in earlier case law, such as post-World War II decisions, and a range of eclectic sources such as the work of International Law Commission, military manuals and Security Council debates"[96]. The judges were ready to accept that the humanitarian considerations that characterize IHL exerted pressure for the creation of customary law, even when they had to ignore or downplay contrary States' practice.

> "Judges, scholars, governments, and nongovernmental organizations are often prepared to accept a rather large gap between practice and the norms concerned without questioning their binding character."[97]

As the ICTY accepted in the *Kupreškić* case, ruling on the prohibition of reprisals against civilians during NIACs, "[because of] the pressure exerted by the requirements of humanity and the dictates of public conscience, a customary rule of international law has emerged"[98]. This approach is explained by Kirgis, who states that "when issues of armed force are involved, it may well be that the need for stability explains an international decision maker's primary reliance on normative words rather than on a combination of words and consistent deeds"[99].

---

96. William Schabas, "Customary Law or 'Judge-Made' Law: Judicial Creativity at the UN Criminal Tribunals", in Jose Doria *et al.* (eds.), *supra* footnote 77, p. 77, at p. 100.
97. Theodor Meron, "The Humanization of Humanitarian Law", 94 *Am. J. Int'l L.* (2000), 239, at 244.
98. *Prosecutor* v. *Kupreškić*, IT-95-16-T, Trial Chamber, 14 January 2000, para. 531.
99. Frederic Kirgis, *supra* footnote 84.

It is clear that despite the great effort by the judges to anchor their dynamism in the traditional customary law elements, it is not easy to find a consistent methodology in their approach. That is why there are proposals that "customary international law in the context of international criminal law means something different than customary international law in the context of traditional public international law"[100]. Besides the problems already mentioned related to the criminalization process and the content of the criminal rules, another less controversial issue is the jurisdiction over war crimes.

Notwithstanding the fact that every State has an interest in prosecuting war crimes[101], there is no specific treaty provision regulating the conduct of hostilities which establishes universal jurisdiction over them. For example, the provisions of the 1949 Geneva Conventions' provisions refer only to the *aut dedere aut judicare* principle, which is applicable only for the grave breaches of the conventions specifically enumerated in them. Moreover, "[c]ustomary international law as reflected by the practice of states does not . . . mean that universal jurisdiction has been applied in national prosecutions" in the judgment of such an expert as Bassiouni[102]. Academics' and experts' writings have been decisive in the recognition of universal jurisdiction over war crimes, as the same writer observes[103]. It is obvious that this treaty-based "quasi universal" jurisdiction, due to the universal ratification of the Geneva Conventions, transforms the permissive character of universal jurisdiction into an obligatory one, at least for the grave breaches[104]. For the rest of the war crimes, the jurisdictional issues remain muddy.

In accordance with the ICRC study on customary international law,

---

100. See *supra* footnote 96, at p. 101.

101. For an excellent overview regarding the criteria that a crime must meet in order to be subject to universal jurisdiction, see James Paul Benoit, "The Evolution of Universal Jurisdiction over War Crimes", 53 *Naval L. Rev.* (2006), 259, at 262.

102. M. Cherif Bassiouni, "The History of Universal Jurisdiction", in Stephen Macedo (ed.), *Universal Jurisdiction — National Courts and the Prosecution of Serious Crimes under International Law*, University of Pennsylvania Press, Philadelphia, 2006, p. 39, at p. 51.

103. *Ibid.* For the just opposite thesis, that despite their ambiguous language the grave breaches provisions of the Geneva Conventions create truly universal jurisdiction, see Roger O'Keefe, "The Grave Breaches Regime and Universal Jurisdiction", 7 *JICJ* (2009), 811.

104. Some claim that there is a two-way relationship between universal jurisdiction and the obligation to prosecute or extradite. For example, in a different context, that of piracy, Chicca claims that universal jurisdiction may create an obligation to extradite or prosecute, due to an emerging customary nature of the *aut dedere aut judicare* principle in relation to piracy, despite the non-universal membership to the SUA Convention. For an elaborate analysis see Matteo Del Chicca, "Universal Jurisdiction as Obligation to Prosecute or Extradite", 11 *WMU J. Maritime Affairs* (2012), 83, at 91.

"States have the right to vest universal jurisdiction in their national courts over war crimes"[105].

By contrast, the United States maintains that State practice does not support the contention that under customary international law other war crimes, except grave breaches, carry permissive universal jurisdiction[106].

As has been already mentioned, real life cases regarding criminal trials for punishment of the perpetrators of war crimes during armed conflicts at sea are rather rare and they concern attacks against protected persons at sea. In *The Llandovery Castle* case the German Reichsgericht in Liepzig found the accused guilty for opening fire on lifeboats of a torpedoed hospital ship[107]. The *Peleus* trial dealt with the elimination of the shipwrecked survivors of *Peleus* by members of the crew of the German U-Boat 852, during World War II. The British Military Court at Hamburg found the accused guilty and rejected the plea of superior orders and the defence of military necessity[108].

The most famous case, however, where the content of the law regulating naval warfare came at the forefront, was adjudicated by the International Military Tribunal in Nuremberg, with the charges against Admirals Doenitz and Raeder. The accused were acquitted for unrestricted submarine warfare against enemy merchant ships in view of their armament and although they were found guilty regarding the attacks on neutral merchant vessels, the Tribunal did not take into account their conviction in assessing the sentences.

More recently in the *Miodrag Jokic* case, the ICTY dealt with the naval bombardment of Dubrovnik in contravention of the rules protecting cultural objects.

SECTION 5 **THE *MAVI MARMARA* INCIDENT**

The *Mavi Marmara* incident is the best example to illustrate the previously indentified issues concerning the application of the concept of war crimes in the context of maritime operations. It is beyond the scope of the present chapter to narrate the events of 31 May 2010 concerning the interception by Israeli forces of the flotilla bound for Gaza, which resulted in the death of nine people, and has already

105. See *supra* footnote 34, at p. 604 (Rule 157).

106. For an analysis see James G. Stewart, "The Future of the Grave Breaches Regime", 7 *JICJ* (2009), 855, at 870.

107. The main points of the judgment are available at http://www.gwpda.org/naval/lcastl12.htm, visited 20 August 2012.

108. For more about the case see United Nations War Crimes Commission, *Law Reports of Trials of War Criminals Vol. I*, London, 1947, at p. 1.

been extensively dealt with[109]. This section will focus more on the serious legal issues that this incident raised in relation to the above discussion over the concept of war crimes in the naval warfare.

Firstly, the issue of the determination of the applicable international law paradigm, which governed the conduct of the Israel Defense Forces: the various commissions that dealt with the matter oscillated between the law enforcement and the armed conflict paradigm. In accordance with the Turkish Report, the armed conflict paradigm had no application in the incident; therefore the interception should have been evaluated by the law enforcement paradigm[110]. In sharp contrast, the Turkel Report and the Palmer Report gave pre-eminence to the armed conflict paradigm and the naval blockade[111].

The selection of the pertinent international law paradigm has inevitable repercussions on the manner of the enforcement action of the naval forces. The mainstream approach is that "under the laws of peace or war much the same standards should be considered to apply"[112]. According to this approach, the standard established by ITLOS in the *M/V "Saiga" (2)* case[113] should, by analogy, apply to wartime

109. Turkey and Israel conducted their own independent enquiries. The Turkish Commission released its report (hereafter "Turkish Report"), in February 2011 (Turkish National Commission of Inquiry, "Report on the Israeli Attack on the Humanitarian Aid Convoy to Gaza on 31 May 2010", available at http://www.mfa.gov.tr/data/Turkish%20Report%20Final%20-%20UN%20Copy.pdf, visited 2 September 2012). The Israeli Commission, known as Turkel Commission published its report (hereafter "Turkel Report") in January 2011 (The Turkel Commission, "The Public Commission to Examine the Maritime Incident of 31 May 2010", available at http://www.turkel-committee.gov.il/files/wordocs/8808report-eng.pdf, visited 2 September 2012). These two national reports were reviewed by a high-level committee appointed by the UNSG which issued its report (hereafter "Palmer Report"), in September 2011 ("Report of the Secretary-General's Panel of Inquiry on the 31 May 2010 Flotilla Incident", available at http://www.un.org/News/dh/infocus/middle_east/Gaza_Flotilla_Panel_Report.pdf visited 2 September 2012). The UN Human Rights Council also established an independent Fact Finding Mission, which released its report (hereafter FFM Report) in September 2010 (UN doc. A/HRC/15/21 available at http://www2.ohchr.org/english/bodies/hrcouncil/docs/15session/A.HRC.15.21_en.PDF).

110. Turkish Report, Conclusions Nos. 29 and 30, at p. 115. That is why the report speaks about the "laws of peace time" that govern the high seas and the "long-standing universally accepted rule" of the freedom of navigation on the high seas. The drafters of the report dedicated eight pages (from 50 to 57) in analysing the law enforcement paradigm during peace time.

111. Palmer Report, paras. 69-82, at pp. 36-45, and Turkel Report, paras. 29-55, at pp. 38-61.

112. See *supra* footnote 72, at p. 211.

113. "[T]he use of force should be avoided as far as possible and, where . . . unavoidable, it must not go beyond what is reasonable and necessary in the circumstances . . . It is only after the appropriate actions fail that the pursuing may, as a last resort use force . . . Even then . . . all efforts should be made to ensure that life is not endangered." (*M/V "Saiga"*

operations. This approach is tacitly adopted in the Turkish Report[114] and implied in the Palmer Report[115].

Even if the factual circumstances of the *Mavi Marmara* incident invite the convergence of the law enforcement and the armed conflict paradigms regarding the applicable standards for the execution of the boarding operation, this approach cannot be generalized. Wartime operations usually allow for a more rapid escalation of force. Enforcing a blockade is a military operation conducted in a war environment, where the naval unit enforcing the blockade has to deal with various threats. The *modus operandi* of such an operation cannot be equated with the way a "police operation" is enforced. In any case, a ship attempting to breach a blockade becomes a military target liable to attack, subject of course to the principles of necessity and proportionality governing the conduct of hostilities. This is not to say that the *"Saiga"* standard is rendered useless. It is that the necessity to use force must be evaluated in accordance with *jus in bello*, and the, sometimes inevitable, civilian life losses in accordance with the principles of distinction and proportionality. This reasoning is followed by the Turkel Report[116], although it is difficult to reconcile the military realities of the specific operation with the rapid escalation of the force used by the Israelis.

The incident also highlighted the underdevelopment of the laws governing armed conflicts at sea. The immaturity of the laws regulating naval warfare, compared with the laws of land warfare, has already been analysed. Another serious question is whether the bridging of the regulatory gap between IACs and NIACs in land warfare has been equally followed in naval warfare. Taking into account the existing state of the law, it had to be expected that diametrically different legal approaches would have been adopted regarding the evaluation of the incident. The Turkish Report concludes that naval blockades are applicable only in IACs[117]. Belligerent rights against neutral shipping cannot be exercised on the high seas during NIACs. Indeed, this approach is supported by eminent academics[118]. Furthermore the Turkish approach continues that because of the non-international character of the conflict between Israel and Hamas the blockade of the Gaza Strip is violating international law[119].

(No. 2) (Saint Vincent and Grenadines v. *Guinea)*, Judgment of 1 July 1999, para. 155).

114. Turkish Report, at p. 86.
115. Palmer Report, paras. 104-133, at pp. 51-61.
116. Turkel Report, paras. 178-179, at pp. 223-224.
117. Turkish Report, at pp. 60-62.
118. See *supra* footnote 71.
119. Turkish Report, at p. 63.

The Turkel Report adopts a diametrically opposite legal evaluation which has also basis in legal theory[120]. Blockade is available both in IACs and NIACs. Despite the fact that the Turkel Commission classifies the conflict between Israel and Hamas as an international one, it continues that the difficulty in characterizing modern armed conflicts as IACs or NIACs, on the one hand, and the tendency to bridge the regulatory gap between IACs and NIACs, on the other, allows it to conjecture that

> "it is likely there will be a willingness on the part of courts and other bodies to recognize that the rules governing the imposition and enforcement of a naval blockade are applicable to non-international armed conflicts"[121].

The Palmer Report dismisses entirely the availability of blockades in NIACs. Considering, without, however, sufficient legal analysis[122] the conflict as an international one, it concludes that the blockade was in conformity with international law[123]. The FFM Report does not deal with the question of the classification of the conflict or whether blockade is an available method of warfare during NIACs. It holds that it is illegal, because "it inflicts disproportionate damage on the civilian population"[124] and "amounts to collective punishment in violation of Israel's obligations under international humanitarian law"[125].

These assertions, especially the latter one, prompt the question of the impact of the humanitarian principles on the traditional law of blockade. The traditional customary requirements for a lawful imposition of blockade, namely notification, effectiveness and impartiality, do not provide for any sanction on the lawfulness of a blockade based on the humanitarian impact upon the blockaded population. Contemporary development of humanitarian law, however, could not ignore the effect of the blockades on the civilian population[126]. The San Remo Manual seems to modernize the law applicable to blockades, emphasizing the humanitarian principles that the traditional paradigm did not accommodate[127]. The inability of the traditional approach to meet the current legal stan-

120. See *supra* footnote 72.
121. Turkel Report, para. 42, at p. 49.
122. As it is explicitly stated in the report "[t]oo much legal analysis threatens to produce political paralysis" (Palmer Report, para. 15, at p. 10) and also "[i]n this context, the debate on Gaza's status, in particular its relationship to Israel, should not obscure the realities. The law does not operate in a political vacuum" (Palmer Report, para. 73, at p. 41).
123. Palmer Report, para. 73, at p. 41.
124. FFM Report, paras. 52-53, at p. 13.
125. FFM Report, paras. 54, at p. 13.
126. Especially Articles 54 and 70 of Additional Protocol I
127. Articles 102 to 104 of the Manual.

dards is widely accepted. That is why all the reports incorporated in their enquiries the considerations of the impact of the blockade on the population of the Gaza Strip.

The Turkel Report, which emphasized the traditional requirements [128], extensively analysed the humanitarian obligations of Israel, basing its analysis on the provisions of the San Remo Manual [129], taking a more conservative approach than the FFM Report regarding the impact of the humanitarian considerations on the assessment of the blockade. Suffice it here to highlight the different analysis of the proportionality principle. As is observed in the Turkel Report, the current development of humanitarian law calls for a disproportionality test, requiring the damage to be excessive related to the military advantage anticipated [130]. The FFM Report concludes that the damage is disproportionate without assessing whether it is excessive or not [131]. Moreover, the Turkel Report adopts a restrictive interpretation of the notion of collective punishment [132], in sharp contrast with the FFM Report [133]. The Turkish Report held that the Israeli blockade violates the principle of proportionality, reaching the conclusion that the damage to the civilian population caused by the blockade is excessive and constitutes collective punishment [134]. The Palmer Report, on the other hand, admits that the imposition of a blockade would be illegal if it was intended to collectively punish the civilian population or if it violated the proportionality principle [135]. Nevertheless, it finds that these conditions are not met in the present case.

It is obvious that the law of blockade is in a state of flux. The traditional paradigm is unable to meet the contemporary requirements of humanitarian law; it has to be enriched with the humanitarian principles. The question is whether the law will adopt the progressive approach of the FFM Report and the Turkish Report, on the one hand, or the more restrictive approach of the Turkel Report on the other [136]. Taking into account the scant practice regarding naval blockades and the absence of treaty-based law, it is impossible to draw definite conclusions, without any judicial decision clarifying the exact content of the customary law.

---

128. Turkel Report, paras 57-60, at pp. 61-64.
129. Turkel Report, paras. 75-97, at pp. 82-102.
130. Turkel Report, paras. 87-97, at pp. 90-101.
131. FFM Report, *supra* footnote 124.
132. Turkel Report, paras. 101-107, at pp. 104-109.
133. FFM Report, *supra* footnote 125.
134. Turkish Report, Conclusions Nos. 38 and 39, at p. 116.
135. Palmer Report, paras. 77-79, at pp. 42-44.
136. For an extensive analysis of the issues related to the traditional technical requirements of the law of blockade vis-à-vis the modern approach that encompasses also humanitarian considerations see Martin David Fink, "Contemporary Views on the Lawfulness of Naval Blockades", *Aegean Rev. Law Sea* (2011), 191.

It is not surprising that the differences in evaluating the substantive law that regulated the incident prompted different reactions on the issue of individual criminal responsibility. According to the Turkel Report, the naval blockade itself and the actions taken to enforce it were found to be legal[137]. The FFM Report, in sharp contrast with the previous assessment, argues for the commission of war crimes, namely willful killing, torture or inhuman treatment and wilfully causing great suffering or serious injury to body or health against the passengers of the flotilla, who are characterized as civilians. Article 147 of the Fourth Geneva Convention regarding its "grave breaches" serves as the legal basis for the alleged crimes[138]. In this specific point, it is interesting that the FFM Report, as already noted, does not analyse whether the conflict between Israel and Hamas is classified as IAC or NIAC. Taking into account that "grave breaches" are committed only during IACs[139], it may be inferred that the Mission regards the conflict to be an international one.

Additionally, there is no analysis in the Report of the characterization of the passengers of the flotilla as civilians. Even if it is assumed that the passengers were civilians, it is doubtful whether the Fourth Geneva Convention is applicable in this case, taking into account that it was intended to protect only enemy nationals within the national territory of the adverse party. The Palmer Report concludes that "the loss of life and injuries resulting from the use of force by Israeli forces during the take-over of the 'Mavi Marmara' was unacceptable", but refrained from characterizing Israeli actions as war crimes[140]. As is obvious, different legal evaluations of the interception of the flotilla resulted in divergent approaches regarding the potential commitment of war crimes by the Israeli forces.

SECTION 6 **CONCLUSION**

Undoubtedly, the current development of IHL regulating armed conflicts at sea and concomitantly its enforcement through

137. Turkel Report, para. 255, at pp. 278-279. Interesting is the distinction made in the report regarding the passengers on board *Mavi Marmara*. The report distinguishes between the IHH activists and the rest of the passengers, characterized as civilians, who did not confront the Israeli forces that took over the ship. The above-mentioned passengers, according to the report, did not take direct part in the hostilities, despite the fact that they voluntarily participated in an attempt to breach a blockade (whether lawfully or unlawfully established), an assertion that it is arguable.

138. FFM Report, paras. 65, 182 and 265 at pp. 15, 40 and 53 respectively.

139. For the relation between grave breaches and internal armed conflicts, see Lindsay Moir, "Grave Breaches and Internal Armed Conflicts", 7 *JICJ* (2009), 763.

140. Palmer Report, para. 134, at p. 61.

ICL leaves much to be desired. Although this is an unfortunate situation, taking into account that our civilization cannot tolerate the existence of aspects of human life that are not regulated sufficiently by law, it does have positive aspects. The modern maritime environment and the focus of most of the navies to the enforcement of public order at sea have reduced dramatically the pressure to shed light over the "gray areas" of IHL, as, for example, armed conflicts at sea. This has rendered insignificant any need for instituting criminal procedures against its violations. In sharp contrast with the atrocities that took place in the context of land warfare during the 1990s, and fuelled the rapid change of IHL and ICL concerning this aspect of conflict, seas remained relative calm.

This does not mean that the potential application of IHL concerning naval warfare is not relevant. As the *Mavi Marmara* incident corroborated, there are still cases which raise thorny questions regarding the law of war at sea. As long as naval warfare remains a possible method of warfare, the need for its regulation will be essential for the international community. Any meaningful attempt to address the gaps of the relevant law must obtain the consent of the major naval powers[141]. This notwithstanding, such a development does not appear possible. Progress regarding regulation of naval warfare has always followed major conflicts in order to remedy the abuses that occurred during them. Let's hope that there will not be such a need again.

Postscript

After the completion of the first draft of this chapter, an interesting development took place regarding the *Mavi Marmara* incident. On 14 May 2013 the Union of the Comoros, flag State of the *Mavi Marmara*, referred the interception of the flotilla by Israeli forces to the ICC. Subsequently, the Office of the Prosecutor announced that it is conducting a preliminary examination in order to establish whether the criteria for opening an investigation are met.

From the standpoint of the present writer, the referral is significant because it is partly based on the allegation that the Israeli forces committed war crimes when they encountered the flotilla. Although the fate of the legal action of the island nation is uncertain, for legal as well as political reasons, the referral brings to the forefront the potential commission of war crimes at sea, and serves as a stimulus for the international community to tackle the weaknesses of the war crimes concept in naval warfare, as already identified in the chapter.

141. J. Ashley Roach, "The Law of Naval Warfare at the Turn of Two Centuries", 94 *Am. J. Int'l L.* (2000), 64, at 77.

CINQUIÈME PARTIE

PART V

Responsabilité et compétence

Responsibility and Jurisdiction

15 La responsabilité de l'Etat dans le cadre des opérations d'interdiction maritime

Kiara Neri *

SECTION 1 INTRODUCTION

L'un des plus grands défis du droit de la mer contemporain, sinon le plus grand, est de réguler le conflit entre ses deux préoccupations majeures: la préservation de la liberté de navigation et la protection de la sécurité en mer. Le droit international doit trouver un équilibre raisonnable entre ces deux considérations. Si la liberté de la navigation conserve, plus que jamais, une importance économique cruciale pour les Etats de la communauté internationale, elle se heurte néanmoins de plein fouet aux nécessités grandissantes de sécurité et de sûreté.

Les espaces maritimes sont en effet très marqués par la recrudescence des activités illicites et dangereuses. Là où le golfe de Guinée, le golfe d'Aden et l'Asie du Sud-Est sont très marqués par la piraterie maritime et ses déclinaisons, la mer des Caraïbes doit faire face à un trafic organisé de stupéfiants et la mer Méditerranée aux problématiques d'immigration clandestine. Les espaces maritimes sont néanmoins unis par les défis, ceux de la lutte contre la criminalité organisée en mer. Pour combattre ces activités, les Etats comme la communauté internationale ont développé et renforcé leurs activités de surveillance des espaces maritimes et des navires. Le droit international a également évolué, conférant aux Etats qui luttent contre les activités illicites en mer de nouveaux titres d'intervention. La multiplication des compétences des Etats en mer soulève alors la question de la gestion des dommages éventuels survenus lors des opérations d'interdiction maritime entreprises pour lutter contre la criminalité. Sujet classique[1] mais néanmoins brûlant d'actualité, il

---

* Maître de conférences et enseignant-chercheur, Université Jean-Moulin Lyon III. Chercheur au centre de droit international de la même université. Enseignant-chercheur, Université catholique de Lyon.

1. Voir, par exemple, le «Quintuple Treaty» de 1841 qui prévoyait que les juridictions nationales doivent accorder une compensation au capitaine ou au propriétaire du navire s'il était stoppé dans le cadre de l'interdiction de l'escla-

reste peu traité par la doctrine[2] et la jurisprudence. Le développement d'un droit clair et prévisible de la responsabilité pour les opérations d'interdiction maritime permettrait par ailleurs de fournir un équilibre à la conciliation entre l'exigence de sécurité et l'exigence de liberté qui tiraille le droit de la mer[3].

La responsabilité internationale de l'Etat et ses contours ont toujours passionné les internationalistes. Déjà en 1930, la Société des Nations réunissait une conférence sur ce thème. Mais c'est principalement la Commission du droit international des Nations Unies (CDI) qui lancera la réflexion des juristes sur le thème de la responsabilité. Il fut l'un des quatorze sujets sélectionnés par la première CDI de Hersh Lauterpacht. La question se révéla rapidement multiple et le travail de la commission se subdivisa dans trois grandes directions: la responsabilité de l'Etat pour fait internationalement illicite[4], la responsabilité de l'Etat pour les activités non prohibées par le droit international[5] et la responsabilité des organisations internationales[6]. Il conviendra ainsi d'appréhender la réparation des dommages subis lors d'opérations d'interdiction maritime à la lumière des principes directeurs dégagés par la CDI à cette occasion, ainsi que de la jurisprudence internationale. Par ailleurs, les conventions maritimes applicables à la lutte contre la criminalité en mer prévoient elles aussi des régimes conventionnels spécifiques de responsabilité permettant de réparer les dommages subis au cours de ces opérations[7].

Il convient néanmoins d'exclure du champ de l'étude le droit maritime et la responsabilité des personnes privées, telle que la responsabi-

---

vage, sans fondement. Article XIII du Traité entre l'Autriche, la France, la Grande-Bretagne et la Russie sur la répression de la traite des esclaves d'Afrique, 20 décembre 1841.

2. A l'exception de l'ouvrage de Ph. Wendel, *State Responsibility for Interferences with the Freedom of Navigation in Public International Law*, Berlin, Springer, 2007.

3. *Ibid.*, pp. 51-55.

4. Projet d'articles sur la responsabilité de l'Etat pour fait internationalement illicite, résolution 56/83 de l'Assemblée générale en date du 12 décembre 2001 (rectifié par document A/56/49 Corr.3/(Vol. I)). Ci-après «Projet d'articles sur la responsabilité de l'Etat».

5. Le Projet a été subdivisé en deux: Projet d'articles sur la prévention des dommages transfrontières résultant d'activités dangereuses, *Annuaire de la Commission du droit international, 2001*, vol. II(2), et Projets de principes sur la répartition des pertes en cas de dommage transfrontière découlant d'activités dangereuses, et commentaires y relatifs, *Annuaire de la Commission du droit international, 2006*, vol. II(2).

6. Projet d'articles sur la responsabilité des organisations internationales, *Annuaire de la Commission du droit international*, *2011*, vol. II.

7. Voir l'article 55 du Projet d'articles sur la responsabilité de l'Etat consacré à la *lex specialis* applicable aux cas où les conditions de l'existence d'un fait internationalement illicite, le contenu ou la mise en œuvre de la responsabilité internationale d'un Etat sont régis par des règles spéciales de droit international.

lité traditionnelle du propriétaire du navire, du capitaine, mais également les obligations d'assurance[8]. De nombreuses conventions internationales prévoient en effet la responsabilité des acteurs privés de la sphère maritime. Par exemple, en matière de transport de passagers, la responsabilité du transporteur est prévue en cas de dommages matériels ou physiques[9]. En matière environnementale, la Convention internationale sur la responsabilité civile pour les dommages dus à la pollution par les hydrocarbures, du 29 novembre 1969, prévoit les modalités d'engagement de la responsabilité des personnes privées. L'on retrouve également, dans le même cadre, l'obligation de mettre en place des fonds de compensation[10].

L'on se limitera à la responsabilité internationale de l'Etat pour les dommages découlant des opérations d'interdiction maritime qu'il mène, afin de lutter contre la criminalité en mer. Ainsi circonscrit, le sujet soulève encore de nombreuses interrogations peu tranchées quant au fait générateur de la responsabilité, notamment au regard de la nécessité d'établir la violation d'une obligation internationale (section 2); ou quant à l'attribution de la responsabilité, parmi la multitude d'acteurs de la lutte contre la criminalité en mer: Etat du pavillon, Etat côtier, organisations internationales (section 3). Il convient de revenir également sur les règles d'engagement de la responsabilité, notamment les possibilités offertes aux personnes privées (section 4) et sur la réparation du préjudice, quelle que soit la forme qu'elle revêt (section 5).

SECTION 2 LE FAIT GÉNÉRATEUR DE LA RESPONSABILITÉ : LES OPÉRATIONS D'INTERDICTION MARITIME

L'interdiction ou interception[11] maritime est entendue comme incluant à la fois l'arraisonnement et la visite des navires soup-

8. G. Nakhleh et M. Quimbert, «Maritime Law», dans J. Crawford, A. Pellet et S. Olleson (dir. publ.), *The Law of International Responsibility*, Oxford, 2010, pp. 195-902.

9. Convention d'Athènes du 13 décembre 1974 sur le transport de passagers et leurs bagages en mer, et ses protocoles de 1976 et 1990.

10. Voir la Convention internationale portant création d'un Fonds international d'indemnisation pour les dommages dus à la pollution par les hydrocarbures, 18 décembre 1971; la Convention de 1992 sur la responsabilité civile et la Convention de 1992 portant création du Fonds, adoptée le 27 novembre 1992, et son protocole de 2003.

11. Les termes sont interchangeables. Voir W. Heintschel von Heinegg, «Maritime Interception/Interdiction Operations», dans T. D. Gill et D. Fleck (dir. publ.), *The Handbook of International Law of Military Operations*, Oxford, New York, Oxford University Press, 2010, p. 376.

çonnés de se livrer à une activité interdite, et quand les soupçons sont fondés, l'arrestation de l'équipage et la saisie du navire et/ou de la cargaison[12]. L'expression regroupe alors le droit d'approche, le droit de visite, le droit d'enquête et le droit de saisie: «Maritime interception operations may range from querying the master of the vessel to stopping, boarding, inspecting, searching, and potentially even seizing the cargo or the vessel.»[13] Il s'agit néanmoins d'un concept opérationnel[14] et non juridique. D'une manière générale, il est clair que l'Etat ne peut intervenir que lorsque le droit international lui confère un titre pour ce faire. En temps de paix, le titre d'intervention sera issu du droit de la mer, tandis que, en temps de guerre, il sera issu du droit international des conflits armés en mer[15].

La mise en œuvre de ce cadre juridique peut alors donner lieu à des questions de responsabilité, en matière de lutte contre la criminalité en mer, notamment en cas de dommages causés au navire intercepté ou à son équipage. Classiquement, le fait générateur de la responsabilité, en droit international, est la commission d'un fait internationalement illicite. Dans le cadre des opérations d'interdiction maritime, cela implique alors que l'intervention elle-même ou son déroulement soit contraire au droit international (paragraphe 1). Il conviendra également de soulever l'éventualité d'une responsabilité sans violation du droit international, mais simplement pour «erreur d'appréciation» ou «si les soupçons se révèlent dénués de fondement», ce que le droit conventionnel et la jurisprudence semblent prévoir (paragraphe 2). Une autre interrogation reste celle de la nécessité de l'existence d'un dommage en tant que condition pour l'engagement de la responsabilité. Le droit international général ne l'impose pas nécessairement pour caractériser un fait internationalement

---

12. D. Guilfoyle, *Shipping Interdiction and the Law of the Sea*, Cambridge, Cambridge University Press, 2009, p. 4.

13. W. Heintschel von Heinegg, «Maritime Interception/Interdiction Operations», *loc. cit.*, p. 375.

14. L'interception est, dans ce cadre, définie par le Haut Commissariat aux réfugiés comme

> «toute mesure appliquée par un Etat en dehors de son territoire national en vue de prévenir, d'interrompre ou d'arrêter un mouvement de personnes en route vers un pays de destination mais dépourvues des documents nécessaires pour franchir les frontières par terre, air ou mer» (UNHCR's Note, Interception of Asylum-Seekers and Refugees: The International Framework and Recommendations for a Comprehensive Approach, EC/50/SC/CRP.17).

15. W. Heintschel von Heinegg considère que l'expression «Maritime Interception Operation» ne peut être employée que pour désigner des situations qui interviennent en temps de paix ou de «crise», mais pas en temps de guerre. Toutefois, si les régimes juridiques applicables diffèrent, l'acte en lui même reste similaire (W. Heintschel von Heinegg, «Maritime Interception/Interdiction Operations», *loc. cit.*, p. 376).

illicite[16]. Toutefois, en matière d'opération d'interdiction maritime, la formulation des dispositions conventionnelles suscitées implique l'existence d'un tel dommage, relié aux actes de l'Etat intervenant par un lien de causalité[17]. Par exemple, le Conseil d'Etat français a refusé d'indemniser les propriétaires d'un navire arraisonné dans les terres australes françaises en l'absence de preuve de l'existence d'un dommage[18].

Paragraphe 1 **La violation d'une obligation internationale**

En principe, la violation d'une obligation internationale est nécessaire pour engager la responsabilité internationale de l'Etat. Telle est la teneur de l'article premier du projet d'article de la CDI sur la responsabilité internationale de l'Etat de 2001 : « [t]out fait internationalement illicite de l'Etat engage sa responsabilité internationale », or ce fait se définit comme « un comportement consistant en une action ou une omission ... attribuable à l'Etat en vertu du droit international et constitu[ant] une violation d'une obligation internationale de l'Etat »[19]. L'obligation internationale apparaît alors comme « le pivot de l'illicéité »[20], cette dernière se définissant comme la violation d'une obligation. Ici, le fait internationalement illicite sera constitué par la violation des règles du droit de la mer (A), mais également du droit des conflits armés en mer (B), du droit international des droits de l'homme ou encore du droit des réfugiés (C).

---

16. Voir le commentaire de l'article 2 du Projet d'articles sur la responsabilité de l'Etat, préc., pp. 75-76 : « On a parfois dit que la responsabilité internationale ne peut être engagée par le comportement d'un Etat qui manque à ses obligations que s'il existe un autre élément, en particulier celui du « dommage » causé à un autre Etat. Mais la nécessité de tenir compte de tels éléments dépend du contenu de l'obligation primaire, et il n'y a pas de règle générale à cet égard. »

17. La nécessité du lien de causalité est un principe général du droit international. Voir sur ce point A. M. Honoré, « Causation and Remoteness of Damage », dans A. Tunc (dir. publ.), *International Encyclopedia of Comparative Law*, vol. 11, Tübingen, Mohr, 1983, pp. 40 ss., et Bin Cheng, *General Principles of Law As Applied by International Courts and Tribunals*, Londres, Stevens, 1953, p. 253. Selon l'auteur, « the duty to make reparation extends only to those damages which are legally regarded as the consequences of an unlawful act ».

18. CE, 26 février 1982, *Affaire Maria* : « il ne resulte pas de l'instruction que les requérants aient subi du fait des operations consécutives à cet arraisonnement un préjudice autre qu'éventuel ».

19. Projet d'articles sur la responsabilité de l'Etat (préc.), art. 2.

20. J. Salmon, « Les obligations quantitatives et l'illicéité », dans L. Boisson de Chazournes et V. Gowlland-Debbas (dir. publ.), *L'ordre juridique international, un système en quête d'équité et d'universalité, Liber Amicorum Georges Abi-Saab*, Kluwer Law International, 2001, pp. 305-325 (spéc. p. 305).

A. *La violation d'une obligation internationale issue du droit de la mer*

i) *La violation des obligations négatives de l'Etat*

Le droit international de la mer fournit un cadre juridique pour l'intervention. Il recèle de nombreux titres d'intervention sectoriels. En principe, l'Etat côtier est compétent pour intervenir dans les eaux qui relèvent de sa souveraineté (ports, eaux intérieures, eaux archipélagiques et mer territoriale[21]). Dans les zones qui relèvent simplement de sa juridiction, il dispose de «droits souverains» sectoriels. Dans la zone contiguë, il peut intervenir en matière sanitaire, fiscale, douanière ou d'immigration[22], tandis que, dans la ZEE, il ne dispose d'une compétence de police qu'en matière de pêche, de conservation des ressources naturelles et de préservation de l'environnement[23]. Au-delà, c'est l'Etat du pavillon qui est compétent pour intervenir sur ses navires[24]. Certaines exceptions à cette règle existent. En matière de piraterie, de transport d'esclaves et de navires sans nationalité, une compétence universelle d'intervention existe en haute mer[25]. La compétence des Etats tiers en haute mer a été étendue par nombre de conventions sectorielles, mais qui exigent toujours, pour la plupart, l'autorisation préalable expresse de l'Etat du pavillon[26]. La compétence de police de l'Etat côtier peut également s'étendre à la haute mer en cas d'exercice du droit de poursuite[27] ou en cas de menace grave de pollution[28].

Le non-respect par l'Etat intervenant des règles ainsi posées constitue

21. La souveraineté de l'Etat sur sa mer territoriale ou ses eaux archipélagiques est limitée par le droit de passage inoffensif. Voir les articles 17-26 de la Convention des Nations Unies sur le droit de la mer, 10 décembre 1982, Montego Bay (CMB), pour la mer territoriale et les articles 52 et 53 CMB pour les eaux archipélagiques.

22. CMB, art. 33.

23. CMB, art. 56. Pour plus de détails, voir Gahlen, chapitre 3 dans ce volume.

24. CMB, art. 94.

25. CMB, art. 110.

26. Voir l'article 17 de la Convention des Nations Unies contre le trafic illicite de stupéfiants et de substances psychotropes, Vienne, 20 décembre 1988, entrée en vigueur le 11 novembre 1990 (ci-après «Convention de Vienne); l'article 21 de l'Accord de 1995 sur les stocks chevauchants; l'article 8 de la Convention pour la répression d'actes illicites contre la sécurité de la navigation maritime, 10 mars 1988, entrée en vigueur le 1 mars 1992 (ci-après «Convention SUA»), etc.

27. CMB, art. 111.

28. Voir l'article premier de la Convention sur l'intervention en haute mer en cas d'accident entraînant ou pouvant entraîner une pollution par les hydrocarbures, Bruxelles, 29 novembre 1969. La Convention permet l'intervention en haute mer pour combattre les conséquences de l'accident, mais ne permet pas d'engager des poursuites pénales.

une violation de ses obligations internationales. Ces violations revêtent des formes très différentes et doivent donc être distinguées. L'illicéité peut se loger dans l'intervention elle-même, contraire au droit de la mer, ou bien dans sa mise en œuvre par l'Etat intervenant. Dès lors, il convient de distinguer les violations qui découlent d'un défaut de compétence de l'Etat intervenant de celles qui découlent d'un excès de pouvoir.

a) La violation des obligations internationales de l'Etat par excès de compétence

Il s'agit ici des cas dans lesquels l'Etat intervient alors qu'il n'en a pas la compétence au regard des règles du droit de la mer.

Il peut s'agir dans un premier temps de la *compétence d'intervention elle-même*, à savoir que l'Etat ne disposait pas d'un titre, en vertu du droit international pour arraisonner et visiter le navire. Par exemple, dans l'affaire *Saïga 2*, le Tribunal international du droit de la mer (TIDM) a jugé que l'intervention de la Guinée sur le navire était en elle-même contraire au droit international, puisqu'elle était insusceptible de se rattacher à un titre de compétence valable[29]. Les affaires du *Estai*[30] et du *Erlangen*[31] en matière de pêcheries et celle du *Torrey Canyon*[32] en matière de pollution en sont également de bons exemples. Le Canada, l'Islande et le Royaume-Uni ont, respectivement, procédé à un arraisonnent et une visite d'un navire étranger en haute mer en dehors de tout droit d'intervention conféré par le droit international ou l'Etat du pavillon. L'intervention britannique sur le *Torrey Canyon* semble néanmoins avoir été justifiée par l'état de nécessité, situation excluant ainsi l'illicéité[33]. L'état de nécessité avait également été invoqué par le Canada dans l'affaire de l'*Estai*[34], mais cette justification rencontra, à

29. Voir TIDM, affaire *Saïga 2* (préc.), par. 136 et 150.

30. La loi canadienne du 12 mai 1994 sur la protection des pêches côtières autorisait les gardes-côtes canadiens à intervenir sur des navires étrangers en haute mer. Elle a été mise en œuvre notamment le 9 mars 1995, à l'encontre du navire de pêche espagnol *Estai*.

31. Voir *infra*.

32. En mars 1967, le pétrolier libérien *Torrey Canyon* s'échoua sur des rochers au large des eaux territoriales britanniques, et de grandes quantités de pétrole se déversèrent en mer, constituant une menace pour les côtes anglaises. Le Gouvernement britannique décida de bombarder le navire afin de détruire le pétrole resté à bord.

33. Article 25 du Projet d'articles sur la responsabilité de l'Etat (préc.); l'exemple du *Torrey Canyon* est donné par la CDI dans le cadre du commentaire de l'article 25, p. 213.

34. CIJ, affaire de la *Compétence en matière de pêcheries (Espagne c. Canada)*, 4 décembre 1998, par. 20, et le contre-mémoire du Canada (février 1996), par. 17 à 45.

l'opposé de l'affaire britannique, une très vive contestation de la part des autres Etats, notamment européens. De manière générale, le consentement, la force majeure, la légitime défense, la détresse, les contre-mesures, le respect d'une norme impérative et l'état de nécessité sont autant de circonstances excluant l'illicéité d'une opération d'interdiction maritime [35]. Leur invocation est néanmoins encadrée par des critères très stricts de telle sorte qu'elles ne sont que très rarement acceptées par la jurisprudence internationale.

La contravention aux règles du droit de la mer ne constitue pas non plus un fait internationalement illicite si l'Etat agit en vertu d'une autorisation du Conseil de sécurité des Nations Unies. Ainsi, la résolution 1816 (2008) et les résolutions qui lui ont succédé autorisent, avec l'accord du gouvernement de transition somalien [36], les Etats tiers à procéder à des opérations d'interdiction maritime dans les eaux territoriales somaliennes. Plus largement, le Conseil a autorisé les Etats à déroger aux règles d'intervention du droit de la mer dans le cadre de la surveillance des embargos. Par exemple, le Conseil a pu autoriser les Etats à déroger à la règle de la compétence souveraine de l'Etat côtier sur ses eaux territoriales [37], ou encore à la règle de la compétence exclusive de l'Etat du pavillon [38]. Les mesures adoptées dans le cadre de la surveillance des embargos n'ont pas pour objet la lutte contre la criminalité en mer, mais l'exemple de la piraterie ouvre la voie à l'adoption de mesures dérogatoires aux règles du droit de la mer en matière d'activités illictes. Dans tous ces cas, l'autorisation du Conseil de sécurité, en vertu de l'article 103 de la Charte, prime les obligations internationales de l'Etat issues du droit de la mer.

Dans un second temps, même si l'Etat intervenant agit en vertu d'un titre d'intervention valide, il n'a pas nécessairement la compétence pour prendre des mesures supplémentaires à l'encontre du navire, comme

35. Voir les articles 20 à 26 du Projet d'articles sur la responsabilité de l'Etat (préc.).

36. L'autorisation ainsi délivrée par les autorités somaliennes était une base juridique suffisante, en droit international, pour permettre l'action des Etats tiers dans les eaux somaliennes.

37. Conseil de sécurité, résolution 820 (1993), 17 avril 1993, par. 28 et 29. Le Conseil a autorisé les Etats présents dans la région à intervenir sur les navires suspects dans ces zones.

38. Conseil de sécurité, résolution 787 (1992), 16 novembre 1992, par. 10. Le Conseil a décidé

> « que tout navire dans lequel une personne ou une entreprise de la République fédérative de Yougoslavie ou y exerçant son activité détient un intérêt majoritaire ou prépondérant sera considéré, aux fins de l'application des résolutions pertinentes du Conseil de sécurité, comme un navire de la République fédérative de Yougoslavie, indépendamment du pavillon sous lequel il navigue ».

procéder à sa fouille, à sa saisie ou encore à l'arrestation de l'équipage. De tels cas peuvent se produire lorsque le droit de la mer requiert l'autorisation préalable de l'Etat du pavillon. Cette autorisation peut être assortie de conditions, notamment au regard des mesures que l'Etat intervenant pourra adopter à l'encontre du navire ou de son équipage[39]. C'est par ailleurs ce que la Cour européenne des droits de l'homme a reproché à la France dans l'affaire *Medvedyev*[40]. Les juges de Strasbourg ont engagé la responsabilité internationale de la France à l'encontre de l'équipage du *Winner* pour avoir procédé à leur détention sans autorisation expresse du Cambodge, sur ce point. L'autorisation du Cambodge ne visait en effet que de manière large le pouvoir d'« intercepter, contrôler et engager des poursuites judiciaires » contre le *navire*, mais ne prévoyait pas de manière précise le sort de l'*équipage*, ni de privation de liberté.

Les conventions applicables vont parfois prévoir une obligation de réparation en cas de violation des règles établies par le droit de la mer. Elles constituent alors des régimes conventionnels spécifiques qui serviront de *lex specialis* par rapport au droit général de la responsabilité. Par exemple, dans le cadre du droit de poursuite, l'article 111, paragraphe 8, de la CMB prévoit une obligation de compensation lorsque l'interception a eu lieu dans des circonstances ne justifiant pas son exercice[41]. Dans le même sens, l'article 106 relatif à la piraterie oblige l'Etat intervenant à compenser le dommage subi si l'intervention a été réalisée « sans motif suffisant », à savoir en violation des règles de visite contenues dans la CMB. Elle implique ainsi l'existence d'un fait internationalement illicite constitué par la violation des règles relatives à la piraterie.

b) La violation des obligations internationales de l'Etat par excès de pouvoir

Dans cette hypothèse, l'Etat intervenant est compétent en vertu du droit de la mer, de l'autorisation de l'Etat du pavillon ou du Conseil de sécurité[42], mais, dans l'exercice de son droit, il viole les règles juridiques de mise en œuvre. Deux cas de figure sont ici envisagés : *le recours à une force excessive* et *le non-respect des obligations de l'Etat en matière de droit de l'homme et de droit des réfugiés*. La seconde

39. Voir par exemple l'article 8, paragraphe 5, du Protocole de Palerme.
40. CEDH, *Medvedyev c. France*, 29 mars 2010, requête nº 3394/03, par. 99.
41. Voir par exemple R. C. Reuland, « The Customary Right of Hot Pursuit into the High Seas: Annotations on Article 111 of the Law of the Sea Convention », *Virginia Journal of International Law*, 1992-1993, p. 587.
42. Cette hypothèse s'applique aussi en cas d'existence d'une circonstance excluant l'illicéité de l'opération d'interdiction ; voir les articles 20 à 25 du Projet d'articles de la CDI sur la responsabilité de l'Etat (préc.).

hypothèse sera examinée plus loin. La première implique la violation des règles de proportionnalité et de nécessité dans la mise en œuvre par l'Etat intervenant de ses pouvoirs de police. Ces règles sont rappelées, de manière sectorielle, par la Convention SUA[43] et l'Accord sur les stocks chevauchants[44]. Elles sont consacrées par la jurisprudence arbitrale[45], mais également par le TIDM dans l'affaire *Saïga*[46]. Les conventions relatives au droit de la mer prévoient également l'engagement de la responsabilité de l'Etat. Il est parfois délicat de distinguer, au sein de ces régimes spécifiques, ce qui relève des violations par excès de compétence ou par excès de pouvoir. Par exemple, la Convention internationale sur l'intervention en haute mer en cas d'accident entraînant ou pouvant entraîner une pollution par hydrocarbures prévoit, dans son article VI, que « [t]oute Partie à la Convention qui a pris des mesures en contravention avec les dispositions de la présente Convention, causant à autrui un préjudice, est tenue de le dédommager »[47]. Telle est également la position de l'Accord sur les stocks chevauchants, qui énonce que les Etats sont responsables des pertes ou dommages qui leur sont imputables lorsque ladite mesure est illicite ou va au-delà de ce qui est raisonnablement nécessaire[48]. L'engagement de la responsabilité de l'Etat nécessite ainsi un acte contraire aux dispositions de l'Accord ou un acte disproportionné, en violation de son article 22 qui prévoit les procédures en matière d'arraisonnement et d'inspection.

Le TIDM consacre dans le même temps la procédure coutumière à respecter avant tout recours à la force dans les espaces marins. Il convient ainsi d'émettre un ordre sonore ou visuel de stopper, en utilisant des signaux reconnus internationalement. Si cela s'avère insuffisant, le TIDM reconnaît que certaines mesures peuvent être adoptées, y compris des coups de feu tirés par-dessus l'étrave du navire. C'est uniquement lorsque ces mesures s'avèrent inefficaces « que le navire poursuivant peut, en dernier ressort, faire usage de la force. Même, dans un tel cas, un avertissement adéquat doit être émis en direction du navire et tout doit être mis en œuvre pour veiller à ne pas mettre de vie en danger. »[49]

---

43. Protocole de 2005 à la Convention SUA (préc.), art. 8 *bis*, par. 9.
44. Article 22 de l'Accord sur les stocks chevauchants (préc.).
45. Voir sentence arbitrale, affaire du *SS I'm Alone (Canada c. Etats-Unis d'Amérique)*, 5 janvier 1935, *Recueil des sentences arbitrales (RSA)*, vol. III, pp. 1609-1618 ; sentence arbitrale, affaire du *Red Crusader (Danemark c. Royaume-Uni)*, 23 mars 1962, *IRL*, vol. 35, p. 485.
46. TIDM, affaire *Saïga 2* (préc.), par. 155 et 156.
47. Convention internationale sur l'intervention en haute mer en cas d'accident entraînant ou pouvant entraîner une pollution par les hydrocarbures (préc.).
48. Article 21, paragraphe 18, de l'Accord sur les stocks chevauchants (préc.).
49. *Ibid.*, par. 156.

ii) *La violation des obligations positives de l'Etat*

Les obligations de l'Etat en droit de la mer en général, et en droit des interdictions maritimes en particulier, ne sont pas simplement des obligations dites « négatives », mais peuvent également prendre la forme d'obligations de faire, ou obligations « positives »[50]. L'omission ou l'abstention de l'Etat peut alors constituer une violation de ses obligations internationales. Ce sont des obligations de diligence, qui s'apparentent à des obligations de moyen. Le droit de la mer recèle, de manière sectorielle, un certain nombre d'obligations de ce type, qu'elles aient pour objet de contraindre l'Etat à exercer ses compétences de police sur les zones maritimes relevant de sa juridiction ou sur les navires battant son pavillon.

a) La violation des obligations de prévenir

De manière générale, le droit international met dans certains cas à la charge de l'Etat des obligations de contrôle des activités se déroulant sur son territoire[51]. L'affaire relative à la *Fonderie de Trail*[52] a dégagé, dans ce cadre, le principe de l'utilisation non dommageable du territoire[53]. Ainsi, tout Etat a l'obligation internationale de veiller à ce que les activités se déroulant sous sa juridiction ne portent pas atteinte au territoire d'un autre Etat. Cette solution, adoptée dans une affaire relative à l'environnement, a pu être étendue à la lutte contre certaines activités illicites telles que le terrorisme. Ainsi, le Conseil de sécurité, dans sa célèbre résolution 1373 (2001), a-t-il pu décider que tous les Etats « [e]mpêchent que ceux qui financent, organisent, facilitent ou commet-

50. Sur la distinction entre ces deux types d'obligations internationales, voir J. Combacau, « Obligations de résultat et obligations de comportement. Quelques questions et pas de réponse », *Mélanges offerts à Paul Reuter, le droit international : unité et diversité*, Paris, Pedone, 1981, pp. 181-204.

51. Cela soulève également l'épineuse question de la capacité à exercer les fonctions étatiques. Pour mémoire, l'article 4 de la Charte des Nations Unies pose comme condition à l'adhésion d'être capable de s'acquitter des obligations de la Charte et disposé à le faire. Dans le même sens, la jurisprudence classique rappelle le « droit » et « le devoir de déployer les activités étatiques », sentence arbitrale, *Ile de Palmas* (préc.), *RSA*, t. II, p. 839. Voir également CIJ, affaire du *Détroit de Corfou* (préc.), p. 4. Pour une application de ces principes à la mer, voir M. Voelckel, « Les zones économiques exclusives et leur surveillance : le droit de la mer entre normativité et effectivité », *loc. cit.*, pp. 11-29.

52. Sentence arbitrale, affaire relative à la *Fonderie de Trail (Etats-Unis/Canada)*, 16 avril 1938 et du 11 mars 1941.

53. Plus largement, l'Etat a un devoir de diligence pour contrôler les activités sur son territoire afin qu'il ne soit pas utilisé pour commettre des actes contraires aux droits d'autres Etats. Voir, parmi tant d'autres : R. Kolb, « La légitime défense des Etats au XXIe siècle et pendant l'époque de la Société des Nations », *loc. cit.*, p. 39.

tent des actes de terrorisme n'utilisent leurs territoires respectifs pour commettre de tels actes contre d'autres Etats ou contre les citoyens de ces Etats». Pour ce faire, les Etats ont également une obligation de coopération dans la prévention de certains actes illicites comme le terrorisme[54].

Dès lors, pour certains auteurs, tels que Claus Dieter Classen, l'exclusivité issue de la souveraineté est «inseparably connected with an obligation: the obligation to protect the rights of other states within the national territory and in particular their right to integrity and inviolability in times of peace»[55]. Cette interprétation est partagée par d'autres auteurs, comme Tammy Sittnick, pour qui il existe, en matière de terrorisme maritime une obligation positive à la charge des Etats de prendre toutes les mesures nécessaires pour prévenir la commission de tels actes[56]. Dès lors, en ne mettant pas tout en œuvre pour permettre l'intervention dans leurs eaux territoriales contre le terrorisme, l'Indonésie et la Malaisie auraient violé leur obligation internationale: «Malaysia's and Indonesia's refusal to consider available options for improving security in the strait arguably constitutes a breach of their international responsability to prevent terrorism.»[57] Selon cette interprétation, les deux Etats pourraient alors engager leur responsabilité pour manquement à leur obligation de prévention[58]. Cette affirmation repose sur le refus de la Malaisie et de l'Indonésie d'autoriser des patrouilles étrangères dans leurs eaux territoriales, lieu de la commission de la plupart des attaques contre les navires. L'obligation de coopération en matière de terrorisme reste soumise au consentement de l'Etat côtier ou de l'Etat du pavillon, et ne semble pas aller jusqu'à imposer aux Etats d'accepter l'aide extérieure et de recourir à des puissances étrangères pour sécuriser leur

54. Voir par exemple le point 3 de la résolution 1373 (2001), 28 septembre 2001, S/RES/1373 (2001).

55. C. D. Classen, «Failed States and the Prohibition of the Use of Force», dans SFDI, *Les nouvelles menaces contre la paix et la sécurité internationales, actes de la journée franco-allemande*, Paris, Pedone, p. 137.

56. Voir les article 8 *bis* et 13 de la Convention SUA telle que modifiée par le Protocole de 2005. Cette obligation de prévention est classique au sein de conventions internationales relatives au terrorisme tel que l'article 10, paragraphe 1, de la Convention pour la répression d'actes illicites dirigés contre la sécurité de l'aviation civile, Montréal, 23 septembre 1971 ; l'article 4 de la Convention sur la prévention et la répression des infractions contre les personnes jouissant d'une protection internationale, y compris les agents diplomatiques, New York, 14 décembre 1973, ou encore l'article 4 de la Convention internationale contre la prise d'otages, New York, 17 décembre 1979.

57. T. M. Sittnick, «States Responsibility and Maritime Terrorism in the Strait of Malacca: Persuading Indonesia and Malaysia to Take Additional Steps to Secure the Strait», *Pacific Rim Law and Policy Journal*, vol. 14, 2005, p. 762.

58. *Ibid.*, p. 769.

territoire maritime[59]. De la même manière, il est délicat d'identifier une obligation d'intervention à la charge des Etats, qui pourrait, en cas d'incapacité matérielle, se transformer en une obligation de « laisser intervenir » les Etats tiers[60].

Néanmoins, il est désormais acquis que les Etats ont une obligation, en vertu du droit international, de surveiller certaines activités se déroulant sur leur territoire. La Cour internationale de justice semble lui accorder une portée générale en proclamant « l'obligation pour tout Etat de ne pas laisser utiliser son territoire aux fins d'actes contraires aux droits d'autres Etats »[61].

b) La violation des obligations de réprimer

L'obligation de prévenir un acte illicite va souvent de pair avec l'obligation de le réprimer. Ainsi, par exemple, la Convention SUA, après avoir défini les actes portant atteinte à la sécurité maritime à son article 3, prévoit que « [t]out Etat Partie réprime les obligations prévues à l'article 3 par des peines appropriées qui prennent en considération la nature grave de ces infractions »[62]. Pour tous les actes énumérés par l'article 3 dont le terrorisme, la piraterie et le vol à main armée font partie, les cent cinquante sept Etats Parties à la Convention SUA ont donc l'obligation de réprimer ces infractions, dès lors que la personne soupçonnée est présente sur leur territoire.

En matière de lutte contre le trafic de stupéfiants, la Convention de Vienne impose aux Etats Parties d'adopter les mesures nécessaires pour pénaliser la production, la fabrication, l'extraction, la préparation, l'offre, la mise en vente, la distribution, la vente, la livraison, le courtage, l'expédition, le transport, l'importation de stupéfiants[63]. L'Etat doit également adopter les mesures nécessaires pour établir sa compétence si l'infraction « a été commise sur son territoire ; [ou] à bord d'un navire battant son pavillon »[64]. De même, la Convention MARPOL prévoit dans le domaine de la lutte contre la pollution en mer, dans son article 4, une obligation similaire de pénalisation et de répression[65] qui s'inscrit

59. Voir *infra* note 76.
60. *Ibid.*
61. CIJ, affaire du *Détroit de Corfou (Royaume-Uni c. Albanie)*, 9 avril 1949, *CIJ Recueil 1949*, p. 22.
62. Convention SUA (préc.), art. 5.
63. Convention de Vienne, art. 4, par. 1, al. *a)*, point i). A ce jour la Convention compte cent quatre-vingt-cinq Etats Parties.
64. *Ibid.*, art 4, par. 1, al. *a)*, points i et ii).
65. Art. 4, par. 2 :

> « Toute violation des dispositions de la présente Convention commise dans la juridiction d'une Partie à la Convention est sanctionnée par la légis-

dans le cadre de l'obligation générale de protéger et de préserver le milieu marin issue de l'article 192 de la CMB.

En matière de terrorisme, la résolution 1373 (2001) prévoit dans le même sens que les Etats» veillent à ce que toutes personnes qui participent au financement, à l'organisation, à la préparation ou à la perpétration d'actes de terrorisme ou qui y apportent un appui soient traduites en justice, ... et à ce que la peine infligée soit à la mesure de la gravité de ces actes»[66].

L'on notera également que cette obligation reste une obligation de résultat, dès lors l'Etat a simplement l'obligation de soumettre l'individu à des poursuites pénales, et non d'aboutir effectivement à l'engagement du procès pénal ou à une condamnation. Dans certains cas, les poursuites pénales ne peuvent pas aboutir à cause d'une immunité ou d'une absence de preuve sans que cela ne soit une violation de l'obligation de réprimer[67].

*c) La violation des obligations d'*intervenir

Il s'agit de l'obligation positive la plus difficile à identifier au sein du droit de la mer. Néanmoins, plusieurs pistes vers l'identification d'une réelle obligation d'intervention doivent être suivies, notamment au regard des obligations de l'Etat du pavillon. Le droit de la mer prévoit en effet qu'il exerce sa juridiction sur ses navires[68]. La question qui se pose est de savoir si cette juridiction s'accompagne d'une obligation positive de l'exercer en procédant à des opérations d'interdiction maritime sur les navires battant son pavillon. C'est certainement en matière de terrorisme que l'obligation apparaît le plus clairement, notamment au regard des différentes résolutions du Conseil de sécurité des Nations Unies, imposant aux Etats de réprimer les actes de terrorisme, au

lation de cette Partie. Chaque fois qu'une telle infraction se produit, la Partie doit: *a)* soit engager des poursuites conformément à sa législation, *b)* soit fournir à l'Autorité dont dépend le navire les preuves qui peuvent être en sa possession pour démontrer qu'il y a eu infraction.» (Convention internationale pour la prévention de la pollution par les navires, Londres, 2 novembre 1973 (ci-après «MARPOL»), telle qu'amendée par les protocoles successifs du 17 février 1978 et du 26 septembre 1997, entrés en vigueur respectivement le 2 octobre 1983 et le 19 mai 2005.)

66. Résolution 1373 (2001) (préc.), point 2 *e)*.

67. Voir la décision du procureur d'Amsterdam de ne pas poursuivre le général Pinochet et la décision de la cour d'appel qui valide cette décision, Court of Appeal of Amsterdam, *The Chili Komitee c. Public Prosecutor*, 14 janvier 1995, dans L. A. N. M. Barnhoorn, «Netherlands Judicial Decisions Involving Questions of Public International Law, 1995-1996», *Netherlands Yearbook of International Law*, 1997, p. 363.

68. CMB, art. 94.

premier rang desquelles la résolution 1373 (2001). A l'occasion de cette résolution, le Conseil décide que les Etats «prennent les mesures voulues pour empêcher que des actes de terrorisme ne soient commis»[69]. Dans ce cadre, le Président Wolfrum a pu relever que l'Etat du pavillon a l'obligation d'intervenir sur ses navires. La violation de cette obligation pouvant entraîner, selon l'ancien Président du TIDM, une intervention de la part d'un Etat tiers[70]. Dans le même sens, Giorgio Gaja a pu considérer que «the existence of a duty for the territorial State or the flag State to combat terrorist acts when they occur leaves little room for doubt»[71].

L'existence d'une telle obligation relance le débat sur les contre-mesures en matière d'interdiction maritime. En effet, certains auteurs ont pu soutenir que la violation par l'Etat compétent de son obligation d'intervention, si tant est qu'elle existe réellement, donnerait naissance à un droit pour l'Etat lésé de procéder à des contre-mesures, au titre de l'article 22 du Projet d'articles de la CDI. Selon les rédacteurs de l'article 22, des contre-mesures auront plus de chances de satisfaire aux conditions de nécessité et de proportionnalité si elles visent la même obligation ou une obligation étroitement connexe à celle qui les a déclenchées[72]. Ainsi, en l'espèce, la contre-mesure pourrait être l'arraisonnement, la visite ou l'arrestation de navires battant le pavillon de l'Etat responsable ou se situant dans une zone relevant de sa juridiction. Cette affirmation se heurte néanmoins à l'interdiction faite à l'Etat qui a recours aux contre-mesures d'employer la force armée. Or, si les mesures d'interdiction maritime sont, en principe, des mesures de police non constitutives d'un emploi de la force armée au sens de l'article 2, paragraphe 4, de la Charte, les frontières ne sont pas toujours très nettes[73].

69. Conseil de sécurité, résolution 1373 (2001) (préc.), par. 2, al. *b)*.

70. R. Wolfrum, «La lutte contre le terrorisme en mer: moyens et limites du droit international», allocution du Président du TIDM (www.itlos.org.doc):

> «Cette argumentation est valable également quand l'Etat du pavillon n'est pas en mesure de réagir tandis que les navires d'Etats tiers le sont. L'atteinte à la souveraineté de l'Etat dont le navire en question bat le pavillon peut se justifier tout au moins par le fait que ledit Etat du pavillon est tenu sur le plan international d'intervenir aux fins de réprimer le terrorisme.» (P. 17.) (Sur l'obligation de coopération et sa portée, voir *infra*.)

71. G. Gaja, «Measures Against Terrorist Acts Under International Law», dans N. Ronzitti (dir. publ.), *Maritime Terrorism and International Law*, Dordrecht, Boston, Londres, Martinus Nijhoff, 1990, pp. 15-23 (spéc. pp. 17-18).

72. Voir sentence arbitrale, *Accord relatif aux services aériens*, *RSA*, vol. XVIII, 1979, p. 416, et J. Crawford, *Les articles de la CDI sur la responsabilité de l'Etat*, Paris, Pedone, p. 337.

73. Voir sur ce point D. Guilfoyle, «Interdicting Vessels to Enforce the Common Interest: Maritime Countermeasures and the Use of Force», *ICLQ*, 2007, pp. 69-82.

Dès lors, il paraît délicat de considérer l'arraisonnement, la visite ou encore l'arrestation d'un navire en mer comme des contre-mesures valables au regard du droit international. L'Etat lésé devra se contenter de mesures d'ordre économique ou diplomatiques, proches, dans leur nature, de celles adoptées par le Conseil de sécurité au titre de l'article 41 et considérées comme « n'impliquant pas l'emploi de la force ».

En tout état de cause, la généralisation de l'obligation d'intervention en mer est délicate. S'il est clair que certaines obligations positives conventionnelles existent, elles ne visent jamais explicitement l'exercice des pouvoirs de police. Il s'agit, en général, pour l'Etat d'établir sa compétence pénale aux fins de répression des contrevenants, et non pas de déployer sa compétence de police opérationnelle en mer. La Convention SUA précise à cet égard que l'Etat du pavillon est en droit de refuser à un Etat Partie qui en fait la demande l'arraisonnement et la fouille du navire battant son pavillon[74]. L'on en déduit sans mal que l'obligation de coopération dans la prévention et la répression des crimes n'implique pas d'obligation d'intervention, et encore moins d'obligation d'autoriser les Etats tiers à intervenir[75].

B. La violation d'une obligation issue du droit des conflits armés en mer

Le droit applicable aux conflits armés en mer a été codifié[76] dans le Manuel de San Remo de 1994. Il contient alors l'expression des règles de conduite des hostilités en mer. Il modifie les équilibres du droit de la mer et permet aux belligérants d'intercepter des navires ne battant pas leur pavillon, en dehors des eaux relevant de leur juridiction. Ainsi, le droit international confère, par exemple, aux belligérants le droit d'intercepter un navire qui tente de franchir un blocus ou une zone d'exclusion valablement mise en place[77]. L'article 146 synthétise les divers titres d'interventions à l'égard des navires tiers :

---

74. Convention SUA telle que modifiée par l'article 8 du Protocole de 2005, art. 8*bis*, par. 5, al. *c)*, point iv).

75. Voir *supra* note 61.

76. Sur la valeur juridique de ce Manuel, voir L. Doswald-Beck (dir. publ.), *San Remo Manual on International Law Applicable to Armed Conflicts at Sea*, Cambridge University Press, 1995, ou L. Doswald-Beck, « Le Manuel de San Remo sur le droit international applicable aux conflits armés sur mer. Historique — Elaboration du Manuel de San Remo et objectif visé — Contenu du Manuel de San Remo », *Revue internationale de la Croix-Rouge*, 1995, n° 816, pp. 635-647.

77. Voir l'article 98 du Manuel de San Remo. Sur les zones d'exclusion, voir les articles 105 et suivants du Manuel, et K. Neri, *L'emploi de la force en mer*, Bruxelles, Bruylant, 2013, par. 255 ss.

«Les navires de commerce neutres peuvent être capturés hors des eaux neutres s'ils se livrent à l'une des activités mentionnées au paragraphe 67 ou s'il est établi par une visite et une perquisition ou par tout autre moyen qu'ils: *a)* transportent de la contrebande; *b)* font route à seule fin de transporter des passagers individuels appartenant aux forces armées ennemies; *c)* agissent directement sous contrôle, ordres, affrètement, emploi ou direction ennemie; *d)* présentent des documents irréguliers ou frauduleux, ne disposent pas des pièces requises, ou détruisent, rendent illisibles ou dissimulent des documents; *e)* violent les règles établies par un belligérant dans la zone immédiate des opérations navales; ou *f)* violent ou tentent de violer un blocus.»

Par ailleurs, les belligérants ont un droit coutumier de contrôler les navires et aéronefs neutres dans le voisinage immédiat des opérations navales[78]. Ainsi, l'article 118 du Manuel de San Remo rappelle que, «[d]ans l'exercice de leurs droits lors d'un conflit armé international sur mer, les navires de guerre et les aéronefs militaires belligérants bénéficient d'un droit de visite et de perquisition des navires de commerce en dehors des eaux neutres lorsqu'il y a raisonnablement lieu de supposer qu'ils pourraient être capturés», à l'exception des navires neutres se rendant dans des ports neutres[79] ou naviguant en convoi sous la protection d'un navire de guerre neutre[80].

Le Manuel de San Remo ne prévoit pas explicitement d'obligation d'indemniser les navires capturés sans motif valable ou à tort. Toutefois, il est clair que, comme toute règle de droit international public, la violation des obligations de l'Etat en vertu du droit de la guerre sur mer peut entraîner la mise en œuvre de la responsabilité internationale de l'Etat. Par exemple, dans l'affaire de la Flottille de la Paix, l'opération menée par Israël ne remplissait pas nécessairement les critères posés par le droit international humanitaire, tant en matière de blocus que de proportionnalité. Dès lors, sa responsabilité peut être engagée sur ce fondement[81]. Le rapport Palmer, issu du panel d'enquête des Nations Unies, reconnaît partiellement la responsabilité d'Israël dans cette affaire, pour non-respect du principe de proportionnalité[82]. Israël avait invoqué la légitime défense pour justifier l'emploi de la force en haute mer contre la Flottille de la Paix composée de navires transportant de l'aide huma-

78. Manuel de San Remo, art. 108.
79. *Ibid.*, art. 120, al. *a)*.
80. *Ibid.*, art. 120, al. *b)*.
81. Voir D. Guilfoyle, «The *Mavi Marmara* Incident and Blockade in Armed Conflict», *BYBIL*, 2010, pp. 171-223.
82. Report of the Secretary-General's Panel of Inquiry on the 31 May 2010 Flotilla Incident, juillet 2011.

nitaire vers Gaza, soumise à un blocus. L'abordage du navire *Mavi Marmara* avait causé la mort, le 31 mai 2010, de neuf ressortissants turcs.

Néanmoins, la question de la licéité du blocus en lui-même est vigoureusement discutée. L'on notera simplement que le blocus est largement condamné, d'une part, par les instances onusiennes[83] — à l'exception du panel d'enquête désigné par le Secrétaire général — et, d'autre part, par les Etats, notamment parce que le blocus, pour être licite, doit être mis en place dans le cadre d'un conflit armé[84], doit avoir un objectif militaire et être proportionné[85] ; et permettre l'approvisionnement des populations civiles en « nourriture et autres biens nécessaires à [leur] survie »[86]. Les deux derniers points semblent être problématiques dans le cas du blocus de Gaza[87].

C. La violation d'une obligation internationale issue du droit international des droits de l'homme ou du droit des réfugiés

Le droit international des droits de l'homme prévoit la responsabilité de l'Etat en cas de violation d'un droit ou d'une liberté. En matière d'opérations d'interdiction maritime, l'intégralité du droit international des droits de l'homme est applicable et s'impose à l'Etat intervenant[88] si les individus sont placés « sous sa juridiction »[89]. L'Etat intervenant pourra voir sa responsabilité engagée pour des actes commis dans les zones maritimes relevant de sa souveraineté. Se pose alors la question des actes commis en haute mer, ou en dehors du territoire de l'Etat. Les juridictions internationales relatives aux droits de l'homme

83. Par le Conseil de sécurité (résolution 1860), mais également par le Secrétaire général et le Haut Commissaire des Nations Unies aux droits de l'homme, Navi Pillay, communiqué de presse, Centre d'actualité des Nations Unies, 31 mai 2010. Le Secrétaire général de la Ligue arabe, Amr Moussa, a, dans le même sens, réclamé le 13 juin 2010 la levée du blocus imposé par Israël à la bande de Gaza. Voir *Le Monde*, 13 juin 2010. Le rapport du Panel conclut, quant à lui, que « Israel's naval blockade was legal » (préc., par. 81).

84. Les critiques se cristallisaient également sur l'existance d'un conflit armé international entre Israël et le Hamas. Voir, sur ce point, D. Guilfoyle, « The *Mavi Marmara* Incident and Blockade in Armed Conflict », *loc. cit.*

85. Manuel de San Remo (préc.), art. 102.

86. *Ibid.*, art. 103 et 104.

87. Voir notamment la Déclaration de M. Natalegawa (Indonésie), lors des débats sur la résolution 1860.

88. En temps de guerre ou de crise, des dérogations à certaines règles sont permises. Voir notamment l'article 15 de la Convention européenne des droits de l'homme.

89. Formulation de l'article premier de la Convention européenne des droits de l'homme.

reconnaissent sans peine une application extraterritoriale, en mer, des traités internationaux relatifs aux droits de l'homme, si les faits se sont déroulés sur des navires gouvernementaux[90], ou si les agents de l'Etat exercent sur les individus un contrôle et une autorité suffisante[91].

Ainsi, la Cour européenne des droits de l'homme a, par exemple, reconnu la responsabilité de la France dans le cadre d'une opération de lutte contre le narcotrafic[92], de l'Italie pour une interception de migrants[93] ou encore du Portugal pour avoir refusé l'entrée dans ses eaux à un navire pour des raisons politiques[94]. Les dispositions déclarées violées par la Cour européenne étaient respectivement l'article 5, paragraphe 1, exigeant que toute privation de liberté soit prévue par la loi ; l'article 3 interdisant la torture et les traitements inhumains et dégradants et l'article 4 prohibant les expulsions collectives ; et l'article 10 protégeant la liberté d'expression. Certaines juridictions nationales ont, dans le même sens, sanctionné des opérations maritimes lorsqu'elles contreviennent aux droits fondamentaux des individus. Par exemple, en matière de piraterie, les juridictions allemandes ont décidé que les conditions de remise de certains pirates au Kenya par la marine allemande constituaient une violation de leurs droits fondamentaux[95].

Les juridictions internationales relatives aux droits de l'homme ont également eu à appliquer le droit des réfugiés. A cette occasion, la responsabilité de l'Etat pour violation de ses obligations internationales au regard du droit des réfugiés a pu être mise en œuvre[96]. Par exemple, la Commission interaméricaine a jugé, en faisant application de l'article 33 de la Convention de Genève sur le droit des réfugiés interdisant le refoulement, que les Etats-Unis avaient violé leurs obligations internationales en refusant aux occupants haïtiens des navires interceptés en haute mer

90. CEDH, affaire *Hirsi Jamma et autres c. Italie*, 23 février 2012, requête nº 27765/09, par. 74 ss. Les navires étaient des navires gouvernementaux italiens ; dès lors, à partir du moment où ils sont montés à bord des navires des forces armées italiennes et jusqu'à leur remise aux autorités libyennes, les requérants se sont trouvés sous le contrôle continu et exclusif, tant *de jure* que *de facto*, des autorités italiennes.

91. CEDH, affaire *Medvedyev et autres c. France*, 29 mars 2010, requête nº 3394/03. Voir également M. Den Heijer, *Europe and Extraterritorial Asylum*, Hart Publishing, 2012, pp. 15 ss.

92. CEDH, affaire *Medvedyev et autres c. France*, 29 mars 2010, requête nº 3394/03.

93. CEDH, affaire *Hirsi Jamma et autres c. Italie* (préc.).

94. CEDH, affaire *Women on Waves et autres c. Portugal*, 3 février 2009, requête nº 31276/05.

95. Tribunal administratif de Cologne, 11 novembre 2011.

96. Pour les obligations internationales de l'Etat envers les réfugiés en mer, voir M. Pallis, « Obligations of States towards Asylum Seekers at Sea: Interactions and Conflicts between Legal Regimes », *International Refugee Law Review*, vol. 14, 2002, pp. 329-364.

le droit de déposer une demande d'asile[97]. Les décisions des juridictions internes américaines et australiennes semblent néanmoins aller dans un sens contraire, considérant respectivement que les dispositions de la Convention de Genève sur les réfugiés n'ont pas d'effet extraterritorial[98], et que le fait de garder des migrants à bord d'un navire pendant plusieurs semaines n'est pas constitutif d'une privation de liberté[99]. Largement critiquées par la doctrine[100], ces décisions ne semblent néanmoins pas refléter le droit international positif.

La responsabilité de l'Etat intervenant est ainsi mise en jeu lorsqu'il enfreint, lors de son opération d'interdiction maritime, une obligation issue du droit international des droits de l'homme ou du droit des réfugiés.

Paragraphe 2 **La responsabilité sans violation d'une obligation internationale de l'Etat**

La responsabilité internationale de l'Etat pour un comportement conforme au droit international existe de manière ponctuelle. Elle est par exemple prévue par le Traité de 1967 sur l'espace extra-atmosphérique ou encore par la Convention de 1972 sur la responsabilité internationale pour les dommages causés par les objets spatiaux[101]. Il s'agit d'une responsabilité pour des activités dangereuses qui causent des dommages inévitables, notamment en matière environnementale[102]. A ce titre elle est largement limitée[103].

En droit de la mer, une telle responsabilité sans fait internationalement illicite existe dans le cadre des opérations d'interdiction mari-

97. CIADH, *The Haitian Center for Human Rights* et al. *c. United States*, 13 mars 1997, affaire n° 10 675, rapport n° 51/96, par. 177.

98. Voir US Supreme Court, *Sale c. Haitian Centers Council* (113 S.Ct, 2549, 1993).

99. Voir Federal Court of Australia, *Ruddock c. Vadarlis* (2001) 183 ALR 1, 10.

100. W. Kirtley, « Tampa Incident: The Legality of Ruddock *v.* Vadarlis under International Law and the Implications of Australia's New Asylum Policy », *Columbia Journal of Transnational Law*, 2002-2003, pp. 251 et s.

101. Voir, sur ce point, M. Forteau, « Space Law », dans J. Crawford, A. Pellet et S. Olleson (dir. publ.), *The Law of International Responsibility, op. cit.*, pp. 903-914.

102. Voir P. M. Dupuy, « La responsabilité internationale des Etats pour les dommages d'origine technologique et industrielle », Paris, Pedone, 1976, p. 222, et A. Kiss, « La réparation pour atteinte à l'environnement », dans SFDI, *La responsabilité dans le système international*, Paris, Pedone, 1991, pp. 225-238.

103. Voir M. Montjoie, « The Concept of Liability in the Absence of an Internationally Wrongful Act », dans J. Crawford, A. Pellet et S. Olleson (dir. publ.), *The Law of International Responsibility, op. cit.*, pp. 503-514; Ph. Guttinger, « Allocation of Responsibility for Harmful Consequences of Acts not Prohibited by International Law », dans J. Crawford, A. Pellet et S. Olleson (dir. publ.), *The Law of International Responsibility, op. cit.*, pp. 515-520.

time[104]. Par exemple, les articles 22 de la Convention de Genève sur la haute mer[105] et 110, paragraphe 3, de la CMB prévoient une compensation du navire si «les soupçons se révèlent dénués de fondement». L'obligation d'indemnisation existe alors même que l'Etat intervenant s'est conformé aux règles de visite et d'intervention prévues par la CMB. Selon certains auteurs[106], la rédaction de l'article 110, paragraphe 3, est inspirée de l'affaire du *Marianna Flora*, jugée par la Cour suprême des Etats-Unis. Dans cette affaire, la Cour avait considéré que «the party seizes at his peril, and is liable to costs and damages if he fails to establish the forfeiture»[107]. Cette responsabilité permet de préserver le principe de liberté de la navigation et d'éviter les abus du droit de visite[108]. La formulation de l'article 9, paragraphe 2, du Protocole de Palerme, très similaire à l'article 110, paragraphe 3, de la CMB, suggère également que l'obligation de compensation existe même en l'absence d'acte illicite de la part de l'Etat intervenant[109]. Dans le même sens, l'article 8 *bis*, paragraphe 10, alinéa *b)*, point i), du Protocole relatif à la Convention SUA prévoit que les Etats Parties sont responsables des dommages ou pertes qui leur sont imputables lorsque «les motifs de ces

---

104. Voir, en ce sens, M. Sorensen, «Principes de droit international public», *RCADI*, tome 100 (1960), p. 221; M. B. Akehurst, «International Liability for Injurious Consequences Arising Out of Acts not Prohibited by International Law», *Netherlands Yearbook of International Law*, 1985, p. 10, ou encore T. Treves, «La navigation», dans R.-J. Dupuy et D. Vignes (dir. publ.), *Traité du nouveau droit de la mer*, Paris, Economica, 1985, p. 700.

105. Voir I. Bownlie, *System of the Law of Nations, States Responsibility, Part 1*, Oxford University Press, 1983, réimprimé en 2001, p. 49. L'auteur considère que l'article 22 est le premier exemple de responsabilité pour un acte qui n'est pas interdit par le droit international.

106. Ph. Wendel, *State Responsibility for Interferences with the Freedom of Navigation in Public International Law, op. cit.*, p. 113.

107. Supreme Court, The *Marianna Flora*, 24 US 11 Wheat. 11 (1826), cité par Ph. Wendel, *State Responsibility for Interferences with the Freedom of Navigation in Public International Law, op. cit.*, p. 113.

108. Voir les commentaires de l'article 46 du Projet d'articles sur la responsabilité de l'Etat (préc.):

> «L'Etat auquel appartient le navire de guerre devra indemniser le navire de commerce pour tout retard occasionné par l'action de ce bâtiment, et cela non seulement lorsque l'arrêt a eu lieu sans motifs valables, mais dans les cas où les soupcons ne sont pas fondés et où le navire n'a commis aucun acte qui soit de nature à faire naître les soupcons. Afin d'éviter des abus en ce qui concerne le droit de visite, cette sanction sévère semble justifiée.» (*Annuaire de la CDI*, 1956-II, p. 284.)

Voir également la position de l'Afrique du Sud qui considérait que l'absence de responsabilité serait une dérogation au principe de la liberté de la navigation en haute mer, *Annuaire de la CDI*, 1956-II, p. 79.

109. Pour une interprétation conforme, voir Ph. Wendel, *State Responsibility for Interferences with the Freedom of Navigation in Public International Law, op. cit.*, p. 123.

mesures se révèlent dénués de fondement, à condition que le navire n'ait commis aucun acte justifiant les mesures prises».

L'obligation de réparer dès lors que les soupçons se sont révélés «sans fondement» est néanmoins soumise à une condition, celle du comportement du navire visé. Cette condition suggère que seuls les dommages causés à des navires dont le comportement ne nécessitait pas une intervention peuvent être indemnisés. Cela limite considérablement la portée de la responsabilité sans fait illicite, si tant est qu'elle existe réellement [110]. En effet, dans bien des cas, l'Etat ne peut intervenir sur un navire que s'il est en mesure de justifier une suspicion. Or, les soupçons se déduisent précisément, la plupart du temps, du comportement du navire [111]. Philippe Wendel classe néanmoins ces dispositions dans la catégorie de celles permettant une responsabilité sans comportement illicite de l'Etat, en se fondant sur les travaux préparatoires de ces instruments, semblant démontrer la volonté des rédacteurs de prévoir ce type de responsabilité sans violation du droit international [112].

La jurisprudence canadienne fournit un exemple topique. Dans la fameuse affaire de l'*Estai*, la Cour fédérale avait accordé la somme de 137 058,57 dollars avec intérêts alors même qu'elle avait rejeté la totalité des allégations d'illicéité de l'intervention sur le navire espagnol. La réparation allouée correspondait, en réalité, à l'endommagement de la coque du navire par les glaces rencontrées lors de son rapatriement par les autorités canadiennes depuis son point de saisie jusqu'à Saint John's. Ainsi, «indépendamment du caractère licite ou non de la saisie, ces dommages étaient attribuables à la négligence des préposés et des mandataires de la Couronne fédérale» [113]. La décision sera infirmée par la Cour fédérale d'appel. Toutefois, les raisons de ce revirement ne se trouvent pas dans le fond du droit, mais dans le simple fait que les juges ont considéré que les requérants avaient abandonné ce grief [114].

Il convient de noter que cette responsabilité sans violation d'une obligation internationale est souvent exclue dans le cadre des opérations

110. Il existe une controverse sur l'existence même d'une responsabilité sans fait internationalement illicite de l'Etat, une intervention injustifiée étant en elle-même illicite, même sans faute commise par l'Etat.

111. Le fait de commettre un acte illicite est de nature à rendre le comportement du navire «suspect»; voir notamment l'arrêt du Conseil d'Etat français, 26 février 1982, affaire *Marie*, n° 18239. Le Conseil d'Etat énonce que seules les activités licites entravées peuvent donner lieu à réparation de la part de l'Etat français.

112. Ph. Wendel, *State Responsibility for Interferences with the Freedom of Navigation in Public International Law, op. cit.*, pp. 120-123. Cette volonté est très claire notamment pour l'article 22 de la Convention sur la haute mer.

113. *Canada (Procureur général) c. Hijos*, 2007 CAF 20 (CanLII), http://canlii.ca/t/1r3z5, consulté le 23 août 2012, par. 41 et 42.

114. *Ibid.*, par. 92.

menées par les Nations Unies. Les accords conclus par les Nations Unies avec les Etats hôtes dans le cadre d'opérations de maintien de la paix excluent les réparations pour des dommages et préjudices issus des «nécessités opérationnelles»[115], à savoir les dommages résultant «d'actions nécessaires entreprises par une force de maintien de la paix dans l'exercice de son mandat»[116].

SECTION 3 L'ATTRIBUTION DE LA RESPONSABILITÉ À L'ÉTAT EN MATIÈRE D'OPÉRATION D'INTERDICTION MARITIME

Les opérations d'interdiction maritime menées de manière unilatérale soulèvent des problématiques classiques d'attribution de la responsabilité à l'Etat, notamment en termes de détermination des critères pour qu'un navire et son équipage soient considérés comme agissant au nom de l'Etat (paragraphe 1). En revanche, cette hypothèse ne soulève que très peu de questions quant à la répartition de la responsabilité. Au contraire, les opérations multilatérales, en constante augmentation, nous amènent à nous interroger sur la répartition de la responsabilité entre Etats participants, mais également entre les Etats et les organisations internationales impliquées, telles que l'Union européenne, l'OTAN ou les Nations Unies (paragraphe 2).

Paragraphe 1 **Le cas des opérations unilatérales: l'attribution de la responsabilité à l'Etat**

L'Etat intervenant semble, à première vue, être l'entité responsable d'éventuels dommages commis lors de l'interception[117]. Par exemple, l'article 22 de la Convention de Genève sur la haute mer a été interprété par la CDI comme imposant à l'Etat «à qui appartient le navire de guerre» de verser une compensation au navire marchand[118]. Dans le même sens, l'article 106 de la CMB est ainsi formulé: «Lorsque la saisie d'un navire ou aéronef suspect de piraterie a été effectuée sans

115. F. Ducroquetz, *L'Union européenne et le maintien de la paix*, thèse, Université de Lille 2, 2010, p. 186.

116. Assemblée générale, *Rapport du Secrétaire général sur le financement de la force de protection des Nations Unies,* 50e session, A/51/389, 20 septembre 1996, par. 13.

117. S. Talmon, «Responsibility of International Organizations: Does the European Community Require Special Treatment», dans M. Ragazzi (dir. publ.), *International Responsibility Today — Essays in Memory of Oscar Schachter*, Leyde, Nijhoff, 2005, p. 411.

118. *Annuaire de la CDI,* 1956-II, p. 284.

motif suffisant, l'Etat qui y a procédé est responsable vis-à-vis de l'Etat dont le navire ou l'aéronef a la nationalité de toute perte ou de tout dommage causé de ce fait.» L'engagement de la responsabilité de l'Etat intervenant sera néanmoins subordonné aux règles d'attribution d'un comportement à l'Etat, issues du droit de la responsabilité. Il ne sera responsable que des actes qui lui sont attribuables, à savoir, dans un premier temps, les actes de ses organes et ses agents[119]. Un navire de guerre ou un autre navire gouvernemental est considéré comme un organe de l'Etat et leur personnel comme des agents de l'Etat. Leurs comportements lui sont donc attribuables sans difficulté.

Néanmoins, en pratique, d'autres questions se posent quant à l'attribution à l'Etat intervenant de la responsabilité en matière d'interdiction maritime. En particulier, celle de la persistance d'une responsabilité de l'Etat du pavillon qui autorise une intervention (A), ainsi que celle de l'attribution à l'Etat de comportements de personnes privées (B).

A. La persistance d'une responsabilité de l'Etat du pavillon

La formulation de l'article 21, paragraphe 18, de l'Accord sur les stocks chevauchants renvoie clairement au droit de la responsabilité et aux règles d'attribution d'un fait à l'Etat. Il énonce en effet que «[l]es Etats sont responsables des pertes ou dommages qui leur sont imputables». Ainsi, si un fait internationalement illicite est attribuable à l'Etat du pavillon, sa responsabilité peut être engagée. Une formulation similaire est adoptée par le Protocole relatif à la Convention SUA.

La question de la persistance d'une responsabilité de l'Etat du pavillon se pose au regard du contrôle qu'il conserve sur l'interception maritime. En effet, à l'exception des cas de compétence universelle d'intervention telle que la piraterie[120], son autorisation est nécessaire préalablement à l'intervention. Elle peut également être assortie de conditions, comme le rappelle l'article 8, paragraphe 5, du Protocole de Palerme: «Un Etat du pavillon peut ... subordonner son autorisation à des conditions arrêtées d'un commun accord entre lui et l'Etat requérant, notamment en ce qui concerne la responsabilité et la portée des mesures effectives à prendre.» Le Protocole de 2005 ajoute également que «le fait d'autoriser l'arraisonnement n'engage pas a priori la responsabilité de

119. Article 4 du Projet d'articles sur la responsabilité de l'Etat (préc.), considéré par la CIJ comme ayant une valeur coutumière: CIJ, *Différend relatif à l'immunité de juridiction d'un rapporteur spécial de la Commission des droits de l'homme*, avis consultatif du 29 avril 1999, par. 62.

120. Voir dans ce volume, Grymaneli, chapitre 5.

l'Etat du pavillon»[121]. L'emploi des termes a priori indique qu'une responsabilité est envisageable, mais qu'elle ne peut naître uniquement de l'autorisation d'intercepter donnée à un Etat tiers[122]. Si l'autorisation en elle-même n'est pas suffisante pour engager la responsabilité de l'Etat du pavillon, d'autres facteurs sont susceptibles de s'ajouter. Lors des négociations, certains Etats ont pu avancer que «the Flag State could only be liable if, for example, it was acting as the boarding State, or the damage or loss was attributable to a condition it imposed on the boarding authorization, or if it granted authorization on grounds that proved to be unfounded»[123]. Dans le même sens, l'Accord relatif au trafic illicite de stupéfiants, mettant en œuvre l'article 17 de la Convention de Vienne, prévoit que la «responsabilité de tout dommage [...] incombe à l'Etat requérant, lequel peut demander une indemnisation à l'Etat requis lorsque le dommage résulte d'une négligence ou autre faute imputable à celui-ci»[124].

La responsabilité naîtrait alors de la participation de l'Etat du pavillon à l'intervention, en offrant son aide ou assistance[125], ou en conservant un certain contrôle sur l'opération d'interdiction maritime[126]. Si cette responsabilité semble envisageable en théorie, elle semble limitée par le type d'obligation à la charge des Etats pavillonnaires si bien que la pratique ne nous fournit, pour l'instant, aucun exemple exploitable. Pour mettre en œuvre la responsabilité de l'Etat du pavillon, il faut justifier de la violation de l'une de ses obligations internationales. Si l'on reprend la classification précédemment évoquée, il ne peut difficilement s'agir d'un excès de compétence puisque ce n'est pas l'Etat du pavillon qui intervient directement, mais plutôt d'un excès de pouvoir, dans la mise en œuvre de l'interception. L'hypothèse la plus viable serait celle de la responsabilité de l'Etat du pavillon pour les violations des droits de l'homme commises par l'Etat intervenant. Cette situation hypothétique est néanmoins susceptible d'évoluer rapidement, à la lumière du développement des Shiprider Agreements. Cette pratique, initiée par les Etats-Unis d'Amérique dans les Caraïbes[127], consiste en la conclusion d'accords bilatéraux avec les Etats de la région[128]. Ils permettent aux

121. Art. 8*bis*, par. 10, al. *b)*.

122. Voir Ph. Wendel, *State Responsibility for Interferences with the Freedom of Navigation in Public International Law, op. cit.*, p. 129.

123. IMO Report of the Working Group, Doc. LEG/SUA/WG.2/4, 9 février 2005, par. 32.

124. Accord du Conseil de l'Europe, *STEI*, n° 156 (préc.), art 26, par. 3.

125. Article 16 du Projet d'articles sur la responsabilité de l'Etat (préc.).

126. Article 17 du Projet d'articles sur la responsabilité de l'Etat (préc.).

127. Initialement dans le cadre du trafic de drogue, mais cette pratique s'est développée dans d'autres cadres comme l'immigration clandestine.

128. Des Shiprider Agreements ont été conclus entre les Etats-Unis et les pays riverains suivants: Bahamas, Haïti, la Jamaïque, République dominicaine,

navires de police américains d'intervenir dans la mer territoriale d'un autre Etat avec lequel il existe un accord bilatéral, afin de procéder aux mesures coercitives s'imposant à l'encontre du navire. Cette possibilité est accordée par l'Etat contractant en raison de la présence de l'un de ses agents à bord du navire américain qui va poursuivre le navire suspect. Par une certaine «fiction juridique», «l'exercice du pouvoir de coercition de l'Etat côtier sur sa mer territoriale est préservé»[129].

Au regard de la responsabilité, il existe bien un agent étranger à bord du navire étatique qui procède à l'intervention. Il faut alors se demander si l'Etat côtier procède, dans ce cadre, à une délégation d'une partie de ses prérogatives de puissance publique. Dans l'affirmative, l'Etat côtier pourrait alors être responsable des dommages causés par l'Etat intervenant en vertu de cette délégation et en application de l'article 5[130] du projet d'articles de la CDI. Initialement prévu pour permettre l'attribution des actes d'entités non étatiques à l'Etat, lorsqu'ils exercent des prérogatives de puissance publique, la lettre de l'article 5 n'exclut pas formellement l'attribution de comportements d'entités étatiques étrangères. Son esprit ne semblant néanmoins pas pouvoir permettre une telle interprétation[131], il faudrait alors se tourner vers les articles du chapitre IV du projet, spécialement consacrés à la responsabilité de l'Etat du fait d'un autre Etat. Agissant comme une *lex specialis*, les règles applicables lorsque deux appareils étatiques sont en cause relèvent alors des articles 16 à 19, et non de l'article 5. Ainsi, les choses seraient claires: l'attribution du comportement d'une personne à l'Etat relève du chapitre II (art. 4-11), alors que l'attribution d'un comportement d'un autre Etat relève du chapitre IV. Toutefois, la lecture extensive que la CIJ elle-même fait de ces articles, notamment en appliquant le chapitre IV à des comportements d'entités non étatiques[132], nous amène à nous interroger sur cette possibilité, qui reste pour le moment uniquement théorique.

Turques-et-Caïques, la Barbade, Antilles néerlandaises, la Dominique, la Grenade, îles Vierges britanniques, Saint-Kitts-et-Nevis, Sainte-Lucie, Saint-Vincent-et-les Grenadines, Trinité-et-Tobago, Belize, Costa Rica, Panama, Suriname. Voir A. Bellayer-Roille, «La lutte contre le narcotrafic en mer Caraïbe: une coopération internationale à géométrie variable», *loc. cit.*, p. 370.

129. A. Bellayer-Roille, «La lutte contre le narcotrafic en mer Caraïbe: une coopération internationale à géométrie variable», *loc. cit.*, p. 370.

130. «Le comportement d'une personne ou entité qui n'est pas un organe de l'Etat au titre de l'article 4, mais qui est habilitée par le droit de cet Etat à exercer des prérogatives de puissance publique, pour autant que, en l'espèce, cette personne ou entité agisse en cette qualité, est considéré comme un fait de l'Etat d'après le droit international.»

131. J. Crawford, *Les articles de la CDI sur la responsabilité de l'Etat*, *op. cit.*, pp. 119 ss.

132. CIJ, *Application de la convention pour la prévention et la répression du crime de génocide*, 26 février 2007.

Le cadre légal naturel reste néanmoins le chapitre IV. Dans ce cadre, si un agent donne l'autorisation d'arraisonner les navires suspects dans la mer territoriale depuis le navire de guerre d'un Etat tiers, il conserve un certain contrôle sur l'opération ou, tout au moins, donne des directives au navire hôte, au sens de l'article 17 du projet d'articles de la CDI. Toutefois, pour tomber sous le coup de cet article, donner des directives, ici une autorisation d'intervention, n'est pas suffisant. Il faut également que les actes illicites aient été commis sous le contrôle de l'Etat de l'agent embarqué. Tel n'est pas le cas dans le cadre des Shiprider Agreements. L'article 17 vise en effet des cas de figure largement historiques comme des protectorats, ou bien, plus actuels, comme des cas d'occupation militaire, bien loin des préoccupations de l'intervention maritime [133]. En revanche, la délivrance d'une autorisation de commettre un acte que l'Etat embarqué sait illicite pourrait être constitutive d'une «assistance» dans la commission d'un acte internationalement illicite, aux termes de l'article 16, pourvu que l'Etat embarqué soit conscient de l'illicéité de l'acte commis et que cet acte aurait de la même manière été contraire au droit international s'il l'avait commis lui-même [134]. Traduction internationale de la notion de complicité [135], cette clause peut notamment jouer, dans le cas des opérations d'interdiction maritimes, uniquement en matière de droits de l'homme. Par exemple, si l'on peut établir qu'un Etat, dans une pratique constante, viole les droits fondamentaux des individus interceptés, alors, délivrer à un tel Etat une autorisation d'intervention tomberait sous le coup de la complicité.

La pratique des Shiprider Agreements doit également être lue à la lumière de l'article 6 du projet d'article de la CDI, qui revient sur la possibilité d'attribuer à l'Etat la responsabilité du comportement d'un organe mis à sa disposition par un autre Etat. Deux interrogations majeures naissent de l'application de cette règle aux opérations d'interdiction maritimes. La première revient à se demander si l'autorisation donnée par l'Etat du pavillon peut s'apparenter à une mise à disposition. La réponse semble devoir être négative, puisque, pour que le comporte-

133. Voir le commentaire de l'article 17 dans J. Crawford, *Les articles de la CDI sur la responsabilité de l'Etat*, *op. cit.*, pp. 182 ss.

134. Conditions posées par l'article 16 et reprises par la CIJ dans l'affaire relative à l'*Application de la convention pour la prévention et la répression du crime de génocide (Bosnie Herzégovie c. Serbie-et-Monténégro)*, 26 février 2007, par. 420 ss.

135. La CIJ a considéré, dans l'affaire Bosnie c. Serbie de 2007 précitée, que l'article 16 reflétait le droit international coutumier (voir par. 420). Sur la complicité en droit international, lire B. Graefrarth, «Complicity in the Law of International Responsibility», *RBDI*, 1996, pp. 370 ss., ou Ch. Dominicié, «Attribution of Conduct to Multiple States and the Implication of a State in the Act of Another State», dans J. Crawford, A. Pellet et S. Olleson (dir. publ.), *The Law of International Responsibility, op. cit.*, pp. 281-296.

ment de l'organe ou de l'agent de l'Etat intervenant soit attribuable à l'Etat côtier sur ce fondement, il faudrait qu'il ait agi « sous la direction et le contrôle exclusifs de celui-ci » [136]. La situation des interceptions maritimes sur autorisation de l'Etat côtier ne semble donc pas entrer dans cette catégorie. L'exemple des mesures prises par l'Italie pour contrôler l'immigration illégale en mer en vertu d'un accord avec l'Albanie est avancé par la CDI, qui considère avec la CEDH qu'elles n'étaient pas imputables à l'Albanie, même si elle les a autorisées [137]. En résumé, il n'apparaît pas que le navire de guerre dans son ensemble soit placé sous la direction et sous le contrôle exclusif de l'agent étranger embarqué. A l'inverse, l'agent embarqué n'est pas placé sous le contrôle exclusif du navire de guerre sur lequel il se trouve. Dès lors, les actes illicites de l'agent embarqué seront difficilement attribuables, sur ce fondement, à l'Etat du navire hôte, et inversement. En revanche, l'agent embarqué engage la responsabilité de son Etat s'il autorise une intervention, une visite, une arrestation ou une saisie en violation des règles du droit de la mer, par exemple, en violation du droit de passage inoffensif dans la mer territoriale [138].

B. L'attribution à l'Etat du comportement de personnes privées

i) *En temps de paix*

L'article 4 du projet d'articles sur la responsabilité de l'Etat prévoit que seul le comportement de ses organes et agents est attribuable à l'Etat. Or, les navires privés et leurs équipages n'entrent pas dans cette définition [139]. L'actualité internationale et le développement exponentiel de pratiques telles que le recours aux sociétés militaires et de sécurité privées (SMP) nous amènent néanmoins à examiner de plus près cette

---

136. Projet d'articles sur la responsabilité de l'Etat, et commentaires y relatifs (préc.), p. 100.

137. CEDH, affaire *Viron Xhavara* (préc.), par. 1 :

> « La Cour note d'emblée que le naufrage du *Kater I Rades* a été directement provoqué par le navire de guerre italien *Sibilla*. Par conséquent, toute doléance sur ce point doit être considérée comme étant dirigée exclusivement contre l'Italie. Le fait que l'Albanie est partie à la Convention italo-albanaise [valant autorisation permanente] ne saurait, à lui seul, engager la responsabilité de cet Etat au regard de la Convention pour toute mesure adoptée par les autorités italiennes en exécution de l'accord international en question. »

138. CMB, art. 17 ss.

139. Voir O. de Frouville, « Private Individuals », dans J. Crawford, A. Pellet et S. Olleson (dir. publ.), *The Law of International Responsibility, op. cit.*, pp. 257-280.

possibilité, notamment au regard des portes laissées ouvertes par le projet d'articles de la CDI pour l'attribution à l'Etat d'actes de personnes privées. L'article 5 du projet d'articles permet l'attribution du comportement d'une personne privée à l'Etat si elle exerce des prérogatives de puissance publique, tandis que l'article 8 [140] prévoit l'attribution des actes privés si les personnes sont placées sous la direction ou le contrôle de l'Etat. L'article 9 [141] peut également, dans une moindre mesure, être utile dans le cas de sociétés militaires privées puisqu'il permet l'attribution à l'Etat du comportement d'entités privées en cas d'absence ou de carence des autorités officielles.

C'est à la lumière de ces règles d'attribution que la pratique contemporaine favorisant le recours aux SMP doit être lue. La SMP, ou «société commerciale qui fournit contre rémunération des services militaires ou de sécurité par l'intermédiaire de personnes physiques ou morales» [142], symbole du «phénomène de l'externalisation des missions de sécurité et de défense» [143], est en effet vue comme une solution par bien des acteurs maritimes. Au premier chef, par les utilisateurs de la mer, armateurs et sociétés commerciales qui font transiter leurs navires par des zones peu fiables en termes de sécurité. Face à l'inaction ou l'impuissance de l'Etat côtier et la désorganisation de la communauté internationale, les sociétés militaires privées sont considérées comme un moyen d'assurer la défense et la protection des navires marchands [144].

Certains Etats ont directement recours aux SMP en mer, afin d'assurer la sécurité des espaces maritimes. C'est parfois un moyen, pour les Etats qui ne disposent pas de forces maritimes suffisantes, de tenter de reprendre le contrôle de leurs espaces maritimes. La Somalie a, par exemple, eu recours à ces contrats. Les sociétés Topcat Marine security Inc., Scopex et Phoenix ont conclu des contrats avec le Gouvernement de

140. L'article 8 est ainsi formulé:

> «Le comportement d'une personne ou d'un groupe de personnes est considéré comme un fait de l'Etat d'après le droit international si cette personne ou ce groupe de personnes, en adoptant ce comportement, agit en fait sur les instructions ou les directives ou sous le contrôle de cet Etat.»

141. «Le comportement d'une personne ou d'un groupe de personnes est considéré comme un fait de l'Etat d'après le droit international si cette personne ou ce groupe de personnes exerce en fait des prérogatives de puissance publique en cas d'absence ou de carence des autorités officielles et dans des circonstances qui requièrent l'exercice de ces prérogatives.»

142. Définition issue du projet de convention sur les sociétés militaires et de sécurité privées présenté au Conseil des droits de l'homme par le Groupe de travail sur l'utilisation de mercenaires, art. 2, al. *a)*, A/HRC/15/25, p. 23.

143. J.-D. Rosi, «Sociétés militaires et de sécurité privées: les mercenaires des temps modernes?», *Les Cahiers du RMES*, vol. IV, n° 2, p. 109.

144. K. Neri, *L'emploi de la force en mer*, Bruxelles, Bruylant, 2013.

transition somalien pour faire cesser la piraterie au large de la Somalie[145]. En enchaînant ainsi les contrats avec diverses SMP, la Somalie tente de s'organiser pour améliorer sa capacité à combattre les actes de violence commis dans ses eaux territoriales, avec, apparemment, un succès fort mitigé. La question qui se pose est celle de savoir si les actes des personnels des SMP en mer peuvent être imputables à l'Etat. Même si, dans le cas de la Somalie, ce sont les autorités gouvernementales qui ont eu recours à ces sociétés privées, elles étaient matériellement dans l'impossibilité d'exercer sur elle un contrôle suffisant pour que leurs actes leur soient attribuables aux termes de l'article 8 du projet d'articles[146]. Il faudrait alors se tourner vers les possibilités ouvertes par les articles 5 et 9. L'article 5 prévoit en effet que le comportement des SMP serait attribuable à l'Etat si celui-ci les a habilitées à exercer des prérogatives de puissance publique. Il y a alors ici une référence au droit interne de l'Etat concerné[147]. S'il contient cette autorisation, alors les actes des SMP pourront lui être attribués. La délégation doit viser non pas seulement des missions d'assistance de navires en danger, mais bien des prérogatives de puissance publique, telle que des pouvoirs d'arrestation des membres de l'équipage ou de saisie des cargaisons. Cette interprétation semble être en accord avec les objectifs poursuivis par l'article 5, notamment « de faire en sorte que soit pris en compte le phénomène de plus en plus répandu des entités para-étatiques qui exercent des prérogatives de puissance publique à la place d'organes de l'Etat »[148]. Dans le cas précis de la Somalie, Etat défaillant, l'on pourrait également imaginer l'applicabilité de l'article 9, étant donné la carence des autorités étatiques pour lutter contre la criminalité en mer. Il semble néanmoins que cette possibilité doive être écartée, puisque l'applicabilité de l'article 9 est subordonnée à l'exercice de fonctions publiques par une entité privée, menée de sa propre initiative[149]. Tel n'est pas le cas dans l'exemple somalien, les SMP ayant été recrutées par les autorités gouvernementales.

D'autres Etats ont recours aux SMP, non pas pour compenser leur

---

145. F. Martineau et A. Salliou, « Défense et sécurité », *loc. cit.*, 2005, p. 496. « Le Français *Secopex* va assurer la sécurité maritime en Somalie », *Mer et marine*, 3 juin 2008, et F. Laurent et A. Garcia, « Défense et sécurité », 2008, *loc. cit.*, p. 648. Voir F. Parodi, « Les Etats face à l'activité des sociétés militaires et de sécurité privées », *loc. cit.*, p. 501 (n. 3).

146. Voir *infra* note 154.

147. Voir J. Crawford, *Les articles de la CDI sur la responsabilité de l'Etat*, p. 120.

148. Projet d'articles sur la responsabilité de l'Etat, et commentaires y relatifs (préc.), pp. 96-97. Les commentaires visent clairement « les entreprises de sécurité privées ».

149. *Ibid.*, p. 116.

défaillance, mais dans le cadre d'une délégation de compétences, notamment en matière de lutte contre la piraterie maritime. Dans ce cas, l'applicabilité de l'article 5 du projet d'articles semble pouvoir être discutée. Certains Etats comme les Etats-Unis d'Amérique auraient eu recourt à ces sociétés pour lutter contre les violences illicites en mer, en particulier la piraterie et le terrorisme maritime [150]. Dans un tel cas, l'habilitation du droit interne de l'Etat mandant permettrait de lui attribuer les actes des personnels des SMP [151]. Toutefois, les commentaires de la CDI relatifs au projet de 2001 laissent à penser que la situation des sociétés militaires privées doive être gérée selon les règles établies à l'article 8. En effet, il fait référence à des « individus ou groupes de personnes privées qui … sont employés comme auxiliaires ou sont envoyés comme « volontaires » dans des pays voisins, ou qui effectuent des missions particulières à l'étranger sur instructions de l'Etat » [152].

Si le principe apparaît bien établi [153], le degré de contrôle que l'Etat doit exercer sur les personnes privées pour que leurs actes leurs soient attribuables en vertu de l'article 8 reste controversé. Il apparaît néanmoins que si le comportement des SMP et de leur personnel est placé sous le contrôle effectif de l'Etat mandant, alors leurs actes leurs sont attribuables. Dans le cadre d'opérations d'interdiction maritime, le comportement des SMP sera attribuable à l'Etat s'il a par exemple ordonné l'interception illicite qui a causé un dommage, et si elle s'est déroulée sous son contrôle opérationnel total. Les critères établis par la Cour internationale de justice quant au degré de contrôle de l'Etat sur les forces non étatiques pour permettre de lui attribuer leurs actes sont en effet très stricts. Elle exige un contrôle stratégique et tactique [154], ou que

150. « Au cours de l'année 2007, la société militaire privée américaine spécialisée dans les opérations maritimes, Pistris Incorporated, s'est vu délivrer des lettres de marque en bonne et due forme de la part du président Georges W. Bush en vue de mener la guerre de course contre les auteurs d'actes de violence privée en mer dans l'océan Indien. » (J.-P. Pancracio.) Catheline Remy remet néanmoins en cause la véracité de cette information, faute de n'avoir pu être vérifiée. Voir C. Remy, « Les sociétés militaires privées dans la lutte contre la piraterie », *Pyramides*, 2012, pp. 119-138.

151. Lecture de l'article 5 du Projet d'articles partagée par C. Laly-Chevalier, « Lutte contre la piraterie maritime et droits de l'homme », *RBDI*, p. 13.

152. Projet d'articles sur la responsabilité de l'Etat, et commentaires y relatifs (préc.), p. 110.

153. Voir, par exemple, les affaires *Zafiro*, *RSA*, vol. VI (1925), p. 160 ; *Stephens*, *RSA*, vol. IV (1927), p. 267 ; *Lehigh Valley Railroad Company, and others*, *RSA*, vol. VIII (1930), p. 84, et vol. VIII (1939), p. 458. Voir également, plus récemment, la jursiprudence *Tadic* du TPIY (Chambre d'appel, *Le Procureur c. Dusko Tadic*, 2 octobre 1995, IT-94-1-T) et *Nicaragua* de la CIJ (*Activités militaires et paramilitaires au Nicaragua et contre celui-ci*, Nicaragua c. Etats-Unis d'Amérique, 27 juin 1986).

154. CIJ, *Nicaragua* (préc.), par. 110.

les actes illicites aient été «ordonnés» ou «imposés»[155] par l'Etat. Il convient en effet de démontrer que «ces instructions ont été données, à l'occasion de chacune des opérations au cours desquelles les violations alléguées se seraient produites, et non pas en général, à l'égard de l'ensemble des actions menées par les personnes ou groupes de personnes ayant commis lesdites violations»[156]. Ces critères rendent l'attribution des actes des personnels des SMP en mer, en vertu de l'article 8, très difficile à mettre en œuvre[157]. Les critères issus de la jurisprudence pourraient néanmoins être assouplis dans le cas de SMP, dans la mesure où ces sociétés ne poursuivent aucun objectif propre, qui pourrait être distinct de celui de l'Etat[158].

ii) *En temps de guerre*

La question de l'attribution des actes des SMP à l'Etat qui délivre l'autorisation, dans le cadre d'un conflit armé, doit être soulevée indépendamment de la licéité elle-même du recours à ces sociétés[159]. Le droit international humanitaire apporte un premier élément de réponse, puisqu'il considère que les membres des SMP, recrutés par un Etat pour participer directement aux hostilités et sous son commandement, peuvent être qualifié des membres des forces armées au sens de l'article 43 du Premier Protocole additionnel et de l'article 4 (par. A, al. 1) de la troisième Convention de Genève[160]. De même, le CICR a identifié, dans

155. CIJ, *Nicaragua* (préc.), par. 115.

156. CIJ, *Application de la convention pour la prévention et la répression du crime de génocide* (préc.), par. 400.

157. Pour une analyse des critères d'attribution, voir A. Cassese, «The Nicaragua and Tadic Tests Revisited in Light of the ICJ Judgment on Genocide in Bosnia», *EJIL*, 2007, vol. 18, nº 4, pp. 649-668.

158. Voir sur ce point l'opinion dissidente du juge Al-Khasawneh dans l'affaire relative à l'*Application de la convention pour la prévention et la répression du crime de génocide* (préc.): »Dans la présente affaire, il y avait unité d'objectifs, unité ethnique et idéologie commune, de sorte qu'un contrôle effectif sur des acteurs non étatiques n'était pas nécessaire» et

> «Dans l'affaire *Nicaragua*, la Cour a noté que les Etats-Unis d'Amérique et les *contras* partageaient le même objectif, à savoir le renversement du Gouvernement nicaraguayen. Cet objectif pouvait toutefois être atteint sans la commission de crimes de guerre ou de crimes contre l'humanité. Les *contras* auraient pu ne s'en prendre qu'à des cibles militaires dans la poursuite de leurs objectifs. Ainsi, pour pouvoir attribuer des crimes contre l'humanité commis dans la poursuite d'un objectif commun, la Cour avait *dit que les crimes* eux-mêmes devaient être l'objet du contrôle.»

159. Voir sur ce point K. Neri, *L'emploi de la force en mer*, *op. cit.*, par. 285 ss.

160. Voir L. Doswald Beck, «Private Military Companies under International Humanitarian Law», dans S. Chesterman et C. Lehnardt (dir. publ.), *From Mercenaries to Market. The Rise and Regulation of Private Military Companies*, Oxford University Press, 2007. *Contra*, voir F. Parodi, «Les sociétés militaires

sa règle numéro 139, une règle coutumière qui impose aux Etats de respecter et faire respecter le droit international humanitaire par «les personnes ou groupes agissant en fait sur ses instructions ou ses directives ou sous son contrôle»[161]. Ainsi, lorsqu'un conflit armé est en cause, le comportement des SMP semble pouvoir être attribuable à l'Etat qui les a engagées si elles sont placées sous son commandement ou sous son contrôle. Une telle interprétation semble être confirmée par l'affaire *Stephens*, dans laquelle le tribunal considéra qu'un membre d'une milice devait être assimilée à un membre des forces armées puisqu'il était placé sous le contrôle d'un sergent de l'armée mexicaine et qu'il exerçait des activités de soldat[162].

Paragraphe 2 **Le cas des opérations multilatérales: les règles de répartition de la responsabilité**

A. La répartition de la responsabilité entre Etats

Les opérations multilatérales sont de plus en plus nombreuses en mer, notamment dans le cadre de coalitions ou d'opérations multilatérales autorisées. Tel est par exemple le cas de l'opération *Enduring Freedom*[163], du projet commun de garde-côtes de l'Afrique de l'ouest[164], ou encore de l'opération au large de la Somalie, autorisée par le Conseil de sécurité[165]. Le droit international de la responsabilité n'exclut pas une responsabilité conjointe si plusieurs Etats entreprennent une action commune qui viole une obligation internationale[166] ou cause

et de sécurité privées», dans IREDIES, *Les menaces contre la paix et la sécurité internationales: nouveaux défis et nouveaux enjeux*, Université Paris 1 Panthéon Sorbonne, p. 157.

161. Henckaert et Doswald Beck, *Droit international humanitaire coutumier*, n° 54, p. 651.

162. Sentence arbitrale, *Charles Stephens and Bowman Stephens (Etats-Unis d'Amérique c. Mexique)*, 15 juillet 1927, *RSA*, vol. IV, p. 265.

163. Voir W. Heintschel von Heinegg, «Maritime Interception/Interdiction Operations within the Framework of Operation Enduring Freedom», dans SFDI, *Les nouvelles menaces contre la paix et la sécurité internationales: journée franco-allemande*, Paris, Pedone, 2004, pp. 149-164.

164. OMAOC, Assemblée générale, Mémorandum d'entente du réseau sous-régional intégré de garde-côtes des Etats d'Afrique de l'Ouest et du Centre, Dakar, 31 juillet 2008, MOWCA/XIII GA.08/8.

165. Voir la résolution 1816 (2008) du Conseil de sécurité. Pour un commentaire, D. Guilfoyle , «Piracy off Somalia: UN Security Council Resolution 1816 and IMO Regional Counter-Piracy Efforts», *ICLQ*, 2008, vol. 57,, n° 3, pp. 690-699.

166. Voir M. L. Padelletti, *Pluralità di Stati nel fatto illecito internazionale*, Milan, Giuffrè, 1990, ou Ch. Dominicié, «Attribution of Conduct to Multiple States and the Implication of a State in the Act of Another State», *loc. cit.*, p. 282.

un dommage en mer. Dans le même sens, une responsabilité conjointe peut être recherchée si un Etat a participé à l'opération illicite en mer.

Ainsi, dans le cas de figure, très fréquent dans le cas d'opérations multilatérales sous commandement unifié, où un Etat exerce le commandement que d'autres sont amenés à exécuter, le simple fait d'avoir reçu des directives dans la commission d'un fait internationalement illicite ne constitue pas une circonstance excluant l'illicéité [167]. Ainsi, si le comportement qui a causé le dommage en mer est imputable à l'Etat, il ne pourra se décharger de sa responsabilité en invoquant que l'ordre opérationnel est venu d'ailleurs.

Les cas de mise en œuvre d'une telle responsabilité sont rares [168], mais seront certainement plus nombreux dans un futur proche, étant donné la multiplication des opérations de ce type, notamment en mer.

B. La répartition de la responsabilité dans le cadre d'opérations décidées ou menées par des organisations internationales

La globalisation de la criminalité en mer a amené la communauté internationale à s'organiser pour lutter efficacement contre les dangers qu'elle cause. Ainsi, les organisations internationales, universelles ou régionales, vont se lancer dans la lutte pour la sécurité des espaces maritimes. L'Union de l'Europe occidentale (UEO), l'OTAN, l'Union européenne ou encore les Nations Unies ont mis en place des opérations partiellement ou totalement maritimes avec des compétences en matière d'interception des navires. La question de la répartition de la responsabilité entre ces organisations et leurs Etats membres se pose alors de manière criante (i)), de même que la répartition de la responsabilité entre les organisations intervenantes (ii)).

i) *La répartition de la responsabilité entre l'organisation internationale et ses Etats membres*

Les règles relatives à la responsabilité des organisations internationales contenues dans le récent projet de la CDI indiquent que l'organisation est responsable des actes qui lui sont attribuables et qui constituent une violation d'une obligation internationale de l'organisation [169].

167. *Op. cit. supra* note 166.

168. Voir les tentatives avortées à l'encontre des forces de l'OTAN dans l'affaire kosovarde : CIJ, *Licéité de l'emploi de la force*, 15 décembre 2004, ou encore l'affaire *Bankovic* devant la CEDH. Voir également l'affaire relative à *Certaines terres à phosphates à Nauru*, 26 juin 1992.

169. Articles 3 et 4 du Projet d'articles sur la responsabilité des organisations internationales (préc.).

Les actes de ses organes ou de ses agents lui sont attribuables, dans le cadre de leurs fonctions[170], mais également le comportement d'autres entités si elles sont placées sous son contrôle effectif[171]: «Lorsqu'un organe ou un agent est mis à la disposition d'une organisation internationale, il apparaît que la question décisive en ce qui concerne l'attribution d'un comportement déterminé est de savoir qui exerce effectivement un contrôle sur le comportement en question.»[172] Ainsi, «loin de conduire à l'attribution automatique à l'ONU de tout comportement sur le terrain, la combinaison de ces critères permet d'attribuer aux agents d'exécution des autorisations du Conseil de sécurité le comportement sur lequel ils exercent en réalité un degré suffisant de contrôle effectif »[173].

Un équilibre semble avoir été trouvé pour la répartition de la responsabilité dans le cadre des opérations décidées par les Nations Unies: les opérations multilatérales autorisées par le Conseil de sécurité relèvent de la responsabilité des Etats ou des organisations régionales qui les mettent en œuvre, parce qu'elles exercent un contrôle effectif. A l'opposé, les opérations de maintien de la paix relèvent de la responsabilité de l'ONU en tant qu'organe subsidiaire de leur organe créateur — le plus souvent, le Conseil de sécurité[174]. Elles engagent alors en principe la responsabilité de l'ONU en cas de dommages. Des commissions de réparations ont par ailleurs été mises en place par les Nations Unies dans ce cadre. Leur impact maritime est moins évident, mais il n'est pas exclu qu'une opération de maintien de la paix (OMP) soit dotée de compétences maritimes, notamment afin de s'assurer du respect d'un embargo décrété par le Conseil[175]. En tout état de cause, un fort consensus sur ces questions avait été relevé par la CDI, ainsi que par la doctrine[176].

Les affaires *Behrami* et *Saramati* jugées par la CEDH[177] sèment néanmoins le trouble en remettant en cause cet équilibre. Les juges de Strasbourg considèrent que le fait que le Conseil de sécurité «détien[ne] l'au-

---

170. Article 6 du Projet d'articles sur la responsabilité des organisations internationales (préc.).

171. *Ibid.*, art. 7.

172. Rapport de la CDI, doc. A/59/10 (2004), chapitre V, commentaire de l'article 5 (par. 7).

173. Voir L. A. Sicilianos, «L'(ir)responsabilité des forces multilatérales?», *International Law and the Quest for Its Implementation: Liber Amicorum Vera Gowlland-Debbas*, Brill, 2010, p. 108.

174. *Ibid.*, pp. 95-125.

175. Tel a par exemple été le cas de la FINUL; voir la résolution du Conseil de sécurité 1701 (2006), par. 11 et 14.

176. L. A. Sicilianos, «L'(ir)responsabilité des forces multilatérales?», *loc. cit.*, p. 170.

177. A. Clapham «The Subject of Subjects and the Attribution of Attribution», *International Law and the Quest for Its Implementation: Liber Amicorum Vera Gowlland-Debbas*, Brill, 2010, pp. 45-58.

torité et le contrôle ultimes»[178] suffit pour considérer que l'action des Etats ou des entités de mise en œuvre est «attribuable» à l'ONU. Du coup il y a fort à parier que la solution sera identique (puisqu'elle a déjà été confirmée par la Cour[179]) si la CEDH venait à connaître d'affaires survenues dans le cadre de l'opération Atalanta de l'Union européenne à laquelle nombre d'Etats du Conseil de l'Europe participent. Même si la jurisprudence *Al Jedda* semble, à première vue, contredire la position de la Cour dans l'affaire *Behrami*, puisqu'elle refuse d'attribuer les actes des soldats britanniques aux Nations Unies et engage la responsabilité du Royaume-Uni, elle n'arrive à cette solution qu'au terme d'un raisonnement confus qui ne tranche pas entre contrôle ultime et contrôle effectif. Elle se contente de relever que ni l'un ni l'autre n'étaient remplis en l'espèce[180]. Ainsi, elle conclurait selon toute vraisemblance à l'attribution du comportement illicite à l'ONU et déclarerait la requête irrecevable.

Toutefois, la jurisprudence de la CEDH n'a pas été reprise dans le projet final de la CDI. Son rapporteur a, en effet, considéré que:

> «à en juger par la façon généralement positive dont les Etats ont réagi à l'égard du critère énoncé à l'article 5 et par l'absence de toute critique de ce critère dans toutes les décisions judiciaires dont il est fait état plus haut, il n'y a pas lieu d'apporter des modifications à l'article 5. Certes, la Cour européenne des droits de l'homme a retenu un critère d'attribution différent et est parvenue, en ce qui concerne l'attribution du comportement de contingents nationaux alloués à une force autorisée par l'ONU, à une conclusion autre que celle à laquelle on serait parvenu sur la base de l'article 5, comme le précise le commentaire. Il reste que, sans pour autant minimiser l'importance de pareille jurisprudence, on pourrait difficilement accepter sur la seule foi du jugement rendu dans *Behrami* et *Saramati*, que le critère y appliqué peut être

178. K. M. Larsen, «Attribution of Conduct in Peace Operation: the "Ultimate Authority and Control" Test», *EJIL*, 2008, pp. 509 ss.

179. CEDH, *Gajic c. Allemagne*, 28 août 2007; CEDH, *Kasumaj c. Grèce*, 5 juillet 2007, et *Beric et consorts c. Bosnie-Herzégovine*, 16 octobre 2007.

180. « Le Conseil de sécurité n'exerçait ni un contrôle effectif ni l'autorité et le contrôle ultimes sur les actions et omissions des soldats de la force multinationale et que, dès lors, l'internement du requérant n'est pas imputable à l'ONU», CEDH, *Al Jedda c. Royaume-Uni*, 7 juillet 2011, requête n° 27021/08. Voir également la décision de la House of Lords, qui juge que le Royaume-Uni pouvait légalement, quand cela était motivé par des raisons impératives de sécurité, exercer le pouvoir de détention prévu par la résolution 1546 du Conseil de sécurité (en vertu de l'article 103), mais devait s'assurer que les droits des détenus, prévus à l'article 5.1 de la Convention, n'étaient pas enfreints à un degré plus élevé que ceux inhérents à ce genre de détention.

considéré comme une règle universelle. Par ailleurs, sur le plan des principes, l'approche adoptée par la Cour européenne des droits de l'homme n'est pas convaincante. Elle conduirait à attribuer à l'ONU un comportement que l'Organisation n'a pas expressément autorisé et dont elle n'a guère connaissance, voire aucune connaissance du tout.» [181]

Reste néanmoins à savoir si le comportement en question constitue une violation d'une obligation internationale de l'Organisation. A cet égard, la CIJ a indiqué, dans son avis consultatif sur l'*Interprétation de l'accord du 25 mars 1951 entre l'OMS et l'Egypte*, que l'organisation internationale est « lié[e] par toutes les obligations que lui imposent les règles générales du droit international, son acte constitutif ou les accords internationaux auxquels [elle] est partie » [182]. En matière d'interdiction maritime, les organisations internationales impliquées ne sont pas liées par les mêmes obligations conventionnelles que leurs Etats membres, issues de la CMB [183] et des traités sectoriels. Il faudrait alors rechercher au cas par cas si une règle coutumière ou conventionnelle lui confère une obligation internationale. Tel sera par exemple le cas des règles coutumières régissant l'emploi de la force ou, encore, des règles contenues dans le droit interne de l'organisation, primaire ou dérivé. Dans ce sens, l'Union européenne sera par exemple liée, en matière de droits de l'homme, par sa Charte des droits fondamentaux [184].

ii) *La répartition de la responsabilité entre organisations internationales impliquées dans des interdictions maritimes*

La question de la répartition de la responsabilité entre organisations doit être posée, notamment entre l'ONU et les organisations régionales qui mènent les opérations autorisées. En principe, les forces nationales sont placées sous le contrôle politique et la direction stratégique de l'organisation régionale si le commandement militaire de l'opération est

181. Assemblée générale, *Commission du droit international — Septième rapport sur la responsabilité des organisations internationales — Giorgio Gaja, Rapporteur général*, adopté à sa soixante et unième session, Genève, 4 mai-5 juin et 6 juillet-7 août 2009, A/CN.4/610, 27 mars 2009, 44 pages, p. 13, par. 30.

182. CIJ, *Interprétation de l'accord du 25 mars 1951 entre l'OMS et l'Egypte, avis consultatif*, 20 décembre 1980, par. 37.

183. L'Union européenne est partie à la CMB depuis le 1er avril 1998, mais elle n'est liée que par les dispositions relatives à la conservation et la gestion des ressources de la pêche, à la protection et la préservation du milieu marin, et, dans une certaine mesure, au regard des dispositions des parties X et XI de la CMB.

184. Voir l'article 51 de la Charte des droits fondamentaux de l'Union européenne, 7 décembre 2000, *JO*, 18 décembre 2000/C, 364/01.

attribué à l'organisation régionale. Ainsi, les contingents qui la composent n'acceptent aucune instruction de leur Etat d'origine ou de l'ONU, mais acceptent les instructions du Commandant nommé par l'organisation régionale[185]. Dans le cadre de l'Union européenne et de la force Atalanta, si

> «[l]es forces déployées sont les forces de l'organisation régionale, composées d'un agrégat de contingents nationaux, mais arborant les couleurs et les signes distinctifs de l'organisation européenne, et l'ensemble du personnel bénéficie des immunités accordées aux membres de la Force de l'UE par l'organisation régionale [et que] les opérations sont financées par l'organisation régionale (et non pas l'ONU)»[186],

alors, seule la responsabilité de l'organisation régionale devrait être recherchée, mais en aucun cas une responsabilité de l'ONU, qui n'exerce pas de véritable contrôle sur l'opération. L'opération Atalanta menée par l'Union européenne au large de la Somalie et dans le golfe d'Aden semble remplir ces critères et être en mesure d'engager la responsabilité internationale de l'Union, s'il existe un lien juridique suffisant unissant l'Union européenne aux opérations.

> «Par exemple, le fait que les décisions soient prises par le Conseil (institution de l'UE) par des actions communes (actes juridiques qui lient les Etats membres) sur la base de l'article 14 TUE (actuellement des décisions sur la base de l'article 25 TUE), que les opérations soient placées sous le contrôle et la direction stratégique du COPS, que le Conseil (sur avis du COPS) peut décider d'un changement du mandat de l'opération et y mettre un terme, que le Conseil puis le COPS se chargent de la nomination du Commandant de l'opération/Chef de la mission, le fait que les membres des forces bénéficient de privilèges et d'immunités accordés à l'UE et négociés par elle, que les forces portent les insignes de l'UE et agissent sous le drapeau de l'UE, pourraient signifier que les opérations sont des organes subsidiaires de l'UE.»[187]

En principe, donc, les dommages causés par les membres de l'opération Atalanta sont imputables à l'Union, en cas de violation d'une de ses obligations internationales.

Au-delà des opérations autorisées à proprement parler, le Conseil a pu, dans le domaine maritime, autoriser les Etats membres ou des orga-

185. F. Ducroquetz, *L'Union européenne et le maintien de la paix*, *op. cit.*, p. 165.
186. *Ibid.*
187. *Ibid.*, p. 170.

nisations régionales à prendre des mesures dérogatoires aux règles classiques du droit de la mer pour intercepter des navires soupçonnés de violer un embargo[188]. Dans ce cas, le Conseil de sécurité ne conserve qu'un contrôle distant sur les opérations d'interdiction menées en mer par les Etats membres ou par les organisations régionales, comme la CEDEAO en Sierra Leone[189] ou l'OTAN et l'UEO en Yougoslavie[190]. Ainsi, les actes illicites ou causant des dommages ne sauraient, en application des règles dégagées par la CDI, être attribuables à l'ONU.

Il convient enfin de noter que la possibilité d'une attribution conjointe à l'organisation et aux Etats membres participants à l'opération subsiste: «conduct does not necessarily have to be attributed exclusively to one subject only ... one could envisage cases in which conduct should be simultaneously attributed to an international organization and one or more of its members»[191]. Dans le même sens: «Detecting state responsibility does not foreclose the possibility that there have also been violations of international law by other entities. Likewise attributing responsibility to an international organization should not blind us to the possibility that other entities might also be attributed their own amount of blame.»[192] Cela permet de surmonter les difficultés liées à l'engagement de la responsabilité internationale des organisations internationales.

SECTION 4 L'ENGAGEMENT DE LA RESPONSABILITÉ

Il convient de rechercher dans le droit de la mer ainsi que dans le droit de la responsabilité les conditions pour qu'un Etat puisse, pour lui-même ou au titre de la protection diplomatique, engager la responsabilité internationale de l'entité qui a causé les dommages (paragraphe 1). Toutefois, la formulation de certaines dispositions conventionnelles suggère la possibilité, pour des acteurs privés victimes d'un dommage, d'engager directement la responsabilité de l'Etat (paragraphe 2).

188. Voir *supra* notes 38-39 et texte.

189. Le Conseil a autorisé la CEDEAO à «utiliser la force pour assurer le respect de l'embargo, y compris en interrompant la navigation maritime» (résolution 1132 (1997), 8 octobre 1997, S/RES/1132 (1997)).

190. L'UEO et OTAN, dans le cadre des résolutions 757 (1992) puis 820 (1993) et de l'embargo complet sur Belgrade, ont en effet lancé deux opérations distinctes mais coordonnées: opération Sharp Vigilance de l'UEO et Maritime Monitor de l'OTAN. Voir la déclaration du Conseil des ministres de l'UEO, 10 juillet 1992, Agence Europe, 11 juillet 1992, p. 3, et la déclaration du Conseil des ministres de l'OTAN, 10 juillet 1992, Agence Europe, 11 juillet 1992, p. 4.

191. Giorgio Gaja, UN doc. A/CN.4.541, 2 avril 2004, par. 6.

192. A. Clapham «The Subject of Subjects and the Attribution of Attribution», *loc. cit.*, p. 58.

Paragraphe 1 L'engagement de la responsabilité par l'Etat lésé

L'engagement de la responsabilité par l'Etat lésé est un point classique du droit de la responsabilité internationale. En cas d'interception en mer, l'Etat lésé peut être l'Etat du pavillon (A) ou l'Etat côtier (B).

A. L'Etat du pavillon

Il s'agit de l'hypothèse la plus courante. Par exemple, la CMB énonce clairement, en matière de saisie arbitraire d'un navire, que, « [l]orsque la saisie d'un navire ou aéronef suspect de piraterie a été effectuée sans motif suffisant, l'Etat qui y a procédé est responsable vis-à-vis de l'Etat dont le navire ou l'aéronef a la nationalité de toute perte ou de tout dommage causé de ce fait »[193]. Ainsi, ce sera à l'Etat du pavillon de réagir à une violation de ses droits, en l'occurrence l'entrave dans sa liberté de navigation, prévue dans l'article 87 de la CMB. Il apparaît alors que la violation de cette liberté constitue un dommage au sens individuel au regard de l'article 42 du projet d'articles et lui permet ainsi d'engager la responsabilité internationale de l'Etat intervenant.

Les moyens de cette réaction diffèrent. Il peut s'agir, au moins dans un premier temps, d'une simple protestation par la voie diplomatique. Tel était par exemple la solution adoptée par l'Argentine pour protester contre l'intervention chilienne sur le navire de pêche argentin *Cruz del Sur* dans les eaux argentines, qui mena à la confiscation par le Chili des fruits de sa pêche[194]. De la même manière, l'Allemagne a protesté par voie diplomatique auprès de l'Islande après l'emploi de la force par les garde-côtes islandais, en haute mer, contre des navires de pêche allemands, notamment[195] l'*Erlangen*, causant de nombreux dégâts matériels et faisant un blessé grave[196]. Toujours en matière de pêcheries, l'incident entre la France et l'Espagne dans le golfe de Gascogne, qui avait fait huit blessés parmi les membres d'équipage du *Valle Axtondo*, a été réglé par un échange de notes entre les deux Etats[197].

---

193. CMB, art. 106.

194. Note du 27 août 1967 du ministre des affaires étrangères argentin à l'ambassadeur chilien en Argentine, reproduite dans I. Bownlie, *System of the Law of Nations, States Responsibility, Part 1, op. cit.*, pp. 90-103.

195. Dans la même journée, cinq autres navires allemands avaient fait l'objet d'interception en haute mer par les gardes-côtes islandais : le *Flensburg*, le *Tiko 1*, le *Sirius*, le *Sagitta Maris* et *l'Arcturus*.

196. Note verbale du 1er décembre 1972 de l'ambassade de la République fédérale d'Allemagne au ministre des affaires étrangères islandais, reproduite dans I. Brownlie, *System of the Law of Nations, States Responsibility, Part 1*, *op. cit.*, pp. 101-103.

197. L'arraisonnement de deux chalutiers espagnols, le *Burgoa Munde* et le *Valle Atxondo*, par la marine française blessa huit membres d'équipage. Voir

Les Etats ont parfois également recours à la saisine du Conseil de sécurité pour protester contre un acte commis à l'encontre d'un de leurs navires. Dans ce cas, l'invocation de la responsabilité de l'Etat intervenant n'est pas toujours formulée de manière directe, les Etats devant justifier, pour saisir le Conseil, de l'existence d'une question relative à la paix et à la sécurité internationales. C'est alors le plus souvent en ces termes que le Conseil est saisi de questions d'interdiction maritimes. Cuba a, par exemple, sollicité une convocation du Conseil de sécurité suite au «harcèlement» d'un navire marchant cubain, en haute mer, par les garde-côtes américains[198], tandis que la Corée du Sud l'a saisi de l'attaque de la corvette *Cheonan*, navire de guerre coulé le 26 mars 2010 par une torpille nord-coréenne, entraînant la mort de quarante-six membres d'équipage[199].

L'Etat du pavillon peut également utiliser la voie juridictionnelle pour mettre en jeu la responsabilité de l'Etat intervenant, sous réserve, bien entendu, du respect des règles de compétence des juridictions internationales. Il peut agir en son nom propre pour obtenir réparation de la violation de sa liberté de navigation, ou dans le cadre de la protection diplomatique en lieu et place du propriétaire du navire. L'affaire *Saïga 2* devant le TIDM en est l'exemple le plus abouti. Le prétoire de la Cour internationale de Justice accueille souvent des différends relatifs au droit de la mer, mais rarement des opérations d'interdiction maritimes. Hormis l'affaire de l'*Estai*, qui s'est heurté à une décision d'incompétence[200], la Cour a eu à juger de la politique d'intervention de l'Islande en matière de pêcheries, à l'encontre de navires étrangers pêchant au large de ses côtes. L'Islande avait, dans les années soixante-dix, adopté un règlement étendant sa compétence exclusive en matière de pêcheries à une zone de cinquante milles nautiques. Cet instrument faisait l'objet d'une mise en œuvre par les autorités islandaises qui interceptaient tout navire étranger pêchant dans cette zone. La Cour a condamné cette pratique, considérant que la législation islandaise n'était pas opposable aux autres Etats. En

---

R. Jeannel, «L'incident de pêche franco-espagnol du 7 mars 1984 dans le golfe de Gascogne», *AFDI*, 1986, p. 737.

198. Lettre datée du 2 février 1990, adressée au Président du Conseil de sécurité par le représentant permanent de Cuba auprès de l'Organisation des Nations Unies, S/21120.

199. Lettre adressée le 4 juin 2010 au Conseil de sécurité par le représentant permanent de la République de Corée auprès de l'Organisation des Nations Unies, S/2010/281.

200. Le Canada avait émis une réserve en acceptant la juridiction obligatoire de la Cour, relative à la police des pêches. Il a exclu, par une notification du 10 mai 1994, à savoir juste avant l'entrée en vigueur de la loi litigieuse, les différends auxquels pourraient donner lieu les mesures de gestion et de conservation adoptées par le Canada dans la zone de l'OPAN. CIJ, *Affaire de la compétence en matière de pêcheries* (préc.).

conséquence, le Gouvernement islandais n'était pas en droit d'exclure unilatéralement les navires de pêche étrangers, en l'occurrence allemands et britanniques[201]. D'autres cas sont néanmoins assez proches, notamment l'affaire du *Détroit de Corfou* et celle des *Plates-formes pétrolières*, où des navires de guerre, respectivement britanniques et américains, avaient été endommagés. Les dommages ont entraîné l'engagement de la responsabilité de l'Albanie, d'une part, et de l'Iran, d'autre part.

Les juridictions internationales relatives aux droits de l'homme qui sont ouvertes aux affaires interétatiques peuvent également théoriquement être saisies de ces questions si des droits humains sont en jeu. Cela n'a pour l'instant jamais été le cas, probablement au regard du caractère régional de ces juridictions, qui limite leur champ d'application et leurs Etats Parties. Mais c'est l'arbitrage international qui reste la source la plus conséquente d'affaires relatives à des opérations d'interdiction maritimes. L'on retrouve, par exemple, les célèbres sentences arbitrales du *SS I'm Alone*[202] et du *Red Crusader*[203], qui fixent la responsabilité de l'Etat intervenant en matière de proportionnalité et de nécessité de l'emploi de la force pour intercepter un navire en mer. Les affaires *Costa Rica Packet*[204], *Manouba*[205] ou encore *James Hamilton*[206] sont

---

201. CIJ, *Compétence en matière de pêcheries (Royaume-Uni c. Islande et Allemagne c. Islande)*, 25 juillet 1974.

202. Sentence arbitrale, *SS «I'm Alone»* (préc.). Dans cette affaire, le navire *I'm Alone* avait été coulé intentionnellement par les Etats-Unis et le Tribunal arbitral considéra que cet acte n'était pas nécessaire et donc contraire au droit international.

203. Sentence arbitrale, *The Red Crusader* (préc.). Il s'agissait d'un emploi excessif de la force armée, le *Niels Ebbesen* ayant tiré sans avertissement au canon, en mettant en danger des vies humaines à bord du *Red Crusader* sans nécessité démontrée. La commission a considéré que d'autres moyens auraient pu être employés pour stopper le *Red Crusader*.

204. Sentence arbitrale, *Baleinier «Costa Rica Packet» (Grande-Bretagne c. Pays-Bas)*, 25 février 1897, *JDI*, 1897, p. 624.

205. Le *Manouba*, navire français transportant des représentants du Croissant-Rouge ottoman, fut saisi le 18 janvier 1912 par un vaisseau de guerre italien, et conduit à Cagliari. La Cour permanente d'arbitrage a retenu la responsabilité de l'Italie pour une interception illicite du navire français et l'a condamné à verser au Gouvernement de la République française 4000 francs au titre des pertes et dommages. Sentence arbitrale, *Manouba (France, Italie)*, 6 mai 1913, *RSA*, vol. XI pp. 463-479.

206. Sentence arbitrale, *Navires «Cape Horn Pigeon», «James Hamilton Lewis», «C. H. White» et «Kate and Anna» (Etats-Unis d'Amérique c. Russie)*, *RSA*, vol. IX, pp. 51-78. Il s'agissait de la saisie et de la confiscation, en haute mer, de navires baleiniers américains par des croiseurs russes, considérant qu'il se livrait à une activité de chasse aux phoques illicite. Dans l'affaire du *Cape Horn Pigeon*, les autorités russes ont reconnu leur responsabilité dans cette erreur et accepté de verser une réparation. La sentence arbitrale porte sur le montant de la réparation. Dans l'affaire du *James Hamilton Lewis*, l'intervention en haute mer sur un navire étranger a été reconnue contraire au droit international.

autant d'autres exemples du succès classique de l'arbitrage en matière d'interception maritime.

L'on ne peut exclure totalement la possibilité d'une action de l'Etat de la nationalité de l'équipage, au titre de la protection diplomatique de ses nationaux, même si l'Etat du pavillon exerce en principe sa juridiction « sur tout navire battant son pavillon, ainsi que sur le capitaine, les officiers et l'équipage pour les questions d'ordre administratif, technique et social concernant le navire »[207].

B. L'Etat côtier

L'Etat côtier est l'Etat lésé au regard du droit international dans deux cas : lorsque l'opération d'interdiction maritime a lieu dans une zone pour laquelle il dispose de droits exclusifs, et lorsque l'interception a causé des dommages environnementaux à ses côtes.

Dans un premier temps, l'Etat côtier est considéré comme l'Etat lésé si l'opération d'interdiction maritime a lieu dans une zone relevant de sa souveraineté ou de sa juridiction. Il en est ainsi d'une intervention d'un Etat tiers dans ses eaux territoriales. Il peut également s'agir d'une intervention dans la zone contiguë ou la ZEE d'un Etat, dans un domaine pour lequel il dispose de droits exclusifs d'intervention. Tel est le cas de la pêche et de la conservation dans la ZEE[208] ou encore des contrôles sanitaires ou d'immigration dans la zone contiguë[209]. La jurisprudence internationale classique nous offre un exemple parfaitement clair de l'engagement de la responsabilité internationale de l'Etat qui intervient, sans autorisation, dans les eaux territoriales d'un autre Etat : l'affaire du *Détroit de Corfou*. La CIJ a en effet condamné le Royaume-Uni pour avoir procédé, sans autorisation, au déminage des eaux du détroit, relevant de la souveraineté de l'Albanie[210]. Sans qu'elle n'ait fait l'objet d'un règlement juridictionnel, l'intervention américaine du 24 mars 2008 à l'entrée du canal de Suez en est également un bon exemple. Un navire américain civil, affrété par l'US Navy, avait effectué des tirs de semonce contre un navire dans le canal et conduit à la mort d'une personne. Cette intervention avait été menée dans les eaux égyptiennes, sans l'accord des autorités. Les Etats-Unis ont officiellement présenté leurs excuses et reconnu leur responsabilité, notamment en dédommageant les familles des victimes[211].

---

207. CMB, art. 94, par. 2, al. *b)*.
208. CMB, art. 56, par. 1.
209. CMB, art. 33.
210. CIJ, *Détroit de Corfou* (préc.).
211. F. Laurent et A. Garcia, « Défense et sécurité », *Annuaire du droit de la mer*, 2008, p. 659.

Dans un second temps, dans l'hypothèse d'un dommage environnemental, c'est souvent l'Etat côtier qui est lésé. Si ce dommage est causé par une intervention d'un Etat tiers sur un navire au large de ses côtes, alors la responsabilité de cet Etat peut être engagée. L'exemple le plus parlant reste sans doute celui de la guerre entre l'Iran et l'Iraq, qui a été le cadre de nombreuses interventions sur des pétroliers et des installations pétrolières en mer, causant des dommages environnementaux sans précédent. L'Iran a par exemple protesté contre ces pratiques auprès du Conseil de sécurité des Nations Unies, considérant qu'elles constituaient une violation, par l'Iraq, de ses obligations internationales au regard du droit de la mer, du droit des conflits armés, mais également de la Convention de Koweït sur la protection des eaux du Golfe[212].

Paragraphe 2 L'engagement de la responsabilité par la personne privée victime du dommage

Une personne privée peut, ponctuellement, être en mesure de demander compensation pour les dommages causés au navire ou à l'équipage. En effet, les dispositions compensatoires de la CMB semblent, tout comme celles des conventions sectorielles, aller dans le sens d'une reconnaissance de ce droit aux personnes privées, notamment en attribuant le droit à obtenir une compensation « au navire », voire même aux personnes lésées elles-mêmes[213] (A). L'intérêt de ce questionnement est majeur : si un tel droit existe en droit international au profit des entités privées, alors le droit interne des Etats doit prévoir les recours adaptés pour permettre la réparation (B).

A. La personne privée destinataire des obligations de compensation

L'engagement de la responsabilité internationale est ouvert aux personnes privées, dans des cas limités aux personnes dont les intérêts économiques ont été lésés, ou aux personnes dont les droits

---

212. Note verbale datée du 20 avril 1983, adressée au Secrétaire général par le représentant permanent de la République islamique d'Iran auprès de l'Organisation des Nations Unies, A/38/163, S/15723 ; lettre datée du 14 octobre 1983, adressée au Secrétaire général par le représentant permanent de la République islamique d'Iran auprès de l'Organisation des Nations Unies, S/16049, ou lettre datée du 23 décembre 1983, adressée au Secrétaire général par le Représentant permanent de l'Iraq auprès de l'Organisation des Nations Unies, A/38/767, S/16238.

213. Ph. Wendel, *State Responsibility for Interferences with the Freedom of Navigation in Public International Law, op. cit.*, pp. 68-69. E. J. Molenaar, « Multilateral Hot Pursuit and Illegal Fishing in the Southern Ocean : The Pursuit of the *Viarsa 1* and the *South Tomi* », *International Journal of Maritime and Coastal Law*, 2004, pp. 19 ss.

fondamentaux ont été violés. Les personnes privées sont en effet les destinataires des obligations de compensation prévues par les conventions maritimes. Elles prévoient une compensation pour «toute perte» ou «tout dommage»[214] subi par le navire ou son équipage. Il peut s'agir d'un simple retardement du navire[215], mais également d'un préjudice financier né d'une perte de profits attendus[216], de l'endommagement ou de la perte du navire et/ou de la cargaison[217], de la détention de l'équipage[218] ou encore des mauvais traitements qu'il a pu subir[219]. Sur ce point, l'arbitre dans l'affaire du *Lusitania* a considéré que le droit international prend en compte la souffrance morale. En effet, «le seul fait qu'ils sont difficiles à mesurer ou à estimer en valeurs monétaires ne les rend pas moins réels et n'est pas une raison qui puisse empêcher une victime d'être indemnisée sous la forme de dommages et intérêts»[220]. Les pertes en vies humaines sont malheureusement souvent à déplorer, comme lorsque deux militaires italiens constituant une équipe de protection embarquée et assurant la sécurité du pétrolier *Enrica Lexie* ouvrent le feu, en haute mer[221], sur ce qu'ils croient être une embarcation pirate en phase d'attaque de leur navire. Deux des occupants du navire, qui

214. Vocabulaire commun aux articles 110, paragraphe 3, 106 et 111, paragraphe 8, de la CMB; 21, paragraphe 18, de l'Accord sur les stocks chevauchants, et 9, paragraphe 2, du Protocole de Palerme.

215. TIDM, *Saïga 2* (préc.), par. 175, al. *c)*.

216. B. Graefrath, «Responsibility and Damages Caused: Relations between Responsibility and Damages», *RCADI*, tome 185 (1984), p. 96. Pour une mise en œuvre, voir les affaires *Cape Horn Pigeon* et *Montijo*, ou encore *Betsey*, reproduites dans J. B. Moore, *History and Digest of the International Arbitrations to Which the United States Has Been a Party*, Washington, Government Printing Office, 1898.

217. Voir, par exemple, la compensation financière accordée par la TIDM dans l'affaire *Saïga* pour les «[d]ommages subis par le *Saïga*, y compris les coûts de réparation du navire, pour un montant de 202 764 dollars, majoré d'intérêts à raison de 6%, exigibles à compter du 31 mars 1998», par. 175.

218. Sur les dommages causés aux individus, voir Ch. Tomuschat, «Individuals», dans J. Crawford, A. Pellet et S. Olleson (dir. publ.), *The Law of International Responsibility, op. cit.*, pp. 985-992.

219. Pour des exemples de compensation financière accordée pour une détention de l'équipage, voir Commission mixte des réclamations anglo-vénézuélienne, affaire *Topaze (Belgique c. Venezuela)*, 1903, *RSA*, vol. IX, pp. 387-389, ou sentence arbitrale *Walker Faulkner c. Mexico*, 2 novembre 1926, *RSA*, vol. IV, pp. 67-74. En cas de mauvais traitements, la compensation pécunière a souvent été alourdie, en particulier dans la sentence arbitrale *William McNeil (Royaume-Uni c. Mexique)*, *RSA*, vol. V, 19 mai 1931, pp. 164-168. Voir également l'affaire *Saïga*. Le TIDM a accordé une indemnisation pour la détention du capitaine et des membres d'équipage, ainsi que pour les dommages corporels subis par l'officier en second, par. 175, al. *e)-j)*.

220. Sentence arbitrale, affaire *Lusitania*, 1er novembre 1923, Nations Unies, *RSA*, vol. VII, 1923, p. 40.

221. Ce point est contesté par les autorités indiennes qui considèrent que le navire italien était dans leurs eaux territoriales.

s'est révélé être un navire de pêche, sont tués[222]. Dans le même sens, un pêcheur indien a été tué et deux autres grièvement blessés par l'intervention, le 16 juillet 2012, du pétrolier-ravitailleur *USNS Rappahannock* sur cette embarcation qui n'avait pas «répondu aux avertissements et alors qu'elle se rapprochait rapidement»[223].

Après examen des dispositions compensatoires des conventions maritimes, il apparaît que le propriétaire du navire ou les membres d'équipage qui ont subi un dommage dans le cadre d'opérations d'interdiction maritime illicites ou infondées ont un droit à demander une compensation dans le cadre de l'article 110, paragraphe 3, et 111, paragraphe 8, de la CMB, 9, paragraphe 2, du Protocole de Palerme et 8*bis*, paragraphe 10, alinéa *b)*. du Protocole à la Convention SUA. Dans l'affaire *Saïga 2*, les deux parties, dans leurs arguments oraux, s'accordaient pour considérer que l'article 111, paragraphe 8, de la CMB comporte une obligation à la charge de l'Etat intervenant de verser une compensation au navire en cas de dommage[224]. Dans le même sens, dans l'affaire *US c. Cadena*, la Cour d'appel (Fifth Circuit) considère que l'article 22, paragraphe 3, de la Convention de Genève sur la haute mer ouvre un droit à obtenir une compensation «pour les citoyens ou navires des nations membres»[225]. Il s'agissait d'une affaire née de la demande de compensation, formulée par un navire saisi par les garde-côtes américains à 200 milles nautiques de leurs côtes. En l'espèce, la compensation n'avait pas été accordée parce que l'Etat du pavillon n'était pas partie à la Convention de Genève.

Lors du conflit indépendantiste algérien, la France avait procédé à la visite d'un grand nombre de navires dans une zone d'environ 50 kilomètres des côtes algériennes. Dans certains cas, la France a versé une compensation financière à des propriétaires de navires, lorsque la détention s'est trouvée infondée[226]. Tel était, par exemple, le cas du navire

222. L'incident s'est déroulé le 15 février 2012 et a donné suite à des poursuites pénales en Inde.

223. Justification donnée par la cinquième flotte américaine, «Un navire américain mitraille des pêcheurs indiens», publié le 16 juillet 2012 et mis à jour le 16 juillet 2012.

224. TIDM, *Saïga 2*, arguments oraux de Saint-Vincent-et-les-Grenadines, 19 mars 1999, *ITLOS Pleadings 1999*, pp. 1208 ss., et arguments oraux de la Guinée, 20 mars 1999, *ITLOS Pleadings 1999*, pp. 1265-1266.

225. *United States* v. *Cadena*, 585 F.2d 1252, 1261 (5th Cir. 1978), cité par Ph. Wendel, *State Responsibility for Interferences with the Freedom of Navigation in Public International Law*, *op. cit.*, p. 73.

226. Néanmoins, dans la plupart des cas, la France a refusé cette compensation. Voir notamment Tribunal d'appel de Paris, 22 octobre 1962, *Société Ignazio Messina c. Ministre des armées «Marine»*. Pour un commentaire, voir L. Lucchini, «Les mesures de surveillance maritime au cours des opérations d'Algérie», *AFDI*, 1962, pp. 920-928.

Helga Böge[227]. Selon Philippe Wendel, « this could indicate that France considers Art. 110, para. 3 LOSC to constitute an individual right of private entities »[228].

Le droit international impose donc à l'Etat intervenant, dans certains cas, d'octroyer une compensation aux personnes privées qui ont subi un dommage et, par voie de conséquence, de prévoir une voie de recours dans leur droit interne.

B. La personne privée titulaire d'un recours juridictionnel

Certaines conventions maritimes, tel le Protocole de 2005 à la Convention SUA, prévoient expressément l'obligation pour les Etats parties de prévoir des voies de recours pertinentes, dans leur droit interne, pour permettre la réparation du dommage[229]. Tel est également le cas de la Convention des Nations Unies sur le droit de la mer, qui prévoit, en matière d'environnement marin[230], que, lorsque les mesures sont « illicites ou vont au-delà de celles qui sont raisonnablement nécessaires, eu égard aux renseignements disponibles »[231], les Etats doivent prévoir « des voies de recours devant leurs tribunaux pour les actions en réparation de ces pertes ou dommages »[232].

En matière de droits de l'homme, les conventions internationales applicables imposent aux Etats de prévoir, dans leur droit interne, un recours effectif en cas d'atteinte à un droit protégé. Tel est le cas, par exemple, de l'article 2, paragraphe 3, du Pacte international relatif aux droits civils et politiques, mais également des articles 13, 5 et 6 de la Convention européenne des droits de l'homme, 47 de la Charte des droits fondamentaux de l'Union européenne et 7 et 25 de la Convention interaméricaine des droits de l'homme. La jurisprudence des cours tant européennes[233] qu'américaines[234] va également dans ce sens, en matière

227. W. Heintschel von Heinegg, « Visit, Search, Diversion, and Capture in Naval Warfare: Part II, Developements Since 1945 », *Canadian Yearbook of International Law*, 1992, p. 101.

228. Ph. Wendel, *State Responsibility for Interferences with the Freedom of Navigation in Public International Law, op. cit.*, p. 75.

229. Art. 8 *bis*, par. 10, al. *b)*.

230. Sur la responsabilité internationale de l'Etat pour les dommages causés à l'environnement marin, voir T. M. Ndiaye, « La responsabilité internationale des Etats pour dommages au milieu marin », *International Law: New Actors, New Concepts — Continuing Dilemmas, Liber Amicorum Božidar Bakotić*, Martinus Nijhoff Publishers, 2010, pp. 265-279.

231. CMB, art. 232.

232. *Ibid.*

233. CEDH, 23 février 2012, affaire *Hirsi Jamma et autres c. Italie* (préc.).

234. Com. IADH, 13 mars 1997, *The Haitian Center for Human Rights* et al. *c. United States* (préc.).

d'interdiction maritime. Il ne s'agit toutefois pas d'une obligation d'établir une compétence universelle civile, mais bien d'offrir un recours devant ses juridictions internes seulement lorsque les autorités étatiques nationales sont en cause. Telle est la portée de l'affaire *Jones c. Saudi Arabia* jugée par la House of Lords britannique. L'ancienne Cour a considéré que l'article 14 de la Convention des Nations Unies contre la torture qui impose au Etats parties de prévoir, dans leur droit interne, un recours effectif, ne s'applique que si les actes ont été commis au Royaume-Uni ou par le Royaume-Uni[235].

Certaines voies de recours devant les juridictions internationales existent afin de mettre en œuvre de manière directe la responsabilité de l'Etat intervenant. Elles sont pour l'instant limitées au domaine des droits de l'homme. La plupart des comités des Nations Unies[236] ainsi que des cours régionales et sous-régionales[237] peuvent désormais recevoir des pétitions ou recours individuels.

SECTION 5 LA RÉPARATION

Selon une règle bien établie du droit international, un Etat qui a subi un préjudice à la suite d'un acte illicite d'un autre Etat est en droit d'obtenir réparation du préjudice qu'il a subi, et « la réparation doit, autant que possible, effacer toutes les conséquences de l'acte illicite et rétablir l'état qui aurait vraisemblablement existé si ledit acte n'avait pas été commis »[238]. Les articles 34 à 39 du projet d'article de la CDI relatifs à la réparation ont été largement acceptés comme étant constitutif d'une coutume internationale[239].

---

235. House of Lords, *Jones (Respondent) c. Ministry of Interior Al-Mamlaka Al-Arabiya AS Saudiya (the Kingdom of Saudi Arabia) (Appellants)*, 14 juin 2006, [2006] UKHL 26 :

> « Article 14 requires every state party to ensure that a victim of an act of torture obtains redress and has a right to a fair and adequate compensation. But this article is, as the Court of Appeal held, plainly concerned with acts of torture within the jurisdiction of the state concerned ... There is nothing in the Torture Convention which creates an exception to state immunity in civil proceedings. »

236. Comité des droits de l'homme, Comité contre la torture, Comité pour l'élimination de la discrimination à l'égard des femmes, Comité pour l'élimination de la discrimination raciale, Comité sur les travailleurs migrants, Comité des droits des personnes handicapées et Comité des disparitions forcées.

237. Une déclaration d'acceptation de la juridiction de la Cour pour les requêtes individuelles est parfois encore nécessaire, comme devant la Cour africaine des droits de l'homme et des peuples.

238. CPJI, *Usine de Chorzów (Allemagne c. Pologne)*, arrêt du 13 septembre 1928, p. 47. Voir TIDM, affaire *« Saïga 2 »*, par. 170.

239. Ch. Dominicié, « The International Responsibility of the United Nations for Injuries Resulting from Non-Military Enforcement Measures », dans

Dès lors, ainsi que le rappelait Paul Reuter, « la responsabilité internationale apparaît sous la forme simple de l'obligation de réparer toute violation de droit commise par un Etat à l'égard d'un autre Etat »[240]. La réparation occupe donc une place centrale dans le droit de la responsabilité. Il en va de même dans le cadre des opérations d'interdiction maritimes, mais elle peut se présenter sous plusieurs formes : restitution en nature, indemnisation, satisfaction et assurances et garanties de non-répétition[241]. Les modalités de la réparation varient notamment sous l'influence du dommage que l'on entend compenser. Alors que la réparation du préjudice subi par l'Etat peut se contenter d'une satisfaction (paragraphe 1), celui causé aux personnes privées nécessite dans la plupart des cas une compensation financière (paragraphe 2).

Paragraphe 1 **La réparation du préjudice de l'Etat**

Le dommage subi par l'Etat du pavillon par une intervention illicite ou injustifiée est une pure violation de ses droits, au regard du droit international. Dès lors, la reconnaissance de la violation est une réparation suffisante[242]. Par exemple, les termes du TIDM dans l'affaire *Saïga 2* sont clairs :

> « Pour ce qui concerne les demandes en réparation de Saint-Vincent-et-les-Grenadines relatives à la violation de ses droits, au sujet des navires battant son pavillon, le Tribunal a déclaré aux paragraphes 136 et 159 que la Guinée a agi de manière illicite et a violé les droits de Saint-Vincent-et-les Grenadines en procédant à l'arraisonnement du *Saïga* dans les circonstances de l'espèce et en faisant usage d'une force excessive. Le tribunal estime que ces constatations constituent une réparation adéquate. »[243]

Dans le même sens, la Cour permanente d'arbitrage, dans l'affaire du *Carthage*, avait refusé d'accorder à la France une indemnisation financière, considérant que la reconnaissance de la violation du droit international ainsi que la compensation des personnes privées étaient suffisantes[244].

M. Ragazzi (dir. publ.), *International Responsibility Today — Essays in Memory of Oscar Schachter*, Leyde, Nijhoff, 2005, p. 368.

240. P. Reuter, *Droit international public*, Paris, PUF, 6e éd., 1983, p. 40. Sur cette question, voir également E. Decaux, « Responsabilité et réparation », SFDI, *La responsabilité dans le système international, op. cit.*, pp. 147-190.

241. Articles 34 à 39 du Projet d'articles sur la responsabilité de l'Etat (préc.).

242. Voir J. Crawford et S. Olleson, « The Nature and Forms of International Responsibility », dans M. D. Evans (dir. publ.), *International Law*, Oxford University Press, 2003, pp. 467-468.

243. TIDM, *Saïga 2*, par. 176.

244. CPA, affaire du *Carthage* et affaire du *Manouba (France c. Italie)*, jugées le 6 mai 1913, *AJIL*, 1913, p. 623 ss.

De la même manière, l'Etat côtier qui est atteint dans l'exclusivité de sa compétence sur ses eaux territoriales ne souffre pas d'un autre préjudice que celui de la violation de son droit. Dès lors, une satisfaction sera considérée comme suffisante par les juridictions internationales, à l'instar de la CIJ dans l'affaire du *Détroit de Corfou* qui reconnait la violation des droits de l'Albanie et indique que cette constatation en elle-même est une satisfaction appropriée[245]. En revanche, le dommage écologique ou environnemental subi par l'Etat côtier devra faire l'objet d'une réparation pécuniaire[246].

Paragraphe 2 **La réparation du préjudice des personnes privées**

Il convient de distinguer entre l'obligation de réparation de l'Etat dans le cadre de sa responsabilité pour fait internationalement illicite et celle naissant dans le cadre de dommages causés par un comportement conforme au droit international. Les modalités de la réparation ainsi que son calcul restent subordonnés aux circonstances de l'espèce, dont la nature de l'obligation internationale de l'Etat responsable fait partie.

Dans le cadre de la responsabilité pour fait internationalement illicite, le droit général de la responsabilité impose à l'Etat de rétablir la situation qui existerait si l'acte illicite n'avait pas eu lieu[247]. Si elle est « matériellement impossible » ou si elle impose « une charge hors de toute proportion avec l'avantage qui dériverait de la restitution plutôt que de l'indemnisation »[248], l'Etat responsable doit alors indemniser l'Etat lésé[249]. Selon la CPJI, si la restitution en nature n'est pas possible, il convient de procéder au « paiement d'une somme correspondant à la valeur qu'aurait la restitution en nature [et à une] allocation s'il y a lieu, de dommages-intérêts pour les pertes subies et qui ne seraient pas couverte par la restitution en nature ou le paiement qui en prend la place »[250].

La restitution peut tout simplement être celle du navire[251] ou de

245. CIJ, *Détroit de Corfou* (préc.), dispositif.

246. Par exemple, dans l'affaire de la *Fonderie de Trail* (préc.), la sentence impose une réparation pécuniaire. Voir la partie 5 de la sentence.

247. Article 35 du Projet d'articles sur la responsabilité de l'Etat (préc.).

248. *Ibid.*

249. Voir CPJI, *Usine de Chorzów* (préc.), p. 47 ; les commentaires de l'article 36 du Projet d'articles ou encore P.-M. Dupuy, « Le fait générateur de la responsabilité internationale des Etats », *Recueil des cours*, tome 188 (1984), p. 94.

250. CPJI, *Usine de Chorzów* (préc.), p. 47.

251. Voir l'incident du *Giaffarieha*, avec la capture en mer Rouge par un navire de guerre égyptien de quatre navires marchands du port de Massawa, battant pavillon italien, Società Italiana per l'Organizzazione Internazionale, Consiglio Nazionale delle Ricerche, *La prassi italiana di diritto internazionale*, première série (Dobbs Ferry, Oceana, 1970), vol. II, pp. 901 et 902.

l'équipage (sa libération). Lorsque des dommages humains ont eu lieu, le préjudice est extrapatrimonial. Selon la CDI, il « s'entend généralement de la perte d'un être cher, du *pretium doloris*, ainsi que de l'atteinte à la personne, à son domicile ou à sa vie privée »[252]. Au même titre que le préjudice matériel, le préjudice extrapatrimonial est susceptible d'évaluation financière et peut faire l'objet d'une demande en indemnisation. Tel était le cas dans l'affaire du *Lusitania*[253]. Ainsi, l'on notera par exemple le versement fait par Cuba aux Bahamas à la suite d'un bombardement aérien d'un navire bahamien, causant des pertes de vies humaines[254]. Dans le même sens, Israël a versé une indemnité aux Etats-Unis pour une attaque lancée en 1967 contre le *USS Libertya*, causant des pertes en vies humaines au sein de l'équipage[255]. Dans le même sens, dans les affaires jugées par la Cour européenne des droits de l'homme, des satisfactions équitables ont été accordées aux requérants, si une violation a été reconnue[256].

Les obligations de l'Etat pour un comportement qui n'est pas contraire au droit international sont moins étendues. Il n'existe alors qu'une obligation d'indemnisation du dommage subi[257]. L'obligation de compensation implique alors l'obligation d'indemniser l'intégralité du dommage subi, « in terms of money »[258]. La CPJI, dans l'affaire *Chorzów*, avait laissé entendre que, en cas d'acte licite qui cause un dommage, la compensation de la valeur « au moment de la dépossession, plus les intérêts jusqu'au jour du paiement » était suffisant. Cette jurisprudence classique, relative à l'expropriation, a été confirmée par le droit international ultérieur[259].

---

252. Projet d'articles sur la responsabilité de l'Etat et commentaires y relatifs, p. 271.

253. Nations Unies, *RSA*, vol. VII, 1923, p. 32. Les juridictions internationales ont fréquemment accordé des indemnités pour préjudice moral causé à des particuliers. Tel a été le cas par exemple dans les affaires suivantes : *Chevreau (France c. Royaume-Uni)*, *RSA*, vol. II, p. 1113 ; *Gage*, *RSA*, vol. X, 1903, p. 226 ; *Di Caro*, *RSA*, vol. X, 1903, p. 597 ; *Héritiers de Jean Maninat*, *RSA*, vol. X, 1903, p. 55.

254. « Chonique des faits internationaux », *RGDIP*, 1981, p. 540.

255. *Ibid.*, p. 562.

256. Par exemple, dans l'affaire *Hirsi Jamaa*, la CEDH a accordé 15 000 euros à chaque requérant, pour dommage moral.

257. Voir B. Graefrath, « Responsibility and Damage Caused : Relations between Responsibility and Damages », *RCADI* (tome 185), 1984, p. 107.

258. *Ibid.*, p. 90.

259. Le droit international connaît également la réparation d'un dommage causé par une activité licite dans le cadre du droit international de l'environnement ou plus largement des activités dangereuses. Le Projet de la CDI de 2006 prévoit que

> « [c]haque Etat devrait prendre toutes les mesures nécessaires pour veiller à ce qu'une indemnisation prompte et adéquate soit accordée aux victimes de

SECTION 6 **CONCLUSION**

Si l'on souscrit aux propos de Jules Basdevant, selon lesquels « les règles de la responsabilité sont en quelque sorte les règles clés de tout ordre juridique » et que l'on « peut affirmer que la valeur pratique d'un ordre juridique déterminé dépend de l'efficacité et de l'étendue des règles sur la responsabilité »[260], alors il est crucial, pour le droit international des opérations d'interdiction maritimes, que les règles régissant la responsabilité des acteurs soient clairement déterminées. Le principe de la responsabilité de l'Etat pour les dommages qu'il cause lors d'opérations de police en mer est clair, tout comme l'obligation de réparation qui l'accompagne. Néanmoins, le contenu exact des obligations internationales des Etats et des organisations internationales, des règles d'attribution et d'engagement de la responsabilité de l'Etat reste largement imprécis. Le droit de la responsabilité de l'Etat pour les dommages causés lors d'opérations d'interdiction maritimes semble alors parsemé de nombreuses inconnues. Ces inconnues font également la richesse du droit de la mer contemporain, confronté à l'évolution des activités illicites et de la pratique que les Etats et les organisations internationales développent corrélativement, afin de lutter contre la criminalité en mer.

> dommages transfrontières causés par des activités dangereuses se déroulant sur son territoire ou placées sous sa juridiction ou son contrôle ».

Le Projet d'articles prévoit que c'est toutefois à l'exploitant, et non à l'Etat, de pourvoir à cette indemnisation (art. 4, par. 2).

260. J. Basdevant, « Actes de la Conférence SDN », 1930, cité par J.-P. Quéneudec, *La responsabilité internationale de l'Etat pour les fautes personnelles de ses agents*, Paris, LGDJ, 1966, p. 5.

16 Shiprider Institution: Questions of Jurisdiction and State Responsibility

Isaias Yemane Tesfalidet *

SECTION 1 INTRODUCTION

The term "shiprider" is used in a variety of contexts, but in this chapter we are concerned with the institution of *shipriders*, whereby a law enforcement official of one State embarks on a law enforcement vessel of another State as one form of the co-operative arrangements adopted by States for the suppression and prosecution of criminal acts at sea. This chapter will focus on two distinct but inter-related legal issues raised by the emergence of the shiprider institution as a juridical entity in international law: jurisdiction and State responsibility. Jurisdiction, especially the exclusive jurisdiction of the flag State on the high seas, can be modified either by the existence of certain facts or by some *legal* act. Some of the facts that modify the allocation of jurisdiction on the high seas are criminal acts, such as piracy and slave-trade. Modification of jurisdictional allocation by *legal act* among States is accomplished when States voluntarily enter into international agreements. The agreements providing for shipriders are one such legal act. This modification of the jurisdictional allocation in turn affects the determination of State responsibility as State responsibility is linked to the exercise of jurisdiction[1].

The treaties creating the shiprider institution are commonly referred to as "Shiprider Agreements"; but the creation of the shiprider institution is in fact but one element of more comprehensive agreements

---

* J.S.D. Candidate at the Yale Law School in New Haven, Connecticut, United States. LL.B., University of Asmara, Faculty of Law (Eritrea), and LL.M., Yale Law School. Staff Attorney at the Office of the Legal Advisor to the Office of the President of Eritrea (2006-2009). The author would like to thank participants of the Doctoral Colloquium at the Yale Law School for useful comments where early drafts of this chapter were presented.

1. See, James Crawford, "Opinion: Third Party Obligations with respect to Israeli Settlements in the Occupied Palestinian Territories", available online at http://www.tuc.org.uk/tucfiles/342/LegalOpinionIsraeliSettlements.pdf (last accessed 20 January 2013) observing that "a State cannot be responsible for acts conducted by entities outside its control and outside of its jurisdiction".

addressing criminal law enforcement co-operation at sea, for instance: "Co-Operation in Suppressing Illicit Maritime Drug Trafficking"[2], "Integrated Cross-border Maritime Law Enforcement Operations"[3], "and Maritime Counter-drug Operations"[4]. In this chapter, shiprider agreements will be used for convenience.

Typically the shiprider is described as: "a designated law enforcement official of a contracting party embarked on a law enforcement vessel of another party pursuant to a bilateral or multilateral agreement"[5]. Although they are not without controversy[6], the shiprider agreements are lauded as innovative tools for enhancing effective co-operation for the suppression and prosecution of criminal acts at sea, for which there would otherwise be impunity, either because of the gaps in jurisdictional

---

2. See, e.g., Agreement between Barbados and the United States concerning Cooperation in Suppressing Illicit Maritime Drug Trafficking, 1997, 1997 *UST LEXIS* 5.

3. See, e.g., Framework Agreement on Integrated Cross-Border Maritime Law Enforcement Operations between the Government of the United States of America and the Government of Canada, signed at Detroit 26 May 2009, 2009 *Digest* 469-470. Text available at http://www.state.gov/s/l/2009/ch12/index.htm and http://www.state.gov/documents/organization/153586.pdf.

4. Agreement between the United States and Trinidad and Tobago concerning Maritime Counter-Drug Operations, signed at Port of Spain 4 March 1996; *TIAS* 12732.

5. See, e.g., *ibid.*

6. The main criticism of the shiprider agreements, which might be specific to the context of the United States arrangements with Caribbean and Latin American countries, focuses on the unequal bargaining between the United States and the Caribbean and Latin American countries as well as the lopsided nature of the control mechanism in place to ascertain compliance with the agreements. The arrangements are viewed by many as entailing extremely high sovereignty costs for the Caribbean and Latin America States by effectively providing a cloak of legality to what the United States was already doing without these agreements. See, for example, Tyrone Ferguson, "Shiprider Revisited: Security and Transnational Crime in the Caribbean", *Caribbean Dialogue: A Journal of Contemporary Caribbean Policy Issues*, Vol. 8, No. 3, pp. 29-27, 39-40 (2003) (hereinafter, Tyrone Ferguson, "Shiprider Revisited" (2003), available online at http://journals.sta.uwi.edu/cd/index.asp?action=fullTextPermaLink&articleId=176&galleyId=159 (last accessed on 16 January 2013). Note, however, that Ferguson concedes "a convincing case can be made that Shiprider has resulted in more drug seizures". Tyrone Ferguson, "Shiprider Revisited" (2003) at p. 41, footnote 40. See also Michelle Williams, "Caribbean Shiprider Agreements: Sunk by Banana Trade War?", 31 *UMIAIALR* 163 (Spring 2000); John Jeremie, "The Caribbean: Small Caribbean States and the New Pax Americana", *Journal of Financial Crime*, Vol. 6, Issue 3, pp. 284-287, 286 (1999) (arguing that, "The Shiprider Agreement when tested against our core criteria of reciprocity, fairness and precedent fails uniformly"); Dr. Kathy-Ann Brown, "The Shiprider Model: An Analysis of the U.S. Proposed Agreement concerning Maritime Counter-Drug Operations in Its Wider Legal Context", *Contemporary Caribbean Legal Studies*, No. 1, at p. 2 (1997) (hereinafter, Dr. Kathy-Ann Brown, "The Shiprider Model" (1997) (referring to the shiprider agreements as "controversial arrangement").

authority or lack of resources[7]. In short, this is due to the fact that States cannot exert enforcement jurisdiction in the territorial waters of other States, no matter which criminal activity takes place therein as well as to the fact that many coastal States lack the necessary capacity to patrol their waters and exercise their inherent powers. Hence, as Brian Robinson observes,

> "[t]hese shiprider agreements are critical in providing our partners around the world with meaningful maritime law enforcement experience, as well as assets from which foreign partners can exercise their own maritime law enforcement authority and develop maritime domain awareness in home waters. This engagement can result in the prosecution of a wide range of illegal activity, such as fisheries violations, illicit drug trafficking, and a host of other offenses, making the global commons a safer place."[8]

Accordingly, the United States Bureau for International Narcotics and Law Enforcement Affairs notes:

> "to increase its operational law enforcement reach, the Coast Guard embarks deployable Law Enforcement Detachments (LEDETs) on U.S. Navy and Allied warships, and embarks partner nation 'shipriders' aboard Coast Guard vessels, consistent with Memorandums of Understanding, bilateral agreements and other arrangements in force;
>
> . . . While these agreements greatly increase the operational reach of U.S. assets, they also enable partner nation assets to better patrol and respond to threats in their own sovereign waters. Frequent U.S. Government success in exercising these agreements has led to enhanced global governance."[9]

---

7. See, e.g., Ellict Abrahams, "The Shiprider Solution: Policing the Caribbean", *The National Interest*, 1 March 1996, available online at http://nationalinterest.org/print/article/the-shiprider-solution-policing-the-caribbean-487?page=show (last visited on 27 December 2012); Richard Halloran, "The Rising East: Change Comes to the U.S. Coast Guard in the Pacific", *Civil Beat*, 09/04/2012, http://www.civilbeat.com/articles/2012/09/04/17002-the-rising-east-change-comes-to-us-coast-guard-in-the-pacific/ (last accessed on 12 January 2013) (quoting Rear Admiral Charles Ray, District Commander of the Fourteenth Coast Guard District, as saying "Having shipriders from Pacific Island nations aboard U.S. cutters has made enforcing international agreements increasingly effective").

8. LCDR Brian W. Robinson, "You Want Authority with That?: How I Learned to Stop Worrying and Love Shipriders", in *Proceedings of the Marine Safety & Security Council, The Coast Guard Journal of Safety and Security at Sea*, 62-68, at 63 (Summer 2009) (hereinafter, Brian W. Robinson, "You Want Authority with That?").

9. United States Department of State, Bureau of International Narcotics and Law Enforcement Affairs, *International Narcotics Control Strategy Report,*

According to these agreements, the shiprider is granted authority to authorize or request a range of law enforcement actions (by law enforcement assets of other States) to be conducted in maritime zones or against vessels and persons which would normally fall under the jurisdiction of his or her State[10]. As one United States Manual notes:

> "Shiprider agreements *provide standing authorization and procedures to embark foreign law enforcement personnel on USCG cutters, and sometimes aboard U.S. or foreign naval vessels with embarked law enforcement detachments (LEDET). Shipriders are critical to the success of USCG law enforcement missions*."[11]

Also, in recent years, the shiprider institution has been promoted as a preferred co-operative arrangement in the fight against piracy off the coast of Somalia as reflected in a number of UN Security Council resolutions[12] and in regional arrangements[13]. To the knowledge of the author, there has been only one relevant arrangement in the framework of Southern African Development Community (SADC). More specifically, South Africa has signed a Memorandum of Understanding with Mozambique on 1 June 2011, which provides for joint patrols in the area, including the embarkation of Mozambique agents on South

---

Vol. 1 (March 2012), at p. 52 (hereinafter, INCSR 2012, Vol. 1 (2012)), also available online at http://www.state.gov/documents/organization/187109.pdf (last accessed on 11 January 2013).

10. The other arrangements for co-operation in this area are the traditional request for assistance, authorization on an *ad hoc* basis for specific requests by other States, joint patrol or co-ordinated efforts. Consent from master of a ship is also another.

11. United States Homeland Security, US Coast Guard, *U.S. Coast Guard Foreign Affairs Policy Manual*, COMDTINST M5710.5 (January 2012) available online at http://www.uscg.mil/directives/cim/5000-5999/CIM_5710_5.pdf (last accessed on 11 January 2013).

12. See, e.g., UNSC res. 1851 (2008), 16 December 2008, ("*Invit[ing]* all States and regional organizations fighting piracy off the coast of Somalia to conclude special agreements or arrangements with countries willing to take custody of pirates in order to embark law enforcement officials ('shipriders') from the latter countries"); United Nations Office of Drugs and Crime, "'Ship riders': Tackling Somali Pirates at Sea", Press Release, 20 January, 2009, available online at http://www.unodc.org/unodc/en/frontpage/ship-riders-tackling-somali-pirates-at-sea.html (last accessed on 11 January 2013). See also Beck Pemberton, "'Pirate Jurisdiction': Fact, Fiction, and Fragmentation in International Law, One Earth Future Foundation, Working Paper", at p. 20 available at http://oneearthfuture.org/images/imagefiles/Piracy%20Jurisdiction%20-%20Pemberton.pdf (last accessed on 15 January 2013).

13. International Maritime Organization (IMO), Code of Conduct concerning the Repression of Piracy and Armed Robbery against Ships in the Western Indian Ocean and the Gulf of Aden, known as Djibouti Code of Conduct, adopted on 29 January 2009 (hereinafter, Djibouti Code of Conduct (2009)), entered into force on 29 January 2009, available online at http://www.imo.org/OurWork/Security/PIU/Pages/DCoC.aspx (last accessed on 12 January 2013).

African warships, with a view to repressing piratical activities in the region[14].

This chapter covers only cases where a shiprider is embarked on another State's law enforcement vessel and law enforcement action is taken pursuant to his or her authority. Arrangements providing for joint patrols but not for shiprider embarkation, Vessel Protection Detachments (VPDs), Law Enforcement Detachments (LEDETs) on US Navy and Allied warships escort services, and private armed guards on board commercial vessels fall outside the purview of this contribution. A few remarks in regard to these arrangements are, however, in order:

Firstly, in the United States practice and manuals, the term shiprider sometimes refers to US Coast Guard personnel embarked on board US naval ships to conduct law enforcement activities because the United States Navy cannot undertake law enforcement action. These are referred to as LEDETs — "USCG personnel [authorized] to carry out drug interdiction operations from naval surface vessels provided by the Department of Defense" because Department of Defense personnel are prohibited "from directly engaging in law enforcement activities"[15]. The shiprider established by treaty between or among sovereign nations should not be confused with, for example, the US Coast Guard practice, whereby its law enforcement officers are placed on board merchant vessels for training purposes under a mutual training programme called "Merchant Marine Indoctrination Ship Rider Program" whereby

> "Coast Guard members . . . join a vessel's crew while underway and act as a riding observer, the program gives the ship rider practical knowledge of the performance and operating characteristics of various vessels, equipment, waterways, and crews operating within the maritime industry"[16].

Reference should also be made to the VPDs, which are a practice that has developed in recent years along with the rise in pirate attacks off the coast of Somalia. VPDs are usually small teams of armed, regular soldiers or marines placed on board merchant ships under the command

14. See Memorandum of Understanding on Piracy and Trans-Border Crime between South Africa and Mozambique, signed at 1 June 2011. For more information see online at http://www.info.gov.za/speech/DynamicAction?pageid=461&sid=18794&tid=34350.

15. United States Coast Guard, *Coast Guard Law Enforcement Detachments: A History*, http://www.uscg.mil/history/articles/LEDET_History.asp (last accessed 21 January 2013).

16. For detailed description, see United States Coast Guard, "Coast Guard Merchant Marine Indoctrination (MMI) Ship Rider Program, Commandant Instruction 16705.1" (8 November 2011) available online at http://www.uscg.mil/directives/ci/16000-16999/CI_16705_1.pdf (last accessed on 1 October 2012).

of their own Government. Shipriders should be distinguished from VPDs, as the latter will be on board vessels flying the same flag with the VPD unit[17]. In addition, VPDs are not authorized to arrest or exercise any kind of jurisdiction over suspected pirates, but only to protect the merchant vessel from piratical attacks.

This chapter is further divided into three main sections.

Section 2 gives a general introduction, providing definitions, overview of the various bilateral and multilateral agreements providing for shipriders with a focus on jurisdictional and State responsibility clauses as well as an overview of the practice of shiprider agreements.

Section 3 will discuss jurisdictional issues raised by shiprider authorized law enforcement operations including visit, boarding, search, seizure, arrest, detention and ultimately prosecution of persons suspected of engaging in criminal acts at sea. The main issues that arise in this context are those that may lead to overlapping or conflicting jurisdiction. This section will also address the waiver of jurisdiction by States pursuant to a shiprider agreement.

Section 4 of this chapter will discuss issues of State responsibility. After a brief review of the potential primary norms that may be implicated during shiprider operations (ranging from human rights issues, claims for loss of property, damage or injury to persons to breach of treaty or customary law obligations either by the shiprider's State or the host vessel's State), this section will discuss questions of attribution of conduct and shared responsibility.

At the outset, it is in order to note that the aim of this contribution is not a critique of the shiprider institution; instead, it will attempt to provide a framework within which disagreements about jurisdictional competences and issues of State responsibility are to be resolved.

SECTION 2 **SHIPRIDER INSTITUTION IN INTERNATIONAL LAW AND PRACTICE**

Paragraph 1 **Shiprider Agreements and International Law**

In general, law enforcement action on the seas involves the exercise of jurisdictional authority by coastal States, flag States and third States[18]. These States are granted different jurisdictional authorities

17. See, e.g., at http://internationalsecuritydiscipulus.wordpress.com/2012/09/26/dutch-use-of-vessel-protection-detachments-in-the-indian-ocean/.

18. Douglas Guilfoyle, *Shipping Interdiction and the Law of the Sea* (2009), p. 5.

in the different maritime zones depending on the character of the ship and persons, the suspected activity involved as well as their location. The prevention, detection, suppression and prosecution of criminal activities on the seas involve various operational acts. These include visiting, boarding, searching and seizing a vessel. These enforcement actions are taken pursuant to the relevant rules of international law dealing with the allocation of jurisdictional competence. These rules are either embodied in international conventions [19] or exist as part of customary international law [20]. The standard or default allocation of jurisdictional authority can be modified by either a permissive rule of international law or by agreement by the relevant States [21]. An example of the latter type of modifying act is the signing of shiprider agreements which establish the institution of "shiprider".

The shiprider is authorized to grant authorization to his or her host vessel to exercise law enforcement action on board a ship which would otherwise be outside the jurisdiction of the State of the host vessel. Although the scope and content of the authority of the shiprider might differ from one agreement to the other, the basic structure is the same. These shiprider agreements cover criminal acts that would normally fall under the jurisdiction of the coastal State, flag State or the third State only. Thus, the shiprider agreements are designed to advance co-operation and co-ordination efforts required by or provided for in other more general conventions or treaties promulgated to fight criminal activities at sea.

Currently, there are a large number of bilateral and multilateral instruments that provide for shiprider arrangements that vary in terms of form, geographic and thematic scope, number of parties involved as well as the nature of obligations assumed by the parties involved. In terms of form, they come either as treaties, memoranda of understanding or standard-setting codes of conduct [22].

When it comes to bilateral shiprider agreements, the United States has by far the largest number of these co-operative arrangements. According to the 2012 *International Narcotics Control Strategy Report*, the United States has a record of

> "44 maritime counterdrug bilateral agreements or operational

---

19. For example the United Nations Convention on the Law of the Sea, Art. 97, 10 December 1982, 1833 *UNTS* 397 (hereinafter, UNCLOS).
20. Such as the right of hot pursuit (codified in Article 111 of UNCLOS).
21. PCIJ, the case of the *SS "Lotus"* (*France* v. *Turkey*), Judgment, *PCIJ, Ser. A, No. 10* (1927), p. 2, at pp. 18-19.
22. See United States Department of States, Bureau of International Narcotics and Law Enforcement Affairs, *International Narcotics Control Strategy Report*, Vol. 1, p. 52 (March 2012).

> procedures in place [with its] partner nations. . . . While individual agreements are specifically tailored for each country, each generally contains all or some of the basic provisions [including] ship boarding, shiprider . . ."[23].

In fact, it can be fairly asserted that shiprider agreements are the creation of the United States. As Douglas Guilfoyle writes, "Ship-rider agreements first emerged in US bilateral drug interdiction treaties."[24]

These agreements are largely based on the "Six Part Model of Bilateral Maritime Law Enforcement Agreement" developed by the United States, which in turn was based on the United States-United Kingdom Agreement historically known as Liquor Treaties[25]. The six part model agreement provides for the six types of law enforcement co-operation arrangements mentioned above, namely, ship-boarding, entry-to-investigate, overflight, shiprider, pursuit, order-to-land[26]. It should be noted here that not all the agreements that the United States entered into contains all of these provisions[27].

---

23. United States Department of States, Bureau of International Narcotics and Law Enforcement Affairs, *International Narcotics Control Strategy Report*, Vol. 1, p. 52 (March 2012). The United States also maintains

> "non-binding operational procedures with Mexico, Ecuador and Peru to facilitate communications between operation centers for confirmation of registry requests and for permission to stop, board, and search suspect vessels [which] provide a process for joint operations in lieu of a formal bilateral agreement. One example of these standard operating procedures (SOP) is the Maritime Operations Letter of Intent (LOI) signed by the Mexican Navy, Canadian Forces, U.S. Northern Command, and the Coast Guard." *(Ibid.)*

24. Douglas Guilfoyle, "Piracy off Somalia: UN Security Council Resolution 1816 and IMO Regional Counter-Piracy Efforts", 57 (3) *ICLQ* (2008), 690-699, 698. See also Douglas Guilfoyle, *Shipping Interdiction and the Law of the Sea*, p. 91 (2009), noting:

> "Seven US bilateral narcotics interdiction treaties and one multilateral convention provide for ship-riders, a designated official of one state who can travel aboard the other party's law enforcement vessels and provide on-the-spot consent to interdiction of their state's flag vessels and enforce the flag state's criminal law once aboard."

25. See, generally, Philipp Wendel, *State Responsibility for Interferences with the Freedom of Navigation in Public International Law*, Berlin, Heidelberg, Springer-Verlag, 2007; and Dr. Kathy-Ann Brown, "The Shiprider Model" (1997).

26. See J. Kramek, "Bilateral Maritime Counter-Drug and Immigrant Interdiction Agreements: Is This the World of the Future?", 31 *U. Miami I-ALR* (2000), 121, 133.

27. See relevant analysis and relevant chart (valid as of 1999) with the categorization of the agreements to the respective models in J. Kramek, *op. cit.*, 150. Also see L. Davis-Mattis, "International Drug Trafficking and the Law of the Sea", 14 *Ocean Yearbook* (2000) 381.

In terms of regional and multilateral agreements, the first to include such provisions was the Agreement concerning Co-operation in Suppressing Illicit Maritime and Air Trafficking in Narcotic Drugs and Psychotropic Substances in the Caribbean Area. This Agreement entered into force on the 18 September 2008[28], and emerged from the practical experiences of the States and territories of the region, including the development of an extensive network of bilateral agreements to counter drug trafficking. According to this Agreement, each party is required to designate law enforcement officials to embark on the vessels of other parties in order to facilitate the timely provision of authorizations and the exercise of relevant national law enforcement powers within zones of jurisdiction of the former party (Art. 9). Under this provision, duly authorized law enforcement officials may enforce the laws of the designating party both in the waters of that party or seaward of such waters, "in the exercise of the right of hot pursuit or otherwise in accordance with international law", such as in the proper exercise of contiguous zone jurisdiction. In addition, they may authorize the entry of the vessel on which they are embarked into the territorial sea of the designating party and authorize the conduct of counter-drug patrols and boarding of suspect vessels therein[29].

In the same region that the aforementioned Agreement operates, namely the Caribbean basin, the CARICOM Member States decided in 2008 to have an all-encompassing maritime security agreement[30]. This Agreement stipulates that each State party may designate under Article VI Security Force Officials, which would have the authority to conduct routine patrols and law enforcement operations in the territorial waters of another State party, either on a Security Force vessel of their own nationality or on board another State party's security vessel[31].

The shiprider is mainly used in interdiction operations against drug trafficking; however, it is increasingly being used against illegal fishing[32],

28. The text and a short commentary is found in W. Gilmore, *Agreement concerning Co-operation in Suppressing Illicit Maritime and Air Trafficking in Narcotic Drugs and Psychotropic Substances in the Caribbean Area* (2005) (hereinafter: Caribbean Agreement).

29. See further analysis in E. Papastavridis, *The Interception of Vessels on the High Seas: Contemporary Challenges to the Legal Order of the Oceans*, Oxford, Hart Publishing, 2013, at p. 221.

30. CARICOM Maritime and Airspace Security Cooperation Agreement, signed at Bolans, Antigua and Barbuda on 4 July 2008; available at www.caricom.org/jsp/secretariat/legal_instruments/agreement_maritime_airspace_security_cooperation.pdf.

31. See also Articles VII and VIII of the CARICOM Agreement.

32. For example, China and Japan have a Memorandum of Understanding with the United States on illegal fishing. See the Memorandum of Understanding between the Government of the United States of America and the Gov-

illegal migration[33] and protection of the environment such as pollution control[34].

Paragraph 2 The Basic Shiprider Model: Law and Practice

A typical shiprider agreement recalls in its preamble the various provisions of the United Nations Convention on the Law of the Sea (UNCLOS), the 1988 Vienna Convention and other bilateral or multilateral treaties that call for enhanced co-operation among the contracting States.

For example, the United States-Barbados shiprider agreement of 25 June 1997 was entered into

> "*Having regard to* the urgent need for international co-operation in suppressing illicit traffic by sea, which is recognized in the *1961 Single Convention on Narcotic Drugs* and its *1972 Protocol,* in the *1971 Convention on Psychotropic Substances,* in the *1982 United Nations Convention on the Law of the Sea,* in the *1988 United Nations Convention against Illicit Traffic in Narcotic Drugs and Psychotropic Substances*."[35]

The agreement further recalls the

> "1996 United Nations International Drug Control Programme (UNDCP) Regional Meeting Plan of Action for Drug Control Co-ordination and Co-operation in the Caribbean and the Treaties

---

ernment of the People's Republic of China on Effective Cooperation and Implementation of United Nations General Assembly Resolution 46/215 of 20 December 1991 (Washington DC, 3 December 1993) available online at http://iea.uoregon.edu/pages/MarineMammals/engine/Documents/1-0629-0630.htm (last accessed 21 January 2013); Japanese Coast Guard-U.S. Coast Guard Memorandum of Cooperation (signed at the North Pacific Coast Guard Forum on 13 September 2010). See also, Richard Halloran, "The Rising East: Change Comes to U.S. Coast Guard in the Pacific (09/04/2012)" (the Coast Guard also works with the Chinese in the North Pacific Coast Guard Forum to reduce illegal fishing. Last month, a US cutter with a Chinese "shiprider" aboard seized a stateless vessel that was fishing with drift nets in the North Pacific) available online at http://www.civilbeat.com/articles/2012/09/04/17002-the-rising-east-change-comes-to-us-coast-guard-in-the-pacific/ (Last visited 3 November 2012). On fishing as a criminal act at sea, see Oanta, Chapter 4, *supra*.

33. See, e.g., Agreement between the Government of the United States of America and the Government of the Dominican Republic concerning Maritime Migration Law Enforcement, signed at Washington, 20 May 2003; entered into force 20 May 2003. *TIAS* 03-520, 2003 *USL LEXIS* 32. On criminal law enforcement efforts against migrant smuggling, see Guggisberg, Chapter 6, *supra*.

34. On the criminalization of maritime pollution by coastal States, see Gahlen, Chapter 3, *supra*.

35. See *supra* footnote 2 (emphasis added).

> between the Government of Barbados and the Government of the United States of America on Mutual Legal Assistance in Criminal Matters, and Extradition, signed at Bridgetown, on the 28th day of February, 1996."[36]

Similar provisions are to be found in the various bilateral agreements entered into by the United States with various Caribbean countries, Canada and other States.

The standard shiprider arrangement involves embarkation of a law enforcement official of one State on board law enforcement vessels of another State with certain enumerated authorities mainly relating to granting permission to conduct certain types of law enforcement action[37].

Pursuant to the extant shiprider agreements, all the law enforcement actions taken are under the jurisdiction, direction and control, and authority of the shiprider when conducted against ships flying the shiprider's flag or in maritime zones under the jurisdiction of the shiprider's State[38]. The host vessel officers can only act pursuant to the request and authorization of the shiprider. The types of actions that can be requested include making available the equipment, information and other resources of the host vessel for the shiprider to use; or operate such equipment to the

36. Preamble; *supra* footnote 2.

37. Douglas Guilfoyle, "Piracy off Somalia: UN Security Council Resolution 1816 and IMO Regional Counter-Piracy Efforts", 57 (3) *ICLQ* (2008), 690-699, 698 (noting, "[shiprider arrangments] . . . involve placing a designated law enforcement officer from one party ('the ship-rider') aboard the vessel of another party ('the host State'). The ship-rider is then able to board the vessels of their flag State and enforce flag-State law once aboard, possibly with the assistance of host State officers. Ship-riders may also have the power to authorise pursuit of a vessel into the territorial waters of their designating State. In practice, most formal ship-rider agreements include provisions allowing for the exercise of such boarding and pursuit powers in limited cases even when no ship-rider is embarked"). See also Douglas Guilfoyle, *Shipping Interdiction and the Law of the Sea* (2009), p. 91, noting:

> "Seven US bilateral narcotics interdiction treaties and one multilateral convention provide for ship-riders, a designated official of one state who can travel aboard the other party's law enforcement vessels and provide on-the-spot consent to interdiction of their state's flag vessels and enforce the flag state's criminal law once aboard."

38. For example, the Agreement between the United States and Trinidad and Tobago stipulates that qualified authorized officers ("shipriders") of the latter State may board a US vessel for the purpose of authorizing the US Coast Guard to pursue a vessel that is fleeing into Trinidad and Tobago waters as well as to conduct counter drug patrols in Trinidad and Tobago waters. See Agreement between the Government of the United States of America and the Government of Trinidad and Tobago concerning maritime counter-drug operations, signed at Port of Spain, 4 March 1996; entered into force 4 March 1996. *TIAS* 12732, 1996 *UST LEXIS* 59, 2473 *UNTS* 307.

benefit of the shiprider to assist him to conduct law enforcement functions.

Usually contained under an article entitled "Authority of Law Enforcement Officials on Board the Other Party's Vessels", are details of what the shiprider can or cannot do while on board the host vessel. As provided in Article 4 of the respective United States-Barbados Agreement (1997):

> "When the law enforcement officials of one Party are embarked on the other Party's vessel, and the enforcement action being carried out is pursuant to the authority of such law enforcement officials, any boarding, search or seizure of property, any detection of a person, and any use of force pursuant to this Agreement, whether or not involving firearms, shall be carried out by such officials."[39]

The exceptions provided for under this clause are when crew members are expressly requested to assist and the laws and procedures of both Parties apply[40].

Another example of exception, (which, however, is the rule in the case concerned) is included in the Djibouti Code of Conduct. Article 7 (4) provides:

> "Embarked officers may assist the host Participant and conduct operations from the host Participant ship or aircraft if expressly requested to do so by the host Participant, and only in the manner requested. Such request may only be made, agreed to, and acted upon in a manner that is not prohibited by the laws and policies of both Participants."[41]

Although the shiprider clauses are almost self-contained, there are

---

39. See *supra* footnote 2.

40. *Ibid.*, Article 4 (a).

41. Article 7 (4) of Djibouti Code of Conduct (2009). See also, Robin Geiss and Anna Petri, *Piracy and Armed Robbery at Sea*, OUP, 2011, p. 91, noting at footnote 379:

> "It is interesting to note, that while Art. 7 U.S. Model Maritime Agreement foresees that a request for assistance in carrying out enforcement measures is made by the shiprider, the Djibouti Code of Conduct reverses this role, in that the embarked officer may assist the host vessel, if expressly requested by the host. This may be due to the specific use of shipriders in the counter-piracy context, where the shiprider is not acting in their own territorial waters, but in an area under Somalia's jurisdiction. In Somali waters, a shiprider (for example from Kenya) has no better right or higher authority to act that the host vessel's officials. Rather, under the Djibouti Code of Conduct the shiprider is seen as a guest on the ship who is dependent on an invitation to act from his host ship master or captain."

other clauses that permeate the agreements in which the shiprider provisions appear. The clauses that affect the interpretation of the shiprider's authority are those clauses that pertain to dispute resolution, jurisdiction with regard to detained persons and property.

While the relationship between the shiprider and the host vessel is primarily governed by the shiprider agreement itself, it should be remembered that the shiprider and the host vessel operate under the laws and procedures of their respective countries. Therefore, the various manuals prepared by the States pertaining to maritime law enforcement operations form an important part of the law governing shiprider embarked operations[42].

For example, the 2012 *U.S. Coast Guard Foreign Affairs Policy Manual* states:

> "Shiprider agreements *provide standing authorization and procedures to embark foreign law enforcement personnel on USCG cutters,* and sometimes *aboard U.S. or foreign naval vessels with embarked law enforcement detachments (LEDET).* Due to the complexity of bilateral agreements and subtle but significant differences from one bilateral agreement to another, *personnel must be intimately familiar with the text of the controlling bilateral agreement*."[43]

The practice is to be gleaned from reports and case law. The extant case law is very impoverished. The cases that exist refer to the Agreements but there seems to be no controversy involving law enforcement action with a shiprider on board. In other words, there are no cases where defendants have contested that the boarding (interdiction) was unlawful because the shiprider's authority contravenes some rule of international law or somehow the shiprider did not have the authority or exceeded the authority he had. In the *United States* v. *Perlaza* case, for example, the Court determined with ease that the United States acquired jurisdiction pursuant to the Bilateral Agreement between the United States and Colombia through a telephone transmitted consent[44].

42. I thank Professor Eugene Fidell for supplying me with a copy of the law enforcement Manual of the United States Coast Guard, although, as he puts it the Manual "is sanitized".

43. United States Homeland Security, US Coast Guard, *U.S. Coast Guard Foreign Affairs Policy Manual*, COMDTINST M5710.5 (January 2012) available online at http://www.uscg.mil/directives/cim/5000-5999/CIM_5710_5.pdf (last visited on 13 October 2012).

44. *United States* v. *Perlaza*, 439 F. 3d 1149, 1168 (14 March 2006) (stating, "The *Gran Tauro* was, without dispute, a Colombian vessel, and the Colombian government gave the *De Wert's* and *Valley Forge's* LEDET teams telephonic consent under the Bilateral Agreement to board the *Gran Tauro*. This satisfied the Government's statutory jurisdiction obligations under § 1903(c)").

SECTION 3 SHIPRIDER INSTITUTION AND QUESTIONS OF JURISDICTION

Paragraph 1 Introduction

The existing jurisdictional authority for the suppression, detection, investigation and prosecution of criminal acts at sea falls under the jurisdiction of the flag State, coastal State or, sometimes, the State of nationality of the crew and passengers. The shiprider institution as conceived in the existing agreements, UN Security Council resolutions, memoranda of understanding follow, and do not modify to any significant degree, the existing allocation — under customary or conventional international law. The dominant UNCLOS dispensation, primarily based on the nationality and territoriality principles, primarily allocates criminal law enforcement jurisdiction to the flag and coastal States[45]. While the flag State exercises exclusive criminal jurisdiction over vessels flying its flag while they are on the high seas, the coastal State exercises criminal jurisdiction over acts committed in its territory — internal waters or territorial waters[46]. On the high seas, Article 97, UNCLOS, provides that "no arrest or detention of the ship, even as a measure of investigation, shall be ordered by any authorities other than those of the flag state". However, the exclusive flag State jurisdiction on the high seas is not an absolute rule; incidents such as transporting slaves, acts of piracy, unauthorized broadcasting permit other States to exercise jurisdiction[47].

Jurisdiction is defined as: "a state's power under international law to govern persons and property by its [national] law and to make, apply, enforce rules of conduct"[48].

Jurisdiction is generally divided between prescriptive and enforcement jurisdiction, with enforcement jurisdiction being deemed to include *adjudicative jurisdiction* as one form of enforcement jurisdiction[49]. In this chapter, the discussion is restricted only to enforcement jurisdiction.

States assert enforcement jurisdiction on the basis of territoriality or on the basis of permission of the territorial State or some other

45. See Maria Gavouneli, *Functional Jurisdiction in the Law of the Sea*, Martinus Nijhoff, 2007, p. 6, footnotes 11-15.

46. *Ibid.*, p. 10

47. *Ibid.*, p. 6.

48. Douglas Guilfoyle, *Shipping Interdiction and the Law of the Sea* (2009), 7.

49. For discussion on the relationship between adjudicative jurisdiction and enforcement jurisdiction see R. Rayfuse, "Regulation and Enforcement in the Law of the Sea", 24 *AYIL* (2005), 181-200, 182.

permissive rule of international law (as with, for example, piracy and slavery)[50].

Under UNCLOS, "a coastal state can enforce its criminal law against ships bound for, or leaving, its internal waters"[51]. One consequence of this jurisdictional allocation of authority among various States is that the State entitled to exercise enforcement jurisdiction is responsible for any breaches of international law that result in damage or injury to nationals, property or other protected interests of other States during the exercise of that jurisdiction. As we will see later in this section, the shiprider arrangement *per se* does not seem to modify in any significant manner this traditional allocation of jurisdiction. An examination, detailed below, of the various shiprider agreements reveals that the provisions closely follow the existing jurisdictional norms. However, there are some instances where the jurisdictional allocation might be complicated by the application of the shiprider agreements in practice.

---

50. Douglas Guilfoyle, *Shipping Interdiction and the Law of the Sea* (2009), p. 8. See also Maria Gavouneli, *Functional Jurisdiction and the Law of the Sea*, Martinus Nijhoff, 2007, pp. 6-10.

51. Douglas Guilfoyle, *op. cit.*, footnote 50, p. 11. Article 27 of UNCLOS, entitled *Criminal Jurisdiction on Board a Foreign Ship*, provides:

> "1. The criminal jurisdiction of the coastal State should not be exercised on board a foreign ship passing through the territorial sea to arrest any person or to conduct any investigation in connection with any crime committed on board the ship during its passage, save only in the following cases:
>
> *(a)* if the consequences of the crime extend to the coastal State;
>
> *(b)* if the crime is of a kind to disturb the peace of the country or the good order of the territorial sea;
>
> *(c)* if the assistance of the local authorities has been requested by the master of the ship or by a diplomatic agent or consular officer of the flag State; or
>
> *(d)* if such measures are necessary for the suppression of illicit traffic in narcotic drugs or psychotropic substances.
>
> 2. The above provisions do not affect the right of the coastal State to take any steps authorized by its laws for the purpose of an arrest or investigation on board a foreign ship passing through the territorial sea after leaving internal waters.
>
> 3. In the cases provided for in paragraphs 1 and 2, the coastal State shall, if the master so requests, notify a diplomatic agent or consular officer of the flag State before taking any steps, and shall facilitate contact between such agent or officer and the ship's crew. In cases of emergency this notification may be communicated while the measures are being taken.
>
> 4. In considering whether or in what manner an arrest should be made, the local authorities shall have due regard to the interests of navigation.
>
> 5. Except as provided in Part XII or with respect to violations of laws and regulations adopted in accordance with Part V, the coastal State may not take any steps on board a foreign ship passing through the territorial sea to arrest any person or to conduct any investigation in connection with any crime committed before the ship entered the territorial sea, if the ship, proceeding from a foreign port, is only passing through the territorial sea without entering internal waters."

On the high seas the fundamental principle governing enforcement jurisdiction is that it may not be exercised without the consent of the flag state. Douglas Guilfoyle writes:

> "As exceptions to the general rule, flag states may exercise criminal jurisdiction over acts committed aboard their flag vessels in international waters ('the high seas'), and under certain circumstances so can non-flag states."[52]

The consent of the flag State may be granted either by a pre-existing international agreement or on an *ad hoc* basis. It is usually included in the agreements that they grant the right of visit as such, or it may be requested by the boarding state after the visit and search of the delinquent foreign-flagged vessel.

According to Papastaviridis,

> "If the flag state accords its consent for the exercise of enforcement jurisdiction, this would entail measures such as bringing the vessel to a port of the boarding state, arrest of the suspects on board, initiation of criminal proceedings and confiscation of the illicit cargo and of the vessel itself."[53]

The generally accepted rule under international law is that flag States have "exclusive jurisdiction" over their flag vessels on the high seas while "[c]oastal states may have jurisdiction over a vessel present within certain regulatory zones adjacent to their coasts"[54].

Paragraph 2 **Shiprider Operations: Who Exercises Jurisdiction?**

In principle, the shiprider exercises territorial and/or nationality based jurisdiction when he or she authorizes or carries out enforcement action against vessels suspected of criminal activity. His or her jurisdiction is based on the territoriality principle in the sense that he or she can authorize enforcement action against vessels flying foreign flags only within the maritime zones that fall within the jurisdiction of his or her State of nationality. Alternatively, the shiprider's jurisdiction is based on the nationality principle in the sense that he or she is authorized to carry out enforcement action or authorize enforcement action against vessels flying the flag of his or her State of nationality on the high seas. In the latter case, the shiprider exercises the exclusive juris-

52. Douglas Guilfoyle, *op. cit.* footnote 50, p. 9.
53. See *supra* footnote 29, at p. 81.
54. Douglas Guilfoyle, *Shipping Interdiction and the Law of the Sea* (2009), p. 9.

diction of the flag State; he/she acts as an organ of the flag State delegated to exercise the inherent jurisdiction of the latter State over the vessel claiming its nationality.

Where the shiprider grants permission for the exercise of enforcement jurisdiction by its host vessel in the shipriders' territorial waters, and this exercise of jurisdiction is against a foreign flagged vessel (one that has neither the nationality of the shiprider or the host vessel), certain legal consequences might result with regard to the arrest of the suspected persons. The following scenario is to the point.

Let's assume a Jamaican shiprider on a US ship in Jamaican waters. Assume further that permission is granted by the shiprider (in Jamaican territorial waters) for the United States to board and search a Nigerian ship. Drugs are found. There is evidence the drugs were bound for (and only for) Mexico. Can the United States prosecute? What would be the basis of its exercise of prescriptive jurisdiction? In the drugs context — the United States usually asserts a broad effects doctrine jurisdiction on the theory that the Caribbean drug trade ultimately impacts the United States. But if all the evidence is that the drugs were going to Mexico (such that there is no effect on the United States) — can the United States, which has contributed to the arrest of the Nigerians, prosecute them? They are not US nationals, the "victims" of the crime will not be US citizens, there is no effect on the United States. And if the United States does prosecute — has it exercised excessive prescriptive jurisdiction and consequently enforcement jurisdiction (when and if it imprisons the Nigerians on the basis of a judgment which actualizes the exercise of prescriptive jurisdiction) such that US responsibility is engaged vis-à-vis Nigeria?

It is first worth noting that the actual arrest is conducted by the Jamaican shiprider; the US vessel was allowed to patrol in Jamaican waters and assisted in the arrest under the authority of the Jamaican shiprider. The interdiction of the suspected vessel was therefore lawful, given that the Jamaicans could have exercised enforcement jurisdiction in their own territorial waters pursuant to Article 27, UNCLOS, and are consequently in a position to give permission to the United States to exercise that jurisdiction in their place. Nonetheless, this evidently does not suffice for the prosecution on the part of the United States. Any further exercise of enforcement jurisdiction should be done either by the coastal State, Jamaica, or the flag State, Nigeria. For the United States to prosecute the arrested Nigerians there is need for the consent of either of these States.

If the United States were to prosecute in these circumstances, the exercise of its prescriptive jurisdiction would be excessive and prima facie illegal. The only plea that the US courts could make in such case would be of universal jurisdiction. As the law stands, the preponderant view is that drug trafficking is not included in the list of the international crimes for which universal jurisdiction is afforded[55]. In the words of Gavouneli, "interestingly enough and contrary to popular belief, neither slavery and slave related practices nor drug trafficking are covered . . ."[56]. Nonetheless, there has been a recent case that held that drug trafficking is a universal crime[57], while there is certainly a trend towards this direction and the possibility that in the near future such argument would gain the acceptance of international doctrine[58].

Difficulties (such as those above) regarding the exercise of jurisdiction are complicated by the simple fact that there is no rule in general international law which provides for any hierarchy among relevant jurisdictional claims. It would be particularly helpful to have treaty provisions regulating such concurrent claims. In the absence of such provisions, any conflict could be resolved by the application of comity or through bona fide negotiations[59].

SECTION 4 STATE RESPONSIBILITY

Paragraph 1 Authority of Shiprider as an Organ of the State

The provisions of the Agreements providing for shipriders generally follow the traditional rules on jurisdiction and seem to be very cautious of the possibility of international responsibility for

55. For example, during the drafting of the ICC Statute, the participants debated but ultimately rejected a proposal to include drug trafficking in the Court's jurisdiction. See relevant analysis in A. Geraghty, "Universal Jurisdiction and Drug Trafficking", 16 *Florida JIL* (2004), 371, 387.

56. M. Gavouneli, *Functional Jurisdiction in the Law of the Sea*, Leiden, Martinus Nijhoff, 2007, at pp. 27-28.

57. See, e.g., *United States* v. *Salcedo-Ibarra*, 2009 WL 1953399 (M.D. Fla. 6 July 2009).

58. Even in the *Marino-Garcia* decision, it was acknowledged that "There is a growing consensus among nations to include drug trafficking as a universally prohibited crime"; at p. 1382. Also, in the recent Jones Act it is stressed that "Congress finds and declares that trafficking in controlled substances aboard vessels is a serious international problem, is universally condemned, and presents a specific threat to the security and societal well-being of the United States"; see §70501. See also the Princeton Principles of Universal Jurisdiction (2001), which even though they did not include drug trafficking in the list of relevant crimes, leave the door open for such development (Principle No. 2). Per is also C. E. Sorensen, "Drug Trafficking on the High Seas: A Move towards Universal Jurisdiction under International Law", 4 *Emory International Law Review* (1990), 225.

59. See Papastavridis, *supra* footnote 29, at p. 255.

internationally wrongful acts. For example, almost all of the agreements make an explicit mention that the law enforcement action should be the responsibility of the shiprider.

The shiprider exercises the authority of his or her State. His or her actions are, therefore, assessed as, and imputable to, those of the State of which he or she is a national. As a juridical entity created by treaty between sovereign nations, the shiprider institution is also subject to the relevant rules of international law pertaining to organs created by treaty. Here it needs to be underscored that the shiprider is not an entity of the two States. Therefore, interdiction conducted with a shiprider on board does not fall under either joint action or action through a joint organ. If anything, the shiprider is to be treated as the regular law enforcement organs of the State that authorizes/designates him. Accordingly, the applicable rules of international law relating to responsibility of States for internationally wrongful acts is that which relates to the acts or omissions of organs of a State[60].

There may, however, be instances where the shiprider requests assistance from the crew of the host vessel as provided for in the various agreements regarding shipriders. These agreements make it clear that such assistance is provided upon the specific request of the embarked officer. Hence, as examined further below, the correct analytical framework is that provided under Article 16 of the ILC Articles on State Responsibility, namely, responsibility of a State for aid or assistance in the wrongful act of another State. It might also be possible to argue that the same circumstances might give rise to scrutiny under the provisions of Article 6 of the ILC Articles on State Responsibility because the State of the host vessel is placing the vessel at the disposal of the shiprider and by extension at the disposal of the State of the shiprider[61].

Paragraph 2 **The Rules on State Responsibility**

Under the law of State responsibility, every internationally wrongful act of a State entails its international responsibility[62], while the conditions required to establish such an act are twofold: first, the conduct in question must be attributable to the State under international law and secondly, for responsibility to attach to the act of the

60. Article 4, ILC Articles on Responsibility of States for Internationally Wrongful Acts, UN General Assembly, *Official Records*, 56th Session, Supp. No. 10 at UN doc A/56/10; at 31 (hereinafter, ILC Articles); available at http:// untreaty.un.org/ilc/texts/instruments/english/ commentaries/9_6_2001.pdf.

61. *Infra* footnote 72 and accompanying text.

62. See Article 1 of ILC Articles. On State responsibility generally as it applies to the suppression of maritime criminality, see Neri, Chapter 15, *infra*.

State, the conduct must constitute a breach of an international legal obligation in force for that State at that time[63]. Thus, the whole edifice of State responsibility is premised upon the existence of a primary rule establishing an obligation under international law for a State[64]. In the present context, the relevant primary rules would consist mainly of the law of the sea and the international human rights law.

State responsibility rules govern both the determination of the existence of liability and available remedies. The first aspect is concerned with the establishment of the existence of wrongful conduct and which State is responsible. The second aspect, described as a general rule, is the obligation to make reparation[65]. It is to be noted that the rules on State responsibility do not necessarily deal with the quantum of damages (amount of compensation); what they do deal with is the nature of the available reparation whether compensation, satisfaction.

At the outset, we distinguish between questions of responsibility as between the contracting parties to the shiprider agreement, and questions of responsibility vis-à-vis third States. The first scenario is governed by the text of the agreement and by general rules of international law. The shiprider agreements the United States has negotiated with Caribbean and other States contain some provisions that attempt to allocate *ex ante* responsibility for wrongful conduct by any of the contracting States[66]. Also, the shiprider agreement provides for the full range of possible dispute settlement mechanisms should disputes arise regarding the interpretation and application of the agreement[67].

The second aspect, instances in which rights and obligations of third States or their nationals are affected, raises more pressing questions.

Guilfoyle sets out the classificatory problem as follows:

> "A basic question of classification arises under the law of state responsibility. If a boarding party is considered to be *solely the organ of its sending state, its wrongful acts entail only the boarding state's responsibility*. If it is considered an *organ acting 'on*

63. See Article 2 of ILC Articles.
64. See Articles on Responsibility of States for Internationally Wrongful Acts with Commentaries, in *Yearbook of the International Law Commission* (2001-II), Part Two, at p. 31 (hereinafter, ILC Articles Commentary). On the distinction between "primary" and "secondary" rules see also A. Cassese, *International Law*, 2nd ed., Oxford, OUP, 2005, at p. 244, and U. Linderfalk, "State Responsibility and the Primary-Secondary Rules Terminology", 78 *Nordic Journal of International Law* (2009), 53.
65. See Article 31, ILC Articles.
66. See, for example, Article 19 of the United States-Barbados shiprider agreement.
67. See, for example, Article 20 of the United States-Barbados shiprider agreement.

joint behalf' of the boarding and flag state, it might incur their joint responsibility. If it is considered to be an organ placed 'at the disposal of' the flag state, the flag state will bear sole responsibility for its acts."[68]

For a State's responsibility to be engaged two elements must be present: breach and attribution[69]. The more pressing question in the context of interdiction operations conducted with a shiprider on board relates to attribution of conduct. In the context of maritime law enforcement operations conducted pursuant to shiprider authority, a key provision is this of Article 6, relating to "Conduct of organs placed at the disposal of a State by another State". Article 6 provides:

> "The conduct of an organ *placed at the disposal of a State* by another State shall be considered an act of the former State under international law if the organ is *acting in the exercise of elements of the governmental authority* of the State at whose disposal it is placed." (Emphasis added.)

Paragraph 1 of the Commentary to Article 6 of ILC Articles explains:

> "Article 6 deals with the limited and precise situation in which an organ of a State is effectively put at the disposal of another State so that the organ may temporarily act for its benefit and under its authority. In such a case, the organ, originally that of one State, acts exclusively *for the purposes of and on behalf of another State and its conduct is attributed to the latter State alone.*" (Emphasis added.)

Paragraph 2 of the Commentary to Article 6 further clarifies:

> "The notion of an organ 'placed at the disposal of' the receiving State is a specialized one, implying that the organ is acting with the consent, under the authority of and for the purposes of the receiving State. Not only must the organ be appointed to perform functions appertaining to the State at whose disposal it is placed, but in performing the functions entrusted to it by the beneficiary State, the organ must also act in conjunction with the machinery of that State and under its exclusive direction and control, rather than on instructions from the sending State. *Thus article 6 is not concerned with ordinary situations of inter-State cooperation or*

68. Guilfoyle, *supra* footnote 24, pp. 332-333.
69. Article 1-2, ILC Articles; see further J. Crawford, *The International Law Commission's Articles on State Responsibility*, Cambridge, Cambridge University Press, 2002.

collaboration, pursuant to treaty or otherwise."[70] (Emphasis added.)

Paragraph 3 The Rules on State Responsibility as Applied to Shiprider Operations

Examination of the relevant provisions of the agreements providing for shipriders is imperative in deciding whether the shiprider institution is a case of "organ placed at the disposal of another state" or "aid and assistance in the commission of a wrongful act".

Article 7 of the United States-Jamaica Agreement is a representative sample.

> "1. . . .
>
> *a*. enforce the laws of Jamaica in Jamaican waters and seaward therefrom, in the exercise of the right of hot pursuit or otherwise in accordance with international law; and
>
> *b*. authorize the entry of the vessel into and its navigation within Jamaican waters.
>
> 2. All activities, including boardings, searches, seizures, detentions and enforcement of Jamaican law under this Article relating to suspect vessels shall *be the responsibility of the Jamaican law enforcement officials and carried out by them*. Such operations shall be conducted in accordance with Jamaican law. In order to carry out their responsibilities, *the Jamaican law enforcement officials may request the Commanding Officer of the U.S. law enforcement vessel to take navigational measures or allow the Jamaican law enforcement officials to use the vessel's systems to communicate with the suspect vessel. Jamaican law enforcement officials may also request or authorize the Commanding Officer of the U.S. law enforcement vessel to use its equipment and available capabilities in order to provide information for the detection, identification and location of vessels and aircraft engaged in illicit traffic*.
>
> 3. All law enforcement activities under this Article shall be under the control and direction of Jamaican law enforcement officials and shall be conducted in accordance with Jamaican law."[71]

The "two cases relating to the exercise by Swiss police in Liechten-

70. ILC Articles, *supra* footnote 60, Commentary to Article 6, para. 2.
71. Article 7 of the United States-Jamaica Agreement.

stein of "delegated" powers"[72] discussed by the ILC in its commentary to Article 6 are useful contrast with the shiprider scenario. In these cases the European Commission of Human Rights found that:

> "At the relevant time Liechtenstein was not a party to the Convention for the Protection of Human Rights and Fundamental Freedoms (European Convention on Human Rights), so that if the conduct was attributable only to Liechtenstein no breach of the Convention could have occurred. The Commission held the case admissible, on the basis that under the treaty governing the relations between Switzerland and Liechtenstein of 1923, Switzerland exercised its own customs and immigration jurisdiction in Liechtenstein, albeit with the latter's consent and in their mutual interest. The officers in question were governed exclusively by Swiss law and were considered to be exercising the public authority of Switzerland. In that sense, they were not 'placed at the disposal' of the receiving State."[73]

For example, in the Barbados-United States Agreement it is provided that "any boarding, search or seizure of property, any detention of a person, and any use of force . . . shall be carried out by such officials [shiprider]" unless the other Party's officials are requested to assist or are acting in self-defence[74]. According to this formulation, responsibility for any wrongful conduct during the operation will be attributable to the shiprider's State, unless the host State's officials are directly involved in the enforcement operations, in which case that State would also bear responsibility for any internationally wrongful acts committed.

But even where the host State's officials are not directly involved, the host State might nevertheless be held responsible for "complicity" under Article 16 of the ILC Articles[75]. With regard to the responsibility for "aiding or assisting", it is well worth observing that under the US Model Maritime Agreement, for example, which has informed many shiprider

---

72. ILC Commentary to Article 6, ILC Articles, *supra* footnote 60, para. 7, citing *X and Y* v. *Switzerland*, Application Nos. 7289/75 and 7349/76, decision of 14 July 1977; Council of Europe, European Commission of Human Rights, *Decisions and Reports*, Vol. 9, p. 57; and *Yearbook of the European Convention on Human Rights*, 1977, Vol. 20 (1978), p. 372, at pp. 402-406.

73. ILC Commentary to Article 6, ILC Articles, *supra* footnote 72, para. 7.

74. See Article 4 of the Barbados-United States Agreement.

75. Article 16 ILC Articles provides that:

> "A State which aids or assists another State in the commission of an internationally wrongful act by the latter is internationally responsible for doing so if:
>
> *(a)* that State does so with knowledge of the circumstances of the internationally wrongful act; and
>
> *(b)* the act would be internationally wrongful if committed by that State."

agreements, it is envisaged that crew members of the host vessel may assist the shiprider in carrying out enforcement actions, if the latter expressly requests such assistance[76]. The host State thus may become responsible for its own act in deliberately assisting the sending State to breach an international obligation by which they are both bound[77]. Under Article 16 of the ILC Articles, a State may be responsible for its "aid or assistance", provided that the aid must have been given

> "(1) with a view to facilitating the commission of the specific act in question; (2) with an awareness of the circumstances making the act wrongful; and (3) the completed act must be such that it would have been wrongful had it been committed by the assisting State itself"[78].

Accordingly, should a breach of an obligation incumbent upon States under the law of the sea or of human rights law occur, the "host State" may also be held responsible for assisting in the commission of such breach, provided that it had knowledge of the breach in question and assisted the shiprider in this regard.

It is also possible that both the sending State and the host State will be responsible for different violations in the course of interdiction operations. *Ex hypothesis*, there might be a shiprider interdiction operation, in which, on the one hand, there would be a disproportionate use of force by the officers of the host State's warship in violation of the relevant legal framework and on the other, a subsequent human rights violation committed under the authority of the shiprider and under directions of the sending State. In such cases, the host State would incur responsibility for the violation of the relevant obligations under the law of the sea and the sending State would incur separate responsibility for the violation of the relevant obligation under international human rights law.

SECTION 5 CONCLUDING REMARKS

It is submitted that the mechanism of shipriders raises many perplexing legal issues that need careful consideration. Suffice to

---

76. See Article 7 of the US Model Maritime Agreement concerning Cooperation to Suppress Illicit Traffic by Sea, reprinted in Kramek, *supra*, footnote 26, Appendix B. See also Geiss/Petrig, 91.

77. See Crawford, *supra* footnote 71, p. 151.

78. See ILC Articles Commentary, 66. On complicity in international law in general, see also H. Aust, *Complicity and the Law of State Responsibility*, Cambridge, Cambridge University Press, 2011, and J. Quigley, "Complicity in International Law: A New Direction in the Law of State Responsibility", 57 *BYIL* (1987), 57.

mention, first, the question of the assertion of jurisdiction. This issue becomes even more tantalizing in the case where more than one State makes claims to assert jurisdiction over the arrested criminals. There is no hierarchy in making such jurisdictional claims.

Secondly, there is the major problem of international responsibility, including cases of shared international responsibility, namely the possibility of both the shiprider's home State and the flag State of the warship incurring responsibility for an internationally wrongful act in the course of a shiprider operation. In assessing the question of international responsibility in the course of shiprider operations, due regard should be paid to the question of who exerts control over the wrongful conduct in question, as the above-mentioned ILC instruments dictate.

Notwithstanding these legal conundrums, the institution of shiprider is a key mechanism in fighting transnational organized crimes at sea, mainly drug trafficking, piracy, illicit migration and illegal fishing. More and more treaties, both multilateral and bilateral, adopt these mechanisms and call for such co-operation of the contracting States. The more advanced co-operation in this regard is noticed in the Caribbean region; however, the recent calls for such operations in the context of the fight against piracy are telling as to the efficacy of shipriders on the international plane.

BIBLIOGRAPHIE SÉLECTIVE

SELECTED BIBLIOGRAPHY

R. J. W. Ridderhof, R. Steenhard
avec la contribution de/with contributions by
L. E. Deeks

Note introductive

La présente bibliographie a été préparée sur la seule base des matériaux de la Bibliothèque du Palais de la Paix à l'usage des chercheurs du Centre d'étude et de recherche de droit international et de relations internationales de l'Académie de droit international de La Haye. L'information bibliographique d'origine, publiée en 2012, a été complétée en mai 2013.

Introductory Note

This bibliography has been compiled exclusively from materials available in the Peace Palace Library for the use of the researchers of the Centre for Studies and Research in International Law and International Relations of the Hague Academy of International Law. Originally published in 2012, its bibliographic content has been extended and updated in May 2013.

Sommaire

1. Opérations d'interdiction maritime : règles et procédures 638
2. La multiplication de régimes juridiques portant sur la criminalité en mer 640
3. Pêche illicite, non déclarée et non réglementée 644
4. Trafic de stupéfiants maritime 650
5. Terrorisme maritime 651
6. Prolifération des armes de destruction massive (ADM) 656
7. Le trafic des êtres humains ; l'esclavage 657
8. Le trafic illicite de migrants 658
9. L'obligation d'assistance et de sauvetage 661
10. Violations grave du droit de la guerre maritime 662
11. Coopération interétatique dans la répression de la criminalité en mer 663
12. La compétence universelle relative à la criminalité en mer 669
13. La compétence nationale en matière de pollution maritime 672
14. Piraterie et droit de la mer 674
15. La compétence nationale en matière de piraterie 681
16. Les vols à main armée en mer 687
17. Opérations d'interdiction maritime et droits de l'homme 691
18. Les questions de compétence par rapport aux initiatives dites « Shiprider » 693
19. Le droit applicable relatif aux sociétés militaires et de sécurité privées 693
20. La responsabilité de l'Etat et l'obligation de réparer le prejudice causé par des opérations d'interdiction maritime 696

Summary

1. Maritime Interdiction Operations: Rules and Procedures 638
2. Proliferation of Legal Regimes Addressing Crimes at Sea 640
3. Illegal, Unreported and Unregulated Fishing 644
4. Drug Trafficking 650
5. Maritime Terrorism. 654
6. Proliferation of Weapons of Mass Destruction 656
7. Human Trafficking; Slave Trade 657
8. Migrant Smuggling. 658
9. Search and Rescue Operations. 661
10. War Crimes during Armed Conflict at Sea 662
11. International Co-operation in the Suppression of Crimes at Sea 663
12. Universal Jurisdiction and Crimes at Sea 669
13. Enforcement Jurisdiction over Maritime Pollution 672
14. Piracy under International Law of the Sea 674
15. Domestic Enforcement Jurisdiction over Piracy 681
16. Armed Robbery at Sea 687
17. Maritime Interdiction and Human Rights 691
18. Ship-Rider Institution and Jurisdictional Questions. 693
19. Private Armed Guards and Applicable Law 693
20. State Responsibility and Reparation for Maritime Interdiction Operations. 696

1 Opérations d'interdiction maritime : règles et procédures

Maritime Interdiction Operations : Rules and Procedures

Alessio, W. d', « I percorsi della sicurezza in mare : dalla salvaguarda della vita umana alla difesa dai rischi di terrorismo internazionale », *Studi in onore di Umberto Leanza III*, Naples, Editoriale scientifica, 2008, pp. 1605-1644.

Becker, M. A., "The Shifting Public Order of the Oceans : Freedom of Navigation and the Interdiction of Ships at Sea", *Harvard International Law Journal,* 46 (2005), No. 1, pp. 131-230.

Brown, Th. M., "For the 'Round and Top of Sovereignty' : Boarding Foreign Vessels at Sea on Terror-Related Intelligence Tips", *Journal of International Maritime Law*, 16 (2010), No. 1, pp. 45-75, and *Naval Law Review*, 59 (2010), pp. 63-103.

Burkhardt, L., "Rules of Engagement zur Pirateriebekämpfung : Inhalte und Verfahren", in Weingärtner (ed.), *Die Bundeswehr als Armee im Einsatz : Entwicklungen im nationalen und internationalen Recht*, Baden-Baden, Nomos, 2010, pp. 125-141.

Caligiuri, A., "Observations sur la poursuite et justice des pirates", dans J. M. Sobrino Heredia, *Sûreté maritime et violence en mer/Maritime Security and Violence at Sea*, Bruxelles, Bruylant, 2011, pp. 251-269.

Fastenrath, U., "Zur Verfassungsmäßigkeit unilateraler Pirateriebekämpfung durch die deutsche Marine", in H. Hestermeyer *et al.*, *Coexistence, Cooperation and Solidarity : Liber Amicorum Rüdiger Wolfrum*, Leiden, Nijhoff, 2012, pp. 1935-1957.

Fink, M. D., "The Right of Visit for Warships : Some Challenges in Applying the Law of Maritime Interdiction on the High Seas", *Revue de droit militaire et de droit de la guerre*, 49 (2010), Nos. 1-2, pp. 7-45.

Fouche, H., and J. Meyer, "Investigating Sea Piracy : Crime Scene Challenges", *WMU Journal of Maritime Affairs*, 11 (2012), No. 1, pp. 33-50.

Gumiero, G., « Operazione antipirateria dell'Unione Europea Atalante : periodo di guida italiana della forza marittima — EUNAVFOR — in mare », dans A. Uricchio *et al.* (dir. publ.), *Nuove piraterie e ordinamenti giuridici interni e internazionali : atti del Convegno tenuto a Taranto il 16 e 17 giugno 2009*, Bari, Cacucci, 2011, pp. 77-88.

Guilfoyle, D., *Shipping Interdiction and the Law of the Sea*, Cambridge, Cambridge University Press, 2009.

—, "Human Rights Issues and Non-Flag State Boarding of Suspect Ships in International Waters", in Clive R. Symmons (ed.), *Selected Contemporary Issues in the Law of the Sea*, Leiden, Nijhoff, 2011, pp. 83-104.

—, "Interdicting Vessels to Enforce the Common Interest : Maritime Countermeasures and the Use of Force", *The International and Comparative Law Quarterly*, 56 (2007), No. 1, pp. 69-82.

Heintschel von Heinegg, W., "Maritime Interception/Interdiction Operations", in T. D. Gill and D. Fleck (eds.), *The Handbook of the International Law of Military Operations*, Oxford, Oxford University Press, 2010, pp. 375-393.

—, « Maritime Interception/Interdiction Operations within the Framework of Operation Enduring Freedom », dans Société française pour le droit international, *Les nouvelles menaces contre la paix et la sécurité internationales : journée franco-allemande/New Threats to International Peace and Security*, Paris, Pedone, 2004, pp. 149-164.

Jorge Urbina, J., « La contribution du Conseil de sécurité à la coopération internationale pour la lutte contre la piraterie dans le golfe d'Aden et au large des côtes de la Somalie », dans J. M. Sobrino Heredia, *Sûreté maritime et violence en mer/Maritime Security and Violence at Sea*, Bruxelles, Bruylant, 2011, pp. 283-300.

Kraska, J., "Broken Taillight at Sea: The Peacetime International Law of Visit, Board, Search, and Seizure", *Ocean and Coastal Law Journal*, 16 (2011), No. 1, pp. 1-46.

Laurent, F., et A. Garcia, « Défense et sécurité », *Annuaire du droit de la mer*, 15 (2010), pp. 475-524.

Leandro, A., « L'azione delle organizzazioni internazionali in materia di pirateria marittima », dans A. Uricchio *et al.* (dir. publ.), *Nuove piraterie e ordinamenti giuridici interni e internazionali : atti del Convegno tenuto a Taranto il 16 e 17 giugno 2009*, Bari, Cacucci, 2011, pp. 121-140.

McLaughlin, R., "United Nations Mandated Naval Interdiction Operations in the Territorial Sea?", *International and Comparative Law Quarterly*, 51 (2002), No. 2, pp. 249-278.

—, *United Nations Naval Peace Operations in the Territorial Sea*, Leiden, Nijhoff, 2009.

Møller, B., "Militia and Piracy in the Horn of Africa: External Responses", in R. Bereketeab, *The Horn of Africa: Intra-state and Inter-state Conflicts and Security*, London, Pluto Press, 2013, pp. 178-196.

Moreno Lax, V., "The EU Regime on Interdiction, Search and Rescue, and Disembarkation: The Frontex Guidelines for Intervention at Sea", *International Journal of Marine and Coastal Law*, 25 (2010), No. 4, pp. 621-635.

Neri, K., *L'emploi de la force en mer*, Bruxelles, Bruylant, 2013.

Papastavridis, E., "Enforcement Jurisdiction in the Mediterranean Sea: Illicit Activities and the Rule of Law on the High Seas", *International Journal of Marine and Coastal Law*, 25 (2010), No. 4, pp. 569-599.

—, "Interception of Human Beings on the High Seas: A Contemporary Analysis under International Law", *Syracuse Journal of International Law and Commerce*, 36 (2009), No. 2, pp. 145-228.

—, *The Interception of Vessels on the High Seas: Contemporary Challenges to the Legal Order of the Oceans*, Oxford, Hart Publishing, 2013.

—, "Piracy of Somalia: The 'Emperors and the Thieves of the Oceans' in the 21st Century", in A. Abass (ed.), *Protecting Human Security in Africa*, Oxford, Oxford University Press, 2010, pp. 122-154.

—, "The Right of Visit on the High Seas in a Theoretical Perspective: Mare Liberum versus Mare Clausum Revisited", *Leiden Journal of International Law*, 24 (2011), No. 1, pp. 45-69.

Rubio Fernandez, E. M., « Bilan de la réglementation juridique internationale de l'assistance aux victimes de la violence sur mer, spécialement de la piraterie ou du vol à main armée », dans J. M. Sobrino Heredia, *Sûreté maritime et violence en mer/Maritime Security and Violence at Sea*, Bruxelles, Bruylant, etc., 2011, pp. 301-322.

Sánchez Barrueco, M. L., "The European Strategy against Piracy off the Somali Coast: A Multi-Pillar Response to a Cross-Pillar Concern", in J. M. Sobrino Heredia, *Sûreté maritime et violence en mer/Maritime Security and Violence at Sea*, Bruxelles, Bruylant, etc., 2011, pp. 323-342.

Spagnolo, A., « Il trasferimento di presunti pirati nell'ambito dell'operazione "Atalanta": gli accordi tra l'Unione europea e i Paesi terzi », *Studi sull'integrazione europea,* 7 (2012), Vol. 2-3, pp. 651-668.

Surbun, V., "The Developing Jurisprudence to Combat Modern Maritime Pricacy: A Crime of the High Seas?", *Comparative and International Law Journal of Southern Africa*, 43 (2010), No. 1, pp. 1-22.

Tajani, A., « Il contrasto alla pirateria marittima: l'impegno delle istituzioni comunitarie e internazionali », *Nuove piraterie e ordinamenti giuridici interni e internazionali : atti del Convegno tenuto a Taranto il 16 e 17 giugno 2009*, Bari, Cacucci, 2011, pp. 21-41.

Tondini, M., "The Legality of Intercepting Boat People under Search and Rescue and Border Control Operations: With Reference to Recent Italian

Interventions in the Mediterranean Sea and the ECtHR Decision in the Hirsi Case, *Journal of International Maritime Law*, 18 (2012), No. 1, pp. 59-74.

WALKER, R., "International Law of the Sea: Applying the Doctrine of Hot Pursuit in the 21st Century", *Auckland University Law Review,* 17 (2011), pp. 194-218.

WILSON, D. G., "Interdiction on the High Seas: The Role and Authority of a Master in the Boarding and Searching of His Ship by Foreign Warships", *Naval Law Review*, 55 (2008), pp. 157-211.

YONG JOONG LEE, E., "Military Rescue Operation for the Hostages taken by Somali Pirates: Was the Korean Navy's 'Daybreak in the Gulf of Aden' Legitimate?", *Journal of East Asia and International Law*, 5 (2012), No. 1, pp. 37-60.

2 La multiplication de régimes juridiques portant sur la criminalité en mer

Proliferation of Legal Regimes Addressing Crimes at Sea

ALCAIDE FERNÁNDEZ, J., "'Hostes Humani Generis': Pirates, Slavers, and Other Criminals", in Bardo Fassbender and Anne Peters (eds.), *The Oxford Handbook of the History of International Law*, Oxford, Oxford University Press, 2012, pp. 120-144.

ANDERSON, J., "A Sea of Change Reforming the International Regime to Prevent, Suppress and Prosecute Sea Piracy", *Journal of Maritime Law and Commerce*, 44 (2013), No. 1, pp. 47-68.

ANDREONE, G., «Protection et sécurité des transports maritimes», dans J. M. Sobrino Heredia, *Sûreté maritime et violence en mer/Maritime Security and Violence at Sea*, Bruxelles, Bruylant, etc., 2011, pp. 465-473.

ARROYO ZAPATERO, L., et A. NIETO MARTÍN (dir. publ.), *Piratas, mercenarios, soldados, jueces y policías: nuevas desafíos del derecho penal europeo e internacional*, Cuenca, Ed. de la Universidad de Castilla-La Mancha, 2010.

BECKMAN, R. C., "Do We Need a New Convention on Piracy and Armed Robbery against Ships?", in Aldo Chircop *et al.* (eds.), *The Regulation of International Shipping: International and Comparative Perspectives: Essays in Honor of Edgar Gold*, Leiden, etc., Nijhoff, 2012, pp. 77-96.

BENTO, L., "Towards an International Law of Piracy Sui Generis: How the Dual Nature of Maritime Piracy Enables Piracy to Flourish", *Berkeley Journal of International Law*, 29 (2011). No. 2, pp. 399-455.

BERG, J., "You're Gonna Need a Bigger Boat: Somali Piracy and the Erosion of Customary Piracy Suppression", *New England Law Review*, 44 (2010), No. 2, pp. 343-386.

BLANCO-BAZÁN, A., "Protection and Safety in Maritime Transport: Measures by International Maritime Organizations", in J. M. Sobrino Heredia, *Sûreté maritime et violence en mer/Maritime Security and Violence at Sea*, Bruxelles, Bruylant, etc., 2011, pp. 381-410.

BOON, K. E., A. HUQ and D. C. Lovelace (eds.), *Piracy and International Maritime Security*, New York, NY, etc., Oxford University Press, 2011.

BURKHARDT, L., "Rules of Engagement zur Pirateriebekämpfung: Inhalte und Verfahren", in Weingärtner (ed.), *Die Bundeswehr als Armee im Einsatz: Entwicklungen im nationalen und internationalen Recht*, Baden-Baden, Nomos, 2010, pp. 125-141.

CALIGIURI, A., «Observations sur la poursuite et justice des pirates», dans J. M. Sobrino Heredia, *Sûreté maritime et violence en mer/Maritime Security and Violence at Sea*, Bruxelles, Bruylant, etc., 2011, pp. 251-269.

CAMPBELL, P., "A Modern History of the International Legal Definition of Piracy", in Bruce A. Elleman, Andrew Forbes, and David Rosenberg (eds.)

Piracy and Maritime Crime: Historical and Modern Case Studies, Newport, RI, Naval War College Press, 2010, pp. 19-32.

CANINAS, O. P., "Pirataria marítima moderna: história, situação atual e desafios", *Revista da Escola de Guerra Naval*, 14 (2009), pp. 101-122.

CASSUTO, Th., «La lutte contre la piraterie maritime: nouvelles perspectivies», *Actualité juridique pénale*, 251 (2012), n° 5, pp. 277-280.

CHANG, D., "Piracy Laws and the Effective Prosecution of Pirates", *Boston College International and Comparative Law Review*, 33 (2010), No. 2, pp. 273-288.

CHI, M., "Finding out the 'Achilles Heels': Piracy Suppression under International Law and Chinese Law", *Journal of East Asia and International Law,* 5 (2012), No. 1, pp. 7-36.

CUDENNEC, A., «Terrorisme et piraterie maritimes: l'affirmation du statut de l'UE sur la scène internationale», dans J. M. Sobrino Heredia, *Sûreté maritime et violence en mer/Maritime Security and Violence at Sea*, Bruxelles, Bruylant, etc., 2011, pp. 191-209.

DAVENPORT, T., "Legal Measures to Combat Piracy and Armed Robbery in the Horn of Africa and in Southeast Asia: A Comparison", *Studies in Conflict and Terrorism*, 35 (2012), Nos. 7-8, pp. 570-587.

DIAZ, L. M., and B. H. DUBNER, "An Examination of the Evolution of Crimes at Sea and the Emergence of the Many Legal Regimes in Their Wake", *North Carolina Journal of International Law and Commercial Regulation*, 34 (2009), No. 2, pp. 521-568.

DUBNER, B. H., "On the Definition of the Crime of Sea Piracy Revisited: Customary vs. Treaty Law and the Jurisdictional Implications Thereof", *Journal of Maritime Law and Commerce,* 42 (2011), No. 1, pp. 71-100.

DUBNER, B. H., and J. P. HENN, "On Selecting a Judicial System(s) to Try Sea Pirates: An Interesting/Necessary Exercise But Is It Enough to Deter the Attacks/Hijackings?", *Journal of Maritime Law and Commerce*, 42 (2011), No. 4, pp. 569-605.

DUTTON, Y. M., "Maritime Piracy and the Impunity Gap: Domestic Implementation of International Treaty Provisions", in Michael J. Struett, Jon D. Carlson and Mark T. Nance (eds.), *Maritime Piracy and the Construction of Global Governance*, New York, NY, Routledge, 2013, pp. 71-95.

ELAGAB, O., "Somali Piracy and International Law: Some Aspects", *Australian and New Zealand Maritime Law Journal*, 24 (2010), pp. 59-75.

FAKHRY, A., "Piracy across Maritime Law: Is There a Problem of Definition?", in Aldo Chircop *et al.* (eds.), *The Regulation of International Shipping: International and Comparative Perspectives: Essays in Honor of Edgar Gold*, Leiden, etc., Nijhoff, 2012, pp. 97-117.

FINK, M. D., and R. J. GALVIN, "Combating Pirates off the Coast of Somalia: Current Legal Challenges", *Netherlands International Law Review*, 56 (2009), No. 3, pp. 367-395.

FOUCHÉ, H., "Harmonized Legal Framework for Africa as an Instrument to Combat Sea Piracy", in A. Petrig (ed.), *Sea Piracy Law: Selected National Legal Frameworks and Regional Legislative Approaches/Droit de la piraterie maritime: cadres juridiques nationaux et approches legislatives régionales*, Berlin, Duncker & Humblot, 2010, pp. 139-159.

GABEL, G. D., "Smoother Seas Ahead: The Draft Guidelines as an International Solution to Modern-Day Piracy", *Tulane Law Review*, 81 (2007), No. 5-6, pp. 1433-1466.

GARCÍA ALFARAZ, A. I., «Apuntes para una reflexión sobre el delito de piratería maritime», dans Laura Zúñiga Rodríguez, Concepción Gorjón Barranco, Julio Fernández García (dir. publ.), *La reforma penal de 2010*, Salamanca, Ratio Legis, 2011, pp. 201-245.

GARCÍA GARCÍA-REVILLO, M., "Roundtable on the Judicial Ways to Face the Violence at Sea", in J. M. Sobrino Heredia, *Sûreté maritime et violence en mer/Maritime Security and Violence at Sea*, Bruxelles, Bruylant, etc., 2011, pp. 493-496.

GATTINI, A., "Somalia: Purposes and Limits of State Fiction in International Law", in Th. Giegerich und A. Proelß (eds), *Krisenherde im Fokus des Völkerrechts*, Berlin, Duncker und Humblot, 2010, pp. 151-165.

GAUCI, G., "Piracy: Legal and Theoretical Problems", in Proshanto K. Mukherjee, Maximo Q. Mejia and Gotthard M. Gauci (eds.), *Maritime Violence and Other Security Issues at Sea*, 2002, pp. 39-53.

GAUTIER, Ph., «Le rôle du Tribunal international du Droit de la Mer face à la violence en mer», dans J. M. Sobrino Heredia, *Sûreté maritime et violence en mer/Maritime Security and Violence at Sea*, Bruxelles, Bruylant, etc., 2011, pp. 483-492.

GEISS, R., and A. PETRIG, *Piracy and Armed Robbery at Sea: The Legal Framework for Counter-Piracy Operations in Somalia and the Gulf of Aden*, Oxford, etc., Oxford University Press, 2011.

GOLITSYN, V., "Maritime Security: Case of Piracy", in H. Hestermeyer *et al.*, *Coexistence, Cooperation and Solidarity: Liber Amicorum Rüdiger Wolfrum*, Leiden, etc., Nijhoff, 2012, pp. 1157-1176.

GRAZIANI, F., *Il contrasto alla pirateria marittima nel diritto internazionale*, Naples, Editoriale Scientifica, 2009.

HAYWOOD, R., and R. SPIVAK, *Maritime Piracy*, London, etc., Routledge, 2012.

HEINTSCHEL VON HEINEGG, W., "Repressing Piracy and Armed Robbery at Sea: Towards a New International Legal Regime", *Israel Yearbook on Human Rights*, 40 (2010), pp. 219-241.

HEINZE, E. A., "A 'Global War on Piracy?' International Law and the Use of Force against Sea Pirates", in Michael J. Struett, Jon D. Carlson and Mark T. Nance (eds.), *Maritime Piracy and the Construction of Global Governance*, New York, NY, Routledge, 2013, pp. 47-70.

IBRAHIM, A. A., «Le cadre juridique relatif à la piraterie maritime à Djibouti», in A. Petrig (ed.), *Sea Piracy Law: Selected National Legal Frameworks and Regional Legislative Approaches/Droit de la piraterie maritime: cadres juridiques nationaux et approches legislatives régionales*, Berlin, Duncker & Humblot, 2010, pp. 83-124.

ISANGA, J. M., "Countering Persistent Contemporary Sea Piracy: Expanding Jurisdictional Regimes", *American University Law Review*, 59 (2010), No. 5, pp. 1267-1320.

IYI, J.-M., "Somali Piracy, UNSC Resolutions 1816-1851: Dilemma of State Failure and the Burden of Legitimacy", *African Yearbook on International Humanitarian Law*, 2011, pp. 47-78.

JENISCH, U., "Piracy, Navies and the Law of the Sea: The Case of Somalia", *WMU Journal of Maritime Affairs*, 8 (2009), No. 2, pp. 123-143.

KAMULI, R., "Tanzania's Legal Framework on Sea Piracy: An Obligatory but Inconsistent Model", in A. Petrig (ed.), *Sea Piracy Law: Selected National Legal Frameworks and Regional Legislative Approaches/Droit de la piraterie maritime: cadres juridiques nationaux et approches legislatives régionales*, Berlin, Duncker & Humblot, 2010, pp. 39-81.

KEMPE, M., and O. GÄNSWEIN, "Die Rückkehr der Universalfeinde: Terroristen als 'hostes humani generis' und was Piraten damit zu tun haben", *Zeitschrift fur Neuere Rechtsgeschichte*, 32 (2010), No. 2, pp. 91-106.

KLEIN, N., *Maritime Security and the Law of the Sea*, Oxford, etc., Oxford University Press, 2011.

LE HARDŸ DE BEAULIEU, L. (dir. publ.), *Criminalité et trafics maritimes: des enjeux politiques aux conséquences juridiques*, Namur, Presses universitaires de Namur, 2008.

LÓPEZ RUEDA, F. C., «Piratería maritíma, terrorismo y figuras afines», *Anuario de derecho maritime*, 29 (2012), pp. 55-123.

MCGAHAN, K., and T. LEE, "Frames, Humanitarianism, and Legitimacy:

Explaining the Anti-piracy Regime in the Gulf of Aden", in Michael J. Struett, Jon D. Carlson and Mark T. Nance (eds.), *Maritime Piracy and the Construction of Global Governance*, New York, NY, Routledge, 2013, pp. 149-167.

MANJIAO, C., "A Note on China's Legal and Operational Responses to International Piracy", *Ocean Development and International Law*, 44 (2013), No. 1, pp. 113-122.

MUKHERJEE, P. K., "Transformation of Conventions into National Legislation: Piracy and Suppression of Unlawful Acts", in Proshanto K. Mukherjee, Maximo Q. Mejia and Gotthard M. Gauci (eds.), *Maritime Violence and Other Security Issues at Sea*, 2002, pp. 71-99.

MURDOCH, A., "Recent Legal Issues and Problems Relating to Acts of Piracy of Somalia", in C. R. Symmons (ed.), *Selected Contemporary Issues in the Law of the Sea*, Leiden, etc., Nijhoff, 2011, pp. 139-168.

NANCE, M. T., and M. J. STRUETT, "Conflicting Constructions: Maritime Piracy and Cooperation under Regime Complexes", in Michael J. Struett, Jon D. Carlson and Mark T. Nance (eds.), *Maritime Piracy and the Construction of Global Governance*, New York, NY, Routledge, 2013, pp. 125-148.

NERI, K., *L'emploi de la force en mer*, Bruxelles, Bruylant, 2013.

NOYES, J. E., "Unit Self-Defense at Sea: Views from the United States and the International Court of Justice", in E. Franckx, Ph. Gautier (eds.), *The Exercise of Jurisdiction over Vessels: New Developments in the Fields of Pollution, Fisheries, Crimes at Sea and Trafficking of Weapons of Mass Destruction*, Brussels, Bruylant, 2010, pp. 185-212.

OLIVEIRA, F. B. de, *A liberdade de circulação nos mares e as «novas Ameaças»: a pirataria marítima, a tutela jurídico-penal*, Lisbonne, Livraria Petrony, 2010.

PELLEGRINO, F., "Historical and Legal Aspects of Piracy and Armed Robbery against Shipping", *Journal of Maritime Law and Commerce*, 43 (2012), No. 3, pp. 429-446.

PEREZ, N., «L'appréhension des actes de piraterie au large de la Somalie par le droit international», *Les menaces contre la paix et la sécurité internationales: nouveaux défis et nouveaux enjeux*, Paris, IREDIES, 2010, pp. 205-219.

PETRIG, A. (ed.), *Sea Piracy Law: Selected National Legal Frameworks and Regional Legislative Approaches/Droit de la piraterie maritime: cadres juridiques nationaux et approches legislatives régionales*, Berlin, Duncker & Humblot, 2010.

PHILLIPS, R. L., *Pirate Accessory Liability — Developing a Modern Legal Regime Governing Incitement and Intentional Facilitation of Maritime Piracy*, Rochester, NY, Social Science Research Network, 2012.

ROACH, J. A., "Countering Piracy off Somalia: International Law and International Institutions", *American Journal of International Law*, 104 (2010), No. 3, pp. 397-416.

ROUGER, M. (dir. publ.), *La piraterie maritime,* Colloque des entretiens de Royan, Bruxelles, Larcier, 2011.

SÁNCHEZ RAMOS, B., "Action Undertaken by the International Maritime Organization in the Struggle against Maritime Piracy and Armed Robbery", in J. M. Sobrino Heredia, *Sûreté maritime et violence en mer/Maritime Security and Violence at Sea*, Bruxelles, Bruylant, etc., 2011, pp. 211-233.

SHEARER, I., "Piracy", *Max Planck Encyclopedia of Public International Law*, 2010.

SHNIDER, S., "Universal Jurisdiction over 'Operation of a Pirate Ship': The Legality of the Evolving Piracy Definition in Regional Prosecutions", *North Carolina Journal of International Law and Commercial Regulation*, 38 (2012), No. 2, pp. 473-359.

SOBRIDO PRIETO, M., «The European Union and Maritime Security-Related Criminal Law», dans J. M. Sobrino Heredia, *Sûreté maritime et violence en mer/Maritime Security and Violence at Sea*, Bruxelles, Bruylant, etc., 2011, pp. 453-463.

SOMERS, E., «Piraterie maritime et droit international», dans L. Le Hardÿ de Beaulieu (dir. publ.), *Criminalité et trafics maritimes: des enjeux politiques aux conséquences*, Namur, Presses universitaires de Namur, 2008, pp. 11-29.

—, "Can the Law Contribute to Solving the Problem of Piracy?", in Kris Bernauw *et al.*, *Free on Board: Liber Amoricorum Marc A. Huybrechts*, Antwerp, etc., Intersentia, 2011, pp. 497-515.

STERIO, M., "International Law in Crisis: Piracy off the Coast of Somalia", *Case Western Reserve Journal of International Law*, 44 (2011), Nos. 1-2, pp. 291-301.

STILES, K. W., "Disaggregating Delegation: Multiplying Agents in the International Maritime Safety Regime", in Joel E. Oestreich (ed.), *International Organizations as Self-directed Actors: A Framework for Analysis*, London, Routledge, pp. 168-194.

STRUETT, M. J., J. D. CARLSON and M. T. NANCE (eds.), *Maritime Piracy and the Construction of Global Governance*, New York, NY, Routledge, 2013.

URBINA, J. J., «El régimen jurídico internacional de la piratería y los problemas que plantea su persecución en las costas de Somalia y el Golfo de Aden», dans R. Castillejo Manzanares (dir. publ.), *La persecución de los actos de piratería en las costas somalíes*, Valence, Tirant lo Blanch, 2011, pp. 34-66.

URICCHIO, A., *et al.* (dir. publ.), *Nuove piraterie e ordinamenti giuridici interni e internazionali: atti del Convegno tenuto a Taranto il 16 e 17 giugno 2009*, Bari, Cacucci, 2011.

WALKER, R., "International Law of the Sea: Applying the Doctrine of Hot Pursuit in the 21st Century", *Auckland University Law Review*, 17 (2011), pp. 194-218.

WAMBUA, P. M., "The Legal Framework for Adjudication of Piracy Cases in Kenya: Review of the Jurisdictional and Procedural Challenges and the Institutional Capacity", in A. Petrig (ed.), *Sea Piracy Law: Selected National Legal Frameworks and Regional Legislative Approaches/Droit de la piraterie maritime: cadres juridiques nationaux et approches legislatives régionales*, Berlin, Duncker & Humblot, 2010, pp. 1-37.

ZOU, K., "Crackdown on Piracy in Southeast Asian Seas: Need a More Effective Legal Regime?", in Shicun Wu and Keyuan Zou, *Maritime Security in the South China Sea: Regional Implications and International Cooperation*, Farnham, Ashgate, 2009, pp. 135-155.

3 Pêche illicite, non déclarée et non réglementée Illegal, Unreported and Unregulated Fishing

ANDREONE, G., "Illegal, Unreported, Unregulated Fishing", in Gianfranco Tamburelli (ed.), *The Antarctic Legal System and Environmental Issues*, Milan, Giuffrè, 2006, pp. 121-131.

ANDREWS-CHOUICHA, E. (dir. publ.), *Pourquoi la pêche pirate perdure: les ressorts économiques de la pêche illégale, non déclarée et non réglementée*, Paris, OCDE, 2005.

— (ed.), *Why Fish Piracy Persists: The Economics of Illegal, Unreported and Unregulated Fishing*, Paris, OECD, 2005.

ANSELL, N., D. ARDILL and H. GREIDANUS, "Using Technology in Combating IUU Fishing: The Potential of Satellite Remote Sensing", in Davor Vidas (ed.), *Law, Technology and Science for Oceans in Globalisation: IUU Fishing, Oil Pollution, Bioprospecting, Outer Continental Shelf*, Leiden, etc., Nijhoff, 2010, pp. 197-210.

AQORAU, T., "Illegal Fishing and Fisheries Law Enforcement in Small Islands Developing States: The Pacific Islands Experience", *The International Journal of Marine and Coastal Law*, 15 (2000), No. 1, pp. 37-63.

—, "Illegal, Unreported and Unregulated Fishing in the Western and Cental Pacific Ocean (WCPO): Some Legal and Policy Issues Surrounding Control of Nationals and Charter Vessels under the New Legal Regime in the WCPO", *Ocean Yearbook*, 21 (2007), pp. 177-201.

ARENAS MEZA, M., «Las medidas relativas al estado del puerto y su actual regulación en el derecho internacional de las pesquerías: insuficiencias y perspectivas de future», dans Jorge Pueyo Losa and Julio Jorge Urbina (dir. publ.), *La cooperación internacional en la ordenación de los mares y océanos*, Madrid, Lustel, 2009, pp. 185-222.

BAIRD, R. J., *Aspects of Illegal, Unreported and Unregulated Fishing in the Southern Ocean*, Dordrecht (etc.), Springer, 2006.

—, "Australia's Response to Illegal Foreign Fishing: A Case of Winning the Battle but Losing the Law?", *International Journal of Marine and Coastal Law*, 23 (2008), No. 1, pp. 95-124.

BAIRD, R. J., N. SLICER and G. L. LUGTEN, *Australia and Southern Ocean IUU Fishing* (Hobart), University of Tasmania Law School Press, 2007.

BALTON, D. A., "Global Review of Illegal, Unreported and Unregulated Fishing Issues: What's the Problem?", in *Fish Piracy: Combating Illegal Unreported and Unregulated Fishing*, Paris, OECD, 2004, pp. 49-50.

—, "IUU Fishing and State Control over Nationals", in *Fish Piracy: Combating Illegal Unreported and Unregulated Fishing*, Paris, OECD, 2004, pp. 51-56.

BENDER, P., "A State of Necessity: IUU Fishing in the CCAMLR Zone", *Ocean and Coastal Law Journal*, 13 (2008), No. 2, pp. 233-280.

BENDER, P., and G. LUGTEN, "Taxing Illegal Fishing: A Proposal for Using Taxation Law to Reduce Profiteering from IUU Fishing Offences", *International Journal of Marine and Coastal Law*, 22 (2007), No. 4, pp. 517-544.

BESLIER, S., "Exercise of Jurisdiction over Vessels: New Developments in the Sector of Fisheries", in E. Franckx and Ph. Gautier (eds.), *The Exercise of Jurisdiction over Vessels: New Developments in the Fields of Pollution, Fisheries, Crimes at Sea and Trafficking of Weapons of Mass Destruction*, Brussels, Bruylant, 2010, pp. 47-55.

BEURIER, J.-P., «Déroutement et saisie des navires de pêche», *Annuaire de droit maritime et océanique*, 22 (2004), pp. 383-393.

BRAY, K., "Illegal, Unreported, and Unregulated Fishing", in M. H. Nordquist and J. N. Moore (eds.), *Current Fisheries Issues and the Food and Agriculture Organization of the United Nations*, The Hague, etc., Martinus Nijhoff Publishers, 2000, pp. 115-135.

BROWELEIT, J., "The Draft 2009 FAO Legally-Binding Port State Measures Agreement: An Evaluation of Its Potential to Combat Illegal, Unreported and Unregulated Fishing", in *Antarctic and Southern Ocean Law and Policy Occasional Papers*, Vol. 13, Hobart, University of Tasmania, Law School, 2009, pp. 21-45.

CHANG, D., "Measures Taken by Chinese Taipei in Combating FOC/IUU Fishing", in *Fish Piracy: Combating Illegal Unreported and Unregulated Fishing*, Paris, OECD, 2004, pp. 365-368.

CULLEN, P., "Privatized Maritime Security Governance in War-torn Sierra Leone", in C. Berube and P. Cullen (eds.), *Maritime Private Security: Market Responses to Piracy, Terrorism and Waterborne Security Risks in the 21st Century*, London, etc., Routledge, 2012, pp. 101-112.

DIAZ, L. M., and B. H. DUBNER, "Foreign Fishing Piracy vs. Somalia Piracy — Does Wrong Equal Wrong", *Barry Law Review*, 14 (2010), No. 1, pp. 73-96.

DOULMAN, D. J., "FAO Action to Combat IUU Fishing: Scope of Initiatives and Constraints on Implementation ", in Davor Vidas (ed.), *Law, Technology and Science for Oceans in Globalisation: IUU Fishing, Oil Pollution, Bioprospecting, Outer Continental Shelf*, Leiden, etc., Nijhoff, 2010, pp. 131-155.

EDESON, W., "The International Plan of Action on Illegal Unreported and Unregulated Fishing: The Legal Context of a Non-Legally Binding Instrument", *The International Journal of Marine and Coastal Law*, 16 (2001), No. 4, pp. 603-623.

ERCEG, D., "Deterring IUU Fishing through State Control over Nationals", *Marine Policy*, 30 (2006), No. 2, pp. 173-179.

FITZPATRICK, K., "Can Admiralty Law Be Used as a Tool to fight Illegal, Unreported and Unregulated Fishing?", in *Antarctic and Southern Ocean Law and Policy Occasional Papers*, Vol. 12, Hobart, Tasmania, University of Tasmania, Faculty of Law, 2008, pp. 55-77.

"Food and Agriculture Organization: International Plan of Action to Prevent, Deter and Eliminate Illegal, Unreported and Unregulated Fishing approved by FAO Committee on Fisheries, 2 March 2001", *The International Journal of Marine and Coastal Law*, 16 (2001), No. 4, pp. 660-678.

FOX, J. J., "Legal and Illegal Indonesian Fishing in Australian Waters", in R. Cribb and M. Ford (eds.), *Indonesia beyond the Water's Edge: Managing an Archipelagic State*, Singapore, Institute of Southeast Asian Studies, 2009, pp. 195-220.

FRANCKX, E., and Ph. GAUTIER (eds.), *The Exercise of Jurisdiction over Vessels: New Developments in the Fields of Pollution, Fisheries, Crimes at Sea and Trafficking of Weapons of Mass Destruction*, Brussels, Bruylant, 2010.

—, "The Protection of Biodiversity and Fisheries Management: Issues Raised by the Relationship between CITES and LOSC", in David Freestone, Richard Barnes and David M. Ong (eds.), *The Law of the Sea: Progress and Prospects*, Oxford, etc., Oxford University Press, 2006, pp. 210-232.

—, "'Reasonable Bond' in the Practice of the International Tribunal for the Law of the Sea", *California Western International Law Journal*, 32 (2002), No. 2, pp. 303-342.

GAUTIER, Ph., "Comments on Flag State's Responsibility, Enforcement Measures against IUU Fishing Activities, and the Settlement of Disputes", in E. Franckx and Ph. Gautier (eds.), *The Exercise of Jurisdiction over Vessels: New Developments in the Fields of Pollution, Fisheries, Crimes at Sea and Trafficking of Weapons of Mass Destruction*, Brussels, Bruylant, 2010, pp. 81-96.

GIANNI, M., "IUU Fishing and the Cost to Flag of Convenience Countries", in *Fish Piracy: Combating Illegal Unreported and Unregulated Fishing*, Paris, OECD, 2004, pp.285-288.

GIANNI, M., and W. SIMPSON, "Flags of Convenience, Transhipment, Re-supply and At-Sea Infrastructure in Relation to IUU Fishing", in *Fish Piracy: Combating Illegal Unreported and Unregulated Fishing*, Paris, OECD, 2004, pp. 79-104.

HANAFUSA, K., and N. YAGI, "Efforts to Eliminate IUU Large-Scale Tuna Longline Vessels", in *Fish Piracy: Combating Illegal Unreported and Unregulated Fishing*, Paris, OECD, 2004, pp.255-279.

HATCHER, A., "Incentives for Investment in IUU Fishing Capacity", in *Fish Piracy: Combating Illegal Unreported and Unregulated Fishing*, Paris, OECD, 2004, pp. 239-253.

HAWARD, M., "IUU Fishing: Contemporary Practice", in A. G. Oude Elferink and D. R. Rothwell, *Oceans Management in the 21st Century: Institutional Frameworks and Responses*, Leiden, etc., Nijhoff, 2004, pp. 87-106.

HAYASHI, M. , "Illegal, Unreported and Unregulated (IUU) Fishing: Global and Regional Responses", in D. D. Caron and H. N. Scheiber, *Bringing New Law to Ocean Waters*, Leiden, etc., Nijhoff, 2004, pp. 95-123.

—, "International Measures to Combat Illegal, Unreported and Unregulated (IUU) Fishing and Japan", *The Japanese Yearbook of International Law*, 51 (2008), pp.57-75.

HOYDAL, K., "IUU Fishing in the NEAFC Area: How Big Is the Problem and What Have We Done?", in *Fish Piracy: Combating Illegal Unreported and Unregulated Fishing*, Paris, OECD, 2004, pp. 159-165.

IYI J.-M., "Somali Piracy, UNSC Resolutions 1816-1851: Dilemma of State

Failure and the Burden of Legitimacy", *African Yearbook on International Humanitarian Law*, 2011, pp. 47-78.

JOYNER, Ch. C., and L. AYLESWORTH, "Managing IUU Fishing in the Southern Ocean: Rethinking the Plight of the Patagonian Tootfish", *Ocean Yearbook*, 22 (2008), pp. 249-290.

KABAI, M., "International Legal Instruments and Measures Providing Protection against Illegal Unregulated and Unreported Fishing (IUU): South African Milieu", *Journal of African and International Law*, 5 (2012), No. 3, pp. 509-535.

KAYE, S., "IUU Fishing in the Southern Ocean: Challenge and Response", in G. Triggs and A. Riddell, *Antarctica: Legal and Environmental Challenges for the Future*, London, British Institute of International and Comparative Law, 2007, pp. 39-59.

KINSEY, Ch., "Private Security Fighting Pirates and Illegal Fishing in Puntland", in Claude Berube and Patrick Cullen, *Maritime Private Security: Market Responses to Piracy, Terrorism and Waterborne Security Risks in the 21st Century*, London, etc., Routledge, 2012, pp. 126-137.

KURUC, M., "Monitoring, Control and Surveillance Tools to Detect IUU Fishing and Related Activities", in Davor Vidas (ed.), *Law, Technology and Science for Oceans in Globalisation: IUU Fishing, Oil Pollution, Bioprospecting, Outer Continental Shelf*, Leiden, etc., Nijhoff, 2010, pp. 101-108.

LITTLE, L., and M. A. ORELLANA, "Can CITES Play a Role in Solving the Problem of IUU Fishing? The Trouble with Patagonian Toothfish", *Colorado Journal of International Environmental Law and Policy Yearbook* (2005), pp. 21-122.

LOBACH, T., "Combating IUU Fishing: Interaction of Global and Regional Initiatives", in Vidas (ed.), *Law, Technology and Science for Oceans in Globalisation: IUU Fishing, Oil Pollution, Bioprospecting, Outer Continental Shelf*, Leiden, etc., Nijhoff, 2010, pp. 109-129.

MANZOLI, J.-M., «La lutte contre la pêche illicite dans la zone économique exclusive des Terres australes et antarctiques françaises», *Revue de droit international, de sciences diplomatiques et politiques*, 85 (2007), n° 1, pp. 1-39.

MARTIN-CASTEX, B., "Potential Link between IUU Fishing and the Status of Safety-Related International Instruments Applicable to Fishing Vessels and Fisheries", in *Fish Piracy: Combating Illegal Unreported and Unregulated Fishing*, Paris, OECD, 2004, pp. 309.

MILLER, D. G. M., N. SLICER and E. N. SABOURENKOV, "IUU Fishing in Antarctic Waters: CCAMLR Actions and Regulations", in Davor Vidas (ed.), *Law, Technology and Science for Oceans in Globalisation: IUU Fishing, Oil Pollution, Bioprospecting, Outer Continental Shelf*, Leiden, etc., Nijhoff, 2010, pp. 175-196.

MILLER, D. G. M., "Occupying the High Ground: Technology and the War on IUU Fishing", in Davor Vidas (ed.), *Law, Technology and Science for Oceans in Globalisation: IUU Fishing, Oil Pollution, Bioprospecting, Outer Continental Shelf*, Leiden, etc., Nijhoff, 2010, pp. 77-99.

MOLENAAR, E. J., "Multilateral Hot Pursuit and Illegal Fishing in the Southern Ocean: The Pursuits of the Viarsa 1 and the South Tomi", *International Journal of Marine and Coastal Law*, 19 (2004), No. 1, pp. 19-42.

—, "Participation, Allocation and Unregulated Fishing: The Practice of Regional Fisheries Management Organisations", *International Journal of Marine and Coastal Law*, 18 (2003), No. 4, pp. 457-480.

—, "Regional Fisheries Management Organizations: Issues of Participation, Allocation and Unregulated Fishing", in A. G. Oude Elferink and D. R. Rothwell, *Oceans Management in the 21st Century: Institutional Frameworks and Responses*, Leiden, etc., Nijhoff, 2004, pp. 69-86.

MYOE, M. A., "Myanmar's Maritime Challenges and Priorities", in Joshua

H. Ho and Sam Bateman (eds.), *Maritime Challenges and Priorities in Asia: Implications for Regional Security*, London, Routledge, 2012, pp. 83-105.

NDIAYE, T. M., "Illegal, Unreported and Unregulated Fishing: Responses in General and West Africa", *Chinese Journal of International Law*, 10 (2011), No. 2, pp. 373-405.

NEUMANN, T., and T. R. Salomon, "Fishing in Troubled Waters — Somalia's Maritime Zones and the Case for Reinterpretation", *ASIL Insights*, 16 (2012), No. 9, Washington, DC, American Society of International Law (PDF).

OANTA, G. A., « The European Union's System to Prevent, Deter and Eliminate Illegal, Unreported and Unregulated Fishing », dans J. M. Sobrino Heredia, *Sûreté maritime et violence en mer/Maritime Security and Violence at Sea*, Bruxelles, Bruylant, etc., 2011, pp. 103-114.

ORGANISATION FOR ECONOMIC CO-OPERATION AND DEVELOPMENT, *Fish Piracy: Combating Illegal Unreported and Unregulated Fishing*, Paris, OECD, 2004.

PALMA, M. A., M. TSAMENYI and W. R. EDESON, *Promoting Sustainable Fisheries: The International Legal and Policy Framework to Combat Illegal, Unreported and Unregulated Fishing*, Leiden, etc., Nijhoff, 2010.

PAPASTAVRIDIS, E., *The Interception of Vessels on the High Seas: Contemporary Challenges to the Legal Order of the Oceans*, Oxford, Hart Publishing, 2013.

POLACHECK, T., "Assessment of IUU Fishing for Southern Bluefin Tuna", *Marine Policy*, 36 (2012), No. 5, pp. 1150-1165.

RAYFUSE, R. G., "Non-flag State Enforcement and Protection of the Marine Environment: Responding to IUU Fishing", in M. H. Nordquist, T. T. B. Koh and J. N. Moore, *Freedom of Seas, Passage Rights and the 1982 Law of the Sea Convention*, Leiden, etc., Nijhoff, 2009, pp. 573-600.

RIDDLE, K., "Illegal, Unreported, and Unregulated Fishing: Is International Cooperation Contagious?", *Ocean Development and International Law*, 37 (2006), Nos. 3-4, pp. 265-297.

RIGG, K., R. PARMENTIER and D. CURRIE, "Halting IUU Fishing: Enforcing International Fisheries Agreements", in *Fish Piracy: Combating Illegal Unreported and Unregulated Fishing*, Paris, OECD, 2004, pp. 369-399.

ROS, N., « La lutte contre la pêche illicite », dans Gemma Andreone, Andrea Caligiuri et Giuseppe Cataldi (dir. publ.), *Droit de la mer et émergences environnementales/Law of Sea and Environmental Emergencies*, Rome, Editoriale Scientifica, 2012, pp. 69-122.

ROTHWELL, D. R., "Law Enforcement in Antarctica", in A. D. Hemmings, D. R. Rothwell and K. N. Scott (eds.), *Antarctic Security in the Twenty-First Century: Legal and Policy Perspectives*, Abingdon, etc., Routledge, 2012, pp. 135-153.

ROTHWELL, D. R., and T. STEPHENS, "Illegal Southern Ocean Fishing and Prompt Release: Balancing Coastal and Flag State Rights and Interests", *The International and Comparative Law Quarterly*, 53 (2004), No. 1, pp. 171-187.

SOBRINO HEREDIA, J. M., « Pabellones de conveniencia y pesca ilegal », dans J. Branco de Sampaio, F. Mayor Zaragoza et M. Oreja Aguirre, *Soberanía del Estado y Derecho internacional: homenaje al profesor Juan Antonio Carrillo Salcedo*, Seville, etc., Universidad de Sevilla, Secretariado de Publicaciones, etc., 2005, pp. 1331-1348.

SOBRINO HEREDIA, J. M., et A. REY ANEIROS, "Plan de acción internacional para prevenir, desalentar y eliminar la pesca ilegal, no declarada y no reglementada", *Revista española de derecho internacional*, 54 (2002), nº 1, pp. 481-487.

SODIK, D. M., "Analysis of IUU Fishing in Indonesia and the Indonesian Legal Framework Reform for Monitoring, Control and Surveillance of Fishing Vessels", *International Journal of Marine and Coastal Law*, 24 (2009), No. 1, pp. 67-100.

—, "Analysis of IUU Fishing in Indonesia for the Reform of Fisheries Legislative and Institutional Frameworks", *Ocean Yearbook*, 23 (2009), pp. 309-344.

—, "IUU Fishing and Indonesia's Legal Framework for Vessel Registration and

Fishing Vessel Licensing", *Ocean Development and International Law*, 40 (2009), No. 3, pp. 249-267.
—, "Non-Legally Binding International Fisheries Instruments and Measures to Combat Illegal, Unreported and Unregulated Fishing", *Australian International Law Journal*, 15 (2008), No. 1, pp. 129-164.
—, "Post-LOSC Legal Instruments and Measures to Address IUU Fishing", *Asian Yearbook of International Law*, 15 (2012), pp. 71-124.
SONG, Y.-H., "The Efforts of ICCAT to Combat IUU Fishing: The Roles of Japan and Taiwan in Conserving and Managing Tuna Resources", *International Journal of Marine and Coastal Law*, 24 (2009), No. 1, pp. 101-140.
STOKKE, O. S., "Trade Measures and the Combat of IUU Fishing: Institutional Interplay and Effective Governance in the Northeast Atlantic", *Marine Policy*, 33 (2009), No. 2, pp. 339-349.
STOKKE, O. S., and D. VIDAS, "Regulating IUU Fishing or Combating IUU Operations?", in *Fish Piracy: Combating Illegal Unreported and Unregulated Fishing*, Paris, OECD, 2004, pp. 19-48.
SUMAILA, U. R., J. ALDER and H. KEITH, "Global Scope and Economics of Illegal Fishing", *Marine Policy*, 30 (2006), No. 6, pp. 696-703.
SWAN, J., "Port State Measures to Combat IUU Fishing: International and Regional Developments", *Sustainable Development Law and Policy*, 7 (2006), No. 1, pp. 38-43.
SYMMONS, C. R., "Use of Law of Piracy to Deal with Violent Inter-Vessel Incidents at Sea beyond the 12-Mile Limit: The Irish Experience", in C. R. Symmons (ed.), *Selected Contemporary Issues in the Law of the Sea*, Leiden, etc., Nijhoff, 2011, pp. 169-193.
TSAMENYI, M., "The European Council Regulation on Illegal, Unreported and Unregulated Fishing: An International Fisheries Law Perspective", *International Journal of Marine and Coastal Law*, 25 (2010), No. 1, pp. 5-31.
TREVES, T, "Jurisdiction over Vessels in the Areas of Pollution and Fisheries: General Report", in E. Franckx and Ph. Gautier (eds.), *The Exercise of Jurisdiction over Vessels: New Developments in the Fields of Pollution, Fisheries, Crimes at Sea and Trafficking of Weapons of Mass Destruction*, Brussels, Bruylant, 2010, pp. 1-28.
—, «La pesca ilegal, no declarada y no reglamentada: estado del pabellón, estado costero y estado del Puerto», dans Jorge Pueyo Losa et Julio Jorge Urbina (dir. publ.), *La cooperación internacional en la ordenación de los mares y océanos*, Madrid, Iustel, 2009, pp. 135-158.
—, "Some International Law Aspects of the Use of Vessel Monitoring Systems for Preventing Illegal Unreported Unregulated Fishing", in T. M. Ndiaye, R. Wolfrum and C. Kojima (eds.), *Law of the Sea, Environmental Law and Settlement of Disputes: Liber Amicorum Judge Thomas A. Mensah*, Leiden, etc., Nijhoff, 2007, pp. 811-820.
UNITED NATIONS OFFICE ON DRUGS AND CRIME, *Transnational Organized Crime in the Fishing Industry* (issue paper), Vienna, UNODC, 2011.
VIDAS, D., "Law, *Technology and Science for Oceans in Globalisation: IUU Fishing, Oil Pollution, Bioprospecting, Outer Continental Shelf*, Leiden, etc., Nijhoff, 2010.
—, "IUU Fishing or IUU Operations?: Some Observations on Diagnosis and Current Treatment", in D. D. Caron and H. N. Scheiber (eds.), *Bringing New Law to Ocean Waters*, Leiden, etc., Nijhoff, 2004, pp. 125-144.
WAGNER, B., "ILO Submission to the Workshop on IUU Fishing Activities", in *Fish Piracy: Combating Illegal Unreported and Unregulated Fishing*, Paris, OECD, 2004, pp. 281-283.
WARNER-KRAMER, D., "Control Begins at Home: Tackling Flags of Convenience and IUU Fishing", *Golden Gate University Law Review*, 34 (2004), No. 3, pp. 497-529.
WYNHOVEN, U. A., "OECD Instruments and IUU Fishing", in *Fish Piracy:*

Combating Illegal Unreported and Unregulated Fishing, Paris, OECD, 2004, pp. 333-364.

4 Trafic de stupéfiants maritime
Drug Trafficking

ANDERSON, D. A., "A European Perspective on Crimes at Sea and Trafficking in Weapons of Mass Destruction", in E. Franckx and Ph. Gautier (eds.), *The Exercise of Jurisdiction over Vessels: New Developments in the Fields of Pollution, Fisheries, Crimes at Sea and Trafficking of Weapons of Mass Destruction*, Brussels, Bruylant, 2010, pp. 171-184.

AUNE, B. R., "Maritime Drug Trafficking: An Underrated Problem", *Bulletin on Narcotics,* 42 (1990), No. 1, pp. 63-72.

—, «Contrebande de drogues par mer et patrouilles maritimes: un problème dont on a sous-estimé l'importance», *Bulletin des stupéfiants*, 42 (1990), No. 1, pp. 69-79.

BENNETT, A., "That Sinking Feeling: Stateless Ships, Universal Jurisdiction, and the Drug Trafficking Vessel Interdiction Act", *Yale Journal of International Law*, 37 (2012), No. 2, pp. 433-461.

BLAKESLEE, F. S., "United States v. Maynard and Enforcement of United States Drug Trafficking Laws on the High Seas: How Far Does United States Jurisdiction Really Reach?", *Pace Yearbook of International Law*, 2 (1990), pp. 169-194.

CELLE, P., and P. PALERMO, "Lotta al traffio di stupefacenti e diritti umani in alto mare", *Diritto marittimo*, 114 (2012), No. 1, pp. 120-142.

CHALK, P., *Grey-Area Phenomena in Southeast Asia: Piracy, Drug Trafficking and Political Terrorism*, Canberra, Strategic and Defence Studies Centre, Research School of Pacific and Asian Studies, Australian National University, 1997.

CURTIS, R. C., "The Outer Limits of Jurisdiction on the High Seas: United States v. Romero-Galue and United States v. Alvarez-Mena", *Wisconsin International Law Journal*, 5 (1986), pp. 222-240.

DAVIS-MATTIS, L., "International Drug Trafficking and the Law of the Sea: Outstanding Issues and Bilateral Responses with Emphasis on U.S.-Caribbean Agreements", *Ocean Yearbook*, 14 (2000), pp. 360-385.

ERRIGO, E., and I. MARINELLI, "Il traffico internazionale via mare di armi e stupefacenti: profili giuridice e poteri degli stati", in G. Reale (ed.), *Il contrasto alle attività illecite in mare*, Naples, Edizioni scientifiche italiane, 2011, pp. 189-220.

GILMORE, W. C., "Drug Trafficking at Sea: The Case of R. v. Charrington and Others", *International and Comparative Law Quarterly,* 49 (2000), No. 2, pp. 477-489.

—, "Narcotics Interdiction at Sea: The 1995 Council of Europe Agreement", *Marine Policy,* 20 (1996), No. 1, pp. 3-14.

—, "Drug Trafficking by Sea: The 1988 United Nations Convention against Illicit Traffic in Narcotic Drugs and Psychotropic Substances", *Marine Policy*, 15 (1991), No. 4, pp. 272-288.

GONZALEZ-PINTO, J., "Interdiction of Narcotics in International Waters", *University of Miami International and Comparative Law Review*, 15 (2008), No. 3, pp. 443-478.

HAUGHTON, S. A., "The Jamaica-Britain Border and Drug Trafficking", *Round Table*, 96 (2007), No. 390, pp. 279-303.

KONTOROVICH, E., "The 'Define and Punish' Clause and the Limits of Universal Jurisdiction", *Northwestern University Law Review*, 103 (2009), No. 1, pp 149-203.

KRAMEK, J. E., "Bilateral Maritime Counter-Drug and Immigrant Interdiction Agreements: Is This the World of the Future?", *The University of Miami Inter-American Law Review*, 31 (2000), No. 1, pp. 121-161.

KRUIT, P. J. J. VAN DER, *Maritime Drug Interdiction in International Law*, S.l., s.n., 2007.

MERRIAM, M. J., "United States Maritime Drug Trafficking Search and Seizure Policy: An Erosion of United States Constitutional and International Law Principles", *Suffolk Transnational Law Review*, 19 (1996), No. 2, pp. 441-472.

PAPASTAVRIDIS, E., *The Interception of Vessels on the High Seas: Contemporary Challenges to the Legal Order of the Oceans*, Oxford, Hart Publishing, 2013.

—, "Enforcement Jurisdiction in the Mediterranean Sea: Illicit Activities and the Rule of Law on the High Seas", *International Journal of Marine and Coastal Law*, 25 (2010), No. 4, pp. 569-599.

REALE, G. (dir. publ.), *Il contrasto alle attività illecite in mare*, Naples, Edizioni scientifiche, 2011.

SCHAMP, F., «Commerce maritime illégal et criminalité: le commerce de la drogue», dans L. Le Hardÿ de Beaulieu (dir. publ.), *Criminalité et trafics maritimes: des enjeux politiques aux conséquences juridiques,* Namur, Presses universitaires de Namur, 2008, pp. 75-79.

SORENSEN, C. E., "Drug Trafficking on the High Seas: A Move toward Universal Jurisdiction under International Law", *Emory International Law Review*, 4 (1990), No. 1, pp. 207-230.

TVEDT, O, "Drug Trafficking, Refugees, and Illegal Immigrants", in Proshanto K. Mukherjee, Maximo Q. Mejia and Gotthard M. Gauci (eds.), *Maritime Violence and Other Security Issues at Sea*, 2002, pp. 165-191.

UNITED NATIONS OFFICE ON DRUGS AND CRIME, *Transnational Organized Crime in the Fishing Industry* (issue paper), Vienna, UNODC, 2011.

VELUT, J.-L., «Protection de l'environnement et lutte contre les activités illicites: de l'évolution de la norme juridique à l'action en mer: l'exemple de la Méditerranée (1)», *Le droit maritime français*, 63 (2011), n° 726, pp. 518-533.

WILSON, B., "Submersibles and Transnational Criminal Organizations", *Ocean and Coastal Law Journal*, 17 (2011), No. 1, pp. 35-63.

5 Terrorisme maritime
Maritime Terrorism

ALESSIO, W. D'. «I percorsi della sicurezza in mare: dalla salvaguarda della vita umana alla difesa dai rischi di terrorismo internazionale», dans *Studi in onore di Umberto Leanza III*, Naples, Editoriale Scientifica, 2008, pp. 1605-1644.

ANDERSON, D. A., "A European Perspective on Crimes at Sea and Trafficking in Weapons of Mass Destruction", in E. Franckx and Ph. Gautier (eds.), *The Exercise of Jurisdiction over Vessels: New Developments in the Fields of Pollution, Fisheries, Crimes at Sea and Trafficking of Weapons of Mass Destruction*, Brussels, Bruylant, 2010, pp. 171-184.

BANLAOI, R. C., "The Abu Sayyaf Group: Threat of Maritime Piracy and Terrorism", in Peter Lehr (ed.), *Violence at Sea: Piracy in the Age of Global Terrorism*, New York, Routledge, 2007, pp. 121-137.

BATEMAN, S., "Outlook: The New Threat of Maritime Terrorism", in Peter Lehr (ed.), *Violence at Sea: Piracy in the Age of Global Terrorism*, New York, Routledge, 2007, pp. 241-262.

BECKMAN, R., and T. DAVENPORT, "Maritime Terrorism and the Law of the Sea: Basic Principles and New Challenges", in Myron H. Nordquist *et al.* (eds.), *The Law of the Sea Convention: US Accession and Globalization*, Leiden, Nijhoff, 2012, pp. 229-257.

BERTIN-MOUROT, E., F. LELIEUR et E. TERROIR, *Terrorisme et piraterie*, Paris, L'Harmattan, 2005.

Berube, C., and P. CULLEN (eds.), *Maritime Private Security: Market Responses to Piracy, Terrorism and Waterborne Security Risks in the 21st Century*, London, Routledge, 2012.

BLANCO-BAZÁN, A., "Protection and Safety in Maritime Transport: Measures by International Maritime Organizations", in J. M. Sobrino Heredia, *Sûreté maritime et violence en mer/Maritime Security and Violence at Sea*, Bruxelles, Bruylant, etc., 2011, pp. 381-410.

BOON, K. E., A. HUQ and D. C. LOVELACE (eds.), *Piracy and International Maritime Security*, New York, NY, etc., Oxford University Press, 2011.

BRINKTRINE, R., "Der Einsatz privater Sicherheitsdienste zum Schutz von Piraterie und maritimen Terrorismus: die staats- und verwaltungsrechtliche Sicht", in R. Stober (ed.), *Der Schutz vor Piraterie und maritimem Terrorismus zwischen internationaler, nationaler und unternehmerischer Verantwortung: brauchen wir zukünftig den Einsatz privater Sicherheitsdienste zum Schutz vor Piraterie?*, Cologne, Heyman, 2010, pp. 39-52.

BUZAWA, A. D., "Cruising with Terrorism: Jurisdictional Challenges to the Control of Terrorism in the Cruising Industry", *Tulane Maritime Law Journal*, 32 (2007), No. 1, pp. 181-202.

CHALK, P., "Maritime Terrorism: Scope, Dimensions and Potential Threat Contingencies", in Claude Berube and Patrick Cullen (eds.), *Maritime Private Security: Market Responses to Piracy, Terrorism and Waterborne Security Risks in the 21st Century*, London, Routledge, 2012, pp. 153-180.

CHEN, J., "The Emerging Nexus between Piracy and Maritime Terrorism in Southeast Asia Waters: A Case Study on the Gerakan Aceh Merdeka (GAM)", in Peter Lehr (ed.), *Violence at Sea: Piracy in the Age of Global Terrorism*, New York, Routledge, 2007, pp. 139-154.

CHIARA NOTO, M., «La repressione del terrorismo marittimo e del traffico illecito di armi di distruzione di massa dopo l'entrata in vigore della Convenzione SUA 2005», *La Comunità internazionale*, 6 (2011), n° 2, pp. 283-300.

CUDENNEC, A., «Terrorisme et piraterie maritimes: l'affirmation du statut de l'UE sur la scène internationale», dans J. M. Sobrino Heredia, *Sûreté maritime et violence en mer/Maritime Security and Violence at Sea*, Bruxelles, Bruylant, etc., 2011, pp. 191-209.

—, «Terrorisme et piraterie maritimes: l'UE affirme son statut d'acteur maritime international», *Revue du Marché commun et de l'Union européenne*, 2009, n° 532, pp. 599-607.

DAVIS, A. M., *Terrorism and the Maritime Transportation System: Are We on a Collision Course?*, Livermore, CA, WingSpan, 2008.

DIAZ, L. M., and B. H. DUBNER, "On the Problem of Utilizing Unilateral Action to Prevent Acts of Sea Piracy and Terrorism: A Proactive Approach to the Evolution of International Law", *Syracuse Journal of International Law and Commerce*, 32 (2004), No. 1, pp. 1-50.

—, "On the Evolution of the Law of International Sea Piracy: How Property Trumped Human Rights, the Environment and the Sovereign Rights of States in the Areas of the Creation and Enforcement of Jurisdiction", *Barry Law Review*, 13 (2009), No. 1, pp. 175-208.

DIREK, O. F., M. D. A. HAMILTON, K. S. OPENSHAW and P. C. R. TERRY, "Somalia and the Problem of Piracy in International Law", *USAK Yearbook of International Politics and Law*, 4 (2011), pp. 223-254.

DONG, W., and J. XIN, "China's Maritime Security: Priorities and Challenges", in Joshua H. Ho and Sam Bateman (eds.), *Maritime Challenges and Priorities in Asia: Implications for Regional Security*, London, Routledge, 2012, 181-200.

EICHSTAEDT, P. H., *Pirate State: Inside Somalia's Terrorism at Sea*, Chicago, IL, Lawrence Hill Books, 2010.

ESPALIÚ BERDUD, C., "The Crime of Maritime Piracy in the 2010 Reform of the Spanish Penal Code", *Spanish Yearbook of International Law*, 16 (2012), pp 55-93.

GARCIA-CORROCHANO MOYANO, L., «Le traitement de la piraterie et le terrorisme dans les espaces maritimes de l'Union des Nations de l'Amérique du

Sud-UNASUR», dans J. M. Sobrino Heredia, *Sûreté maritime et violence en mer/Maritime Security and Violence at Sea*, Bruxelles, Bruylant, etc., 2011, pp. 271-281.

GIL PÉREZ, J., «La piratería en el estrecho de Malaca: lecciones para el caso somalí», in Jesús Ramón Bacas Fernández *et al.* (dir. publ.), *Crisis somalí, piratería e intervención internacional*, Madrid, Instituto Universitario General Gutiérrez Mellado-UNED, 2009, pp. 97-123.

GINKEL, B. VAN, and F. P. VAN DER PUTTEN (eds.), *The International Response to Somali Piracy: Challenges and Opportunities*, Leiden, etc., Nijhoff, 2010.

GRAY, J., M. MONDAY AND G. STUBBLEFIELD, *Maritime Terror: Protecting Yourself, Your Vessel, and Your Crew against Piracy*, Boulder, CO, Paladin, 2011.

GUILFOYLE, D., "The Legal Challenges in Fighting Piracy", Bibi van Ginkel and Frans-Paul van der Putten (eds.), *The International Response to Somali Piracy: Challenges and Opportunities*, Leiden, Nijhoff, 2010, pp. 127-152.

HALBERSTAM, M., "Terrorism on the High Seas: The Achille Lauro, Piracy and the IMO Convention on Maritime Safety", *American Journal of International Law*, 82 (1988), pp. 269-310.

HALLWOOD, P., and TH. J. MICELI, "The Economics of International Cooperation in the Apprehension and Prosecution of Maritime Pirates", *Ocean Development and International Law*, 43 (2012), No. 2, pp. 188-200.

HAYWOOD, R., and R. SPIVAK, *Maritime Piracy*, London, etc., Routledge, 2012.

HELLER-ROAZEN, D., *The Enemy of All: Piracy and the Law of Nations*, New York, Zone Books, 2009.

—, traduit de l'anglais par Françoise et Paul Chemla, *L'ennemi de tous: le pirate contre les nations*, Paris, Seuil, 2010.

HERBERT-BURNS, R., "Compound Piracy at Sea in the Early Twenty-first Century: A Tactical to Operational-Level Perspective on Contemporary, Multiphase Piratical Methodology", in Peter Lehr, *Violence at Sea: Piracy in the Age of Global Terrorism*, New York, Routledge, 2007, pp. 95-120.

HUGUES, E., «Le terrorisme maritime, une nouvelle forme de guerre», *Outre-Terre: Revue européenne de géopolitique*, 25-26 (2010), pp. 83-99.

JOYNER, C. C., "Suppression of Terrorism on the High Seas: The 1988 IMO Convention on the Safety of Maritime Navigation", *Israel Yearbook on Human Rights,* 19 (1990), pp. 341-369.

—, "Navigating Troubled Waters — Somalia, Piracy, and Maritime Terrorism", *Georgetown Journal of International Affairs*, 10 (2009), No. 1, pp. 83-92.

—, "The 1988 IMO Convention on the Safety of Maritime Navigation: Towards a Legal Remedy of Terrorism at Sea", *German Yearbook of International Law*, 31 (1989), pp. 230-262.

KIM, S. K., "Maritime Security Initiatives in East Asia: Assessment and the Way Forward", *Ocean Development and International Law*, 42 (2011), No. 3, pp. 227-244.

KLEIN, N., J. MOSSOP and D. R. ROTHWELL (eds.), "Maritime Security: International Law and Policy Perspectives from Australia and New Zealand", London, Routledge, 2011.

—, "The Right of Visit and the 2005 Protocol on the Suppression of Unlawful Acts against the Safety of Maritime Navigation", *Denver Journal of International Law and Policy*, 35 (2007), No. 2, pp. 287-332.

KOLB, A. S., T. R. SALOMON and J. UDICH (eds.), "Paying Danegeld to Pirates: Humanitarian Necessity or Financing Jihadists", *Max Planck Yearbook of United Nations Law*, 15 (2011), pp. 105-164.

KONTOROVICH, E., "'A Guantánamo on the Sea': The Difficulty of Prosecuting Pirates and Terrorists", *California Law Review*, 98 (2010), No. 1, pp. 243-275.

LE HARDŸ DE BEAULIEU, L., «Le terrorisme maritime», dans L. Le Hardÿ de Beaulieu (dir. publ.), *Criminalité et trafics maritimes: des enjeux politiques aux conséquences juridiques*, Namur, Presses universitaires de Namur, 2008, pp. 31-50.

LEHR, P. (ed.), *Violence at Sea: Piracy in the Age of Global Terrorism*, New York, Routledge, 2007.

LEHR, P., and H. Lehmann, "Somalia: Pirates' New Paradise", in Peter Lehr, *Violence at Sea: Piracy in the Age of Global Terrorism*, New York, Routledge, 2007, pp. 1-22.

LENNOX-GENTLE, T., "Piracy, Sea Robbery, and Terrorism: Enforcing Laws to Deter Ransom Payments and Hijacking", *Transportation Law Journal*, 37 (2010), No. 3, pp. 199-218.

LÓPEZ RUEDA, F. C., « Piratería maritíma, terrorismo y figuras afines », *Anuario de derecho maritime*, 29 (2012), pp. 55-123.

MACDORMAN, T. L., "Maritime Terrorism and the International Law of Boarding of Vessels at Sea: A Brief Assessment of the New Developments", in David D. Caron and Harry N. Scheiber (eds.), *The Oceans in the Nuclear Age: Legacies and Risks*, Leiden, Nijhoff, 2010, pp. 239-264.

MAK, J. N., "Pirates, Renegades, and Fishermen: The Politics of 'Sustainable' Piracy in the Strait of Malacca", in Peter Lehr, *Violence at Sea: Piracy in the Age of Global Terrorism*, New York, Routledge, 2007, pp. 199-223.

—, "Maritime Security and the ARF: Why the Focus on Dialiogue rather than Action", in J. Haacke and N. M. Morada, *Cooperative Security in the Asia-Pacific: The ASEAN Regional Forum*, London, etc., Routledge, 2011, pp. 172-198.

MCLAUGHLIN, R., "Terrorism as a Central Theme in the Evolution of Maritime Operations Law since 11 September 2011", *Yearbook of International Humanitarian Law*, 14 (2012), pp. 391-409.

MELLOR, J. S. C., "Missing the Boat: The Legal and Practical Problems of the Prevention of Maritime Terrorism", *American University International Law Review*, 18 (2002), No 2, pp. 341-397.

MURPHY, M. N., "Piracy and UNCLOS: Does International Law Help Regional States Combat Piracy?", in Peter Lehr (ed.), *Violence at Sea: Piracy in the Age of Global Terrorism*, New York, Routledge, 2007, pp. 155-182.

—, *Somalia: the New Barbary? Piracy and Islam in the Horn of Africa*, New York, NY, Columbia University Press, 2011.

—, *Contemporary Piracy and Maritime Terrorism: The Threat to International Security*, London, etc., Routledge, 2012.

ODIER, F., « Piraterie, terrorisme : une ménace pour les navires, un défi pour le droit de la mer », *Annuaire du droit de la mer*, 10 (2005), pp. 263-274.

ONG-WEBB, G. G., "Piracy in Maritime Asia: Current Trends", in Peter Lehr (ed.), *Violence at Sea: Piracy in the Age of Global Terrorism*, New York, Routledge, 2007, pp. 37-93.

ONG-WEBB, G. G. (ed.), *Piracy, Maritime Terrorism and Securing the Malacca Straits*, Leiden, International Institute for Asian Studies, 2006.

ORIOLO, A., "The Multilateral Approach of the EU Maritime Security Policy: The Fight against Piracy, Terrorism and Violence at Sea", *The Global Community*, 1 (2009), pp. 251-266.

PONTECORVO, C. M., "Failing Somalia, Trapped in the Vicious Circle of Unsolved Old Issues and Rampant New Piracy: Current Legal Challenges (Part II)", in Giancarlo Guarino and Ilaria D'Anna (eds.) *International Institutions and Co-operation: Terrorism, Migrations, Asylum: 2nd Naples Colloquium, 9-11 December 2010*, Naples, Satura Editrice, 2011, pp. 67-130.

POWER, J., "Maritime Terrorism: A New Challenge to National and International Security", *Barry Law Review*, 10 (2008), pp. 111-138.

ROSENBERG, D., "The Maritime Borderlands: Terrorism, Piracy, Pollution, and Poaching in the South China Sea", in James Clad, Sean M. McDonald, and Bruce Vaughn (eds.), *The Borderlands of Southeast Asia: Geopolitics, Terrorism and Globalization*, Washington, DC, National Defense University Press, 2011, pp. 107-126.

ROTHWELL, D. R., and N. Klein, "Maritime Security and the Law of the Sea",

Natalie Klein, Joanna Mossop and Donald R. Rothwell (eds.), *Maritime Security: International Law and Policy Perspectives from Australia and New Zealand*, Abingdon, Routledge, 2010, pp. 22-36.

SAKHUJA, V., "Sea Piracy in South Asia", in Peter Lehr (ed.), *Violence at Sea: Piracy in the Age of Global Terrorism*, New York, Routledge, 2007, pp. 23-36.

SALONIO, L., and R. Sinha, "International, Regional and National Approaches towards Maritime Security Issues of Terrorism", in Proshanto K. Mukherjee, Maximo Q. Mejia and Gotthard M. Gauci (eds.), *Maritime Violence and Other Security Issues at Sea*, 2002, pp. 221-252.

SEIDEL, G., "Völkerrechtliche Aspekte des Kampfes gegen Piraterie und maritimen Terrorismus unter Einbeziehung privater Sicherheitsdienste", in R. Stober (ed.), *Der Schutz vor Piraterie und maritimem Terrorismus zwischen internationaler, nationaler und unternehmerischer Verantwortung: brauchen wir zukünftig den Einsatz privater Sicherheitsdienste zum Schutz vor Piraterie?*, Cologne, Heyman, 2010, pp. 19-38.

SHANOR, C. A., "Terrorism, Historical Analogies, and Modern Choices", *Emory International Law Review*, 24 (2010), No. 2, pp. 589-617.

SITTNICK, T. M., "State Responsibility and Maritime Terrorism in the Strait of Malacca: Persuading Indonesia and Malaysia to Take Additional Steps to Secure the Strait", *Pacific Rim Law and Policy Journal*, 14 (2005), pp. 743-769.

SNODDON, R., "Piracy and Maritime Terrorism: Naval Responses to Existing and Emerging Threats to the Global Seaborne Economy", in Peter Lehr (ed.), *Violence at Sea: Piracy in the Age of Global Terrorism*, New York, Routledge, 2007, pp. 225-240.

SOBRINO, J. M., «Le terrorisme et la piraterie maritime», dans J. M. Sobrino Heredia, *Sûreté maritime et violence en mer/Maritime Security and Violence at Sea*, Bruxelles, Bruylant, etc., 2011, pp. 155-190.

SOBRINO HEREDIA, J. M., *Sûreté maritime et violence en mer/Maritime Security and Violence at Sea*, Bruxelles, Bruylant, etc., 2011.

STEVENSON, J., "Jihad and Piracy in Somalia", *Survival*, 52 (2010), No. 1, pp. 27-38.

STILLWELL, N., "Robbers or Robinhoods: A Study of the Somali Piracy Crisis and a Call to Develop an International Framework to Combat Maritime Terrorism", *Loyola Maritime Law Journal*, 7 (2009), pp. 127-146.

STOBER, R. (ed.), *Der Schutz vor Piraterie und maritimem Terrorismus zwischen internationaler, nationaler und unternehmerischer Verantwortung: brauchen wir zukünftig den Einsatz privater Sicherheitsdienste zum Schutz vor Piraterie?*, Cologne, Heymann, 2010.

TARASENKO, S.,"The United Nations' Role in Combatting Piracy and Terrorism at Sea", in Myron H. Nordquist *et al.* (eds.), *The Law of the Sea Convention: US Accession and Globalization*, Leiden, Nijhoff, 2012, pp. 143-153.

TASSEL, Y., «Terrorisme, piraterie et guerre sous le rapport de l'assurance maritime», *Annuaire de droit maritime et oceanique*, 23 (2006), pp. 77-94.

TREVES, T., "Violenza in mare: iniziative dopo l'11 settembre 2001", *Studi in onore di Umberto Leanza III*, Naples, Editoriale scientifica, 2008, pp. 1817-1823.

TÜRK, H., "The Resurgence of Piracy: A Phenomenon of Modern Times", *University of Miami International and Comparative Law*, 17 (2009), No. 1, pp. 1-42.

—, "Combating Terrorism at Sea: The Suppression of Unlawful Acts against the Safety of Maritime Navigation", in Myron H. Nordquist *et al.* (eds.), *Legal Challenges in Maritime Security*, Leiden, etc., Nijhoff, 2008, pp. 41-78.

TURNER, R. F., "State Responsibility and the War on Terror: The Legacy of Thomas Jefferson and the Barbary Pirates", *Chicago Journal of International Law*, 4 (2003), No. 1, pp. 121-140.

VALLON, F., *La mer et son droit, entre liberté et consensualisme, l'impossible gestion de la piraterie et du terrorisme*, Paris, Publibook, 2011.

VÁZQUEZ GÓMEZ, E. M., «Terrorism and Piracy», dans J. M. Sobrino Heredia, *Sûreté maritime et violence en mer/Maritime Security and Violence at Sea*, Bruxelles, Bruylant, etc., 2011, pp. 343-346.

ZOU, K., "Maritime Security and Multilateral Interactions between China and Its Neighbours", in Guoguang Wu and Helen Lansdowne (eds.), *China Turns to Multilateralism: Foreign Policy and Regional Security*, London, etc., Routledge, 2008, pp. 147-172.

6 Prolifération des armes de destruction massive (ADM) Proliferation of Weapons of Mass Destruction

ALLEN, Ch., "Countering Proliferation: WMD on the Move", *Georgia Journal of International and Comparative Law*, 40 (2011), No. 1, pp. 15-35.

ANDERSON, D. A., "A European Perspective on Crimes at Sea and Trafficking in Weapons of Mass Destruction", in E. Franckx and Ph. Gautier (eds.), *The Exercise of Jurisdiction over Vessels: New Developments in the Fields of Pollution, Fisheries, Crimes at Sea and Trafficking of Weapons of Mass Destruction*, Brussels, Bruylant, 2010, pp. 171-184.

BECKER, M. A., "The Shifting Public Order of the Oceans: Freedom of Navigation and the Interdiction of Ships at Sea", *Harvard International Law Journal*, 46 (2005), No. 1, pp. 131-230.

BECKMAN, R., and T. Davenport, "Maritime Terrorism and the Law of the Sea: Basic Principles and New Challenges", in Myron H. Nordquist *et al.* (eds.), *The Law of the Sea Convention: US Accession and Globalization*, Leiden, Nijhoff, 2012, pp. 229-257.

BYERS, M., "Policing the High Seas: The Proliferation Security Initiative", *American Journal of International Law*, 98 (2004), No. 3, pp. 526-545.

CHIARA NOTO, M., «La repressione del terrorismo marittimo e del traffico illecito di armi di distruzione di massa dopo l'entrata in vigore della Convenzione SUA 2005», *La Comunità internazionale*, 6 (2011), n° 2, pp. 283-300.

FRANCKX, E., and PH. GAUTIER (eds.), *The Exercise of Jurisdiction over Vessels: New Developments in the Fields of Pollution, Fisheries, Crimes at Sea and Trafficking of Weapons of Mass Destruction*, Brussels, Bruylant, 2010.

FROWEIN, J. A.,"The Security Council and the Security on the Seas", in Holger Hestermeyer *et al.* (eds.), *Law of the Sea in Dialogue*, Heidelberg, Springer, 2011, pp. 179-189.

GUILFOYLE, D., "Maritime Interdiction of Weapons of Mass Destruction", *Journal of Conflict and Security Law*, 12 (2007), No. 1, pp. 1-35.

—, "Interdicting Vessels to Enforce the Common Interest: Maritime Countermeasures and the Use of Force", *The International and Comparative Law Quarterly*, 56 (2007), No. 1, pp.69-82.

—, "Maritime Interdiction of Weapons of Mass Destruction", *Journal of Conflict and Security Law*, 12 (2007), No. 1, pp. 1-35.

—, "The Proliferation Security Initiative: Interdicting Vessels in International Waters to Prevent the Spread of Weapons of Mass Destruction", *Melbourne University Law Review*, 29 (2005), No. 3, pp. 733-764.

HODGKINSON, S. L., "Challenges to Maritime Interception Operations in the War on Terror: Bridging the Gap", *American University International Law Review*, 22 (2007), No. 4, pp. 583-671.

JIMENEZ KWAST, P., "Maritime Interdiction of Weapons of Mass Destruction in an International Legal Perspective", *Netherlands Yearbook of International Law*, 38 (2007), pp. 163-241.

KEYUAN, Z., "Maritime Enforcement of United Nations Security Council Resolutions: Use of Force and Coercive Measures", *International Journal of Marine and Coastal Law*, 26 (2011), No. 2, pp. 235-261.

KIM, S. K., "Maritime Security Initiatives in East Asia: Assessment and the Way Forward", *Ocean Development and International Law,* 42 (2011), No. 3, pp. 227-244.

KLEIN, N., *Maritime Security and the Law of the Sea*, Oxford, Oxford University Press, 2011.

KRASKA, J., "Broken Taillight at Sea: The Peacetime International Law of Visit, Board, Search, and Seizure", *Ocean and Coastal Law Journal*, 16 (2011), No. 1, pp. 1-46.

MACDORMAN, T. L., "Maritime Terrorism and the International Law of Boarding of Vessels at Sea: A Brief Assessment of the New Developments", in David D. Caron and Harry N. Scheiber (eds.), *The Oceans in the Nuclear Age: Legacies and Risks*, Leiden, Nijhoff, 2010, pp. 239-264.

OXMAN, B. H., "Crimes at Sea and Trafficking of Weapons of Mass Destruction: General Report", in E. Franckx and Ph. Gautier (eds.), *The Exercise of Jurisdiction over Vessels: New Developments in the Fields of Pollution, Fisheries, Crimes at Sea and Trafficking of Weapons of Mass Destruction*, Brussels, Bruylant, 2010, pp. 137-150.

PAPASTAVRIDIS, E., *The Interception of Vessels on the High Seas: Contemporary Challenges to the Legal Order of the Oceans*, Oxford, Hart Publishing, 2013.

—, "Enforcement Jurisdiction in the Mediterranean Sea: Illicit Activities and the Rule of Law on the High Seas", *International Journal of Marine and Coastal Law*, 25 (2010), No. 4, pp. 569-599.

ROACH, J. A., "An American Perspective on Crimes at Sea and Trafficking of Weapons of Mass Destruction" in E. Franckx and Ph. Gautier (eds.), *The Exercise of Jurisdiction over Vessels: New Developments in the Fields of Pollution, Fisheries, Crimes at Sea and Trafficking of Weapons of Mass Destruction*, Brussels, Bruylant, 2010, pp. 151-169.

7 Le trafic des êtres humains; l'esclavage
Human Trafficking; Slave Trade

ABAD CASTELOS, M., "Measures Taken by International Organizations to Combat Illicit Human Trafficking and Transnational Organized Crime", in J. M. Sobrino Heredia, *Sûreté maritime et violence en mer/Maritime Security and Violence at Sea*, Bruxelles, Bruylant, etc., 2011, pp. 47-68.

ARIAS FERNÁNDEZ, G., "FRONTEX and Illegal Immigration in the European Union", in J.M. Sobrino Heredia, *Sûreté maritime et violence en mer/Maritime Security and Violence at Sea*, Bruxelles, Bruylant, etc., 2011, pp. 29-46.

CASADO RAIGÓN, R., «Trafic illicite des personnes et criminalité transnationale organisée», dans J. M. Sobrino Heredia, *Sûreté maritime et violence en mer/Maritime Security and Violence at Sea*, Bruxelles, Bruylant, etc., 2011, pp. 3-18.

COHEN, M., "Analogy between Piracy and Human Trafficking: A Theoretical Framework for the Application of Universal Jurisdiction", *Buffalo Human Rights Law Review*, 16 (2010), pp. 201-236.

DEL VALLE-GALVEZ, A., «Mesures nationales sur le trafic illicite de personnes et la criminalité transnationale organisée», dans J. M. Sobrino Heredia, *Sûreté maritime et violence en mer/Maritime Security and Violence at Sea*, Bruxelles, Bruylant, etc., 2011, pp. 19-28.

EBERL, O., "Dialektik des Abolitionismus: die völkerrechtliche Ächtung des Sklavenhandels und die europäische Expansion im 19. Jahrhundert", in Rainer Klump and Miloÿés Vec (eds.), *Völkerrecht und Weltwirtschaft im 19. Jahrhundert,* Baden-Baden , Nomos, 2012, pp. 197-219.

FERNÁNDEZ SÁNCHEZ, P. A., "Illegal Trafficking of People of the High Seas", in

J. M. Sobrino Heredia, *Sûreté maritime et violence en mer/Maritime Security and Violence at Sea*, Bruxelles, Bruylant, etc., 2011, pp. 69-84.

FERNÁNDEZ SÁNCHEZ, P. A., « Tráfica ilegal de personas y cooperacíon marítima internacional », dans Jorge Pueyo Losa and Julio Jorge Urbina (dir. publ.), *La cooperación internacional en la ordenación de los mares y océanos*, Madrid, Lustel, 2009, pp. 363-396.

FIADINO, A., "Il divieto di tratta de esseri umani via mare", dans G. Reale (dir. publ.), *Il contrasto alle attività illecite in mare*, Naples, Edizioni scientifiche italiane, 2011, pp. 105-158.

LIROLA DELGADO, L., « España y la lucha contra el tráfico ilícito de inmigrantes por mar », dans Jorge Pueyo Losa et Julio Jorge Urbina (dir. publ.), *La cooperación internacional en la ordenación de los mares y océanos*, Madrid , Iustel, 2009, pp. 397-429.

—, "Spain and the Smuggling of Immigrants by Sea: An Analysis in the Light of the Palermo Protocol", in J. M. Sobrino Heredia, *Sûreté maritime et violence en mer/Maritime Security and Violence at Sea*, Bruxelles, Bruylant, etc., 2011, pp. 85-102.

MENEFEE, S. P., "The Smuggling of Refugees by Sea: A Modern Day Maritime Slave Trade", *Regent Journal of International Law*, 2 (2003-2004), No. 1, pp. 1-28.

MORGAN, Ph. D., *Maritime Slavery*, London, etc., Routledge, 2012.

NESSEL, L. A., "Externalized Borders and the Invisible Refugee", *Columbia Human Rights Law Review*, 40 (2009), No. 3, pp. 625-699.

PALLIS, M., "Obligations of States towards Asylum Seekers at Sea: Interactions and Conflicts between Legal Regimes", *International Journal of Refugee Law*, 14 (2002), No. 2-3, pp. 329-364.

PAPASTAVRIDIS, E., "Enforcement Jurisdiction in the Mediterranean Sea: Illicit Activities and the Rule of Law on the High Seas", *International Journal of Marine and Coastal Law*, 25 (2010), No. 4, pp. 569-599.

—, "'Fortress Europe' and FRONTEX: Within or Without International Law?", *Nordic Journal of International Law,* 79 (2010), No. 1, pp. 75-111.

—, "Interception of Human Beings on the High Seas: A Contemporary Analysis under International Law", *Syracuse Journal of International Law and Commerce*, 36 (2009), No. 2, pp. 145-228.

QUINDIMIL LÓPEZ, J. A., "The United Nations and the Fight against Transnational Organised Crime: The Application of the Palermo Protocol to the Smuggling of Migrants by Sea", in J. M. Sobrino Heredia, *Sûreté maritime et violence en mer/Maritime Security and Violence at Sea*, Bruxelles, Bruylant, etc., 2011, pp. 115-130.

REALE, G. (dir. publ.), *Il contrasto alle attività illecite in mare*, Naples, Edizioni Scientifiche, 2011.

REY ANEIROS, A., "Illegal Human Trafficking and Transnational Organized Crime", in J. M. Sobrino Heredia, *Sûreté maritime et violence en mer/Maritime Security and Violence at Sea*, Bruxelles, Bruylant, etc., 2011, pp. 145-151.

ROBINSON, B. W., "Smuggled Masses: The Need for a Maritime Alien Smuggling Law Enforcement Act", *Army Lawyer*, 2010 (2010), No. 8, pp. 20-40.

SOBRINO HEREDIA, J. M., *Sûreté maritime et violence en mer/Maritime Security and Violence at Sea*, Bruxelles, Bruylant, etc., 2011.

STANSLAS, P. T., "Transborder Human Trafficking in Malaysian Waters: Addressing the Root Causes", *Journal of Maritime Law and Commerce*, 41 (2010), No. 4, pp. 595-606.

UNITED NATIONS OFFICE ON DRUGS AND CRIME, *Transnational Organized Crime in the Fishing Industry* (issue paper), Vienna, UNODC, 2011.

ZINSMEISTER, J. E., "In Rem Actions under U.S. Admiralty Jurisdiction as an Effective Means of Obtaining Thirteenth Amendment Relief to Combat Modern Slavery", *California Law Review*, 93 (2005), No. 4, pp. 1249-1284.

8 Le trafic illicite de migrants
Migrant Smuggling

ABAD CASTELOS, M., "Measures Taken by International Organizations to Combat Illicit Human Trafficking and Transnational Organized Crime", in J. M. Sobrino Heredia, *Sûreté maritime et violence en mer/Maritime Security and Violence at Sea*, Bruxelles, Bruylant, etc., 2011, pp. 47-68.

ANDREONE, G., et G. CATALDI, «Regards sur les évolutions du droit de la mer en Méditerranée», *Annuaire français de droit international,* 56 (2010), pp. 1-39.

ARIAS FERNÁNDEZ, G., "FRONTEX and Illegal Immigration in the European Union", in J. M. Sobrino Heredia, *Sûreté maritime et violence en mer/Maritime Security and Violence at Sea*, Bruxelles, Bruylant, etc., 2011, pp. 29-46.

BARNES, R., "The International Law of the Sea and Migration Control", Bernard Ryan and Valsamis Mitsilegas, *Extraterritorial Immigration Control: Legal Challenges*, Leiden, etc., Nijhoff, 2010, pp. 103-149.

BLOUW, N. DE, "Drowning Policies: A Proposal to Modify the Dublin Agreement and Reduce Human Rights Abuses in the Mediterranean", *California Western International Law Journal,* 40 (2010), No. 2, pp. 335-368.

BROLAN, C., "An Analysis of the Human Smuggling Trade and the Protocol against the Smuggling of Migrants by Land, Air and Sea (2000) from a Refugee Protection Perspective", *International Journal of Refugee Law*, 14 (2002), No. 4, pp. 561-596.

BROWN, D. L., "Crooked Straits: Maritime Smuggling of Humans from Cuba to the United States", *University of Miami Inter-American Law Review*, 33 (2002), No. 2-3, pp. 273-293.

BULGHERINI, E. T., «Il traffico via mare di clandestini», *Studi in onore di Umberto Leanza III*, Naples, Editoriale scientifica, 2008, pp. 1837-1866.

CASADO RAIGÓN, R., «Trafic illicite des personnes et criminalité transnationale organisée», dans J. M. Sobrino Heredia, *Sûreté maritime et violence en mer/ Maritime Security and Violence at Sea*, Bruxelles, Bruylant, etc., 2011, pp. 3-18.

DEL VALLE-GALVEZ, A., «Mesures nationales sur le trafic illicite de personnes et la criminalité transnationale organisée», dans J. M. Sobrino Heredia, *Sûreté maritime et violence en mer/Maritime Security and Violence at Sea*, Bruxelles, Bruylant, etc., 2011, pp. 19-28.

FERNÁNDEZ SÁNCHEZ, P. A., "Illegal Trafficking of People of the High Seas", in J. M. Sobrino Heredia, *Sûreté maritime et violence en mer/Maritime Security and Violence at Sea*, Bruxelles, Bruylant, etc., 2011, pp. 69-84.

—, «Tráfica ilegal de personas y cooperacíon marítima internacional», dans Jorge Pueyo Losa and Julio Jorge Urbina (dir. publ.), *La cooperación internacional en la ordenación de los mares y océanos*, Madrid , Iustel, 2009, pp. 363-396.

GAMMELTOFT-HANSEN, T., "The Refugee, the Sovereign, and the Sea: European Union Interdiction Policies", in Rebecca Adler-Nissen and Thomas Gammeltoft-Hansen (eds.), *Sovereignty Games: Instrumentalizing State Sovereignty in Europe and Beyond*, New York, Palgrave Macmillan, 2008, pp. 171-195.

GOODWIN-GILL, G. S., "The Right to Seek Asylum: Interception at Sea and the Principle of Non-Refoulement", *International Journal of Refugee Law*, 23 (2011), No. 3, pp. 443-457.

HINRICHS, X., "Measures against Smuggling of Migrants at Sea: A Law of the Sea Related Perspective", *Revue belge de droit international*, 36 (2003), No. 2, pp. 413-451.

KLEPP, S., "A Double Bind: Malta and the Rescue of Unwanted Migrants at Sea, a Legal Anthropological Perspective on the Humanitarian Law of the Sea", *International Journal of Refugee Law,* 23 (2011) No. 3, pp. 538-557.

KRAMEK, J. E., "Bilateral Maritime Counter-Drug and Immigrant Interdiction Agreements: Is This the World of the Future?", *The University of Miami Inter-American Law Review*, 31 (2000), No. 1, pp. 121-161.

KRIEKEN, P. VAN, "Migrant's Rights and the Law of the Sea: Further Efforts to Ensure Universal Participation", *International Migration,* 45 (2007), No. 1, pp. 209-224.

LIGUORI, A., «La Corte europea dei diritti dell'uomo condanna l'Italia per i respingimenti verso la Libia del 2009: il caso Hirsi», *Rivista di diritto internazionale,* 95 (2012), n° 2, pp. 415-443.

LIROLA DELGADO, I., «España y la lucha contra el tráfico ilícito de inmigrantes por mar», dans Jorge Pueyo Losa et Julio Jorge Urbina (dir. publ.), *La cooperación internacional en la ordenación de los mares y océanos*, Madrid , Lustel, 2009, pp. 397-429.

MALLIA, P., *Migrant Smuggling by Sea: Combating a Current Threat to Maritime Security through the Creation of a Cooperative Framework*, Leiden, Nijhoff, 2010.

MATHEW, P., "Legal Issues concerning Interception", *Georgetown Immigration Law Journal*, 17 (2003), No. 2, pp. 221-250.

MILTNER, B., "Irregular Maritime Migration: Refugee Protection Issues in Rescue and Interception", *Fordham International Law Journal*, 30 (2006), No. 1, pp. 75-125.

MORENO LAX, V., "The EU Regime on Interdiction, Search and Rescue, and Disembarkation: The Frontex Guidelines for Intervention at Sea", *International Journal of Marine and Coastal Law*, 25 (2010), No. 4, pp. 621-635.

—, "Seeking Asylum in the Mediterranean: Against a Fragmentary Reading of EU Member States' Obligations Accruing at Sea", *International Journal of Refugee Law,* 23 (2011), No. 2, pp. 174-220.

MYOE, M. A., "Myanmar's Maritime Challenges and Priorities", in Joshua H. Ho and Sam Bateman (eds.), *Maritime Challenges and Priorities in Asia: Implications for Regional Security*, London, Routledge, 2012, pp. 83-105.

NESSEL, L. A., "Externalized Borders and the Invisible Refugee", *Columbia Human Rights Law Review*, 40 (2009), No. 3, pp. 625-699.

OBOKATA, T., "The Legal Framework concerning the Smuggling of Migrants at Sea under the UN Protocol on the Smuggling of Migrants by Land, Sea and Air", in B. Ryan and V. Mitsilegas (eds.), *Extraterritorial Immigration Control: Legal Challenges*, Leiden, etc., Nijhoff, 2010, pp. 151-166.

OLLUS, N., "Protocol against the Smuggling of Migrants by Land, Air and Sea, Supplementing the United Nations Convention against Transnational Organized Crime: A Tool for Criminal Justice Personnel", *Resource Material Series*, 62 (2004), pp. 31-43.

PAPASTAVRIDIS, E., "Enforcement Jurisdiction in the Mediterranean Sea: Illicit Activities and the Rule of Law on the High Seas", *International Journal of Marine and Coastal Law*, 25 (2010), No. 4, pp. 569-599.

—, "'Fortress Europe' and FRONTEX: Within or Without International Law?", *Nordic Journal of International Law*, 79 (2010), No. 1, pp. 75-111.

—, "Interception of Human Beings on the High Seas: A Contemporary Analysis under International Law", *Syracuse Journal of International Law and Commerce*, 36 (2009), No. 2, pp. 145-228.

PARISCIANI, E., «I respingimenti in Libia tra contrasto all'immigrazione clandestina e rispetto dei diritti umani», dans Maurizio Simoncelli (dir. publ.), *Dove i diritti umani non esistono più: la violazione dei diritti umani nelle guerre contemporanee,* Rome, Ediesse, 2010, pp. 153-177.

QUINDIMIL LÓPEZ, J. A., "The United Nations and the Fight against Transnational Organised Crime: The Application of the Palermo Protocol to the Smuggling of Migrants by Sea", in J. M. Sobrino Heredia, *Sûreté maritime et violence en mer/Maritime Security and Violence at Sea*, Bruxelles, Bruylant, etc., 2011, pp. 115-130.

REY ANEIROS, A., "Illegal Human Trafficking and Transnational Organized Crime", in J. M. Sobrino Heredia, *Sûreté maritime et violence en mer/Maritime Security and Violence at Sea*, Bruxelles, Bruylant, etc., 2011, pp. 145-151.

ROBINSON, B. W., "Smuggled Masses: The Need for a Maritime Alien Smuggling Law Enforcement Act", *Army Lawyer*, 2010 (2010), No. 8, pp. 20-40.

RONZITTI, N., "Coastal State Jurisdiction over Refugees and Migrants at Sea", in N. Ando, E. McWhinney, R. Wolfrum and B. B. Röben (eds.), *Liber Amicorum Judge Shigeru Oda* (Vol. 2), The Hague, etc., Kluwer Law International, 2002, pp. 1271-1286.

SOBRINO HEREDIA, J. M., *Sûreté maritime et violence en mer/Maritime Security and Violence at Sea*, Bruxelles, Bruylant, etc., 2011.

TONDINI, M., "The Legality of Intercepting Boat People under Search and Rescue and Border Control Operations: With Reference to Recent Italian Interventions in the Mediterranean Sea and the ECtHR Decision in the Hirsi Case", *Journal of International Maritime Law*, 18 (2012), No. 1, pp. 59-74.

TREVISANUT, S., "Search and Rescue Operations in the Mediterranean: Factor of Cooperation or Conflict?", *International Journal of Marine and Coastal Law*, 25 (2010), No. 4, pp. 523-542.

TRIANDAFYLLIDOU, A., and T. MAROUKIS, *Migrant Smuggling: Irregular Migration from Asia and Africa to Europe*, Basingstoke, etc., Palgrave Macmillan, 2012.

TVEDT, O, "Drug Trafficking, Refugees, and Illegal Immigrants", in Proshanto K. Mukherjee, Maximo Q. Mejia and Gotthard M. Gauci (eds.), *Maritime Violence and Other Security Issues at Sea*, 2002, pp. 165-191.

UNITED NATIONS OFFICE ON DRUGS AND CRIME, *Transnational Organized Crime in the Fishing Industry* (issue paper), Vienna, UNODC, 2011.

—, *Smuggling of Migrants by Sea* (issue paper), Vienna, UNODC, 2011.

VAUGHAN-WILLIAMS, N., "Off-Shore Biopolitical Border Security: The EU's Global Response to Migration, Piracy, and 'Risky' Subjects", in L. Bialasiewicz (ed.), *Europe in the World: EU Geopolitics and the Transformation of European Space*, Farnham, etc., Ashgate, 2011, pp. 185-200.

9 L'obligation d'assistance et de sauvetage
Search and Rescue Operations

ABBOTT, Ch. J., "Hijacked: Somalia Sanctions Hold U.S. Ship Owners Hostage", *Suffolk Transnational Law Review*, 35 (2012), No. 1, pp. 101-120.

ALESSIO, W. D'. "I percorsi della sicurezza in mare: dalla salvaguarda della vita umana alla difesa dai rischi di terrorismo internazionale", *Studi in onore di Umberto Leanza III*, Naples, Editoriale Scientifica, 2008, pp. 1605-1644.

DAVIES, M., "Obligations and Implications for Ships Encountering Persons in Need of Assistance at Sea", *Pacific Rim Law and Policy Journal*, 12 (2003), pp. 109-141.

JENISCH, U., "Piracy, Navies and the Law of the Sea: The Case of Somalia", *WMU Journal of Maritime Affairs*, 8 (2009), No. 2, pp. 123-143.

KENNEY, F. J., and V. Tasikas, "The Tampa Incident: IMO Perspectives and Responses on the Treatment of Persons Rescued at Sea", *Pacific Rim Law and Policy Journal*, 12 (2003), pp. 143-177.

KLEIN, N., "The Right of Visit and the 2005 Protocol on the Suppression of Unlawful Acts against the Safety of Maritime Navigation", *Denver Journal of International Law and Policy*, 35 (2007), No. 2, pp. 287-332.

KLEPP, S., "A Double Bind: Malta and the Rescue of Unwanted Migrants at Sea, a Legal Anthropological Perspective on the Humanitarian Law of the Sea", *International Journal of Refugee Law*, 23 (2011) No. 3, pp. 538-557.

MILTNER, B., "Irregular Maritime Migration: Refugee Protection Issues in Rescue and Interception", *Fordham International Law Journal*, 30 (2006), No. 1, pp. 75-125.

MOEN, A. E., "For Those in Peril on the Sea: Search and Rescue under the Law of the Sea Convention", *Ocean Yearbook*, 24 (2010), pp. 377-410.

MORENO LAX, V., "The EU Regime on Interdiction, Search and Rescue, and

Disembarkation: The Frontex Guidelines for Intervention at Sea", *International Journal of Marine and Coastal Law*, 25 (2010), No. 4, pp. 621-635.
—, "Seeking Asylum in the Mediterranean: Against a Fragmentary Reading of EU Member States' Obligations Accruing at Sea", *International Journal of Refugee Law*, 23 (2011), No. 2, pp. 174-220
NESSEL, L. A., "Externalized Borders and the Invisible Refugee", *Columbia Human Rights Law Review*, 40 (2009), No. 3, pp. 625-699.
PALLIS, M., "Obligations of States towards Asylum Seekers at Sea: Interactions and Conflicts between Legal Regimes", *International Journal of Refugee Law*, 14 (2002), Nos. 2-3, pp. 329-364.
PAPASTAVRIDIS, E., "The Right of Visit on the High Seas in a Theoretical Perspective: Mare Liberum versus Mare Clausum Revisited", *Leiden Journal of International Law*, 24 (2011), No. 1, pp. 45-69.
—, "Piracy of Somalia: The 'Emperors and the Thieves of the Oceans' in the 21st Century", in Ademola Abass (ed.), *Protecting Human Security in Africa*, Oxford, Oxford University Press, 2010, pp. 122-154.
PUGASH, J. Z., "The Dilemma of the Sea Refugee: Rescue without Refuge", *Harvard International Law Journal*, 18 (1977), pp. 577-604.
RAPP, G. C., "Salvage Awards on the Somali Coast: Who Pays for Public and Private Rescue Efforts in Piracy Crises", *American University Law Review*, 59 (2010), No. 5, pp. 1399-1424.
ROBINSON, B. W., "Smuggled Masses: The Need for a Maritime Alien Smuggling Law Enforcement Act", *Army Lawyer*, 2010 (2010), No. 8, pp. 20-40.
RUBIO FERNANDEZ, E. M., « Bilan de la réglementation juridique internationale de l'assistance aux victimes de la violence sur mer, spécialement de la piraterie ou du vol à main armée », dans J. M. Sobrino Heredia, *Sûreté maritime et violence en mer/Maritime Security and Violence at Sea*, Bruxelles, Bruylant, etc., 2011, pp. 301-322.
SAM-LEFEBVRE, A., « Quelles réponses face à la recrudescence de la malveillance », *Annuaire de droit maritime et oceanique*, 28 (2010), pp. 163-174.
TONDINI, M., "The Legality of Intercepting Boat People under Search and Rescue and Border Control Operations: With Reference to Recent Italian Interventions in the Mediterranean Sea and the ECtHR Decision in the Hirsi Case", *Journal of International Maritime Law*, 18 (2012), No. 1, pp. 59-74.
TREVISANUT, S., "Search and Rescue Operations in the Mediterranean: Factor of Cooperation or Conflict?", *International Journal of Marine and Coastal Law*, 25 (2010), No. 4, pp. 523-542.
UNITED NATIONS OFFICE ON DRUGS AND CRIME, *Smuggling of Migrants by Sea* (issue paper), Vienna, UNODC, 2011.
VASILOGEORGI, I. M., "Delimination of IMO-ICAO Search and Rescue Regions: A Case of Jurisdictional Compilation and Complication", *Annals of Air and Space Law*, 36 (2011), pp. 251-278.
YONG JOONG LEE, E., "Military Rescue Operation for the Hostages taken by Somali Pirates: was the Korean Navy's 'Daybreak in the Gulf of Aden' Legitimate?", *Journal of East Asia and International Law*, 5 (2012), No. 1, pp. 37-60.

10 Violations grave du droit de la guerre maritime
War Crimes during Armed Conflict at Sea

DEL CHICCA, M., "Universal Jurisdiction as Obligation to Prosecute or Extradite", *WMU Journal of Maritime Affairs*, 11 (2012), No. 1, pp. 83-93.
DUTTON, Y. M., "Bringing Pirates to Justice: A Case for Including Piracy within the Jurisdiction of the International Criminal Court", *Chicago Journal of International Law*, 11 (2010), No. 1, pp. 197-241.
GUILFOYLE, D., "The Laws of War and the Fight against Somali Piracy: Combatants or Criminals", *Melbourne Journal of International Law*, 11 (2010), pp. 141-153.

KONTOROVICH, E., "'A Guantánamo on the Sea': The Difficulty of Prosecuting Pirates and Terrorists", *California Law Review*, 98 (2010), No. 1, pp. 243-275.

LILJEDAHL, J., "Transnational and International Crimes: Jurisdictional Issues", in Proshanto K. Mukherjee, Maximo Q. Mejia and Gotthard M. Gauci (eds.), *Maritime Violence and Other Security Issues at Sea*, 2002, pp. 115-131.

PAPASTAVRIDIS, E., *The Interception of Vessels on the High Seas: Contemporary Challenges to the Legal Order of the Oceans*, Oxford, Hart Publishing, 2013.

RODRÍGUEZ-VILLASANTE Y PRIETO, J. L., «Aspectos jurídicos-penales del crímen internacional de piratería», dans R. Castillejo Manzanares (dir. publ.), *La persecución de los actos de piratería en las costas somalíes*, Valencia, Tirant lo Blanch, 2011, pp. 113-144.

11 Coopération interétatique dans la répression de la criminalité en mer

International Co-operation in the Suppression of Crimes at Sea

ANDREONE, G., «Protection et sécurité des transports maritimes», dans J. M. Sobrino Heredia, *Sûreté maritime et violence en mer/Maritime Security and Violence at Sea*, Bruxelles, Bruylant, etc., 2011, pp. 465-473.

ARSANJANI, M. H., and W. M. REISMAN, "East African Piracy and the Defense of World Public Order", in Holger Hestermeyer *et al.* (eds.), *Law of the Sea in Dialogue*, Heidelberg, etc., Springer, pp. 137-159.

BACAS FERNÁNDEZ, J. R., «La participación europea en la lucha internacional contra la piratería en el cuerno de África: la operación Atalanta», dans Jesús Ramón Bacas Fernández *et al.* (dir. publ.), *Crisis somalí, piratería e intervención internacional*, Madrid, Instituto Universitario General Gutiérrez Mellado-UNED, 2009, pp. 149-174.

BACAS FERNÁNDEZ, J. R., *et al.* (dir. publ.), *Crisis somalí, piratería e intervención internacional*, Madrid, Instituto Universitario General Gutiérrez Mellado-UNED, 2009.

BACOT-DÉCRIAUD, M., «Des coups d'épée dans l'eau: l'UE et la lutte internationale contre la piraterie maritime», dans A. Macleod (dir. publ.), *Les défis de la sécurité internationale à l'aube d'un monde pluripolaire*, Bruxelles, Bruylant, 2011, pp. 191-206.

—, «Les Etats et l'Union européenne confrontés au «Jolly Roger»: Etats et piraterie», dans Josiane Tercinet (dir. publ.), *États et sécurité internationale*, Bruxelles, Bruylant, pp 255-262.

BECKMAN, R. C., and J. A. ROACH (eds.), *Piracy and International Maritime Crimes in ASEAN: Prospects for Cooperation*, Cheltenham, Elgar, 2012.

BLANCO-BAZÁN, A., "Protection and Safety in Maritime Transport : Measures by International Maritime Organizations", in J. M. Sobrino Heredia, *Sûreté maritime et violence en mer/Maritime Security and Violence at Sea*, Bruxelles, Bruylant, etc., 2011, pp. 381-410.

BUEGER, C., "Drops in the Bucket? A Review of Onshore Responses to Somali Piracy", *WMU Journal of Maritime Affairs,* 11 (2012), No. 1, pp. 15-31.

BUEGER, C., and J. STOCKBRUEGGER, "Security Communities, Alliances, and Macrosecuritization: The Practices of Counter-Piracy Governance", in Michael J. Struett, Jon D. Carlson and Mark T. Nance (eds.), *Maritime Piracy and the Construction of Global Governance*, New York, NY, Routledge, 2013, pp. 99-124.

BUGNON, C., «L'action contre les actes de piraterie maritime: à propos de l'affaire du voilier ponant», *Annuaire de droit maritime et océanique*, 28 (2010), pp. 133-162.

BURKHARDT, L., "Rules of Engagement zur Pirateriebekämpfung: Inhalte und Verfahren", in Weingärtner (ed.), *Die Bundeswehr als Armee im Einsatz: Ent-*

wicklungen im nationalen und internationalen Recht, Baden-Baden, Nomos, 2010, pp. 125-141.

CALIGIURI, A., «Observations sur la poursuite et justice des pirates», dans J. M. Sobrino Heredia, *Sûreté maritime et violence en mer/Maritime Security and Violence at Sea*, Bruxelles, Bruylant, etc., 2011, pp. 251-269.

CARAFANO, J. J., R. WEITZ and M. E. ANDERSEN, *Maritime Security: Fighting Piracy in the Gulf of Aden and Beyond*, Washington, DC, Heritage Foundation, 2007.

CHALK, P., "Piracy off the Horn of Africa: Scope, Dimensions, Causes and Responses", *Brown Journal of World Affairs*, 16 (2010), No. 2, pp. 89-108.

—, "Assessing the Utility of Current Counterpiracy Initiatives off the Horn of Africa", *Studies in Conflict and Terrorism*, 35 (2012), Nos. 7-8, pp. 553-561.

CHI, M., "Finding out the 'Achilles Heels': Piracy Suppression under International Law and Chinese Law", *Journal of East Asia and International Law*, 5 (2012), No. 1, pp. 7-36.

CLIFT, R., et S. CORDONNIER, «La piraterie somalienne: le prix d'une vie», *Le droit maritime français*, 64 (2012), nº 736, pp. 408-411.

CONING, E. DE, and G. STØLSVIK, "Combating Organised Crime at Sea: What Role for the United Nations Office on Drugs and Crime? Current Legal Developments: United Nations Office on Drugs and Crime", *International Journal of Marine and Coastal Law*, 28 (2013), No. 1, pp. 189-204.

CORTI, S., «Somalia: tra guerra e pirateria», dans Maurizio Simoncelli (dir. publ.), *Dove i diritti umani non esistono più: la violazione dei diritti umani nelle guerre contemporanee*, Rome, Ediesse, 2010, pp. 125-151.

CUDENNEC, A., «Terrorisme et piraterie maritimes: l'UE affirme son statut d'acteur maritime international», *Revue du Marché commun et de l'Union européenne,* 2009, nº 532, pp. 599-607.

DAVENPORT, T., "Legal Measures to Combat Piracy and Armed Robbery in the Horn of Africa and in Southeast Asia: A Comparison", *Studies in Conflict and Terrorism*, 35 (2012), Nos. 7-8, pp. 570-587.

DU CASTEL, V., «Piraterie maritime: nouvelles géostratégies en construction», *Revue Défense nationale* (2010), nº 734, pp. 81-87.

ELAGAB, O., "Somali Piracy and International Law: Some Aspects", *Australian and New Zealand Maritime Law Journal*, 24 (2010), pp. 59-75.

ERICKSON, A. S., "Maritime Security Cooperation in the South China Sea Region", in Shicun Wu and Keyuan Zou, *Maritime Security in the South China Sea: Regional Implications and International Cooperation*, Farnham, Ashgate, 2009, 51-80.

ESPALIÚ BERDUD, C., «La operación Atalanta de la Unión Europea en el marco de la lucha contra la piratería marítima», *Revista de las cortes generales*, 79 (2010), pp. 103-159.

FANTAUZZI, R., "Rascals, Scroundels, Villains, and Knaves: The Evolution of the Law of Piracy from Ancient Times to the Present", *International Journal of Legal Information*, 39 (2011), No. 3, pp. 346-383.

FISCHER-LESCANO, A., and L. KRECK, "Piracy and Human Rights: Legal Issues in the Fight against Piracy within the Context of the European 'Operation Atalanta'", *German Yearbook of International Law*, 52 (2010), pp. 525-561.

FOUCHE, H., and J. Meyer, "Investigating Sea Piracy: Crime Scene Challenges", *WMU Journal of Maritime Affairs*, 11 (2012), No. 1, pp. 33-50.

GARCIA-CORROCHANO MOYANO, L., «Le traitement de la piraterie et le terrorisme dans les espaces maritimes de l'Union des Nations de l'Amérique du Sud-UNASUR», dans J. M. Sobrino Heredia, *Sûreté maritime et violence en mer/Maritime Security and Violence at Sea*, Bruxelles, Bruylant, etc., 2011, pp. 271-281.

GEISS, R., and A. PETRIG, "UN-mandatierte Piraterie-Bekämpfung im Golf von Aden: langfristige Lösungen müssen gefunden werden", *Vereinte Nationen*, 58 (2010), No. 1, pp. 3-8.

GINKEL, B. VAN, and F.-P. VAN DER PUTTEN (eds.), *The International Response to Somali Piracy: Challenges and Opportunities*, Leiden, etc., Nijhoff, 2010.

GOODWIN, D., *Pirates, Profits and Politics: The Dilemma of Gunboat Diplomacy*, Camberley, Royal Military Academy Sandhurst, 2011.

GÓMEZ RIVERO, C., «La represión penal de la piratería: bases para la oportunidad de una reforma», dans Luis Arroyo Zapatero et Adán Nieto Martín (dir. publ.), *Piratas, mercenarios, soldados, jueces y policías: nuevas desafíos del derecho penal europeo e internacional*, Cuenca, Ed. de la Universidad de Castilla-La Mancha, 2010, pp. 53-75.

GOVERN, K. H., "National Solutions to an International Scourge: Prosecuting Piracy Domestically as a Viable Alternative to International Tribunals", *University of Miami International and Comparative Law Review*, 19 (2011), No. 1, pp. 1-56.

GRAZIANI, F., *Il contrasto alla pirateria marittima nel diritto internazionale*, Naples, Editoriale scientifica, 2009.

GUILFOYLE, D., "Combating Piracy: Executive Measures on the High Seas", *Japanese Yearbook of International Law*, 53 (2010), pp. 149-177.

—, "Piracy off Somalia: UN Security Council Resolution 1816 and IMO Regional Counter-Piracy Efforts", *International and Comparative Law Quarterly*, 57 (2008), No. 3., pp. 690-699.

GULLESTRUP, G., and M.-B.U. STUMBAUM, "Coping with Piracy: The European Union and the Shipping Industry", in B. van Ginkel and F.-P. van der Putten (eds.), *The International Response to Somali Piracy: Challenges and Opportunities*, Leiden, etc., Nijhoff, 2010, pp. 105-125.

HÄUSSLER, U., "Crisis Response Operations in Maritime Environments", in M. Odello and R. Piotrowicz (eds.), *International Military Missions and International Law*, Leiden, etc., Nijhoff, 2011, pp. 161-210.

HODGKINSON, S. L, K. M. KELLY, Th. H. VAN HORN and G. P., NOONE, "Piracy: New Efforts in Addressing this Enduring Problem", *Tulane Maritime Law Journal*, 36 (Winter 2011), No. 1, pp. 65-122.

HODGKINSON, S. L., "International Law in Crisis: Seeking the Best Prosecution Model for Somali Pirates", *Case Western Reserve Journal of International Law*, 44 (2011), Nos. 1-2, pp. 303-316.

HOLMES, J. R., "The Interplay between Counterpiracy and Indian Ocean Geopolitics", in B. van Ginkel and F.-P. van der Putten (eds.), *The International Response to Somali Piracy: Challenges and Opportunities*, Leiden, etc., Nijhoff, 2010, pp. 153-177.

HOMAN, C., and S. KAMERLING, "Operational Challenges to Counterpiracy Operations off the Coast of Somalia", in B. van Ginkel and F.-P. van der Putten (eds.), *The International Response to Somali Piracy: Challenges and Opportunities*, Leiden, etc., Nijhoff, 2010, pp. 65-103.

HOUGHTON, M. C., "Walking the Plank: How United Nations Security Council Resolution 1816, While Progressive, Fails to Provide a Comprehensive Solution to Somali Piracy", *Tulsa Journal of Comparative and International Law*, 16 (2009), No. 2, pp. 253-286.

HOWARD, J. H., "Southeast Asian SLOC Security", in Shicun Wu and Keyuan Zou, *Maritime Security in the South China Sea: Regional Implications and International Cooperation*, Farnham, Ashgate, 2009, 157-176.

ISANGA, J. M., "Countering Persistent Contemporary Sea Piracy: Expanding Jurisdictional Regimes", *American University Law Review*, 59 (2009-2010), No. 5, pp. 1267- 1320.

IYI, J.-M., "Somali Piracy, UNSC Resolutions 1816-1851: Dilemma of State Failure and the Burden of Legitimacy", *African Yearbook on International Humanitarian Law*, 2011, pp. 47-78.

JENISCH, U., "Piracy, Navies and the Law of the Sea: The Case of Somalia", *WMU Journal of Maritime Affairs*, 8 (2009), No. 2, pp. 123-143.

JOHNSON, D., and M. VALENCIA (eds.), *Piracy in Southeast Asia: Status, Issues, and Responses*, Singapore, Institute of Southeast Asian Studies, 2005.

JORGE URBINA, J., «La contribution du Conseil de sécurité à la coopération internationale pour la lutte contre la piraterie dans le Golfe d'Aden et au large des côtes de la Somalie», dans J. M. Sobrino Heredia, *Sûreté maritime et violence en mer/Maritime Security and Violence at Sea*, Bruxelles, Bruylant, etc., 2011, pp. 283-300.

KARAGIANNIS, S., «La sécurité maritime et l'Union européenne: l'exemple de la lutte contre la piraterie au large des côtes somaliennes», dans Josiane Auvret-Finck (dir. publ.), *L'Union européenne et la lutte contre le terrorisme: état des lieux et perspectives*, Bruxelles, Larcier, 2011, pp. 217-249.

KONTOROVICH, E., "United States v. Shi. 525 F. 3d 709, cert. denied, 129 S. Ct. 324 (2008): United States Court of Appeals for the Ninth Circuit Opinion on Piracy as an Offense within Universal Jurisdiction and on Application of the Convention for the Suppression of Unlawful Acts against the Safety of Maritime Navigation: United States Court of Appeals for the Ninth Circuit, April 24, 2008", *American Journal of International Law*, 103 (2009), No. 4, pp. 734-740.

—, "Exchange of Letters between the European Union and the Government of Kenya on the Conditions and Modalities for the Transfer of Persons Suspected of Having Committed Acts of Piracy", *International Legal Materials*, 48 (2009), No. 4, pp 747-759.

—, "'A Guantánamo on the Sea': The Difficulty of Prosecuting Pirates and Terrorists", *California Law Review*, 98 (2010), No. 1, pp. 243-275.

KÖNIG, D., *Die Bekämpfung von Terroristen und Piraten: ist der Einsatz der deutschen Marine im Rahmen von OEF, PSI und Operation Atalanta mit dem Völkerrecht vereinbar?*, Trier, Institut für Rechtspolitik (IRP) an der Universität Trier, 2009.

KRASKA, J., "Contemporary Maritime Piracy: International Law, Strategy and Diplomacy at Sea", Santa Barbara, CA, Praeger, 2011.

—, "Brandishing 'Legal Tools' in the Fight against Maritime Piracy", in Myron H. Nordquist *et al.* (eds.), *The Law of the Sea Convention: US Accession and Globalization*, Leiden, Nijhoff, 2012, pp. 258-290.

—, "I.O. 2.0: Indian Ocean Security and the Law of the Sea", *Georgetown Journal of International Law*, 43 (2012), No. 2, pp. 433-493.

KRASKA, J., and B. WILSON, "The Pirates of the Gulf of Aden: The Coalition Is the Strategy", *Stanford Journal of International Law*, 45 (2009), No. 2, pp. 243-286.

—, "Piracy Repression, Partnering and the Law", *Journal of Maritime Law and Commerce*, 40 (2009), No. 1, pp. 43-58.

LANDSIDLE, J., "Enhancing International Efforts to Prosecute Suspected Pirates", *Case Western Reserve Journal of International Law*, 44 (2011), Nos. 1-2, pp. 317-323.

LARIK, J., and Q. WEILER, "Going Naval in Troubled Waters: The EU, China and the Fight against Piracy off the Coast of Somalia", in J. Men and B. Barton (eds.), *European Union in Africa: Partners or Competitors?*, Farnham, etc., Ashgate, 2011, pp. 81-103.

LAURENT, F., et A. Garcia, «Défense et sécurité», *Annuaire du droit de la mer*, 15 (2010), pp. 475-524.

LEHR, P., "Maritime Piracy as a U.S. Foreign Policy Problem: The Case of the 'Maersk Alabama'", in Ralph G. Carter (ed.), *Contemporary Cases in U.S. Foreign Policy: From Terrorism to Trade*, Washington, DC, CQ Press, pp. 200-228.

LISS, C., *Oceans of Crime: Maritime Piracy and Transnational Security in Southeast Asia and Bangladesh*, Leiden, etc., International Institute for Asian Studies, 2011.

MACKINLAY, A., *La lucha contra la piratería en aguas del Océano Índico: la necesidad de una aproximación integral*, Madrid, Real Instituto Elcano, 2010.

MALLIA, P., "The Fight against Piracy and Armed Robbery against Ships off the Coast of Somalia: International Cooperation Illustrated", in A. Martínez

Gutiérrez (ed.), *Serving the Rule of International Maritime Law: Essays in Honour of Professor David Joseph Attard*, London, etc., Routledge, 2010, pp. 216-232.

—, *Migrant Smuggling by Sea: Combating a Current Threat to Maritime Security through the Creation of a Cooperative Framework*, Leiden, Nijhoff, 2010.

MARTIN-CASTEX, B., et G. LOONIS-QUÉLEN, «L'Organisation maritime internationale et la piraterie ou le vol à main armée en mer: le cas de la Somalie», *Annuaire français de droit international*, 54 (2009), pp. 77-117.

MASETTI, G., et F. ORSINI, *La Missione Atalanta e la politica estera dell'Unione Europea: entrata in vigore del Trattato di Lisbona, azione esterna e capacità di protezione navale*, Rome, Aracne, 2010.

MASSARELLA, C., "UN Security Council Resolution 1976 (2011) and Efforts to Support Piracy Prosecutions", *International Journal of Marine and Coastal Law*, 26 (2011), No. 4, pp. 679-685.

MCGAHAN, K., and T. LEE, "Frames, Humanitarianism, and Legitimacy: Explaining the Anti-piracy Regime in the Gulf of Aden", in Michael J. Struett, Jon D. Carlson and Mark T. Nance (eds.), *Maritime Piracy and the Construction of Global Governance*, New York, NY, Routledge, 2013, pp. 149-167.

MEJIA, M., "Regional Cooperation in Combating Piracy and Armed Robbery against Ships: Learning Lessons from ReCAAP", in A. Petrig (ed.), *Sea Piracy Law: Selected National Legal Frameworks and Regional Legislative Approaches/Droit de la piraterie maritime: cadres juridiques nationaux et approches legislatives régionales*, Berlin, Duncker & Humblot, 2010, pp. 125-137.

MENEFEE, S. P., "Predicting Piracy: Can We Anticipate the Future of Maritime Crime?", in Myron H. Nordquist *et al.* (eds.), *The Law of the Sea Convention: US Accession and Globalization*, Leiden, Nijhoff, 2012, pp. 291-303.

MIDDLETON, R., *Piracy in Somalia: Threatening Global Trade, Feeding Local Wars*, London, Royal Institute of International Affairs, 2008.

—, "More than Just Pirates: Closing the Space for Somali Pirates through a Comprehensive Approach", in B. van Ginkel and F.-P. van der Putten (eds.), *The International Response to Somali Piracy: Challenges and Opportunities*, Leiden, etc., Nijhoff, 2010, pp. 13-30.

MUKHERJEE, P. K., M. Q. MEJIA and G. M. GAUCI (eds.), *Maritime Violence and Other Security Issues at Sea*, Malmö, World Maritime University, 2002.

MURPHY, M. N., "International Cooperation against Piracy: China's Role, Problems and Prospects", *WMU Journal of Maritime Affairs,* 11 (2012), No. 1, pp. 71-81.

NANCE, M. T., and M. J. STRUETT, "Conflicting Constructions: Maritime Piracy and Cooperation under Regime Complexes", in Michael J. Struett, Jon D. Carlson and Mark T. Nance (eds.), *Maritime Piracy and the Construction of Global Governance*, New York, NY, Routledge, 2013, pp. 125-148.

NERI, K., *L'emploi de la force en mer*, Bruxelles, Bruylant, 2013.

ODIER, F., «Convention relative à la répression d'actes illicites contre la sécurité de la navigation maritime», *Annuaire du droit de la mer*, 10 (2005), pp. 299-306.

OLIVEIRA, G. C. DE, "Naval Peacekeeping and Piracy: Time for a Critical Turn in the Debate", *International Peacekeeping*, 19 (2012), No. 1, pp. 48-61.

ORIOLO, A., "The Multilateral Approach of the EU Maritime Security Policy: The Fight against Piracy, Terrorism and Violence at Sea", *The Global Community*, 1 (2009), pp. 251-266.

—, "Pirateria, terrorismo e sicurezza dei mari nella nuova politica marittima dell'Unione Europea", dans Angela Del Vecchio (dir. publ.), *La politica marittima comunitaria*, Rome, Aracne, 2009, pp. 113-137.

PARADISO, D. P., "Come All Ye Faithful: How the International Community has Addressed the Effects of Somali Piracy but Fails to Remedy Its Cause", *Penn State International Law Review*, 29 (2010), No. 1, pp. 187-210.

PEPPETTI, J. D., "Building the Global Maritime Security Network: A Multinational Legal Structure to Combat Transnational Threats", *Naval Law Review*, 55 (2008), pp. 73-156.

PHAM, J.-P., "The Failed State and Regional Dimensions of Somali Piracy", in B. van Ginkel and F.-P. van der Putten (eds.), *The International Response to Somali Piracy: Challenges and Opportunities*, Leiden, etc., Nijhoff, 2010, pp. 31-64.

PUEYO LOSA, J., et J. J. URBINA (eds.), *La cooperación internacional en la ordenación de los mares y océanos*, Madrid, Iustel, 2009.

RAHMAN, C., "The International Politics of Combating Piracy in Southeast Asia", in Peter Lehr (ed.), *Violence at Sea: Piracy in the Age of Global Terrorism*, New York, Routledge, 2007, pp. 183-198.

REALE, G. (dir. publ.), *Il contrasto alle attività illecite in mare*, Naples, Edizioni Scientifiche, 2011.

REGUEIRO DUBRA, R., «El uso de la fuerza en el mar y la operación Atalanta de la Unión Europea», dans Jesús Ramón Bacas Fernández *et al.* (dir. publ.), *Crisis somalí, piratería e intervención internacional*, Madrid, Instituto Universitario General Gutiérrez Mellado-UNED, 2009, pp. 125-148.

ROACH, J. A., "Countering Piracy off Somalia: International Law and International Institutions", *American Journal of International Law*, 104 (2010), No. 3, pp. 397-416.

—, "General Problematic Issues on Exercise of Jurisdiction over Modern Instances of Piracy", in Clive R. Symmons (ed.), *Selected Contemporary Issues in the Law of the Sea*, Leiden, etc., Nijhoff, 2011, pp. 119-137.

RUBIO FERNANDEZ, E. M., «Bilan de la réglementation juridique internationale de l'assistance aux victimes de la violence sur mer, spécialement de la piraterie ou du vol à main armée», dans J. M. Sobrino Heredia, *Sûreté maritime et violence en mer/Maritime Security and Violence at Sea*, Bruxelles, Bruylant, etc., 2011, pp. 301-322.

SAKHUJA, V., «Les menaces et défis auxquels se heurte la chaîne logistique maritime», *Forum du disarmament*, 2010, n° 2, pp. 3-13.

SALVATIERRA, M., *El próspero negocio de la piratería en África*, Madrid, Catarata, 2010.

SÁNCHEZ BARRUECO, M. L., "The European Strategy against Piracy off the Somali Coast: A Multi-Pillar Response to a Cross-Pillar Concern", in J. M. Sobrino Heredia, *Sûreté maritime et violence en mer/Maritime Security and Violence at Sea*, Bruxelles, Bruylant, etc., 2011, pp. 323-342.

—, "Reflections on the EU Foreign Policy Objectives behind the Integrated Approach in the Response to Priacy off Somalia", *Croation Yearbook of European Law and Policy*, 5 (2009), pp. 195-238.

SARTRE, P., «La communauté internationale face à la piraterie en mer», *Annuaire français de relations internationales*, 11 (2010), pp. 803-817.

SAWYER, M., "International Conference on Piracy at Sea 2011", *WMU Journal of Maritime Affairs*, 11 (2012), No. 1, pp. 143-147.

SHARAMO, R., and B. MESFIN (ed.), *Regional Security in the post-Cold War Horn of Africa*, Pretoria, Institute for Security Studies, 2011.

YANN-HUEI SONG, "Regional Maritime Security Inititiative (RMSI) and Enhancing Security in the Straits of Malacca: Littoral States' and Regional Responses", in Shicun Wu and Keyuan Zou, *Maritime Security in the South China Sea: Regional Implications and International Cooperation*, Farnham, Ashgate, 2009, 109-134.

SPAGNOLO, A., «Il trasferimento di presunti pirati nell'ambito dell'operazione "Atalanta": gli accordi tra l'Unione europea e i Paesi terzi», *Studi sull' integrazione europea*, 7 (2012), Vols. 2-3, pp. 651-668.

STAVRIDIS, J. G., and R. E. LEBRON, "Taming the Outlaw Sea", *Naval War College Review*, 63 (2010), No. 4, pp. 73-83.

STRUETT, M. J., J. D. CARLSON and M. T. NANCE (eds.), *Maritime Piracy and the Construction of Global Governance*, New York, NY, Routledge, 2013.

SURBUN, V., "The Developing Jurisprudence to Combat Modern Maritime Pricacy: A Crime of the High Seas?", *Comparative and International Law Journal of Southern Africa*, 43 (2010), No. 1, pp. 1-22.

SYRING, T., "'Candide', or Pessimism: Fighting Piracy and Transnational Crime in Uncharted Waters", *Interdisciplinary Political Studies*, 2 (2012), No. 1, pp. 48-58.

TARASENKO, S., "The United Nations' Role in Combatting Piracy and Terrorism at Sea", in Myron H. Nordquist *et al.* (eds.), *The Law of the Sea Convention: US Accession and Globalization*, Leiden, Nijhoff, 2012, pp. 143-153.

TREVIÑO RUIZ, J. M., *La seguridad marítima y la piratería*, Madrid, Real Instituto Elcano (ARI), 2010.

UNITED NATIONS OFFICE ON DRUGS AND CRIME, *Smuggling of Migrants by Sea* (issue paper), Vienna, UNODC, 2011.

URBINA, J. J., «El régimen jurídico internacional de la piratería y los problemas que plantea su persecución en las costas de Somalia y el Golfo de Aden», dans R. Castillejo Manzanares (dir. publ.), *La persecución de los actos de piratería en las costas somalíes*, Valencia, Tirant lo Blanch, 2011, pp. 34-66.

—, «La cooperación internacional en la prevención y control de los actos de piratería en el actual derecho del mar», dans Jorge Pueyo Losa and Julio Jorge Urbina (dir. publ.), *La cooperación internacional en la ordenación de los mares y océanos*, Madrid , Iustel, 2009, pp. 321-362.

VAUGHAN-WILLIAMS, N., "Off-Shore Biopolitical Border Security: The EU's Global Response to Migration, Piracy, and 'Risky' Subjects", in L. Bialasiewicz (ed.), *Europe in the World: EU Geopolitics and the Transformation of European Space*, Farnham, etc., Ashgate, 2011, pp. 185-200.

WILSON, B., "Somali Piracy Challenge: Operational Partnering, the Rule of Law, and Capacity Building", *Loyola University Chicago International Law Review*, 9 (2011), No. 1, pp. 45-70.

WITHERBY SEAMANSHIP INTERNATIONAL, *Best Practice Management Practices to Deter Piracy off the Coast of Somalia and in the Arabian Sea Area: Suggested Planning and Operational Practices for Ship Operators, and Masters of Ships transiting the Gulf of Aden and the Arabian Sea*, Edinburgh, Witherby Seamanship International, 2010.

WOOLLEY, C. R., "Piracy and Sovereign Rights: Addressing Piracy in the Straits of Malacca without Degrading the Sovereign Rights of Indonesia and Malaysia", *Santa Clara Journal of International Law*, 8 (2010), No. 2, pp. 447-472.

YAKEMTCHOUK, R., «Les Etats de l'Union européenne face à la piraterie maritime somalienne», *Revue du Marché commun et de l'Union européenne*, 2009, nº 530, pp. 441-450.

ZOU, K., "Maritime Security and Multilateral Interactions between China and its Neighbours", in Guoguang Wu and Helen Lansdowne (eds,), *China Turns to Multilateralism: Foreign Policy and Regional Security*, London, etc., Routledge, 2008, pp. 147-172.

12 La compétence universelle relative à la criminalité en mer

Universal Jurisdiction and Crimes at Sea

BENNETT, A., "That Sinking Feeling: Stateless Ships, Universal Jurisdiction, and the Drug Trafficking Vessel Interdiction Act", *Yale Journal of International Law*, 37 (2012), No. 2, pp. 433-461.

BONT, S. DE, "Murky Waters: Prosecuting Pirates and Upholding Human Rights Law", *Journal of International Law and International Relations*, 7 (Fall 2011), No. 1, pp. 104-145.

CALIGIURI, A., "Observations sur la poursuite et justice des pirates", dans

J. M. Sobrino Heredia, *Sûreté maritime et violence en mer/Maritime Security and Violence at Sea*, Bruxelles, Bruylant, etc., 2011, pp. 251-269.

CASTILLEJO MANZANARES, R. (dir. publ.), *La persecución de los actos de piratería en las costas somalíes*, Valencia, Tirant lo Blanch, 2011.

CHANG, D., "Piracy Laws and the Effective Prosecution of Pirates", *Boston College International and Comparative Law Review*, 33 (2010), No. 2, pp. 273-288.

COHEN, M., "Analogy between Piracy and Human Trafficking: A Theoretical Framework for the Application of Universal Jurisdiction", *Buffalo Human Rights Law Review*, 16 (2010), pp. 201-236.

DEL CHICCA, M., "Universal Jurisdiction as Obligation to Prosecute or Extradite", *WMU Journal of Maritime Affairs*, 11 (2012), No. 1, pp. 83-93.

DOBY, D., "Piracy 'Jure Gentium': The Jurisdictional Conflict of the High Seas and Territorial Waters", *Journal of Maritime Law and Commerce*, 41 (2010), No. 4, pp. 561-580.

DOEG, B. K., "PMCs on the High Seas: The Solution to Somali Piracy or a Failure to Learn from History", *National Security and Conflict Law Review*, 1 (2010-2011), pp. 139-164.

DUTTON, Y. M., "Bringing Pirates to Justice: A Case for Including Piracy within the Jurisdiction of the International Criminal Court", *Chicago Journal of International Law*, 11 (2010), No. 1, pp. 197-241.

—, "Pirates and Impunity: Is the Threat of Asylum Claims a Reason to Allow Pirates to Escape Justice?", *Fordham International Law Journal*, 34 (2011), No. 2, pp. 236-295.

—, "Maritime Piracy and the Impunity Gap: Insufficient National Laws or a Lack of Political Will", *Tulane Law Review*, 86 (2012), No. 5, pp. 1111-1162.

—, "Maritime Piracy and the Impunity Gap: Domestic Implementation of International Treaty Provisions", in Michael J. Struett, Jon D. Carlson and Mark T. Nance (eds.), *Maritime Piracy and the Construction of Global Governance*, New York, NY, Routledge, 2013, pp. 71-95.

FANTAUZZI, R., "Rascals, Scroundels, Villains, and Knaves: The Evolution of the Law of Piracy from Ancient Times to the Present", *International Journal of Legal Information*, 39 (2011), No. 3, pp. 346-383.

GOLITSYN, V., "Maritime Security: Case of Piracy", in H. Hestermeyer *et al.* (eds.), *Coexistence, Cooperation and Solidarity: Liber Amicorum Rüdiger Wolfrum*, Leiden, etc., Nijhoff, 2012, pp. 1157-1176.

GRAZIANI, F., *Il contrasto alla pirateria marittima nel diritto internazionale*, Naples, Editoriale Scientifica, 2009.

HODGKINSON, S. L., "International Law in Crisis: Seeking the Best Prosecution Model for Somali Pirates", *Case Western Reserve Journal of International Law*, 44 (2011), Nos. 1-2, pp. 303-316.

ISANGA, J. M., "Countering Persistent Contemporary Sea Piracy: Expanding Jurisdictional Regimes", *American University Law Review*, 59 (2009-2010), No. 5, pp. 1267- 1320.

KELLEY, R. P., "UNCLOS, but No Cigar: Overcoming Obstacles to the Prosecution of Maritime Piracy", *Minnesota Law Review*, 95 (2010-2011), No. 6, pp. 2285-2317.

KONTOROVICH, E., "The Piracy Analogy: Modern Universal Jurisdiction's Hollow Foundation", *Harvard International Law Journal*, 45 (2004), No. 1, pp. 183-237.

—, "The 'Define and Punish' Clause and the Limits of Universal Jurisdiction", *Northwestern University Law Review*, 103 (2009), No. 1, pp 149-203.

—, "United States v. Shi. 525 F. 3d 709, cert. denied, 129 S. Ct. 324 (2008): United States Court of Appeals for the Ninth Circuit Opinion on Piracy as an Offense within Universal Jurisdiction and on Application of the Convention for the Suppression of Unlawful Acts against the Safety of Maritime Navigation: United States Court of Appeals for the Ninth Circuit, April 24, 2008", *American Journal of International Law*, 103 (2009), No. 4, pp.734-740.

—, "'A Guantánamo on the Sea': The Difficulty of Prosecuting Pirates and Terrorists", *California Law Review*, 98 (2010), No. 1, pp. 243-275.

KONTOROVICH, E., and S. ART, "An Empirical Examination of Universal Jurisdiction for Piracy", *American Journal of International Law*, 104 (2010), No. 3, pp. 436-453.

LELARGE, A., « La Somalie entre anarchie et piraterie », *Journal du droit international*, 137 (2010), nº 2, pp. 449-474.

LILJEDAHL, J., "Transnational and International Crimes: Jurisdictional Issues", in Proshanto K. Mukherjee, Maximo Q. Mejia and Gotthard M. Gauci (eds.), *Maritime Violence and Other Security Issues at Sea*, 2002, pp. 115-131.

MANJÓN-CABEZA OLMEDA, A.,« Alcance de la jurisdicción universal española tras la modificación operada por la L. O. 1/2009 de 3 de noviembre », dans R. Castillejo Manzanares (dir. publ.), *La persecución de los actos de piratería en las costas somalíes*, Valencia, Tirant lo Blanch, 2011, pp. 146-206.

MARTIN, J.-Ch., « La répression des actes de piraterie maritime : développements récents en matière de poursuites et détention des pirates somaliens », *Annuaire français de droit international,* 56 (2010), pp. 497-527.

MERTEN, D., "Pirates: Towards an International Criminal Law?" *Een kwestie van grensoverschrijding: Liber Amicorum P. E. L. Janssen*, Nijmegen, Wolf Legal Publishers, 2009, 189-194.

MIDDELBURG, A., *Piracy in a Legal Context: Prosecution of Pirates Operating off the Somali Coast*, Nijmegen, Wolf Legal Publishers, 2011

PHILIP-GAY, M., « Compétence universelle et piraterie maritime : vers un alignement du régime de compétence en matière de piraterie sur celui des autres crimes internationaux ? », dans Guillaume Protière (dir. publ.) *Espaces du droit et droits des espaces*, Paris, L'Harmattan, 2010, pp. 91-103.

ROACH, J. A., "Countering Piracy off Somalia: International Law and International Institutions", *American Journal of International Law*, 104 (2010), No. 3, pp. 397-416.

SATKAUSKAS, R., "Piracy at Sea and the Limits of International Law", *Aegean Review of the Law of the Sea and Maritime Law,* 1 (2011), No. 2, pp. 217-235.

SHNIDER, S., "Universal Jurisdiction over 'Operation of a Pirate Ship': The Legality of the Evolving Piracy Definition in Regional Prosecutions", *North Carolina Journal of International Law and Commercial Regulation*, 38 (2012), No. 2, pp. 473-359.

SORENSEN, C. E., "Drug Trafficking on the High Seas: A Move toward Universal Jurisdiction under International Law", *Emory International Law Review*, 4 (1990), No. 1, pp. 207-230.

STERIO, M., "International Law in Crisis: Piracy off the Coast of Somalia", *Case Western Reserve Journal of International Law*, 44 (2011), Nos. 1-2, pp. 291-301.

STRUETT, M. J., J. D. CARLSON and M. T. NANCE (eds.), *Maritime Piracy and the Construction of Global Governance*, New York, NY, Routledge, 2013.

SYRING, T., "A Pirate and a Refugee: Reservations and Responses in the Fight against Piracy", *ILSA Journal of International and Comparative Law*, 17 (2011), No. 2, pp. 437-457.

THEDWALL, G., "Choosing the Right Yardarm: Establishing and International Court for Piracy", *Georgetown Journal of International Law*, 41 (2010), No. 2, pp. 501-523.

TUERK, H., "Maritime Protection and Violence at Sea: Remarks", in J. M. Sobrino Heredia, *Sûreté maritime et violence en mer/Maritime Security and Violence at Sea*, Bruxelles, Bruylant, etc., 2011, pp. 477-482.

—, "The Resurgence of Piracy: A Phenomenon of Modern Times", *University of Miami International and Comparative Law*, 17 (2009), No. 1, pp. 1-42.

YAO, H., "Universal Jurisdiction over Piracy and East Asian Practice", *Chinese Journal of International Law*, 11 (2012), No. 4, pp. 623-655.

13 La compétence nationale en matière de pollution maritime

Enforcement Jurisdiction over Maritime Pollution

BANG, H., "Is Port State Control an Effective Means to Combat Vessel-Source Pollution? An Empirical Survey of the Practical Exercise by Port States of Their Powers of Control", *International Journal of Marine and Coastal Law*, 23 (2008), No. 4, pp. 715-759.

—, "Port State Jurisdiction and Article 218 of the UN Convention on the Law of Sea", *Journal of Maritime Law and Commerce*, 40 (2009), No. 2, pp. 291-313.

BECKMAN, R., "Singapore Strives to Enhance Safety, Security, and Environmental Protection in Its Port and in the Straits of Malacca and Singapore", *Ocean and Coastal Law Journal*, 14 (2009), No. 2, pp. 167-200.

BECKMAN, R. C., "The Regulation of Ship-Source Pollution in Straits Used for International Navigation", in Myron H. Nordquist, Tommy T. B. Koh and John Norton Moore (eds.), *Freedom of Seas, Passage Rights and the 1982 Law of the Sea Convention*, Leiden, etc., Nijhoff, 2009, pp. 311-337.

BERNHARDT, J. P. A., "A Schematic Analysis of Vessel-Source Pollution: Prescriptive and Enforcement Regimes in the Law of the Sea Conference", *Virginia Journal of International Law*, 20 (1980), pp. 265-311.

CANDIDO, N., « Attività d'indagine sui rifiuti transfrontalieri », dans A. Uricchio *et al.* (dir. publ.), *Nuove piraterie e ordinamenti giuridici interni e internazionali: atti del Convegno tenuto a Taranto il 16 e 17 giugno 2009*, Bari, Cacucci, 2011, pp. 471-479.

CHRISTODOULOU-VAROTSI, I., "Recent Developments in the EC Legal Framework on Ship-Source Pollution: The Ambivalence of the EC's Penal Approach", *Annuaire de droit maritime et océanique*, 26 (2008), pp. 219-234.

DARMODY, J., "The Oil Pollution Act's Criminal Penalties: On a Collision Course with the Law of the Sea", *Boston College Environmental Affairs Law Review*, 21 (1993), No.1, pp. 89-144.

DEL VECCHIO, A., « Protection et sécurité dans les transports maritimes: les mesures de l'Union européenne », dans J. M. Sobrino Heredia, *Sûreté maritime et violence en mer/Maritime Security and Violence at Sea*, Bruxelles, Bruylant, etc., 2011, pp. 357-377.

DUSSOL, B., et Ch. NITHART, « Le cargo de la honte: l'effroyable odyssée du *Probo Koala* », Paris, Stock, 2010.

FRANCKX, E., *Contemporary Regulation of Marine Living Resources and Pollution: Proceedings of the Classes of Excellence and Final Conference Held at the Occasion of the International Francqui Chair Attributed to Professor Dermott Devine*, Antwerp, Apeldoorn, Maklu, 2007.

—, "Marine Environmental Jurisdictional Issues: Coastal States", in Myron H. Nordquist, John Norton Moore and Said Mahmoudi, *The Stockholm Declaration and Law of the Marine Environment*, The Hague, etc., Nijhoff, 2003, pp. 287-298.

—, "Vessel-source Pollution and Coastal State Jurisdiction: General Framework", *South African Yearbook of International Law*, 24 (1999), pp. 1-34.

FRANCKX, E. (ed.), *Vessel-Source Pollution and Coastal State Jurisdiction: The Work of the ILA Committee on Coastal State Jurisdiction Relating to Marine Pollution* (1991-2000), The Hague, etc., Kluwer Law International, 2001.

FRANCKX, E., and Ph. GAUTIER (eds.), *The Exercise of Jurisdiction over Vessels: New Developments in the Fields of Pollution, Fisheries, Crimes at Sea and Trafficking of Weapons of Mass Destruction*, Brussels, Bruylant, 2010.

GULLO, B. S., "The Illegal Discharge of Oil on the High Seas: The U.S. Coast Guard's Ongoing Battle against Vessel Polluters and a New Approach Toward Establishing Environmental Compliance", *Military Law Review*, 209 (2011), pp. 122-185.

HEDEMANN-ROBINSON, M., "The EU and Environmental Crime: The Impact of the ECJ's Judgment on Framework Decision 2005/667 on Ship-Source Pollution", *Journal of Environmental Law*, 20 (2008), No. 2, pp. 279-292.

HOMER, A. W., "Red Sky at Morning: The Horizon for Corporations, Crew Members, and Corporate Officers as the United States Continues Aggressive Criminal Prosecution of Intentional Pollution from Ships", *Tulane Maritime Law Journal*, 32 (2007), No. 1, pp. 149-180.

KÖNIG, D., "The EU Directive on Ship-Source Pollution and on the Introduction of Penalties for Infringements: Development or Breach of International Law?", in Tafsir Malick Ndiaye and Rüdiger Wolfrum (eds.), *Law of the Sea, Environmental Law and Settlement of Disputes: Liber Amicorum Judge Thomas A. Mensah*, Leiden, etc., Nijhoff, 2007, pp. 767-785.

MANIRABONA, A. M., «L'affaire Trafigura: vers la répression de graves atteintes environnementales en tant que crimes contre l'humanité?», *Revue de droit international et de droit comparé*, 88 (2011), n° 4, pp. 535-576.

MUKHERJEE, P. K., "The Penal Law of Ship-Source Marine Pollution: Selected Issues in Perspective", in Tafsir Malick Ndiaye and Rüdiger Wolfrum (eds.), *Law of the Sea, Environmental Law and Settlement of Disputes: Liber Amicorum Judge Thomas A. Mensah*, Leiden, etc., Nijhoff, 2007, pp. 463-498.

PARENTE, F., «Le piraterie ambientale da traffico illecito dei rifuti: tecniche risarcitorie e sottosistemi normativi», dans A. Uricchio *et al.* (dir. publ.), *Nuove piraterie e ordinamenti giuridici interni e internazionali: atti del Convegno tenuto a Taranto il 16 e 17 giugno 2009*, Bari, Cacucci, 2011, pp. 429-448.

ROSENBERG, D., "The Maritime Borderlands: Terrorism, Piracy, Pollution, and Poaching in the South China Sea", in James Clad, Sean M. McDonald and Bruce Vaughn (eds.), *The Borderlands of Southeast Asia: Geopolitics, Terrorism and Globalization*, Washington, DC, National Defense University Press, 2011, pp. 107-126.

SCHOFIELD, C., "Plundered Waters: Somalia's Maritime Resource Insecurity", in T. Doyle and M. Risely, *Crucible for Survival: Environmental Security and Justice in the Indian Ocean Region*, New Brunswick, NJ, Rutgers University Press, 2008, pp. 102-115.

SELVAGGI, N., «Profili penali del traffico di rifiuti», dans A. Uricchio *et al.* (dir. publ.), *Nuove piraterie e ordinamenti giuridici interni e internazionali: atti del Convegno tenuto a Taranto il 16 e 17 giugno 2009*, Bari, Cacucci, 2011, pp. 465-470.

SMITH, N., "Piratical Jurisdiction: The Plundering of Due Process in the Case of Lei Shi", *Emory International Law Review*, 23 (2009), No. 2, pp. 693-738.

SUÁREZ, J., "Protection and Safety in Maritime Transport: National Measures", in J. M. Sobrino Heredia, *Sûreté maritime et violence en mer/Maritime Security and Violence at Sea*, Bruxelles, Bruylant, etc., 2011, pp. 349-356.

SYMEONIDOU-KASTANIDOU, E., "Ship-Source Marine Pollution: The ECJ Judgments and Their Impact on Criminal Law", *European Journal of Crime, Criminal Law and Criminal Justice*, 17 (2009), No. 4, pp. 335-357.

TAN, A. K., "The EU Ship-Source Pollution Directive and Coastal State Jurisdiction over Ships", *Lloyd's Maritime and Commercial Law Quarterly*, (2010), No. 3, pp. 469-488.

—, *Vessel-Source Marine Pollution: The Law and Politics of International Regulation*, Cambridge, etc., Cambridge University Press, 2006.

—, "The EU Ship-Source Pollution Directive and Recent Expansions of Coastal State Jurisdiction", in Davor Vidas (ed.), *Law, Technology and Science for Oceans in Globalisation: IUU Fishing, Oil Pollution, Bioprospecting, Outer Continental Shelf*, Leiden, etc., Nijhoff, 2010, pp. 291-305.

THOUVENIN, J.-M., «Pas de refuge pour la grande piraterie», dans Rafael Casado Raigón et Giuseppe Cataldi (dir.), *L'évolution et l'état actuel du droit interna-*

tional de la mer : mélanges de droit de la mer offerts à Daniel Vignes, 2009, pp. 865-885.

TREVES, T, "Jurisdiction over Vessels in the Areas of Pollution and Fisheries: General Report", in E. Franckx and Ph. Gautier (eds.), *The Exercise of Jurisdiction over Vessels: New Developments in the Fields of Pollution, Fisheries, Crimes at Sea and Trafficking of Weapons of Mass Destruction*, Brussels, Bruylant, 2010, pp. 1-28.

UDELL, R. A., "United States Criminal Enforcement of Deliberate Vessel Pollution: A Document-based Approach to MARPOL", in Davor Vidas (ed.), *Law, Technology and Science for Oceans in Globalisation: IUU Fishing, Oil Pollution, Bioprospecting, Outer Continental Shelf*, Leiden, etc., Nijhoff, 2010, pp. 269-290.

URICCHIO, V. F., « Il traffico illegale dei rifiuti e l'intensificazione dei controlli ambientali », dans A. Uricchio *et al.* (dir. publ.), *Nuove piraterie e ordinamenti giuridici interni e internazionali : atti del Convegno tenuto a Taranto il 16 e 17 giugno 2009*, Bari, Cacucci, 2011, pp. 459-463.

UHLMANN, D. M., "After the Spill Is Gone: The Gulf of Mexico, Environmental Crime, and the Criminal Law", *Michigan Law Review*, 109 (2011), No. 8, pp. 1413-1462.

VANDERZWAAG, L., and A. DANIEL, "International Law and Ocean Dumping: Steering a Precautionary Course aboard the 1996 London Protocol, but Still an Unfinished Voyage", in Aldo Chircop, Ted L. McDorman and Susan J. Rolston, *The Future of Ocean Regime-building: Essays in Tribute to Douglas M. Johnston*, Leiden, etc., Nijhoff, 2009, pp. 515-550.

VANHEULE, B., "Criminal Sanctions in Relation to Ship-Source Pollution", in Norman A. Martínez Gutiérrez (ed.), *Serving the Rule of International Maritime Law: Essays in Honour of Professor David Joseph Attard*, London, etc., Routledge, 2010, pp. 54-74.

—, "Penalties against Ship-Source Pollution" in Kris Bernauw *et al.* (eds.), *Free on Board: Liber Amicorum Marc A. Huybrechts*, Antwerp, etc., Intersentia, 2011, pp. 689-710.

VELUT, J-L., « Protection de l'environnement et lutte contre les activités illicites : de l'évolution de la norme juridique à l' action en mer : l'exemple de la Méditerranée (1) », *Le droit maritime français*, 63 (2011), n° 726, pp. 518-533.

WANG, Ch.-P., "A Review of the Enforcement Regime for Vessel-Source Oil Pollution Control", *Ocean Development and International Law*, 16 (1986), No. 4, pp. 305-339.

ZHU, L., A. K. Y. NG and M. ZHANG, "Some Thoughts on Civil Liability for Maritime Piracy-Caused Oil Pollution ", *Journal of International Maritime Law*, 18 (2012), No. 4, pp. 306-315.

14 Piraterie et droit de la mer
Piracy under International Law of the Sea

ADEMUN-ODEKE, A., "Somali-Piracy: Jurisdiction over Foreign Pirates in Domestic Courts and Third States under International Law", *The Journal of International Maritime Law*, 17 (2011), No. 2, pp. 121-146.

ANDREAS, A. VON, "Die moderne Piraterie und das Völkerrecht", *Archiv des Völkerrechts*, 47 (2009), No. 4, pp. 454-480.

ARSANJANI, M. H., and W. M., REISMAN, "East African Piracy and the Defense of World Public Order", in Holger Hestermeyer *et al.* (eds.), *Law of the Sea in Dialogue*, Heidelberg, etc., Springer, pp. 137-159.

AUST, H. P., "Pirateriebekämpfung im Lichte von Grundgesetz und Völkerrecht auf dem verwaltungsgerichtlichen Prüfstand", *Deutsches Verwaltungsblatt*, 127 (2012), No. 8, pp. 484-490.

BAUTISTA JIMÉNEZ, J. M., « Questions anciennes (déjà oubliées), nouvelles (à la souveraineté) : les voleurs de la mer et la réaction de la communauté internationale », dans J. M. Sobrino Heredia, *Sûreté maritime et violence en mer/Maritime Security and Violence at Sea*, Bruxelles, Bruylant, etc., 2011, pp. 235-250.

BECKMAN, R., and T. DAVENPORT, "Maritime Terrorism and the Law of the Sea: Basic Principles and New Challenges", in Myron H. Nordquist *et al.* (eds.), *The Law of the Sea Convention: US Accession and Globalization*, Leiden, Nijhoff, 2012, pp. 229-257.

BECKMAN, R. C., and J. A. ROACH (eds.), *Piracy and International Maritime Crimes in ASEAN: Prospects for Cooperation*, Cheltenham, Elgar, 2012.

BECKMAN, R. C., "Do We Need a New Convention on Piracy and Armed Robbery against Ships?", in Aldo Chircop *et al.* (eds.), *The Regulation of International Shipping: International and Comparative Perspectives: Essays in Honor of Edgar Gold*, Leiden, etc., Nijhoff, 2012, pp. 77-96.

BELLAYER-ROILLE, A., « Montée en puissance de la lutte contre la « piraterie » maritime « sus à l'hostis humani generis ! », *Annuaire de droit maritime et océanique*, 27 (2009), pp. 309-331.

BEREKETEAB, R., *The Horn of Africa: Intra-State and Inter-State Conflicts and Security*, London, Pluto Press, 2013.

BEVILACQUA, G., « Il problema della repressione del reato di pirateria marittima e il necessario bilanciamento tra le esigenze di esercizio effetivo della giurisdizione e di garanzia dei diritti individuali », *Diritto marittimo*, 114 (2012), n° 3, pp. 664-686.

BLANCO-BAZÁN, A., "Protection and Safety in Maritime Transport : Measures by International Maritime Organizations", in J. M. Sobrino Heredia, *Sûreté maritime et violence en mer/Maritime Security and Violence at Sea*, Bruxelles, Bruylant, etc., 2011, pp. 381-410.

BONT, S. DE, "Murky Waters: Prosecuting Pirates and Upholding Human Rights Law", *Journal of International Law and International Relations*, 7 (Fall 2011), No. 1, pp. 104-145.

BRIGNARDELLO, M., « Nozione di pirateria marittima e sue implicazioni », dans Francesco Berlingieri (dir. publ.), *Scritti in onore di Francesco Berlingieri* (vol. I), Gênes, Il diritto marittimo, 2010, pp. 224-246.

CALIGIURI, A., « Observations sur la poursuite et justice des pirates », dans J. M. Sobrino Heredia, *Sûreté maritime et violence en mer/Maritime Security and Violence at Sea*, Bruxelles, Bruylant, etc., 2011, pp. 251-269.

CHANG, D., "Piracy Laws and the Effective Prosecution of Pirates", *Boston College International and Comparative Law Review*, 33 (2010), No. 2, pp. 273-288.

CHI, M., "Finding out the 'Achilles Heels': Piracy Suppression under International Law and Chinese Law", *Journal of East Asia and International Law*, 5 (2012), No. 1, pp. 7-36.

CUDENNEC, A., « Terrorisme et piraterie maritimes: l'affirmation du statut de l'UE sur la scène internationale », dans J. M. Sobrino Heredia, *Sûreté maritime et violence en mer/Maritime Security and Violence at Sea*, Bruxelles, Bruylant, etc., 2011, pp. 191-209.

DANIELS, Ch. L., *Somali Piracy and Terrorism in the Horn of Africa*, Lanham, MD, etc., Scarecrow Press, 2012.

DEL CHICCA, M., "Universal Jurisdiction as Obligation to Prosecute or Extradite", *WMU Journal of Maritime Affairs*, 11 (2012), No. 1, pp. 83-93.

DINSTEIN, Y., "Piracy 'Jure Gentium'", in H. Hestermeyer *et al.*, *Coexistence, Cooperation and Solidarity: Liber Amicorum Rüdiger Wolfrum,* Leiden, etc., Nijhoff, 2012, pp. 1125-1145.

DIAZ, L. M., and B. H. DUBNER, "On the Evolution of the Law of International Sea Piracy: How Property Trumped Human Rights, the Environment and the Sovereign Rights of States in the Areas of the Creation and Enforcement of Jurisdiction", *Barry Law Review*, 13 (2009), No. 1, pp. 175-208.

DIAZ, L. M., and B. H. DUBNER, "An Examination of the Evolution of Crimes at Sea and the Emergence of the Many Legal Regimes in Their Wake", *North Carolina Journal of International Law and Commercial Regulation*, 34 (2009), No. 2, pp. 521-568.

DIAZ, L. M., and B. H. DUBNER, "On the Problem of Utilizing Unilateral Action to Prevent Acts of Sea Piracy and Terrorism: A Proactive Approach to the Evolution of International Law", *Syracuse Journal of International Law and Commerce*, 32 (2004), No. 1, pp. 1-50.

DIREK, O. F., M. D. A. HAMILTON, K. S. OPENSHAW and P. C. R TERRY, "Somalia and the Problem of Piracy in International Law", *USAK Yearbook of International Politics and Law*, 4 (2011), pp. 223-254.

DOBY, D., "Piracy 'Jure Gentium': The Jurisdictional Conflict of the High Seas and Territorial Waters", *Journal of Maritime Law and Commerce*, 41 (2010), No. 4, pp. 561-580.

DUBNER, B. H., *The Law of International Sea Piracy*, The Hague, etc., Martinus Nijhoff, 1980.

DUBNER, B. H., and J. P. HENN, "On Selecting a Judicial System(s) to Try Sea Pirates: An Interesting/Necessary Exercise but Is It Enough to Deter the Attacks/Hijackings?", *Journal of Maritime Law and Commerce*, 42 (2011), No. 4, pp. 569-605.

ESPALIÚ BERDUD, C., "The Crime of Maritime Piracy in the 2010 Reform of the Spanish Penal Code", *Spanish Yearbook of International Law*, 16 (2012), pp 55-93.

—, «La operación Atalanta de la Unión Europea en el marco de la lucha contra la piratería marítima», *Revista de las cortes generales*, 79 (2010), pp. 103-159.

FAKHRY, A., "Piracy across Maritime Law: Is There a Problem of Definition?", in Aldo Chircop *et al.* (eds.), *The Regulation of International Shipping: International and Comparative Perspectives: Essays in Honor of Edgar Gold*, Leiden, etc., Nijhoff, 2012, pp. 97-117.

FANTAUZZI, R., "Rascals, Scroundels, Villains, and Knaves: The Evolution of the Law of Piracy from Ancient Times to the Present", *International Journal of Legal Information*, 39 (2011), No. 3, pp. 346-383.

GABEL, G. D., "Smoother Seas Ahead: The Draft Guidelines as an International Solution to Modern-Day Piracy", *Tulane Law Review*, 81 (2007), Nos. 5-6, pp. 1433-1466.

GARCIA-CORROCHANO MOYANO, L., «Le traitement de la piraterie et le terrorisme dans les espaces maritimes de l'Union des Nations de l'Amérique du Sud-UNASUR», dans J. M. Sobrino Heredia, *Sûreté maritime et violence en mer/Maritime Security and Violence at Sea*, Bruxelles, Bruylant, etc., 2011, pp. 271-281.

GARCÍA GARCÍA-REVILLO, M., "Roundtable on the Judicial Ways to Face the Violence at Sea", in J. M. Sobrino Heredia, *Sûreté maritime et violence en mer/Maritime Security and Violence at Sea*, Bruxelles, Bruylant, etc., 2011, pp. 493-496.

GATHII, J. T., "Jurisdiction to Prosecute Non-National Pirates Captured by Third States under Kenyan and International Law", *Loyola of Los Angeles International and Comparative Law Review*, 31 (2009), No. 3, pp. 363-404.

—, "Kenya's Piracy Prosecutions", *American Journal of International Law*, 104 (2010) No. 3, pp. 416-436.

GAUTIER, Ph., «Le rôle du Tribunal international du droit de la mer face à la violence en mer», dans J. M. Sobrino Heredia, *Sûreté maritime et violence en mer/Maritime Security and Violence at Sea*, Bruxelles, Bruylant, etc., 2011, pp. 483-492.

GEISS, R., and A. Petrig, *Piracy and Armed Robbery at Sea: The Legal Framework for Counter-Piracy Operations in Somalia and the Gulf of Aden*, Oxford, etc., Oxford University Press, 2011.

GOLITSYN, V., "Maritime Security: Case of Piracy", in H. Hestermeyer *et al.*, *Coexistence, Cooperation and Solidarity: Liber Amicorum Rüdiger Wolfrum*, Leiden, etc., Nijhoff, 2012, pp. 1157-1176.

GUILFOYLE, D., "Combating Piracy: Executive Measures on the High Seas", *Japanese Yearbook of International Law*, 53 (2010), pp. 149-177.

—, *Shipping Interdiction and the Law of the Sea*, Cambridge, Cambridge University Press, 2009.

—, "The Legal Challenges in Fighting Piracy", Bibi van Ginkel and Frans-Paul van der Putten (eds.), *The International Response to Somali Piracy: Challenges and Opportunities*, Leiden, Nijhoff, 2010, pp. 127-152.

GUILFOYLE, D., *et al.*, "Piracy off Somalia: The Challenges for International Law", *Proceedings of the Annual Meeting American Society of International Law*, 103 (2009), pp. 89-99.

HALLWOOD, P., and Th. J. Miceli, "The Economics of International Cooperation in the Apprehension and Prosecution of Maritime Pirates", *Ocean Development and International Law*, 43 (2012), No. 2, pp. 188-200.

HÄUSSLER, U., "Crisis Response Operations in Maritime Environments", in M. Odello and R. Piotrowicz (eds.), *International Military Missions and International Law*, Leiden, etc., Nijhoff, 2011, pp. 161-210.

HEINTSCHEL VON HEINEGG, W., "Repressing Piracy and Armed Robbery at Sea: Towards a New International Legal Regime", *Israel Yearbook on Human Rights*, 40 (2010), pp. 219-241.

—, "The Special Issue of Piracy", in M. Odello and G. L. Beruto (eds.), *Non-State Actors and International Humanitarian Law: Organized Armed Groups: A Challenge for the 21st Century*, Milan, Angeli, 2010, pp. 170-177.

HODGKINSON, S. L., K. M. KELLY, Th. VAN HORN, and G. P. NOONE, "Piracy: New Efforts in Addressing this Enduring Problem", *Tulane Maritime Law Journal*, 36 (2011), No. 1, pp. 65-122.

HOESSLIN, K. VON, "Piracy and Armed Robbery at Sea in Southeast Asia: Organized and Fluid", *Studies in Conflict and Terrorism*, 35 (2012), Nos. 7-8, pp. 542-552.

HOUGHTON, M. C., "Walking the Plank: How United Nations Security Council Resolution 1816, While Progressive, Fails to Provide a Comprehensive Solution to Somali Piracy", *Tulsa Journal of Comparative and International Law*, 16 (2009), No. 2, pp. 253-286.

ISANGA, J. M., "Countering Persistent Contemporary Sea Piracy: Expanding Jurisdictional Regimes", *American University Law Review*, 59 (2009-2010), No. 5, pp. 1267- 1320.

JENISCH, U., "Piracy, Navies and the Law of the Sea: The Case of Somalia", *WMU Journal of Maritime Affairs*, 8 (2009), No. 2, pp. 123-143.

JORGE URBINA, J., «La contribution du Conseil de sécurité à la coopération internationale pour la lutte contre la piraterie dans le Golfe d'Aden et au large des côtes de la Somalie», dans J. M. Sobrino Heredia, *Sûreté maritime et violence en mer/Maritime Security and Violence at Sea*, Bruxelles, Bruylant, etc., 2011, pp. 283-300.

KARIM, Md. S., "Is There an International Obligation to Prosecute Pirates?", *Netherlands International Law Review,* 58 (2011), No. 3, pp. 387-407.

KELLEY, R. P., "UNCLOS, but No Cigar: Overcoming Obstacles to the Prosecution of Maritime Piracy", *Minnesota Law Review*, 95 (2010-2011), No. 6, pp. 2285-2317.

KLEINEN, J., and M. OSSEWEIJER (eds.), *Pirates, Ports, and Coasts in Asia: Historical and Contemporary Perspectives*, Leiden, etc., International Institute for Asian Studies (etc.), 2010

KOLB, A. S., Th. NEUMANN and T. R. SALOMON, "Die Entführung deutscher Seeschiffe: Flaggenrecht, Strafanwendungsrecht und diplomatischer Schutz", *Zeitschrift für ausländisches öffentliches Recht und Völkerrecht,* 71 (2011), No. 2, pp. 191-246.

KONTOROVICH, E., "'A Guantánamo on the Sea': The Difficulty of Prosecuting Pirates and Terrorists", *California Law Review*, 98 (2010), No. 1, pp. 243-275.

KRASKA, J., "Brandishing 'Legal Tools' in the Fight against Maritime Piracy", in Myron H. Nordquist *et al.* (eds.), *The Law of the Sea Convention: US Accession and Globalization*, Leiden, Nijhoff, 2012, pp. 258-290.

LE HARDŸ DE BEAULIEU, L., «La piraterie maritime à l'aube du XXIe siècle», *Revue générale de droit international public*, 115 (2011), n° 3, pp. 653-674.

LEANZA, U., «La pirateria marittima: diritto consuetudinario, diritto convenzionale e norme nazionali», dans A. Uricchio *et al.* (eds.), *Nuove piraterie e ordinamenti giuridici interni e internazionali: atti del Convegno tenuto a Taranto il 16 e 17 giugno 2009*, Bari, Cacucci, 2011, pp. 89-112.

LECLERCQ, J.-F., «La lutte contre la piraterie moderne entravant la circulation maritime et le droit fondamental des Nations Unies», *Revue de droit international et de droit comparé*, 88 (2011), n° 1, pp. 7-52.

—, "The Fight against Modern Piracy Impeding Maritime Traffic and Hampering United Nations Fundamental Rights", *European Transport Law,* 46 (2011), No. 4, pp. 359-401.

MALLIA, P., "The Fight against Piracy and Armed Robbery against Ships off the Coast of Somalia: International Cooperation Illustrated", in A. Martínez Gutiérrez (ed.), *Serving the Rule of International Maritime Law: Essays in Honour of Professor David Joseph Attard*, London, etc., Routledge, 2010, pp. 216-232.

MARTIN, J.-Ch., «La répression des actes de piraterie maritime: développements récents en matière de poursuites et détention des pirates somaliens», *Annuaire français de droit international*, 56 (2010), pp. 497-527.

MASSARELLA, C., "UN Security Council Resolution 1976 (2011) and Efforts to Support Piracy Prosecutions", *International Journal of Marine and Coastal Law*, 26 (2011), No. 4, pp. 679-685.

MATHONNET, D.,«De quelques remèdes à la piraterie maritime», *Le droit maritime français*, 63 (2011), n° 726, pp. 534-543.

MENEFEE, S. P., "A Model National Law on Acts of Piracy or Maritime Violence", in Proshanto K. Mukherjee, Maximo Q. Mejia and Gotthard M. Gauci (eds.), *Maritime Violence and other Security Issues at Sea*, 2002, pp. 101-114.

MENSAH, Th. A., "Piracy at Sea: A New Approach to an Old Menace", in Holger Hestermeyer *et al.* (eds.), *Law of the Sea in Dialogue*, Heidelberg, Springer, 2011, pp. 161-177.

MIDDELBURG, A., *Piracy in a Legal Context: Prosecution of Pirates Operating off the Somali Coast*, Nijmegen, Wolf Legal Publishers, 2011.

MANJIAO, C., "A Note on China's Legal and Operational Responses to International Piracy", *Ocean Development and International Law*, 44 (2013), No. 1, pp. 113-122.

MØLLER, B., "Militia and Piracy in the Horn of Africa: External Responses", in R. Bereketeab, *The Horn of Africa: Intra-state and Inter-state Conflicts and Security*, London, Pluto Press, 2013, pp. 178-196.

MURDOCH, A., "Recent Legal Issues and Problems Relating to Acts of Piracy of Somalia", in C. R. Symmons (ed.), *Selected Contemporary Issues in the Law of the Sea*, Leiden, etc., Nijhoff, 2011, pp. 139-168.

MURPHY, M., "Piracy and UNCLOS: Does International Law Help Regional States Combat Piracy?", in Peter Lehr (ed.), *Violence at Sea: Piracy in the Age of Global Terrorism*, New York, Routledge, 2007, pp. 155-182.

NEUHOLD, H., "The Return of Piracy: Problems, Parallels, Paradoxes", in H. Hestermeyer *et al.*, *Coexistence, Cooperation and Solidarity: Liber Amicorum Rüdiger Wolfrum,* Leiden, Nijhoff, 2012, pp. 1239-1258.

NTOVAS, A., "UN Resposes to Piracy", *Shipping and Trade Law*, 10 (2010), No. 8, pp. 4-6.

OBOKATA, T., "Maritime Piracy as a Violation of Human Rights: A Way Forward for Its Effective Prevention and Suppression?", *The International Journal of Human Rights*, 17 (2013), No. 1, pp. 18-34.

OKANO, M., "Is International Law Effective in the Fight against Piracy?", *Japanese Yearbook of International Law,* 53 (2011), pp. 178-201.

OLIVEIRA, F. B. DE, *A liberdade de circulação nos mares e as «novas Ameaças»: a pirataria marítima, a tutela jurídico-penal*, Lisbonne, Livraria Petrony, 2010.

ÖZÇAYIR, Z. O., "Piracy Part I", *Journal of International Maritime Law*, 15 (2009), No. 3, pp. 274-282.

—, "Piracy Part II", *Journal of International Maritime Law*, 16 (2010), No. 2, pp. 161-168.

PAPASTAVRIDIS, E., "The Right of Visit on the High Seas in a Theoretical Perspective: Mare Liberum versus Mare Clausum Revisited", *Leiden Journal of International Law*, 24 (2011), No. 1, pp. 45-69.

—, "Enforcement Jurisdiction in the Mediterranean Sea: Illicit Activities and the Rule of Law on the High Seas", *International Journal of Marine and Coastal Law*, 25 (2010), No. 4, pp. 569-599.

—, "Piracy of Somalia: The 'Emperors and the Thieves of the Oceans' in the 21st Century", in Ademola Abass (ed.), *Protecting Human Security in Africa*, Oxford, Oxford University Press, 2010, pp. 122-154.

PARADISO, D. P., "Come All Ye Faithful: How the International Community has Addressed the Effects of Somali Piracy but Fails to Remedy Its Cause", *Penn State International Law Review*, 29 (2010), No. 1, pp. 187-210.

PASSMAN, M. H., "Protections Afforded to Captured Pirates under the Law of War and International Law", *Tulane Maritime Law Journal,* 33 (2008), No. 1, pp. 1-40.

PARSONS, D. M., "Protecting the Booty: Creating a Regulatory Framework to Govern Increased Use of Private Security Companies in the Fight against Pirates", *Tulane Maritime Law Journal*, 35 (2010), No. 1, pp. 153-181.

PÉROUSE DE MONTCLOS, M.-A., "Maritime Piracy in Nigeria: Old Wine in New Bottles?", *Studies in Conflict and Terrorism,* 35 (2012), Nos. 7-8, pp. 531-541.

PETRIG A. (ed.), *Sea Piracy Law: Selected National Legal Frameworks and Regional Legislative Approaches/Droit de la piraterie maritime: cadres juridiques nationaux et approches legislatives régionales*, Berlin, Duncker & Humblot, 2010.

PHILLIPS, R. L., *Pirate Accessory Liability — Developing a Modern Legal Regime Governing Incitement and Intentional Facilitation of Maritime Piracy*, Rochester, NY, Social Science Research Network, 2012.

REALE, G., «La pirateria marittima: evoluzione del fenomeno criminale ed efficacia attuale degli strumenti di contrasto disponibili», dans G. Reale (dir. publ.), *Il contrasto alle attività illecite in mare*, Naples, Edizioni scientifiche italiane, 2011, pp. 13-77.

REALE, G. (ed.), *Il contrasto alle attività illecite in mare*, Naples, Edizioni scientifiche, 2011.

ROACH, J. A., "Countering Piracy off Somalia: International Law and International Institutions", *American Journal of International Law*, 104 (2010), No. 3, pp. 397-416.

ROACH, J. A., and R. W. SMITH, *Excessive Maritime Claims*, Leiden, etc., Nijhoff, 2012.

RODRÍGUEZ-VILLASANTE Y PRIETO, J. L., «Aspectos jurídicos-penales del crímen internacional de piratería», dans R. Castillejo Manzanares (dir. publ.), *La persecución de los actos de piratería en las costas somalíes*, Valencia, Tirant lo Blanch, 2011, pp. 113-144.

ROTHWELL, D. R., and N. KLEIN, "Maritime Security and the Law of the Sea", Natalie Klein, Joanna Mossop and Donald R. Rothwell (eds.), *Maritime Security: International Law and Policy Perspectives from Australia and New Zealand*, Abingdon, Routledge, 2010, pp. 22-36.

RUBIO FERNANDEZ, E. M., «Bilan de la réglementation juridique internationale de l'assistance aux victimes de la violence sur mer, spécialement de la piraterie ou du vol à main armée», dans J. M. Sobrino Heredia, *Sûreté maritime et violence en mer/Maritime Security and Violence at Sea*, Bruxelles, Bruylant, etc., 2011, pp. 301-322.

SÁNCHEZ BARRUECO, M. L., "The European Strategy against Piracy off the Somali Coast: A Multi-Pillar Response to a Cross-Pillar Concern", in J. M. Sobrino Heredia, *Sûreté maritime et violence en mer/Maritime Security and Violence at Sea*, Bruxelles, Bruylant, etc., 2011, pp. 323-342.

SÁNCHEZ RAMOS, B., "Action Undertaken by the International Maritime Organization in the Struggle against Maritime Piracy and Armed Robbery", in J. M. Sobrino Heredia, *Sûreté maritime et violence en mer/Maritime Security and Violence at Sea*, Bruxelles, Bruylant, etc., 2011, pp. 211-233.

SATKAUSKAS, R., "Piracy at Sea and the Limits of International Law", *Aegean Review of the Law of the Sea and Maritime Law*, 1 (2011), No. 2, pp. 217-235.

SHEARER, I., "Piracy", *Max Planck Encyclopedia of Public International Law*, 2010.

SHNIDER, S., "Universal Jurisdiction over 'Operation of a Pirate Ship': The Legality of the Evolving Piracy Definition in Regional Prosecutions", *North Carolina Journal of International Law and Commercial Regulation*, 38 (2012), No. 2, pp. 473-359.

SOBRINO HEREDIA, J. M., «Le terrorisme et la piraterie maritime», dans J. M. Sobrino Heredia, *Sûreté maritime et violence en mer/Maritime Security and Violence at Sea*, Bruxelles, Bruylant, etc., 2011, pp. 155-190.

—, *Sûreté maritime et violence en mer/Maritime Security and Violence at Sea*, Bruxelles, Bruylant, etc., 2011.

SOMERS, E., «Piraterie maritime et droit international», dans L. Le Hardÿ de Beaulieu (dir. publ.), avec les contributions de Ph. Gautier *et al.*, *Criminalité et trafics maritimes: des enjeux politiques aux conséquences*, Namur, Presses universitaires de Namur, 2008, pp. 11-29.

—, "Can the Law Contribute to Solving the Problem of Piracy?" in Kris Bernauw *et al.*, *Free on Board: Liber Amoricorum Marc A. Huybrechts*, Antwerp, etc., Intersentia, 2011, pp. 497-515.

STERIO, M., "International Law in Crisis: Piracy off the Coast of Somalia", *Case Western Reserve Journal of International Law*, 44 (2011), Nos. 1-2, pp. 291-301.

SURBUN, V., "The Developing Jurisprudence to Combat Modern Maritime Pricacy: A Crime of the High Seas?", *Comparative and International Law Journal of Southern Africa*, 43 (2010), No. 1, pp. 1-22.

STRUETT, M. J., J. D. CARLSON and M. T. NANCE (eds.), *Maritime Piracy and the Construction of Global Governance*, New York, NY, Routledge, 2013.

SYMMONS, C. R., "Use of Law of Piracy to Deal with Violent Inter-Vessel Incidents at Sea beyond the 12-Mile Limit: The Irish Experience", in C. R. Symmons (ed.), *Selected Contemporary Issues in the Law of the Sea*, Leiden, etc., Nijhoff, 2011, pp. 169-193.

SYRING, T., "A Pirate and a Refugee: Reservations and Responses in the Fight against Piracy", *ILSA Journal of International and Comparative Law*, 17 (2011), No. 2, pp. 437-457.

TAJANI, A., «Il contrasto alla pirateria marittima: l'impegno delle istituzioni comunitarie e internazionali», *Nuove piraterie e ordinamenti giuridici interni e internazionali: atti del Convegno tenuto a Taranto il 16 e 17 giugno 2009*, Bari, Cacucci, 2011, pp. 21-41.

TARASENKO, S.,"The United Nations' Role in Combatting Piracy and Terrorism at Sea", in Myron H. Nordquist *et al.* (eds.), *The Law of the Sea Convention: US Accession and Globalization*, Leiden, Nijhoff, 2012, pp. 143-153.

THEDWALL, G., "Choosing the Right Yardarm: Establishing and International

Court for Piracy", *Georgetown Journal of International Law*, 41 (2010), No. 2, pp. 501-523.

TREVES, T., "Piracy, Law of the Sea, and Use of Force: Developments off the Coast of Somalia", *European Journal of International Law*, 20 (2009), No. 2, pp. 399-414.

TUERK, H., "Maritime Protection and Violence at Sea: Remarks", in J. M. Sobrino Heredia, *Sûreté maritime et violence en mer/Maritime Security and Violence at Sea*, Bruxelles, Bruylant, etc., 2011, pp. 477-482.

—, *Reflections on the Contemporary Law of the Sea*, Leiden, etc., Nijhoff, 2012.

—, "The Resurgence of Piracy: A Phenomenon of Modern Times", *University of Miami International and Comparative Law*, 17 (2009), No. 1, pp. 1-42.

URBINA, J. J., «La cooperación internacional en la prevención y control de los actos de piratería en el actual derecho del mar», dans Jorge Pueyo Losa et Julio Jorge Urbina (dir. publ.), *La cooperación internacional en la ordenación de los mares y océanos*, Madrid , Iustel, 2009, pp. 321-362.

URICCHIO, A., *et al.* (dir. publ.), *Nuove piraterie e ordinamenti giuridici interni e internazionali: atti del Convegno tenuto a Taranto il 16 e 17 giugno 2009*, Bari, Cacucci, 2011.

UYKUR, T., "An Overview of Two Contemporary Issues in the Law of the Sea: Islands within the Context of Delimitation and Combating Piracy off the Coasts of Somalia", in Myron H. Nordquist *et al.* (eds.), *The Law of the Sea Convention: US Accession and Globalization*, Leiden, Nijhoff, 2012, pp. 551-568.

VALLON, F., *La mer et son droit, entre liberté et consensualisme, l'impossible gestion de la piraterie et du terrorisme*, Paris, Publibook, 2011.

VÁZQUEZ GÓMEZ, E. M., "Terrorism and Piracy", in J. M. Sobrino Heredia, *Sûreté maritime et violence en mer/Maritime Security and Violence at Sea*, Bruxelles, Bruylant, etc., 2011, pp. 343-346.

WILSON, D. G., "Interdiction on the High Seas: The Role and Authority of a Master in the Boarding and Searching of His Ship by Foreign Warships", *Naval Law Review*, 55 (2008), pp. 157-211.

WOOLLEY, C. R., "Piracy and Sovereign Rights: Addressing Piracy in the Straits of Malacca without Degrading the Sovereign Rights of Indonesia and Malaysia", *Santa Clara Journal of International Law*, 8 (2010), No. 2, pp. 447-472.

WORLD BANK, *The Pirates of Somalia: Ending the Threat, Rebuilding a Nation*, Washington, DC, World Bank, 2013.

YAO, H., "Universal Jurisdiction over Piracy and East Asian Practice", *Chinese Journal of International Law*, 11 (2012), No. 4, pp. 623-655.

15 La compétence nationale en matière de piraterie
Domestic Enforcement Jurisdiction over Piracy

ADEMUN-ODEKE, A.,"Jurisdiction by Agreement over Foreign Pirates in Domestic Courts: In re Mohamud Mohamed Dashi", *University of San Francisco Maritime Law Journal*, 24 (2011-2012) , No. 1, pp. 35-64.

—, "Somali-Piracy: Jurisdiction over Foreign Pirates in Domestic Courts and Third States under International Law", *Journal of International Maritime Law*, 17 (2011), No. 2, pp. 121-146.

AMBANI, O., "Prosecuting Piracy in the Horn of Africa: The Case of Kenya", in Chacha Murungu and Japhet Biegon (eds.), *Prosecuting International Crimes in Africa*, Pretoria, Pretoria University Law Press, 2011, pp. 233-246.

AUST, H. P., "Pirateriebekämpfung im Lichte von Grundgesetz und Völkerrecht auf dem verwaltungsgerichtlichen Prüfstand", *Deutsches Verwaltungsblatt*, 127 (2012), No. 8, pp. 484-490.

BAHAR, M., "Attaining Optimal Deterrence at Sea: A Legal and Strategic Theory for Naval Anti-Piracy Operations", *Vanderbilt Journal of Transnational Law,* 40 (2007), No. 1, pp. 1-86.

BUEGER, C., "Drops in the Bucket? A Review of Onshore Responses to Somali Piracy", *WMU Journal of Maritime Affairs*, 11 (2012), No. 1, pp. 15-31.

CALIGIURI, A., «Observations sur la poursuite et justice des pirates», dans J. M. Sobrino Heredia, *Sûreté maritime et violence en mer/Maritime Security and Violence at Sea*, Bruxelles, Bruylant, etc., 2011, pp. 251-269.

CASTILLEJO MANZANARES, R., «Jurisdicción española para perseguir actos de piraterá: especial referencia al caso Alakrana», dans R. Castillejo Manzanares (dir. publ.), *La persecución de los actos de piratería en las costas somalíes*, Valencia, Tirant lo Blanch, 2011, pp. 207-235.

CASTILLEJO MANZANARES, R. (dir. publ.), *La persecución de los actos de piratería en las costas somalíes*, Valencia, Tirant lo Blanch, 2011.

CHI, M., "Finding out the 'Achilles Heels': Piracy Suppression under International Law and Chinese Law", *Journal of East Asia and International Law*, 5 (2012), No. 1, pp. 7-36.

DEANS, A., "Suing Organized Piracy: An Application of Maritime Torts to Pirate Attacks, and Subsequent Civil Actions against the Supporters of Organized Piracy", *Roger Williams University Law Review*, 16 (2011), No. 3, pp. 655-686.

DEL CHICCA, M., «La pirateria marittima di fronte ai giudici di Stati membri dell'Unione Europea», *Rivista di diritto internazionale*, 95 (2012), n° 1, pp. 104-119.

DOEG, B. K., "PMCs on the High Seas: The Solution to Somali Piracy or a Failure to Learn from History", *National Security and Conflict Law Review*, 1 (2010-2011), pp. 139-164.

DUBNER, B. H., and S. FREDERICKSON, "On the Legal Issues regarding the Prosecution of Sea Pirates (Including Human Rights): A Case of History Repeating Itself", *Temple International and Comparative Law Journal*, 26 (2012), No. 2, pp. 233-262.

DUMOUCHEL, A. C., et S. TOUZÉ (dir. publ.), «Contenu et dernières avancées du projet de loi français de lutte contre la piraterie», *Le droit maritime français*, 62 (2010), n° 720, pp. 961-970.

DUTTON, Y. M., "Maritime Piracy and the Impunity Gap: Insufficient National Laws or a Lack of Political Will", *Tulane Law Review*, 86 (2012), No. 5, pp. 1111-1162.

—, "Maritime Piracy and the Impunity Gap: Domestic Implementation of International Treaty Provisions", in Michael J. Struett, Jon D. Carlson and Mark T. Nance (eds.), *Maritime Piracy and the Construction of Global Governance*, New York, NY, Routledge, 2013, pp. 71-95.

ESPALIÚ BERDUD, C., "The Crime of Maritime Piracy in the 2010 Reform of the Spanish Penal Code", *Spanish Yearbook of International Law*, 16 (2012), pp. 55-93.

ESSER, R., and S. FISCHER, "Festnahme von Piraterieverdächtigen auf Hoher See: Geltung des § 127 StPO im Rahmen der Operation Atalanta", *Zeitschrift für Internationale Strafrechtsdogmatik*, 4 (2009), No. 13, pp. 771-783.

FANTAUZZI, R., "Rascals, Scroundels, Villains, and Knaves: The Evolution of the Law of Piracy from Ancient Times to the Present", *International Journal of Legal Information*, 39 (2011), No. 3, pp. 346-383.

FASTENRATH, U., "Zur Verfassungsmäßigkeit unilateraler Pirateriebekämpfung durch die deutsche Marine", in H. Hestermeyer *et al.*, *Coexistence, Cooperation and Solidarity: Liber Amicorum Rüdiger Wolfrum*, Leiden, etc., Nijhoff, 2012, pp. 1935-1957.

FELDTMANN, B., "Should We Rule out Criminal Law as a Means of Fighting Maritime Piracy? An Essay on the Challenges and Possibilities of Prosecuting Somali Pirates", in Ulrika Andersson, Christoffer Wong, Helén Örnemark

Hansen, *Festskrift till Per Ole Träskman,* Stockholm, Norstedts Juridik, pp. 179-188.

FINK, M. D., and R. J. GALVIN, "Combating Pirates off the Coast of Somalia: Current Legal Challenges", *Netherlands International Law Review*, 56 (2009), No. 3, pp. 367-395.

FOUCHE, H., and J. MEYER, "Investigating Sea Piracy: Crime Scene Challenges", *WMU Journal of Maritime Affairs*, 11 (2012), No. 1, pp. 33-50.

"Framework Agreement on Integrated Cross-Border Maritime Law Enforcement Operations between the Government of the United States of America and the Government of Canada", in Jack W. Harris (ed.), *Maritime Law: Issues, Challenges and Implications*, New York, Nova Science, 2011, pp. 133-143.

FISCHER-LESCANO, A., and L. KRECK, "Piracy and Human Rights: Legal Issues in the Fight against Piracy within the Context of the European 'Operation Atalanta'", *German Yearbook of International Law*, 52 (2010), pp. 525-561.

FRITZ, D., "Child Pirates from Somalia: A Call for the International Community to Support the Further Development of Juvenile Justice Systems in Puntland and Somalia", *Case Western Reserve Journal of International Law*, 44 (2012), No. 3, pp. 891-919.

GARCIA-CORROCHANO MOYANO, L., « Le traitement de la piraterie et le terrorisme dans les espaces maritimes de l'Union des Nations de l'Amérique du Sud-UNASUR », dans J. M. Sobrino Heredia, *Sûreté maritime et violence en mer/Maritime Security and Violence at Sea*, Bruxelles, Bruylant, etc., 2011, pp. 271-281.

GATHII, J. T., "Kenya's Piracy Prosecutions", *American Journal of International Law*, 104 (2010) No. 3, pp. 416-436.

—, "Jurisdiction to Prosecute Non-National Pirates Captured by Third States under Kenyan and International Law", *Loyola of Los Angeles International and Comparative Law Review*, 31 (2009), No. 3, pp. 363-404.

GÓMEZ RIVERO, C., « La represión penal de la piratería: bases para la oportunidad de una reforma », dans Luis Arroyo Zapatero et Adán Nieto Martín (dir. publ.), *Piratas, mercenarios, soldados, jueces y policías: nuevas desafíos del derecho penal europeo e internacional*, Cuenca, Ed. de la Universidad de Castilla-La Mancha, 2010, pp. 53-75.

GOVERN, K. H., "National Solutions to an International Scourge: Prosecuting Piracy Domestically as a Viable Alternative to International Tribunals", *University of Miami International and Comparative Law Review*, 19 (2011), No. 1, pp. 1-56.

HEINTSCHEL VON HEINEGG, W., "The Special Issue of Piracy", in M. Odello and G. L. Beruto (eds.), *Non-State Actors and International Humanitarian Law: Organized Armed Groups: A Challenge for the 21st Century*, Milan, Angeli, 2010, pp. 170-177.

HELFMAN, T., "Marauders in the Courts: Why the Federal Courts Have Got the Problem of the Maritime Piracy (Partly) Wrong", *Syracuse Law Review*, 62 (2012), No. 1, pp. 53-74.

HODGKINSON, S. L., K. M. KELLY, Th. VAN HORN and G. P. NOONE, "Piracy: New Efforts in Addressing This Enduring Problem", *Tulane Maritime Law Journal*, 65 (2011), No. 1, pp. 65-122.

IBRAHIM, A. A., "Le cadre juridique relatif à la piraterie maritime à Djibouti", in A. Petrig (ed.), *Sea Piracy Law: Selected National Legal Frameworks and Regional Legislative Approaches/Droit de la piraterie maritime: cadres juridiques nationaux et approches legislatives régionales*, Berlin, Duncker & Humblot, 2010, pp. 83-124.

ISANGA, J. M., "Countering Persistent Contemporary Sea Piracy: Expanding Jurisdictional Regimes", *American University Law Review*, 59 (2009-2010), No. 5, pp. 1267- 1320.

JANSSENS, P.-A., « La loi française de lutte contre la piraterie maritime à l'épreuve des mesures pionnières adoptées par la Belgique», *Le droit maritime français*, 63 (2011), n° 726, pp. 544-551.

—, "La Belgique en passe de juger son premier (présumé) pirate: état d'une législation pionnière en matière de piraterie maritime", *European Transport Law*, 46 (2011), No. 2, pp. 117-127.

Jimenez Kwast, P., "Maritime Law Enforcement and the Use of Force: Reflections on the Categorisation of Forcible Action at Sea in the Light of the Guyana/Suriname Award", *Journal of Conflict and Security Law*, 13 (2008), No. 1, pp. 49-91.

Juanes Peces, A, «Competencia de la audiencia nacional en los delitos de piratería», dans R. Castillejo Manzanares (dir. publ.), *La persecución de los actos de piratería en las costas somalíes*, Valencia, Tirant lo Blanch, 2011, pp. 237-243.

Kamuli, R., "Tanzania's Legal Framework on Sea Piracy: An Obligatory but Inconsistent Model", in A. Petrig (ed.), *Sea Piracy Law: Selected National Legal Frameworks and Regional Legislative Approaches/Droit de la piraterie maritime: cadres juridiques nationaux et approches legislatives régionales*, Berlin, Duncker & Humblot, 2010, pp. 39-81.

Karim, Md. S., "Is There an International Obligation to Prosecute Pirates?", *Netherlands International Law Review*, 58 (2011), No. 3, pp. 387-407.

Kelley, R. P., "UNCLOS, but No Cigar: Overcoming Obstacles to the Prosecution of Maritime Piracy", *Minnesota Law Review*, 95 (2010-2011), No. 6, pp. 2285-2317.

Kimball, J. D., «The Prosecution of Pirates under United States Law», dans Francesco Berlingieri (dir. publ.), *Scritti in onore di Francesco Berlingieri* (Vol. II), Gênes, Il diritto marittimo, 2010, pp. 615-622.

Klein, N., "Legal Implications of Australia's Maritime Identification System", *International and Comparative Law Quarterly*, 55 (2006), No. 2, pp. 337-368.

Kleinen, J., and M. Osseweijer (eds.), *Pirates, Ports, and Coasts in Asia: Historical and Contemporary Perspectives*, Leiden, etc., International Institute for Asian Studies, etc., 2010.

Kolb, A. S., Th. Neumann and T. R. Salomon, "Die Entführung deutscher Seeschiffe: Flaggenrecht, Strafanwendungsrecht und diplomatischer Schutz", *Zeitschrift für ausländisches öffentliches Recht und Völkerrecht*, 71 (2011), No. 2, pp. 191-246.

Kress, C., "Die moderne Piraterie, das Strafrecht und die Menschenrechte: Gedanken aus Anlass der deutschen Mitwirkung an der Seeoperation Atalanta", in Weingärtner (ed.), *Die Bundeswehr als Armee im Einsatz: Entwicklungen im nationalen und internationalen Recht*, Baden-Baden, Nomos, 2010, pp. 95-123.

Ladiges, M., "Festnahme und Strafvervolging von Piraten: Anmerkung zu dem Urteil des VG Köln vom 11. November 2011: 25 K 4280/09", *Neue Zeitschrift für Wehrrecht*, 54 (2012), No. 2, pp. 56-63.

Landsidle, J., "Enhancing International Efforts to Prosecute Suspected Pirates", *Case Western Reserve Journal of International Law*, 44 (2011), Nos. 1-2, pp. 317-323.

Lavrisha, D. A., "Pirates, Ye Be Warned: A Comparative Analysis of National Piracy Laws", *University of Toledo Law Review*, 42 (2010), No. 1, pp. 255-282.

Leanza, U., «La pirateria marittima: diritto consuetudinario, diritto convenzionale e norme nazionali», dans A. Uricchio *et al.* (dir. publ.), *Nuove piraterie e ordinamenti giuridici interni e internazionali: atti del Convegno tenuto a Taranto il 16 e 17 giugno 2009*, Bari, Cacucci, 2011, pp. 89-112.

Leclercq, J. F., «La répression en droit belge des actes de piraterie moderne entravant le tranport maritime, exemple d'une Union fédérale réussie», *Revue de droit international et de droit comparé*, 89 (2012), n° 2, pp. 241-260.

—, «La notion de piraterie en droit maritime belge: transport et assurance», *Le droit maritime français*, 62 (2010), n° 720, pp. 951-960.

LELARGE, A., «La Somalie entre anarchie et piraterie», *Journal du droit international*, 137 (2010), n° 2, pp. 449-474.

LE GOURIELLEC, S., «Base militaire à Djibouti: le paradoxe de la puissance japonaise», *Revue Défense nationale* (2010), n° 734, pp. 88-92.

LE HARDŸ DE BEAULIEU, L., «La nouvelle législation belge relative à la piraterie maritime», *Revue internationale de droit comparé*, 62 (2010), n° 3, pp. 741-753.

LESIEUR, F., "Commentaire sur la nouvelle loi française relative à la lutte contre la piraterie et à l'exercice des pouvoirs de police de l'Etat en mer", *Journal of East Asia and International Law*, 4 (2011), No. 1, pp. 115-129.

MANJIAO, C., "A Note on China's Legal and Operational Responses to International Piracy", *Ocean Development and International Law*, 44 (2013), No. 1, pp. 113-122.

MANUSAMA, K. M., "Prosecuting Pirates in the Netherlands: The Case of the MS Samanyolu", *Revue de droit militaire et de droit de la guerre*, 49 (2010), Nos. 1-2, pp. 141-168.

MENEFEE, S. P., "Anti-piracy Law in the Year of the Ocean: Problems and Opportunity", *ILSA Journal of International and Comparative Law,* 5 (1999), No. 2, pp. 309-318.

—, "A Model National Law on Acts of Piracy or Maritime Violence", in Proshanto K. Mukherjee, Maximo Q. Mejia and Gotthard M. Gauci (eds.), *Maritime Violence and Other Security Issues at Sea*, 2002, pp. 101-114.

MICHEL, B., «Les lois du 30 décembre 2009 relatives à la lutte contre la piraterie maritime», *Revue de droit pénal et de criminologie*, 90 (2010), n°s 7-8, pp. 854-877.

MIDDELBURG, A., *Piracy in a Legal Context: Prosecution of Pirates Operating off the Somali Coast*, Nijmegen, Wolf Legal Publishers, 2011.

MOMTAZ, D., «L'apport du Conseil de sécurité à la lutte contre l'impunité des pirates opérant au large des côtes de Somalie», *Annuaire du droit de la mer*, 15 (2010), pp. 239-248.

MUTETI, A. M., "Prosecution of Piracy Cases — the Kenya Experience", *Commonwealth Law Bulletin*, 39 (2013), No. 1, pp. 73-77.

NARAIN, A., "Preparing for Piracy Trials in Mauritius", *Commonwealth Law Bulletin*, 39 (2013), No. 1, pp. 53-58.

NTOVAS, A. X. M., "Towards the Establishment of Specialised Anti-Piracy Courts", *Shipping and Trade Law*, 12 (2012), No. 6, pp. 1-4.

ÖZÇAYIR, Z. O., "Ransom Payments and the US Executive Order on Somalian Piracy: Piracy Part III", *Journal of International Maritime Law*, 16 (2010), No. 4, pp. 323-328.

PANOSSIAN, A., «L'action du Conseil de sécurite en Somalie: entre lutte contre la piraterie et restauration de l'Etat», *L'observateur des Nations Unies*, 28 (2010), n° 1, pp. 221-254.

PAPASTAVRIDIS, E., "Enforcement Jurisdiction in the Mediterranean Sea: Illicit Activities and the Rule of Law on the High Seas", *International Journal of Marine and Coastal Law*, 25 (2010), No. 4, pp. 569-599.

PEREZ, N., «L'appréhension des actes de piraterie au large de la Somalie par le droit international», dans *Les menaces contre la paix et la sécurité internationales: nouveaux défis et nouveaux enjeux*, Paris, IREDIES, 2010, pp. 205-219.

PÉROUSE DE MONTCLOS, M.-A., "Maritime Piracy in Nigeria: Old Wine in New Bottles?", *Studies in Conflict and Terrorism*, 35 (2012), Nos. 7-8, pp. 531-541.

PETRIG A. (ed.), *Sea Piracy Law: Selected National Legal Frameworks and Regional Legislative Approaches/Droit de la piraterie maritime: cadres juridiques nationaux et approches legislatives régionales*, Berlin, Duncker & Humblot, 2010.

REALE, G., «La pirateria marittima: evoluzione del fenomeno criminale ed efficacia attuale degli strumenti di contrasto disponibili», dans G. Reale (dir. publ.), *Il contrasto alle attività illecite in mare*, Naples, Edizioni scientifiche italiane, 2011, pp. 13-77.

REALE, G. (dir. publ.), *Il contrasto alle attività illecite in mare*, Naples, Edizioni scientifiche, 2011.

ROACH, J.A., "Countering Piracy off Somalia: International Law and International Institutions", *American Journal of International Law*, 104 (2010), No. 3, pp. 397-416.

—, "General Problematic Issues on Exercise of Jurisdiction over Modern Instances of Piracy", in Clive R. Symmons (ed.), *Selected Contemporary Issues in the Law of the Sea*, Leiden, Nijhoff, 2011, pp. 119-137.

RODRÍGUEZ-VILLASANTE Y PRIETO, J. L., «Aspectos jurídicos-penales del crímen internacional de piratería», dans R. Castillejo Manzanares (dir. publ.), *La persecución de los actos de piratería en las costas somalíes*, Valencia, Tirant lo Blanch, 2011, pp. 113-144.

—, «Problemas jurídico-penales e internacionales del crimen de piratería: una laguna imperdonable de nuestro Código Penal y, ¿por qué no decirlo? un crimen de la competencia de la Corte Penal Internacional», *Revista española de derecho military* (2009), n° 93, pp. 187-222.

RUBIN, A. P., *The Law of Piracy*, Irvington-on-Hudson, NY, Transnational, 1998.

SHANOR, C. A., "Terrorism, Historical Analogies, and Modern Choices", *Emory International Law Review*, 24 (2010), No. 2, pp. 589-617.

SHNIDER, S., "Universal Jurisdiction over 'Operation of a Pirate Ship': The Legality of the Evolving Piracy Definition in Regional Prosecutions", *North Carolina Journal of International Law and Commercial Regulation*, 38 (2012), No.2, pp. 473-359.

STERIO, M., "Fighting Piracy in Somalia (and Elsewhere): Why More is Needed", *Fordham International Law Journal*, 33 (2010), No. 2, pp. 372-408.

—, "Piracy off the Coast of Somalia: The Argument for Pirate Prosecutions in the National Courts of Kenya, the Seychelles, and Mauritius", *Amsterdam Law Forum*, Vol. 4 (2012), No. 2, pp. 104-124.

SWANSON, S. R., "Terrorism, Piracy, and the Alien Tort Statute", *Rutgers Law Journal*, 40 (2008), No. 1, pp. 159-218.

TOTTEN, Ch., and M. BERNAL, "Somali Piracy: Jurisdictional Issues, Enforcement Problems and Potential Solutions", *Georgetown Journal of International Law*, 41 (2010), No. 2, pp. 377-424.

TSURUTA, T., "The Japanese Act on the Punishment of and Measures against Piracy, *Aegean Review of the Law of the Sea and Maritime Law,* 1 (2011), No. 2, pp. 237-245.

URICCHIO, A., *et al.* (dir. publ.), *Nuove piraterie e ordinamenti giuridici interni e internazionali: atti del Convegno tenuto a Taranto il 16 e 17 giugno 2009*, Bari, Cacucci, 2011.

WAMBUA, P. M., "The Legal Framework for Adjudication of Piracy Cases in Kenya: Review of the Jurisdictional and Procedural Challenges and the Institutional Capacity", in A. Petrig (ed.), *Sea Piracy Law: Selected National Legal Frameworks and Regional Legislative Approaches/Droit de la piraterie maritime: cadres juridiques nationaux et approches legislatives régionales*, Berlin, Duncker & Humblot, 2010, pp. 1-37.

—, "The Jurisdictional Challenges to the Prosecution or Piracy Cases in Kenya: Mixed Fortunes for a Perfect Model in the Global War against Piracy", *WMU Journal of Maritime Affairs*, 11 (2012), No. 1, pp. 95-113.

WITTENBERG, M., "Operation ATALANTE: Ingewahrsamnahme und Strafverfolgung von mutmaßlichren Piraten: Theorie und Praxis", *Neue Zeitschrift für Wehrrecht*, 53 (2011), No. 2, pp. 62-72.

16 Les vols à main armée en mer
Armed Robbery at Sea

ABBOTT, Ch. J., "Hijacked: Somalia Sanctions Hold U.S. Ship Owners Hostage", *Suffolk Transnational Law Review*, 35 (Winter 2012), No. 1. pp. 101-120.

ABHYANKAR, J., "Piracy and Maritime Violence: A Global Update", in Proshanto K. Mukherjee, Maximo Q. Mejia and Gotthard M. Gauci (eds.), *Maritime Violence and other Security Issues at Sea*, 2002, pp. 9-25.

ADEMUN-ODEKE, A., "Somali Piracy — Effects on Oceanborne Commerce and Regional Security and Challenges to International Law and World Order", *Australian and New Zealand Maritime Law Journal*, 25(2011), No. 1, pp. 134-160.

ALCAIDE FERNÁNDEZ, J., "'Hostes Humani Generis': Pirates, Slavers, and Other Criminals", in Bardo Fassbender and Anne Peters (eds.), *The Oxford Handbook of the History of International Law*, Oxford, Oxford University Press, 2012, pp. 120-144.

ARTEAGA, F., *La lucha contra la piratería en Somalia: el problema persiste a pesar del esfuerzo militar* (ARI), Madrid, Real Instituto Elcano (ARI), 2011.

BACAS FERNÁNDEZ, J. R., *et al.* (dir. publ.), *Crisis somalí, piratería e intervención internacional*, Madrid, Instituto Universitario General Gutiérrez Mellado-UNED, 2009.

BAHADUR, J., *Deadly Waters: Inside the Hidden World of Somalia's Pirates*, London, Profile Books, 2011.

BATEMAN, S., "Piracy and Armed Robbery against Ships in Indonesian Waters" in Robert Cribb and Michele Ford (eds.), *Indonesia beyond the Water's Edge: Managing an Archipelagic State*, Singapore, Institute of Southeast Asian Studies (ISEAS), 2009, pp. 117-133.

—, "Sea Piracy: Some Inconvenient Truths", *Disarmament Forum*, 2010, No. 2, pp. 13-24.

—, «La piraterie maritime: des vérités qui dérangent», *Forum du désarmement*, 2010, n° 2, pp. 15-28.

BAUTISTA JIMÉNEZ, J. M., «Questions anciennes (déjà oubliées), nouvelles (à la souveraineté): les voleurs de la mer et la réaction de la communauté internationale», dans J. M. Sobrino Heredia, *Sûreté maritime et violence en mer/Maritime Security and Violence at Sea*, Bruxelles, Bruylant, etc., 2011, pp. 235-250.

BECKMAN, R. C., "Do We Need a New Convention on Piracy and Armed Robbery against Ships?", in Aldo Chircop *et al.* (eds.), *The Regulation of International Shipping: International and Comparative Perspectives: Essays in Honor of Edgar Gold*, Leiden, etc., Nijhoff, 2012, pp. 77-96.

BLANCO-BAZÁN, A., "Protection and Safety in Maritime Transport : Measures by International Maritime Organizations", in J. M. Sobrino Heredia, *Sûreté maritime et violence en mer/Maritime Security and Violence at Sea*, Bruxelles, Bruylant, etc., 2011, pp. 381-410.

CALIGIURI, A., «Observations sur la poursuite et justice des pirates», dans J. M. Sobrino Heredia, *Sûreté maritime et violence en mer/Maritime Security and Violence at Sea*, Bruxelles, Bruylant, etc., 2011, pp. 251-269.

CANINAS, O. P., «Pirataria marítima moderna: história, situação atual e desafios», *Revista da Escola de Guerra Naval*, 14 (2009), pp. 101-122.

CARAFANO, J. J., R. WEITZ and M. E. ANDERSEN, *Maritime Security: Fighting Piracy in the Gulf of Aden and Beyond*, Washington, DC, Heritage Foundation, 2007.

CÉCILE, J.-J., *Pirates en eaux somaliennes*, Paris, Nouveau Monde, 2010.

CHALK, P., "Piracy off the Horn of Africa: Scope, Dimensions, Causes and Responses", *Brown Journal of World Affairs*, 16 (2010), No. 2, pp. 89-108.

CHALK, P., and S. J. HANSEN, "Present Day Piracy: Scope, Dimensions, Dangers, and Causes", *Studies in Conflict and Terrorism*, 35 (2012), Nos. 7-8, pp. 497-506.

CORMIER-SALEM, M.-C., et T. DAHOU, *Gouverner la mer: Etats, pirates, sociétés*, Paris, Karthala, 2009.

CORTI, S., «Somalia: tra guerra e pirateria», dans Maurizio Simoncelli (dir. publ.), *Dove i diritti umani non esistono più: la violazione dei diritti umani nelle guerre contemporanee*, Rome, Ediesse, 2010, pp. 125-151.

DIREK, O. F., M. D. A., HAMILTON, K. S. OPENSHAW and P. C. R. TERRY, "Somalia and the Problem of Piracy in International Law", *USAK Yearbook of International Politics and Law*, 4 (2011), pp. 223-254.

DONG, W., and J. XIN, "China's Maritime Security: Priorities and Challenges", in Joshua H. Ho and Sam Bateman (eds.), *Maritime Challenges and Priorities in Asia: Implications for Regional Security*, London, Routledge, 2012, 181-200.

DUBNER, B. H., and J. P. HENN, "On Selecting a Judicial System(s) to Try Sea Pirates: An Interesting/Necessary Exercise but Is It Enough to Deter the Attacks/Hijackings?", *Journal of Maritime Law and Commerce*, 42 (2011), No. 4, pp. 569-605.

DUBNER, B. H., and R. RATURI, "On the Economics of International Sea Piracy: A Case of History Repeating Itself", *Michigan State International Law Review*, 20 (2012), No. 3, pp. 745-773.

EKLÖF, S., *Pirates in Paradise: A Modern History of Southeast Asia's Maritime Marauders*, Copenhagen, NIAS Press, 2006.

EL-KHAWAS, M. A., and J. NDUMBE ANYU (eds.), *Case Studies of Conflict in Africa: The Niger Delta, the Bakassi Peninsula, and Piracy in Somalia*, Lewiston, NY, etc., Mellen, 2012.

ELLEMAN, B. A., A. FORBES and D. ROSENBERG (eds.), *Piracy and Maritime Crime: Historical and Modern Case Studies*, Newport, RI, Naval War College Press, 2010.

FANTAUZZI, R., "Rascals, Scroundels, Villains, and Knaves: The Evolution of the Law of Piracy from Ancient Times to the Present", *International Journal of Legal Information*, 39 (2011), No. 3, pp. 346-383.

FOUCHÉ, H., "Harmonized Legal Framework for Africa as an Instrument to Combat Sea Piracy", in A. Petrig (ed.), *Sea Piracy Law: Selected National Legal Frameworks and Regional Legislative Approaches/Droit de la piraterie maritime: cadres juridiques nationaux et approches législatives régionales*, Berlin, Duncker & Humblot, 2010, pp. 139-159.

FRÉCON, E., "Piracy and Armed Robbery at Sea along the Malacca Straits: Initial Impressions from Fieldwork in the Riau Islands", in Graham Gerard Ong-Webb (ed.), *Piracy, Maritime Terrorism and Securing the Malacca Straits*, Singapore, etc., ISEAS, Institute of Southeast Asian Studies, etc., 2006, pp. 68-83.

—, «Géopolitique de la piraterie au Sud-Est asiatique: conflits de représentations», *Outre-Terre: Revue européenne de géopolitique*, 25-26 (2010), pp. 101-123.

GABEL, G. D., "Smoother Seas Ahead: The Draft Guidelines as an International Solution to Modern-Day Piracy", *Tulane Law Review*, 81 (2007), Nos. 5-6, pp. 1433-1466.

GEISS, R., and A. PETRIG, *Piracy and Armed Robbery at Sea: The Legal Framework for Counter-Piracy Operations in Somalia and the Gulf of Aden*, Oxford, etc., Oxford University Press, 2011.

GIL PÉREZ, J., "La piratería en el estrecho de Malaca: lecciones para el caso somalí", dans Jesús Ramón Bacas Fernández *et al.* (dir. publ.), *Crisis somalí, piratería e intervención internacional*, Madrid, Instituto Universitario General Gutiérrez Mellado-UNED, 2009, pp. 97-123.

GOLITSYN, V., "Maritime Security: Case of Piracy", in H. Hestermeyer *et al.*, *Coexistence, Cooperation and Solidarity: Liber Amicorum Rüdiger Wolfrum*, Leiden, etc., Nijhoff, 2012, pp. 1157-1176.

GRAY, J., M. MONDAY and G. STUBBLEFIELD, *Maritime Terror: Protecting Yourself, Your Vessel, and Your Crew against Piracy*, Boulder, CO, Paladin, 2011.

HANSEN, S. J., "The Dynamics of Somali Piracy", *Studies in Conflict and Terrorism*, 35 (2012), Nos. 7-8, pp. 523-530.

HAYWOOD, R., and R. SPIVAK, *Maritime Piracy*, London, etc., Routledge, 2012.

HEINTSCHEL VON HEINEGG, W., "Repressing Piracy and Armed Robbery at Sea: Towards a New International Legal Regime", *Israel Yearbook on Human Rights*, 40 (2010), pp. 219-241.

HELLER-ROAZEN, D., *The Enemy of All: Piracy and the Law of Nations*, New York, Zone Books, 2009.

HELLER-ROAZEN, D., traduit de l'anglais par Françoise et Paul Chemla, *L'ennemi de tous: le pirate contre les nations*, Paris, Seuil, 2010.

HO, J., "Combating Piracy and Armed Robbery in Asia: Boosting ReCAAP's Role", in Myron H. Nordquist, Tommy T. B. Koh and John Norton Moore (eds.), *Freedom of Seas, Passage Rights and the 1982 Law of the Sea Convention*, Leiden, Nijhoff, 2009, pp. 619-623.

INTERNATIONAL CHAMBER OF SHIPPING, *Pirates and Armed Robbers: Guidelines on Prevention for Masters and Ship Security Officers*, London, International Shipping Federation (ICS/ISF), 2004.

JOHNSON, D., and M. VALENCIA (eds.), *Piracy in Southeast Asia: Status, Issues, and Responses*, Singapore, Institute of Southeast Asian Studies, 2005.

JORGE URBINA, J., «La contribution du Conseil de sécurité à la coopération internationale pour la lutte contre la piraterie dans le Golfe d'Aden et au large des côtes de la Somalie», dans J. M. Sobrino Heredia, *Sûreté maritime et violence en mer/Maritime Security and Violence at Sea*, Bruxelles, Bruylant, etc., 2011, pp. 283-300.

KAMERLING, S., and F. P. VAN DER PUTTEN, "An Overseas Naval Presence without Overseas Bases: China's Counter-Piracy Operation in the Gulf of Aden", *Journal of Current Chinese Affairs*, 40 (2011), No. 4, pp. 119-146.

KEMPE, M., and O. GÄNSWEIN, "Die Rückkehr der Universalfeinde: Terroristen als 'hostes humani generis' und was Piraten damit zu tun haben", *Zeitschrift fur Neuere Rechtsgeschichte*, 32 (2010), No. 2, pp. 91-106.

KIOURKTSOGLOU, G., and A. D. COUTROUBIS, "Is Somali Piracy a Random Phenomenon?", *WMU Journal of Maritime Affairs*, 11 (2012), No. 1, pp. 51-70.

KLEIN, N., *Maritime Security and the Law of the Sea*, Oxford, etc., Oxford University Press, 2011.

KONTOROVICH, E., "'A Guantánamo on the Sea': The Difficulty of Prosecuting Pirates and Terrorists", *California Law Review*, 98 (2010), No. 1, pp. 243-275.

KVASHNY, K. E., *Modern Maritime Piracy in Asia: A Case Study of Transnational Organized Crime*, Ann Arbor, MI, UMI, 2003.

KRASKA, J., "Brandishing 'Legal Tools' in the Fight against Maritime Piracy", in Myron H. Nordquist *et al.* (eds.), *The Law of the Sea Convention: US Accession and Globalization*, Leiden, Nijhoff, 2012, pp. 258-290.

KRITSIOTIS, D., "The Contingencies of Piracy", *California Western International Law Journal,* 41 (2011), No. 2, pp. 305-343.

KRASKA, J., "Freakonomics of Maritime Piracy", *Brown Journal of World Affairs*, 16 (2010), No. 2, pp. 109-120.

LAURENT, F., et A. GARCIA, «Défense et sécurité», *Annuaire du droit de la mer*, 15 (2010), pp. 475-524.

LEHR, P., "Maritime Piracy as a U.S. Foreign Policy Problem: The Case of the 'Maersk Alabama'", in Ralph G. Carter (ed.), *Contemporary Cases in U.S. Foreign Policy: From Terrorism to Trade*, Washington, DC, CQ Press, pp. 200-228.

LENNOX-GENTLE, T., "Piracy, Sea Robbery, and Terrorism: Enforcing Laws to Deter Ransom Payments and Hijacking", *Transportation Law Journal*, 37 (2010), No. 3, pp. 199-218.

LISS, C., *Oceans of Crime: Maritime Piracy and Transnational Security in*

Southeast Asia and Bangladesh, Leiden, etc., International Institute for Asian Studies, 2011.

MALLIA, P., "The Fight against Piracy and Armed Robbery against Ships off the Coast of Somalia: International Cooperation Illustrated", in A. Martínez Gutiérrez (ed.), *Serving the Rule of International Maritime Law: Essays in Honour of Professor David Joseph Attard*, London, Routledge, 2010, pp. 216-232.

MARLEY, D. F., *Modern Piracy: A Reference Handbook*, Santa Barbara, etc., ABC-CLIO, 2011.

MARTIN-CASTEX, B., et G. LOONIS-QUÉLEN, «L'Organisation maritime internationale et la piraterie ou le vol à main armée en mer: le cas de la Somalie», *Annuaire français de droit international,* 54 (2009), pp. 77-117.

MCKINNON, A., "Maritime Piracy: A Hong Kong Perpective", *Hong Kong Law Journal*, 41 (2011), No. 3, pp. 635-657.

MEJIA, M., "Regional Cooperation in Combating Piracy and Armed Robbery against Ships: Learning Lessons from ReCAAP", in A. Petrig (ed.), *Sea Piracy Law: Selected National Legal Frameworks and Regional Legislative Approaches/Droit de la piraterie maritime: cadres juridiques nationaux et approches legislatives régionales*, Berlin, Duncker & Humblot, 2010, pp. 125-137.

MEJIA, M. Q., "Defining Maritime Violence and Maritime Security", in Proshanto K. Mukherjee, Maximo Q. Mejia and Gotthard M. Gauci (eds.), *Maritime Violence and Other Security Issues at Sea*, 2002, pp. 27-38.

MURPHY, M. N., *Somalia: The New Barbary? Piracy and Islam in the Horn of Africa*, New York, NY, Columbia University Press, 2011.

MURPHY, M. N., *Contemporary Piracy and Maritime Terrorism: The Threat to International Security*, London, etc., Routledge, 2012.

NDUMBE ANYU, J., and S. M. MOKI, "Piracy along the African Coast and Its Implications for Global Security", in M. A. El-Khawas and J. Ndumbe Anyu (eds.), *Case Studies of Conflict in Africa: The Niger Delta, the Bakassi Peninsula, and Piracy in Somalia*, Lewiston, NY, etc., Mellen, 2012, pp. 73-109.

NEUMANN, Th., and T. R. SALOMON, "Kein Krieg vor Somalia", *Humanitäres Völkerrecht*, 24 (2011), No. 3, pp. 165-172.

PAPASTAVRIDIS, E., *The Interception of Vessels on the High Seas: Contemporary Challenges to the Legal Order of the Oceans*, Oxford, Hart Publishing, 2013.

PARSONS, D. M., "Protecting the Booty: Creating a Regulatory Framework to Govern Increased Use of Private Security Companies in the Fight against Pirates", *Tulane Maritime Law Journal*, 35 (2010), No. 1, pp. 153-181.

PAYNE, J. C., *Piracy Today: Fighting Villainy on the High Seas*, Dobbs Ferry, NY, Sheridan House, 2010.

PELLEGRINO, F., "Historical and Legal Aspects of Piracy and Armed Robbery against Shipping", *Journal of Maritime Law and Commerce*, 43 (2012), No. 3, pp. 429-446.

PETRIG A. (ed.), *Sea Piracy Law: Selected National Legal Frameworks and Regional Legislative Approaches/Droit de la piraterie maritime: cadres juridiques nationaux et approches législatives régionales*, Berlin, Duncker & Humblot, 2010.

Piracy off the Coast of Somalia: Tenth Report of Session 2010-12, House of Commons, Foreign Affairs Committee, London, Stationery Office, 2012.

RAYMOND, C. Z., "Piracy and Armed Robbery in the Malacca Strait: A Problem Solved?", in Bruce A. Elleman, Andrew Forbes and David Rosenberg (eds.), *Piracy and Maritime Crime: Historical and Modern Case Studies*, Newport, RI, Naval War College Press, 2010, pp. 109-120.

ROUGER, M. (dir. publ.), *La piraterie maritime*, Colloque des entretiens de Royan, Bruxelles, Larcier, 2011.

RUBIN, A. P., *The Law of Piracy*, Irvington-on-Hudson, NY, Transnational, 1998.

RUBIO FERNANDEZ, E. M., «Bilan de la réglementation juridique internationale de l'assistance aux victimes de la violence sur mer, spécialement de la piraterie ou du vol à main armée», dans J. M. Sobrino Heredia, *Sûreté maritime et violence en mer/Maritime Security and Violence at Sea*, Bruxelles, Bruylant, etc., 2011, pp. 301-322.

SALVATIERRA, M., *El próspero negocio de la piratería en África*, Madrid, Catarata, 2010.

SAM-LEFEBVRE, A., «Quelles réponses face à la recrudescence de la malveillance», *Annuaire de droit maritime et océanique*, 28 (2010), pp. 163-174.

SÁNCHEZ BARRUECO, M. L., "The European Strategy against Piracy off the Somali Coast: A Multi-Pillar Response to a Cross-Pillar Concern", in J. M. Sobrino Heredia, *Sûreté maritime et violence en mer/Maritime Security and Violence at Sea*, Bruxelles, Bruylant, etc., 2011, pp. 323-342.

SÁNCHEZ RAMOS, B., "Action Undertaken by the International Maritime Organization in the Struggle against Maritime Piracy and Armed Robbery", in J. M. Sobrino Heredia, *Sûreté maritime et violence en mer/Maritime Security and Violence at Sea*, Bruxelles, Bruylant, etc., 2011, pp. 211-233.

SANTOS, E. M. R., "Piracy and Armed Robbery against Ships in the Philippines", in Graham Gerard Ong-Webb (ed.), *Piracy, Maritime Terrorism and Securing the Malacca Straits*, Singapore, etc., ISEAS, Institute of Southeast Asian Studies, etc., 2006, pp. 37-51.

SOBRINO HEREDIA, J. M., *Sûreté maritime et violence en mer/Maritime Security and Violence at Sea*, Bruxelles, Bruylant, etc., 2011.

SÖRENSON, K., *State Failure on the High Seas: Reviewing the Somali Piracy*, Stockholm, Swedish Defence Research Agency (FOI), 2008.

STEHR, M., *Piraterie am Horn von Afrika: Bedrohung der zivilen Seeschifffahrt vor Somalia, 2005-2010*, Berlin, Köster, 2011.

SUGIKI, A., "Piracy in a Failed State: How State-Building Can Stabilize the Situation off the Somali Coast?", *Journal of East Asia and International Law,* 5 (2012), No. 1, pp. 61-92.

SYRING, T., "A Pirate and a Refugee: Reservations and Responses in the Fight against Piracy", *ILSA Journal of International and Comparative Law*, 17 (2011), No. 2, pp. 437-457.

—, "'Candide', or Pessimism: Fighting Piracy and Transnational Crime in Uncharted Waters", *Interdisciplinary political studies*, 2 (2012), No. 1, pp. 48-58.

UYKUR, T., "An Overview of two Contemporary Issues in the Law of the Sea: Islands within the Context of Delimitation and Combating Piracy off the Coasts of Somalia", in Myron H. Nordquist *et al.* (eds.), *The Law of the Sea Convention: US Accession and Globalization*, Leiden, Nijhoff, 2012, pp. 551-568.

VÁZQUEZ GÓMEZ, E. M., "Terrorism and Piracy", in J. M. Sobrino Heredia, *Sûreté maritime et violence en mer/Maritime Security and Violence at Sea*, Bruxelles, Bruylant, etc., 2011, pp. 343-346.

WIJK, R., D. ANDERSON and S. HAINES, "The New Piracy: Three Contexts (Forum)", *Survival*, 52 (2010), No. 1, pp. 39-54.

WITHERBY SEAMANSHIP INTERNATIONAL, *Best Practice Management Practices to Deter Piracy off the Coast of Somalia and in the Arabian Sea Area: Suggested Planning and Operational Practices for Ship Operators, and Masters of Ships Transiting the Gulf of Aden and the Arabian Sea*, Edinburgh, Witherby Seamanship International, 2010.

WOODWARD, P., *Crisis in the Horn of Africa: Politics, Piracy and the Threat of Terror*, London, Tauris, 2013.

17 Opérations d'interdiction maritime et droits de l'homme

Maritime Interdiction and Human Rights

BEVILACQUA, G., «Il problema della repressione del reato di pirateria marittima e il necessario bilanciamento tra le esigenze di esercizio effetivo della giurisdizione e di garanzia dei diritti individuali», *Diritto marittimo*, 114 (2012), n° 3, pp. 664-686.

BLOUW, N. DE, "Drowning Policies: A Proposal to Modify the Dublin Agreement and Reduce Human Rights Abuses in the Mediterranean", *California Western International Law Journal*, 40 (2010), No. 2, pp. 335-368.

BODINI, S. P., "Fighting Maritime Piracy under the European Convention on Human Rights", *European Journal of International Law*, 22 (2011), No. 3, pp. 829-848.

BONT, S. DE, "Murky Waters: Prosecuting Pirates and Upholding Human Rights Law", *Journal of International Law and International Relations*, 7 (Fall 2011), No. 1, pp. 104-145.

CELLE, P., et P. PALERMO, « Lotta al traffio di stupefacenti e diritti umani in alto mare », *Diritto marittimo*, 114 (2012), n° 1, pp. 120-142.

DIAZ, L. M., and B. H. DUBNER, "On the Evolution of the Law of International Sea Piracy: How Property Trumped Human Rights, the Environment and the Sovereign Rights of States in the Areas of the Creation and Enforcement of Jurisdiction", *Barry Law Review*, 13 (2009), No. 1, pp. 175-208.

DUBNER, B. H., and S. FREDERICKSON, "On the Legal Issues regarding the Prosecution of Sea Pirates (Including Human Rights): A Case of History Repeating Itself", *Temple International and Comparative Law Journal*, 26 (2012), No. 2, pp, 233-262.

DUTTON, Y. M., "Pirates and Impunity: Is the Threat of Asylum Claims a Reason to Allow Pirates to Escape Justice?", *Fordham International Law Journal*, 34 (2011), No. 2, pp. 236-295.

FISCHER-LESCANO, A., and L. KRECK, "Piracy and Human Rights: Legal Issues in the Fight against Piracy within the Context of the European 'Operation Atalanta' ", *German Yearbook of International Law*, 52 (2010), pp. 525-561.

GUILFOYLE, D., "Human Rights Issues and Non-Flag State Boarding of Suspect Ships in International Waters", in Clive R. Symmons (ed.), *Selected Contemporary Issues in the Law of the Sea*, Leiden, Nijhoff, 2011, pp. 83-104.

—, "The Legal Challenges in Fighting Piracy", Bibi van Ginkel and Frans-Paul van der Putten (eds.), *The International Response to Somali Piracy: Challenges and Opportunities*, Leiden, Nijhoff, 2010, pp. 127-152.

—, "Counter-Piracy Law Enforcement and Human Rights", *International and Comparative Law Quarterly*, 59 (2010), No. 1, pp. 141-169.

HEINTSCHEL VON HEINEGG, W., "The Special Issue of Piracy", in M. Odello and G. L. Beruto (eds.), *Non-State Actors and International Humanitarian Law: Organized Armed Groups: A Challenge for the 21st Century*, Milan, Angeli, 2010, pp. 170-177.

KRESS, C., "Die moderne Piraterie, das Strafrecht und die Menschenrechte: Gedanken aus Anlass der deutschen Mitwirkung an der Seeoperation Atalanta", in Weingärtner (ed.), *Die Bundeswehr als Armee im Einsatz: Entwicklungen im nationalen und internationalen Recht*, Baden-Baden, Nomos, 2010, pp. 95-123.

LALY-CHEVALIER, C., « Lutte contre la piraterie maritime et droits de l'homme », *Revue belge de droit international*, 42 (2009), n° 1, pp. 5-51.

LIGUORI, A., « La Corte europea dei diritti dell'uomo condanna l'Italia per i respingimenti verso la Libia del 2009: il caso Hirsi », *Rivista di diritto internazionale*, 95 (2012), n° 2, pp. 415-443.

MATHEW, P., "Legal Issues concerning Interception", *Georgetown Immigration Law Journal*, 17 (2003), No. 2, pp. 221-250.

MOMTAZ, D., « L'apport du Conseil de sécurité à la lutte contre l'impunité des pirates opérant au large des côtes de Somalie », *Annuaire du droit de la mer*, 15 (2010), pp. 239-248.

NESSEL, L. A., "Externalized Borders and the Invisible Refugee", *Columbia Human Rights Law Review*, 40 (2009), No. 3, pp. 625-699.

NEUMANN, Th., and T. R. SALOMON, "Kein Krieg vor Somalia", *Humanitäres Völkerrecht*, 24 (2011), No. 3, pp. 165-172.

OBOKATA, T., "Maritime Piracy as a Violation of Human Rights: A Way Forward for Its Effective Prevention and Suppression?", *The International Journal of Human Rights*, 17 (2013), No. 1, pp. 18-34.

PAPASTAVRIDIS, E., *The Interception of Vessels on the High Seas: Contemporary Challenges to the Legal Order of the Oceans*, Oxford, Hart Publishing, 2013.

—, "Enforcement Jurisdiction in the Mediterranean Sea: Illicit Activities and the Rule of Law on the High Seas", *International Journal of Marine and Coastal Law*, 25 (2010), No. 4, pp. 569-599.

PARISCIANI, E., «I respingimenti in Libia tra contrasto all'immigrazione clandestina e rispetto dei diritti umani», dans Maurizio Simoncelli (dir. publ.), *Dove i diritti umani non esistono più: la violazione dei diritti umani nelle guerre contemporanee*, Rome, Ediesse, 2010, pp. 153-177.

PASSMAN, M. H., "Protections Afforded to Captured Pirates under the Law of War and International Law", *Tulane Maritime Law Journal*, 33 (2008), No. 1, pp. 1-40.

TONDINI, M., "The Legality of Intercepting Boat People under Search and Rescue and Border Control Operations: With Reference to Recent Italian Interventions in the Mediterranean Sea and the ECtHR Decision in the Hirsi Case", *Journal of International Maritime Law*, 18 (2012), No. 1, pp. 59-74.

18 Les questions de compétence par rapport aux initiatives dites «Shiprider»

Shiprider Institution and Jurisdictional Questions

DAVIS-MATTIS, L., "International Drug Trafficking and the Law of the Sea: Outstanding Issues and Bilateral Responses with Emphasis on U.S.-Caribbean Agreements", *Ocean Yearbook*, 14 (2000), pp. 360-385.

HAUGHTON, S. A., "Bilateral Diplomacy: Rethinking the Jamaica-US Shiprider Agreement", *The Hague Journal of Diplomacy*, 3 (2008), No. 3, pp. 253-276.

HENKE, H., "Between Rocks and a Hard Place: The 'Shiprider Controversy' and the Question of Caribbean Sovereignty", *International Studies*, 35 (1998), No. 4, pp. 423-437.

KRAMEK, J. E., "Bilateral Maritime Counter-Drug and Immigrant Interdiction Agreements: Is This the World of the Future?", *The University of Miami Inter-American Law Review*, 31 (2000), No. 1, pp. 121-161.

WILLIAMS, M., "Caribbean Shiprider Agreements: Sunk by Banana Trade War?", *The University of Miami Inter-American Law Review*, 31 (2000), No. 1, pp 163-195.

19 Le droit applicable relatif aux sociétés militaires et de sécurité privées

Private Armed Guards and Applicable Law

ARROYO ZAPATERO, L., A. NIETO MARTÍN, M. MUÑOZ DE MORALES and M. BAILONE (dir. publ.) *Piratas, mercenarios, soldados, jueces y policías: nuevas desafíos del derecho penal europeo e internacional*, Cuenca, Ed. de la Universidad de Castilla-La Mancha, 2010.

BERUBE, C. G., "Anti-Piracy Escorts in the Gulf of Aden: Problems and Prospects", in C. Berube and P. Cullen (eds.), *Maritime Private Security: Market Responses to Piracy, Terrorism and Waterborne Security Risks in the 21st Century*, London, Routledge, 2012, pp. 74-85.

BERUBE, C., and P. CULLEN, "The Future of Private Security at Sea: Conclusion", in C. Berube and P. Cullen (eds.), *Maritime Private Security: Market Responses to Piracy, Terrorism and Waterborne Security Risks in the 21st Century*, London, Routledge, 2012, pp. 217-223.

BERUBE, C., and P. CULLEN (eds.), *Maritime Private Security: Market Responses to Piracy, Terrorism and Waterborne Security Risks in the 21st Century*, London, Routledge, 2012.

BRINKTRINE, R., "Der Einsatz privater Sicherheitsdienste zum Schutz von Piraterie und maritimen Terrorismus: die staats- und verwaltungsrechtliche Sicht", in R. Stober (ed.), *Der Schutz vor Piraterie und maritimem Terrorismus zwischen internationaler, nationaler und unternehmerischer Verantwortung: brauchen wir zukünftig den Einsatz privater Sicherheitsdienste zum Schutz vor Piraterie?*, Cologne, Heyman, 2010, pp. 39-52.

CARAFANO, J. J., "The United States' Use of Maritime Private Security from the War of Independence to the 21st Century", in C. Berube and P. Cullen (eds.), *Maritime Private Security: Market Responses to Piracy, Terrorism and Waterborne Security Risks in the 21st Century*, London, Routledge, 2012, pp. 13-24.

CULLEN, P., "Privatized Maritime Security Governance in War-torn Sierra Leone", in C. Berube and P. Cullen (eds.), *Maritime Private Security: Market Responses to Piracy, Terrorism and Waterborne Security Risks in the 21st Century*, London, etc., Routledge, 2012, pp. 101-112.

—, "Surveying the Market in Maritime Private Security Services", in C. Berube and P. Cullen (eds.), *Maritime Private Security: Market Responses to Piracy, Terrorism and Waterborne Security Risks in the 21st Century*, London, etc., Routledge, 2012, pp. 25-37.

—, "Private Security Companies in the Malacca Straits: Mapping New Patterns of Security Governance", in Alejandro Colás and Bryan Mabee (eds.), *Mercenaries, Pirates, Bandits and Empires: Private Violence in Historical Context*, London, Hurst, 2010, pp. 187-212.

DEWITT, B., "Integrating Private Security into Port Security in a Post-9/11 Environment", in C. Berube and P. Cullen (eds.), *Maritime Private Security: Market Responses to Piracy, Terrorism and Waterborne Security Risks in the 21st Century*, London, etc., Routledge, 2012, pp. 193-204.

DOEG, B. K., "PMCs on the High Seas: The Solution to Somali Piracy or a Failure to Learn from History", *National Security and Conflict Law Review*, 1 (2010-2011), pp. 139-164.

GINKEL, B. VAN, F-P. VAN DER PUTTEN and W. MOLENAAR, *State or Private Protection against Maritime Piracy?: A Dutch Perspective*, The Hague, Clingendael Institute, 2013.

HANSEN, S., "Private Security, Maritime Protection and Surveillance in Somaliland", in C. Berube and P. Cullen (eds.), *Maritime Private Security: Market Responses to Piracy, Terrorism and Waterborne Security Risks in the 21st Century*, London, Routledge, 2012, pp. 113-125.

HARRELSON, J., "Blackbeard Meets Blackwater: An Analysis of International Conventions that Address Piracy and the Use of Private Security Companies to Protect the Shipping Industry", *American University International Law Review*, 25 (2010), No. 2, pp. 283-312.

JEFFREY, R. S., "An Efficient Solution in a Time of Economic Hardship: The Right to Keep and Bear Arms in Self-Defense against Pirates", *Journal of Maritime Law and Commerce*, 41 (2010), No. 4, pp. 507-540.

HAWKES, R., "Securing the Offshore Oil Industry in the Gulf of Guinea", in C. Berube and P. Cullen (eds.), *Maritime Private Security: Market Responses to Piracy, Terrorism and Waterborne Security Risks in the 21st Century*, London, etc., Routledge, 2012, pp. 138-149.

KINSEY, Ch., "Private Security Fighting Pirates and Illegal Fishing in Puntland", in C. Berube and P. Cullen, *Maritime Private Security: Market Responses to Piracy, Terrorism and Waterborne Security Risks in the 21st Century*, London, etc., Routledge, 2012, pp. 126-137.

KRAHMANN, E., "Commercial Risk Consulting and Management in the Maritime Sector", in C. Berube and P. Cullen, *Maritime Private Security: Market Responses to Piracy, Terrorism and Waterborne Security Risks in the 21st Century*, London, etc., Routledge, 2012, pp. 181-192.

KRASKA, J., and B. WILSON, "Piracy Repression, Partnering and the Law", *Journal of Maritime Law and Commerce*, 40 (2009), No. 1, pp. 43-58.

KOUAR, M., « La sûreté est-elle privatisable ? », *Outre-Terre : Revue européenne de géopolitique,* 25-26 (2010), pp. 49-74.

LAURENT, F., et A. GARCIA, « Défense et sécurité », *Annuaire du droit de la mer*, 15 (2010), pp. 475-524.

LE MIERE, Ch., "Policing the Waves: Maritime Paramilitaries in the Asia-Pacific", *Survival*, 53 (2011), No. 1, pp. 133-146.

LISS, C., "Commercial Anti-Piracy Escorts in the Malacca Strait", in C. Berube and P. Cullen, *Maritime Private Security: Market Responses to Piracy, Terrorism and Waterborne Security Risks in the 21st Century*, London, etc., Routledge, 2012, pp. 51-64.

—, "Private Military and Security Companies in the Fight against Piracy in Southeast Asia", in G. G. Ong-Webb (ed.), *Piracy, Maritime Terrorism and Securing the Malacca Straits*, Singapore, etc., ISEAS, 2006, pp. 103-133.

MARTIN, J. S., "Fighting Piracy with Private Security Measures: When Contract Law Should Tell Parties to Walk the Plank", *American University Law Review*, 59 (2009-2010), pp. 1363-1398.

MINEAU, M. L., "Pirates, Blackwater and Maritime Security: The Rise of Private Navies in Response to Modern Piracy", *Journal of International Business and Law*, 9 (2010), No. 1, pp. 63-78.

PARSONS, D. M., "Protecting the Booty: Creating a Regulatory Framework to Govern Increased Use of Private Security Companies in the Fight against Pirates", *Tulane Maritime Law Journal*, 35 (2010), No. 1, pp. 153-181.

REMY, C., « Les sociétés militaires privées dans la lutte contre la piraterie », *Pyramides*, 21 (2012), pp. 119-138.

RICHARD, Th. T., "Reconsidering the Letter of Marque: Utilizing Private Security Provider against Piracy", *Public Contract Law Journal*, 39 (2010), No. 3, pp. 411-464.

RODDEN, G., and J. WALSH,"Legal Issues of Private Armed Security on Commercial Ships", *Federal Lawyer*, 58 (2011), No. 4 (2011), pp. 30-56.

RONZITTI, N., "The Use of Private Contractors in the Fight against Piracy: Policy Options", in F. Francioni and N. Ronzitti (eds.), *War by Contract: Human Rights, Humanitarian Law, and Private Contractors*, Oxford, etc., Oxford University Press, 2011, pp. 37-51.

ROUGER, M. (dir. publ.), *La piraterie maritime*, Colloque des entretiens de Royan, Bruxelles, Larcier, 2011.

SÁNCHEZ PATRÓN, J. M., « Piratería marítima, fuerza armada y seguridad privada », *Revista Electrónica de Estudios Internacionales*, 23 (2012), pp. 1-20.

SEIDEL, G., "Völkerrechtliche Aspekte des Kampfes gegen Piraterie und maritimen Terrorismus unter Einbeziehung privater Sicherheitsdienste", in R. Stober (ed.), *Der Schutz vor Piraterie und maritimem Terrorismus zwischen internationaler, nationaler und unternehmerischer Verantwortung: brauchen wir zukünftig den Einsatz privater Sicherheitsdienste zum Schutz vor Piraterie?*, Cologne, Heyman, 2010, pp. 19-38.

SPEARIN, Ch., "Private Gunboats on the Horizon? Private Security and Contemporary Naval Presence", in C. Berube and P. Cullen, *Maritime Private Security: Market Responses to Piracy, Terrorism and Waterborne Security Risks in the 21st Century*, London, etc., Routledge, 2012, pp. 38-48.

—, "A Private Security Solution to Somali Piracy? The U.S. Call for Private Security Engagement and the Implications for Canada", *Naval War College Review*, 63 (2010), No. 4, pp. 56-71.

STOBER, R. (ed.), *Der Schutz vor Piraterie und maritimem Terrorismus zwischen internationaler, nationaler und unternehmerischer Verantwortung: brauchen wir zukünftig den Einsatz privater Sicherheitsdienste zum Schutz vor Piraterie?*, Cologne, Heymann, 2010.

STRUWE, L. B., "Private Security Companies (PSCs) as a Piracy Countermeasure", *Studies in Conflict and Terrorism*, 35 (2012), Nos. 7-8, pp. 588-596.

TEMPEST, M., "Legal Considerations for Private Naval Company Armed Anti-Piracy Escorts", in C. Berube and P. Cullen, *Maritime Private Security: Market Responses to Piracy, Terrorism and Waterborne Security Risks in the 21st Century*, London, etc., Routledge, 2012, pp. 86-97.

VAN HOOK, G. E., "Private Security at Sea: A Customer's Perspective", in C. Berube and P. Cullen (eds.), *Maritime Private Security: Market Responses to Piracy, Terrorism and Waterborne Security Risks in the 21st Century*, London, etc., Routledge, 2012, pp. 65-73.

XINNING, G., *Anti-Terrorism, Maritime Security, and ASEAN-China Cooperation: a Chinese Perspective*, Singapore, ISEAS, 2005.

20 La responsabilité de l'Etat et l'obligation de réparer le prejudice causé par des opérations d'interdiction maritime

State Responsibility and Reparation for Maritime Interdiction Operations

BODINI, S. P., "Fighting Maritime Piracy under the European Convention on Human Rights", *European Journal of International Law*, 22 (2011), No. 3, pp. 829-848.

BROWN, Th. M., "For the 'Round and Top of Sovereignty': Boarding Foreign Vessels at Sea on Terror-Related Intelligence Tips", *Journal of International Maritime Law*, 16 (2010), No. 1, pp. 45-75, and *Naval Law Review*, 59 (2010), pp. 63-103.

CRAWFORD, J., A. PELLET, S. OLLESON and K. PARLETT, *The Law of International Responsibility*, Oxford, Oxford University Press, 2010.

DECAUX, E., «Responsabilité et réparation: rapport général», dans Société française pour le droit international, Université du Maine, Le Mans, *La responsabilité dans le système international: colloque du Mans*, Paris, Pedone, 1991, pp. 147-190.

GUILFOYLE, D., *Shipping Interdiction and the Law of the Sea*, Cambridge, Cambridge University Press, 2009.

HEINTSCHEL VON HEINEGG, W., "Maritime Interception/Interdiction Operations", in T. D. Gill and D. Fleck (eds.), *The Handbook of the International Law of Military Operations*, Oxford, Oxford University Press, 2010, pp. 375-393.

—, "Maritime Interception/Interdiction Operations within the Framework of Operation Enduring Freedom", in Société française pour le droit international, *Les nouvelles menaces contre la paix et la sécurité internationales: journée franco-allemande/New Threats to International Peace and Security*, Paris, Pedone, 2004, pp. 149-164.

PALLIS, M., "Obligations of States towards Asylum Seekers at Sea: Interactions and Conflicts between Legal Regimes", *International Journal of Refugee Law*, 14 (2002), No. 2-3, pp. 329-364.

SILVA, M., "Somalia: State Failure, Piracy, and the Challenge to International Law", *Virginia Journal of International Law*, 50 (2010), No. 3, pp. 553-578.

SITTNICK, T. M., "State Responsibility and Maritime Terrorism in the Strait of Malacca: Persuading Indonesia and Malaysia to Take Additional Steps to Secure the Strait", *Pacific Rim Law and Policy Journal*, 14 (2005), pp. 743-769.

TURNER, R. F., "State Responsibility and the War on Terror: The Legacy of Thomas Jefferson and the Barbary Pirates", *Chicago Journal of International Law*, 4 (2003), No. 1, pp. 121-140.

TABLE

INDEX

Solène Guggisberg

Table analytique des matières 699

Analytical Index 717

TABLE ANALYTIQUE DES MATIÈRES

La présente table couvre les articles dans les deux langues
(Index in English : see p. 717)

A. A. C. GRÈCE (CEDH), 464, 478-479

ACCIDENT DE L'*AMOCO CADIZ*, 473

ACCIDENT DE L'*ERIKA*, 113-114, 119-120, 124, 129, 142, 473

ACCIDENT DE L'*EXXON VALDEZ*, 142, 473

ACCIDENT DU *PRESTIGE*, 97, 108, 129, 142, 144, 473-474

ACCIDENT DU *TORREY CANYON*, 97, 473, 563

ACCORD D'APPLICATION DE LA FAO DE 1993, 48, 159-160, 163, 165, 171

ACCORD DE 1997 ENTRE LES ÉTATS-UNIS ET LA BARBADE, 610, 618-620, 628, 631

ACCORD DE COOPÉRATION SUR LA SUPPRESSION DU TRAFIC ILLICITE MARITIME ET AÉRONAUTIQUE DE STUPÉFIANTS ET DE SUBSTANCES PSYCHOTROPES DANS LA RÉGION DES CARAÏBES
Voir *Trafic de drogue*

ACCORD DE LA FAO RELATIF AUX MESURES DU RESSORT DE L'ÉTAT DU PORT DE 2009, 6-7, 152-153, 156, 171-175, 194-195

ACCORD DE NEW YORK DE 1995, 6, 11, 49-50, 155, 159-160, 163-177, 189-191

ACCORD DE SAN JOSÉ
Voir *Trafic de drogue :* Accord de coopération sur la suppression du trafic illicite maritime et aéronautique de stupéfiants et de substances psychotropes dans la région des caraïbe

ACCORD ENTRE LES ÉTATS-UNIS ET LA JAMAÏQUE, 630

ACCORDS D'ARRAISONNEMENT
Voir *Accords ou schémas de* ship-boarding

ACCORDS OU SCHÉMAS DE *SHIP-BOARDING*, 18, 26-28, 50-51, 192, 502, 511, 614-622

ACTE DE VIOLENCE EN MER, 25, 41, 44-47, 202-208, 212, 215, 217-218, 220-221, 233, 290-294, 297, 302, 305, 308, 317, 341, 360, 363, 375-376, 423, 438-439, 451, 494, 586-587

ACTEURS NON ÉTATIQUES, 20, 24-27, 60, 74, 83, 91, 321-322, 347-348, 351, 490-499, 510-519, 582, 587-588
Voir aussi *Sociétés privées de sécurité maritime*

ADMISSIBILITÉ DES PREUVES
voir *Preuves*

AFFAIRE DE LA FLOTTILLE DE LA PAIX
Voir *Incident du* Mavi Marmara

AFFAIRE DE L'*ERIKA* (Cour de cassation)
Voir *Accident de l'*Erika

AFFAIRE DE L'*ESTAI*, 49, 563, 578, 597

AFFAIRE DU *CAP ANAMUR*, 423-424

AFFAIRE DU *DÉTROIT DE CORFOU (ROYAUME-UNI C. ALBANIE)* (CIJ), 7, 301, 567, 569, 598-599, 606

AFFAIRE DU *MAERSK ALABAMA*, 344, 355, 367-368

AFFAIRE DU *RED CRUSADER (DANEMARK C. ROYAUME-UNI)*, 566, 598

AFFAIRE *ERLANGEN*, 563, 596

AFFAIRE *KADI ET AL BARAKAAT INTERNATIONAL FOUNDATION*, 508-509

AFFAIRE *SS I'M ALONE*, 566, 598

AFFAIRE *TADIĆ* (TPIY), 525-526, 530, 587-588

AFFAIRE *TORREY CANYON*
Voir *Accident du* Torrey Canyon

AFFAIRES *M/V SAIGA* (TIDM), 13, 54, 167, 402, 439, 548-549, 563, 566, 597, 601-602, 604-605

AFRIQUE OCCIDENTALE, 4, 26, 28, 36, 43, 150-151, 179, 199, 207, 245, 277, 297, 299, 340-341, 353, 368-369, 376, 557, 589, 595, 625

AGENCES PRIVÉES DE SÉCURITÉ
Voir *Sociétés privées de sécurité maritime*

AL-JEDDA C. ROYAUME-UNI (CEDH), 75, 436, 592

ALLÉGATIONS DE COMPÉTENCES
Voir *Titres de compétence*

AL-SKEINI ET AUTRES C. ROYAUME-UNI (CEDH), 77, 433-435, 461

ANDRONICOU ET CONSTANTINOU C. CHYPRE (CEDH), 439

APPLICABILITÉ EXTRATERRITORIALE DES DROITS HUMAINS
Voir *Droits humains*

ARMES BIOLOGIQUES, CHIMIQUES OU BACTÉRIOLOGIQUES
Voir *Armes de destruction massive*

ARMES DE DESTRUCTION MASSIVE (ADM), 3, 9-10, 12, 14, 18, 20-27, 59-60, 66-67, 73-75, 80, 83, 89, 91-92, 107, 454, 472, 485-521
armes biologiques, chimiques ou bactériologiques, 20, 24, 74, 107, 485-500, 505, 510, 518-520
Traité sur la non-prolifération des armes nucléaires de 1968, 490-492, 498, 512-519
transport d'ADM par mer, 9, 22, 24-27, 59-60, 74, 89, 91, 489-490, 496-497, 501-502, 507, 510, 516-519

ARMES NUCLÉAIRES
Voir *Armes de destruction massive*

ARMURERIES FLOTTANTES, 339, 359-360

ARRESTATION, 11, 13, 22, 25, 37, 44, 50-51, 65-67, 70, 72, 151, 186, 209, 218, 227, 233-236, 245, 260, 267-268, 303-305, 317, 319, 332-335,

ARRÊT *SALE C. HAITIAN CENTERS COUNCIL*, 275-276, 576

ARTICLE 103 DE LA CHARTE DES NATIONS UNIES, 65, 67-68, 75, 507-509, 564, 592

ATTENTATS DU 11 SEPTEMBRE 2001, 20, 489-490, 493, 496

ATTRIBUTION DE COMPORTEMENT
voir *Responsabilité de l'Etat*

AUT DEDERE, AUT JUDICARE, 26, 80-83, 86-87, 209, 211-212, 229-232, 312, 320-331, 546

BANKOVIC ET AUTRES C. BELGIQUE (CEDH), 76, 280, 433-435, 590

BEHRAMI ET SARAMATI C. FRANCE (CEDH), 435, 591-593

BLADET TROMSO ET STENSAAS C. NORVÈGE (CEDH), 467

BLANCHIMENT D'ARGENT, 211, 213, 326-327, 334

BLANCHIMENT DU PRODUIT DU CRIME
Voir *Blanchiment d'argent*

BLOCUS NAVAL, 20, 548-552, 572-574

BMI, 206, 342

CAPITAINE DE NAVIRE, 6, 8, 28, 38-41, 66, 102, 111, 118-119, 121, 123-125, 130, 137-140, 143, 145-147, 237, 241, 299, 304, 316-317, 325, 341, 348-349, 352-355, 365, 372-375, 382-383, 387, 403, 410-411, 419-422, 425-426, 430, 471, 474, 557, 559-560, 599, 601, 612, 620, 623

CARAÏBES, 4-5, 26-28, 32-33, 41, 194, 245, 265-266, 275-277, 381, 418, 575-576, 581-582, 597, 607, 610-611, 617-619, 621, 625, 628, 633

CARICOM
Voir *Caraïbes*

CEDEAO
Voir *Afrique occidentale*

COUR EUROPÉENNE DES DROITS DE L'HOMME (CEDH), 42, 75-77, 90-91, 237, 251, 253-256, 270, 274, 279-280, 282-283, 395, 406-407, 433-435, 443, 446-447, 449, 454, 457-481, 565, 575, 584, 590-593, 603, 607

CENTRE DE COORDINATION DES OPÉRATIONS DE SAUVETAGE (RCC)
Voir *Recherche et sauvetage*

CHAMBRE INTERNATIONALE DE LA MARINE MARCHANDE (ICS), 339, 441, 443, 368, 403

CHEVAUCHEMENT DE COMPÉTENCES, 13, 62, 64, 99-100, 112-115, 129-130, 232-235, 272, 303, 316, 347, 358, 503, 614, 626

COMITÉ INTERNATIONAL DE LA CROIX-ROUGE (CICR), 526-529, 533, 539, 544, 547, 588-589

CIRCONSTANCES EXCLUANT L'ILLICÉITÉ
Voir *Responsabilité de l'Etat*

CNUDM, 3-52, 54-74, 79-85, 88-89, 92-93, 99-116, 120-123, 126-135, 139-140, 143, 151-152, 158-168, 170-171, 183-194, 202-209, 215-226, 233-235, 237, 249, 258-260, 263-272, 278, 288-289, 292-293, 303-304, 309, 313-320, 333-336, 341, 346-348, 353, 355-364, 371, 375, 383-384, 388-389, 409-413, 431, 434, 442-443, 457, 465, 468, 474-475, 478, 502-508, 562-566, 570, 577, 579, 584, 593, 596-597, 599-603, 615, 618, 622-623, 625

CODE DE CONDUITE DE DJIBOUTI, 235, 290, 293, 376, 407, 612, 620

CODE DE CONDUITE INTERNATIONAL POUR LES PRESTATAIRES PRIVÉS DE SERVICES DE SÉCURITÉ
Voir *Sociétés privées de sécurité maritime*

CODE FRONTIÈRES SCHENGEN, 385-387, 392, 394, 426

CODE INTERNATIONAL POUR LA SÉCURITÉ DES NAVIRES ET DES INSTALLATIONS PORTUAIRES, 348, 355, 372,

CODE OF PRACTICE FOR THE INVESTIGATION OF THE CRIMES OF PIRACY AND ARMED ROBBERY AGAINST SHIPS
Voir *Piraterie*

COMITÉ 1540, 92, 495, 500-501, 510

COMITÉ DE LA SÉCURITÉ MARITIME, 299, 348-350, 396-400

COMPAGNIE DE NAVIGATION DE LA RÉPUBLIQUE ISLAMIQUE D'IRAN C. TURQUIE (CEDH), 470-472

COMPENSATION
Voir *Réparation*

COMPÉTENCE EXTRATERRITORIALE
Voir *Titres de compétence*

COMPÉTENCE QUASI UNIVERSELLE
Voir *Titres de compétence*

COMPÉTENCE UNIVERSELLE
Voir *Titres de compétence*

CONCEPTION, CONSTRUCTION ET ARMEMENT DES NAVIRES, 57, 101-103, 115, 129-130, 360

CONFÉRENCE MARITIME INTERNATIONALE ET BALTIQUE (BIMCO), 339, 341, 352, 356-357

CONFLIT ARMÉ INTERNATIONAL, 526-527, 533-534, 539-541, 549-550, 552, 573-574, 588-589

CONFLIT ARMÉ NON INTERNATIONAL, 307, 525-526, 529-531, 539-541, 545, 549-550, 552

CONSEIL DE SÉCURITÉ DES NATIONS UNIES, 9, 21, 23-25, 43, 46, 53, 59-60, 65-68, 73-75, 78-79, 84, 91-92, 199-201, 203, 206, 208, 211-212, 217-218, 221, 224, 226, 236, 291, 296-302, 304, 307-309, 311, 332-334, 340, 364, 397, 431, 435-436, 447, 454-455, 485, 489, 491-495, 499, 501, 506, 508-510, 513-514, 517-518, 524, 529, 545, 567, 570-571, 589-591, 595, 597, 600, 611-612, 616, 619, 622

CONSERVATION DES RESSOURCES BIOLOGIQUES, 8, 13, 49, 56, 158-162, 168, 184, 188, 195, 288

CONTRE-MESURES, 191-194, 389, 564, 571-572

CONTRÔLE DE L'ÉTAT PORTUAIRE, 7, 99-100, 173, 194-195

CONTRÔLE EFFECTIF, 77, 164-166, 169, 250, 270, 274, 276, 283, 433, 435-436, 438, 461, 587, 591-592

CONVENTION INTERNATIONALE CONTRE LA PRISE D'OTAGES DE 1979
Voir *Otages*

CONVENTION CTO
Voir *Criminalité transnationale organisée:* Convention des Nations Unies contre la criminalité transantionale organisée

CONVENTION DE 1951 SUR LES RÉFUGIÉS
Voir *Demandeurs d'asile*

CONVENTION DE L'ASEAN CONTRE LE TERRORISME
Voir *Extradition*

CONVENTION DES NATIONS UNIES CONTRE LA CORRUPTION DE 2003
Voir *Corruption*

CONVENTION DES NATIONS UNIES CONTRE LA CRIMINALITÉ TRANSNATIONALE ORGANISÉE DE 2000
Voir *Criminalité transnationale organisée*

CONVENTION DES NATIONS UNIES DE 1988 CONTRE LE TRAFIC ILLICITE DE STUPÉFIANTS ET DE SUBSTANCES PSYCHOTROPES
Voir *Trafic de drogue*

CONVENTION INTERNATIONALE DE 1989 SUR L'ASSISTANCE, 382-383, 419-422

CONVENTION INTERNATIONALE POUR LA RÉPRESSION DES ACTES DE TERRORISME NUCLÉAIRE DE 2005
Voir *Terrorisme*

CONVENTION INTERNATIONALE POUR LA RÉPRESSION DU FINANCEMENT DU TERRORISME DE 1999
Voir *Terrorisme*

CONVENTION INTERNATIONALE SUR LA PRÉPARATION, LA LUTTE ET LA COOPÉRATION EN MATIÈRE DE POLLUTION PAR LES HYDROCARBURES
Voir *Pollution*

CONVENTION INTERNATIONALE SUR LA RECHERCHE ET LE SAUVETAGE EN MER DE 1979
Voir *Convention SAR*

CONVENTION POUR LA RÉPRESSION D'ACTES ILLICITES CONTRE LA SÉCURITÉ DE LA NAVIGATION MARITIME DE 1988
Voir *Convention SUA*

CONVENTION POUR LA RÉPRESSION D'ACTES ILLICITES DIRIGÉS CONTRE LA SÉCURITÉ DE L'AVIATION CIVILE DE 1971, 229, 568

CONVENTION POUR LA RÉPRESSION DE LA CAPTURE ILLICITE D'AÉRONEFS DE 1970, 229

CONVENTION SAR DE 1979, 39-40, 385, 387-401, 404-408, 411-413, 460

CONVENTIONS DE GENÈVE DE 1958, 17, 19, 44, 162, 164, 167-168, 189, 203, 222, 225, 288, 292, 308

CONVENTION SUA DE 1988, 25-26, 63-64, 67-68, 80-83, 86, 202, 204, 206-211, 228-232, 237, 293-294, 314, 320-325, 332, 334-336, 360, 431, 490, 497, 518, 546, 562, 566, 568-569, 572
protocole SUA de 2005, 4, 12, 14, 21, 25-26, 80, 82-83, 92, 207, 490-492, 495-502, 510-518, 566-569, 572, 577, 580, 603

CONVOI
Voir *Navire d'escorte*

CORRUPTION, 153, 179, 196, 211, 314, 326

CONVENTION DES NATIONS UNIES CONTRE LA CORRUPTION DE 2003, 314, 326-327, 329-330

CÔTE SOMALIENNE
Voir *Somalie*

COUR DE JUSTICE DE L'UNION EUROPÉENNE, 116, 119, 122, 168, 182, 217, 256, 386, 508-509

COUR DE JUSTICE DES COMMUNAUTÉS EUROPÉENNES
Voir C*our de justice de l'Union européenne*

COUR INTERNATIONALE DE JUSTICE, 7, 49, 60-62, 71, 83-84, 86, 167, 170, 223, 234, 246, 274, 301, 389, 400, 412, 487-488, 516, 534, 543, 563, 567, 569, 580, 582-583, 587-588, 590, 593, 597-599, 606

COUR PÉNALE INTERNATIONALE, 20, 113-114, 214-215, 454, 523, 525, 530, 541, 553, 626

CRIME ENVIRONNEMENTAL
Voir *Protection de l'environnement*

CRIMES DE GUERRE, 20, 55, 62, 84-85, 213, 215, 223, 253, 523-553, 588

CRIMINALITÉ TRANSNATIONALE ORGANISÉE, 4-5, 35, 52-43, 64, 79, 80, 82-83, 87, 153-154, 180-181, 185, 211-213, 228-229, 231, 239-242, 247-248, 261, 264, 269-271, 277, 285, 314, 325-330, 334-335, 422-425, 576
Convention des Nations Unies contre la criminalité transnationale organisée de 2000, 4, 64, 80, 82-83, 181, 211-213, 218, 228-229, 242, 247-248, 261, 264, 269-271, 277, 314, 320, 325-331, 334, 422-424, 460

CRITÈRE D'INTENTION, 51, 57-58, 69, 105, 118-126, 136-138, 144, 180-181, 192, 203, 206-208, 211-212, 219-220, 247-248, 284, 290, 292, 322, 357, 468-469, 494-495, 504

DÉBARQUEMENT
Voir *Lieu sûr*

DÉCHARGES
Voir *Pollution*

DÉCISION 2010/252/UE DU CONSEIL, 386-387, 392, 394-395, 426

DÉCISION-CADRE 2005/667/JAI, 116, 138

DÉFINITION D'UN OBJECTIF MILITAIRE
Voir *Principe de distinction*

DEMANDEURS D'ASILE, 35-36, 39, 42, 85, 239-240, 243-244, 250-256, 259, 261-262, 275, 279, 283-284, 381, 386, 391-395, 401, 403, 407, 418, 423, 426-427, 448, 451, 464-465, 478-479, 560, 575-576
Convention sur les réfugiés de 1951, 251-253, 261, 274-275, 392, 431, 448, 451, 575-576

DÉTACHEMENT CHARGÉ DE L'EXÉCUTION DE LA LOI, 611-613, 621

DÉTACHEMENTS DE PROTECTION DES NAVIRES, 346, 356, 361, 368-370, 613-614

DÉTERMINATION DU STATUT DE RÉFUGIÉ
Voir *Demandeurs d'asile*

DÉTRESSE EN MER, 6, 38-39, 57-58, 105, 119, 240, 383-387, 391, 394, 401, 403-410, 413-416, 420-422, 425-426, 460, 564

DÉTROITS INTERNATIONAUX, 9-10, 341, 361-362, 568
détroit de Malacca, 46, 294, 340, 362, 568

DIFFICULTÉ DE PREUVE
Voir *Preuve*

DIRECTIVE 2005/35/EC, 116, 121-123, 130-131

DISSUASION NUCLÉAIRE, 487-489, 511, 513-515

DOCTRINE DES EFFETS
Voir *Titres de compétence*

DOMMAGE ENVIRONNEMENTAL
Voir *Protection de l'environnement*

DOUBLE INCRIMINATION, 327, 329

DROIT À LA LIBERTÉ ET À LA SÉCURITÉ DE LA PERSONNE
Voir *Droits humains*

DROIT À LA VIE
Voir *Droits humains*

DROIT À UN RECOURS EFFECTIF
Voir *Droits humains*

DROIT AU RESPECT DE LA VIE PRIVÉE
Voir *Droits humains*

DROIT DE POURSUITE, 11, 18-19, 68-70, 74, 78, 188-189, 207, 268-269, 277, 281, 313, 565, 615, 617, 630

DROIT DE PROPRIÉTÉ
Voir *Droits humains*

DROIT DE QUITTER SON PROPRE PAYS ET LIBERTÉ DE MOUVEMENT
Voir *Droits humains*

DROIT DE RECONNAISSANCE, 15-17

DROIT DE VISITE, 15-23, 25, 29-30, 32-33, 36-37, 40, 65, 67, 70-72, 88-89, 134-135, 185, 188-189, 244-245, 265-271, 346, 460, 524, 559-560, 563, 565, 571-573, 577, 584, 602, 614-615, 624
droit de visite des belligérants, 16, 20, 524

DROIT INTERNATIONAL HUMANITAIRE, 84, 304, 306-307, 352, 364, 406, 409, 427, 431-432, 488, 494, 515, 523, 525, 527-553, 573, 588-589

DROIT PÉNAL INTERNATIONAL, 53, 67, 92, 525, 541-542, 546, 552-553

DROITS HUMAINS, 46, 52, 55, 72, 75-78, 85, 90-92, 196, 200, 236-237, 240-241, 246, 250-258, 262, 273-276. 278-285, 365, 304-307, 350-352, 367, 401-402, 407, 409, 412, 427, 429-456, 457-481, 531, 561, 565, 574-576, 581, 585, 592-593, 598, 614, 628, 632
applicabilité extraterritoriale des droits humains, 76-78, 274-276, 279-280, 283, 432-435, 453, 461, 479-480, 575-576
droit à la liberté et à la sécurité de la personne, 90-91, 181, 252, 261, 275, 277, 440-445, 473-479, 565, 575-576
droit à la vie, 76, 275, 305, 438-439, 461, 531
droit à un recours effectif, 254, 480-481, 603-604
droit au respect de la vie privée, 437, 467, 607
droit de propriété, 447, 460, 469-472
droit de quitter son propre pays et liberté de mouvement , 257-258, 277-278
garanties procédurales, 244-255, 283, 443-447, 472
interdiction de la torture, des traitements ou peines cruels, inhumains ou dégradants , 86, 90, 215, 230, 237, 251-253, 305, 431, 439, 447-453, 459-464, 552, 575, 604
interdiction des expulsions collectives, 256-257, 274, 283, 472, 479-480
liberté d'expression, 460, 465-469, 575

DROITS SOUVERAINS, 12-13, 70, 106, 160-161, 164, 503, 562

DRUG TRAFFICKING VESSEL INTERDICTION ACT (loi relative à l'interception des navires utilisés pour le trafic de drogue)
Voir *Trafic de drogue*

DUE DILIGENCE, 168-169, 352-354

EAUX INTÉRIEURES, 5-8, 18, 21, 33, 46, 56, 65, 67, 69, 99, 105, 121, 191, 248, 290, 293, 300-303, 306, 308-310, 504, 206, 216, 358, 369, 500, 503, 507, 562, 622-623

EMBARGO, 360, 414, 485, 564, 591, 595

EMISSIONS NON AUTORISÉES, 3, 17, 21, 30, 71, 88-89, 189, 317-319, 502, 622

EMPLOI DE LA FORCE, 25, 58-60. 76-77, 191-194, 203, 345, 347, 349-351, 353-356, 361, 363-364, 369, 371-375, 438-439, 494, 504, 523, 525-528, 531, 545, 548-549, 552, 566, 571, 573, 593, 595-596, 598, 605, 620, 631-632

ENTRAIDE JUDICIAIRE, 52, 311-336, 619

ESCLAVAGE, 3, 12, 16-17, 21, 30, 36, 38, 72, 79-80, 88-89, 189, 214-215, 242-243, 249, 267-268, 305, 317-319, 455, 457, 502, 558, 562, 609, 622-623, 626

ÉTAT CÔTIER, 3, 6-14, 18-19, 21, 33, 37-40, 46-47, 51, 56-63, 65-70, 75, 78-79, 81, 88, 98-107, 110-115, 120-121, 126-135, 143, 145, 147, 149, 151-152, 154, 157, 159-161, 164, 167, 170, 172, 183, 186-189, 196-197, 204, 225, 235, 244, 257-265, 268, 276-281, 300-303, 307, 309-310, 316, 333, 348, 350, 355, 358-362, 369, 382, 387-389, 394, 403, 409-413, 426, 460, 465, 468, 503-507, 517, 528, 559, 562, 564, 568, 582, 584-585, 596, 599-600, 606, 611, 614-615, 618, 622-623, 625
intérêts du littoral, 66, 98-99, 103, 105, 111-113, 127, 129, 132, 358-359, 599-600

ÉTAT DE DÉTENTION, 86-87, 322-324, 327, 335

ÉTATS-UNIS C. IBARGUEN-MOSQUERA, 30

ÉTATS-UNIS C. SAID, 220

ÉTATS-UNIS C. ALI, 219, 232

ÉTATS-UNIS C. DIRE, 216, 221

ÉTATS-UNIS C. SMITH, 220-221, 443

EU NAVFOR, 43, 45, 341, 346, 366, 431, 435, 455, 523, 529, 592, 594

EUROSUR, 418

EXPULSION, 86, 250-257, 274-275, 283-284, 462-463, 472-473, 479-480, 575

EXTRADITION, 25-26, 52, 64, 82, 86-87, 218, 229-233, 251, 311-336, 442, 447, 449, 473, 546, 619
Convention de l'ASEAN contre le terrorisme, 332
London Scheme of Extradition, 331-332

FAIT GÉNÉRATEUR
Voir *Responsabilité de l'Etat*

FRONTEX, 5, 36, 244-245, 277, 280, 386, 394-395, 417-418, 427, 454

GARANTIES PAR UN PAYS TIERS (p. ex. GARANTIES DIPLOMATIQUES), 237, 255, 449-453

GARANTIES PROCÉDURALES
Voir *Droits humains*

GARDES ARMÉS PRIVÉS
Voir *Sociétés privées de sécurité maritime*

GOLFE D'ADEN
Voir *Somalie*

GOLFE DE GUINÉE
Voir *Afrique occidentale*

GROUPE INTERINSTITUTIONS (UNHCR, UNDOALOS, UNODC, OHCHR, IOM, IMO), 401-402, 406

GUARDCON, 352, 355-357, 375

GUERRE NAVALE, 19, 523-553, 572-574, 588-589

HARVARD DRAFT CONVENTION ON PIRACY
Voir *Piraterie*

HAUTE MER, 3, 7-30, 32-33, 36-38, 41, 44, 48-50, 54, 61, 68-75, 81-84, 88-89, 111-112, 121, 126, 150, 152, 157-170, 176, 184-185, 188-194, 197, 203-212, 216-225, 244-251, 257-258, 263, 265-283, 288, 292-293, 298, 307-310, 312, 316-319, 358-360, 375, 384, 419-421, 434, 444, 448, 454-457, 463, 476, 500-502, 511, 521, 540-541, 549, 562-563, 566, 573-579, 596-602, 609, 622-624

HIRSI JAMAA ET AUTRES C. ITALIE (CEDH), 251, 254-256, 274, 283, 407, 448, 463-464, 479, 607

HOSTILITÉS EN MER
Voir *Guerre navale*

INCIDENT DE L'*ALMEZAAN*, 358, 365-366, 371

INCIDENT DE L'*ACHILLE LAURO,* 23, 63, 207, 321

INCIDENT DU *BBC CHINA*, 490, 498, 502

INCIDENT DU *MAVI MARMARA*, 20, 525, 531, 547-553, 573-574

INCIDENT DU *MV ENRICA LEXIE*, 366-367, 371, 601-602

INCIDENT DU *MV TAMPA*, 35, 39, 239, 250, 258

INCIDENT DU *WINNER*
Voir *Medvedyev et autres c. France*)

INDEMNISATION, 88-89, 130, 198-140, 147, 347, 352, 458, 471, 474, 557-559, 561, 565, 573, 577-578, 581, 600-608, 628

INFRACTION DE PROLIFÉRATION, 489, 491, 499, 501, 504, 510

INFRACTIONS DOCUMENTAIRES, 115, 117, 125-128, 138, 182, 247

INITIATIVE DE SÉCURITÉ CONTRE LA PROLIFÉRATION (ISP), 3, 9, 20-21, 26, 490, 498, 500-502, 521

INTERDICTION DE LA TORTURE, DES TRAITEMENTS OU PEINES CRUELS, INHUMAINS OU DÉGRADANTS
Voir *Droits humains*

INTERDICTION DES EXPULSIONS COLLECTIVES
Voir *Droits humains*

INTÉRÊTS DU LITTORAL
Voir *Etat côtier*

INTERPOL, 154, 179

IPOA-IUU, 47, 152, 155-157, 171-172, 196

JAMES ET AUTRES C. ROYAUME-UNI (CEDH), 469-470

JUS AD BELLUM, 77, 523-524, 538

JUS IN BELLO, 77, 84, 306-307, 486, 488, 521, 523-524, 528, 530, 533, 538, 542, 549, 560-561, 572, 600

LÉGITIME DÉFENSE, 16, 111, 356, 368, 373-375, 488, 523-524, 538, 540, 564, 567, 573, 631

LIBERTÉ DE LA HAUTE MER, 14-15, 111, 161, 265

LIBERTÉ D'EXPRESSION
Voir *Droits humains*

LIEN SUBSTANTIEL, 164, 166-169, 196

LIEU SÛR, 6, 36, 39-40, 255, 286, 349, 359, 387, 390-403, 406, 408-413, 426-427, 464
projet de protocole d'entente pour la Méditerranée sur le débarquement, 391, 396-409, 427

LONDON SCHEME OF EXTRADITION
Voir *Extradition*

M/V *PINAR E*, 390

M/V SO SAN, 22, 490

MALTE, 27, 29, 113-114, 251, 262, 273, 390, 393, 395-399, 403-409, 413, 416-417, 427, 463

MANDAT D'ARRÊT EUROPÉEN, 332

MANGOURAS C. ESPAGNE (CEDH), 474-475

MANQUE DE MAINTENANCE, 102-103, 129, 145-147

MANUEL DE SAN REMO, 523, 533-540, 544, 550-551, 572-574

MANUEL INTERNATIONAL DE RECHERCHE ET DE SAUVETAGE AÉRONAUTIQUES ET MARITIMES
Voir *Recherche et sauvetage*

MARE CLAUSUM, 190, 287

MARE LIBERUM, 55, 190, 287

MARÉES NOIRES
Voir *Pollution*

MARINE MARCHANDE ARMÉE, 536-537

MARPOL 73/78, 7, 52, 97-98, 102-103, 105-113, 116-138, 142, 146-148, 473, 569-570

MÉDITERRANÉE, 5, 35-37, 42, 133, 146, 162, 194, 239-240, 245, 251, 254-255, 277, 381-382, 390-391, 393-409, 413-418, 423-427, 448-452, 463-465, 479-480, 557, 575, 584

MEDVEDYEV ET AUTRES C. FRANCE (CEDH), 91, 238, 266, 270, 433-434, 438, 440-446, 454-455, 476-478, 565, 575

MER TERRITORIALE, 3, 7-12, 18-19, 21, 25, 28, 32-33, 37, 43, 46-47, 51, 56-59, 61, 63, 65-69, 73-82, 85, 98, 100-106, 112, 114-115, 127-128, 132, 134-135, 139-140, 145, 160, 188, 204-207, 215-216, 225, 244-245, 248, 257-265, 268-269, 276-283, 288-290, 293, 297-310, 312, 316, 333, 335, 340, 347, 358-362, 367-370, 384, 391, 395, 397, 405, 426, 432, 448-450, 460, 465, 468-469, 475-476, 500, 503-507, 517, 529, 540, 562-564, 568, 582-584, 586, 599, 601, 606, 611, 617, 619-625

MESURES DE MARCHÉ, 153-154, 159, 171-178, 196

MESURES DES BELLIGÉRANTS, 19-20, 533-541, 549, 572-573

MODES OPÉRATOIRES NORMALISÉS POUR LES CAPITAINES DE NAVIRE (SOPS), 403, 529, 616

NAVIGABILITÉ, 34, 37, 239, 367, 381, 385-386, 409-410

NAVIRE APATRIDE, 34, 37, 185, 266-267, 271-272, 367, 381, 385-386, 409, 562

NAVIRE D'ESCORTE, 340, 345-347, 356, 359, 361-362, 369, 412, 573, 613

NAVIRE « LEFT-TO-DIE », 240, 414-417

NAVIRES NEUTRES, 19, 524, 532, 534, 540-541, 547, 549, 573

NAVIRES SURCHARGÉS/INNAVIGABLES
Voir *Navigabilité*

NÉCESSITÉ ET PROPORTIONNALITÉ, 111, 177, 196, 263, 329, 363, 373-375, 384, 439, 447, 471, 508, 531, 540-541, 547, 549-551, 563-566, 571, 573-574, 579, 598, 632

NON-REFOULEMENT
Voir *Refoulement*

OACI, 388

OBLIGATION DE PORTER SECOURS, 38, 333, 382-387, 416, 419-422, 426, 460

OBLIGATION DE POURSUIVRE OU D'EXTRADER
Voir *Aut dedere aut judicare*

OBLIGATIONS *ERGA OMNES*, 158, 168, 191, 193, 512

OBSERVATION GÉNÉRALE DU COMITÉ DES DROITS DE L'HOMME, 251, 258, 274, 433, 452

ÖCALAN C. TURQUIE (CEDH), 433, 442

OCÉAN INDIEN, 22, 26, 43, 45, 162, 194, 290, 297, 340, 357, 366-367, 587, 602, 612

OMAOC, 341, 589

OMI, 21, 25, 39, 43, 46-47, 52, 64, 199, 205, 208, 217, 289-291, 296-299, 336, 339-341, 345, 347-351, 353, 355, 357, 359, 363-364, 373, 376, 382, 385, 388, 392-408, 425-426, 470, 612

OPÉRATION ATALANTE
Voir *EU NAVFOR*

OPÉRATION DE POLICE, 10, 15, 33, 36, 85, 98, 228, 244, 316, 360, 411, 430, 438, 523-531, 549, 562, 566-567, 571-572, 582, 608, 610, 614, 617, 622-626, 629

OPÉRATION D'INTERDICTION MARITIME, 4, 85, 244-245, 429-456, 524, 557-561, 564, 570-571, 574, 576, 579-595, 597-599, 602, 605, 608

OPÉRATION *ENDURING FREEDOM*, 25, 490, 540, 589

OPÉRATION *UNIFIED PROTECTOR*, 393, 397-398, 416-417

OPÉRATIONS DE RENVOI, 35, 42, 245, 256

ORGANISATION INTERNATIONALE DE NORMALISATION, 350

ORGPS, 48, 50, 154-160, 162-164, 166, 173-174, 177, 187, 189-190-191, 193, 195-196

OTAGES, 43, 80, 82, 90, 202, 207, 210-212, 228-229, 231-232, 297, 304-305, 307, 309, 320-324, 332, 334, 363, 439, 442, 568
Convention internationale contre la prise d'otages de 1979, 210-211, 229, 231, 320-324, 332, 334,

OTAN, 35, 43, 341, 393-394, 397-398, 414-417, 431, 435, 493, 579, 590, 595

PACTE INTERNATIONAL RELATIF AUX DROITS CIVILS ET POLITIQUES DE 1966, 251, 257, 273, 305, 432-434, 451, 603

PAMUK ET AUTRES, 37, 267, 269

P&I, 352, 354, 357

PARTAGE DES CHARGES, 395, 407-409, 426-427

PASSAGE INOFFENSIF, 7-9, 36, 56-61, 69, 74, 101-106, 244, 258-263, 277-278, 281, 303, 360-362, 465, 468, 503-509, 562, 584

PASSEURS
Voir *Trafic de migrants :* trafiquants de migrants

PAVILLON DE COMPLAISANCE, 18, 160, 163-166, 178, 185, 188, 191, 196, 420

PAVILLON DE NON-RESPECT
Voir *Pavillon de complaisance*

PAYS TIERS SÛR, 225-226, 286, 393, 406, 446, 448, 452

PÊCHE ILLÉGALE, 4, 6, 8, 11, 13, 18, 47-51, 149-197, 424, 617-618, 633

PÊCHE *INN*
Voir *Pêche illégale*

PERSONNEL ARMÉ DE SÉCURITÉ SOUS CONTRAT PRIVÉ
Voir *Sociétés privées de sécurité maritime*

PERTES MARITIMES, 316-317, 531

PÉTROLE ET GAZ , 3, 10, 51-52, 97, 113, 120-121, 133, 138, 142, 342, 369, 405, 563, 600-602

PIRATERIE, 3, 4, 8, 12, 14, 16-18, 21, 23, 30, 43-47, 70-75, 78-79, 84, 88-90, 180, 188-189, 199-238, 271-272, 289-290, 294-295, 299-326, 333-336, 339-377, 389, 431, 434, 436-437, 442-443, 445, 447, 449-455, 457, 477-478, 502, 524, 529-530, 546, 557, 562-565, 569, 575, 579-580, 586-587, 596, 601, 609, 612-614, 620, 622-623, 633
Code of Practice for the Investigation of the Crimes of Piracy and Armed Robbery against Ships, 47, 205, 208, 217
Harvard Draft Convention on Piracy, 203, 205, 214, 237

POLLUTION, 6-10, 12-13, 51-52, 57-58, 63, 66, 69, 97-148, 173, 180, 182, 298, 457, 473-474, 559, 562-563, 566, 569-570
Convention internationale sur la préparation, la lutte et la coopération en matière de pollution par les hydrocarbures de 1990, 52
décharges, 7, 10, 13, 51, 97, 110, 117, 120-121, 124, 126-127, 132, 134-137, 144
marées noires, 139, 142, 147, 473

PORT, 5-7, 21, 46, 51, 56, 67, 79, 99-100, 127-128, 132-136, 140-147, 152-154, 156, 159, 170-176, 183, 194-196, 241, 333, 339, 342, 348, 350, 355-359, 361, 365, 369, 372, 374, 383, 390, 398, 409, 413, 423, 425, 445-446, 453, 463, 470, 501, 503, 562, 573, 606, 623-624

PORT DE COMPLAISANCE, 176

PREUVE, 87, 131-138, 143-144, 161, 231, 255, 267, 284, 389, 417, 463, 570

PRÉVISIBILITÉ, 147, 222, 270-271, 282, 440-444

PRINCIPE DE DISTINCTION, 534-539, 549, 574

PRINCIPE DE NATIONALITÉ
Voir *Titres de compétence :* principe de personnalité

PRINCIPE DE PERSONNALITÉ
Voir *Titres de compétence*

PRINCIPE DE PROTECTION
Voir *Titres de compétence*

PRINCIPE DE TERRITORIALITÉ
Voir *Titres de compétence*

PRINTEMPS ARABE, 35, 381, 402, 408, 427

PRIVATION DE LIBERTÉ
Voir *Droits humains :* droit à la liberté et à la sécurité de la personne

PROCÈS DE NUREMBERG, 523, 547

PROJET DE CONVENTION DES NATIONS UNIES SUR LA RÉGLEMENTATION, LA LICENCE, LE CONTRÔLE ET LA SURVEILLANCE DES SOCIÉTÉS MILITAIRES ET DE SÉCURITÉ PRIVÉES
Voir *Sociétés privées de sécurité maritime*

PROJET DE PROTOCOLE D'ENTENTE POUR LA MÉDITERRANÉE SUR LE DÉBARQUEMENT
Voir *Lieu sûr*

PROMPTE MAINLEVÉE, 70, 186-187

PROPRIÉTAIRE DE NAVIRE, 100, 102, 113, 118-119, 121, 123-125, 130, 141, 144, 148, 299, 344, 347-349, 352-354, 357, 362, 368-369, 375, 419, 421-422, 430, 436, 460, 463, 475, 557, 559, 561, 597, 585, 602

PROTECTION DE L'ENVIRONNEMENT, 8, 12-13, 51-52, 57, 97-101, 107-108, 126-128, 131, 135, 139-141, 144-145, 147, 149, 168-170, 175, 179-184, 194, 196, 317, 342, 347, 372, 376, 420, 474-475, 559, 562, 567, 576, 599-600, 603, 606-607, 618

PROTOCOLE DE 2000 CONTRE LE TRAFIC ILLICITE DE MIGRANTS PAR TERRE, AIR ET MER À LA CONVENTION DES NATIONS UNIES CONTRE LE CRIME TRANSNATIONAL ORGANISÉ
Voir *Trafic de migrants*

PROTOCOLE DE 2005 À LA CONVENTION POUR LA RÉPRESSION D'ACTES ILLICITES CONTRE LA SÉCURITÉ DE LA NAVIGATION MARITIME
Voir *Convention SUA :* Protocole SUA de 2005

PROTOCOLE SUA DE 2005
Voir *Convention SUA de 1988*

PROTOCOLE DE 2000 VISANT À PRÉVENIR, RÉPRIMER ET PUNIR LA TRAITE DES PERSONNES, EN PARTICULIER DES FEMMES ET DES ENFANTS
Voir *Traite de personnes*

PUSH-BACK
Voir *Opérations de renvoi*

RAPPORT PALMER
Voir *Incident du* Mavi Marmara

RECHERCHE ET SAUVETAGE, 39-40, 118, 125, 381-427, 460, 463,
Centre de coordination des opérations de sauvetage (RCC), 387, 391, 403, 406, 411, 416
Manuel international de recherche et de sauvetage aéronautiques et maritimes, 388
régions de recherche et de sauvetage, 387-395, 403-409, 413, 426-427
sous-comité de l'OIM des radiocommunications et de la recherche et du sauvetage (COMSAR), 396-397, 399-400, 404

RECOURS À LA FORCE
Voir *Emploi de la force*

REFOULEMENT, 85, 250-256, 259, 262-263, 274-283, 392, 394, 407, 447-452, 463-464, 472, 479-481, 575-576

RÉFUGIÉS
Voir *Demandeurs d'asile*

RÉGION D'INFORMATION DE VOL, 404-405

RÉGIONS À HAUT RISQUE, 339-341, 345, 348-349, 353, 355-357, 363

RÉGIONS DE RECHERCHE ET DE SAUVETAGE
Voir *Recherche et sauvetage*

RÈGLEMENT DU CONSEIL (EC) NO. 1005/2008, 156, 177-178, 182-183, 185, 191, 195

RÈGLEMENT DU CONSEIL (EC) N° 1224/2009, 177, 191

RÈGLEMENT DUBLIN II, 407

RÈGLES APPLICABLES POUR RECOURIR À LA FORCE
Voir *Règles d'engagement*

RÈGLES D'ENGAGEMENT, 4, 353-354, 363, 371, 373-374, 454

RÈGLES ET NORMES INTERNATIONALES GÉNÉRALEMENT ACCEPTÉES (RNIGA), 102-103, 108-110, 114, 116, 120-121, 128-130

RÉPARATION, 88-89, 130, 141-142, 375, 458, 472, 557-559, 561, 565, 571, 577-579, 591, 597-598, 600-607, 628

RÉSOLUTIONS DE L'ASSEMBLÉE GÉNÉRALE DES NATIONS UNIES, 153, 155, 179, 200, 210-211, 248, 250, 270, 291, 296-298, 424, 426, 495, 558, 618, 627

RÉSOLUTIONS DU CONSEIL DE SÉCURITÉ DES NATIONS UNIES, 9-10, 21, 23-25, 43, 46, 59-60, 66-67, 73-75, 79, 84, 91-92 201, 203, 208, 218, 226, 236, 291, 299, 301-302, 308-309, 311-313, 321, 332-334, 340, 364, 394, 397, 431, 435, 447, 454, 506, 508-509, 513-514, 524, 570-571, 589, 591, 612, 622
- résolution 1373, 21, 23, 567-568, 570-571
- résolution 1540, 9-10, 24-25, 59-60, 74, 91-92, 485, 489-495, 498-502, 506-511, 513, 515-518
- résolution 1816, 23, 73-74, 206-207, 298, 340, 564
- résolution 1851, 298, 311-312, 333-334, 529-530
- résolution 1897, 73, 298, 301-302, 304, 333
- résolution 1973, 397-398
- résolution 1976, 308, 334
- résolution 2020, 46, 73, 221, 298, 334
- résolution 2077, 199

RESPONSABILITÉ CIVILE, 97, 99, 130, 141-142, 147, 161, 375, 422, 473-474, 558-559

RESPONSABILITÉ DE L'ÉTAT, 84-90, 92, 157, 169, 192-193, 196, 225, 270, 351-352, 366-367, 371, 382, 409-413, 489, 518, 557-608, 626-632
- attribution de comportement, 90, 280, 371, 410-412, 430, 435, 559, 579-595, 608, 614, 629
- circonstances excluant l'illicéité, 192, 270-271, 385, 564-565, 590
- fait générateur, 559-579

RESPONSABILITÉ POUR DES ACTIVITÉS LICITES DANGEREUSES, 576-579, 607

RESTITUTION
Voir *Réparation*

RUSES DE GUERRE, 536-537

SANCTIONS CIVILES
Voir *Responsabilité civile*

SANCTUARISATION, 487, 513

SATISFACTION
Voir *Réparation*

SHCHUKIN ET AUTRES C. CHYPRE (CEDH), 462

SHIPRIDER, 28, 33, 72, 173, 191-192, 277, 333-334, 340, 347, 377, 581-583, 609-633

SITUATION OBJECTIVE (EN DROIT INTERNATIONAL PUBLIC), 512-514

SOCIÉTÉS PRIVÉES DE SÉCURITÉ MARITIME, 90, 339-377, 584-589, 594
Code de conduite international pour les prestataires privés de services de sécurité, 350
projet de convention des Nations Unies sur la réglementation, la licence, le contrôle et la surveillance des sociétés militaires et de sécurité privées, 351-352

SOERING C. ROYAUME-UNI (CEDH), 251, 447, 451, 462

SOFT LAW, 172-173, 299, 348-351, 394-395, 400-401, 426, 431, 534

SOLAS CONVENTION DE 1974, 7, 21, 39-40, 102-103, 108-109, 116, 129-130, 372, 375, 384, 393, 396, 401, 404, 406-408, 411, 420-421, 431

SOMALIE, 18, 23, 43-47, 73-75, 84, 199-211, 217-226, 232, 235-237, 251, 290, 297-300, 307, 311, 313-314, 319-321, 332-335, 340-350, 356-358, 360, 364-365, 367-368, 370, 413, 445, 449, 455, 463, 529-530, 557, 564, 585-586, 589, 594, 612-613, 620

SOUS-COMITÉ DE L'OIM DES RADIOCOMMUNICATIONS ET DE LA RECHERCHE ET DU SAUVETAGE (COMSAR)
Voir *Recherche et sauvetage*

SOUTAGE/ DÉTOURNEMENT DE PÉTROLE, 3, 51

SOUVERAINETÉ, 5-8, 19, 31, 33, 49, 55-59, 74-75, 99-101, 107, 109-111, 127,131, 151-152, 159, 169-170, 183-188, 197, 244, 250, 258, 287-288, 301, 312, 328, 358-361, 369, 499-504, 509-510, 562, 568, 571, 574, 599

SUBSTANCES RADIOACTIVES, 107, 496-497

SYSTÈME MONDIAL DE DÉTRESSE ET DE SÉCURITÉ EN MER, 404, 420-421

TÉMOIGNAGES, 52, 87, 135-136, 250, 284, 312, 331, 333, 335, 453, 480

TERRORISME, 3, 6, 8, 11-12, 14, 18, 20-25, 37, 59, 74, 87-88, 204, 207, 210-211, 225, 229, 231-232, 289, 297, 307, 309, 313-314, 320-322, 328, 332, 335, 425, 489, 492-500, 503-504, 508, 514-521, 567-571, 587
Convention internationale pour la répression des actes de terrorisme nucléaire de 2005 , 494-495, 498, 500, 514, 517, 562
Convention internationale pour la répression du financement du terrorisme de 1999, 314, 322-324, 334

TIDM, 54, 166-167, 186-188, 289, 295, 402, 439, 548, 563, 566, 571, 597, 601-602, 604-605

TITRES DE COMPÉTENCE,
allégations de compétences, 3, 10-11, 14, 26, 29-30, 44-45, 154, 445, 550, 552, 633
compétence extraterritoriale, 56, 61-65, 71-72, 76, 80, 111-112, 214, 226, 228, 245, 274-276
compétence quasi universelle, 228-231, 235, 264, 270, 282, 320-325, 546
compétence universelle, 44-47, 62, 71, 76, 79-84, 89-90, 184, 189, 199, 209, 213, 216-219, 222-235, 246, 272, 282-283, 443, 546-547, 562, 580, 604, 626
doctrine des effets, 62-63, 71-72, 89, 625
principe de personnalité, 47, 62, 64, 68, 70-71, 76, 80-81, 84, 178, 184, 191, 209, 222-224, 229, 231, 246, 264, 270-272, 282, 622, 624
principe de protection, 9, 62, 76-77, 184, 229, 246, 269, 272-273
principe de territorialité, 55-61, 63, 81, 184, 209, 222, 228-229, 246, 259-261, 269-273, 276, 280, 622, 624

TOW-BACK, 245, 256, 394, 448

TPIR, 523, 525, 541-542

TPIY, 523, 525, 541-542, 544-545, 547, 587

TRAÇABILITÉ, 177-178, 196

TRAFIC DE DROGUE, 3-8, 11-14, 18, 27-34, 37, 41, 66, 88, 91, 236, 239, 270-273, 285-286, 289, 307, 314-319, 441, 454-457, 475-477, 511, 524, 557, 562, 569, 575, 581-582, 610-611, 615-619, 623, 625-626, 633
Accord de coopération sur la suppression du trafic illicite maritime et aéronautique de stupéfiants et de substances psychotropes dans la région des Caraïbes, 28, 32, 475-476, 617
Convention des Nations Unies de 1988 contre le trafic illicite de stupéfiants et de substances psychotropes, 28-34, 441, 457, 475, 562, 618
Drug Trafficking Vessel Interdiction Act (loi relative à l'interception des navires utilisés pour le trafic de drogue), 28, 30, 246, 272

TRAFIC DE MIGRANTS, 3-4, 8, 10-12, 14, 34-42, 59, 66-67, 69, 79-80, 82-83, 85, 88-89, 239-286, 289, 307, 326, 381, 384, 390, 393-396, 398, 401-418, 422-427, 454, 460-465, 472, 478-480, 524, 575
Protocole de 2000 contre le trafic illicite de migrants par terre, air et mer à la Convention des Nations Unies contre le crime transnational organisé, 4, 10, 35, 40, 67, 80, 82-83, 242-243, 246-249, 251, 253, 260-261, 264, 266-267, 282-283, 326, 420, 422-424, 460, 565, 570, 580, 601-602
trafiquants de migrants, 28, 34-42, 239, 241, 248, 250, 261, 269-272, 281-286, 422-425, 461

TRAFIC DE STUPÉFIANTS
Voir *Trafic de drogue*

TRAITE DE PERSONNES, 4, 12, 17, 34-42, 66-67, 80, 240-245, 249-250, 267-269, 277, 283, 299, 425, 457, 558

PROTOCOLE DE 2000 VISANT À PRÉVENIR, RÉPRIMER ET PUNIR LA TRAITE DES PERSONNES, EN PARTICULIER DES FEMMES ET DES ENFANTS, 242-243, 249, 268, 283, 325
Voir *Traite de personnes*

TRAITE DES ESCLAVES
Voir *Esclavage*

TRAITÉ SUR LA NON-PROLIFÉRATION DES ARMES NUCLÉAIRES DE 1968
Voir *Armes de destruction massive*

TRAITÉS D'EXTRADITION
Voir *Extradition*

TRANSIT, 9-10, 28, 36, 43, 263, 277-278, 281, 341, 344, 349, 355, 357-362, 370, 377, 395, 426, 504-507, 517, 585

TRANSPORT D'ADM PAR MER
Voir *Armes de destruction massive*

TRANSPORT D'ESCLAVES
Voir *Esclavage*

UNHCR, 35, 39, 245, 252, 254-256, 262, 275, 280, 381, 392, 401-403, 407, 413, 426, 463, 560

UNODC, 27, 34, 46, 154, 179-181, 239-243, 247-248, 250, 253, 259, 271, 276-277, 284-285, 333, 402, 423-425, 460, 476, 612

US NAVY, 528, 534-535, 599, 611-613

VOL À MAIN ARMÉE, 3, 8, 43, 46-47, 58, 66, 69, 78, 180, 205-209, 217-218, 221, 287-310, 314, 333, 335, 341, 350, 362, 569

W*OMEN ON WAVES ET AUTRES C. PORTUGAL* (CEDH), 442, 467-468, 575

ZEE, 3, 7, 9, 11-14, 19, 25, 32, 36, 49, 61, 63, 68, 70, 88, 105-111, 113, 115, 117-121, 126, 128-129, 132, 134-135, 150, 152, 160-161, 164, 170, 186-189, 204, 216, 265, 289, 383-384, 562, 599

ZONE CONTIGUË, 10-12, 18-19, 28, 32, 36, 61, 68-70, 88, 263-265, 268, 281, 288, 360, 562, 599, 617

ANALYTICAL INDEX

This index covers items in both languages
(*Table en français : voir p. 699*)

A. *A.* V. *GREECE* (ECTHR), 464, 478-479

ACT OF VIOLENCE AT SEA, 25, 41, 44-47, 202-208, 212, 215, 217-218, 220-221, 233, 290-294, 297, 302, 305, 308, 317, 341, 360, 363, 375-376, 423, 438-439, 451, 494, 586-587

ADMISSIBILITY OF EVIDENCE
See *Evidence*

AGREEMENT CONCERNING CO-OPERATION IN SUPPRESSING ILLICIT MARITIME AND AIR TRAFFICKING IN NARCOTIC DRUGS AND PSYCHOTROPIC SUBSTANCES IN THE CARIBBEAN AREA
See *Drug Trafficking*

AGREEMENT ON PORT STATE MEASURES OF THE FAO OF 2009, 6-7, 152-153, 156, 171-175, 194-195

AL-JEDDA V. *UNITED KINGDOM* (ECTHR), 75, 436, 592

ALMEZAAN INCIDENT, 358, 365-366, 371

AL-SKEINI AND OTHERS V. *UNITED KINGDOM* (ECTHR), 77, 433-435, 461

AMOCO CADIZ ACCIDENT, 473

ANDRONICOU AND CONSTANTINOU V. *CYPRUS* (ECTHR), 439

ARAB SPRING, 35, 381, 402, 408, 427

ARMED MERCHANT MARINE, 536-537

ARMED ROBBERY AT SEA, 3, 8, 43, 46-47, 58, 66, 69, 78, 180, 205-209, 217-218, 221, 287-310, 314, 333, 335, 341, 350, 362, 569

ARREST, 11, 13, 22, 25, 37, 44, 50-51, 65-67, 70, 72, 151, 186, 209, 218, 227, 233-236, 245, 260, 267-268, 303-305, 317, 319, 332-335

ASEAN CONVENTION ON COUNTER-TERRORISM (ACCT)
See *Extradition*

ASSERTION OF JURISDICTION
See *Titles of Jurisdiction*

ASYLUM SEEKERS, 35-36, 39, 42, 85, 239-240, 243-244, 250-256, 259, 261-262, 275, 279, 283-284, 381, 386, 391-395, 401, 403, 407, 418, 423, 426-427, 448, 451, 464-465, 478-479, 560, 575-576
Refugee Convention of 1951, 251-253, 261, 274-275, 392, 431, 448, 451, 575-576

ATTRIBUTION OF CONDUCT
See *State Responsibility*

AUT DEDERE AUT JUDICARE, 26, 80-83, 86-87, 209, 211-212, 229-232, 312, 320-331, 546

BALTIC AND INTERNATIONAL MARITIME COUNCIL (BIMCO), 339, 341, 352, 356-357

BANKOVIC AND OTHERS V. *BELGIUM* (ECTHR), 76, 280, 433-435, 590

BBC CHINA INCIDENT, 490, 498, 502

BEHRAMI AND SARAMATI V. *FRANCE* (ECTHR), 435, 591-593

BELLIGERENT MEASURES, 19-20, 533-541, 549, 572-573

BELLIGERENT RIGHT OF VISIT
See *Right of Visit*

BIOLOGICAL, CHEMICAL OR BACTERIOLOGICAL WEAPONS
See *Weapons of Mass Destruction*

BLADET TROMSO AND STENSAAS V. *NORWAY* (ECTHR), 467

BURDEN-SHARING, 395, 407-409, 426-427

CAP ANAMUR CASE, 423-424

CARIBBEAN, 4-5, 26-28, 32-33, 41, 194, 245, 265-266, 275-277, 381, 418, 575-576, 581-582, 597, 607, 610-611, 617-619, 621, 625, 628, 633

CARICOM
See *Caribbean*

CIRCUMSTANCES PRECLUDING WRONGFULNESS
See *State Responsibility*

CIVIL RESPONSIBILITY, 97, 99, 130, 141-142, 147, 161, 375, 422, 473-474, 558-559

CIVIL SANCTIONS
See *Civil Reparations*

COASTAL STATE, 3, 6-14, 18-19, 21, 33, 37-40, 46-47, 51, 56-63, 65-70, 75, 78-79, 81, 88, 98-107, 110-115, 120-121, 126-135, 143, 145, 147, 149, 151-152, 154, 157, 159-161, 164, 167, 170, 172, 183, 186-189, 196-197, 204, 225, 235, 244, 257-265, 268, 276-281, 300-303, 307, 309-310, 316, 333, 348, 350, 355, 358-362, 369, 382, 387-389, 394, 403, 409-413, 426, 460, 465, 468, 503-507, 517, 528, 559, 562, 564, 568, 582, 584-585, 596, 599-600, 606, 611, 614-615, 618, 622-623, 625
interest of coastal State, 66, 98-99, 103, 105, 111-113, 127, 129, 132, 358-359, 599-600

CODE OF PRACTICE FOR THE INVESTIGATION OF THE CRIMES OF PIRACY AND ARMED ROBBERY AGAINST SHIPS
See *Piracy*

COMITY 1540, 92, 495, 500-501, 510

COMPENSATION
See *Reparation*

CONSERVATION OF LIVING RESOURCES, 8, 13, 49, 56, 158-162, 168, 184, 188, 195, 288

CONTIGUOUS ZONE, 10-12, 18-19, 28, 32, 36, 61, 68-70, 88, 263-265, 268, 281, 288, 360, 562, 599, 617

CONVENTION FOR THE SUPPRESSION OF UNLAWFUL ACTS AGAINST THE SAFETY OF CIVIL AVIATION OF 1971, 229, 568

CONVENTION FOR THE SUPPRESSION OF UNLAWFUL ACTS AGAINST THE SAFETY OF MARITIME NAVIGATION OF 1988
See *SUA Convention of 1988*

CONVENTION FOR THE SUPPRESSION OF UNLAWFUL SEIZURE OF AIRCRAFT OF 1970, 229

CONVOY
See *Escort Vessel*

CORFU CHANNEL CASE *(UNITED KINGDOM* V. *ALBANIA)* (ICJ), 7, 301, 567, 569, 598-599, 606

CORRUPTION, 153, 179, 196, 211, 314, 326
United Nations Convention against Corruption of 2003, 314, 326-327, 329-330

COUNCIL DECISION 2010/252/EU, 386-387, 392, 394-395, 426

COUNCIL REGULATION (EC) NO. 1005/2008, 156, 177-178, 182-183, 185, 191, 195

COUNCIL REGULATION (EC) NO. 1224/2009, 177, 191

COUNTERMEASURES, 191-194, 389, 564, 571-572

COURT OF JUSTICE OF THE EUROPEAN COMMUNITIES
See *Court of Justice of the European Union*

COURT OF JUSTICE OF THE EUROPEAN UNION, 116, 119, 122, 168, 182, 217, 256, 386, 508-509

CRITERION OF INTENTION, 51, 57-58, 69, 105, 118-126, 136-138, 144, 180-181, 192, 203, 206-208, 211-212, 219-220, 247-248, 284, 290, 292, 322, 357, 468-469, 494-495, 504

CUSTODIAL STATE, 86-87, 322-324, 327, 335

DEFINITION OF A MILITARY OBJECTIVE
See *Principle of Distinction*

DEPRIVATION OF LIBERTY
See *Human Rights*: right to liberty and security of person

DESIGN, CONSTRUCTION AND ARMAMENT, 57, 101-103, 115, 129-130, 360

DIRECTIVE 2005/35/EC, 116, 121-123, 130-131

DISCHARGES
See *Pollution*

DISEMBARKATION
See *Place of Safety*

DISTRESS AT SEA, 6, 38-39, 57-58, 105, 119, 240, 383-387, 391, 394, 401, 403-410, 413-416, 420-422, 425-426. 460, 564

DJIBOUTI CODE OF CONDUCT, 235, 290, 293, 376, 407, 612, 620

DOCUMENTARY VIOLATION, 115, 117, 125-128, 138, 182, 247

DRAFT REGIONAL MEMORANDUM OF UNDERSTANDING FOR THE MEDITERRANEAN ON DISEMBARKATION
See *Place of Safety*

DRUG TRAFFICKING, 3-8, 11-14, 18, 27-34, 37, 41, 66, 88, 91, 236, 239, 270-273, 285-286, 289, 307, 314-319, 441, 454-457, 475-477, 511, 524, 557, 562, 569, 575, 581-582, 610-611, 615-619, 623, 625-626, 633
Agreement concerning Co-operation in Suppressing Illicit Maritime and Air Trafficking in Narcotic Drugs and Psychotropic Substances in the Caribbean Area, 28, 32, 475-476, 617
Drug Trafficking Vessel Interdiction Act, 28, 30, 246, 272
United Nations Convention against Illicit Traffic in Narcotic Drugs and Psychotropic Substances of 1988, 28-34, 441, 457, 475, 562, 618

DUAL CRIMINALITY, 327, 329

DUBLIN II REGULATION, 407

DUE DILIGENCE, 168-169, 352-354

DUTY TO RENDER ASSISTANCE, 38, 333, 382-387, 416, 419-422, 426, 460

ECOWAS
See *West Africa*

EEZ, 3, 7, 9, 11-14, 19, 25, 32, 36, 49, 61, 63, 68, 70, 88, 105-111, 113, 115, 117-121, 126, 128-129, 132, 134-135, 150, 152, 160-161, 164, 170, 186-189, 204, 216, 265, 289, 383-384, 562, 599

EFFECTIVE CONTROL, 77, 164-166, 169, 250, 270, 274, 276, 283, 433, 435-436, 438, 461, 587, 591-592

EFFECTS DOCTRINE
See *Titles of Jurisdiction*

EMBARGO, 360, 414, 485, 564, 591, 595

ENRICA LEXIE INCIDENT, 366-367, 371, 601-602

ENVIRONMENTAL CRIME
See *Protection of the Environment*

ENVIRONMENTAL DAMAGE
See *Protection of the Environment*

ERGA OMNES OBLIGATIONS, 158, 168, 191, 193, 512

ERIKA ACCIDENT AND CASE, 113-114, 119-120, 124, 129, 142, 473

ERLANGEN CASE, 563, 596

ESCORT VESSEL, 340, 345-347, 356, 359, 361-362, 369, 412, 573, 613

ESTAI CASE, 49, 563, 578, 597

EU NAVFOR, 43, 45, 341, 346, 366, 431, 435, 455, 523, 529, 592, 594

EUROPEAN ARREST WARRANT, 332

EUROPEAN COURT OF HUMAN RIGHTS (ECTHR), 42, 75-77, 90-91, 237, 251, 253-256, 270, 274, 279-280, 282-283, 395, 406-407, 433-435, 443, 446-447, 449, 454, 457-481, 565, 575, 584, 590-593, 603, 607

EUROSUR, 418

EVIDENCE, 87, 131-138, 143-144, 161, 231, 255, 267, 284, 389, 417, 463, 570

EVIDENTIARY DIFFICULTIES
See *Evidence*

EXPULSION, 86, 250-257, 274-275, 283-284, 462-463, 472-473, 479-480, 575

EXTRADITE OR PROSECUTE OBLIGATION
See *Aut Dedere Aut Judicare*

EXTRADITION, 25-26, 52, 64, 82, 86-87, 218, 229-233, 251, 311-336, 442, 447, 449, 473, 546, 619
Asean Convention on Counter-Terrorism (ACCT), 332
London Scheme of Extradition, 331-332

EXTRADITION TREATIES
See *Extradition*

EXTRATERRITORIAL APPLICATION OF HUMAN RIGHTS
See *Human Rights*

EXTRATERRITORIAL JURISDICTION
See *Titles of Jurisdiction*

EXXON VALDEZ ACCIDENT, 142, 473

FAO COMPLIANCE AGREEMENT OF 1993, 48, 159-160, 163, 165, 171

FLAG OF CONVENIENCE, 18, 160, 163-166, 178, 185, 188, 191, 196, 420

FLAG OF NON-COMPLIANCE
See *Flag of Convenience*

FLIGHT INFORMATION REGION, 404-405

FLOATING ARMORIES, 339, 359-360

FORESEEABILITY
See *Predictability*

FRAMEWORK DECISION 2005/667/JAI, 116, 138

FREEDOM OF SPEECH
See *Human Rights*

FREEDOM OF THE HIGH SEAS, 14-15, 111, 161, 265

FRONTEX, 5, 36, 244-245, 277, 280, 386, 394-395, 417-418, 427, 454

GENERALLY ACCEPTED INTERNATIONAL RULES AND STANDARDS, 102-103, 108-110, 114, 116, 120-121, 128-130

GENEVA CONVENTIONS OF 1958, 17, 19, 44, 162, 164, 167-168, 189, 203, 222, 225, 288, 292, 308

GENUINE LINK, 164, 166-169, 196

GLOBAL MARITIME DISTRESS AND SAFETY SYSTEM (GMDSS), 404, 420-421

GUARDCON, 352, 355-357, 375

GULF OF ADEN
See *Somalia*

GULF OF GUINEA
See *West Africa*

HARVARD DRAFT CONVENTION ON PIRACY
See *Piracy*

HIGH RISK AREAS, 339-341, 345, 348-349, 353, 355-357, 363

HIGH SEAS, 3, 7-30, 32-33, 36-38, 41, 44, 48-50, 54, 61, 68-75, 81-84, 88-89, 111-112, 121, 126, 150, 152, 157-170, 176, 184-185, 188-194, 197, 203-212, 216-225, 244-251, 257-258, 263, 265-283, 288, 292-293, 298, 307-310, 312, 316-319, 358-360, 375, 384, 419-421, 434, 444, 448, 454-457, 463, 476, 500-502, 511, 521, 540-541, 549, 562-563, 566, 573-579, 596-602, 609, 622-624

HIRSI JAMAA AND OTHERS V. *ITALY* (ECTHR), 251, 254-256, 274, 283, 407, 448, 463-464, 479, 607

HOSTAGES, 43, 80, 82, 90, 202, 207, 210-212, 228-229, 231-232, 297, 304-305, 307, 309, 320-324, 332, 334, 363, 439, 442, 568
International Convention against the Taking of Hostages of 1979, 210-211, 229, 231, 320-324, 332, 334

HOSTILITIES AT SEA
See *Naval Warfare*

HOT PURSUIT, 11, 18-19, 68-70, 74, 78, 188-189, 207, 268-269, 277, 281, 313, 565, 615, 617, 630

HRC GENERAL COMMENTS, 251, 258, 274, 433, 452

HUMAN RIGHTS, 46, 52, 55, 72, 75-78, 85, 90-92, 196, 200, 236-237, 240-241, 246, 250-258, 262, 273-276, 278-285, 365, 304-307, 350-352, 367, 401-402, 407, 409, 412, 427, 429-456, 457-481, 531, 561, 565, 574-576, 581, 585, 592-593, 598, 614, 628, 632
extraterritorial application of human rights, 76-78, 274-276, 279-280, 283, 432-435, 453, 461, 479-480, 575-576
freedom of speech, 460, 465-469, 575
procedural guarantees, 244-255, 283, 443-447, 472
prohibition of collective expulsion, 256-257, 274, 283, 472, 479-480
prohibition of torture or other inhuman or degrading treatment or punishment, 86, 90, 215, 230, 237, 251-253, 305, 431, 439, 447-453, 459-464, 552, 575, 604
right to an effective remedy, 254, 480-481, 603-604
right to leave one's own country and freedom of movement, 257-258, 277-278
right to liberty and security of person, 90-91, 181, 252, 261, 275, 277, 440-445, 473-479, 565, 575-576
right to life, 76, 275, 305, 438-439, 461, 531
right to property, 447, 460, 469-472
right to respect for private life, 437, 467, 607

ICAO, 388

ICCPR OF 1966, 251, 257, 273, 305, 432-434, 451, 603

ICTR, 523, 525, 541-542

ICTY, 523, 525, 541-542, 544-545, 547, 587

ILLEGAL FISHING, 4, 6, 8, 11, 13, 18, 47-51, 149-197, 424, 617-618, 633

IMB, 206, 342

IMO, 21, 25, 39, 43, 46-47, 52, 64, 199, 205, 208, 217, 289-291, 296-299, 336, 339-341, 345, 347-351, 353, 355, 357, 359, 363-364, 373, 376, 382, 385, 388, 392-408, 425-426, 470, 612

INCIDENT OF THE *ACHILLE LAURO*, 23, 63, 207, 321

INDIAN OCEAN, 22, 26, 43, 45, 162, 194, 290, 297, 340, 357, 366-367, 587, 602, 612

INNOCENT PASSAGE, 7-9, 36, 56-61, 69, 74, 101-106, 244, 258-263, 277-278, 281, 303, 360-362, 465, 468, 503-509, 562, 584

INTERAGENCY GROUP (UNHCR, UNDOALOS, UNODC, OHCHR, IOM, IMO), 401-402, 406

INTEREST OF COASTAL STATE
See *Coastal State*

INTERNAL WATERS, 5-8, 18, 21, 33, 46, 56, 65, 67, 69, 99, 105, 121, 191, 248, 290, 293, 300-303, 306, 308-310, 504, 206, 216, 358, 369, 500, 503, 507, 562, 622-623

INTERNATIONAL AERONAUTICAL AND MARITIME SEARCH AND RESCUE MANUAL (IAMSAR MANUAL)
See *Search and Rescue*

INTERNATIONAL ARMED CONFLICT, 526-527, 533-534, 539-541, 549-550, 552, 573-574, 588-589

INTERNATIONAL CHAMBER OF SHIPPING (ICS), 339, 441, 443, 368, 403

INTERNATIONAL CODE OF CONDUCT FOR PRIVATE SECURITY SERVICE PROVIDERS (ICOC)
See *Private Maritime Security Companies*

INTERNATIONAL COMITY OF THE RED CROSS (ICRC), 526-529, 533, 539, 544, 547, 588-589

INTERNATIONAL CONVENTION AGAINST THE TAKING OF HOSTAGES OF 1979
See *Hostages*

INTERNATIONAL CONVENTION FOR THE SUPPRESSION OF ACTS OF NUCLEAR TERRORISM OF 2005
See *Terrorism*

INTERNATIONAL CONVENTION FOR THE SUPPRESSION OF THE FINANCING OF TERRORISM OF 1999
See *Terrorism*

INTERNATIONAL CONVENTION ON MARITIME SEARCH AND RESCUE OF 1979
See *SAR Convention of 1979*

INTERNATIONAL CONVENTION ON OIL POLLUTION PREPAREDNESS, RESPONSE AND CO-OPERATION OF 1990
See *Pollution*

INTERNATIONAL CONVENTION ON SALVAGE OF 1989, 382-383, 419-422

INTERNATIONAL COURT OF JUSTICE, 7, 49, 60-62, 71, 83-84, 86, 167, 170, 223, 234, 246, 274, 301, 389, 400, 412, 487-488, 516, 534, 543, 563, 567, 569, 580, 582-583, 587-588, 590, 593, 597-599, 606

INTERNATIONAL CRIMINAL COURT, 20, 113-114, 214-215, 454, 523, 525, 530, 541, 553, 626

INTERNATIONAL CRIMINAL LAW, 53, 67, 92, 525, 541-542, 546, 552-553

INTERNATIONAL HUMANITARIAN LAW, 84, 304, 306-307, 352, 364, 406, 409, 427, 431-432, 488, 494, 515, 523, 525, 527-553, 573, 588-589

INTERNATIONAL ORGANIZATION FOR STANDARDIZATION (ISO), 350

INTERNATIONAL SHIPS AND PORT SECURITY FACILITY CODE (ISPS CODE), 348, 355, 372

INTERNATIONAL STRAITS, 9-10, 341, 361-362, 568
Malacca Straits, 46, 294, 340, 362, 568

INTERPOL, 154, 179

IPOA-IUU, 47, 152, 155-157, 171-172, 196

ISLAMIC REPUBLIC OF IRAN SHIPPING LINES V. *TURKEY* (ECTHR), 470-472

ITLOS, 54, 166-167, 186-188, 289, 295, 402, 439, 548, 563, 566, 571, 597, 601-602, 604-605

IUU FISHING
See *Illegal Fishing*

JAMES AND OTHERS V. *UK* (ECTHR), 469-470

JUS AD BELLUM, 77, 523-524, 538

JUS IN BELLO, 77, 84, 306-307, 436, 488, 521, 523-524, 528, 530, 533, 538, 542, 549, 560-561, 572, 600

KADI AND AL BARAKAAT INTERNATIONAL FOUNDATION CASE, 508-509

LACK OF MAINTENANCE, 102-103, 129, 145-147

LAUNDERING OF THE PROCEEDS OF CRIMES
See *Money Laundering*

LAW ENFORCEMENT DETACHMENTS, 611-613, 621

LAW ENFORCEMENT OPERATION, 10, 15, 33, 36, 85, 98, 228, 244, 316, 360, 411, 430, 438, 523-531, 549, 562, 566-567, 571-572, 582, 608, 610, 614, 617, 622-626, 629

LEFT-TO-DIE BOAT, 240, 414-417

LIABILITY FOR DANGEROUS LICIT ACTIVITIES, 576-579, 607

LONDON SCHEME OF EXTRADITION
See *Extradition*

M/V PINAR E, 390

M/V SAIGA CASES (ITLOS), 13, 54, 167, 402, 439, 548-549, 563, 566, 597, 601-602, 604-605

M/V SO SAN, 22, 490

MAERSK ALABAMA CASE, 344, 355, 367-368

MALACCA STRAITS
See *International Straits*

MALTA, 27, 29, 113-114, 251, 262, 273, 390, 393, 395-399, 403-409, 413, 416-417, 427, 463

MANGOURAS V. *SPAIN* (ECTHR), 474-475

MARE CLAUSUM, 190, 287

MARE LIBERUM, 55, 190, 287

MARITIME CASUALTIES, 316-317, 531

MARITIME INTERDICTION OPERATION (MIO), 4, 85, 244-245, 429-456, 524, 557-561, 564, 570-571, 574, 576, 579-595, 597-599, 602, 605, 608

MARITIME SAFETY COMMITTEE, 299, 348-350, 396-400

MARKET MEASURES, 153-154, 159, 171-178, 196

MARPOL 73/78, 7, 52, 97-98, 102-103, 105-113, 116-138, 142, 146-148, 473, 569-570

MAVI MARMARA INCIDENT, 20, 525, 531, 547-553, 573-574

MEDITERRANEAN SEA, 5, 35-37, 42, 133, 146, 162, 194, 239-240, 245, 251, 254-255, 277, 381-382, 390-391, 393-409, 413-418, 423-427, 448-452, 463-465, 479-480, 557, 575, 584

MEDVEDYEV AND OTHERS V. *FRANCE* (ECTHR), 91, 238, 266, 270, 433-434, 438, 440-446, 454-455, 476-478, 565, 575

MIGRANT SMUGGLING, 3-4, 8, 10-12, 14, 34-42, 59, 66-67, 69, 79-80, 82-83, 85, 88-89, 239-286, 289, 307, 326, 381, 384, 390, 393-396, 398, 401-418, 422-427, 454, 460-465, 472, 478-480, 524, 575
- migrant smugglers, 28, 34-42, 239, 241, 248, 250, 261, 269-272, 281-286, 422-425, 461
- Protocol of 2000 against Smuggling of Migrants by Land, Sea and Air, Supplementing the United Nations Convention against Transnational Organized Crime, 4, 10, 35, 40, 67, 80, 82-83, 242-243, 246-249, 251, 253, 260-261, 264, 266-267, 282-283, 326, 420, 422-424, 460, 565, 570, 580, 601-602

MONEY LAUNDERING, 211, 213, 326-327, 334

MOWCA, 341, 589

MUTUAL LEGAL ASSISTANCE, 52, 311-336, 619

NATIONALITY PRINCIPLE
See *Titles of Jurisdiction:* personality principle

NATO, 35, 43, 341, 393-394, 397-398, 414-417, 431, 435, 493, 579, 590, 595

NAVAL BLOCKADE, 20, 548-552, 572-574

NAVAL WARFARE, 19, 523-553, 572-574, 588-589

NECESSITY AND PROPORTIONALITY, 111, 177, 196, 263, 329, 363, 373-375, 384, 439, 447, 471, 508, 531, 540-541, 547, 549-551, 563-566, 571, 573-574, 579, 598, 632

NEUTRAL SHIPPING, 19, 524, 532, 534, 540-541, 547, 549, 573

NEW YORK AGREEMENT OF 1995, 6, 11, 49-50, 155, 159-160, 163-177, 189-191

NON-INTERNATIONAL ARMED CONFLICT, 307, 525-526, 529-531, 539-541, 545, 549-550, 552

NON-REFOULEMENT
See *Refoulement*

NON-STATE ACTORS, 20, 24-27, 60, 74, 83, 91, 321-322, 347-348, 351, 490-499, 510-519, 582, 587-588
See also *Private Maritime Security Companies*

NUCLEAR DETERRENCE, 487-489, 511, 513-515

NUCLEAR WEAPONS
See *Weapons of Mass Destruction*

NUREMBERG TRIALS, 523, 547

OBJECTIVE SITUATION (IN PUBLIC INTERNATIONAL LAW), 512-514

ÖCALAN V. *TURKEY* CASE (ECTHR), 433, 442

OIL AND GAS, 3, 10, 51-52, 97, 113, 120-121, 133, 138, 142, 342, 369, 405, 563, 600-602

OIL BUNKERING, 3, 51

OIL SPILLAGE
See *Pollution*

OPERATION ATALANTA
See *EU NAVFOR*

OPERATION ENDURING FREEDOM, 25, 490, 540, 589

OPERATION UNIFIED PROTECTOR, 393, 397-398, 416-417

OVERLAP OF JURISDICTION, 13, 62, 64, 99-100, 112-115, 129-130, 232-235, 272, 303, 316, 347, 358, 503, 614, 626

P&I, 352, 354, 357

PALMER REPORT
See Mavi Marmara *Incident*

PAMUK AND OTHERS, 37, 267, 269

PEACE FLOTILLA CASE
See Mavi Marmara *Incident*

PERSONALITY PRINCIPLE
See *Titles of Jurisdiction*

PIRACY, 3, 4, 8, 12, 14, 16-18, 21, 23, 30, 43-47, 70-75, 78-79, 84, 88-90, 180, 188-189, 199-238, 271-272, 289-290, 294-295, 299-326, 333-336, 339-377, 389, 431, 434, 436-437, 442-443, 445, 447, 449-455, 457, 477-478, 502, 524, 529-530, 546, 557, 562-565, 569, 575, 579-580, 586-587, 596, 601, 609, 612-614, 620, 622-623, 633
Code of Practice for the Investigation of the Crimes of Piracy and Armed Robbery against Ships, 47, 205, 208, 217
Harvard Draft Convention on Piracy, 203, 205, 214, 237

PLACE OF SAFETY, 6, 36, 39-40, 255, 286, 349, 359, 387, 390-403, 406, 408-413, 426-427, 464
Draft Regional Memorandum of Understanding for the Mediterranean on Disembarkation, 391, 396-409, 427

POLLUTION, 6-10, 12-13, 51-52, 57-58, 63, 66, 69, 97-148, 173, 180, 182, 298, 457, 473-474, 559, 562-563, 566, 569-570
discharges, 7, 10, 13, 51, 97, 110, 117, 120-121, 124, 126-127, 132, 134-137, 144
International Convention on Oil Pollution Preparedness, Response and Co-operation of 1990, 52
oil spillage, 139, 142, 147, 473

PORT, 5-7, 21, 46, 51, 56, 67, 79, 99-100, 127-128, 132-136, 140-147, 152-154, 156, 159, 170-176, 183, 194-196, 241, 333, 339, 342, 348, 350, 355-359, 361, 365, 369, 372, 374, 383, 390, 398, 409, 413, 423, 425, 445-446, 453, 463, 470, 501, 503, 562, 573, 606, 623-624

PORT OF CONVENIENCE, 176

PORT STATE CONTROL, 7, 99-100, 173, 194-195

PREDICTABILITY, 147, 222, 270-271, 282, 440-444

PRESTIGE ACCIDENT, 97, 108, 129, 142, 144, 473-474

PRINCIPLE OF DISTINCTION, 534-539, 549, 574

PRINCIPLE OF TERRITORIALITY
See *Titles of Jurisdiction*

PRIVATE ARMED GUARDS
See *Private Maritime Security Companies*

PRIVATE MARITIME SECURITY COMPANIES, 90, 339-377, 584-589, 594
International Code of Conduct for Private Security Service Providers (ICOC), 350
UN Draft Convention on the Regulation, Oversight and Monitoring of Private Military and Security Companies, 351-352

PROCEDURAL GUARANTEES
See *Human Rights*

PROHIBITION OF COLLECTIVE EXPULSION
See *Human Rights*

PROHIBITION OF TORTURE OR OTHER INHUMAN OR DEGRADING TREATMENT OR PUNISHMENT
See *Human Rights*

PROLIFERATION SECURITY INITIATIVE, 3, 9, 20-21, 26, 490, 498, 500-502, 521

PROLIFERATION VIOLATION, 489, 491, 499, 501, 504, 510

PROMPT RELEASE, 70, 186-187

PROTECTION OF THE ENVIRONMENT, 8, 12-13, 51-52, 57, 97-101, 107-108, 126-128, 131, 135, 139-141, 144-145, 147, 149, 168-170, 175, 179-184, 194, 196, 317, 342, 347, 372, 376, 420, 474-475, 559, 562, 567, 576, 599-600, 603, 606-607, 618

PROTECTIVE PRINCIPLE
See *Titles of Jurisdiction*

PROTOCOL OF 2005 TO THE CONVENTION FOR THE SUPPRESSION OF UNLAWFUL ACTS AGAINST THE SAFETY OF MARITIME NAVIGATION
See *SUA Convention of 1988*: SUA Protocol of 2005

PROTOCOL OF 2000 AGAINST SMUGGLING OF MIGRANTS BY LAND, SEA AND AIR, SUPPLEMENTING THE UNITED NATIONS CONVENTION AGAINST TRANSNATIONAL ORGANIZED CRIME
See *Migrant Smuggling*

PROTOCOL OF 2000 TO PREVENT, SUPPRESS AND PUNISH TRAFFICKING IN PERSONS, ESPECIALLY WOMEN AND CHILDREN
See *Trafficking in People*

PUSH-BACK OPERATIONS, 35, 42, 245, 256

QUASI-UNIVERSAL JURISDICTION
See *Titles of Jurisdiction*

RADIOACTIVE MATERIAL, 107, 496-497

RED CRUSADER CASE (*DENMARK* V. *UNITED KINGDOM*), 566, 598

REFOULEMENT, 85, 250-256, 259, 262-263, 274-283, 392, 394, 407, 447-452, 463-464, 472, 479-481, 575-576

REFUGEE
See *Asylum Seekers*

REFUGEE CONVENTION OF 1951
See *Asylum Seekers*

REFUGEE STATUS DETERMINATION
See *Asylum Seekers*

REPARATION, 88-89, 130, 141-142, 375, 458, 472, 557-559, 561, 565, 571, 577-579, 591, 597-598, 600-607, 628

RESCUE CO-ORDINATION CENTRE (RCC)
See *Search and Rescue*

RESTITUTION
See *Reparation*

RFMOS, 48, 50, 154-160, 162-164, 166, 173-174, 177, 187, 189-190-191, 193, 195-196

RIGHT OF APPROACH, 15-17

RIGHT OF VISIT, 15-23, 25, 29-30, 32-33, 36-37, 40, 65, 67, 70-72, 88-89, 134-135, 185, 188-189, 244-245, 265-271, 346, 460, 524, 559-560, 563, 565, 571-573, 577, 584, 602, 614-615, 624
belligerent right of visit, 16, 20, 524

RIGHT TO AN EFFECTIVE REMEDY
See *Human Rights*

RIGHT TO LEAVE ONE'S OWN COUNTRY AND FREEDOM OF MOVEMENT
See *Human Rights*

RIGHT TO LIBERTY AND SECURITY OF PERSON
See *Human Rights*

RIGHT TO LIFE
See *Human Rights*

RIGHT TO PROPERTY
See *Human Rights*

RIGHT TO RESPECT FOR PRIVATE LIFE
See *Human Rights*

RULES FOR THE USE OF FORCE (RUF)
See *Rules of Engagement*

RULES OF ENGAGEMENT, 4, 353-354, 363, 371, 373-374, 454

RUSES OF WAR, 536-537

SAFE THIRD COUNTRY, 225-226, 286, 393, 406, 446, 448, 452

SALE V. *HAITIAN CENTERS COUNCIL* CASE, 275-276, 576

SALVAGE CONVENTION OF 1989
See *International Convention on Salvage of 1989*

SAN JOSE AGREEMENT
See *Drug Trafficking:* Agreement concerning Co-operation in Suppressing Illicit Maritime and Air Trafficking in Narcotic Drugs and Psychotropic Substances in the Caribbean Area

SAN REMO MANUAL, 523, 533-540, 544, 550-551, 572-574

SANCTUARIZATION, 487, 513

SAR CONVENTION OF 1979, 39-40, 385, 387-401, 404-408, 411-413, 460

SATISFACTION
See *Reparation*

SCHENGEN BORDERS CODE, 385-387, 392, 394, 426

SEARCH AND RESCUE, 39-40, 118, 125, 381-427, 460, 463
International Aeronautical and Maritime Search and Rescue Manual (IAMSAR Manual), 388
search and rescue regions (SRR), 387-395, 403-409, 413, 426-427
Rescue Co-ordination Center (RCC), 387, 391, 403, 406, 411, 416
Sub-Committee of the IMO on Radiocommunications and Search and Rescue (COMSAR), 396-397, 399-400, 404

SEAWORTHINESS, 34, 37, 239, 367, 381, 385-386, 409-410

SELF-DEFENCE, 16, 111, 356, 368, 373-375, 488, 523-524, 538, 540, 564, 567, 573, 631

SHCHUKIN AND OTHERS V. *CYPRUS* (ECTHR), 462

SHIP-BOARDING AGREEMENTS OR SCHEMES, 18, 26-28, 50-51, 192, 502, 511, 614-622

SHIPMASTER, 6, 8, 28, 38-41, 66, 102, 111, 118-119, 121, 123-125, 130, 137-140, 143, 145-147, 237, 241, 299, 304, 316-317, 325, 341, 348-349, 352-355, 365, 372-375, 382-383, 387, 403, 410-411, 419-422, 425-426, 430, 471, 474, 557, 559-560, 599, 601, 612, 620, 623

SHIP-OWNER, 100, 102, 113, 118-119, 121, 123-125, 130, 141, 144, 148, 299, 344, 347-349, 352-354, 357, 362, 368-369, 375, 419, 421-422, 430, 436, 460, 463, 475, 557, 559, 561, 597, 585, 602

SHIP-RIDER, 28, 33, 72, 173, 191-192, 277, 333-334, 340, 347, 377, 581-583, 609-633

SLAVE TRADE
See *Slavery*

SLAVERY, 3, 12, 16-17, 21, 30, 36, 38, 72, 79-80, 88-89, 189, 214-215, 242-243, 249, 267-268, 305, 317-319, 455, 457, 502, 558, 562, 609, 622-623, 626

SOERING V. *UNITED KINGDOM* (ECTHR), 251, 447, 451, 462

SOFT LAW, 172-173, 299, 348-351, 394-395, 400-401, 426, 431, 534

SOLAS CONVENTION OF 1974, 7, 21, 39-40, 102-103, 108-109, 116, 129-130, 372, 375, 384, 393, 396, 401, 404, 406-408, 411, 420-421, 431

SOMALI COAST
See *Somalia*

SOMALIA, 18, 23, 43-47, 73-75, 84, 199-211, 217-226, 232, 235-237, 251, 290, 297-300, 307, 311, 313-314, 319-321, 332-335, 340-350, 356-358, 360, 364-365, 367-368, 370, 413, 445, 449, 455, 463, 529-530, 557, 564, 585-586, 589, 594, 612-613, 620

SOVEREIGN RIGHTS, 12-13, 70, 106, 160-161, 164, 503, 562

SOVEREIGNTY, 5-8, 19, 31, 33, 49, 55-59, 74-75, 99-101, 107, 109-111, 127, 131, 151-152, 159, 169-170, 183-188, 197, 244, 250, 258, 287-288, 301, 312, 328, 358-361, 369, 499-504, 509-510, 562, 568, 571, 574, 599

SS I'M ALONE CASE, 566, 598

STANDARD OPERATING PROCEDURES FOR SHIPMASTERS (SOPS), 403, 529, 616

STATE RESPONSIBILITY, 84-90, 92, 157, 169, 192-193, 196, 225, 270, 351-352, 366-367, 371, 382, 409-413, 489, 518, 557-608, 626-632
attribution of conduct, 90, 280, 371, 410-412, 430, 435, 559, 579-595, 608, 614, 629
circumstances precluding wrongfulness, 192, 270-271, 385, 564-565, 590
wrongful act, 559-579

STATELESS VESSEL, 34, 37, 185, 266-267, 271-272, 367, 381, 385-386, 409, 562

SUA CONVENTION OF 1988, 25-26, 63-64, 67-68, 80-83, 86, 202, 204, 206-211, 228-232, 237, 293-294, 314, 320-325, 332, 334-336, 360, 431, 490, 497, 518, 546, 562, 566, 568-569, 572
SUA Protocol of 2005, 4, 12, 14, 21, 25-26, 80, 82-83, 92, 207, 490-492, 495-502, 510-518, 566-569, 572, 577, 580, 603

SUB-COMMITTEE OF THE IMO ON RADIOCOMMUNICATIONS AND SEARCH AND RESCUE (COMSAR)
See *Search and Rescue*

T*ADIĆ* CASE (ICTY), 525-526, 530, 587-588

TAMPA INCIDENT, 35, 39, 239, 250, 258

TERRITORIAL SEA, 3, 7-12, 18-19, 21, 25, 28, 32-33, 37, 43, 46-47, 51, 56-59, 61, 63, 65-69, 73-82, 85, 98, 100-106, 112, 114-115, 127-128, 132, 134-135, 139-140, 145, 160, 188, 204-207, 215-216, 225, 244-245, 248, 257-265, 268-269, 276-283, 288-290, 293, 297-310, 312, 316, 333, 335, 340, 347, 358-362, 367-370, 384, 391, 395, 397, 405, 426, 432, 448-450, 460, 465, 468-469, 475-476, 500, 503-507, 517, 529, 540, 562-564, 568, 582-584, 586, 599, 601, 606, 611, 617, 619-625

TERROR ATTACKS OF 11 SEPTEMBER 2001, 20, 489-490, 493, 496

TERRORISM, 3, 6, 8, 11-12, 14, 18, 20-25, 37, 59, 74, 87-88, 204, 207, 210-211, 225, 229, 231-232, 289, 297, 307, 309, 313-314, 320-322, 328, 332, 335, 425, 489, 492-500, 503-504, 508, 514-521, 567-571, 587
International Convention for the Suppression of Acts of Nuclear Terrorism of 2005, 494-495, 498, 500, 514, 517, 562
International Convention for the Suppression of the Financing of Terrorism of 1999, 314, 322-324, 334

THIRD COUNTRY ASSURANCE (E.G. DIPLOMATIC ASSURANCES), 237, 255, 449-453

TITLES OF JURISDICTION,
assertion of jurisdiction, 3, 10-11, 14, 26, 29-30, 44-45, 154, 445, 550, 552, 633
effects doctrine, 62-63, 71-72, 89, 625
extraterritorial jurisdiction, 56, 61-65, 71-72, 76, 80, 111-112, 214, 226, 228, 245, 274-276
personality principle, 47, 62, 64, 68, 70-71, 76, 80-81, 84, 178, 184, 191, 209, 222-224, 229, 231, 246, 264, 270-272, 282, 622, 624
principle of territoriality, 55-61, 63, 81, 184, 209, 222, 228-229, 246, 259-261, 269-273, 276, 280, 622, 624
protective principle, 9, 62, 76-77, 184, 229, 246, 269, 272-273
quasi-universal jurisdiction, 228-231, 235, 264, 270, 282, 320-325, 546
universal jurisdiction, 44-47, 62, 71, 76, 79-84, 89-90, 184, 189, 199, 209, 213, 216-219, 222-235, 246, 272, 282-283, 443, 546-547, 562, 580, 604, 626

TORREY CANYON ACCIDENT, 97, 473, 563

TOW-BACK, 245, 256, 394, 448

TRACEABILITY, 177-178, 196

TRAFFICKING IN PERSONS, 4, 12, 17, 34-42, 66-67, 80, 240-245, 249-250, 267-269, 277, 283, 299, 425, 457, 558
Protocol of 2000 to Prevent, Suppress and Punish Trafficking in Persons, Especially Women and Children, 242-243, 249, 268, 283, 325

TRANSIT, 9-10, 28, 36, 43, 263, 277-278, 281, 341, 344, 349, 355, 357-362, 370, 377, 395, 426, 504-507, 517, 585

TRANSNATIONAL ORGANIZED CRIME, 4-5, 35, 52-43, 64, 79, 80, 82-83, 87, 153-154, 180-181, 185, 211-213, 228-229, 231, 239-242, 247-248, 261, 264, 269-271, 277, 285, 314, 325-330, 334-335, 422-425, 576
United Nations Convention against Transnational Organized Crime of 2000, 4, 64, 80, 82-83, 181, 211-213, 218, 228-229, 242, 247-248, 261, 264, 269-271, 277, 314, 320, 325-331, 334, 422-424, 460

TRANSPORT OF SLAVES
See *Slavery*

TRANSPORT OF WMD BY SEA
See *Weapons of Mass Destruction*

TREATY ON THE NON-PROLIFERATION OF NUCLEAR WEAPONS
See *Weapons of Mass Destruction*

UNAUTHORIZED OR ILLEGAL BROADCASTING, 3, 17, 21, 30, 71, 88-89, 189, 317-319, 502, 622

UNCLOS, 3-52, 54-74, 79-85, 88-89, 92-93, 99-116, 120-123, 126-135, 139-140, 143, 151-152, 158-168, 170-171, 183-194, 202-209, 215-226, 233-235, 237, 249, 258-260, 263-272, 278, 288-289, 292-293, 303-304, 309, 313-320, 333-336, 341, 346-348, 353, 355-364, 371, 375, 383-384, 388-389, 409-413,

431, 434, 442-443, 457, 465, 468, 474-475, 478, 502-508, 562-566, 570, 577, 579, 584, 593, 596-597, 599-603, 615, 618, 622-623, 625

UN DRAFT CONVENTION ON THE REGULATION, OVERSIGHT AND MONITORING OF PRIVATE MILITARY AND SECURITY COMPANIES
See *Private Maritime Security Companies*

UNHCR, 35, 39, 245, 252, 254-256, 262, 275, 280, 381, 392, 401-403, 407, 413, 426, 462, 560

UNITED NATIONS CHARTER ARTICLE 103, 65, 67-68, 75, 507-509, 564, 592

UNITED NATIONS CONVENTION AGAINST CORRUPTION OF 2003
See *Corruption*

UNITED NATIONS CONVENTION AGAINST ILLICIT TRAFFIC IN NARCOTIC DRUGS AND PSYCHOTROPIC SUBSTANCES OF 1988
See *Drug Trafficking*

UNITED NATIONS CONVENTION AGAINST TRANSNATIONAL ORGANIZED CRIME OF 2000
See *Transnational Organized Crime*

UNITED NATIONS GENERAL ASSEMBLY RESOLUTIONS, 153, 155, 179, 200, 210-211, 248, 250, 270, 291, 296-298, 424, 426, 495, 558, 618, 627

UNITED NATIONS SECURITY COUNCIL, 9, 21, 23-25, 43, 46, 53, 59-60, 65-68, 73-75, 78-79, 84, 91-92, 199-201, 203, 206, 208, 211-212, 217-218, 221, 224, 226, 236, 291, 296-302, 304, 307-309, 311, 332-334, 340, 364, 397, 431, 435-436, 447, 454-455, 485, 489, 491-495, 499, 501, 506, 508-510, 513-514, 517-518, 524, 529, 545, 567, 570-571, 589-591, 595, 597, 600, 611-612, 616, 619, 622

UNITED NATIONS SECURITY COUNCIL RESOLUTIONS, 9-10, 21, 23-25, 43, 46, 59-60, 66-67, 73-75, 79, 84, 91-92 201, 203, 208, 218, 226, 236, 291, 299, 301-302, 308-309, 311-313, 321, 332-334, 340, 364, 394, 397, 431, 435, 447, 454, 506, 508-509, 513-514, 524, 570-571, 589, 591, 612, 622
- Resolution 1373, 21, 23, 567-568, 570-571
- Resolution 1540, 9-10, 24-25, 59-60, 74, 91-92, 485, 489-495, 498-502, 506-511, 513, 515-518
- Resolution 1816, 23, 73-74, 206-207, 298, 340, 564
- Resolution 1851, 298, 311-312, 333-334, 529-530
- Resolution 1897, 73, 298, 301-302, 304, 333
- Resolution 1973, 397-398
- Resolution 1976, 308, 334
- Resolution 2020, 46, 73, 221, 298, 334
- Resolution 2077, 199

UNITED STATES V. *ALI*, 219, 232

UNITED STATES V. *DIRE*, 216, 221

UNITED STATES V. *IBARGUEN-MOSQUERA*, 30

UNITED STATES V. *SAID*, 220

UNITED STATES V. *SMITH*, 220-221, 443

UNITED STATES-BARBADOS 1997 AGREEMENT, 610, 618-620, 628, 631

UNITED STATES-JAMAICA AGREEMENT, 630

UNIVERSAL JURISDICTION
See *Titles of Jurisdiction*

UNODC, 27, 34, 46, 154, 179-181, 239-243, 247-248, 250, 253, 259, 271, 276-277, 284-285, 333, 402, 423-425, 460, 476, 612

UNSEAWORTHY VESSELS
See *Seaworthiness*

UNTOC
See *Transnational Organized Crime:* United Nations Convention against Transnational Organized Crime of 2000

US NAVY, 528, 534-535, 599, 611-613

USE OF FORCE, 25, 58-60, 76-77, 191-194, 203, 345, 347, 349-351, 353-356, 361, 363-364, 369, 371-375, 438-439, 494, 504, 523, 525-528, 531, 545, 548-549, 552, 566, 571, 573, 593, 595-596, 598, 605, 620, 631-632

VESSEL PROTECTION DETACHMENTS, 346, 356, 361, 368-370, 613-614

WAR CRIMES, 20, 55, 62, 84-85, 213, 215, 223, 253, 523-553, 588

WEAPONS OF MASS DESTRUCTION (WMD), 3, 9-10, 12, 14, 18, 20-27, 59-60, 66-67, 73-75, 80, 83, 89, 91-92, 107, 454, 472, 485-521
- biological, chemical or bacteriological weapons, 20, 24, 74, 107, 485-500, 505, 510, 518-520
- transport of WMD by sea, 9, 22, 24-27, 59-60, 74, 89, 91, 489-490, 496-497, 501-502, 507, 510, 516-519
- Treaty on the Non-proliferation of Nuclear Weapons of 1968, 490-492, 498, 512-519

WEST AFRICA, 4, 26, 28, 36, 43, 150-151, 179, 199, 207, 245, 277, 297, 299, 340-341, 353, 368-369, 376, 557, 589, 595, 625

WINNER INCIDENT
See *Medvedyev and Others* v. *France*

WITNESSES, 52, 87, 135-136, 250, 284, 312, 331, 333, 335, 453, 480

WOMEN ON WAVES AND OTHERS V. *PORTUGAL* (ECTHR), 442, 467-468, 575

WRONGFUL ACT
See *State Responsibility*

PUBLICATIONS DE L'ACADÉMIE
DE DROIT INTERNATIONAL
DE LA HAYE

PUBLICATIONS OF THE
HAGUE ACADEMY OF INTERNATIONAL
LAW

RECUEIL DES COURS

Depuis 1923, les plus grands noms du droit international ont professé à l'Académie de droit international de La Haye. Tous les tomes du *Recueil* qui ont été publiés depuis cette date sont disponibles, chaque tome étant, depuis les tout premiers, régulièrement réimprimé sous sa forme originale.

Depuis 2008, certains cours font l'objet d'une édition en livres de poche (voir ci-après).

En outre, toute la collection existe en version électronique. Tous les ouvrages parus à ce jour ont été mis en ligne et peuvent être consultés moyennant un des abonnements proposés, qui offrent un éventail de tarifs et de possibilités.

INDEX

A ce jour, il a paru sept index généraux. Ils couvrent les tomes suivants:

1 à 101	(1923-1960)	379 pages	ISBN 978-90-218-9948-0
102 à 125	(1961-1968)	204 pages	ISBN 978-90-286-0643-2
126 à 151	(1969-1976)	280 pages	ISBN 978-90-286-0630-2
152 à 178	(1976-1982)	416 pages	ISBN 978-0-7923-2955-8
179 à 200	(1983-1986)	260 pages	ISBN 978-90-411-0110-5
201 à 250	(1987-1994)	448 pages	ISBN 978-90-04-13700-4
251 à 300	(1995-2002)	580 pages	ISBN 978-90-04-15387-7

A partir du tome 210 il a été décidé de publier un index complet qui couvrira chaque fois dix tomes du *Recueil des cours*. Le dernier index paru couvre les tomes suivants:

311 à 320 (2004-2006) 392 pages Tome 320A ISBN 978-90-04-19695-7

COLLOQUES

L'Académie organise également des colloques dont les débats sont publiés. Les derniers volumes parus de ces colloques portent les titres suivants: *Le règlement pacifique des différends internationaux en Europe: perspectives d'avenir* (1990); *Le développement du rôle du Conseil de sécurité* (1992); *La Convention sur l'interdiction et l'élimination des armes chimiques: une percée dans l'entreprise multilatérale du désarmement* (1994); *Actualité de la Conférence de La Haye de 1907, Deuxième Conférence de la Paix* (2007). (Voir ci-après.)

CENTRE D'ÉTUDE ET DE RECHERCHE

Les travaux scientifiques du Centre d'étude et de recherche de droit international et de relations internationales de l'Académie de droit international de La Haye, dont les sujets sont choisis par le Curatorium de l'Académie, faisaient l'objet, depuis la session de 1985, d'une publication dans laquelle les directeurs d'études dressaient le bilan des recherches du Centre qu'ils avaient dirigé. Cette série a été arrêtée et la dernière brochure parue porte le titre suivant: *Les règles et les institutions du droit international humanitaire à l'épreuve des conflits armés récents*. Néanmoins, lorsque les travaux du Centre se révèlent particulièrement intéressants et originaux, les rapports des directeurs et les articles rédigés par les chercheurs font l'objet d'un ouvrage collectif qui est publié dans la collection Les livres de droit de l'Académie (voir ci-après).

Les demandes de renseignements ou de catalogues et les commandes doivent être adressées à

MARTINUS NIJHOFF PUBLISHERS

B.P. 9000, 2300 PA Leyde Pays-Bas **http://www.brill.nl**

COLLECTED COURSES

Since 1923 the top names in international law have taught at the Hague Academy of International Law. All the volumes of the *Collected Courses* which have been published since 1923 are available, as, since the very first volume, they are reprinted regularly in their original format.

Since 2008, certain courses have been the subject of a pocketbook edition (see below).

In addition, the total collection now exists in electronic form. All works already published have been put "on line" and can be consulted under one of the proposed subscription methods, which offer a range of tariffs and possibilities.

INDEXES

Up till now seven General Indexes have been published. They cover the following volumes:

1 to 101	(1923-1960)	379 pages	ISBN 978-90-218-9948-0
102 to 125	(1961-1968)	204 pages	ISBN 978-90-286-0643-2
126 to 151	(1969-1976)	280 pages	ISBN 978-90-286-0630-2
152 to 178	(1976-1982)	416 pages	ISBN 978-0-7923-2955-8
179 to 200	(1983-1986)	260 pages	ISBN 978-90-411-0110-5
201 to 250	(1987-1994)	448 pages	ISBN 978-90-04-13700-4
251 to 300	(1995-2002)	580 pages	ISBN 978-90-04-15387-7

From Volume 210 onwards it has been decided to publish a full index covering, each time, ten volumes of the *Collected Courses*. The latest Index published covers the following volumes:

311 to 320 (2004-2006) 392 pages Volume 320A ISBN 978-90-04-19695-7

WORKSHOPS

The Academy publishes the discussions from the Workshops which it organizes. The latest titles of the Workshops already published are as follows: *The Peaceful Settlement of International Disputes in Europe: Future Prospects* (1990) ; *The Development of the Role of the Security Council* (1992); *The Convention on the Prohibition and Elimination of Chemical Weapons: A Breakthrough in Multilateral Disarmament* (1994); *Topicality of the 1907 Hague Conference, the Second Peace Conference* (2007). (See below.)

CENTRE FOR STUDIES AND RESEARCH

The scientific works of the Centre for Studies and Research in International Law and International Relations of the Hague Academy of International Law, the subjects of which are chosen by the Curatorium of the Academy, have been published, since the Centre's 1985 session, in a publication in which the Directors of Studies reported on the state of research of the Centre under their direction. This series has been discontinued and the title of the latest booklet published is as follows: *Rules and Institutions of International Humanitarian Law Put to the Test of Recent Armed Conflicts*. Nevertheless, when the work of the Centre has been of particular interest and originality, the reports of the Directors of Studies together with the articles by the researchers form the subject of a collection published in the series The Law Books of the Academy (see below).

TABLE PAR TOME DES COURS PUBLIÉS CES DERNIÈRES ANNÉES

INDEX BY VOLUME OF THE COURSES PUBLISHED THESE LAST YEARS

Tome/Volume 354 (2011)

Lamm, C. B.: Internationalization of the Practice of Law and Important Emerging Issues for Investor-State Arbitration (Opening Lecture), 9-64.

Briggs, A.: The Principle of Comity in Private International Law, 65-182.

Davey, W. J.: Non-discrimination in the World Trade Organization: The Rules and Exceptions, 183-440.

(ISBN 978-90-04-22728-6)

Tome/Volume 355 (2011)

Chemillier-Gendreau, M.: A quelles conditions l'universalité du droit international est-elle possible ? (conférence inaugurale), 9-40.

Xue Hanqin: Chinese Contemporary Perspectives on International Law — History, Culture and International Law, 41-234.

Arrighi, J. M.: L'Organisation des Etats américains et le droit international, 235-438.

(ISBN 978-90-04-22729-3)

Tome/Volume 356 (2011)

Talpis, J.: Succession Substitutes, 9-238.

Lagrange, E.: L'efficacité des normes internationales concernant la situation des personnes privées dans les ordres juridiques internes, 239-552.

(ISBN 978-90-04-22730-9)

Tome/Volume 357 (2011)

Dugard, J.: The Secession of States and Their Recognition in the Wake of Kosovo, 9-222.

Gannagé, L.: Les méthodes du droit international privé à l'épreuve des conflits de cultures, 223-490. (ISBN 978-90-04-22731-6)

Tome/Volume 358 (2011)

Brand, R. A.: Transaction Planning Using Rules on Jurisdiction and the Recognition and Enforcement of Judgments, 9-262.

Hafner, G.: The Emancipation of the Individual from the State under International Law, 263-454. (ISBN 978-90-04-22732-3)

Tome/Volume 359 (2012)

Opertti Badán, D.: Conflit de lois et droit uniforme dans le droit international privé contemporain: dilemme ou convergence ? (conférence inaugurale), 9-86.

Chen Weizuo: La nouvelle codification du droit international privé chinois, 87-234.

Kohler, Ch.: L'autonomie de la volonté en droit international privé: un principe universel entre libéralisme et étatisme, 285-478.

(ISBN 978-90-04-25541-8)

Tome/Volume 360 (2012)

Basedow, J.: The Law of Open Societies — Private Ordering and Public Regulation of International Relations. General Course on Private International Law, 9-516.

(ISBN 978-90-04-25550-0)

Tome/Volume 361 (2012)

Pinto, M. C. W.: The Common Heritage of Mankind: Then and Now, 9-130.

Kreindler, R.: Competence-Competence in the Face of Illegality in Contracts and Arbitration Agreements, 131-482.

(ISBN 978-90-04-25552-4)

Tome/Volume 362 (2012)

Arsanjani, M. H.: The United Nations and International Law-Making (Opening Lecture), 9-40.

Alland, D.: L'interprétation du droit international public, 41-394.

(ISBN 978-90-04-25554-8)

Tome/Volume 363 (2012)

Sur, S.: La créativité du droit international. Cours général de droit international public, 9-332.

Turp, D.: La contribution du droit international au maintien de la diversité culturelle, 333-454.

(ISBN 978-90-04-25556-2)

Tome/Volume 364 (2012)

Gaja, G.: The Protection of General Interests in the International Community. General Course on Public International Law (2011), 9-186.

Glenn, H. P.: La conciliation des lois. Cours général de droit international privé (2011), 187-470.

(ISBN 978-90-04-25557-9)

Tome/Volume 365 (2013)

Crawford, J.: Chance, Order, Change: The Course of International Law. General Course on Public International Law, 9-390.

(ISBN 978-90-04-25560-9)

Tome/Volume 366 (2013)

Hayton, D.: "Trusts" in Private International Law, 9-98.

Hobér, K.: *Res Judicata* and *Lis Pendens* in International Arbitration, 99-406.

(ISBN 978-90-04-26395-6)

Tome/Volume 367 (2013)

Kolb, R.: L'article 103 de la Charte des Nations Unies, 9-252.

Nascimbene, B.: Le droit de la nationalité et le droit des organisations d'intégration régionales. Vers de nouveaux statuts de résidents ?, 253-454.

(ISBN 978-90-04-26793-0)

LES LIVRES DE POCHE DE L'ACADÉMIE

POCKETBOOKS OF THE ACADEMY

(Par ordre chronologique de parution) (By chronological order of publication)

Gaillard, E.: Aspects philosophiques du droit de l'arbitrage international, 2008, 252 pages.
(ISBN 978-90-04-17148-0)

Schrijver, N.: The Evolution of Sustainable Development in International Law: Inception, Meaning and Status, 2008, 276 pages.
(ISBN 978-90-04-17407-8)

Moura Vicente, D.: La propriété intellectuelle en droit international privé, 2009, 516 pages.
(ISBN 978-90-04-17907-3)

Decaux, E.: Les formes contemporaines de l'esclavage, 2009, 272 pages.
(ISBN 978-90-04-17908-0)

McLachlan, C.: *Lis Pendens* in International Litigation, 2009, 492 pages.
(ISBN 978-90-04-17909-7)

Carbone, S. M.: Conflits de lois en droit maritime, 2010, 312 pages.
(ISBN 978-90-04-18688-0)

Boele-Woelki, K.: Unifying and Harmonizing Substantive Law and the Role of Conflict of Laws, 2010, 288 pages.
(ISBN 978-90-04-18683-5)

Onuma, Y.: A Transcivilizational Perspective in International Law, 2010, 492 pages.
(ISBN 978-90-04-18689-7)

Bucher, A.: La dimension sociale du droit international privé. Cours général, 2011, 552 pages.
(ISBN 978-90-04-20917-6)

Thürer, D.: International Humanitarian Law: Theory, Practice, Context, 2011, 504 pages.
(ISBN 978-90-04-17910-3)

Alvarez, J. E.: The Public International Law Regime Governing International Investment, 2011, 504 pages.
(ISBN 978-90-04-18682-8)

Wang, G.: Radiating Impact of WTO on Its Members' Legal System: The Chinese Perspective, 2011, 384 pages.
(ISBN 978-90-04-21854-3)

Bogdan, M.: Private International Law as Component of the Law of the Forum, 2012, 360 pages.
(ISBN 978-90-04-22634-0)

Davey, W. J.: Non-discrimination in the World Trade Organization: The Rules and Exceptions, 2012, 360 pages.
(ISBN 978-90-04-23314-0)

Xue Hanqin : Chinese Contemporary Perspectives on International Law — History, Culture and International Law, 2012, 288 pages.

(ISBN 978-90-04-23613-4)

Reisman, W. M.: The Quest for World Order and Human Dignity in the Twenty-first Century : Constitutive Process and Individual Commitment. General Course on Public International Law, 2012, 504 pages.

(ISBN 978-90-04-23615-8)

Dugard, J.: The Secession of States and Their Recognition in the Wake of Kosovo, 2013, 312 pages.

(ISBN 978-90-04-25748-1)

Gannagé, L.: Les méthodes du droit international privé à l'épreuve des conflits de cultures, 2013, 372 pages.

(ISBN 978-90-04-25750-4)

Kohler, Ch.: L'autonomie de la volonté en droit international privé : un principe universel entre libéralisme et étatisme, 2013, 288 pages.

(ISBN 978-90-04-25752-8)

Kreindler, R.: Competence-Competence in the Face of Illegality in Contracts and Arbitration Agreements, 2013, 504 pages.

(ISBN 978-90-04-25754-2)

Crawford, J.: Chance, Order, Change : The Course of International Law. General Course on Public International Law, 2014, 540 pages.

(ISBN 978-90-04-26808-1)

Brand, R. A.: Transaction Planning Using Rules on Jurisdiction and the Recognition and Enforcement of Judgments, 2014, 360 pages.

(ISBN 978-90-04-26810-4)

Kolb, R.: L'article 103 de la Charte des Nations Unies, 2014, 360 pages.

(ISBN 978-90-04-27836-3)

Benvenisti, E.: The Law of Global Governance, 2014, 336 pages.

(ISBN 978-90-04-27911-7)

LES LIVRES DE DROIT DE L'ACADÉMIE

THE LAW BOOKS OF THE ACADEMY

(Par ordre chronologique de parution) (By chronological order of publication)

Dupuy, R.-J. (dir. publ./ed.): Manuel sur les organisations internationales/A Handbook on International Organizations. (1988, 714 pages.)
(ISBN 978-90-247-3658-4)

Dupuy, R.-J., and D. Vignes (eds.): A Handbook on the New Law of the Sea. (2 volumes)
Volume 1: 1991, 900 pages. (ISBN 978-0-7923-0924-3)
Volume 2: 1991, 882 pages. (ISBN 978-0-7923-1063-1)

Carreau, D., et/and M. N. Shaw (dir. publ./eds.): La dette extérieure/The External Debt. (1995, 818 pages.)
(ISBN 978-90-411-0083-2)

Dupuy, R.-J. (dir. publ./ed.): Manuel sur les organisations internationales/A Handbook on International Organizations. (2e éd./2nd ed., 1998, 1008 pages.)
(ISBN 978-90-411-1119-7)

Eisemann, P. M., et/and M. Koskenniemi (dir. publ./eds.): La succession d'Etats : la codification à l'épreuve des faits/State Succession: Codification Tested against the Facts. (2000, 1058 pages.)
(ISBN 978-90-411-1392-4)

Caron, D. D., et/and Ch. Leben (dir. publ./eds.): Les aspects internationaux des catastrophes naturelles et industrielles/The International Aspects of Natural and Industrial Catastrophes. (2001, 912 pages.)
(ISBN 978-90-411-1485-3)

Bothe, M., et/and P. H. Sands (dir. publ./eds.) : La politique de l'environnement. De la réglementation aux instruments économiques/Environmental Policy. From Regulation to Economic Instruments. (2002, 958 pages.)
(ISBN 978-90-411-1604-8)

Forlati Picchio, L., et/and L.-A. Sicilianos (dir. publ./eds.): Les sanctions économiques en droit international/Economic Sanctions in International Law. (2004, 912 pages.)
(ISBN 978-90-04-13701-1)

Boisson de Chazournes, L. et/and S. M. A. Salman (dir. publ./eds.): Les ressources en eau et le droit international/Water Resources and International Law. (2005, 848 pages.)
(ISBN 978-90-04-13702-8)

Mahiou, A., et/and F. Snyder (dir. publ./eds.): La sécurité alimentaire/Food Security and Food Safety. (2006, 992 pages.)
(ISBN 978-90-04-14543-6)

Kahn, Ph., et/and T. W. Wälde (dir. publ./eds.): Les aspects nouveaux du droit des investissements internationaux/New Aspects of International Investment Law. (2007, 1072 pages.)

(ISBN 978-90-04-15372-1)

Glennon, M. J., et/and S. Sur (dir. publ./eds.): Terrorisme et droit international/ Terrorism and International Law. (2008, 864 pages.)

(ISBN 978-90-04-16107-8)

Nafziger, J. A. R., et/and T. Scovazzi (dir. publ./eds.): Le patrimoine culturel de l'humanité/The Cultural Heritage of Mankind. (2008, 1168 pages.)

(ISBN 978-90-04-16106-1)

Momtaz, D., et/and M. J. Matheson (dir. publ./eds.): Les règles et institutions du droit international humanitaire à l'épreuve des conflits armés récents/Rules and Institutions of International Humanitarian Law Put to the Test of Recent Armed Conflicts. (2010, 1072 pages.)

(Relié/Hard-back: ISBN 978-90-04-17283-8)
(Broché/Soft-cover: ISBN 978-90-04-18697-2)

Maljean-Dubois, S., et/and L. Rajamani (dir. publ./eds.): La mis en œuvre du droit international de l'environnement/Implementation of International Environmental Law. (2011, 864 pages.)

(Relié/Hard-back: ISBN 978-90-04-20892-6)
(Broché/Soft-cover: ISBN 978-90-04-20916-9)

Foblets, M. C., et/and N. Yassari (dir. publ./eds.): Approches juridiques de la diversité culturelle/Legal Approaches to Cultural Diversity. (2013, 1024 pages.)

(Relié/Hard-back: ISBN 978-90-04-25015-4)
(Broché/Soft-cover: ISBN 978-90-04-25016-1)

Papastavridis, E. D., et/and K. N. Trapp (dir. publ./eds.): La criminalité en mer/Crimes at Sea (2014), 784 pages.

(Relié/Hard-back: ISBN 978-90-04-26805-0)
(Broché/Soft-cover: ISBN 978-90-04-26807-4)

Sarooshi, D. (dir. publ./eds.): Mesures de réparation et responsabilité à raison des actes des organisations internationales/Remedies and Responsibility for the Actions of International Organizations (2014), 736 pages.

(Relié/Hard-back: ISBN 978-90-04-26802-9)
(Broché/Soft-cover: ISBN 978-90-04-26804-3)

COLLOQUES

WORKSHOPS

Colloque/Workshop 1968

Kojanec, G. (dir. publ./ed.): Les accords de commerce international/International Trade Agreements. (1969, 374 pages.)

(ISBN 978-90-286-1672-1)

Colloque/Workshop 1971

Rideau, R. (dir. publ./ed.): Les aspects juridiques de l'intégration économique/ Legal Aspects of Economic Integration. (1972, 620 pages.)

(ISBN 978-90-286-0053-9)

Colloque/Workshop 1973

Kiss, A.-C. (dir. publ./ed.): La protection de l'environnement et le droit international/ The Protection of the Environment and International Law. (1975, 650 pages.)

(ISBN 978-90-286-0494-0)

Colloque/Workshop 1978

Dupuy, R.-J. (dir. publ./ed.): Le droit à la santé en tant que droit de l'homme/The Right to Health as a Human Right. (1979, 513 pages.)

(ISBN 978-90-286-1028-6)

Colloque/Workshop 1979

Dupuy, R.-J. (dir. publ./ed.): Le droit au développement au plan international/The Right to Development at the International Level. (1980, 458 pages.)

(ISBN 978-90-286-0990-7)

Colloque/Workshop 1980

Dupuy, R.-J. (dir. publ./ed.): Le nouvel ordre économique international. Aspects commerciaux, technologiques et culturels/The New International Economic Order. Commercial, Technological and Cultural Aspects. (1981, 395 pages.)

(ISBN 978-90-247-2602-8)

Colloque/Workshop 1981

Dupuy, R.-J. (dir. publ./ed.): La gestion des ressources pour l'humanité: le droit de la mer/The Management of Humanity's Resources: The Law of the Sea. (1982, 448 pages.)

(ISBN 978-90-247-2762-9)

Colloque/Workshop 1982

Dupuy, R.-J. (dir. publ./ed.): Le règlement des différends sur les nouvelles ressources naturelles/The Settlement of Disputes on the New Natural Resources. (1983, 487 pages.)

(ISBN 978-90-247-2901-2)

Colloque/Workshop 1983

Dupuy, R.-J. (dir. publ./ed.): L'avenir du droit international dans un monde multiculturel/The Future of International Law in a Multicultural World. (1984, 510 pages.)

(ISBN 978-90-247-3070-4)

Colloque/Workshop 1984

Dupuy, R.-J. (dir. publ./ed.): L'avenir du droit international de l'environnement/The Future of the International Law of the Environment. (1985, 536 pages.)

(ISBN 978-90-247-3239-5)

Colloque/Workshop 1985

Bardonnet, D. (dir. publ./ed.): L'adaptation des structures et méthodes des Nations Unies/The Adaptation of Structures and Methods at the United Nations. (1986, 434 pages.)

(ISBN 978-90-247-3441-2)

Colloque/Workshop 1990

Bardonnet, D. (dir. publ./ed.): Le règlement pacifique des différends internationaux en Europe: perspectives d'avenir/The Peaceful Settlement of International Disputes in Europe: Future Prospects. (1991, 704 pages.)

(Relié/Hard-back. ISBN 978-0-7923-1572-8)
(Broché/Soft-cover. ISBN 978-0-7923-1573-5)

Colloque/Workshop 1992

Dupuy, R.-J. (dir. publ./ed.): Le développement du rôle du Conseil de sécurité/The Development of the Role of the Security Council. (1993, 514 pages.)

(ISBN 978-0-7923-2318-1)

Colloque/Workshop 1994

Bardonnet, D. (dir. publ./ed.): La Convention sur l'interdiction et l'élimination des armes chimiques: une percée dans l'entreprise multilatérale du désarmement/The Convention on the Prohibition and Elimination of Chemical Weapons: A Breakthrough in Multilateral Disarmament. (1995, 712 pages.)

(ISBN 978-90-411-0154-9)

Colloque/Workshop 2007

Daudet, Y. (dir. publ./ed.): Actualité de la Conférence de La Haye de 1907, Deuxième Conférence de la Paix/Topicality of the 1907 Hague Conference, the Second Peace Conference. (2008, 528 pages.)

(ISBN 978-90-04-17421-4)

Centre 2012/7-14-6